ENGLAND'S
WHO'S WHO

Pitch Publishing Ltd
A2 Yeoman Gate
Yeoman Way
Durrington
BN13 3QZ

Email: info@pitchpublishing.co.uk
Web: www.pitchpublishing.co.uk

First published by Pitch Publishing 2013
Text © 2013 Tony Matthews

A CIP catalogue record for this book is available from the British Library.

13-digit ISBN: 978-1909178632
Design and typesetting by Duncan Olner
Printed in the UK by CPI Group (UK), Croydon CRO 4YY

ENGLAND'S
WHO'S WHO

THE WHO'S WHO OF ENGLAND INTERNATIONAL FOOTBALLERS 1872-2013

TONY MATTHEWS

FOREWORD
by Gordon Taylor, O.B.E., Chief Executive of the Professional Footballers' Association

Every boy's dream is to be a professional footballer or certainly it was in the area of Ashton-under-Lyne that I grew up in. At a time of the Busby Babes, half of the City of Manchester was watching the Revie Plan and the other half Duncan Edwards – a keen rivalry not so different to that of today.

Playing football morning, afternoon and night through the holidays, imagining ourselves as one of the heroes whose autographs we collected, with every game a Cup final.

We never quite got as far as imagining ourselves as international players! That really was reaching for the stars, albeit my heroes such as Nat Lofthouse (the 'Lion of Vienna'), Tom Finney and Stanley Matthews all played with distinction for England who amazingly managed to lose to the USA the first time they entered the World Cup in 1950. We reached the quarter-finals in 1954, having lost twice to the mighty Hungarian team in home and away friendly internationals earlier that season, failed to get beyond the group stage in 1958 (beaten in a play-off) but did better in 1962, when again we made the last eight.

By now the maximum wage was removed and in 1966, England became World champions, winning the Jules Rimet trophy on home soil at Wembley. It was certainly a great afternoon all round, especially for one of my contemporaries and boyhood friends from Bolton Wanderers, Alan Ball, who played a prominent role in the 4-2 extra-time victory over West Germany.

We have, of course, aspired to great things since then. In 1986 we lost in the World Cup quarter-finals, came so close to glory when reaching the semi-finals of the 1990 World Cup in Italy, the 1996 European Championships in England and the World Cup again in South Africa in 2012, while in between times, in the 2002 World Cup in Japan, we were in front against Brazil, only to lose against ten men in the end.

Whilst not achieving the distinction of playing for England, it has been a real pleasure to be on the FA Council and a member of the International Committee, allowing me to travel with the team all over the world, and of course to see youngsters coming through, the likes of Steven Gerrard, Wayne Rooney, Ashley Cole and Frank Lampard to become the same that my boyhood heroes were.

The latest generation will be watching the likes of Jack Wilshere and Danny Welbeck, players I feel they can be proud of, and maybe they can be key players of the Roy Hodgson era, just like Johnny Haynes, Finney, Matthews, Lofthouse and others were for Walter Winterbottom.

This epic publication by Tony Matthews is a very impressive 364 page, 350,000 word catalogue, covering each and every player who has won at least one full cap for England - from those who appeared in the very first international way back in 1872 against Scotland, to those who wore the 'Three Lions' in the latest game against Brazil in Rio in June 2013.

This book is a must for football lovers and historians. It covers all the one game wonders to the icons who gained more than 100 caps, led initially by the great Billy Wright, followed by Bobby Moore, Bobby Charlton, goalkeeper Peter Shilton (with a record 125 international appearances) and David Beckham, and of course the latest duo of Steven Gerrard and Ashley Cole.

On the 150th anniversary of the Football Association it is a wonderful time to be reminded that whilst our League football is amongst the most competitive and attractive in the world and the Premier League is being watched by more countries than any other country in the world, nevertheless it is nice that international football remains a barometer for the quality of players we are capable of producing. The club v. country battle has always been blamed for a lack of international success but maybe things will now change with the introduction of the Elite Player Performance Plan and here's hoping that all the players in this book will have laid the foundations for us to scale world heights once again and next time, with goal-line technology now in place, we won't have any worries about whether the ball was over the line or not!

Gordon Taylor

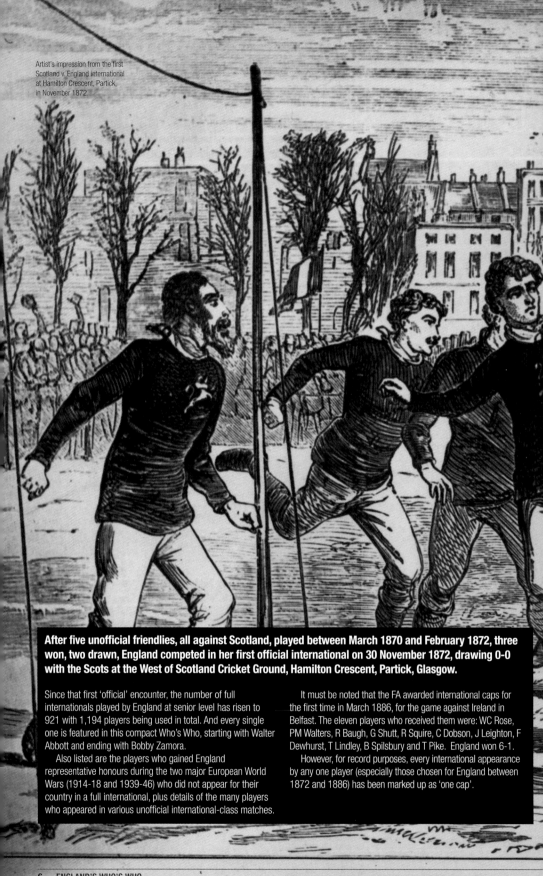

Artist's impression from the first Scotland v. England international at Hamilton Crescent, Partick, in November 1872.

After five unofficial friendlies, all against Scotland, played between March 1870 and February 1872, three won, two drawn, England competed in her first official international on 30 November 1872, drawing 0-0 with the Scots at the West of Scotland Cricket Ground, Hamilton Crescent, Partick, Glasgow.

Since that first 'official' encounter, the number of full internationals played by England at senior level has risen to 921 with 1,194 players being used in total. And every single one is featured in this compact Who's Who, starting with Walter Abbott and ending with Bobby Zamora.

Also listed are the players who gained England representative honours during the two major European World Wars (1914-18 and 1939-46) who did not appear for their country in a full international, plus details of the many players who appeared in various unofficial international-class matches.

It must be noted that the FA awarded international caps for the first time in March 1886, for the game against Ireland in Belfast. The eleven players who received them were: WC Rose, PM Walters, R Baugh, G Shutt, R Squire, C Dobson, J Leighton, F Dewhurst, T Lindley, B Spilsbury and T Pike. England won 6-1.

However, for record purposes, every international appearance by any one player (especially those chosen for England between 1872 and 1886) has been marked up as 'one cap'.

THE FOOTBALL MATCH AT

.—ENGLAND v. SCOTLAND.

INTRODUCTION

The England international football team is controlled by the Football Association, the governing body for football in England. England is the joint oldest national team in the world, alongside Scotland.

The two countries first met each other in an unofficial friendly match in March 1870. The game ended in a 1-1 draw and after four more friendly encounters had taken place - three won by England, 1-0, 2-1 and 1-0, with one more draw - the first full international was staged on 19 November 1872, which also resulted in a draw (0-0).

Since the latter, England has fulfilled a further 920 full internationals, winning over 520 of them and scoring over 2,000 goals while awarding caps to 1,194 players, and this does not include the 45 or so whose only appearance in an England shirt came in Wartime and/or Victory internationals during season 1918-19 or between 1939 and 1946.

For seven years, 1872-79, England played exclusively against Scotland at senior level, before taking in the other two Home Nations - Ireland and Wales – when the British International Championship commenced, although they did entertain the touring Canadians in 1891 (won 6-1).

England joined FIFA in 1906 and two years later ventured abroad for the first time, undertaking a tour of Central Europe in June 1908. They played four friendlies against Austria (two), Bohemia and Hungary, winning all four and scoring a total of 28 goals.

Since then over 85 other countries have taken on England at full international level (see full details on page 358).

From 1888 until Wembley Stadium was utilised for the first time in 1924, England played the majority of their home matches on the ground of a Football League club... thus taking the game to the loyal and ardent supporters spread all over the country.

England withdrew from FIFA in April 1920, rejoined in 1924, pulled out again in 1928 and did not re-enter until after World War Two. During that time, in March 1923, Belgium became the first continental country to play in England; they lost 6-1 at Highbury.

As a result of their non-membership of FIFA, England missed out on playing in the first three World Cup competitions, 1930, 1934 and 1938. They finally entered in 1950, but, as all serious fans know, they suffered a disastrous result, losing 1-0 to the U.S.A. and failed to get past the first round.

A year earlier, on 21 September 1949, England suffered her first home defeat by a non-Home nation, when the Republic of Ireland upsets the odds with a 2-0 victory at Goodison Park.

Four years later, England were thumped 6-3 by the 'magical Magyars' of Hungary – their first defeat at Wembley by a team from outside the British Isles - and to make matters worse, the return match in Budapest, played the following May, saw Koscis, Puskas, Hidegkuti, Boszik and Co. win 7–1, which still stands today as England's worst ever defeat.

After the latter game, England's bewildered centre-half Syd Owen said: "It was like playing people from outer space".

In the 1954 World Cup in Switzerland, two goals by Ivor Broadis saw him become the first England player to score twice in a game at the World Cup finals. He beat Nat Lofthouse by 30 minutes as both netted braces in a thrilling 4–4 draw against Belgium. After reaching the quarter-finals for the first time, England lost 4–2 to Uruguay.

Walter Winterbottom was appointed as England's first-ever full-time manager in the summer of 1946. Prior to that the team had been chosen by a committee and, indeed, a committee still had a big say in which players were selected right up until Alf Ramsey took over in 1963.

Winterbottom did well and guided England to two World Cups, in 1958 and 1962.

The 1966 World Cup was hosted in England and Ramsey steered the hosts through to the final for the first time. In front of a 92,000 sun-drenched crowd at Wembley, England beat West Germany 4-2 after extra-time with the West Ham striker Geoff Hurst scoring a hat-trick – the first ever in a World Cup final.

As holders, England qualified for the next tournament in Mexico in 1970. They looked strong and reached the quarter-finals only to be knocked out by West Germany who gained sweet revenge for that defeat four years earlier.

England, in fact, went 2–0 up but eventually lost 3–2 after extra-time. Unfortunately they failed to qualify for the 1974 and 1978 tournaments, leading to Ramsey's dismissal.

Under his successor, Ron Greenwood, England successfully qualified for the 1982 World Cup in Spain (the first time they had done so competitively since 1962) but were eliminated from a second qualifying round, which comprised further group matches, without losing a game all tournament!

Bobby Robson was next in charge and under his control the team fared much better in 1986 when again they

reached the World Cup quarter-finals before losing 2–1 to Argentina in a game made famous by Maradona's two goals – one a brilliant individual effort, the other deliberate handball!

Two years later England had a disastrous Euro '88 tournament, losing every match but it was a different story in the 1990 World Cup when they claimed their second-best finishing position, taking fourth place after losing in the semi-finals, again to West Germany, this time by 4-3 in their first-ever penalty shoot-out.

During the 1990s, England had four different managers, and each one stayed in office for a relatively brief period of time.

Graham Taylor was Robson's successor, but he departed after England failed to qualify for the 1994 World Cup. Terry Venables replaced him.

At Euro '96, staged in England, Venables led England to their best performance in this competition, reaching the semi-finals. He resigned, however, following investigations into his financial activities.

Stepping up next was another former Tottenham Hotspur player, Glenn Hoddle, who similarly left the job for non-footballing reasons after just one international tournament - the 1998 World Cup - in which England were eliminated in the second round, again by Argentina, again in a penalty shoot-out (after a 2–2 draw).

Kevin Keegan took over from Hoddle and he guided England to Euro 2000, but performances were disappointing and he resigned on the night Germany

won the last international staged at the 'old' Wembley, 1-0 in a World Cup qualifier in October 2001.

Sven-Göran Eriksson – the first non-Englishman to mange England - was next in office. He held his position for five years, until 2006, and despite controversial press coverage of his personal life, he was consistently popular with the majority of Three Lions fans.

He twice guided England to the quarter-finals of the World Cup, in 2002 and 2006, and in fact, lost only five competitive matches during his tenure as England rose to number four in the World ranking under his guidance. His contract was extended by the Football Association by two years but perhaps surprisingly, he was fired at the conclusion of the 2006 World Cup.

Into the hot-seat stepped Steve McClaren, appointed officially as head coach. His reign yielded little success as England failed to qualify for Euro 2008.

McClaren was sacked unanimously by The Football Association on 22 November 2007 after only 16 months in charge. This made him the shortest-serving full time England manager since the inauguration of the post in 1946.

He was replaced in mid-December 2007 by the former Real Madrid and AC Milan manager Fabio Capello. Capello, an Italian, took charge of his first game on 6 February 2008 against Switzerland, in which England won 2–1.

Thereafter, England won all but one of their qualifying games for the 2010 World Cup, the 5–1 victory over Croatia at Wembley ensuring the team a place in the finals with two games to spare, a feat that had never been achieved before.

However, at the 2010 World Cup, England disappointed. They drew their opening two games but still qualified for the knockout stage only to lose 4–1 to their arch-rivals Germany, their heaviest defeat in a World Cup finals match.

After that Capello guided England through the qualifying rounds and into Euro 2012 proper before quitting his post.

Former international and U21 manager Stuart Pearce stepped in to hold the fort as caretaker-manager until the appointment of Roy Hodgson in May 2012.

Vastly experienced, the 64 year-old saw England start well under his control, although there was bitter disappointment when the team was defeated by Italy on penalties in the quarter-finals of the Euro Championships in Poland/Ukraine.

Thereafter, it was all hands to the pump and after an impressive qualifying campaign, and a series of competitive friendlies, when Hodgson introduced several young players, England found themselves in a great position to book their place in the 2014 World Cup finals in Brazil.

Bibliography

- A Century of English International Football 1872-1972
  (Morley Farror & Doug Lamming, published by Robert Hale, 1972)
- England – The Football Facts
  (Nick Gibbs, published by Facer, 1988)
- The Essential History of England
  (Andrew Mourant & Jack Rollin, published by Headline, 2002)
- The PFA Premier & Football League Players' Records 1946-98
  (Edited by Barry Hugman, published by Queen Anne Press, 1998)
- Football League Players' Records 1888 to 1939
  (Michael Joyce, published by Soccer Data, 2002)
- The History of the World Cup
  (Brian Glanville, published by Times Newspapers, 1973)
- Carling Football Fact Book
  (Henry Russell, published by Stopwatch, 1998)
- European Football Yearbooks
  (Edited by Mike Hammond, published by Sports Projects 1991-98)
- The Football League Jubilee Book
  (Ivan Sharpe, published by Stanley Paul, 1963)
- Soccer Shorts (Jack Rollin, published by Guinness Books, 1988)
- The Encyclopaedia of Association Football
  (Maurice Golesworthy, published by Robert Hale, 1969)
- The Datasport Book of Wartime Football: 1939-46
  (Gordon Andrews, published by Gardenia Press, 1989)
- England v Scotland
  (Brian James, published by Pelham Books, 1969)
- Soccer At War: 1939-45
  (Jack Rollin, published by Willow Books, 1985)
- Forgotten Caps
  (Bryan Horsnell & Doug Lamming, published by Yore, 1995)
- The Breedon Book of Football Managers
  (Dennis Turner & Alex White, published by Breedon, 1993)
- The Guinness Book of Soccer Facts & Feats
  (Jack Rollin, published by Guinness Books, 1980)
- England, England! (Dean Hayes, published by Sutton, 2004)
- England Player By Player
  (Graham Betts, published by Green Umbrella, 2006)

Wembley Stadiums

The original and first Wembley Stadium was built in Brent, North London, initially constructed for the British Empire Exhibition. After the 1923 FA Cup final between Bolton Wanderers and West Ham United had taken place there in front of a huge crowd which some sources believe topped the 200,000 mark, England played their first match at the stadium on 12 April 1924 against Scotland (1-1) with Billy Walker of Aston Villa scoring his country's first goal in front of just 37,250 paying spectators.

It was then four years before the second international was staged there, and this time a crowd of 80,868 saw Scotland, dubbed the 'Wembley Wizards' whip England 5-1 on 31 March 1928.

For the next 22 years, Wembley remained the venue for matches against Scotland only. But from 1950 until 2001, Wales, Northern Ireland, the Republic of Ireland and scores of other countries played under the twin towers.

The '1923' Wembley was demolished after standing for 78 years and from 2001 to 2007, England's home internationals were played on many different Premiership and Football League grounds up and down the country before the 'new' Wembley stadium, owned by the Football Association via its subsidiary Wembley National Stadium Limited, was built with an all-seated capacity of 90,000.

- **The A-Z of Football**
  (In house, published by Marks & Spencer, 2008)
- **The England Football Miscellany**
  (John White, published by Carlton Books, 2006)
- **Association Football And The Men Who Made It**
  (Alfred Gibson & William Pickford, four volumes, published by Caxton, 1906)
- **Association Football**
  (Aubrey Fabian & Geoffrey Green, four volumes, published by Caxton, 1960)
- **We Are The Champions**
  (Maurice Golesworthy, published by Pelham, 1972)

- **Rothman's Football Yearbook, 1970 to 2003**
  (Published by Headline)
- **Sky Sports Football Yearbook 2004-13**
  (Published by Headline)
- **The PFA Footballers' Who's Who 1995 to 2011**
  (Edited by Barry Hugman,
  Published by Stanley Paul & Queen Anne Press)
- **The News of the World Football Annual**
  (Various issues from 1946 to 2004,
  Published by the News of the World)

I have also referred to several club and international programmes, 1905-2013; football club yearbooks/annuals, 1905 to 2012; *The Sports Argus*, *The Sporting Star*, *Birmingham Post & Mail* and the *Express & Star* (four Midland-published newspapers); *Charles Buchan's Football Monthly*, 1950-74; *Memorable Football Firsts*, published for *Shoot/Goal* magazines by IPC Magazines, 1975; *Soccer Sensations*, a series compiled for *Shoot Magazine* by IPC Magazines, 1977 and many scrapbooks borrowed from supporters which contain hundreds of match reports and stories/articles on players.

Photography: Action Images, Colorsport, Getty Images, Ian Summers (Bluwater photography, Spain)

Throughout this book, the years to the right of the player's name indicate the seasons when he played for his country (i.e. 1876-79 means seasons 1876-77 to 1878-79) and after that, in circles, are the number of caps won and, where applicable, goals scored by each player.

ABBOTT, Walter 1901-02 ①

Born: Small Heath, Birmingham, 7 December 1877
Died: Birmingham, 1 February 1941
Career: Rosewood Victoria (August 1894), Small Heath (professional, April 1896), Everton (July 1899), Burnley (July 1908), Birmingham (July 1910, retired, May 1911); later worked in the motor car industry in Birmingham.

Walter Abbott was a strong, purposeful, hard-shooting inside-forward who later developed into a very reliable wing-half. He still holds the record for most goals in a season for Small Heath (Birmingham) of 42 in 1898-99 and won the FA Cup with Everton in 1906. Capped against Wales at Wrexham, as a late replacement for the injured Bill Bannister in March 1902, Abbott also represented the Football League on four occasions.

A'COURT, Alan 1957-59 ⑤ ①

Born: Rainhill, Lancs, 30 September 1934
Died: Bebington, Lancs, 14 December 2009
Career: Prescot Grammar School, Prescot Celtic (August 1950), Prescot Cables (July 1951), Liverpool (professional, September 1952), Tranmere Rovers (£4,500, October 1964), Norwich City (player/trainer-coach, July 1966), Chester (assistant-manager/coach, October 1968), Crewe Alexandra (assistant-manager, February-June 1969), Stoke City (coach, July 1969-April 1972), Ndola United/Zambia (coach, May-July 1972), Stoke City (assistant-coach, August 1972-May 1978; also caretaker-manager for two games, January 1978), Crewe Alexandra (assistant-manager, July 1978-May 1980); joined the sports staff at North Staffordshire Polytechnic, which later became Staffordshire University; Nantwich Town (manager); later ran a tobacconist/newsagent shop near Birkenhead and Bebington on Merseyside.

A fast-raiding outside-left who could cross accurately on the run, Alan A'Court scored on his international debut against Northern Ireland in November 1957 when he replaced the injured Tom Finney. His next three caps all came in the 1958 World Cup finals when once again he stood in for Finney and in the 2-2 draw with Austria, it was his shot which was parried by 'keeper Szanwald, only for Haynes to net the rebound. A Second Division championship winner with Liverpool in 1962, he was sidelined by injury for the whole of the 1963-64 season when the First Division trophy was lifted. He was sold to Tranmere Rovers for £4,500 after netting 63 goals in 381 appearances during his 11 years at Anfield. A'Court died of cancer.

ADAMS, Tony Alexander, MBE 1987-2001 ⑥⑥ ⑤

Born: Romford, Essex, 10 October 1966
Career: Arsenal (apprentice, April 1983, professional, January 1984, retired, June 2002, Wycombe Wanderers (manager, November 2003-November 2004), Feyenoord/Holland (coach, July 2005), FC Utrecht/Holland (coach, January-February 2006), Arsenal (part-time scout, season 2005-06), Portsmouth (assistant-manager/coach, June 2006, caretaker-manager, October 2008, then manager to February 2009); Gabala FC/Azerbaijan, manager-coach, May 2010-November 2011)

Tony Adams was a durable, wholehearted centre-half, totally committed who made 673 appearances for Arsenal, helping the Gunners win two First Division titles, two Premierships, the League Cup twice, the FA Cup three times and the European Cup-Winners' Cup once. As partner to Terry Butcher, he gained his first cap against Spain in Madrid in February 1987 when Gary Lineker scored all of England's goals in a 4-1 win, and thereafter remained a regular in the squad until 2001, although he was omitted from the 1990 World Cup team and given a three-month prison sentence for a drink driving offence later that same year.

Known for his lionhearted, hand on heart pre-match dressing room 'speeches' Adams was involved in a number of terrific battles with some of the game's greatest strikers and was very rarely given a tough time, although he was certainly turned inside out by Holland's Marco van Basten at Euro '88. He was forever dangerous at set pieces and his delightful flick-on for Alan Shearer's goal in the Euro '96 semi-final against Germany was something special.

Adams, in fact, scored at both ends of the field in the England-Holland international at Wembley in March 1988. He deflected Ruud Gullit's shot past Peter Shilton for a first-half equaliser and then levelled things up later on for his own team with a header from Trevor Steven's free-kick.

Adams was also the last England player to score at the 'old' Wembley Stadium when he netted the second goal in a 2-0 win over Ukraine in May 2000. This was also his first goal since scoring in the friendly against Saudi Arabia in November 1988, thus giving him the record for the longest gap between goals for England. His captaincy was also inspirational, especially under manager Terry Venables. Adams, who played in 60 internationals at Wembley – more than any other player – also starred in 18 Youth, four B and five U21 internationals. His international career at senior level spanned 13 years and 232 days (1987-2000). And in fact, Adams was the first footballer to play for England who was born after the 1966 World Cup success.

His Arsenal testimonial match helped raise £500,000 for his charity, the Sporting Chance Clinic, which was founded in September 2000, as a result of his own experiences with alcoholism and drug addiction.

Tony Adams

ADCOCK, Hugh 1929-30 ⑤ ①

Born: Coalville, Leics, 10 April 1903
Died: Coalville, 16 October 1975
Career: Coalville All Saints School, Coalville Town (1918), Loughborough Corinthians (April 1921), Leicester City (March 1923), Bristol Rovers (July 1935), Folkestone (September 1936), Ibstock Penistone Rovers (August 1938, retired May 1939), Coalville Town (trainer, mid to late 1940s), Whitwick Colliery FC (trainer/part-time manager, season 1948-49); also a licensee at Sileby, Leicestershire and later a maintenance engineer in Coalville.

Hughie Adcock was a powerhouse down the right-wing, strong and mobile, a regular goalscorer, who helped Leicester win the Second Division title in 1925. He made his England debut in a 4-1 friendly win over France in Paris in May 1929, laid on two goals in his next international 48 hours later when Belgium were battered 5-1 in Brussels and following good displays against Spain in Madrid (lost 4-3) and Ireland in Belfast (won 3-0) he scored in his last England game, a 6-0 drubbing of Wales at Stamford Bridge in November 1929. Sammy Crooks (Derby) subsequently took over on England's right-wing. Adcock, who exhibited undiminished enthusiasm for more than 30 years, made 460 appearances during his time with Leicester. His cousin was Joe Bradford, ex-Birmingham and England centre-forward.

AGBONLAHOR, Gabriel 2008-09 ③

Born: Lambeth, London, 13 December 1987
Career: Aston Villa (apprentice, June 2003, professional, March 2005), Watford (loan, September 2005), Sheffield Wednesday (loan, October-December 2005).

Blessed with speed, strength, an abundance of tricks and a powerful shot, 'Gabby' Agbonlahor was chosen to play for Nigeria against Rwanda in an U20 international on 20 September 2006 but turned down the chance, pledging his future to England for whom he gained the first of 15 U21 caps a week later v. Germany. In February 2008, he was named in Fabio Capello's full England squad for the first time but it was nine months before he won his first senior cap, also against Germany, receiving high praise from John Terry. His second cap came his way against the European champions Spain early in 2009 and since then he has been a regular member of the squad, but missed out on the 2010 World Cup finals. 'Aggers' had netted 76 goals in 296 appearances for Aston Villa up to May 2013, and is the Midland club's top scorer in the Premiership with 63.

Gabriel Agbonlahor

ALCOCK, Charles William 1874-75 ① ①

Born: Sunderland, 2 December 1842
Died: Brighton, 26 February 1907
Career: Forest School, Harrow School, Wanderers (seasons 1866-73); also Surrey; FA Committee member (1866-69, honorary secretary, 1870-86, honorary treasurer 1877, secretary 1887-95 and vice-President, April 1896-February 1907); FA Cup final referee 1875 and 1879; secretary of Surrey County Cricket Club (February 1872 until his death); also employed as a reporter/journalist for many years; formed Forest FC (Chingford, Essex) with his brother John in 1859.

Charles Alcock, the first official secretary of the Football Association, is widely regarded as being the father of the English national team. It was his letter to *The Sportsman*, a leading London newspaper dealing with football, dated 5 February 1870, which sparked off a series of five friendly matches between England and Scotland, all of which took place in England with both teams being made up of players who were resident of the home country. However, come 1872 it was agreed that a true test of the two nations' footballing ability could only be gauged if Scotland chose their players from teams north of the border.

An FA Cup winner with the Wanderers in the first-ever final of 1872, Alcock was a hard-working, forceful centre-forward who loved to run at defenders, and never worried about trying a shot at goal from any distance with either foot.

He missed the very first two official internationals between England and Scotland due to injury, but did attend the first game, acting as his country's match umpire. He finally gained his only senior cap as captain against the Scots in March 1875 when he scored England's second goal with a toe-ender from Pelham von Donop's low corner in a 2-2 draw at The Oval.

Alcock – a football, and indeed cricket man, through and through – was instrumental in creating the FA Cup competition (1871) and after retiring as a player he refereed two finals, those of 1875 and 1879. Earlier he had created the first-ever *Football Annual*, published in 1868 and also edited the *Cricket Newspaper* for almost a quarter-of-a-century as well as being editor-in-chief of *James Lillywhite's Cricketers' Annual* from 1872 to 1900. He is buried in West Norwood cemetery, London.

ALDERSON, John Thomas 1922-23 ①

Born: Crook, County Durham 28 November 1891
Died: Sunderland, 17 February 1972
Career: Crook Town (August 1908), Shildon Athletic (July 1910), Middlesbrough (amateur, July 1912), Shildon Athletic (November 1912), Newcastle United (£30, February 1913), Crystal Palace (£50, May 1919), Pontypridd (July 1924), Sheffield United (May 1925), Exeter City (May 1929, retired, injured, May 1930), Torquay United (trainer/coach, November 1930-34), Worcester City (player, September 1931), Crook Town (August 1932, retired, May 1933); became a farmer in the North-east of England.

A well-built, consistent goalkeeper, Jack Alderson's only game for England was against France in Paris in May 1923. Brought in at the last minute following the withdrawal of the West Brom number one, Hubert Pearson, he performed well in a 4-1 win. A Third Division Championship winner with Crystal Palace in 1921, he saved 11 out of 12 penalties (two in one match) for the Eagles for whom he made over 200 appearances.

ALDRIDGE, Albert James 1888-89 ②

Born: Walsall, 18 April 1864
Died: Great Barr, Birmingham, 29 May 1891
Career: Pleck Council School/Walsall, Walsall Swifts (August 1885), West Bromwich Albion (amateur, March 1886, professional, July 1886), Walsall Town Swifts (July 1888), Aston Villa (August 1889, retired through ill-health, March 1891).

An FA Cup finalist in 1887 and a winner in 1888 with Albion, Albert Aldridge was a tough-tackling, resolute and unyielding full-back. He partnered PM Walters in his first international, a 5-0 win over Scotland at Hampden Park in March 1888 and from his long downfield 'punt' John Goodall scored England's fourth goal. He was only 27 when he died.

ALLEN, Albert Arthur 1887-88 ① ③

Born: Aston, Birmingham, 7 April 1867
Died: Edgbaston, Birmingham, 13 October 1899
Career: St. Phillips FC/Aston (seasons 1882-84), Aston Villa (amateur, August 1884, professional, August 1885, retired through ill-health, May 1891)

Albert Allen, rather on the small side, was a modest and unassuming player, yet a prolific goalscorer who scored a hat-trick in his only international v. Ireland in Belfast in March 1888 when he deputised for the injured John Goodall. A live-wire poacher, two of his goals were short-range tap-ins after the Irish 'keeper had failed to clear his lines. Albert was also the scorer of Aston Villa's first hat-trick in League football against Notts County in 1889.

ALLEN, Anthony 1959-60 ③

Born: Stoke-on-Trent, 27 November 1939
Career: Broom Street School/Stoke, Wellington Road School/Hanley, Stoke Boys' Brigade FC (1954-55), Stoke City (amateur, April 1955, professional, November 1956), Bury (£10,000, October 1970), Hellenic FC/South Africa (season 1971-72), Stafford Rangers (seasons 1972-75).

A sure-footed, reliable full-back, Tony Allen made 473 appearances for Stoke, gaining a Second Division Championship winner's medal in 1963. A Youth international, he also represented his country in seven U23 matches and gained his three senior caps in the space of five weeks, October-November 1959, when, as Jimmy Armfield's replacement, he partnered Don Howe against Wales, Sweden and Northern Ireland. Tony loved to get forward and developed an excellent left-wing understanding with winger Eddie Holliday.

ALLEN, Clive Darren 1984-88 ⑤

Born: Stepney, East London, 20 May 1961
Career: Havering Schools, Essex Schools, London Schools, Queens Park Rangers (apprentice, June 1976, professional, September 1978), Arsenal (£1.23m, June 1980), Crystal Palace (£1.25m, June 1980), Queens Park Rangers (£700,000, June 1981), Tottenham Hotspur (£700,000, August 1984), Bordeaux/France (£1m, March 1988), Manchester City (£1.1m, July 1989), Chelsea (£250,000, December 1991), West Ham United (£250,000, March 1992), Millwall (£75,000, May 1995), Carlisle United (briefly, 1995); Tottenham Hotspur (Youth Development coach, August 1995; twice served as caretaker-manager, 2007 & 2008, also acted as assistant-manager, then coach at White Hart Lane); engaged as a Sky TV football analyst; played American football for London Monarchs in the NFL (Europe.)

An exceptional striker, Clive Allen scored 232 goals in 485 appearances in almost 20 years as a player, including a record 49 for Spurs in 1986-87, setting a new League Cup record with 12 goals in the process. He was also voted 'Footballer of the Year' despite finishing up on the losing side in the FA Cup final (v. Coventry City).

Besides his full caps for England, Allen also played in four Schoolboy, four Youth and three U21 internationals and represented the Football League. As a member of Bobby Robson's squad for the tour of South America in the summer of 1984, he made his senior debut as a second-half substitute in place of Tony Woodcock against Brazil (when John Barnes scored that magnificent goal) and also played against Uruguay and Chile, managing to miss three clear-cut chances against the latter country. He claimed his last two caps in 1987 and 1988 against Turkey (when he had a goal disallowed) and Israel, being replaced in both games.

Allen failed to make a single League or Cup appearance for Arsenal (only three friendly outings) and left Highbury for Crystal Palace within a fortnight! At the time of his transfer to QPR (1980), the fee involved was the highest any British club had paid for a teenager.

Allen's father, Les, was a member of the legendary Tottenham team which clinched the League and FA Cup double in 1961 (the Cup success occurring exactly two weeks before Allen junior's birth). He is also the brother of former player Bradley Allen and cousin of Football League manager Martin Allen and the much-travelled midfielder Paul Allen while his son, Oliver, assisted Stevenage Borough.

Allen holds the unique distinction of playing for more London based football clubs than any other footballer in history.

ALLEN, Henry 1887-90 ⑤

Born: Walsall, 19 January 1866
Died: Wolverhampton, 23 February 1895
Career: Walsall Town Swifts (April 1883), Wolverhampton Wanderers (professional, August 1886, retired, injured, October 1894); became a coal merchant and later a Wolverhampton-based licensee.

An FA Cup runner-up with Wolves in 1889 and a winner in 1893 (his superb goal beat Everton at Fallowfield) Harry Allen was a solid, unflagging defender, a demanding captain whose heading ability was first-class. With so many excellent centre-halves around at the same time, he shared the centre-half spot in the national team with West Bromwich Albion's Charlie Perry and Johnny Holt of Everton. England scored 18 goals and conceded six when Allen was in the side.

ALLEN, James Phillips 1933-34 ②

Born: Poole, Dorset, 16 October 1909
Died: Portsmouth, 1 February 1995
Career: Longfleet St Mary's School/Poole, Poole Central (1926), Poole Town (August 1927), Portsmouth (£1,200, July 1932), Aston Villa (£10,775, June 1934, retired, injured, May 1944); guested for Birmingham, Chelsea, Crystal Palace, Fulham, Luton Town, Portsmouth and Southampton during WW2; Aston Villa (colts' coach, September 1946), Colchester United (manager, July 1948-April 1953); also employed as Sports & Welfare officer at Gaskell & Chambers, before becoming a licensee in Southsea.

An FA Cup finalist in 1934 and a Second Division Championship winner in 1938, Jimmy Allen was a big, strong and thoroughly sporting centre-half, a real 'stopper' who made 160 appearances for Aston Villa. He partnered Alf Strange of Sheffield Wednesday in the England defence in his two internationals, having an excellent debut in a 3-0 win over Ireland at Windsor Park, although he was given a testing time by the Welsh front three in his second outing at Newcastle a month later. He also represented the Football League and as manager guided Colchester into the Football League.

ALLEN, Ronald 1951-55 ⑤ ②

Born: Fenton, Stoke-on-Trent, 15 January 1929
Died: Great Wyrley, Walsall, 9 June 2001
Career: Hanley High School/Stoke, Bucknall Boys' Brigade FC, Wellington Scouts, Staffs County Youths (rugby union, 1941-42), Northwood Mission (August 1942), Port Vale (amateur, March 1944, professional, March 1946), West Bromwich Albion (£20,050, March 1950), Crystal Palace £4,500, player-coach, May 1961, retired as a player, May 1965); Wolverhampton Wanderers (coach, July 1965, manager, January 1966-November 1968), Athletic Bilbao/Spain (manager, March 1969-November 1971), Sporting Lisbon/Portugal (manager, April 1972-May 1973), Saudi Arabia (coach, briefly, mid-1973), Walsall (manager, June-December 1973), West Bromwich Albion (scouting advisor, January-June 1977, manager, June-December 1977), Saudi Arabia (national team coach, December 1977), Panathinaikos/Greece (coach/manager, June-September 1980), West Bromwich Albion (manager, July 1981-May 1982, then general manager to May 1983; later returned to club as part-time coach, 1990-95); also sales director of Black Country engineering company, specializing in oil rigs.

Ronnie Allen played in all five forward positions during an excellent career which saw him score 276 goals in 637 matches, including an Albion record of 234 in 415 outings. He netted twice in the 1954 FA Cup final and actually played his last game of football, as a substitute, for WBA in a friendly against Cheltenham in 1995, aged 66.

He won his first full cap at outside-right against Switzerland in Zurich in May 1952, when Tom Finney switched to the left. He gave a lively performance in a 3-0 win. Playing his other four games at centre-forward, he scored, along with his Albion team-mate Johnny Nicholls in a 4-2 win over Scotland at Hampden Park in April 1954 and following some fine combination work between Len Shackleton and Tom Finney, he netted with a crisp right-footed half volley in a 3-1 victory over the reigning World Champions West Germany at Wembley eight months later. After an excellent season with West Bromwich Albion, Allen was named as an England 'possible' ahead of the 1954 World Cup in Switzerland. Unfortunately he didn't make the final squad of 17, Nat Lofthouse and Tommy Taylor being preferred ahead of him by manager Walter Winterbottom. Besides his five full caps, Allen played once for England B and he also represented the Football League and the FA XI. He was 72 when he died in the Hardwick Court Nursing Home, Great Wyrley.

ALSFORD, Walter John 1934-35 ①

Born: Edmonton, London, 6 November 1911
Died: Bedford, 3 June 1968
Career: Edmonton Schools, London Schools, Tottenham Hotspur (amateur, May 1929); played briefly for Northfleet (two spells) and Cheshunt; Tottenham Hotspur (professional, August 1930), Nottingham Forest (January 1937-May 1938); later served as a guest for Aldershot, Arsenal, Nottingham Forest and Doncaster Rovers during WW2; later a licensee in Nottingham, Brighton and Bedford.

A stylish wing-half and fine passer of the ball, steady and controlled, Walter Alsford made 100 appearances for Spurs but for all his efforts won only one cap, replacing Wilf Copping in a 2-0 defeat by Scotland at Hampden Park in front of 129,613 spectators. Unfortunately it was Jackie Bray of Manchester City who clinched the vacant left-half position in the end.

AMOS, Andrew Reverend 1884-86 ② ①

Born: Southwark, London, 20 September 1863
Died: Rotherhithe, London, 2 October 1931
Career: Charterhouse School (1882-83), Clare College/Cambridge (seasons 1883-86), Old Carthusians (mid-1880s), Hitchin Town (briefly), Corinthians (seasons 1885-90), Hertfordshire (1880s); ordained in 1887, he was the Minister in South East London from 1889, being Rector of Rotherhithe from 1922 until his death in 1931; also served as an Alderman on the Bermondsey Borough Council.

An efficient half-back, good in the air, Andrew Amos was a smart passer of the ball who gave excellent service to his forwards. He won his first cap against Scotland at The Oval (1-1) and his second against Wales at Wrexham a year later, scoring an excellent goal in a 3-1 win.

ANDERSON, Rupert Darnley, OBE 1878-79 ①

Born: Liverpool, 29 April 1859
Died: Stafford, 23 December 1944
Career: Eton College (season 1878-79), Trinity Hall/Cambridge University (seasons 1879-83), Old Etonians (seasons 1878-81); an orange planter in Florida for many years, he also lived in Farnham and Staffordshire and was awarded the OBE for his services in the Territorial Army and RAF during the 1914-18 War.

Although gaining his only cap as a late replacement for injured goalkeeper, the Reverend Blackmore, Rupert Anderson did very well in a hard-earned 2-1 win over Wales at The Oval. His true position was that of a hard-shooting, attacking inside-forward and he scored plenty of goals at university level. Unfortunately he missed Old Etonians' 1879 FA Cup final victory through injury.

ANDERSON, Stanley 1961-62 ②

Born: Horden, County Durham, 27 February 1933
Career: Horden Colliery Welfare (1947), Springwell United (1948), Sunderland (amateur, June 1949, professional, February 1951), Newcastle United (£19,000, November 1963), Middlesbrough (£11,500, player-coach, November 1965, manager, April 1966), AEK Athens/Greece (coach, January 1973), Panathinaikos/Greece (coach, May 1974), Queens Park Rangers (assistant-coach, May 1974, then assistant-manager, June-November 1974), Manchester City (scout, December 1974), Doncaster Rovers (manager, February 1975), Bolton Wanderers (coach, November 1978, manager, February 1980-May 1981); thereafter an occasional scout in the North-East of England, mainly for Newcastle United.

Stan Anderson was a cultured, whole-hearted wing-half who amassed over 600 appearances for the three North-east clubs, gaining a Second Division Championship medal with Newcastle in 1965. Capped at Schoolboy and Youth team levels, he also played in four U23 internationals, being sent off against Bulgaria in 1957. His two senior outings for England came in the 3-1 home win over Austria when he replaced Bobby Robson, and a 2-0 defeat by Scotland, both games ahead of the World Cup finals. He was taken to Chile by Walter Winterbottom as reserve to Bobby Moore, Robson, Ron Clayton and Ron Flowers.

ANDERSON, Vivian Alexander, MBE 1978-87 ③⓪ ②
Born: Nottingham, 29 August 1956
Career: Fairham Comprehensive School/Nottingham, Manchester United (trial, May-June 1971), Nottingham Forest (apprentice, November 1972, professional, August 1974), Arsenal (£250,000, July 1984), Manchester United (£250,000, July 1987), Sheffield Wednesday (free, January 1991), Barnsley (free, player-manager, July 1993), Middlesbrough (assistant-manager, May 1994-July 2001); inducted into the English Football Hall of Fame in 2004 in recognition of his impact on the English League; later ran a sports travel agency; was a goodwill ambassador for the Football Association and now runs a sport media business with former Nottingham Forest and England team-mate Tony Woodcock.

Viv Anderson was the first black player to win a full England cap, doing so on a frozen Wembley pitch against Czechoslovakia in November 1978....and he played a prominent part in the game's only goal, scored by Steve Coppell in the 68th minute. An attacking right-back, full of endeavour, Anderson eventually took over from Phil Neal to form a fine partnership with Kenny Sansom.

He didn't play in the 1986 World Cup finals, but returned soon afterwards to score in the 2-0 European Championship qualifying victory over Yugoslavia at Wembley. Unfortunately a leg injury ended his international career. Besides his senior caps, he also represented his country in one U21 and seven B internationals.

Anderson made 768 appearances for his six League clubs, including 430 for Forest. He gained a First Division, two European Cup, European Super Cup and League Cup winner's medals during a wonderful career. Anderson received his MBE in January 2000.

Said Anderson after his first England game in 1978: "Whether you are white, brown, purple or blue, it's the same. When you are fortunate enough to make an England debut at Wembley, it's the greatest feeling in the world!"

ANDERTON, Darren Robert 1994-2002 ③⓪ ⑦
Born: Southampton, 3 March 1972
Career: Itchen Saints (1986), Portsmouth (apprentice, April 1988, professional, April 1988), Tottenham Hotspur (£1.75m, June 1992), Birmingham City (free, August, 2004), Wolverhampton Wanderers (free, August, 2005), Bournemouth (free, September 2006, retired, December 2008).

A strong, well-built utility forward who preferred to raid down the flanks, Darren Anderton, who was nicknamed 'Sick note' and 'Shaggy' gained Youth honours as a junior before going on to add one B and 12 U21 caps to those he won at senior level, gained over an eight-year period.

He made his full England debut in a 1-0 win over Denmark in March 1994 (Terry Venables' first game in charge) and scored a brilliant goal in his second outing in a 5-0 win over Greece at Wembley two months later. On the night, the Greeks had no answer to Anderton's pace and skill down the right flank and he had a hand in two of the other four goals.

A key member of England's Euro '96 team, he also played in all five matches in the 1998 World Cup finals in France and but for injuries would have surely won more caps at senior level. He was actually capped by six different England managers. Anderton netted 79 goals in 563 club appearances (all competitions). His scored a brilliant winning goal in his last match for Bournemouth against Chester City.

ANGUS, John 1960-61 ①
Born: Amble, Northumberland, 2 September 1938
Career: Amble Boy's Club (seasons 1952-54), Burnley (amateur, April 1954, professional, September 1955, retired, May 1972); later ran a sea-front café at Amble before working as a maintenance engineer in his native town.

John Angus was an adventurous, hard-tackling full-back who gained his only cap, behind his Burnley team-mate Brian Miller, against Austria in Vienna in May 1961. Called in to replace Middlesbrough's Mick McNeill who withdrew through injury, he lacked confidence at times as the Austrians eased to a 3-1 win. A one club man, Angus made 521 appearances for the Clarets whom he served for 18 years, gaining a League Championship medal in 1960, followed by a FA Cup runner's-up medal two years later. He was also a very good county golfer with a handicap of 8.

ARMFIELD, James Christopher, CBE, DL, OBE 1958-66 ㊸
Born: Denton, Lancs, 21 September 1935
Career: Rovoe Junior and Arnold Grammar Schools/Blackpool, St. Peter's and Highfield Youth Clubs/Blackpool, Blackpool (amateur, May 1952, professional, September 1954, player-coach, February-May 1971), Bolton Wanderers (manager, May 1971-October 1974), Leeds United (manager, October 1974-August 1978); appointed Head of FA Coaching Department; later a journalist and respected broadcaster after leaving Elland Road.

'Gentleman Jim' Armfield was one of the first over-lapping full-backs in the Football League and probably on the international circuit as well. Solidly built and quick over the ground, he exhibited a firm tackle, he made his international debut as Don Howe's partner against Brazil in front of 160,000 fans in the giant Maracana Stadium in Rio on England's tour to South America at the end of the 1958-59 season. Playing out of position, he had a tough time against the reigning World Cup holders, tricky winger Julinho causing him problems all through the game.

He later replaced Howe at right-back and held that position until George Cohen came along in 1964. On his own admittance, his worst England performance was against France in February 1963 (Alf Ramsey's first game in charge) when the visitors won 5-2.

Darren Anderton

"I couldn't do a thing right" he said. Another poor show came against Scotland at Wembley two months later when he 'gifted' the first goal to Jim Baxter in a 2-1 defeat.

"I was castigated by Gordon Banks for passing across the penalty-area" said Armfield.

In the 3-0 defeat by Spain in Madrid in May 1960, Armfield played 'magnificently' to control Gento. In the end the team ran out of steam as the Spaniards scored twice late on to clinch a hollow victory.

The recipient of nine U23 caps and a Football League representative, Armfield made 627 appearances for Blackpool, won the Third Division Championship as Bolton's manager in 1973 and

guided Leeds to the European Cup final in 1975. He was awarded the CBE on January 2000, made a Freeman of Blackpool in the summer of 2003, became a High Sheriff of Lancashire in May 2005 and received with the OBE in 2010.

Armfield was guest of honour at the 2012 FA Cup final and duly presented the trophy to Chelsea's winning captain, John Terry.

ARMITAGE, George Henry 1925-26 ①
Born: Stoke Newington, 17 January 1898
Died: Aylesford, Kent, 28 August 1936
Career: Wordsworth Road School, Hackney/London, Wimbledon (briefly, season 1923-24), Charlton Athletic (amateur, March 1924), Leyton (January 1931, retired May 1933; joined club's committee).

George Armitage was a fine, dominating defender who won five caps as an amateur before appearing for the senior side against Ireland in October 1925. Chosen at a time when the centre-half position was causing some concern, he was, in fact, the seventh different player to be selected as pivot in seven internationals over a period of 18 months. He made 182 appearances for Charlton, gaining a Third Division Championship winner's medal in 1929. A tuberculosis victim and a patient at Preston Hall Sanatorium near Maidstone, Armitage was only 38 when he died, his body being found on the railway lines at Aylesford.

ARMSTRONG, David 1979-84 ③
Born: Durham, 26 December 1954
Career: Middlesbrough (amateur, September 1968, apprentice, July 1970, professional, January 1972), Southampton (August 1981), Sheffield Wednesday (July 1987), AFC Bournemouth (August 1987), Netley Central Sports (coach, July 1989), Andover Town (commercial manager, January 1991, manager, February-April 1991, combining both jobs), AFC Bournemouth (community officer, July 1991); later Waterlooville FC (general manager), Reading (Community officer); also sports liaison officer for Hampshire Schools and an occasional radio reporter covering Saints' games.

A naturally left-sided player with a terrific engine and good ball skills, David Armstrong gained the first of his three caps against Australia in Sydney in May 1980 at a time when manager Ron Greenwood was switching his team around ahead of the European Championships.

He was substituted in all of his three internationals. The recipient of four U21 and two England B caps, Armstrong scored 73 goals in 416 games for Middlesbrough and 80 in 289 for Southampton. He holds the Boro' record for most consecutive appearances with 305 in the League and 358 in all competitions between March 1972 and August 1980. He was awarded a testimonial at the age of 25.

ARMSTRONG, Kenneth 1954-55 ①
Born: Bradford, 3 June 1924
Died: New Zealand, 15 June 1984
Career: Bradford Rovers (August 1939), Army football (1943-46), Chelsea (professional, December 1946-May 1957); emigrated to New Zealand where he played, in turn, for Eastern Union FC, North Shore United and Gisborne, retiring in May 1965); later elected chief coach of the country's FA.

A League Championship winner with Chelsea in 1955, Ken Armstrong was a tenacious yet constructive right-half, consistent and durable who skippered the Blues on several occasions while making 402 appearances. His only cap came in the 7-2 win over Scotland at Wembley in April 1955 when he partnered Duncan Edwards in midfield.

The Glasgow Herald reporter wrote: "McMillan, the Scottish inside-left, had a poor game against the tight-marking and very effective Armstrong who made a first-class debut in international football." Armstrong also played in three B internationals, represented the Football League and gained 14 caps for New Zealand between 1958 and 1963. And following his death, at the age of 60, his ashes were flown back to London and scattered over the Stamford Bridge pitch.

ARNOLD, John 1932-33 ①
Born: Cowley, Oxford, 30 November 1907
Died: Southampton, 3 April 1984
Career: Cowley Elementary, Oxford Schools, Oxford City (seasons 1925-28), Southampton (professional, September 1928), Fulham (February 1933, retired May 1945); Southampton (guest during WW2); also an England Test cricketer v. New Zealand in 1931; he played for Oxfordshire and Hampshire Counties and on retiring in 1950, had scored 21,831 runs in 396 matches for Hants, including 37 centuries. He became a first-class umpire in 1961 and stood by the wickets until 1982. He was also licensee of the Criterion Pub in St Mary's, Southampton for several years.

A natural left-footer, stocky, mobile and assertive, Johnny Arnold played superbly on the left-wing in an international trial before winning his only cap in a 2-1 defeat by Scotland in front of 134,810 fans at Hampden Park in April 1933. Unfortunately, said wrote reporter, "He made a far from memorable debut, missing two easy chances from close range, both shots going wide of the posts." He scored 63 goals in 213 games for Fulham and 46 in 110 for Southampton.

ARTHUR, William John Herbert 1884-87 ⑦
Born: Blackburn 14 February 1863
Died: Blackburn, 27 November 1930
Career: Lower Bank Academy/Blackburn (seasons 1877-79), King's Own (season 1879-80), Blackburn Rovers (August 1880), Southport Central (May 1890), Blackburn Rovers (season 1891-92); later worked as a commercial traveller

Initially a wing-half and an amateur throughout his career 'Herbie' Arthur developed into an exceptionally fine goalkeeper – the first international 'keeper in Blackburn's history. There was a little flamboyance about his style, often leaping through the air to keep his goal in tact. He conceded only four goals in seven international appearances, producing a brilliant display to keep out the Welsh in England's 3-1 victory at Wrexham in March 1886. He gained three FA Cup winner's medals with Blackburn in the mid-1880s and represented Lancashire in several county matches.

ASHCROFT, James 1905-06 ③
Born: Liverpool, 12 September 1878
Died: Birkenhead, 9 April 1943
Career: Wilsby's United (season 1893-94), Anfield Recreationalists (seasons 1894-96), Garston Copper Works (1896), Liverpool (trial, 1897), Everton (amateur, season 1898-99), Gravesend United (August 1899), Woolwich Arsenal (June 1900), Blackburn Rovers (May 1908), Tranmere Rovers (May 1913, retired, May 1915).

Jimmy Ashcroft was a goalkeeper who made difficult saves look easy. A safe handler of the ball, good with both high and low shots, he played in all three Home international matches at the end of the 1905-06 season before losing his place to Liverpool's Sam Hardy. He hardly had a save to make on his debut in a 5-0 win over Ireland in Belfast in February 1906, produced three terrific saves in the 1-0 victory over Wales, but he was certainly at fault for Scotland's first goal in their 2-1 win in his third game. He safely gathered a rising shot from Howie, but as he attempted to throw the ball out to a colleague, he stepped back over his the line and conceded an own-goal. *The Times* reporter stated "The incident rather damaged his reputation."
   Ashcroft made 303 appearances for Arsenal and 129 for Blackburn, and was also unlucky to lose in three FA Cup semi-finals, two with the Gunners and one with Rovers.

ASHMORE, George Samuel Austin 1925-26 ①
Born: Plymouth, 5 May 1898
Died: Handsworth, Birmingham, 19 May 1973
Career: Plymouth Schools (aged 13), Nineveh Wesley FC/Birmingham (from 1913), West Bromwich Albion (professional, November 1919), Chesterfield (October 1931, retired, May 1935); later worked for the MEB in Birmingham for over 25 years.

An agile goalkeeper, alert and confident, George 'Cap' Ashmore was the fifth goalkeeper used by England in successive matches when he made his debut in a 5-3 win over Belgium in Antwerp in May 1926. He amassed 268 appearances for Albion and over 75 for Chesterfield.

ASHTON, Claude Thesiger 1925-26 ①
Born: Calcutta, India, 19 February 1901
Died: Caernarvon, Wales, 31 October 1942
Career: Winchester College (years, 1918-20), Trinity College/Cambridge University (1921-23), Corinthians (seasons 1920-25), Old Wykehamists (season 1921-22); a Cambridge 'Blue' at football, cricket and hockey, he also played for Essex CCC and after retiring from football in 1933, joined Beckenham Hockey club and later played in England trials. A chartered accountant by profession, he was later on the stock exchange.

Capped by England 12 times as an amateur, mainly as a wing-half, Claude Ashton won his only full cap as a centre-forward in the 0-0 draw with Ireland in Belfast in October 1925 when he didn't have the greatest of games, missing two chances, the first from Syd Puddefoot's cross and the second after Aston Villa's Billy Walker had sent him clean through on goal. Ashton appeared in every position for the Corinthians, even in goal. He was strong at dribbling, possessed a powerful shot but was said to be weak at heading. He was killed in a flying accident whilst serving with the RAF.

ASHTON, Dean 2007-08 ①
Born: Crewe, 24 November 1983
Career: Stoke City (youth team, season 1998-99), Crewe Alexandra (apprentice, May 1999, professional, November 2000), Norwich City (£3m, January 2005), West Ham United (£7.25m, January 2006, retired, injured, December 2009); now out of football, living in Norwich.

An injury-prone 6ft 1in striker, strong and willing, Dean Ashton progressed through the England Youth set up, racking up an impressive goal-to-game ratio. In August 2006, he was first called into the full senior squad for the friendly against Greece. However, during a training session 24 hours before the match, he was involved in a heavy tackle with Shaun Wright-Phillips and broke an ankle. Ruled out for over a year, he missed the whole of the 2006-07 campaign. Then, a few days before an international with Estonia, he was injured again, sidelined this time for six weeks with a sprained medial knee ligament. Finally, in May 2008, Ashton made his long-awaited England debut, more than two years after his first call up, in the friendly against Trinidad & Tobago, under new manager Fabio Capello. Sadly though, a year later the unlucky Ashton announced his retirement from competitive football due to a persisting ankle problem. He scored 111 goals in 280 club appearances.
   In January 2011, West Ham, seeking compensation for Ashton, prepared a writ against the FA for £10.5m.

ASHURST, William 1922-25 ⑤
Born: Willington, County Durham, 4 May 1894
Died: Nottingham, 26 January 1947
Career: Willington Council School, Durham City (July 1914), Leeds City (July 1919), Lincoln City (£500, October 1919), Notts County (£1,000, June 1920), West Bromwich Albion (£2,500, November 1926, also acted as club coach), Newark Town (August 1928), Bestwood Colliery FC (June 1929, retired, May 1930); later worked as a machine operator in Nottingham.

A dour, relentless, crisp-tackling defender, Billy Ashurst was one of six different right-backs used by England between May 1923 and May 1925, when he also had four different partners in five outings. He made 222 appearances for Notts County, helping them win the Second Division Championship in 1923. His brother Elias played for Birmingham in the 1920s.

ASTALL, Gordon 1955-56 ② ②
Born: Horwich, Lancs, 22 September 1927
Career: Bolton Wanderers (trial, aged 14), Royal Marines (1943), Southampton (amateur, July 1945), Bolton Wanderers (second trial, 1946), Plymouth Argyle (professional, November 1947), Birmingham City (£14,000, October 1953), Torquay United (July 1961, retired, May 1963); Upton Vale/Devon (coach, late 1960s/early 70s); also worked for insurance company in Devon; lives in Torquay.

Sturdy in build, difficult to stop when in full flow, Gordon Astall's two caps came on England's end-of-season tour in May 1956 against Finland and West Germany when regular wingers Stan Matthews and Tom Finney did not travel….and he scored in each game. He also played in one B international and twice for the Football League. A Third Division (South) winner with Plymouth (1952), Astall helped Blues win the Second Division (1955) and reach the finals of the FA Cup and Fairs Cup (1956 and 1958 respectively). He netted over 100 goals in a fine career and at 2012 was one of England's oldest former players.

ASTLE, Jeffrey 1968-70 Ⓢ

Born: Eastwood, Nottingham, 13 May 1942
Died: Netherseal, Burton-on-Trent, 19 January 2002
Career: Devonshire Drive Junior and Walker Street Secondary Modern Schools/Nottingham, West Notts Juniors, Holy Trinity Youth Club, Notts County (trial, 1956), Coventry City (trial 1956), John Player FC/Nottingham, Notts County (amateur, May 1957, professional, July 1960), West Bromwich Albion (£25,000, September 1964) Hellenic FC/South Africa (May 1974), Dunstable Town (July 1974), Weymouth (£15,000, July 1975), Atherstone Town (October 1976), Hillingdon Borough (loan, February-May 1977 when he retired); later ran his own industrial window cleaning business, appeared regularly on the TV programme *Fantasy Football* (with Frank Skinner and David Baddiel and went into variety with his own 'Roadshow'.

Known as 'The King' at West Bromwich Albion, Jeff Astle scored 174 goals in 361 games for the Baggies, helping them win the League Cup in 1966 and the FA Cup two years later. Blessed with great heading ability, he was no slouch on the floor, although he did miss a great chance to equalise in a 1970 World Cup group game against Brazil, firing high and wide from a good position. "How did you miss?" agonised Alan Ball as he sat by the pool next morning at the Guadalajara Hilton.

Earlier in the game, Jeff had nodded a cross down for Ball but he threw away the chance with a casual shot.

Although a talismanic striker at The Hawthorns, he never adapted to international football, simply because his club (Albion) played a completely different style of football. Capped for the first time against Wales in May 1969, he was 'lively' throughout and after his drive had been cleared off the line, Francis Lee fired in the rebound for a 2-1 win.

However, with so many other good strikers around including Geoff Hurst, Mick Jones, Peter Osgood and even Bobby Charlton, Astle was always fighting for a place in the team. Besides his full caps, he also played for an England XI and the Football League, and was voted 'Midland Footballer of the Year' in 1968 before becoming the first player to score in both a League Cup final and FA Cup final at Wembley.

A surgeon said that Astle died from 'footballer's migraine, caused by repeatedly heading the ball.'

ASTON, John 1948-51 ⑰

Born: Prestwich, Manchester, 3 September 1921
Died: Manchester, 31 July 2003
Career: Ravensbury Street School, Crossley Lads (1935), Clayton Methodists (1936), Royal Marines (aged 15), Mujacs FC (1937), Manchester United (amateur, January 1938, professional, December 1939); guest for Hamilton Academical, Hyde United, Plymouth Argyle and Portsmouth during WW2; retired as a player, May 1954, became junior coach at Old Trafford, later chief scout (August 1970-December 1972).

A former Marine commando, Johnny Aston won the FA Cup (1948) and the First Division Championship (1952) with Manchester United. Able to occupy both full-back positions and also the centre-forward berth, such was his adaptability, he was a whole-hearted footballer who scored 30 goals in 282 appearances for the Reds. Taking over from George Hardwick, he made his international debut against Denmark in September 1948 and played in the 1950 World Cup finals in Brazil, including that horrendous defeat by the USA. In fact, he was one of three defenders who hesitated inside the penalty-area before the crucial goal was scored and was dropped for the last game against Spain!

ATHERSMITH, William Charles Harper 1891-1900 ⑫ ③

Born: Bloxwich, Staffs, 10 May 1872
Died: Shifnal, Shropshire, 18 September 1910
Career: Walsall Road Council School/Bloxwich, Bloxwich Wanderers (1887), Bloxwich Strollers (1888), Unity Gas Works (1890), Saltley FC (briefly), Aston Villa (February 1891), Birmingham (June 1901-May 1905), Bloxwich Strollers (August 1906, retired May 1907); Grimsby Town (trainer, June 1907-May 1909); was also involved in an unsanctioned Tagg & Campbell tour to Germany in 1905 for which he was suspended for one year.

The recipient of four League Championship and two FA Cup winner's medals with Aston Villa for whom he scored 86 goals in 311 appearances, Charlie Athersmith was one of the fastest wingers in the game in the 1890s. He centred the ball with unerring precision, was clever, witty and packed a powerful shot, a superb outside-right who contested that outside-right position in the England team for almost a decade with West Bromwich Albion's wizard Billy Bassett. In fact, if Bassett had played in a different era then one suspects that Athersmith would have won far more caps than he did. He was brilliant when Ireland were thrashed 13-2 in February 1899, having a hand in six of the goals. He also played nine times for the Football League.

ATYEO, Peter John Walter 1955-57 ⑥ Ⓢ

Born: Dilton Marsh, Wiltshire, 7 February 1932
Died: Bristol, 16 June 1993
Career: Dilton Junior & Trowbridge High Schools, Westbury United (1949), Portsmouth (amateur, season 1950-51), Bristol City (professional, June 1951, retired, May 1966); a qualified teacher, he continued to teach at Warminster School for several years.

A Third Division (S) winner with Bristol City in 1955, John Atyeo, not all that skilful, was a superb marksman with an enviable physique who scored 359 goals in 656 appearances in 15 years at Ashton Gate. Gaining his six caps (November 1955-May 19570, he netted on his debut, after a brilliant seven-man, 10 pass move, in a 4-1 win over Spain at Wembley when partnering Tom Finney on the right-wing, but a year later, in a 4-2 win over Brazil, he missed a second-half penalty, as did Roger Byrne. If Atyeo had been with a bigger club, he would surely have gained more honours as he never let England down - his goal tally proves this. And the brace he netted against the Republic of Ireland in a World Cup qualifier in May 1957, when Manchester United's Tommy Taylor joined him up front, were splendid efforts.

AUSTIN, Sydney William 1925-26 ①

Born: Arnold, Nottinghamshire, 29 April 1900
Died: Kidderminster, 2 April 1979
Career: Arnold United (season 1918-19), Sheffield United (August 1919), Arnold St Mary's (October 1919), Norwich City (October 1920), Manchester City (May 1924), Chesterfield (December 1931), Kidderminster Harriers (seasons 1932-36).

A fast-raiding winger with a 'clinking shot' Billy Austin scored regularly throughout his career, ending with almost 100 goals to his name in more than 350 club appearances. He played in the 1928 FA Cup final for Manchester City and gained his only England cap against Ireland in Belfast in October 1925, at a time when the outside-right position was causing some concern, six different players having been used in the previous nine internationals.

BACH, Philip 1898-99 ①

Born: Ludlow, Shropshire, 9 September 1872
Died: Middlesbrough, 30 December 1937
Career: Middlesbrough Juniors (1886), Middlesbrough (1887), Reading (May 1895), Sunderland (June 1897), Bristol City (May 1900, retired, May 1904); Middlesbrough (director, February 1911, chairman, July 1911-May 1925 and again from August 1931 to May 1935), FA Councillor (1925-37), FA Selection committee member (October 1929 until his death); also served on the Football League management Committee; was a hotel proprietor in Cheltenham and then Middlesbrough.

Phil Bach was a consistent right-back, sound rather than brilliant who made only 46 League appearances in seven years (1897-1904) but was good enough to play for England on his own pitch at Sunderland in February 1899 when he assisted in two of the goals in a record 13-2 win over Ireland.

BACHE, Joseph William 1902-11 ⑦ ④

Born: Stourbridge, 8 February 1880
Died: Aston, Birmingham, 10 November 1960
Career: Bewdley Victoria (1895), Stourbridge (July 1897), Aston Villa (professional, December 1900), Notts County (guest, 1915-16), Mid-Rhondda (player-manager, July 1919), Grimsby Town (player-coach, July 1920), Rot-Weiss FC Frankfurt/Germany (coach-trainer, May 1921-April 1927), Aston Villa (reserve team coach, July 1927), Mannheim FC/Germany (coach, July 1928), Rot-Weiss FC Frankfurt (coach, August 1929-May 1930); later hospital clerical worker, licensee and manager of gent's outfitters shop

Joe Bache was a cultured inside or outside-left who had few equals in the art of dribbling, although at times he could be rather selfish! An England international trialist in 1902, due to the enormous talent of players available for selection, he gained his first and last caps eight years apart, scoring in his first matches, against Wales (twice), Ireland and Scotland. He netted 184 goals in 474 appearances during his 19 years with Aston Villa, collecting a League Championship and two FA Cup winner's medals in the process.

BADDELEY, Thomas 1902-04 ⑤

Born: Bycars, Stoke-on-Trent, 2 November 1874
Died: Hartshill, Stoke-on-Trent, 24 September 1946
Career: Bycars Juniors (1888), Burslem Swifts (professional, August 1890), Burslem Port Vale (September 1893), Wolverhampton Wanderers (£50, October 1896), Bradford Park Avenue (May 1907), Stoke (March-April 1910), Whitfield Colliery FC (September 1910, retired, early 1911)

Goalkeeper Tom Baddeley, only 5ft 9ins tall, had outstanding ability. Quite brilliant at closing down opponents, he was a fine shot-stopper who could throw a ball, right-handed, well over the halfway line. One of several exceptionally fine 'keepers eager to represent England in the early 1900s, he was outstanding on his debut in a 4-0 win over Ireland in February 1903 but surprisingly won only five caps. Baddeley also represented the Football League and during his career amassed a total of 367 League appearances.
   Three of Baddeley's brothers were also professional footballers.

BAGSHAW, John James 1919-20 ①

Born: Derby, 25 December 1885
Died: Nottingham, 25 August 1966
Career: Graham Street Primitives/Derby (1903), Fletcher's Athletic/Derby (1904), Derby County (August 1906), Notts County (WW1 guest, signed permanently for £500, February 1920), Watford (£200, July 1921), Ilkeston United (August 1922), Grantham (July 1924, retired May 1925); later Nottingham Forest (trainer, during WW2); then scout for Notts County, Coventry City and Nottingham Forest; also worked in the lace trade and for Raleigh Industries, Nottingham.

A centre or wing-half, perceptive, hard-working, quick over the ground, sound in distribution and tackling, Jim Bagshaw's only England cap came against Ireland in Belfast in October 1919 when most players were still regaining full fitness after the war. He also played in a Victory international against Wales a week before, and twice helped Derby win the Second Division Championship (1912 and 1915).

BAILEY, Gary Richard 1984-85 ②

Born: Ipswich, 9 August 1958
Career: Witts University/South Africa (seasons 1974-77), Manchester United (professional, January 1978-September 1987), Kaiser Chiefs/South Africa (seasons 1988-90); now presenter of South African TV's version of Match of the Day and was an ambassador in that country's successful bid to host the 2010 World Cup

Gary Bailey, the son of the former Ipswich Town goalkeeper Roy Bailey, was effectively reserve to Peter Shilton in the international pecking order. He gained his two caps against the Republic of Ireland at Wembley in March 1985 (won 2-1, although his error led to Liam Brady scoring) and versus Mexico in South America three months later (lost 1-0). Tall and agile, he made 373 appearances during his time at Old Trafford, helping United win the FA Cup in 1983 and 1985. He also played for England at U21 and B team levels and in fact, will be remembered for playing up until what seemed like his thirties in the U21 side. He won the nickname 'Dracula' due to his inability to deal with crosses.

Gary Bailey

BAILEY, Horace Peter 1907-08 ⑤

Born: Derby, 3 July 1881
Died: Biggleswade, 1 August 1960
Career: Derby County (September 1899), Ripley Athletic (August 1903), Leicester Imperial (September 1905), Leicester Fosse (January 1907), Derby County (April 1909), Birmingham (September 1910, retired, June 1913); later employed as a rating officer for the Midland Railway Company, based in Derby

An exceptionally agile, bold and confident goalkeeper with massive hands, Horace Bailey won eight amateur caps (1908-13) as well as his senior caps. As deputy for Sam Hardy, he had virtually nothing to do during his five major internationals (his last four were on tour to Bohemia in 1908) as England scored a total of 35 goals while Bailey conceded just three. Unfortunately he was Leicester's 'keeper when Nottingham Forest won 12-0 in a League game in 1908.

BAILEY, Michael Alfred 1963-66 ⑤

Born: Wisbech, 27 February 1942
Career: Precasters FC/Gorleston (1955), Gorleston Juniors (1956), Charlton Athletic (amateur, May 1957, professional, March 1959), Wolverhampton Wanderers (£40,000, February 1966-January 1977), Minnesota Kicks/USA (£15,000, player/assistant-coach, June 1977-May 1978), Hereford United (player-manager, June 1978-October 1979), Charlton Athletic (chief scout, October 1979, manager, March 1980-June 1981), Brighton & Hove Albion (manager, June 1981-December 1982), OFI Crete/Greece (coach, briefly in season 1983-84), Bexley FC (player-manager, seasons 1985-86), New Valley FC (co-manager with Ken Hunt, season 1987-88), Fisher Athletic (manager, November 1989-January 1991), Portsmouth (reserve team manager-coach, seasons 1991-93); also served as a scout for Blackburn Rovers, Derby County, Everton and Newcastle United.

Full of drive and enthusiasm, Mike Bailey was a forceful, hard-tackling wing-half who captained Wolves in the 1972 UEFA and 1974 League Cup finals. He made his international debut in the 10-0 win over the USA in New York in May 1964, replacing Liverpool's Gordon Milne. His second outing followed in November 1964 against Wales when manager Alf Ramsey was undecided as to who was the best right-half in the country! He eventually settled for Nobby Stiles. Bailey, who also gained five U23 caps, made 436 appearances for Wolves and 169 for Charlton. He was voted Midland Footballer of the Year in 1967.

BAILEY, Norman Coles 1877-87 ⑲ ②

Born: Streatham, London, 23 July 1857
Died: Bow, London, 13 January 1923
Career: Westminster School (1874), Old Westminsters (seasons 1875-78), Clapham Rovers (seasons 1878-85), Corinthians (seasons 1886-89), Wanderers (1880s), Swifts (1880s), Surrey County; member of FA Committee (August 1882-June 1884) and FA vice-president (seasons 1887-90); admitted a solicitor in 1880, practised in London with the firm Bailey, Shaw & Gillett.

Strong in all facets of half-back play, Norman Bailey was a safe, sound and highly efficient footballer who loved to join in the attack. One of the great players of his era, he was a regular in the England team for nine years from March 1878 to March 1887 and played in ten consecutive internationals against Scotland, his first ending in a 7-2 defeat. He captained the side on several occasions and was said to have been the first orthodox left-half in the game.
    The spectators watching England in those days certainly got excellent value for money as no less than 98 goals were scored in the 19 internationals Bailey played in. He was an FA Cup winner with Clapham Rovers in 1880.

BAILY, Edward Francis 1949-53 ⑨ ⑤

Born: Clapton, London, 6 August 1925
Died: Welwyn Garden City, Herts, 13 October 2010
Career: Hackney Schools, Middlesex Schools, Tottenham Juniors (1940), Finchley (1942), Tottenham Hotspur (amateur, 1943), Chelsea (amateur, 1944), Hotspur (amateur, February 1946, professional, October 1946), Port Vale (January 1956), Nottingham Forest (October 1956), Leyton Orient (player-coach, December 1958), Tottenham Hotspur (assistant-manager, October 1963); later scout for West Ham United (September 1974-May 1976) and England; also P.E. teacher at Bishop Stopford School, Enfield

During his career, Eddie Baily, nicknamed 'The Cheekie Chappie', scored 97 goals in 458 senior appearances for his four clubs, gaining both Second and First Division Championship winner's medals with Spurs in 1950 and 1951 respectively. Short and stocky, with a tincture of Cockney pertness always present, his inside-forward play had a touch of panache about it – and he made an impressive start to his England career, in the 1-0 defeat by Spain in a World Cup encounter in Rio de Janeiro in July 1950, replacing the axed Roy Bentley following the disastrous defeat by the USA. He later partnered his Spurs club-mate Les Medley on the left-wing in games against Wales (twice), Yugoslavia and Austria and scored the first of his five international goals with a superbly executed hook shot in a 4-1 win over Northern Ireland in Belfast six months after his debut. Baily also played in three B internationals, represented the Rest of the United Kingdom (v. Wales), starred for the Football League fives times and an England XI once.

BAIN, John 1876-77 ①

Born: Bothwell, Lanarkshire, 15 July 1854
Died: Marlborough, 7 August 1929
Career: Sherborne School (1869), Winchester College (1871), New College Oxford (seasons 1874-79); called to the bar at Lincoln's Inn in 1880; Master at Marlborough College from 1879-83 and again from 1886-1913 when he retired.

An all-action forward, forever involved in the action, John Bain's only England appearance was against Scotland in March 1877 when he failed to impress in a 3-1 defeat.

BAINES, LEIGHTON JOHN 2009-13 ⑯ ①

Born: Kirby, Liverpool, 11 December 1984
Career: Wigan Athletic (apprentice, April 2001, professional, January 2003), Everton (£6m, August 2007)

Following an injury to Ashley Cole and the decision by Wayne Bridge 'not to play' the Everton left-back was handed his England debut my Fabio Capello against Egypt at Wembley in March 2010 – and he did well in a 3-1 win before a crowd of over 80,000.
    Baines, who had been called into the full England squad for the first time in March 2009, is small in stature but quick over the ground and delivers a telling cross. He made 162 appearances for Wigan and helped the Latics win the Division Two championship before his transfer to Goodison Park in 2007. He has now made over 400 appearances at club level, including 246 for Everton and has also starred in 16 U21 internationals, scoring a vital goal against Germany in October 2006, securing a 1–0 win in the first leg of a UEFA European U21 Championship play-off. He was in England's squad at Euro 2012 as cover for Ashley Cole.

BAKER, Alfred 1927-28 ①

Born: Ilkeston, 27 April 1898
Died: Islington, London, 1 April 1955
Career: Chaucer Street School/Ilkeston, Ilkeston FC (briefly), Cossall St Catherine's FC/Long Eaton, Eastwood Rangers (season 1913-14); WW1 guest for Chesterfield, Crystal Palace and Huddersfield Town; Arsenal (professional, May 1919, retired May 1931); became groundsman at a sports club ground in South London; Arsenal scout during 1940s.

A hard-working right-half who won his only England cap in November 1927 against Wales during a time when Willis Edwards was out injured, Alf Baker also played in three international trials, represented the Football League twice and won the FA Charity Shield with a Prof. XI in 1924. He scored 26 goals in 351 games for Arsenal and appeared in two FA Cup finals, losing in 1927 and winning in 1930.

BAKER, Benjamin Howard 1920-26 ②

Born: Aigburth, Liverpool, 12 February 1892
Died: Warminster, 10 September 1987
Career: Marlborough Old Boys (1909), Northern Nomads (1911), Blackburn Rovers reserves (season 1913-14), Corinthians (season 1914-15), Preston North End (briefly, April 1915), Lancashire County (season 1919-20), Liverpool (March 1920), Everton (November 1920), Northern Nomads (February 1921), Chelsea (October 1921), Corinthians (March 1926), Everton (July 1926), Oldham Athletic (March 1929), Corinthians (September 1930, retired, April 1931); an all round sportsman, he starred as the British record holder in the high jump at the 1912 and 1920 Olympics, played cricket for Liverpool CC (scoring two centuries), kept goal for a local water polo team and competed in several lawn tennis tournaments, almost qualifying for the Wimbledon men's singles in 1925.

An amateur throughout his career, Howard Baker had trials for England as a centre-half before becoming an exceptionally fine goalkeeper. He went on to win ten caps at amateur level and two for the senior side, the latter against Belgium in Brussels in May 1921 and Ireland in Belfast four years later, keeping a clean sheet both times. During that time England used no fewer than 12 different 'keepers, Baker perhaps being one of the best!

BAKER, Joseph Henry 1959-66 ⑧ ③

Born: Liverpool, 17 July 1940
Died: Wishaw, Lanarkshire, 6 October 2003
Career: Coltness United (season 1954-55), Chelsea (trial, May-June 1955), Hibernian (amateur, August 1955), Armadale Thistle/Edinburgh (July 1956), Hibernian (professional, July 1957), AC Torino/Italy (May 1961), Arsenal (£70,000, July 1962), Nottingham Forest (£65,000, March 1966), Sunderland (£5,000, July 1969), Hibernian (free, January 1971), Raith Rovers (free, June 1972-May 1974), Fauldhouse United (manager-coach, season 1980-81), Albion Rovers (coach, season 1981-82 and again from June 1984 to May 1991)

Joe Baker was the first footballer ever to play in an international match in his native city for an away country – starring at centre-forward for Scotland against England in a Schoolboy international in 1955. Then, four years later, in November 1959, he became the first player to win a full England cap while on the books of a Scottish club (Hibernian), scoring a 'brilliantly worked goal' in a 2-1 win over Northern Ireland. He lost his place to Bobby Smith of Spurs and with the likes of Gerry Hitchens, Ray Pointer, Alan Peacock and Johnny Byrne around at the same time, his opportunities were somewhat limited.

Playing on with a damaged shoulder in the 1-1 draw with Scotland in April 1960, a month later Baker was excellent in the 3-3 draw with Yugoslavia at Wembley. He came close to scoring on several occasions and it was his thumping 89th minute drive which led to England's late, yet deserved equalizer. With the crossbar wobbling, Johnny Haynes pounced to tuck away the loose ball. Then, just a minute later, Baker headed against the bar, but on this occasion there was no-one around to pick up the pieces. Although he didn't score, Baker was one of England's star players on the day.

Five years later, in November 1965, when deputizing for the hospitalised Jimmy Greaves, Baker scored a 19th minute goal in a 2-1 victory.

Besides his senior caps, he also played in six U23 internationals and was in Alf Ramsey's original squad of 40 for the 1966 World Cup. He once scored nine times for Hibs in a Scottish Cup-tie against Peebles Rovers in 1961 and played alongside Denis Law in Italy. His career realised 356 goals (all levels), including 113 for Hibs, 100 for Arsenal, 49 for Forest and 12 for Sunderland.

BALL, Alan James 1964-75 ⑦② ⑧

Born: Farnworth near Bolton, 12 May 1945
Died: Warsash, Hampshire, 25 April 2007
Career: Oswestry Boys High School, Wolverhampton Wanderers (trial, May 1960), Bolton Wanderers (amateur, October 1960), Blackpool (amateur, September 1961, professional, May 1962), Everton (£110,000, August 1966), Arsenal (£220,000, December 1971), Southampton (£60,000, December 1976), Philadelphia Fury/USA (player-coach, May 1978), Vancouver Whitecaps/Canada (June 1979), Blackpool (player-manager, July 1980-February 1981), Southampton (March 1981), Eastern AA/Hong Kong (October 1982), Bristol Rovers (January 1983), Portsmouth (manager, May 1984-January 1989), Colchester United (assistant-manager, February-October 1989), Stoke City (assistant-manager, October-November 1989, manager, November 1989-February 1991), Exeter City (manager, July 1991-January 1994), England (assistant-coach, February-August 1992), Southampton (manager, January 1994-July 1995), Manchester City (manager, July 1995-November 1996), Portsmouth (manager, February 1998-December 1999).

Alan Ball, a tireless midfield firebrand, a veritable little dynamo, 'Mr. Perpetual Motion' who covered acres of ground during the course of a game, was an inspirational choice by England boss Alf Ramsey in the 1966 World Cup. Having made his debut as an inside-forward against Yugoslavia in May 1965, scored his first international goal in a 2-1 win in Sweden soon afterwards and missed a penalty in a pre-tournament warm-up game against Finland in Helsinki, Ball was chosen to

Alan Ball

play on the right-wing during the latter stages of competition.

It was a master plan by Ramsey. Ball was terrific against Argentina, Portugal and West Germany in the final, causing problems for all the left-backs who tried to mark him! He was certainly at his best against the Germans, and the sight of him running up and down the wing with his socks round his ankles endeared him to the public. It was his cross which led to Geoff Hurst scoring that dubious yet all-important third goal. "He trod on every blade of grass that afternoon," wrote one reporter.

After the game, manager Alf Ramsey said to Ball, 21 at the time: "Young man, you will never play a better game of football than you did today."

Although one feels that his performance against Scotland at Wembley in May 1975, certainly matched that effort against the Germans. Partnering Gerry Francis in midfield, he ran the Scots ragged as England stormed to a 5-1 win. He was also in 'top form' when England were defeated 2-1 in Brazil in June 1969. "Pele never had a kick due to the policing of Ball," wrote one reporter.

Ball also competed well in the 1970 World Cup tournament in Mexico. In the third group game against Brazil he struck the bar as England tried in vain to grab an equalizer.

In the international match with Scotland at Wembley in May 1971, Ball's suicidal back-pass gifted Hugh Curran a first-half equaliser, but after that he produced a storming performance, having a hand in one of Martin Chivers's two goals to set up a 3-1 win.

Ball was sent off playing for England against Poland in a World Cup qualifier in Chorzow in January 1973. He grabbed Polish defender Cmikiewicz round the neck after he had laid Martin Peters on the deck. At that time he was only the second player to be sent off in England's history.

After that misdemeanour, Ball was out of the team for almost a year, returning in April 1974 against Portugal. Later handed the captaincy – he led England in the 100th international at Wembley v. West Germany in March 1975 (won 2-0). He then lost that honour and also his place in the team to Gerry Francis. Ball's wife told him of the changeover after she had received a call from a journalist, asking her for a reaction to the decision made by manager Revie. That didn't go down too well. "I cherished that England captaincy," said Ball. "I was still convinced that I was as good as any midfield player he (Revie) had available." The pair never got on after that episode.

Besides his senior honours, ginger-top Ball also played in eight U23 internationals, represented the Football League and during a wonderful career amassed in excess of 900 club appearances, (743 in the Football League), scoring 190 goals. He won the First Division title with Everton in 1970 and was twice an FA Cup runner-up. As a manager he guided Portsmouth into the First Division in 1987. He sadly died from a heart attack, aged 61.

BALL, John 1927-28 ①

Born: Hazel Grove, Stockport, 29 September 1899
Died: Perry Barr, Birmingham, 11 May 1989
Career: Silverwood Colliery FC (seasons 1915-19), Sheffield United (professional, May 1919), Bristol Rovers (May 1921), Wath Athletic (June 1922), Bury (May 1923), West Ham United (May 1929), Coventry City (May 1930), Stourbridge (July 1931, retired, injured, May 1935).

A former miner, John Ball was called up to replace the injured Arthur Rigby of Blackburn Rovers for his only cap against Ireland in Belfast in October 1927. He gave a creditable performance as a makeshift goalkeeper after Ted Hufton of West Ham had gone off with a broken arm in the second-half. He produced a series of fine saves in a 2-0 defeat. A powerful centre-forward or inside-left, he spent the majority of his career with Bury and overall scored a total of 110 goals in 269 League games for his five major clubs.

BALL, Michael John 2000-01 ①

Born: Crosby, Liverpool, 2 October 1979
Career: Liverpool (junior, July 1994), FA School of Excellence (seasons 1994-96), Everton (professional, June 1996), Glasgow Rangers (£6.5m, October 2001), PSV Eindhoven/Holland (£500,000, July 2005), Manchester City (January 2007, released July 2009), Wigan Athletic (trial, January 2010), Blackpool (trial, September-October 2010), Leicester City (trial, July 2011, signed August 2011, dismissed January 2012)

A highly-competitive full-back, who struggled with injuries from 2008 onwards, Michael Ball made his England debut in the 3-0 friendly victory over Spain at Villa Park in February 2001, coming on as a second-half substitute for Chris Powell...one of 18 players used by boss Sven Göran Eriksson during that game. He also represented his country at Schoolboy, Youth and U21 levels and as a teenager played with Michael Owen and Steven Gerrard in Liverpool's 'A' team. Ball helped Rangers win the Scottish League and League Cup double in 2005 and gained a Dutch Eredivisie championship winner's medal with PSV in 2006.

On 23 January 2012, Ball was fined £6,000 by the Football Association for homophobic comments made on Twitter about Antony Cotton when the actor was a contestant on I'm a Celebrity... Get Me Out of Here! The next day, his club, Leicester City, sacked him.

BALMER, Walter William 1904-05 ①

Born: West Derby, Liverpool, 29 September 1875
Died: Huddersfield, 1 February 1941
Career: Aintree Church (1892), South Shore FC (1895), Everton (August 1897), Croydon Common (June 1908, retired, May 1913); Huddersfield Town (coach, seasons 1919-21); later worked as a newsagent.

Able to play in both full-back positions, Billy Balmer was a thickset, durable defender with a bone-shaking tackle who played in successive FA Cup finals for Everton in 1906 and 1907, gaining a winner's medal in the latter. He was called into the England team for the home game against Ireland at Middlesbrough in February 1905, when Bob Crompton cried off with an ankle injury.

BAMBER, John 1920-21 ①

Born: Peasley Cross near St Helens, 11 April 1895
Died: Peasley Cross, 4 August 1971
Career: St Helens Recreationalists (seasons 1911-13), Heywood (August 1913), Liverpool (professional, December 1915), Leicester City (February 1924), Tranmere Rovers (July 1927), Prescot Cables (August 1930, retired, April 1932).

Strongly built with a crisp tackle, Jack Bamber was regarded as one of the best wing-halves in the First Division during the immediate post WW1 era and was rewarded for his fine efforts with an England call-up against Wales in March 1921, preferred at right-half ahead of Aston Villa's Andy Ducat and Bert Smith of Tottenham Hotspur. He also represented the Football League and toured South Africa with the FA whilst at Anfield.

BAMBRIDGE, Arthur Leopold 1879-84 ③ ①

Born: Windsor, 16 June 1861
Died: Caen, France, 27 November 1923
Career: St Mark's School/Windsor (seasons 1874-76), Swifts (seasons 1876-78), Clapham Rovers (seasons 1878-81); also played for Berkshire and Corinthians (seasons 1880-82); travelled the world studying art and produced a few minor paintings; brother of E.C. and E.H.

A valuable, perceptive and exceptionally versatile player, Arthur Bambridge gained his three caps in different positions, those of left-back (on his debut against Wales in March 1880), outside-right v. Wales in February 1883 and inside-right versus Ireland in February 1884. He possessed terrific speed and had the ability to cross the ball with unerring accuracy when on the run.

BAMBRIDGE, Edward Charles 1878-87 ⑱ ⑫

Born: Windsor, 30 July 1858
Died: Wimbledon, 8 November 1935
Career: St Mark's School/Windsor (seasons 1870-73), Windsor Home Park (seasons 1873-75), Swifts (seasons 1875-88); also played for Streatham FC, Berkshire County, Upton Park, Clapham Rovers, Corinthians between 1877 and 1886; FA Committee member (seasons 1883-86), later honorary secretary of Corinthians (seasons 1923-32).

The greatest outside-left of his day, Edward Bambridge was tremendously quick, could dribble with the ball at pace and possessed a stinging shot in both feet. Referred to as England's 'counter weapon' he scored twice on his international debut, in a 5-4 win over Scotland at The Oval in April 1879. His first effort was brilliant ... 'possibly the finest ever scored in football' thought Gibson and Pickard. He ran practically the full length of The Oval pitch, passing player after player, before cleverly placing his shot beyond Parlane, a giant of a man, in the Scotland goal. England, 4-1 down at half-time, were now back in the game and after Goodyer and Bailey had brought the scores level, Bambridge darted away again to win the match with only minutes to spare.

He scored two more goals in the same fixture a year later, but this time the score-line was reversed at the First Hampden Park. Bambridge, who was on target in each of his first four England games, captained his country in his 16th international, a 7-0 victory over Ireland at Sheffield in February 1887.

Two of his sons, Rupert and Frederick, were killed in France during the Great War. His grandson, Anthony Charles Bambridge, was managing director of Colmans Foods in the 1970s.

BAMBRIDGE, Ernest Henry 1875-76 ①

Born: Windsor, 16 May 1848
Died: Southend-on-Sea, 16 October 1917
Career: St Mark's School/Windsor (seasons 1860-63), Swifts (seasons 1863-77); also played for Windsor Home Park, East Sheen, Berkshire County, Corinthians between 1882 and 1880; FA Committee member (seasons 1876-82); Corinthians committee member (seasons 1882-84); later a stock exchange clerk in Central London.

A versatile forward able to score goals at will, Ernest Bambridge thrived on hard work and gained his only cap against Scotland in March 1876. He was killed during the Great War.

BANKS, Gordon, OBE 1962-72 ㉓

Born: Tinsley, Sheffield, 30 December 1937
Career: Sheffield & District Schools, Millspaugh Steelworks FC/Sheffield (2 spells), Rawmarsh Welfare (August 1952), Chesterfield (amateur, April 1954, professional, September 1955), Leicester City (£7,000, May 1959), Stoke City (£52,000, April 1967), Fort Lauderdale Strikers/USA (free, March 1977), St Patrick's Athletic (briefly), Stoke City (coach, May 1978), Port Vale (coach, December 1978, reserve team manager-coach, October-December 1979), Telford United (scout, coach and general manager, season 1980-81), Leicester City (fund raising committee, 1986); later appointed president of Stoke City football club; also runs his own Sports Promotion Agency.

Unquestionably the best England goalkeeper of all-time, Gordon Banks was dependable, brave, unruffled, a superb handler of the ball and had outstanding reflexes. His 'blinding' save from Pele's header in a temperature of 98 degrees in the Mexico World Cup finals of 1970, is still rated as the greatest ever and people and players are still trying to work out how he did it.

The save came in the 11th minute from a Jairzinho cross. Banks, on his line, flung himself across his goal to flip Pele's powerful downward header over the bar. It was an amazing stop, and some years later Pele himself agreed it was the 'finest save he has ever witnessed.' But Banks himself said it wasn't the best save he ever made. The one he placed top of his list came from a bullet header from Wyn Davies while playing for Stoke City against Newcastle United in December 1968 when he somehow tipped the ball over the bar from two yards to earn the Potters a 1-0 win.

Banks's consistent performances led to the re-wording of a common English idiom used in everyday speech to 'Safe as the Banks of England.'

Taking over from Ron Springett, he suffered a 2-1 home defeat by Scotland in April 1963 in his first international and after his second game, a 1-1 draw with Brazil, he received a rollicking from manager Alf Ramsey for 'falling for Pepe's three-card trick' when he curled in a beauty from outside the area.

Banks took note and went on to win 73 caps in ten years (keeping 35 clean sheets) with only injury and illness forcing him out of the action. Banks, in fact, was the first 'new' goalkeeper chosen by Alf Ramsey and after playing well in a 1-1 draw with Brazil and likewise in a 4-2 victory over Czechoslovakia soon after the Scotland match, he said: "The foundations for a club-style spirit have been laid."

However, Banks didn't always get on with Ramsey. They had several arguments and following a 4-3 victory over Portugal in Lisbon in May 1964, Ramsey blamed him for two of the goals and promptly dropped him for the next match against the Republic of Ireland, bringing in the untried Tony Waiters.

But he was soon back in the team and produced some brilliant displays, playing a major part in the 1966 World Cup triumph when he conceded only three goals. However, like all goalkeepers, Banks had his off days. He had an indifferent game against Scotland at Wembley in April 1967 when he allowed Jim McCalliog's shot to squeeze past him inside his near post; gave away a 'silly' goal in the 2-2 draw with the Soviet Union eight months later and was at fault (by his own admission) for Switzerland's two equalisers in a 3-2 win in Basle in October 1971. He also 'slipped on the treacherous mud and icy surface' at Hampden Park to allow Scotland's John Hughes to equalise in a 1-1 in February 1968. In between times, however, he was brilliant, especially when Wales were whipped 3-0 at Ninian Park. He next pulled off a stunning save from Amancio's lightning back-heeler in the 1-0 win over Spain in April 1968 and followed up by saving Carlos Alberto's penalty in a 2-1 defeat by Brazil in front

of 160,000 fans in the Maracana Stadium in Rio de Janeiro in June 1969 - this was his only spot-kick save for his country.

In the 1970 World Cup, he was again 'quite outstanding' and it was a pity that a stomach bug (Montezumah's revenge had never been harsher) ruled him out the quarter-final clash with West Germany, because one felt – and no disrespect to his replacement Peter Bonetti – that if he had played England would probably have repeated their 1966 final victory and gone on to retain the trophy. We shall never know. Ramsey said: "Of all the players to lose, we had to lose him."

An interesting snippet concerning Banks materialized from the game against Malta at Wembley in May 1971. England won comfortably by 5-0, but Banks only touched the ball four times in the entire game, all from back passes.

Banks has the best 'goals against' average in World Cup finals for his country, with 0.43 goals conceded per 90 minutes played in nine matches at the 1966 and 1970 finals. Shilton's record was 0.56.

Besides winning 73 full caps, Banks also represented his country in two U23 matches and played for the Football League six times before his international career came to a premature end in 1972 when he was being pushed all the way by Ray Clemence and Peter Shilton.

Twice a League Cup winner, in 1964 and 1972, Banks was named both 'Footballer of the Year' and 'Sportsman of the Year' in 1972 and was awarded the OBE in 1970 and made over 600 club and international appearances during his lengthy career.

In 2004, Banks was named by Pelé as one of the top 125 greatest living footballers and was also elected in a poll by the IFFHS as the second best goalkeeper of the 20th Century, behind the Russian Lev Yashin, and ahead of Italy's Dino Zoff and soon afterwards he sold his World Cup winner's medal at Christies for £124,750

BANKS, Herbert Ernest/Edward 1900-01 ①

Born: Coventry, 3 June 1874
Died: Smethwick, 8 April 1947
Career: Leamington Spa junior football, Coventry Highfield FC (1894); served with the 72nd Regt. Seaforth Highlanders in India; Everton (professional, October 1896), St Mirren (loan, January 1897), Third Lanark (August 1897), Millwall Athletic (March 1899), Aston Villa (April 1901), Bristol City (November 1901), Watford (May 1903), Coventry City (August 1904), Stafford Rangers (December 1905), Verity's Athletic (October 1906; reinstated as an amateur, May 1907, retired, April 1910); later worked for a Birmingham-based engineering firm.

Short, heavily built with a strong left foot shot, inside-forward Bert Banks was Millwall's first-ever international, capped as a late replacement for the injured G.O. Smith against Ireland in March 1901, following an impressive two-goal trial. Two years earlier he had been suspended by his club (Millwall) for being overweight. During his career Banks scored 70 goals in more than 200 club appearances, and as a soldier, twice helped his regiment win the Simla Cup in India.

BANKS, Thomas 1957-59 ⑥

Born: Farnworth, Lancashire, 10 November 1929
Career: Farnworth Boys' Club (1943), Partridge's XI (August 1945), Bolton Wanderers (amateur, May 1947, professional, October 1947), Altrincham (August 1961), Bangor City (March 1963, retired, May 1965); became a building contractor in Bolton.

Tommy Banks, the hard man of the Bolton defence, won all his caps at left-back as partner to Don Howe. He played in all four matches in the 1958 World Cup in Sweden after replacing Jim Langley, and had a terrific game in the 0-0 draw with Brazil in Gothenburg when he was effectively a 'covering sweeper' behind Billy Wright. A real

down to earth character, he had a reputation of being a no-nonsense take-the-man tackler and a famous remark of his was: "Tha'd better not try to get past me unless tha' wants gravel rash." He made 255 appearances for Bolton, gaining an FA Cup winner's medal in 1958 and also represented the Football League. As a youngster he played for both England Boys and Great Britain Boys' Clubs. He also participated in Army football and helped Bangor win the Welsh Cup in 1964.

As recounted in Declan Hill's book 'The Fix', Banks also had a small but influential role in the fight to acquire better pay and conditions for football players in the 1961 labour dispute with the Football League.

BANNISTER, William 1900-02 ②

Born: Burnley, 26 December 1878
Died: Leicester, 26 March 1942
Career: Earley FC (August 1896), Burnley (professional, August 1899), Bolton Wanderers (£100, November 1901), Woolwich Arsenal (£250, December 1902), Leicester Fosse (£300, May 1904), Burnley (£1,000, September 1910), Leicester Imperial (free, August 1912, retired, May 1914); thence a licensee in Burnley, later likewise in Leicester.

Bill Banister was a tough, towering centre-half, competent in all aspects of defensive play whose two caps were gained against Wales in March 1901 and Ireland a year later, being a winner on each occasion. Around this time England were struggling to find a reliable centre-half and Bannister was one of six different players tried in that position over the course of three seasons.

BARCLAY, Robert 1931-36 ③ ②

Born: Scotswood, 27 October 1906
Died: Halifax, 13 July 1969
Career: Scotswood United Church (1920), Bell's Close Juniors (1921), Allendale (1923), Scotswood (1925), Derby County (professional, February 1927), Sheffield United (June 1931), Huddersfield Town (March 1937, retired, May 1944).

Bobby Barclay was a neat, tidy inside-forward, deft in footwork, with a strong shot which it is said he used 'too sparingly.' Although a shade on the small side he was never afraid to mix it with bigger opponents and overall had a decent career, playing in two losing FA Cup finals in three years (1936 and 1938). He scored with a deflected shot off Allan Craig on his international debut against Scotland at Wembley in April 1932, won 3-0, and netted the winner in his second game against Ireland later in the year. He was unlucky to have so many other quality centre-halves playing at the same time.

BARDSLEY, David John 1992-94 ②

Born: Manchester, 11 September 1964
Career: Blackpool (apprentice, August 1980, professional, November 1982), Watford (£150,000, November 1983), Oxford United (£265,000, September 1987), Queens Park Rangers (£500,000, September 1989), Blackpool (free, July 1998), Northwich Victoria (season 1999-2000); later opened his own soccer School before moving to America where, in March 2007, he become director of Ajax's Youth Academy in Florida.

After representing his country at Youth team level, full-back David Bardsley gained two full caps, both under his former club manager Graham Taylor, the first as a substitute for Lee Dixon in 1-0 defeat by Spain in September 1992 when he was injured and as a result missed two League games, and his second in a 1-1 World Cup qualifying draw with Poland in May 1993. He made almost 300 League and Cup appearances for QPR despite being sidelined for 20 months up to February 1998.

BARHAM, Mark Francis 1982-83 ②

Born: Folkestone, 12 July 1962
Career: Norwich City (apprentice, June 1978, professional, April 1980), Huddersfield Town (£100,000, July 1987), Middlesbrough (November 1988), West Bromwich Albion (free, September 1989), Brighton & Hove Albion (loan, January-March 1990, signed permanently, December 1990), Shrewsbury Town (non-contract, September-December 1992); then over the next seven years was manager, in turn, of Kitchee FC, Sittingbourne, Southwick and Fakenham Town, the latter to May 1999; now assists in Norwich City's Corporate hospitality suite on matchdays and runs his own tool hire business in Norwich.

A right-sided midfielder with good skills, Mark Barham won his England caps on the summer tour to Australia in 1983, featuring in a 0-0 draw in Sydney and a 1-0 win in Brisbane, where he had a hand in Paul Walsh's second-half goal. He made over 200 appearances for Norwich with whom he gained Second Division and League Cup winner's medals.

Barham played roller-hockey for England as a youngster while his father won the News of the World amateur golf tournament.

BARKAS, Samuel 1935-38 ⑤

Born: Wardley Colliery, Northumberland, 29 December 1909
Died: Bradford, 10 December 1989
Career: Middle Dock FC (1925), Bradford City (professional, August 1928), Manchester City (April 1934, retired, May 1947); Workington (manager, May 1947), Wigan Athletic (manager, April-September 1957); Manchester City (scout, seasons 1957-59), Leeds United (scout, seasons 1959-61); later worked in Bradford City's pools and lottery department.

A stylish left-back who always tried to use the ball constructively, rather than booting it downfield, Sam Barkas would certainly have gained more caps but for the presence of Arsenal's Eddie Hapgood. However, the fact that he was a defender was underlined when he deputised for the injured Ray Bowden on tour against Belgium in Brussels in May 1936. A total of 27 goals were scored in the five internationals Barkas played in. He helped Manchester City win the First and Second Division Championships either side of the war. Barkas and his Manchester City team-mate Eric Brook, were injured in a three-car pile-up at Wath-on-Dearne, Yorkshire, on their way to play in the Wartime international against Scotland at Newcastle in December 1939. The pair were replaced by two Newcastle players, Joe Richardson and Tom Pearson, the latter being a Scot who was subsequently capped against England and Belgium in 1947.

BARKER, John William 1934-37 ⑪

Born: Denaby, 27 February 1907
Died: Derby, 20 January 1982
Career: Denaby Rovers (seasons 1923-26), Denaby United (seasons 1926-28), Derby County (£200, professional, April 1928, retired April 1946); Bradford City (manager, May 1946-January 1947), Dundalk (manager, January 1947-October 1948), Oldham Athletic (trainer-coach, November 1948-January 1949); Derby County (manager, November 1953-April 1955); also worked at Rolls Royce factory (Derby) and as a fitter's mate at the Derby Carriage & Wagon Railway works.

Jack Barker, one of the best centre-halves in the Football League during the mid-1930s, made 353 appearances for Derby. Blessed with attacking flair, he figured in the hotly-contested and violent match against Italy in November 1934 which was dubbed 'The Battle of Highbury' losing a tooth and also suffering a nasty cut over his right eye. Barker captained England in his final match against Wales in October 1936. He died just short of his 76th birthday, losing a fight against cancer and a spinal problem.

BARKER, Richard Raine 1894-95 ①

Born: Kensington, London, 29 May 1869
Died: Dover, Kent, 1 October 1940
Career: Repton School (seasons 1886-88), Casuals (seasons 1888-94), Corinthians (seasons 1894-97); an engineer by profession, he was manager of the Bromley Electric Light Co.

A useful left-half, strong in the tackle, but lacking speed, Dick Barker was once described as being 'much too slow for an international.' His only cap came in a 2-0 win over Wales at the Queens Club (London).

BARKER, Robert Clifton 1872-73 ①

Born: Wouldham, Kent, 19 June 1847
Died: Paddington, London, 11 November 1915
Career: Marlborough College (seasons 1861-66, where he also played rugby), Hertfordshire Rangers (seasons 1866-74); also Middlesex County (season 1868-69), Kent County (seasons 1868-70); after retiring, he became chief assistant engineer to the London, Chatham and Dover Railway and then the South Eastern Railway

Bob Barker was a well-built forward and, because of his rugby experience, was selected to play in goal in England's first ever international against Scotland in November 1872 when Alex Morten was unavailable. He played well in the first half, kept a clean-sheet, but during the second period he switched positions with outside-left William Maynard.

BARLOW, Raymond John 1954-55 ①

Born: Swindon, 17 August 1926
Died: Bridgend, Wales, 13 March 2012
Career: Sandford Street School/Swindon, Swindon Town (trial, 1942), Garrard's FC/Swindon (August 1942), West Bromwich Albion (amateur, June 1944, professional, November 1944), Swindon Town (WW2 guest, season 1945-46), Birmingham City (June 1960), Stourbridge FC (August 1961, retired, May 1962); later a proprietor of tobacco/ confectionery shop in West Bromwich and a post office in Stourbridge; also played for West Bromwich Albion Old Stars (seasons 1969-81).

Big, tall and upright, Ray Barlow was initially an inside-forward who developed into a brilliant left-half and later a centre-half. He made 482 appearances for WBA, gaining an FA Cup winner's medal in 1954. Unfortunate to have Jimmy Dickinson around at the same time, Barlow's only cap was gained against Northern Ireland in Belfast in October 1954 when he starred in a 2-0 win. In fact, along with Barlow, three other players made their one and only appearances for England in this same international - Bill Foulkes, Johnny Wheeler and Brian Pilkington.

BARMBY, Nicholas Jonathan 1995-2003 ㉓ ④

Born: Hull, 11 February 1974
Career: Tottenham Hotspur (apprentice, May 1989, professional, April 1991), Middlesbrough (£5.25m, August 1995), Everton (£5.75m, November 1996), Liverpool (£6m, July 2000), Leeds United (£2.75m, August 2002), Nottingham Forest (loan, February-March 2004), Hull City (free, July 2004, player-caretaker-manager, November 2011, retired as player, January 2012, appointed manager, January 2012, sacked May 2012).

Attacking midfielder Nick Barmby scored the first goals of both Glenn Hoddle's and Sven-Göran Eriksson's reigns as England manager - in a 3–0 victory over Moldova in a World Cup qualifier in 1996 and in a 3–0 friendly win over Spain in 2003. He also appeared in Euro '96 and Euro 2000 and starred in that memorable 5–1 victory over Germany in September 2001. He made his international debut in the 0-0 draw with Uruguay at Wembley in March 1995, coming on as a substitute for Peter Beardsley.

A League Cup and UEFA Cup winner with Liverpool in 2001, Barmby's transfer money, over the years, has amounted to £21.75 million. In 2009, he netted his 100th career goal, reached the milestone of 500 club appearances and became only the fifth player to score for six different clubs in the Premiership. He also represented his country at both schoolboy and youth team levels before gaining four U21 and two B caps.

Barmby and striker Andy Cole became the first two graduates from the FA's National School of Excellence to play for England at senior level when they entered the action as second-half substitutes against Uruguay in May 1995.

He lost his appeal for 'unfair dismissal' as manager of Hull City in 2012, having been replaced by Steve Bruce.

BARNES, John Charles Bryan, MBE 1985-96 ㉙ ⑫

Born: Kingston, Jamaica, 7 November 1963
Career: Sudbury Court FC/Jamaica (August 1979), Watford (free, July 1981), Liverpool (£900,000, June 1987), Newcastle United (free, August 1997), Charlton Athletic (free, February-May 1999), Celtic (player, head coach-manager, August 1999-February 2000); Jamaica (national team manager, September 2008-May 2009), Tranmere Rovers (manager, June-October 2009); became a Sky Sport football analyst

A positive outside-left, elegant and unflurried, John Barnes was a key figure in Graham Taylor's successful Watford team of the early 1980s, helping the Hornets gain promotion, finish runners-up in the First Division and reach the FA Cup final in three years.

He was given his England debut by Bobby Robson as a second-half replacement for his Vicarage Road team-mate Luther Blissett in the 0-0 with Northern Ireland in Belfast in May 1983. A year later, in June 1984, he scored one of the most breathtaking, individual goals ever seen at international level, when he outpaced, bamboozled and bewildered at least five Brazilians before scoring during an encounter at the Estádio do Maracanã Stadium in Rio de Janeiro. The 44th minute 'Made in Brazil' goal brought him worldwide fame but also a sense of heavy expectation, with the media and fans who expected him to produce moments like that every time he wore the 'three lions' shirt!

In his early England days, along with fellow black player Mark Chamberlain, Barnes was subjected to threats from racist groups, being personally abused by National Front supporters when flying back from South America after that 2-0 victory over Brazil in June 1984. The racists claimed that England had only won 1-0, because his goal 'didn't count.' Bobby Robson did not use John until the quarter final stage of the 1986 World Cup. Coming on when trailing 2-0 to Argentina with 15 minutes to go, he set up a goal for Gary Lineker and created another chance which Lineker missed as England went out of the competition. A regular starter at both Euro '88 and the World Cup two years later, he sustained a groin injury in the latter tournament against Belgium as England went out on penalties in the semi-final against Germany.

After a poor performance by the whole team in a 1994 World Cup qualifier against San Marino at Wembley, Barnes was booed by a section of England supporters, but he shrugged that aside and continued his international career into the mid-1990s. Today he remains as England's most-capped black player (79), his last coming in September 1995 in that 0-0 draw with Colombia at Wembley…a game that will always be remembered because of the eccentric 'Scorpion Kick' performed by the Colombian goalkeeper, Rene Higuita. At club level, Barnes amassed a total of 781 appearances and scored 198 goals. He gained two FA Cup, one League Cup and two League Championship winner's medals with Liverpool. Unfortunately, he failed as a manager, although he did lead Jamaica to Caribbean Cup glory in 2008!

In fact, his much-hyped reign as head-coach/manager of Celtic (under Kenny Dalglish) included a shock Scottish Cup defeat by Inverness Caledonian Thistle in February 2000 which gave birth to this famous headline in *The Sun* newspaper: "Super Caley go ballistic, Celtic are atrocious." Barnes was sacked shortly afterwards!

Awarded the MBE in October 1998 for services to football, Barnes' social awareness and responsibility were demonstrated when he visited Burundi as an unofficial ambassador for Christian Aid. In the latter part of 2007, Barnes competed in the fifth BBC series of Strictly Come Dancing with his partner Nicole Cutler. They finished in seventh place. He was also the first male celebrity to receive a ten from the judges, which he got for his salsa.

In 1990, ahead of the World Cup, Barnes supplied a rap for the song 'World in Motion' by New Order which was a UK Number 1 and is still regarded by many as the best football song ever made.

John Barnes MBE

BARNES, Peter Simon 1977-82 (22) (3)

Born: Chorlton, Manchester, 10 June 1957
Career: Chorlton High Grammar School, Manchester & District Boys, Gatley Rangers/Manchester (season 1970-71), Manchester City (apprentice, June 1971, professional, August 1974), West Bromwich Albion (£748,000, July 1979), Leeds United (£930,000, August 1981), Real Betis/Spain (loan, August 1982), West Ham United (briefly), Melbourne JUST/Australia (April 1984), Manchester United (loan, May 1984), Coventry City (£65,000, May 1984), Manchester United (free, July 1985), Bolton Wanderers (loan, October-November 1987), Port Vale (loan, December 1987), Manchester City (January 1987), Hull City (March 1988), Drogheda United (April-May 1988), Sporting Farense/Portugal (August-September 1988), Bolton Wanderers (November 1988), Sunderland (February 1989), Tampa Bay Rowdies/USA (loan, April-August 1989), Northwich Victoria (August 1990), Wrexham (September 1990), Radcliffe Borough (November 1990-May 1991), Mossley FC (July-October 1991), Cliftonville/Ireland (November 1992); then Stockport County and Hamrun Sports/Malta (season 1993-94), Manchester City (part-time coach and Youth Development officer, August 1994), Runcorn (manager, August 1996-March 1997); later Gibraltar (coaching), Manchester's City (Academy coach), Norway (coaching); also worked as a broadcaster for Piccadilly Radio (Manchester).

A record signing and sale by West Bromwich Albion, left-winger Peter Barnes was a regular in the England side during Ron Greenwood's reign as manager but fell from favour once Bobby Robson had taken over in 1982. The son of the former Manchester City wing-half Ken Barnes, he was apparently unpopular with his team-mates, who took advantage of his club troubles by pressuring Greenwood to drop him. On his day he could be a match-winner. He had pace, good control and could shoot, and would often go past his full-back on the outside before getting in an accurate cross. Occasionally though, he was far too over-elaborate with his footwork. He made his England debut against Italy in November 1977 and won his last cap against Holland in May 1982. All his three international goals came in victories – 3-1 over Wales in 1978, 3-1 versus Scotland in 1979 and 3-0 v. Bulgaria, also in 1979. In 1976, Barnes was voted PFA 'Young Footballer of the Year' and gained a League Cup winner's medal with Manchester City, scoring as a 19 year-old in the final against Newcastle United. He also represented England at Youth and U21 levels, gaining nine caps in the latter category.

BARNET, Horace Hutton 1881-82 (1)

Born: Kensington, London, 6 March 1856
Died: Knightsbridge, London, 29 March 1941
Career: served in and played for the Royal Engineers (seasons 1876-1905); also played for Corinthians (seasons 1882-86).

An outside-right, with good pace and clever footwork, Horace Barnet played his part in England's record-breaking 13-0 win over Ireland in February 1882, having a hand in five of the goals. At times he annoyed his colleagues with some indifferent shooting and centring. He played in the 1878 FA Cup final and attained the rank of Colonel while serving with the Royal Engineers.

BARRASS, Malcolm Williamson 1952-53 (3)

Born: Blackpool, 15 December 1924
Career: Ford Motor Works Toolshop FC/Manchester (from 1940), Bolton Wanderers (professional, February 1944), Sheffield United (September 1956), Wigan Athletic (player-manager, July 1958-January 1959), Nuneaton Borough (player-coach, March 1959-May 1960), Pwllheli (player, February-May 1961), Hyde (trainer, June 1962-May 1964).

Originally an inside-forward, capped in that position against Wales in a Victory international at The Hawthorns in 1945, Malcolm Barrass was successfully converted into a strong-tackling centre-half and went on to win the first of three full caps as England's pivot in October 1951 in a 1-1 draw with Wales when he competently dealt with the threat of Trevor Ford. Portsmouth's Jack Froggatt was all set to play in that game but cried off at the last minute, allowing Malcolm to fill the gap. A Football League (North) Cup winner with Bolton in 1945, he played in the now-legendary 'Matthews' FA Cup Final of 1953, one of 357 senior appearances he made for the Burnden Park club (27 goals). His father, Matt, was also a professional footballer with Blackpool, Sheffield Wednesday and Manchester City while his grandson, also named Matt, has played for Bury and Ratcliffe Borough.

BARRETT, Albert Frank 1929-30 (3)

Born: Stratford, London, 11 November 1903
Died: Cape Town, South Africa, 8 December 1989
Career: Park School/West Ham, West Ham Boys, Fairburn House Boys' Club, Middlesex Wanderers (August 1919), Leytonstone (February 1921), West Ham United (November 1921), Southampton (February 1925), Fulham (June 1925); Leytonstone (coach, August 1937-September 1939); later secretary of a wholesale firm in Romford Market; emigrated to South Africa in winter of 1954.

Easily spotted on the field by his blond, almost white hair Albert 'Snowball' Barrett was a classy left-half, strong and efficient, unruffled, attack-minded with expert passing ability. His only game in an England shirt was against Ireland in October 1929 when he deputized for the injured Joe Peacock of Middlesbrough. He made one of the goals in a 3-0 win. A Schoolboy international at the age of 14, he toured South Africa with the FA XI in the summer of 1929, won a Third Division (South) Championship medal in 1936 and during his career made over 300 appearances at club level.

BARRETT, Earl Delisser 1991-93 ③

Born: Rochdale, 28 April 1967
Career: Manchester City (apprentice, May 1983, professional, April 1985), Chester City (loan, March-April 1986), Oldham Athletic (November 1987), Aston Villa (£1.7m, February 1992), Everton (£1.7m, January 1995), Sheffield United (loan, January 1998), Sheffield Wednesday (February 1998, retired, injured, July 1999); subsequently obtained a degree in sports science and is now working towards his coaching badges; engaged by Manchester City as an Events Organiser; part of a consortium considering investing in Port Vale (2008); U16 coach at Oldham Athletic (2008-09) and in July 2009 was engaged as U14 Academy coach at Stoke City.

Earl Barrett's form for Oldham earned him the call-up to Graham Taylor's England team but, like many other players, he failed to provide answers to the troublesome right-back position. He never played in any worthwhile matches – in just three pointless summer friendlies. The first in June 1991 against New Zealand in Auckland, when he deputised for centre-half Mark Wright, the second v. Brazil in Washington and third versus Germany in Detroit, both in June 1993 when he stepped in for Lee Dixon. Barrett won the Second Division with Oldham in 1991, the League Cup with Aston Villa in 1994 and also represented his country in four B and four U21 internationals. He amassed over 400 club appearances during his 16-year career.

BARRETT, James William 1928-29 ①

Born: Stratford, London, 19 January 1907
Died: Stratford, London, 25 November 1970
Career: Park School/West Ham, Fairburn House Boys' Club (August 1921), West Ham United (professional, August 1923, retired during WW2; appointed A team coach and later club groundsman)

A larger than life character, 'Big Jim' Barrett's international career lasted for just eight minutes. He injured his right knee in a midfield tackle during the game against Ireland at Liverpool in October 1928 and never got another call. During his West Ham career, Barrett scored 53 goals in 467 first-class appearances and 15 in 71 Wartime games. His son, Jimmy, played for West Ham, Nottingham Forest and Birmingham City.

BARRY, Gareth 1999 to date ㊳ ②

Born: Hastings, 23 February 1981
Career: Brighton & Hove Albion (trial, 1995), Aston Villa (apprentice, April 1996, professional, February 1998), Manchester City (£12m, June 2009)

Gareth Barry made 27 appearances for England's U21 side, a total later equalled by Jamie Carragher and surpassed by Scott Carson, Tom Huddlestone, Fabrice Muamba and James Milner. Used initially in the senior side as a second-half substitute against Ukraine in May 2000 by manager Kevin Keegan, he was the 1,100th player to gain a full England cap and is the only player to date to have been selected for international duty by each of the last eight England managers. Part of the squad at Euro 2000, he did not feature in any of the side's games, but then, after a four-year international exile, he was recalled in February 2007 and hasn't looked back since. One of Fabio Capello's 'reliable regulars' he can play at left-back, on the left-side of midfield or in the

centre. He has been immense in the England engine-room, forming a wonderful partnership with Steven Gerrard and Frank Lampard, and in June 2008, he had the pleasure of captaining the team in the second half of his 20th international against Trinidad & Tobago. Two years later he played in the World Cup finals in South Africa and in November 2011 his first-half header was deflected into the net by Daniel Majstorovic to give England a 1-0 home friendly win over Sweden. It was the 2,000th goal scored by England at full international level.

Barry made 440 appearances for Aston Villa before his £12 million transfer to Manchester City in the summer of 2009. He has also played for England at Youth and B team level but sadly missed Euro 2012 through injury.

BARRY, Leonard James 1927-29 ⑤

Born: Sneiton, Notts, 27 October 1901
Died: Mapperley, Notts, 17 April 1970
Career: Sneiton Boys' School, Mundella Grammar School, RAF Cranwell (1918-19), Notts County (amateur, May 1920, professional, April 1923), Leicester City (£3,500, September 1927), Nottingham Forest (August 1933, retired, May 1934); later worked on transport at RAF Chilwell and at Langar and Newton Aerodromes.

An accomplished left-winger with neat control, speed and excellent crossing ability, Len Barry loved to cut inside and have a shot at goal. He played for England against Ireland as an amateur in 1923 before going on to win five full caps, sharing his duties at the time with Jimmy Ruffell of West Ham. He had a hand in two of George Camsell's four goals in a 5-1 win over Belgium in Brussels in May 1929. He made 214 appearances for Leicester and 153 for Notts County.

BARSON, Frank 1919-20 ①

Born: Grimethorpe, Sheffield, 10 April 1891
Died: Winson Green, Birmingham, 13 September 1968
Career: Grimethorpe Road County School, Albion FC/Sheffield (1909), Cammell Laird FC/Sheffield (1910), Barnsley (August 1911), Burnley (WW1 guest, season 1916-17), Aston Villa (£2,850, October 1919), Manchester United (August 1922), Watford (May 1928), Hartlepool United (player-coach, May 1929), Wigan Borough (July 1930), Rhyl Athletic (player-manager, June 1931); Stourbridge (manager, July-August 1935), Aston Villa (coach, head trainer, October 1935), Solihull Town (B team manager, season 1940-41), Swansea Town (trainer, July 1947-February 1954), Lye Town (trainer, September 1954, manager, October 1954-April 1956); was a bailiff during WW2.

Frank Barson was a bastion in defence and regarded as one of the 'hard men' of English football. Quite regularly he was escorted out of grounds by policemen protecting him from groups of angry opposition fans. Opposing crowds loathed him, yet he still continued to be aggressive, never changing his style. In fact, he said soon after retiring: "I've been brought up to play hard and saw nothing wrong with an honest to goodness shoulder charge."

Sent off at least 12 times during his career, including a dismissal in his very last League game for Wigan Borough against Accrington Stanley on Boxing Day 1930, his longest suspension was for seven months, following an incident involving a Fulham player when he was with Watford in 1928 and he was banned for eight weeks for knocking Manchester City's Sam Cowan unconscious during the 1926 FA Cup semi-final.

Barrel-chested and a blacksmith by trade, Barson's only England cap came against Wales at Highbury in March 1920 when he had a rather poor game in a 2-1 defeat. An FA Cup winner that season with Villa who had paid a record £2,700 for him from Barnsley, he made over 350 appearances at club level during his 19-year career.

Gareth Barry

BARTON, John 1889-90 ① ①

Born: Blackburn, 5 October 1866
Died: Blackburn, 22 April 1910
Career: Witton FC (September 1883), Blackburn West End (August 1885), Blackburn Rovers (professional, August 1887, retired, injured, April 1892); Preston North End (trainer); then a licensee in Blackburn.

Twice an FA Cup winner with Blackburn (1890 and 1891) right-half Jack Barton modelled his play on that of his fellow wing-half James Forrest. A steady but efficient footballer, he passed the ball with precision and was certainly no slouch when it came to tackling. He played 'outstandingly well' and scored in his only game for England in a 9-1 victory over Ireland in Belfast in March 1890, when four of his Blackburn team-mates also starred. Badly injured playing for Blackburn at Aston Villa in September 1891, he never recovered and retired at the end of the season.

BARTON, Joseph Anthony 2006-07 ①

Born: Huyton, Merseyside, 2 September 1982
Career: Manchester City (apprentice, April 1999, professional, July 2001), Newcastle United (£5.8m, July 2007), Queen's Park Rangers (August 2011), Olympique Marseille/France (loan, August 2012-May 2013)

Before joining Newcastle Joey Barton made over 150 appearances for Manchester City, played twice for England at U21 level and gained one full cap against Spain in February 2007. What a hilarious call up this was. Okay, Barton was a professional footballer but to select him just weeks after berating several England players for releasing books after their poor showing at 2006 World Cup was ridiculous. It got worse. Having lambasted key players prior to selection, Barton failed to do his talking on the Old Trafford pitch, being bereft of ideas as Spain won 1-0.

His life in general has been marred by numerous controversial incidents and disciplinary problems, being convicted twice on charges of violence. In May 2008, he was sentenced to six months imprisonment for common assault and affray during an incident outside a McDonald's restaurant in Liverpool (he served 77 days in all). In July 2008 Barton was given a four-month suspended sentence after admitting assault occasioning actual bodily harm on former team-mate Ousmane Dabo during a training ground dispute. This incident effectively ended his Manchester City career. Then, just three days after his release, he was charged with violent conduct by the FA for the assault on Dabo. Earlier, in 2004, he was also involved in an incident where he stubbed out a cigar onto the eyes of reserve team player Jamie Tandy during a Christmas party at the Lucid nightclub. This resulted in permanent scarring for the victim, although his vision was to return to normal. On 13 May 2012, on the final day of the season, with QPR requiring at least a draw in their match away at Manchester City or for Bolton to lose or draw to guarantee their Premier League safety, Barton was sent off in the 55th minute for violent conduct after elbowing Carlos Tevez in the face. Immediately after being shown a red card, Barton then kicked Sergio Aguero in the back of the knee and attempted to head-butt City captain Vincent Kompany. At this point, Barton had to be dragged from the pitch by his former team-mate Micah Richards as he argued with Manchester City players and staff and attempted to square-off with striker Mario Balotelli. QPR went on to concede two late goals

and lose the match 3–2, thus handing City the title. Bolton, however, were unable to capitalize, drawing 2-2 at Stoke, thus ensuring QPR's safety. Barton took to Twitter after the game and admitted to trying to "take [one] of their players with me." The FA responded by issuing two charges of violent conduct against him, for the kick and the attempted head-butt, the initial foul already carrying with it a charge of violent conduct. Barton accepted the charge for kicking Agüero but denied the charge for attempting to head-butt Kompany. QPR also began an internal investigation into his behaviour, amid speculation that he will be stripped of the captaincy and fined and possibly shown the door by the club either by being sold, released on a free transfer or having his contract terminated for gross misconduct. Barton has been widely condemned in the media for his actions and for attempting to defend himself on Twitter, where he also attacked BBC *Match of the Day* pundits Gary Lineker and Alan Shearer, his manager at Newcastle.

On 23 May, Barton attended an FA hearing where he was found guilty on all three accounts of violent conduct, handed a twelve-match ban and fined £75,000. A month later, QPR announced the results of their internal investigation and as a result, Barton was stripped of the captaincy and fined six weeks' wages, believed to be between £420,000 and £500,000. The fiery midfielder was also removed from the Rangers' pre-season tour of Asia and in a statement the club said that they had... "Also reached an agreement with Barton that if he seriously breaches the club's disciplinary procedures again, the club reserves the right to terminate his contract." Barton responded by saying that "My behaviour was wrong and I accept the punishment that has been imposed upon me as a result."

BARTON, Percival Archibald 1920-25 ⑦

Born: Edmonton, London, 19 August 1893
Died: Bordesley Green, Birmingham, 21 October 1961
Career: Montague Road School/Edmonton, Tottenham Thursday (1910), Edmonton Amateurs (1911), Sultan FC (1912), Birmingham (professional, January 1914), Tottenham Hotspur (WW1 guest, 1915), Stourbridge (August 1929, retired, June 1933).

A Second Division Championship winner with Birmingham in 1921, Percy Barton was an industrious player, clever in breaking up attacks who occupied both wing-half positions and that of full-back. He made 349 appearances for Blues, scoring 14 goals, one a 30-yard header v. Wolves. The first of his seven England caps was gained against Belgium in May 1921 and his last v. Ireland in October 1924.

BARTON, Warren Dean 1994-96 ③

Born: Stoke Newington, London, 19 March 1969
Career: Leytonstone (1985), Dagenham (1987), Maidstone United (£10,000, July 1989), Wimbledon (£300,000, June 1990), Newcastle United (£4.5m, June 1995), Derby County (free, February 2002), Queens Park Rangers (free, October 2003), Wimbledon (player-coach, February 2004), Milton Keynes Dons (player-coach, July 2004), Dagenham & Redbridge (player, September 2004, retired as a player, May 2005); engaged by Dagenham & Redbridge as a coach and also by Brighton and Hove Albion as a part-time consultant; LA Galaxy/USA (U18 coach, season 2008-09); San Diego Flash/USA (as a partner and technical adviser, January 2010; later named president and head coach of the club, March 2010); also worked as a soccer pundit for the Fox TV channel and Asian TV companies as well as running his own travel agency company.

An attacking full-back who played in three B internationals before gaining his three full caps, Warren Barton spent his best years with Wimbledon and Newcastle and in all amassed well over

Joey Barton

550 senior appearances at club level and was the most expensive defender in League football when he joined Newcastle in 1995. He made his senior debut for England in the infamous February 1995 friendly away match against the Republic of Ireland which was abandoned after only 27 minutes because of rioting extreme-right political activists. Later that year, he earned his second and third caps against Sweden and Brazil respectively, coming on as a very late substitute for John Scales in the latter.

BASSETT, William Isaiah 1887-96 ⑯ ⑧
Born: West Bromwich, 27 January 1869
Died: West Bromwich, 9 April 1937
Career: Christ Church School/West Bromwich, Oak Villa (1883), West Bromwich Strollers (not Albion, 1884), Old Church FC (1885), West Bromwich Albion (professional, August 1886, retired, April 1899; appointed coach at the club); qualified as a Football League linesman (1903-04); became a West Bromwich Albion director (August 1905, then Chairman from August 1908 until his death); also a member of the Football Council, the Football League Management committee and the International selection committee, he was associated with football for 55 years.

Standing just 5ft 5ins tall and of slight physique, Billy Bassett was one of the greatest outside-rights of the Victorian era. He was fast and tricky, had fine judgment and was dangerous in front of goal. He made his England debut against Ireland with Preston's Bob Holmes in March 1888, having given the North End left-back a testing time in the FA Cup final just seven days earlier.

He won half of his caps against Scotland and in a 4-1 victory at Ibrox Park in 1892, was described in an after-match report as being the 'smartest forward on the pitch.' He had a hand in two of the goals that afternoon and afterwards Walter Arnott, the defender who was given the job of marking him, said: "I simply couldn't cope with his footwork or his speed." And one neutral reporter covering that game admitted 'It was the finest display he had ever witnessed by a team of footballers.'

When Scotland won 3-2 in April 1889, Bassett was the pick of the English forwards, scoring both his team's goals – a low shot after a fine dribble and shot, the second a tap-in after a scrimmage.

Twice an FA Cup winner with Albion (in 1888 and 1892), Bassett also represented the Football League on three occasions and played for an England XI, the Football League and the FA. He scored 77 goals in 311 appearances in his 13 years as a player with West Bromwich Albion (1886-99).

BASTARD, Segar Richard 1879-80 ①
Born: Bow, London, 25 January 1854
Died: Epsom, Surrey, 20 March 1921
Career: Upton Park (1870), Corinthians (seasons 1872-82), Essex (seasons 1872-74); also Essex County cricketer; an FA Committee member, and FA referee; later became a racehorse owner.

An all-round sportsman, who competed well in cricket, rugby and football matches, Dick Bastard was a strong-running right-winger with a fair turn of speed. He played in the 5-4 defeat by Scotland in March 1880 – two years after refereeing the FA Cup final. Indeed, he is one of only two men ever to play for England and take charge of a Cup final and referee an international match (Charles Clegg being the other). Bastard died at Epsom railway station, after attending a race meeting.

BASTIN, Clifford Sydney 1931-38 ㉑ ⑫
Born: Exeter, Devon, 14 March 1912
Died: Exeter, 4 December 1991
Career: Ladysmith Road School/Exeter, Exeter Schools, Exeter St Mark's (1924), Exeter St James (1925), Exeter City (June 1926), Arsenal (£2,000, May 1929, retired, January 1947); later a licensee at Heavitree near Exeter.

As a mere stripling, Cliff 'Boy' Bastin was a wonderful, direct outside-left who later performed splendidly as an inside-forward and wing-half. Blessed with a natural body-swerve, he possessed a powerful shot, used when least expected, but his outstanding characteristic was an ice-cool temperament. Deafness which first affected him as a young man, meant he was ineligible for military service and as a result he made the most of playing football. He had already played for England Schoolboys v. Wales in 1926 before gaining the first of his senior caps against the same country in November 1931. Deputising for Eric Houghton, he assisted in one of the goals in a 3-1 win. In fact, before he had reached the age of 20, Bastin had starred in international football and won the League and FA Cup with Arsenal, yet it wasn't until May 1933 that he made the outside-left position his own at Highbury. And there were some pretty decent wingers around at the same time!

In May 1938, having given the Nazi salute along with his team-mates before kick-off, Bastin was outstanding in England's 6-3 win over Germany in Berlin's packed Olympic Stadium. He scored after 12 minutes and had a hand in two more goals as Germany's 16-match unbeaten run came to a stuttering end.

Bastin, who scored 178 goals in 396 competitive games for the Gunners, also collected four more League Championship winning medals and tasted FA Cup final glory for a second time.

BAUGH, Richard 1885-90 ②

Born: Wolverhampton, 14 February 1864
Died: Wolverhampton, 14 August 1929
Career: St Luke's School/Blakenhall, Rose Villa (1880), Wolverhampton Rangers (August 1882), Stafford Road (seasons 1884-86), Wolverhampton Wanderers (professional, May 1886), Walsall (September 1896, retired, injured, May 1897).

Twice an FA Cup finalist and a winner in 1893, Dickie Baugh was a redoubtable full-back, dour, zealous and quick to clear. An excellent club man, he served Wolves for 10 years from 1886, making 227 appearances. Impressive on his England debut in a 6-1 win over Ireland in March 1886, he had to wait four years for his second cap, also against Ireland. He was not really tested but was involved in the build-up to two goals in another resounding victory, this one by 9-1. His son, Dickie Baugh junior, played for Wolves, West Bromwich Albion and Exeter City.

BAYLISS, Albert Edward James Matthias 1890-91 ①

Born: Tipton, 14 January 1863
Died: West Bromwich, 19 August 1933
Career: Great Bridge & Horseley Heath Council School, Great Bridge Unity (1878), Tipton Providence (1879), Wednesbury Old Athletic (seasons 1880-84), West Bromwich Albion (amateur, August 1884, professional, August 1885, retired, March 1892; was appointed club director in 1891, remained on board until 1905; made a Life Member, August 1909).

'Gentleman' Jem Bayliss ('Jem' coming from the initials of three of his Christian names) won his only cap against Ireland in March 1891. That day he played right-half, and with his Albion team-mates, Charlie Perry and Billy Bassett also in the team, England romped to a 6-1 victory at Molineux. Prior to that Bayliss had played at centre-forward and had appeared in three successive FA Cup finals, gaining a winner's medal in 1888. Whilst on holiday in Gibraltar six years after winning his only cap, Bayliss was informed that his obituary had been printed in a local paper back in the Midlands, stating he had died from typhoid fever. Despite being rather upset, he got back home, cut the notice from the page and kept it until his 'declared' death in 1933 – some 36 years later!

BATTY, David 1990-98 ㊷

Born: Leeds, 2 December 1968
Career: Allerton Grange School/Leeds, Leeds & West Yorkshire Schools, Tingley Athletic (1984), Leeds United (apprentice, April 1985, professional, August 1987), Blackburn Rovers (£2.75m, September 1993), Newcastle United (£3.75m, March 1996), Leeds United (£4.4m, December 1998-May 2004); later Harrogate Town (vice-president); also involved in advertising campaigns for Cancer Research along with Les Ferdinand, Alan Hansen and John Hartson to raise the awareness of prostate cancer.

A hard-working midfielder, David Batty was the player who missed the last and vital penalty in the shoot-out with Argentina in the second round of the 1998 World Cup in France – it was the first spot-kick he had ever taken!

A year later, he became the eighth England player to get sent off in a major international when he took the 'walk of shame' during the European Championship clash with Poland in Warsaw in September 1999. England's 10 men held on for a 0-0 draw.

He became an established England player under Graham Taylor, having won the first of his 42 caps as a late second-half substitute for Dennis Wise against the USSR in May 1991. Manager Hoddle preferred him in midfield to Steve McManaman and it paid off when England beat Georgia 2-0 (away) in a vital World Cup qualifier in November 1996.

Batty also represented his country at B and U21 levels and made over 470 senior appearances for his three League clubs, gaining both the First and Second Division Championship winner's medals with Leeds.

BAYNHAM, Ronald Leslie 1955-56 ③

Born: Erdington, Birmingham, 10 June 1929
Career: Erdington Rovers (August 1946), Bromford Amateurs (June 1948), Worcester City (August 1949), Luton Town (professional, November 1951, retired, May 1965); later worked as a painter and decorator in Bedfordshire.

Ron Baynham had another England international goalkeeper with him at Luton – Bernard Streten. But he was the younger and held off the challenge of his more senior colleague and went on to appear in over 400 games for the Hatters, gaining an FA Cup runners-up medal in 1959. Honoured by England at B team level, he twice represented the Football League and won his three full caps against Denmark, Northern Ireland and Spain in the space of six weeks in October/November 1955 when called in to replace Bert Williams. England won all three games and Baynham was hardly troubled, although he did save brilliantly from Charlie Tully in the 3-0 win over the Irish and produced three excellent saves in the 4-1 victory over the Spaniards at Wembley.

BEARDSLEY, Peter Andrew, MBE 1985-96 ⑤⑨ ⑨

Born: Longbenton, Newcastle-upon-Tyne, 18 January 1961
Career: Wallsend Boys' Club (1976), Newcastle United (trial,
1977), Carlisle United (professional, August 1979), Vancouver
Whitecaps/Canada (May 1981), Manchester United (£300,000,
September 1982), Vancouver Whitecaps (May 1983), Newcastle
United (£120,000, September 1983), Liverpool (£1.9m, July 1987),
Everton (£1m, August 1991), Newcastle United (£1.45m, June
1993), Bolton Wanderers (£450,000, August 1997), Manchester
City (loan, February-March 1998), Fulham (March 1998), Hartlepool
United (December 1998, released, May 1999), Melbourne Knights/
Australia (briefly); England (assistant-manager/coach, 1999-2000),
Newcastle United (Academy coach, from July 2000; acted as
caretaker-manager in 2010, before Alan Pardew's appointment).

Peter Beardsley was an exceptionally fine footballer, quick-witted,
sharp with a wonderful technique. He amassed a terrific record
of almost 1,000 appearances (for clubs and country) and netted
over 275 goals. Strike-partner to some of the game's greatest
goalscorers, namely Ian Rush, Kevin Keegan, Tony Cottee, Gary
Lineker and Alan Shearer, he partnered the latter two several times
on the international front.

One of the best players on the pitch when England battered
Turkey 8-0 in a European Championship qualifier at Wembley in
1987, he was also outstanding in the next match against Yugoslavia
(won 4-1), had the pleasure of scoring the only goal of the Rous Cup
game against Scotland at Wembley in 1988 before striking home
a real beauty in a 5-0 romp over Greece in 1994. He won his first
cap as a substitute against Egypt in January 1986, scored his first
goal in a 3-0 win over Mexico in Los Angeles four months later and
collected his last cap, also as a 'sub' against China in Beijing in
1996, replacing Nick Barmby.

Beardsley also played in two B internationals, won two League
Championships and the FA Cup with Liverpool and helped Fulham
capture the Second Division title under his old buddy Keegan.

BEASANT, David John 1989-90 ②

Born: Willesden, London, 20 March 1959
Career: Old Uffintonians, Legionnaires FC (1975), Edgware Town
(1976), Wimbledon (£1,000, August 1979), Newcastle United
(£800,000, June 1988), Chelsea (£275,000, January 1989),
Grimsby Town (loan, October 1992), Wolverhampton Wanderers
(loan, January 1993), Southampton (£300,000, November 1993),
Nottingham Forest (free, August 1997), Portsmouth (free, August
2001), Tottenham Hotspur (free, November 2001), Portsmouth
(free, January 2002), Bradford City (free, September 2002), Wigan
Athletic (October 2002), Brighton & Hove Albion (January 2003),
Fulham (August 2003); later Wycombe Wanderers (coach), Northern
Ireland (assistant-manager/coach), Fulham (reserve team player
and goalkeeping coach); The Glenn Hoddle Soccer Academy/Spain
(goalkeeping coach, since 2009)

Goalkeeper Dave Beasant squeezed
himself a couple of England caps on the
basis of being able to kick the ball long
distances – and the dropping of a bottle
of salad cream on his foot was pure farce!
Never likely to oust Peter Shilton, his
international outings were as substitute
(for 'Shilts') in friendlies against Italy and
Yugoslavia at Wembley late in 1989. A
Fourth Division Championship and FA Cup
winner with the Dons, he saved John Aldridge's penalty in the latter
final of 1988. Beasant also helped Chelsea win the Second Division
title in 1989 and the Full Members' Cup a year later. He was in
Forest's team that took the First Division crown in 1998 and was
44 when he retired in 2003, having made 897 appearances (774 in
the Football League/Premiership, placing him 10th in the overall list)
during his nomadic career.

BEASLEY, Albert Edward 1938-39 ① ①

Born: Stourbridge, 27 July 1913
Died: Taunton, Somerset, 3 March 1986
Career: Brierley Hill Schools, Cookley FC (August 1929), Stourbridge
(July 1930), Arsenal (£550, as a professional, May 1931),
Huddersfield Town (£750, October 1936), Arsenal (WW2 guest,
seasons 1940-42 and October-November 1945), Fulham (£400,
December 1945), Bristol City (player-manager, July 1950, retired
as a player, May 1952, continued as manager to January 1958);
Birmingham City (joint manager, February 1958, sole manager,
September 1958-May 1960), Fulham (scout, season 1960-61),
Dover Athletic (manager, June 1961-April 1964); worked for the
Royal Mint during WW2.

Initially a forceful, direct winger and thereafter an attacking left-half,
'Pat' Beasley won the League title twice with Arsenal (1934 and
1935) and also lost in the FA Cup final with Huddersfield (1938). He
won his only cap, awarded against Scotland in April 1939, when as
a late replacement for the injured 'JR' Smith, he scored in a 2-1 win
at Hampden Park in front of 149,269 spectators. John Macadam of
the *Daily Mail* described it as a 'simple goal' – the ball flew high into
the net from five yards after Third Lanark's full-back Carrabine had
missed Tommy Lawton's square pass. Beasley also helped Fulham
win the Second Division Championship and as a manager, steered
Bristol City to Third Division (South) glory in 1955 and Birmingham
City to the Fairs Cup final in 1960.

BEATS, William Edwin 1900-02 ②

Born: Wolstanton, Staffs, 13 November 1871
Died: Reading, 6 April 1939
Career: Pothill Victoria (August 1887), Port Vale Rovers (1889), Burslem Port Vale (1891), Wolverhampton Wanderers (£80, June 1895), Bristol Rovers (May 1903), Port Vale (August 1906), Reading (May 1907, retired April 1911), Reading (trainer, May 1911), Bristol Rovers (trainer, season 1913-14), Reading (trainer, August 1914-April 1917); later licensee of the Truro Inn, Castle Street, Reading (until 1936).

Billy Beats, quiet and unassuming, was an opportunist goalscorer, who invariably popped up in the right place at the right time. He always showed commendable unselfishness and netted over 150 goals in an excellent career, 73 in 199 appearances for Wolves (1895-1903) and 43 in 117 outings for Port Vale. He played in the 1896 FA Cup final and skippered Bristol Rovers to the Southern League Championship in 1905.

Although not on target in either of his two games for England, he assisted in three of the goals when Wales were hammered 6-0 at Newcastle in March 1901 and played his part when England gained a 1-1 draw in the re-arranged game with Scotland at Villa Park in May 1902. The 'first' match, played a month earlier at Ibrox Park was abandoned when part of the terracing collapsed with horrific consequences…26 people lost their lives and almost 600 more were badly injured. Beats and Steve Bloomer actually assisted the police, stewards and first aid workers by moving some of the injured into the centre of the pitch.

BEATTIE, James Scott 2002-04 ⑤

Born: Lancaster, 27 February 1978
Career: Blackburn Rovers (apprentice, April 1993, professional, March 1995), Southampton (£1m, July 1998), Everton (£6m, January 2005), Sheffield United (£4m, August 2007), Stoke City (£3.5m, January 2009), Glasgow Rangers (August 2010), Blackpool (loan, January-May 2011); contract terminated by Glasgow Rangers (August 2011); AFC Bournemouth (trial, November 2011), Sheffield United (November 2011, released, May 2012), Accrington Stanley (November 2012, then player-coach/player-manager, May 2013)

James Beattie won his first cap in the friendly against Australia in February 2003, during his most successful season with Southampton. The Aussies won 3-1 and the result was described (by the Australian media) as 'one of the biggest upsets in soccer history.' At first Beattie combined well with Michael Owen, but overall his contribution (however limited the opportunity) was felt to be disappointing. He was replaced at half-time by Francis Jeffers. Selected four times more by his country, three as a substitute, he has also gained U21 caps (one goal). He was not selected for Euro 2004, Sven Göran Eriksson preferring Heskey instead. Beattie has made almost 500 appearances at club level (231 for Saints). It must have been hard playing in the same era as Shearer and Owen but, really, was Beattie ever considered a genuine replacement for either?

He was the first player signed by Rangers for two years when he moved to Ibrox Park in 2010.

BEATTIE, Thomas Kevin 1974-78 ⑨ ①

Born: Carlisle, 18 December 1953
Career: Ipswich Town (apprentice, April 1970, professional, July 1971), Colchester United (non-contract, July 1982), Middlesbrough (November 1982, retired, injured, October 1983), Sandvikens IF/Sweden (November 1983), Kongsverg/Norway (player-coach, August 1984, retired May 1985); now out of football, living in Suffolk.

Kevin Beattie, equally comfortable as a central defender or left-back, made his England debut in April 1975 against Cyprus in a European Championship qualifier which ended in a 5-0 win. Little more than a month later, he scored with a stunning, looping header when Scotland was thrashed 5-1 at Wembley. This stunning effort was later chosen as one of England's fifty greatest goals. He won his nine caps over a period of 2½ years when at times he battled for a place with his Ipswich team-mate Mick Mills. This was small return for a man who was dubbed 'the new Bobby Moore' and 'better than Duncan Edwards'. Indeed, Sir Bobby Robson said some years later, he expected Beattie to become England's most capped player ever. He nicknamed him 'The Diamond' on the grounds that he had discovered a gem.

Other admirers included Bill Shankly - who tried to sign him for Liverpool - Don Revie and Sir Alf Ramsey, who gave him his U23 debut after he had played less than 10 games as a professional. Beattie was also the inaugural winner of the PFA Young Player of the Year award.

A persistent knee injury forced Beattie to pull out of numerous England squads and for a large part of his career he was only able to make sporadic appearances. Capped twice as a Youth by England and nine times at U23 level, Beattie played a starring role when Ipswich won the FA Cup in 1978 but missed their 1981 UEFA Cup triumph after breaking an arm in the FA Cup semi-final defeat by Manchester City a few weeks earlier. During his career Beattie missed a number of games after suffering serious burns at a family bonfire. He scored 32 goals in 307 games for Ipswich (1971-82). He also starred in the 1981 war film *Escape to Victory* with Pele, Bobby Moore, Ossie Ardiles, Mike Summerbee, Sylvester Stallone and several of his fellow Ipswich Town colleagues including internationals Russell Osman and John Wark.

James Beattie

BECKHAM, David Robert Joseph, OBE (114) (17)

Born: Leytonstone, London, 2 May 1975
Career: Ridgeway Park & Chingford Foundation Schools, Bradenton Preparatory Academy; Manchester United (schoolboy forms, May 1989), Brimsdown Rovers (August 1989), Leyton Orient (trial, March 1991), Norwich City (trial, April 1991), Tottenham Hotspur (School of Excellence, May 1991), Manchester United (apprentice, July 1991, professional, January 1993), Preston North End (loan, February-March 1995); transferred to Real Madrid/Spain (£25m, July 2003), LA Galaxy/USA (£35m, July 2007 – secured on a five-season contract worth £175m; left December 2012); also AC Milan/Italy (loan, January-May 2009 and again, January-March 2010); trained with Tottenham Hotspur (January-February 2011); engaged by England as P.R officer and advisor (to Fabio Capello) at the 2010 World Cup in South Africa; served as vice-President and chief spokesman of England's 2018 World Cup bid Committee; Paris Saint-Germain/France (January-May 2013); also appointed as China's first Football Ambassador (March 2013).

David Beckham made his England debut in September 1996, in a World Cup qualifier against Moldova. He went on to play in all the remaining qualifying matches ahead of the finals in France but was stunned when manager Glenn Hoddle publicly accused him of not concentrating on the tournament. In fact, he did not start in either of the first two matches but was selected for the third against Colombia and scored his first England goal with a free-kick in a 2–0 victory. Then, to his dismay and that of his team-mates and the

England supporters, he received a red card in a clash with Argentinian Diego Simeone in a second round tie in St Etienne. Beckham, after he had been fouled, kicked out at the Argentinian whilst lying on the floor. Simeone said later he tried to get Beckham sent off by over-reacting to the kick. At the time, Beckham was only the fifth player to be sent off playing for England; Ray Wilkins had been the last 12 years earlier.

The match against Argentina ended in a draw but England lost in a penalty shoot-out. Many fans and journalists blamed Beckham for England's elimination and he became the target of criticism and abuse, including the hanging of an effigy outside a London pub, while the *Daily Mirror* printed a dartboard with a picture of him centred on the bullseye. Beckham also received death threats after returning home. The abuse that Beckham received from the fans peaked during England's 3–2 defeat by Portugal in UEFA Euro 2000, despite him creating two goals. A boisterous group of supporters taunted him throughout the match and Beckham responded by raising his middle finger and, while the gesture attracted some criticism, many of the newspapers that had previously encouraged his vilification asked their readers to stop abusing him.

In mid November 2000, a few weeks after Kevin Keegan had resigned as England manager, Beckham was promoted to captain by the caretaker-boss Peter Taylor. He retained the role under Sven-Göran Eriksson and helped England qualify for the 2002 World Cup finals.

One of his, and the team's best performances, came when Germany were thrashed 5–1 in Munich but the final step in his conversion from villain to hero happened in England's 2–2 draw with Greece at Old Trafford in October 2001.

England needed to win or draw the match in order to qualify outright for the World Cup, but were 2–1 down with time running out. Then, with just seconds remaining, Teddy Sheringham was fouled 25 yards out from goal. Beckham took the free-kick and scored with a majestic, curling strike, which by now was his trademark. England had qualified and shortly afterwards, he was voted the BBC Sports Personality of the Year for 2001, while once again finished runner-up to Portugal's Luís Figo in the FIFA World Player of the Year poll.

Beckham was only 75 per cent fit when the 2002 World Cup came round. He played in the first match against Sweden and scored a winning penalty against Argentina in the second. But England themselves went out soon afterwards, beaten in the quarter-finals by the eventual winners Brazil.

The following month, at the opening ceremony of the 2002 Commonwealth Games in Manchester, Beckham escorted Kirsty Howard as she presented the Jubilee Baton to the Queen.

Euro 2004 was a huge disappointment for Beckham. He had a penalty saved in the 2–1 defeat by France and missed another in the quarter-final shoot-out against Portugal, as England slipped out of the competition.

Beckham became a UNICEF Goodwill Ambassador in January 2005 and was involved in promoting London's successful bid for the 2012 Summer Olympic Games.

In October 2005, he was sent off for a second time in an international match, on this occasion against Austria. This was the first time an England captain had been dismissed and he also became the first (and only) player to be red-carded twice while playing for England. He retained the captain's armband, nevertheless, and led his country for the 50th time in a friendly against Argentina the following month, celebrating with a 3-2 victory courtesy of two late Michael Owen goals.

In England's opening game at the 2006 World Cup, against Paraguay, Beckham's free-kick led to an own-goal by Carlos Gamarra as England won 1–0. In the next match against Trinidad and Tobago, his crosses created late goals for Peter Crouch and Steven Gerrard in a 2-0 win.

Beckham curled in a 59th minute free-kick to knock Ecuador out in the second round and by doing so became the first ever English player to score in three separate World Cups. Unfortunately he was ill and missed the quarter-final encounter with Portugal which England again lost on penalties (3-1). Watching from the dug-out, Beckham was visibly shaken and emotional for not being able to play in that game, being in tears at one point.

A day after England had been eliminated from the World Cup a tearful Beckham announced he had stepped down as England captain.

He said "It has been an honour and privilege to captain my country… I feel the time is right to pass on the armband as we enter a new era under Steve McClaren." He was succeeded by Chelsea captain John Terry.

Beckham was omitted from the England team for the next match but was recalled by McClaren for the game against Brazil – England's first match at the new Wembley Stadium. He put in a positive performance and set up a goal for John Terry.

In August 2007, Beckham starred in the friendly against Germany and by doing so became the first player to appear for England while with a non-European club (Los Angeles Galaxy).

Three months later he won his 99th cap against Croatia but sadly England lost 3-2 and failed to qualify for the Euro 2008 finals. Despite this disappointment, Beckham had no plans to retire and after being passed over initially by new England coach Fabio Capello, his former boss at Real Madrid, he finally reached the milestone of 100 international appearances for his country when he played against France in Paris in March 2008. Sir Bobby Charlton presented Beckham with his 100th cap, before the next international against the USA.

Remaining in Capello's squad after that, he played his part in helping England qualify for the 2010 World Cup finals in South Africa, and he even regained the captaincy, albeit only briefly!

In March 2009, Beckham, on as a second-half substitute against Slovakia, overtook Bobby Moore to become England's most-capped outfield player with 109 to his name. Now lying second (behind Peter Shilton) in the list of all-time England appearance-makers, he won 68 of his 115 caps in competitive matches (a record) while 55 were gained when he was playing outside the English Premiership. He also holds another record – that of receiving most yellow cards, 17.

Besides his England duties, Beckham, who made his Football League debut whilst on loan to Preston in 1995, scored 85 goals in 394 appearances for Manchester United with whom he was associated from 1991 to 2003. He helped the Reds win six Premiership titles, the FA Cup twice, the European Champions League, two FA Community Charity Shields and the FA Youth Cup. He joined Real Madrid for £25 million in the summer of 2003 and four years later gained a La Liga Championship winner's medal before switching his allegiance to the Californian-based soccer club LA Galaxy, signing a contract believed to be worth £175m. While in America he helped 'Galaxy' win three MLS Conference titles, the Regional play-off victories, the MLS Cup twice (in 2011 and 2012, thus making it a Hollywood ending in his last game in the final against Houston Dynamo on 1 December) and two MLS Supporters' Shields. He also had two loan spells with Italian giants AC Milan, and at May 2013, after his last outing for PSG, Beckham had appeared in 846 games for club and country and scored 146 goals.

On 31 January 2013, after training with Arsenal, Beckham signed a five-month deal with Paris Saint-Germain, stating that his entire salary (£3.2m) would be donated to a local children's charity. He helped PSG win the French league title, thus becoming the first Englishman to win a League championship in four different countries.

Married to former 'Posh Spice' Victoria Adams since 1999, the Beckhams have four children and own a joint estate worth £195m. Awarded the OBE in the Queen's birthday honours list in June 2003, Beckham was disappointed not to be included in Team GB's squad for the 2012 Olympic Games in London. Beckham retired as a player in May 2013.

BECTON, Francis 1894-97 ② ②

Born: Preston, 11 May 1873
Died: Liverpool, 6 November 1909
Career: Fishwick Ramblers (April 1892), Preston North End (August 1893), Liverpool (March 1895), Sheffield United (October 1898), Bedminster (May 1899), Preston North End (June 1900), Swindon Town (May 1901), Ashton Town (August 1903), New Brighton Tower (August 1904, retired, ill-health, April 1905).

A clever, scheming inside-forward 'Frank' Becton scored twice on his international debut when Ireland got whipped 9-0 at Derby in March 1895. A few weeks earlier he had netted a hat-trick for Preston against West Brom and soon after starring for England he joined Liverpool. His early death came from tuberculosis.

BEDFORD, Henry 1922-25 ② ①

Born: Calow near Chesterfield, 15 October 1899
Died: Derby, 24 June 1976
Career: Grassmoor Ivanhoe/Chesterfield (1914), Nottingham Forest (professional, October 1918), Blackpool (£1,500, March 1921), Derby County (£3,000, September 1925), Newcastle United (£4,000, December 1930), Sunderland (£3,000, January 1932), Bradford Park Avenue (£1,000, May 1932), Chesterfield (free, June 1933), Heanor Town (player-trainer, August 1934); Newcastle United (coach-trainer, October 1937), Derby County (masseur, May 1938), Belper Town (manager, January 1954), Heanor Town (manager, March 1955-March 1956); later a licensee in Derby and an assistant at The Baseball Ground, he worked for Rolls Royce, Derby for 23 years.

Any lack of ball finesse by Harry Bedford was more than atoned for by his dashing and fearless style and his powerful shooting. He scored over 300 goals in 486 League appearances over a period of 14 years (1919-33). Very underrated, he made his international debut against Sweden in Stockholm in May 1923, laying on a goal for Billy Walker in a 4-2 victory. His second cap followed in October 1924 when he scored in a 3-1 win over Ireland at Goodison Park. Bedford also netted four times when the Football League beat the Irish League 5-0 in Belfast in October 1924.

BELL, Colin, MBE 1968-76 ㊽ ⑨

Born: Heselden, County Durham, 26 February 1946
Career: Horden Schools, Horden Colliery (1961), Sunderland (trial, 1962), Newcastle United (trial, 1962), Bury (professional, August 1963), Manchester City (£47,500, March 1966), San Jose Earthquakes/USA (August 1979, retired, November 1979); later returned to Manchester City as a part-time coach (1990); became a restaurateur in partnership with former Burnley player Colin Waldron.

Known as 'Nijinsky' by the Manchester City fans, Colin Bell was always full of running, a great all-round inside-right, a forager who came up with some cracking goals. A League Championship, FA Cup, European Cup Winners' Cup and League Cup winner with City for whom he netted 152 goals in 501 appearances, Bell was at Maine Road for 13 years (1966-79). In 1970, along with his team-mate Francis Lee, he earned a place in the England squad for the World Cup finals in Mexico. To help the players acclimatise to the heat, an inter-squad mini-Olympics was organised – and Bell won every event. During the World Cup itself, Bell played in three games, against Brazil, Czechoslovakia and West Germany. He replaced Bobby Charlton in the 3-2 quarter-final defeat by Germany. But the substitution was deemed, by some, to be the turning point of the game! However, Charlton later argued that it was not the substitution which changed

the game, and pointed out that Germany scored their first goal before he was substituted, and also the Germans had gained a habit of coming back in games. Making his international debut against Germany in June 1968 (lost 1-0) he remained a regular in the squad for six years, captaining the side in a surprise 1-0 defeat by Northern Ireland in 1972. But despite his success, Bell was upset that he was unable to better make his name on the world stage, especially when England failed to qualify for the World Cup in 1974. When his former manager at Manchester City Joe Mercer took over as caretaker-manager from Sir Alf Ramsey in 1974, he chose Bell to play in every game that he was in charge. Rated as one of England's finest ever midfield players, being described by one commentator as 'the most finished article in the modern game', Bell's finest performances for his country included scoring in the 7-0 thrashing of Austria in September 1973, helping England defeat the then World Champions Germany 2-0 in March 1975 (this being the 100th international game played at the old Wembley Stadium) and the 5-1 slaughter of Scotland in May 1975 when he also found the net.

Bell's autobiography entitled 'Colin Bell: Reluctant Hero' was published in 2005.

BENNETT, Walter 1900-01 ②

Born: Mexborough, Yorkshire, 11 June 1874
Died: Denaby, 6 April 1908
Career: Mexborough (July 1889), Sheffield United (professional, February 1896), Bristol City (April 1905), Denaby United (May 1907); killed when a pit-roof collapsed on top of him while working down a mine in Denaby.

Although a short, heavy, aggressive outside-right, Walter 'Cocky' Bennett was also clever on the ball and on his day was one of England's best; on other occasions he was temperamental.
He was outstanding on his debut against Wales in March 1901, setting up two of Steve Bloomer's four goals in a 6-0 victory, and in his second international against Scotland four weeks later, The Times reporter wrote: "Bennett surprised everyone with his ball control on a pitch all but waterlogged by heavy morning rain." This game ended 2-2.
He helped Sheffield United win the League Championship in 1898 and the FA Cup in 1899 and 1902, while with Bristol City he gained a Division Two winner's medal.

BENSON, Robert William 1912-13 ①

Born: Swalwell, Whitehaven, 9 February 1883
Died: Islington, London, 19 February 1916
Career: Dunston Villa (1898), Shankhouse FC (1899), Swalwell FC (1900), Newcastle United (£150, professional, December 1902), Southampton (£150, September 1904), Sheffield United (£150, May 1905), Arsenal (£200, November 1913, retired, April 1914).

Having toured South Africa with the FA in 1910 and represented the Football League, Bob Benson was awarded his only England cap against Ireland in Belfast in 1913 when he deputised for the injured Jesse Pennington. He was given a testing time by Everton's outside-right John Houston as the Irish won 2-1.
In February 1916, Benson was a spectator at Highbury, waiting for the Arsenal-Reading Combination game to kick-off when the Gunners found out they were a man short. Although he had not played for two years, Benson volunteered to make up the team. Just before half-time he left the field feeling unwell. Sadly he died soon afterwards from a burst blood vessel. He was only 33.

BENT, Darren Ashley 2005-12 ⑬ ④

Born: Wandsworth, London, 6 February 1984
Career: Ipswich Town (apprentice, June 1980, professional, July 2001), Charlton Athletic (£2.5m, June 2005), Tottenham Hotspur (£16.5m, June 2007), Sunderland (£10m, August 2009), Aston Villa (£22m, January 2011)

Having been capped by England at Youth, U19 and U21 levels, Darren Bent eventually made his senior debut in March 2006 in the friendly against Uruguay at Anfield, but was not included in the World Cup squad when it was announced two months later. He came on as an 80th minute substitute in the 3–2 defeat by Croatia in November 2007 which ended England's dream of qualifying for Euro 2008. Named in the initial squad of 30 for the 2010 World Cup, owing to Carlton Cole's injury, he was left out of Fabio Capello's final 23, but after some impressive displays, first for Sunderland and then for Aston Villa, he was recalled to the England team for the friendly with Denmark in February 2011, scoring the equaliser in a 2-1 win.
Bent is the England's U21 joint second top-scorer (with Frank Lampard and James Milner) with nine goals from 14 appearances. Injury unfortunately ruled him out of Euro 2012.

Darren Bent

BENTLEY, David Michael 2007-09 ⑦

Born: Peterborough, 27 August 1984
Career: Arsenal (apprentice, August 2000, professional, August 2001), Norwich City (loan, June 2004-May 2005), Blackburn Rovers (loan, August 2005, signed permanently, January 2006), Tottenham Hotspur (£1.5m, July 2008), Birmingham City (loan, January-May 2011), West Ham United (season-long loan, August 2011-May 2012), Blackburn Rovers (loan, January-May 2013).

The similarities with David Beckham start and finish with the fact they're both called David. A wide-player, preferring the right flank, he's nowhere near as good as the former Manchester United star and his dead-ball capabilities are only moderate. Bentley was tormented by the England boo-boys after rejecting a call-up to the U21s. For all his natural ability it's difficult to forget that Arsene Wenger gladly let him go from Arsenal, and Wenger doesn't let quality players leave without a fight. Selected for the Euro 2008 qualifiers against Israel and Russia, he made his senior debut as a substitute for Shaun Wright-Phillips against Israel and was jeered by some of the fans. He started an England game for the first time in the friendly against Switzerland in February 2008. Unfortunately his seven appearances for the national side to date have been wholly forgettable. A former Youth international, he gained one B and seven U21 caps.

BENTLEY, Roy Thomas Frank 1948-55 ⑫ ⑨

Born: Bristol, 17 May 1924
Career: Portway School/Bristol, Bristol Rovers (amateur forms, August 1937), Bristol City (groundstaff/amateur, July 1938, professional, August 1941), Newcastle United (£8,500, June 1946), Chelsea (£12,500, January 1948), Fulham (£8,600, September 1956), Queens Park Rangers (May 1961, retired, December 1962); Reading (manager, January 1963-February 1969), Bradford City (scout, March-May 1969), Swansea City (manager, August 1969-October 1972), Thatcham Town (manager, seasons 1973-76), Reading (secretary, June 1978-February 1984), Aldershot (secretary, January 1985-August 1986).

Centre-forward Roy Bentley was an England international for six years. He made his debut against Sweden in May 1949 – when he dribbled through before setting up Tom Finney for the 67th minute winner - and played in the 1950 World Cup, including the infamous 1-0 defeat by the USA, having netted the winning goal against Scotland at Hampden Park to confirm England's qualification for that tournament and at the same time, deny the Scots a place in the finals, for which he was dubbed 'The man who robbed Scotland of Rio.' In fact, Bentley later admitted that his strike against the Scots was the best goal he ever scored in his entire career. Initiated by two craftsmen – Jimmy Dickinson and Wilf Mannion – Bobby Langton then set up Bentley who finished in style.
After being forgiven for his past in the World Cup defeat by the USA in 1950, Bentley came back with a bang in November 1954 when he scored a hat-trick in a 3-2 win over Wales on a saturated Wembley pitch. He was 30 years, 177 days old at the time – making him the oldest player ever to net a treble for England.
Also on target in his last international against Portugal in May 1955 (lost 3-1) the tall Chelsea striker was perhaps unfortunate to have Nat Lofthouse and Stan Mortensen playing at the same time. He scored 150 goals in 357 appearances for Chelsea, gaining a League Championship winner's medal in 1955.

BERESFORD, Joseph 1933-34 ①

Born: Chesterfield, 26 February 1906
Died: Aston, Birmingham, 26 February 1978
Career: Bentley Toll Bar School/Chesterfield (1917-20), Doncaster Schools (1918-20), Bentley New Village Old Boys (1921), Ashern Working Men's Club/Doncaster (March 1922), Bartley Colliery (season 1922-23), Mexborough Athletic (August 1923), Mansfield Town (May 1926), Aston Villa (May 1927), Preston North End (September 1935), Swansea Town (December 1937), Stourbridge (August 1938), Sutton Town (September 1939, retired, May 1941); returned with Hartlepool United (guest, 1943); later ran a fish shop in Stourbridge and also worked for I.C.I. Witton/Birmingham for eleven years.

The scorer of 73 goals in 251 appearances for Aston Villa (1927-35), Joe Beresford was a 'human dynamo' in the attack, a fitting partner to 'Pongo' Waring and Billy Walker. He won his only England cap (behind his club colleague Tom Gardner) against Czechoslovakia in Prague in May 1934 when he partnered Sammy Crooks of Derby on the right-wing.

BERRY, Arthur 1908-09 ①

Born: Liverpool, 3 January 1888
Died: Liverpool, 15 March 1953
Career: Denstone School (rugby union XV 1904-05, captain 1905-06), Wrexham (March 1907), Wadham College/Oxford University (1907-08), Liverpool (April 1908 and October 1908), Wrexham (March 1909), Everton (August 1909), Fulham (September 1909), Wrexham (December 1909 and November 1911-April 1912), Oxford City (May 1912), Liverpool (October 1912), Wrexham (October 1912), Oxford City (January 1913), Wrexham (April 1914), Northern Nomads (August 1914, retired, October 1914); practised as a solicitor and was called to the Bar at Gray's Inn in October 1914.

Capped 32 times as an amateur by England (1908-13), Arthur Berry was one of the finest right-wingers of his era. One contemporary summed up his direct style as 'a complete art without tinsel or gaudiness.' His only senior outing for his country was in the 4-0 win over Ireland at Bradford in February 1909 when, as one reporter wrote: "He was often collared by McCartney, the Ireland left full-back, but he and Woodward worked well together down the right. He was unlucky with one shot that looped over the crossbar."

Berry played in the 1913 Amateur Cup final for Oxford City and also won soccer gold medals for the United Kingdom at the 1908 and 1912 Olympic Games. His father, Edwin, who played for Everton, became a Liverpool director and Chairman of the club (1904-09).

BERRY, John Reginald 1952-56 ④

Born: Aldershot, 1 June 1926
Died: Farnham, Surrey, 16 September 1994
Career: St Joseph's School/Aldershot, Aldershot Schoolboys, Aldershot YMCA, Army football (Royal Artillery), Birmingham City (professional, December 1944), Manchester United (£25,000, August 1951, retired, due to injuries received in Munich air crash in 1958); later ran a sports outfitters shop in the south of England.

Johnny Berry was a casualty of the Munich air disaster in February 1958. Aged 31 at the time, he spent two months in hospital with multiple injuries: a fractured skull, broken jaw, broken elbow, broken pelvis and a broken leg. All his teeth had to be removed while treating his jaw injuries. In fact, when he woke up Berry was totally unaware of

the plane crash, his injuries having caused a slight form of amnesia. One month after he regained consciousness he found out about the crash while reading a newspaper. He never played football again. Prior to that disaster, as one of the Busby Babes, Berry had won three League titles with Manchester United for whom he scored 44 goals in 273 appearances.

A Football League representative and an England B player, Berry's four senior caps came on the South American tour in May 1953 against Argentina, Chile and Uruguay, when he played on the left-wing in place of Jack Froggatt, and versus Sweden in May 1956 when he replaced the injured Stan Matthews on the right. He would surely have gained more honours had not Matthews and Tom Finney been around at the same time.

BERTRAND, Ryan Dominic 2012-13 ②

Born: Southwark, London, 5 August 1989
Career: Gillingham (youth team player, April 2004), Chelsea (signed for £125,000 as a trainee, July 2005, professional, August 2006), AFC Bournemouth (loan, November 2006-January 2007), Oldham Athletic (loan, August 2007-January 2008), Norwich City (loan, January-May 2008 and again, July 2008-May 2009), Reading (loan, July 2009-May 2010), Nottingham Forest (loan, August 2010-January 2011).

A very competent left-back, quick over the ground, strong in the tackle with good vision, Ryan Bertrand made over 150 club appearances as a loan player before making his Chelsea Premiership debut in April 2011. The following season he was given eight more Premiership outings by the Stamford Bridge club, which saw him produce some superb performances, resulting in selection for Great Britain's 2012 Olympic team. Shortly afterwards Bertrand collected his first full England cap in the 2-1 win over the World cup runners-up Italy in Berne, Switzerland. As youngster, he had represented his country at five other levels – from U17 to U21.

BESTALL, John Gilbert 1934-35 ①

Born: Beighton, Yorkshire, 24 June 1900
Died: Doncaster, 11 April 1985
Career: Crooksmoor School/Sheffield, Beighton Miners' Welfare, Rotherham United (1924), Grimsby Town (November 1926, retired, May 1936); Birmingham (coach, June 1938, then chief scout, August 1944-February 1946), Doncaster Rovers (manager, March 1946-April 1949), Blackburn Rovers (manager, June 1949-May 1953), Nelson (manager, July 1953-November 1954), Doncaster Rovers (chief scout, August 1958, then manager, March 1959-August 1960, reverting to coach until May 1962).

Jackie Bestall, who captained Grimsby to the Second Division Championship in 1934, gained his only cap in February 1935 against Northern Ireland at Goodison Park at the age of 34 years, 226 days - the sixth oldest player to make his England debut. Partnering Arsenal's Ted Drake in attack that day, he also became the first Grimsby player to win a full cap. Bestall also represented the Football League on three occasions while scoring 83 goals in 457 appearances for the Mariners between 1926 and 1938, and vied with 'wee' Alex James as being the smallest forward in league football in the 1930s. In tribute to his career he had a lounge at Blundell Park and the smallest road in Grimsby and Cleethorpes named after him.

Ryan Bertrand

BETMEAD, Harry Archibald 1936-37 ①

Born: Grimsby, 11 April 1912
Died: Hertford, 26 August 1984
Career: Grimsby Sunday school football, Hay Cross FC (seasons 1927-30), Grimsby Town (professional, October 1930, retired, December 1947); also played cricket for Lincolnshire.

Replacing Alf Young of Huddersfield Town at centre-half, Harry Betmead starred in his only game for England, in an 8-0 win over Finland in Helsinki in May 1937. Although he had very little to do that afternoon, he marshalled his defence superbly and even found time to venture upfield and strike the crossbar with a header. Two years later he toured South Africa with the FA playing in two Test Matches.
    A member of the same Grimsby team as Jackie Bestall, he appeared in 315 games for the Mariners up to 1947.

BETTS, Morton Peto 1876-77 ①

Born: Bloomsbury, London, 30 August 1847
Died: Menton, France, 19 April 1914
Career: Harrow School, Harrow Chequers (1862), Wanderers (seasons 1864-73); also assisted West Kent, Essex and Old Harrovians; FA Committee member (seasons 1870-72) and 1881-90), FA vice-president (season 1890-91); played cricket for Essex (briefly), Middlesex and Kent; Essex CCC (secretary, seasons 1887-90)

A leading sportsman of the late 19th century, Morton Betts was credited with the first and winning goal in an FA Cup Final…for the Wanderers against the Royal Engineers in 1872. He played under the pseudonym A.H. Chequer because he was already registered with Harrow Chequers, a team associated with Harrow School. However, they had withdrawn prior to the first game, so under the rules of the time, Betts could not play with another club in the same tournament. He did though, and his 'goal' was a simple 'tap-in' after Robert Vidal had 'dribbled' through the Royal Engineers' defence. Switching between football and cricket duties frequently, Betts usually played soccer as a full-back, though his only appearance for England, in a 2-1 defeat by Scotland, in March 1877, was as a goalkeeper. A report in *Bells Life* stated: 'Betts played well, although at times a certain amount of looseness was noticeable.'

BETTS, William 1888-89 ④

Born: Sheffield, 26 March 1864
Died: Sheffield, 8 August 1941
Career: Pitsmoor FC (August 1878), Parkwood Rovers (December 1878), Clarence FC (season 1879-80), Pyebank Rovers (season 1880-81) Heeley (April 1881), Sheffield Wednesday (April 1881-October 1883), Lockwood Brothers (November 1883-May 1885); Sheffield Wednesday (July 1885-May 1897); later Wednesday's groundsman and also assistant trainer; played cricket for Yorkshire colts.

A versatile half-back, strong in the air and on the ground, Billy Betts made 143 appearances in two spells with the Owls, scoring four goals. He won his only cap for England against Wales in February 1889 when he starred in a 4-1 win at Stoke… at a time when several changes were being made in the middle-line. He played in the 1890 FA Cup final.

BEVERLEY, Joseph 1883-84 ③

Born: Blackburn, 12 November 1856
Died: Blackburn, 21 May 1897
Career: St John's School/Blackburn, Black Star FC/Blackburn, Blackburn Olympic (founder member, April 1876), Blackburn Rovers (October 1882), Blackburn Olympic (August 1884), Blackburn Rovers (October 1887-May 1889); later worked at Albion Mill, Blackburn, where he died following an accident.

An FA Cup winner with Blackburn Rovers in 1884, Joe Beverley could play at left-back, centre and left-half, centre-forward or inside-left. Quick over the ground, with a good passing ability, he won his three caps in the space of three weeks in February/March 1884 as full-back partner to Alf Dobson of Notts County, having a hand in two of the goals when Ireland were whipped 8-1 in Belfast on his debut.

BIRKETT, Ralph James Evans 1935-36 ①

Born: Newton Abbot, Devon, 9 January 1913
Died: Torquay, Devon, 8 July 2002
Career: Woodthorpe School/Ashford, Middlesex Schools, Ashford FC (1928), Dartmouth United (amateur, August 1928), Torquay United (amateur, August 1929, professional, March 1930), Arsenal (£2,000, April 1933), Middlesbrough (£5,000, March 1935), Newcastle United (£5,900, July 1938); served in India as an Army PT Instructor during WW2; also played as a guest for Darlington, Fulham, Chester, Middlesbrough, Chelsea, Reading and Torquay United during WW2 (retired May 1946).

An outside-right, and the recipient of a First Division Championship medal with Arsenal in 1934, Ralph Birkett was a regular scorer throughout his 17-year career. Twice a Football League representative, he gained his only England cap against Ireland in Belfast in October 1935 when he and Sam Tilson kicked the ball over the line together for the second goal in a 3-1 win, but it was awarded to Tilson in the end. Birkett was chosen for the next international against Germany but was injured and his place went to Stanley Matthews. He never got another senior call, although he did play and score in a Wartime international against Scotland at Newcastle in February 1941.

BIRKETT, Reginald Halsey 1878-79 ①

Born: Westminster, London, 28 March 1849
Died: Holborn, London, 30 June 1898
Career: Lancing College (seasons 1865-68), Lancing Old Boys seasons 1868-70), Clapham Rovers (football and rugby union, seasons 1871-81), Surrey (between 1872 and 1878); also played rugby for England v. Scotland (1871-76); Rugby Union committee member (1877-83); he worked as a hide and skin broker in London and died in the city following an accident sustained whilst suffering from delirium during an attack of typhoid fever.

An FA Cup finalist in 1879 and winner in 1880, Reg Birkett was effectively a fearless goalkeeper who actually played in every outfield position during his varied career. His international cap came against Scotland in April 1879 when he conceded four first-half goals before England stormed back to win a memorable match 5-4.
    His brother Louis and his son John were also England rugby internationals.

BIRLEY, Francis Hornby, J.P. **1873-75** ②

Born: Chorley, Lancs, 14 March 1850
Died: Dormansland, Surrey, 1 August 1910
Career: Winchester College, University College/Oxford University (1866-74), Wanderers (1875-78), Middlesex (1870s); also played cricket for Lancashire and Surrey; worked as a barrister, Inner Temple, from January 1876.

Both of Francis Birley's caps were won against Scotland - the first in March 1874, when the Scots managed a 2–1 victory to avenge their 1873 defeat; the second twelve months later when he played with four of his Wanderers team-mates at The Oval. This time the game ended 2–2, Birley's club-mates Charles Wollaston and Charles Alcock scoring the goals. An FA Cup winner three times and a finalist once, Birley occupied all three half-back positions, being described as 'two-footed, difficult to beat and who played the game with unbounded enthusiasm.'

BIRTLES, Garry **1979-81** ③

Born: Nottingham, 27 July 1956
Career: Long Eaton Rovers (August 1971), Long Eaton United (July 1973), Nottingham Forest (£2,000, professional, December 1976), Manchester United (£1.25m, October 1980), Nottingham Forest (£250,000, September 1982), Notts County (June 1987), Grimsby Town (August 1989-May 1992), Gresley Rovers (player/joint-manager with Paul Futcher, November 1995-May 1999); he now co-commentates on Sky Sports, having previously reported on and analysed Nottingham Forest matches on local radio; he also writes a weekly column for Nottingham's local newspaper *The Nottingham Evening Post*.

A fast and dangerous striker, Gary Birtles scored 96 goals in 283 appearances for Nottingham Forest with whom he gained a League Cup and two European Cup winner's medals. He also played in one B, two U21 and three full internationals for England whilst at The City Ground. He failed to hit it off at Old Trafford but managed 12 goals in 82 games for Notts County. His senior caps for his country came in the space of five months in 1980 against Argentina (when, as a substitute, he replaced team-mate Trevor Francis), versus Italy (when he started up front alongside his former Forest colleague Tony Woodcock) and v. Romania (when again he partnered Woodcock). There were so many good strikers around at the same time as Birtles, thus limiting his opportunities.

BISHOP, Sidney Macdonald **1926-27** ④ ①

Born: Stepney, London, 10 February 1900
Died: Chelsea, London, 4 May 1949
Career: Lexford School/Ilford (to August 1914), served in RAF (years 1916-18), Crystal Palace (trial, 1919), Ilford (briefly), West Ham United (May 1920), Leicester City (November 1926), Chelsea (£3,800, June 1928, retired, May 1933).

A wing-half or inside-forward with an unflurried demeanour, Sid Bishop helped West Ham gain promotion to the First Division and also appeared in the first FA Cup final at Wembley Stadium in 1923. Nicknamed 'Sticks' he made 172 appearances for the Hammers and 109 for Chelsea and won all his four caps with Leicester, the first in a 2-1 win over Scotland at Hampden Park in April 1927. *The Daily Express* reporter at this game wrote: 'I noticed that the knees of some of the players, Edwards and Bishop among them, were chattering. It may only have been due to cold, but I have my doubts.' Then, on the end-of-season tour, Bishop helped England thrash Belgium 9-1, scored in the 86th minute in a 5-2 win over Luxembourg and was prominent in a resounding 6-0 victory over France.

BLACKBURN, James Thomas Alfred **1900-04** ③ ①

Born: Mellor near Blackburn, 12 September 1878
Died: Ilford, Essex, October 1952
Career: Mellor FC (seasons 1894-97), Blackburn Rovers (professional, July 1897), West Ham United (May 1905, retired May 1913); later Barking FC (coach, seasons 1931-33) after serving in the Merchant Navy.

Outside-left 'Fred' Blackburn scored on his international debut – in a 2-2 draw with Scotland at Crystal Palace in March 1901. 'He touched the ball home in the 19th minute from what appeared an offside position, inches from the goal-line' reported *The Times*. Difficult to dispossess but erratic in shooting, he helped England beat Ireland 1-0 twelve months later and Scotland by the same score in April 1904 when his cross was missed by full-back Watson, allowing Steve Bloomer to score in the 18th minute.
Blackburn also represented the English League and played in a North versus South fixture. He made 237 Southern League appearances for West Ham, scoring 24 goals.

BLACKBURN, George Frederick **1923-24** ①

Born: Willesden Green, London, 18 March 1899
Died: Cheltenham, 3 July 1957
Career: Pound Lane School/Willesden, London Juniors, London FA, Willesden Juniors, Middlesex FA, St Francis's FC, Hampstead Town (January 1916), Army football/Essex Yeomanry (1917-19), Hampstead Town (August 1919), Aston Villa (amateur, December 1920, professional, January 1921), Cardiff City (£1,000, June 1926), Mansfield Town (£100, June 1931), Cheltenham Town (player-manager, July 1932, retired, May 1934), Moor Green (coach, August 1934), Birmingham (trainer, July 1937, coach, August 1946-May 1948).

A very useful left-half, tireless, tenacious and wholehearted, George Blackburn, who had twice been named as a reserve, won his only England cap against France in Paris in May 1924 when he was chosen ahead of Birmingham's Percy Barton who had played in the previous three internationals.

Blackburn, an FA Cup finalist in 1924, made 145 appearances for Aston Villa and 116 for Cardiff, but missed the 1927 FA Cup final with the latter club, although he did gain two Welsh Cup winner's medals.

BLENKINSOP, Ernest 1927-33 ㉖

Born: Cudworth, Barnsley, Yorkshire, 20 April 1900
Died: Sheffield, 24 April 1969
Career: Brierley Colliery FC (1917), Cudworth United Methodists (August 1919), Hull City (professional, October 1921), Sheffield Wednesday (£1,150, January 1923), Liverpool (£6,500, March 1934), Cardiff City (player-coach, November 1937), Buxton (August 1939); played as a guest during WW2 for Hurst FC, Halifax Town, Bradford City and Bradford Park Avenue (retired May 1945); Sheffield FC (coach, briefly), later Sheffield Wednesday (scout); became a licensee in Sheffield.

A Second Division and twice a First Division Championship winner with Sheffield Wednesday in 1926, 1929 and 1930 respectively, Ernie Blenkinsop served England admirably for five years. Captain of both club and country, he made his international debut against France in March 1928 and played his last game against Scotland in April 1933. England was undefeated in 21 of his 26 games and scored 82 goals, Ernie having a hand in at least 10 of them. Along with his Wednesday team-mates Alf Strange and Bill Marsden, he was brilliant in the 5-2 win over Scotland at Wembley in 1930, confirmed by J. H Freeman of the *Daily Mail* who wrote: 'The virtues of club pairs and threes in international matches have often been extolled. On this occasion the Wednesday players deserved all the praise they got.'

A left-back with a polished style, he was 'judicious in tackling, cool under pressure and placed his clearances with unfailing accuracy.' He made well over 500 appearances in club football (425 for Wednesday).

BLISS, Herbert 1920-21 ①

Born: Willenhall, Staffs, 29 March 1890
Died: Bournemouth, 14 June 1968
Career: Willenhall Pickwick (seasons 1905-09), Willenhall Swifts (August 1909), Tottenham Hotspur (professional, April 1912), Clapton Orient (December 1922), Bournemouth (July 1925, retired, May 1926)

An inside forward with a reputation for speed, accurate passing and riffling shots on goal, Bert Bliss scored 106 goals in 215 appearances for Spurs. A member of the team which gained promotion to the First Division in 1920 and won the FA Cup the following year, his direct play and accurate passing was a notable feature of the game. Bliss played once for England, with three of his club-mates, Jimmy Dimmock, Arthur Grimsdell and Bert Smith, against Scotland in April 1921 (two weeks before the FA Cup final). It was a bad day all round as the Scots won 3-0 at Hampden Park...'Bliss and Dimmock failing to reproduce their club form' wrote John Crockett in the *Daily Mail*.

BLISSETT, Luther Loide 1982-84 ⑭ ③

Born: Falmouth, Jamaica, 1 February 1958
Career: Watford (apprentice, April 1973, professional, July 1975), AC Milan (£1m, June 1983), Watford (£550,000, August 1984), Bournemouth (£60,000, November 1985), Watford (£40,000, August 1991), West Bromwich Albion (loan, October-November 1992), Bury (free, August 1993), Derry City (loan, September 1993),

Mansfield Town (free, December 1993), Southport (loan, March-May 1994), Wimbourne Town (briefly), Fakenham Town (player-coach, August 1994, retiring as a player, May 1995); Watford (assistant-manager/coach, February 1996), York City (coach, May 2002-May 2003), Portsmouth (coach, seasons 2003-05), Chesham United (manager, February-April 2006); quit football to concentrate on his involvement with the Windrush Motorsport project/Le Mans 24-hour race; returned with Hemel Hempstead Town (coach, March 2010).

Luther Blissett's England career may have started well - all three of his international goals came in one game against Luxembourg in December 1982. In fact, he became the first black player to net for England at senior level in that 9-0 win over Luxembourg, which is the highest score for a European Championship match.

However, the fact he went on to win just 14 caps speaks volumes. He only started five times for his country. His move to AC Milan coincided with a total draining of confidence from the target-man and the tabloids nicknamed him 'Luther Miss-it.' Blissett, who also won one B and four U21 caps, scored 213 goals in 584 League games in an excellent club career. He is Watford's all-time record appearance-maker and goalscorer.

BLOCKLEY, Jeffrey Paul 1972-73 ①

Born: Leicester, 12 September 1949
Career: New Parks Secondary School/Leicester, Leicester & Blaby Schools, Blaby Boys' Club (1964), Midland Athletic (1965), Coventry City (apprentice, October 1966, professional, June 1967), Arsenal (£200,000, October 1972), Leicester City (£100,000, January 1975), Derby County (loan, January-February 1978), Notts County (June 1978), Enderby Town (player-coach, July 1980), Gloucester City (June 1981, retired as a player, May 1983), Leicester United (manager, July 1983), Shepshed Charterhouse (manager, May 1984), Hinckley Athletic (manager, April-May 1989); now runs his own engineering business, Transmech, in the East Midlands.

Jeff Blockley, a central defender, was called up by England as a late replacement for Roy McFarland just days after moving to Arsenal from Coventry City in 1972 but the 1-1 draw against Yugoslavia at Wembley proved to be his only cap. His stay at Arsenal was also unsuccessful and Bertie Mee later said signing Blockley was 'the worst mistake he ever made as manager.' He did, however, gain six U23 caps and amassed over 400 club appearances during his career.

BLOOMER, Stephen 1894-1907 ㉓ ㉘

Born: Cradley Heath, West Midlands, 20 January 1874
Died: Derby, 16 April 1938
Career: Derby Schools, Derby Swifts (April 1890), Tutbury Hawthorn (August 1891), Derby Midland (semi-professional, October 1891), Derby County (professional, August 1892), Middlesbrough (March 1906), Derby County (September 1910, retired, January 1914); Britannia Berlin '92/Germany (coach, July 1914); interned at Ruhleben, Spandau prisoner-of-war camp during WW1; Baluu-Wit Amsterdam (coach, seasons 1918-21); Canada (as coach, February-May 1921), Real Union FC/Spain (manager-coach, seasons 1923-26), Derby County (reserve team coach and general assistant, seasons 1926-30); also played cricket and baseball (for the Derby Baseball club, British champions, 1895, '97 & '98).

Steve Bloomer was slight, pale-faced, an unlikely athlete really, but he was 'full of wire and whipcord, as hard as nails and a predator of the highest order.' One of England's greatest-ever goalscorers, the Black Country-born centre-forward made his 23 international appearances over a period of 12 years. He netted twice on his debut in a 9-0 win over Ireland in March 1895, drove in a fine through pass from Holt in a 3-0 win over Scotland at Goodison Park in his second game and subsequently scored 19 times in his first 10 matches for his country, one of his best being the winner against Scotland at Celtic Park in April 1904 when he was quick to take advantage of a mistake by Watson.

In March 1896, Bloomer notched a five-timer in a 9-1 win over Wales and in March 1901 scored four times when the same opposition was battered 6-0 - thus becoming the first player to score two hat-tricks for England and was also the first to score four goals for his country twice. He eventually bagged a grand total of 28 international goals... netting in ten consecutive matches over a period of four years between 9 March 1895 and 20 March 1899 – a record.

During his international career Bloomer – who was England's most-capped player until 1911 when Bob Crompton won his 23rd - was on the losing side just twice and many of his club colleagues played alongside him at international level, namely John Goodall, Frank Becton, Jack Reynolds, Ernest Needham, Fred Spiksley, Sam Wolstenholme and Vivian Woodward.

Bloomer, who helped England win the British Home Championship eight times, scored 332 goals in 525 appearances for Derby and 62 in 130 for Middlesbrough and during his career as a whole, he struck no less than 430 goals in 684 competitive matches – what a record! And he was the first player to score at West Bromwich Albion's current ground, The Hawthorns, doing so for Derby in September 1900.

As a coach, he guided Real Union to victory in Spain's Campeonato de Guipuzcoa and Copa Del Rey Cup final of 1923-24.

Besides being a brilliant footballer, Bloomer also excelled at cricket, once scoring 204 and taking 6-15 in the same match; he clocked 9.6 seconds for the 75-yard sprint and won honours at baseball. In late 1937, while severely ill, Derby County paid for him to go on a cruise to Australia and New Zealand. He died three weeks after returning home in April 1938. His grave can be visited in Nottingham Road Cemetery, Derby.

In January, 2009 after a long and sustained period of campaigning, a bust of Bloomer was finally unveiled inside Derby County's home ground, at Pride Park.

BLUNSTONE, Frank 1954-56 ⑤

Born: Crewe, 17 October 1934
Career: Bedford Street School/Crewe, Cheshire FA, Crewe Alexandra (amateur, August 1951, professional, January 1952). Chelsea (£7,000, February 1953, retired, injured, June 1964, appointed club's youth team coach); Brentford (manager, December 1969-June 1973), Manchester United (youth team manager/coach, January 1974-June 1977), Derby County (assistant-manager/coach, September 1977-May 1979), Ethnikos FC/Greece (coach, August 1979), Aris Thessalonica/Greece (coach, March-July 1980), Brentford (youth team manager, seasons 1980-82), Sheffield Wednesday (youth team manager-coach, July 1982, then caretaker-manager, briefly in season 1983-84); now lives at Weston near Crewe.

Frank Blunstone made his international debut against Wales in November 1954, creating two goals for his Chelsea team-mate Roy Bentley in a 3-2 win on a rain-soaked Wembley pitch. He also played in England's famous 7-2 win over Scotland at Wembley in April 1955 when he gave an immaculate display of direct wing-play. The *Herald* correspondent covering the game wrote: 'Scotland's right-back Cunningham was so outclassed by Blunstone that it is remarkable that the outside-left did not score half a dozen goals.' Blunstone, who twice came back after breaking a leg and was once described by Jimmy Greaves as having a heart the size of a cabbage, scored 54 goals in 347 appearances for Chelsea between 1953 and 1964, gaining a League Championship winner's medal in 1955. On retiring, he joined the coaching staff at Stamford Bridge and later, as Brentford's manager, he took the Bees to promotion to the Third Division in 1972.

BOND, Richard 1904-10 ⑧ ②

Born: Garstang, Lancs, 14 December 1883
Died: Lancaster, 25 April 1955
Career: Royal Artillery football (seasons 1899-1902), Preston North End (professional, August 1902), Bradford City (£950, May 1909); taken as a prisoner-of-war during WW1; Blackburn Rovers (August 1922), Lancaster Town (August 1923, retired, May 1924); returned with Garstang FC (August 1926, retired, May 1925-27); later ran a fried fish business before becoming a Preston publican.

A superficial observer might find it strange that Dicky Bond, a wiry, slippery, clever outside-left, could withstand over 20 years in top flight football (1902-23), for he was slight of frame, stood 5ft 5ins tall and weighed barely 10st.

He made his first international appearance for England while at Preston in February 1905 against Ireland and in fact, both his goals were scored against the Irish in a 5-0 win in February 1906. He contest the right-wing position with Jack Rutherford of Newcastle United and John Sharp of Everton.

BONETTI, Peter Phillip 1966-70 ⑦

Born: Putney, London, 27 September 1941
Career: St Mary's School/Worthing, Worthing Roman Catholic Youth Club (1956), Chelsea (amateur, May 1958, professional, April 1959, released, May 1975; re-signed, October 1975-May 1979), Worthing (briefly), Dundee United (August 1979, retired, September 1979); moved to the Isle of Mull; Chelsea (coach, December 1979), later goalkeeping coach at Birmingham City, and also England; now lives in Birmingham.

Peter Bonetti's international career was somewhat unfortunate. He emerged in an era of talented English goalkeepers and thus faced stiff competition for a place in the side, particularly from Ron

Springett and Gordon Banks early on, and later from Peter Shilton, which limited him to just seven caps. A non-playing member of Alf Ramsey's 1966 World Cup winning squad, his career with England is largely remembered for one match - the 1970 World Cup quarter-final against West Germany in Mexico when, unproven in big internationals, he was thrust into the starting line-up as a late replacement for Banks who was suffering from a stomach bug. England lost 3-2 after extra-time, having been 2-0 up at one stage. After the game, Bonetti was made one of the scapegoats, although he could be reasonably faulted for only one of the three goals conceded. That was his only appearance in the World Cup and his last for England. He had conceded only one goal in his previous six internationals. He had made his debut in a 2-0 win over Denmark on a bumpy pitch in Copenhagen in July 1966.

Spectacularly agile with outstanding reflexes, Bonetti – nicknamed 'The Cat' - made 729 appearances for Chelsea, helping the Blues win the FA Cup, League Cup and European Cup Winners' Cup.

Following a Football Association-led campaign to persuade FIFA to award all the squad members from 1966 with World Cup winner's medals, Bonetti duly received his from Gordon Brown at a ceremony at number 10 Downing Street in June 2009.

BONSOR, Alexander George 1872-75 ② ①
Born: Bermondsey, London, 7 October 1851
Died: Knightsbridge, London, 17 August 1907
Career: Eton College (seasons 1866-71), Old Etonians (seasons 1871-77); also played for Wanderers (seasons 1871-74), Surrey (1870s); became a brewer with Combe & Delafield, later incorporated in Watneys.

Alex Bonsor was a big, strong forward, with good dribbling skills. A winner with Wanderers in the first two FA Cup finals, 1872 and 1873, he later played in two losing finals with Old Etonians, scoring in both. His two caps were both against Scotland. He scored 10 minutes into his debut in March 1873 (won 4-2) and in his second game in March 1875 (which ended 2-2), he actually kept goal for the first 15 minutes until first choice 'keeper Billy Carr turned up…. and he kept a clean sheet. Bonsor also played in one 'unofficial' international.

BOOTH, Frank 1904-05 ①
Born: Hyde, Cheshire, autumn, 1882
Died: Manchester, 22 June 1919
Career: Hyde (seasons 1898-1900), Glossop (August 1900), Stockport County (May 1901), Manchester City (April 1902), Bury (January 1907), Clyde (June 1909), Manchester City (July 1911, retired, injured, May 1912).

Frank 'Tabby' Booth, a slim and lively winger who enjoyed hugging the touchline, became the seventh different player used by England in the then problematic outside-left position in 10 internationals when he played in a 1-1 draw against a moderate Irish side at Middlesbrough in February 1905. He made 107 appearances in his two spells with Manchester City, and played in the 1904 FA Cup final victory over Bolton Wanderers.

One of the players sold by City after the 1906 bribery 'scandal' he later took advantage of the FA amnesty and returned to Hyde Road via Clyde. However, he was only a shadow of the player who had served City so well during the early years of the 20th century.

BOOTH, Thomas Edward 1897-1903 ②
Born: Pim Mill Brow, Ardwick, Manchester, 25 April 1874
Died: Manchester, 7 September 1939
Career: Hooley Hill (1888), Ashton North End (August 1892), Rest of Lancashire (season 1893-94), Blackburn Rovers (professional, May 1896), Everton (April 1900-May 1908), Preston North End (briefly), Carlisle United (November 1908, retired, injured, May 1910).

An unspectacular but still worthy and consistent defender, in essence a first-rate club man, Tommy Booth scored 11 goals in 185 games for Everton and 11 in 120 for Blackburn and unfortunately missed successive FA Cup finals with the Merseysiders. He made his international debut against Wales at Wrexham in March 1898 when he partnered West Brom's Tom Perry at the heart of the defence in a 3-0 win. His second cap followed five years later in a 2-1 defeat by Scotland at Sheffield, when, reported the *Daily Record* 'Booth failed to cope with the tall, long-legged Hamilton who had a fine game for the Scots.'

BOTHROYD, Jay 2010-11 ①
Born: Islington, London, 5 May 1982
Career: Arsenal (academy, May 1998, professional, July 1999), Coventry City (£1m, July 2000), Perugia/Italy (July 2003), Blackburn Rovers (loan, September-December 2004), Charlton Athletic (free, August 2005), Wolverhampton Wanderers (free, July 2006), Stoke City (loan, March-April 2008), Cardiff City (£300,000, August 2008), Queen's Park Rangers (free, July 2011).

One of many strikers who played for England between 2008 and 2011, Jay Bothroyd is a fine front man who during his career has served alongside some excellent strikers. Quick over the ground, with an eye for goal, he made his senior international debut as a second-half substitute against France in November 2010 - the first Cardiff City player to represent England at senior level in the club's 111-year history. He was also the first Football League player to win a full cap since David Nugent in 2007.

He failed to make the grade with Arsenal, did well with Coventry and even better with Cardiff City before joining Premiership new-boys QPR in 2011. In October 2008, it was revealed that Bothroyd was on the verge of a possible call-up to play for Jamaica, as he qualified via his grandparents. However, he wanted to play for England and was capped at youth and U21 levels before making the senior team.

BOULD, Stephen Andrew 1993-95 ②
Born: Stoke-on-Trent, 16 November 1962
Career: Stoke City (apprentice, May 1978, professional, November 1980), Torquay United (loan, October-November 1982), Arsenal (£390,000, June 1988), Sunderland (£400,000, July 1999, retired, May 2000); Arsenal (U18 Academy head coach, from season 2001-02 onwards).

Steve Bould, Arsenal's 6ft 4in centre-back, made his England debut against Greece in May 1994, at the age of 31 which tells you two things: his manager was desperate and there were quite a few injuries to others in his position. Honest, reliable and well-liked, he was abandoned after gaining just two caps as Terry Venables preferred the younger Gareth Southgate. Bould made 211 appearances for Stoke and 373 for the Gunners with whom he won three League titles, the FA Cup and the European Cup Winners' Cup. He also played for England's B team.

BOWDEN, Edwin Raymond 1934-36 ⑥ ①
Born: Looe, Cornwall, 13 September 1909
Died: Plymouth, Devon, 23 September 1998
Career: Liskeard Secondary Council School, Looe FC (seasons 1924-26), Plymouth Argyle (professional, September 1926), Arsenal (£7,000, March 1933), Newcastle United (£5,000, November 1937, retired, injured, September 1939); later ran a sports outfitters shop in Plymouth.

Ray Bowden won his first England cap against Wales in Cardiff in September 1934, partnering Stanley Matthews on the right-wing in a 4-0 win. Two months later, he was one of the seven Arsenal players who played against the World champions Italy in the 'Battle of Highbury' match, which England won 3-2. In fact, one report stated 'The right-wing of Matthews and Bowden was useless.' In his six internationals, Bowden scored once, in a 2-1 defeat by Wales at Molineux in February 1936.

Charlie Buchan noted 'Bowden is a great player with the ball'. A stylist inside-forward, he scored 10 goals in one game for Looe and 100 in one season. In his professional career which was dogged by injury and illness, he netted almost 150 times in close on 350 appearances. He helped Plymouth win the Third Division (South) title and gained an FA Cup and two League Championship winner's medals with Arsenal. He also played in one unofficial international, represented the FA on tour to Canada/North America in 1931 (when he scored 15 goals) and was an England trialist.

BOWER, Alfred George 1923-27 ⑤
Born: Bromley, Kent, 10 November 1895
Died: Croydon, 30 June 1970
Career: Charterhouse School, Old Carthusians (1911), Corinthians (December 1918), Chelsea (August 1923-April 1925), Corinthians (July 1925), Casuals (August 1928, retired, April 1934); FA Councillor (seasons 1928-33); later a member of the Stock Exchange and Welfare Officer in Croydon.

Full-back Alf 'Baishe' Bower, tall and strong, won 13 amateur and five full caps for England, doing so at a time when it was becoming increasingly rare for an amateur to play in senior internationals. He won his first cap against Northern Ireland in October 1923, his second a month later in Belgium and his last three as captain v. Belgium at The Hawthorns in December 1924, when he starred in a 4-0 win and against Wales in February 1925 and again in February 1927. He seemed to lose confidence when worried by captaincy cares, but one thing no-one can take away from him, is that he was the last amateur to skipper the full England team.

BOWERS, John William Anslow 1933-34 ③ ②
Born: Santon near Scunthorpe, 22 February 1908
Died: Lichfield, Staffs, 4 July 1970
Career: Appleby Works/Scunthorpe, Scunthorpe & Lindsey United (professional, December 1927), Derby County (May 1928), Leicester City (November 1936, retired May 1943); Notts County (coach, August 1943), Derby County (assistant-trainer from 1945, then physiotherapist until 1965)

An opportunist centre-forward always pestering defenders, Jack Bowers was a consistent scorer throughout his career, netting 183 goals (including 16 hat-tricks) in 220 appearances for Derby County alone. He twice represented the Football League and won his three England caps during his time at The Baseball Ground, scoring on his international debut in a 3-0 win over Ireland in Belfast in October 1933. After going close in a 2-1 defeat by Wales in his next outing, he was on target again with a late header in a 3-0 victory over Scotland at Wembley in April 1934, Arthur Simmons of the *Daily Express* describing it as 'a face-saver for the ineffectual Derby County centre-forward.'

A Second Division Championship winner with Leicester in 1937, Bowers' son, also named Jack, played for Derby between 1957 and 1966.

BOWLES, Stanley 1973-77 ⑤ ①
Born: Manchester, 24 December 1948
Career: Manchester City (apprentice, June 1965, professional, January 1967), Bury (loan, July-August 1970), Crewe Alexandra (September 1970), Carlisle United (£12,000, October 1971), Queens Park Rangers (£110,000, September 1972), Nottingham Forest (£225,000, December 1979), Orient (July 1980), Brentford (£40,000, October 1981-May 1984), Epping Town (season 1984-85); later returned to Brentford (part-time coach, mid-1990s); became an after-dinner speaker.

A natural-born footballer with flair and ability, Stan Bowles scored 127 goals in 507 League games for eight different clubs over a period of 16 years (1967-83). A colourful character both on and off the field, he represented the Football League and netted once in his five games for England, in a 2-0 win over Wales in May 1974.

Not a huge favourite of caretaker-manager Joe Mercer, Bowles 'walked out in a huff' after being substituted against Northern Ireland and was then dropped for the next game against Scotland in May 1974. He had to wait two-and-a-half years for his next cap (v. Italy in November 1976). Three months later, in February 1977, he played against Holland wearing a Gola boot on his left foot and an Adidas on his right. He didn't score as the Dutch won 2-0.

One football fan once remarked: 'If Stan Bowles could pass a betting shop the same way he passes a ball he'd be a world beater.'

BOWSER, Sidney 1919-20 ①
Born: Handsworth, Birmingham, 6 April 1891
Died: Acocks Green, Birmingham, 10 February 1961
Career: Astbury Richmond/Handsworth (season 1905-06), Willenhall Town (July 1906), Birmingham (trial, April-May 1907), Willenhall Town (August 1907), West Bromwich Albion (professional, July 1908), Belfast Distillery (free, April 1913), West Bromwich Albion (free, February 1914), Walsall (August 1924, retired, May 1927); later a licensee in Dudley for 25 years.

Sid Bowser divided his talents between two completely different roles – those of inside-left and centre-half. Tenacious and resilient in both, he helped West Brom win the Second and First Division Championships in 1911 and 1920 and in his two spells at The Hawthorns made 371 appearances, scoring 72 goals, including a hat-trick from centre-half v. Bradford City in 1919. He played for the Irish League before gaining his solitary England cap as a defender against Ireland in Belfast in October 1919, being the fourth different player to occupy the centre-half position in consecutive internationals.

BOWYER, Lee David 2002-03 ①

Born: Canning Town, London, 3 January 1977
Career: Senrab FC (Sunday League team), Charlton Athletic (apprentice, April 1992, professional, April 1994), Leeds United (£2.6m, July 1996), West Ham United (£100,000, January 2003), Newcastle United (free, July 2003), West Ham United (£250,000, June 2006), Birmingham City (free, January 2009), Ipswich Town (free, July 2011, released May 2012)

I can honestly say that Lee Bowyer, although voted PFA 'Young Player of the Year' in 1999, has never been the most popular figure in English football. His checkered career is typified by an FA ruling, stating that he could not appear for the national side while he had a court case hanging over him (and there have been a few of those, sadly). The fact he managed to pilfer an England cap does not encourage anger, just bemusement. That was awarded against Portugal in September 2002 by Sven Göran Eriksson. He set up a goal for his Leeds team-mate Alan Smith in a 1-1 draw at Villa Park. Bowyer, who also won 13 U21 caps as an aggressive midfielder, was the most yellow-carded player in the Premiership in season 2010-11. His club record at May 2013 stood at 604 appearances and 99 goals (489/68 at League level).

BOYER, Philip John 1975-76 ①

Born: Nottingham, 25 January 1949
Career: Musters Road School/Nottingham, Rushcliffe Representative XI, Derby County (August 1965, professional, November 1966), York City (£3,000, July 1968), AFC Bournemouth (£20,000, December 1970), Norwich City (£145,000, February 1974), Southampton (£130,000, August 1977), Manchester City (£220,000, November 1980), Bulova/Hong Kong (loan, February 1982-April 1983), Grantham Town (July 1983), Stamford (1984), Shepshed Charterhouse (1985), Grantham Town (player/assistant-manager, December 1985-February 1987), Spalding (player, briefly), Harrowby Town (manager, season 1987-88); also engaged as a scout by Blackpool and Northampton Town (late 1980s).

Phil Boyer had two wonderfully exciting seasons playing alongside Ted MacDougall at Norwich and as a result was capped by England boss Don Revie against Wales at Wrexham in March 1976, doing well in a 2-1 win. Playing together, Boyer and 'Super Mac' scored a total of 195 competitive goals as strike partners with four different clubs in ten years: 1968-78. Boyer, who also gained two U23 caps, missed the 1981 FA Cup final through injury; the most disappointing moment of his career!

BOYES, Walter Edward 1938-39 ③

Born: Killamarsh, Sheffield, 5 January 1913
Died: Swansea, 16 September 1960
Career: Sheffield Boys, Woodhouse Mills United (1929), West Bromwich Albion (professional, February 1931), Everton (£6,000, February 1938); WW2 guest for Aldershot, Brentford, Clapton Orient, Leeds United, Manchester United, Middlesbrough, Millwall, Newcastle United, Preston North End and Sunderland; Notts County (player-coach, June 1949), Scunthorpe United (player-trainer, June 1950-May 1953), Retford Town (player-manager, August 1954), Hyde Town (player-manager, May 1958), Swansea Town (trainer, July 1959, retired from football through ill-health, May 1960); also sports master at Oakwood Collegiate School, Sheffield (1952-58) and later worked as an aide-teacher at various schools in the Sheffield area.

As a West Brom player, Wally Boyes starred at outside-left, inside-left and left-half and scored in the 1935 FA Cup final. That same year he won his first England cap against Holland in Amsterdam when his Hawthorns club-mate 'W.G.' Richardson lined up at centre-forward. In 1938-39 Boyes helped Everton win the League title and appeared in two more internationals, against Wales at Cardiff and versus the Rest of Europe at Highbury, producing some exhilarating runs down the left flank in the latter game which England won 3-0. Boyes, who was only 5ft 4ins tall, also played in one unofficial international (v. Scotland in August 1935) and twice represented the Football League.

In 1927-28, he scored 17 goals for Sheffield Boys in a 31-2 win over Rotherham Juniors.

BOYLE, Thomas Wilkinson 1912-13 (1)

Born: Platts Common, Hoyland near Barnsley, 29 January 1886
Died: Goosenargh, Lancashire, 2 January 1940
Career: Hoyland Star (1903), Elsecar (1905), Barnsley (professional, May 1906), Burnley (record £1,150, September 1911; appointed player-coach, May 1922), Wrexham (free, May 1923, retired May 1924); coached in Germany (seasons 1924-26)

An FA Cup and League Championship winner with Burnley in 1914 and 1921 respectively, Tom Doyle was an exceptionally fine centre-half, strong in the air and on the ground. He was selected for his only international appearance against Ireland in February 1913 when Billy Wedlock of Bristol City had to withdraw through injury. He didn't fare too well against the tricky Billy Gillespie who scored both the Irish goals in a 2-1 win. Boyle died of 'General paralysis of the Insane' in Whittingham Mental Hospital, Lancashire.

BRABROOK, Peter 1958-60 (3)

Born: Greenwich, London, 8 November 1937
Career: Windsor & Napier Schools, East Ham, Middlesex FA, Ford United, Chelsea (amateur, March 1953, professional, March 1955), West Ham United (£35,000, October 1962), Leyton Orient (July 1968), Romford (August 1971), Woodford Town (August 1972, retired, May 1974); later West Ham United (Academy coach); also ran a butcher's ship in Hornchurch and worked for the paper tycoon, Neville Ovendon.

Peter Brabrook, quick and strong with a powerful shot, played on both wings, winning his three England caps on the right, his first in a 1-0 pool 2 play-off defeat by Russia in the World Cup in Gothenburg in June 1958. Replacing the injured Bryan Douglas, and chosen ahead of Bobby Charlton, he gave a 'somewhat uneven performance' twice hitting the woodwork and missing a chance at the far post created by Broadbent's fine pass. However, he still kept his place for the next international against Northern Ireland. His last cap followed versus Spain in Madrid in May 1960. He won the FA Cup with the Hammers in 1964 and the Third Division Championship with Orient in 1970 and also represented his country in three Youth and nine U23 matches.

BRACEWELL, Paul William 1984-85 (3)

Born: Heswall, Cheshire, 19 July 1962
Career: Stoke City (apprentice, July 1978, professional, February 1980), Sunderland (£225,000, July 1983), Everton (£250,000, May 1984), Sunderland (loan, August 1989, signed for £250,000, September 1989), Newcastle United (£250,000, June 1992), Sunderland (£50,000, player-coach, May 1995), Fulham (£75,000, player-coach, October 1997, retired as a player, May 1999; later coach/assistant-manager, then manager, May 1999-July 2000), England (U16 and U20 coach), Halifax Town (manager, October 2000-September 2001), Walsall (assistant-manager/coach, February 2004-May 2005).

Midfielder Paul Bracewell gained his first England cap as a second-half substitute for Bryan Robson against West Germany in Mexico City in June 1985. He then set up two goals in his next game against the USA in Los Angeles, one of them being scored by his club-mate Gary Lineker. A steadying influence on the game, he won the League title and European Cup Winners' Cup with Everton, the First and Second Division titles with Newcastle and Sunderland, played in four losing FA Cup finals, amassed 720 club appearances, and also played 13 times for his country at U21 level.

BRADFORD, Geoffrey Reginald William 1955-56 (1) (1)

Born: Frenchay, Bristol, 18 July 1927
Died: Bristol, 30 December 1994
Career: Soundwell School/Bristol, Soundwell FC (August 1945), Bristol Rovers (professional, June 1949, retired, May 1964); later employed as a tanker driver for an oil company at Avonmouth.

Geoff Bradford, who scored a record 355 goals in 626 games for Bristol Rovers, helping them win the Third Division (South) title, was a strong, hard-working inside-forward. A series of leg injuries failed to affect his potency unduly and one feels that if he had been with a more fashionable club he would have gained more than just the one cap. That came in a friendly against Denmark in Copenhagen in October 1955 when, replacing Dennis Wilshaw and partnering Tom Finney on the left-wing, he scored in a 5-1 win. Even against the modest opposition, he was hardly international class and was not chosen again, yet is the only Rovers player ever to play for England.

BRADFORD, Joseph 1923-31 (12) (7)

Born: Peggs Green, Leicester, 22 January 1901
Died: Edgbaston, Birmingham, 6 September 1980
Career: Coalville FC (1912), Peggs Green Victoria (August 1913), Aston Villa (trial, April 1919), Derby County (trial, May 1919), Birmingham (£125, professional, February 1920), Bristol City (free, May 1935, retired May 1937); Arsenal (scout, 1940s), Sutton Town FC (president, from 1951); was also a licensee in Birmingham, Droitwich and Stourbridge, worked in Pools office at St Andrew's and also ran a sports shop in Sutton Coldfield.

Joe Bradford was 'a dashing centre-forward' who scored three goals in his first two internationals, including one on his debut against Ireland in October 1923 when he was introduced in place of Aston Villa's Billy Walker. He was in the team thrashed 5-1 by Scotland (the 'Wembley Wizards') in 1928 and two years later helped reap revenge when England won 5-2, also at Wembley when, wrote J. H. Freeman in the *Daily Mail*, "Watson, Jack and Bradford formed a formidable triple strike-force, Bradford laying on goals for Watson and Rimmer.

Bradford scored a record 267 goals in 445 appearances for Birmingham (1920-35), helping them win the Second Division Championship and reach the FA Cup final. He also represented the Football League on five occasions, striking home five goals for them in a 7-2 win over the Irish League in September 1929.

His brother, William, played for Walsall and his cousin, Hugh Adcock, for Leicester City and England.

BRADLEY, Warren 1958-59 (3) (2)

Born: Hyde, Cheshire, 20 June 1933
Died: Manchester, 6 June 2007
Career: Hyde Grammar School, Cheshire Schools, Cheshire County Youths, Durham University, Durham City (1953), Bolton Wanderers (amateur, August 1954), Bishop Auckland (amateur, June 1955), Manchester United (amateur, February 1958, professional, November 1958), Bury (March 1962), Northwich Victoria (July 1963), Macclesfield Town (November 1963), Bangor City (May 1964), Macclesfield Town (April 1966, retired, May 1967); was a schoolteacher by profession.

Twice an FA Amateur Cup winner with Bishop Auckland, pint-sized outside-right Warren Bradley also made 11 appearances for

England as an amateur (1957-59). Shrewd and clever, he was confident on the ball and few were quicker off the mark. Replacing Bryan Douglas, he gained the first of his three full caps in May 1959 against Italy at Wembley, scoring in a 2-2 draw. He also netted in his third international when the USA were battered 8-1 in Los Angeles later in the month. He was the 777th player capped by England.

BRADSHAW, Francis ① ③

Born: Sheffield, 31 May 1884
Died: Taunton, Somerset, 23 May 1950
Career: Oxford Street Sunday School/Sheffield, Sheffield Schools, Sheffield Wednesday (amateur, April 1904, professional, September 1904), Northampton Town (July 1910), Everton (November 1911), Arsenal (June 1914, retired, May 1923); Aberdare Athletic (manager, July 1923-May 1924); FA coach (Somerset), later worked for the British Aeroplane Company.

One of only five players (and the last so far) to score a hat-trick on his England debut, Frank Bradshaw achieved the feat against Austria in Vienna in June 1908 when he deputised from George Hilsdon of Chelsea in an 11-1 victory. Initially a potent, brainy and dangerous inside-left, he also had a hand in four of the other eight goals that afternoon. He received a second call-up for the Ireland game in February 1909 but had to withdraw through injury and never got another chance. Bradshaw, an FA Cup winner with Sheffield Wednesday who later moved to left-half and then full-back, also represented the Southern League once and the Football League on five occasions as well as starring in an international trial.

BRADSHAW, Thomas Henry 1896-97 ①

Born: Liverpool, 24 August 1873
Died: Tottenham, London, 25 December 1899
Career: Liverpool Nomads (August 1889), Northwich Victoria (May 1891), Liverpool (August 1893), Tottenham Hotspur (May 1898), Thames Ironworks, now West Ham United (July 1899, retired, ill-health, November 1899).

An ingenious and fleet-footed outside-left, Tom Bradshaw gained his solitary England cap in February 1897 when he starred in a 6-0 win over Ireland at Nottingham, being the fifth different player to occupy that position in five matches. Liverpool's first ever international, he twice helped the Merseysiders win the Second Division Championship, played for the South against the North and also for an England XI versus a Scotland XI to raise funds for the Players' Union.
    He was only 26 when he died and shortly afterwards Spurs met Thames Ironworks in a match to raise funds for his dependants.

BRADSHAW, William 1909-13 ④

Born: Padiham, Lancs, May 1884
Died: Blackburn, 12 April 1955
Career: Padiham FC (seasons 1900-02), Accrington Stanley (April 1902), Blackburn Rovers (May 1903), Rochdale (player-manager, April-September 1920).

Twice a League Championship winner with Blackburn, Bill Bradshaw was a very efficient, hard-working left-half and expert from the penalty spot. His four England games spanned three years. He was brilliant in the 6-1 win over Ireland in February 1912 when he joined forces with his club-mates Bob Crompton and Jack Simpson, and then he played behind two more of his Blackburn colleagues, Edwin Latheron and Joe Hodkinson, when England defeated Wales 4-3 in March 1913. He also represented the Football League three times.

BRANN, George 1885-91 ③ ①

Born: Eastbourne, 23 April 1865
Died: Surbiton, Surrey, 14 June 1954
Career: Ardingley College (seasons 1883-85), Swifts (seasons 1886-92); also played for Corinthians (1886-93) and Slough (late 1880s); played cricket for Sussex (291 matches, 11,205 runs, 24 centuries and 69 wickets) and was a fine golfer too.

An amateur outside or inside-right and a leading player of his day, George Brann's first cap was against Scotland in Glasgow in March 1886 when he set up Tinsley Lindley to lob in England's goal in the 1-1 draw. Retained for the next match against Wales two days later, he scored in a 3–1 victory, before making his final appearance also against Wales in March 1891.

BRAWN, William Frederick 1903-04 ②

Born: Wellingborough, 1 August 1878
Died: Holborn Hill, London, 18 August 1932
Career: Rock Street School/Wellingborough, Wellingborough Schools, Wellingborough White Star, Wellingborough Principals, Wellingborough, Northampton Town (July 1895), Sheffield United (professional, January 1900), Aston Villa (December 1901), Middlesbrough (March 1906), Chelsea (November 1907), Brentford (August 1911, retired, May 1919); WW1 guest for Tottenham Hotspur (November 1918); later engaged as an advisory manager at Brentford; also licensee of the King's Arms, Boston Road, Brentford.

An FA Cup winner with Aston Villa in 1905, outside-right Billy Brawn was 6ft 2in tall and 13st in weight - one of the biggest and heaviest wingers in the game at that time. Replacing Harry Davis of Sheffield Wednesday, his two England caps came in successive internationals against Wales and Ireland in February and March 1904, when he played in the same forward-line as his team-mate Joe Bache in both matches and also with Villa colleague Alex Leake in his second. A very fine player, Brawn retired with over 350 club appearances under his belt.

BRAY, John 1934-37 ⑥

Born: Oswaldtwistle, Lancs, 22 April 1909
Died: Manchester, 20 November 1982
Career: St Andrew's School/Oswaldtwistle, Clayton Olympia (1926), Manchester Central (August 1928), Manchester City (£1,000, October 1929, retired, March 1946); Watford (manager, March 1947-January 1948), Nelson (coach, February-September 1948); played cricket for Accrington (Lancashire League).

Jackie Bray, who brought a degree of constructiveness to his performances at left-half, loved to drive forward at every opportunity. An FA Cup and League Championship winner with Manchester City in 1934 and 1937, he had to fight for a place in the England team with Wilf Copping and Horace Burrows, and was rewarded with six caps, the first in a 4-0 win over Wales in September 1934 when he laid on a goal for his club-mate Sam Tilson. He did likewise in his next international against Ireland (won 3-0) while in his last, against Scotland in April 1937 at Hampden Park which attracted a record crowd of 149,547, he struggled to contain the threat posed by Jimmy Delaney and Tommy Walker down Scotland's right. He also played in the unofficial jubilee international v. Scotland in 1935.

BRAYSHAW, Edward 1886-87 ①

Born: Kirkstall, Leeds, 7 November 1863
Died: Wortley, Sheffield, 20 November 1908
Career: Walkley All Saints, Sheffield Wednesday (August 1884-April 1891), Lockwood Brothers/Sheffield (season 1891-92), Sheffield Rovers (August 1892), Grimsby Town (season 1893-94); later a licensee in Sheffield.

The son of a Sheffield detective, right-back or centre-half Teddy Brayshaw was a Football Alliance winner with Wednesday and starred in his only game for England, a 7-0 defeat of Ireland at Sheffield in February 1887. Surprisingly, he was never selected again, despite his excellent club form. A huge favourite with the fans, he was ranked among the club's best and helped the Owls win several local competitions. He also had a trial for England. Sadly his last days were spent in a South Yorkshire Asylum.

BRIDGE, Wayne Michael 2001-10 ㉝ ①

Born: Southampton, 5 August 1980
Career: Southampton (apprentice, August 1996, professional, January 1998), Chelsea (£7m, July 2003), Fulham (loan, January-March 2006), Manchester City (£10m, January 2009), West Ham United (loan, January-May 2011), Sunderland (loan, January-May 2012), Brighton & Hove Albion (loan, July 2012-May 2013), Reading (June 2013)

During his time with Southampton, Wayne Bridge's three managers, Dave Jones, Glenn Hoddle and Stuart Gray, all predicted he would play for England. They were right, as the left-back quickly gained U21 recognition, followed by a senior call from Sven-Göran Eriksson against the Netherlands in February 2002. He proved himself as an international and appeared twice as a substitute in the World Cup finals that year, although he missed out on Euro 2004 when Ashley Cole was preferred. During qualification for the 2006 World Cup, however, Bridge was occasionally given the role of playing in the problematic left midfield position, but lost out in the end to his Chelsea team-mate Joe Cole when he was injured. Thereafter he played in both the 2008 European Championship and 2010 World Cup qualifying groups but is now basically understudy to Ashley Cole. Bridge helped Chelsea win the Premiership title, the League Cup twice and the FA Cup in the space of three years. He also has eight U21 caps to his credit, has made 451 club appearances and helped Brighton reach the 2013 Championship play-offs.

BRIDGES, Barry John 1964-66 ④ ①

Born: Horsford near Norwich, 29 April 1941
Career: Norfolk Boys (season 1955-56), Chelsea (amateur, July 1956, professional, May 1958), Birmingham City (£55,000, May 1966), Queens Park Rangers (£5,000, August 1968), Millwall (free, September 1970), Brighton & Hove Albion (free, September 1972), Highland Park/South Africa (summer, 1974), St Patrick's Athletic (player-manager, August 1976, retired as a player, June 1977, remained as manager to May 1978), Sligo Rovers (manager, season 1978-79); thereafter Dereham Town (manager), Kings Lynn (manager), Horsford United (manager); later ran hotel in Brighton, then worked as a milkman in his native Horsford.

Barry Bridges gained the first of his four caps against Scotland in April 1965 when he partnered Jimmy Greaves and Johnny Byrne in attack in the 2-2 draw at Wembley. He came close to scoring in the first half but missed a late chance which would have given his side victory. He scored his only England goal in a 1-1 draw with Yugoslavia a month later and was named in the preliminary squad of forty players selected by Alf Ramsey ahead of the 1966 World Cup, but failed to make the final 22.
Bridges played in six Schoolboy and two Youth internationals and also represented the Football League. A League Cup winner with Chelsea, he scored 215 goals in 567 League games for his five major clubs.

BRIDGETT, George Arthur 1904-09 ⑪ ③

Born: Forsbrook, Stoke-on-Trent, 11 October 1882
Died: Newcastle-under-Lyme, Staffs, 26 July, 1954
Career: St Peter's School/Stoke, Burslem Park Boys (1897), Trentham FC (1899), Stoke (professional, August 1902), Sunderland (November 1902-May 1912), South Shields (player-manager, July 1912), North Shields (player-manager, August 1914), Port Vale (guest, April 1917, signed permanently, November 1923), Sandbach Ramblers (May 1924, retired, May 1926).

A quick and direct outside-left with a powerful shot in both feet, Arthur Bridgett was never on the losing side for England, 10 of his international appearances ending in victories. His three goals were all scored away from home - in the 6-1 and 11-1 wins in Austria in June 1908 and in the 4-2 victory over Hungary in May 1909. A deeply religious man who never played on Christmas Day or Good Friday, Bridgett also played for the Football League XI and was 41 when he played for Port Vale.

BRINDLE, Thomas 1879-80 ② ①

Born: Darwen, 8 January 1861
Died: Blackburn, 15 April 1905
Career: Darwen (seasons 1878-86), Blackburn Olympic (August 1886-April 1887), Darwen (May 1887), West Bromwich Albion (May 1891, retired October 1891, injured)

A strong-kicking, powerfully built left-back, Tom Brindle made his international debut in a thrilling 5-4 defeat to Scotland in March 1880. The Times correspondent, covering the game wrote: 'On a heavy pitch England's big defender Brindle was given a hard time throughout by John McPherson, the Vale of Leven left-winger, who assisted in three of his side's goals.' Brindle then became the first full-back to score for England in open play when he fired in from 'distance' in the 3-2 win over Wales at Wrexham two days later.

BRITTLETON, James Thomas 1911-14 ⑤

Born: Winsford, Cheshire, 23 April 1882
Died: Winsford, 22 February 1955
Career: Winsford Juniors (from August 1897), Winsford Celtic (February 1899), Winsford United (August 1901), Stockport County (May 1903), Sheffield Wednesday (£300, January 1905), Stoke (May 1920), Winsford United (player-coach, August 1924, retired, April 1926).

An FA Cup winner with Sheffield Wednesday in 1907, right-half Tom Brittleton had a remarkably long throw, sometimes hurling the ball up to 40 yards. Indefatigable, he possessed a fearsome tackle and made 512 appearances in the Football League, his last at the age of 40 for Stoke. He made an impressive international debut against Ireland in February 1912 (won 6-1) and was outstanding when England defeated Scotland 1-0 at Stamford Bridge twelve months later, the *Daily Mail* reporter stating: 'Although not a great game, the best feature was the five-star showing of England's half-back line of Brittleton, McCall and Watson.'

BRITTON, Clifford Samuel 1934-37 ⑨ ①

Born: Hanham, Bristol, 27 August 1909
Died: Anlaby, Hull, 1 December 1975
Career: Hanham Athletic (1923), Hanham United Methodists (1924), Bristol, St George (1925), Bristol Rovers (amateur, April 1926, professional, August 1928), Everton (June 1930, retired October 1945); Burnley (manager, October 1945-September 1948), Everton (manager, September 1948-February 1956), Preston North End (manager, August 1956, resigned April 1961), Hull City (manager, July 1961, general manager, November 1969, retired, October 1971).

Cliff Britton was an excellent right-half of great style and polish who enjoyed moving forward with the ball. An FA Cup winner with Everton in 1933, he had a fine international debut against Wales the following year, starring in a 4-0 win, and followed up with another splendid performance in the 'Battle of Highbury' two months later when England beat the World champions Italy 3-2. His only England goal was scored in a 6-2 win over Hungary in December 1936 when he moved forward to strike the ball home after Ted Drake had won a header. Britton also played in the unofficial Jubilee match against Scotland in 1935 and in 12 Wartime internationals (1941-44) when he was part of a wonderful middle-line along with Stan Cullis and Joe Mercer. He made 242 appearances for Everton, gaining Second Division and FA Cup winner's medals. He was the 600th player to win a full England cap.

BROADBENT, Peter Frank 1958-60 ⑦ ②

Born: Elvington, Kent, 15 May 1933
Career: Dover (August 1949), Brentford (professional, May 1950) Wolverhampton Wanderers (£10,000, February 1951), Shrewsbury Town (free, January 1965), Aston Villa (October 1966), Stockport County (October 1969), Bromsgrove Rovers (October 1970, retired, May 1971); later ran a baby-wear shop in Halesowen (to 1998).

Inside-forward Peter Broadbent was a brainy and thoughtful footballer who created chances galore for his colleagues at Molineux during the 1950s when Wolves won three League Championships and the FA Cup under manager Stan Cullis. Unfortunately there was room for only one 'play-maker' in the England team – Johnny Haynes – and therefore he was restricted to just seven caps, the first in the 1958 World Cup pool 2 play-off against Russia which

ended in a 1-0 defeat. His two international goals both came in the 2-2 draw with Wales six months later. Standing in for Johnny Haynes, he lobbed 'keeper Jack Kelsey to equalize Derek Tapscott's early goal before levelling things up again late on with a back-post header from Alan A'Court's left-wing cross.

Broadbent was also capped once by England at both B and U23 levels and twice represented the Football League. He netted 145 goals in 497 appearances for Wolves.

BROADIS, Ivan Arthur 1951-54 ⑭ ⑧

Born: Isle of Dogs, Poplar, London, 18 December 1922
Career: Finchley (1938), Northfleet (1939); WW2 guest for Millwall, Manchester United, Blackpool, Carlisle United and Bradford Park Avenue; Carlisle United (player-manager, August 1946), Sunderland (£18,000, January 1949), Manchester City (£25,000, October 1951), Newcastle United (£17,500, October 1953), Carlisle United (£3,500, player-coach, July 1955), Queen of the South (June 1959, retired as a player, May 1960, remained as coach until May 1962); later a Carlisle-based sports journalist for newspapers on Tyneside and Cumbria.

Ivor Broadis put a great deal of effort into his inside-forward play. Quick over the ground, with good balance and technique, he gained his first cap in the 2-2 draw with Austria in November 1951 and his last in a 4-2 World Cup defeat by Uruguay in June 1954. He was one of the few players to perform in Budapest when England crashed 7-1 to Hungary in May 1954, scoring his country's consolation goal. He then went out and netted twice in the next game, a 4-4 draw with Belgium in the World Cup. Quite outspoken at times, Broadis once said: "I'm hard to please. I am a rebel. But it's better to speak your mind than be a slave."

Aged only 23 when he was appointed manager of Carlisle United in August 1946, Broadis made almost 500 appearances at club level, representing the Football League as a Manchester City player.

BROCKBANK, John 1872-73 ①

Born: Whitehaven, Cumberland, 22 August 1848
Died: Fulham, London, 4 February 1896
Career: Shrewsbury School (early 1860s), Trinity College/Cambridge University (seasons 1870-76); an actor by profession, also played cricket for the MCC.

A fast-raiding forward, two-footed with excellent ball skills, Jack Brockbank always played with his right knee heavily bandaged. Nevertheless, he was a fine footballer who played in England's first-ever international, a 0-0 draw with Scotland at The West of Scotland cricket ground, Partick, in November 1872. The *Bell's Life* correspondent wrote: 'The magnificent dribbling of Brockbank was greatly admired by the immense concourse of spectators.'

BRODIE, John Brant 1889-91 ③ ①

Born: Wightwick near Wolverhampton, 30 August 1862
Died: Wolverhampton, 16 February 1925
Career: St Luke's School/Blakenhall, Wolverhampton Wanderers (founder member of the club, January 1877), West Bromwich Albion (guest, July 1886), retired as a player (May 1891); also Saltley College/Birmingham (pupil-teacher), later headmaster of St Peter's School/Wolverhampton; a qualified referee, he was a director of Wolverhampton Wanderers FC (August 1913 until his death in 1925).

Very popular during his playing days (and afterwards) the versatile Jack Brodie occupied six different positions during his career. Basically a forward, he made his England debut as leader of the attack in March 1889, scoring as captain in a 6-1 win over Ireland at Anfield. His second appearance was against Scotland the following month (lost 3-2) when he appeared on the right-wing. After the match, the *North British Daily Mail* reporter wrote 'Brodie of Wolverhampton was far too clever for the Scots at times and caused plenty of anxiety in their defence'. His third and final game was also versus Ireland in March 1891 when he played left-half in a 6-1 victory on his home ground at Molineux. Brodie scored 44 goals in 65 senior appearances for Wolves for whom he played in the 1889 FA Cup final defeat by Preston.

BROMILOW, Thomas George 1921-26 ⑤

Born: Liverpool, 7 October 1894
Died: Nuneaton, Warwickshire, 4 March 1959
Career: Fonthill Road School/Liverpool, West Dingle FC, United West Dingle Presbyterian Club, Army football (1915-18), Liverpool (professional, April 1919, retired, May 1930), FC Amsterdam/Holland (coach, season 1931-32), Burnley (manager, October 1932-May 1935), Crystal Palace (manager, July 1935, resigned, June 1936; returned as manager, December 1936-May 1939), Leicester City (manager, July 1939-May 1945), coached in Holland (season 1945-46), Newport County (manager, May 1946-January 1950), Leicester City (chief scout and trainer, July 1950 until his death).

Twice a League Championship winner with Liverpool, Tom Bromilow carried out his duties at left-half with 'style and artistry, being especially notable for his anticipation and attacking flair.' He gained his first cap on his own patch (Anfield) against Wales in March 1921 when he worked 'overtime' to keep the visiting forwards at bay in a 0-0 draw. He later created two goals in the 6-1 victory over Belgium in March 1923.

Bromilow, who made 375 appearances for Liverpool (1919-30), also represented the Football League on five occasions. Bromilow died suddenly on a train in 1959 while scouting for Leicester City, on his way home from a cup-tie between Wrexham and Merthyr Tydfil.

BROMLEY-DAVENPORT, Brigadier-General Sir William, MP, DL, KCB, CMG, CBE, DSO, TD 1883-84 ② ②

Born: Reading, 21 January 1862
Died: Macclesfield, 6 February 1949
Career: Eton College (seasons 1879-82), Balliol College/Oxford University (1882-84), Old Etonians (seasons 1884-86); Macclesfield MP (1886-1906); Secretary to War Office (1903-05); Lieutenant of Cheshire (1920-49); served in Staffordshire Yeomanry in South Africa (1900); Brigadier in Command 22nd Mounted Brigade, Egypt (1916); assistant-Director of Labour, France (1917).

William Bromley-Davenport was a centre-forward, strong and direct, a clever dribbler with a fair amount of pace. He won his first cap in a 1-0 defeat by Scotland in mid March 1884 – 'Being unlucky not to score' stated the *Bell's Life* reporter - and two days later scored twice in a 4-0 win over Wales.

BROOK, Eric Fred 1929-38 ⑱ ⑩

Born: Mexborough, Yorkshire, 27 November 1907
Died: Wythenshawe, Manchester, 29 March 1965
Career: Dolcliffe Road School/Mexborough, Oxford Road YMCA, Swinton Primitives (1923), Mexborough (June 1924), Wath Athletic (August 1925), Barnsley (professional, February 1926), Manchester City (£6,000, with Fred Tilson, March 1928, retired injured, May 1940); later worked as a coach driver, crane operator and licensee.

Ostensibly an outside-left who also appeared as an inside-forward, Eric Brook was an ebullient character with a powerful left-foot shot. He made his England debut in a 3-0 win over Ireland in October 1929 but had to wait almost four years for his second cap v. Switzerland when he starred in a 4-0 win. First choice for the next three years, he scored in all four internationals in 1933-34 and over the course of time had several left-wing partners including Bastin, Hall and Westwood. One of Brook's finest hours in an England shirt came in the 'Battle of Highbury' encounter with Italy in 1934 when he scored two goals in the first quarter-of-an-hour, a bullet header from Britton's cross and a thunderbolt free-kick from 20 yards. The Manchester City player should have had a hat-trick that day but saw a first minute penalty saved by Ceresoli and then, as freelance reporter Archie Ledbrooke wrote: "The Italian goalkeeper later produced the best single save I had ever seen in a quarter of a century when he thwarted Brook."

Brook, who played in one Wartime international v. Wales in 1939, scored 178 goals in almost 500 appearances for Manchester City (1927-39), only missing games through international calls and an appendicitis operation in November 1937. An FA Cup and First Division Championship winner in 1934 and 1937 respectively, he retired following a wartime motor car accident.

BROOKING, Sir Trevor David, MBE, CBE 1973-82 ㊼ ⑤

Born: Barking, Essex, 2 October 1948
Career: Ripple Infants and Ilford County High Schools, West Ham United (apprentice, July 1965, professional, October 1966-May 1984); assisted Cork City (November 1985-May 1986); later West Ham United (caretaker-manager, 2003, and director); joined the Football Association as Director of Football Development (December 2003); also runs his own company Colbrook Plastics Ltd.; was Chairman of the Eastern Region Council for Sport and Recreation (1978-97) and Chairman of Sport England (1999-2002) and has worked in TV and radio; now lives in Brentwood, Essex.

Creative midfielder Trevor Brooking – who 'had brains in his boots' said one journalist - appeared in only two major tournaments for England - Euro 1980 and the 1982 World Cup. In the former, he played in the opening game against Belgium (1-1), but was dropped for the second match against the host nation Italy (lost 1-0). He was re-instated to the starting eleven against Spain and scored the first goal in a 2-1 win. Due to an injury his action in the 1982 World Cup was limited to playing just once as a substitute against Spain. This was a game England had to win to qualify for the semi-final but they were held to a 0-0 draw by the host country. One of Brooking's best performances for England came in a 3-1 win over Hungary in a World Cup qualifier in June 1981. He scored twice, his second a rasping left-footer which he hit so hard that the ball lodged in the stanchion holding up the frame of the goal. He also netted a beauty in a 2-0 win over Scotland in May 1980.

Upright, honest and polite, he scored 102 goals in 635 games for the Hammers (1967-84), gained two FA Cup winner's medals, scoring with a rare header to settle the 1980 final against Arsenal and collected a Second Division Championship winner's medal in 1981. He also starred for England at Youth team level and played twice for the U23s. He was awarded the MBE in 1981, the CBE in 1999 and Knighted in 2004.

BROOKS, John 1956-57 ③ ②

Born: Reading, 23 December 1931
Career: Reading & Berkshire Schools, Coley Old Boys, Mount Pleasant FC, Reading (amateur, February 1949, professional, April 1949), Tottenham Hotspur (February 1953), Chelsea (£20,000, plus Les Allen, December 1959), Brentford (September 1961), Crystal Palace (January 1964), Stevenage Town (October 1964), Cambridge City (1965), FC Toronto/Canada (1966), Knebworth Town (player-manager, season 1967-68); later a stockbroker's messenger in the City; he is now living in Bournemouth.

Johnny Brooks was a skilful, creative inside-forward whose career spanned almost 20 years during which time he netted over 100 goals in 375 appearances, winning the Fourth Division with Brentford in 1963. Partnering Stan Matthews on the right-wing, he scored on his England debut v. Wales in November 1956 (won 3-1), struck again in his next match v. Yugoslavia (3-0), firing high into the net after a smart pass from Johnny Haynes, but missed two easy chances in his third outing when Denmark were beaten 5-2 in a World Cup qualifier at Molineux. Brooks' son, Shaun, played for Crystal Palace and Leyton Orient.

BROOME, Frank Henry 1937-39 ⑦ ③

Born: Berkhamsted, Herts, 11 June 1915
Died: Bournemouth, 10 September 1994
Career: Berkhamsted Victoria Church of England School, Boxmoor United Juniors (1927), Berkhamsted Town (1928), Boxmoor United (September 1929-May 1932), Berkhamsted Town (August 1932), Aston Villa (professional, November 1934); WW2 guest for Aldershot, Birmingham, Charlton Athletic, Chelmsford City, Chesterfield, Northampton Town, Nottingham Forest, Notts County, Revo Electric FC, Watford, Wolverhampton Wanderers and Worcester City; Derby County (September 1946), Notts County (in exchange for Harry Brown, October 1949), Brentford (July 1953), Crewe Alexandra (October 1953), Shelbourne (February 1955, retired, May 1955); Notts County (assistant-trainer, June 1955, caretaker-manager, January-May 1957, assistant-manager, June-December 1957), Exeter City (manager, January 1958-May 1960), Southend United (manager, May-December 1960), Bankstown/NSW/Australia (manager-coach, July 1961-October 1962), Corinthians/Sydney/Australia (manager-coach, November 1962), Melita Eagles/Sydney (part-time coach, early 1967), Exeter City (manager, May 1967-February 1969); coached in the Middle East (early 1970s).

Small, frail yet thrustful, Frank Broome was a respected goalscoring forward, blessed with great acceleration, he often left defenders standing! In fact, he was quite elusive and often wandered effectively around the pitch in an attempt to shake off his 'policeman' defender. He appeared in four different positions for England, scoring on his debut against Germany in Berlin in 1938 when, prior to kick-off, and having first refused to give the Nazi salute (towards Herr Hitler), Broome and 'most' of his team-mates reluctantly rose their right arms. But on the pitch it was a different story – as all the England players raised both their arms in delight after thrashing the Germans 6-3!

Some years later Broome said: "I was intent on scoring in that game…I wanted to show who was boss."

He played for the FA XI in 1944 and 1951, gained Second Division and Wartime League Cup winner's medals with Villa in 1938 and 1944, helped Wolves win the War Cup final in 1942 and was a Third Division (South) Championship winner with Notts County in 1950. His career realized 255 goals in 606 appearances.

BROWN, Anthony 1970-71 (1)

Born: Oldham, 3 October 1945
Career: St Columba's/Manchester, St Peter's/Wythenshawe and St Clare's/Blakely Schools; Manchester District & Lancashire Schools, West Bromwich Albion (apprentice, April 1961, professional, October 1963), Jacksonville/New England Tea Men/USA (loan, May-July 1981), Torquay United (October 1981), Jacksonville Teamen (loan, May-July 1982), Stafford Rangers (February-April 1983); West Bromwich Albion (Schoolboy & Junior coach, February 1984, senior coaching staff, June 1984-May 1986), Birmingham City (assistant-manager/coach, June 1987-May 1989); played for West Bromwich Albion All Stars (seasons 1979-88); also employed as a sales rep. by a West Bromwich-based electrical company; currently engaged by local radio station and contributes to West Bromwich Albion's official matchday programme.

Despite scoring a record 279 goals in 720 games for West Bromwich Albion, Tony 'Bomber' Brown appeared for England just once, in the 0-0 draw with Wales at Wembley in May 1971. He spent 74 minutes on the pitch alongside Geoff Hurst who would become his team-mate at The Hawthorns four years later. Brown gained that solitary cap after finishing the season as the First Division's leading scorer. A League Cup and FA Cup winner in 1966 and 1968, Brown served Albion as a player for 20 years (1961-81). He was voted Midland Footballer of the Year on three occasions, played for Young England (v. England) and twice represented the Football League.

Since retiring he has undergone two hip operations. His son is a champion amateur golfer.

BROWN, Arthur Alfred 1881-82 (3) (4)

Born: Aston, Birmingham, 15 March 1859
Died: Aston, Birmingham, 11 July 1909
Career: Aston Park School, Florence FC (1874), Aston Unity (1876), Aston Villa (August 1878), Mitchell St. George's (August 1879), Birchfield Trinity (November 1879), Birmingham Excelsior (January 1880), Aston Villa (February 1880, retired through ill-health, May 1886; remained at club as a steward until 1908)

Arthur 'Digger' Brown gained his first England cap in a 13-0 win over Ireland in February 1882. Playing alongside his club-mate colleague Howard Vaughton, the Villa duo bagged nine of the goals between them, Brown scoring four. After that impressive display, Brown 'seemed set for a lengthy international career' but was selected only twice more by England, in the 1882 defeats by Wales and Scotland. His international career lasted just 23 days.

BROWN, Arthur Samuel 1903-06 (2) (1)

Born: Gainsborough, 6 April 1885
Died: Gainsborough, 27 June 1944
Career: Gainsborough Church Lads' Brigade (1900), Gainsborough Trinity (amateur, February 1902, professional, April 1902), Sheffield United (£350, May 1902), Sunderland (£1,000, June 1908), Fulham (October 1910), Middlesbrough (July 1912-May 1913); also a sculptor (a monumental mason).

A centre-forward chiefly noted for his opportunism which was outstanding, Arthur Brown had a decent career, especially with Sunderland (23 goals in 55 games) and Sheffield United (104 in 187). Deputising for Vivian Woodward, he won his first cap at the age of 18 against Wales in February 1904 and his second v. Ireland in February 1906. He scored with a 'clever shot' in a 5-0 win over the Irish in Belfast.

BROWN, George 1926-33 (9) (4)

Born: Mickley, Northumberland, 22 June 1903
Died: Stirchley, Birmingham, 10 June 1948
Career: Mickley Juniors, Mickley Colliery, Huddersfield Town (trial, March 1921, signed as a professional, April 1921), Aston Villa (£5,000, August 1929), Burnley (£1,400, October 1934), Leeds United (£3,100, September 1935), Darlington (£1,000, player-manager, October 1936-October 1938); Sutton Town (guest, season 1939-40), Shirley NFS (guest, season 1940-41); became a Birmingham licensee, at The Star Vaults, Aston and then The Plume of Feathers, Stratford Rod, Shirley, the latter until his death.

A forceful, all-action inside-right or centre-forward, good on the ball, George 'Bomber' Brown, had a huge reputation for scoring goals, yet failed to find the net in each of his first three internationals as England drew 3-3 with both Ireland (when he partnered his cousin Joe Spence on the right-wing) and Wales and beat Scotland 2-1. He finally got off the mark with two excellent strikes in a 9-1 win over Belgium in May 1927 and followed up soon afterwards with two more in a 6-0 defeat of France. 'Dixie' Dean played alongside him in both of these high-scoring matches, the Everton star netting five times.

Brown gained three successive League winner's medals with Huddersfield for whom he scored 159 goals in 229 games. He also represented the Football League.

BROWN, James 1880-85 (5) (3)

Born: Blackburn, 31 July 1862
Died: Blackburn, 4 July 1922
Career: St John's School/Blackburn, Mintholme College (1876-79), Blackburn Rovers (July 1879, retired, injured, May 1889); became a solicitor's managing clerk.

Although small and light for a centre-forward, Jim Brown was extremely fast and elusive with a terrific shot. A star performer in Blackburn's three FA Cup final triumphs in the mid-1880s, he made his England debut as an 18 year-old against Wales in February 1881 and scored twice in his second international, a rousing 13-0 win over Ireland twelve months later, when he played alongside his namesake Arthur. He was also on target once in the 4-0 victory over the Irish in February 1885 when three of his Rovers team-mates also appeared. Brown and another of his Rovers colleagues, Jim Lofthouse, then played together in the 1-1 draw with Scotland at The Oval in March 1885. The Bell's Life reporter wrote: '...they gave the English attack a degree of style and comprehension which had long been lacking.'

BROWN, John Henry 1927-30 (6)

Born: Worksop, Notts, 19 March 1899
Died: Sheffield, 9 April 1962
Career: Manton Colliery (1917), Worksop Town (August 1919), Sheffield Wednesday (£360, February 1923), Hartlepools United (September 1937, released after a fortnight); became a licensee and also worked for The Sheffield Drill and Twist Company.

A broad-shouldered, hefty goalkeeper, Jack Brown was 'efficient, sound and dependable who often advanced well out of his area to avert danger.' Five of his six caps were gained at the end of the 1926-27 season after England had used no less than eight different 'keepers in their previous ten internationals. Unfortunately on his debut he was badly hurt in the draw with Wales and conceded three goals, but was quite outstanding when Scotland were defeated 2-1 at Hampden Park six weeks later, the 'Broadcaster' saying 'His masterly display helped carry England to victory.' Harry Hibbs was just starting to hit form following Brown's last England game against Ireland in October 1929. An FA Cup winner with Wednesday in 1935, Brown made 509 appearances for the Owls between 1923 and 1937.

BROWN, Kenneth 1959-60 ①

Born: Forest Gate, Essex, 16 February 1934
Career: Lymington Secondary Modern School, Dagenham Schools, Neville United (seasons 1949-51), West Ham United (professional, October 1951), Torquay United (May 1967), Hereford United (June 1969), Bournemouth (trainer-coach, May 1970-December 1973), Norwich City (assistant-manager, December 1973-October 1980, than manager, November 1980-November 1987), Shrewsbury Town (caretaker-manager, November-December 1987), Plymouth Argyle (manager, July 1988-February 1990); later England (scout), also deeply involved with the Lakenham Leisure Centre, Norwich.

A very capable centre-half, creative and firm, seldom drawn out of position, Ken Brown's only England cap was won against Northern Ireland at Wembley in November 1959, at a time when manager Walter Winterbottom was searching for a replacement for the retired Billy Wright. Although he gave a solid performance in the 2-1 victory, he was quickly dumped as the selectors continued their search for Billy Wright's replacement.

Brown gave the Hammers tremendous service. He appeared in 455 games between 1953 and 1967, helping them win the Second Division Championship, the FA Cup and European Cup Winners' Cup in 1958, 1964 and 1965 respectively. He also won the League Cup as manager of Norwich City.

BROWN, Wesley Michael 1998-2010 ㉓ ①

Born: Longsight, Manchester, 13 October 1979
Career: Manchester United (apprentice, August 1994, professional, November 1996), Sunderland (undisclosed fee, July 2011).

Versatile defender Wes Brown was capped by England at Schoolboy, Youth and U21 levels (eight caps gained in the latter category) before making his full international debut in April 1999 against Hungary in Budapest when he partnered his Manchester United team-mate Phil Neville at full-back. Subsequently plagued by injury he was in and out of the team but after playing exceptionally well in 2005-06, he hoped to make it into the squad for the World Cup finals, but in the end was not selected. Chosen again by Steve McClaren, Brown played against Andorra in the 2008 European Championship qualifiers, taking over from club-mate Rio Ferdinand to partner John Terry at the heart of the defence, and then he himself replaced Terry in the friendly against Brazil in June 2007, almost conceding an own goal in the first minute! Fabio Capello named him as a starter in both of his first two games in charge against Switzerland and France and he finally scored his first international goal in the 2-2 friendly draw with the Czech Republic in August 2008, stealing in front of a defender to head in David Beckham's corner.

At the time of his transfer to Sunderland in 2011 on a four-year contract, Brown had made 361 appearances for Manchester United whom he helped win six Premiership titles, two Champions League finals and both the FA Cup and League Cup. He retired from international football in August 2010.

Wesley Brown

BROWN, William 1923-24 ① ①

Born: Fencehouses near Chester-le-Street, County Durham, 22 August 1899
Died: Hetton, County Durham, 7 January 1985
Career: Hetton FC (August 1919), West Ham United (August 1920), Chelsea (February 1924), Fulham (June 1929), Stockport County (August 1930), Hartlepools United (May 1931), Annfield Plain (1932), Blackhall Colliery Welfare (seasons 1932-34); later engaged as a baths superintendent at Easington Colliery, County Durham; also stood as a cricket umpire for many years.

Inside-right Billy Brown's first-class career lasted twelve years, 1920-32, during which time he scored 44 goals in 147 club games, including an appearance for West Ham in the first Wembley Cup final of 1923. His highly effective skilful play earned him an England cap against Belgium in Brussels in November 1923 when, playing in a multi-changed side, he found the net in a 2-2 draw. Surprisingly, he made only 116 League appearances during his career.

BRUTON, John 1927-29 ③

Born: Westhoughton, Lancs, 21 November 1903
Died: Bournemouth, 13 March 1986
Career: Westhoughton Sunday school football, Hindley Green, Bolton Wanderers (trial), Wigan Borough (trial), Horwich R.M.I. (August 1924), Burnley (March 1925), Blackburn Rovers (December 1929), Preston North End (August 1939, retired during WW2); Blackburn Rovers (assistant-secretary, September 1947, then manager, December 1947-May 1949), Bournemouth (manager, March 1950-March 1956); later scout for Portsmouth, Bournemouth and Blackburn Rovers.

A decidedly clever and quick outside-right, with an easy, yet deceptive running style, Jack Bruton was a constant threat to opposing full-backs. He assisted in the two goals when France were blitzed 5-2 on his England debut in May 1928 and did well in his second outing against Belgium two days later, but found it hard going against the tough-tackling yet outstanding Scottish left-back Joe Nibloe when England lost 1-0 at Hampden Park the following year. Bruton scored 44 goals in 176 appearances for Burnley and 115 in 344 games for Blackburn.

BRYANT, William Ingram 1924-25 ①

Born: Ghent, Belgium, 1 March 1899
Died: Whitham, Essex, 21 January 1986
Career: St Olave's Grammar School/Chelmsford, Clapton Orient (professional, August 1919), Millwall Athletic (June 1925), Clapton Orient (May 1931, retired May 1933); became a reporter and later a director of a wholesale seed company in Essex.

Billy Bryant won the FA Amateur Cup with Clapton in 1924 and 1925 and the Third Division (South) championship with Millwall in 1928. One of three Clapton players to win full caps for England in the 1920s (the others were Stan Earle and Vivian Gibbins). An astute, 6ft 1in tall centre-half, strong in the air and on the ground, he remained an amateur throughout his career and won seven caps at this level. His senior game for England came in the 3-2 win over France in Paris in May 1925 when one of his long clearances set up a goal for his colleague Gibbins. He netted 30 times in 140 games for Millwall (1925-31).

BUCHAN, Charles Murray 1912-24 ⑥ ④

Born: Plumstead, London, 22 September 1891
Died: Monte Carlo, France, 25 June 1960
Career: Bloomfield Road School/Woolwich, High School Council School/Plumstead, Woolwich Polytechnic, Plumstead St Nicholas Church (1905), Plumstead FC (1906), Woolwich Arsenal (amateur, December 1908), Northfleet (November 1909), Leyton (March 1910), Sunderland (£1,200, March 1911); commissioned in Sherwood Foresters, served with Grenadier Guards in France (WW1); member of Players' Union Committee (1923-25), Arsenal (£2,000 plus £100 per goal, July 1925, retired, May 1928); served in Home Guard (WW2); ran a sports shop in Sunderland; played cricket for East Bolden (1919) and Durham County (1920 and 1921); became a football journalist with the *Daily News* (later renamed the *News Chronicle*); wrote one of the first coaching manuals and also commentated for the BBC; in 1947, he co-founded the Football Writers' Association and from 1951 until his death, edited his own football magazine, *Charles Buchan's Football Monthly*. His autobiography *A Lifetime in Football* was published in 1955.

Charlie Buchan was a 'top drawer player' yet he was only ever awarded six caps. In all probability his independence of mind and willingness to speak it provided the explanation.
  A marvellous inside-right or centre-forward, Buchan's subtleties were said to 'bewilder his team-mates as well as the opposition.' A wonderful footballer, he mastered every trick in the game, was tall and agile, brilliant in the air and also on the ground.
  He grew up in Greenwich and played his early football on Plumstead common before signing for Arsenal at the age of 18, only to leave Highbury after a row with his manager over expenses and didn't return until 1925. He went on to score 56 goals in 120 games for the Gunners and 222 in 411 for Sunderland with whom he won a League Championship medal in 1913. He also netted in the 10th minute of his England debut against Ireland in Belfast in February 1913, but the hosts, down to 10 men, hit back to win 2-1 to record their first ever victory over the English!
  Buchan also found the net in his next outing v. Wales and followed up later with further goals against Belgium and France in 1921 and 1923. Overlooked for the next five matches, his last appearance for his country was in the first international staged at Wembley against Scotland in April 1924.
  It ended in a 1-1 draw, but *The Times* said: 'He (Buchan) was outstanding…only the close attentions of Scottish centre-half Morris prevented him from leading his country to victory.'
  Buchan, who also played in one Victory international v. Wales in October 1919, received the Military Medal for service in France during WW1.

BUCHANAN, Walter Scott 1875-76 ①

Born: Hammersmith, London, 1 June 1855
Died: Hammersmith, 11 November 1926
Career: Clapham Rovers (seasons 1873-77); also played for Barnes and Surrey (1870s)

A light-weight forward and clever dribbler, Walter Buchanan played in the 3-0 defeat by Scotland in March 1876…and according to *Bell's Life* '…once or twice found open space but was speedily closed down by the stern Caledonians.'

BUCKLEY, Major Franklin Charles 1913-14 ①

Born: Urmston, Manchester, 9 November 1883
Died: Walsall, 22 December 1964
Career: Urmston Boys, Aston Villa (April 1903), Brighton & Hove Albion (May 1905), Manchester United (June 1906), Manchester City (September 1907), Birmingham (July 1909), Derby County (May 1911), Bradford City (May 1914); served in the Army in WW1, attaining the rank of Major while engaged with the First Footballers' Battalion (17th Middlesex Regiment), Norwich City (player-manager, March 1919-July 1920); worked as a commercial traveller in London until July 1923; Blackpool (manager, July 1923-May 1927), Wolverhampton Wanderers (secretary-manager, May 1927-March 1944), Notts County (manager, March 1944-May 1946), Hull City (manager, May 1946-March 1948), Leeds United (manager, May 1948-April 1953), Walsall (manager, April 1953, retired from football, September 1955).

A well-built, fair-haired centre-half, Frank Buckley served with six different clubs in six years and only found something approaching stability with Birmingham. In 1909 he joined Derby County and two years after helping the Rams win the Second Division title, he gained his sole England cap in 1914, deputising for Preston's Joe McCall in a shock 3-0 defeat by Ireland at Ayresome Park, when Billy Gillespie and Billy Lacey gave the home defence an exceptionally tough time.
As a manager, Buckley guided Wolves to the First Division Championship in 1932, the FA Cup final in 1939 and victory in the Wartime Cup in 1944.
  His brother, Chris Buckley, played for Manchester City, Brighton, Aston Villa, Arsenal, Birmingham, Manchester United and Coventry City; was an Aston Villa director in 1936-37, and also club chairman

BULL, Stephen George, MBE 1987-91 ⑬ ④

Born: Tipton, West Midlands, 28 March 1965
Career: Wednesbury Oak Primary, Willingsworth High School/Tipton, Ocker Hill Infants, Bustleholme Boys/West Bromwich, Tipton Town (August 1979), Red Lion FC (seasons 1981-83), Newey Goodman FC (September 1983), Tipton Town (October 1983), West Bromwich Albion (amateur, July 1984), Tipton Town (August-September 1984), West Bromwich Albion (professional, September 1984), Wolverhampton Wanderers (£70, with Andy Thompson, November 1986), Hereford United (player-coach, July 1999, retired as player, July 2001), Wolverhampton Wanderers (P.R. officer, August 2001), Stafford Rangers (manager, February-December 2008); gained his UEFA 'B' coaching badge in 2005-06.

Steve Bull was a bold, strong-running centre-forward who, after leaving The Hawthorns, went on to become Wolves' greatest-ever striker, scoring 306 goals in 559 appearances spread over 13 years (1986-99). He hit the 50-goal mark twice in successive seasons (1987-89), becoming the first player to claim a century of goals in just two campaigns for 60 years (since George Camsell in the 1920s), and struck 17 hat-tricks. He helped the Molineux club gain promotion from the Fourth to the Second Division in successive seasons and win the Sherpa Van Trophy at Wembley. The first Third Division player capped by England

Steve Bull

since Peter Taylor in 1976, 'Bully' scored on his England debut against Scotland at Hampden Park in May 1989 (won 2-0) and his effort in the friendly against Czechoslovakia soon afterwards was subsequently voted as number 37 of England's 50 'Greatest Goals'.

Bull also netted a late equaliser against Tunisia in Tunis (1-1). He was sent on in place of Gary Lineker as England's battled to get on level terms and so avoid a shock defeat.

Named in Bobby Robson's World Cup squad for Italia '90, he played four times in Italy - three as a substitute - and his last match in an England shirt was in October 1990 against Poland, chosen by his future Wolves manager, Graham Taylor. All told, 'Bully' netted nine goals in 23 appearances for his country at full, U21, A and B team levels.

He is the cousin of Gary Bull who played as a striker for Barnet, Nottingham Forest and Birmingham City among others.

BULLOCK, Frederick Edwin 1920-21 ①
Born: Hounslow, Middlesex, 19 June 1886
Died: Huddersfield, 15 November 1922
Career: Isleworth Schools, Hounslow Town (1903), Ilford (1909), Huddersfield Town (professional, December 1910-May 1922); was licensee of The Slubbers Arms in Huddersfield at the time of his death

Captain of England's amateur team, capped in 1911, Fred Bullock was a strong-tackling left-back who made 215 appearances for Huddersfield between 1910 and 1921. He was forced to retire through injury just six months after he had helped England beat Ireland 2-0 at Sunderland when he 'played well' at a time when the search was on for a replacement for the long-serving Jesse Pennington.

Bullock was the 400th England player to win a full cap.

BULLOCK, Norman 1922-27 ③ ②
Born: Monton Green, Eccles, Lancs, 8 September 1900
Died: Manchester, 22 October 1970
Career: Broughton St. John's (1914), Sedgley Park Amateurs (1915), Prestwich Amateurs (1919), Bury (professional, February 1921, player-manager, May 1934, retired as a player, May 1938, remained as manager to June 1938), Chesterfield (manager, June 1938-May 1945), Bury (manager, July 1945-December 1949), Leicester City (manager, December 1949-February 1955); also worked as an analytical chemist.

Taking over from Vic Watson, Norman Bullock found the net on his England debut in a 6-1 win over Ireland in March 1923 and scored in his third and last international also against the Irish three-and-a-half years later, helping his side earn a 3-3 draw at Liverpool. A legend at Gigg Lane, the versatile Bullock scored 127 goals in 537 appearances for Bury between 1920 and 1934. He was in football management for 21 years.

BURGESS, Henry 1930-31 ④ ④
Born: Alderley Edge, Cheshire, 20 August 1904
Died: Wilmslow, Cheshire, 6 October 1957
Career: Wilmslow Albion (1918), Alderley Edge FC (1919), Nantwich Ramblers (1922), Stockport County (May 1925), Sandbach Ramblers (loan, briefly, 1926), Sheffield Wednesday (£3,500, August 1929), Chelsea (£1,000, March 1935); WW2 guest for Brentford, Brighton & Hove Albion, Fulham, Reading, Southampton and Stockport County; retired, injured, May 1942; worked for the Ministry of Defence, also a licensee in Stockport.

A solid, stockily-built inside-forward with good dribbling skills, Harry Burgess was a regular scorer throughout his career which realized 186 goals in 510 appearances for his three League clubs, helping Wednesday win the League title in 1930. He won all his England caps in the same season, 1930-31, scoring twice on his debut in a 5-1 win over Ireland when, deputizing for Joe Bradford, he partnered Eric Houghton on the left-wing and then repeated the feat with two goals in his final game against Belgium in Brussels. Burgess, however, had a poor game in the 2-0 defeat by Scotland at Hampden Park, 'Broadcaster' in the *Daily Express* saying 'I have rarely seen an international team that seemed so unlikely to get goals…Meiklejohn and Miller had Dean and Burgess in their pockets.'

BURGESS, Herbert 1903-06 ④
Born: Openshaw, Manchester, 30 October 1883
Died: Manchester, 2 August 1954
Career: Gorton St Francis (1897), Openshaw United (1898), Edge Lane FC (also 1898), Moss Side (April 1899), Glossop (April 1900), Manchester City (July 1903), Manchester United (December 1906, retired, injured, May 1910); subsequently coached in Austria, Denmark, Hungary, Italy, Spain and Sweden; Ashton National (trainer, October 1934-May 1936); later a licensee near Old Trafford.

An FA Cup winner with Manchester City in 1904 and a League Championship winner with United four years later, Bert Burgess, despite his size (5ft 5ins) was a superb left-back, blessed with great anticipation, a stout tackle and powerful kick.

First capped in a 2-2 draw with Wales in February 1904 when he 'didn't have a good game' Burgess played a lot better in his next international a fortnight later against Ireland (won 3-1) and did even better in his third outing when Scotland were defeated 1-0 at Celtic Park in April, Bedouin of the *Daily Record* saying 'England's strength stemmed from the back line of Crompton and Burgess…England has not been served by a more effective pair of backs since the days of the Walters brothers.'

Burgess also represented the Football League on seven occasions and played in an international trial.

BURNUP, Cuthbert James 1895-96 ①
Born: Blackheath, Kent, 21 November 1875
Died: Golder's Green, Middlesex, 5 April 1960
Career: Malvern College (seasons 1890-94), Clare College/Cambridge University (1894-99); also played for Old Malvernians (1894-86) and Corinthians (1895-1901); played cricket for Kent (scoring over 13,000 runs, 26 centuries); later engaged in commerce and stock broking in the City of London.

True to his name, Cuthbert Burnup was a whole-hearted outside-left, a good dribbler with a terrific turn of speed, but he didn't play well as Steve Bloomer's deputy in his only game for England, a 2-1 defeat by Scotland in April 1896. 'Burnup and Wood on England's left-wing were not strong enough to cause problems for the Scottish defenders…Burnup was out of his depth,' reported the *Daily Mail*.

An interesting fact from his cricketing days is that Burnup bowled a ball for the MCC in 1900 which was hit for 10 by Samuel Hill-Wood of Derbyshire – a record for most runs scored off one ball in a first-class match.

BURROWS, Horace 1933-35 ③

Born: Sutton-in-Ashfield, Notts, 11 March 1910
Died: Sutton-in-Ashfield, 22 March 1969
Career: Notts Schools, Sutton Junction (1927), Coventry City (professional, February 1930), Mansfield Town (May 1930), Sheffield Wednesday (£200, May 1931-May 1942); WW2 guest for Millwall; served in El Alamein during the war; Ollerton Colliery (player-manager, season 1945-46); later ran a sports outfitters in his home town.

A left-half with a cogent tackle, Horace Burgess scored eight goals in 261 appearances for Sheffield Wednesday, collecting aa FA Cup winner's medal in1935. He won two of his three England caps on the European tour in May 1934, replacing Wilf Copping against Czechoslovakia and Hungary. His last game was the 1-0 win over Holland in Amsterdam a year later, when he performed with 'great commitment.'
  Burgess's son, Adrian, played for Mansfield Town, Plymouth Argyle, Southend United and Northampton Town.

BURTON, Frank Ernest 1888-89 ①

Born: Nottingham, 18 March 1865
Died: Bingham, Notts, 10 February 1948
Career: Nottingham High School, Notts County (professional, October 1886-October 1887), Nottingham Forest (November 1887, retired, injured, November 1891); became managing-director and then chairman of the family grocery business, Joseph Burton & Sons Ltd.; was also the High Sheriff of Nottingham (1938-39).

Capped as a Forest player in the 6-1 win over Ireland at Goodison Park in March 1889, Frank Burton was said to have played 'a keen game at inside-right, carrying raids to enemy territory with dash and verve.'
  Burton scored five goals on his FA Cup debut for Notts County in October 1886.

BURY, Lindsay 1877-79 ②

Born: Withington, Manchester, 9 July 1857
Died: Bradford, 30 October 1935
Career: Eton College (1875-76), Trinity College/Cambridge University (1877-81); also appeared for Old Etonians (seasons 1878-80 and 1882-84); played cricket for Hampshire; FA Committee member 1878-89; also worked as an orange planter in Florida (USA).

Reputed to be the strongest full-back of his period, 'Lyn' Bury was sure-footed and 'kicked the ball an admirable length.' An FA Cup winner with Old Etonians, he represented England in two internationals at The Oval, against Scotland in March 1877 and Wales in March 1879. His 'buddy' was fellow 'Etonian' Rupert Anderson.

BUTCHER, Terence Ian 1980-90 ⑦⑦ ③

Born: Singapore, 28 December 1958
Career: Fen Park Primary and Lowestoft Grammar Schools, Lowestoft Schools, Ashlea Boys Club/Lowestoft, Suffolk County Boys (U15s and U19s), Ipswich Town (apprentice, April 1975, professional, December 1976), Glasgow Rangers (£725,000, July 1986), Coventry City (£400,000, player-manager, November 1990-January 1992); out of football for 13 months; Sunderland (player-manager, February-November 1993); Raith Rovers (player/reserve team coach, January 1997-May 1998), Dundee United (player/youth team coach, August 1998-October 2001); also Clydebank (briefly as coach); Motherwell (coach/assistant-manager, October 2001-April 2002, then manager, June 2006), Sydney FC/Australia (head coach/manager, July

2006-February 2007), Partick Thistle (coach/assistant-manager, March 2007), Brentford (manager, April-December 2007); Scotland (coach/assistant-manager to George Burley, during season 2008-09), Inverness Caledonian Thistle (manager, January 2009 to date); worked for BBC Sport during the 2006 World Cup; also used as an in-game commentator in the first Pro-Evolution Soccer Video game and the Nintendo 64 game, International Superstar 2000 along with main presenter Chris James.

Terry Butcher's impressive displays for Ipswich were noticed by England boss Ron Greenwood who handed him his debut (along with his club colleague Russell Osman) in a friendly against Australia in May 1980.
  Two years later, 6ft 4in Butcher was the youngest member of the back four which featured at the World Cup in Spain in 1982. He remained as first choice centre back for the rest of the decade, playing in the World Cup again four years later when he infamously tried to tackle Diego Maradona with some desperation as the Argentina skipper slotted in his wondrous second goal in the quarter-final, which England lost 2-1.
  Butcher won his 50th cap in April 1987, having a 'storming game' in a 2-0 win over Northern Ireland in Belfast. However, a broken leg meant that he was not in the side torn apart in all three group games of Euro '88, his absence proving crucial as manager Bobby Robson was forced to rely on the then inexperienced defensive partnership of Tony Adams and Mark Wright.
  In September 1989, while playing for England in a vital World Cup qualifier in Sweden, Butcher suffered a deep cut to his forehead early in the game. He had some impromptu stitches inserted and, head swathed in bandages, continued playing. His constant heading of the ball disintegrated the bandages and reopened the cut to the extent that his white England shirt was entirely red by the end of the game. A proper Man. This match remains his defining moment as one of the great footballing heroes, especially as England got the draw they needed to qualify for the 1990 competition, and is often used when referencing Butcher even today. And with 'Butch' at the back England made it through to the semi-finals of the 1990 World Cup. He also took over the captaincy after an injury ended Bryan Robson's tournament prematurely. That memorable image of Butcher and team-mate Chris Waddle dancing in triumph in front of the England fans after beating Belgium in the second round, was later printed on a T-shirt with the heading 'Let's All Have A Disco'.
  Butcher, who also won one B and seven U21 caps for England but surprisingly never played in the European Championships, appeared in 579 club games (445 in the League), scoring 34 goals. He won the UEFA Cup with Ipswich and three Scottish League titles and two League Cups with Rangers, and at present is England's 14th most capped player. He hasn't succeeded (yet) as a manager.
  In April 1988 Butcher was convicted of disorderly conduct and breach of the peace due to his behaviour in an Old Firm match in November 1987. He was fined £250. Six months later, in October 1988, he was the subject of a police investigation when he kicked the referee's room door off its hinges after a match at Aberdeen. No criminal charges were brought, but Butcher was fined £1,500 by the SFA.

Terry Butcher

BUTLAND, Jack 2012-13 ①

Born: Clevedon near Bristol, 10 March 1993
Career: Clevedon Community School, Jamie Shore Academy/Bristol, Clevedon United (season 2005-06), Birmingham City (initially on schoolboy forms, 2007, trainee, July 2009, professional, March 2010), Cheltenham Town (loan, September-December 2011 and February-May 2012), Stoke City (£3.5m, January 2013), Birmingham City (loan, January-May 2013).

 When he made his full England debut (in place of the injured Joe Hart) in England's 2-1 friendly win over Italy in Berne, Switzerland in 2012, Jack Butland became his country's youngest-ever goalkeeper at the age of 19 years and 158 days, taking over the mantle from Billy Moon who was a shade over two months older when he played against Wales in 1888. Shot-stopper Butland, 6ft 4ins tall and weighing over 12st, represented Team GB at the London Olympics, having made only 24 League Two appearances for Cheltenham Town as a loanee. He has also been capped by England at youth, U20 and U21 levels.

BUTLER, John Dennis 1924-25 ①

Born: Colombo, Ceylon, 14 August 1894
Died: Kensington, London, 5 January 1961
Career: West London Schools, Fulham Thursday (February 1913), Dartford (August 1913), Fulham Wednesday (October 1913), Arsenal (professional, March 1914); served in the Royal Field Artillery in France during WW1; Torquay United (£1,000, June 1930, retired, April 1932); Royal Daring FC/Brussels (coach, July 1932-April 1939); also Belgium national team coach (seasons 1932-39), Leicester City (trainer-coach, October 1940-February 1946), FC Copenhagen/Denmark (coach, March-June 1946), Torquay United (manager, June 1946-May 1947), Crystal Palace (manager, May 1947-May 1949), Royal Daring FC/Brussels (manager, May 1949-April 1950); coached in Denmark (August 1950-May 1953), Colchester United (manager, June 1953-January 1955).

Described as being 'a centre-half of willowy build whose weight gave him command in the air' Jack Butler was also steady and controlled on the ground and was a smart passer too. He made almost 300 appearances for Arsenal (1914-30) and gained his only England cap (as defensive partner to Fred Ewer) against Belgium at The Hawthorns in December 1924 when he 'never put a foot wrong' in a 4-0 win.

BUTLER, William 1923-24 ①

Born: Atherton, Lancs, 27 March 1900
Died: Durban, South Africa, 11 July 1966
Career: Howe Bridge FC (1913), Atherton Colliery (1914), Bolton Wanderers (professional, May 1921), Reading (June 1933, then manager, August 1935-February 1939), Guildford City (manager, June 1939-May 1945), Torquay United (manager, June 1945-May 1946), Johannesburg Rangers/South Africa (manager, seasons 1946-48); became Pietermaritzburg & District FA football coach, and later chief coach in Rhodesia with the Rhodesian FA.

A dribbling outside-right with good speed, Billy Butler gained three FA Cup winner's medals with Bolton in the 1920s. He spent 12 years at Burnden Park during which time he scored 74 goals in 449 appearances for the Wanderers. He played in the first international match at Wembley, a 1-1 draw with Scotland in April 1924, but didn't have a great game, *The Times* reporter noting: 'He was never happy and his inside partner David Jack, also played well below par.'

BUTT, Nicholas 1996-2005 ㊉

Born: Manchester, 21 January 1975
Career: Oldham & District Schools, Greater Manchester Schools, Manchester United (apprentice, July 1991, professional, January 1993), Newcastle United (£2.5m, July 2004), Birmingham City (loan, August 2005-March 2006); released by Newcastle United (May 2010), South China FC/Hong Kong (November 2010-May 2011); now soccer analyst and summariser on the ESPN football show

Hard-working midfielder Nicky Butt made his international debut as a substitute for Steve McManaman against Mexico in March 1997. He immediately became a squad regular, providing reliable back-up for the central midfield positions. An injury to first choice midfielder Steven Gerrard before the 2002 World Cup gave Butt his chance in the starting line-up alongside his club-mates David Beckham and Paul Scholes. He played exceptionally well and was named 'best player in the tournament' by Brazilian legend Pelé - a compliment to his performance in the unattractive holding role. After the World Cup he returned to his role as a squad player, covering for Gerrard and Frank Lampard. Selected for Euro 2004, he unfortunately missed the tournament through injury. His last England game was in a friendly against Spain in November 2004.

Butt also represented England at Schoolboy and Youth team levels and played in seven U21 matches. He scored 26 goals in 387 appearances for Manchester United (1993-2004), gaining Champions League, six Premiership and two FA Cup winner's medals. And when he left Newcastle in 2010, his record in English football read 35 goals in 590 club games.

BYRNE, Gerald 1963-66 ②

Born: Liverpool, 29 August 1938
Career: Liverpool Schools, Liverpool (amateur, August 1953, professional, August 1955, retired, injured, December 1969; joined the Anfield coaching staff, remained at club until 1974).

A resilient full-back, strong going forward, resolute in defence, Gerry Byrne is best remembered for playing 117 minutes of the 1965 FA Cup final with a broken collar-bone, his courage being rewarded with a winner's medal. He made 333 appearances for Liverpool who he served as player and coach for 25 years (1953-78). He gained two England caps, the first along with his Anfield team-mate Jimmy Melia against Scotland at Wembley in April 1963, when he partnered Jimmy Armfield in a 2-1 defeat; the second versus Norway in June 1966 when his right-back colleague was George Cohen. Chosen in Alf Ramsey's original 40-strong squad ahead of the World Cup, Byrne failed to make the final 22.

BYRNE, John Joseph 1961-65 ⑪ ⑧

Born: West Horsley, Surrey, 13 May 1939
Died: Cape Town, South Africa, 27 October 1999
Career: Effingham School, Epsom Town (1954), Guildford City Youth (1955-56), Crystal Palace (professional, July 1956), West Ham United (£65,000, March 1962), Crystal Palace (February 1967), Fulham (March 1968), emigrated to South Africa in 1968; joined Durban City (May 1969, manager May 1972), Hellenic (player-coach, seasons 1972-84), Cape Town Spurs (coach, seasons 1984-88), later Michau Warriors/Port Elizabeth (temporary coach, season 1997-98).

An FA Cup winner with West Ham in 1964, Johnny 'Budgy' Byrne was a skilful, often brilliant, occasionally undisciplined centre-forward who it was said 'required little space in which to manoeuvre.' He gained his 11 England caps over a period of three-and-a-half years and was the 800th player to play for his country at senior level, having an impressive debut in the 1-1 draw with Northern Ireland in November 1961. He then netted twice in his second outing when Switzerland were battered 8-1 in Zurich in June 1963. Five more goals followed in his next four internationals including a hat-trick in a 4-3 victory over Portugal in Lisbon in May 1964 when he outshone both Jimmy Greaves and Bobby Charlton, striking home his third goal in the 87th minute to win the match, and two more in a 2-1 victory over the tough-tackling Uruguayans at Wembley in May 1964. Unfortunately he wasn't selected again after hobbling off with a badly injured knee during the 2-2 draw with Scotland in April 1965.

The first-ever Fourth Division player to win an U23 cap, Byrne also represented his country at Youth team level and in September 1966, he bagged four goals for the Football League in a 12-0 win over the Irish League at Plymouth. He scored 171 goals in a combined total of 411 League appearances for his three major English clubs. He actually played his last game of football in South Africa in 1980, coming on as a late substitute for Hellenic against Dynamos just short of his 51st birthday.

BYRNE, Roger William 1953-58 ㉝

Born: Gorton, Manchester, 8 February 1929
Died: Munich, Germany, 6 February 1958
Career: Burnage Grammar School/Manchester, Ryder Brow Youth Club/Gorton (1944), Manchester United (professional, March 1949 until his death)

Roger Byrne, sadly, was one of the eight Manchester United players that lost their lives in the Munich air disaster on 6 February 1958. Club captain from 1953 (until his death) and despite being right-footed, he played as an outside-left and wing-half before Matt Busby converted him into a traditional left-back, similar to a modern day sweeper. Considered one of the most gifted footballers of his time, Byrne's tackling could be suspect and his aerial ability was described as 'no better than average' but his incredible work ethic and footballing intelligence allowed him to position himself and react to danger swiftly. Innovatively, he was also adept in joining in an attack at a time when full-backs were expected to hold their ground and defend.

Perhaps his best asset was his ability to inspire players with his charismatic leadership. Listed among Manchester United's greatest captains, Byrne made 277 appearances for the Reds, gaining three League Championship winner's medals and an FA Cup runners-up prize. A regular member of Walter Winterbottom's England team during the 1950s, he was expected to captain the team at the 1958 World Cup. Gaining his caps in consecutive internationals between April 1954 and November 1957, Byrne made an impressive debut in a 4-2 win over Scotland at Hampden Park (likened to the great Eddie Hapgood by Daily Mail writer Roy Peskett) and over the next three years or so he had five different partners - Ron Staniforth, club-mate Bill Foulkes, Jimmy Meadows, Jeff Hall (in 17 games) and finally Don Howe. He had the misfortune to be one of the players 'tortured' 7-1 by the Hungarians in Budapest in May 1954 and he also had a tough time when England were held 4-4 by the Rest of The World three weeks later. But after that he hardly put a foot wrong, producing some wonderful displays especially when the Scots were crushed 7-2 at Wembley in April 1955. The report in the Glasgow Herald after this rout, stated: 'Byrne and his Manchester United colleague Duncan Edwards were brilliant down England's left… three of the goals came from attacks started by Byrne.'

However, in the 4-2 win over Brazil at Wembley in 1956, Byrne was one of two England players to miss a penalty - the other was John Atyeo - and six months later, in the 3-0 win over Yugoslavia, he had another spot-kick saved, this time by Vladimir Beara. All of Byrne's 33 caps came in succession – a record for an England player's career from debut.

Stanley Matthews said Byrne could have been England's best-ever full-back but for the Munich air crash.

CAHILL, Gary 2010-12 ⑮ ②

Born: Dronfield, Sheffield, 19 December 1985
Career: AFC Dronfield/Sheffield, Derby County (Academy), Aston Villa (apprentice, April 2001, professional, December 2003), Burnley (loan, November 2004-May 2005), Sheffield United (loan, September-October 2007), Bolton Wanderers (£4.5m, January 2008), Chelsea (£7m, January 2012)

A tall, commanding defender, sure-footed with excellent positional sense, Gary Cahill was called up to the England squad for the match against Kazakhstan in June 2009 following the withdrawal of Rio Ferdinand but had to wait over a year for his first cap, coming on as a second half substitute for Michael Dawson in a 4-0 win over Bulgaria in September 2010 at Wembley – and by doing so, he became the first Bolton player to represent England at senior level since Michael Ricketts in 2002. Cahill had made three U20 and three U21 appearances for his country before his big-money move to Chelsea in 2012. He subsequently helped the Blues win the FA Cup, the Champions League and the Europa League, yet missed Euro 2012. He was initially named in Roy Hodgson's squad but in early June, during a 1–0 friendly win over Belgium at Wembley, he was pushed by opposing striker Dries Mertens and collided with his own goalkeeper Joe Hart, sustaining a double fracture of the jaw. He was replaced by Liverpool's Martin Kelly.

Gary Cahill

CALLAGHAN, Ian Robert, MBE 1965-78 ④

Born: Liverpool, 10 April 1942
Career: St Patrick's RC School/Liverpool, Liverpool & Merseyside Boys, Liverpool (£10 signing-on fee, amateur, May 1957, professional, March 1960), Swansea City (September 1978-January 1981), Cork Hibernian (February-March 1981), Sandefjord/Norway (April-June 1981), Crewe Alexandra (October 1981, retired, February 1982); became an after-dinner speaker.

Ian Callaghan always put maximum effort into his performances on the right-wing. A direct player who crossed the ball precisely (given the chance) he later switched to midfield where he became far more aggressive. Described by his manager at Liverpool, Bill Shankly, as 'the model professional' he scored 69 goals in 856 appearances for the Reds whom he served for 21 years from 1957. The recipient of five First Division, one Second Division, two FA Cup, two UEFA Cup and European Cup winner's medals, he also gained several runners-up prizes, was awarded the MBE in 1973 and voted FWA 'Footballer of the Year' in 1974.

Having been capped for the first time against Finland in June 1966 (won 3-0) Callaghan, along with his Anfield team-mates Roger Hunt and Gerry Byrne, was then named in Alf Ramsey's squad for the 1966 World Cup finals. He played in the 2-0 group game win over France, but ultimately was left out of the side as the competition progressed as Ramsey preferred Alan Ball in an innovative system which did not deploy a natural winger. England, referred to as 'wingless wonders', went on to win the trophy. Callaghan then waited 11 years and 49 days for his third cap v. Switzerland in September 1977 when five of his Liverpool team-mates also played. This was a record for the gap between international appearances. He duly collected his fourth and last cap against Luxembourg a month later. Callaghan also played in four U23 internationals.

CALVEY, John 1901-02 ①

Born: South Bank, Middlesbrough, 23 June 1875
Died: Poplar, London, 3 January 1937
Career: South Banks Juniors (1891), Millwall Athletic (May 1895), Nottingham Forest (August 1899), Millwall Athletic (September 1904-May 1905); later worked in London's dockland.

Centre-forward or inside-right Jack Calvey scored 57 goals in 150 appearances for Nottingham Forest in five seasons: 1899-1904. A weighty, exciting player who often bustled his way past defenders, he won his only cap in March 1902, partnering Steve Bloomer in attack when England beat Ireland 1-0 in Belfast.

CAMPBELL, Austen Fenwick 1928-32 ⑧

Born: Hamsterley, County Durham, 5 May 1901
Died: Hull, 8 September 1981
Career: Spen Black & White, Leadgate Park (1917), Coventry City (seasons 1919-21), Leadgate Park (June 1921), Blackburn Rovers (February 1923), Huddersfield Town (September 1929), Hull City (November 1935-May 1936).

Surprisingly fast over the ground for a left-half, the stylish Austen Campbell was a hard-worker who, once in control of the ball, passed it with great 'efficiency and smoothness'. An FA Cup winner with Blackburn in 1928 and a runner-up with Huddersfield two years later, he made his England debut against Ireland in October 1928 and played his last game in December 1931 against Spain when he had a hand in two of the goals in a 7-1 victory.

CAMPBELL, Fraizer Lee 2011-12 ①

Born: Huddersfield, 13 September 1987
Career: Manchester United (apprentice, June 2003, professional, March 2006), Hull City (loan, October 2007-May 2008), Tottenham Hotspur (loan, September 2009-January 2010), Sunderland (£3.5m, July 2009).

Owing to the number of quality strikers at the club, Fraizer Campbell made only two Premiership appearances during his association with Manchester United, although he did play for England at Youth and U21 levels, having 14 outings in the latter category. He did well at Hull before his transfer to Sunderland, gaining his first full cap as an 80th minute substitute against Holland at Wembley in February 2012, replacing Danny Welbeck in a 3-2 defeat.

CAMPBELL, Sulzeer Jeremiah 1995-2007 ⑦③ ①

Born: Plaistow, London, 18 September 1974
Career: Tottenham Hotspur (apprentice, April 1991, professional, September 1992), Arsenal (free, July 2001), Portsmouth (free, August 2006), Notts County (free, August 2009), Arsenal (free, January 2010), Newcastle United (free, July 2010, released, May 2011); thereafter engaged as a soccer pundit.

A well-built central defender who could also fill in as a full-back, Sol Campbell had his good and bad days as an England player.

He certainly 'scored' what should have been the winning goal against Argentina in the World Cup in St Etienne in June 1998, but his header was ruled out (wrongly in my opinion) for a foul on the 'keeper by Alan Shearer....and all this, after he had netted in the opening group game against Sweden.

Two years after winning his first full cap, Campbell became England's second-youngest captain, after Bobby Moore, when he led his country against Belgium in the King Hassan II Cup in Casablanca in May 1998, at the age of 23 years and 248 days. Then, in 2006, he became the only player to have represented England in six consecutive major tournaments, playing in the final stages of the 1996, 2000 and 2004 European Championships and in the 1998, 2002 and 2006 World Cups.

Campbell, who helped England win the U18 Youth tournament in 1993, has also played 11 times for his country's U21 side (2 goals scored) and in two B internationals.

Campbell, who played in only one League game for Notts County in 2009 when Sven-Göran Eriksson was at Meadow Lane, became only the fourth player (behind David James, Gary Speed and Ryan Giggs) to appear in 500 Premiership games when he turned out for Newcastle against West Bromwich Albion in December 2010. At 2011 he had made a total of 644 appearances at club level.

In 2009 Campbell launched his charity 'Kids Go Live' which allows inner city children to see a variety of live sporting events such as Wimbledon, The Olympics and rugby internationals.

Sol Campbell

CAMSELL, George Henry 1928-36 ⑨ ⑱

Born: Framwellgate Moor, County Durham, 27 November 1902
Died: Middlesbrough, 7 March 1966
Career: Durham Chapel Club (1921), Tow Law Town (1922), Esh Winning (1923), Durham City (June 1924), Middlesbrough (£500, October 1925, retired during WW2, appointed chief scout and coach; then club's assistant-secretary, October 1956-December 1963).

George Camsell, a wonderful centre-forward, strong and mobile, scored 345 goals in 453 appearances for Middlesbrough, including a staggering 64 in League and Cup in season 1926-27 when 'Boro won the Second Division championship and 37 the following term. He also netted a club record 24 hat-tricks and scored in ten successive campaigns (1926-36). The driving force of the attack, his enthusiasm and commitment was infectious, but surprisingly he won only nine caps for England – simply because Dixie Dean and a few other quality marksmen were scoring just as many goals at the same time as Camsell!

For the record, the Middlesbrough ace found the net in each of his nine internationals, banging in goals in a 5-1 win over Belgium and a hat-trick in a 6-0 demolition of Wales in the space of six months in 1929.

Camsell was associated with Middlesbrough for 38 years.

CAPES, Arthur John 1902-03 ①

Born: Burton-on-Trent, Staffs, 23 February 1875
Died: Burton-on-Trent, 26 February 1945
Career: Burton Wednesday FC (seasons 1892-94), Burton Wanderers (September 1894), Nottingham Forest (July 1896), Stoke (August 1902), Bristol City (June 1904), Swindon Town (August 1905, retired, injured, May 1906); later worked in the beer trade.

Not the most competent of inside-lefts, Arthur 'Sailor' Capes was, nevertheless, a hard-worker who scored his fair share of goals - 98 in 352 club appearances spread over 12 years (1894-1906). An FA Cup winner with Forest in 1898, he gained his only England cap against Scotland at Bramall Lane in April 1903, partnering John Cox of Liverpool on the left-wing. The *Scottish Daily Record* stated: 'The English attack, sparkling with bright forward movement, played through the Scottish half-backs brilliantly…Capes was in the thick of the action early on but faded like his colleagues as the Scots went on to win 2-1.' Capes also represented the Football League.

CARR, John 1905-07 ②

Born: Seaton Burn, Northumberland,
7 October 1878
Died: Newcastle-upon-Tyne, 17 March 1948
Career: Seaton Burn (1895), Newcastle United (November 1897, retired, May 1912, appointed assistant-trainer), Blackburn Rovers (manager, February 1922-December 1926); became a licensee near the Greenmarket, Newcastle; also played cricket for Northumberland.

Starting out as a half-back, Jack Carr switched to full-back where he performed with great ability. Well-built, strong in the tackle, he had expert judgment and once scored a goal from fully 40 yards while playing for Seaton Burn. He netted five times in 278 appearances for Newcastle, helping the Geordies win two League Championships and the FA Cup

between 1905 and 1910. His two England caps both came against Ireland, the first at Ayresome Park in February 1905 when he deputised for Burgess and the second two years later at Liverpool when he partnered the great Bob Crompton.

CARR, John 1920-23 ②

Born: South Bank, Middlesbrough, 26 November 1892
Died: Darlington, 10 May 1942
Career: South Bank East End (June 1906), South Bank (August 1908), Middlesbrough (professional, February 1911), Blackpool (May 1930), Hartlepools United (player-coach, July 1931, then manager, April 1932-April 1935), Tranmere Rovers (manager, July 1935-November 1936); out of football for two years; Darlington (manager, October 1938-May 1942)

Jackie Carr could play, and play well, either at inside or outside-right. A schemer and maker of goals rather than a scorer himself, he was provider-in-chief over many years for a succession of quality Middlesbrough marksmen, including George Camsell. Twice a Second Division Championship winner in 1927 and 1929, Carr gained his first England cap against Ireland in Belfast in October 1919 and his second against Wales in Cardiff in March 1923 when he had a hand in Harry Chambers' goal. Both games ended in draws.

CARR, William Henry 1874-75 ①

Born: Sheffield, 12 November 1848
Died: Sheffield, 22 February 1924
Career: Walkley FC (seasons 1865-68), Owlerton (player-secretary, seasons 1868-75), Sheffield Wednesday (seasons 1875-77), Sheffield FA (seasons 1877-79)

Bill Carr, 6ft 3ins tall and 13st in weight, played equally well as a defender or goalkeeper. He gained his only cap 'between the posts' against Scotland at The Oval in March 1875 – but the 'committee' wasn't too pleased, as he turned up at the ground 15 minutes late, forcing England to play with only 10 men until his arrival. The score-sheet was blank at the time, but Carr, who produced some 'clever saves' was perhaps at fault for Scotland's second equaliser in the 2-2 draw when he failed to deal with a corner-kick from which Peter Andrew scored. He wasn't selected again.

CARRAGHER, James Lee Duncan 1998-2010 ㊳

Born: Bootle, Merseyside, 28 January 1978
Career: FA School of Excellence (Lilleshall), Liverpool (apprentice, April 1994, professional, October 1996, retired May 2013).

One of the best defenders in the Premiership between 2003 and 2013, strong on the ground and in the air, 'Scouser' Jamie Carragher spent 19 years with Liverpool, during which time he amassed 737 appearances for the Anfield club. He has two FA Cup, two League Cup, UEFA Cup, Champions League and two Super Cup winner's medals to his credit and besides his 38 full caps, he's also represented his country at Youth team level and in three B and 27 U21 internationals (joint sixth highest with Gareth Barry). Indeed, the latter tally stood as a record until eclipsed in 2007 by goalkeeper Scott Carson.

In April 1999, Carragher won his first cap, as a substitute against Hungary, making his full début versus Holland at White Hart Lane two years later. Having helped England crush Germany 5-1 in the Olympiastadion, he missed the 2002 World Cup through injury, but travelled to Euro 2004, only to

Jamie Carragher

lose out to Ledley King. Selected in the squad for the 2006 World Cup, he was not in the original starting eleven, but came into the team following Gary Neville's injury. The versatile Carragher has played at centre-back, right-back, left-back and as a defensive midfielder for England, but despite his tally of caps, he was never a regular in the starting eleven. In July 2006, Carragher was one of three players to have a penalty saved by Ricardo Pereira, as England, again, succumbed on penalties to exit the 2006 World Cup in the quarter finals against Portugal. Carragher, who had been brought on as a substitute for Aaron Lennon late in he game, scored with his first attempt but was forced to re-take his spot-kick by the referee, who had not blown his whistle. Carragher then saw his second effort saved. He announced his retirement from international football in 2007, saying that he had been unhappy at the failure of successive England managers to pick him at centre-back, preferring to use him as cover along the back four and even as a holding midfielder. 'This was a wrong decision' said several of his Liverpool team-mates. However, Carragher was persuaded by England boss Fabio Capello to return and subsequently played in the 2010 World Cup in South Africa.

Carragher became the first British player to appear in 150 European games when he lined up for Liverpool against Zenit St Petersburg in the Europa League in February 2013.

CARRICK, Michael 2000-13 ㉙
Born: Wallsend-on-Tyne, 28 July 1981
Career: West Ham United (apprentice, August 1996, professional, August 1998), Swindon Town (loan, November-December 1999), Birmingham City (loan, February-March 2000), Tottenham Hotspur (£3m, August 2004), Manchester United (£14m, August 2006)

A very efficient, creative midfielder, hard-working with good passing ability and a terrific engine, Michael Carrick, a former Youth international, played in one B and 14 U21 internationals and has now amassed 538 club appearances, 307 for United (at May 2013).

A four-time Premiership winner with Manchester United, he has also helped the Reds win the Champions League.

Having made two substitute appearances in 2001, Carrick was given his first England start in May 2005 during the tour of the United States, being considered by manager, Sven-Göran Eriksson as 'a good option as a holding midfielder'. A year later, he was named in the squad for the 2006 World Cup and played in the 1-0 win over Ecuador.

However, despite his consistent club form Carrick has been generally overlooked by the respective England managers, rarely starting games under Eriksson, Steve McClaren and Fabio Capello. In fact, he hardly figured for 16 months, although he was named in Capello's squad for the game against the Czech Republic only to withdraw through injury. Returning to the side in November 2008 in a 2-1 win over Germany in Berlin, he was effectively considered a 'reserve' to Messrs. Barry, Gerrard, Lampard and even Hargreaves, but battled on and was in the England squad at the 2010 World Cup.

CARROLL, Andrew Thomas 2010-12 ⑨ ②
Born: Gateshead, 6 January 1989
Career: Newcastle United (apprentice, April 2005, professional, July 2006), Preston North End (loan, August-September 2007, Liverpool (£35m, January 2011), West Ham Utd (loan, August 2012-May 2013; signed for £15m, June 2013)

A tall, robust, pony-tailed striker – likened to those good old-fashioned centre-forwards of yesteryear - Andy Carroll made his England debut as a substitute in a 2-1 defeat by France at Wembley in November 2010. Later admitting he wasn't 100 per cent fit, he nevertheless proved to be the only positive performer of the night, working his socks off, providing some smart flick-ons and not looking at all out of place. Four months later, after he had moved from Newcastle to Liverpool, he was back at Wembley for his full debut, scoring in a 1-1 draw with Ghana.

A hero at St James' Park, he netted 33 goals in 91 first-class appearances for the Magpies before making a record-breaking move to Anfield early in 2011. An England youth team player, Carroll has also appeared in five U21 internationals and was a member of Roy Hodgson's squad at Euro 2012 where he scored with a fine header against Sweden in a group game.

CARSON, Scott Paul 2006-08 ④

Born: Whitehaven, 3 September 1985
Career: Leeds United (apprentice, April 2001, professional, September 2002), Liverpool (£750,000, January 2005), Sheffield Wednesday (loan, March-May 2006), Charlton Athletic (loan, August 2006-May 2007), Aston Villa (loan, August 2007-May 2008), West Bromwich Albion (£3.25m, July 2008), Bursaspor/Turkey (free transfer, June 2011).

A catastrophic mistake by Scott Carson on his first competitive start for his country against Croatia at Wembley in November 2007 knocked the stuffing out of England as they attempted to qualify for Euro 2008. Well positioned, he seemed capable of dealing with a 30-yard shot by Niko Kranjcar, but the ball dipped and bounced before him, which he could only parry into the net to give Croatia the lead. A second goal followed before England pulled level only for the unfortunate Carson to concede a third goal as England crashed out of the competition. Coach Steve McClaren was sacked the next day, after commentators had criticised him for selecting an inexperienced goalkeeper for such an important match.

Carson was only 18 when he won the first of his then record 29 U21 caps, a total since beaten by three outfield players. He gained his last against the hosts, Holland, in the semi-final of the U21 European Championships in 2007. The game finished 1–1 after extra-time but in the resultant penalty shoot-out, Carson saved one of the 16 spot-kicks he faced and also scored one himself, but England still lost 13–12. Carson was subsequently overtaken by James Milner as England's most-capped player at U21 level.

Earlier, in the summer of 2005, Carson toured the USA with the full England squad and a year later, came on as substitute for Robert Green in the 'B' international against Belarus. Selected continuously thereafter in the senior squad, he made his full England debut against Austria in November 2007, keeping a clean sheet. A week later, he played in his first competitive match (v. Croatia, above). Then manager Fabio Capello named him in his first England squad for the friendly against Switzerland in February 2008 but he did not win his third England cap until November 2008, against Germany in Berlin when he came on for the second half. In doing so he became the first West Bromwich Albion goalkeeper to play for England since Harold Pearson in 1932, and the first Baggies player to win a full cap since 1984. Carson was recalled to the senior squad in March 2011 (following an injury to Ben Foster).

Carson made over 200 club appearances in English football, gaining a Super Cup winner's medal with Liverpool in 2005 and promotion to the Premiership with WBA in 2010.

CARTER, Horatio Stratton 1934-47 ⑬ ⑦

Born: Hendon, Sunderland, 21 December 1913
Died: Willerby, Hull, 9 October 1994
Career: Hendon School/Sunderland, Whitburn St. Mary's, Sunderland Forge, Esh Winning (September 1931), Sunderland (professional, November 1931); WW2 guest for Cardiff City, Hartlepools United, Huddersfield Town, Nottingham Forest and Notts County; Derby County (December 1945), Hull City (March 1948, player/assistant-manager, resigned as manager, September 1951, continued as a player until April 1952); Cork Athletic (January 1953, retired, May 1953); Leeds United (manager, May 1953-June 1958); out of football for 20 months; Mansfield Town (manager, February 1960), Middlesbrough (manager, January 1963-February 1966); played cricket for Derbyshire and also for Durham v. Australia; later a sports shop manager, then a confectionery shop proprietor in Hull.

Raich Carter's international career covered 13 years and 34 days and only three players can better that – Stanley Matthews, Tony Adams and David Beckham. During that time he won only 13 caps, despite being regarded as one of the finest inside-forwards in League football in the 1930s. A great executioner and tactician, he had only one flaw, that of being rather impatient with those who he felt did not match up to his high standards! He drew up a fine understanding with Stan Matthews on England's right-wing, and later with Tom Finney. Indeed, Sir Stan was among Carter's many admirers, saying: "I felt [he] was the ideal partner for me... Carter was a supreme entertainer who dodged, dribbled, twisted and turned, sending bewildered left-halves madly along false trails. Inside the penalty box with the ball at his feet and two or three defenders snapping at his ankles, he'd find the space to get a shot in at goal... Bewilderingly clever, constructive, lethal in front of goal, yet unselfish. Time and again he'd play the ball out wide to me and with such service I was in my element."

Carter's first game with Finney was against Northern Ireland in September 1946 when he was 'quite brilliant, constantly changing tack, feinting and double-feinting throughout the 90 minutes.' He scored the opening goal – England's first at senior level since WW2 - and laid on two more in a resounding 7-2 win.

Eight months later in the clash with Scotland at Wembley and with the scores level at 1-1 with barely seconds remaining, Carter raced clear but with only the keeper to beat he suddenly stopped, claiming he had heard a whistle…which in fact came from the crowd! Then, when France were defeated 3-0 in May 1947, he gave a repeat performance of his display against the Irish, one reporter saying 'Carter gave a perfect display of ball control…a most talented ball player if ever I saw one.'

Besides his senior appearances for England, Carter also played in 17 Wartime internationals (scoring 18 goals). He was on the losing side just one, in his last game against France in Paris in May 1946. The French goalkeeper Da Rui was carried off the pitch shoulder high after his team's 2-1 victory and was later given a 10 out of 10 rating in the local newspaper, L'Equipe.

Carter's Wartime goal-tally included a hat-trick against Wales in May 1945, four days before V.E. Day was declared. He also starred in two international trials, hitting four goals in his second at Roker Park, played in one unofficial international and represented his country at schoolboy level.

In club football, Carter netted 128 times in 278 games for Sunderland, 50 in 83 for Derby and 62 in 150 for Hull City. He won the League title and FA Cup with the Wearsiders in 1936 and 1937, the Third Division (North) Championship with Hull in 1949 and the FA League of Ireland Cup with Cork in 1953.

CARTER, Joseph Henry 1926-29 ③ ④

Born: Aston, Birmingham, 27 July 1899
Died: Handsworth, Birmingham, 21 January 1977
Career: Farm Street Council and Hockley Hill Schools/Birmingham, Westbourne Celtic (1918), West Bromwich Albion (professional, April 1921), Sheffield Wednesday (for six days, February 1936), Tranmere Rovers (£450, May 1936), Walsall (£200, November 1936), Vono Sports (player-manager, August 1938, retired, May 1942); later licensee of the Grove Inn, Handsworth, Birmingham.

Inside-right Joe Carter, who gave West Bromwich Albion 15 years of magnificent service (1921-36), was tall and wiry, a good dribbler with a superb body swerve and powerful shot. He scored 155 goals

in 451 appearances for the Baggies, whom he helped complete the FA Cup and promotion double in 1931 and reach the 1935 FA Cup final. He was also the first Albion player to be sent off at The Hawthorns, dismissed against Blackburn Rovers in September 1931.

A scorer on his international debut against Belgium in Brussels in May 1926 (won 5-3), Carter was on target against the same opposition in a 5-1 victory three years later when he netted his country's 500th goal at senior level. He then struck twice in his third outing shortly afterwards when Spain won 4-3 in suffocating heat in Madrid. Carter was one of the better players that afternoon, one reporter stating: 'He was always a danger with his clever footwork and angled shooting. He was certainly England's best forward.'

CATLIN, Arthur Edward 1936-37 ⑤

Born: South Bank, Middlesbrough, 11 January 1911
Died: Sheffield, 28 November 1990
Career: Middlesbrough Schools, South Bank FC (junior, summer, 1926), Sheffield Wednesday (amateur, April 1930, professional, October 1930, retired, May 1945, then club scout, later chief scout until 1965); also played club cricket; later a licensee and also proprietor of a Blackpool boarding house.

A very thoughtful and composed left-back, Ted Catlin was also extremely skilful. He cleared his lines effectively and was rarely guilty of a mistimed tackle. An FA Cup winner with Wednesday in 1935, he made 228 appearances for the Owls in 15 years before retiring to join the club's scouting staff.

Deputising for Arsenal's Eddie Hapgood, Catlin's full England caps were won against Wales, Ireland and Hungary in 1936 and Norway and Sweden in 1937. His team scored 20 goals in those five matches, of which Catlin helped set up just two with well placed clearances down field. He also represented the Football League and was an international trialist. At cricket, his best bowling figures were 9-39 and his top score was 88 not out.

CAULKER, Stephen Roy 2012-13 ① ①

Born: Feltham, Middlesex, 21 December 1991
Career: Tottenham Hotspur (trainee, June 2007, professional, July 2009), Yeovil Town (loan, July 2009-May 2010), Bristol City (loan, September 2010-March 2011), Swansea City (loan, July 2011-May 2012)

Steven Caulker, the 6ft 3in tall, confident Tottenham Hotspur centre-back, scored on his England debut in a 4-2 defeat by Sweden in Stockholm in November 2012. One of six 'new' faces used by manager Roy Hodgson that night, he coped well against one of the best strikers in world football, Zlatan Ibrahimovic, who went on to net all of his country's four goals, three after Caulker had been substituted for Ryan Shawcross!

Caulker, who had scored in the Premiership against both Chelsea and Manchester United before winning his first senior cap, had not even played for Spurs before being called up to represent Team Great Britain at the 2012 London Olympics, although he had represented his country at youth and U21 levels and made a total of 99 League appearances while on loan to Yeovil Town, Bristol City and Swansea City during seasons 2009-12.

CHADWICK, Arthur 1899-1900 ②

Born: Church, Lancs, 31 July 1875
Died: Exeter, Devon, 21 March 1936
Career: Church (1890), Accrington (1892), Burton Swifts (May 1895), Southampton (May 1897), Portsmouth (May 1901), Northampton Town (June 1904), Accrington (August 1906), Exeter City (April 1908, then manager, May 1910-December 1922), Reading (manager, January 1923-April 1925), Southampton (manager, October 1925-April 1931).

Initially a right-half, Arthur Chadwick developed into a big, powerful centre-half, one of the best in the country. However, he was not always at ease when facing a clever dribbler but nevertheless was a class defender. He helped Saints win the Southern League three times and the FA Cup once in the space of four years. His two England caps were won against Scotland and Wales in March and April 1900. Unfortunately he was 'seriously at fault' for two of the goals in Scotland's 4-1 win at Celtic Park. A report in the *Football Sun* stated: 'McColl proved an uncomfortable thorn in the side of the English centre-half Chadwick, a newcomer to the team…the ball seemed too clever for him.' McColl scored a hat-trick and could easily have doubled his goal-tally. Against Wales he was 'out of his depth' according to reporter C.W. Alcock but also said that he came close to scoring twice! The game ended in a 1-1 draw.

In January 1899, in a match at Sheppey United, Chadwick became the first Saints player to be sent off in a Southern League match. He collapsed and died while watching Exeter play Clapton Orient in 1936.

CHADWICK, Edgar Wallace 1890-97 ⑦ ②

Born: Blackburn, 14 June 1869
Died: Blackburn, 14 February 1942
Career: Rising Sun FC/Blackburn, St George's Mission/Blackburn, Little Dots FC/Blackburn (1885), Blackburn Olympic (season 1886-87), Blackburn Rovers (professional, July 1887), Everton (August 1888), Burnley (May 1889), Southampton (August 1900), Liverpool (May 1902), Blackpool (May 1904), Glossop (May 1905), Darwen (July 1906, retired April 1908); coached in Germany and also England (amateur team coach, briefly), Holland (national team manager, 1908-13); also coached FC The Hague, Haarlem FC, Vitesse Arnhem and Sport Rotterdam/Holland (between 1908-15); became a Blackburn-based baker after WW1.

Cousin of Arthur (above), Edgar Chadwick, 5ft 6ins tall, was a very talented inside-left, quick, cunning, excellent at passing and he could shoot. When England were scheduled to play Scotland at Ewood Park, Blackburn in 1891, thousands of Rovers supporters stayed away because not one member of their team was in the England XI. However, England won the game 2-1 and to help smooth things over, Blackburn-born Chadwick (then of Everton) scored the deciding goal.

A year later, in April 1892, he scored a brilliant 35-second goal (from Jack Southworth's left-wing cross) in a 4-1 win over the Scots at Ibrox Park.

Chadwick, who also represented the Football League and Football Alliance, was the recipient of First Division and Southern League Championship winner's medals with Everton and Southampton respectively, making well over 550 appearances as a player, including 300 for Everton (110 goals scored). As a manager he guided the Netherlands to the bronze medal in both the 1908 and 1912 Olympic Games and Sparta Rotterdam to the Dutch League title in 1915. He was the first Englishman to coach abroad.

Stephen Caulker

CHAMBERLAIN, Mark Valentine 1982-85 ⑧ ①

Born: Stoke-on-Trent, 19 November 1961
Career: Port Vale (apprentice, April 1977, professional, April 1979), Stoke City (£135,000, August 1982), Sheffield Wednesday (£300,000, September 1985), Portsmouth (£200,000, August 1988), Brighton & Hove Albion (free, August 1994), Exeter City (free, August 1995), Fareham Town (player-manager/coach, March 1997, later Director of Football, June 2000), East Timor/South-east Asia (national team, assistant-manager/coach, April-August, 2008), Portsmouth (coach, September 2008)

A very fast, direct winger, who tended to over-run the ball at times, Mark Chamberlain had an excellent career… and he was the second black player (Luther Blissett was the first) to score a senior goal for England, doing so on his debut as a second-half substitute in a 9-0 win over Luxembourg at Wembley in December 1982. He also represented his country as a Schoolboy and Youth team player before winning four caps at U21 level. During his 20-year career he appeared in well over 600 competitive games including 518 in the Football League (69 goals scored).

His brother, Neville, also played for Port Vale and Stoke City while his highly-rated son is Alex Oxlade-Chamberlain.

CHAMBERS, Henry 1920-24 ⑧ ⑤

Born: Willington Quay, Co. Durham, 17 November 1896
Died: Shrewsbury, 29 June 1949
Career: Tynemouth School/Willington, Willington United Methodists (1911), North Shields Athletic (1913), Liverpool (professional, April 1915); WW1 guest for Belfast Distillery and Glentoran; West Bromwich Albion (£2,375, March 1928), Oakengates Town (player-manager, June 1929), Hereford United (player-manager, January 1933, retired as a full-time player, May 1934, continued as manager until May 1948).

Harry Chambers was a brainy footballer who played initially as an inside-left or centre-forward before becoming a centre-half with WBA. As hard as nails, he was predominantly left-footed and would regularly have a shot at goal from any distance. Capped twice as a Schoolboy (in 1911), Chambers failed to score in either of his first two full internationals against Wales and Scotland in 1921 but then five times in his next four, including two that beat Ireland at The Hawthorns in October 1922. His last international goal was a real cracker, in a 6-1 victory over Belgium in March 1923.

Chambers, who won the Irish Cup with Glentoran and successive League Championship medals with Liverpool in 1922 and 1923, scored 151 goals in 338 appearances for the Merseysiders whom he served for 13 years (1915-28). Chambers played his last game for Hereford at the age of 51.

CHANNON, Michael Roger 1972-78 ㊻ ㉑

Born: Orcheston, Wiltshire, 28 November 1948
Career: Shrewton U/11s (season 1958-59), Amesbury Secondary School, Salisbury and Wiltshire Schools (season 1962-63), Southampton (apprentice, March 1964, professional, December 1965), Durban Celtic/South Africa (loan, 1974), Manchester City (£300,000, July 1977), Cape Town City/South Africa (loan, 1978), Southampton (September 1979), Newcastle KB United/Australia (loan, 1981), Gosnells City (loan, 1981), Caroline Hills/

Hong Kong (loan, 1982), Newcastle United (August 1982), Bristol Rovers (October 1982), Norwich City (December 1982), Durban City (loan, 1983), Miramar Rangers, 1983), Portsmouth (August 1985), Finn Harps/Ireland (August 1986, retired May 1987); has been a successful racehorse trainer since 1990.

A big, strongly-built forward with good pace and powerful shot, Mick Channon was the player most-capped by England boss Don Revie. He made his international debut in the 1-1 draw with Yugoslavia in October 1972, scored the first of his 21 goals in his second game against Scotland in February 1973 (won 5-0 at Wembley) and collected his 46th and last cap in the 0-0 draw with Switzerland in September 1977.

He also scored in the sixth minute of manager Joe Mercer's

last match in charge – a 2-2 draw with Yugoslavia in Belgrade in June 1974 – and found the net in a 2-1 defeat by the ten men of Czechoslovakia in Bratislava in October 1975.

He was also a provider – setting up all of Malcolm Macdonald's five goals in a 5-0 drubbing of Cyprus at Wembley in April 1975.

He struck two fine goals himself in a 4-0 win over Northern Ireland in May 1976 – soon after helping Southampton win the FA Cup - and four days later netted against Scotland - this time from the penalty spot – in what was the infamous 2-1 defeat when Scottish supporters invaded the Wembley pitch in celebration, ripping up clods of turf for souvenirs and pulling down one of the crossbars.

As captain of England against Italy in New York in May 1976, Channon scored twice in a 3-2 win and ten months later, he was the player fouled by Dresch, the Luxembourg defender, who was sent off in the 85th minute of England's 5-0 win in March 1977 to become the second player dismissed at Wembley.

At club level, Channon – known for his swirling arm 'windmill celebration' - made over 850 appearances in all competitions and netted almost 300 goals. In the Football League alone he scored 232 times in 717 appearances, and won the FA Cup with Southampton in 1976 and the League Cup with Norwich City in 1985. He also gained nine U23 caps and twice represented the Football League.

Among the owners who have had their horses with Channon are old colleagues and acquaintances from his footballing days including Kevin Keegan, Alan Ball, Sir Alex Ferguson and Chris Cattlin.

CHAPPELL, Frederick Patey Maddison 1872-73 ①
Born: Chiswick, London, 22 July 1849
Died: Hammersmith, London, 25 September 1907
Career: Marlborough Grammar School, Brasenose College/Oxford University (seasons 1865-72), Wanderers (seasons 1872-75), Crystal Palace (season 1875-76); called to the Bar in 1876 but disbarred in October 1884 at his own request to become a solicitor (from December 1884).

Fred Chappell played under the name of Maddison in the first-ever England-Scotland game in November 1872 and his dribbling was 'greatly admired by the immense concourse of spectators.' A right-half who could also appear in the forward-line, he was fearless and was not averse to using his weight, he won the FA Cup with Oxford University in 1874 and the Wanderers in 1876.

Some reference books list this player as MADDISON, Frederick Brunning.

CHARLES, Gary Andrew 1980-81 ②
Born: Newham, London, 13 April 1970
Career: Newham & District Schools, Arsenal (trial, 1985), Leyton Orient (trial, 1986), Nottingham Forest (apprentice, June 1986, professional, November 1987), Leicester City (loan, March-May 1989), Derby County (£750,000, July 1983), Aston Villa (£1.45m, January 1995), Benfica/Portugal (£1.5m, January 1999), West Ham United (£1.2m, October 1999), Birmingham City (loan, September-October 2000), returned to West Ham United (retired, May 2002); out of football for nine years; Lincoln City (coach, October 2011).

An attacking right-back with good pace and the ability to recover quickly, Gary 'Fluff' Charles was the unfortunate victim of Paul Gascoigne's reckless challenge in the 1991 FA Cup final when Spurs beat Nottingham Forest. His two full caps were awarded on tour against New Zealand and Malaysia in June 1991, replacing Paul Parker as partner to his Forest club-mate Stuart Pearce.

A fractured ankle effectively ended his career after 216 League appearances. He also gained six U21 caps.

After quitting football in 2002, Charles struggled with alcoholism and has served four prison sentences – for drunken driving, cutting off his electronic tag to go on holiday to the Costa del Sol, attending court drunk and for a serious public order offence. In 2005, he was charged with assaulting a woman in a taxi office in Clay Cross, Derbyshire but when the jury failed to reach a verdict, a retrial was ordered and he was subsequently fined and given a suspended sentence and a community service order.

He eventually returned to the game as coach under manager David Holdsworth at Lincoln City in 2011.

CHARLTON, John, OBE, DL **1964-70** ㉟ ⑥

Born: Ashington, Northumberland, 8 May 1935
Career: Ashington YMCA (1950), Ashington Welfare (1951); National Service with Household Cavalry; Leeds United (professional, May 1952, retired, May 1973); Middlesbrough (manager, May 1973-April 1977), Sheffield Wednesday (manager, October 1977-May 1983), Newcastle United (manager, June 1984-August 1985), Middlesbrough (caretaker-manager, March-April 1984), Republic of Ireland (manager, February 1986, resigned July 1996).

Jack Charlton, the tall, rugged and uncompromising Leeds United centre-half, was the linchpin of the toughest and most durable defence in the country and he took over the same mantle in the England team.

Described as being 'Gangling, awkward and headstrong' he was almost 30 when Alf Ramsey handed him his international debut against Scotland at Wembley in April 1965, joining forces with 'our kid' Bobby to become the first set of brothers to play together for England since Frank and Fred Forman in April 1899.

'Niggling injuries' caused Charlton to miss several internationals in the late 1960s. Indeed, he told reporters: "In other circumstances they might not have been enough to stop me playing for my club, Leeds, but if a big match came round then I was told by the boss, Don Revie, to pull out."

All of Charlton's 35 appearances for England were at centre-half. He was on the losing side just once, against Austria in 1965, while 23 of the games he played in England kept a clean sheet.

He made his debut in the 2-2 draw with Scotland at Wembley in April 1965 and played very well against the likes of Ian St John and Denis Law. Brian James wrote in the *Daily Mail*: "This lanky streak from Leeds was suitably tough and predictably calm in a first-cap situation that would have tested the most experienced international."

Thereafter he was 'a rock at the back' and despite having to deal with some exceedingly clever centre-forwards, he was never really given a roasting. He formed an excellent partnership with Bobby Moore and although pushed hard and long by Everton's Brian Labone, 'Big Jack' or 'the Giraffe' stood his ground and produced some terrific performances. His last cap was gained in the 1-0 win over Czechoslovakia in the 1970 World Cup in Mexico.

Charlton scored his first England goal in the 3-0 win over Finland in June 1966 – a freak effort in the last minute. His last decided the match with Portugal in December 1969 - a powerful header from brother Bobby's corner in treacherous conditions at Wembley. In between times he collected a World Cup winner's medal – although his heart was in his mouth in the semi-final when he gave away a penalty as England eventually saw off Portugal 2-1 before going on to beat West Germany in the final.

A Leeds player for 20 years (1952-72) Charlton made 773 appearances, 629 in the Football League, and he scored 96 goals, a wonderful return for a defender! He won First and Second Division Championship medals, triumphed in FA Cup, League Cup and two Inter-Cities Fairs Cup finals, collected a plethora of runners-up medals in various competitions and was voted FWA Footballer of the Year in 1967. And besides his senior caps, Charlton also played in one unofficial international and represented the Football League on six occasions. As a manager he steered Middlesbrough to the Second Division title in 1974 and took Eire into the quarter-finals of the World Cup in 1990.

Personal honours awarded to him include the OBE and, in 1996, that of honorary Irish citizenship – which amounted to full Irish citizenship and is the highest honour the Irish state gives and is rarely granted. In 1994 he was made a Freeman of the City of Dublin and simultaneously was given an honorary doctorate by the University of Limerick. Three years later, 'Big Jack' was appointed a deputy Lieutenant of Northumberland.

Charlton also has a life-size statue at Cork Airport in Ireland, representing him sitting down in his fishing gear displaying a salmon.

CHARLTON, Sir Robert, OBE, CBE 1957-70 (106) (49)

Born: Ashington, Northumberland, 11 October 1937
Career: East Northumberland Schools, Manchester United (amateur, January 1953, professional, October 1954), Preston North End (manager, May 1973-August 1975 which included a spell as player-manager from May 1974), Waterford/Ireland (player, January-March 1976), Wigan Athletic (director and briefly caretaker-manager during season 1982-83), Manchester United (director, June 1984 to date; also acts as United's Ambassador, with Bryan Robson).

Bobby Charlton was a vital cog in the engine-room of Alf Ramsey's World Cup winning side in 1966. He scored a brilliant right-footed rocket in the 2-0 win over Mexico at the group stage and struck two hammer blows in the semi-final defeat of Portugal. And with a total of 49 international goals for his country, Charlton remains, to this day, as England's leading scorer.

He is also the fourth most-capped player with 106 to his name, gained over a period of 12 years between April 1958 and June 1970, collecting his 100th against Northern Ireland in May 1969. He played in three World Cup final tournaments (1962-66-70) and he also represented his country in three different decades: 1950s, '60s and '70s.

Injured in the Munich air crash in February 1958, Charlton had recovered sufficiently to make his international debut as a 20 year-old in a 4-0 win over Scotland at Hampden Park two months later. That afternoon he scored a classic goal. Finney made a clever, twisting run down the left and swung over a tempting cross. Charlton, lurking on the edge of the penalty-area, moved in, made contact with the ball and volleyed unerringly past Tommy Younger in the Scots goal. What a start!

Eighteen days later Charlton cracked in both goals in a 2-1 win over Portugal, at which point some pundits believed 'the power of his shooting might be a potent, perhaps indispensable weapon.' And so it proved.

Two more goals followed in the 3-3 draw with Northern Ireland in October 1958 - both of them thunderbolts - and three weeks later he struck another when the Soviet Union were crushed 5-0 at Wembley.

He managed only one goal in his next six games but got back on track with a hat-trick in the 8-1 win over the USA in May 1959. His treble came in the second-half – all fired home from outside the penalty-area.

Three more trebles were to follow – against Luxembourg in October 1960 (won 9-0), v. Mexico in May 1961 (won 8-0) and versus Switzerland in June 1963 (won 8-1).

In April 1960, he netted against Scotland for the second time, this one a penalty, but he also missed from the spot with a twice-taken kick in the 1-1 draw in Glasgow.

In a 4-0 win over Wales at Ninian Park in October 1963, Charlton netted his 31st England goal, moving ahead of Tom Finney and Nat Lofthouse in the national scoring charts.

Leading up to the 1966 World Cup, Charlton had not been in good scoring form. Indeed, he had only found the back of the net on six occasions in his previous 22 outings but he netted a brilliant goal in the group win over Mexico and then secured England's place in the final with a brace against Portugal in the semis. He and his brother then scored a goal apiece when England beat Wales

5-1 at Wembley four months after their World Cup triumph, and in January 1969, against Romania at Wembley, Charlton, playing in his 90th international, skippered England for the first time and saw his brother Jack score in the 1-1 draw.

As the years ticked by Charlton continued to hammer shots past hapless goalkeepers, scoring in his 100th international against Northern Ireland at Wembley in April 1970 (won 3-1). He eventually finished up with a record of almost a goal every two games. In fact, his tally of 49 remains an England record to this day...and some feel it will never be broken.

One of the game's greatest players, Charlton served Manchester United for 20 years, from 1953 to 1973, and during that time scored 253 goals in 766 first-team appearances.

He helped the Reds win three FA Youth Cup finals, three League Championships, the FA Cup and the coveted European Cup, and he was voted FWA 'Footballer of the Year' in 1966. He also represented his country in four Schoolboy, five Youth and six U23 internationals as well as playing for the Rest of Europe, the United Kingdom, an England Select XI, the Three (v. the Six), England (v. Young England), the FA, in eight Inter-League games, in one unofficial international and twice for the Army. And if all his games were added together (including those he starred in for Preston and England), then Charlton's overall appearance tally would be around the 1,000 mark.

A member of the Laureus World Sports Academy, Charlton helped to promote Manchester's bids for the 1996 and 2000 Olympic Games and the 2002 Commonwealth Games, England's bid for the 2006 World Cup and London's successful bid for the 2012 Olympic Games. He received a knighthood in 1994 and was an Inaugural Inductee to the English Football Hall of Fame in 2002. On accepting his award he commented: "I'm really proud to be included in the National Football Museum's Hall of Fame. It's a great honour. If you look at the names included I have to say I couldn't argue with them. They are all great players and people I would love to have played with."

Charlton is also the (honorary) president of the national Football Museum, an organisation about which he said: "I can't think of a better Museum anywhere in the world."

On 14 December 2008 Charlton was awarded the prestigious BBC Sports Personality of the Year Lifetime Achievement Award and three months later, on 2 March 2009, he was handed the Freedom of the city of Manchester, stating: "I'm just so proud, it's fantastic. It's a great city. I have always been very proud of it."

Now closely linked with a number of charitable activities including fund raising for cancer hospitals, Charlton became involved in the cause of landmine clearance after visits to Bosnia and Cambodia and readily supports the Mines Advisory Group as well as founding his own charity, Find A Better Way, which funds research in to improved civilian landmine clearance.

The Charltons, Bobby and brother Jack, were related to 'Wor' Jackie Milburn.

CHARNLEY, Raymond Ogden 1962-63 ①

Born: Lancaster, 29 May 1935
Died: Blackpool, 15 November 2009
Career: Bolton-le-Sands FC (1950), Preston North End Amateurs (1951), Morecambe (part-time professional, August 1954), Blackpool (£750, professional, May 1957), Preston North End (£11,000, December 1967), Wrexham (£10,000, July 1968), Bradford Park Avenue (January 1969), Morecambe (June 1970, retired, May 1971)

Ray Charnley, ideally built for a centre-forward, he was big and strong, had good pace, was excellent in the air and was a consistent scorer throughout his career. His only cap came in the 1-1 draw with France in a European Nations Cup qualifier at Hillsborough in October 1962, being chosen ahead of Alan Peacock and Gerry Hitchens who had both fared poorly in the World Cup in Chile. Unfortunately he did not play well against the French and never got another chance. Charnley spent most of his career with Blackpool for whom he scored 222 goals in 407 appearances between 1957 and 1968.

CHARSLEY, Charles Christopher 1882-83 ①

Born: Leicester, 7 November 1864
Died: Weston-super-Mare, 10 January 1945
Career: St Patrick's Court FC/Stafford, Stafford Town (1881), Stafford Rangers (August 1883), Aston Villa (guest, 1886), Small Heath (September 1886), West Bromwich Albion (August-December 1891), Small Heath (December 1891 and again, December 1893-May 1894); became a police constable in 1884, served initially with the City of Birmingham force before becoming Chief Constable of Coventry in 1899, holding office until 1918; later Weston-super-Mare borough councillor (November 1933, until his death in 1945); also acted as deputy Mayor of Weston-super-Mare in 1939-40.

An amateur throughout his career, goalkeeper Chris Charsley was sound rather than brilliant. Tall and brave, he lost eight teeth in one game when playing for West Bromwich Albion. He helped Small Heath (now Birmingham City) win the Second Division title and later gain promotion. With Toone (Notts County) and Rowley (Stoke) both sidelined, Charsley was called up for his only England cap against Ireland in February 1893. He played well in a 6-1 victory.

CHEDGZOY, Samuel 1919-25 ⑧

Born: Ellesmere Port, Cheshire, 27 January 1890
Died: Montreal, Canada, 15 January 1967
Career: Burnell's Ironworks/Ellesmere Port (1908), Everton (professional, December 1910), New Bedford FC/USA (May 1926-May 1930), Carsteel FC/Montreal, Canada (August 1931-May 1940)

A swift and resourceful right-winger with a useful shot, Sam Chedgzoy was one of the first players to start the practice of dribbling the ball forward from a corner-kick, but the law soon changed, making the taker kick the ball just once. He scored 38 goals in 300 games for Everton between 1910 and 1926 when he moved to America. He played his last game of football at the age of 50.

As an England winger, Chedgzoy played in the second full international after WW1 against Wales at Highbury but was pressed hard for a place in the side by Wallace (Aston Villa) and Rawlings (Preston). Maintaining his form, he appeared in five internationals in 18 months before losing his place, only to be recalled later when the right-wing position was causing the selectors some concern. His best performance in an England shirt came in the 2-2 draw with Scotland at Hampden Park in April 1923, giving left-back Jimmy Blair of Cardiff City 'some anxious moments.'

CHENERY, Charles John 1872-74 ③ ①

Born: Lambourn, Berkshire, 1 January 1850
Died: Mansfield, Australia, 17 April 1928
Career: Crystal Palace (the original club, seasons 1865-75), Surrey FC (season 1875-76); also represented Wanderers (as player, seasons 1871-74, acted as secretary for season 1871-72); represented London (1870s); also played cricket for Northamptonshire and Surrey between 1872 and 1874; emigrated to Australia in 1878, settling in Mansfield, Victoria.

Described as being 'an admirable forward, a dribbling artist and one who played at full stretch until the last minute' Charlie Chenery, however, had 'no joy' against the tough-tackling Queen's Park full-back William Ker in England's first-ever international against Scotland in November 1872. A year later, however, he played well, scored a fine goal and helped his side to a 4-2 win. His third and final game was also against the Scots in March 1874 when once again he had a tough time against a tight-marking, strong-tackling full-back in Third Lanark's John Hunter. Chenery also played in one unofficial international v. Scotland in February 1872.

CHERRY, Trevor John 1975-80 ㉗

Born: Huddersfield, 23 February 1948
Career: Newsham County Secondary Modern school/Huddersfield, Huddersfield YMCA (1963), Huddersfield Town (professional, July 1965), Leeds United (£100,000, June 1972), Bradford City (player-manager, December 1982, retiring as a player, May 1985, remaining as manager until January 1987); Huddersfield Town (associate director, 1990s); awarded an honorary degree by the University of Huddersfield in November 2005; now runs a promotions and hospitality business, a waste paper company and a five-a-side football centre.

Trevor Cherry won his first full cap in March 1976 against Wales. Three years later – and six days after making three goal-line clearances to earn a 0-0 draw with Brazil in Rio de Janeiro – he became only the third England player to receive his marching orders in a major international when he was sent off in the 1-1 friendly draw with Argentina in Buenos Aires in June 1977. Cherry lost two teeth after being punched in the mouth by Daniel Bertoni, who had been felled by a nasty tackle from Cherry. Bertoni was also shown a red card for retaliation. Cherry's England career continued throughout the rest of the 1970s, even after his mentor Don Revie had left the job. And when England qualified for a major tournament - their first in ten years - Cherry made the squad of 22 which travelled to Italy for the 1980 European Championships. His input on the pitch, however, was limited to a single substitute appearance against Spain in a group game. England were eliminated at this stage and it proved to be Cherry's final cap. He had captained the team in his penultimate game against Australia.

A versatile footballer, able to play in both full-back positions and at centre-half, he was a Second Division Championship winner with Huddersfield in 1970, won the First Division title with Leeds in 1974 and during his career appeared in 895 senior games, 485 for Leeds, scoring a total of 46 goals. He also played in one unofficial international for England. He was given an honorary degree by the University of Huddersfield in November 2005.

CHILTON, Allenby Cedric 1950-52 ②

Born: South Hylton, County Durham, 16 September 1918
Died: Humberside, 15 June 1996
Career: Ford School/South Hylton, Sunderland & Durham Schools,
Seaham Colliery (1934), Liverpool (amateur, September-November
1938), Manchester United (November 1938); served in the
Durham Light Infantry in WW2; also guest for Airdrieonians, Cardiff
City, Charlton Athletic, Hartlepools United, Newcastle United and
Middlesbrough; Grimsby Town (player-manager, March 1955, retired
as a player, October 1956, continued as manager until April 1959);
Wigan Athletic (manager, May 1960-May 1961), Hartlepools United
(scout, season 1961-62, then manager, July 1962-May 1963).

A key figure at the heart of Manchester United's defence in the
early 1950s, Allenby Chilton stood over six feet tall, weighed 13st,
tackled like a Trojan and was diligent in virtually everything he did.
He won the League Cup South with Charlton (1944) and the FA Cup
(1948) and League Championship (1952) with United for whom
he made 390 senior appearances in 17 years (1938-55). He led
Grimsby to the Third Division (North) title in 1955. Chilton gained his
two England caps in the 4-1 win over Northern Ireland in Belfast in
October 1950 and the 2-2 draw with France at Highbury in October
1951, partnering Billy Wright on both occasions. He had a nightmare
afternoon against the French centre-forward Jacques Grumellon.

CHIPPENDALE, Henry 1893-94 ①

Born: Blackburn, 2 October 1870
Died: Blackburn, 29 September 1952
Career: Blackburn Oak Rangers (1887), Nelson (1889), Blackburn
Rovers (professional, August 1891, retired, injured, May 1897);
later employed at Hornby's Brockhouse Mill, Blackburn; became a
linesman before being added to the Football League's list in 1908.

Quite tall for an outside-right, Harry Chippendale had good pace,
could whip over a dangerous cross on the run and packed a
powerful shot which he used far too sparingly. His only England
cap was won against Ireland in March 1894 when he partnered his
Blackburn team-mate Jimmy Whitehead in the 1-1 draw in Belfast.

CHIVERS, Martin Harcourt 1970-74 ㉔ ⑬

Born: Southampton, 27 April 1945
Career: Foundry Lane Junior and Taunton Grammar Schools/
Southampton, Hampshire County Schools, CPC Sports/
Southampton, Southampton (professional, September 1962),
Tottenham Hotspur (£125,000 plus Frank Saul, January 1968),
FC Servette/Switzerland (£80,000, July 1976), Norwich City (July
1978), Brighton & Hove Albion (March 1979); Frankston City/
Australia (loan, mid-1980), Dorchester Town (player-manager,
August 1980), Vard FC/Norway (player-coach, season 1981-82),
Barnet (player-manager, October 1982-May 1984); later ran a
hotel/restaurant in Hertfordshire; also matchday host at Tottenham
Hotspur and worked on BBC Radio 5; appointed the FA's National
Development Manager, May 2008.

Exceptionally nimble for a big man, Martin Chivers when in full flow
was difficult to dispossess. Strong and mobile, he played at inside-
right and centre-forward, but was often seen as a lethargic and lazy
player, yet his pace and natural strength established 'Big Chiv' as a
star of the Spurs side and indeed England during the early 1970s.
In 1971 he scored both goals in Spurs' League Cup final win over
Aston Villa, made his international debut against Malta and followed
up by netting on his full England debut against Greece (won 3-0)
before gaining a UEFA Cup winner's medal in 1972 and a second

League Cup winner's prize a year later.
After scoring twice in a 5-0 win over Scotland and likewise in a 2-1
win over Northern Ireland at Everton, Chivers received the last of his
full England caps against Poland in an infamous World Cup qualifier
in October 1973. But despite netting six goals for his country during
the calendar year, he was a casualty of his country's failure to qualify
for the finals and would later be ignored by caretaker-manager Joe
Mercer and future boss Don Revie. The scorer of 97 goals in 175
games for Southampton and 202 in 415 first-team matches for
Spurs (1967-76), Chivers also gained 17 England U23 caps.

CHRISTIAN, Edward 1878-79 ①

Born: Malvern, Worcestershire, 14 September 1858
Died: Gloucester, 3 April 1934
Career: Eton College, Trinity College/Cambridge University (seasons
1874-76), Old Etonians (seasons 1876-80); worked in Ceylon from
1881-1904.

A very competent full-back, adept with both feet, Ted Christian won
the FA Cup with Old Etonians in 1879, the same year he gained
his only England cap when he partnered Harold Morse in a 5-4 win
against Scotland at The Oval. At fault for the Scots' second goal, he
did a good job generally, marking Dr. John Smith, the fleet-footed
right-winger from Edinburgh University quite well.

CLAMP, Harold Edwin 1957-58 ④

Born: Coalville, Leics, 14 September 1934
Died: Wolverhampton, 10 November 1995
Career: Bridge Road School/Coalville, Leicestershire County Schools, Wolverhampton Wanderers (amateur, September 1949; played for Wolves' nursery team, Wath Wanderers; turned professional at Molineux, April 1952), Arsenal (£12,000, November 1961), Stoke City (£14,000, September 1962), Peterborough United (October 1964), Worcester City (August 1965-May 1966); out of football for a year; Lower Gorna FC (September 1967, retired, May 1970); also played for Wolves Old Stars (1979-84); later ran his own business in Wolverhampton.

True to his name, Eddie Clamp, a tall, well-built, strong-looking wing-half certainly 'clamped down' on a lot of things in midfield. One of the 'best players on the pitch' when winning his first cap against Russia in the friendly ahead of the game of the 1958 World Cup in Sweden, Clamp then played in the opening pool 2 game against the same opposition in Gothenburg when he lined up alongside his Molineux team-mates Billy Wright and Bill Slater. Again he did well in a bruising 2-2 draw when wingers, Bryan Douglas and Tom Finney both had 'chunks kicked out of them.' His last two caps followed in the drawn games against Brazil and Austria before England went out of the tournament losing in a play-off against the Russians.

'Chopper' Clamp spent most of his career with Wolves for whom he scored 25 goals in 241 games between 1949 and 1961, gaining three League Championship winning medals in the 1950s and an FA Cup winner's medal in 1960. He helped Stoke win the Second Division title in 1963 when he played with Stan Matthews and two other former England internationals in Tony Allen and Dennis Viollet.

CLAPTON, Daniel Robert 1958-59 ①

Born: Stepney, London, 22 July 1934
Died: Hackney, London, 16 June 1986
Career: Hackney Schools, Leytonstone (amateur, August 1949), Arsenal (trial, August 1953, professional, August 1953), Luton Town (£6,000, September 1962), Sydney Corinthians/Australia (October 1964-December 1970); became a licensee in Hackney, London.

A right-winger with a dashing style, Danny Clapton had all the tricks of the trade and gave Arsenal excellent service for nine years. He joined the Gunners in 1953 and went on to score 27 goals in 225 League and Cup games while also playing once for England, in the 2-2 draw with Wales at Villa Park in November 1958. Arsenal took on Juventus at Highbury in a friendly later that same day and Clapton played in that match as well, alongside goalkeeper Jack Kelsey who earlier in the day starred for Wales.

CLARE, Thomas 1888-94 ④

Born: Congleton, Cheshire, 12 March 1865
Died: Ladysmith, Vancouver, Canada, 27 December 1929
Career: Congleton Schools, Talke Rangers (1880), Goldenhill Wanderers (1882), Burslem Port Vale (February 1884), Stoke (July 1884), Burslem Port Vale (guest, November 1884); returned to Stoke, then to Burslem Port Vale (as player-coach, July 1897), Manchester City (trial, March 1898), Burslem Port Vale (April 1898, retired as a player, April 1899, re-signed as player-coach, August 1900, continued as coach, until 1905, then secretary-manager, July 1905-May 1906); emigrated to Canada, summer, 1907.

'A right-back of thoughtful bent' Tommy Clare was quick and resolute, good in the air and strong on the ground. Hardly ever 'roasted' by a winger, he gave Stoke excellent service for 13 years during which time he appeared in 251 first-class matches. He earned his first England cap against Ireland in March 1889 at Anfield when the selectors made eleven changes to the side that had beaten Wales the previous week, Clare being one of nine making their international debuts, among them his Stoke team-mate, Bill Rowley in goal. England won the match 6-1.

Clare's next England appearance came three years later, also against Ireland in Belfast when he was joined again by Rowley and also by the Potters' left-back Alf Underwood. This time the score-line was much closer, England winning 2-0.

Clare's last two England games were against Wales in March 1893 (won 6–0) and Scotland in April 1894 (2–2 draw).

CLARKE, Allan John 1969-76 ⑲ ⑩

Born: Willenhall, Staffordshire, 31 July 1946
Career: South East Staffordshire Boys, Birmingham & District Schools, Walsall (apprentice, July 1961, professional, August 1963), Fulham (£35,000, March 1966), Leicester City (£150,000, June 1968), Leeds United (£165,000, July 1969), Barnsley (player-manager, May 1978-October 1980), Leeds United (manager, October 1980-June 1982), Scunthorpe United (manager, February 1983-August 1984), Barnsley (manager, July 1985-November 1989), Lincoln City (manager, June-November 1990); now living in Scunthorpe.

Slim-looking but deceptively strong, Allan Clarke made scoring look easy at club level. He had quick reflexes, a sharp mind and was there when it mattered most – on hand to put the ball into the net. Nicknamed 'Sniffer' he notched over 250 goals for his five clubs, having his best spell at Leeds for whom he struck 151 goals in 366 appearances, gaining League, FA Cup and Fairs Cup winner's medals in the 1970s.

Clarke was the last player to make his England debut in a World Cup final tournament – replacing the 'rested' Geoff Hurst for the third and crucial group three encounter against Czechoslovakia in Mexico in June 1970. He played as well as anyone in stifling conditions and celebrated the occasion by scoring, with 'singular coolness' the winning penalty four minutes into the second-half after a Czech defender had handled.

Clarke, in fact, found the net in each of his first four internationals, but he also missed from the spot in a 5-0 home win over Malta, while his 80th minute winner against Northern Ireland in Belfast soon afterwards, came after George Best's 'famous' disallowed goal when the Manchester United winger flicked the ball away from Gordon Banks as he was about to clear his lines.

'Clarkey' followed up by netting twice in a 5-0 thumping of Scotland at Hampden Park in February 1973. The Scots were punished for every mistake, especially by Clarke who had a hand in two of the other three goals. Later in the year, Clarke was in the team which needed to beat Poland at Wembley to qualify for the 1974 World Cup finals. A goal down, England were awarded a penalty from which Clarke coolly scored, but he was among many players that night who were thwarted by the brilliant Polish goalkeeper Jan Tomaszewski. And in the end the 1-1 draw was not enough and England went out.

Four of Clarke's brothers – Derek, Frank, Kevin and Wayne – were all professional footballers.

Allan Clarke

CLARKE, Henry Alfred 1953-54 ①

Born: Woodford Green, Essex, 23 February 1923
Died: Romford, Essex, 16 April 2000
Career: Woodford Schools, RAF football, Lovells Athletic (1947), Tottenham Hotspur (professional, March 1949, retired, May 1957, became club coach), Llanelli (player-manager, February 1959), Romford (manager, season 1960-61); later worked for a security company.

A tall, lanky centre-half, masterful in the air, perhaps not as strong on the ground, Harry Clarke's distribution, for a defender, was of the highest quality. He joined Spurs in March 1949 and played 322 matches as a centre-half up to 1956. The backbone of the famous push-and-run side, he featured in all 42 matches of the Championship winning season of 1950–51. His only England cap was gained in April 1954 when he starred in a 4-2 win over Scotland at Hampden Park, having been brought in to replace Blackpool's Harry Johnston. Unfortunately Clarke never got another chance, Sid Owen taking over before he was replaced by Billy Wright. He won the Welsh Cup with Lovells Athletic in 1948.

Clarke's son-in-law was John White, the former Spurs and Scotland player who was killed by lightning on a golf course.

CLAY, Thomas 1919-22 ④

Born: Leicester, 19 November 1892
Died: Southend-on-Sea, Essex, 21 February 1949
Career: Fosseway School/Leicester, Belvoir Sunday school, Leicester Fosse (professional, April 1911), Tottenham Hotspur (January 1914); WW1 guest for Notts County); Northfleet (player-coach, June 1929-May 1931), St Albans City (trainer-coach, July 1931-May 1933); later a publican in St Albans before returning to his original trade as a bricklayer.

Said to be 'a right-back strategist who more than balanced any deficiency in speed by an innate positional sense', Tommy Clay often cleared his lines by driving the ball out of defence low rather than giving it 'some welly.'

He spent 15 years at White Hart Lane (1914-29) during which time he made 506 first team appearances for Spurs, scoring 38 goals. In March 1921 he kept goal for the full 90 minutes when Spurs beat Sunderland 1-0 in a League game at Sunderland.

After a successful international trial, he won his first England cap in March 1920 against Wales at Highbury. Soon afterwards he collected the Second Division Championship trophy and then, in 1921, gained an FA Cup winner's medal while also adding to his tally of caps and representing the Football League. His last England game was against Scotland at Villa Park in April 1922 when he and Frank Moss teamed up well to contain the threat of the Scots' tantalizing left-wing duo of Tommy Cairns and Alan Morton.

CLAYTON, Ronald 1955-60 ㉟

Born: Preston, 5 August 1934
Died: Blackburn, 29 October 2010
Career: Ribberton Avenue Methodists and Fishwick Secondary Modern schools/Preston, Blackburn Rovers (amateur, July 1949, professional, August 1951), Morecambe (player-manager, August 1959-August 1970), Great Harwood (October 1970, retired, April 1971); became a newsagent in Blackburn, and later a company representative.

Ronnie Clayton was a neat, tidy and utterly reliable right-half of all-round ability. He made his debut for Blackburn at the age of 17 and stayed around for 18 years, amassing 665 appearances for the Ewood Park club. His performances were of the highest order, one of the great wing-halves of his era and one believes that if he

had been with a more fashionable club then he would certainly have gained more caps than he did. His international debut came in November 1955 against Northern Ireland at Wembley when goalkeeper Ron Baynham and left-winger Bill Perry were also winning their first caps.

He was outstanding when Spain were defeated 4-1 in his second game and when Finland were whipped 5-1 in Helsinki in May 1956, some reporters named him as 'man of the match.' A year later he played his part in a 2-1 victory over Scotland at Wembley, helping set up a goal for Derek Kevan. With England boss Walter Winterbottom choosing to play three Wolves half-backs in the 1958 World Cup finals, Clayton appeared only once in the tournament, in the play-off defeat by the Soviet Union. Nevertheless, he continued to be part of the international set-up and produced a wonderful display when England gained sweet revenge over the Russians with a 5-0 win at Wembley four months later.

In a tour game in Rio de Janeiro in June 1959, Clayton clattered into Pele who was carried off on a stretcher for treatment. The Brazilian superstar was soon back, however, and with the crowd making Clayton's life a misery, he guided his team to a comfortable 2-0 win.

The Blackburn skipper, who had earlier been badly burned while sunbathing, played with massive blisters on his back in the next game against Mexico. They burst during the second-half and at the end of the game a Mexican doctor bathed his back with methylated spirits. Directed straight to bed, Clayton then found he was sharing a room with six complete strangers. Amazingly five days later he was fit enough to play against the USA and starred in an 8-1 win in Los Angeles.

Clayton, who took over the England captaincy from Billy Wright, won his 35th and final cap in the 3-3 draw with Yugoslavia in May 1960, after which he was replaced in the team by Bobby Robson while handing over the captaincy to Johnny Haynes.

Besides his senior outings, Clayton also played in one B and six U23 internationals.

CLEGG, Sir John Charles 1872-73 ①

Born: Sheffield, 15 June 1850
Died: Sheffield, 26 June 1937
Career: Sheffield FC (1866), Norfolk FC (1868), Perseverance FC (1869); Sheffield FA (season 1870-71), Sheffield Wednesday (seasons 1871-74); refereed the 1882 and 1892 FA Cup finals, also the England-Scotland match in 1886; FA Committee member (1885, chairman 1889, vice-President 1889-1923); also Chairman of Sheffield Wednesday FC and Sheffield United; became a professional solicitor (1872), practising in Sheffield with Clegg & Sons; also worked as a highway rate collector and was Mayor of Sheffield three times; knighted in June 1927 for services to football with his brother W.E. (below).

Charles Clegg was a tremendous dribbler, fast, direct and shrewd, and when it came to shooting and passing he was on par with some of the best in the game. He played in the first ever England-Scotland international in November 1872, and as the reporter in *Bell's Life* in London stated "…he had a distinctive weight advantage over his opponents and came close to scoring a goal on at least two occasions."

Clegg – known as 'The Great Old Man of Football' - also played in one unofficial international v. Scotland in February 1872, scoring in a 1-0 win. He was the first England player to be knighted for services to the game of football.

CLEGG, Sir William Edwin, OBE 1878-79 ②

Born: Sheffield, 21 April 1852
Died: Sheffield, 22 August 1932
Career: Sheffield Albion (1868), Sheffield FC (1869), Perseverance FC (1871), Norfolk FC (1873), Sheffield Wednesday (August 1874, retired, injured, January 1880), Sheffield FA; became a director of both Sheffield Wednesday and Sheffield United; also vice-president of the Sheffield & Hallamshire FA; admitted a solicitor in 1874, he too practised at the family firm of Clegg & Sons in Sheffield; became Lord Mayor of Sheffield in 1893, holding office for six years; knighted in 1906 for services to football, he was awarded the OBE in 1918 for his work on Sheffield munitions Tribunal; also a fine sprinter in his day.

William Clegg junior played most of his football as a wing-half. He was safe and reliable and like his brother was also a fine passer of the ball. After doing well in his first international against Scotland in March 1873 when he had two goal-bound efforts saved by goalkeeper Gardner, Clegg was selected to play against Wales at The Oval in January 1879. However, he was busily checking through some paperwork ahead of the trial of Charles Pearce and had to delay his departure from Sheffield to London until the Saturday morning. Unfortunately a heavy snowfall overnight meant that Clegg did not arrive for the match until 20 minutes after kick-off. In the meantime, due to the severe weather conditions, the respective captains had agreed to play only half-an-hour each-way. So Clegg missed only 10 minutes of the first-half as England scrambled a 2-1 win.

As a solicitor, Clegg's most notable case was defending murderer and cat burglar, Charles Peace, who was subsequently hanged in 1879.

CLEMENCE, Raymond Neal, MBE 1972-84 ⑥①

Born: Skegness, Lincolnshire, 5 August 1948
Career: Skegness Schoolboy football, Skegness Youth Club (1963), Notts County (amateur, non-contract, August 1964), Scunthorpe United (professional, August 1965), Liverpool (£18,000, June 1967), Tottenham Hotspur (£300,000, August 1981, retired, March 1988; appointed reserve team coach, June 1989, upgraded to first team coach, May 1992; also caretaker-manager with Doug Livermore, briefly); Barnet (joint-manager, with Gary Phillips, January 1994-July 1996); England (goalkeeping coach, August 1996-December 2007); retained on coaching staff as Head of the FA's Development Team, acting as assistant goalkeeping coach); also worked as a TV football pundit/analyst.

One of the best goalkeepers in the world during the 1970s, Ray Clemence would have won many more caps were it not for the fact that at international level he was forced to compete or even alternate with the equally talented Peter Shilton.

The six foot 'stopper' made his international debut with his club-mate Kevin Keegan, against Wales in a World Cup qualifier at Ninian Park in November 1972. This was also Alf Ramsey's 100th game in charge of England. Clemence played very well, making two excellent saves in a hard-earned 1-0 win. Thereafter he rarely let his country down, producing several outstanding performances between the posts, none more than when he kept five clean sheets in a row in 1974-75 and six out of seven in 1977-78. He conceded only 54 goals in his 61 internationals spread over eleven years. However, a skeleton in Clemence's cupboard is the game against Scotland at Hampden Park in May 1976. That day, he let a half-hit shot from his Liverpool team-mate Kenny Dalglish slip through his legs in the 49th minute as the Scots squeezed out a 2-1 win at Hampden Park to ruin England's 500th international match celebration. "That was the worst moment of my career," said Clemence after the game.

"I thought I had the ball covered but it bobbled and the next thing I knew it had gone through my legs and was in the net."

Against the Scots at Wembley in May 1979, Clemence produced a 'miracle' save from a deflected shot by Joe Jordan. Committed diving to his left, he then twisted in mid-air and somehow turned the ball away with his right fist. "The best save I have ever seen" said Scots' midfielder John Wark after the game which England won 3-1.

In the European Championship clash with Spain in Naples in June 1980, Clemence conceded a penalty early in the second-half from which Cardenosa equalised (1-1). The Spaniards were then awarded a second spot kick six minutes later from which Dani 'scored'. But the referee ordered the kick to be retaken and this time Clemence produced a superb save as England went on to record a 2-1 win.

At club level, Clemence helped Liverpool win six League Championships, two UEFA Cups, three European Cups, the League Cup, FA Cup and European Super Cup before gaining a second FA Cup winner's medal with Spurs. During his career he appeared in 1,114 competitive games - 665 for Liverpool (1967-81), 330 for Spurs (1981-88), 53 for Scunthorpe and 66 for England (61 full, 4 U23 and one unofficial international). He was awarded the MBE in 1987. His son, Stephen, is also a professional footballer.

CLEMENT, David Thomas 1975-77 ⑤

Born: Battersea, London, 2 February 1948
Died: Reading, 31 March 1982
Career: South London Schools, Queens Park Rangers (apprentice, April 1963, professional, July 1965), Bolton Wanderers (£170,000, June 1979), Fulham (October 1980), Wimbledon (October 1981 until his death).

A very useful right-back, good at going forward, better at tracking back and defending, Dave Clement made his international debut as a second-half substitute for Trevor Cherry against Wales in March 1976. He then made his first start against the same country two months later but with Cherry and Todd pressing him hard he was given only three more caps by manager Don Revie.

Clement, who made 476 appearances for QPR between 1966 and 1979, also represented England at Youth level. At the age of 34 and suffering from depression after badly breaking his leg, he believed his career was finished and committed suicide by poisoning himself with weed killer.

His son Neil, also a full-back, was only three at the time of his death. He played for Chelsea, Reading, QPR and WBA.

CLEVERLEY, Thomas William 2012-13 ⑨
Born: Basingstoke, 12 August 1989
Career: Manchester United (trainee, July 2005, professional, July 2007), Leicester City (loan, January-May 2009), Watford (loan, August 2009-May 2010), Wigan Athletic (loan, August 2010-May 2011)

Energetic midfielder Tom Cleverley bided his time at Old Trafford, being loaned out by manager Sir Alex Ferguson to 'gain experience' before producing some solid and worthwhile performances albeit as a substitute in United's first team at the end of the 2011-12 season. His efforts resulted in his selection in the Great Britain team at the 2012 London Olympics and soon afterwards he won his first full England cap against Italy and added a second versus Moldova soon afterwards, having previously represented his country at youth, U20 and U21 levels.

CLOUGH, Brian Howard, OBE 1959-60 ②
Born: Middlesbrough, 21 March 1935
Died: Derby, 20 September 2004
Career: Great Broughton FC/Yorkshire, Billingham Synthonia (1950), Middlesbrough (amateur, November 1951, professional, May 1952), Sunderland (£45,000, July 1961, retired, injured, November 1964; engaged as a coach until May 1965); Hartlepools United (manager, October 1965), Derby County (manager, June 1967-October 1973), Brighton & Hove Albion (manager, November 1973-July 1974), Leeds United (manager, July-September 1974), Nottingham Forest (manager, January 1975-May 1993); handed the Freedom of the City of Nottingham in 1993 and the Freedom of Derby ten years later.

In his prime Brian Clough had few equals and certainly no superiors in the art of goalscoring. A dynamic, all-action 'straight-for-goal' centre-forward, he was strong in the air and on the ground, had good pace and ability and packed a powerful right-foot shot. But unfortunately there were many more exceptionally fine marksmen around at the same time and as a result 'Cloughie' gained only two full caps, both in October 1959, the first against Wales in Cardiff, the second against Sweden at Wembley. He also played in one B and two U23 internationals and twice represented the Football League, netting all his side's goals in a 5-0 win over the Irish League in September 1959. He was forced to retire with a knee injury having scored 204 goals in 222 games for Middlesbrough and 63 in 74 for Sunderland.

Charismatic, outspoken and often controversial, Clough is widely considered to be one of the greatest managers ever and certainly the greatest Englishman never to manage England! Asked what he thought of the England hierarchy, the FA if you like, he replied: "I'm sure they knew that if they took me on and gave me the job, I'd want to run the show. They were shrewd because that's exactly what I would have done."

I know for a fact that if they had appointed him he would have scared a lot of people to death – but England I feel would have won the World Cup!

As a club manager, Clough was in charge for 1,140 matches (505 wins, 291 draws, 344 defeats). He won the Second and First Division Championships with Derby and then, while in charge of Nottingham Forest, lifted the European Cup twice, the Super Cup, the First Division title, the League Cup three times, the FA Charity Shield, the Simod Cup and the ZDS Cup. Regarded as one of the game's greatest-ever managers, 'Cloughie' transformed Derby from a modest Second Division team into the 'best' in England. He replaced Don Revie at Leeds but lasted only 44 days and later received £20,000 compensation for unfair dismissal! And as Forest boss, he won everything except the FA Cup. His son, Nigel (see below) also played for England and became a League club manager.

CLOUGH, Nigel Howard 1988-92 ⑭

Born: Sunderland, 19 March 1966
Career: Allestree School/Derby, Heanor Town (1982), Nottingham Forest (professional, September 1984), Liverpool (£2.275m, June 1993), Manchester City (£1.5m, January 1996), Nottingham Forest (loan, December 1996-January 1997), Sheffield Wednesday (loan, September-October 1997), Burton Albion (player-manager, October 1998-January 2009); Derby County (manager, January 2009, while also registering himself as a player; retired as a player, May 2011)

Nigel Clough was nothing like his father. He was more laid back but still a fine marksman who played a withdrawn role rather than being the main striker. Good on the ball, he could also play in midfield and his passing was first-class. He made almost 540 appearances in club football, 412 for Forest for whom he also netted 131 goals. In his two spells at The City Ground, he gained two League Cup winner's medals and also helped the Reds lift both the Simod and ZDS Cups at Wembley. He then guided Burton to the NPLP and Conference titles and saw the non-League club draw with Manchester United in the FA Cup, before taking over as boss of his father's former club, Derby County.

When he was first capped by Bobby Robson against Chile at Wembley in May 1989, Clough junior emulated the achievement of George Eastham junior by following his own father who had represented his country in 1959-60. He played out the full 90 minutes and according to one reporter, 'did okay' in a 0-0 draw. His other 13 caps were gained under manager Graham Taylor, his last against Germany in Detroit in the US Cup in June 1993. Clough also played in three B internationals (one goal scored) and in 15 U23 matches (3 goals).

COATES, Ralph 1969-71 ④

Born: Hetton-le-Hole, County Durham, 26 April 1946
Died: Bedfordshire, 17 December 2010
Career: Lambton & District Schools, Hetton Schools, County Durham Schools, Hetton Juniors, Eppleton Colliery Welfare (season 1960-61), Burnley (amateur, October, professional, June 1963), Tottenham Hotspur (£190,000, May 1971), St George FC/Sydney, Australia (loan, summer 1978), Leyton Orient (November 1978), Hertford Heath (1979), Ware (1980), Nazeing (1981); became manager of a Hertfordshire leisure complex; also matchday host at Tottenham Hotspur.

Not the greatest footballer around but one of the gutsiest, Ralph Coates worked overtime up and down the flank, scurrying away, harassing opponents all through a game. A real workhorse, he occupied four front-line positions, missing out at centre-forward. With Spurs, he won the UEFA Cup in 1972 and a year later scored the winning goal after coming on as a substitute in the League Cup final victory over Norwich. He netted 32 goals in 261 appearances for Burnley and 24 in 248 for Spurs. He won eight England U23 caps and played four times for the Football League before moving to White Hart Lane. Making his full international debut against Northern Ireland in April 1970, taking over from Francis Lee, his other three caps followed a year later against Greece and Malta in European Championship qualifiers and v. Wales at Wembley when he had a poor game and was replaced by Allan Clarke. Coates died in hospital, following a series of strokes.

COBBOLD, William Neville 1882-87 ⑨ ⑦

Born: Long Melford, Suffolk, 4 February 1863
Died: West Wrattling, Cambridgeshire, 8 April 1922
Career: Cranbrook School, Charterhouse School, Jesus College/Cambridge University (1882-86), Old Carthusians (1886-88), Wrattling Park (1888-89), Corinthians (various years, 1886-89); also played cricket for Kent and West Wrattling; was a schoolteacher by profession.

Believed to have been the best 'footballing' forward of the early-to-mid 1880s, William 'Nuts' Cobbold combined his speed with magnificent dribbling and fine shooting and was every rarely knocked off the ball.

One article stated: "To his abilities as a runner and a dribbler, moreover, must be added great prowess as a goalscorer. Cobbold was renowned for his marksmanship, and it was commented that, given two feet of goal to aim at 'Nuts' would invariably hit the target. The striker had, most contemporaries agreed, one of the fiercest shots yet seen. He could shoot in any position and he sent the ball in like a charge from a hundred-ton gun."

Cobbold anticipated the professional game in one respect (noted Edward Grayson, the historian of the early amateurs), "for in order to avoid getting hurt, he turned out swathed in rubber bandages and ankle guards. He belonged, nonetheless, resolutely to the earliest period of Association Football, disdaining - in common with many footballers of his generation - the aerial game, then regarded as a novel and distasteful innovation, and eliminating all heading from his play."

Cobbold scored twice on his England debut (including his country's 50th goal) in a 7-0 win over Ireland in February 1883 and followed up with another goal in his second international against Scotland a fortnight later. His other four goals (two 2s) came in another 7-0 drubbing of Ireland in February 1887 and in a 4-0 win over Wales later that same month.

His nickname of 'Nuts' was given to him during his school days… "Possibly because he was the very best Kentish cob quality, all kernel and extremely hard to crack" thought C.B. Fry.

COCK, John Gilbert, DCM, MM **1919-20** ② ②

Born: Hayle, Cornwall, 14 November 1893
Died: Kensington, London, 19 April 1966
Career: West Kensington United (August 1908), Forest Gate (April 1910), Old Kingstonians (December 1912), Brentford (amateur, March 1914), Huddersfield Town (professional, April 1914); Army service (1915-18); Chelsea (£2,500, October 1919), Everton (January 1923), Plymouth Argyle (March 1925), Millwall (November 1927), Folkestone (July 1931), Walton FC/Surrey (October 1932, retired May 1933); out of game for several years; Millwall (manager, November 1944-August 1948); later ran a pub in New Cross, London.

Perfectly proportioned for his role as a centre-forward, Jack Cock was an exceptionally fit player who was going as strong at the end of a game as he was when it started. He was fast, held the ball up well, could use his head and both feet and scored plenty of goals. Having already played in one Victory international (v. Wales in October 1919) Cock scored on his full England debut against Ireland later that same month, netting after just 30 seconds, which is currently the third-fastest timed England goal of all time. It was also the first goal scored by England at senior level after WW1.

Leading the line with competence and aggression, he was on target again in his second international against Scotland at Hillsborough at the end of that season when, in the middle of a downpour, he opened the scoring in the 10th minute. He went on to play his part in an exciting 5-4 victory. Cock, who twice represented the Football League and certainly had his best years at club level with Chelsea, netted a career total of 234 League goals in 391 appearances. Two of his brothers, Don and Herbert, were also professional footballers.

Owing to his good looks and a tenor voice, Cock appeared regularly on the music hall stage during his playing days and often sang as he ran onto the pitch. He also starred in several films, including 'The Winning Goal' (1920) and 'The Great Game' (1930).

COCKBURN, Henry **1946-52** ⑬

Born: Ashton-under-Lyne, 14 September 1921
Died: Ashton-under-Lyne, 4 February 2004
Career: Goslings United/Manchester (seasons 1937-39), Manchester United (amateur, September 1943, professional, August 1944); guest for Accrington Stanley (season 1944-45); Bury (free, October 1954), Peterborough United (July 1956), Corby Town (July 1959), GKN Sankeys/Wellington (May 1960, retired, January 1961); Oldham Athletic (assistant-trainer/coach, February 1961), Huddersfield Town (assistant-trainer/coach, September 1964, senior coach, June 1969-May 1975); also played cricket for Ashton CC.

The 'Mighty Atom' in the Manchester United midfield in the early 1950s, Henry Cockburn, although on the small side and rather frail, was combative, aggressive, dominant when required, good in the air despite his height, and above all a very good footballer. He would run his socks off, and kept on running while others sagged.

He spent 11 years at Old Trafford (1943-54) during which time he scored four goals in 275 senior appearances, helping United win the FA Cup in 1948 and the League Championship in 1952. He lost his first team place to Duncan Edwards.

First capped in September 1946 against Northern Ireland (won 7-2), he was outstanding when Scotland were defeated 2-0 in April 1948 and again when Italy were thrashed 4-0 the following month. Another fine performance from the 'little man' came against Switzerland in December 1948 when he had a hand in two goals in a resounding 6-0 win.

Cockburn also represented England at B team level.

COHEN, George Reginald, MBE **1963-68** ㊲

Born: Kensington, London, 22 October 1939
Career: Hammersmith Schools, West London Boys, All-London Schools, Middlesex Youth, Fulham (amateur, June 1955, professional, October 1956, retired, injured, March 1969; then Youth team manager, January 1970-June 1971); England U23 (coach, early 1970s), Tonbridge FC (manager, briefly, 1973); ran a sports shop before becoming a property developer in Tunbridge Wells, Kent.

After Jimmy Armfield had been given a tough time by Rangers winger Davey Wilson in an embarrassing 1-0 defeat by Scotland at Hampden Park in April 1964, the following month boss Alf Ramsey handed George Cohen his England debut against Uruguay. Replacing the injured Jimmy Armfield, he partnered Ray Wilson and did exceedingly well in a 2-1 win, held his place and played in 21 of the next 23 internationals. Armfield, in fact, appeared twice more before the 1966 World Cup, but Cohen was Ramsey's first choice by the time the competition started.

He went out and produced some immaculate performances in Ramsey's revolutionary team which played without conventional wide men, allowing for extra strength in midfield and relying on young, stamina-based players like Martin Peters and Alan Ball to drift from centre to flank and back again as required. When these players were occupied in more central positions or chasing high up the flank and needing support, this was where attacking full back Cohen proved his worth. His unfussy displays were rightly seen as just as vital as the attention-grabbing displays from the likes of Bobby Charlton. Cohen maintained his form and continued to impress down the right flank. In the aftermath of the rough quarter-final victory over Argentina, Ramsey ran to Cohen in order to prevent him swapping shirts with one of his opponents. Three days later, one of Cohen's overlapping runs and clever near-post passes contributed to Charlton's clincher as the hosts edged past the splendid, if rather enigmatic Portugal in the semi-finals.

In the final against West Germany, Cohen won his 30th cap as vice-captain and was his usual immaculate self, though in a game full of incident and iconic individual contributions, his only notable moment of the match was managing to block the vicious last minute free-kick from Lothar Emmerich which subsequently found its way across the England six-yard box for Wolfgang Weber to bang in the equaliser which forced extra-time. England as we know went on to win 4-2. Cohen played in seven of the next eight internationals before Ramsey decided to bring in younger players for the 1968 European Championships. Cohen's 37th and final England appearance came in a 2-0 win over Northern Ireland at Wembley in November 1967. And in fact he was the first of England's 1966 XI to cease playing for his country. Also capped eight times at U23 level, Cohen was certainly a big favourite of Alf Ramsey's.

Fulham was Cohen's only major League club. He spent 14 years at Craven Cottage (1954-69) during which time he scored six goals in 459 senior appearances.

His main return to the public eye came in the 1980s when he fought and won his battle with stomach cancer which lasted for 14 years.

In 2000, Cohen suffered personal heartbreak when his brother Peter, a night club owner and father of England rugby player Ben Cohen, his nephew, was killed. Three men were acquitted of murder and manslaughter, yet were only jailed for violent disorder. Ben later helped win the 2003 Rugby Union World Cup.

In 2010, Cohen criticised changes to the design of footballs following the intense criticism of the Adidas Jabulani used at that year's World Cup finals in South Africa. Cohen was quoted: "Designers have constantly tried to create more goals by using lighter and lighter balls. It was thought they would fly further and everyone loves to see a 30-yard screamer bend into the top corner. But things have gone too far."

COLCLOUGH, Horace 1913-14 ①

Born: Meir, Stoke-on-Trent, 12 July 1891
Died: Stoke-on-Trent, 11 April 1941
Career: Crewe Alexandra (semi-professional, August 1906), Crystal Palace (May 1912, retired, injured, May 1917)

Left-back Harry Colclough made 87 appearances for Palace in three seasons (1912-15) but due to the presence, and form, of Jesse Pennington, his international career was restricted to just one cap, awarded against Wales in March 1914. Solid in all aspects of defending, he kicked long and true and although perhaps a shade slow at times, his positional sense was second to none.

His brother, Ephraim, played for Stoke, Watford and Brighton & Hove Albion.

COLE, Andrew Alexander 1994-2002 ⑯ ①

Born: Nottingham, 15 October 1971
Career: Arsenal (apprentice, April 1988, professional, October 1989), Fulham (loan, September 1991), Bristol City (loan, March 1992, for £500,000, May 1992), Newcastle United (£1.75m, March 1993), Manchester United (£7m, January 1995), Blackburn Rovers (£7.5m, December 2001), Fulham (free, July 2004), Manchester City (free, July 2005), Portsmouth (free, August 2006), Birmingham City (loan, March-May 2007), Sunderland (free, August 2007), Burnley (loan, January-March 2008), Nottingham Forest (free, July 2008, retired, November 2008); MK Dons (coach, August 2009), Huddersfield Town (coach, September 2009), Manchester United (assistant-coach, December 2010).

One of the finest goalscoring predators of his era, Andy Cole had everything – pace, control, strength and, above all, a wonderful knack of knowing where the net was – even with his back to goal and marked by six defenders!

He gained his first four England caps under four different managers for an average of one manager per appearance, an average that can only be bettered if the Football Association takes to firing and hiring England managers at half-time.

He made his debut as a substitute (for Teddy Sheringham) against Uruguay under Terry Venables in March 1995, appeared next against Italy in 1997 when Glenn Hoddle was in charge, made his third appearance against France under caretaker-boss Howard Wilkinson in 1999 and collected his fourth cap against Poland under Kevin Keegan.

Hoddle, in defence of his decision not to select Cole for the 1998 World Cup, said he needed six or seven chances to score one goal!

The second-highest scorer in Premier League history, Cole netted 187 times in the top flight, placing him behind Alan Shearer's tally of 260 goals. He also shares the record with Shearer for netting 34 goals in a single campaign. In a wonderful career which saw him serve with 12 different clubs, scoring for six of them in the Premiership, Cole notched a total of 290 goals in 646 appearances. He won the First Division with Newcastle, five Premierships, two FA Cups, two Charity Shields, the European Champions League and the Intercontinental Cup with Manchester United and the League Cup with Blackburn as well as being voted PFA Young Player of the Year and winning the Golden Boot award in 1993-94. He also netted five goals in United's 9-0 Premier

League defeat of Ipswich Town in March 1995, a feat only achieved since by three other England internationals, Jermain Defoe (Spurs), Shearer (Blackburn) and Teddy Sheringham (Manchester United).

Besides his senior caps for England, Cole also played in eight U21 internationals (4 goals scored) and in one B team game (one goal).

Born-again Christian Cole and Nick Barmby were the first two graduates from the FA's National School of Excellence to win a full cap for England (v. Uruguay in 1995).

In 2000, Cole visited Zimbabwe and later returned to set up his own charity foundation called the 'Andy Cole Children's Foundation' which helped AIDS orphans. He is also a distant relation of Mariah Carey.

COLE, Ashley 2000-13

Born: Stepney, London, 20 December 1980
Career: Senrab FC (London-based Sunday League team), Arsenal (apprentice, April 1997, professional, November 1998), Crystal Palace (loan, February-May 2000), Chelsea (£5m, August 2006, with William Gallas moving to the Gunners)

Now England's most capped left-back and most capped black player, Ashley Cole earned his 100th against Brazil at Wembley in February 2013. Cole has pace, good footwork and the ability to get forward down the flank. However, he has admitted that he has 'occasionally lacked concentration' which has led to goals being scored against his team.

An England Youth international, capped at the 1999 FIFA World Youth Championship alongside Peter Crouch and Andrew Johnson, he also made four appearances at U21 level, scoring once, before making his senior debut against Albania in March 2001.

He played in the 2002 World Cup and Euro 2004 Championships, being named with three other England players in the all-star squad for the latter tournament, and was an ever-present in the 2006 World Cup. Against Ecuador in the second round, it was his terrific block-tackle which deflected Carlos Tenorio's shot onto the crossbar which earned his side a 1-0 victory. But in the end England were knocked out on penalties by Portugal in the quarter-finals.

Andrew Cole

Moving on… his ridiculous square pass across the field in England's World Cup qualifying game against Kazakhstan at Wembley in October 2008 led to an equalising goal and as a result he was booed when in possession right through to the final whistle. *The Guardian* reported: "Cole, for his part, committed an error of such dimensions that it was hard at first to be sure what he had even been trying to do."

Thankfully England went on to win 5-1 and his error was soon forgotten!

Then, a year later, he was caught in possession for Ukraine's winning goal in the World Cup qualifier in October 2009. He lost the ball to Roton when trying to dribble out of the penalty-area and when Nazarenko fired in a left foot rocket, it deflected off Cole past substitute 'keeper David James.

That last error was unexpected for he had been, by far, England's most consistent defender over the previous 12 months, producing some brilliant displays. Cole went on to play in the World Cup finals in South Africa but was stuck on 99 caps (and no goals scored) for quite some time, as manager Roy Hodgson chose to persevere with the Everton left-back Leighton Baines instead.

At club level, he made 228 appearances for Arsenal and 14 for Palace and has now amassed over 550 for Chelsea. He has a record seven FA Cup winner's medals to his name (three with the Gunners, four with Chelsea), plus a Champions League, Europa League, three Premiership, a League Cup and three Charity Shield winner's prizes.

Cole married 'Girls Aloud' singer and X-Factor judge, Cheryl Tweedy in 2006 but the couple divorced in 2010.

COLE, Carlton Michael Okirie 2008-10 ⑦

Born: Croydon, Surrey, 12 November 1983
Career: Chelsea (apprentice, April 1999, professional, October 2000), Wolverhampton Wanderers (loan, October 2002-January 2003), Charlton Athletic (loan, August-November 2003), Aston Villa (loan, July 2004-March 2005), West Ham United (£2m, July 2006).

Born to Nigerian and Sierra Leonean parents, Carlton Cole rejected the chance to play for either of those two countries and became a regular in England's U21 side, scoring six goals in 19 appearances. Peter Taylor, then the U21 manager, claimed that Cole had 'The potential to break into the full England squad.'

Then, in August 2008, Nigeria's coach Shaibu Amodu surprisingly called Cole into his squad ahead of a vital World Cup qualifier against South Africa. However, it was later reported that Cole was ineligible to play for Nigeria anyway, as he was at the time, too old to switch from one country to another.

Six months later Cole won his first full England cap, taking the field as a 75th minute substitute in a 2-0 defeat by Spain in February 2009. Cole did well enough and was subsequently named in the squad for the following games against Slovakia and Ukraine in the spring of 2009. All of his seven caps to date have come as a substitute.

Despite a few injury problems in recent years, so far at club level, Cole has netted 73 goals in more than 300 appearances, having his best spell with West Ham for whom he has scored 58 times in 235 games since joining from Chelsea in 2006. He missed the World Cup finals in 2010 through injury. In the summer of 2011 the Hammers turned down a £4m offer for Cole from the Turkish club, Galatasaray. They didn't regret the decision as Cole helped the London club gain promotion back to the Premiership in 2012.

The striker is one of a number of Premier League players that use Twitter to communicate with fans. In April 2011 he was fined £20,000 by the Football Association for comments he made on the site during England's friendly with Ghana in March 2011. He admitted a charge of improper conduct over the 'tweet': *"Immigration has surrounded the Wembley premises! I knew it was a trap! The only way to get out safely is to wear an England jersey and paint your face with the St George's flag!"*

COLE, Joseph John 2000-10 ㊏ ⑩

Born: Paddington, London, 8 November 1981
Career: St Mary's Primary and Haversток Schools/Camden, St Aloysius College/North London, West Ham United (apprentice, April 1997, professional, December 1998), Chelsea (£6.6m, August 2003), Liverpool (free, July 2010), Lille/France (loan, August 2011-May 2012), West Ham United (free, January 2013)

Joe Cole made his international debut against Mexico in May 2001. He was a member of England's 2002 FIFA World Cup squad but did not start any games, making only one substitute appearance. A member of Sven-Göran Eriksson's party at Euro 2004, he did not get a game but his displays in the friendlies leading up to the 2006 World Cup enhanced his reputation ahead of the summer's finals in Germany.

In May 2006, Cole was confirmed in the England squad for the 2006 World Cup, ahead of Chelsea team-mate Shaun Wright-Phillips. He played on the left side of midfield in England's opening game win over Paraguay before helping his side draw 2-2 with Sweden, scoring with a superb volley in the 34th minute and then setting up an 85th equaliser for Steven Gerrard. At the end of the match, Budweiser presented Cole with the 'Man of the Match' award. Injuries, though, were beginning to interrupt his progress. He played in the 1–1 draw with the Netherlands, crossing for Wayne Rooney to score, but after another injury blow, he was out for seven months before returning for the friendly against Brazil at Wembley in June 2007. Soon afterwards he scored his seventh international goal, in a 3-0 European Championship qualifying win in Estonia.

In February, 2008, Cole starred in the 2-1 friendly win over Switzerland, setting up a goal for Jenas with 'a quick bit of trickery'. He received the Man of the Match award for his performance.

Six months later, Cole scored a late equalizer to salvage a 2-2 draw against the Czech Republic at Wembley and he struck twice in the next fixture – Fabio Capello's first in charge - when Andorra were defeated 2-0 in the opening match for the 2010 World Cup qualifiers.

In England's next qualifying game against Croatia, he suffered a head injury in a clash with defender Robert Kovac which resulted in the Croatian's sending off.

Sidelined with a ruptured cruciate ligament for the second half of 2008-09 and for the first part of 2009-10, Cole was 'sorely missed' on England's left flank.

Cole, who brings his own particular brand of magic to the game, represented England at Schoolboy and Youth team levels and has one B and eight U21 caps in his locker. For West Ham he netted 13 goals in 150 appearances, 40 in 278 for Chelsea and three in 32 for Liverpool. Thrice a Premiership winner with Chelsea, he also helped the Blues twice win the FA Cup (completing the double in 2010), the League Cup twice and the Charity Shield twice. As a Hammer he won the FA Youth Cup.

Jo Cole

COLEMAN, Ernest Herbert 1920-21 ①

Born: Steyning, Sussex, 19 October 1889
Died: Hove, Sussex, 15 June 1958
Career: Steyning Schools, Croydon Amateurs (August 1905), Dulwich Hamlet (amateur, August 1912, retired, May 1925; served on club's committee for 10 years; was an accountant by profession.

Goalkeeper Ernie Coleman was a prominent inter-war amateur whose displays between the posts where sometimes described as 'brilliant'. He made hard saves look easy but occasionally made simple saves look hard! His senior international debut for England was against Wales in March 1921 when he kept a clean sheet in a goalless draw. He also won four caps for his country at amateur level (1920-22) and gained an FA Amateur Cup winner's medal with Dulwich Hamlet in 1920.

COLEMAN, John George 1906-07 ①

Born: Kettering, 26 October 1881
Died: Amsterdam, Holland, 20 November 1940
Career: Kettering Town (1899), Northampton Town (professional, June 1901), Woolwich Arsenal (with Everard Lawrence, May 1902), Everton (£700, February 1908), Sunderland (May 1910), Fulham (June 1911), Nottingham Forest (June 1914); joined Football Battalion in 1915; Tunbridge Wells Rangers (September 1920-May 1921), Maidstone United (manager-coach, season 1921-22); coached in Holland (seasons 1927-29); later employed as a window cleaner

'Tim' Coleman was an inside-forward blessed with craft and deft ball control who seemed to bring the best out of his team-mates. He gained his only cap against Ireland at Goodison Park in February 1907, helping England win 1-0. He also represented the Football League on three occasions. At club level, Coleman scored 188 goals in 406 League games over a period of 15 years (1901-15 inclusive).
While at Everton, Coleman was notable for being one of the few players, along with most of the Manchester United team, to maintain their membership of the Players' Union (the forerunner of the PFA) in defiance of FA rules. After a standoff, the FA backed down.

COLLYMORE, Stanley Victor 1994-98 ③

Born: Swynnerton near Stafford, Staffs, 22 January 1971
Career: Broomhill Primary and Sherbrook Comprehensive Schools/Cannock, Longmoor Boys, Walsall (apprentice, June 1989), Wolverhampton Wanderers (non-contract, July 1989), Stafford Rangers (July 1990), Crystal Palace (£100,000, December 1990), Southend United (£100,000, November 1992), Nottingham Forest (£2.25m, July 1993), Liverpool (£8.5m, June 1995), Aston Villa (£7m, May 1997), Fulham (loan, July-November 1999), Leicester City (£250,000, rising to £500,000, February 2000), Bradford City (free, October 2000), Real Oviedo/Spain (February 2001, retired, May 2001); also starred in film *Basic Instinct 2* (with Sharon Stone); has since worked on radio, TV and in the media as a soccer pundit/summariser.

A robust centre-forward, good in the air, strong on the ground, Stan Collymore at times was terrific; on other occasions he was plain ordinary. On his day he certainly gave defenders a torrid time and scored some cracking goals. At club level, he netted 125 in 317 senior appearances, including 99 in 251 League games.
Known as 'Stan the Man' he gained his first England cap in a 2-1 win over Japan at Wembley in June 1995, when he partnered Alan Shearer in attack. His other two followed, both as a substitute, in the 3-1 defeat by Brazil a

week later and in the 4-0 win over Moldova in a World Cup qualifier in September 1997.
In October 2008, in a landmark case that may have set a precedent for cases in the future, Collymore won more than £1.5m in damages from his financial advisers, for the poor investment advice he had been given since retiring from professional football in 2001. The judge ruled that Collymore had, indeed, been given advice that was in breach of statutory obligations.

COMMON, Alfred 1903-06 ③ ②

Born: Millfield, County Durham, 25 May 1880
Died: Darlington, 3 April 1946
Career: Millfield BC, South Hylton Juniors (August 1896), Jarrow (July 1897), Sunderland (professional, August 1900), Sheffield United (£520, November 1901), Sunderland (£500, plus Arthur Lewis, June 1904), Middlesbrough (£1,000, February 1905), Arsenal (£250, August 1910), Preston North End (£200, December 1912, retired, May 1914); became a local referee before managing the Alma Hotel at Cockerton and a pub in Darlington until 1943.

The game's first £1,000 footballer when transferred from Sunderland to Middlesbrough in 1904, Alf Common was a jovial, loquacious character, able to play as an inside or centre-forward. Aggressive and powerful with strong shoulders, he was forever a threat near goal. Defenders hated him! He won the FA Cup with Sheffield United and the Second Division Championship with Preston and during a wonderful club career scored 134 goals in 419 competitive matches.
He also netted on his England debut in a 2-2 draw with Wales in February 1904 and hit the net again in his second game when Ireland were defeated 3-1 a month later. His third international appearance followed v. Wales in March 1906 when he laid on the winning goal for Sammy Day. Common was the first Middlesbrough player to represent the Football League.

COMPTON, Leslie Harry 1950-51 ②

Born: Woodford, Essex, 12 September 1912
Died: Essex, 27 December 1984
Career: Middlesex Schools, Bell Lane Old Boys (1926), Hampstead Town (August 1927), Arsenal (amateur, August 1930, professional, February 1932, retired, July 1953; then coach at Highbury until May 1956); played county cricket for Middlesex (seasons 1938-66, appearing in 276 first-class matches, amassing 5,814 runs, average 16.75, with a highest score of 107 n.o.); later a publican in North London, he also worked as a rep. for a wine and spirits company and was a prominent player for a North London bowls club.

Although big and strong, Leslie Compton was an extremely cool centre-half, almost unbeatable in the air but at times a tad too casual on the ground. In the late 1930s he established himself as a full-back and during five Wartime internationals was also used as a makeshift centre-forward, twice playing in the same team as his brother Denis in 1943. Compton – the 700th player to win a full England cap - was 38 years and 64 days old when he made his international debut, alongside another county cricketer, Willie Watson, in a 4-2 victory over Wales at Roker Park, Sunderland in November 1950. He did well in that game but a week later, playing on his own patch at Highbury, he conceded an own-goal in

Stan Collymore

the 2-2 draw with Yugoslavia and was never chosen again. Compton made 401 appearances for Arsenal (all competitions including wartime) and won the League Championship and the FA Cup with the Gunners in 1948 and 1950. On the cricket field he was a batsman-wicketkeeper and an occasional bowler. He played in 274 matches for Middlesex, scoring 5,814 runs at an average of 16.75 with a top knock of 107. His best bowling figures were 2-21. Sadly, he had a foot amputated in 1982.

CONLIN, James 1905-06 ①

Born: Durham, 6 July 1881
Died: Flanders, France, 23 June 1917
Career: Captain Colt's Rovers, Cambuslang, Hibernian (August 1898), Falkirk (January 1900), Albion Rovers (March 1901), Bradford City (August 1904), Broadheath (briefly, May 1906), Manchester City (July 1906), Birmingham (September 1911), Airdrieonians (September 1912), Broxburn United (registered from August 1913, until his death); killed whilst serving with the Highland Light Infantry in Flanders in 1917.

A diminutive outside-left, one of the smallest players of his era, Jimmy Conlin was continually under the hammer from the bigger and more bruising defenders who opposed him, but he always had a smile on his face – more so, after having jinked past or around them to create a chance! A born footballer, he was a wonderful crosser of the ball and was never afraid to cut inside and have a crack at goal. His only England cap came in the 2-1 defeat by Scotland at Hampden Park in April 1906. He was battered and bruised that afternoon, knocked to the ground at regular intervals by the tough-tackling right-back Don McLeod of Celtic, but got up and kept on going, grinning all over his face. A real character, he twice represented the Football League and won the Second Division Championship with Manchester City in 1910. Conlin lost his life while serving with the Highland Light Infantry in France during WW1.

CONNELLY, John Michael 1959-66 ⑳ ⑦

Born: St. Helens, Lancs, 18 July 1938
Died: Brierfield near Burnley, 25 October 2012
Career: St. Helens Town (1954), Burnley (trial, September-October 1956, professional, November 1956), Manchester United (£56,000, April 1964), Blackburn Rovers (£40,000, September 1966), Bury (free, June 1970, retired, June 1973); ran a fish and chip shop (Connelly's Plaice) in Brierfield near Burnley for 31 years.

John Connelly could play on both wings – and at times he was exceptionally good. He had a direct style, was two-footed, crossed the ball well and was always looking for the opportunity to shoot at goal.

He had made his international debut as a Burnley player in October 1959 against Wales at Ninian Park and was a member of the squad that went to the World Cup in Chile in 1962 but was not selected to play. Four years later, having scored against Wales at Wembley in November 1962 – the last goal of Walter Winterbottom's reign as team manager – Connelly was named in Alf Ramsey's 22-man squad for the 1966 World Cup. He played in the opening 0-0 draw with Uruguay, but unfortunately he failed miserably and when Ramsey decided to do away with a winger, it marked the end of his England career!

Connelly won the League Championship with both Burnley (1960) and Manchester United (1965) and also played in one U23 international. Connelly scored 105 goals in 265 appearances for Burnley and 35 in 113 for United – his two 'best' club returns.

Following an FA led campaign to persuade FIFA to award World Cup winning medals to all the squad members of 1966, Connelly was presented with his award by Gordon Brown at a ceremony at number 10 Downing Street in June 2009.

COOK, Thomas Edwin Reed 1924-25 ①

Born: Cuckfield, Sussex, 5 February 1901
Died: Brighton, 15 January 1950
Career: Brighton Municipal School, Cuckfield FC (1919), Brighton & Hove Albion (August 1921-May 1929); coached cricket in South Africa (1929-30); Northfleet FC (September 1930), Bristol Rovers (October 1931, retired, May 1933); Brighton & Hove Albion (manager, May-November 1947); also played cricket for Sussex (seasons 1922-37... a right-handed batsman, he played in 460 games, scored 20,198 runs with 32 hundreds); managed the Prince Albert Hotel, in Simonstown, South Africa (1937-38).

Although his entire club career was spent in the Third Division (South) Tommy Cook was nevertheless a terrific centre-forward, very effective, highly constructive, with a strong shot. He inspired players around him and his attitude towards the game was first-class. In his only international against Wales in February 1925, he played well in a 2-1 win.

Cook was a prolific run-maker in the cricket seasons of 1933 and 1934 when Sussex finished runners-up in the County Championship.

He served in both World Wars but suffered serious injuries in the latter. He sadly committed suicide three weeks before his 49th birthday.

COOPER, Colin Terence 1994-96 ②

Born: Sedgfield, County Durham, 28 February 1967
Career: Middlesbrough (apprentice, June 1983, professional, July 1984), Millwall (£300,000, July 1991), Nottingham Forest (£1.7m, June 1993), Middlesbrough (£2.5m, August 1998), Sunderland (loan, March 2004); returned to Middlesbrough (retired May 2006, appointed reserve team coach, June 2006, first team coach, December 2006, assistant-manager, June 2009, caretaker-manager for four days, October 2009, left club, May 2010); Bradford City (assistant-manager, March 2011, caretaker-manager, August 2011); Middlesbrough (coach, September 2011); Hartlepool United (manager, May 2013).

A very capable defender, cool and consistent, Colin Cooper's form for Nottingham Forest earned him an England call-up in June 1995 for the game against Sweden at Leeds. He struggled at the back alongside Gary Pallister in the 3-3 draw and did likewise in his next game against Brazil at Wembley three days later. He wasn't considered again. Cooper made over 700 appearances during his career (606 in the Football League). He won the First Division Championship with Forest and he also played eight times for England at U21 level. He certainly loves Middlesbrough!

COOPER, Norman Charles 1892-93 ①

Born: Norbiton, Kingston-upon-Thames, Surrey, 12 July 1870
Died: Hampden Park, East Sussex, 30 July 1920
Career: Brighton College (seasons 1886-90), Jesus College/ Cambridge University (1890-93), played for Corinthians (seasons 1891-95), Old Brightonians (1890s), represented Sussex (between 1888 and 1893); played cricket for Cambridge University (1890s).

A very neat and stylish wing-half, highly accomplished, Norman Cooper tackled well and passed with authority. He played for England just once – against Ireland at Perry Barr, Birmingham in February 1893 when he 'did a sound job' in a 6-1 win.

COOPER, Terence 1968-75 (20)

Born: Knottingly, Yorkshire, 12 July 1945
Career: Brotherton School/Castleford (to 1960), Ferrybridge
Amateurs (May 1960), Wolverhampton Wanderers (March
1961), Wath Wanderers (April 1961), Leeds United (apprentice,
May 1961, professional, July 1962), Middlesbrough (£50,000,
March 1975), Bristol City (£20,000, July 1978), Bristol Rovers
(player-coach, August 1979, manager, April 1980-October 1981),
Doncaster Rovers (November 1981), Bristol City, (player-manager,
May 1982-March 1988, also appointed club director); Exeter
City (manager, May 1988), Birmingham City (manager, August
1991-November 1993; also club director); Exeter City (manager,
January 1994-June 1995), Southampton (assistant-manager, then
overseas scout until retiring, May 2007); now lives in Tenerife.

Terry Cooper, an outside-left-cum-left-
back, provided a 'sparky presence' when
making his England debut alongside
Keith Newton in a 5-0 win over France
at Wembley in March 1969. Then, in the
1970 World Cup he again produced three
exciting performances, with some zestful,
overlapping displays, having perhaps
his best game in the 1-0 opening group
win over Romania. Unfortunately he was
given a tough time in the quarter-final against West Germany where
Grabowski was always a threat, setting up the all-important winning
goal for Gerd Muller in the 110th minute. Despite that 'uneasy
game' Cooper played in a further eight internationals, his last
against Portugal in a European Championship qualifier in November
1974. A broken leg effectively ended his international career.

As a timid youngster Cooper went along to Elland Road, with his
boots in a paper bag, and asked for a trial. He impressed enough to
be given a two-year contract.

He did very well with Leeds, winning two League Championship,
two Fairs Cup and a League Cup winner's medal while also making
351 first-class appearances over a period of 14 years (1961-75).

As a manager he guided Bristol City to victory in the Freight Rover
Trophy in 1986 and Exeter to the Fourth Division title in 1990.

His son, Mark, was also a professional footballer in the lower
echelons of the Football League, and is now a club manager.

COOPER, Thomas 1927-35 (15)

Born: Fenton, Stoke-on-Trent, 9 April 1904
Died: Aldeburgh, Suffolk, 25 June 1940
Career: Longton FC (1920), Trentham FC (1922), Port Vale (£20
as a professional, August 1924), Derby County (£2,000, March
1926), Liverpool (£7,500, December 1934), WW2 guest for
Wrexham (September 1939 until his death); killed whilst serving in
the Military Police.

A wonderfully consistent full-back,
accurate with his tackling, sound in
kicking and clearing his lines, a writer said
of Tom 'Snowy' Cooper in 1929: 'He feeds
his forwards as well as a half-back.'

He played against eight different
countries during his international career
and featured in the first defeat inflicted
upon England by a foreign country when
Spain won 4-3 in Madrid in May 1929. He
also played in the 2-1 defeat by Ireland in October 1927 - the last
time the Irish had beaten England in Belfast prior to their 1-0 victory
in a World Cup qualifier in September 2005.

Cooper was given the ultimate honour of captaining his
country twice in his last two appearances – in a 2-1 defeat by
Czechoslovakia in May 1934 and in a 4-0 win over Wales four
months later. One feels he would have been selected for more
representative matches if it hadn't have been for the number of
injuries he received. These included having both knee cartilages
removed, three cracked ankle bones, two broken toes, a dislocated
shoulder and concussion, suffered several times!

Cooper made 33 appearances for Port Vale, 266 for Derby and
160 for Liverpool.

He lost his life in a motor cycling accident with a lorry whilst
serving as an army dispatch rider with the Military Police during WW2.

COPPELL, Stephen James, BSc. 1976-84 (42) (7)

Born: Liverpool, 9 July 1955
Career: Quarry Bank Grammar School/South Liverpool, Liverpool
University, Tranmere Rovers (amateur, June 1973, professional,
January 1974), Manchester United (£60,000, February 1975,
retired, injured, October 1983); Crystal Palace (manager,
June 1984-May 1993; Manager/Director of Football, June
1995-February 1996); Manchester City (manager for 33 days,
October-November 1996), Crystal Palace (Chief Scout, December
1996, manager, February 1997-March 1998 and again, January
1999-August 2000), Brentford (manager, May 2001-June 2002),
Swindon Town (assistant-manager, July-October 2002), Brighton
& Hove Albion (manager, October 2002-October 2003), Reading
(manager, October 2003-May 2009), Bristol City (manager, May-
August 2010); Crawley Town (Director of Football, April 2012);
also Chairman of the Professional Footballers' Association (Players'
Union); graduated as a Bachelor of Science in Economics from
Liverpool University.

Outside-right Steve Coppell was a real 'line hugger' and he proved a great outlet for Manchester United. Fast and tricky, he was a fine crosser of the ball and at times was a star when it came to shooting! He scored 70 goals in 393 appearances during his eight years at Old Trafford (1975-83), helping United win the Second Division title and FA Cup in 1975 and 1977 respectively.

Coppell won his first England cap in a 2-0 win over Italy at Wembley in November 1976. He stayed in the plans of new manager Ron Greenwood, playing in several friendly matches during 1978 and scoring the only goal of the game - his first for England - in a victory over Scotland at Hampden Park.

He remained a regular for his country over the next 12 months, scoring against Czechoslovakia and Northern Ireland.

A week after losing the 1979 FA Cup final with Manchester United, Coppell was back at Wembley, scoring one goal and making another in a 3-1 win over Scotland. He continued to impress for his country and his habit of scoring against the Scots continued in 1980 with a fine goal in a 2-0 win at Hampden Park prior to the European Championships, during which he featured in the opening two group matches, though England failed to progress further.

Coppell's 42nd and last England appearance was against Luxembourg in December 1983 when he found the net once in a rather 'humiliating' 9-0 victory. He also gained one U23 cap.

First appointed manager of Crystal Palace at the age of 28 (making him one of the youngest-ever in the Football League) he did reasonably well at Selhurst Park, guiding the Eagles to the 1990 FA Cup final and into two play-offs. Then in 2006, he took Reading into the Premiership (top flight) for the first time in the club's 135-year history as League Championship winners. Coppell was in charge for 988 games as a manager.

On 10 April 2012, Coppell was appointed Director of Football at Crawley Town, naming Craig Brewster as the club's manager. A month later Crawley clinched promotion to the Football League.

COPPING, Wilfred 1932-39 ⑬

Born: Middlecliffe, Kent, 17 August 1909
Died: Prittlewell, Southend-on-Sea, 12 June 1980
Career: Houghton Council School/Kent, Deane Valley Old Boys (1925), Middlecliffe Rovers (1926), Dartford Rovers (1928), Barnsley (trial, April-May 1929), Leeds United (amateur, March 1929, professional, June 1930), Arsenal (£8,000, June 1934), Leeds United (free, March 1939); WW2 guest for Arsenal; served in Army as a Company Sergeant Major instructor in North Africa; (retired from football, May 1942); Royal Beerschot/Belgium FC and also Belgian national team coach (seasons 1943-45) British Army FC (trainer, season 1945-46); Southend United (trainer, June 1946-July 1953), Bristol City (trainer, July 1954-October 1956), Coventry City (trainer, November 1956-May 1959); moved to Southend and worked for Ford Motor Company, Dagenham until August 1972.

A left-half of 'grim mien' Wilf Copping never shaved before a match… turning out rough and ready, hoping to frighten the opposition forwards! He was very dark skinned and he was tough, real tough, and some said 'The tougher the game, the tougher Wilf played.' Completely fearless, yet humble, he had two lethal weapons – a rasping two-footed tackle and a mighty shoulder charge. He put them both to good use when England 'fought' it out with Italy in the 'Battle of Highbury' in 1934. In that 3-2 victory he was utterly fearless and was involved in several tough, bone-crunching challenges. Six of his Arsenal colleagues also played against the Italians.

A genuine tough guy, a pocket-size battleship, Copping was as hard as nails, a never-give-in destructor, ferocious in the tackle and quick to use the ball once he'd won it. In the next international (after the Italian job) he crunched and munched at the Ireland forwards as England won 2-1 at Goodison Park, Peter Docherty feeling the pain most of all, saying: "That bloke Copping certainly gave me some stick, but it was all fair and above board. I had no complaints."

He was also a 'star performer' when Scotland were defeated 3-0 at Wembley in April 1934. The *Daily Express* reporter, Arthur Simmons wrote: "English pivot Hart, from Leeds, found himself chasing shadows…but his club-mate Copping stuck to his position and destroyed several Scottish attacks."

Indeed, hard-man Copping, never shirked a challenge in any of his 20 England matches and at the end of the day several of his opponents knew they had been in a contest.

Besides his England honours, Copping also played twice for the Football League, collected one Wartime cap, won two League titles, the FA Cup and two FA Charity Shields with Arsenal for whom he made 192 first-team appearances.

CORBETT, Bertram Oswald 1900-01 ①

Born: Thame, Oxfordshire, 15 May 1875
Died: Whaddon Manor, Portesham, Dorset, 30 November 1967
Career: Thame Grammar School, Oriel College/Oxford University (seasons 1894-97), Corinthians (player, seasons 1897-1906, acting as secretary for two seasons, 1902-04), Casuals (at various times in 1890s), Reading (1900), Slough (seasons 1899-1901); also played cricket for Buckinghamshire and Derbyshire (1910) and hockey for England; was a teacher by profession, first at Brighton College, then in Derbyshire and finally at a preparatory school in Dorset.

A speedy outside-left, great dribbler and with an excellent shot, Bertie Corbett was one of the great Corinthian footballers of his day. Yet, surprisingly he gained only one England cap, starring, and laying on two of Steve Bloomer's four goals, in the 6-0 win over Wales at St James' Park, Newcastle in March 1901. At the time England were struggling to fill the left-wing position and, in fact, they used no less than 15 different players in that position in 20 internationals spread over four years.

Corbett was the editor of 'Annals of the Corinthian Football Club' published in 1906. His brother John also played cricket while another brother Reg (below) played football.

CORBETT, Reginald 1902-03 ①

Born: Thame, Oxfordshire, April 1879
Died: Dorchester, 2 September 1967
Career: Malvern College (seasons 1895-98), Old Malvernians (seasons 1898-1902), Corinthians (seasons 1902-05); schoolteacher by profession, first in Derbyshire and later in Dorset (like his brother).

Able to play as an inside or outside-left, Reg Corbett preferred the latter position but was rather erratic at times. He had a good scoring record over the years and once struck five goals in a game for Old Malvernians. Like his brother he too was chosen to play in one international, lining up against Wales at Fratton Park, Portsmouth in March 1903 when he partnered Aston Villa's Joe Bache, also a debutant, on the left-wing in a 2-1 win.

An FA Amateur Cup winner with Old Malvernians in 1902, Corbett also retired to live in Dorset.

CORBETT, Walter Samuel 1908-09 ③

Born: Wellington, Shropshire, 26 November 1880
Died: Aston, Birmingham, 21 November 1960
Career: Vicarage Road Council School/Kings Heath, Birmingham; King Edward VI Grammar School/Birmingham; Thornhill FC, Asbury Richmond, Headingly FC and Soho Villa FC (all junior clubs in Handsworth, Birmingham), Aston Villa (trial, 1901-02), Birmingham & District Juniors, Bournbrook FC/Birmingham (August 1901-May 1903), Aston Villa (December 1902), Queens Park Rangers (guest, early September 1907), Birmingham (late September 1907), Wellington Town (guest, April 1909, signed, June 1911), Wolverhampton Old Church (August 1913, retired, May 1915); became manager of a Birmingham Export House and later worked in the wages department of the Birmingham Transport offices.

One of the best amateur full-backs of his time, Walter Corbett had good speed, was quick in recovery and kicked well, hardly ever losing direction. Besides gaining three senior caps for England, he also starred in 16 amateur internationals (debut v. Ireland in December 1906), helped the United Kingdom win the soccer gold medal at the 1908 Olympic Games (three games) and played for the mixed Amateurs and Professional XI on a short summer tour in 1906 when he partnered Bob Crompton who also played alongside him in two of his three major internationals.

"One of the most gentlemanly players one could hope to meet in a long day's march" according to the *Sports Argus*, Corbett rarely did a 'dirty trick' on the field.

Taken on England's first-ever European tour in June 1908, as cover for Jesse Pennington, Corbett stood in for the West Bromwich Albion left-back in three friendly wins over Austria (6-1), Hungary (7-1) and Bohemia (4-0). He was impressive in every game and one reporter stated: "The crowd saw an exceptionally fine player out there today... clean-kicking, strong in the tackle with a wonderful technique."

CORRIGAN, Joseph Thomas 1975-82 ⑨

Born: Manchester, 18 November 1948
Career: Sale FC (1964), Manchester City (professional, January 1967), Seattle Sounders/USA (£30,000, June 1982), Brighton & Hove Albion (free, September 1983), Norwich City (loan, September 1984), Stoke City (loan, September-November 1984); retired February 1985; later engaged as a goalkeeping coach by Liverpool, Celtic, Chester City, Stockport County and West Bromwich Albion; retired from football in 2010.

A well-built, strong-looking and very efficient goalkeeper, 'Big Joe' Corrigan made all his nine appearances for England while playing at Manchester City. He was part of the 1982 World Cup squad but found his chances limited due to the form of Peter Shilton and Ray Clemence. It was a pity, because he was a very fine 'keeper.

He made his debut as a substitute for Jimmy Rimmer in a 3-2 win over Italy in New York in May 1976 and made his first start two years later in the 1-1 draw with Brazil at Wembley. He only conceded seven goals for his country, keeping three clean-sheets in three outings against Wales in 1979, 1981 and 1982.

Corrigan made 603 appearances in his 17 years at Maine Road (1966-83) and over 700 during his career (553 in the Football League). He helped City win the First Division Championship, the League Cup twice, the FA Charity Shield and the European Cup Winners' Cup. He also represented England in three U21, one U23 and 10 B internationals and played for the Football League and an FA XI. After retiring he became a highly-respected goalkeeping coach.

COTTEE, Anthony Richard 1987-89 ⑦

Born: Plaistow, London, 11 July 1965
Career: Plaistow & District Schools, West Ham United (apprentice, July 1980, professional, September 1982), Everton (£2.3m, August 1988), West Ham United (in exchange for David Burrows, September 1994), MPPJ Selangor/Malaysia (March 1997), Leicester City (£500,000, August 1997), Birmingham City (loan, November-December 1997), Norwich City (free, September 2000), Barnet (player-manager, October 2000), Millwall (free, March 2001, retired, July 2001); became a soccer pundit on Sky TV.

An instinctive striker, nimble and alert, Tony Cottee was a first-class poacher who continually found the back of the net from well inside the penalty-area! In a wonderful club career which spanned 20 years (1981-2001), he scored 292 goals in 713 games, with 240 coming in 603 League matches. He won the League Cup with Leicester in 2000 and the both Malaysian FA Cup and national Cup with Selangor.

He broke into the England team while with the Hammers but - despite his impressive goalscoring record in League football - he never scored for his country in the seven matches he played in over a period of three years. In fact, he came on as a substitute in his first six games before making his first and last start against Scotland at Hampden Park in the 2-0 Rous Cup win in May 1989 when he partnered John Fashanu in attack. He was even taken off in that game, meaning he never once contested a full 90 minutes for his country. Cottee also represented England at Youth team level and appeared in eight U21 internationals (one goal).

Cottee played for a different team in each of the top four divisions of English football in 2000-01, a rare achievement, last performed by goalkeeper Eric Nixon in 1986–87.

Cottee also diligently maintained a scrapbook containing press cuttings of every goal he scored throughout his playing career.

COTTERILL, George Huth 1890-93 ④ ②

Born: Brighton, 4 April 1868
Died: Llandaff, Glamorgan, 1 October 1950
Career: Brighton College (seasons 1882-86), Trinity College/
Cambridge University (seasons 1887-91), Old Brightonians
(seasons 1888-90); also played for Weybridge and Burgess Hill FC,
Corinthians (seasons 1887-98), Surrey, Sussex; also played rugby
for Richmond and Surrey and cricket for Cambridge University and
Sussex, and also competed in athletics.

A giant of a centre-forward, 6ft 3in tall, 14st in weight, George Cotterill
feared no one! Yet, despite his size, he was a good dribbler and
combined well with his fellow forwards. After some wonderful displays
for both the Corinthians and Cambridge University, he made his
international debut in March 1891 while still at University. In fact, for
the second year running, England played both Wales and Ireland on the
same day, and, for the match against the Irish at Molineux, the selectors
chose a predominantly Midlands based team, with five players making
their debut, inside-right Cotterill being one of them – and he scored in
a 6–1 win. Eight months later he played for England in an 'unofficial'
match against Canada, when he scored in another 6–1 victory.
    Fellow Corinthian CB Fry, who also played in that match, said
"Cotterill was the best player on the field."
    In 1892-93 Cotterill toured Northern England and Scotland with
the Corinthians and played five games in eight days in December
and January against professional teams scoring five times. On his
return he captained England in wins over Ireland (6-1) and Scotland
(5-2). He netted the second goal against the Scots to bring the
scores level after 58 minutes and set them on course to win the
Home International Championship for the third consecutive season.
    Cotterill retired in 1898 having scored 53 goals in 65 matches in
13 years with the Corinthians.
    Lieutenant Cotterill served in the 2nd Volunteer Battalion of the
Queens Royal West Country Regiment, was a Captain and later
Major in the 11th battalion, the Lancashire Fusiliers.
    *His father, George Edward Cotterill, also played cricket for
Cambridge University, Cambridgeshire and Sussex while his uncle,
Joseph Cotterill also played for Sussex.*

COTTLE, Joseph Richard 1908-09 ①

Born: Bedminster, Bristol, October 1886
Died: Bristol, 3 February 1958
Career: Eclipse FC (1901), Dolphin FC/Bristol (1902), Bristol City
(August 1904, retired April 1911); entered the building trade and
later became a Bristol licensee.

A full-back with tremendous drive and endeavour, Joe Cottle loved
to get forward – sometimes to the annoyance of his manager! Full
of grim determination, he played the game with gusto and was a big
favourite with the supporters of Bristol City for whom he made 204
appearances. His only England cap was against Ireland in Bradford
in February 1909 when, as Bob Crompton's partner, he 'never put a
foot wrong' in a 4-0 win.

COWAN, Samuel 1925-31 ③

Born: Chesterfield, 10 May 1901
Died: Haywards Heath, Sussex, 4 October 1964
Career: Ardwick Juniors (1915), Bullcroft Colliery (seasons 1918-
20), Denaby United (seasons 1920-23), Doncaster Rovers (June
1923), Manchester City (£1,500, December 1924), Bradford City
(£2,000, October 1935), Mossley (player-manager, July 1937,
retired as a player, May 1938); Brighton & Hove Albion (coach, June

1938); Manchester City (manager, November 1946-June 1947);
became a physiotherapist in Brighton, acting as masseur to Sussex
CCC and also the MCC (touring Australia in 1962-63).

Sam Cowan was a hefty centre-half who
was best when on the attack, as he loved
to drive forward with the ball. Captain
of Manchester City for many years, his
enthusiasm and commitment was much
appreciated by his team-mates and
supporters alike. He scored 24 goals in
407 appearances during his 11 seasons
at Maine Road (1924-35). He played in
three FA Cup finals, losing two before
winning in 1934. Earlier, in 1928, he helped City win the Second
Division Championship. And before that, he scored a hat-trick of
headers for Doncaster v. Halifax Town in March 1924.
    His three England caps were won over a period of five years; his
first in a 5-3 win over Belgium in Antwerp in May 1926 when he
assisted in three of the goals; his second against Austria in Vienna
in May 1930 (0-0) and his last, also against Belgium in Brussels
in May 1931 (4-1). Cowan died whilst refereeing a junior football
match at Haywards Heath.

COWANS, Gordon Sidney 1982-91 ⑩ ②

Born: West Cornworth, County Durham, 27 October 1958
Career: County Durham & District Schools, Aston Villa (apprentice,
July 1974, professional, August 1976), Bari/Italy (£450,000
with Paul Rideout, June 1985), Aston Villa (£250,000, July
1988), Blackburn Rovers (£200,000, November 1991), Aston
Villa (free, July 1993), Derby County (£80,000, February 1994),
Wolverhampton Wanderers (£20,000, December 1994), Sheffield
United (free, December 1995), Bradford City (free, July 1996),
Stockport County (free, March 1997), Burnley (player/reserve-team
coach, August 1997-May 1998); Aston Villa (assistant-manager/
coach, August 1998 onwards)

Midfielder Gordon 'Sid' Cowans had a
magical left foot. He could deliver an inch-
perfect pass and his presence in the Aston
Villa side of the 1980s was vitally important.
Unfortunately for him he failed to hold down
a regular place in the England team, making
only 10 appearances and scoring two goals
between February 1983 and November
1990 – due perhaps to the enormous
amount of midfield talents available at the
time to managers Bobby Robson and Graham Taylor.
    He made his international debut against Wales at Wembley when
only 24,000 fans bothered to turn up to see England win 2-1. He
scored his first goal in a 2-0 win over Scotland at the same venue
four months later when partnering Bryan Robson and Glenn Hoddle
in the 'engine-room' and he was also on target in the 4-0 thrashing
of Egypt in Cairo in January 1986 when he was pushing hard for a
place in the World Cup squad, which he didn't win!
    Cowan, in his three spells at Villa Park, scored 59 goals in 528
appearances, gaining FA Youth Cup, League Cup, First Division,
European Cup and Super Cup winner's medals. He also represented
his country at Youth level and in two B and five U21 internationals.
His career on the whole realised 825 appearances and 75 goals,
and at 2012 Cowans had been associated with Aston Villa for a total
of 29 years (in 4 separate spells).

COWELL, Arthur 1909-10 ①

Born: Blackburn, 20 May 1886
Died: Darwen, 12 February 1959
Career: Blackburn St Peter's (1899), Nelson (from 1901), Blackburn Rovers (May 1905, retired, injured, May 1920, then club trainer from June 1920); Wrexham (trainer, July 1937, manager, August 1938-March 1939); became a newsagent in Kirkham, then Darwen.

Full-back Arthur Cowell partnered the great Bob Crompton at Blackburn Rovers for many years. A polished defender, rather on the short side, he was blessed with persistence and fine judgment and could manoeuvre the ball around in the smallest of spaces. His only England appearance was against Ireland in Belfast in February 1910, when he deputised for Jesse Pennington in the 1-1 draw.

Cowell made 306 appearances for Blackburn, helping them win two League Championships before WW1. His cousin was Albert Edward Houlker.

COX, John Thomas 1900-03 ③

Born: Liverpool, 21 December 1877
Died: Walton-on-Thames, Surrey, 11 November 1955
Career: South Shore Standard/Blackpool (1892), South Shore (August 1895), Blackpool (professional, August 1897), Liverpool (February 1898), Blackpool (free, player-manager, August 1909, retired ill-health, May 1911)

Jack Cox was a mercurial outside-left, fast and clever who, when in the mood, could give his marking full-back a headache! Unfortunately he tended to overdo the clever stuff at times, and was known to beat his opponent twice and sometimes three times before crossing the ball, much to the detriment of teamwork. Cox helped Liverpool secure the League Championship in 1901 and 1906 and the Second Division title in 1905. In all he scored 80 goals in 360 appearances for the Merseysiders whom he served for more than 11 years.

This sort of form caught the eye of the England selectors who awarded him his first cap against Ireland at The Dell in March 1901. After playing 'an exceedingly good, powerful game' in a 3-0 win, he went on to represent England in successive internationals against Scotland - a 2-2 draw at Ibrox Park in May 1902, when he partnered Everton's Settle on the left-wing, and a 2-1 defeat at 12 months later when his inside partner was Capes of Stoke. The report of the latter contest in the *Scottish Daily Record* thought "Cox made his presence felt…and his curling shots worried 'keeper Doig." It was an astute cross from Cox which gave Vivian Woodward his goal before the Scots hit back with two in two minutes after half-time.

COX, John David 1891-92 ①

Born: Spondon, Derbyshire, October 1867
Died: Toronto, Canada, 16 June 1957
Career: Spondon FC (April 1886), Long Eaton Rangers (August 1889), Derby County (professional, May 1891); emigrated to Canada, late December 1899.

A strong-running, hard-tackling right-half who was a wonderful passer of the ball, Jack Cox scored seven goals in 238 appearances for Derby County, playing in two successive losing FA Cup finals. His only England cap was gained against Ireland in Belfast in March 1892 when he played 'competently' in a 2-0 win.

Known as 'Squire Spondon' Cox surprisingly moved to Canada soon after playing his last game for Derby v. Liverpool on Christmas Day, 1899, to work as a painter and decorator, but returned to England to fight for his country during WW1. He later went back to Canada, residing with his family in Toronto until his death.

CRABTREE, James William 1893-1902 ⑭

Born: Burnley, 23 December 1871
Died: Moseley, Birmingham, 28 June 1908
Career: Burnley Royal Swifts (September 1885), Burnley Rossendale (August 1889), Heywood Central (August 1890), Burnley (professional, August 1892), Aston Villa (£250, August 1895), Plymouth Argyle (January 1904), Oreston Rovers (May 1904, retired, May 1905); coached briefly at non-League level; also licensee of the Royal Victoria Cross, Lozells, Birmingham (April 1906, until his death).

A naturally gifted footballer, Jimmy Crabtree played at left-half and left-back and gave Aston Villa excellent service for nine seasons (1895-1904) during which time he made 200 appearances and scored seven goals, helping Villa win the FA Cup and four League Championships, including the double, in the last five seasons of the 19th century.

Unfortunately he had the tendency to hold the ball far too long, but that apart he was a pure master, yet was reputed to be very sensitive to criticism. He played in front of Howard Spencer for Villa, and went on to share the captaincy of the club with him.

Crabtree won the first of his 14 England caps against Ireland in Belfast in March 1894, playing behind his Villa team-mates Jack Devey and Dennis Hodgetts and putting in a 'decent performance' in the 2-2 draw.

In his next international, also against Ireland a year later, he helped set up four of the goals in a 9-0 win and four years later when the hapless Irish were whipped 13-2, he was brilliant, being involved in the build up to seven of the goals, although he did miss a penalty (the first England player to do so at senior level). He also played his part, from left-back, when Scotland were defeated 2-1 on his home patch at Villa Park in April 1899, keeping Rangers' right-winger Johnny Campbell 'quiet all afternoon.'

Crabtree also represented the Football League on six occasions.

This was a feature in the first edition of The Villa News and Record, printed on 1 September 1906… "One of England's greatest players. Shone in any position. Great as a half-back, but greater, possibly, as a back, kicking cleanly and with rare precision. A keen, skilful tackler, clever at close quarters and equally reliable in the open, cool, resourceful and brainy. Excelled in the finer points of the game, and one of the most versatile players England has boasted. For many seasons unrivalled in his position."

CRAWFORD, John Forsyth 1930-31 ①

Born: Jarrow, Northumberland, 26 September 1896
Died: Epsom, Surrey, 27 September 1975
Career: Jarrow Celtic (August 1910), Palmer's Works FC/Jarrow (September 1912), South Shields (trial, 1913), Jarrow Celtic (April 1914); served in Royal Navy during WW1; Hull City (professional, March 1920), Chelsea (£3,000, May 1923), Queens Park Rangers (May 1934, retired, May 1937; club coach to September 1939); Maldon Town (part-time coach, seasons 1945-48); worked at the Ford Motor car factory, Dagenham until his retirement in 1961.

Spent his long career playing on both wings, preferring perhaps the left where he won his three caps. Somewhat diminutive, only 5ft 3ins tall and relatively lightweight at 8st 6lbs, yet full of tricks, Jack Crawford was a fine crosser of the ball and when he chose to let fire, his shot was hard and true. He made his international debut against Scotland at Hampden Park in March 1931 and according to 'Broadcaster' in the *Daily Express* he found it difficult' against the Clyde right-back Danny Blair who closed him down quickly at every opportunity. He made 126 appearances for Hull and 308 for Chelsea.

CRAWFORD, Raymond 1961-62 ② ①

Born: Portsmouth, 13 July 1936
Career: Hilsea Junior & Portsmouth Senior Schools, Portsmouth (amateur, July 1952, professional, December 1954), Ipswich Town (£6,500, September 1958), Wolverhampton Wanderers (£55,000, September 1963), West Bromwich Albion (£30,000, February 1965), Ipswich Town (£15,000, March 1966), Charlton Athletic (March 1969), Kettering Town (November 1969), Colchester United (June 1970), Durban City/South Africa (August 1971), Brighton & Hove Albion (player-coach, November 1971, retired as a player, May 1973); Portsmouth (coach, June 1973), FC Eden/New Zealand (coach, August 1974), Portsmouth (Youth team manager-coach, July 1975-June 1978), Fareham Town (manager, August 1978), Winchester City (manager, May 1981-June 1983); represented Malaysia FA when on National service in the mid-1950s; now resides in Portsmouth.

Ray Crawford was a wonderfully consistent goalscorer, a thrustful, opportunist centre-forward with two good feet and a decent head! He bagged a grand total of 355 goals in 616 games during a near 20-year career, a record 228 of his goals coming with Ipswich, whom he helped win the Second and First Division Championships in successive seasons (1961 and 1962). He also netted five times when Ipswich beat Floriana of Malta 10-0 in a European Cup game in 1962.
    Unfortunately, his international career was surprisingly brief, winning only two caps. He made his England debut against Northern Ireland in November 1961 and played in his second game against Austria in April 1962 when he opened the scoring in a 3-1 win. It can be argued that Crawford's low amount of caps was due to the fact that he was around when Jimmy Greaves was also creating a reputation as a prolific goalscorer. Twice a Football League representative, he also played for the FA.
    In 2007, he published his autobiography entitled 'Curse of the Jungle Boy.'

CRAWSHAW, Thomas Henry 1894-1904 ⑩ ①

Born: Sheffield, 27 December 1872
Died: Wharncliffe, Sheffield, 25 November 1960
Career: Park Grange FC (1888), Attercliffe (1890), Heywood Central (August 1892), Sheffield Wednesday (professional, May 1894-June 1908), Chesterfield (July 1908), Castleford Town (July 1911, retired, May 1913); Glossop (secretary-manager, September 1913-April 1914); later ran a newsagents shop in Bramall Lane and was also landlord of two pubs in Sheffield.

In his prime Tom Crawshaw was, without doubt, the best centre-half in the Football League. A hard grafter, superb with his head, he tackled fair and square, a wonderfully alert footballer who passed with thought and precision. Unfortunately he was badly injured early in the game against Scotland in April 1897. He was off the field for quite a while before returning to the heart of the defence, albeit in a lot of pain. Nevertheless he battled on gamely and although England lost 2-1 he certainly 'man of the match' as far as some observers were concerned, *The Times* saying 'he was full of resource.'
    Crawshaw had made his international debut in March 1895 in a 9–0 win over Ireland at the County Ground, Derby.
    Following the Scotland game, above, he had a four-year absence from international football until March 1901, although only ten matches were played in this time. He marked his return by scoring in a 3–0 victory over Ireland in March 1901. His final appearance was also against Ireland in Belfast in March 1904.
    Crawshaw netted 24 goals in 466 appearances for Sheffield Wednesday between 1894 and 1908, helping the Owls win the FA Cup in 1896 and 1907, the First Division title in 1903 and 1904 and the Second Division Championship in 1900. He made eight appearances for the Football League.

CRAYSTON, John William 1935-38 ⑧ ①

Born: Grange-over-Sands, Lancashire, 9 October 1910
Died: Sutton Coldfield, 5 December 1992
Career: Barrow Schoolboys, Ulverston Town (May 1927), Barrow (professional, October 1928), Bradford Park Avenue (June 1930), Arsenal (£5,250, May 1934, retired, injured, January 1944; appointed club coach, later assistant-manager, June 1947, caretaker-manager, then manager from November 1956-May 1958; Doncaster Rovers (manager, July 1958, secretary-manager, March 1959-June 1961); later ran a newsagents shop in Streetly, Sutton Coldfield until 1980.

A supremely cultured right-half, an excellent passer of the ball as well as being a firm tackler, Jack Crayston could also throw the ball a long way, which proved a great weapon in his Arsenal days when Ted Drake was playing centre-forward. He made 284 first-team appearances for Arsenal between 1934 and 1944, helping the Gunners twice win the League Championship and also the FA Cup in the space of three seasons: 1935-38.
    A non-smoker and teetotaller, 'Gentleman Jack' made his England debut against Germany at Tottenham in December 1935 – playing alongside three other Arsenal players, full-backs George Male and Eddie Hapgood and winger Cliff Bastin. This in fact was England's 200th official international. He performed well and appeared in the next four internationals including the 1-1 draw with Scotland at Wembley in April 1936 when the pitch was 'too perfect, too lush' to play proper football. His last three caps were all won in 1937-38 when he scored his only England goal, in a thrilling 5-4 victory over Czechoslovakia at White Hart Lane when he played behind hat-trick hero Stan Matthews.
    Crayston also appeared in one Wartime international v. Wales in 1939, played for an England XI against the Anglo-Scots and represented the Football League.

CREEK, Frederick Norman Smith, MM, MBE 1922-23 ① ①

Born: Darlington, 12 January 1898
Died: Salisbury, Wiltshire, 26 July 1980
Career: Darlington Grammar School; served in the Royal Flying Corps (WW1); Trinity College/Cambridge University (seasons 1919-22); associated with the Corinthians (initially as a player, then as player-coach, seasons 1920-34); also registered with Darlington (amateur, May 1922-April 1924); England Amateur team (manager, 1940s); Great Britain Olympic team (manager, late 1950s-mid 1960s); FA coach (1946-60); was a sports and geography teacher at Dauntsey's School, Wiltshire (1923-54); also played cricket for Wiltshire; was a cricket correspondent for the *Daily Telegraph*, and wrote various books including *A History of the Corinthian Football Club* (1933) and *Centre Half - Attack or Defence?*.

A centre-forward, rather on the lean side, Norman Creek received a fair buffeting from the hefty defenders of his day but he battled on gamely, showing a fair degree of keenness and initiative while scoring his fair share of goals.
    His solitary appearance for England came in May 1923 when he scored in a 4–1 victory over France, although he also won five caps for his country as an amateur, scoring four goals on his debut.
    After the cessation of hostilities, he attended Cambridge University where he won his first 'Blue' in 1920. Injury prevented him playing in 1921, but he earned his second 'Blue' the following year. He was awarded the MBE in 1943 and the Military Cross a year later.

CRESSWELL, Warneford 1920-30 ⑦

Born: South Shields, 5 November 1897
Died: South Shields, 20 October 1973
Career: Stanhope Road School/South Shields, North Shields Athletic (April 1913); WW1 guest for Heart of Midlothian and Hibernian; South Shields (professional, August 1919), Sunderland (£5,500, March 1922), Everton (£7,000, February 1927, retired, April 1936); Port Vale (manager-coach, May 1936-April 1937), Northampton Town (manager, April 1937-September 1939), Dartford (manager, season 1939-40); became a licensee in South Shields after WW2.

Warney Cresswell, who occupied both full-back positions, played the game with coolness and vigilance. Nicknamed the 'Iceberg' he was hardly ever flustered and was perhaps unlucky, inasmuch that there were so many other excellent backs around at the same time as himself. He won his first England cap against Wales in 1921 and got a wonderful write-up in the press after the 0-0 draw but the selectors forgot him for the next few years, eventually recalling him for the clash with France in Paris in May 1923 when he again performed well in a 4-1 win. His last five caps were spread over six years when on three occasions his full-back partner was Sam Wadsworth.

Cresswell made 190 appearances for Sunderland (1922-27) and 306 for Everton (1927-36). He helped the Merseysiders win the First Division in 1928 and 1932, the Second Division in 1931 and the FA Cup in 1933. He also represented England as a Schoolboy and played five times for the Football League.

CROMPTON, Robert 1901-14 ㊶

Born: Blackburn, 26 September 1879
Died: Blackburn, 16 March 1941
Career: Moss Street School/Blackburn, Rose & Thistle FC (August 1892), Blackburn Trinity (September 1894), Blackburn Rovers (professional, September 1896, retired, May 1920); WW1 guest for Blackpool; Blackburn Rovers (manager, December 1926-February 1931; also director from June 1921-March 1931), Bournemouth & Boscombe Athletic (manager, June 1935-February 1936), Blackburn Rovers (honorary manager, April 1938 until his death).

One of the great names in the annals of English international football, Bob Crompton was a superbly-gifted right-back, robust yet scrupulously fair, quick, alert and a timely tackler who gave Blackburn Rovers 24 years' wonderful service (1896-1920), during which time he scored 14 goals in 576 appearances, skippering the team to two League Championship triumphs in 1912 and 1914.

Referred to in several reference books, magazines and programmes, as perhaps the 'greatest Rover of them all', Crompton was first capped by England against Wales at The Racecourse Ground, Wrexham in March 1902. He played a 'blinder' and retained his place for the next three games, against Ireland and Scotland twice, including the Ibrox Park disaster game, before playing against both Wales and Scotland again, the latter at Bramall Lane, Sheffield on 4 April 1903 when he contained the wing threat of Newcastle's left-winger Bobby Templeton.

He was the only player to captain England more than 20 times before WW1.

Injury caused him to miss all three internationals in 1904-05 but was back on duty in February 1906 for the clash with Ireland in Belfast, and he remained first choice at right-back for the next eight years, captaining his country on 22 occasions in the process.

He also formed, what many believe, has been England's best-ever full-back partnership of himself and the ever-reliable West Bromwich Albion skipper Jesse Pennington. They first played together against Wales in March 1907 and went on to appear in 23 internationals as England's right and left backs.

Crompton won his 41st and final England cap against Scotland at Hampden Park in April 1914, when he also lined up alongside his great pal 'Peerless' Pennington for the last time. For the record, Crompton suffered only six defeats in his England career, the worst being 3-0 against Ireland in February 1914.

He never ventured far enough upfield to score a goal, but he did concede two own-goals – after just 40 seconds in the 1-1 draw v. Scotland in April 1907 and in the 8-2 win over Hungary in May 1909, although the latter he knew nothing about. He also had the misfortune to give away three penalties!

Time and again match reports covered Crompton in glory. When Scotland were defeated 2-0 at Crystal Palace in April 1909, Bedouin of the *Scottish Daily Record* said: "He was the master – his vitality was amazing." And when the Scots were held to a 1-1 draw at Hampden Park in March 1912 it was Crompton and Pennington, in their sixth season as partners, who saved England from likely defeat. Scotland in fact switched winger Quinn from right to left in order to 'bash Crompton' wrote the *Daily Mirror* reporter, but the only bashing that went on was when Quinn was 'unceremoniously downed' by the English skipper.

Crompton also knew how to handle the wing threat of canny Irishman Frank Thompson and the tricky Welshman Bob Evans, but occasionally he was given a testing time by the skill and pace of a few darting outside-lefts in club football, although generally speaking overall there weren't too many wingers who got the better of the imperious Bob Crompton, who sadly died while watching Blackburn play Barnsley while he was still in charge at Ewood Park.

It is believed that Crompton was the first footballer to drive his own car to a game, doing so in 1908.

CROOKS, Samuel Dickinson 1929-37 ㉖ ⑦

Born: Bearpark, County Durham, 16 January 1908
Died: Belper, Derbyshire, 5 February 1981
Career: Durham County Boys, Bearpark Colliery (April 1922), Brandon Juniors (August 1923), Tow Law Town (July 1924), Durham City (professional, November 1926), Derby County (April 1927); WW2 guest for Nottingham Forest; Derby County (continued as a player until June 1947, then coach to August 1949), Retford Town (player-manager, December 1949-May 1950); Shrewsbury Town (manager, May 1950-June 1954), Gresley Rovers (manager, May 1955-April 1957), Burton Albion (manager, August 1957-April 1958), Gresley Rovers (manager, July 1958-May 1959), Heanor Town (manager, June 1959-May 1960); Derby County (chief scout, July 1960-May 1967); ran a sports clothing store in Derby; also served for 14 years as secretary of the Association Football Players' Union.

Sprightly, long-serving outside-right of Derby County, Sammy Crooks had a direct approach, was skilful, pacy, crossed superbly on the run and packed a fine shot. He scored 111 goals in 445 games for the Rams between 1927 and 1947 but sadly missed the 1946 FA Cup final victory over Charlton through injury.

He was England's right-winger on 26 occasions and played for times for the Football League in an era when there was an abundance of direct and good outside-rights including Stan Matthews and Joe Hulme. Only the Arsenal full-back Eddie Hapgood played more times for England between the wars than Crooks.

His first appearance for England was in a 5-2 victory against Scotland at Wembley in April 1930. He was the 'chief tormentor' of a troubled Scottish defence and gave left-back Tommy Law an afternoon he would never forget! The *Daily Mail* reporter wrote: "We had the unedifying spectacle, in the first half, of Law running here, there and everywhere, but rarely able to lay the elusive Crooks to the heels. Law's discomfort was complete."

Indeed, Crooks had a hand in England's four first-half goals and he came close to scoring himself after the break with a wicked shot that clipped the outside of 'keeper Harkness's post.

After this impressive display, Crooks became a regular fixture in the national side. He created chances for his colleagues in every game and found time to score seven goals himself, including two extra-special efforts in a 7-1 defeat of Spain at Highbury in December 1931. His final England appearance came in a 6-2 victory over Hungary in December 1936 when he played alongside his Derby County colleagues Raich Carter and Eric Keen. He helped set up two of Ted Drake's three goals in this match.

CROUCH, Peter James 2004-13 42 22

Born: Macclesfield, 30 January 1981
Career: North Ealing Primary & Drayton Manor High Schools, Tottenham Hotspur (apprentice, April 1996, professional, July 1998), Dulwich Hamlet (loan, March-April 2000), IFK Hassleholm (loan, May-June 2000), Queens Park Rangers (£60,000, July 2000), Portsmouth (£1.25m, July 2001), Aston Villa (£4m, March 2002), Norwich City (loan, September 2003-January 2004), Southampton (£2m, July 2004), Liverpool (£7m, July 2005), Portsmouth (£9m, July 2008), Tottenham Hotspur (approx. £10m, July 2009), Stoke City (£10m, August 2011).

Peter Crouch played in the 1999 World Youth Championship with Ashley Cole and Andrew Johnson and starred in six U21 internationals before gaining his first full cap in May 2005 under Sven-Göran Eriksson in the 3-2 win over Colombia in New Jersey. At 6ft 6¾in, he became the tallest player ever to star for England at senior level, taking over the mantle jointly held by weighty goalkeeper 'Fatty' Foulke from the 1890s and defender Zat Knight who had played in the previous game.

Crouch next appeared in the World Cup qualifying campaign but in the win over Poland, he was booed by his own supporters. In March 2006 he scored his first England goal, the equaliser in a 2–1 win over Uruguay when bizarrely wearing two different squad numbers on his shirt - 21 on the front and 12 on the back.

Two months later Crouch was included in the 23-man squad for the 2006 World Cup, and was expected to play a significant part due to Wayne Rooney's foot injury.

In the build-up to the tournament he netted in a 3-1 win over Hungary, celebrating with his robotic dance-style jig and soon afterwards he bagged a hat-trick and missed a penalty in a 6-0 win over Jamaica.

Crouch then partnered Michael Owen in England's attack in the first two World Cup games against Paraguay and Trinidad and Tobago, scoring in the latter but the goal provoked some controversy as replays showed Crouch to be pulling on Brent Sancho's long hair, holding the defender down, to gain an advantage.

A second minute 'sub' in the third game versus Sweden, replacing the injured Owen, he also came off the bench following Wayne Rooney's sending-off in the quarter-final defeat by Portugal.

After the tournament, retired English referee Graham Poll claimed that FIFA had specifically warned referees at the event to pay close attention to Crouch, claiming that "he's a real pain and he's getting away with too much."

He continued to score goals – notching two in a 4–0 win over Greece and two in a 5–0 drubbing of Andorra in a Euro 2008 qualifier to become the first player ever to reach ten goals for England within a single calendar year.

Peter Crouch

He was top scorer in the qualifying campaign with five goals and then, under Fabio Capello, he carried on his good work in 2010 World Cup qualifying victories over Ukraine and Belarus – which took his tally to 18 goals in just 17 international starts. Unfortunately he hardly figured in the finals in South Africa.

Not the quickest striker around, Crouch has certainly proved to be the perfect target man for the wide player delivering high crosses into the danger-zone, and there's no doubt that his scoring record at club and international level is excellent, as he has now netted over 160 goals in almost 550 appearances as a professional. He is also one of only five players to have scored for six different clubs in the Premiership. He helped Norwich win the Division One title in 2004 and Liverpool the FA Cup and Charity Shield in 2006 and has also represented England in one B international. He became Stoke's record buy from Spurs in 2011 on a four-year contract with the fee likely to rise to £12m.

CROWE, Christopher 1962-63 ①

Born: Newcastle-upon-Tyne, 11 June 1939
Died: Bristol, 12 May 2003
Career: St John's School/Edinburgh, Edinburgh Boys & Scotland Schools, Leeds United (junior, July 1954, professional, June 1956), Blackburn Rovers (£25,000, March 1960), Wolverhampton Wanderers (£30,000, February 1962), Nottingham Forest (£30,000, August 1964), Bristol City (£15,000, January 1967), Walsall (September 1969), Aubur FC/Sydney, Australia (May 1970), Bath City (February 1971, retired, May 1971).

An adroit, lightly-built inside-forward with clever footwork and a useful engine, Chris Crowe's only cap came in the 1-1 draw with France at Hillsborough in a European Championship qualifier in October 1962 when he partnered Birmingham City's Mike Hellawell on the right-wing. He also made eight Youth and four U23 appearances (2 goals) for England and, owing to being raised north of the border, he represented Scotland as a schoolboy. Crowe spent his best years with Leeds United (1954-60) for whom he scored 27 goals in 100 appearances.

CUGGY, Francis 1912-14 ②

Born: Walker, Northumberland, 16 June 1889
Died: Walker, Northumberland, 27 March 1965
Career: Walker Boys Club (August 1903), Willington Athletic (July 1906), Sunderland (professional, August 1909, Wallsend (player-manager, May 1921-September 1923); Celta Vigo/ Spain (coach for five years, November 1923-September 1928); later worked in the Wearside shipyards.

Unruffled, tireless and somewhat robustic, Frank Cuggy was the apex of Sunderland's celebrated centre-field triangle of himself, Jackie Mordue and Charlie Buchan which was so prominent during the early 1900s. He served the Wearsiders for 12 years, 1909-21, during which time he scored four times in 187 appearances, gaining a League Championship winner's medal in 1913.

Both Cuggy's appearances for England came against Ireland. The first was in February 1913 at Windsor Park, Belfast when he teamed up with his Sunderland colleagues Buchan and Mordue, and although Buchan scored early in the game, England lost 2–1. His second game followed a year later on St Valentine's Day 1914, when this time he was joined by his Roker Park team-mate Henry Martin who was making his England debut. This match, at Ayresome Park, ended in another Ireland victory, this time 3–0. It was the first time an England team had lost on home soil to the Irish.

CULLIS, Stanley 1937-39 (12)

Born: Ellesmere Port, Cheshire, 25 October 1915
Died: Malvern, 27 February 2001
Career: Cambridge Road School/Ellesmere Port, Ellesmere Port Wednesday (August 1930), Bolton Wanderers (trial, April-May 1931), Wolverhampton Wanderers (professional, February 1934, coached briefly in Norway, 1946, retired August 1947); WW2 guest for Aldershot, Fulham, Gillingham and Liverpool; also played for the British Wanderers in Turkey; Wolverhampton Wanderers (assistant-manager to Ted Vizard, August 1947, then manager, June 1948-September 1964), Birmingham City (manager, December 1965-March 1970); later ran a travel agency (in Malvern), was a member of the Midland Sports Council and a columnist in a local Midlands paper.

Centre-half Stan Cullis was described as a 'beefy stopper' who would whack the ball clear if danger threatened. Yet he hated wasting the ball and tried to hang on to it as long as possible, sometimes to the exasperation of his colleagues and manager!

He knew what he wanted to do, and would regularly come out of a ruck of players with the ball, arms out, full of authority.

He won his first senior cap in October 1937 in a 5–1 success against Ireland, and when England played Germany in Berlin in May 1938, Cullis was the only player who refused to join the rest of his team-mates in performing a Nazi salute prior to the match. He was a rock (as usual) as England beat the Germans 6–3 but was dropped from the team for the next game v. Switzerland!

England's youngest-ever captain when he led the team in his 12th and final international against Romania in Bucharest in May 1939 at the age of 23, Cullis was by far the best central defender anywhere in the world during the late 1930s. Although he continued to play for club and country after that, appearing in 20 Wartime internationals (10 as captain), the hostilities in Europe seriously disrupted his career and he eventually retired in 1947, having appeared in 171 games for Wolves. Then, as manager, he guided the Molineux club to three League Championship triumphs in the 1950s and to two FA Cup final victories in 1949 and 1960. He also played for the Football League XI.

He later took Birmingham City to the semi-finals of both the League Cup and FA Cup.

Cullis was injured in an off-the-ball incident during the WW2 international against Scotland at Hampden Park in April 1943. The defender was carried to the touchline while his team-mates protested rigorously to referee Mr. Peter Craigmyle, stating that he had been punched on the back of the head by an opponent.

CUNLIFFE, Arthur 1932-33 (2)

Born: Blackrod near Wigan, Lancs, 5 February 1909
Died: Bournemouth, 28 August 1986
Career: Adlington FC (junior, May 1923), Chorley (August 1927), Blackburn Rovers (professional, January 1928), Aston Villa (joint signing with Ronnie Dix, May 1933), Middlesbrough (December 1935), Burnley (April 1937), Hull City (June 1938); WW2 guest for Aldershot, Brighton & Hove Albion, Fulham, Reading, Rochdale and Stoke City; Rochdale (free, August 1946, retired to become trainer, May 1947-May 1950); Bournemouth (trainer, July 1950, then physiotherapist, April 1971-May 1974).

Arthur Cunliffe started off as a right-winger before making his name on the opposite flank. Lightning quick, he had great control, could beat his full-back on the inside or out, centred with wonderful accuracy and when given the chance, his shooting was as good as any other forward. His two England caps were gained in season 1932-33, the first

in a 1-0 win over Northern Ireland in the October, the second a month later in the 0-0 draw with Wales. He was unfortunate to have the likes of Cliff Bastin and Eric Houghton around at the same time. In his club career, Cunliffe netted 76 times in 221 appearances, having his best years with Blackburn for whom he struck 47 goals in 129 games (1928-33). He served Bournemouth for almost 25 years. His cousin was Jimmy Cunliffe (see below).

CUNLIFFE, Daniel 1899-1900 (1)

Born: Bolton, 11 June 1875
Died: Heywood, Lancs, 28 December 1937
Career: Little Lever (August 1892), Middleton Borough (July 1894), Oldham County (August 1896), Liverpool (professional, July 1897), New Brighton Tower (May 1898), Portsmouth (May 1899), New Brighton Tower (May 1900), Portsmouth (May 1901), New Brompton/Gillingham (May 1906), Millwall Athletic (June 1907), Heywood (September 1909), Rochdale (May 1912-May 1914); did not play after WW1.

A stocky, well-built inside-right, difficult to knock off the ball, Danny Cunliffe was a frequent scorer throughout his career. His form for Portsmouth earned him selection for England against Ireland at Lansdowne Park, Dublin in March 1900. Confidently expecting an easy match after five successive victories, including a 13–2 drubbing of the Irish the previous year, the selectors handed debuts to five players and it was Cunliffe, playing against his club-mate and Pompey goalkeeper Matt Reilly, who had a hand in one of the goals in England's 2–0 victory. He scored 178 goals in 451 games in his two spells with Portsmouth, helping them win the Southern League title in 1902.

CUNLIFFE, James Nathaniel 1935-36 (1)

Born: Blackrod near Wigan, Lancs, 5 July 1912
Died: Bolton, 21 November 1986
Career: Adlington FC (August 1928), Everton (professional, May 1930), Rochdale (September 1946, retired, injured, November 1946)

'Nat' Cunliffe, cousin of Arthur (above) was an all-purpose forward who used to bob up anywhere in the attack. He was quick and clever and scored plenty of goals. Capped by England in the 3-2 defeat by Belgium in Brussels in May 1936, he had a 'decent enough' game but was never considered for international duty again.

Partnering Dixie Dean in attack, he scored 76 goals in 187 appearances during his 16 years at Goodison Park (1939-46).

CUNNINGHAM, Laurence Paul 1978-81 (6)

Born: Archway, London, 8 March 1956
Died: near Madrid, Spain, 15 July 1989
Career: Stroud Green School/Archway, Highgate Wood Boys, Haringey Schools, South East Counties Schools, North London Boys, Arsenal (schoolboy forms, June 1971), Leyton Orient (apprentice, August 1972, professional, July 1974), West Bromwich Albion (£110,000, March 1977), Real Madrid/Spain (£995,000, June 1979), Manchester United (loan, March-April 1983), Sporting Gijon/Spain (loan, August-September 1983), Olympique Marseille/France (loan, August 1984-March 1985), Leicester City (loan, November 1985-May 1986), Rayo Vallecano/Spain (free, August 1986-June 1987), Real Betis/Spain (trial, August-September 1987), RSC Charleroi/Belgium (free, October-December 1987), Wimbledon (non-contract, January-May 1988), Rayo Vallecano (free, August 1988 until his death)

Laurie Cunningham

West Bromwich Albion were one of the most attractive and exciting teams in the Football League in the late 1970s and Laurie Cunningham soon attracted attention. He was the first black player to wear an England shirt at senior level when he starred for the U21 side against Scotland at Bramall Lane in April 1977, scoring to mark the occasion. He subsequently earned the first of his six full caps in the Home International against Wales two years later and, in fact, became the first black player to appear at senior level for his country, as Viv Anderson had made his debut six months earlier in a friendly. In June 1979, Cunningham won his second and third caps against Sweden and Austria respectively and followed up with three more in 1980 against the Republic of Ireland, Spain and Romania. He deserved more, for he was a terrific footballer, blessed with pace, skill and shooting ability. Referred to as the 'Black Pearl' and 'Black Beauty' he helped Real Madrid achieve the double (La Liga and Spanish Cup) in his first season, gained a second Cup winner's medal two years later, won the FA Cup with Wimbledon in 1987 and besides his full caps, he collected six at U21 level and also played for England B. He probably played his best football with WBA, for whom he netted 30 goals in 114 appearances (1977-79), but he also did well with Real Madrid, although in the 2nd leg of a UEFA Cup quarter-final clash with FC Kaiserslautern in 1982, he was sent off shortly before half time for retaliation, as the Germans won 5-0 to inflict upon Real their worst-ever defeat in a major European competition (up to that time).

Tragically, Cunningham was killed in a car crash on the outskirts of Madrid in July 1989. He was 33. He left behind his Spanish wife and a young son.

CURLE, Keith 1991-92 ③

Born: Bristol, 14 November 1963
Career: Bristol Rovers (apprentice, August 1979, professional, November 1981), Torquay United (£5,000, November 1983), Bristol City (£10,000, March 1984), Reading (£150,000, October 1987), Wimbledon (£500,000, October 1988), Manchester City (£2.5m, August 1991), Wolverhampton Wanderers (£650,000, August 1996), Sheffield United (free, July 2000, appointed player-coach, September 2000), Barnsley, Mansfield Town (player-manager, December 2002-December 2004), Chester City (manager, May 2005-February 2006), Torquay United (head-coach/manager, February-May 2007), Crystal Palace (coach/assistant-manager, October 2007), Queens Park Rangers (coach/assistant-manager, March 2010), Notts County (manager, February 2012, sacked February 2013).

A defender with a good aerial presence and a strong presence on the ground, Keith Curle was perhaps a surprise choice by England manager Graham Taylor when he made his international debut as a substitute in the 2-2 draw with the C.I.S. in Moscow in April 1992. He started the next game, a 1-0 win over Hungary, and was then named in the squad for Euro '92 as 'experienced' defensive cover, but played, alongside Des Walker, in the opening 0-0 draw with Denmark, but took no further part in the action after that as England crashed out at the first stage.

Curle made well over 700 League appearances during his 24-year career (1981-2005), having his best spells with Bristol City, Manchester City and Wolves. He won the Associate Members' Cup with Bristol City and the Full Members' Cup with Reading. He also gained four England B caps.

Curle was voted by the supporters of West Bromwich Albion as their 'Player of the Year' in 1997-98 ... for scoring an own-goal which gave the Baggies a 1-0 derby win over Wolves at the start of the season.

CURREY, Edmund Samuel 1889-90 ② ③

Born: Lewes, Sussex, 28 June 1868
Died: Hammersmith, London, 12 March 1920
Career: Charterhouse School, Magdalen College/Oxford University (seasons 1887-90), Old Carthusians (season 1887-88), assisted Corinthians and Sussex (seasons 1888-91); admitted a solicitor in 1895 and practised in London until his death.

A centre or inside-forward with a real attacking flair, Ted Currey was a typical Carthusian footballer, blessed with aggression and commitment. He scored twice on his England debut in a 3-2 win over Wales at Wrexham in March 1890 and in his second international, a 1-1 draw with Scotland at Hampden Park a month later, he was on target again with 'an obliquely angled shot which went in off the inside of the far post with Wood following the ball over the line.'

Some record books show Wood as the goalscorer in this game and not Currey.

CURRIE, Anthony William 1971-79 ⑰ ③

Born: Edgware, Middlesex, 1 January 1950
Career: Childshill Junior & Whitefield Secondary Schools/Cricklewood, Hendon Schools/Boys (season 1964-65), Queens Park Rangers (amateur, November 1964), Chelsea (youth team player, August 1965), Watford (apprentice, February 1966, professional, May 1967), Sheffield United (£26,500, May 1967), Leeds United (£240,000, June 1976), Queens Park Rangers (£400,000, August 1979), Toronto Nationalists/Canada (£60,000, May-June 1983), Chesham United (August 1983), Southend United (September 1983), Chesham United (November 1983), Torquay United (non-contract, February 1984), Tranmere Rovers (October-November 1984), Stockport County (briefly), Dunstable Town (season 1984-85), Hendon (season 1985-86), Goole Town (player-coach, August 1986); Sheffield United (Football in the Community Officer, February 1988 to date)

A very composed footballer, the blond-haired Tony Currie was introduced into England's midfield for his international debut by Alf Ramsey against Northern Ireland in May 1972. He was then surprisingly overlooked for a year before returning in June 1973 against the Soviet Union. He played well in a 2-1 win and had a 'decent' game against Italy shortly afterwards before scoring his first England goal with a rasping drive from 18 yards in a resounding 7-0 win over Austria in the September. In this game England showed a lot more fluency and sharpness than had been displayed for quite a while, Currie commanding midfield with some authority. However, there is no doubt that Currie's best performance in an England shirt was in the 1-1 draw with Brazil at Wembley in April 1978 when he was 'head and shoulders above any other player in terms of skill and ball control.' The following month he scored a 'cracking goal' in the 4-1 home win over Hungary.

Currie's international career continued until June 1979 when manager Ron Greenwood opted for a more attacking line-up.

Besides his full caps, Currie also played in four Youth and 13 U23 internationals and represented the Football League, and at club level he amassed a total of 528 League appearances and scored 80 goals. His best years were spent with Sheffield United for whom he netted 66 times in 376 games (1967-76).

Tony Currie

CURSHAM, Arthur William 1875-83 ⑥ ②

Born: Wilford, Nottinghamshire, 14 March 1853
Died: Florida, USA, 24 December 1884
Career: Oakham School, Nottingham Law Club (September 1869), Notts County (August 1871-May 1884), Sheffield FC (briefly, August 1884); a colliery owner in Derbyshire, also played cricket for Derbyshire and Nottinghamshire; emigrated to USA (Florida) in November 1884

An energetic, fast-raiding outside-right who at times could overrun the ball, Arthur Cursham is the elder brother of H.A.

He played for Notts County between 1876 and 1883 and made his England debut in March 1876 in a 3-0 home defeat by Scotland. It is understood that Cursham actually took a photograph of the other ten members of the team in which he played (he was presumably behind the camera). Cursham went on to appear in five more internationals, three against the Scots and two against Wales. He captained his country and scored in a 7-2 defeat by the Scots at First Hampden in March 1878 and helped himself to a goal in a 5-3 win over the Welsh at The Oval in February 1883. Cursham died from yellow fever at the age of 31.

CURSHAM, Henry Alfred 1879-84 ⑧ ⑤

Born: Wilford, Nottinghamshire, 27 November 1859
Died: Holme, Pierrepoint, Nottinghamshire, 6 August 1941
Career: Repton School, Notts County (July 1877-May 1882), Corinthians (August 1882-April 1886), Grantham (season 1886-87), Thursday Wanderers (season 1887-88), Sheffield FC (briefly in 1888-89); worked as an insurance broker, appeared in two county cricket matches for Notts (24 years apart) and also played rugby for Nottinghamshire v. Bedfordshire in February 1892.

Unlike his brother, Harry Cursham was a more compact footballer, a close dribbler with a delicate touch. However, he is hardly a household name today but no player in the history of the FA Cup has scored more goals in the competition than the former Notts County player who, in a ten-year period from 1877 to 1887, notched a total of 49, 48 in the competition proper and one in a 4th round qualifying tie against Staveley. His biggest haul was six against Wednesbury Strollers in an 11-1 win. Cursham is also County's all-time record scorer, bagging 208 goals between 1877 and 1891. He accrued eight caps for the England, the first in a 3-2 victory against Wales in 1880. He scored his first international goal in his second match when Ireland were blitzed 13-0 in Belfast in 1882, added a second to his tally in the 5-3 defeat by Wales at Wrexham in 1882, and ended with a terrific hat-trick when the Irish were drubbed 8-1 in Belfast early in 1884.

DAFT, Henry Butler 1888-92 ⑤ ③

Born: Radcliffe-on-Trent, Notts, 5 April 1866
Died: High Cross, Herts, 12 January 1945
Career: Trent College/Nottingham (1883-85), Notts County (amateur, March 1885, professional, August 1890), Nottingham Forest (January 1893), Notts County (August 1893), Newark Town (January 1895); assisted Corinthians (seasons 1887-90); played for Nottinghamshire in county matches; also played county cricket for Nottinghamshire and lacrosse for the North of England.

Harry Daft he was certainly not! This speed-merchant on the left-wing could be brilliant at times and he gave many full-backs the runaround. He scored 81 goals in 179 appearances in two spells for Notts County between 1885 and 1895, gaining an FA Cup winner's medal in 1894. He made his international debut in March 1889 against Ireland, playing as well as anyone in a 'comfortable' 6-1 victory and setting up two of John Yates' three goals. The following season, he played against Wales (won 3-1) and Scotland

(drew 1-1) and two weeks before the 1891 FA Cup final defeat by Blackburn, he won his fourth cap against Ireland, scoring in the 6-1 win. At the end of the 1891-92 season, Daft made his final appearance for England, captaining the team and scoring both goals in a 2-0 win over the Irish in Belfast. As an all-round cricketer, he played 200 games for Nottinghamshire, scoring 4,370 runs at an average of 15.89 and taking 86 wickets at 26.03 each.

DALEY, Anthony Mark, BSc 1991-92 ⑦

Born: Lozells, Birmingham, 18 October 1967
Career: Aston Manor & Holte Comprehensive Schools/Birmingham, Birmingham Boys, Aston Villa (apprentice, June 1983, professional, May 1985), Wolverhampton Wanderers (£1.25m, June 1994); had loan spells with FC Madeira/Portugal and Hapoel Haifa/Israel (season 1997-98), Watford (July 1998), Walsall (June 1999), Nailsworth FC (briefly) Forest Green Rovers (October 1999, retired, injured, July 2002); Aston Villa (fitness coach, August 2002-May 2003), Sheffield United (fitness coach, June 2003-August 2007), Wolverhampton Wanderers (fitness coach, season 2007-08); gained a Bachelor of Science degree in Sports and Exercise Science at Coventry University.

Tony Daley had pace, plenty of it, but all too often he was blocked off by his marking full-back. When running into space he was mighty dangerous and the fans loved it when he was in full flight. Unfortunately he suffered a serious leg injury soon after joining Wolves from Aston Villa in 1994 and never really regained full fitness.

Daley won his seven England caps under former club manager Graham Taylor. He made his debut as a substitute in a vital 1-1 draw in Poland in November 1991 that saw England qualify for the 1992 European Championships in Sweden. He then played well in the friendlies against C.I.S., Hungary, Brazil and Finland and was subsequently chosen for the squad in Sweden. He appeared in two of England's three games there, missing two clear chances in the 2-1 defeat by the host nation in Stockholm, but after the tournament he never played for his country again, new manager Terry Venables preferring John Barnes as his main winger.

Daley spent eleven years with Aston Villa (1983-94) during which time he scored 38 goals in 290 appearances, gaining a League Cup winner's medal in his last season. He also played in one B international.

DANKS, Thomas 1884-85 ①

Born: Nottingham, 30 May 1863
Died: Nottingham, 27 April 1908
Career: Wilford FC/Nottingham (June 1879), Nottingham Forest (December 1882-February 1889); had loan spells with Sherwood FC/Nottingham (1883), Notts County (1884) and Burslem Port Vale (September 1888); later worked as an ironmonger in Nottingham.

A very unselfish player, centre-forward Tommy Danks played superbly at club level, albeit before the Football League came into being, but sadly he was 'out of his depth' in his only England game against Scotland which ended in a 1-1 draw at The Oval in March 1885.

DAVENPORT, James Kenyon 1884-90 ② ②

Born: Bolton, 23 March 1862
Died: Bolton, 29 September 1908
Career: Gilnow Rangers/Bolton (August 1879), Bolton Wanderers (August 1883), Southport Central (November 1892-May 1894); represented Lancashire County (1890s); worked as a fitter in Bolton.

An admirable servant to Bolton Wanderers for whom he scored 36 goals in 77 games between 1883 and 1892, the versatile Jim Davenport could occupy any forward position and in the late 1880s was regarded as one the fastest players in the North of England. He 'impressed' on his England debut in the 1-1 draw with Wales at Blackburn in March 1885, when he became the first Bolton player to win a full cap. In his second international, five years later, he scored twice in a 9-1 win over Ireland in Belfast, but surprisingly he was never selected again.

DAVENPORT, Peter 1984-85 ①

Born: Birkenhead, 24 March 1961
Career: Cammell Laird FC (August 1980), Nottingham Forest (professional, January 1982), Manchester United (£570,000, March 1986), Middlesbrough (£750,000, November 1988), Sunderland (£350,000, July 1990), Airdrieonians (free, June 1993), St. Johnstone (August 1994), Stockport County (free, March 1995), Southport (player/assistant-manager, September 1995), Macclesfield Town (player-coach, August 1997, manager, January 2000-January 2001), Congleton Town (April 2001), Bangor City (manager, May 2001-May 2005), Colwyn Bay (manager, May 2006-January 2007), Southport (manager, January 2007-April 2008), Bradford Park Avenue (assistant-manager, May 2010).

Peter Davenport's international career ended after just 18 minutes! He was a second-half substitute for Mark Hateley in the international against the Republic of Ireland at Wembley in March 1985 which England won 2-1.

A tall, mobile striker, he had a decent career in top-class football, scoring over 130 goals in almost 550 competitive matches. He also played for England's B team.

DAVIES, Kevin Cyril 2010-11 ①

Born: Sheffield, 26 March 1977
Career: Chesterfield (apprentice, June 1992, professional, April 1994), Southampton (£750,000, May 1997), Blackburn Rovers (£7.25m, June 1998), Southampton (August 1999), Millwall (loan, September-October 2002), Bolton Wanderers (free, July 2003).

Having been capped at both Youth and U21 levels, Kevin Davies – regarded as one of the last of the genuine old-style British centre-forwards - became the oldest player to make his full England debut since 38 year-old Arsenal defender Leslie Compton in November 1950, when he came on as a second-half substitute in the 0-0 European Championship qualifier against Montenegro at Wembley in October 2010, at the age of 33 years and 200 days.

Six feet tall, strong and aggressive, the former Chesterfield FA Cup semi-finalist (1997) had scored over 125 goals in almost 650 appearances for five clubs and his country at 2011, including 25 in 125 outings in his two spells with Saints. He has also won a number of 'Player of the Year' awards with Bolton.

DAVIS, George Henry 1903-04 ② ①

Born: Alfreton, Derbyshire, 5 June 1881
Died: Wimbledon, London, 28 April 1969
Career: Alfreton Town (May 1897), Derby County (professional, December 1899-May 1908), Alfreton Town (August 1908-April 1912), Calgary Hillhurst FC/Canada (May 1912, retired as a player, May 1915); later coached in Manitoba and made his fortune in the hotel business; returned to Nottingham in 1955.

A useful outside-left, virile and compact, George Davis trained diligently despite suffering several knee and ankle injuries. He made his England debut in the 2-2 draw with Wales at Wrexham in February 1904 and netted with a deflected shot in his second international when Ireland were defeated 3-1 a fortnight later. The scorer of 29 goals in 155 appearances in eight years for Derby, Davis was 41 when he gained a Cup winner's medal with his Canadian club in 1922.

DAVIS, Henry 1902-03 ③ ①

Born: Wombwell, Yorkshire, 20 November 1879
Died: Sheffield, 18 October 1945
Career: Ardsley FC (June 1895), Barnsley (professional, April 1898), Sheffield Wednesday (£200, January 1900, retired, May 1909; became assistant-trainer); became a Sheffield licensee and later a newsagent.

At 5ft 4ins, Harry Davis was one of the smallest players in the professional game around the turn of the 20th century. Nicknamed 'Joe Pluck', his late goal earned Barnsley their first-ever League victory over Luton Town in 1898 and during his nine years at Hillsborough (1900-09) he helped Wednesday win the Second Division Championship in 1900 and back to back First Division titles in 1903 and 1904. He scored 67 goals in 267 appearances for the Owls with whom he won his three England caps, all in the Home International Championship of 1902-03. He had the pleasure of scoring on his debut against Ireland in the February, made a goal in the 2-1 win over Wales at Portsmouth but was 'kept quiet' by Sunderland's burly left-back Jim Watson in the 2-1 defeat by Scotland on his home ground at Hillsborough. Davis also represented the Football League as an 'Owl'. A broken leg, suffered in 1907, effectively ended his career.

DAVISON, John Edward 1921-22 ①

Born: Gateshead, 2 September 1887
Died: Wortley, Sheffield, 6 January 1971
Career: Gateshead St Chad's (August 1903), Gateshead Town (September 1905), Sheffield Wednesday (£300, April 1908-June 1926); played briefly for Sheffield FC (in season 1919-20); Mansfield Town (player-manager, June 1926-December 1927), Chesterfield (manager, December 1927-June 1932), Sheffield United (manager, June 1932-August 1952), Chesterfield (manager, August 1952-May 1958, then chief scout for three years)

Considered to be one of the shortest of all England goalkeepers at 5ft 7ins, Teddy Davison, placid, gentle, acrobatic and plucky, was blessed with greater muscular strength than was imagined. He made his international debut against Wales in March 1922 and kept a clean sheet in a 1–0 win. He was also picked eight times for Sheffield's representative side and toured Australia with the FA in 1925. He made 424 appearances for Sheffield Wednesday between 1908 and 1926; guided Chesterfield to the Third Division (North) title and took Sheffield United to the 1936 FA Cup final and as a manager he 'found' future England World Cup winning goalkeeper Gordon Banks and signed Jimmy Hagan for the Blades.

DAWSON, Jeremiah 1921-22 ②

Born: Cliviger, Burnley, 18 March 1888
Died: Cliviger, Burnley, 8 August 1970
Career: Portsmouth Rovers/Todmorden (August 1903), Holme FC (July 1904), Cliviger FC (August 1905), Burnley (professional, February 1907, retired, May 1929; became club scout); also played for Burnley cricket club.

Jerry Dawson is mostly remembered for one match, the 1914 FA Cup final, even though he did not play in it. The day before the game, he told manager John Haworth that he didn't think he would make it to the end of the game. As there were no substitutes in those days, that would have left Burnley without a goalkeeper. Burnley still lifted the trophy and, as a sign of respect of his unselfishness, Dawson was presented with a winner's medal along with the rest of the team. In his time at Turf Moor (1906-29) Dawson played in 569 games, gained a League Championship winner's medal in 1921 and was capped twice by England, against Ireland in Belfast in October 1921 (1-1 draw) and v. Scotland at Villa Park six months later when his intended clearance struck full-back Sam Wadsworth and dropped into the path of Andrew Wilson who scored the only goal of the game. Dawson, who was unlucky to have that great 'keeper Sam Hardy around at the same time, also represented the Football League against the Scottish League at Ibrox Park in 1913 and received a standing ovation from the crowd after 'a magnificent display of goalkeeping.'

DAWSON, Michael Richard 2010-11 ②

Born: Northallerton, Yorkshire, 18 November 1983
Career: Wensleydale School/Leyburn, Northallerton Juniors (season 1996-97), Richmond FC (junior, August 1997), Nottingham Forest (schoolboy forms, April 1998, apprentice, April 1999, professional, November 2000), Tottenham Hotspur (£8m, with Andy Reid, January 2005)

Central defender Matt Dawson made his England debut as a second-half substitute for John Terry in the 2-1 friendly win over Hungary at Wembley in August 2010. However, it was his mistake (a mistimed lunge at Zoltan Gera) which resulted in the Magyars' goal, yet he (according to TV pictures) got back into position and actually cleared Jagielka's deflection off the line, although the assistant referee thought otherwise, and signalled that the ball had crossed the line! He gained his second cap, alongside Terry in a 2-1 win over Denmark in February 2011.

DAY, Samuel Hulme 1905-06 ③

Born: Peckham Rye, London, 29 December 1878
Died: Canterbury, Kent, 21 February 1950
Career: Malvern College (seasons 1896-98), Queen's College/Cambridge University (seasons 1898-1902); also played for Corinthians (1902-12, acting as player-secretary for a short time); also assisted Old Malvernians (seasons 1900-02); graduated from University, became a teacher at Westminster School and later headmaster of Heatherdown Preparatory School, Ascot; also played county cricket for Kent (1897-1919).

A quick-moving lightweight inside-forward, skilful with a powerful right-foot shot, Sammy Day won his three England caps against Ireland (won 5-0), Wales (won 1-0) and Scotland (lost 1-2) in February, March and April 1905. He scored in each of his first two matches but missed two easy chances against the Scots at Hampden Park when, it is thought, over 100,000 spectators attended an international match for the first time.

Day, who helped Old Malvernians win the FA Amateur Cup in 1902, also gained five Amateur caps for England, and he scored 7,722 runs for Kent in 22 seasons of county cricket (1897-1919).

DEAN, William Ralph 1926-33 ⑯ ⑱

Born: Birkenhead, Merseyside, 22 January 1907
Died: Liverpool, 1 March 1980
Career: Albert Industrial & Laird Street Schools/Birkenhead, Birkenhead Schoolboys, Moreton Bible Class, Wirral Railways, Heswall FC (season 1921-22), Pensby United (September 1922), Tranmere Rovers (amateur, November 1923, professional, February 1925), Everton (£2,500, March 1925), Notts County (£3,000, March 1938), Sligo Rovers (January 1939), Hurst FC (July 1939); WW2 guest for York City; (retired April 1941); became a licensee in Chester, gave up in 1962 through poor health; later worked for Littlewoods Pools company until his retirement in January 1972

'Dixie' Dean announced his arrival on the international scene with two superb goals in the 3-3 draw with Wales at Wrexham in February 1927. Then against Scotland a fortnight later, he showed his splendid opportunism by netting two more in double-quick time in a 2-1 win. He equalised Alan Morton's first-half effort with a clinical finish after being sent clear by Sid Bishop while his second was a great solo effort. This is how it was described by Broadcaster in the *Daily Express*: "One defender came for him, then another, and then another. They all seemed to be round him, but although he (Dean) did not seem to be travelling much faster than they were, he stuck to the ball like a leech, kept them off somehow and, as the goalkeeper came out, slipped the ball neatly past him for the winner."

In fact, hot-shot Dean found the net twelve times in his first five internationals, including hat-tricks in wins over Belgium (9-1) and Luxembourg (5-2). He also scored four times for the Football League in a 9-1 win over the Irish League in September 1927, adding a few more to his tally at this level as the years rolled by. In fact, Dean scored 64 first-class goals in the calendar year of 1927.

Not for the want of trying, Dean failed to find the net in his next three full internationals, but bagged five more goals in the following three games before adding just one more to his tally in his remaining five internationals.

Imperious in the air, able to shoot with both feet, his positional sense was second to none and his successor at Goodison Park, Tommy Lawton, thought he was 'the most complete centre-forward you could possibly wish to meet.'

The scorer of 60 League goals for Everton when

William 'Dixie' Dean

they won the First Division title in 1927-28 (a record no-one will ever beat) he hated his nickname 'Dixie', always telling people to call him Bill. A year earlier a motor cycle accident had left him unconscious and with several head injuries, it was feared he might not play football again. But through sheer guts and willpower he was back in the reserves within three months and went on playing – and scoring – for many more years. In fact, he bagged 383 goals in 433 games for Everton up to 1938. He added a second League Championship winner's medal to his tally in 1932, having collected a Second Division winner's prize in 1931. He also scored when the Blues won the 1933 FA Cup final. A great practical joker, Dean sent a telegram to Elisha Scott, the Liverpool goalkeeper, on the eve of the Merseyside derby in September 1931. It read 'Sleep well – I'll keep you awake tomorrow.' And he did! He scored a hat-trick in a 3-1 win at Anfield, one of a record 34 trebles he bagged for club and country.

DEANE, Brian Christopher 1991-93 ③

Born: Leeds, 7 February 1968
Career: Leeds City Boys (season 1983-84), Leeds United (junior, April 1984), Doncaster Rovers (apprentice, December 1985, professional, February 1986), Sheffield United (£30,000, July 1988), Leeds United (£2.9m, July 1993), Benfica/Portugal (£1m, January 1998), Middlesbrough (£3m, October 1998), Leicester City (£150,000, November 2001), West Ham United (free, October 2003), Leeds United (free, July 2004), Sunderland (free, March 2005), Perth Glory/Australia (July 2005), Sheffield United (December 2005, retired, May 2006); now a Sports Consultant for Blacks Solicitors LLP in Leeds.

Brian Deane's three England caps were won as a Sheffield United player in the early 1990s. His debut was as a half-time substitute in a tour match against New Zealand at Mount Smart Stadium, Auckland in June 1991, while his second outing was also against New Zealand at Athletic Park shortly afterwards. He had to wait until September 1992 for his third cap, won against Spain in Santander.

A tall, traditional target man, Deane scored 45 goals in 201 games in his three spells with Leeds and 119 in 273 outings for Sheffield United. In all, for his eight League clubs, he bagged well over 250 goals in more than 800 senior appearances and had the honour of scoring the first goal in the English Premier League for Sheffield United against Manchester United after just five minutes of the opening game of the 1992-93 season at Bramall Lane. He also gained three England B caps.

DEELEY, Norman Victor 1958-59 ②

Born: Wednesbury, Staffs, 30 November 1933
Died: Wednesbury, 7 September 2007
Career: Wolverhampton Wanderers (amateur, April 1949, professional, December 1950), Leyton Orient (£1,200, February 1962), Worcester City (July 1964), Bromsgrove Rovers (August 1967), Darlaston (September 1971, retired, April 1974); became manager of Caldmore Community Programme Agency, Walsall and also served Walsall FC as a matchday steward.

Norman Deeley scored two goals when Wolves beat Blackburn 3-0 in the 1960 FA Cup final. The impish winger also won three League titles with the Molineux club for whom he netted 73 times in 237 appearances before transferring to Leyton Orient in 1962. His two caps came on England's South American tour in May 1959, the first in a 2-0 defeat by the reigning World champions Brazil in front of 160,000 fans inside the giant Maracana Stadium in Rio de Janeiro when his right-wing partner was club-mate Peter Broadbent; the second in a 4-1 reverse against Peru in Lima. He had earlier

represented his country at Schoolboy level - as a 4ft 4in tall wing-half (1.32m) in 1947-48. He helped Orient clinch promotion to the top flight in 1963 before moving into non-League football. Playing fields in his native Wednesbury were later named after him in tribute to his football career. His son Andy has represented New Zealand at international level.

DEFOE, Jermain Colin 2003-13 (54) (19)

Born: Beckton, Newham, London, 7 October 1982
Career: St Joachim Primary School/Custom Hill & St Bonaventure's
Roman Catholic Comprehensive School/Forest Gate, London;
Senrab FC (Sunday League team); FA National School of Excellence
at Lilleshall/Shropshire (1997); Idsall School (1997-98), Charlton
Athletic (apprentice, April 1998), West Ham United (£400,000,
October 1999), AFC Bournemouth (loan, October 2000-May 2001),
Tottenham Hotspur (£7m, February 2004), Portsmouth (£9m,
January 2008), Tottenham Hotspur (£15m, January 2009).

Jermain Defoe's form for AFC Bournemouth in 2000–01 resulted
in an England U21 call-up against Mexico and he marked his debut
with the second goal in a 3–0 victory. He went on to win 23 caps
at this level, scoring seven goals, before making his senior bow in
a 1–0 defeat by Sweden in March 2004, when he came on as an
early substitute for the injured Darius Vassell. England manager
Sven-Göran Eriksson singled out Defoe's display for praise in an
otherwise poor performance, saying, "He did very well - I liked what
I saw. He showed that he can do very well even in international
football and that he is technically very good. Jermain is quick and he
knows where the goal is, so I liked him very much."

He was not, however, selected for Euro 2004 but was back in
contention soon afterwards, making his first start in a World Cup
qualifier against Poland, scoring in a 2–1 win.

As he did six months earlier, Eriksson paid tribute to Defoe,
saying, "Jermain is a great talent. It couldn't have been much better
for him. He did very well. He scored one goal and created other
chances as well. He is a great player who will always score goals."

Despite appearing regularly for England in World Cup qualifying
and friendly matches, Defoe was not named in the provisional
squad for the 2006 World Cup in Germany, being put on standby as
cover for Wayne Rooney who was, at the time, struggling with injury.
Rooney was subsequently declared fit and Defoe missed out. He
confessed that he was baffled by his omission, saying, "I don't know
why I'm not out there. I've been involved in every squad for the last
two years and feel I've played a part in helping us to qualify. I have
never felt fitter and sharper than I was in training and believe I could
have scored goals in the tournament. It's a strange
decision and everybody I speak to thinks so as well."

Eriksson said he did not think that Defoe would
have been a better option than 17 year-old Theo
Walcott, who was included in the squad.

Steve McClaren, who took over as England
manager after the World Cup, selected
Defoe for his first match against Greece
in August 2006 and since then the
striker has continued to appear, on
and off, for England, making an
impact in the qualifying games
for both Euro 2008 and the World
Cup in 2010.

He was initially omitted from Fabio Capello's
squad but after scoring on his Portsmouth debut
he was recalled in place of the injured Gabriel
Agbonlahor. He quickly knocked in some
important goals, including two against
Trinidad and Tobago and one in the 5-1
victory over Kazakhstan in October 2008,
having come on as a late sub for Rooney.

He also netted twice in three minutes
against Andorra in a World Cup qualifier,
did likewise in the 2–2 draw against the

Jermaine Defoe

Netherlands and scored the winning goal against Slovenia in the 2010
World Cup finals in South Africa before sadly England exited at the
second hurdle.

In September 2010 he whipped in his first international hat-trick
as England started their 2012 European Championship qualifying
campaign off in style by beating Bulgaria 4-0 at Wembley. He hardly
figured, however, in the finals in Poland/Ukraine.

Defoe does hold an English international record – that of appearing
most times as a substitute at senior level, 33 (at June 2013).

Besides his U21 and senior appearances for England, Defoe has
also represented his country in three Youth and two B internationals.
At club level, at the end of season 2012-13, he had scored 210
goals in 512 appearances, including 133 in 340 games for Spurs.
He also netted the 14,000th goal in Premiership football, for Spurs
v. Birmingham City in December 2005.

*Defoe played for the same Sunday League team (Senrab FC) as
Lee Bowyer, Ashley Cole, Ledley King and John Terry.*

DE PARAVICINI, Percy John, JP, MVO, CVO 1882-83 (3)

Born: Bow, London, 15 July 1862
Died: Hill Fields, Pangbourne, 11 October 1921
Career: Aldin House School/Slough, Eton College (season 1880-81),
Trinity College/Cambridge University (seasons 1881-83); also
played for Old Etonians, Windsor, Berkshire-Buckinghamshire
and Corinthians, the latter (seasons 1884-86); served on the FA
Committee (1885-86); also a fine cricketer, playing for Cambridge
and Middlesex.

A speedy, two-footed defender, Percy de Paravicini appeared in two
FA Cup finals for Old Etonians, gaining a winner's medal in 1882.
In that final, along with Arthur Kinnaird, he managed to contain the
sprightly Blackburn Rovers forwards after Reg Macaulay had scored
the all-important goal in the 8th minute.

In February and March 1883, de Paravicini was selected for all
three England internationals, against Scotland, Wales and Ireland.
The Welsh were defeated 5–0, the Irish 7–0 but the Scots managed
to sneak home 3-2 despite some splendid defensive play by de
Paravicini. He played in 121 matches for Middlesex CCC (1881-92)
and was decorated with the Victoria Order (MVO) in 1908 and the
CVO in 1921.

DEVEY, John Henry George 1891-94 (2) (1)

Born: Newtown, Birmingham, 26 December 1866
Died: Aston, Birmingham, 13 October 1940
Career: Aston Brook School/Birmingham, Montrose
Youth Club/Aston (August 1881), Wellington
Road FC (September 1882), Excelsior FC/
Birmingham (April 1883), Aston Unity (July
1885), Aston Manor (August 1886), West
Bromwich Albion (briefly, during season 1889-
90), Mitchell St George's (August 1890), Aston
Villa (professional, March 1891, retired, April
1901; club coach, seasons 1901-03, then a
director at Villa Park, June 1904-September
1934); also ran a sports outfitters shop in
Lozells, Birmingham and played county cricket for
Warwickshire (seasons 1888-97).

One of Aston Villa's greatest captains, Jack Devey was a skilful inside
right/centre-forward who, surprisingly, gained only two England caps,
both against Ireland, in a 2-0 win in March 1892 and a 2-2 draw in
March 1894, scoring in the latter.

Exceptionally clever with head and feet, he was a prolific marksman, bagging 186 goals in 308 appearances during his ten years with the Villa with whom he won five League Championship and two FA Cup winner's medals, helping his club achieve the double in 1897. As a Warwickshire cricketer, Devey scored over 6,500 runs and hit eight centuries.

Four of his five brothers - Ted and Will for Small Heath and Harry and Bob for Villa – were footballers while a fifth, Abel, played cricket for Staffordshire.

DEVONSHIRE, Alan Ernest 1979-84 ⑧
Born: Park Royal, London, 13 April 1956
Career: Crystal Palace (schoolboy forms), Southall & Ealing Borough Boys (1971), Southall FC (August 1974), West Ham United (£5,000, October 1976), Watford (July 1990, retired, May 1992); Maidenhead United (manager, seasons 1996-2003), Hampton & Richmond Borough (manager, July 2003), Braintree (manager, May 2011)

A wide midfielder, Alan Devonshire scored 32 goals in 446 appearances for West Ham whom he served for 14 years, helping the Hammers win the FA Cup in 1980 and the Second Division Championship the following year. A serious knee injury, suffered in 1984, effectively ended his England career after he had played in one B and eight full internationals, the first against Northern Ireland in May 1980 when he played alongside his club-mate Trevor Brooking in the 1-1 draw at Wembley. His last appearance was in the 4-0 European Championship qualifying win in Luxembourg in November 1983 when his continuous running down the flank caused problems galore for the home side.

Devonshire's father, Les, was a professional footballer while Alan himself has a race horse named after him.

DEWHURST, Frederick 1885-89 ⑨ ⑩
Born: Fulwood near Preston, 16 December 1863
Died: Preston, 21 April 1895
Career: Preston junior football, Preston North End (amateur, August 1882, retired, May 1890); also played for Corinthians (seasons 1886-89) and Lancashire; was a schoolteacher at Preston Catholic Grammar School.

An amateur throughout his career, outside-left Fred Dewhurst scored in eight of his nine internationals for England. Five of his 10 goals came against Ireland, including one on his debut in a 6-1 win in March 1886. He also notched two against Scotland, his second in a splendid 5-0 victory at Hampden Park in March 1888. After Lindsay had saved from Goodall, the *North British Daily Mail* reporter wrote: "But Dewhurst was following up and lofted a goal over the 'keeper's head."

Dewhurst's main claim to fame was his goal for Preston in the 5-2 victory over Burnley in their opening game in the inaugural season of the Football League on 8 September 1888. Although Aston Villa's Gershom Cox had conceded an own-goal against Wolves a few minutes earlier, Dewhurst's effort was the first 'intentional' goal in the newly-formed competition. He gained an FA Cup winner's medal in 1889 and was the first Preston player to appear in a representative match when he lined up for Lancashire against London for the benefit of the Moorfield Colliery Relief Fund.

DEWHURST, Gerald Powys 1894-95 ①
Born: Greenwich, London, 14 February 1872
Died: Liverpool, 29 March 1956
Career: Repton College (seasons 1889-90), Trinity College/ Cambridge University (seasons 1890-94); also played for Corinthians (seasons 1892-95) and Liverpool Ramblers (seasons 1894-95); a cotton merchant by profession, based in Liverpool.

The weighty Gerald Dewhurst had one major fault – he held on to the ball far too long! Otherwise, he was a fine inside-forward, fast over the ground with a powerful right-foot shot. His only England appearance was in the 1-1 draw with Wales at The Queens Club, London in March 1895.

DICKINSON, James William, MBE 1948-57 ㊽
Born: Alton, Hants, 24 April 1925
Died: Alton, Hants, 8 November 1982
Career: Alton Secondary Modern School, Alton Youth Club (from August 1940), Portsmouth (amateur, October 1943, professional, January 1944, retired, May 1965); became the club's public relations officer, then Chief Executive, part-time secretary and finally manager (May 1977-May 1979).

Jimmy Dickinson amassed almost 850 first team appearances for Portsmouth in 22 years, 764 coming in the Football League, the second highest total for any one club, behind John Trollope who played in 770 games for Swindon Town. Dickinson, in fact, was the first footballer to amass 750 League appearances.

A quiet, super-efficient left-half who occasionally lined up at centre-half and left back, Dickinson helped Pompey win successive League Championships in 1949 and 1950 and the Second Division title in 1962. His brilliant performances in 1948-49 earned him a call-up to the England team, making his debut against Norway in May 1949. He went on to win 48 caps, making him Portsmouth's most capped English player of all-time. Never once booked or sent off, he was known as 'Gentleman Jim' and some of his performances at international level were excellent, but occasionally he did make the odd mistake!

He lost possession and conceded a throw-in just seconds after the start of the Hungary game at Wembley in November 1953. An England player never touched the ball again as the Magyars 'cut through the defence like a knife through butter' setting up Nandor Hidegkuti to fire a rocket high past a static Gil Merrick in goal.

After that Dickinson and his team-mates found it tough to contain Sandor Kocsis as Hungary out-paced, out-manoeuvred and out-thought England on their way to a resounding 6-3 win. He was also in the side which crashed 7-1 in Budapest six months later when he confessed that he was 'dog tired' after chasing around trying to get hold of the ball.

Playing against Belgium in the opening game of the 1954 World Cup in Switzerland and with extra-time fast running out, England were leading 4-3 but then inexplicably, Dickinson headed a looping free-kick into his own net to deny his team victory. "I completely misjudged the flight of the ball" he said afterwards.

Stanley Matthews, who confessed that Dickinson was one of the best left-halves he had seen play, wrote in his autobiography, "Jim was a gentleman, very strong in the tackle... his distribution was not special, and defending was the highlight of his make-up... a good marker of his inside-forward."

Dickinson, who also represented England in three B internationals and played for the Football League side on 11 occasions, was awarded the MBE in 1964. He suffered three heart attacks, prior to his death in 1982, and as a tribute the famous 'Pompey Chimes' rang hauntingly around St Mary's Church in the Portsmouth district of Fratton at a packed memorial service for the much-loved legend.

DIMMOCK, James Henry 1920-26 ③
Born: Edmonton, London, 5 December 1900
Died: Enfield, Middlesex, 23 December 1972
Career: Montague Road School, Park Avenue FC (August 1915), Gothic Works FC (late 1915), Edmonton Ramblers (March 1916), Tottenham Hotspur (amateur, July 1916, professional, May 1919); WW1 guest for Clapton Orient; Thames FC (August 1931), Clapton Orient (September 1932), Ashford (March 1934, retired, May 1934); later worked in the road haulage business.

Jimmy Dimmock holds a unique place in the history of Tottenham Hotspur by being the only player in the club's history to play 400 League games and score 100 League goals while adding 12 goals in 38 FA Cup matches to his tally.
    He also remains (at 20 years 139 days) the youngest Spurs player ever to appear in an FA Cup final, doing so in 1921 when Wolves were defeated by his solitary goal at Stamford Bridge. A week before the final Dimmock made his international debut against Scotland at the age of 20 years and 125 days to become the youngest Spurs player (at that time) to play for his country. His White Hart Lane colleague Bert Bliss also made his debut in this game but unfortunately their club form let them down badly as the Scots racked up a convincing 3-0 victory at Hampden Park. Surprisingly, he had to wait five years to gain his other two caps, against Wales (lost 3-1) and Belgium (won 5-3) in 1926. Dimmock, who also played in two international trials, sadly lost both his legs before his death in 1972.

DITCHBURN, Edwin George 1948-57 ⑥
Born: Gillingham, Kent, 24 October 1921
Died: Ipswich, Suffolk, 26 December 2005
Career: Kent Schools, Northfleet Paper Mills FC (August 1936), Tottenham Hotspur (groundstaff, May 1937, amateur, June 1938), Northfleet FC (loan, season 1938-39), Tottenham Hotspur (professional, May 1939); guest for Aberdeen, Birmingham City and Dartford during WW2; Romford (April 1959, then player-manager, July 1959-March 1965, player-coach, April-May 1965), Brentwood Town (August 1965, retired, May 1966); later ran a sports-outfitters business, a toys and games shop and also worked in printing.

The son of a professional boxer, goalkeeper Ted Ditchburn made over 500 first-team appearances for Spurs (including Wartime) during his 22 years' association with the London club. An ever present when Spurs gained promotion as Division Two champions in 1950 he then helped the team win the League a year later. He developed the 'short throw' that provided the starting block for Spurs' famous 'push and run' style of the early 1950s.
    Ditchburn, who had to fight for an England place with the likes of Bert Williams and Gil Merrick, gained six caps. His first, with club-mate Alf Ramsey, came in a 6-0 win over Switzerland at Highbury in December 1948; his last in a 5-2 win over Denmark in a World Cup qualifier at Molineux in December 1956 when he made four 'brilliant saves' according to the reporter in the local *Express & Star*. In between Ditchburn went to the 1950 World Cup as cover for the aforementioned Williams but never played. A broken finger ended his first-class career in August 1958.

DIX, Ronald William 1938-39 ① ①
Born: Bristol, 12 September 1912
Died: Bristol, 2 April 1998
Career: South Central Schools/Bristol, Bristol Schools, Gloucestershire Schools, Bristol Rovers (amateur, July 1927, professional, September 1929), Blackburn Rovers (May 1932), Aston Villa (with Arthur Cunliffe, May 1933), Derby County (February 1937),Tottenham Hotspur (June 1939); WW2 guest for Blackpool, Bradford Park Avenue, Bristol City, Chester, Liverpool Wrexham, York City and Liverpool; Reading (November 1947, retired, June 1949); went into business in Bristol.

A stocky, clever inside-forward of high consistency, Ronnie Dix holds the record for being the youngest goalscorer in Football League history, when he netted for Bristol Rovers v. Norwich City in March 1928, at the age of 15 years and 180 days. The recipient of one England cap, he replaced Len Goulden for the friendly against Norway at St James' Park, Newcastle in November 1938 and celebrated the occasion by scoring in a 4-0 win. In his club career Dix netted over 150 times in more than 450 senior appearances, having his best years with Bristol Rovers, Aston Villa and Derby. He represented England as a Schoolboy and helped Blackpool win the Wartime League North Cup in 1943.

DIXON, John Auger 1884-85 ①
Born: Grantham, 27 May 1861
Died: Nottingham, 8 June 1931
Career: Grantham Grammar, Nottingham High & Chigwell Schools, Notts County (amateur, June 1883, professional, August 1885, retired, injured, May 1888), also played for Corinthians seasons 1886-88; cricketer for Nottinghamshire (seasons 1882-1905); later an England Test selector and director of Dixon & Parke Ltd., clothing manufacturers of Nottingham.

A sprightly, hard-working inside or outside-left, Jack Dixon played once for England, replacing the injured Edward Bambridge in the 1-1 draw with Wales at Blackburn in March 1885. He played in 253 matches as captain and all-round cricketer for Notts (1882-1905), amassing 9,527 runs at an average of 24.18 and top-scoring with 268 not out v. Surrey in 1897, while taking 184 wickets at 27.60 apiece with a best return of 5-28 and securing 180 catches, the majority close to the wicket.

DIXON, Kerry Michael 1984-87 ⑧ ④
Born: Luton, 24 July 1961
Career: Chesham United (junior, August 1976), Tottenham Hotspur (apprentice, July 1977, professional, July 1978), Dunstable Town (1979), Reading (£20,000, July 1980), Chelsea (£150,000, August 1983, plus another £25,000, December 1983), Southampton (£575,000, July 1992), Luton Town (free, February 1993), Millwall (£25,000, March 1995), Watford (£25,000, January 1996), Doncaster Rovers (free, player-manager, August 1996-May 1997), Basildon United (briefly, August-October 1997), Boreham Wood (November 1997-May 1999), Hitchin Town (coach, 1999), Letchworth Town (manager, seasons 2000-02), later coach and/or manager at Hitchin Town (again), Dunstable Town (joint-manager), Icknield U14's (coach); also ran a football School in Dunstable and currently assists Pat Nevin and Ron Harris with organised tours of Stamford Bridge.

Kerry Dixon

Kerry Dixon's scoring feats for Chelsea earned him an England call-up against Mexico in an international tournament in June 1985, coming on as a second-half substitute for Glenn Hoddle in a 1-0 defeat in Mexico City. Three days later, the impressive striker scored twice and set up Bryan Robson for the other goal in England's 3-0 win over West Germany and he followed up with two more goals four days later in the 5-0 battering of the USA in Los Angeles. A member of the World Cup set-up in 1986, he played in five more internationals over the next fifteen months, but failed to find the net, and with Gary Lineker, Peter Beardsley and Mark Hateley seemingly ahead of him in the pecking order, his international career came to an abrupt end. At club level, Dixon was around for 16 years, during which time he scored 276 goals in 771 games, including 231 in 593 League matches. He had his best spell with Chelsea (1983-92) for whom he struck 191 goals in 421 appearances, helping the Blues twice win the Second Division Championship and the Full Members' Cup. He also played for England's U21 team.

DIXON, Lee Michael 1989-1998 ㉒

Born: Manchester, 17 March 1964
Career: Manchester & District Schools, Burnley (apprentice, May 1980, professional, July 1982), Chester City (free, February 1984), Bury (free, July 1985), Stoke City (£40,000, July 1986), Arsenal (£400,000, January 1988, retired, June 2002); now a BBC TV *Match of the Day* and *Football Focus* football pundit; plays golf at the Woburn club, has business interest in the Riverside Brasserie in Bray, Berkshire (originally with chef Heston Blumenthal) and has a holiday home in Marazion, Cornwall.

A fine attacking right-back, with strength, ability and courage, Lee Dixon made his England debut in April 1990 in a World Cup warm-up friendly against Czechoslovakia. He played well, but there was little hope of him being in the squad for the tournament as he was at least third in the list behind Gary Stevens and Paul Parker. Only injury to one of these two would have opened a door for Dixon to go to Italy and that didn't happen as the pair stayed fully fit throughout the competition. After the World Cup, new manager Graham Taylor immediately introduced Dixon, who scored a goal at Wembley in only his sixth international, an important 1-1 Euro 92 qualifying draw with the Republic of Ireland at Wembley in March 1991. In the same season, Arsenal's notoriously mean defence (with David Seaman keeping goal) won the League championship for the second time in three years. Dixon played in all the Euro 92 qualifiers, through which England qualified for the finals in Sweden. But as the finals approached, Dixon suffered an injury, allowing Stevens a route back into the side as the deadline for squad announcement approached. Taylor, though, named Dixon instead of Stevens in his provisional squad, but ultimately neither went to the tournament. Dixon pulled out injured, so Stevens was recalled, only for the Rangers full-back also to withdraw through injury. England ended up with no recognised right back in their squad and didn't get past the group stages. After the summer recess, a fit-again Dixon was back in the England team while also defending the League title within the familiar and feared Arsenal defence. Over the next few years England were over-blessed with right-backs

– Earl Barrett, Rob Jones, Warren Barton, Gary and Phil Neville, even Sol Campbell and Rio Ferdinand – leaving Dixon to fiddle his thumbs and hope! He eventually got a recall, playing for his country for the last time in a 2-0 home defeat by France in 1999 – five years after winning his 21st cap in a 7-1 win over San Marino, the year England failed again to qualify for the World Cup finals.

As a 'Gunner' he was suspended for the 1993 FA Cup final against Sheffield Wednesday, having being sent off in the semi-final victory over Spurs at Wembley. However, the game ended in a draw and Dixon played in the replay which Arsenal won 2-1.

All told, he appeared in 614 competitive matches for Arsenal (1988-2002), many of them as Nigel Winterburn's full-back partner. He helped the Gunners win two First Division titles, two Premierships, the FA Cup on three occasions, the League Cup, the European Cup Winners' Cup and twice lift the FA Charity Shield. He also played in four B internationals and during a wonderful career he amassed 860 club and international appearances – a magnificent record.

DOBSON, Alfred Thomas Carrick 1881-84 ④

Born: Sherwood, Nottinghamshire, 28 March 1859
Died: Basford, Nottingham, 22 October 1932
Career: Downside College near Bath, Notts County (amateur, August 1877-May 1885); also played for Corinthians (seasons 1881-85); a keen cyclist, he was associated with W.E. & F. Dobson, lace manufacturers and doublers in Nottingham and later a director of Wrights & Dobson Brothers (dyers, bleachers and dressers) also in Nottingham.

Although he suffered with poor eyesight, Alf Dobson was a safe full-back, fast and a good tackler whose myopia was not an undue handicap as it did not prevent him from gaining four England caps, the first in a 13-0 thrashing of Ireland in February 1882 when two of his 50-yard clearances led to goals. Two years later he played against the Irish again, starring in a 4-0 win.

DOBSON, Charles Frederick 1885-86 ①

Born: Basford, Nottingham, 9 September 1862
Died: Ealing, London, 18 May 1939
Career: Stoneyhurst College/Lancashire, Notts County (amateur, March 1880-April 1889); also played for Corinthians (seasons 1881-87); like his elder brother (above) he too, was associated with the family firm W.E. & F. Dobson; also a member of the Nottinghamshire County tennis and golf clubs.

A competitive, hard-working wing-half, Charlie Dobson won his only cap against Ireland in Belfast in March 1886, when he 'passed forward' to Ben Spilsbury to score one of his four goals in a resounding 6-1 victory.

Lee Dixon

DOBSON, John Martin 1973-75 ⑤

Born: Rishton near Blackburn, Lancs, 14 February 1948
Career: Clitheroe Grammar School, Lancashire Youths, Bolton Wanderers (apprentice, April 1963, professional, July 1966), Burnley (free, August 1967), Everton (£300,000, August 1974), Burnley (£100,000, August 1979), Bury (player-manager, March 1984-March 1989, retired as a player, May 1986); Northwich Victoria (manager for 39 days, June-July 1991), Bristol Rovers (manager for 12 games, July-October 1991), Burnley (Youth Development Officer, 1990s, then caretaker-manager, January 2010, later engaged on club's coaching staff).

Popularly known as 'Sir Dobbo', Martin Dobson was a tall, upright midfielder, a great 'thinker' who had a long and successful career which spanned almost 20 years, during which time he amassed 661 League appearances and scored 96 goals. In fact, after failing to get a game with Bolton, he played in 499 games for Burnley, helping the Clarets win the Second and Third Division championships. He gained the first of his five England caps in April 1974, in a 0-0 draw with Portugal – selected because of FA Cup commitments of other players. He impressed manager Sir Alf Ramsey enough to retain his place throughout the year, being one of the best midfielders on the pitch when England drew 2-2 with Argentina at Wembley. After that game Dobson said: "We hit the woodwork more times than a team of lumberjacks."
    Dobson also represented the Football League and England U23s.

DOGGART, Alexander Graham William 1923-24 ①

Born: Bishop Auckland, 2 June 1897
Died: Lancaster Gate, Bayswater, London, 7 June 1963
Career: Darlington Grammar School, Bishop's Stortford School (seasons 1912-16), Kings College/Cambridge University (1920-22); also played for Corinthians (seasons 1920-32), Darlington (briefly) and Bishop Auckland; member of the FA Council (becoming vice-president then chairman); also played cricket for Cambridge University, Durham County and Middlesex, and was on the committees of both the MCC and Sussex CC; a charted accountant by profession.

Brilliant at close dribbling, Alex Doggart had a wonderful left foot and regularly topped the scoring charts for the Corinthians; indeed he was perhaps the amateur club's greatest-ever scorer, bagging 160 goals in 170 matches. He was capped at inside-left against Belgium in Antwerp in November 1923 and had a hand in one of the goals in a 2-2 draw. Doggart, who also played in four Amateur internationals, died while attending an FA committee meeting. His brother, Jimmy, became a distinguished ear, nose and throat surgeon while his eldest son, Hubert, became a schoolmaster and cricketer who played in two Test Matches for England.

DORIGO, Anthony Robert 1989-91 ⑮

Born: Melbourne, Australia, 31 December 1965
Career: Birmingham & District Schools, Aston Villa (apprentice, July 1981, professional, July 1983), Chelsea (£475,000, July 1987), Leeds United (£300,000, May 1991), Torino/Italy (free, June 1997), Derby County (free, October 1998), Stoke City (free, July 2000, retired, May 2002); worked for a vehicle leasing firm, later a soccer pundit on Italian football on 'Bravo' and Channel 5; was involved in property developing in Portugal; now holds a UEFA Pro Licence, the highest-level managerial qualification in association football and is the Managing-Director of Pro-Vision Football Ltd (with 360 players listed).

Left-back Tony Dorigo was a class act who made his England debut as a second-half substitute for Stuart Pearce in the 2-1 win over Yugoslavia at Wembley in December 1989. A year earlier he had been a surprise inclusion in the squad for the European Championships as cover for Kenny Sansom, after regular deputy Pearce pulled out through injury. He was also part of the 1990 World Cup squad, playing in the third place play-off defeat by Italy before winning his fifth and final cap against Hungary two months later. He made well over 600 appearances for his six major clubs, 535 in the League, and helped Chelsea win the Second Division Championship and the ZDS Cup and Leeds United the First Division title. He also played for England in 11 U21 and seven B internationals.

DORRELL, Arthur Reginald 1924-26 ④ ①

Born: Small Heath, Birmingham, 30 March 1896
Died: Alum Rock, Birmingham, 13 September 1942
Career: Belper Road & Loxton Street Schools/Leicester, Carey Hall Sunday School/Leicester, RASC/Army (from 1916), Aston Villa (professional, May 1919), Port Vale (June 1931, retired, August 1932); was landlord of The Pelham Arms, Alum Rock, Birmingham (1932 until his death).

Arthur Dorrell was a fast and clever outside-left who formed a famous wing-partnership with Billy Walker. Among the most unemotional of players, Dorrell won his first cap, alongside Walker, in a comprehensive 4-0 victory over Belgium at The Hawthorns in December 1924. The pair played together in the next match (a 2-1 win over Wales) and later in the year they lined up against France in Paris and Ireland in Belfast, Dorrell scoring an excellent goal in the 3-2 win over the French.
    During his 12 years with Villa (1919-31) he scored 65 goals in 390 appearances, gaining an FA Cup winner's medal in 1920. He also represented the Football League. His father, William, also played for Villa and his brother for Hinckley Athletic.

DOUGLAS, Bryan 1957-63 ㊱ ⑪

Born: Blackburn, 27 May 1934
Career: St Bartholomew's Junior & Blakey Moor Secondary Modern Schools/Blackburn, Lower Darwen Youth Club (April 1950), Blackburn Rovers (professional, April 1952), Great Harwood (June 1969, retired May 1991); became a sales representative with a stationery company; now lives in Darwen.

Some people say that Bryan Douglas was one of the finest ball-playing wingers of the late 1950s/early '60s. A terrific little player, with bags of skill, he could play on both flanks and also inside-right. He scored 111 goals in 503 appearances for Blackburn up to 1969, helping them gain promotion in 1958 and reach the FA Cup final two years later. Inheriting the mantle of Messrs. Matthews and Finney in the England team, he won the first of his 36 caps against Wales in Cardiff in October 1957 when he had a 'storming game' and scored twice in an emphatic 4-0 win.
    When France were thumped 4-0 at Wembley in November 1957, Douglas was again brilliant. He set up three goals with measured crosses from the right and despite being one of the smallest players on the pitch he rose majestically to head in a high centre from his club colleague Ronnie Clayton in a 4-0 thrashing of Scotland at Hampden Park in April 1958.

He played in three of the four World Cup games in Sweden in the summer but soon afterwards lost his place in the forward-line when manager Walter Winterbottom decided to give chances to a host of right-wingers including Warren Bradley, Doug Holden, Norman Deeley and John Connelly. Recalled to duty at the end of the 1959-60 season, Douglas then held his place, injuries apart, right through to the last World Cup game v. Brazil in June 1962. After that, under Alf Ramsey, he appeared in just three more internationals, scrambling a dramatic late equaliser in his penultimate game with the World champions Brazil at Wembley in May 1963. He also netted in his last international, an 8-1 drubbing of Switzerland a month later. Douglas, who was a great favourite with the supporters, also played in one B and five U23 internationals and represented the Football League.

DOWNING, Stewart 2004-13 ㉞

Born: Middlesbrough, 22 July 1984
Career: Middlesbrough (apprentice, July 1999, professional, July 2001), Sunderland (loan, October-December 2003), Aston Villa (£12m, July 2009)

Wide player Stewart Downing made his England debut in February 2005 against the Netherlands at Villa Park, coming on as a second-half substitute for Shaun Wright-Phillips. Unfortunately he suffered a set-back in May 2005 when he was injured in training on tour in the USA. Sidelined for quite some time, he recovered in time to feature

in the 2006 World Cup, primarily as a back-up for Joe Cole, coming on in the second-half against Paraguay and Trinidad and Tobago. He made his first start in August 2006 against Greece, having a hand in three of the goals in a 4-0 win.

He played in three Euro 2008 qualifiers, but his performances drew criticism from the press, many stating that he was only being selected due to his 'friendship' with manager Steve McClaren. However, Downing was subsequently selected by Fabio Capello for the game in France in March 2008 and also, alongside with his Middlesbrough team-mate David Wheater, for the friendlies against the USA and Trinidad and Tobago, receiving the nod ahead of Ashley Young in the latter when he assisted in the first two goals, winning praise from the press who had previously slated him and also from his Italian boss who 'was most impressed by Downing.'

In February 2011, Downing was back on the international scene, playing the last 25 minutes of the 2-1 win in Denmark.

He also starred for his country in the 2003 European U19 Championships, gained eight U21 and two B caps, but didn't play in Euro 2012, being an unused substitute.

After scoring 22 goals in 234 appearances for Middlesbrough, Downing joined Aston Villa in the summer of 2009 but missed the first half of the season with a broken foot.

DOWNS, Richard Walter 1920-21 ①

Born: Middridge, Newton Aycliffe, County Durham, 13 August 1886
Died: Hove, Sussex, 24 March 1949
Career: Newton Aycliffe Youths, Crook Town (amateur, June 1901), Shildon Athletic (1906), Barnsley (professional, May 1908), Everton (£3,000, March 1920), Brighton & Hove Albion (August 1924, retired May 1925); coached in Europe during the late 1920s.

Renowned for his sliding tackles and fly-kick volleys, full-back Dickie Downs whose muscular legs were like tree-trunks, skippered Barnsley for several years and helped them win the FA Cup in 1912 before moving to Goodison Park. His first season with Everton was a huge success and after a successful international trial, he won his only cap against Ireland in October 1920 at Roker Park. He did well in a 2-0 win. He also represented the Football League on two occasions.

DOYLE, Michael 1975-77 ⑤

Born: Manchester, 25 November 1946
Died: Ashton-under-Lyne, 27 June 2011
Career: Stockport Boys (season 1961-62), Manchester City (apprentice, April 1962, professional, May 1964), Stoke City (£50,000, June 1978), Bolton Wanderers (£10,000, January 1982), Rochdale (August 1983, retired, May 1984); became sales manager for the sports company, Slazenger, also commentator on local radio.

Hard-tackling defensive right-half Mick Doyle made 572 appearances for Manchester City between 1964 and 1978. He helped City win both the First and Second Division titles, two League Cups, the FA Cup, European Cup Winners' Cup and FA Charity Shield, scoring in the 1970 League Cup final win over West Bromwich Albion and skippering the team to victory in the Cup Winners' Cup final against Real Madrid. He won the first of his five England caps against Wales in March 1976, being one of seven debutants named by Don Revie in a 2-1 win at Wrexham. His last outing was in the 2-0 defeat by Holland eleven months later when England's defence was given a pasting by Messrs. Cruyff, Neeskens and Co. Doyle also played in one unofficial and eight U23 internationals.

DRAKE, Edward Joseph 1934-38 ⑤ ⑥

Born: Southampton, 16 August 1912
Died: Raynes Park, Merton, London, 30 May 1995
Career: Southampton Schools, Southampton Gas Works FC (August 1928),Winchester City (April 1929), Southampton (professional, November 1931), Arsenal (£6,500, March 1934; served as a Flight Lieutenant in the RAF during WW2; retired, injured, May 1945; appointed coach at Highbury for 1945-46 season); Hendon (manager, August 1946), Reading (manager, June 1947-June 1952), Chelsea (manager, June 1952-September 1961); worked as a turf accountant, 1960s; CF Barcelona/Spain (assistant-manager, January-June 1970); employed as a Life Insurance salesman in London (from 1970); Fulham (reserve team manager, November 1972, Chief Scout, July 1975-June 1985; also club Director from 1979 and later President); played county cricket for Hampshire (seasons 1931-36).

One of the toughest centre-forwards in the game during the 1930s, Ted Drake never gave up, always chasing and harassing defenders. Legendary goalkeeper Frank Swift believed he was one of the best central strikers he's ever faced, saying: "There was no quarter given or asked, but it was a delight to play against him."

Give him a through ball to chase and he'd go after it like a charging bull. He was fearless and strong, and often suffered leg injuries, quite regularly starting a game with bandages on both ankles and knee-caps.

Drake was brought down inside the penalty-area by Italian goalkeeper Ceresoli in the very first minute of his international debut in the 'Battle of Highbury' in November 1934. Brook, however, missed from the spot. Sixty seconds later Drake was involved in a tackle with centre-half Monti and was blamed for breaking the defender's toe. As a result the Italians 'sought retribution'. But Drake had the last laugh, putting his side 3-0 up by half-time after Brook had made amends for his penalty miss with two early goals. The following season Drake played in England's 2-1 victory over Ireland and he also had a particularly good game against Aston Villa in mid-December 1935. He was suffering from a knee injury but his manager George Allison decided to risk him. By half-time he had scored a hat-trick. Drake scored three more in the first 15 minutes of the second-half, and also hit the bar. When he told the referee the ball had crossed the line, the official replied: "Don't be greedy, isn't six enough?". In the very last minute Drake scored again from Cliff Bastin's low cross, to achieve the feat of bagging seven goals in an away League - an amazing achievement, which has never been matched.

Drake returned to the England team against Wales in February 1936 but failed to score and was replaced by George Camsell in the next game against Scotland. Stoke's Freddie Steele also occupied the centre-forward position until Drake regained his place for the game against Hungary in December 1936, rewarding the selectors with a hat-trick in the 6-2 victory. And he followed up with two more goals in a 4-2 win over France in his international in Paris in May 1938.

With Dixie Dean also around at the same time, Drake's England career was relatively short, but it was great while it lasted. For Arsenal, Drake was often brilliant. In his first season at Highbury (1933-34) he helped the Gunners clinch the League title and his goal haul of 44 in 1934-35 remains a club record to this day. He scored the only goal of the 1936 FA Cup final against Sheffield United and gained a First Division championship medal two years later as well as receiving two FA Charity Shield winner's medals. All told he netted 230 goals in 314 games for Arsenal (all competitions including Wartime). Later, as a manager, Drake guided Chelsea to

their first-ever League title in 1955. And it was he who discovered future England internationals Barry Bridges, Peter Bonetti, Jimmy Greaves, Bobby Tambling and Terry Venables. His son, Bobby, played for Fulham in the 1960s.

DUBLIN, Dion 1997-99 ④

Born: Leicester, 22 April 1969
Career: Wigston Fields (August 1986), Oakham United (August 1987), Norwich City (professional, March 1988), Cambridge United (free, August 1988), Barnet (loan, 1988), Manchester United (£1m, August 1992), Coventry City (£2m, September 1994), Aston Villa (£5.75m, November 1998), Millwall (loan, March-May 2002), Leicester City (May 2004), Celtic (January-May 2006), Norwich City (September 2006, retired, May 2008); now works in the media as a pundit for Sky Sports.

It was thought that Dion Dublin, who won the Golden Boot by finishing as the Premier League's joint top scorer in 1997-98, would be in Glenn Hoddle's squad for the World Cup finals in France that summer but he was controversially excluded. The tall striker had earlier made his international debut, along with Michael Owen, in the 2-0 defeat by Chile at Wembley in February 1998 and he also played in the two King Hassan Cup games against Morocco and Belgium before gaining his final cap against the Czech Republic at Wembley in November 1998 when his co-strikers were Ian Wright, Paul Merson and substitute Robbie Fowler. Dublin retired in 2008 with 232 goals to his name in 742 club games. He had his best years with Cambridge United, Coventry and Aston Villa, yet surprisingly his only medal came in 1991 when Cambridge won the Third Division championship.

DUCAT, Andrew 1909-21 ⑥

Born: Brixton, Surrey, 16 February 1886
Died: St John's Wood, Marylebone, London, 23 July 1942
Career: Brewer Road & Crompton House Schools/Southend, Westcliffe Athletic (April 1901), Southend Athletic (August 1903), Woolwich Arsenal (amateur, January 1905, professional, February 1905), Aston Villa (£1,000, June 1912); WW1 guest for Birmingham, Bellis & Morcom FC, Grimsby Town and Alexander Pontorium FC; Fulham (May 1921, retired, May 1924; then manager, May 1924-July 1926), Corinthian Casuals (re-instated as an amateur, August 1926-May 1927); became a sports coach at Eton College; ran a sports outfitter's in Birmingham and also licensee of a pub and a hotel; played county cricket for Surrey (seasons 1906-31).

Andy Ducat started out as a forward but after switching to right half he became a regular in the Arsenal team and during his time with the Gunners, he won three caps for England, with his debut coming in a 6-1 win over Ireland in Belfast in February 1910. In his second international, against Wales the following month, Ducat scored the only goal in a 1-0 win.

In April 1920, he produced one of his best displays for his country, in the 5-4 win over Scotland at Hillsborough. He had a hand in two goals and also struck the outside of a post with a fine right-footed drive from 20 yards. His last England game came in the 2-0 win over Ireland later that year.

He gained an FA Cup winner's medal with Aston Villa in 1920.
Between 1906 and 1931, he scored 23,373 runs for Surrey including 52 centuries with a top score of 306 not out for an average of 38.63. He also took 21 wickets and claimed 205 catches. He played in one Test Match for England v. Australia in 1921.

Sadly, Ducat died playing cricket at Lord's for Surrey Home Guard against Sussex Home Guard. He is the only player to have died during a game at the Middlesex county ground.

DUNN, Arthur Tempest Blakiston 1882-92 ④ ②
Born: Whitby, Yorkshire, 12 August 1860
Died: Ludgrove, London, 20 February 1902
Career: Eton College (seasons 1880-83), Trinity College/Cambridge University (seasons 1883-86); played for Old Etonians (seasons 1881-84), Granta FC (seasons 1884-86), Corinthians (seasons 1886-90); also represented Cambridgeshire and Norfolk; schoolmaster by profession and founder of Ludgrove School in 1892.

A Cambridge 'Blue' and initially a fleet-footed centre-forward, clever at dribbling, with a deadly shot, Arthur Dunn scored twice on his England debut in a 7-0 win over Ireland in February 1883. In fact, he was a winner in each of his four games for his country when a total of 21 goals were scored – although in his last two internationals v. Wales and Scotland in March and April 1892, Dunn played at right-back.
   He appeared in successive FA Cup finals for Old Etonians, gaining a winner's medal in 1882, a loser's prize the following year. After his death the Arthur Dunn Cup was instituted in his memory. This is a competition for old boys of various leading independent schools and was first competed for in 1902.

DUNN, David John Ian 2002-03 ①
Born: Great Harwood, Lancs, 27 December 1979
Career: Blackburn Rovers (apprentice, April 1996, professional, September 1997), Birmingham City (£5.5m, July 2003), Blackburn Rovers (£2.2m, January 2007)

Owing to a long list of midfield players available for selection, David Dunn won only one England cap - in the 1-1 friendly draw with Portugal in September 2002. A hard-working player, he has also represented his country at U21 level, being in the squad for the European Championships in Slovakia in 2000. Dunn has gained both FA Youth and League Cup winner's medals with Blackburn.

DUXBURY, Michael 1983-85 ⑩
Born: Blackburn, 1 September 1959
Career: Manchester United (apprentice, May 1975, professional, October 1976), Blackburn Rovers (August 1990), Bradford City (January 1992-May 1994), Hong Kong Golden FC/Hong Kong

(seasons 1994-96); coached with Manchester United Soccer Schools programme in Hong Kong and Dubai and was also engaged as a P.E. teacher at a Bolton independent school.

Mike Duxbury will always be remembered as being a courageous battler but never those important words like talented or successful. His brief cameo in the England team ended after the arrival of Gary Stevens into the national squad.
   Partnering Kenny Sansom at full-back, he made a 'quiet, untroubled' debut in the 4-0 win in Luxembourg in November 1983 and later added nine more caps to his tally, all in 1984, perhaps having his best games as Kenny Sansom's partner in the 2-0 and 5-0 wins over Brazil in Rio de Janeiro and Finland at Wembley respectively.
   The ever-reliable Duxbury made 382 appearances for Manchester United.

DYER, Kieron Courtney 1999-2008 ㉝
Born: Ipswich, Suffolk, 29 December 1978
Career: Ipswich Town (apprentice, June 1995, professional, January 1997), Newcastle United (£6m, July 1999), West Ham United (£6m, August 2007), Queen's Park Rangers (July 2011), Middlesbrough (January 2013)

After representing his country at Youth, U21 and B levels, attacking midfielder Kieron Dyer made his senior debut for England in the 6-0 win over Luxembourg in September 1999. A year later he appeared in the 2002 World Cup finals and then starred in Euro 2004. However, after almost two years without making an international appearance, his outstanding form for Newcastle earned him a recal to Steve McClaren's squad against Spain in February 2007. He started in place of Wayne Rooney and was the high point in an otherwise lacklustre England performance which ended in a 1-0 defeat. His last cap came in August 2007 v. Germany.
   Dyer, who struggled with injuries for three years from 2008, made 113 appearances for Ipswich, exactly 250 for Newcastle but barely one tenth of that total for West Ham. He joined newly-promoted QPR on the same day as Jay Bothroyd in August 2011.

EARLE, Stanley George James 1923-25 ②
Born: Stratford, London, 6 September 1897
Died: Colchester, Essex, 18 September 1971
Career: Goodwin Road School/West Ham; Clapton (amateur, August 1913); served in Army during WW1; continued to play for Clapton as well as Arsenal (jointly, between March 1922 and July 1924), West Ham United (August 1924), Clapton Orient (May 1932), Walthamstow Avenue (player-coach, August 1933-May 1934); Leyton Orient (manager, July 1934-May 1936); thereafter, ran a business in Brightlingsea, Essex, for several years.

A well-built inside-right who represented England as a Schoolboy (1912) and also as an amateur (1923-24), Stan Earle made an impressive senior debut in a 3-1 win over France in Paris in May 1924… shortly after gaining an FA Amateur Cup winner's medal with Clapton Orient. His father, Harry Earle, a goalkeeper, played for Clapton and Notts County.

EASTHAM, George Edward, OBE 1962-66 ⑲ ②

Born: Blackpool, 23 September 1936
Career: Revoe Primary & Arnold Grammar Schools/Blackpool,
Blackpool & District Schools, Bispham Church team/Blackpool,
Highfield Youth Club (season 1951-52), Blackpool (trial, July-August
1952), Bolton Wanderers (trial, May 1953), Ards (Ireland, amateur,
April 1954, professional, September 1955), Newcastle United (£9,000,
May 1956), Arsenal (£47,500, October 1960), Stoke City (£30,000,
August 1966), Cape Town Spurs/South Africa (loan, player-coach,
February 1971), Hellenic FC/South Africa (player-manager, February
1971), Stoke City (October 1971, then player/assistant-manager until
January 1972, retired as a player, March 1977, continued as manager
until January 1978); emigrated to South Africa in the summer of 1978;
started his own sportswear business in Johannesburg called Hat Trick;
also vice-president of the Arsenal Supporters' club.

When capped by England against Brazil in May 1963, George
Eastham emulated his father by playing for his country in a senior
international (see below). The highly-skilful midfielder helped
orchestrate things from his deep-lying position and was a key figure
in most of the games in which he played. He was outstanding in
quick-fire wins over Czechoslovakia, East Germany, Wales, The Rest
of the World and Northern Ireland during the next six months, starred
against Uruguay, Portugal, the Republic of Ireland (when he scored in
a 3-1 win) and the USA in 1964 and played his part in a very good
2-0 victory over Spain in Madrid in late 1965 when Norman Hunter
became the first player to make his England debut as a substitute.

A League Cup winner at the age of 35 with Stoke in 1972,
Eastham made 239 appearances for the Potters. He was awarded
the OBE in 1975.

EASTHAM, George Richard 1934-35 ①

Born: Blackpool, 13 September 1913
Died: Johannesburg, South Africa, 12 January 2000
Career: Cambridge Juniors/Blackpool (August 1927), South
Shore Wednesday (September 1929), Bolton Wanderers
(professional, May 1932), Brentford (June 1937), Blackpool
(November 1938); WW2 guest for Birmingham, Bolton Wanderers,
Brentford, York City, Mansfield Town, Millwall and Queens Park
Rangers; Swansea Town (August 1947), Rochdale (June 1948),
Lincoln City (December 1948), Hyde United (May 1950), Ards
(player-manager, July 1953, retired as a player, May 1955,
continued as manager until October 1958), Accrington Stanley
(manager, October 1958-June 1959), Lisburn Distillery (manager,
June 1959-March 1964), Ards (manager, November 1964-March
1970), Stoke City (scout, April 1970-October 1971), Hellenic FC/
South Africa (manager, November 1971-May 1972), Glentoran
(manager, seasons 1972-74); returned to live in South Africa.

George 'Diddler' Eastham was a crafty inside-forward whose
only England cap came against Holland in Amsterdam in
May 1935 when he partnered Portsmouth's right-winger
Fred Worrell in the 1-0 win. He made 131 appearances in five
years for Bolton.

ECKERSLEY, William 1950-54 ⑰

Born: Southport, Lancs, 16 July 1926
Died: Blackburn, 25 October 1982
Career: High Park FC/Southport (during WW2), Blackburn Rovers
(amateur, November 1947, professional, March 1948, retired,
injured, February 1961); became a private car driver in Blackburn.

Former lorry driver and one-club man, Bill Eckersley was a slightly-
built, strong and fair tackling left-back who made 432 appearances
for Blackburn Rovers in 14 years. He also gained 17 full caps for
England, making his debut in a 1950 World Cup encounter against
Spain. He partnered Alf Ramsey in several of his internationals but
was unfortunate to come up against one of the finest overseas
right-wingers in the game, Budai, when Hungary crushed England
6-3 at Wembley in November 1953. That, in fact, was Eckersley's
last game for his country; Roger Byrne replaced him.

Stan Matthews once said: "Bill was one of the most difficult
opponents I faced. I never had a good game against him; he always
gave me a tough time. He was a fine defender." His ashes were
scattered over the Ewood Park pitch in an emotional ceremony prior
to a first team game in 1982.

EDWARDS, Duncan 1954-58 ⑱ ⑤

Born: Dudley, Worcs, 1 October 1936
Died: Munich, Germany, 21 February 1958
Career: Wolverhampton Street Secondary Modern Boys' School/
Dudley, Dudley Schools, Brierley Hill & District Schools (seasons
1950-52), Manchester United (amateur, June 1952, professional,
October 1953 until his death)

English football has never sustained a greater individual loss than
was caused by the tragic death of Duncan Edwards. By the time
he was 21, the immensely skilled left-half (or inside-left) was a
permanent fixture in the England team, had already made over
100 appearances for Manchester United, gained two League
Championship winner's medals and played in an FA Cup final.
Hugely talented, as strong as an ox, bold, brave and confident, he
packed a terrific shot and feared no-one.

One of the first graduates of England's U23 set-up, Edwards
made his international debut in that brilliant 7-2 win over
Scotland at Wembley in April 1955 at the
age of 18 years
and 183 days. The *Glasgow Herald*
reporter, covering the match, thought
that Stanley Matthews (the oldest player
on the pitch) and four-goal hero Dennis
Wilshaw were both terrific efforts and he
also praised the young Edwards, saying
'He played with the confidence of a
30 year-old and was the driving force
of the team continually powering his
way into the opposition half.'

Two years later, in the same
fixture, Matthews and Edwards
played together for the last time,
and on this occasion the Scots were
defeated 2-1, Edwards having the
pleasure of scoring the winning goal.
With six minutes remaining, in typical style,
he picked up the ball in centre-field, charged
forward 15 yards, leaving defenders in his wake,
before smashing home a thunderous shot. It flew
past Scotland's 'keeper Tommy Younger like a rocket
and the goal has been ranked as one the best ever
seen at Wembley.

Duncan Edwards

In the summer of 1956 Edwards was again a match-winner with another towering performance against West Germany in Berlin. One of his one-man cavalry charges in the 20th minute, into the heart of the German defence, ended with a crashing shot high into the net to set up a 3-1 win.

Wrote Norman Giller: "He strode onto the pitch like a colossus and dominated the entire game both in defence and midfield."

When England beat Denmark 5-2 in a World Cup qualifier at Molineux in December 1956, Edwards, being watched by his family and friends, scored with two booming shots, had another brilliant effort saved by the 'keeper and almost snapped a post in half with a 25-yard free-kick.

Edwards' last England goal was scored in a 3-2 defeat by Northern Ireland at Wembley in November 1957 and later in the month he played his last international, in a 4-0 victory over France.

Then, as we all know, he was seriously injured in the Munich air crash in February 1958. Sadly, he failed to get out of his hospital bed in Germany and as a result not only Manchester United but also England and world football on the whole, had lost one of the great players of his era.

After playing in a local derby against Manchester City at Old Trafford in February 1955, Edwards was caught by the police riding home on his bicycle without lights. He was fined five shillings (25p) by the courts and two weeks' wages by Manchester United for bringing their name into disrepute.

EDWARDS, John Hawley 1873-74 ①

Born: Shrewsbury, 12 March 1850
Died: Old Colwyn, Denbighshire, 14 January 1893
Career: Shropshire Wanderers (August 1866), Shrewsbury (seasons 1867-70), Wanderers (seasons 1870-76); also played cricket for Shropshire; admitted solicitor in 1871, acted as treasurer to the FWA and clerk of the Shrewsbury magistrate court (1874 until his death).

Jack Edwards was a utility forward and despite being born on the 'Welsh' side of the English-Wales border, made his England debut as a late replacement for John Wylie in a 2-1 defeat by Scotland in March 1874. However, two years later, after certain paper work had been checked, he played for his 'home country' of Wales against Scotland – making him the first dual international. 'There are few better dribblers in this part of the country, his only fault being that he prefers a crooked course not a straight one' wrote a journalist for the *Shrewsbury Chronicle*. Edwards, who won the FA Cup with the Wanderers in 1876, played for Wales against Scotland in Glasgow the following week to become the first player to represent two different countries at international level.

Edwards died from a throat infection at the age of 42.

Bob Evans, Stuart McCrae and John Reynolds later played international football for England and for one other country.

EDWARDS, Willis 1925-30 ⑯

Born: Newton near Alfreton, 28 April 1903
Died: Leeds, 27 September 1988
Career: Newton Rangers (from August 1919), Chesterfield (£10, April 1922), Leeds United (£1,500, March 1925, retired, May 1946; assistant trainer, May 1946, then manager, April 1947-April 1948; assistant-trainer, May 1948-May 1960); worked briefly in a jam factory.

Willis Edwards was an exceptionally talented footballer, a right-half for the connoisseur who served Leeds United for 15 years: 1924-39, during which time he appeared in 444 competitive matches. The 500th player to win a full England cap, he made his debut at the age of 22 against Wales in March 1926 and was arguably the best player in his position between the wars, his trapping, control and distribution being a delight to watch. He was outstanding when England battered Belgium 9-1 in May 1927 and likewise when France were whipped 6-0 later in the month. He also helped destroy the French 5-1 in May 1928 and was by far the game's star player when Wales were blitzed 6-0 in his last international in November 1929.

Edwards also represented the Football League on 11 occasions.

EHIOGU, Ugochuku 1995-2002 ④ ①

Born: Hackney, London, 3 November 1972
Career: West Bromwich Albion (apprentice, April 1988, professional, July 1989), Aston Villa (£40,000, July 1991), Middlesbrough (£8m, October 2000), Leeds United (loan, November 2006-January 2007), Glasgow Rangers (January 2007-January 2008), Sheffield United (January 2008-May 2009), MK Dons (trial, July 2009; retired, August 2009).

Ugo Ehiogu holds the record for most appearances for England without ever starting a game – four between 23 May 1996 and 27 March 2002.

The tall Aston Villa defender made his senior debut against China in Beijing in May 1996, coming on as a second-half substitute for Tony Adams. He bagged his only international goal in a 3-0 win

over Spain on his own patch at Villa Park in February 2001. He also represented England in one B and 15 U21 matches and in fact, was the first black player ever to skipper an England team, leading the U21 side against Holland at Fratton Park Portsmouth, in April 1993.

At club level, he made 302 appearances for Villa and 151 for Middlesbrough, winning the League Cup with both clubs.

ELLERINGTON, William 1948-49 ②

Born: Southampton, 30 June 1923
Career: Barnes School, Sunderland Technical College, Fatfield Juniors (season 1938-39), Sunderland (amateur, June 1939), Southampton (amateur, September 1940, professional, September 1945, player-coach, May 1956, retired as a player, May 1957, first team trainer, from June 1968, then club scout, August 1973-May 1978).

The son of a former Darlington, Middlesbrough and Nelson professional, right-back Bill Ellerington won his two England caps in May 1949, partnering Johnny Aston in wins over Norway in Oslo and France in Paris. He competed with Alf Ramsey at Southampton and they remained close friends for many years. Ellerington, who also represented the Football League twice and played once for England's B team, made 239 senior appearances for Saints. The scout who 'found' Mick Channon, at 2012 he was one of the oldest living former England internationals.

ELLIOTT, George Washington 1912-20 ③

Born: Sunderland, 7 January 1889
Died: Middlesbrough, 27 November 1948
Career: Redcar Crusaders (April 1906), South Bank (July 1907), Middlesbrough (professional, August 1909, retired, August 1925); WW1 guest for Bradford, Fulham and Celtic; became cargo superintendent in Middlesbrough's dockland.

George Elliott retired after scoring 213 goals in 365 games for Middlesbrough whom he served as a cultured inside or centre-forward for 16 years. He won his first England cap, alongside Charlie Buchan, in a 2-1 defeat by Ireland in February 1913. Unfortunately he failed to produce his club form in any of his three internationals.

ELLIOTT, William Henry 1951-53 ⑤ ③

Born: Bradford, 20 March 1925
Died: Sunderland, 21 January 2008
Career: Thornbury Boys & Lapage Street Schools/Bradford, Thornbury Boys FC (August 1938), Bradford Park Avenue (amateur, May 1939, professional, March 1942), Burnley (£23,000, August 1951), Sunderland (£26,000, June 1953), Wisbech Town (July 1959), Libya (national team coach, October 1961-May 1963), Sheffield Wednesday (scout, season 1963-64), US Forces/Germany (coach, seasons 1964-66), Daring FC/Brussels (trainer-manager, July 1966-January 1968), Sunderland (trainer-coach, January 1968-June 1973), FC Brann/Norway (coach, August 1974-September 1978), Sunderland (caretaker-manager, December 1978-May 1979), Darlington (manager, June 1979-June 1983).

Billy Elliott scored in the last minute of his third international against Northern Ireland in October 1952 to earn England a 2-2 draw in a dramatic match in Belfast. Five month earlier he had starred in the famous 3-2 win over Austria in Vienna and in November 1952 he netted twice in a resounding 5-0 win over Belgium. Mainly a direct, penetrative left-winger, he also performed at left-back and left-half where his crisp and timely tackling was a key factor in his play. His club career realised over 500 appearances (443 in the League). He also represented the Football League on four occasions and was the only Burnley player to be sent off in 20 years when he was dismissed in a League game in 1955. Elliott was involved in football for 40 years (1939-79).

EVANS, Robert Ernest 1910-12 ④ ①

Born: Chester, 21 November 1885
Died: Chester, 28 November 1965
Career: Saltney Ferry (April 1899), Bretton FC (August 1900), Saltney Works FC (August 1902), Chester (June 1905), Wrexham (professional, July 1905), Aston Villa (£30, March 1906), Sheffield United (£1,000 plus Peter Kyle, October 1908); WW1 guest for Tranmere Rovers (season 1916-17) and Sandycroft FC (season 1918-19); Crichton's Athletic (£25, May 1921), Brookhirst FC (manager, June 1922-May 1923), Saltney Ferry (May 1923, retired, May 1924); later worked as a welfare supervisor, and played for Shell Mex, Ellesmere Port, and was later trainer to the team which included Joe Mercer.

Bob Evans was a six-foot tall outside-left with a long, raking stride and powerful shot. Prior to playing for England he had lined up in 10 full internationals for Wales (1906-10) before it was discovered he was born on the English side of the border. He scored on his England debut v. Ireland in February 1911 and gained an FA Cup winner's medal with Sheffield United four years later.
John Hawley Edwards, Stuart Macrae and John Reynolds are three other footballers who all represented England and one other country in a full international.

EWER, Frederick Harold 1923-25 ②

Born: West Ham, London, 30 September 1898
Died: Peckham, London, 29 January 1971
Career: East End Boys (seasons 1916-19), London Casuals (August 1919-May 1923), Corinthians (August 1923-May 1932); later a member of the Stock Exchange

Fred Ewer also gained 14 caps as an amateur for England between 1924 and 1930. A wing-half, full of grit and determination, despite suffering many injuries during his career, he always came up smiling. A fighter to the end, he made over 100 appearances for the Corinthians and was outstanding in each of his two full internationals, the first against France in Paris in May 1924 (won 3-1) and his second against Belgium at The Hawthorns nine months later when he laid on two goals in a 4-0 win.

FAIRCLOUGH, Percy 1877-78 ①

Born: Mile End, London, 1 February 1858
Died: Belgravia, London, 22 June 1947
Career: Forest School XI (season 1876-77), Old Foresters (seasons 1877-79), Corinthians (seasons 1879-89); also played for Essex County and London; member of the Stock Exchange for 40 years as partner in the firm Fairclough, Dodd and Jones.

Percy Fairclough was described as a 'ponderous forward with a powerful but erratic kick who had the knack of charging well.' He didn't fare too well in his only international, a 7-2 defeat by Scotland in Glasgow in March 1878. He died as a result of a road accident at the age of 89.

FAIRHURST, David Liddle 1933-34 ①

Born: Blyth, Northumberland, 20 July 1906
Died: Blyth, 26 October 1972
Career: New Delaval Villa (July 1919), Blyth Spartans (August 1922), Walsall (professional, June 1927), Newcastle United (£1,750, March 1929); WW2 guest for Hartlepool United (1939-40) and Wrexham (1943-46); retired from playing, May 1946; Birmingham City (trainer, July 1946, then physiotherapist); later worked in a North-east shipyard and briefly as a miner.

Dave Fairhurst was a reliable and competent left-back, heavy in build who complemented Jimmy Nelson at Newcastle, gaining an FA Cup winner's medal in 1932. He spent 10 years at St James' Park, making 285 appearances for the Geordies. His only England cap came in the 4-1 win over France at White Hart Lane in December 1933 when he deputised for the injured Eddie Hapgood. His father William and brother Bill were also professional footballers.

FANTHAM, John 1961-62 ①

Born: Sheffield, 6 February 1939
Career: Sheffield Wednesday (£10, amateur, April 1954, professional, October 1956), Rotherham United (£5,000, October 1969), Macclesfield Town (season 1971-72), thereafter Hallam FC/Sheffield (coach and assistant-manager); now owns his own machinery business.

With Jimmy Greaves and Gerry Hitchens otherwise engaged with their clubs in Italy and Johnny Haynes out injured, the Sheffield Wednesday forward Johnny Fantham combined with Ray Pointer and Dennis Viollet for his England debut against Luxembourg in a World Cup qualifier at Highbury in September 1961. He played 'okay' in a rather disappointing 4-1 win as the crowd booed and slow-handclapped... considering that in the first game the minnows had been battered 9-0 on their own patch just eleven months earlier. This was Fantham's only cap, although he did play in one U23 international.
He scored 167 goals in 435 senior appearances for Sheffield Wednesday, helping the Owls win the Second Division title in 1959 and reach the FA Cup final in 1966.

FASHANU, John 1989-90 ②

Born: Kensington, London, 18 September 1962
Career: Cambridge United (junior, August 1977), Norwich City (professional, October 1979), Crystal Palace (loan, August 1983), Lincoln City (loan, September-November 1983, signed for £15,000, December 1983), Millwall (£55,000, November 1984), Wimbledon (£125,000, March 1986), Aston Villa (£1.35m, June 1994, retired, May 1996); later a TV personality in *The Gladiators, I'm A Celebrity Get Me Out Of Here* (2003) and *Total Wipeout*; member of a religious sect; promoter of Third World Development in Africa; also Chairman of Barry Town FC (August 2001-August 2003).

Six foot tall striker John Fashanu made his England debut, alongside Nigel Clough, in the 0-0 home draw with Chile in May 1989, thus becoming the first Wimbledon player ever to be capped at senior level. Unfortunately he limped off after 70 minutes to be replaced by Tony Cottee. His second cap followed soon afterwards, in a 2-0 win over Scotland.
Brother of Justin Fashanu, he helped the Dons reach the First Division and win the FA Cup in the late 1980s. He scored 126 goals in 326 games for Wimbledon (1986-94) and was offered the club's presidency by Sam Hammam in an effort to keep him at Plough Lane. In April 2011, Fashanu competed in *Celebrity Total Wipeout* and ultimately won the title, collecting £10,000 for UNICEF.

FELTON, William 1924-25 ①
Born: Heworth, Gateshead, 1 August 1900
Died: Manchester, 22 April 1977
Career: Pelaw Albion (April 1914), Pandon Temperance (August 1915), Pelaw Albion (August 1917), Wardley Colliery (September 1918), Jarrow (May 1919), Grimsby Town (professional, January 1921), Sheffield Wednesday (£1,450, January 1923), Manchester City (March 1929), Tottenham Hotspur (March 1932), Altrincham (May 1934, retired, June 1936).

Bill Felton helped Sheffield Wednesday win the Second Division title in 1926 and Spurs gain promotion to the top flight in 1933. A lusty right-back, quick in recovery with a solid tackle, he partnered Tom Parker of Southampton in his only international v. France in Paris in May 1925. He was also a very fine golfer.

FENTON, Michael 1937-38 ①
Born: Stockton-on-Tees, 30 October 1913
Died: Stockton-on-Tees, 5 February 2003
Career: South Bank East End (from April 1929), Middlesbrough (professional, August 1933, retired, May 1950, having played his last game in January of that year; then club coach and reserve team trainer until May 1965); WW2 guest for Blackpool; later a newsagent in Stockton.

Micky Fenton was a sprightly inside-right or centre-forward. Quick over the ground, he could shoot with both feet and despite being on the small side, withstood all the hard knocks and challenges dished out by sturdy defenders. He scored 162 goals in 269 games for Middlesbrough (1933-51). He made his England debut in the 1-0 defeat by Scotland at Wembley in April 1938 when he was closely marked by the Preston centre-half Tom Smith. He scored in the 3-0 unofficial international victory over Switzerland in Zurich in July 1945 and also played in the 1-0 Victory international defeat by Wales at The Hawthorns in October 1945, as well as taking part in three Test Matches when touring South Africa with the FA in 1939.

FENWICK, Terence William 1983-88 ⑳
Born: Durham, 17 November 1959
Career: Durham & District Schools, Crystal Palace (apprentice, September 1975, professional, December 1976), Queens Park Rangers (December 1980), Tottenham Hotspur (December 1987), Leicester City (loan, October 1990), Swindon Town (season 1993-94); Portsmouth (manager, February 1995-January 1998); Southall (manager from March 1998), Northampton Town (manager, for seven games in 2003); Ashford Town/Kent (Director of Football, August 2004), then coach of San Juan Jabloteh/Trinidad & Tobago (from 2006).

Terry Fenwick came on as a substitute for Alvin Martin in the 80th minute of England's 1-0 defeat by Wales at Wrexham in May 1984 to win the first of his 20 caps. Two years later he was given a 'roasting' by Argentina's star man Maradona in the 1986 World Cup 'Hand of God' game in Mexico. Out of the retaliate-first School of football, Fenwick had decided that a physical assault might be the best way of keeping the little man quiet. Wrong! All he got for his efforts was a booking and a cold star from the master who gave him a lesson on how to play carpet football...and it must be said that Fenwick never really got near him during the 90 minutes, especially when the Argentinian waltzed through the England defence to score his second goal.

Also the recipient of four Youth and eleven U21 caps, Fenwick helped Crystal Palace and QPR win the Second Division title in 1979 and 1986 respectively and played in the 1982 FA Cup final for QPR v. Spurs and in the League Cup final v. Oxford United four years later. His last full international outing was against Israel in February 1988. Fenwick has the unwanted tag of being the most booked/yellow-carded England player in World Cup finals tournaments, receiving three in Mexico, 1986.

He made 551 appearances at club level (455 in the League, 256 for QPR). He was also the first full-back to score a goal from play in an FA Cup final at Wembley, doing so for QPR against his future club, Spurs, in 1982.

In the summer of 2003, Fenwick was lined up to become the new manager of Luton Town but chose not to take the job due to uncertainty over the club's ownership - amid allegations of fraud surrounding Hatters, and former Southall chairman John Gurney. After enduring a fairly torrid time with Southall, through no fault of his own, Fenwick transgressed to become director of football at Ryman League side Ashford Town. Yet, despite plans to reshape the club for bigger things, a lack of private investment and on-field success, meant the Kent club was unable to move forward.

FERDINAND, Leslie, MBE 1993-98 ⑰ ⑤

Born: Acton, London, 8 December 1966

Career: AEL (a KOPA Cypriot team in England, August 1981), Southall (August 1983), Hayes (semi-professional, June 1985), Queens Park Rangers (£30,000, April 1987), Brentford (loan, March-May 1988), Besiktas/Turkey (loan, season 1988-89), Newcastle United (£6m, June 1995), Tottenham Hotspur (£6m, August 1997), West Ham United (January 2003), Leicester City (free, May 2003); Bolton Wanderers (free, August 2004), Reading (January 2005-May 2006), Watford (July 2005, retired, September 2006); Tottenham Hotspur (forward coach, from November 2008); also TV football pundit and Radio 5 match summariser; with fellow former footballers John Barnes and Luther Blissett, he founded Team48 Motorsport, a team which promotes young racing drivers of African-Caribbean background (in 2008, the Team entered the British Touring Car Championship, running Alfa Romeos for white Jamaican Matthew Gore and 18-year-old black Briton Darelle Wilson; Ferdinand is a qualified helicopter pilot and owns at least one helicopter.

Les Ferdinand scored on his England debut in the 6-0 World Cup qualifying victory over San Marino at Wembley in February 1993, also assisting in two of David Platt's four goals in this same match. Then, after failing to hit the target in his next three internationals, he netted in wins over Portugal (3-0) and San Marino (7-1) before cracking in an early, winning goal against Bulgaria at Wembley in March 1996. He also missed from the spot in the penalty shoot-out defeat by Belgium in the King Hassan II Cup in Casablanca in May 1998.

Voted 'Footballer of the Year' in 1996, and also capped once by England at B team level, Ferdinand was a strong, forceful striker, who joined Kevin Keegan's Newcastle from QPR for £6 million in 1995. His career spanned 18 years (1987-2005) during which time he netted 197 goals in 493 appearances at club level, including the 10,000th in the Premiership (for Spurs v. Fulham in December 2001). In fact, Ferdinand netted for six different clubs in the Premiership. He helped Besiktas win the Turkish Cup in 1988.

Popularly nicknamed Sir Les, he was made an MBE in the 2005 Queen's Birthday Honours List. He is Rio Ferdinand's cousin.

FERDINAND, Rio Gavin 1997-2013 ⑧⑴ ③

Born: Peckham, London, 7 November 1978

Career: West Ham United (apprentice, April 1994, professional, November 1995), AFC Bournemouth (loan, November 1996-January 1997), Leeds United (£18m, November 2000), Manchester United (£29.1m, July 2002).

Rio Ferdinand is a very good tackler and passer of the ball, cool under pressure (most of the time) and an excellent reader of the game. However, during the 2008-09 season, he began to have 'lapses in concentration' on the pitch, being responsible for a goal in the friendly against Holland (2-2) and then inexplicably failing to deal with a long ball down the middle during the World Cup qualifier in Ukraine, causing Robert Green to rush off his line and bring down Artem Milevskiy resulting in a red card for the West Ham 'keeper and a penalty for the home side (which was missed). England eventually lost that game 1-0. At the time the press said Ferdinand 'was losing it' and that 'he needed to have a re-think.' He certainly lacked his normal composure in both of those matches. But after taking over the captaincy (from John Terry) his game improved ten-fold and he played his part gallantly in the World Cup finals in South Africa.

Initially selected by Glenn Hoddle for England's World Cup qualifier with Moldova in September 1997, Ferdinand was sent home following a drink driving offence. He had to wait two more months before winning his first full cap v. Cameroon.

At club level, the experienced central defender has now made over 670 appearances, 431 with Manchester United who signed him for a record fee in the summer of 2002. However, a year-and-a-half later, in December 2003, he was banned by the FA for eight months for failing to undergo a drugs test. Ferdinand has so far helped the Reds win six Premiership titles, the League Cup twice, the Champions League, the FIFA Club World Cup and the FA Charity/Community Shield on four occasions. Unfortunately he missed the 2010 World Cup finals through injury.... and how England could have done with him! He also missed Euro 2012, not chosen this time by Roy Hodgson!

Cousin of Les Ferdinand (above), Ferdinand's brother Anton, previously with West Ham, now plays for Sunderland.

As a schoolboy, Rio was approached by the Central School of Ballet and had an invitation to perform at Sadler's Wells Theatre – but he decided not to pursue this venture and became a defender instead of a dancer!

During his spell at Leeds United, Ferdinand suffered a tendon strain in his knee...watching television! As his manager at the time, David O'Leary, explained: "He was watching television and had his foot up on the coffee table. He had it there in a certain position for a number of hours - and strained a tendon behind his knee."

FIELD, Edgar 1875-81 ②

Born: Wallingford, Berkshire, 29 July 1854

Died: Derby, 11 January 1934

Career: Lancing College XI (seasons 1870-74), Clapham Rovers (seasons 1874-83); also represented Reading, Berkshire & Buckinghamshire (seasons 1875-82); a chartered account by trade.

Edgar Field was a tough-tackling, robust full-back, rather on the slow side who starred in two FA Cup finals for Clapton Rovers, gaining a winner's medal in his second, in 1880. He made his England debut in a 3-1 defeat by Scotland in March 1876 but had to wait five years before collecting his second cap, also v. the Scots in March 1881 when he was given a testing time by the Queens Park left-winger Henry McNeill as his side was humiliated 6-1 at The Oval.

Rio Ferdinand

FINNEY, Sir Thomas, OBE, CBE 1946-58 ⑦⑥ ㉚

Born: Preston, 5 April 1922
Career: Deepdale Council & Preston Secondary Modern Schools, Holme Slack FC/Preston (season 1936-37), Preston North End (amateur, May 1937, professional, January 1940, retired May 1960); Distillery/Ireland (as a guest, September 1963); ran his own plumbing and electrical business in Preston for many years.

The first player to win the coveted 'Footballer of the Year' award twice - in 1954 when he captained Preston in the FA Cup final and in 1957 - Tom Finney was preferred by the selectors to Stanley Matthews on England's right-wing several times.

'A slightly-built genius' wrote one journalist, the Preston plumber was able to ride a tackle with ease and scythe, even glide, through the tightest of defences with the ball at his feet. He packed a powerful shot, mainly right-footed, could execute a delicate chip, make an inch-perfect pass and centre on the run as gwell as any winger in the game. He always came up smiling, even after taking a 'hammering' from the rugged defenders who tried to mark him.

Having played in two unofficial internationals against Switzerland in Berne and Zurich in July 1945 (scoring in a 3-0 victory in the latter), Finney then netted on his full England debut in a 7-2 win over Northern Ireland in September 1946 and 48 hours later, in fading light at Dalymount Park, he saved his team's blushes with a scrambled winner eight minutes from the end against the Republic of Ireland. In fact, he found the net eight times in his first eight England games, playing the first five at outside-right.

Asked to turn out on the left-wing in place of the injured Bobby Langton against Portugal in Lisbon in May 1947, Finney replied: "I'll play left-back if necessary. I want to be in the team." He then went out and produced a wonderful virtuoso performance, scored a great goal and assisted in three of the other nine in a resounding 10-0 win. This, in fact, was the first time manager Walter Winterbottom had fielded Finney and Stanley Matthews in the same forward-line.

Another terrific goal followed in an excellent 4-0 win over Italy in Milan in May 1948. Set up by Stan Mortensen, who slipped a fine pass through to him, Finney found the net with a brilliant left-foot drive, sending the ball low into the net past the hapless Bacigalupo.

Six months after completing the 'Italian job' Finney struck the winner against Wales at Villa Park when Kenneth Wolstenholme made his debut as a BBC commentator.

Finney also scored a four-timer in a 5-3 win over Portugal at Kenilworth Road, Luton in May 1950, two of his goals coming from the penalty spot.

Soon afterwards he went to the World Cup in Brazil and admitted he didn't perform well, especially in the 1-0 reverses at the hands of the USA and Spain. "That defeat by the Yanks was a nightmare," he said. "We missed at least six or seven chances and I sent two shots several yards wide when I knew I should have at least made their keeper work."

Against Spain, acrobatic goalkeeper Ramalets twice saved goal-bound efforts from Finney in what was described as a 'not very nice football match.'

After four decent years playing for Preston and England, Finney then did as well as anyone in the 1954 World Cup in Switzerland, but was surprisingly dropped for the Hungary game at Wembley six months later. Feeling rather despondent, he sat and watched from the stands as England got walloped 6-3, and afterwards said: "I came away wondering what we had been doing all those years. The Hungarians were so much better in technique it was untrue."

Finney missed a 5th minute penalty in the 4-1 win over Spain at Wembley in November 1955 but made amends by laying on a goal for John Atyeo and scoring another himself.

His international career covered 12 years and when he netted against Northern Ireland in October 1958, he became England's second oldest goalscorer at the age of 36 years, 182 days. He made his last appearance for his country just 18 days later, in a superb 5-0 win over Russia at Wembley. This victory came just four months after the Russians had held England to a 2-2 draw in the opening pool 2 game of the World Cup in Sweden. Trailing 2-1 with just six minutes remaining of that game, England were awarded a penalty. Up stepped an ice-cool Finney and with consummate ease and accuracy, stroked the ball wide of Lev Yashin to earn a draw. Immediately after the 'goal' the big goalkeeper – known as the 'Man in Black' – raced up to the referee, spun him round like a top but was allowed to stay on the field. Finney himself damaged a knee in this game and missed the rest of the tournament.

Finney, along with Billy Wright, was the first player to appear in three World Cups for England (1950-54-58).

This is what Finney's great pal and fellow winger Stanley Matthews had to say about the Preston plumber: "Tom was a great player. The secret of his game was that he had that unpredictable change of pace, the same as Cruyff. He kidded every full-back, and when he was outside-right – a position he didn't really like – he could use his left foot on the inside and was a marvellous goalscorer, showing that he could play anywhere effectively for England."

Finney, who also represented the Football League, was a one-club man. He scored 210 goals in 456 appearances for Preston whom he served for 23 years. He helped the Lillywhites win the Football League Wartime Cup in 1941, lift the Second Division championship in 1951 and also guested for the Irish club Distillery v. Benfica in a European Cup match in 1963.

Awarded the OBE in 1961, the CBE in 1992, Finney was subsequently knighted in 1998. He was also made a Freeman of Preston in 1979, the town where he still lives and is believed to be the second oldest former England player alive today, behind goalkeeper Bert Williams, who was born in January 1920.

FLEMING, Harold John 1908-14 ⑪ ⑨

Born: Downton near Salisbury, Wiltshire, 30 April 1887
Died: Swindon, 23 August 1955
Career: Downton Boys Club (seasons 1901-04), Swindon Amateurs (August 1904), Swindon Town (professional, October 1907, retired, August 1924); played cricket for Wiltshire; later ran a football-boot manufacturing business in Swindon.

Inside-right Harold Fleming played all his football for Swindon Town for whom he scored well over 150 goals in more than 400 appearances between 1907 and 1924, gaining two Southern League championship-winning medals in 1911 and 1914. An unorthodox roaming player, predominantly right-footed, he possessed wonderful ball control and regularly changed direction of his run, sending defenders in the wrong direction. One feels he would have gained more caps for England had he been with a more fashionable club. He made the first of his 11 appearances for his country in a 2-0 win over Scotland in April 1909 and won his last cap against the same country in April 1914, netting his ninth goal in a 3-1 defeat. Two years earlier he struck a superb hat-trick in a 6-1 win over Ireland. Fleming also went on two end-of-season tours with the FA, scoring 20 goals in South Africa, in May-July 1910.

FLETCHER, Albert Thomas 1888-90 ②

Born: New Invention, Wolverhampton, 4 June 1867
Died: Wolverhampton, 16 August 1938
Career: Willenhall Pickwick (from August 1882), Wolverhampton Wanderers (August 1885, retired, July 1891; became coach at Molineux, then assistant-trainer and finally head trainer, a position he held for 24 years, from August 1896 to August 1920).

Albert Fletcher served Wolves for 35 years, first as a player, then as a coach, assistant–trainer and finally as head trainer. Joining the club as an 18 year-old, he played at right-half until a broken leg suffered against Aston Villa ended his career in 1891. He appeared in the 1889 FA Cup final defeat by Preston and gained the first of his two England caps in February of that season v. Wales (won 4-1), collecting his second against the Principality in March 1890 when he was 'considerably inspired' in a 3-1 victory.

Some reference books state that Fletcher may have died in Birmingham in 1947 or Warwick in1955

FLOWERS, Ronald 1954-66 ㊾ ⑩

Born: Edlington near Doncaster, 28 July 1934
Career: Edlington Grammar School, Doncaster & Yorkshire Boys, Doncaster Rovers Juniors (July 1949), Wath Wanderers (July 1950), Wolverhampton Wanderers (professional, July 1952), Northampton Town (September 1967, player-manager, May 1968-May 1969), Wellington Town/Telford Town (July 1969 as player-coach-manager, resigned October 1971); ran his own sports shop in Wolverhampton for many years; now lives in Stafford.

Ron Flowers, the tall, blond Wolves wing-half, combined elegance with industry, energy and stamina and linked up superbly in midfield with Johnny Haynes and at times with his club-mate Peter Broadbent.
He could also shoot – and hard! When England thumped the USA 8-1 in Los Angeles in May 1959, Flowers struck home two booming 30-yard pile-drivers. His team-mate, Don Howe, said after the game: "I was amazed that his second effort didn't go straight through the net. It was struck with enormous force."

Ron Flowers

During the first-half of the 2-2 draw with Italy at Wembley in May 1959, Flowers went off with a broken nose, claiming that he had been 'struck by the elbow' of a tough defender.
In a World Cup qualifying draw with Portugal in Lisbon in May 1961, Flowers scored a stunning equalising goal eight minutes from time after Johnny Haynes had rolled a free-kick into his path. 'The ball hit the net like a bullet fired from a gun' said one reporter.
A year later, in England's opening match in group 4 of the 1962 World Cup against Hungary in Chile, Flowers equalised from the spot but then a rudimentary error let in Florian Albert for the winner. And the tall blond also had the pleasure of scoring his country's first goal in the European Nations Cup – another penalty driven home to earn a point against France in a qualifier at Hillsborough in October 1962. In all Flowers was successful with six spot-kicks for England, three in successive games in 1962.
He gained his first cap as a 20 year-old against France in May 1955. His second followed three-and-a-half years later against Wales and after that he was practically a regular in the half-back line right through to the mid-1960s. A member of Alf Ramsey's initial World Cup squad of 40, he failed to make an appearance in the finals, winning his last cap against Norway in June 1966.
Flowers served Wolves for 15 years (1952-67), during which time he scored 37 goals in 515 senior games, gaining an FA Cup and three League championship winning medals under manager Stan Cullis. He also won two England U23 caps and represented the Football League on 13 occasions and led Telford to the final of the FA Vase in 1971.
Flowers' father and brother both played for Doncaster Rovers.

FLOWERS, Timothy David 1993-98 ⑪

Born: Kenilworth, Warwickshire, 3 February 1967
Career: Wolverhampton Wanderers (apprentice, June 1983, professional, August 1984), Southampton (loan, March-April 1986, signed permanently £70,000, June 1986), Swindon Town (loan, March-May 1987 and November-December 1987), Blackburn Rovers (£2.4m, November 1993), Leicester City (£1.1m, July 1999); loan spells with Stockport County (2001), Coventry City (2002) and Manchester City (loan, 2002); retired as a player (May 2003); then part-time goalkeeping coach at Manchester City and Leicester City (during seasons 2003-06); Coventry City (assistant-manager, February 2007-February 2008), Queens Park Rangers (assistant-manager, February 2008-January 2010), Northampton Town (goalkeeping coach, February 2010); also an occasional coach at Kidderminster Harriers; Hull City (assistant-manager, March 2010), Stafford Rangers (manager, season 2010-2011), Northampton Town (assistant-manager/coach, September 2011, caretaker-manager, October-November 2011).

Goalkeeper Tim Flowers made an 'exceptional' debut for England in the 1-1 draw with Brazil in the US Cup in Washington in June 1993. He pulled off at least five excellent saves before conceding an equaliser with 15 minutes remaining. He was also impressive in his next game v. Greece (won 5-0) but was caught out on a couple of occasions when in his sixth international, Sweden forced a 3-3 draw at Elland Road, Leeds in June 1995. With David Seaman pressing hard for a regular place in the England team, Flowers eventually gave way to the Arsenal 'keeper three months later and gained only four more caps after that, despite being on the subs' bench at the 1998 World Cup. At club level, he appeared in well over 600 League and Cup games for his seven employers. A Premiership title winner with Blackburn in 1995

FORMAN, Frederick Ralph 1898-99 ③ ③

Born: Aston-on-Trent, Derbyshire, 8 November 1873
Died: Nottingham, 14 June 1910
Career: Aston-upon-Trent FC (August 1888), Beeston Town (June 1891), Derby County (professional, July 1893), Nottingham Forest (July 1894, retired, May 1903; club committee member, seasons 1903-10); was a railway draughtsman by profession.

Fred Forman, playing in front of his brother Frank (previous column) scored twice on his England debut in a 13-2 win over Ireland in February 1899. Able to play equally well as a half-back, inside-forward or outside-left, he netted in his second game v. Wales a month later and played his last international v. Scotland at the end of that season. A shade lethargic at times, Forman made over 200 appearances in League football, 188 for Nottingham Forest, playing in the same team as his brother almost 120 times.

FORREST, James Henry 1883-90 ⑪

Born: Blackburn, 24 June 1864
Died: Blackburn, 30 December 1925
Career: Imperial United (August 1878), Witton FC (July 1880), King's Own/Blackburn (August 1882), Blackburn Rovers (January 1883, professional, August 1885-May 1895); returned with Darwen (October 1895-May 1896); Blackburn Rovers (director, July 1906 until his death); worked as a tape-sizer in a cotton factory and a shuttle-peg maker in joinery firm; was also a licensee in Blackburn.

Left-half Jim Forrest was the first Blackburn player to wear an England shirt after professionalism was introduced to the game. He lined up in his fourth international against Scotland in March 1885, having made his debut v. Wales twelve months earlier. Wearing a different shirt to the rest of his team-mates, the Scots protested vehemently about his inclusion in the team. However, the game went on and Forrest played his part in the 1-1 draw. He received £1 for playing, but as he was already earning that amount of money as a Rovers player, he didn't get any wages that week!
Forrest was only 12 years of age when he captained Imperial United in 1876. He later gained five FA Cup winner's medals with Blackburn Rovers (1884-85-86-90-91) and scored six goals in 196 games for the Lancashire club. His son, also named James, played for Blackburn when he was a director at Ewood Park.

FORT, John 1920-21 ①

Born: Leigh, 15 April 1888
Died: New Cross, London, 23 November 1965
Career: St Andrew's Mission (August 1904), Atherton FC (July 1907), Exeter City (semi-professional, May 1911), Millwall Athletic (professional, June 1914, retired, May 1930; became coach, then trainer, scout and finally groundsman, serving the club for 50 years, up to 1964)

Stocky right-back Jack Fort's only cap came against Belgium in May 1921 when he partnered Liverpool's Ephraim Longworth in a 2-0 win. He also represented the Southern League and served Millwall for almost 50 years, 16 as a player (1914-30). He helped the Lions win the Third Division (South) championship in 1928 and was, in fact, the first player from a Third Division club to win a full England cap.

and League Cup victor with Leicester in 2000, he was forced to retire with arthritic problems four years later and quickly went into coaching. Flowers holds the record for the fastest dismissal by a goalkeeper in the Premiership...sent off after just 72 seconds when playing for Blackburn v. Leeds United in February 1995. Arthritis problems forced Flowers to retire prematurely. Another ex-Wolves and England star, Steve Bull, also managed Stafford Rangers.

FORMAN, Francis 1898-1903 ⑨ ①

Born: Aston-on-Trent, Derbyshire, 23 May 1875
Died: West Bridgford, Nottingham, 4 December 1961
Career: Aston-on-Trent FC (August 1891), Beeston Town (May 1892), Derby County (professional, March 1894), Nottingham Forest (December 1894, retired, May 1905; then committee member, seasons 1903-06; thereafter Life Member of club); engaged in business as a building contractor in West Bridgford, Nottingham with his brother-in-law and fellow footballer James Linacre.

Frank Forman won the FA Cup with Nottingham Forest in 1898. A born leader, he played as a right-half and centre-half and was one of the finest players of his era. Calm and unruffled, he always tried to use the ball rather than boot it into the air. He scored 30 goals in 260 games for Nottingham Forest and won the first of his nine England caps in March 1898 v. Ireland, claiming his only international goal in his third game, eleven months later, also against the Irish when England won 13-2. Forman was never on the losing side for his country. He was the brother of Fred Forman (next column).

FOSTER, Benjamin Anthony 2006-13 ⑥

Born: Leamington Spa, 3 April 1983
Career: Racing Club Warwick (August 1999), Stoke City (professional, April 2001), Bristol City (loan, March-May 2002), Tiverton Town (season 2002-03), Stafford Rangers (loan, August-September 2004), Kidderminster Harriers (loan, October-November 2004), Wrexham (loan, January-May 2005), Manchester United (£1m, July 2005), Watford (loan, August 2005-May 2006 and again, August 2006-March 2007), Birmingham City (£5.9m, July 2010), West Bromwich Albion (loan, August 2011-May 2012; signed for £4.1m, June 2013).

Goalkeeper Ben Foster won the Football League Trophy with Wrexham in 2005, helped Watford into the FL play-offs, gained successive League Cup winner's medals with Manchester United in 2009 and 2010 and collected a third League Cup winner's prize with Birmingham City in 2011. He served as understudy to Edwin van der Sar and also Tomasz Kuszczak at Old Trafford for three years before moving to St Andrew's, having an excellent first season with Blues. A fine 'keeper, he has now played in five full internationals for England, his first against Spain at Old Trafford in February 2007.

Unfortunately in his third game versus France at Wembley in November 2010 which ended in a 2-1 defeat, he was horribly at fault for the visitors' opening goal - beaten at his near post by Benzema's effort. At the end of the 2012-13 season, Foster had amassed over 250 appearances at club level.

Foster returned to international duty when named in England's squad for World Cup qualifiers against San Marino and Montenegro in March 2013.

FOSTER, Reginald Erskine 1899-1902 ⑤ ③

Born: Malvern, Worcs, 16 April 1878
Died: Worcester, 13 May 1914
Career: Malvern College XI (season 1895-96), University College/Oxford University (seasons 1897-1900); played for Old Malvernians (late 1890s/early 1900s) and Corinthians (seasons 1899-1902); also competent cricketer (8 Tests for England) and a rackets and golf blue at Oxford University; was a stock broker by profession.

Reg 'Tip' Foster was a tall, lanky inside-forward, clever in footwork with supreme ball control and powerful shot. A richly gifted footballer, he won the FA Amateur Cup with the Old Malvernians in 1902. Three of his England caps were gained against Wales, the first in March 1900 and he scored twice (one a real beauty) in a 3-0 win over Ireland in his second international a year later. In the small red ball game, between 1897 and 1912, Foster served Worcestershire and Oxford and amassed 9,037 runs including 22 centuries with a top-score of 287 for England in his first Test v. Australia in 1903. Voted Wisden's Cricketer of the Year in 1901, he later served on the Committee of the MCC for four years to 1907 and again in 1910 until his death from diabetes at the age of 36.

FOSTER, Stephen Brian 1981-82 ③

Born: Portsmouth, 24 September 1957
Career: Hampshire County Schools, Portsmouth (apprentice, June 1973, professional, September 1975), Brighton & Hove Albion (£130,000, July 1979), Aston Villa (£150,000 plus Mark Jones, March 1984), Luton Town (£70,000, November 1984), Oxford United (free, July 1989), Brighton & Hove Albion (free, August 1992, retired, May 1996); became a businessman and in January 2008 he was named as a member of an Anglo-American consortium, which included BBC presenter Nick Owen, bidding to buy his former club Luton Town.

Steve Foster won the first of his three England caps as partner to Dave Watson in the 4-0 home win over Northern Ireland in February 1982. His other two, when he had Phil Thompson alongside him, came against Holland (won 2-0) and Kuwait (1-0), the latter in the World Cup. However, with so many talented defenders around at the same time, his international career was short and sweet. He played in the 1983 FA Cup final replay for Brighton and five years later helped Luton win the League Cup.

In January 2008 Foster was named as a member of an Anglo-American consortium, which includes BBC presenter Nick Owen, bidding to buy his former club Luton Town.

FOULKE, William Henry 1896-97 ①

Born: Dawley, Shropshire, 12 April 1874
Died: Blackpool, 1 May 1916
Career: Alfreton (August 1889), Blackwell Colliery (August 1892), Sheffield United (professional, June 1894), Chelsea (May 1905), Bradford City (April 1906, retired, November 1907); also played cricket for Derbyshire.

Goalkeeper Willie Foulke - known affectionately as 'Tiny' Foulke and 'Fatty' Foulke - won his only cap as a Sheffield United player, when England beat Wales 4-0 in March 1897. It was said at the time that he weighed around 20 stones, making him the heaviest player ever to represent England in a full international. During his career Foulke weighed anything from 15 stone in 1892 to 25 stone when he ended his career in 1907 at Bradford City. Standing 6ft 6in in his bare feet, Foulke was also the tallest player to have appeared for England. And, in fact, he remained as such until defender Zat Knight arrived on the scene in May 2005, and later Peter Crouch. Although regarded as a freak show by many, Foulke was extremely agile for his size and an expert at saving penalties. From 1891 (when the penalty kick was introduced) 'keepers did not have to remain on the goal line when facing a spot-kick and therefore when the player taking it ran up to the ball, Foulke did likewise from his line, and his enormous bulk certainly put opponents off. Foulke played in three FA Cup finals with Sheffield United, gaining winner's medals in 1899 and 1902. He also helped the Blades clinch the League title in 1898. In later years he worked on a 'penny a shot' sideshow on Blackpool beach. He died of pneumonia in a private nursing home.

FOULKES, William Anthony 1955-56 ①
Born: St Helens, Lancs, 5 January 1932
Career: Whiston Boys' Club (August 1946), Manchester United (amateur, March 1950, professional, August 1951, retired, June 1970; became youth coach and assistant-trainer at Old Trafford); Chicago Sting/USA (manager-coach, 1975-77), Tulsa Roughnecks/USA (manager-coach, 1978), San Jose Earthquakes/USA (manager-coach, 1978); Whitney Town, now United (manager, season 1979-80); managed four Norwegian club between 1980 and 1988: IL Byrne, FC Steinkjer, Lillstrom SK and Viking Stavanger; FC Mazda/Japan (manager, December 1988-January 1992); advisory coach for the Manchester FA in 2002-03.

Bill Foulkes, who survived the Munich air crash, gave Manchester United excellent service as a strong, steady and reliable right-back and centre-half, amassing 682 senior appearances between 1952 and 1969. He helped the Reds win four League titles, the FA Cup and also the European Cup. He collected his only England cap (in place of injured right-back Ron Staniforth) in a 2-0 win over Northern Ireland in Belfast in October 1954. He deserved more. Fluent in Japanese, he frequently took visitors from the Far East country around Old Trafford.

FOWLER, Robert Bernard 1995-2002 ㉖ ⑦
Born: Toxteth, Liverpool, 9 April 1975
Career: Liverpool (apprentice, May 1991, professional, April 1992), Leeds United (£12.5m, November 2001), Manchester City (£3m, January 2003-January 2006), Liverpool (free, January 2006), Cardiff City (free agent, July 2007), Blackburn Rovers (free, May-December 2008), North Queensland Fury/Australia (February 2010), Perth Glory/Australia (April 2010), Bury (assistant-manager, April 2011), Muangthong United/Thailand (August 2011), MK Dons (coach), invested in racehorses; media work for Abu Dhabi Sports Channel, Sky Sports and ITV; with a net wealth of £28m, was named in the Sunday Times Rich List as one of the 1,000 wealthiest Britons in 2005.

Everton fan Robbie Fowler made his England debut as a substitute against Bulgaria in March 1996 and scored his first international goal in a 2-0 friendly win over Mexico a year later. A brilliant opportunist marksman, he was perhaps unlucky that there were so many other great strikers around at the same time including Alan Shearer, Teddy Sheringham and Michael Owen, although a serious injury, suffered in February 1998, hit him hard and ruled him out of the World Cup that year. However, he bounced back with confidence

Robbie Fowler

and went on to gain a total of 26 full caps, picking up his last in a 3-0 win over Denmark in 2002.

Fowler netted 163 Premiership goals (only Alan Shearer, Andy Cole and Thierry Henry scored more) in his overall tally of 252 in 589 club matches in the UK, including the fastest hat-trick in Premier League history for Liverpool v. Arsenal in 1993. He also appeared in one unofficial international, gained one B and eight U21 caps, represented England as a Schoolboy and helped his country win the UEFA Youth Cup in 1993. Voted PFA Young Player of the Year in 1995 and 1996, he played in two League Cup winning teams for Liverpool in 1995 and 2001 and was an unused substitute in two other triumphant finals in 2001, the FA Cup and UEFA Cup. He also helped the Merseysiders finish runners-up in the 1996 FA Cup and 2007 Champions League finals. With North Queensland Fury in 2010, he was named Player of the Year and Players' Player of the Year and won the Golden Boot award. His book – Fowler, My Autobiography – was published in September 2005.

FOX, Frederick Samuel 1924-25 ①
Born: Highworth, Swindon, 22 November 1898
Died: High Wycombe, 15 May 1968
Career: Swindon Town (initially, August 1916), Abertillery (August 1919), Preston North End (professional, May 1921), Gillingham (June 1922), Millwall Athletic (May 1925), Halifax Town (June 1927), Brentford (March 1928, retired, injured, April 1931)

Goalkeeper Fred Fox won his only England cap as a Gillingham player in a 3-2 win over France in Paris in May 1925. At the time the number one position was causing some concern with seven different keepers having been used in the previous 10 internationals. If he had plied his trade with a bigger club, then Fox would surely have gained more honours.

FRANCIS, Gerald Charles James 1974-77 ⑫ ③
Born: Chiswick, London, 6 December 1951
Career: Chiswick League football, Queens Park Rangers (apprentice, April 1968, professional, June 1969), Crystal Palace (£462,500, July 1979), Queens Park Rangers (£150,000, February 1981), Coventry City (trial, February 1982, signed for £150,000, March 1982), Exeter City (player-manager, July 1983), Cardiff City (non-contract, September 1984), Swansea City (n/c, October 1984), Portsmouth (n/c, November 1984), Wimbledon (n/c, March 1985), Bristol Rovers (n/c, September 1985; then manager, July 1987); Queens Park Rangers (manager, summer, 1991), Tottenham Hotspur (manager, November 1994), Queens Park Rangers (manager, September 1998-May 2001), Bristol Rovers (manager, briefly in 2001); later Stoke City (senior coach and advisor); also owns an antique shop in Chertsey; investor in West End musical '125th Street'; TV and radio pundit.

Given his international debut by Don Revie against Czechoslovakia at Wembley in October 1974, midfielder Gerry Francis became the 900th player to represent England at senior level. He played 'very well' in a 3-0 win and did likewise in his next game against Portugal. He was then out of the side for the next five matches before returning to help annihilate Scotland 5-1 in May 1975, scoring twice, one a 'delightful header', the other a booming 25-yard shot which took a slight deflection.
After that impressive display he was handed the captaincy (in place of Alan Ball), subsequently handing over the duties to Kevin Keegan. Francis, who also gained six U23 caps, made over 600 appearances during his senior career, 495 of which came in the Football League alone (82 goals scored).

FRANCIS, Trevor John 1976-86 ⑤² ⑫

Born: Plymouth, Devon, 19 April 1954
Career: Ernesettle Youth Club/Plymouth, Plymouth Boys (season 1968-69), Birmingham City (apprentice, June 1969, professional, May 1971), Detroit Express/USA (loan, May-August 1978), Nottingham Forest (£975,000+ Vat & Levy = £1m, February 1979), Detroit Express (loan, June-August 1979), Manchester City (£1.2m, September 1981), Sampdoria/Italy (£800,000, July 1982), Atalanta/Italy (£900,000, July 1986), Glasgow Rangers (free, September 1987), Queens Park Rangers (free, March 1988), Wollongong City/Australia (June-August 1988), Queens Park Rangers player-manager, December 1988), Sheffield Wednesday (free, February 1990, retired as a player, May 1991, manager June 1991-May 1995); spent 1995-96 season working for Sky Sports; Birmingham City (manager, May 1996-October 2001), Crystal Palace (manager, November 2001-April 2003); now a TV soccer pundit and match summariser for Asian networks.

Utility forward Trevor Francis – who became the first £1 million footballer in Britain when he was transferred from Birmingham City to Nottingham Forest in January 1979 - made his England debut in a 2-0 defeat by Holland at Wembley in February 1977. He never really got a look in against an exceptionally strong side which included the two Johannes, Cruyff and Neeskens, in midfield.

Fast and direct, Francis scored his first international goal in the 2-0 win over Spain in Barcelona in March 1980. In fact, he could well have scored a hat-trick that day but for some brilliant saves by Arconada.

His 74th minute goal gave his country their first win over Wales for five years in April 1982 (1-0) before he was replaced by Cyrille Regis. Soon afterwards, in the second half half of a World Cup encounter in Spain, Francis rammed the ball high into the net past Czechoslovakian goalkeeper Semen to set up a 2-0 victory. And then the Nottingham Forest striker scored a 'gem of a goal' in the 27th minute which was enough to beat Kuwait 1-0 in Bilbao.

He added four further goals after that, including two against Denmark in a European Championship qualifier in September 1982.

At club level, Francis bagged a total of 225 goals in 752 senior appearances in club football, scoring the deciding goal in the 1979 European Cup final when Nottingham Forest beat FF Malmo. He won the Scottish League Cup with Rangers in 1988 and as a manager guided Sheffield Wednesday to both the FA Cup and League Cup finals in 1993 and Birmingham City to the 2001 League Cup final, as well as taking the Blues into the First Division play-offs four seasons running. An England Youth international, he also collected five caps at U23 level.

FRANKLIN, Cornelius 1946-50 ②⁷

Born: Stoke-on-Trent, 24 January 1922
Died: Stoke-on-Trent, 9 February 1996
Career: Stoke Schools, Stoke Old Boys (season 1935-36), Stoke City (amateur, April 1936, professional, January 1939); WW2 guest for Gainsborough Trinity; Independiente Santa Fé, Bogota/Colombia (May 1950), Hull City (February 1951), Crewe Alexandra (February 1956), Stockport County (October 1957), Wellington Town (player-coach, July 1959), GKN Sankey's/Wellington (player July 1960, manager July-August 1961, retired, as a player, December 1962); Apoel Nicosia/Cyprus (coach, February-November 1963), Colchester United (manager, November 1963-May 1968); later a licensee in Oswaldtwistle (from January 1969) then at Sandon near Stone, Staffs.

Neil Franklin made defending look easy, a master centre-half. Always wanting the ball, he passed it well and seemed to have all the time in the world. If he was around today, playing as a sweeper, he'd never need to have a bath!

Succeeding Stan Cullis, he made his international debut in a 7-2 win over Northern Ireland in September 1946 and after several inspiring performances he was 'absolutely brilliant' when England beat Italy in Turin in 1948, floating about the pitch, playing the ball with both feet, even beating opponents with ease on the edge of his own penalty-area. He was a terrific player – and it was a body blow when he chose to quit England to try his luck in South America…a big, big mistake! Some said if he had played in the 1950 World Cup, England won have won it.

Besides his full caps – all won in succession – Franklin also played in 10 Wartime and two unofficial internationals (both v. Switzerland in July 1945), gained one B cap and represented the Football League five times. He played in 348 games for Stoke City (1936-50) and his tally included Wartime fixtures.

FREEMAN, Bertram Clewley 1908-12 ⑤ ③

Born: Handsworth, Birmingham, 10 October 1885
Died: Edgbaston, Birmingham, 11 August 1955
Career: Gower Street School/Aston (Birmingham), Gower Street Old Boys, Aston Manor (1903), Aston Villa (professional, April 1904), Woolwich Arsenal (November 1905), Everton (April 1908), Burnley (April 1911), Wigan Borough (September 1921-May 1922), Kettering Town (August 1923), Kidderminster Harriers (March 1924, retired, August 1924)

An FA Cup winner with Burnley in 1914, Bertie Freeman differed from many of his contemporaries, inasmuch that he was a ball player rather than an all-action, robust centre-forward whose League career realised 197 goals in more than 350 appearances. He netted on his international debut in a 2-0 win over Wales at Nottingham in March 1909 and was on target again in the 6-1 and 2-0 wins over Ireland and Wales in February and March 1912. He also represented the Football League on four occasions, scoring four goals in an 8-1 win over the Irish League in October 1909.

FROGGATT, Jack 1949-53 ⑬ ②

Born: Sheffield, 17 November 1922
Died: Portsmouth, 17 February 1993
Career: Served in the RAF; Portsmouth (trial, March-April 1945, semi-professional, September 1945, full-time professional, August 1946), Leicester City (March 1954), Kettering Town (player-coach, November 1957, player-manager, January 1958-September 1961, remained as a player until May 1962); later a publican for 22 years, first in Portsmouth, as mine host of the Manor House in East Cosham and then The Milton Arms near Fratton Park, and later of

The Green Man in Partridge Green, West Sussex. His father and his second cousin Redfern (below) both played for Sheffield Wednesday.

Having played his first two games for England at outside-left against Northern Ireland and Italy, both in November 1949, Jack Froggatt won his third cap as a centre-half against Scotland at Wembley in April 1951. Lawrie Hughes, Allenby Chilton and 38 year-old Leslie Compton had all played there in the previous four internationals, but the FA in a moment of madness, thought that the pace of Froggatt would be advantageous against the nippy Scottish forwards. Unfortunately the Portsmouth player had a torrid afternoon, as did the recalled Billy Wright, the passes of both players continually going astray as England lost 3-2. Thankfully Froggatt quickly forgot that game and went on to produce several outstanding performances.

He played exceedingly well in the 3-2 win over Austria in Vienna in May 1952. Despite conceding a clumsy penalty from which Huber equalised at 1-1, he sent Jackie Sewell through for England's second goal soon afterwards and towards the end defended as well as anyone as the Austrians battled for a third equaliser.

Six months later in a 5-2 win over Wales at Wembley, when he played behind his cousin, Redfern (below) Froggatt was carried off after a collision with Trevor Ford. He returned as a hobbling left-wing passenger and scored his side's third goal with a header shortly before half-time.

His last game in an England shirt was on the left-wing against the USA in June 1953 when he assisted in two of the goals in a resounding 6-3 win in New York.

A back-to-back League championship winner with Portsmouth in 1949 and 1950, Froggatt struck 73 goals in 305 appearances for Pompey between 1945 and 1954 and he helped Leicester win the Second Division title in 1957. He also represented the Football League on four occasions. His father played for Sheffield Wednesday, Notts County and Chesterfield.

FROGGATT, Redfern 1952-53 ④ ②
Born: Sheffield, 23 August 1924
Died: Sheffield, 26 December 2003
Career: Sheffield YMCA (seasons 1939-42), Sheffield Wednesday (professional, July 1942), Stalybridge Celtic (May 1962, retired, April 1964); later worked as a sales representative in Sheffield.

A finely built inside-forward, Redfern Froggatt made his England debut 'in front' of his second cousin Jack (above) in a 5-2 win over Wales at Wembley in November 1952. A fortnight later, in driving sleet, he scored his first international goal in a 5-0 home victory over Belgium and then partnered Jack on the left-wing in his third game, a 2-2 draw with Scotland. He missed a couple of early chances but had a good game overall before 97,000 fans at Wembley. His second international goal was scored in his last game, when England beat the USA 6-3 in June 1953. Capped once by England B, Froggatt also represented the Football League and during his 20 years with Sheffield Wednesday, he scored 148 goals in 458 appearances, helping the Owls win the Second Division championship three times (1952, '56 and '59).

FRY, Charles Burgess 1900-01 ①
Born: Croydon, Surrey, 25 April 1872
Died: Hampstead, London, 7 September 1956
Career: West Kent Boys' Club (September 1884), Repton School (seasons 1887-91), Wadham College (season 1891-92), Oxford University (seasons 1892-95); also played for Old Reptonians and Corinthians (between 1892-1903), assisted Southampton (amateur, December 1900-November 1902), Portsmouth (amateur, December 1902-April 1903); played county cricket for Surrey, Sussex and Hants,

starring in 26 Test Matches for England; played rugby for Blackheath, the Barbarians and Surrey; a schoolmaster by profession, he had a spell in journalism and was an unsuccessful Liberal candidate for Brighton, Banbury and Oxford before taking over the naval training ship, HMS *Mercury*, in 1908 where he remained until 1950.

Charles Fry was a brilliant all-round sportsman who excelled at football, rugby and cricket, on the athletics track, in the long jump and even on the tennis court.

Football was certainly not the principal sport of this exceptionally talented gentleman. He chose to play at right-back and gained just one full cap for England, lining up against Ireland in March 1901. He also helped Southampton reach the 1902 FA Cup final and he also appeared in one unofficial international for his country (v. Canada in 1891). As a cricketer, Fry scored a total of 30,886 runs in first-class matches including 94 centuries and was named as one of Wisden's five cricketers of the year in 1895. The following year he played in his first Test Match v. South Africa. In 1893 he beat the World long jump record with a leap of 23ft 6½ins which stood for several years. In fact, if he had competed in the 1896 Olympic Games he would have won the gold medal. A master at Charterhouse School, Fry wrote his autobiography - *A Life Worth Living* - in 1939.

FURNESS, William Isaac 1932-33 ①
Born: New Washington, County Durham, 8 June 1909
Died: Norwich, 29 August 1980
Career: Washington Colliery (April 1925), Usworth Colliery (May 1926), Leeds United (£50, professional, August 1928), Norwich City (£2,700, June 1937, retired, May 1947; became assistant-trainer, then head trainer and later physiotherapist, remaining at Carrow Road until 1970).

Inside-forward Billy Furness won his only England cap against Italy in May 1933. He was an aggressive player with a good turn of speed and scored 66 goals in 257 appearances for Leeds and 21 in 96 games for Norwich.

GALLEY, Thomas 1936-37 ②
Born: Hednesford, Staffs, 4 August 1915
Died: Cannock, Staffs, 5 May 2000
Career: Hednesford & District Schools (season 1929-30), Cannock Town (amateur, season 1930-31), Notts County (amateur, August 1931), Wolverhampton Wanderers (professional, August 1933); served with the Royal Artillery in France and Germany during WW2 and played as a guest for Aldershot, Clapton Orient, Leeds United and Watford; Grimsby Town (November 1947), Kidderminster Harriers (August 1949), Clacton Town (player-coach, May 1950), retired as a player, May 1955, remained as coach until June 1960).

Tom Galley gained his two caps on England's Scandinavian tour in May 1937. A tall, rangy utility forward who was later converted into a cultured half-back, he scored on his debut in a 6-0 win over Norway in Oslo and then laid on one of Freddie Steele's three goals in a 4-0 victory over Sweden in Stockholm. During his career, Galley spent 13 years with Wolves, during which time he appeared in 278 first team games (57 goals scored) and gained a Wartime League Cup winner's medal in 1942, three years after collecting a runners-up prize following Wolves' surprise 4-1 defeat by Portsmouth. His son, John, a striker, later played for Wolves, Rotherham United, Bristol City, Nottingham Forest, Peterborough United and Hereford United.

GARDNER, Anthony Derek 2003-04 ①

Born: Stone, Staffs, 19 September 1980
Career: Port Vale (apprentice, May 1996, professional, July 1998), Tottenham Hotspur (£1m, January 2000), Hull City (£2.5m, August 2008).

Anthony Gardner was part of the Tottenham Hotspur side that was having a resurgence of form under Maarten Jol but even the club's die-hard fans raised an eyebrow when the former 6ft 5in Port Vale defender was selected for England by manager Sven-Göran Eriksson. He made his substitute debut appearance in the defeat by Sweden in March 2004 and unfortunately he 'did not do the business.' Gardner, who has also played in one U21 international, moved to Hull in 2008, having made 144 appearances for Spurs.

GARDNER, Thomas 1933-35 ②

Born: Huyton near Liverpool, 28 May 1910
Died: Chester, 23 February 1970
Career: Orrell FC (junior, May 1926), Liverpool (amateur, July 1928, professional, April 1929), Grimsby Town (June 1931), Hull City (£2,000, May 1932), Aston Villa (£4,500, February 1934), Burnley (April 1938); WW2 guest for Preston North End, Blackpool, Southport, Manchester United and Blackburn Rovers; Wrexham (December 1945), Wellington Town (August 1947), Oswestry Town (player-manager, June 1950, reverting to player-coach, January 1952), Saltney FC (player, August 1952, retired May 1953), Chester (assistant-trainer/groundsman, July 1954-May 1967); then steward at a social club in Chester (until his death); also owned a hotel in Wrexham (albeit briefly).

A fair-haired, enthusiastic yet very constructive wing-half, Tom 'Ghandi' Gardner spent 43 years in football (1926-69). He possessed a decidedly long throw and many goals were scored from his launches deep into the opposition penalty-area. His two England caps were gained against Czechoslovakia in Prague in May 1934 (lost 2-1) and Holland in Amsterdam twelve months later (won 1-0). He helped Hull win the Third Division (North) championship in 1933 and was a WW2 League Cup winner with Blackpool in 1943.

GARFIELD, Benjamin Walter 1897-98 ①

Born: Higham Ferrers, Nene Valley, Northants, 18 August 1872
Died: Tunbridge Wells, Kent, 10 December 1942
Career: Finedon FC (season 1888-89), Wellingborough (seasons 1889-91), Kettering Town (May 1892), Burton Wanderers (July 1894), West Bromwich Albion (£200, May 1896), Aston Villa (guest, 1900), Brighton & Hove Albion (£100, August 1902), Tunbridge Wells Rangers (August 1905, retired May 1906); became a licensee in Tunbridge Wells, Kent.

Inside or outside-left Ben Garfield scored 38 goals in 117 games for WBA whom he served for six years from 1896, helping the Baggies win the Second Division title in 1902. A year later he gained a Southern League championship winner's medal with Brighton. A surprise choice by England for the Home international against Ireland in Belfast in March 1898, when he partnered Fred Wheldon on the left-wing, Garfield had a 'decent enough game' in a 3-2 win.

GARRATY, William 1902-03 ①

Born: Saltley, Birmingham, 6 October 1878
Died: Aston, Birmingham, 6 May 1931
Career: Church Road & Saltley St Saviour's Schools/Birmingham, Ashted Swifts (August 1892), St Saviour's FC (April 1893), Highfield Villa (August 1894), Lozells FC (September 1895), Aston Shakespeare (May 1896), Aston Villa (professional, August 1897),

Leicester Fosse (£150, September 1908), West Bromwich Albion (£270, October 1908), Lincoln City (£100, May 1910, retired, May 1911); Aston Villa (trainer, April-May 1913); fell seriously ill with pneumonia in April 1915; recovered and later employed as a delivery driver for an Aston-based brewery.

Bill Garraty was a very skilful inside-right or centre-forward who helped Aston Villa win successive League championships in 1899 and 1900, top-scoring in the second season when he also headed the First Division charts. In 1905 he added an FA Cup winner's medal to his tally before leaving Villa Park in 1908 having netted 112 goals in 259 first-class appearances. He won his only England cap in a 2-1 win over Wales at Portsmouth in March 1903 when he played 'up front' with his Villa team-mate Joe Bache. His brother Frank played for Aston Villa's second team in the late 1890s.

GARRETT, Thomas Henry 1951-53 ③

Born: Whiteless, County Durham, 28 February 1927
Died: Wallsend, New South Wales, Australia, 16 April 2006
Career: Horden Colliery FC (season 1941-42), Blackpool (amateur, August 1942, professional, October 1944), Millwall (free, May 1961); Fleetwood Town (August 1962), Mayfield United-Newcastle FC/Australia, (May 1963, retired, October 1964); remained in Australia for the rest of his life.

Very few right-wingers got the better of dashing left-back Tom Garrett who made a sound international debut in place of the injured Bill Eckersley in a 2-1 win over Scotland at Hampden Park in April 1951. He then played well in a 1-1 draw with Italy the following month before winning his final cap against Wales in a World Cup qualifier in October 1953 (won 4-1). Garrett amassed 334 appearances for Blackpool whom he served from 1942 until 1961, gaining an FA Cup winner's medal in 1953. He helped Millwall win the Fourth Division championship in 1962.

GASCOIGNE, Paul John 1988-98 ㊗ ⑩

Born: Gateshead, 27 May 1967
Career: Redheugh Boys' Club/Gateshead (from 1978), Dunston Juniors (season 1982-83), Newcastle United (initially signing schoolboy forms in May 1980, then apprentice, June 1983, professional, May 1985) , Tottenham Hotspur (£2m, July 1988), SS Lazio/Italy (£5.5m, May 1992), Glasgow Rangers (£4.3m, July 1995), Middlesbrough (£3.4m, March 1998), Everton (July 2000), Burnley (free, March 2002), DC United/USA (trial, June-July 2002), Gansu Tianmu/China (player-coach, January-April 2003), Wolverhampton Wanderers (reserves, August-September 2003), Boston United (player-coach, July-October 2004); attended a coaching course in season 2004-05; Algarve United/Portugal (two months, summer 2005), Kettering Town (manager, for 39 days, October-December 2005); out of football for five years; Garforth Town (manager, briefly, October 2010, but was never seen at the club or a match and did not sign a contract); has appeared on the BBC TV quiz show *The Weakest Link*; had his autobiography published in 2004 (*Gazza – My Story*); has promoted two video games; advertised Fabergé brand Brut, was part of the ITV commentary team at the 2002 World Cup and made a pop record – 'Fog on the Tyne Revisited' – with Lindisfarne in 1990, which reached number 2 in the UK charts. As a player he was involved in many off-field incidents and since retiring has suffered from alcoholism, been arrested numerous times for drink driving and acts of violence, monitored for mental illness as well as having to cope with scores of personal and legal problems. Shortly after entering rehab for the 12th time in November 2010, he received an eight-week prison sentence, suspended for one year at Newcastle Magistrates Court.

Paul Gascoigne was on top of his game at Italia '90, producing some superb performances, before his unforgettable tears following the semi-final defeat by West Germany.

Before that tournament, the chunky, beefy Geordie made his England debut as a late substitute (for Peter Beardsley) in a 1-0 win over Denmark at Wembley in April 1988. He quickly began to 'please' the fans by producing some dazzling performances, both at home and away. Indeed, in April 1989, he netted his first international goal, after a magical, ghosting dribble and gliding shot into the far corner in the 5-0 home win over Albania.

He produced a super show in the 4-2 win over Czechoslovakia at Wembley in April 1990. Taking the game by the 'scruff of the neck' he showed skill, power, drive and enthusiasm and laid on goals for Steve Bull and Stuart Pearce before adding a fourth himself with a thumping left foot drive high into the net.

But his stunning goal against Scotland at Euro '96 remains a firm favourite with the fans. That afternoon he was superb and his right-foot volley sewed up a 2-0 victory.

Gascoigne was carried off in successive games in May 1997 – first against South Africa at Old Trafford and then in a World Cup qualifier in Poland. But he was quickly back into the action…never wanting to be sidelined for too long!

Probably England's most 'exciting' player in modern times, simply because of his enthusiasm and commitment, unfortunately 'Gazza' had his off days and his overall brilliance only came in fits and starts. He was actually dropped by manager Graham Taylor for the game against the Republic of Ireland in Dublin in November 1990. And he was sorely missed as the Irish plundered a 1-1 draw.

'Gazza', who also played for his country at Youth team level as well as in four B and 13 U21 internationals, was voted the PFA's 'Young Player of the Year' in 1988. He was signed by Spurs manager Terry Venables (from Newcastle) in 1988 for a then British record fee of £2 million. He helped Spurs win the FA Cup in 1991 - although he was carried off with a cruciate knee ligament injury after an ill-judged lunge at Nottingham Forest full-back Gary Charles - and later played his part as Rangers won two Scottish Premiership titles and also triumphed in both domestic Cup competitions. He then became the first player (albeit as a substitute) to make a club debut in a Wembley Cup final when he came on for Middlesbrough in their League Cup victory over Chelsea in 1998. In a varied yet exciting career, Gascoigne scored over 100 goals in more than 450 club appearances, having his best spells with Newcastle and Spurs. Unfortunately it was all down hill for the reliable Geordie once he had taken off his boots!

GATES, Eric Lazenby 1980-81 ②

Born: Ferryhill, County Durham, 28 June 1955
Career: Ipswich Town (apprentice, May 1971, professional, October 1972), Sunderland (£150,000, August 1985), Carlisle United (free, May 1990 retired, May 1991); later worked for Century FM and BBC Radio Newcastle and became one of the North-east's most popular after dinner speakers with his entertaining personality and stories from his football career.

Eric Gates made his England debut against Norway at Wembley in September 1980. He did well in midfield with Bryan Robson and fellow debutant Graham Rix in a 4-0 win. However, he didn't impress in his second game v. Romania and was never selected again. Overall he had an excellent career, scoring over 160 goals in more than 650 League and Cup games for his three clubs. He helped Ipswich win the UEFA Cup in 1981 and twice finish runners-up in the First Division.

GAY, Leslie Hewitt 1892-94 ③

Born: Brighton, 24 March 1871
Died: Sidmouth, Devon, 1 November 1949
Career: Marlborough College (April 1888), Brighton College XI (seasons 1889-91), Clare College/Cambridge University (seasons 1891-94); played for Old Brightonians (early to mid-1890s), Corinthians (seasons 1891-94); also played cricket for Hampshire and Somerset, appearing in one Test Match for England as a wicket-keeper; a useful golfer who worked in Ceylon as a coffee planter before becoming a land agent in Somerset and Devon.

An utterly fearless goalkeeper, Leslie Gay conceded five goals in his three internationals. He played 'well' on his debut in a 5-2 win over Scotland at the Richmond Athletic Ground, Surrey, in April 1893, produced a fine display in his next game, a 5-1 victory over Wales at Wrexham, but was at fault for one of the goals in his last outing, a 2-2 draw with the Scots at Parkhead in April 1894, failing to hold a weakish shot from McMahon. As a cricketer, his Test Match appearance was against Australia in 1894-95.

This man is the only Gay to play for England at either football or cricket!

GEARY, Fred 1889-91 ② ③

Born: Hyson Green, Nottingham, 23 January 1868
Died: Liverpool, 8 January 1955
Career: Hyson Green Church (seasons 1882-85), Balmoral FC/ Nottingham (August 1885), Notts Rangers (April 1886), Grimsby Town (professional, June 1887), Notts Rangers (August 1888), Notts County (briefly in 1889), Notts Rangers (March-April 1889), Everton (July 1889), Liverpool (£60, May 1895, retired, injured, May 1899); became a licensee in Liverpool.

Fred Geary helped Everton win the First Division championship in 1891 and Liverpool the Second Division title in 1896. A dashing, thrustful, lively centre-forward, he was a splendid marksman although at times could be too hasty in front of goal. He scored a hat-trick on his England debut in a 9-1 win over Ireland in March 1890 but found it much tougher in his second game v. Scotland a year later, although he played well enough in a 2-1 victory. His club career realised over 100 goals in more than 160 senior games, with his best return coming with Everton, 86 goals in 98 appearances.

GEAVES, Captain Richard Lyon 1874-75 ①

Born: Acuna, Mexico, 6 May 1854
Died: Winchester, 21 March 1935
Career: Harrow School (seasons 1870-72), Caius College/Cambridge University (seasons 1872-75); played for Clapham Rovers and Old Harrovians (during seasons 1873-75); served with the 14th Buckingham Prince of Wales Yorkshire Regiment for six years from 1875, attaining the rank of Captain before retiring in 1881; also played cricket and later returned to Mexico in an attempt to bring the game to that country.

A tireless, enthusiastic winger, Dick Geaves was difficult to knock off the ball and was always a threat down the left flank. He twice came close to scoring in his only game for England, a 2-2 draw with Scotland at The Oval in March 1875.

GEE, Charles William 1931-37 ③

Born: Reddish near Stockport, 6 April 1909
Died: Edgeley, Stockport, 11 July 1981
Career: Reddish Green Wesleyans (April 1924), Stockport County (professional, December 1928), Everton (£3,000, July 1930, retired, injured, May 1940); returned to live and work in Stockport.

Centre-half Charlie Gee was as strong as any defender in the game during the 1930s. A highly constructive player, he helped Everton win the Second Division title in 1931 and the First Division a year later, but missed the Merseysiders' FA Cup final victory in 1933 through injury. He made 212 appearances for the Goodison Park club in 10 years. He was outstanding on his England debut in a 3-1 win over Wales in November 1931 and the following month played even better when Spain were battered 7-1 at Highbury. Gee was perhaps unfortunate not to win more caps than he did…as there were so many other fine pivots around at the same time.

GELDARD, Albert 1933-38 ④

Born: Bradford, 11 April 1914
Died: Lancaster, 19 October 1989
Career: Whetley Lane School/Bradford, Manningham Mills FC (junior, August 1927), Bradford Park Avenue (amateur, aged 14, June 1928, semi-professional, April 1930), Everton (professional, November 1932), Bolton Wanderers (£4,500, July 1938, retired, injured, May 1947); returned with Darwen (November 1949-May 1950); also played club cricket in the Yorkshire League and was a member of the Magic Circle.

An England Schoolboy international as a 14 year-old, Albert Geldard played in his first Football League game for Bradford Park Avenue at the age of 15 years, 156 days in September 1929 – the youngest ever debutant at that time. A fast-raiding outside-right, he went on to have a fine career and gained an FA Cup winner's medal with Everton in 1933. His first game in an England shirt was against Italy in May 1933 when he was tightly-marked in a 1-1 draw. A week later he had a hand in two of the goals when Switzerland were whipped 4-0 but disappointed in a 2-0 defeat by Scotland two years later. His final international appearance was against Ireland in October 1937 when he caused havoc at times as England raced to a 5-1 victory. One must remember that when Geldard was playing, there were several pretty useful right-wingers around at the same time including Sammy Crooks, Joe Hulme and a certain Stanley Matthews.
　　Geldard struck over 50 goals in just over 250 appearances in competitive football (233 in the Football League). Without doubt, he had his best spell with Everton – 37 goals in 180 games – and once, as a schoolboy, he scored 22 goals in one Saturday morning match. He was a magician both on and off the field!

GEORGE, Charles Frederick 1976-77 ①

Born: Islington, London, 10 October 1950
Career: Holloway Comprehensive School/London, Islington & District Schools, Middlesex Schools, London Schools, New Middleton FC (season 1965-66), Arsenal (apprentice, May 1966, professional, February 1968), Derby County (£90,000, July 1975), St George's Budapest/Australia (loan, May 1977), Minnesota Kicks/USA (loan, May 1978), Southampton (£400,000, December 1978), Nottingham Forest (loan, January-March 1990), Bulova/Hong Kong (September-October 1981), AFC Bournemouth (early March 1982), Derby County (late March 1982), Bulova (again, summer 1982), Dundee United (trial, September 1982), Coventry City (August 1983, retired, April 1984); lost a finger in a lawnmower accident towards the end of his football career; later ran a pub in New Milton in the New Forest and worked as a mechanic as part-owner of a garage firm before becoming a matchday host at Highbury and running the Arsenal museum.

Charlie George produced a lack-lustre performance when making his England debut in the 1-1 draw with the Republic of Ireland at Wembley in September 1976. He had been overlooked by Alf Ramsey when in his prime with Arsenal and received a belated call from Don Revie. A flamboyant forward who could be brilliant one week and dire the next, George was certainly a favourite with the fans wherever he played. He helped Arsenal win the Inter Cities Fairs Cup in 1970 and complete the double the following year when he scored a dramatic winning goal in the FA Cup final v. Liverpool. George, who was plagued by injury from 1975 onwards, netted 105 goals in 411 games during his club career which spanned 18 years.

GEORGE, William 1901-02 ③

Born: Shrewsbury, 29 June 1874
Died: Aston, Birmingham, 4 December 1933
Career: Woolwich Ramblers (season 1887-88); served in the Army with the Royal Artillery (from October 1888), Trowbridge Town (when on leave, seasons 1895-97), Aston Villa (£50, professional, October 1897), Birmingham (player-trainer, July 1911, retired as a player, May 1913, continued as trainer until May 1915); later worked at the Austin Rover car plant, Longbridge; also played cricket for Warwickshire (between 1901 and 1907), Wiltshire and Shropshire.

Billy George was a huge goalkeeper, 6ft 4ins tall and weighing well over 21 stone at times. He was consistent throughout his career, making 401 appearances for Aston Villa with whom he won the FA Cup and two League championships. Capped three times by England v. Wales, Ireland (when he saved Bob Milne's penalty) and Scotland in season 1901-02, he took over from John Robinson (Southampton) and kept clean sheets in his first two games before conceding two goals in the drawn game with the Scots on his own patch at Villa Park… this being a replay of the abandoned game at Ibrox Park a month earlier when 26 people were killed as terraces collapsed at one end of the ground.
　　Unsighted for the first Scottish goal scored by his Villa team-mate Bobby Templeton after just three minutes, George was later beaten by a header at his near post by Orr before another of his club-mates Albert Wilkes equalised to salvage a point.
　　He made one appearance for Birmingham at the age of 37.
　　When George was 'signed' out of the Army in 1897, there was such a hullabaloo surrounding the transaction that two Aston Villa committee members, George Ramsay, a former England international, and Fred Rinder, along with George himself, were suspended by the FA for a month!

GERRARD, Steven George, MBE 2000-12 (102) (19)

Born: Huyton, Liverpool, 30 May 1980
Career: Liverpool (apprentice, May 1996, professional, February 1998)

A real powerhouse for his club and country, Steven Gerrard has been brilliant over the last three years, driving forward and scoring some cracking goals despite being asked to play on the right, in the centre and on the left of midfield. After suffering a stress fracture at the base of his back during a training session under England manager Kevin Keegan in his first season as a professional at Anfield, Gerrard made his international debut against Ukraine in May 2000 and that summer was called up for Euro 2000, making only one appearance as a substitute in a 1–0 win over Germany before England were eliminated in the group stage. In September 2001 he scored his first England goal in that marvellous 5-1 victory over the Germans in Munich.

He bagged his second goal in the 2-2 draw with Macedonia later that season and since then has figured on the scoresheet at regular intervals, including as captain, netting England's first goal (v. the USA) in the 2010 World Cup finals in South Africa. But he has confessed: 'I should have scored more.' Subsequently skipper of Roy Hodgson's side at Euro 2012, Gerrard was perhaps one of England's better players in Poland and the Ukraine.

In November 2012, he deservedly won his 100th full cap, skippering England in Stockholm. Unfortunately it wasn't a happy night out for the likeable 'Scouser' as the Swedes won 4-2. But he did have the pleasure of seeing the 'best goal' he's ever witnessed, a remarkable overhead kick from 30 yards by Zlatan Ibrahimovic who, in fact, netted all his country's goals in the Friends Arena.

As a Liverpool player, Gerrard was instrumental when the treble of League Cup, FA Cup and UEFA Cup was won in 2001. He was outstanding again in 2003 when the League Cup was lifted for a second time and two years later celebrated with his team-mates when Liverpool won the European Champions League final after storming back from 3-0 down at half-time to beat Milan on penalties after extra-time. Besides his full England caps, Gerrard – who has had to cope with a string of irritating injuries over the last three years - has also represented his country in five Youth and four U21 internationals and was voted PFA Young Player of the Year in 2003. At May 2013, he had scored 159 goals in 631 senior appearances for Liverpool.

Gerrard appeared in the 2011 film, *Will*.

GIBBINS, William Vivian Talbot 1923-25 (2) (3)

Born: Forest Gate, London, 10 August 1901
Died: Walthamstow, London, 21 November 1979
Career: Godwin Road School/London, Clapton (August 1919), West Ham United (December 1923), Clapton (January 1932), Brentford (February 1932), Bristol Rovers (June 1932), Southampton (September 1933), Leyton (March 1934), Catford Wanderers/London (August 1934, retired, May 1939); was a schoolteacher by profession, becoming headmaster of a state school in West Ham.

One of the great non-professional forwards of his generation, Vivian Gibbins retained amateur status throughout his career which spanned 20 years: 1919-39. He helped Clapton win the FA Amateur Cup in 1924 and later played for Leyton in the 1934 final. He won 12 caps for England as an amateur (1925-32) and two at senior level, scoring twice on his debut in a 3-1 win over France in May 1924 and netting against the same opposition in his second international a year later when his side won 2-1. He scored 58 goals in 129 appearances for West Ham.

GIBBS, Kieran James Ricardo 2010-11 (2)

Born: Lambeth, London, 26 September 1989
Career: Arsenal (apprentice, April 2006, professional, September 2007), Norwich City (loan, January-March 2008)

Attacking left-back Kieran Gibbs made his full England debut as a second-half substitute for Ashley Cole in the 2-1 friendly win over Hungary at Wembley in August 2010. He produced a very impressive performance, linking up down the flank with Ashley Young. Three months later he won his second cap, starting in the 2-1 defeat by France when he opposed his Arsenal team-mates Samir Nasri and Bacary Sagna. Unfortunately a lack of match sharpness was exposed although he did have a couple of decent runs down the left wing. Gibbs has also played for his country at youth and U21 levels. He replaced Gael Clichy in the Arsenal team.

GIDMAN, John 1976-77 (1)

Born: Garston, Liverpool, 10 January 1954
Career: Garston Schoolboy football, Liverpool (apprentice, June 1969), Aston Villa (professional, August 1971), Everton (£650,000, plus Pat Heard, October 1979), Manchester United (£450,000, August 1981), Manchester City (free, October 1986), Stoke City (free, August 1988), Darlington (player and assistant-manager, February-May 1989), King's Lynn (manager, briefly, early 1990s); moved to Marbella, Spain to run a café/bar.

An attacking right-back, capped once by England against Luxembourg in a World Cup qualifier in March 1977 when he partnered Trevor Cherry in a 5-0 win at Wembley, John Gidman twice helped Aston Villa win the League Cup, in 1975 and 1977, as well as the FA Youth Cup and Third Division championship. He also played in three Youth and four U23 internationals.

Injuries interrupted him late in his career and he also suffered eye damage from an exploding firework. Undoubtedly a fine player, he was sent off playing for Villa in a UEFA Cup clash against Barcelona in the Nou Camp Stadium in 1978. Gidman, who retired as a player in 1989, amassed a total of 432 League appearances during his career.

GILLARD, Ian Terry 1974-76 (3)

Born: Hammersmith, London, 9 October 1950
Career: London Schools, Tottenham Hotspur (signed schoolboy forms, aged 14, May 1964), Queens Park Rangers (apprentice, March 1967, professional, October 1968), Aldershot (player, July 1982, player-coach, May 1983, retired from football, May 1985).

Strong-tackling left-back Ian Gillard played in three full internationals for England, lining up against West Germany (won 2-0) and Wales (2-2) towards the end of the 1974-75 season when Leicester's Steve Whitworth was his partner and in the 2-1 defeat by Czechoslovakia in a European Championship qualifier in October 1975 when Paul Madeley of Leeds United was on his right.

GILLIAT, Walter Evelyn 1892-93 ① ③
Born: Stoke Poges, Buckinghamshire, 22 July 1869
Died: Woking, 2 January 1963
Career: Charterhouse School (seasons 1884-88), Magdalen
College/Oxford University (seasons 1888-93); also played for Old
Carthusians and Woking (seasons 1892-95); also played cricket for
Buckinghamshire; ordained in 1895 and became curate at Woking and
Tunbridge Wells; later Vicar of Iver 1901, Rector of Sevenoaks 1921-29.

Rated second only to the great William Cobbold, slightly-built
forward Walter Gilliat was a wonderful close dribbler who would
surely have played more times for England had injuries not affected
his game for long periods. His only cap was won against Ireland in
February 1893 and what a game he had! He scored a hat-trick, two
of his goals superb individual efforts, in a resounding 6-1 win.

GODDARD, Paul 1981-82 ① ①
Born: Harlington, Middlesex, 12 October 1959
Career: Queens Park Rangers (apprentice, May 1976, professional,
July 1977), West Ham United (£800,000, August 1980), Newcastle
United (£415,000, November 1986), Derby County (£425,000,
July 1988), Millwall (£800,000, December 1989), Ipswich Town
(free, February 1991; retired May 1994, appointed coach, became
assistant-manager, then caretaker-manager, December 1994,
assistant-coach, January 1995); returned to West Ham United
(as coach and assistant-manager); since 2008, has worked as a
football agent for the Stellar Group.

Debutant striker Paul Goddard (brought on for Cyrille Regis) collected
Glenn Hoddle's inch-perfect pass to net a 69th minute equaliser
for England against Iceland in Reykjavik in June 1982 (1-1). This
gave him the honour (record) of being the only substitute to score
for England on his debut and never win another cap. Also capped
eight times at U21 level, Goddard's League career spanned 16
years (1977-93) during which time he scored a total of 125 goals
in 442 appearances, helping West Ham win the Second Division
championship and reach the League Cup semi-final in 1981.

GOODALL, Frederick Roy 1925-34 ㉕
Born: Dronfield, Yorkshire, 31 December 1902
Died: Shipley, Yorkshire, 19 January 1982
Career: Dronfield Grammar School, Dronfield Woodhouse (junior,
August 1919), Huddersfield Town (£20, professional, August 1921,
retired May 1937); Nottingham Forest (trainer, May 1937-April
1944), Mansfield Town (secretary-manager, August 1945-June
1949), Huddersfield Town (trainer, from August 1949, then youth
team manager, October 1964-July 1965).

Right-back Roy Goodall gained a hat-trick
of First Division championship winner's
medals with Huddersfield (1924-25-26)
and he also played in two losing FA
Cup finals (1928 and 1930) during his
time at Leeds Road when he made 440
appearances for the Terriers. A Football
League representative on eight occasions,
he won his first England cap as partner to
Tommy Mort in the 1-0 defeat by Scotland
at Old Trafford in April 1926…this being the 50th full international
between the two countries. The Times reporter stated that Goodall's
'speed about the penalty area in pursuit of the mercurial Hughie
Gallacher and outside-left Troup' was among the consoling features
for the England supporters.

Despite that decent performance, Goodall missed the next two
games but then came back in April 1927 and later captained the
team. Never overawed by a big occasion, he was without doubt, a
great defender. Fast and clever in his positional play, he believed in the
shoulder charge and his tackling was first-class. Goodall continued
to turn out for England until December 1933, finishing on the losing
side just five times in 25 starts. He did though miss a penalty for his
country in a 2-1 defeat by Wales at Burnley in November 1927.

GOODALL, John 1887-98 ⑭ ⑫
Born: Westminster, London, 19 June 1863
Died: Watford, 20 May 1942
Career: Kilmarnock Burns (August 1878), Kilmarnock Athletic
(August 1879), Great Lever (May 1884), Preston North End
(professional, August 1885), Derby County (May 1889), New
Brighton Tower (June 1899), Glossop (August 1900), Watford
(player-manager, August 1903-May 1907); out of football for three
years; Racing Club Roubaix/France (manager, seasons 1910-12),
Mardy/Wales (manager, May 1912, retired, May 1913); later West
Herts Club, Watford (groundsman, February 1925-May 1928); also
played cricket for Derbyshire and Hertfordshire.

John Goodall – known as 'Johnny All
Good' – and his Preston team-mate Fred
Dewhurst played brilliantly together when
England whipped Scotland 5-0 in Glasgow
in March 1888 – to register their first
victory over their 'Northern' rivals in eight
years. The Scots defenders were 'defeated,
disgraced and annihilated by the powerful
England forwards who may well have
scored four or five goals more.' An inside-
right or centre-forward of unsurpassed excellence, Goodall scored
on his international debut a month earlier in a 5-1 win over Wales,
and in fact he was on target in each of his first three England games
and scored in ten of his first 12, bagging braces in a 4-1 win over the
Scots in April 1892 and in a 9-0 drubbing of Ireland in March 1895.

Goodall was superb at holding a forward-line together and in a
long and varied career he scored well over 200 goals in more than
300 club appearances (182 in 273 in Football League games).
He bagged nine goals in Preston's 26-0 FA Cup win over Hyde in
1887 and did likewise in the club's 16-2 friendly win over Dundee
Strathblane. He also helped Preston complete the League and Cup
double in 1889 and played in two losing Cup finals. He appeared
in his last game for Watford on 14 September 1907 at the age of
44 years, 87 days in a Southern League game against Bradford,
becoming the oldest person ever to have played for the Hornets.

His brother, Archibald, was born in Ireland, and played for that
country as well as Derby County.

GOODHART, Harry Chester 1882-83 ③
Born: Wimbledon, 17 July 1858
Died: Edinburgh, 21 April 1895
Career: Eton College (seasons 1876-78), Trinity College/Cambridge
University (seasons 1878-82), played for Old Etonians (seasons
1882-90); lecturer at Cambridge and later professor of Humanities
at Edinburgh University.

Harry Goodhart played in three FA Cup finals for Old Etonians,
gaining a winner's medal in 1882. A hard-working utility forward, he
lacked pace but nevertheless always gave 100 per cent in whatever
game he played. He won his three England caps in the space of five
weeks towards the end of the 1882-83 season, starring in 5-0 and
7-0 wins over Wales and Ireland respectively.

GOODWYN, Alfred George 1872-73 ①
Born: Calcutta, India, 13 March 1850
Died: Roorkee, East Indies, 14 March 1874
Career: Royal Military Academy/Woolwich (seasons 1869-71), Royal Engineers (August 1871 until his death).

A resolute full-back or right-half, strong and mobile, Alf Goodwyn played in the very first FA Cup final for Royal Engineers in their 1-0 defeat by the Wanderers. The following year he won his first England cap in a 4-2 victory over Scotland at The Oval. Wrote one correspondent: "For England Captain Kenyon-Slaney was of the greatest service...but we must not forget the excellent play of Goodall and Howell."

Having been posted back to India with his regiment, Goodwyn sadly died a day after his 24th birthday from injuries received in a riding accident. His passing came on the morning of the FA Cup final where his colleagues were defeated 2-0 by Oxford University.

Goodwyn died whilst on active service with the Royal Engineers in the East Indies.

GOODYER, Arthur Copeland 1878-79 ①
Born: Nottingham, 2 February, 1854
Died: Denver, Colorado, USA, 8 January 1932
Career: Trent College/Nottingham, Nottingham Forest (November 1878, retired, injured, March 1880); later engaged in the lace trade; emigrated to the USA in 1888; also competed as a useful middle-distance runner.

Arthur Goodyer scored a 'great' goal on his international debut when England edged out brave Scotland 5-4 at The Oval in April 1879. He was one of the star players on a day when both defences took a battering! A useful winger with a good turn of foot, Goodyer was prone to get 'stranded upfield' far too often! He was tragically killed in a car accident.

GOSLING, Robert Cunliffe, JP 1891-95 ⑤ ②
Born: Farnham, Surrey, 15 June 1868
Died: Hassiobury, Essex, 18 April 1922
Career: Eton College (seasons 1886-88), Trinity College/Cambridge University (seasons 1889-91), played for Old Etonians (seasons 1888-90) and Corinthians (seasons 1889-1900); Donor of the Arthur Dunn Cup (an old boys' football trophy); also played cricket for Cambridge University, Essex and Eton (v. Harrow); became Justice of the Peace and High Sheriff of Essex.

Bob Gosling was a quality footballer, strong and fast who could perform equally well as a winger or inside-forward. He gained the first of his five England caps at outside-right in a 2-0 victory over Wales at Wrexham in March 1892 and followed up by scoring in each of his next two internationals v. Scotland (won 5-2) and Wales (won 5-1).

Described by Sir Frederick Wall, the long-serving Secretary of the Football Association, as 'the richest man who ever played football for England', Gosling was the scion of a wealthy Essex family and the oldest of seven brothers (and one of 14 children), four of whom played cricket for Eton against Harrow. Gosling was, recalled the early sportswriter JAH Catton ('Tityrus'), '...the most aristocratic-looking man I ever saw', a view concurred in by his England international colleague C.B. Fry, who described him as 'the best-looking man of my acquaintance' and one of the players whose presence in the Corinthians' side contributed to 'their reputation up North as a team of toffs'.

Secretary Wall also stated that... 'Gosling's bearing lent him an imposing presence on the football field'. He looked 'every inch the high-born...his carriage and gait would have done credit to a court Chamberlain at a levee' and was admirably built, being merely 'bone and muscle, not soft flesh.'

When Gosling died in 1922, he left a fortune which proved to be more than £700,000 (£21.25m at current prices). One of his brothers, William, followed him as High Sheriff of Essex.

GOSNELL, Albert Arthur 1905-06 ①
Born: Colchester, 10 February 1880
Died: Norwich, 6 January 1972
Career: The Albion/Colchester (August 1898), Colchester Town (July 1899), New Brompton (July 1901), Chatham (August 1902), Newcastle United (£10, May 1904), Tottenham Hotspur (£100, July 1910), Darlington (August 1911), Port Vale (August 1912-May 1915), Newcastle United (assistant-trainer, August 1919); Norwich City (manager, January 1921-March 1926), Colchester United (trainer-coach, June 1928-May 1928); also played for Essex County (between 1900 and 1904); became a licensee in Norwich.

Albert Gosnell won two League championships with Newcastle (1905 & 1907) and also played in two losing FA Cup finals. A wonderful outside-left, he replaced Bobby Templeton at St. James' Park where he spent his best years, scoring 18 goals in 124 appearances for the Geordies. His only England cap came against Ireland in February 1906 when he assisted in two of the goals in a resounding 5-0 win in Belfast. He was the ninth different left-winger used by England in just ten internationals over a period of three years.

GOUGH, Harold Cyril 1920-21 ①
Born: Chesterfield, 31 December 1890
Died: Castleford, West Yorkshire, 16 June, 1970
Career: Spital Olympic (from June 1906), Bradford Park Avenue (May 1910), Castleford Town (August 1911), Sheffield United (May 1913; suspended May-December 1924 for becoming a licensee which was against Castleford/Sheffield United rules); Harrogate (October 1926), Oldham Athletic (February 1927), Bolton Wanderers (December 1927), Torquay United (June 1928, retired, injured, May 1930).

Harold Gough helped Sheffield United win the FA Cup in 1915 – just two years after playing in non-League football. A daring, courageous goalkeeper who enjoyed racing out to dive at the feet of opposing forwards, he collected his solitary England cap in a 3-0 defeat by Scotland in Glasgow in April 1921...at a time when the number 1 position was causing some concern. In fact, Gough was the fourth different 'keeper called up in consecutive matches. He was suspended by the Blades for breaking club rules when he took over a public house in 1924.

GOULDEN, Leonard Arthur 1936-39 ⑭ ④
Born: Hackney, London, 16 July 1912
Died: Looe, Cornwall, 14 February 1995
Career: Holborn Street School/London, West Ham Schools, Chelmsford (amateur, May 1928), Leyton (June 1929), Dagenham (briefly), West Ham United (amateur, July 1931, professional, April 1933), Chelsea (WW2 guest, signed for £5,000, August 1945, retired, May 1950; then coach for two seasons, to May 1952); Watford (manager, November 1952-July 1956; acted as general manager, October 1955-February 1956); worked as a sub-master (1956-59); also coached briefly in Libya; Watford (coach, July 1959-May 1962); coached in Libya (again, for two years); Banbury Town/Spencer (secretary-manager, October 1965-March 1967), Oxford United (reserve team coach, January 1969-February 1970); later worked at the US Air Force base in Northamptonshire.

Inside-forward Len Goulden had a magical left-foot and the way he could dribble and twist and give a short ball was fascinating. Quick-witted, he was a born footballer and when he shot at goal his effort was controlled. He served West Ham for 12 years (1933-45) scoring 55 goals in 253 first-team appearances and helping the Hammers win the Wartime League Cup. He was later in Chelsea's team as a guest that won the Football League South Cup in 1945. Goulden netted once on his England debut in a 6-0 win over Norway in Oslo in May 1937. He was outstanding in the 4-0 victory over Sweden a few days later, set up a goal for Mills in a 5-1 triumph over Ireland five months after that and had a helping hand in one of Stanley Matthews' hat-trick goals when Czechoslovakia were defeated 5-4 at Tottenham in December 1937. On target in a 6-3 win over Germany in Berlin in May 1938, he then scored in a 3-0 win over FIFA later in the year before grabbing his fourth and final international goal in a 2-0 victory in Romania in May 1939.

Goulden also scored three goals in six Wartime internationals.

GRAHAM, Leonard 1924-25 ②
Born: Leyton, London, 20 August 1901
Died: Archway, London, 21 December 1962
Career: Capworth United/Leyton (August 1918), Leytonstone (June 1921), Millwall (October 1923, retired, injured, May 1934); gained FA coaching badge; The Hague (coach, seasons 1936-39); later Merchant Taylor School (coach); also played cricket for Essex; became a licensee and then business executive in London.

A Third Division (South) winner with Millwall, Len Graham was a stylish left-half, highly constructive whose two caps were gained against Wales in February 1925 (won 2-1) and Scotland five weeks later. He was given a tough time in the latter international at Hampden Park by the right-wing pairing of Alec Jackson and Willie Russell as the Scots won 2-0 in front of 92,000 spectators.

GRAHAM, Thomas 1930-31 ②
Born: Hamsterley, County Durham, 5 March 1907
Died: Nottingham, 29 March 1983
Career: Hamsterley Swifts (August 1922), Consett Celtic (August 1923), Nottingham Forest (trial, April-May 1926), Newcastle United (trial, summer, 1927), Nottingham Forest (signed, professional, August 1927, retired, May 1944; then club's trainer to 1961, later youth team advisor and part-time scout)

Tommy Graham was a brilliant centre-half who made 391 appearances for Nottingham Forest whom he served in various capacities for 43 years. Despite being on the small side, he was never over-powered in the air and was as good as any defender when the ball was on the ground. He was handed his two England caps against France in Paris in May 1931 when he admitted 'he wasn't at his best' in a 5-2 defeat, and in the 6-2 victory over Ireland in Belfast five months later when he took over from injured captain Alf Strange. Graham also played twice for the Football League.

GRAINGER, Colin 1955-57 ⑦ ③
Born: Havercraft, Yorkshire, 10 June 1933
Career: Rye Hill Junior & South Hindley Secondary Modern Schools, Rye Hill & Havercroft Boys, South Elmshall FC (August 1948), Wrexham (groundstaff, June 1949, professional, February 1951), Sheffield United (£3,000, June 1953), Sunderland (£7,000, February 1957), Leeds United (£15,000, July 1960), Port Vale

(£6,000, October 1961), Doncaster Rovers (free, August 1964), Macclesfield Town (free, July 1966, released November 1966); later Huddersfield Town (scout); also employed in Harrogate by his uncle, Edwin Holliday; became a regional manager and sales representative before earning a living as a professional singer.

Colin Grainer was a sprightly outside-left who scored twice on his England debut in a win over Brazil at Wembley in May 1956. With so many talented left-wingers around at the same time, including Tom Finney, Frank Blunstone and Bill Perry, Grainger did well to keep his place and had outstanding games when West Germany were defeated 3-1 in Berlin three weeks after his debut and Scotland were beaten 2-1 at Wembley in April 1957, *Daily Mail* reporter Roy Peskett writing: "The Sunderland winger certainly gave the Everton right-back Alex Parker plenty to think about with his pace and eagerness to get to the bye-line."

Grainger, who also represented the Football League, scored 55 goals in 355 League games during his career.

GRAY, Andrew Arthur 1991-92 ①
Born: Lambeth, London, 22 February 1964
Career: Lambeth & London Borough Schools, Corinthian Casuals (seasons 1980-82), Dulwich Hamlet (seasons 1982-84), Crystal Palace (£2,000, professional, November 1984, Aston Villa (£150,000, November 1987), Queens Park Rangers (£425,000, February 1989), Crystal Palace (£500,000, August 1989), Tottenham Hotspur (£900,000, February 1992), Swindon Town (loan, December 1992-January 1993), CA Marbella/Spain (season 1994-95), Falkirk (seasons 1994-97), Bury (free, July 1997), Millwall (January 1998, retired, May 1998); later Sierra Leone (head coach, national team coach, seasons 2006-08)

Andy Gray was a surprise selection by England manager Graham Taylor for the European Championship qualifier against Poland in November 1991. He played in midfield with David Platt, Geoff Thomas and David Rocastle but wasn't a success in the 1-1 draw. Also capped twice at U21 level, Gray scored 61 goals in 335 club appearances during his career, helping Aston Villa gain promotion to the top flight and Crystal Palace win the ZDS Cup.

GRAY, Michael 1998-99 ③
Born: Sunderland, 3 August 1974
Career: Manchester United (trial, 1989), Sunderland (apprentice, August 1990, professional, August 1991), Celtic (September 2003), Blackburn Rovers (free, January 2004), Leeds United (free, February 2005), Wolverhampton Wanderers (July 2007), Sheffield Wednesday (loan, January 2009, signed permanently, February 2009), Manchester City (briefly, trial, during season 2009-10, retired)

Left-back Michael Gray made his debut for England against Hungary in April 1999 after being picked by Kevin Keegan despite the fact he was playing in the First Division for Sunderland. He also went on to star against Sweden and Bulgaria and became the last outfield player from outside the top-flight to play for England until Preston's David Nugent in 2007. Capped once at U21 level, Gray has now amassed in excess of 550 senior appearances for his seven clubs and twice helped Sunderland win the First Division title, in 1996 and 2000, having missed a penalty in a shoot-out which denied the Wearsiders a place in the Premiership in 1998.

Gray clocked 1hr 33 mins in the Great North Run in September 2011.

Jimmy Greaves

GREAVES, James Peter 1958-67 ⑤⑦ ㊹

Born: East Ham, London, 20 February 1940
Career: Lakeside Manor Boys' Club, Dagenham Schools, London Schools, Essex Boys, Chelsea (amateur, April 1955, professional, May 1957), AC Milan/Italy £80,000, June 1961), Tottenham Hotspur (£99,999, December 1961 – Spurs manager Bill Nicholson was reluctant to make him a £100,000 footballer), West Ham United (£200,000, March 1970 in cash/player deal involving Martin Peters, valued at £146,000 and Greaves at £54,000, retired, May 1971, but returned with Barnet (free, May 1971), then Brentwood Town (season 1975-76), Chelmsford City (August 1976-May 1977), Barnet (July 1977-May 1979), Woodford Town (July 1979, retired, May 1980); had a successful career as a journalist and TV presenter with ex-Liverpool and Scotland star Ian St John; later a newspaper journalist

Full of humour in and out of the dressing room, on and off the pitch, Jimmy Greaves was one of the greatest goalscorers of the 1950s and '60s – his record proves that.

Top journalist Brian Glanville once wrote: 'His turn of speed was extraordinary; his confidence more remarkable still; his left foot a hammer; his instinct for being in the right place near the goal almost psychic.'

Greaves was a 'pure genius' and in a wonderful career in top-class football which spanned 26 years (1955-81) he scored 554 goals in 750 games at club and international level. In fact, 357 of his goals came in the First Division alone (the top flight of English football).

He wasn't at all happy on England's summer tour to South America in May 1959. He said: "The organization was appalling. We were made to train in the heat of the midday sun ahead of a match kicking off at 4 o'clock. The hotel in Mexico was distinctly poor with three or four players having to share the same bedroom. Some of the team suffered terrible burns, ignorant of the dangers of the strong sun in a rarified atmosphere. We weren't given enough time to acclimatise to the weather or indeed surroundings, and I for one was the subject of a lot of academic training."

Greaves was 19 when he made his England debut in a 4-1 defeat by Lima in Peru on that summer tour. The scorer of a 'neat' goal, he also took quite a bit of 'kicking'.

Greaves, as we all know, was an instinctive goal-poacher. He thought it was funny to be told by manager Walter Winterbottom that he should get 'more coaching in the art of ball control and shooting!'

After Scotland had been thrashed 9-3 at Wembley in April 1961, Brian Woolnough's after-match report in the *Sunday Dispatch* stated: 'Greaves, a sprightly genius, gave a Stefano-class performance of ball control.' He scored a hat-trick that afternoon and also assisted in goals for Bobby Smith and Johnny Haynes.

Greaves, in fact, scored seven goals in the Home International Championship of 1960-61 – the most by an England player in this competition, and over the course of that season he netted 13 times in eight games for his country, including goal number 1,000 versus Wales at Wembley on 23 November 1960.

Playing against the Rest of the World at Wembley in October 1963, Greaves was the star performer in a 2-1 win. He scored once and could well have notched a first-half hat-trick had it not been for an outstanding display by the giant Russian goalkeeper Lev Yashin who saved at least six efforts from Greaves during the course of the afternoon.

The very next month, in-form Greaves scored four times in an 8-3 home win over Northern Ireland and after the game Harry Gregg, the Irish 'keeper, said "I have never faced a more complete finisher…he is a genius."

Almost a year later superman Greaves bagged a hat-trick in 12 first-half minutes in a 4-3 win over the Irish in Belfast. This was the fastest treble by an England player since Willie Hall's effort in 1938.

However, a prolonged bout of jaundice and hepatitis kept Greaves out of the international arena for over seven months, from November 1965 to May 1966. Recalled for a friendly against Yugoslavia, ahead of the World Cup, he scored within nine minutes of a 2-0 win to prove he was ready to be included in Alf Ramsey's squad.

Fully rejuvenated, he then gave a 'comprehensive exhibition of the striker's art' by scoring four times in a 6-1 defeat of Norway – the sixth occasion he had netted three or more goals for his country – and although he didn't find the net in his 50th international v. Denmark in the next game, he was bang in form and ready for action when the World Cup got under way in mid July.

Unfortunately for Greaves, due to some tough, hard, clinical tackling, he was completely snuffed out in the opening three group games, leaving the pitch in the third against France with a badly gashed leg that required six stitches. This put him out of the quarter-final clash with Argentina. Replaced by Geoff Hurst, the West Ham centre-forward headed the winner and kept his place through to the final, leaving Greaves to sit and watch from the sidelines, despite him having been declared fit by the team's physio.

'It would be an understatement to say I was disappointed,' he wrote later. 'I had always anticipated I would be part of the greatest day in the history of our game. Alf came round to me around midday and said, "I've decided on an unchanged team. I know you'll understand."'

In April 1967, Greaves was recalled to the England team (in place of Hunt) for the visit of Scotland to Wembley. It wasn't a happy return for the striker who was handicapped with a leg injury from the 24th minute onwards as the Scots won 3-2 to become the first victors over England since Austria in October 1965.

Apart from his senior duties for his country, Greaves also gained five Youth and 12 U23 caps. As a Spurs player, he gained two FA Cup winner's medals (1962 and 1967), and won the European Cup- Wnners' Cup (1963). After retiring as a player in the mid 1970s, Greaves sadly fell victim to alcoholism which was well-publicised by the media but he regained his self-confidence and formed a great duo on TV with Ian St John in the *Saint and Greavsie* show.

GREEN, Frederick Thomas 1875-76 ①

Born: Dorchester, 21 June 1851
Died: Ealing, Middlesex, 6 July 1928
Career: Winchester College (seasons 1869-74), New College/Oxford University (seasons 1874-78); also played for Wanderers (seasons 1873-78) and Middlesex County (1870s); became a Barrister, later an Inspector of Schools (Middlesex).

The recipient of three FA Cup winner's medals – in 1874 with Oxford University and 1877 and 1878 with Wanderers – sure-footed right-back Tommy Green won his only England cap in a 3-0 defeat by Scotland at Partick in March 1876 when he found outside-left John Baird 'a tricky opponent.'

GREEN, George Henry 1924-28 ⑧

Born: Leamington Spa, 2 May 1901
Died: Warwick, 2 August 1980
Career: Leamington Town (junior, July 1918), Nuneaton Borough (August 1919), Sheffield United (professional, May 1923), Leamington Town (July 1934, retired, May 1936); thereafter worked as a turner and fitter most of his life.

It was rewarding to watch the 'Englishness' of George Green's style. A skilful left-half, George Green won his eight England caps over a period of three years. He made a 'sound' debut in a 3-2 win over France in May 1925 and later produced a 'powerful performance' when the French were defeated 5-1 in May 1928. In between times he contributed greatly in a 5-3 win over Belgium and played decidedly well when England beat the same country 3-1 in his last international.

An FA Cup winner with Sheffield United in 1925, Green spent 11 years at Bramall Lane, making 438 appearances for the Blades. He also represented the Birmingham FA against Scotland in a junior international and played three games for the Football League.

GREEN, Robert 2004-10 ⑫

Born: Chertsey, Surrey, 18 January 1980
Career: Norwich City (apprentice, April 1996, professional, July 1997), West Ham United (£2m, August 2006), Queen's Park Rangers (free, June 2012)

Robert Green could hardly be blamed for the torrid evening he endured in Ukraine in October 2009 when England lost 1-0 in a World Cup qualifier. His night ended prematurely when he was sent off for bringing down Artem Milevskiy in the 13th minute after a mistake by Rio Ferdinand. In fact, in those early minutes the West Ham 'keeper was attacked by flares, conceded a penalty (which was missed) and as a result of his red card, was automatically suspended.

An excellent shot-stopper, usually calm and confident, Green at times, however, has looked unsteady with high, looping crosses, especially when challenged by a sturdy striker and tends to lack communication with his own defenders. But there is no doubting he has done well and at the end of the 2012-13 season had made almost 500 club appearances, 241 for both West Ham and Norwich with whom he won his first full cap against Colombia on England's summer tour to the USA in May 2005. Taken to the World Cup finals in 2010 by Fabio Capello, Green was chosen ahead of David James but a dreadful handling error in the opening group game against the USA cost England a win and as a result he was dropped (replaced by James).

Also honoured at Youth and B team levels, Green helped the Canaries win the First Division championship in 2004 but was relegated from the Premiership with the Hammers in 2011 before helping them regain top-flight status a year later. While acting as reserve 'keeper to Joe Hart at Euro 2012, Green was transferred across London from Upton Park to QPR.

Green's sending-off against Ukraine in 2009 was only the 13th in a full international for England and he was, of course, the first goalkeeper to see red!

GREENHALGH, Ernest Harwood 1872-73 ②

Born: Mansfield, 22 August 1848
Died: Mansfield, 11 July 1922
Career: Mansfield Invicta (briefly in 1867-68), Notts County (February 1869-November 1883); became secretary of Greenhalgh FC (Mansfield); later the proprietor of Field Mill, current ground of Mansfield Town, and worked as a cotton doubler, dyer and bleacher.

Robust right-back Ernie Greenhalgh played in England's first two internationals, both against Scotland, a 0-0 draw at Partick in November 1872 and a 4-2 win at The Oval four months later. He was a Notts County player for 14 years.

GREENHOFF, Brian 1975-80 ⑱

Born: Barnsley, 28 April 1953
Died: Rochdale, 22 May 2013
Career: Barnsley & Yorkshire Schools, Manchester United (apprentice, August 1968, professional, June 1970), Leeds United (£350,000, August 1979-May 1982), Wits University/South Africa (briefly), Bulova/Hong Kong (loan, season 1982-83), RoPs/Finland (free, July 1983), Rochdale (free, December 1983-March 1984), Chadderton FC (coach, season 1984-85); became a licensee in Rochdale, then a sales representative for a sports goods wholesaler; also ran a restaurant in Menorca.

Honoured by England four times at U23 level, defender Brian Greenhoff won his first full cap against Wales in May 1976, playing well alongside Phil Thompson at the back in a hard-earned 1-0 win in Wrexham. He retained his place for the next game (v. Northern Ireland) but missed the next four before returning for the friendly draw with the Republic of Ireland in September. Thereafter he was in and out of the team as Thompson, Roy McFarland and Dave Watson tended to get the nod ahead of him. He made his final England appearance in a 2-1 win in Australia in May 1980.

Greenhoff's elder brother, Jimmy, also played for Leeds United, Manchester United and Rochdale as well as Birmingham City, Stoke City and he was, in fact, a ball-boy at Wembley when Jimmy won a League Cup winner's medal with Leeds in 1968. Eight years later Brian was a loser with Manchester United in the FA Cup final v. Southampton but the following season he celebrated victory in the same competition v. Liverpool. Greenhoff junior made over 350 club appearances during his career, 270 with Manchester United and 78 with Leeds. He also played in one unofficial international.

GREENWOOD, Doctor Haydock 1881-82 ②

Born: Blackburn, 31 October 1860
Died: Holborn, London, 3 November 1951
Career: Malvern College (seasons 1878-80), Blackburn Rovers (August 1880-May 1883); also played for Corinthians (late 1870s)

A strong tackling full-back with a powerful kick, 'Doc' Greenwood was, at times, rather slow to react and was often uncertain with his challenges. But nevertheless, he was a 'good' defender who 'had very little to do' on his England debut when Ireland were whipped 13-0 in Belfast in February 1882 was given a 'roasting' by outside-right Bill Anderson in his next game three weeks later when Scotland romped to a 5-1 win in Glasgow.

Greenwood, who made just 10 first-class appearances for Blackburn Rovers, missed the 1882 Cup final through injury. He was an original committee member of the Corinthians club. Doctor was his real Christian name – not a title.

GREGORY, John Charles 1982-84 ⑥

Born: Scunthorpe, 11 May 1954
Career: Watford (trial, April-May 1969), Northampton Town (apprentice, June 1969, professional, May 1973), Aston Villa (£40,000, June 1977), Brighton & Hove Albion (£250,000, July 1979), Queens Park Rangers (£300,000, June 1981), Derby County (£100,000, November 1985), Portsmouth (player-coach, August 1988, then manager, January 1989-January 1990), Plymouth Argyle (non-contract, player/caretaker-manager, January 1990), Bolton Wanderers (non-contract player, March 1990, retired as a

player, May 1991), Leicester City (coach, June 1991); soccer analyst on Sky TV (seasons 1992-94); Aston Villa (coach, seasons 1994-96), Wycombe Wanderers (manager, October 1996), Aston Villa (manager, February 1998-January 2002), Derby County (manager, January 2002); football analyst for Sky TV (again, seasons 2005-08); Maccabi Ahi Nazareth/Israel (manager, December 2009-April 2010), FC Ashdod/Israel (manager, May 2010-April 2011).

John Gregory made a 'sound rather than spectacular' debut for England in the 0-0 draw with Australia in Sydney in June 1983. He played alongside Mark Barham, Steve Williams and Gordon Cowans in midfield. He added five more caps to his tally after that, playing in his last international against Wales in 1984 (lost 1-0).

Gregory played for QPR in the 1982 FA Cup final and helped the London club win the Second Division title a year later and Derby County likewise in 1987. He accumulated a total of 610 appearances at club level over a period of 21 years: 1969-90.

He left Derby (as manager) under a cloud and later issued a writ against the club.

When he took on the job of manager of Maccabi Ahi in 2009, Gregory signed a six-month contract worth £33,000.

As a manager, Gregory once said: "Strikers win matches, defenders win championships."

GRIMSDELL, Arthur 1919-23 ⑥ ②

Born: Watford, 23 March 1894
Died: Watford, 12 March 1963
Career: Watford Field School, Watford St Stephen's, Watford Boys (season 1907-08), Watford (amateur, July 1909, professional, November 1911), Tottenham Hotspur (March 1912), Clapton Orient (player/secretary-manager, August 1929-April 1930); after coaching schoolboys (in Watford area), became a director of both Clapton Orient and Watford (between August 1945 and May 1951), ran a sports outfitters shop in Romford and played cricket for Hertfordshire.

A long throw expert, Arthur Grimsdell became a wonderfully consistent left-half, determined, aggressive and dominating, who actually started his career at centre-forward, representing England Schoolboys in that position as a 14 year-old. Following a successful international trial, he won the first of his six full caps against Wales in March 1920 - the same year he helped Spurs win the Second Division title. The very next season he captained the White Hart Lane club to victory in the FA Cup final v. Wolves. He also played in two unofficial internationals before breaking his leg in October 1925. Out of action for 18 months, he went on to score 38 goals in 417 games for Spurs before moving to Clapton Orient.

GROSVENOR, Arthur Thomas 1933-34 ③ ②

Born: Netherton, Dudley, 22 November 1908
Died: Dudley, 31 October 1972
Career: Northfield Road School/Dudley, Tippity Green Victoria (August 1923), Vono Works (July 1924), Stourbridge (August 1926), Birmingham (amateur, March 1928, professional, September 1928), Sheffield Wednesday (February 1936), Bolton Wanderers (May 1937), Dudley Town (August 1939, retired, May 1943); later employed as a sheet metal worker in Dudley.

Hardly a prolific scorer, Tom Grosvenor was nonetheless a fine inside-right. Standing 6ft tall and strong in the air, he laid on plenty of chances for his colleagues including several in his three outings for England v. Ireland, Wales and France between October and December 1933, finding the net himself against the Irish and French. He also represented the Football League and spent his best years with Birmingham for whom he netted 18 goals in 115 appearances. His brothers Cliff and Percy were also professional footballers.

GUNN, William 1883-84 ② ①

Born: St Anne's, Nottingham, 4 December 1858
Died: Standard Hill, Nottingham, 29 January 1921
Career: Nottingham Forest (August 1881), Notts County (February 1882, professional from 1885-May 1890); reinstated as an amateur (September 1890); played in Nottingham & District league for five years; was also at Notts County (director from August 1890, club president from July 1920 until his death); played county cricket for Nottinghamshire (April 1880-September 1904 – 363 matches) and in 11 Tests for England (1886-99); a sports outfitter, he was a co-founder of the firm Gunn & Moore in 1885.

A strong, forceful 6ft 4½in forward, Billy Gunn was a regular for Notts County for nine years (1881-90) following his transfer from neighbours Forest. A brilliant footballer, exceptionally fast over the ground, he scored 14 goals in 28 games for the Magpies and gained his two England caps in season 1883-84, making his debut in a 1-0 defeat by Scotland in Glasgow and then scoring in a 4-0 win over Wales in Wrexham two months later. As a cricketer, he was a right-hand batsman, who amassed 25,840 runs, including 48 centuries and eight double-centuries in his 24-year career at Trent Bridge, helping Notts win six County Championships during that time. His top-score in senior cricket was 273 for Notts against Derbyshire in 1901. He was the uncle of George and John Richard Gunn, both Notts cricketers.

GUPPY, Stephen Andrew 1999-2000 ①

Born: Winchester, 29 March 1969
Career: Southampton (trial, summer, 1984), Coldon Common (August 1986), Wycombe Wanderers (September 1989), Newcastle United (£150,000, August 1994), Port Vale (£225,000, November 1994), Leicester City (£950,000, February 1997), Celtic (£350,000, August 2001), Leicester City (free, January 2004), Leeds United (free, August 2004), Stoke City (free, September 2004), Wycombe Wanderers (free, November 2004), Washington DC United/USA March 2006), Stevenage Borough (August 2006), Rochester Rhinos/ USA (player/assistant-coach, March 2008); Colorado Rapids/USA, (assistant-manager/coach, from June 2009).

A GM Vauxhall Conference and twice an FA Trophy winner with Wycombe Wanderers, a direct winger who later switched to full-back, Steve Guppy entered League football with Newcastle at the age of 25 and went on to appear in more than 400 first-class games over the next 12 years, helping Leicester win the League Cup in 2000 and Celtic the Scottish League title in 2002. Naturally left-footed, fast and clever with a good technique, he was drafted into the England team for his first and only cap v. Belgium in October 1999 when he did well at left-wing back in a 2-1 win. Guppy also played for his country's B, U21 and semi-professional sides.

GURNEY, Robert 1934-35 ①

Born: Silkworth, County Durham, 13 October 1907
Died: Sunderland, 21 April 1994
Career: Hetton Juniors (May 1921), Seaham Harbour (August 1922), Bishop Auckland (amateur, April 1924-April 1925), Sunderland (professional, May 1925, retired, May 1946; joined club's training staff); Horden Colliery (manager, June 1947-December 1949), Peterborough United (manager, February 1950-March 1952), Darlington (manager, March 1952-October 1957), Leeds United (scout, December 1957-May 1960), Horden Colliery (manager, seasons 1960-63), Hartlepools United (manager, April 1963-January 1964); then Leeds United (scout for four years); later a representative for a wine and spirit firm.

A local discovery, centre-forward Bob Gurney became one of Sunderland's greatest-ever goalscorers, netting 228 times in 390 appearances for the Wearsiders between 1925 and 1942, gaining League Championship and FA Cup winner's medals in 1936 and 1937 respectively. Two broken legs didn't help his cause on the international front and with Ted Drake, Dixie Dean, George Camsell and Ray Westwood all challenging for the centre-forward spot Gurney won just one full cap against Scotland in April 1935 when almost 130,000 packed into Hampden Park to see the home side win 2-0. Gurney then scored in a 4-2 defeat in an unofficial Jubilee international against the Scots four months later. One of Sunderland's finest footballers, Gurney deserved more honours for sure.

HACKING, John 1928-29 ③

Born: Blackburn, 22 December 1897
Died: Accrington, 1 June 1955
Career: Grimshaw Park Co-operative/Blackburn, Blackpool (professional, January 1919), Fleetwood (July 1925), Oldham Athletic (May 1926), Manchester United (March 1934), Accrington Stanley (player-manager, May 1935, retired as a player, December 1935); Barrow (secretary-manager, May 1949 until his death).

With the likes of Jack Brown and Arthur Hufton and even Harry Hibbs seemingly higher than him in the pecking order of England goalkeepers, Oldham's Jack Hacking still managed to win three full caps, playing in the Home International Championship matches against Ireland (won 2-1), Wales (won 3-2) and Scotland (lost 1-0) in 1928-29. He performed well, especially against the Scots in front of 110,512 fans at Hampden Park where he was beaten by a last minute, wind-assisted goal scored direct from a corner by inside-right Alex Cheyne. This in fact, was the first goal netted direct from a flag-kick in international football. Hacking, who also represented the Football League, made 223 appearances for Oldham.

HADLEY, Harold 1902-03 ①

Born: Barrow-in-Furness, 26 October 1877
Died: West Bromwich, 12 September 1942
Career: Cradley Heath & District Schools, Colley Gate United (August 1891), Halesowen (August 1893), West Bromwich Albion (£100, professional, February 1897), Aston Villa (£250, February 1905), Nottingham Forest (April 1906), Southampton (April 1907), Croydon Common (August 1908), Halesowen (February 1910), Merthyr Town (manager, May 1919-April 1922), Chesterfield (manager, April-August 1922), Merthyr Town (three spells as manager between June 1923 and October 1927), Aberdare Athletic (manager, November 1927-November 1928), Gillingham (manager, briefly in 1928-29), Aberdare Athletic (manager, April 1930-September 1931); out of football for four years; Bangor City (manager, July 1935-April 1936).

Harry Hadley was a very useful, industrious wing-half who made 181 appearances for WBA whom he helped win the Second Division title in 1901. His only England cap came against Ireland at Wolverhampton in February 1903 at a time when the management committee was searching for a long-term replacement for Ernie Needham. As a manager Hadley guided Merthyr into the Football League in 1920. His brother, Ben, also played for WBA.

HAGAN, James 1948-49 ①

Born: Washington, County Durham, 21 January 1918
Died: Sheffield, 26 February 1998
Career: Intermediate School/Washington, Usworth Colliery, West Bromwich Albion (trial, April-May 1931), Liverpool (amateur, January 1932), Derby County (amateur, May 1933, professional, January 1935), Sheffield United (£2,500, November 1938); WW2 guest for Aldershot; retired, as a player, May 1958; Peterborough United (manager, August 1958-October 1962), West Bromwich Albion (manager, April 1963-May 1967); Manchester City (scout, July 1967-February 1969), Benfica/Portugal (manager, March 1970-September 1973), Kuwait National team (coach, seasons 1974-76), Sporting Lisbon/Portugal (manager, August 1976-May 1977), FC Porto/Portugal (manager, seasons 1977-79), Boavista/Portugal (manager, season 1979-80), Vitoria Setubal/Portugal (manager, seasons 1980-82).

Inside-right Jimmy Hagan, quiet, unobtrusive and unselfish, was a master craftsman in deep thinking tactical play who scored after just 50 seconds in England's 5-4 Wartime defeat by Scotland at Hampden Park in April 1942. Both centre-forwards netted hat-tricks in this game (Lawton and Jock Dodds). Hagan won a total of 16 Wartime caps (13 goals scored) but gained only one senior cap, in the 0-0 draw with Denmark in September 1948. He scored 118 goals in 364 appearances for Sheffield United, helping the Blades win the Second Division title in 1953. He also represented the Football League on three occasions. As a manager Hagan took Peterborough into the Football League in 1960 and six years later guided WBA to League Cup glory.

Hagan's father, Alf, played for Newcastle United, Cardiff City and Tranmere Rovers in the 1920s.

HAINES, John Thomas William 1948-49 ① ②

Born: Wickhamford, Worcs, 24 April 1920
Died: Evesham, 19 March 1987
Career: Badsey Council & Evesham Grammar Schools, Evesham Town (August 1935), Cheltenham Town (May 1937), Liverpool (trial, August 1938), Swansea Town (August 1939); WW2 guest for Bradford Park Avenue, Doncaster Rovers, Lincoln City, Notts County and Wrexham; rejoined Swansea Town (August 1945), Leicester City (£10,000, June 1947), West Bromwich Albion (£6,000 in player-exchange deal involving Peter McKennan, March 1948), Bradford Park Avenue (£10,000, December 1949), Rochdale (September 1953), Chester (July 1955), Wellington Town (player-coach, May 1957), Kidderminster Harriers (player, season 1958-59), Evesham Town (August 1959), Bretforton Village FC (August 1960, retired, March 1961).

Inside-left Jackie Haines scored two 'very good' goals in his only game for England in a comfortable 6-0 win over Switzerland at Highbury in December 1948. That same season he helped his club, WBA, gain promotion to the First Division and during a lengthy injury-hit career he stacked up more than 360 club appearances, scoring over 100 goals.

HALL, Albert Edward 1909-10 ①

Born: Wordsley, Stourbridge, 21 January 1882
Died: Stourbridge, 17 October 1957
Career: Amblecote Council School/Stourbridge, Brierley Hill Wanderers (July 1897), Wall Heath (August 1898), Stourbridge (August 1900), Aston Villa (£100, professional, July 1903), Millwall Athletic (December 1913, retired May 1916), returned with Stourbridge (September-November 1919); also played cricket for Stourbridge in the Birmingham League; worked as an enamelware manufacturer.

With Aston Villa for whom he scored 62 goals in 215 appearances, Albert Hall formed a brilliant left-wing partnership with fellow England international Joe Bache, both players gaining League and FA Cup winner's medals. Hall's only international game was against Ireland in February 1910 when he played alongside Bache in a 1-1 draw in Belfast. He was badly gassed while serving with the 5th South Staffordshire Regiment during WW1.

HALL, George William 1933-39 ⑩ ⑨

Born: Newark, Notts, 12 March 1912
Died: Newark, Notts, 22 May 1967
Career: Lover's Lane Primary School/Nottingham, Nottingham Schools, Ransome & Marles FC (April 1929), Notts County (professional, November 1930), Tottenham Hotspur (£2,500, December 1932); WW2 guest for West Ham United; retired, February 1944; Clapton Orient (coach, August 1945, manager, September-November 1945), Chelmsford City (manager, seasons 1946-49), Chingford Town (manager, August 1949-May 1950); became a publican in East London, later returning to Nottinghamshire.

Willie Hall scored five goals from eight shots, including a hat-trick in just 3½ minutes, when England trounced Ireland 7-0 at Maine Road, Manchester in November 1938. He was in quite brilliant form that afternoon, finding the back of the net between the 34th and 38th minutes for his rapid-fire treble… the fastest-ever by an England player and possibly the fastest on record by anyone worldwide in a full international.

Seven months later the Spurs forward equalised against Italy in May 1939 with a superb 86th minute goal to stun the 70,000 Milan crowd. However, the usually reliable inside-forward then missed a penalty in a 1-0 defeat by Wales in one of his two Wartime internationals in April 1940.

He made an impressive international debut against France in December 1933 and also represented the Football League. He helped Notts County win the Third Division (South) title in 1931 and overall his career realised more than 400 senior appearances and over 50 goals. For Spurs alone Hall had 375 games and struck 45 goals. In later life he sadly had both of his legs amputated.

HALL, Jeffrey 1955-57 ⑰

Born: Scunthorpe, 7 September 1929
Died: Selly Oak, Birmingham, 4 April 1959
Career: Bingley & District Schoolboy football, St Anne's FC/Keighley, Wilsden FC (August 1945), Bank Top FC (June 1947), Bradford Park Avenue (amateur, August 1949); REME (during National Service), Birmingham City (professional, May 1950, until his death)

Jeff Hall and Roger Byrne (Manchester United) played together at full-back in 17 successive England internationals – the first against Denmark in Copenhagen in October 1955, the last against the Republic of Ireland in May 1957. Hall was on the losing side only once – versus Wales at Cardiff in October 1955 – and statistically speaking, had the best record in terms of games played won and lost, of any England full-back. A shade on the small side, he always defended sturdily and strongly and was forever game, hardly ever getting a 'roasting' from an opposing left-winger.

Sadly, Hall was only 29 years of age when he died from polio soon after appearing in the last of 264 senior games for Birmingham City with whom he won the Second Division championship in 1955 and reached the FA Cup final the following year.

HALSE, Harold 1908-09 ①

Born: Stratford, East London, 1 January 1886
Died: Colchester, 25 March 1949
Career: Park Road School/Wanstead, Leytonstone & District Schools, Newportians/Leyton (April 1902), Wanstead FC (August 1903), Barking Town (July 1904), Clapton Orient (amateur, August 1905), Southend United (professional, June 1906), Manchester United (£350, March 1908), Aston Villa (£1,200, July 1912), Chelsea (May 1913); WW1 guest for Clapton Orient; Charlton Athletic (July 1921, retired, May 1923; then coach, later scout until 1925); later ran a tobacconist shop in Walton-on-Naze.

An FA Cup winner with Manchester United in 1909, the same year he won his only England cap when playing alongside Vivian Woodward, he scored twice in an 8-1 win over Austria in Vienna. Mercurial inside-right or centre-forward Harold Halse also won the First Division title with United in 1911 and netted six goals for United in their 8-4 FA Charity Cup victory over Swindon Town that same year.

He then played in the 1913 and 1915 FA Cup finals for Aston Villa (winners) and Chelsea (losers) respectively and during his senior career he notched 92 goals in 260 League appearances, having his best spells at Old Trafford and Stamford Bridge. Small and frail looking, he was a rare opportunist who as a junior bagged 200 goals in just two seasons while playing for Southend. He also represented the Football League and captained Charlton in their first season of League football: 1921-22.

HAMMOND, Henry Edward Denison 1888-89 ①

Born: Priston, Somerset, 26 November 1866
Died: Taunton, 16 June 1910
Career: St Edward's School/Oxford, Lancing College (seasons 1882-85), Corpus Christi College/Oxford University (seasons 1886-89), Lancing Old Boys (season 1886-87); played for Corinthians (season 1889-90); Master at Blair Lodge School (1889), schoolmaster at Edinburgh Academy (seasons 1890-99), then Superintendent of British Education Section at Paris Exhibition (1899-1900) and Director General of Education for Rhodesia (from 1900); played county cricket for Somerset; later travelled through Dorset and Somerset, collecting folk songs.

Wing-half Harry Hammond was a powerful player with tremendous stamina. Replacing Harry Allen of Wolves, he won his only England cap in a 3-2 defeat by Scotland at The Oval in April 1889 when he found it 'hard going against a smooth, inter-changing Scottish forward-line.'

Good at all sports, Hammond was a terrific athlete, all-round cricketer and swimmer who also enjoyed bowls, tennis and rowing.

HAMPSON, James 1930-33 ③ ⑤
Born: Little Hulton, Lancs, 23 March 1906
Died: Fleetwood, 10 January 1938
Career: Hulton Council School, Walkden Park FC (April 1920), Little Hulton St John's (August 1923), Manchester United (trial, April-May 1924), Nelson (July 1925), Blackpool (professional, October 1927 until his death).

 Centre-forward Jimmy Hampson helped Blackpool win the Second Division championship in 1930 when he netted 45 goals which remains to this day as a seasonal record for the Seasiders. After making the first of four appearances for the Football League – he later netted two hat-tricks at this level v. the Scottish League in 1930 and the Irish League a year later – Hampson scored on his England debut in a 5-1 win over Northern Ireland in October 1930, following up by netting twice in each of his next two games v. Wales (won 4-0) a month later and Austria (won 4-3) in December 1932. One feels that if he had been with a top-line club then Hampson would have gained many more caps.

Blessed with a deadly right foot and fine head work, he spent 11 years at Bloomfield Road, during which time he struck 252 goals in 373 first-class appearances for Blackpool. Sadly, Hampson was drowned at sea after his yacht had collided with a fishing trawler off the coast of Fleetwood.

HAMPTON, Joseph Harold 1912-14 ④ ③
Born: Wellington, Shropshire, 21 April 1885
Died: Wrexham, 15 March 1963
Career: Wellington Council School, Potter's Bank FC (September 1899), Lilleshall Ironworks (August 1900), Shifnal Juniors (August 1901), Hadley FC (May 1903), Wellington Town (October 1903), Aston Villa (professional, April 1904); WW1 guest for Bellis & Morcom, Birmingham, Blackpool, Derby County, Fulham, Nottingham Forest, Reading and Stoke; Birmingham (February 1920), Newport County (September 1922, retired, May 1923), returned with Wellington Town (January 1924-May 1925), Preston North End (coach, June 1925-January 1926), Lilleshall Town (Birmingham Works football, seasons 1926-28), Birmingham (colts' coach, October 1934-May 1937); later ran the Carlton Café in Queen Street, Rhyl.

'Appy' Harry Hampton, also known as the 'Wellington Whirlwind' (because of the way his used to swing his arms around) was a real terror to opposing goalkeepers and defenders. During the decade leading up to the outbreak of WW1, he was one of the finest centre-forwards in the game. Afraid of no-one, his devil-may-care, strong, forceful, determined style was admired and appreciated by plenty. The idol of the Villa Park crowd, he scored 242 goals in 376 appearances for the Birmingham club between 1904 and 1920, gaining one League championship and two FA Cup winner's medals during that time. He was capped by England on four occasions, scoring on his international debut against Wales in March 1913 (won 4-3). Then, in his second game against Scotland at Stamford Bridge a month later he shoulder-charged the Scots' goalkeeper Jim Brownlie 'over the line' for the winning goal. The Scots weren't too pleased with the referee's decision to allow the goal, claiming a foul on the 'keeper who was adamant that neither the ball nor himself had crossed the line. His other two England outings were against Wales and Scotland the following season.

Hampton also represented the Football League three times (scoring all the goals in a 4-0 win over the Irish League in October 1911), played for Birmingham against London on three occasions and starred in an international trial in 1913. After leaving Villa he helped Birmingham win the Second Division title.

One of the few players to send 22 stone goalkeeper Billy 'Fatty' Foulke into the back of the net, Hampton's brother, George, also played for Aston Villa.

HANCOCKS, John 1948-51 ③ ②
Born: Oakengates, Shropshire, 30 April 1919
Died: Oakengates, 14 February 1994
Career: Oakengates & District Schools, Oakengates Town (August 1934), Walsall (amateur, May 1937, professional, August 1938); WW2 guest for Chester, Crewe Alexandra and Wrexham; Wolverhampton Wanderers (£4,000, May 1946), Wellington Town (player-manager, June 1958, resigned as manager, September 1959, continued as player until December 1959), Cambridge United (Southern League, January 1960), Oswestry Town (June 1960), GKN Sankeys FC (December 1960, retired, May 1962); later worked for Maddocks & Son (ironfounders) in Oakengates.

A member of the great Wolves side of the 1950s, midget winger Johnny Hancocks, who wore a size 2 boot, could play on both flanks but preferred the right. He was fast and tricky and packed a terrific shot in his right foot. He scored 167 goals in 378 games during his time at Molineux, helping Wolves win the FA Cup in 1949 and the First Division championship in 1954.

He netted twice on his England debut in a 6-0 win over Switzerland at Highbury in December 1948 and went on to play against Wales in October 1949 (England's 250th international which was won 4-3) and Yugoslavia a year later (2-2). At his peak at the same time as several other quality wingers – hence his low cap count – Hancocks top-scored with 16 goals on England's tour of North America/Canada in 1950 but was not selected for that year's World Cup. However, he was in the squad four years later, but did not go because he had an aversion to flying, and although he asked the FA if he could travel by rail, this request was refused and Stanley Matthews went instead. Also honoured twice by the Football League, he is regarded as one of Wolves' greatest-ever players.

HAPGOOD, Edris Albert 1932-39 ㉚
Born: Bristol, 24 September 1908
Died: Leamington Spa, 20 April 1973
Career: St Phillip's Adult School/Bristol, Bristol Rovers (trial, May 1927), Kettering Town (August 1927), Arsenal (£950, October 1932); WW2 guest for Birmingham City, Luton Town and Chelsea; (continued playing for Arsenal until retiring in February 1946); Blackburn Rovers (manager, June 1946-February 1947), Shrewsbury Town (player-coach, August 1947-February 1948), Watford (manager, February 1948-March 1950), Bath City (manager, March 1950-February 1956); later ran YMCA hostels in Harwell, Berkshire and Weymouth, Dorset.

An elbowing incident when Eddie Hapgood broke his nose in the 'battle' with Italy at Highbury in November 1934, rattled most of the England players. He was carried off but returned for the second-half, clearly handicapped yet with the stomach to carry on the fight and help his side record a famous 3-2 victory.

Old scars were remembered when the two nations met against in Milan five years later and this time Hapgood's defensive contribution was outstanding as England won 4-0.

Throwing his weight around, however, was not the way Hapgood liked to play. He was a high-class left-back – aloof but brilliant – who liked to play football. His forte was his intercepting and averting trouble, making him living proof that fair play could combine with the uncompromising will to win.

Hapgood was "a classic, a great full-back" said Stanley Matthews. "He used to jockey when facing a tricky winger and often buttoned them up, me included."

Hapgood, who tore the ligaments in his left ankle playing against Yugoslavia in May 1939, made his international debut against the Italians six years earlier and thereafter produced some brilliant displays, playing alongside his Arsenal club-mate George Male on 13 occasions. He went on to captain England in all of his 13 Wartime internationals.

Dedicated (to playing football) Hapgood was smart, well-mannered and never drank or smoked. He formed a terrific full-back partnership with Male at Highbury and during his 19 years with the Gunners (1927-46) he appeared in 542 games, including 102 in WW2. He gained five League championship and two FA Cup winner's medals.

His son, Tony, was also a professional footballer with Burnley and Watford. He died in September 2011.

HARDINGE, Harold Thomas Walter 1909-10 ①

Born: Greenwich, London, 25 February 1886
Died: Cambridge, Kent, 8 May 1965
Career: Blackheath Road School/Greenwich, Eltham FC (April 1901). Tonbridge FC (August 1902), Maidstone United (September 1903), Newcastle United (professional, September 1905), Sheffield United (£350, December 1907), Arsenal (£500, June 1913, retired, May 1921); was a petty officer in the Royal Naval Air Service during WW1; Tottenham Hotspur (assistant-coach and reserve team manager, seasons 1935-37); also played cricket for Kent and England; worked for the sports outfitters, John Wisden Ltd.

Capped by England against Scotland as a Sheffield United player in April 1910, inside-left Wally Hardinge was a subtle, scheming player with pronounced leanings towards individualism – perhaps the reason for why he gained only one cap. He was certainly a clever ball player who made 300 club appearances during his career, including 154 for Sheffield United and 125 for Arsenal. As a Kent cricketer between 1902 and 1933, he scored 33,519 runs, including 35 centuries and top-scoring with 263. He played in one Test match against Australia in 1921.

HARDMAN, Harold Payne 1904-08 ④ ①

Born: Kirkmanshulme, Manchester, 4 April 1882
Died: Sale, Cheshire, 9 June 1965
Career: South Shore High School/Blackpool, Northern Nomads (July 1896), Wordsley Wanderers (August 1897), Chorlton-cum-Hardy (March 1898), South Shore Choristers (August 1899), Blackpool (amateur, July 1900), Everton (amateur, May 1903), Manchester United (amateur, August 1908), Bradford City (amateur, January 1909), Stoke (amateur, February 1910); Manchester United (amateur, September 1913, retired, May 1915; later director, then chairman at Old Trafford, 1951-65); served as an FA, Lancashire FA and Central League Committee member; also a practising solicitor in Manchester.

An amateur throughout his career, outside-left Harold Hardman was one of the most distinguished non-professional footballers of his era. Small, fast and elusive, he won an Olympic soccer gold medal with the United Kingdom in 1908 (v. Denmark), gained 10 amateur and four full caps for England and was an FA Cup winner and loser with Everton in 1906 and 1907. His senior international debut came in the 3-1 win over Wales in March 1905 and his only England goal was enough to beat Ireland two years later. After retiring as a player with more than 250 club appearances under his belt including 156 for Everton (29 goals) Hardman became a director and then chairman of Manchester United whom he served in various capacities for more than 50 years.

HARDWICK, George Francis Moutry 1946-48 ⑬

Born: Saltburn, Cleveland, 2 February 1920
Died: Middlesbrough, 19 April 2004
Career: Lingdale School/Cleveland, South Bank East End (April 1934), Middlesbrough (professional, May 1937); WW2 guest for Chelsea; Oldham Athletic (£15,000 as player-manager, November 1950, retired April 1956); US Army team/Germany (coach, August 1956-May 1957), PSV Eindhoven/Holland (coach, June 1957-May 1959), the Dutch FA (coach, season 1958-59), Middlesbrough (Youth team coach, August 1961-November 1963); also served the Middlesbrough local authority (as football coach, early 1960s), Sunderland (manager, November 1964-May 1965), Gateshead (manager, April 1968-February 1970); later managed a garage and was chairman of a steel company in Saltburn.

Left-back George Hardwick captained England on his senior debut in the first Home International after WW2, leading his country to a 7-2 victory over Northern Ireland.

He remained as skipper right through his international career, which ended when he damaged his right knee in a 2-0 win over the Scots in April 1948, finishing the game hobbling on the left-wing. A cultured and composed player, he also missed a penalty in an 8-2 win over Holland in his fourth international, having previously played in 17 Wartime and two unofficial internationals (both v. Switzerland in July 1945) and captained the Great Britain side against the Rest of Europe in 1947. He made 166 appearances for Middlesbrough (conceding a 50-second own-goal on his League debut v. Bolton in 1937) and 203 for Oldham, helping the Latics win the Third Division (North) championship in 1953.

Hardwick was a hit with the females, his good looks making him the 'George Best' of the 1940s.

HARDY, Henry Jacob 1924-25 ①

Born: Stockport, 4 January 1895
Died: Stockport, 17 February 1969
Career: Alderley Edge FC (August 1912), Stockport County (professional, August 1920), Everton (October 1925), Bury (July 1928, retired, April 1930); became a professional oboe player; later employed as a School caretaker in Stockport.

Regarded as one of the best goalkeepers outside the First Division, Henry Hardy was deft at handling, possessed fine judgment and always looked cool and controlled in his actions. Capped by England against Belgium at The Hawthorns in December 1924 when he made three excellent saves in a 4-0 victory, he twice represented the Football League and made over 300 senior appearances for his three clubs, 274 in the League including 207 for Stockport.

HARDY, Samuel 1906-20 (21)

Born: Newbold, Derbyshire, 26 August 1883
Died: Chesterfield, 24 October 1966
Career: Newbold Church School, Newbold Boys Youth Club (April 1899), Newbold White Star (July 1901), Chesterfield (professional, April 1903), Liverpool (£500, October 1905), Aston Villa (£600, May 1912); Royal Navy barracks/Plymouth and WW1 guest for Plymouth Argyle and Nottingham Forest; joined Nottingham Forest (£1,000, August 1921, retired, May 1925); became a hotelier in Chesterfield and ran his own billiard hall in Alfreton, Derbyshire.

Sam 'Chuffer' Hardy became the first England goalkeeper to win caps in three decades: 1900s, 1910s and 1920s. He was also the first player along with Jesse Pennington to represent their country either side of WW1.

Until the emergence of Harry Hibbs, Hardy was universally regarded as the non-pareil of England goalkeepers. His anticipation was masterful and he very rarely had a bad game... he made the job look easy. He gained his first full cap v. Ireland in February 1907, pulling off three excellent saves in a 1-0 victory and two years later he was quite brilliant in successive victories over Ireland, Wales, Scotland (when he saved Jim Stark's penalty) and Hungary. In his last game, a 5-4 win over Scotland at Hillsborough in April 1920, Hardy admitted that two of the goals he conceded took wicked deflections while *Daily Mail* reporter Alfred Davis wrote: "On a mud heap, Hardy was beaten by two lucky shots and he was unsighted when Miller scored his second goal, as there were far too many players in front of him."

A League championship winner with Liverpool, twice an FA Cup winner with Villa and a Second Division champion with Nottingham Forest, he made over 600 appearances (551 in the League) during a wonderful career which spanned 22 years (1903-25). He also played in three Victory internationals, twice represented the Football League, starred for Birmingham against London and played for England v. the South and North in international trials. At the age of 36 years, 227 days, Hardy is the fourth oldest player ever to win a full England cap (behind Stanley Matthews, Peter Shilton and Leslie Compton).

HARFORD, Michael Gordon 1987-88 (2)

Born: Sunderland, 12 February 1959
Career: Sunderland Schools, Wearside & District Schools, Lambton Star Boys Club (May 1974), Newcastle United (trial, July-August 1975), Sunderland (trial, May-June 1976), Lincoln City (professional, July 1977), Newcastle United (£216,000, December 1980), Bristol City (£160,000, August 1981), Newcastle United (£100,000, early March 1982), Birmingham City (£100,000, mid-March 1982), Luton Town (£250,000, December 1984), Derby County (£450,000, January 1980), Luton Town (£325,000, September 1991), Chelsea (£300,000, August 1992), Sunderland (£250,000, March 1993), Coventry City (£200,000, July 1993), Wimbledon (£75,000, August 1994, then player-coach, May 1997, later player/assistant-manager and also caretaker-manager to May 2001). Luton Town (coach, May 2001-May 2003, then Director of Football, also assistant-manager, caretaker-manager and senior coach), Nottingham Forest (assistant-manager/coach, November 2004, caretaker-manager to February 2005), Swindon Town (assistant-manager/coach, February-April 2005), Rotherham United (manager, April-December 2005), Millwall (coach, January-May 2006), Colchester United (assistant-manager/coach, July 2006), Queens Park Rangers (assistant-manager/coach, June 2007), Luton Town (manager, January 2008-October 2009), Queens Park Rangers (manager, December 2009-March 2010), MK Dons (assistant-manager/coach, May 2012).

A tall striker, good in the air, Mick Harford made his England debut (as a substitute) along with midfielder Steve McMahon, in the 0-0 draw with Israel in Tel Aviv in February 1988. His second cap came in a 1-0 win over Denmark soon afterwards.

Also the recipient of one B cap, Mick gained a League Cup winner's medal in 1988 and scored in the 1989 League Cup final. And he actually helped Luton escape relegation on the last day of the season! When Derby met Luton - who needed the win to stay up - Harford somehow headed the ball from outside his own penalty-area, past England goalkeeper Peter Shilton into his own net to hand the Hatters the victory they required to avoid the drop! Later, in 2009, he guided Luton to victory at Wembley in the final of the Johnstone Paints Trophy but at the end of that season the Kenilworth Road club lost its Football League status after being docked 30 points at the end of the previous campaign.

Harford's playing career at club level, realised 231 goals in 708 appearances, attaining his best statistics with Luton - 93 goals in 217 outings in two spells.

HARGREAVES, Frederick William 1879-82 (3)

Born: Blackburn, 16 August 1858
Died: Blackburn, 5 April 1897
Career: Malvern College (seasons 1876-78), Blackburn Rovers (August 1878-May 1884), represented the Lancashire FA (1870s); also a Lancashire county cricketer

An industrious, shrewd and stern-tackling half-back, Fred Hargreaves was an FA Cup finalist with Blackburn in 1882. By that time he had already gained three England caps (the first two v. Wales) and his third v. Ireland when he had a hand in four of the goals in a rampaging 13-0 win. The brother of John Hargreaves (below), he also played in one county cricket match for Lancashire.

HARGREAVES, John 1881-82 (2)

Born: Blackburn, 13 December 1860
Died: Blackburn, 13 January 1903
Career: Malvern College (seasons 1877-79), Blackburn Rovers (July 1878-May 1884); also played for Lancashire FA (1870s); admitted a solicitor in 1884, he practised in Blackburn until his death.

Inside or outside-left John Hargreaves made his England debut against Wales in February 1881, lining up in front of his brother, Fred, in a 1-0 defeat on his home ground at Blackburn. His second international followed a month later when Scotland won 6-1 at The Oval. He too played in the losing FA Cup final against Old Etonians in 1882 but two years later celebrated with a winner's medal when Rovers beat the Scottish club Queen's Park 2-1.

HARGREAVES, Owen Lee 2001-08 (42)

Born: Calgary, Canada, 20 January 1981
Career: Calgary Foothills FC (junior, August 1994), Bayern Munich (apprentice, May 1997, professional, May 2000), Manchester United (£17m, July 2007), Manchester City (free, August 2011, released, May 2012).

Born in Canada to a Welsh mother and an English father, midfielder Owen Hargreaves was eligible to represent Canada, Wales and England. He chose the latter and donned a 'three lions' shirt for the first time in the U21 team in 2000 before collecting his first

HARPER, Edward Cashfield 1925-26 ①

Born: Sheerness, Kent, 22 August 1901
Died: Blackburn, 22 July 1959
Career: Whitstable Town (August 1918), Sheppey United (May 1921), Blackburn Rovers (professional, May 1923), Sheffield Wednesday (November 1927), Tottenham Hotspur (March 1929), Preston North End (December 1931), Blackburn Rovers (November 1933, then trainer-coach, May 1935-May 1948); worked for English Electric Co. until his death.

Ted Harper was a wonderfully consistent goalscorer. Big and strong, he could match anyone for pace and was certainly a player to be reckoned with. He scored almost 280 goals in more than 350 League and Cup appearances for his four major clubs over a period of 12 years (1923-35), bagging a staggering 122 goals in just 177 games for Blackburn. For all his efforts, he was surprisingly awarded only one England cap, when he played alongside his Blackburn club-mate Syd Puddefoot in a 1-0 defeat by Scotland at Old Trafford in April 1926. He twice came close to equalizing, although *The Times* reporter stated that he 'lacked steam.' Harper broke individual scoring records for Blackburn, Spurs and Preston.

HARRIS, Gordon 1965-66 ①

Born: Worksop, Notts, 2 June 1940
Career: Worksop Schools, Firbeck Colliery (from August 1955), Burnley (professional, January 1958), Sunderland (January 1968), South Shields (July 1972, retired, May 1975)

Initially a somewhat volatile yet lively left-winger, Gordon Harris developed into a highly-efficient inside-forward who later starred as a left-half. He spent a decade with Burnley for whom he appeared in the 1962 FA Cup final, one of 313 senior games for the Turf Moor club (81 goals scored). He also netted 16 times in 135 outings for Sunderland. His only England cap came against Poland in January 1966, when he came into the team as a late replacement for Bobby Charlton in a 1-1 draw at Anfield. Harris also appeared in two U23 internationals (one goal) and twice for the Football League.

HARRIS, Peter Philip 1949-54 ②

Born: Portsea, Portsmouth, 19 December 1925
Died: Hayling Island, 2 January 2003
Career: Milton Junior and Meon Road Senior Schools/Portsmouth, Portsmouth de Havillands Works team (Airspeed FC, seasons 1940-42), Gosport Borough (August 1942-September 1944), Portsmouth (trial, October 1944, professional, November 1944, retired through ill-health, December 1959); later worked for a boat builder, owned a restaurant and club at Hayling Island and worked at a Day Care Centre for mentally handicapped children.

Speedy outside-right Peter Harris made his England debut in the 2-0 defeat by the Republic of Ireland at Goodison Park in September 1949, replacing Tom Finney who switched to the opposite flank. Harris's second appearance followed four-and-a-half years when he had a 'horrible game' in the 7-1 defeat in Hungary in 1954. Playing in fits and starts, he was starved of the ball virtually throughout the second-half.

An excellent club man, he gave Pompey 15 years' dedicated service, scoring 208 goals (193 in the Football League) in 520 appearances, gaining successive First Division championship winner's medals in 1949 and 1950. Harris also represented the Football League on five occasions. A serious chest infection ended his career.

full cap the following year, coming on as a substitute against Holland when playing in the German Bundesliga for Bayern Munich, thus becoming the 1,111th player to represent England at full international level. He is also the only footballer so far to have played for England without having previously lived in the United Kingdom and he's only the second to have done so without having previously played in the English football League system.

Hard-working and a strong tackler, he once held the record for making most substitute appearances for England (25) and, in fact, he was called off the bench no less than 14 consecutive times. A member of England's 2002 World Cup squad, Hargreaves has also won one B and three U21 caps and was a Premiership and Champions League winner with Manchester United in 2008. On his debut for Manchester City v. Birmingham in a Carling Cup-tie in September 2011 – only his sixth game in more than three years – he scored a superb goal in a 2-0 win. Whilst in Germany, he helped Bayern win four Bundesliga titles, the DFB-Pokol three times and the UEFA Champions League, Intercontinental Cup and DFB-Ligapokal all once...and 39 of his England caps came as a Munich player. Unfortunately he was plagued by injury for almost three seasons: 2008-11.

Hargreaves' father played for Bolton Wanderers' youth team and also for Calgary Kickers in the Canadian Soccer League.

HARRIS, Stanley Schute 1903-06 ⑥ ②
Born: Sea Mills, Bristol, 19 July 1881
Died: Farnham, Surrey, 4 May 1926
Career: Westminster School (seasons 1898-1901), Pembroke College/Cambridge University (seasons 1901-05); also represented Old Westminsters, Casuals, Worthing, Portsmouth (registered between September 1905-May 1907), Surrey and Corinthians between 1900 and 1910; played cricket for Gloucestershire, Surrey and Sussex; became headmaster at St Ronan's Preparatory School, Worthing (1904-26).

Stanley Harris was described as being a 'crafty, ball-playing inside-left, splendid at dribbling, shooting and distributing the ball with either the inside or the outside of his foot.'
    He made his senior debut for England in a 1-0 win over Scotland at Celtic Park in April 1906, playing along fellow amateur Vivian Woodward. The *Daily Record's* reporter at the game 'Bedouin' wrote: "At the interval it looked distinctly promising for Scotland, crossing over with no goals against them and the wind at their backs. But they fell all to pieces thereafter, and Harris and Woodward got the inside game in motion and the super-excellence of the amateurs transformed the situation." And it was Harris on whom the most praise was lavished. "The Corinthian was the outstanding forward on the field and he brought to the assistance of his comrades a style of game that harmonised with the old-time game of the best type of Corinthians forward play."
    Harris netted two goals for his country, in wins over Wales and Ireland in 1905 and 1906, and besides his six full caps, he also represented his country in one amateur international when he scored seven times in a 15-0 win over France in Paris in October 1906.

HARRISON, Alban Hugh 1892-93 ②
Born: Bredhurst, Kent, 30 November 1869
Died: Paddington, London, 15 August 1943
Career: Westminster School (seasons 1886-88), Trinity College/Cambridge University (seasons 1888-92); also played for Old Westminsters (August 1889-May 1891) and Corinthians (seasons 1891-94).

Full-back Hugh Harrison was a master of the half-volley clearance. A clever footballer, he gained his two England caps towards the end of the 1892-93 season, starring in a 6-1 win over Ireland at Birmingham on his debut and then having a fine game in a 5-2 victory over Scotland at the Richmond Athletic Ground, Surrey.

HARRISON, George 1920-22 ②
Born: Church Gresley, 18 July 1892
Died: Derby, 12 March 1939
Career: Schoolboy football, Gresley Rovers (August 1909), Leicester Fosse (professional, February 1911), Everton (with Bob Thompson, April 1913), Preston North End (December 1923), Blackpool (November 1931, retired, May 1932); became a licensee in Preston and Church Gresley.

George Harrison was a stocky left-winger, quick and direct who was not easily knocked off the ball. He could unleash a powerful shot and was a noted penalty expert. A League championship winner with Everton in 1915, he won his two England caps five months apart in 1921, making a 'useful' debut in a 2-0 win over Belgium in Brussels in the May and having his second outing in the 1-1 draw with Ireland in Belfast in the October. He scored nine goals in 59 League starts for Leicester, 17 in 171 for Everton, 72 in 274 for Preston and one in 16 for Blackpool.

HARROW, Jack Harry 1922-23 ②
Born: Beddington, Surrey, 8 October 1888
Died: Mitcham, Surrey, 19 July 1958
Career: Mitcham FC (August 1906), Mill Green Rovers (August 1907), Croydon Common (semi-professional, June 1908), Chelsea (£50, professional, March 1911, retired June 1926; engaged on club's training staff until 1938); later employed by Mitcham Council.

An FA Cup finalist with Chelsea in 1915, Jack Harrow started his career as a centre-forward before establishing himself as an international left-back. He had the knack of waiting until the last second before putting in a challenge which he did with precision and commitment. A Football League representative in 1914, he won the first of his two England caps against Northern Ireland in October 1922 when he partnered Joe Smith of West Bromwich Albion. His second came in a 4-2 win over Sweden in Stockholm at the end of the season. Harrow made 333 appearances in 15 years at Stamford Bridge. He was forced to retire after being struck full in the face by a ball which severely damaged his eyesight.

HART, Ernest Arthur 1929-34 ⑧
Born: Overseal, Staffs, 3 January 1902
Died: Ardwick-le-Street near Doncaster, 21 July 1954
Career: Overseal School, Overseal Juniors (May 1915), Woodlands Wesleyans (August 1918), Leeds United (professional, August 1920), Mansfield Town (£350, August 1936, retired, March 1937); Coventry City (scout, briefly), Tunbridge Wells Rangers (manager, July 1938-September 1939); later ran his own haulage business in Doncaster.

Ernie Hart was a splendid centre-half with an attacking bent. Blessed with excellent ball control, he made 472 appearances for Leeds (1920-36), helping them win the Second Division championship in 1924. He made his England debut, alongside his Leeds team-mate Edwards, in a 3-2 win over Wales in Swansea in November 1928 but had to wait almost a year for his second cap. After that he contested the centre-half position with several other defenders, among them Seddon (Bolton), Hill (Newcastle), Webster (Middlesbrough), Leach (Sheffield Wednesday), Graham (Nottingham Forest) and Cowan (Manchester City) before collecting his last cap v. Czechoslovakia in Prague in May 1934. Harrison also played three times for the Football League and toured South Africa with the FA in 1929.

HART, Charles Joseph John 2007-13 ㉜
Born: Shrewsbury, 19 April 1987
Career: Oxon Primary School, Meole Brace Science College, Shrewsbury Town (apprentice, May 2002, professional, August 2004), Manchester City (£600,000, May 2006), Tranmere Rovers (loan, January-March 2007), Blackpool (loan, April-May 2007), Birmingham City (loan, June 2009-May 2010); also a good club cricketer.

Goalkeeper Joe Hart played for England in five Youth and 21 U21 internationals before earning his first full cap as a second-half substitute for David James in a 3-0 win over Trinidad & Tobago in June 2008, and since then, for club and country, he has produced several brilliant displays. Unfortunately, like all keepers from time to time, he had an off-day and it was he who stood between the posts when giant striker Zlatan Ibrahimovic became the first player to score four goals in a full international against England in Sweden's 4-2

HARVEY, Alfred 1880-81 ①

Born: Wednesbury, 12 February 1860
Died: West Bromwich, 10 June 1923
Career: White Cross FC/Wednesbury (season 1874-75), West Bromwich Strollers (season 1875-76), Wednesbury Strollers (August 1876-May 1883), Aston Villa (briefly during season 1883-84), Staffordshire County (1880s).

Fellow England international Charles Alcock described Alf Harvey as being 'a clever, hard-working back, who dodged well.' He was certainly an elusive, dexterous defender and was not the worst player on the pitch when England lost 1-0 to Wales in February 1881 – his only international appearance. His career was cut short through injury.

HARVEY, James Colin 1970-71 ①

Born: Liverpool, 16 November 1945
Career: Liverpool & Merseyside Schools, Everton (apprentice, April 1960, professional, October 1962), Sheffield Wednesday (£70,000, September 1974, retired, injured, March 1976); Everton (youth team coach, July 1976, reserve team coach, then first team coach, August 1983; manager, June 1987-October 1990; returned to club as assistant to manager Howard Kendall, November 1990-December 1993; then coach to May 1994); Mansfield Town (assistant-manager to Andy King, June-October 1994), Oldham Athletic (assistant-manager to Graeme Sharp, November 1994), Everton (youth team coach, January 1995-May 2006), Bolton Wanderers (chief scout, November 2007).

An FA Cup and League championship winner with Everton in 1966 and 1970 respectively, midfielder Colin Harvey formed a terrific combination with Alan Ball and Howard Kendall at Goodison Park (the trio was known as the Holy Trinity). Nicknamed the 'White Pele' by Everton fans and described by commentator Kenneth Wolstenholme as "a beautiful footballer" as a boy, he scored 24 goals in 387 first-class games for the Merseyside club between 1962 and 1974 and gained his only England cap in the 1-0 European qualifying victory over Malta in February 1971 when two of his team-mates, Ball and Joe Royle, also played. Harvey, who spent over 40 years at Goodison Park, off and on, also lined up in one unofficial international. Unfortunately, he achieved very little as a manager.

In 2005, Harvey's autobiography "Everton Secrets" was released.

HASSALL, Harold William 1950-51 ⑤ ④

Born: Tyldesley, Lancs, 4 March 1929
Career: Leigh Grammar School, Astley & Tyldesley Collieries (seasons 1944-46), Huddersfield Town (professional, September 1946), Bolton Wanderers (January 1952, retired, injured, December 1955); qualified as PE teacher and FA coach; member of FIFA coaching list; England Youth team manager; Malaysia national team coach; Preston North End (scout); became senior lecturer at Padgate College of Education, Lancashire; later general secretary of the Amateur Swimming Association.

Tall, long-striding, hard-shooting inside-left Harry Hassall netted a brilliant goal on his international debut, albeit to no avail, as England lost 3-2 to Scotland at Wembley in April 1951. He opened the scoring in the 24th minute with a tremendous right-foot drive from 25 yards from Stan Mortensen's square pass. Right at the death Hassall could have earned his side a draw but his weak shot from 12 yards went straight at goalkeeper Jimmy Cowan. A year later he netted again in a 5-2 win over Portugal in Lisbon and in November 1953, playing alongside his Bolton team-mate Nat Lofthouse, he scored twice in a 3-1 win over Northern Ireland at Goodison Park, this being his last international appearance. He represented the Football League on three occasions, and was an FA Cup finalist in 1953 with Bolton for whom he scored 34 goals in 109 appearances, having earlier netted 26 times in his 78 outings for Huddersfield (1946-52). A serious knee injury ended his career in 1955.

friendly win in Stockholm in November 2012. In fact, Hart's attempted headed clearance late in this game, resulted in the Swede scoring what some have described as the 'greatest goal' ever seen when he netted with a superb overhead bicycle kick from 30 yards.

Hart had earlier been in excellent form when on loan with Birmingham City in 2009-10 which resulted in him being named as third choice England goalkeeper at the World Cup finals in South Africa. Thereafter, he contested the number one position with four other 'keepers before making it his own in 2011, leading him into Euro 2012.

Taking over from Shay Given between the posts at Manchester City, he duly helped the Blues win the Premiership title on the very last day of the 2011-12 season. Hart, who is now rated as one of the best 'keepers in world football, has made almost 300 appearances at club level.

Hart saved Ronaldinho's penalty when England beat Brazil 2-1 at Wembley in February 2013.

HARTLEY, Frank 1922-23 ①

Born: Shipton-under-Wychwood, Oxfordshire, 7 February 1896
Died: Shipton-under-Wychwood, 20 October 1965
Career: Burford Grammar School, Oxford City (amateur, August 1919), Tottenham Hotspur (amateur, November 1922), played for Corinthians (between August 1923 and May 1927), Tottenham Hotspur (professional, February 1928, retired, May 1932); Eton Manor FC (secretary, seasons 1932-36); played cricket and hockey and was a member of a prominent Cotswolds farming family.

Ball-playing inside-forward Frank Hartley's only appearance for England came in a 4-1 friendly win over France in Paris in May 1923 when he set up a goal for his left-wing partner Kenneth Hegan. Also capped seven times at amateur level, Hartley was registered with Spurs, but injuries ruined his first-class career. He had trials for England at field hockey.

HATELEY, Mark Wayne 1984-92 ③② ⑨

Born: Wallasey, Merseyside, 7 November 1961
Career: Coventry City (apprentice, June 1977, professional,
December 1978), Detroit Express/USA (loan, April-June 1980),
Portsmouth (£190,000, June 1983), AC Milan/Italy (£1m, June
1984), AS Monaco/France (June 1987), Glasgow Rangers
(£500,000, June 1990), Queens Park Rangers (£1.5m, November
1995), Leeds United (loan, August-October 1996), Glasgow
Rangers (£300,000, March 1997), Hull City (free, August 1997,
player-manager, December 1998-June 1999), Ross County (season
1999-2000); later covered Scottish games for Setantna TV; also
associated again with Glasgow Rangers (part-time coach)

Mark Hateley's goal was the difference as Bobby Robson's England
beat Northern Ireland 1-0 at Windsor Park to clinch a place in the
1986 World Cup finals, and then, annoyingly, his brilliant diving
header against Mexico in Los Angeles in the finals was missed by
the TV cameras filming the game. One spokesman said 'No-one
expected him to go for it!'

Making his international debut as a substitute against the USSR
at Wembley in June 1984, Hateley brought 'life to the attack' but
failed to get in a worthwhile shot in a 2-0 defeat. He scored against
Brazil in the Maracana Stadium in his second international later in
the month but three days after that he gave away an eighth minute
penalty in a 2-0 defeat by Uruguay in Montevideo. "Acosta fell over
my outstretched leg," said Hateley. "It was never a foul."

Hateley scored twice in a 5-0 win over Finland in October 1984
and followed up with two great headers when England defeated
Mexico 3-0 in Los Angeles in May 1986.

Over the next six years he continued to put himself about and
despite having several different strike-partners, he gave defenders
plenty to think about but unfortunately he was goalless in his last
14 internationals, of which only two were won. At club level, Hateley
netted over 200 goals in more than 500 senior appearances,
including 167 goals in 428 games for his British clubs. He won
the French League title with Monaco and followed up by gaining
six League championship, two Scottish Cups and three League
Cup winner's medals in his two spells at Ibrox Park, teaming up
splendidly with Ally McCoist. In fact, Hateley bagged 113 goals in
220 games for Rangers. He also played in five Youth and 10 U21
internationals and in 1994 became the first English-born player to
win the coveted Scottish Footballer of the Year award.

Hateley's father, Tony, also a striker, had a long career with Notts
County, Aston Villa, Liverpool, Chelsea, Coventry City, Birmingham
City and Oldham Athletic.

HAWKES, Robert Murray 1906-08 ⑤

Born: Breachwood Green, Hertfordshire, 18 October 1880
Died: Luton, 12 September 1945
Career: Luton Higher Grade School, Luton Stanley (June 1895),
Luton Victoria (May 1896), Luton Clarence (August 1898),
Hertfordshire County (August 1899), Luton Town (amateur, June
1901, professional, August 1911), Bedford Town (February 1920,
retired, May 1920); worked in Luton for many years.

Frail-looking left-half Robert Hawkes, who was a fine ball player,
was associated with Luton Town for 19 years. During that time he
amassed over 300 first-team appearances and gained five full and
22 amateur internationals caps for England. His first at senior level
came against Ireland in February 1907 and his last versus Bohemia
in June 1908. He was on the winning side in each of his five games
as England rattled in a total of 29 goals, Hawkes having a hand in
six of them, three in the 11-1 victory over Austria, five days before
his last outing. In 1908 the Luton player helped the United Kingdom
beat Denmark inn the Olympic Games football final.

HAWORTH, George 1886-1890 ⑤

Born: Accrington, 17 October 1864
Died: Bradford, 5 January 1943
Career: Church FC (June 1880), Accrington (May 1883), Blackburn
Rovers (July 1884), Accrington (August 1885-May 1890).

One of Blackburn's finest-ever half-backs, George Haworth gained an
FA Cup winner's medal in 1885 and in an article written 20 years later,
Jimmy Crabtree (also an England international) described him as being
one of the best tacklers and most judicious players of the mid-1880s.

Capped five times by England, Haworth made his debut in a 7-0
win over Ireland in February 1887 and played his last game in the 1-1
draw with Scotland in April 1890 when he marked Jimmy McColl out
of the game.

His uncle, John Haworth, managed Burnley (1910-24).

HAWTRY, John Purvis 1880-81 ②

Born: Eton, Bucks, 19 July 1850
Died: Reading, Berkshire, 17 August 1925
Career: Eton College (seasons 1862-64), Clifton College (seasons
1864-68); later played for Old Etonians (seasons 1870-83),
Remnants FC, Berkshire and Buckinghamshire; retired in May 1885;
became a school teacher at Aldin House, Slough, and thence an
actor and later playwright (working under the name of John Trent-
Hay) before running the newspaper, *Sporting World.*

An FA Cup winner with Old Etonians in 1879, goalkeeper Jack
Hawtry could be brilliant at times but it must be said he was also
one of the most inconsistent of his generation. His two caps were
gained against Wales and Scotland in February and March 1881,
having a nightmare against the Scots in a 6-1 defeat…the heaviest
England has suffered on home soil against their 'north of the border'
opponents. Hawtry also represented London against Birmingham.

HAYGARTH, Edward Brownlow 1874-75 ①

Born: Cirencester, 26 April 1854
Died: Cirencester, 14 April 1915
Career: Lancing College; represented Wanderers, Swifts, Reading and Berkshire County (between August 1870 and May 1880); played cricket for Hants, Gloucestershire and Berkshire; became a solicitor in Cirencester

Ted Haygarth, heavily built and courageous, was regarded as a splendid full-back. He was capped by England as a Swifts player against Scotland in March 1875 and reported *Bell's Life*, 'played a good game' in the 2-2 draw at The Oval. He was a wicket-keeper and under-arm bowler on the cricket field.

HAYNES, John Norman 1954-62 ㊻ ⑱

Born: Kentish Town, London, 17 October 1934
Died: Edinburgh, 18 October 2005
Career: Houndsfield Road & Latymer Grammar Schools/Edmonton, Edmonton Schools, London & Middlesex Boys, Fulham (amateur, July 1950); played for Feltham Boys, Wimbledon juniors and Woodford Town (during seasons 1950-52); Fulham (professional, May 1952, player-manager, briefly, November-December 1968, reverted back to playing until May 1970); also played for Toronto City/Canada (1961), Durban City/South Africa (August 1970-April 1971), Wealdstone (July 1971-May 1972), Durban City (August 1972, retired, May 1973); part-owner of a bookmaker's business; also the face for an 'ad campaign' for Brylcreem.

 Johnny Haynes – rated by some as England's finest-ever playmaker – controlled the midfield for the majority of his international career. Perhaps the most-gifted footballer of his generation he could spray out passes long or short, high or low, splitting a defence in half with his supreme judgment. He could beat an opponent in one quick movement and above all, he was a predator of the highest order, a master of seizing a loose ball in or outside the penalty-area, often clipping it into the net. Indeed, he became the first England player to score a hat-trick against an Eastern European country when his treble helped beat the USSR 5-0 at Wembley in October 1958. This was Haynes' 'finest hour' for besides his treble he also had a hand in the other two goals as the Russians were torn to shreds.

When he won his first senior cap as a 19 year-old in October 1954 against Northern Ireland in Belfast, Haynes became the first English footballer to represent his country at five different levels – Schoolboy, Youth, B, U23 and full – when playing the game against the Irish he was rebuked by Stan Matthews for 'shouting on the field.' Unperturbed he got on with his game and celebrated the occasion by scoring in a 2-0 win.

Haynes was the motor that drove the England midfield…and he certainly silenced the Hampden 'roar' with a last-minute equaliser against Scotland in April 1956.

Badly injured in the game against Yugoslavia seven months later, following a tackle by Belin, Haynes missed the 5-2 win over Denmark at Molineux in the December and also the Scotland game in April 1957 before returning to action in the 5-1 World Cup qualifying win over the Republic of Ireland at Wembley when he was 'quite outstanding.'

Unfortunately after taking over the captaincy from Ronnie Clayton in 1960, his performances suffered at times, although he was still a master tactician right up until his last game for his country against Brazil in the ill-fated 1962 World Cup tournament in Chile.

He scored the 'goal of the game' from fully 25 yards when

England whipped hapless Luxembourg 9-0 away in October 1960 and seven months later led his team to a memorable 3-2 victory over Italy in Rome. After this game he took his players on a lap of honour as the majority of the 100,000 fans whistled and jeered their own players as they trooped off down the tunnel.

His misery was complete that year when he was badly hurt in a car crash in Blackpool. This seriously affected Haynes and, in fact, he played very few games for Fulham in 1962-63 and wasn't selected at all by new England boss Alf Ramsey, not even as a standby-reserve! His international career was over, and this after he had won 32 of his 56 caps playing Second Division football.

A one-club man and the first player to command a salary of £100-a-week, Haynes scored 158 goals in 658 appearances for Fulham between 1952 and 1970. He died in an Edinburgh hospital after a second serious car crash in 2005.

HEALLESS, Henry 1924-28 ②

Born: Blackburn, 10 February 1893
Died: Blackburn, 11 January 1972
Career: Blackburn Athletic (August 1907), Victoria Cross (May 1910), Blackburn Trinity (July 1911), Blackburn Rovers (amateur, November 1914, professional, May 1919, retired, April 1933); Almelo FC/Holland (coach, September 1935-October 1937); Haslingden Grange (reinstated as an amateur, November 1937, retired, May 1949); later Blackburn Rovers (coach, November 1951-May 1953).

After England had been tanked 5-1 by the 'Wembley Wizards' Scotland in April 1928, one reporter stated: 'The three half-backs, Edwards, Wilson and Healless were bewildered and lost from beginning to end.'

Harry Healless, however, was a dour defender with a crunching tackle who made his international debut in a 3-1 win over Northern Ireland at Goodison Park in October 1924. He captained Blackburn for many years, making 396 senior appearances for the club over a period of 19 years, gaining an FA Cup winner's medal in 1928.

He played with his son at the age of 48 for Haslingden Grange and kicked his last ball in earnest at the age of 56.

HECTOR, Kevin James 1973-74 ②

Born: Leeds, 2 November 1944
Career: South Leeds FC (junior, August 1959), Bradford Park Avenue (apprentice, April 1960, professional, July 1962), Derby County (£34,000, September 1966), Vancouver Whitecaps/Canada (January 1978), Burton Albion (loan, season 1978-79), Boston United (loan, season 1979-80), Derby County (free, October 1980-May 1982), Belper Town (August 1982, retired May 1985); became a postman after retiring; also played for Derby County Old Stars.

Kevin Hector gave supporters immense pleasure through his style, his goals and his manner on and off the field. A terrific marksman, sharp and instinctive, he scored 113 goals in 176 consecutive League appearances for Bradford before joining Derby. He went on to amass a club record 589 senior appearances for the Rams (486 in the League) in two spells with the club, netting a total of 201 goals (only Steve Bloomer scored more), 155 in the League while helping Brian Clough's team win the Second Division championship in 1969 and the First Division title in 1972 and 1975. Unfortunately he failed to score in each of his England internationals when he came on as a second-half substitute against Poland in that vital World Cup qualifier at Wembley which ended 1-1 and Italy, lost 1-0. He also represented the Football League. Hector helped Belper Town win the Northern Counties (East) League championship in 1985.

He had the pleasure of scoring his first goal with an overhead kick in a charity match at the age of 59.

HEDLEY, George Albert 1900-01 ①
Born: South Bank, Cleveland, 20 July 1876
Died: Wolverhampton, 16 August 1942
Career: South Bank (May 1895), Sheffield United (professional, May 1898), Southampton (May 1903), Wolverhampton Wanderers (May 1906, retired, April 1913); Bristol City (manager, April 1913-May 1915); became a licensee in Bristol and later ran a boarding house.

George Hedley was a tough, aggressive centre-forward who loved to compete in knock-out competitions! He gained three FA Cup winner's medals (two with Sheffield United, one with Wolves) and he also helped Southampton win the Southern League championship. His career spanned 16 years (1897-1913) during which time he scored 147 goals in 449 club appearances. With two key players sidelined – Steve Bloomer and G.O. Smith – Hedley was handed his only England cap in a 3-0 win over Ireland in March 1901 on his own patch, The Dell, Southampton.

HEGAN, Kenneth Edward, OBE 1922-24 ④ ④
Born: Coventry, 24 January 1901
Died: Warwick, 3 March 1989
Career: Bablake School, RMC Sandhurst (joined May 1916); played football with the 1st Dublin Fusiliers and Royal Army Service Corps; retired with rank of Lieutenant Colonel, July 1949; also played for Corinthians (August 1919-May 1935); awarded OBE for Army service during WW2.

A slender, fast and courageous winger who could man both flanks, Ted Hegan – 'Jackie' to his pals – made the most appearances for England's amateur team between the two World Wars (23). He collected his four full caps over a period of eight months, gaining his first against Belgium in March 1923 when he scored twice in a 6-1 win and his last versus the same country the following November (2-2). In between times he netted two more goals in a 4-1 victory over France and played in the 2-1 defeat by Ireland. He also bagged 37 goals in 138 appearances for the Corinthians.

HELLAWELL, Michael Stephen 1962-63 ②
Born: Keighley, Yorkshire, 30 June 1938
Career: Salts FC (May 1953), Huddersfield Town (amateur, July 1954), Queens Park Rangers (professional, August 1955), Birmingham City (£5,000, May 1957), Sunderland (January 1965), Huddersfield Town (September 1966), Peterborough United (December 1968), Bromsgrove Rovers (August 1969, retired, May 1971); also played cricket for Warwickshire.

Fast-raiding red-haired right-winger Mike Hellawell had an excellent career. He scored over 40 goals in more than 350 club appearances and helped Birmingham win the League Cup in 1963 and reach the final of the Inter Cities Fairs Cup. Replacing Bryan Douglas, he gained his two England caps in October 1962 - in a 1-1 draw with France in a European qualifier at Hillsborough and a 3-1 Home International victory over Northern Ireland in Belfast. His brother, John, played for Darlington and Rotherham United.

HENDERSON, Jordan Brian 2010-11 ⑤
Born: Sunderland, 17 June 1990
Career: Sunderland (apprentice, June 2006, professional, July 2008), Coventry City (loan, January-May 2009), Liverpool (£16m, June 2011)

Jordan Henderson was handed his England debut far too early, selected by Fabio Capello against top-class opposition in France in

November 2010. He struggled to get a foothold on the game from midfield and was shown a yellow card for a rather reckless tackle. Capped at Youth team level, he had played in barely 50 senior games for Sunderland before taking on the French and subsequently being signed by Liverpool boss Kenny Dalglish for a huge fee. Henderson subsequently played for his country at Euro 2012 under new manager Roy Hodgson.

HENDRIE, Lee Andrew 1998-99 ①
Born: Birmingham, 18 May 1977
Career: Birmingham City (juniors, season 1992-93), Aston Villa (apprentice, June 1993, professional, May 1994), Stoke City (two loan spells, between September 2006 and April 2007), Sheffield United (free, July 2007), Leicester City (loan, February 2008), Blackpool (loan, January-March 2008), Derby County (free, September 2009), Brighton & Hove Albion (loan, March-May 2010), Aberdeen (trial, July 2010), Bradford City (free, August 2010), FC Bandung/Indonesia (January-June 2011), Corby Town (trial July 2011), Hinckley Town (trial, August-September 2011), Daventry Town (August 2011), Kidderminster Harriers (non-contract, November 2011), Chasetown (March 2012), Evesham United (May 2012), Redditch United (June 2012)

Hard-working, fiery midfielder Lee Hendrie was honoured by England at Youth, U21 (13 times) and B team levels before winning his only full cap against Czechoslovakia in November 1998 when he came off the subs' bench to replace his Aston Villa team-mate Paul Merson in the 2-0 victory at Wembley. At 2012, he had made well over 420 club appearances, including 308 for Villa for whom he played in the 2000 FA Cup final defeat by Chelsea. He was voted joint 'Young Footballer of the Year' with Robbie Keane in 1999. Hendrie's father, Paul, played for Birmingham City, his cousin John, a Scottish international, assisted Leeds United, Middlesbrough and Newcastle United, among others, and his younger brother Stuart played with him at Daventry. And Hendrie himself was the first England player to be engaged by Kidderminster Harriers since Jesse Pennington was appointed coach in 1923.
In January 2012, prospective businessman Hendrie was declared bankrupt.

HENFREY, Arthur George 1890-96 ⑤ ②
Born: Wellingborough, 2 May 1868
Died: Finedon, Northamptonshire, 17 October 1929
Career: Wellingborough Grammar School, Jesus College/Cambridge University (years 1887-92); also starred for Finedon FC (season 1889-90), Corinthians (1890-1903) and Northamptonshire (1890s); played cricket for Cambridge University and Northants (seasons 1886-97, captain in 1893 and 1894); later worked in local government in Northampton.

The versatile Arthur Henfrey scored as an inside-forward on his international debut v. Ireland in March 1891 (won 6-1) and likewise against Wales in his second game a year later (won 2-0) before gaining his other three caps as a half-back v. Wales in 1895 when he assisted in three of the goals in a 9-1 win, and Wales again and Scotland in 1896. Henfrey also scored in one unofficial international for England.

HENRY, Ronald Patrick 1962-63 ①

Born: Shoreditch, London, 17 April 1934
Career: Harpenden Boys, Hertfordshire Schools, Luton Town (amateur, May 1949), Harpenden Town (August 1951), Redbourne (July 1952), Tottenham Hotspur (amateur, March 1953, professional, January 1955, retired May 1969; thereafter colts' coach); later ran his own nursery business in Hertfordshire.

Ron Henry was the only debutant in Alf Ramsey's first England team – and ironically he played for the same team as Ramsey had done many years before – Tottenham Hotspur. Partnering Jimmy Armfield at full-back, Henry didn't have the greatest of games against flying winger Wisnieski as France won a European Championship qualifier by 5-2 in Paris in February 1963. A double winner with Spurs in 1961 and an FA Cup winner again in 1962, Henry then added a European Cup Winners' Cup medal to his collection the following year. Originally a left-winger, then a left-half, Henry made most of his 287 appearances for Spurs at left-back when he performed with steadiness and consistency for 14 years (1955-69).

HERON, Charles Francis William 1875-76 ①

Born: Uxbridge, Middlesex, 30 January 1853
Died: Christchurch, Dorset, 23 October 1914
Career: Mill Hill School (from Easter 1864), Uxbridge FC (seasons 1870-74), also played for Wanderers (seasons 1875-78), Swifts (briefly), Windsor (1870s); became a wine merchant in Bournemouth

Lightweight Wanderers inside-right Frank Heron, described as being 'an expert dribbler' won his only England cap in a 3-0 defeat by Scotland at Partick in March 1875, lining up in front of his older brother Hubert (below). He won the FA Cup with Wanderers in 1876.

HERON, George Hubert Hugh 1872-78 ⑤

Born: Uxbridge, Middlesex, 30 January 1852
Died: Bournemouth, 5 June 1914
Career: Mill Hill School (from April 1864), Uxbridge FC (seasons 1869-74); also played for Wanderers (seasons 1874-79), Swifts (season 1879-80), Middlesex (1870s); later served on the FA Committee; worked with his brother, as wine merchant in Bournemouth

Three times an FA Cup winner with Wanderers (1876-77-78), Hubert Heron won the first of his five caps in England's second international against Scotland in March 1873. An outside-left, who also played at left-half, he did well in a 4-2 win at The Oval. Indeed, the reporter for *Bell's Life* stated: 'Rather selfish at times, he gave the Scottish right-back Joe Taylor a difficult time'. He had a hand in the fourth goal scored by Charles Chenery.

HESKEY, Emile William Ivanhoe 1998-2010 (62) ⑦

Born: Leicester, 11 January 1978
Career: Ratby Groby Juniors/Leicester (May 1993), Leicester City (apprentice, April 1994, professional, October 1995), Liverpool (£11m, March 2002), Birmingham City (£3.5m, July 2004), Wigan Athletic (£5.5m, July 2006), Aston Villa (£3.5m, January 2009, released, May 2012), Newcastle Jets/Australia (September 2012)

Prior to his big-money move to Liverpool in 2000, Emile Heskey spent six years with Leicester, collecting a League Cup winner's medal in his last season. At Anfield he won multiple honours, including the FA Cup, League Cup and UEFA Cup treble and after that did well with Blues and Wigan (each time under manager Steve Bruce) and Aston Villa, for whom he played in the 2010 League Cup final. A big bold striker of

Antiguan descent, Heskey made his international debut for England in the 1-1 draw with Hungary in Budapest in April 1999 when he came on as a second-half substitute for Kevin Phillips. A regular on the international circuit, scoring his first England goal in a 2-1 win over Malta in Valletta in June 2000, Heskey was one of four players who wore the captain's armband in the game against Serbia & Montenegro at Leicester's Walkers Stadium in February 2003.

Heskey lost his place in the squad after Euro 2004 but was recalled for the Euro 2008 qualifiers in September 2007 and although in and out of the team after that, he was still admired by Fabio Capello and was part of his World Cup squad in South Africa, although it must be said he had a poor tournament! And he knew it – announcing his retirement from international football on his return home. On his release by Aston Villa at the end of the 2011-12 season, Heskey had scored 151 goals in 696 club appearances for his five English clubs. He also won 12 Youth, one B and 16 U21 caps to his credit.

HIBBERT, William 1909-10 ①

Born: Golborne near Wigan, 21 September, 1884
Died: Blackpool, 6 March 1949
Career: Golborne Juniors (September 1898), Newton le Willows (April 1902), Brynn Central (August 1904), Bury (professional, May 1906), Newcastle United (£1,950, October 1911); WW1 guest for Sheffield Wednesday and Leeds City; Bradford City (£700, May 1920), Oldham Athletic (£500, May 1922, retired, April 1923); Fall River Marksmen/USA June 1923), J & P Coats FC/Rhode Island/USA (player-coach, October 1923), Real Gimnástico CF/Spain (player-coach, June 1927, retired, May 1928); Wigan Borough (trainer, briefly 1929); later worked in Blackpool.

Not the biggest or strongest of attackers, Billy Hibbert nevertheless had an excellent career which brought him over 60 goals in almost 200 League and Cup appearances (50 in 159 starts for Newcastle). His solitary cap came against Scotland in April 1910 when partnering Richard Bond of Bradford City on England's right-wing, but he failed to impress in a 2-0 defeat at Hampden Park. Hibbert also represented the Football League on three occasions and toured South Africa with the FA in 1910 when he top-scored with 34 goals, including two sixes v. Western Province (won 13-0) and Klip River District XI (13-3) and hat-tricks v. Griqualand (7-1), South Africa (in a Test Match, 3-0), Port Elizabeth (8-0) and Eastern Province (10-0).

HIBBS, Henry Edward 1929-36 ㉕

Born: Wilnecote, Tamworth, 27 May 1906
Died: Welwyn Garden City, 23 April 1984
Career: Wilnecote Holy Trinity (August 1920), Tamworth Castle (July 1921), Birmingham (amateur, April 1924, professional, May 1924, retired, May 1940); Walsall (manager, August 1944-June 1951), De Havillands FC (permit player, February 1953-May 1954); Ware Town (manager, August 1960-May 1962), Welwyn Garden City (manager, July 1962-May 1964).

A plumber's apprentice, goalkeeper Harry Hibbs had two horrendous seasons in the Birmingham & District Football League, conceding no less than 164 goals. But despite this, he managed to produce some outstanding performances which did not go unnoticed by eagle-eyed scouts from Birmingham. At the age of 17 he was handed a professional contract at St Andrew's and remained with the Midlands club until 1940, amassing 389 appearances and helping Blues reach the 1931 FA Cup final. He was selected for the FA tour to South Africa in the summer of 1929, playing in three Test Matches, and he duly earned the first of his 25 England caps against Wales at Stamford Bridge in November of that same year, saving Fred Keenor's penalty in the process.

Prior to Hibbs's call-up, the England selectors had tried 21 different goalkeepers in 46 internationals over a period of nine years since Sam Hardy's retirement in 1920. Hibbs was almost a 'carbon copy' of Hardy. Unspectacular but extremely reliable, he kept ten clean sheets for his country. The highlight of his managerial career period was to take Walsall into the 1946 Third Division (South) Cup final against Bournemouth at Stamford Bridge. His cousin was the West Bromwich Albion and England goalkeeper Harold Pearson, who played against Blues in the 1931 Cup final.

NB: Hibbs scored from the penalty-spot for the FA XI in a 7-1 win over Vancouver in British Columbia in June 1931.

HILL, Frederick 1962-63 ②

Born: Sheffield, 17 January 1940
Career: Sheffield Schools, Bolton Wanderers (amateur, April 1955, professional, March 1957), Halifax Town (July 1969), Manchester City (May 1970), Cape Town City/South Africa (loan, 1972), Peterborough United (August 1973-May 1975); later assisted Cork Hibernians/Ireland (season 1975-76), Droylsden (season 1976-77), Radcliffe Borough (July 1977, retired, May 1978). Became a licensee in Peterborough.

A strong, skilful inside-forward with loads of ability, Freddie 'The Fox' Hill, who played for England 10 times at U23 level, won the first of his two senior caps in a 3-1 win over Northern Ireland in October 1962 and his second in a 4-0 victory over Wales a month later. Unfortunately he was one of several players competing for a place in the national team, among them Johnny Haynes, Ron Flowers and George Eastham. He spent his best years with Bolton for whom he scored 79 goals in 412 appearances (1957-69). He had over 150 games for his three other clubs and helped Peterborough win the Fourth Division title in 1974.

HILL, Gordon Alex 1975-78 ⑥

Born: Sunbury-on-Thames, Surrey, 1 April 1954
Career: Ashford Youth Club (April 1968), Queens Park Rangers (trial, April-May 1969), Southend United (trial, July-August 1969), Staines Town (August 1970), Slough Town (May 1971), Southall (June 1972), Millwall (professional, January 1973), Chicago Sting/USA (loan, April-August 1975), Manchester United (November 1975), Derby County (April 1978), Queens Park Rangers (November 1979), Montreal Manic/Canada (April 1981), Chicago Sting/USA (March 1982; also played in Indoor League for same club), San Jose Earthquakes/USA (September 1982), New York Arrows/USA (Indoor League, January 1983), Inter-Montreal/Canada (summer, 1983), Kansas Comets/USA (Indoor League, October 1983), Tacoma Stars/USA (Indoor League, December 1984); FC Twente Enschede/Holland (season 1985-86), HJK Helsinki/Finland (August 1986); AFC Bournemouth (trial, late 1986), Northwich Victoria (briefly), Stafford Rangers (December 1987), Northwich Victoria (caretaker-manager, 1988, then coach), Radcliffe Borough (coach, 1989); Nova Scotia Clippers/Canada, player-coach, summer, 1991); managed his own soccer school in Florida for five years; then Chester City (manager, in season 2001-02), Hyde United (briefly as manager, 2002); now head coach of United FC (McKinney, Texas); also runs soccer schools in Cardiff and Newport, Wales.

Gordon Hill was a tricky left-winger with dash and confidence. He gained the first of his six England caps in a 3-2 win over Italy in the US Bicentennial tournament in New York in May 1976 and collected his next five over a period of 18 months when depending on the formation and opposition, he contested for a place in the line-up along with Dennis Tueart, Trevor Francis and Ian Callaghan.

Nicknamed 'Merlin,' Hill helped Manchester United reach successive FA Cup finals, collecting a winner's medal in 1977. He made 225 League appearances at club level between 1973 and 1981 and scored 65 goals. Also capped by England at B and U23 levels, he did extremely well in the USA and Canada during the 1980s.

HILL, John Henry 1924-29 ⑪

Born: Hetton-le-Hole, County Durham, 2 March 1897
Died: Helensburgh, Scotland, 5 April 1972
Career: Durham junior football, Durham City (professional, April 1919), Plymouth Argyle (September 1920), Burnley (£5,450, May 1923), Newcastle United (£8,100, October 1928), Bradford City (£600, June 1931), Hull City (£100, November 1931, retired, April 1934, manager, April 1934-January 1936, later scout, seasons 1948-55); Scarborough Town (Pools Scheme manager, late 1950s).

Jack Hill was a tall, elegant, red-haired right or centre-half whose long legs enabled him to become a rare spoiler. He was a brainy, constructive player who made his international debut behind his Burnley club mate Robert Kelly, against Wales in February 1925 when he starred in a 2-1 win at Swansea. He continued to perform with confidence and was superb in centre-field when Belgium and France were thumped 9-1 and 6-0 respectively in May 1927 and he also caught the eye again when Scotland were defeated 2-1 at Hampden Park a month earlier. Off the field with a bad gash over his left eye which required 10 stitches, Hill returned to the action and 'Broadcaster' reporting for the *Daily Express*, stated: "Strangely it was when Hill resumed for a second time, operating in the unfamiliar position of outside-right, that England began to show their true form."

Hill, who made over 500 club appearances during his career (1920-34), 461 in the League, actually represented the Football League three times and helped Hull win the Third Division (North) championship in 1935.

HILL, Richard Henry 1925-26 ①

Born: Mapperley, 26 November 1893
Died: Coventry, 10 April 1971
Career: Army football (served with the Grenadier Guards), Millwall Athletic (professional, June 1919), Torquay United (July 1930), Newark Town (May 1931, retired June 1932); Mansfield Town (trainer, August 1932), Coventry City (trainer, May 1935), Torquay United (trainer, July 1950-May 1955).

A Third Division (South) championship winner with Millwall, left-back Dicky Hill spent eleven years with the London club during which time he made 392 appearances, many alongside his admirable partner Jack Fort. His only England cap came in the 5-3 win over Belgium in Antwerp in May 1926 when he partnered Tom Lucas of Liverpool. He never got another call, however, due to the consistent form of Herbert Jones (Blackburn) and Ernie Blenkinsopp (Sheffield Wednesday).

HILL, Ricky Anthony 1982-83 ③

Born: Paddington, London, 5 March 1959
Career: Luton Town (apprentice, April 1975, professional, May 1976), Le Havre/France (August 1989), Leicester City (£100,000, August 1990), Tampa Bay Rowdies/USA (May 1991), Hitchin Town (August 1993), Chertsey Town (1994, retired 1995); Cocoa Expos/USA (coach, season 1995-96); Sheffield Wednesday (U19 coach, July 1996), Tottenham Hotspur (U17 coach, June 1998), Luton Town (manager, July-November 2000), San Juan Jabloteh FC/Trinidad & Tobago (manager-coach, from August 2000).

A Youth international, hard-working midfielder Ricky Hill was the first 'new' player chosen by Bobby Robson when he took over as England boss. The Luton Town star made his debut as a second-half substitute for Tony Morley in the 2-2 draw with Denmark in Copenhagen in September 1982. He added two further caps to his collection when he played against West Germany at Wembley (lost 2-1) in October 1982 and Egypt in Cairo in January 1986 (won 4-0).
    Hill netted 54 goals in 436 League appearances for the Hatters whom he helped win the Second Division championship in 1982 and the League Cup in 1988.

HILLMAN, John 1898-99 ①

Born: Tavistock, Devon, 30 October 1870
Died: Burnley, 1 August 1955
Career: Tavistock intermediate League football, Burnley (professional, October 1891), Everton (February 1895), Dundee (July 1896), Burnley (March 1898), Manchester City (January 1902), Millwall (January 1907, retired, elbow injury, April 1908), Burnley (trainer, after WW1); later ran a confectionery shop in Burnley.

Goalkeeper Jack Hillman, 6ft 4ins tall, was blessed with a fine physique and natural agility, being regarded universally as an 'impeccable performer.' Surprisingly he won only one cap for England v. Ireland in February 1899, having very little to do in all fairness as the Irish were battered 13-2 at Sunderland. He was suspended by Dundee in 1897-98 for 'not trying' and during his second spell with Burnley (1899-1900) he was charged by an FA-Football League committee with attempted bribery. Found guilty he was banned for a season. Then, in 1904-05 as Manchester City's goalkeeper, he was one of a number of players, among them Billy Meredith, who were suspended in respect of another bribery scandal. In the end he was one of 17 City players who were sold!
    Hillman, who also represented the Football League, won the Second Division championship and FA Cup with Manchester City in 1903 and 1904 and during his career (1891-1907) he made well over 400 club appearances, 188 for Burnley.

HILLS, Arnold Frank 1878-79 ①

Born: Camden Town, London, 12 March 1857
Died: East Ham, London, 7 March 1927
Career: Harrow School (seasons 1871-73), University College/Oxford (seasons 1874-81); played for Old Harrovians (1870s); later Thames Ironworks FC (managing-director and founder of club in 1895); also a fine track athlete who won the AAA mile title in 1877.

An FA Cup winner with Oxford University in 1877, fleet-footed winger Arnold Hill would race away down the flank with his head bowed and to the annoyance of his team-mates often ran the ball out of play. His only England cap was gained against Scotland at The Oval in April 1879 when he was one of the stars in the second-half as England stormed back from being 4-1 down to win 5-4.

HILSDON, George Richard 1906-09 ⑧ ⑭

Born: Bow, London, 10 August 1885
Died: East Ham, London, 7 September 1941
Career: East Ham Schools, South West Ham (May 1900), Clapton Orient (June 1901), Luton Town (May 1902), West Ham United (August 1903), Chelsea (May 1906), West Ham United (June 1912), Chatham (June 1919), Gillingham (May 1921, retired, November 1921); was badly gassed when serving in France with the British Army during WW1; became a member of Fred Karno's famous travelling circus.

Nicknamed 'Gatling Gun' for his quick-fire shooting, dynamic centre-forward George Hilsdon was strong in all departments. A 'striker' to savour, he scored over 150 goals in more than 275 club appearances over a period of 14 years and in his eight internationals for England he netted almost two goals per game, including a rip-roaring four-timer in a 7-0 victory over Hungary in Budapest in June 1908 when he played alongside his Chelsea team-mate Jimmy Windridge. He had made a moderate debut 16 months earlier against Ireland, missing three easy chances in a 1-0 win at Goodison Park, but over the next two years he was brilliant, claiming five braces to go with his four-timer.

HINCHCLIFFE, Andrew George 1996-99 ⑦

Born: Manchester, 5 February 1969
Career: Manchester City (apprentice, April 1985, professional, February 1986), Everton (£800,000 plus Neil Pointon, July 1990), Sheffield Wednesday (£2.85m, January 1998, retired, injured, March 2002; moved into coaching); now works as a football commentator on Key 103 and Magic 1152 Manchester and also Sky Sports.

Wholehearted and enthusiastic left-back and occasional midfielder Andy Hinchcliffe retired from the game with a serious Achilles heel injury in 2003 with 463 club appearances under his belt, 227 for Everton, with whom he won the FA Cup and Charity Shield in 1995. He won his seven England caps over a period of three years from September 1996, having the honour of never being on the losing side (four wins, three draws). He made an impressive debut in a 3-0 World Cup qualifying victory over Moldova and was 'on top of his game' in his third international v. Georgia and also in his fourth v. Cameroon. When capped against Switzerland in 1998, Hinchcliffe became the first Sheffield Wednesday player for five years to represent England for whom he also gained Youth and U21 honours.

HINE, Ernest William 1928-32 ⑥ ④

Born: Smithy Cross, Barnsley, Yorkshire, 9 April 1901
Died: Huddersfield, 11 April 1974
Career: New Hills FC (August 1918), Staincross Station FC (May 1919), Barnsley (amateur, April 1921, professional, January 1922), Leicester City (£3,000, January 1926), Huddersfield Town (£4,000, May 1932), Manchester United (£2,000, February 1933), Barnsley (£1,500, December 1934, retired, May 1938, then coach, May 1939 onwards).

Opportunist goalscorer Ernie Hine was a good old-fashioned inside or centre-forward with stamina, guts, speed and shooting power. His League career spanned 18 years (1921-39) during which time he netted 287 goals in just over 600 appearances, having his best spell with Leicester (1926-32).

First capped by England in a 2-1 win over Northern Ireland at Goodison Park in October 1928, he netted in a 3-2 victory over Wales at Swansea in his second outing and found the net in his third international versus the Irish in October 1929. His other two goals followed in successive wins over Ireland and Wales in October and November 1931.

Hine also represented the Football League on five occasions and toured Canada/North America with the FA in 1931, top-scoring with 20 goals including one five and two fours.

HINTON, Alan Thomas 1962-65 ③ ①

Born: Wednesbury, Staffs, 6 October 1942
Career: South East Staffs Schools, Birmingham County (trial, summer 1956), West Bromwich Albion (trial, April 1957), Wolverhampton Wanderers (amateur, July 1957, professional, October 1959), Nottingham Forest (January 1964), Derby County (£30,000, September 1967), Dallas Tornado/USA (March 1977), Vancouver Whitecaps/Canada (October 1977), Tulsa Roughnecks/USA (October 1978), Seattle Sounders/USA (November 1979-January 1983), Tacoma Stars/USA (Indoor League, February 1983-November 1984); became top-class coach in the NASL and US Indoor League; now runs his own Real Estate business with his wife in the USA

Former Youth and U23 international Alan Hinton made his England debut on the left flank in the 1-1 draw with France in a European Championship qualifier in October 1962. In his second outing, two years later, he scored in the 2-2 draw with Belgium at Wembley. Partnering another new 'cap' Terry Venables, he equalised in the 77th minute with a deflected shot. His third international followed soon afterwards against Wales (won 2-1). Several football analysts thought that Hinton would have been at home 20 years earlier, for he was a wonderful orthodox winger with pace, a strong shot and wicked crossing ability. His playing career covered 15 years during which time he scored more than 100 goals in well over 400 club appearances and helped Derby win the Second and then First Division championships in 1969 and 1972. He was voted NASL 'Coach of the Year' in 1980.

HIRST, David Eric 1990-92 ③ ①

Born: Cudworth, Yorkshire, 7 December 1967
Career: Barnsley (apprentice, April 1983, professional, November 1985), Sheffield Wednesday (£300,000, August 1986), Southampton (£2m, October 1997), Brunsmeer Athletic (August 1998, retired, May 1999); later employed as a matchday host at Hillsborough and also worked for local radio (sport).

David Hirst, the Sheffield Wednesday striker, was called up for England's tour of Australasia in 1991 but had mixed fortunes. He was 'subbed' at half-time in the first game against Australia and scored in the second match against New Zealand. Hirst earned just one more cap afterwards, joining Alan Shearer up front against France at Wembley in February 1992. An excellent player at club level, he spent his best

years with Sheffield Wednesday for whom he scored 128 goals in 358 appearances (1986-97). He was forced to retire from League football with a knee injury, caused in a freak training ground fall.

HITCHENS, Gerald Archibald 1961-62 ⑦ ⑤

Born: Rawnsley, Staffs, 8 October 1934
Died: Hope, Clwyd, Wales, 13 April 1983
Career: Highley Council School, Highley Youth Club, Highley Village Boys, Highley Miners' Welfare (season 1952-53), Kidderminster Harriers (August 1953), Cardiff City (£1,500, January 1955), Aston Villa (£22,500, December 1957), Inter Milan/Italy (£60,000, June 1961), Torino/Italy (£50,000, November 1962), Atalanta/Italy (£25,000, June 1965), Cagliari/Italy (£5,000, June 1967), Worcester City (free, November 1969), Merthyr Tydfil (free, September 1971, retired, May 1972), went into business in Pontypridd.

Gerry Hitchens made a sensational start to his England career by scoring with his first shot after just 90 seconds of the game against Mexico at Wembley in May 1961. His goal also gave him the honour of being the first overseas-based player to score for England. He later set up two of Bobby Charlton's three goals in a convincing 8-0 victory. In his second international he netted twice in a 3-2 victory over Italy and then, impressing in Serie A with Inter Milan, he was taken to the World Cup finals in 1962, where he played in two games against Hungary and the subsequent winners, Brazil. A Welsh Cup winner with Cardiff in 1956 and a Second Division championship winner with Aston Villa in 1960, he also helped Villa reach the final of the League Cup before moving to Italy. In the summer of 1956 he netted 18 goals in 12 Test Matches for the FA on tour in South Africa and he also starred for England at U23 level. A dashing centre-forward, Hitchens' senior career spanned 15 years (1955-69 inclusive) during which time he netted over 230 goals in more than 450 club appearances, including a splendid five-timer for Villa in an 11-1 Second Division win over Charlton Athletic in November 1959. This feat equalled the club's individual scoring record.

HOBBIS, Harold Henry Frank 1935-36 ② ①

Born: Dartford, 9 March 1913
Died: Eastbourne, Kent, 12 May 1991
Career: Brent Council School/Dartford, Brent School Old Boys (August 1928), Bromley (April 1929), West Ham United (amateur, September 1929), Tottenham Hotspur (amateur, April 1930), Charlton Athletic (amateur, December 1930), Arsenal (amateur, January 1931), Charlton Athletic (amateur, February 1931, professional, March 1931); WW2 guest for Brentford, Bristol City, Cambridge United, Fulham, Ipswich Town, Lovells Athletic, Luton Town, Merthyr Tydfil, Oxford City, Walsall, Watford and West Ham United (retired from League football, May 1948); Tonbridge (player-manager, November 1948); Middlesex Wanderers (coach, briefly, 1949); Crystal Palace (scout), Wolverhampton Wanderers (scout); ran a car hire business, newsagent's and tobacconists shops in Hackney and Bexhill; mine host of 'The Man of Kent' pub, Sydenham, then 'The Valley' (opened in November 1960) licensee in Charlton.

Outside-left Harold Hobbis spent 17 years with Charlton (1931-48) during which time he appeared in 266 first-team games and scored 78 goals, helping the Addicks win the Third Division (South) championship in 1935. Lively and direct, he had a distinctive gait when running and regularly unleashed a powerful shot. He made his international debut v. Austria in Vienna in May 1936 (won 2-1) and found the net in his second outing v. Belgium in Brussels three days later (lost 3-2). With Brook, Cliff Bastin and Joe Johnson all in good form around the same time, Hobbis was at least fourth choice for his country.

He represented an England Amateur XI, had international trials and coached Middlesex Wanderers on tour. His son, Brian, played for Tooting & Mitcham and Crystal Palace colts.

He had earlier netted on his international debut in a 2-0 win over Bulgaria in a European Championship qualifier in November 1979 and thereafter made more goals than he scored, having a hand in three and netting one himself of the nine against hapless Luxembourg at Wembley in December 1982 and two in the second-half of an 8-0 demolition of Turkey in October 1987. He made his last appearance for England in a 3-1 European Championship finals defeat by the Soviet Union in Frankfurt in 1988.

At club level, between 1975 and 1993, Hoddle made 669 first-class appearances and struck 140 goals, spending his best years with Tottenham for whom he bagged 132 goals in 590 games. Voted PFA 'Young Footballer of the Year' in 1979, he helped Spurs gain promotion in 1976, twice helped the Londoners win the FA Cup, scoring the deciding penalty in the 1982 replay against QPR, gained a UEFA Cup winner's medal in 1984 and was also a League championship and French Cup winner with AS Monaco.

As a manager he took Swindon into the Premiership in 1993 and was a runner-up with Chelsea in the FA Cup final a year later and with Spurs in the League Cup final of 2003.

Hoddle's first game in charge of England was against Moldova (away) in a World Cup qualifier in September 1996 (won 3-0). He then led his country in the 1998 World Cup finals in France before his contract was terminated by the FA after he had been in office for just 30 months.

HODGE, Stephen Brian 1985-91 ㉔

Born: Nottingham, 25 October 1962
Career: Nottinghamshire Schools, Nottingham Forest (apprentice, May 1978, professional, October 1980), Aston Villa (£450,000, August 1985), Tottenham Hotspur (£650,000, December 1986), Nottingham Forest (£575,000, August 1988), Leeds United (£900,000, July 1991), Derby County (loan, August-September 1994), Queens Park Rangers (£300,000, October 1994), Watford (free, February 1995), Hong Kong football (January 1996), Leyton Orient (free, August 1997); Walsall (trial, retired, May 1998), Chesterfield (coaching assistant), coached in Iran (December 2002-January 2003); Chesterfield (part-time coach, under Roy McFarland, season 2010-11); also worked at Nottingham Forest (matchday hospitality host) and Notts County (Academy coach with Steve Chettle); also soccer pundit on TalkSport.

Steve Hodge was one of the 'best players on the pitch' and may well have scored a hat-trick when England beat World Cup qualifiers Canada 1-0 in Burnaby in May 1986.

At the World Cup soon afterwards, it was the hard-working midfielder who bagged Diego Maradona's shirt at the end on the infamous 'Hand of God' encounter in Mexico City.

Hodge had made his international debut against USSR as a second-half substitute for Gordon Cowans in a 1-0 friendly win in Tbilisi in March 1986.

A professional footballer for 18 years, from 1980 to 1998, he scored over 100 goals in 515 appearances at club level, helping Forest twice lift the League Cup and win the Simod Cup. He was an FA Cup winner with Spurs in 1991 before helping Leeds claim the last Football League title (before the introduction of the Premiership) in 1992. He also played in two B and eight U21 internationals.

His autobiography – *The Man with Maradona's Shirt* – was published in 2010.

HODDLE, Glenn 1979-88 ㊾ ⑧

Born: Hayes, Middlesex, 27 October 1957
Career: Spinney Dynamos, Harlow & District Schools, Essex Schools, Tottenham Hotspur (apprentice, April 1974, professional, April 1975), AS Monaco/France (£800,000, July 1987-December 1990), Chelsea (non-contract, January 1991), Swindon Town (free as player-manager, March 1991), Chelsea (£75,000, as player-manager, June 1993, retired as a player, May 1994, resigned as manager, June 1996); England (manager/head coach, July 1996, resigned, August 1998); Southampton (manager, January 2000-April 2001), Tottenham Hotspur (manager, April 2001-July 2003); occasional TV match summariser (season 2003-04), Wolverhampton Wanderers (manager, December 2004-June 2006); now runs The Glenn Hoddle Soccer Academy (for released Premiership players) near Malaga, Spain.

A masterful midfielder and scorer of some stunning goals, Glenn Hoddle missed a penalty in the 5-0 win over the USA in Mexico in June 1985 before being substituted by Trevor Steven. And then, just eight months later he netted a late winner from the spot as Israel were defeated 2-1 in Rammat Gan.

HODGETTS, Dennis 1887-94 ⑥ ①

Born: Hockley, Birmingham, 28 November 1863
Died: Aston, Birmingham, 25 March 1945
Career: The Dreadnought (May 1878), Birmingham St George's (August 1879), Great Lever (August 1880), Birmingham St George's (1882), Aston Villa (professional, February 1886), Small Heath/Birmingham (August 1896, retired, August 1898); Aston Villa (coach, seasons 1899-1902; later vice-President from June 1910); was licensee of the Salutation Inn, Summer Lane, Aston and also a champion snooker player.

A born footballer, remarkably clever with his feet, unselfish, powerful in his approach, two-footed with an eye for goal, Dennis Hodgetts spent ten-and-a-half years with Aston Villa during which time he bagged 91 goals in 215 appearances, gaining two League Championship and two FA Cup winner's medals as well as playing in six full internationals for England, making his debut against Wales in February 1888. He then scored in his second outing, a 5-0 romp against Scotland at Hampden Park, the reporter from the *Daily Mail* stating: "A Hodgetts' header, from another corner, gave the visitors their second goal."

HODGKINSON, Alan, MBE 1956-61 ⑤

Born: Laughton, Rotherham, 16 August 1936
Career: Laughton Council, & Dinnington Secondary Modern Schools, Thurscroft Youth Club (April 1950), Worksop Town (August 1951), Sheffield United (amateur, January 1953, professional, September 1953, retired May 1971; became assistant trainer/coach at Bramall Lane); later Gillingham (assistant-manager), Coventry City (goalkeeping coach), Scotland (goalkeeping coach).

Capped seven times at U23 level and a Football League representative, Sheffield United goalkeeper Alan Hodgkinson took over from Ted Ditchburn in England's senior side and made his debut in a 2-1 win over Scotland in front of 97,520 spectators at Wembley in April 1957. That afternoon he produced three excellent saves but right at the death he was barged over the line by Lawrie Reilly as Willie Fernie slipped the loose ball into the net. Thankfully Dutch referee Pieter Roomer was right on the spot to disallow the goal. He conceded a goal in each of his five internationals, having his last game against Wales in November 1960 (won 5-1). Thereafter Eddie Hopkinson, Colin McDonald and then Ron Springett were all ahead of him in the pecking order. Hodgkinson was a very consistent performer who made 576 appearances for the Blades between 1953 and 1971.

HODGSON, Gordon 1930-31 ③ ①

Born: Johannesburg, South Africa, 16 April 1904
Died: Stoke-on-Trent, 14 June 1951
Career: Benoni FC/South Africa (August 1919), Rustenberg/South Africa (April 1921), Pretoria/South Africa (August 1922), Transvaal/South Africa (season 1924-25), Liverpool (December 1925), Aston Villa (£3,000, January 1936), Leeds United (£1,500, March 1937, then player and youth team coach from August 1942); WW2 guest for Hartlepool United; Port Vale (manager, October 1946 until his death); played cricket for Spen Victoria and Transvaal in South Africa and later for Lancashire (56 matches between 1928-32) and Forfarshire (1934-36); he also excelled at baseball.

Gordon Hodgson was a powerfully built inside-forward, thrustful with

an excellent goal return. He played as an amateur for South Africa against England, Scotland, Ireland and Wales before winning three senior caps for his 'adopted' country, England, gaining his first versus Northern Ireland in October 1930 when, as Sammy Crooks's right-wing partner, he played his part in a comprehensive 5-1 win in Sheffield. A month later he netted in a 4-0 victory over Wales at Wrexham.

Hodgson scored 240 goals in 378 appearances for Liverpool, setting a club record for the most in one League season with 36 in 1930-31, bettered some 30 years later by Roger Hunt who struck 41 in 1961-62. Hodgson, who also represented the Football League, sadly died while still serving as Port Vale's manager.

HODKINSON, Joseph 1912-20 ③

Born: Preston, 20 June, 1889
Died: Lancaster, 8 June 1954
Career: Lancaster Town (August 1906), Glossop (professional, July 1909), Blackburn Rovers (January 1913), Lancaster Town (April 1923, retired, January 1925); became a licensee in Lancaster.

A fast and tricky outside-left, Joe Hodkinson won a League championship medal with Blackburn in 1914. He spent 11 years at Ewood Park (1912-23) during which time he netted 20 goals in 244 appearances. He gained the first of his three England caps against Wales in March 1913 when he partnered his club mate Latheron in a 4-3 victory at Bristol. The following month he had a 'good game' when Scotland were defeated 1-0 at Chelsea. Hodkinson also played in one WW1 international.

HOGG, William 1901-02 ③

Born: Hendon, Newcastle-upon-Tyne, 29 May 1879
Died: Sunderland, 30 January 1937
Career: Willington Athletic (May 1896), Sunderland (professional, November 1899), Glasgow Rangers (May 1909), Dundee (May 1913), Raith Rovers (player-manager, June 1914-May 1915); played part-time for Montrose (seasons 1923-25); Sunderland (coach, October 1927-May 1934); worked in engineering in Sunderland (1915-18); also a licensee in Earlsdon, West Stanley, Sunderland and latterly of the Old Mill Inn, Southwick until his death.

A Football League championship winner with Sunderland in 1902 and a triple Scottish League championship winner with Rangers before WW1, speedy outside-right Billy Robb gained his three full England caps in 1901-02 when he was rated as one of the 'Best outside-rights in Britain.' He didn't do too well, however, in his first two internationals v. Wales (0-0) and Ireland (won 1-0) but had a decent game in the re-arranged encounter against Scotland at Villa Park, his corner-kicks leading to goals for Settle and Wilkes in the 2-2 draw. Earlier, Hogg had played in the Ibrox Park disaster game against the Scots which was subsequently declared as an unofficial international. A Football League representative on three occasions, Hogg scored 84 goals in 303 appearances for Sunderland.

HOLDCROFT, George Henry 1936-37 ②

Born: Norton-le-Moor, 23 January 1909
Died: Penworthen, 17 April 1983
Career: Biddulph (August 1924), Norton Druids (May 1925), Whitfield Colliery (December 1925), Port Vale (professional, June 1926), Darlington (May 1928), Everton (August 1931), Preston North End (December 1932; WW2 guest for Accrington Stanley, Barnsley,

Burnley, Bury, Oldham Athletic, Manchester United and Southport; Barnsley (November 1945, retired, injured, May 1947); later returned with Leyland Motors, Morecambe, Chorley.

A resourceful, cool and agile goalkeeper, George Holdcroft was strong on crosses and his anticipation was exceptionally good. Absent from the 1937 FA Cup final through injury, the following year he was outstanding as Preston lifted the trophy with an extra-time win over Huddersfield Town. His performances during season 1936-37 earned him two England caps, against Wales (lost 2-1) and Ireland (won 3-1). He was unlucky to have fellow 'keepers Ted Sagar, George Tweedy and Vic Woodley all on top of their game at the same time.

HOLDEN, Albert Douglas 1958-59 ⑤

Born: Manchester, 28 September 1930
Career: Princess Road School/Manchester, Manchester YMCA (April 1945), Bolton Wanderers (amateur, August 1946, professional, May 1949), Preston North End (November 1962), Hakoah FC/Australia, June 1965, retired May 1967, then coach until July 1968); Auburn FC, Sydney/Australia (coach, season 1969-70), Grimsby Town (trainer-coach, January 1971-May 1973)

Doug Holden played with 'pace and fire' against a defence reluctant to concede an inch, when making his international debut in the 1-0 victory over Scotland at Wembley in April 1959 – the same day that skipper Billy Wright won his 100th cap. He did well in his second game against Italy (2-2) and went on to play in three tour games at the end of that season, including an outing against the reigning World Champions Brazil in front of 160,000 fans in the giant Maracana Stadium in Rio.
    Also an England Youth team player, he was an FA Cup runner-up with Bolton in 1953 before gaining a winner's medal with Preston in 1964, and during his English League career (in England) Holden netted 53 goals in 508 appearances. He also represented Australia 'B' when playing for Hakoah in 1966.

HOLDEN, George Henry 1881-84 ④

Born: West Bromwich, 6 October 1858
Died: West Bromwich, 3 March 1922
Career: St John's School/Wednesbury, Wednesbury Old Park (seasons 1873-76), Wednesbury St James' (season 1876), Wednesbury Old Athletic (September 1878-April 1883), West Bromwich Albion (guest, May 1883), Wednesbury Old Athletic (re-signed, August 1883), Aston Villa (March-April 1885), Wednesbury Old Athletic (season 1885-86), West Bromwich Albion (amateur, July 1886), Wednesbury Old Athletic (June 1887), Derby Midland (August 1888, retired, April 1892); represented the Birmingham County FA and Staffordshire (1880s); later worked as a puddler for the Patent Shaft & Axletree Company and was also a local councillor.

Outside-right George Holden was a clever dribbler, fast and direct who made his international debut in the 6-1 hammering by Scotland at The Oval in March 1881. Three years later he was superb, creating two of the eight goals which England put past Ireland in Belfast and soon afterwards he again inspired his team-mates to a 4-0 win over Wales.
    He was one of the outstanding footballers of his era.

HOLDEN-WHITE, Cecil Henry 1887-88 ②

Born: Notting Hill, London, 3 November 1860
Died: Kensington, London, 21 September 1934
Career: Brentwood School, Clapham Rovers (August 1876), Swifts (September 1878), Corinthians (between August 1882 and April 1891); also assisted Clapton Rovers (April 1886-June 1888); was

an original committee member of the Corinthians in 1882 and became team captain; also an FA committee member, 1883-85; was a businessman in the City of London.

A quick-moving half-back, strong and athletic, Charles Holden-White was a business man in London and played all his football in the capital. He was 'outstanding' on his international debut in a 5-1 win over Wales at Crewe in February 1888 and he linked up extremely well with Dennis Hodgetts and Fred Dewhurst in his second game, a 5-0 victory over Scotland at Hampden Park a month later. His brother was Charles Henry Holden-White.

HOLFORD, Thomas 1902-03 ①

Born: Hanley, Stoke-on-Trent, 28 January 1878
Died: Blurton, Stoke-on-Trent, 6 April 1964
Career: Granville's Night School/Cobridge (1892), Cobridge FC (May 1896), Stoke (professional, May 1898), Manchester City (July 1908); Port Vale (player-manager, May 1914); served in Royal Artillery during the war, also played as a guest for Nottingham Forest; Port Vale (re-signed as a player, May 1919, retired, March 1923 to become trainer; returned for one game as a player in 1924, aged 46; returned as Vale manager, June 1932, sacked, September 1935, served as a scout until 1950 and trainer from July 1939 to July 1946.

A Second Division championship winner with Manchester City in 1904, centre-half Tom Holford was versatile enough to play in any defensive position. Nicknamed 'Dirty Tommy' (although he was never that sort of player), he was a tireless worker with good distribution. Unfortunately at times he tended to sky the ball far too high but was nevertheless a first-class player who won his only England cap against Ireland in February 1903 when he contributed to one of the goals in a 4-0 win at Molineux. Holford scored 33 goals in 269 appearances during his ten years with Stoke (1898-1908) and then had 141 games for Port Vale, lining up in his last game at the age of 46.

HOLLEY, George Henry 1908-13 ⑩ ⑧

Born: Seaham Harbour, County Durham, 25 November 1885
Died: Leeds, 27 August 1942
Career: Seaham Athletic (August 1899), Seaham Villa (July 1900), Seaham White Star (December 1903), Sunderland (professional, November 1904); WW1 guest for Fulham; Brighton & Hove Albion (July 1919, retired, May 1920); Sunderland (coach, July 1920-June 1922), Wolverhampton Wanderers (trainer, August 1922-May 1932); Barnsley (trainer, August 1932-May 1938), Leeds United (trainer, July 1938 until his death).

An FA Cup finalist with Sunderland in 1913, George Holley was a gifted inside-forward who regularly 'bewildered' his opponents with his brilliant dribbling skills. Very consistent, he scored 160 goals in 315 appearances for Sunderland (1904-19) and eight in his 10 outings for England, including a splendid effort on his debut in a 2-0 win over Wales in March 1909. Two months later he netted twice in a resounding 8-2 victory over Hungary in Budapest, repeated the feat 24 hours later when Austria were battered 8-1 in Vienna and later found the net in all three Home International matches against Wales, Ireland and Scotland in 1911-12. This is how his 13th minute equaliser in the latter game was described in the *Daily Mirror*. "Sunderland's Holley received a throw in, headed down to his feet and slammed a close-range shot past the keeper."
    He also netted 20 goals (including three hat-tricks) for the FA team on tour to South Africa in 1910.
    Holley's son, Tom, was a central defender with Barnsley (1932-36) and Leeds United (1936-48).

HOLLIDAY, Edwin 1959-60 ③

Born: Royston, Barnsley, 7 June 1939
Career: Royston Modern School/Barnsley, Middlesbrough (amateur, July 1955, professional, 1956), Sheffield Wednesday (March 1962), Middlesbrough (June 1965), Hereford United (July 1966), Workington (February 1968), Peterborough United (August 1969; retired, injured, May 1971).

A well-balanced, well-built outside-left, able to shoot with both feet, Eddie Holliday played in five U23 internationals before gaining three full caps for England, the first against Wales in October 1959 when Tony Allen, Trevor Smith, John Connelly and Brian Clough were also debutants in a 1-1 draw in Cardiff. He struck 25 goals in 169 games for Middlesbrough. Unfortunately a broken leg, initially suffered in November 1970, subsequently ended his career. Holliday was first cousin to former Leeds United players Dennis, Colin and Jack Grainger.

HOLLINS, John William, MBE 1966-67 ①

Born: Guildford, Surrey, 16 July 1946
Career: Guildford Schoolboys, Chelsea (junior, July 1961, professional, July 1963), Queens Park Rangers (£80,000, June 1975), Arsenal (£75,000, July 1979), Chelsea (player-coach, June 1983, retired as a player, May 1984, continued as coach/assistant-manager to John Neal; manager, June 1985-March 1988), Cobh Ramblers/Ireland (February 1989); ran his own sports promotion and agency company and also worked as a financial advisor (1989-1994); Queens Park Rangers (reserve team coach, February 1995); later Swansea City (manager, July 1998-May 2001), Rochdale (manager, season 2001-02), Stockport County (assistant-manager/coach, 2002, caretaker-manager, October 2003), Stockport Tiger Star FC/China (manager, December 2003-May 2004), Raith Rovers (assistant-manager, briefly, late 2004), Crawley Town (manager, November 2005-October 2006), Weymouth (manager, November-December 2008)

Energetic right-half John Hollins won his only cap in the 2-0 win over Spain at Wembley in May 1967 and it was his deep cross which was headed down by Alan Ball for Roger Hunt whose shot was blocked, allowing Jimmy Greaves to fire in the first goal.

At club level, Hollins helped Chelsea win the League Cup, FA Cup, European Cup Winners' Cup and Second Division championship in 1965, 1970, 1971 and 1984 respectively and overall in his 20-year career, he made over 720 League appearances for his three major clubs (465 for Chelsea alone). He was also capped at Youth, B and U23 levels.

Hollins' son, Chris, a television presenter, won BBC TV's Strictly Come Dancing title in 2009. His brother, Dave, was a Welsh international goalkeeper and his father had played for Stoke and Wolves.

HOLMES, Robert 1887-95 ⑦

Born: Preston, 23 June 1867
Died: Preston, 17 November 1955
Career: Preston Olympic (August 1883), Preston North End (amateur, April 1884, professional, May 1888, retired, April 1903); became a Football League referee; Bradford City (trainer, season 1904-05), Blackburn Rovers (trainer, July 1905-November 1913); also engaged as England amateur team manager (April-May 1908); Public Schools football coach (seasons 1913-15); ran his own business in Preston after WW1.

A key member of Preston's double-winning team of 1888-89 and a League championship winner again in 1890, full-back Bob Holmes was courageous, willing, agile and strong.

He gained his England caps over a period of seven years between March 1888 and March 1895, winning his first and last against Ireland.

HOLT, John 1889-1900 ⑩

Born: Church, Blackburn, 10 April 1865
Died: Liverpool, 24 May 1933
Career: Kings Own Blackburn (August 1881), Blackpool St John's (March 1884), Church FC (August 1885), Blackpool (briefly, early 1886), Bootle (August 1886), Everton (professional, August 1888), Reading (August 1898, retired, May 1900, later club scout); was appointed a director of Reading but was unable to accept the position as the FA refused to reinstate him as an amateur.

One of the best 'marking' defenders during the 1890s, Johnny Holt – known as the 'Little Devil' – made 252 appearances in ten years with Everton (1888-98), gaining a League championship medal in 1891. He was only 5ft 4½ins tall and weighed just over 10 stones, but he loved to 'mix it' with the taller and stronger players and often came out on top.

The first Everton player to gain an England cap, selected initially against Wales in March 1890 (won 3-1) he was never on the losing side at international level and was outstanding in the 2-1, 4-1, 5-2 and 3-0 victories over Scotland between April 1891 and April 1895. In the latter encounter on his own patch at Goodison Park when he lined up alongside Ernest Needham (Sheffield United), he was reported by the *Daily Mirror* to be one of the game's 'best players'. Holt also represented the Football League on two occasions and starred in four tour games with the FA at the end of the 1899-1900 season.

HOPKINSON, Edward 1957-60 ⑭

Born: Wheatley Hill, County Durham, 19 October 1935
Died: Royton, Lancs, 25 April 2004
Career: Chadderton School/Royton, Lancashire County Schools, Haggate Lads' Club (August 1950), Oldham Athletic (amateur, October 1951), Bolton Wanderers (amateur, August 1952, professional, November 1952, retired, May 1970, then coach until May 1974); Stockport County (coach/assistant-manager, July 1974, briefly caretaker-manager, then coach until May 1978), Bolton Wanderers (goalkeeping coach, season 1979-80); became a representative for a chemical company.

After an impressive performance in his first international against Wales in October 1957 when England won 4-0, Bolton's 'keeper Eddie Hopkinson was credited with an 'unfortunate own-goal' in his second game against Northern Ireland at Wembley. Jimmy McIlroy's penalty kick hit a post but the ball rebounded into play, struck 'Hoppy' on the back and went into the net. The Irish went on to win the game 3-2 – their first victory on English soil since 1914.

He later produced three world-class saves when England drew 2-2 with Italy at Wembley in May 1959 but after an 'indifferent tour' to South America and a rather average game against Wales, his international career ended following a horror show performance against Sweden at Wembley soon afterwards when England lost 3-2.

Almost metronomically consistent, colossally determined, and spikily ready to stand up for himself, never being short of a spirited rebuke to forwards whom he felt might have exceeded the limits of fair play, 'Hoppy' was Bolton's number one for 18 years, during which time he appeared in 578 first-class matches. Hopkinson played in the 1953 FA Cup final defeat by Blackpool but celebrated five years later when he gained a winner's medal when the Trotters beat Manchester United. He also represented his country in six U23 internationals, played twice for the Football League and made his senior debut for Oldham at the age of 16 years and 75 days v. Crewe Alexandra in January 1952. His son, Paul, kept goal for Stockport County.

HOSSACK, Anthony Henry 1891-94 ②
Born: Pleck, Walsall, 2 May 1867
Died: Torquay, Devon, 24 January 1925
Career: Chigwell School (seasons 1881-86), Jesus College/ Cambridge University (seasons 1887-91); also appeared for Corinthians (seasons 1891-94); played cricket for Essex; qualified as a solicitor and practised in Dawlish, Devon until his death.

A durable wing-half, fast over 15-20 yards, Harry Hossack was also a strong tackler who never shirked a challenge. He won his England caps both against Wales two years apart, debuting in a 2-0 win in March 1892 and then playing very well in a 5-1 victory in March 1894.

HOUGHTON, William Eric 1930-33 ⑦ ⑤
Born: Billingborough, Lincolnshire, 29 June 1910
Died: Sutton Coldfield, 1 May 1996
Career: Donnington County and Grammar Schools; briefly played for Boston Town, Billingborough Rovers and Billingborough FC between August 1925 and May 1927, Aston Villa (trial, July 1927, professional, August 1927); WW2 guest for Brentford, Coventry City, Hereford United, Kidderminster Harriers, Leicester City, Nottingham Forest and Notts County; joined Notts County (December 1946, retired as a player, April 1949, then manager April 1949-August 1953); Aston Villa (manager, September 1953-November 1958); Nottingham Forest (chief scout, July 1959-November 1960); Rugby Town (secretary-manager, February 1961-March 1964); Aston Villa (scout, October 1964-August 1965); Walsall (scout, September 1965, then a director, late 1960s); Aston Villa (coach and assistant in Youth Development Department, May 1970; club director, September 1972-December 1979; senior vice-president, January 1983 until his death); played minor counties cricket for Lincolnshire and also for Warwickshire v. India in 1946.

A Second Division championship and Wartime (North) Cup winner with Aston Villa in 1938 and 1944 respectively, outside-left Eric Houghton was fast and confident. He could shoot with both feet and is said to have had the hardest shot in the game during the 1930s, at the same time being one of the finest penalty-takers in

Great Britain. His record with Villa, whom he served as a player from 1927-46, was exceptional… 170 goals (79 of them penalties) in 392 first team matches, plus another 87 goals in 151 WW2 matches. And when he returned to the club as manager he guided them to FA Cup glory in 1957. Earlier, in 1950, he took Notts County to the Third Division (South) title.

At international level, Houghton won only seven caps, scoring on his debut in a 5-1 win over Northern Ireland in October 1930. Six months later he netted again in a 4-1 victory over Belgium in Brussels and was on target twice when the Irish were battered 6-2 in Belfast in October 1931. His fifth and final England goal came in the 4-3 win over Austria at Chelsea in December 1932 when he also assisted in one of Jimmy Hampson's two strikes. He probably deserved more caps than he received, but he did have the likes of Cliff Bastin and Eric Brook and to contend with!

Houghton also played for the Football League on four occasions and represented Birmingham County Juniors v. Scotland in 1928 as well as starring for the RAF. His brother, Ron, also played for Notts County.

HOULKER, Albert Edward Kelly 1901-06 ⑤
Born: Blackburn, 27 April 1872
Died: Blackburn, 27 May 1962
Career: Blackburn Hornets (May 1887), Oswaldtwistle Rovers (August 1889), Cobwall FC (May 1891), Park Road (June 1893), Blackburn Rovers (professional, August 1894), Portsmouth (May 1902), Southampton (May 1903), Blackburn Rovers (May 1906-May 1907); out of football for two seasons; returned with Colne FC (July 1909); then WW1 guest for Blackburn Rovers (January 1918); later an overlooker at Garden Street Mill (Blackburn), he also ran his own coal and haulage company until 1947; he was 90 when he died.

Ted Houlker, small and athletic, was a very clever footballer, his tricky tackling dodges often bemusing his opponents and sometimes his own team-mates! He made five appearances for England and during his career played in over 250 competitive games, helping Southampton win the Southern League title in 1904. He was a huge favourite wherever he played because of his pluck and tenacity.

HOWARTH, Robert Henry 1886-94 ⑤
Born: Preston, 20 June 1865
Died: Preston, 20 August 1938
Career: Excelsior (Rugby club, August 1881), Preston North End (amateur, January 1883, professional, August 1885), Everton (November 1891), Preston North End (May 1894, retired, May 1896); also represented Lancashire County (seasons 1885-87); after football he became a solicitor, admitted in 1908, practised in Preston.

Immaculate right-back Bob Howarth, always cool and collected with a solid tackle, was in the Preston side which completed the double in 1889 and won a second League championship medal in 1890. He gained several representative honours but was surprisingly never a regular in the England team, winning only five caps over a period of seven years (February 1887-March 1894). The reporter for the *North British Daily Mail* stated that "His general play was splendid and much admired" when Scotland were beaten 5-0 at Hampden Park in March 1888 and three years later he partnered his Preston team-mate Robert Holmes when the Scots were defeated 2-1 at Blackburn.

He made his debut for Preston in an 18-3 friendly win over Battersea Old Collegians on Shrove Tuesday 1883 and in his two spells with the Lillywhites, made well over 200 appearances, 58 at competitive level.

HOWE, Donald 1957-60 ㉓

Born: Springfield, Wolverhampton, 12 October 1935
Career: St Peter's School/Wolverhampton, Wolverhampton &
District Boys, Wolverhampton Wanderers (trial, September-
October 1950), West Bromwich Albion (amateur, December
1950, professional, November 1952), Arsenal (£40,000, April
1964, retired, injured, May 1967; then coach at Highbury, later
assistant-manager, seasons 1969-71); West Bromwich Albion
(manager, July 1971-April 1975), Galatasaray/Turkey (coach,
May-September 1975), Leeds United (coach, October 1975-June
1977), Arsenal (coach, August-December 1977); England B team
(assistant-manager and coach, January 1978-June 1989); also
Arsenal (manager, December 1983-March 1986); Saudi Arabia
(coach, during 1986-87); Bristol Rovers (part-time coach, July
1987), Wimbledon (assistant-manager/coach, August 1987-July
1989), Queens Park Rangers (assistant-manager, July 1989,
manager-coach, November 1989-May 1991), Wimbledon (coach,
May-October 1991), Barnet (coach, briefly, 1991), Coventry City
(manager, January-July 1992), Chelsea (coach/assistant-manager,
July 1992); also covered Italian Serie 'A football for Channel 4; also
Arsenal (Youth team coach); FA Technical advisor from January
1993); remained as an advisory coach to Arsenal until 2006; now
assists with coaching schemes throughout the UK.

Don Howe made over 350 appearances for WBA between 1951
and 1964 but never won a single medal! His playing career ended
in 1966 after breaking his leg while starring for the Gunners v.
Blackpool. Blessed with deft positional sense, reliability and strength
in tackling and kicking, Howe was England's regular right-back
for just over two years, from October 1957 until November 1959.
Taking over from the ill-fated Jeff Hall, he made an impressive
debut against Wales (won 4-0) and as Roger Byrne's partner he
was on 'top of his game' in future wins over Scotland (also 4-0),
the Soviet Union (5-0) and the USA (8-1). He also played well in the
1958 World Cup finals in Sweden. Howe eventually lost his place to
Jimmy Armfield.
    As a coach, he was at Highbury when Arsenal won the double
in 1971, was a member of the Wimbledon backroom staff when
the Wombles lifted the FA Cup in 1988 and worked under England
managers Ron Greenwood, Bobby Robson (his former team-mate at
West Brom) and Terry Venables.

HOWE, John Robert 1947-49 ③

Born: West Hartlepool, 7 October 1925
Died: Hartlepool, 5 April 1987
Career: Hartlepool junior football, Hartlepool United (professional,
June 1934), Derby County (March 1936); WW2 guest for Aberdeen,
Falkirk, Hearts, St Mirren; Huddersfield Town (October 1949), King's
Lynn (player-manager, July 1951), Long Sutton (player-manager,
August 1955), Wisbech Town (player, briefly, season 1955-56).

When he made his international debut in a 4-0 win over Italy in Turin
in May 1948, fearless and dominant left-back Jack Howe became
the first player to appear in a full international for England wearing
contact lenses. In his second game – a 6-2 win over Northern
Ireland in October 1948 – he twice cleared shots off the line and
also came close to scoring at the other end with a wind-assisted
clearance that swerved past a post.
    At club level when he also appeared at right-back, Howe made
244 appearances for Derby, gaining an FA Cup winner's medal in
1946. He also represented the Scottish League v. the British Army
during WW2. His grandson, Steve Fletcher, is a professional footballer.

HOWELL, Leonard Sidgwick 1872-73 ①

Born: Herne Hill, Kent, 6 August 1848
Died: Lausanne, Switzerland, 7 September 1895
Career: Dulwich Hamlet (briefly, season 1863-64), Winchester
College (seasons 1864-70); played for Wanderers (1871-75), also
Surrey (early 1870s); cricketer for Surrey and MCC.

A sportsman through and through, at college Len Howell enjoyed
football, cricket and athletics, winning the 100 yards and 300
yards and 110 yards hurdles in 1866. He made his debut for the
Wanderers in the 1873 FA Cup final, gaining a winner's medal. A
full-back or half-back, strong in kicking, his solitary appearance
for England had come three weeks before the final, in the second
international match against Scotland played at The Oval in early
March. England, whose line-up included five other players with a
Wanderers influence - Charles Chenery, Robert Vidal, Alexander
Bonsor, William Kenyon-Slaney and Hubert Heron - won the match
4–2. Howell's football career ended following an injury sustained
during the 1873–74 season.
    Also an accomplished cricketer, Howell made nineteen appearances
for Surrey and the MCC between 1869 and 1880. A right-hand bat,
his best year was in 1870 when he scored 163 runs in eight innings,
top-scoring with 96. In later life he became a malt factor.

HOWELL, Raby (Rabbi) 1894-95 ② ①

Born: Wincobank, Sheffield, 12 October 1869
Died: Sheffield, 22 November 1937
Career: Ecclesfield/Sheffield (August 1886), Rotherham Swifts (June
1888), Sheffield United (£250, professional, June 1890), Liverpool
(£200, April 1898), Preston North End (June 1901, retired, injured,
September 1903)

Raby Howell was probably the first Romany gypsy ever to play for
England, gaining the first of his two caps against Ireland in March
1895 when he scored in a 9-0 win. A highly-skilled player despite
his small size (5ft 5ins/1.65 metres) he was described as being 'a
nippy half-back or inside right'. In 1897-98, he gained a League
championship medal with Sheffield United for whom he made over
150 appearances in five years. A broken leg, suffered in 1903,
ended his career. His cousin, Colin Myers, was also a professional
footballer in the 1920s.

HOWEY, Stephen Norman 1994-96 ④

Born: Sunderland, 26 October 1971
Career: Newcastle United (apprentice, October 1986, professional,
December 1989), Manchester City (£2m, August 2000), Leicester
City (£300,000, July 2003), Bolton Wanderers (free, January 2004),
New England Revolution/USA (summer 2004), Hartlepool United
(March 2005); Crook Town (manager, September-November 2006),
Middlesbrough (coach, early 2007), Bishop Auckland (part-time
player-coach, season 2007-08); became co-presenter of Total Sport
on BBC Newcastle with Marco Gabbiadini and Simon Pryde; East

Durham College Football Development
Centre (coach, August 2007, then become
head coach from May 2010)

Initially a striker, Steve Howey was
converted into a centre-back by Newcastle
boss Ossie Ardiles and went on to
represent his country in that position,
gaining four full caps and also playing in
one unofficial international.

Powerful in the air and on the ground, Howey made his debut alongside Neil Ruddock in a 1-0 friendly win over Nigeria at Wembley in November 1994. He later partnered Tony Adams at the heart of the England defence and was in the squad at Euro 96, after making his last appearance v. Bulgaria the previous March.

Howey, whose club career realised over 300 League appearances, now co-presents Total Sport on BBC Newcastle with Marco Gabbiadini and Simon Pryde.

His brother, Lee, was also a footballer, principally with Newcastle's rivals Sunderland.

HUDDLESTONE, Thomas Andrew 2009-11 ④

Born: Sneinton, Nottingham, 28 December 1986
Career: Derby County (apprentice, November 2002, professional, February 2004), Tottenham Hotspur (£1m, July 2005), Wolverhampton Wanderers (loan, October 2005-January 2006)

Tall, well-built, strong, hard-shooting midfielder Tom Huddlestone made his England debut as an 81st minute substitute in the 1-0 friendly defeat by Brazil in November 2009. He then added two further caps to his tally under boss Fabio Capello.

Huddlestone also represented his country as a Youth team player, appeared in 33 U21 internationals (the joint second most with Fabrice Muamba) and in 2012, reached the personal milestone of 250 club appearances.

HUDSON, Anthony Alan 1974-75 ②

Born: Chelsea, London, 21 May 1951
Career: London Schools, Fulham (schoolboy forms, May 1964), Chelsea (schoolboy forms, July 1965, apprentice, April 1966, professional, June 1968), Stoke City (£240,000, January 1974), Arsenal (£200,000, December 1976), Seattle Sounders/USA (October 1978), Hercules FC, Cleveland Force/USA (Indoor League, 1979-80), Alicante/Spain (1980), Chelsea (£23,500, August 1983), Stoke City (January 1984, retired, May 1985); later opened a nightclub in Stoke-on-Trent, penned a column in the *Stoke Evening Sentinel* and *Sporting Life* and worked in the media; now lives in East London; had problems with alcoholism, was declared bankrupt and in December 1997, suffered multiple injuries when run over by a car (spent two months in a coma); his autobiography, entitled *The Working Man's Ballet* was published in 1998 and further books followed: *The Tinker and The Talisman*, self-published in 2003, and *The Waddington Years* released in 2008; in 2006, he joined Radio Napa in Cyprus and covered the World Cup in Germany.

Given his international debut by Don Revie against West Germany in March 1975, Alan Hudson played brilliantly in a 2-0 win and a month later when Cyprus were blitzed 5-0, he helped set up three of Malcolm Macdonald's five goals. A tremendously skilful player, upright with good pace, Hudson was unfortunate to gain only two caps – he deserved more. He won the European Cup Winners' Cup with Chelsea in 1971 and helped Arsenal reach the 1978 FA Cup final. Due to a leg injury, Hudson, who also played in ten U23 internationals, was forced into early retirement at the age of 34, having amassed over 350 club appearances.

His son Anthony Hudson, a former professional footballer, is manager of Real Maryland FC in the USL in the USA.

HUDSON, John 1882-83 ①

Born: Sheffield, 11 August 1860
Died: Sheffield, 10 November 1941
Career: Sheffield Heeley (June 1876), Sheffield FC (August 1878), Sheffield Wednesday (August 1880-May 1886; also acted as club secretary for a short time), Blackburn Olympic (July 1886), Sheffield United (May 1889, retired, injured, May 1891); worked as an engraver in Sheffield for many years.

Jack Hudson's usual position was half-back, although at times he featured prominently at full-back. Very strong defensively, he was a hard tackler who never gave his opponent an inch in which to work. He made his England debut against Ireland in February 1883, deputising for Horace Bailey in a one-sided 7-0 win in Liverpool.

HUDSPETH, Francis Carr 1925-26 ①

Born: Percy Main near Newcastle, Tyneside, 20 April 1890
Died: Burnley, 8 February, 1963
Career: Scotswood (May 1904), Newburn (September 1905), Clare Vale Juniors (July 1906), North Shields Athletic (August 1907), Newcastle United (£100, semi-professional, May 1910); WW1 guest for Leeds City; Stockport County (January 1929), Crook Town (re-instated as an amateur, December 1930, retired, injured, January 1931); Rochdale (trainer, July 1933-May 1934), Burnley (assistant-trainer, June 1934-May 1945).

A defender who spent 19 seasons with Newcastle United, Frank Hudspeth was a popular figure amongst the fans and gained the nickname 'Old Surefoot' for his reliability. Captain of the team for three years, he gained League championship and FA Cup winner's medals and is second only to Jimmy Lawrence for making the most senior appearances for Newcastle – 472. He also scored 37 goals, 25 of them penalties. His only full cap for England was against Ireland in October 1925, although he did play in one Wartime international.

HUFTON, Arthur Edward 1923-29 ⑥

Born: Southwell, Notts, 25 November 1892
Died: Swansea, 2 February 1967
Career: Atlas & Norfolk Works FC (seasons 1909-12), Sheffield United (professional, November 1912), West Ham United (May 1919), Watford (June 1932, retired, May 1934); worked as a press steward at Upton Park for many years and also worked as a car salesman in London's East End; served with the Coldstream Guards during WW1.

A handsome chap, Ted Hufton had the physique a sculptor would have gone crazy about. It was said that he would have made a champion heavyweight boxer given the chance.

A real crowd pleaser, he was a spectacular goalkeeper who took many risks in trying to prevent opponents scoring past him. He certainly could not be faulted for courage. He was a very persuasive man, who kidded an opponent to shoot when he wanted him to!

He won his six caps over a period of six years, challenging the likes of Fox Hardy, Mitchell, Pym, Sewell, Taylor and many others for the number one position. He made his debut in a 2-2 draw with Belgium in Antwerp in November 1923 and played in his last international in a 4-1 win over France in Paris in May 1929. In between times he was 'between the posts' when Scotland (the 'Wembley Wizards') blitzed England 5-1 in 1928 but reports indicated that he saved his side from a much heavier defeat. Playing against Ireland in October 1927 he fractured his right arm and was out of action for more than two months. At club level Hufton made 401 appearances for West Ham between 1919 and 1932, playing in the first Wembley Cup final in 1923. Something of a 'penalty king', he saved over 20 spot-kicks during his career including 11 out of 18 in two seasons with the Hammers.

HUGHES, Emlyn Walter, OBE 1969-80 (62) (1)

Born: Barrow-in-Furness, 28 August 1947
Died: Sheffield, 9 November 2004
Career: North Lancashire Schools, Roose FC/Blackpool (May 1962), Blackpool (apprentice, April 1963, professional, September 1964), Liverpool (£65,000, February 1967), Wolverhampton Wanderers (£90,000, August 1979), Rotherham United (player-manager, July 1981), Hull City (March 1983), Mansfield Town (August 1983), Swansea City (September-October 1983, retired at this point due to injury); also Hull City director (briefly); worked in the media and captained a team on the BBC programme *A Question of Sport*.

Emlyn Hughes made his England debut at left-back in a 1-0 win over Holland in Amsterdam in November 1969, putting in a 'decent performance against a very good Dutch side.' Growing in confidence with every kick, he became a regular in the national team and his cap tally increased accordingly. He scored his only goal for his country in a 3-0 win over Wales in May 1972 and two years later gave away a last minute penalty against Argentina at Wembley. The player he 'fouled' was Mario Kempes who stepped up and duly made it 2-2 from the spot.

Hughes, who captained every club he played for, also skippered his country, doing so in three decades: 1960s, '70s and '80s. Nicknamed 'Crazy Horse' and described as being a 'biggish bundle of dynamic energy' he moved forward into the left-half position as time passed by and scored some stunning goals for Liverpool. He made over 800 appearances during his career (665 for Liverpool), gaining two FA Cup, four League Championship, two European Cup and two UEFA Cup winner's medals during his time at Anfield and a League Cup winner's medal with Wolves. He also won eight U23 caps, represented the Football League on four occasions and was voted FWA 'Footballer of the Year' in 1977.

Hughes' father, Fred, was a Great Britain Rugby League international.

HUGHES, Laurie 1949-50 (3)

Born: Waterloo, Liverpool, 2 March 1924
Died: Liverpool, 9 September 2011
Career: Merseyside Schools, Liverpool junior football, Tranmere Rovers (amateur, May 1942), Liverpool (professional, February 1943, retired after injury problems, May 1960).

The first player to make his England debut in a World Cup finals tournament, centre-half Laurie Hughes starred in the 2-0 win over Chile in Rio de Janeiro in June 1950. He took over from Neil Franklin and in fact was all set to make his first appearance in the friendly against Portugal the previous month, but pulled out at the last minute with an injury, allowing his Liverpool team-mate Bill Jones to step in for his first cap.

Hughes added two more caps to his collection by playing in that shock 1-0 defeat by the USA in Belo Horizonte and versus Spain three days later. After that injuries prevented him from winning more honours.

A strong, uncompromising defender, who could also play wing half, Hughes had the knack of being able to read the game, stopping moves before they caused too many problems. He spent 17 years with Liverpool, but was sidelined for the last three through injury. He appeared in 326 first-class matches for the Merseyside club, gaining a League championship winner's medal in 1947. He also played in one B international.

HULME, Joseph Harold Anthony 1926-33 (9) (4)

Born: Stafford, 26 August 1904
Died: Winchmere Hill, Enfield, 26 September 1991
Career: Stafford YMCA (April 1919), York City (semi-professional, August 1923), Blackburn Rovers (£250, February 1924), Arsenal, (£3,500, February 1926), Huddersfield Town (£500, January 1938, retired, May 1938); engaged with the Police Reserve Unit during WW2; Tottenham Hotspur (assistant-secretary, February 1944, manager, October 1945-May 1949); employed as a sports journalist with the *People* (1949-69); played cricket for Middlesex; lived in Palmer's Green, London for many years.

Joe Hulme usually played on the right-wing and was Herbert Chapman's first major signing in 1926. Known for his pace and ball control, he spent twelve years at Highbury, scoring 125 goals in 374 appearances for the Gunners, gaining two FA Cup and three League championship winner's medals.

He represented the Football League before collecting the first of his nine England caps against Scotland at Hampden Park in April 1927 when he partnered George Brown on the right-flank in a 2-1 win. 'Broadcaster' reporting for the *Daily Express*, said: "Hulme wrought havoc on Thomson, the Scottish left-back, with his pace and uninhibited style." An all-round sportsman, Hulme was also a keen cricketer, and scored over 8,000 runs in 225 games for Middlesex between 1929 and 1939 as a middle-order batsman and medium bowler. After WW2 which he spent working as a policeman, Hulme managed Arsenal's fiercest rivals, Tottenham Hotspur from 1945 to 1949, laying the foundations for their championship-winning side of 1950-51. After that, he became a successful journalist.

HUMPHREYS, Percy 1902-03 (1)

Born: Cambridge, 3 December 1880
Died: Stepney, London, 13 April 1959
Career: Cambridge St Mary's (August 1896), Cambridgeshire (seasons 1896-1900), Queens Park Rangers (May 1900), Notts County (July 1901), Leicester Fosse (June 1907), Chelsea (February 1908), Tottenham Hotspur (December 1909), Leicester Fosse (October

1911), Hartlepools United (player-manager, June 1913-May 1914); Norwich City (player-coach, November 1914); FC Basel/Switzerland (coach, December 1914-May 1915); was not in football after WW1.

A utility forward, tricky, well-built, Percy Humphreys made his presence felt out on the pitch and was the pick of the England side that lost 2-1 against Scotland at Sheffield in April 1903. In club football, he helped Leicester gain promotion in 1908 and scored 73 goals in 202 appearances for Notts County (1901-07). He also represented the Football League.

HUNT, George Samuel 1932-33 ③ ①

Born: Barnsley, 22 February 1910
Died: Bolton, 19 September 1996
Career: Regent Street Congregationalists, Barnsley (trial, April-May 1926), Sheffield United (trial, May 1927), Port Vale (trial, June-July 1928), Chesterfield (professional, September 1929), Tottenham Hotspur (June 1930), Arsenal (October 1937), Bolton Wanderers (February 1938); WW2 guest for Liverpool, Luton Town and Rochdale; Sheffield Wednesday (November 1946, retired, May 1948); Bolton Wanderers (assistant-trainer/coach, May 1948-September 1968); later ran the car wash department at a Bolton garage.

A giant of a man, quite fearless, who played as an inside or centre forward, George Hunt was 19 when he entered League football with Chesterfield. He continued to play until 1948, amassing a League record of 169 goals in 294 appearances. He was adored at White Hart Lane and netted 138 goals in 198 first-team matches for Spurs with whom he gained his three England caps, all at the end of the 1932-33 season against Scotland (scorer of his country's goal in a 2-1 defeat), Italy and Switzerland. He also played in one unofficial international (v. Switzerland in Berne in July 1945). In 1938 he helped Arsenal win the League championship and seven years later starred for Bolton when they won the Wartime League North Cup. Hunt suffered from Alzheimer's disease for the last few years of his life.

HUNT, Rev Kenneth Reginald Gunnery 1910-11 ②

Born: Oxford, 24 February 1884
Died: Heathfield, Wolverhampton, 28 April 1949
Career: Wolverhampton Grammar School, Trent College/Derbyshire (seasons 1901-05), Queen's College/Oxford University (seasons 1905-08); also played for Corinthians (during seasons 1906-07 and 1920-23), Wolverhampton Wanderers (several spells between March 1907 and April 1920), Leyton (occasionally between August 1908 and May 1913), Tottenham Hotspur (WW1 guest, December 1916), Crystal Palace (from August 1912-April 1913) and Oxford City (briefly in season 1921-22); served on the FA Council; ordained in 1909, became Master at Highgate School (1908-45)

The Reverend Kenneth Hunt was the first ordained clergyman ever to appear for England in a full international. He was selected for the game against Wales in March 1911 and helped set up a goal for Vivian Woodward in a 3-1 win. Soon afterwards he played 'very efficiently' in the 1-1 draw with Scotland at Goodison Park. Three years earlier Hunt had scored a beauty for Wolves in their 3-1 FA Cup final victory over Newcastle United.

Besides his two full caps, Hunt won 20 at amateur level (1907-21) and was a gold medal winner as a key member of the United Kingdom XI at the 1908 Olympic Games, playing with Bailey (goal), full-backs Corbett and Smith; Chapman, Hawkes (half-backs) and Berry, Woodward, Stapley, Purnell and Hardman (forwards).

Described as the 'Personification of the muscular Christian' Hunt was a sturdy wing-half who played without fear. He was a striking personality who remained an amateur throughout his playing career. He had 10 different spells with Wolves – his home town club – and also played regularly for Corinthians during the early 1920s.

HUNT, Roger 1961-68 ㉞ ⑱

Born: Golborne, Lancs, 20 July 1938
Career: Culcheth Secondary Modern & Leigh Grammar Schools, Lancashire & District Schools, Croft Youth Club (April 1952), Devizes Town (briefly in season 1956-57), Stockton Heath (August 1957), Liverpool (amateur, August 1958, professional, July 1959), Bolton Wanderers (£31,000, December 1969, retired, May 1972); ran the family haulage and transport business in Culcheth near Manchester until 1995.

Taking over from Johnny Byrne, Roger Hunt scored a 'fine goal' on his England debut in a 3-1 win over Austria at Wembley in April 1962 but missed four easier chances! He took time to establish himself in the team, being called up only twice more in the next two years.

Playing in place of tonsillitis-victim Jimmy Greaves, he netted a spectacular equalizer from 30 yards to set up a 2-1 win over East Germany in Leipzig in June 1963 and then went on to hit the headlines with a flurry of goals... including four in a 10-0 win over the USA in May 1964 and singles against Portugal and Spain in his next four matches.

One reporter wrote: 'He was a slow burning fuse ready to ignite'...and he did just that.

He struck a smart goal which beat Poland in July 1966 and then played his part in the World Cup triumph, netting three times in group matches – once in the 2-0 win over Mexico and twice in the 2-0 victory over France.

However, by the late 1960s, Hunt's game had started to suffer. The Liverpool striker, said by Geoffrey Green of The Times to be 'a doer of good stealth' needed a fillip of some sort. He was being considered as just a workhorse of moderate ability and after playing in successive draws, at home and away, against Romania halfway through the 1968-69 campaign, he asked manager Alf Ramsey to leave him out of the team. Hunt was duly 'axed' and replaced by Francis Lee who became Geoff Hurst's new strike-partner, with Colin Lee aiding and abetting as best he could.

The recipient of a Second Division and two League championship winner's medals with Liverpool, he also helped the Reds lift the FA Cup and reach the European Cup Winners' Cup final. Hunt scored 286 goals in 492 appearances during his ten years at Anfield (1959-69) and followed up by bagging another 25 in 82 games for Bolton (up to 1972). He also represented the Football League on five occasions and played several games for the Army.

HUNT, Stephen Kenneth 1983-84 (2)

Born: Perry Barr, Birmingham, 4 August 1956
Career: Yew Tree Infants & Junior Schools, Aston & Witton Boys,
Warwickshire Schools, Stanley Star (May 1971), Aston Villa
(apprentice, July 1972, professional, January 1974), New York
Cosmos/USA (£50,000, February 1977), Coventry City (£40,000,
August 1978), New York Cosmos (loan, May-August 1982), West
Bromwich Albion (£80,000, March 1984), Aston Villa (£90,000
plus Darren Bradley, March 1986; retired with knee injury, May
1988), Willenhall Town (manager, June 1988), Port Vale (Youth team
coach, July 1989, then Community officer, June 1990-May 1991),
Leicester City (coach, July 1991-April 1992), VS Rugby (manager,
season 1994-95), AP Leamington (manager, season 1996-97),
Hinckley Town (coach, seasons 1997-99), Bembridge FC/Isle of
Wight (coach, August 2003-May 2005)

Unfortunately midfielder Steve Hunt's international career covered
just 50 minutes. He was a second-half substitute against Scotland
at Hampden Park and also against the USSR at Wembley in May and
June 1984. He deserved more, for he was a talented player whose
League career spanned 16 years during which time he netted
almost 70 goals in 402 club appearances. He helped New York
Cosmos to successive NASL championship wins in the late 1970s.

HUNTER, John 1877-82 (7)

Born: Crookes, Sheffield, 20 March 1852
Died: Blackburn, 13 April 1903
Career: Providence FC/Sheffield (August 1868), Sheffield Albion
(May 1872), Sheffield Heeley (May 1875), Sheffield Wednesday
(September 1880), Blackburn Olympic (seasons 1882-86),
Blackburn Rovers (season 1886-87), Heeley FC/Sheffield (August
1887, retired, April 1888); Blackburn Rovers (assistant-trainer/
groundsman, seasons 1888-94); worked as a butcher and silver
cutter while playing football; also trained local cotton works team; a
fine athlete, he became a licensee in Blackburn.

Reputed to be one of the finest half-backs of his time, Jack Hunter
was a powerfully built, strong kicking player who could also play at
full-back. An FA Cup winner with Blackburn Olympic in 1883, he
gained his seven England caps over a period of four years, collecting
his first in a 7-2 defeat by Scotland at the Queens Park ground,
Glasgow in March 1878 when he was given a 'hard time' by the
lively home forwards in gale force conditions. There were always
plenty of goals to be seen when Hunter was around... a total of 45
were scored in his seven England games alone.

HUNTER, Norman 1965-75 (28) (2)

Born: Eighton Banks, Newcastle-upon-Tyne, 29 October 1943
Career: Birtley Secondary Modern School, Birtley Juniors (September
1957), Chester-le-Street (August 1958), Leeds United (apprentice,
November 1960, professional, April 1961), Bristol City (October
1976), Barnsley (player-coach, June 1979, manager September
1980-February 1984, then manager); West Bromwich Albion
(assistant-manager/coach, February 1984), Rotherham United
(manager, June 1985-December 1987), Leeds United (coach,
February-October 1988), Bradford City (assistant-manager, February
1989-February 1990); became a soccer pundit on BBC Radio Leeds;
also sold sporting goods and insurance; also an after-dinner speaker.

The first player to make his England debut as a substitute (v.
Spain in December 1965), Norman Hunter was in and out of the
international spotlight for the next nine years.

And one game he never wants reminding about was that vital
World Cup qualifier against Poland at Wembley in October 1973.
England had to win but only drew 1-1 and missed out on the
finals in Germany. On the hour mark Poland were attacking down
England's right flank. Hunter, playing in place of skipper Bobby
Moore, ran across from centre-field, near the halfway line in an
attempt to block the move. He failed miserably to clear an innocuous
long pass which was drifting down the touchline, allowing the ball
to remain in play. It was quickly switched inside and within seconds
Poland had scored to go 1-0 up. It was a major set-back, but Hunter
battled on, and although Allan Clarke equalised with a penalty, the
Leeds hard man left the pitch with his head bowed low with Ramsey
taking all the flak. England had dominated this game, having 35
attempts on goal.

Hunter, however, battled on as ever and went on to play in three
more internationals after that Poland game.

The first of his two England goals was scored in the 2-1 win over
Spain in Madrid in May 1968 (a low drive with his most under-used
right foot), while his second came in the 1-1 draw with Wales in
January 1973 when, in the 42nd minute, he fired home an equaliser
from distance past his Leeds team-mate Gary Sprake to salvage a
1-1 draw at Wembley.

Besides his senior games for England, the tough-tackling defensive
midfielder Hunter also played for his country at Youth team level,
represented the Football League and starred for a United Kingdom XI.

He made 726 appearances for Leeds between 1960 and 1976,
gaining First and Second Division, FA Cup, League Cup and two Fairs
Cup winner's medals. He was voted PFA Footballer of the Year in 1974.

HURST, Sir Geoffrey Charles, MBE 1965-72 49 24

Born: Ashton-under-Lyne, 8 December 1941
Career: King's Road Secondary Modern School/Chelmsford,
Chelmsford Schools Select, Halstead FC (August 1955), Chelmsford
City (January 1957), West Ham United (amateur, July 1957,
professional, April 1959), Stoke City (£80,000, June 1972), Cape
Town City/South Africa (guest, summer 1973), West Bromwich Albion
(£20,000, August 1975), Cork Celtic (guest, early 1976), Seattle
Sounders/USA (free, February 1976), Telford United (player-manager,
March 1976, retired, May 1977); England (U21 manager-coach,
September 1977, then full team assistant-coach, January 1978-June
1982), Chelsea (assistant-manager/coach, May 1979, then manager,
October 1979-April 1981), Al-Kuwait (coach, summer 1982-May
1984); also played county cricket for Essex; later a sales director of
Motorplan, Essex and Director of Football for McDonalds.

For what he achieved in the 1966 World Cup final, Hurst will always
be part of England folklore.

Having missed out on the opening three group games, only an
injury/illness to Jimmy Greaves gave Geoff Hurst his chance in the
tournament – which he took with head and right foot!

His soaring header from a Peters cross saw off the ten men of
Argentina in the quarter-final; he then played his part by setting up
Bobby Charlton's second goal in the 2-1 semi-final triumph over
Portugal before laying into the Germans in the final.

After the Germans had taken the lead at Wembley, Hurst
equalised with a well-judged, glancing header from Bobby Moore's
perfectly weighted free-kick on 19 minutes. Then, after near misses
at both ends of the field, Hurst saw his 77th minute shot, from Alan
Ball's right-wing corner, balloon up in the air off Weber for Peters to
pounce and drive the ball home. However, the Germans hit back and
grabbed a last minute equaliser to take the final into extra-time. It
was nerve-wracking to say the least. After a pep-talk on the pitch,
England went for the jugular straightaway and Nobby Stiles' long

pass down the right was caught by Alan Ball who crossed for Hurst to swivel and crash the ball against the bar, Roger Hunt putting his arms in the air as it dropped down. Goal or no goal? The Russian linesman, near Ball, said 'Yes' and England led 3-2.

The Germans pushed men forward from that moment on and with time running out and with the Swiss referee Herr Dienst ready to blow for full-time, BBC TV commentator Kenneth Wolstenholme let everyone know 'They think it's all over' just as Moore launched a long downfield pass to Hurst, 40 yards from goal. He controlled the ball, took it forward and then let it fly….it flew high past Tilkowski's right arm…just as Wolstenholme shouted 'It is now.' It was now England 'champions of the World' and Hurst had become the first player in history to score a hat-trick in a World Cup final.

After the game Alan Ball, while discussing the final and elaborating on the cross which set up England's third goal, confessed: 'Geoff and I had built up a perfect understanding with each other. I could find him with a pass in the dark; we had worked on moves so often together, Ramsey knew exactly what we were capable of doing.'

Hurst had made his international debut, ironically, in a 1-0 win over West Germany five months before the World Cup final…and by shear coincidence would make his last appearance for his country against the same opponents in the European Nations Cup in April 1972.

Strong in the shoulder, thick in the thigh, tall, brilliant in the air and blessed with a powerful right foot shot, he scored one other hat-trick for England, in a 5-0 drubbing of France in March 1969, while his two goals in the 4-1 victory over Scotland at Wembley two months later clinched the Home International Championship, having netted his first goal against the Scots in a 4-3 win back in April 1966.

In November 1967, he smashed home a terrific right-foot volley in a 2-0 win over Northern Ireland at Wembley; was right 'on song' with a splendid hat-trick in a 5-0 drubbing of France in March 1969 and netted his last goal with a cannonball shot in the 2-0 win over Greece in Athens in December 1971. Four of his England goals came from the penalty spot.

But like all natural goalscorers, Hurst did have his off days! He was quiet, very quiet in fact, between May 1967 and January 1969, when he mustered only three goals in 12 internationals. But then he scored six in three outings and was back in form!

In the 4-1 win over Scotland at Wembley in May 1969, he crashed home a penalty with one of the most powerful shots ever witnessed. One observer said it was 'awesome', another admitted it was 'like a bullet fired from a gun.'

Moving onto the 1970 World Cup tournament in Mexico, Hurst netted the winning goal in England's opening match against Romania, controlling, turning and firing home after Alan Ball had crossed to the far post. But after that he struggled in the heat, as did several of his colleagues. He played in eight more internationals, his last being the 3-1 home defeat by West Germany in the European Championship qualifier in April 1972, when he was substituted by Rodney Marsh.

In club and international football, Hurst netted 296 goals in 716 appearances including 249 in exactly 500 games for the Hammers whom he served from 1957-72. He also shares the record with Ian Rush for scoring most goals in the League Cup competition (49).

He also played for his country at Youth team level, won four U23 caps and represented the Football League on seven occasions. The recipient of Second Division Championship, FA Cup and European Cup Winners' Cup medals with West Ham, he is the only player ever to score a hat-trick in the two top Divisions of the Football League, in the FA Cup, the League Cup and in a World Cup final.

Hurst often muses on the validity of his second and England's third goal in the 1966 World Cup final, saying: "I have to admit that I had a bit of sympathy for the Germans. They genuinely believed the ball had not crossed the line and they may be right."

Jimmy Armfield reckoned Hurst 'the best centre-forward England ever had.'

INCE, Paul Emerson Carlyle 1992-2000 ⑤③ ②

Born: Ilford, Essex, 21 October 1967
Career: Essex Schools, West Ham United (apprentice, October 1983, professional, July 1985), Manchester United (£2.4m, September 1989), Inter Milan/Italy (£8m, July 1995), Liverpool (£4.2m, July 1997), Middlesbrough (£1m, August 1999), Wolverhampton Wanderers (free, August 2002-July 2006), Swindon Town (player-coach, August-September 2006), Macclesfield Town (player-manager, October 2006-May 2007), Milton Keynes Dons (manager, June 2007-May 2008), Blackburn Rovers (manager, June-December 2008), Milton Keynes Dons (manager, July 2009-May 2010), Notts County (manager, October 2010-April 2011), Blackpool (manager, February 2013)

Midfield anchorman Paul Ince was the first black player to captain England at senior level, doing so in the 2-0 defeat by the USA in the US Cup tournament at Foxboro, Massachusetts in June 1993. And he was also the first black player to be sent off while playing for England at senior level – dismissed against Sweden in a European Championship qualifier in Stockholm in September 1998. England lost that game 2-1.

Ince made his senior debut in September 1992 in a 1-0 friendly defeat by Spain in Santander. Success at international level was not forthcoming, however and he was booked in a crucial World Cup qualifier against Poland, which caused him to be suspended for a critical 2-0 loss to Norway.

Ince scored his first and only international goals in a 7-1 thumping of San Marino in Bologna in another vital World Cup qualifier in November 1993. England needed to win this game by seven clear goals and hope that the Netherlands lost to Poland. Neither occurred, and they failed to qualify.

As a member of Terry Venables' squad at Euro 96, Ince helped England reach the semi-finals before losing to Germany in a penalty shoot-out. In fact, he received criticism for not taking a spot-kick (the vital sixth which was missed by Gareth Southgate) and for spending the whole of the shoot-out sat down in the centre circle with Steve McManaman with their backs to goal.

Surprisingly Ince retained his place for the next six internationals under Glenn Hoddle and during a World Cup qualifier in Moldova, a famous photograph of him was taken as he tried to climb a wall at the stadium, only for Paul Gascoigne to pull his tracksuit trousers down, revealing Ince's bare buttocks in front of an army of cameras.

In the 0-0 draw with Italy soon afterwards (which guaranteed England their World Cup place) Ince started the game wearing a traditional white shirt but finished in a red one…after his jersey had been soaked by his own blood following a deep cut to his head. In the World Cup, England succumbed in the second round to Argentina, after another shoot-out. This time Ince did take a penalty but saw it saved.

Due to a red card received against Sweden in England's first qualifying match for Euro 2000, Ince was suspended for three matches by UEFA but he returned to

Paul Ince

the side for the two legged play-off with Scotland as England made progress and qualified for Euro 2000.

In a warm up friendly against Malta, Ince won his 50th cap and played in all three of England's group games of the tournament – winning a penalty against Romania in the last game. By losing two of their three matches, England were eliminated and as a result Ince immediately retired from the international scene.

Besides his senior honours, he gained one B and two U21 caps and also appeared in one unofficial international.

His career at club level realised 757 appearances and 90 goals. He won two Premier League, 2 FA Cup, League Cup, European Cup Winners' Cup and UEFA Super Cup winner's medals with Manchester United.

The first black manager in the top flight of English football when he was appointed boss of Blackburn Rovers, Ince later guided the MK Dons to victory in the Football League Trophy and League Two championship and when in charge of lowly Notts County, his team knocked Premiership side Sunderland out of the FA Cup, putting one across his former Manchester United team-mate Steve Bruce.

Ince is the cousin to former boxer Nigel Benn, while his son Thomas, a former junior at Liverpool, is now playing for Blackpool and has represented England at three levels: U17 (4 caps), U19 (4) and U21 (8).

IREMONGER, James 1900-02 ②

Born: Norton, West Yorkshire, 5 March 1876
Died: Nottingham, 25 March 1956
Career: Wilford FC (August 1891), Nottingham Jardine's Athletic (May 1894), Nottingham Forest (professional, January 1896, retired, May 1910); Notts County (trainer/coach, seasons 1919-27); also played cricket for Nottinghamshire (later on coaching staff at Trent Bridge).

Jimmy Iremonger was a very tall, well-built full-back with a short-temper and quite regularly spectators delighted in 'getting his rag up.'

A Football League representative on four occasions, he gained only two England caps, the first in a 2-2 draw with Scotland at Crystal Palace in March 1901 when he made two crucial last-ditch tackles to deny both Bob McColl and Alex Smith from winning the game for the Scots.

As a cricketer, Iremonger scored 16,662 runs, including 31 centuries, and took 619 wickets in 334 games for Notts, between 1897 and 1914.

His younger brother, Albert, made 601 appearances in goal for Notts County between 1904 and 1926.

JACK, David Bone Nightingale 1923-33 ⑨ ③

Born: Bolton, 3 April 1899
Died: High Holborn, London, 10 September 1958
Career: Leigh Road Council School/Westcliff-on-Sea, Southend & District Schools, Plymouth Presbyterians (August 1914); served in Royal Navy during WW1. Also a guest player for Chelsea; Plymouth Argyle (professional, August 1919), Bolton Wanderers (£3,500, December 1920), Arsenal (£10,890, October 1928, retired, May 1934); Southend United (secretary-manager, May 1934-August 1940); Middlesbrough (manager, September 1944-April 1952), Shelbourne/Ireland (manager, August 1953-April 1955); also manager of the Sunderland greyhound stadium; served with the Inland Revenue for many years and was also a journalist.

David Jack scored the first-ever goal at Wembley – for Bolton in their 2-0 win over West Ham in the 1923 FA Cup final – his shot knocking out a spectator who was pinned up against the net!

With an ice cool brain, brilliant close control and powerful shot, Jack was a terrific marksman who, during a 15-year playing career, netted well over 300 goals in more than 500 club appearances, gaining a second Cup winner's medal with Bolton in 1926 and three League championship winner's medals with Arsenal in the 1930s. He had moved to Highbury for a then record fee of £10,890 in October 1928 to become the first 'five figure' footballer.

Surprisingly he was awarded only nine full England caps, collecting his first against Wales in March 1924 and his last versus Austria in December 1932. He played in the first Wembley international v. Scotland in 1924 (1-1) and was outstanding when France were thumped 5-1 in Paris four years later, scoring once and having a hand in two more goals. He also netted with a terrific diving header to earn England a 3-3 draw in Germany in 1929. It was a pity that so many other great forwards were around at the same time as Jack. His father, Bob, had two spells as manager of Plymouth before and after WW1.

JACKSON, Elphinstone 1890-91 ①

Born: Calcutta, India, 9 October 1868
Died: Calcutta, India, 11 December 1945
Career: Lancing College (seasons 1885-89), Oriel College/Oxford University (seasons 1889-92); also played for Corinthians (season 1889-90); son of a High Court Judge, he returned to India on leaving University and was a founder member of the Indian FA in 1893.

Captain of both his college and university teams, stern-tackling full-back 'Elph' Jackson who could head a ball as hard as some players could kick one, played 'very well' in his only international for England, in a 4-1 win over Wales at Sunderland in March 1891.

JAGIELKA, Philip Nikodem 2008-12 ⑱ ①

Born: Manchester, 17 August 1982
Career: Hales Barn United (1996), Sheffield United (apprentice, August 1998, professional, May 2000), Everton (£4m, July 2007)

Of Polish descent, versatile defender Phil Jagielka has so far played for England in one B, six U21 and 18 senior internationals. He won his first full cap against Trinidad and Tobago in June 2008, coming on as a second-half substitute, and after that played a friendly against the European Champions Spain in February 2009.

Sadly injury ruled him out of the 2010 World Cup. He then had the misfortune to be credited with an own-goal when he returned to international duty in a 2-1 friendly victory over Hungary in August 2010 (see Matt Dawson).

Later in the year he was used as a right-back replacement for Glenn Johnson but didn't have the greatest of games, especially against France when both Benzema and Malouda were thorns in his side! He was also included in the England squad for Euro 2012 (not called into action).

He made 287 appearances for Sheffield United before his £4 million transfer to Everton in 2007. His brother Steve is currently with Hednesford Town.

In September 2009, three men broke into Jagielka's £2 million home in Cheshire while he was watching his side play Hull City on the television. He was forced to hand over jewellery and the keys to his Range Rover, which was among a number of luxury cars in his driveway. He was recovering from injury at the time of the incident.

JAMES, David Benjamin 1996-2010 ⑤⓪

Born: Welwyn Garden City, Hertfordshire, 1 August 1970
Career: Frederic Osborn School/Welwyn Garden City, Watford (apprentice, August 1986, professional, July 1988), Liverpool (£1m, July 1992), Aston Villa (£1.8m, June 1999), West Ham United (£3.5m, July 2000), Manchester City (£1.3m, January 2004), Portsmouth (£1.2m, August 2006), Bristol City (free, August 2010, released, May 2012), Bournemouth (season 2012-13), IVB/Iceland (player-coach, April-May 2013)

Despite there being the fear that he is never more than a shot or cross away from dropping a clanger, David James's sheer presence between the posts has over the years, added that little extra assurance to England's defence.

After making one U21 appearance for his country whilst at Watford, James made his full debut under Glenn Hoddle in a friendly against Mexico in March 1997 as a Liverpool player, a game in which he kept his first international clean sheet in a 2–0 win. For several years, however, he acted as understudy to regular 'keeper, David Seaman and when he was dropped after making a mistake against FYR Macedonia in 2002, James became England's new number one. He retained his place in the team even though his club, West Ham, were relegated in 2003, and was the only player from outside the top flight to win an England cap between 1999 and 2007. He went on to play in all of his country's senior matches in Euro 2004 before being axed after an error in a 2–2 World Cup qualifying draw with Austria in September 2004, his place going to Tottenham's Paul Robinson.

James returned as a half-time substitute and conceded all four goals in the 4–1 drubbing by Denmark in a friendly in August 2005 — their worst defeat in 25 years. However, he still remained part of the senior squad, and was selected as the second-choice 'keeper behind Robinson for the 2006 World Cup in Germany, though he did not play. Dropped again at the start of Steve McClaren's reign, he was not called up in 2006-07 but returned again for the friendly with Germany in August 2007 and by doing so he became the first Portsmouth player to play for the senior England team since Mark Hateley in 1984. Scott Carson was then chosen ahead of both James and Robinson for the decisive Euro 2008 qualifier against Croatia in November 2007 which England lost 3-2.

After McClaren had been replaced by Fabio Capello, James was re-established between the posts, although he was challenged by Robert Green. Injuries though, interrupted his game, yet he was still rated as the best 'keeper in England and was duly named in the World Cup squad for South Africa at the age of 39.

As the 2012-13 season ended, James was well on his way to reaching the personal milestone of 1,000 club and international appearances. He also holds the distinction of twice having been the record holder for consecutive Premier League appearances, with 159 during his Liverpool days, 1994-98, and 166 while playing for Manchester City and Portsmouth, 2006-08; these streaks were eventually topped by Chelsea's Frank Lampard and Aston Villa's Brad Friedel, respectively. In February 2009, James set a new Premier League record of 535 appearances, eventually taking his tally to 572 (only Ryan Giggs has made more). The record holder for most clean-sheets in Premiership and Championship football (173), he won the League Cup with Liverpool in 1995 and the FA Cup with Portsmouth in 2008. He also has five Youth, two B and 10 U21 caps to his credit.

James, an accomplished artist, now lives in Chudleigh, Devon and in 2010 joined

Bristol City – so as to be nearer his family home.

James once pulled a muscle in his back when reaching for a television remote control and was forced out of matches. He also missed a match at Liverpool suffering from an RSI injury to his thumb which he blamed on his excessive computer-game habit.

JARRETT, Reverend Beaumont Griffith 1875-78 ③

Born: Camberwell, London, 18 July 1855
Died: Louth, Lincolnshire, 11 April 1905
Career: Harrow School, Christ's College/Cambridge University (seasons 1874-78); also played for Old Harrovians (1874-79), Grantham (season 1879-80); served on the FA Council (years 1876-78); ordained in 1878; spent many years working in the Ministry in Lincoln.

'Beau' Jarrett was described as a 'brilliant half-back' who was England's best player when making his international debut in a 3-0 defeat by Scotland at Partick in March 1876. In fact, Jarrett won all his caps against the Scots, who won the other two matches by 3-1 and 7-2. Jarrett was, in fact, selected by Wales for their inaugural match against Scotland in 1876 but did not play. Then someone found out he was born in England!

JARVIS, Matthew Thomas 2010-11 ①

Born: Middlesbrough, 22 May 1986
Career: Millwall (youth team player), Gillingham (apprentice, June 2002, professional, May 2004), Wolverhampton Wanderers (June 2007), West Ham United (£7.5m, August 2012).

After some very impressive displays for Wolves in the Premiership, clever and fast-raiding right (or left) winger Matt Jarvis was called into the England squad by manager Fabio Capello for the European Championship encounter with Wales in March 2011. He did not figure in the game but four days later he made his full international debut as a second-half substitute in the 1-1 friendly draw with Ghana at Wembley.

He was the first Wolves player to win a full England cap since Steve Bull in 1990 and before his transfer to Molineux, Jarvis had scored 16 goals in 122 appearances for the Gills. He then netted 21 times in 175 outings for Wolves, whom he helped win the Championship in 2009.

JEFFERIS, Frank 1911-12 ②

Born: Fordingbridge, Hants, 3 July 1884
Died: New Cross, London, 21 May 1938
Career: Fordingbridge Turks (May 1902), Southampton (trial, March 1905, signed for £5, April 1905), Everton (£1,500, March 1911), Preston North End (January 1920, player-coach, July 1922); Southport (player-coach, June 1923), Preston North End (reserve team coach, October 1925), Southport (coach, May 1926; played twice in 1927 in an emergency); Millwall Athletic (trainer, May 1936 until his death in 1938)

League championship winner with Everton in 1915, inside-forward Frank Jefferis had a long and varied career. He was a graceful footballer, neat and tidy, who certainly at club level, brought the best out of his fellow attackers. His two England caps both came in March 1912, partnering John Simpson of Blackburn Rovers on the right-wing in a 2-0 win over Wales at Wrexham and a 1-1 draw with Scotland at Hampden Park. In the latter game the *Daily Mirror* stated: 'Freeman was the pick of the English forwards but support was sadly lacking'... hinting that Jefferis didn't have a good game!

David James

JEFFERS, Francis 2002-03 ① ①

Born: Liverpool, 25 January 1981
Career: Everton (apprentice, April 1997, professional, February 1998), Arsenal (£8m, June 2001), Everton (loan, September 2003-May 2004), Charlton Athletic (£2.6m, August 2004), Rangers (loan, August-December 2005), Blackburn Rovers (free, July 2006), Ipswich Town (loan, March-May 2007), Sheffield Wednesday (£700,000, August 2007), Motherwell (January 2011), Newcastle United Jets/Australia.

Utility forward Franny Jeffers, who gained Schoolboy and Youth caps and appeared in 16 U21 internationals (scoring 13 goals, a record he shares with Alan Shearer) had an average first senior game for England against Australia in February 2003, although he did score in a 3-1 defeat. His career, in all fairness, has been plagued by injury and we will never know what he might have achieved if he had been fit and scoring regularly. Owing to these niggling injuries, between 1998 and 2013 he made just 286 first-class appearances for his seven clubs (52 goals scored).

JENAS, Jermaine Anthony 2002-10 ㉑ ①

Born: Nottingham, 18 February 1983
Career: Nottingham Forest (apprentice, June 1999, professional, February 2000), Newcastle United (£5m, February 2002), Tottenham Hotspur (£7m, August 2005), Aston Villa (loan, August 2011-May 2012), Queens Park Rangers (January 2013)

Tall, energetic, with good passing skills and a powerful right-foot shot, midfielder Jermaine Jenas made his senior debut (along with Jeffers, above) against Australia in February 2003 and for the next five years was a key member of the senior squad while performing exceedingly well for Tottenham Hotspur with whom he gained a League Cup winner's medal in 2008.

Jenas also won nine U21 caps and scored in a 2-1 defeat by Belarus in a B international in May 2006 – arranged by manager Sven-Göran Eriksson as a World Cup warm-up friendly. In 2009-10 Jenas reached the personal milestone of 350 club appearances.

JENKINSON, Carl Daniel 2012-13 ①

Born: Harlow, Essex, 8 February 1992
Career: Davenant Foundation School, Charlton Athletic (trainee, April 2009, professional, March 2010), Welling United (loan, January 2010), Eastbourne Borough (loan, November 2010-January 2011), Arsenal (£1.2 million, June 2011)

Born to an English father and Finnish mother, attacking right-back Carl Jenkinson had already played for England's U17 team and for Finland at U19 and U21 levels before winning his first full international cap as a second-half substitute for Glen Johnson in England's 4-2 friendly defeat in Sweden in November 2012. Good on the ball with an appetite for hard work, he made just eight League appearances for Charlton before his big-money move to the Emirates where initially he acted as cover for Frenchman Bacary Sagna.

JEZZARD, Bedford Alfred George 1953-56 ②

Born: Clerkenwell, London, 19 October 1927
Died: Fulham, London, 21 May 2005
Career: Croxley Green School, Croxley Green Juniors (May 1942), Old Merchant Taylor's Sports ground (assistant groundsman, seasons 1946-47), Watford (amateur), Fulham (amateur, June 1948, professional, October 1948, retired, injured, August 1957; joined coaching staff, then manager, June 1958, general manager, October 1964, resigned December 1964); later a licensee in Hammersmith, London.

A hapless debutant in Budapest in May 1954 when England were crushed 7-1 by a rampant Hungary, Bedford Jezzard hardly got a kick and one reporter wrote: "The Fulham centre-forward made a best-forgotten debut." In November 1955 he was recalled to the attack and played alongside his club-mate Johnny Haynes in a 3-0 win over Northern Ireland at Wembley. His career ended a year later due to an ankle injury.

During his time with Fulham (1948-57) Jezzard, a speedy, thrustful inside or centre-forward, scored 154 goals in 306 appearances, helping the Cottagers win the Second Division championship in 1949. He had been ill with multi-infarct dementia for some time before his death.

JOHNSON, Adam 2009-12 ⑫ ②

Born: Sunderland, 14 July 1987
Career: Middlesbrough (apprentice, July 2003, professional, May 2005), Leeds United (loan, October-December 2006), Watford (loan, September-December 2007), Manchester City (£7m, February 2010), Sunderland (£10m, August 2012)

A left-sided midfielder with good pace, plenty of skill and a strong shot, Adam Johnson made his senior international debut as an 84th minute substitute for James Milner in a 3-1 win over Mexico in May 2010, having earlier represented his country at youth team level and in 19 U21 matches.

He made 120 appearances for Middlesbrough (16 goals scored) before his big money move to The City of Manchester Stadium, and after helping City win the FA Youth Cup, the FA Cup in 2011 and the Premiership title twelve months later, as well as netting 15 times in 97 outings, he switched his allegiance to Sunderland on a four-year contract.

JOHNSON, Andrew 2004-08 ⑧

Born: Bedford, 10 February 1981
Career: Mark Rutherford Upper School (Bedford), Luton Town (academy), Birmingham City (apprentice, July 1997, professional, March 1998), Crystal Palace (£750,000, August 2002), Everton (£6m, June 2006), Fulham (£10.5m, August 2008)

Striker Andy Johnson has pace, skill and a strong shot but injuries have seriously affected his game since 2009.

An England U20 player with Birmingham City, he was selected in the team for the 1999 FIFA World Youth Championship alongside Stuart Taylor, Ashley Cole, Peter Crouch and Matthew Etherington but failed to impress.

Second top goalscorer in the Premier League in 2004-05 (behind Thierry Henry), Johnson made his full international debut in the 0-0 friendly draw against the Netherlands in February of that season, replacing Wayne Rooney in the 61st minute. His second cap followed soon afterwards, in a 2-1 win over the USA during a tour of America in the summer of 2005 and when Steve McClaren took over as England boss, Johnson got further opportunities to play for his country in the Euro 2008 qualifiers against Andorra, Macedonia and Israel, making his first competitive start for England in the latter. His last cap was as a substitute v. West Germany at Wembley in August 2007.

Although struggling with injuries from time to time, at club level Johnson has proved very effective, scoring a goal every three games - almost 150 in 450 outings up to May 2013. He helped Crystal Palace reach the Premiership (via the Play-offs) in 2004 and was in Fulham's losing Europa Cup final team of 2010.

NB: With a grandfather born in Poland, in 2004, Johnson was given the chance to play international football for Poland. He declined. Johnson is now the Patron of Football for Cancer.

JOHNSON, David Edward 1974-80 ⑧ ⑥

Born: Liverpool, 23 October 1951
Career: Everton (juniors, season 1966-67), Ipswich Town (apprentice, April 1967, professional, April 1969), Ipswich Town (November 1972), Liverpool (£200,000, August 1976), Everton (August 1982), Barnsley (loan, February-March 1984), Manchester City (March 1984), Tulsa Roughnecks/USA (June-September 1984), Preston North End (non-contract, October 1984-March 1985), Naxxar Lions/Malta (season 1985-86); Barrow AFC (player-manager), later worked as a matchday host in the corporate lounges at Anfield; also worked for BBC Radio Merseyside.

Hard-working striker David Johnson made a memorable debut for England, scoring both goals in a 2-2 draw with Wales at Wembley in May 1975 when he partnered Mick Channon in attack. His second strike came late on when he headed home substitute Brian Little's cross to salvage a draw.

Having been dropped, he was then recalled in place of the injured Trevor Francis for the game against Argentina at Wembley in May 1980…and responded in style by scoring twice in a 3-1 win. His final cap came in the 1-1 draw with Belgium in the European Championship in June 1980.

Overall Johnson had a fine career, netting 110 goals in 409 League appearances. He won three League titles and the European Cup with Liverpool.

Johnson was the first player to score for both clubs in the Merseyside League derby.

JOHNSON, Edward 1879-84 ② ②

Born: Nechells, Birmingham, 9 June 1862
Died: Stoke-on-Trent, 30 June 1901
Career: Saltley College/Birmingham (August 1880), Stoke (September 1881, retired, injured, April 1885); represented Staffordshire (1882-85); also Stoke St Peter's (club committee member, seasons 1886-89); Staffordshire County (FA Committee member, seasons 1889-1898).

As a fast, direct and clever winger, Teddy Johnson represented the Birmingham FA and Staffordshire before making his international debut in a 3-2 win over Wales in March 1880. He had to wait four years before winning his second cap, scoring twice in an 8-1 win over Ireland in February 1884. Unfortunately, he let himself and his team-mates down by holding on to the ball far too long.

JOHNSON, Glen McLeod 2003-13 ㊽ ①

Born: Greenwich, London, 23 August 1984
Career: West Ham United (apprentice, August 2000, professional, August 2001), Millwall (loan, October 2002-January 2003), Chelsea (£6m, July 2003), Portsmouth (loan, July 2006-May 2007 and signed for £4m, August 2007), Liverpool (£18.5m, June 2009)

One of England's best attacking outlets in several internationals, right-back Glen Johnson has good pace, boundless energy and smart footwork, but defensively he occasionally suffers positional lapses yet still makes some vitally important tackles and when he gets forward he can whip in a splendid cross while also laying on plenty of chances for his colleagues.

Capped at Youth team level and on 14 occasions as an U21 player, he made his full international debut against Denmark in November 2003 and six months later struck home a brilliant goal, left footed, when England beat Mexico 3-1 in a friendly at Wembley. When free from injury, he has been a regular member of the senior squad ever since and played in all four 2010 World Cup games in South Africa and in every match at Euro 2012.

Following his big-money transfer from West Ham, he helped Chelsea win the League Cup and Premiership in 2005 and then, during his loan spell with Portsmouth, gained an FA Cup winner's medal in 2008. He won the League Cup with Liverpool in 2012.

JOHNSON, Joseph Alfred 1936-39 ⑤ ②

Born: Grimsby, 4 April 1911
Died: West Bromwich, 8 August 1983
Career: Grimsby Council School, Cleethorpes Royal Saints (August 1926), Scunthorpe & Lindsey United (professional, April 1928), Bristol City (£1,200, May 1931), Stoke (£2,500, April 1932), West Bromwich Albion (£6,500, November 1937); WW2 guest for Crewe Alexandra, Leicester City and Notts County; Hereford United (free, May 1946), Northwich Victoria (August 1948, retired, May 1950); returned to West Bromwich where he ran the café and tea rooms in Dartmouth Park.

Joe Johnson was an excellent left-winger whose scoring record was first-class for a player in his position. Possibly the highlight of his career came in April 1937 when he produced a terrific display for England against Scotland in front of 149,547 fans at Hampden Park. Johnson's clubmates from Stoke, Stanley Matthews and Freddie Steele, also competed in this game which England lost, somewhat unluckily, by 3-1.

Challenging Cliff Bastin and Eric Brook for a place in the England team, Johnson's international debut had come six months earlier in November 1936 against Ireland on his home patch at The Victoria Ground and his two goals for his country were scored in a 4-0 win over Sweden in Stockholm and an 8-0 walloping of Finland in Helsinki in May 1937. His best years at club level were spent with Stoke (1932-37).

JOHNSON, Seth Art Maurice 2000-01 ①

Born: Selly Oak, Birmingham, 12 March 1979
Career: Holmes Chapel Comprehensive School/Cheshire, Crewe Alexandra (apprentice, June 1995, professional, July 1996), Derby County (£3m, May 1999), Leeds United (£7m, October 2001), Derby County (free, August 2005-June 2007), Leyton Orient (trial, season 2007-08), Cambridge United (briefly, 2008, retired, May 2008).

Hard-running right-sided midfielder Seth Johnson was a surprise second-half substitute (for Gareth Barry) in England's 1-0 defeat by Italy in Turin in November 2000. He was one of 16 players used in the friendly and didn't play at all well and was never selected again. He suffered horrendous injuries during his career and over a period of 13 years, scored 16 goals in 275 League appearances, helping Derby County win promotion to the Premiership in 2007.

JOHNSON, Thomas Clark Fisher 1925-33 ⑤ ⑤

Born: Dalton-in-Furness, near Barrow, 19 August 1901
Died: Liverpool, 29 January 1973
Career: Dalton Athletic (August 1916), Dalton Casuals (November 1916), Manchester City (amateur, May 1918, professional, February 1919), Everton (£6,000, March 1930), Liverpool (March 1934), Darwen (August 1936, retired, May 1937)

The recipient of Second Division championship winner's medals with both Manchester City and Everton, Tommy Johnson also won the FA Cup with the Merseysiders and in a lengthy career, mainly as an inside-left, he scored 238 goals in 552 club appearances. His record with City was 166 goals in 354 first-class matches, for Everton it was 64 in 159 games and for Liverpool eight in 39.

With so many talented goal-getters around at the same time, Johnson won only five full caps for England in six-and-a-half years, scoring on his debut in a 5-3 win over Belgium in Antwerp in May 1926. He then netted twice in each of his next two internationals v. Wales (won 6-0) and Spain (7-1). He was injured in his last game against Ireland in October 1932.

JOHNSON, William Harrison 1899-1903 ⑤ ①

Born: Ecclesfield, Yorkshire, 4 January 1876
Died: Sheffield, 17 July 1940
Career: Atlas & Norfolk Works FC (May 1891), Ecclesfield Church (August 1894), Sheffield United (professional, August 1895, retired, injured, May 1909; remained on club's training staff until 1935)

In 1900, the *Sporting Sun* stated that Bill Johnson was 'watchful and alert…among the best wing-halves in England.'

Twice an FA Cup winner with Sheffield United for whom he made 275 appearances in 12 years (1897-1909), he gained the first of his six England caps against Ireland in March 1900, scoring in a 2-0 win. After that he played twice against both Wales and Scotland and once more against the Irish. In his second game against the Scots at Celtic Park in April 1900 when he played in the same half-back line as his club-mate Ernest Needham, he was 'watchful and alert' but was still given a 'hard time' by Bob McColl and Jock Campbell as

England crashed to a 4-1 defeat. His two sons, Harry and Tom, both went on to play for Sheffield United, the club their father served for 38 years as a player and then trainer.

JOHNSTON, Henry 1946-54 ⑩

Born: Droylsden, Manchester, 26 September 1919
Died: Manchester, 12 October 1973
Career: Fairfield Road Council School/Droylsden, Lancashire Boys, Droylsden Athletic (May 1934), Blackpool (amateur, June 1935, professional, September 1936, retired, November 1955); Reading (manager, November 1955-January 1963), Blackpool (chief scout, also twice caretaker-manager before leaving Bloomfield Road in May 1972); later ran a newsagents business in Blackpool.

'Harry' Johnson, one of several outstanding defenders who starred for England during the late 1940s, played with distinction and consistency in all three half-back positions and to prove he was a fine player he was voted Footballer of the Year in 1951. A first-class strategist, notably constructive, he preferred the centre-half role from where he captained the Seasiders to FA Cup glory in 1953. Johnston, who made 438 first-class appearances during his 19 years at Bloomfield Road, gained a Wartime League North Cup winner's medal in 1943 and all but scored on his England debut against Holland at Huddersfield in November 1946. Replacing Henry Cockburn, he starred alongside Neil Franklin and Billy Wright in a resounding 8-2 win. However, after good displays in following games against Scotland in 1947 (1-1), Chile in 1953 (won 2-1), and in World Cup qualifying victories in 1953 v. Wales (4-1) and Northern Ireland (3-1) his tenth and last international appearance was a disaster, being one of the defenders given a roasting by Ferenc Puskas and his 'marvellous Magyars' in the 6-3 massacre by Hungary at Wembley in November 1953. He was one of four Blackpool players who lined up against Hungary. He played behind Tommy Lawton for Lancashire Boys aged 14 and served in the RAF as a PT instructor in Egypt during WW2.

JONES, Alfred 1881-83 ③

Born: Walsall, 3 August 1861
Died: Walsall, 12 February 1930
Career: Pleck (April 1878), Walsall Town Swifts (September 1879), Great Lever (August 1882), Walsall Town Swifts (June 1883), Aston Villa (briefly during season 1885-86), Burnley (for a month in 1886), Walsall Town (August-November 1887).

Described as being a 'sterling right or left-back with many qualities' Alf Jones was blessed with steadiness and a strong tackle. Very thoughtful in his defensive play, he was the first Walsall player to win a full cap when making his England debut against Scotland in March 1882. Unfortunately he had an 'unimpressive game' as the Scots won 5-1 at Hampden Park. But despite all this, Jones was retained in defence for the next match against Wales two days later. England were expected to claim a 'comfortable victory' but the Welsh side 'fought magnificently to secure a 5-3 victory' with Jones scoring an own goal in the 60th minute. He won his final cap in a 3-2 defeat by Scotland in March 1883.

JONES, Harry 1922-23 ①

Born: Blackwell, Derbyshire, 24 May 1891
Died: Nottingham, winter 1950
Career: Blackwell Boys Brigade, Blackwell Wesley Guild (August 1909), Blackwell Colliery (June 1910), Nottingham Forest (July 1911, retired, injured, March 1924); returned with Sutton Town (December 1924, retired again, April 1925).

A resolute, tough and unyielding full-back, Harry Jones was also an excellent passer who maintained a high level of consistency throughout his career. He made 239 appearances for Nottingham Forest between 1911 and 1924, helping the club win the Second Division championship in 1924. The previous season he had been one of six 'new caps' in the England team that beat France 4-1 in Paris. He partnered Warney Cresswell and scribed one reporter: "Jones looked comfortable throughout the game."

JONES, Herbert 1926-28 ⑤

Born: Blackpool, 3 March 1896
Died: Fleetwood, Lancs, 11 September 1973
Career: South Shore Strollers (May 1918), Fleetwood Town (May 1920), Blackpool (professional, June 1922), Blackburn Rovers (December 1925), Brighton & Hove Albion (May 1934), Fleetwood Town (July 1935, retired, May 1936).

An FA Cup winner with Blackburn in 1928, left-back Bert Jones was a wonderful positional player, dauntless, fleet-footed who put plenty of thought into his game. He made his England debut in a 2-1 win over Scotland in April 1927 and a year later won his last cap against the same country (lost 2-1). He partnered Roy Goodall (Huddersfield) in five of his six internationals, producing solid performances in away wins over Belgium (9-1) and Luxembourg (5-2). He played football until he was 40.

JONES, Michael David 1964-70 ③

Born: Worksop, Notts, 24 April 1945
Career: Priory Primary & Senior Schools/Worksop, Worksop Boys, Sheffield junior football, Rotherham Boys, Dinnington Miners' Welfare (April 1961), Sheffield United (professional, November 1962), Leeds United (£100,000, September 1967, retired, injured, October 1975); ran a market stall with his son, selling sportswear in Nottingham; now works in hospitality at Leeds United.

Mick Jones led England's attack for the first time in the 1-0 win over West Germany in Nuremberg in May 1965. He played as well as the other front men and went on to win two more caps, against Sweden four days later and Holland in January 1970. At club level, the burly, aggressive striker, hard and totally committed, became the bludgeon of the Leeds attack, forming an excellent partnership with Allan Clarke. He helped Don Revie's team twice win the Fairs Cup as well as the League championship and the FA Cup, scoring the winning goal in the final of the latter competition in 1972 against Arsenal. He netted 187 goals in 485 senior appearances for his two English clubs, having his best years at Elland Road (111 goals in 313 outings).

JONES, Philip Anthony 2011-13 ⑦

Born: Preston, 21 February 1992
Career: Balshaw's CE High School, Leyland, Ribblesdale Wanderers (August 2001), Blackburn Rovers (schoolboy forms, summer 2002, professional, February 2009), Manchester United (£16.5m, February 2011)

Phil Jones made just 35 Premiership appearances for Blackburn Rovers before his big-money move to Old Trafford in 2011. Primarily a central defender, he is equally adapt as a right back or defensive midfielder. In August 2010 he was called up to the England U21 squad, starting the game against Uzbekistan before being substituted in the 46th minute by Liverpool's Martin Kelly. Later he captained the team in the final 2011 U21 European Championship qualifier against the Czech Republic in Denmark. He went on to make his debut at right-back in the Euro 2012 qualifying draw in Montenegro in 7 October 2011 after which coach Fabio Capello said: 'He's born with talent.' He was subsequently named in Roy Hodgson's 23-man squad for Euro 2012. Unfortunately injuries affected his game in recent times.

JONES, Robert Marc 1991-95 ⑧

Born: Wrexham, 5 November 1971
Career: Ellesmere Port Youth Centre, Holton Boys (seasons 1986-88), Crewe Alexandra (apprentice, May 1988, professional, December 1988) Liverpool (October 1991-June 1999), West Ham United (July 1999, retired, injured, August 1999); now runs a children's nursery in Warrington.

Right-back Rob Jones made a 'sound rather than impressive' England debut in the 0-0 draw with France at Wembley in February 1992. A very confident player who loved to drive forward, he was never on the losing side for his country and was outstanding in the wins over Poland and Greece in his second and third internationals. Jones, who played for Wales as a schoolboy before representing England's Youth team and later gaining two U21 caps, became Crewe's second youngest-ever player in 1988. He won the FA Cup and League Cup with Liverpool for whom he made 243 senior appearances in his eight years at Anfield but only played in one InterToto Cup game for West Ham. Jones' grandfather was ex-Liverpool player William Henry Jones (next column).

JONES, William 1900-01 ①

Born: Brighton, Sussex, 6 March 1876
Died: Swindon, 11 November 1908
Career: Heaton Rovers (April 1892), Bristol Rovers (briefly, during season 1894-95), Willington Athletic (August 1895), Loughborough Town (professional, May 1896), Bristol City (July 1897), Tottenham Hotspur (May 1906), Swindon Town (May 1907, retired, May 1908).

During his varied career, Bill Jones played as an inside-left and right-half, gaining his only England cap in the latter position as a Bristol City player when he deputised for Harry Johnson of Sheffield United in a 3-0 win over Ireland at Southampton in March 1901. A timely tackler and good distributor, he played most of his football in the Southern League. He died of typhoid at the age of 32.

JONES, William Henry 1949-50 ②

Born: Whaley Bridge, Derbyshire, 13 May 1921
Died: Chester, 26 December 2010
Career: Hayfield St Matthews FC/Derbyshire (August 1936), Liverpool (professional, September 1938); WW2 guest for Leeds United, Reading and York City; Ellesmere Port Town (player-manager, May 1954-June 1958); Liverpool (scout, early 1960s-mid-1970s)

A month or so after playing in the FA Cup final for Liverpool, centre-half Bill Jones made a surprise England debut in the 5-3 win over Portugal in Lisbon in May 1950. Brought in at the last minute after his Anfield team-mate Lawrie Hughes had pulled out with a leg injury, Jones did well and retained his place for the next game against Belgium in Brussels. But he struggled to contain a lively centre-forward and despite England's 4-1 win, he was not included in the squad for the World Cup which started in Brazil a month later. The recipient of one B cap and a Football League representative, Jones made 278 first-class appearances during his 16 years at Anfield. Jones was 89 when he did of natural causes in Countess of Chester Hospital in 2010.

JOY, Bernard 1935-36 ①

Born: Fulham, London, 29 October 1911
Died: Kenton, London, 18 July 1984
Career: London University (two years, 1927-29), Corinthian Casuals (amateur, August 1929-May 1948); also played for Southend United (amateur, between August 1931 and April 1933), Fulham (May 1934). Arsenal (May 1935-May 1947); served as a flight lieutenant in the RAF during the war; became a schoolmaster in Hounslow, Middlesex (1936 onwards); engaged periodically as a sports journalist with *The Star* and *Evening Standard,* also an author.

The last amateur to appear for England in a full international was Bernard Joy of the Corinthians, who earned his only cap in the 3-2 defeat by Belgium in Brussels in May 1936. Registered to play for Arsenal at the time, wing-half Joy developed a similar 'third back' style to his Arsenal predecessor Herbie Roberts. Big and strong, he represented England in 12 amateur internationals, in one Wartime fixture (at centre-half in a 6-2 win over Scotland at Wembley in front of 90,000 fans in October 1944), played in the 1936 Olympic Games, won the FA Amateur Cup with the Casuals in 1936 and the League Championship and Football League South Wartime Cup with Arsenal in 1938 and 1943. He wrote the book *Forward Arsenal* (a complete record of Arsenal).

KAIL, Edgar Isaac Lewis 1928-29 ③ ②

Born: Dulwich, London, 26 November 1900
Died: Dulwich, London, 10 June 1976
Career: Goodrich Road School/South London, Dulwich Hamlet (August 1915-May 1934); also represented Surrey County; became a representative for a London-based wines and spirits company.

Edgar Kail became the first amateur from non-League football to win a full England cap. The Dulwich Hamlet inside-right scored twice on his senior debut in a 4-1 win over France in Paris in May 1929. One of four players who made their first starts for their country in that game, Kail was also capped by England as a Schoolboy, played in 21 Amateur internationals (seasons 1921-33) and gained two FA Amateur Cup winner's medals with Dulwich Hamlet in 1920 and 1932. Occasionally said to be 'too greedy with the ball'.

KAY, Anthony Herbert 1962-63 ① ①

Born: Attercliffe, Sheffield, 13 May 1937
Career: Sheffield junior football, Sheffield Wednesday (professional, May 1954), Everton (£60,000, December 1962; suspended, April 1965); later lived in Spain (briefly); became a groundsman in London; now resides on Merseyside.

Dynamic, forceful and unyielding, midfielder Tony Kay's red hair matched his play. He made his England debut against Switzerland in Basle in June 1963 – and he scored to celebrate the occasion in an 8-1 win. Unfortunately a year later, along with his then Sheffield Wednesday team-mates Bronco Layne and Peter Swan, his career was wrecked by a bribery scandal which led to a term on imprisonment. Only 28 years of age when he walked free from incarceration, Kay should have been at the peak of his powers for both club and country. As time passed by he would return to competitive football on occasion at amateur level, but remained an outcast to the game at which he had once been a star. Later while working and living in Spain where he spent twelve years, he avoided arrest for selling a counterfeit diamond. On his return to the UK Kay was fined £400 and as time passed by he was employed as a groundsman in South-East London.

Kay spent eight years at Hillsborough during which time he made 203 appearances, following up with another 57 for Everton. He won the Second Division championship with the Owls and the First with the Toffees.

KEAN, Frederick William 1922-29 ⑨

Born: Sheffield, 3 April 1899
Died: Sheffield, 28 October 1973
Career: Hallam FC (August 1914), WW1 guest for Portsmouth (1917), Sheffield Wednesday (free, July 1920), Bolton Wanderers (September 1928), Luton Town (June 1931), Sutton Town (player-coach, November 1935-May 1937); became a licensee in Sheffield.

A Second Division championship winner with Wednesday and an FA Cup winner with Bolton, Fred Kean was a tall, upright player who occupied the right-half and centre-half positions with authority. Strong in the air and on the ground, he was a real tough footballer who made his international debut in a 6-1 victory over Belgium at Highbury in May 1923 when he made two important goal-line clearances and one of his long downfield passes led to one of Ted Hegan's two goals. He won only five more caps over the next six years, competing for a place with the likes of Tommy Magee, Frank Moss and Willis Edwards. During his 16-year career, Kean made over 400 appearances at club level, 247 for Sheffield Wednesday.

KEEGAN, Joseph Kevin, OBE 1972-82 ㊛ ㉑

Born: Armthorpe, Doncaster, 14 February 1951
Career: Enfield House Youth Club (April 1966), Peglar's Brass Works, Lonsdale Hotel FC (Doncaster Sunday League, during season 1966-67), Coventry City (trial), Scunthorpe United (apprentice, December 1967, professional, December 1968), Liverpool (£33,000, May 1971), SV Hamburg/Germany (£500,000, June 1977), Southampton (£400,000, July 1980), Bankstown City/Australia (briefly), Newcastle United (£100,000, August 1982, retired, May 1984; spent eight years out of game, returned as Newcastle manager (February 1992-January 1997); TV pundit; Fulham (Chief Operating Officer, September 1997, then manager, season 1998-99); also England (manager, February 1999 when still manager of Fulham, resigned, October 2000); Manchester City (manager, May 2001, resigned March 2005).

During Joe Mercer's short reign as England boss, he recalled Kevin Keegan to the team but almost immediately had to deal with an unsavoury and rather ugly incident inside Belgrade airport in June 1974. The versatile forward was one of several players gaming around near the luggage carousel and was singled out by the police who marched him off and allegedly 'roughed him up.' As cool as you like, Mercer intervened and sorted the incident, just in time to prevent the rest of the players refusing to compete in the friendly against Yugoslavia.

So annoyed was he at being left out of the England-Wales game at Wembley in May 1975 by new boss Don Revie, that he packed his bags and stormed off. Some managers would never have picked him again.

But Revie knew he was a 'class act' and soon afterwards caught up with Keegan and told him he had only been 'rested' ahead of the Scotland match. As fresh as a daisy, Keegan went out and helped pulverize the Scots as England stormed to a 5-1 victory.

A player with a whole-hearted approach, Keegan seemed always full of running. He was terrific in the air (for a small man), sharp on the ground and had good pace which allowed him to free himself from the tight-marking defenders.

He was handed his first England start against Wales at Cardiff in November 1972. Conspicuous with his bubble-permed hair, he had a golden opportunity to mark his debut with a goal but allowed Gary Sprake to snatch the ball away from him as he attempted to dribble round the 'keeper. England still won the game 1-0.

The usually reliable 'K.K.' missed a penalty in the 2-1 win over Switzerland in Basle in September 1975 but two years later he was brilliant when Italy were defeated 2-0 in a World Cup qualifier at Wembley. He headed home Trevor Brooking's cross in the 11th minute and then he set Brooking clear to score the clinching goal with nine minutes remaining.

Keegan headed two excellent goals and also hit the woodwork when England beat Denmark 4-3 in Copenhagen in September 1978. Five months later he was irrepressible after bravely heading England into an early lead against Northern Ireland at Wembley. He then laid on the first of Bob Latchford's two goals and back-headed a corner to Dave Watson to fire home another as the Irish were humbled 4-0.

The little 'terrier' was at it again against the Republic of Ireland at Wembley in February 1980. Playing with pace and power, improvisation and skill, he bagged both goals in a 2-0 win.

Having been handed the captaincy in 1976, he retired from international football after the 1982 World Cup, having led his country 31 times (the fourth most). Surprisingly, though, Keegan managed only one World Cup appearance and this was limited to just 26 minutes when he came on as a substitute in the final game against the host nation Spain when he missed a headed chance to break the deadlock.

Following a successful start to the 1982-83 season with Newcastle United, there was much controversy when newly appointed England boss Bobby Robson did not select him for international duty. And there his England career ended, having scored 21 goals in 63 matches (an average of one every three). He also netted twice in one unofficial international as well as gaining five caps at U23 level.

Voted PFA 'Footballer of the Year' in 1976 and 1982, Keegan also won the European Footballer and German Player of the Year awards and helped Liverpool lift the European Cup, the UEFA Cup twice, the FA Cup and three League titles, while celebrating Bundesliga success with Hamburg. For his five clubs, Keegan struck 298 goals in 838 club and international appearances, spending his best years with Liverpool (100 goals in 323 games). He also

had the humiliation of being sent off, along with Billy Bremner of Leeds United, during the 1974 FA Charity Shield game at Wembley. As a manager he became a folk hero at St James' Park, steering Newcastle to the First Division championship and twice to the runners-up spot in the Premier League. He then guided Fulham to the Second Division title before having 18 months (and 18 games) in charge of England, resigning after a 1-0 World Cup qualifying defeat by Germany in October 2000 - the last game played at the 'old' Wembley.

In April 1991 Keegan was attacked while sleeping in his Range Rover by the M25 at Reigate Hill in Surrey. His assailants later admitted in court that they needed money for a drugs debt and had no idea they were attacking Keegan.

In July 2008, Flybe International announced the naming of one of their new Bombardier Q400 aircraft in honour of Keegan's service to Newcastle United, both as a player and as a manager. The plane is used on the regular service from Newcastle International Airport to London Gatwick.

KEEN, Errington Ridley Liddell 1932-37 ④

Born: Walker-on-Tyne, County Durham, 4 September 1910
Died: Fulham, London, 2 July 1984
Career: Newcastle Schools, Nun's Moor FC/Newcastle (April 1925), Newcastle Swifts (August 1926), Newcastle United (September 1927), Derby County (player-exchange deal involving Harry Bedford, December 1930), Chelmsford City (player-manager, May 1938), Hereford United (player-manager, July 1939); WW2 guest for Notts County, Rochdale, Everton, Fulham, Millwall, Liverpool, Lincoln City, Charlton Athletic and Leeds United, the latter in December 1945; Bacup Borough (July 1946), Hull City (November-December 1946); IFK Norrkoping/Sweden (August 1949, retired, April 1950); later coach in Hong Kong, managed in Egypt, also returned as manager of Norrkoping IF and Besiktas/Turkey (manager)

Easily recognisable by his blond hair, Errington Keen was a stylish left-half, sure-footed, quick in the tackle who loved to join the attack. A player for 20 years, he had his best spell with Derby County for whom he made 237 appearances in eight years: 1930-38. He made an impressive international debut in a 4-3 win over Austria at Stamford Bridge in December 1932 but had to wait four years before winning his second cap, in a 2-1 defeat by Wales. After a 'steady game' in a 3-1 victory over Ireland a month later he was one of the 'best players on the field' when Hungary were defeated 6-2 at Highbury in his last game in December 1936.

KELLY, Martin Ronald 2011-12 ①

Born: Bolton, 27 April 1990
Career: Liverpool (trainee, June 2006, professional, December 2007), Huddersfield Town (loan, March-May 2009)

An attacking right full-back, Martin Kelly won his first England cap as an 88th minute substitute for Manchester United's Phil Jones against Norway in Oslo in May 2012 having made just 24 Premiership appearances for Liverpool. He had earlier represented his country at youth, U20 and U21 levels.

KELLY, Robert 1919-28 ⑭ ⑦

Born: Ashton-in-Makerfield, 16 November 1893
Died: Fylde, Lancs, 22 September 1969
Career: Ashton White Star (May 1908), Ashton Central (August 1910), Earlstown Rovers (August 1912), St Helens Town (August 1913), Burnley (£275, professional, November 1913); served in Army during WW1; Sunderland (£6,550, December 1925), Huddersfield Town (£3,500, February 1927), Preston North End (£1,200, February 1932), Carlisle United (player-manager, March 1935-November 1936), Stockport County (manager, November 1936-January 1938), Sporting Club de Portugal (trainer-coach, August 1946); coached in FC St Gallen/Switzerland (coach, seasons 1949-51), SC Heerenveen/Holland (coach, season 1954-55); also coached in Channel Islands (mid-1950s), Barry Town/Suffolk (manager, December 1960-May 1961).

A League championship winner with Burnley in 1921 and twice an FA Cup finalist with Huddersfield, outside-right Bob Kelly scored twice on his England debut in a rousing 5-4 victory over Scotland at Hillsborough in April 1920. Alf Davis, reporting for the *Daily Mail*, wrote: "On a mud heap of a pitch, England proved better in attack than defence…Morris and Kelly were the outstanding figures. Playing in an international for the first time they showed the cool skill and resource of veterans combined with pace, dash and fine shooting power."

Kelly was regarded as being one of the 'best players' in League football between the two Wars. He possessed wonderful close ball control, was remarkably fast over 20-30 yards, passed with confidence and could shoot hard and straight.

He scored almost 180 goals in 663 appearances for his five League clubs, having his best return with Burnley (97 goals in 299 outings).

KENNEDY, Alan Phillip 1983-84 ②

Born: Sunderland, 31 August 1954
Career: Wearside junior football, Newcastle United (apprentice, July 1971, professional, September 1972), Liverpool (£330,000, August 1978), Sunderland (£100,000, September 1985), Husqvarna/Sweden (September 1987), Beerschot/Belgium (October 1987), Hartlepool United (non-contract, November 1987), Grantham Town (briefly, early December 1987), Wigan Athletic (one-week trial, signed December 1987), Sunderland (March 1988), Colne Dynamos (August 1988), Wrexham (March-December 1990), Morecambe (March 1991), Netherfield (player-manager, July 1991-August 1992), Northwich Victoria (October 1992), Radcliffe Borough (December 1992), Netherfield (player-manager, November 1993), Barrow (player-coach, August 1994, retired, March 1996); now an occasional after-dinner speaker, living in Ormskirk.

An England U23 and B international, strong-kicking left-back Alan Kennedy gained two full caps for his country, lining up alongside Viv Anderson and then Mike Duxbury in games against Northern Ireland and Wales in 1983-84 under manager Bobby Robson.

However, with Kenny Sansom around he never really got a chance to establish himself as a regular in the team. He had earlier been named in the senior squad in 1975 but a knee injury prevented him from making his international debut. He played his best football at Anfield and helped Liverpool win the European Cup twice, the League Championship four times and the League Cup thrice, being a vital member of the Reds treble-winning team of 1984. Kennedy made over 680 club appearances (357 for Liverpool) during his lengthy time in the game. His younger brother, Keith, also played for Newcastle (1968-72) as well as for Bury, Mansfield Town and Barrow.

KENNEDY, Raymond 1975-80 ⑰ ③

Born: Seaton Delaval, Northumberland, 28 July 1951
Career: South Northumberland Schools, Port Vale (trial, July-August 1966), New Hartley Juniors/Seaton Delaval (season 1966-67), Port Vale (apprentice, August 1967, released, January 1968), Arsenal (apprentice, May 1968, professional, November 1968), Liverpool (£180,000, July 1974), Swansea City (£160,000, January 1982-October 1983), Hartlepool United (November 1983-May 1985); Sunderland (part-time coach, February 1987, first team coach, April 1897-May 1991); became a licensee in Hartlepool until Parkinson's Disease forced him into retirement.

Attacking midfielder Ray Kennedy was a double winner and the recipient of a Fairs Cup winner's medal with Arsenal before leaving Highbury for Anfield. He then went on to collect four more League championship, a UEFA Cup, League Cup, three European Cup and European Super Cup medals with Liverpool. It was he who netted the vital winning goal for the Gunners v. Spurs to clinch the League and FA Cup double in 1971. He later won the Welsh Cup with Swansea. Kennedy won the first of his 17 full caps under Don Revie as a left sided midfielder v. Wales in March 1976, scoring the opening goal in a 2-1 win at Wrexham. Then, under new boss Ron Greenwood, he was forced to compete with Trevor Brooking for that position. In fact, he strongly believed that Greenwood favoured his old West Ham protégé Brooking and this led to Kennedy informing Greenwood in late 1980 that he no longer wished to play for England. Kennedy's other two 'international' goals came in the 5-0 and 2-0 World Cup qualifying wins over Luxembourg in March and October 1977. During his club career the powerfully built Kennedy scored over 150 goals in over 660 club appearances, including 72 in 392 games for Liverpool. Sadly, he is now suffering from Parkinson's Disease.

KENYON-SLANEY, Colonel William Stanley (Slaney) 1872-73 ① ②

Born: Rajkot, Gujarat, India, 24 August 1847
Died: Newport, Shropshire, 24 April 1908
Career: Eton College, Christ Church College/Oxford University (from August 1868), Old Etonians (seasons 1870-77); also played for Wanderers (1870s); served in Grenadier Guards for 21 years (1867-88); was MP for Newport, Shropshire (1886 until his death); elected a Privy Councillor (1904); also played cricket and was a member of the MCC committee for eight years.

William Kenyon-Slaney, the first footballer born outside the United Kingdom to represent England in a full international, captained his country in the second international against Scotland in March 1873 and was described as being 'of the greatest service' to his side. He played with élan and dash, and had the pleasure of scoring England's first 'official' international goal in the aforementioned fixture at The Oval 'passing the ball between the goal posts' from a throw-in in the opening minute. He later struck home the decisive third goal after the Scots had pulled back to 2-2. England eventually won 4-2. Served in the Grenadier Guards under the command of Sir Garnet Wolseley, participating in the Battle of Tel el-Kebir during the Arabi Revolt and was decorated for his efforts.

KEOWN, Martin Raymond 1991-2002 ㊸ ②

Born: Oxford, 24 July 1966
Career: Arsenal (apprentice, June 1982, professional, February 1984), Brighton & Hove Albion (loan, February 1985), Aston Villa (£200,000, June 1986), Everton (£750,000, August 1989), Arsenal (£2m, February 1993-May 2004), Leicester City (free, July 2004), Reading (free, January 2005, retired, May 2005); Newbury (coach, season 2005-06), Arsenal (coach, season 2006-07), Oxford University Blues (coach, season 2007-08); became a soccer pundit on BBC TV and also covered Champions League matches for Irish broadcasters.

After a solid, resilient performance on his debut for England in a 2-0 win over France at Wembley in February 1992, central defender Martin Keown scored a spectacular equaliser from distance in his second game to earn a 2-2 draw with Czechoslovakia in Prague a month later and then in his third game, a 0-0 draw with Finland in Helsinki in mid-October, he became the 100th player to captain a full England team.

With an injury to Mark Wright, Keown was subsequently called up into the squad for Euro '92, and played in all three matches.

However, Keown's early ascension to the England team under Graham Taylor did not continue under Terry Venables, who ignored him completely. Keown earned a recall from Glenn Hoddle in 1997, and went to the 1998 World Cup, but did not play. He then became a regular under Kevin Keegan (captaining the side against Finland) and played in two of England's Euro 2000 matches. By the time Sven-Göran Eriksson took over as manager, Keown's age was against him, though he went to the 2002 World Cup, but was once again a non-playing squad member. Keown had played at both U16 and U18 levels for his country and, when at the age of 17, it was learnt that both his parents were Irish, Jack Charlton enquired about his availability to play for the Republic of Ireland but found that he was not eligible due to his underage games.

Keown made almost 800 appearances for his six clubs (586 in the League) in a career which spanned 21 years (1984-2005). He certainly played his best football with Arsenal, drawing up an excellent partnership at the heart of the defence with Tony Adams. He won the Premiership, FA Cup and Charity Shield three times each with the Gunners between 1998 and 2004 and also played in four Youth, one B and eight U21 internationals.

KEVAN, Derek Tennyson ⑭ ⑧

Born: Ripon, 6 March 1935
Died: Birmingham, 4 January 2013
Career: Ripon Secondary Modern School, Harrogate & District Schools, Ripon YMCA, Ripon City (August 1950), Sheffield United (trial, April-May 1951), Bradford Park Avenue (amateur, July 1951, professional, October 1952), West Bromwich Albion (£3,000, April 1953), Chelsea (£50,000, March 1963), Manchester City (£35,000, August 1963), Crystal Palace (free, July 1965), Peterborough United (free, March 1966), Luton Town (free, December 1966), Stockport County (free, March 1967), Macclesfield Town (free, August 1968), Boston United (briefly), Stourbridge (August 1969), Ansells FC/Birmingham (December 1969, retired, June 1975); also played for West Bromwich Albion All Stars (seasons 1972-85, then manager, September 1985-May 1993); employed in West Bromwich Albion's lottery department (1983-84); worked as a licensee (in Birmingham), for a brewery and as a delivery driver; now resides in Castle Bromwich, Birmingham.

Yorkshireman Derek Kevan, a big man with a big heart, was a muscular, weighty centre-forward, nicknamed 'The Tank' who scored on his international debut against Scotland at Wembley in April 1957. After fluffing two easy chances in the first-half, he bravely dived forward to head home the equalizer from Colin Grainger's left-wing cross in the 62nd minute to set up a 2-1 win.

The following year he was on target twice in a 4-0 win over Scotland at Hampden Park and soon afterwards scored the equalizer - and hit both posts - in a 1-1 friendly draw with the USSR in Moscow before netting in his first game in the World Cup against the tough-tackling Russians in Sweden in June 1958 – another fine header from Bryan Douglas's flick-on in the 68th minute. It brought England back into the game at 2-1 and a late Tom Finney penalty salvaged a point in a 2-2 draw. After coming close on two occasions to breaking the deadlock in the 0-0 draw with Brazil in the next game, Kevan then used his bulldozing tactics to disrupt the Austrian defence in the third match in Boras when he struck a late equaliser to earn another 2-2 draw. Soon afterwards, Bobby Robson thought he had won the game but his effort was ruled out after Kevan had been penalized for a foul on the goalkeeper – a challenge which would have been acceptable in the English League (and even today).

Kevan, replacing Jimmy Greaves, missed three gilt-edged scoring opportunities when Mexico were hammered 8-0 at Wembley in May 1961.

Perhaps not the most polished of strikers, nevertheless 'The Tank' gave his all at both club and international level. He had his critics as his bustling style was not viewed with unalloyed approval by the certain members of the media but no one could deny he made his presence felt.

Kevan scored 235 goals in 440 League matches, having, by far, his best spell with West Bromwich Albion for whom he netted 173 times in 291 first-class appearances in ten years.

KIDD, Brian 1969-70 ② ①

Born: Collyhurst, Manchester, 29 May 1949
Career: St Patrick's School (Collyhurst), Manchester Schoolboys, Manchester United (associated schoolboy, December 1963, apprentice, August 1964, professional, June 1966), Arsenal (£110,000, August 1974), Manchester City (£100,000, July 1976), Everton (£150,000, March 1979), Bolton Wanderers (£110,000, May 1980); Atlanta Chiefs/USA (loan, April-August 1981), Fort Lauderdale Strikers/USA (January-February 1982), Minnesota Strikers/USA (May 1984, retired, July 1984); Barrow (manager, August 1984), Swindon Town (coach/assistant-manager, April 1985), Preston North End (coach/assistant-manager, then manager, January-March 1986), Manchester United (junior coach, Director of School of Excellence, May 1988, youth development officer, October 1990, then assistant-manager, 1995), Blackburn Rovers (manager, December 1998-November 1999), Leeds United (Director of Football/ assistant-manager, 2000), England (coach/assistant-manager, season 2003-04), Sheffield United (assistant-manager, seasons 2006-08), Portsmouth (assistant-manager, 2008-09), Manchester City (Academy coach, Technical Advisor, early 2009, then assistant-manager to Roberto Mancini, July 2009, then caretaker-manager, May 2013).

Brian Kidd came to prominence on his 19th birthday in front of almost 100,000 fans at Wembley when he scored in the 1968 European Cup final for Manchester United in their 4-1 extra-time win over Benfica. The strong, hard-running, highly-effective striker subsequently earned his England caps two years later, against Northern Ireland and Ecuador, scoring in a 2-0 win over the latter. He also represented his country at Youth and U23 levels and played for the Football League XI.

Kidd who maintained a healthy goalscoring ratio throughout his career, netted over 300 goals, including 152 in 461 League starts for his major clubs. Manchester United won eight trophies (including the double twice) when Kidd was engaged as a coach and assistant-manager at Old Trafford under Alex Ferguson.

KING, Ledley Brenton 2002-10 ⑳ ②
Born: Bow, London, 12 October 1980
Career: Blessed John Roche RC school (now closed), Senrab FC
(London Sunday League team, seasons 1994-96); also Tower
Hamlets Boys' XI; Tottenham Hotspur (apprentice, July 1996,
professional, July 1998, retired, injured, July 2012; continued to act
as a club ambassador at White Hart Lane).

Injuries have seriously affected Ledley
King's club and international career. The 6ft
2in tall Spurs defender made his England
debut in place of his Spurs team-mate Sol
Campbell in a 2-1 defeat by Italy in March
2002. He was then called up for the friendly
against Portugal in February 2004 when he
had the pleasure of netting his first goal in
a 1-1 draw in Faro. After that he deputised
for John Terry against France in Euro 2004,
man-marking Thierry Henry out of the game and not putting a foot
wrong. Unfortunately a fractured foot put him out of the 2006 World Cup.
King who has occasionally filled in as a holding midfielder, continued
to make the England squad when healthy and fit but he knew he was
perhaps fourth choice in the pecking order behind Terry, Rio Ferdinand
and Matthews Upson. In March 2009, King was given a shock recall
by head coach Fabio Capello for the games against Slovakia and
Ukraine. However, after being assessed by England's medical staff,
he was forced to pull out with a chronic knee condition. At the time
Capello commented: "Without doubt, King is one of the best central
defenders in England. He's a very interesting player - one of the
best centre-backs - but I don't know the future as injuries can ruin a
player's career." Subsequently taken to the 2010 World Cup finals,
King was injured in the first game against the USA. Also capped by
his country at Youth, B and U21 levels, King went on to amass 315
senior appearances for Spurs, scoring 15 goals.

KING, Canon Robert Stuart 1881-82 ①
Born: Leigh-on-Sea, Essex, 4 April 1862
Died: Leigh-on-Sea, 6 March 1950
Career: Felsted School (years 1878-80), Hertford College/Oxford
University (seasons 1881-85), Upton Park (briefly, in 1885), Grimsby
Town (during 1885-86), Essex County (1880s); ordained in 1887, he
was Rector of Leigh-on-Sea from 1892 until shortly before his death.

An excellent half-back, strong in the air, accurate with his passing,
Robert King was composed in everything he did. He gained his only
England cap, along with six other players, in a 13-0 win over Ireland
in Belfast in February 1882, having a hand in two of the goals as
well as striking an upright with a 20 yard toe-poke.

KINGSFORD, Robert Kennett 1873-74 ① ①
Born: Sydenham Hill, Surrey, 23 December 1849
Died: Adelaide, Australia, 14 October 1895
Career: Marlborough College (two years, 1866-68), Old Malburnians
(seasons 1868-72), Wanderers (player, seasons 1872-76, also
secretary from June 1874); Surrey County (1870s); also played cricket
for Surrey; became a law student before immigrating to Australia.

Robert Kingsford scored on his England debut against Scotland
in March 1874 when he 'chested' home an attempted clearance
by goalkeeper Gardner. A mobile forward, he won the FA Cup with
Wanderers in 1873 and the following season was top-scorer in
the country with over 20 goals (in all competitions). He succeeded
Charles Alcock as secretary of Wanderers.

KINGSLEY, Matthew 1900-01 ①
Born: Turton, Lancs, 10 October, 1875
Died: Atherton, Lancs, 27 March 1960
Career: Edworth FC (May 1891), Blackburn Rovers (briefly, winter,
1893), Turton FC (April 1894), Darwen (professional, July 1896),
Newcastle United (£150, April 1898), West Ham United (May 1904),
Queens Park Rangers (June 1905-April 1906); out of football for 18
months; Rochdale (October 1907), Barrow (May 1908, retired, May
1909).

The first Newcastle player to win a full cap Matt Kingsley was a
very efficient goalkeeper, who regularly chose to punch the ball to
safety rather than catch it. It was said that he could fist the ball up
to 40 yards, often setting up an attack. With so many other 'keepers
around at the same time, he made his England debut in a 6-0 win
over Wales on his home ground (St James' Park) in March 1901.
He also represented the Football League on three occasions, was an
international trialist and made over 400 club appearances (at various
levels) between 1895 and 1908, including 189 for Newcastle.

KINSEY, George 1891-96 ④
Born: Burton-on-Trent, Staffs, 20 June 1866
Died: Burton-on-Trent, 10 January 1911
Career: Burton Crusaders (August 1883), Burton Swifts (September
1885), Mitchell St George's/Birmingham (May 1888), Wolverhampton
Wanderers (professional, July 1891), Aston Villa (£500, June 1894),
Derby County (May 1895), Notts County (March 1897), Eastville
Rovers/Bristol (May 1897), Burton Swifts (September 1900), Gresley
Rovers (August 1901), Burton Early Closing (September 1902 when
re-instated as an amateur; retired, May 1906); became a licensee in
Burton-on-Trent.

George Kinsey was a solid left-half who occasionally turned out at
left-back. He played his best football with Wolves, gaining an FA Cup
winner's medal in 1893 and representing England twice, collecting
his first cap against Wales in March 1892 (won 2-0) and his second
versus Scotland in April 1893 (won 5-2). After leaving Molineux he
did reasonably well with Derby with whom he won two more caps
in March 1896, playing behind his club colleague Steve Bloomer
in successive wins over Ireland (2-0) and Wales (9-1). In fact, he
helped set up two of Bloomer's five goals against the Welsh.

KIRCHEN, Alfred John 1936-37 ③ ②
Born: Shouldham, Norfolk, 26 April 1913
Died: Norwich, 18 August 1999
Career: Middleton School/King's Lynn (August 1924), King's Lynn
Schools (season 1926-27), King's Lynn Old Boys (August 1927),
Norfolk County (late 1920s), Shouldham FC (September 1931),
Norwich City (amateur, October 1933, professional, November
1933), Arsenal (£6,000, March 1935, retired, injured, September
1943); served in the RAF as a PT instructor during WW2; Norwich
City (trainer, July 1946-March 1947, later director of club); also
worked as a farmer in Norfolk.

Alf Kirchen won his three caps in the space of a fortnight during
England's Scandinavian tour in May 1937. He scored in emphatic
6-0 and 8-0 wins over Norway and Finland respectively and also
starred in a 4-0 victory over Sweden. A well-built, decidedly quick
outside-right, difficult to knock off the ball, Kirchen gained First
Division and Wartime League Cup and League South Cup winner's
medals with Arsenal whom he served for eight years, scoring 45
goals in 101 first-class appearances and 80 in 113 WW2 matches.

KIRKE-SMITH, Reverend Arnold 1872-73 ①

Born: Ecclesfield, Yorks, 23 April 1850
Died: Boxworth, Cambs, 8 October 1927
Career: Cheltenham College, University College/Oxford (seasons 1871-74), Sheffield FC (season 1874-75); ordained in 1875, he later became Vicar of Biggleswade, Eaton Socon, Somersham and Boxworth, the latter from 1889 until his death, aged 77.

Brought in as a 'late replacement' for England's first international against Scotland in November 1872, Arnold Kirke-Smith was a powerful attacker, 'a magnificent dribbler' who tended to run with his head down and was often criticized for his 'greediness.' He played in the 1873 FA Cup final for Oxford University.
The international jersey worn by Kirke-Smith against the Scots in 1872 was auctioned off in 1998 for £21,275.

KIRKLAND, Christopher Edmund 2006-07 ①

Born: Barwell, Leicester, 2 May 1981
Career: Heathfield School, Leicestershire Schools; trained with Coventry City and Leicester City (during season 1996-97); Blackburn Rovers (trial, April 1997), Coventry City (apprentice, May 1997, professional, May 1998), Liverpool (£6m, August 2000), West Bromwich Albion (loan, June-October 2005), Yeovil Town (loan, one game, 2005), Wigan Athletic (July 2006), Leicester City (loan, December 2010), Doncaster Rovers (loan, October 2011), Sheffield Wednesday (free, May 2012)

Chris Kirkland, 6ft 3ins tall, may well have become England's number one goalkeeper but for a spate of annoying injuries. Very agile, a fine shot-stopper (he was regarded as one of the best in the game in 2005-06), he had already won two youth and eight U21 caps before making his full international debut as a second-half substitute against Greece in August 2006. A League Cup winner with Liverpool in 2003, he reached the milestone of 200 club appearances in 2010, and has expressed a wish to be a fireman after he retires from football.... although a problematic back may prevent this from happening.
When Kirkland was just eleven years old, his father and some family friends placed bets of £100 each at odds of 100/1 that he would play for England before he reached the age of 30. He did just that and the syndicate banked £10,000 each.

KIRTON, William John 1921-22 ①

Born: Newcastle-upon-Tyne, 2 December 1896
Died: Sutton Coldfield, 27 September 1970
Career: Todd's Nook School/North Shields, North Shield Schools, Pandon Temperance (before WW1), Leeds City (professional, May 1919), Aston Villa (£500, October 1919), Coventry City (£1,700, September 1928), Kidderminster Harriers (September-October 1930), Leamington Town (November 1930, retired, July 1931); later ran a newsagent's shop in Kingstanding, Birmingham.

A wonderfully consistent inside-right, Billy Kirton won the FA Cup with Aston Villa in 1920 and scored 59 goals in 261 appearances during his nine years at Villa Park. After a successful international trial, he scored on his England debut when partnering Everton's Sam Chedgzoy in the 1-1 draw with Ireland in Belfast in October 1921. He deserved more caps but missed out because there were so many other talented players around at the same time. A teetotaller and non-smoker, Kirton was also a fine golfer with a handicap of 8.

KNIGHT, Arthur Egerton 1919-20 ①

Born: Godalming, Surrey, 7 September 1887
Died: Portsmouth, 10 March 1956
Career: King Edward VI Grammar School/Guildford, Guildford Schools, Godalming FC (seasons 1903-08), Portsmouth (August 1908-20); also represented Corinthians (seasons 1921-31) and Surrey (1920s); played cricket for Hampshire; was a captain in the 6th Hampshire Territorials during WW1; worked for a Portsmouth-based wine company for many years.

An amateur throughout his career, tough-tackling left-back Arthur Knight gained 30 caps as a non-professional between 1910 and 1923. He helped Great Britain win the Olympic gold medal at soccer in 1912 and Portsmouth lift the Southern League championship in 1920. He was registered with Pompey for 12 years and made 219 first team appearances. He stepped in for the injured Jesse Pennington for his only senior game for England, partnering the great Bob Crompton in the 1-1 draw with Ireland in Belfast in October 1919. A fine cricketer, Knight spent 10 years with Hampshire.

KNIGHT, Zatyiah 2004-05 ②

Born: Solihull, 2 May 1980
Career: Rushall Olympic (August 1996), West Bromwich Albion (trial, April-May 1998), Fulham (professional, February 1999), Peterborough United (loan, February-May 2000), Aston Villa (£4m, August 2007), Bolton Wanderers (July 2009)

Capped four times at U21 level, Zat Knight made his full international debut in the 2-1 friendly win against the USA in Chicago in May 2005 when he came on as a second-half substitute for Sol Campbell. He was, at the time, the tallest outfield player ever to appear for England at 6ft 6ins. He amassed 181 senior appearances for Fulham before his transfer to Villa Park.

KNOWLES, Cyril Barry 1967-68 ④

Born: Fitzwilliam, Yorkshire, 13 July 1944
Died: Middlesbrough, Cleveland, 31 August 1991
Career: South Emshall Schools, Manchester United (schoolboy forms, June 1959), Hemsworth FC (season 1959-60), Blackpool (trial, April 1961), Wolverhampton Wanderers (trial, July-August 1961), Middlesbrough (professional, October 1962), Tottenham Hotspur (May 1964, retired, May 1976); Hertford Town (manager, seasons 1976-77); also acted as Spurs scout in Yorkshire; Doncaster Rovers (coach, August 1977), Middlesbrough (coach, July 1981, assistant-manager, February 1982), Darlington (manager), Torquay United (manager, May 1983-March 1987), Torquay United (manager, June 1987-October 1989), Hartlepool United (manager, December 1989-June 1991)

Right-back Cyril Knowles made his England debut in a 2-2 draw with the USSR on a snow covered pitch at Wembley in November 1967. He had a good game in difficult conditions but with George Cohen, Keith Newton and Ray Wilson seemingly ahead of him in the selection poll, he was only called up three more times, for the European Championship qualifier against Spain and the friendlies against Sweden and West Germany at the end of that season.
  Tall, long legged, strong and dependable, Knowles, who actually started out as a left-winger, loved to overlap and he helped Spurs win the FA Cup in 1967, the League Cup in 1971 and the UEFA Cup a year later. The success of a TV advert for bread led to him gaining the catchphrase 'Nice One Cyril.' He made 546 club appearances (507 for Spurs) before retiring to go into management, taking charge of clubs on a low budget. Sadly Knowles died from a brain tumour at the age of 47. His brother, Peter, played for Wolves and later became a Jehovah's Witness.

KONCHESKY, Paul Martyn 1962-05 (2)

Born: Barking, Essex, 15 May 1981
Career: Charlton Athletic (apprentice, June 1996, professional, May 1998), Tottenham Hotspur (loan, September-December 2003), West Ham United (£1.5m, July 2005), Fulham (£2m, July 2007), Liverpool (£3.5m, August 2010), Nottingham Forest (loan, January 2011 for 93 days), Leicester City (£1.5m, July 2011).

Shaven-haired left-back Paul Konchesky, then of Fulham, made his England debut as a second-half substitute in that shocker of a friendly when Australia beat England 3-1 at Upton Park in February 2003.... being one of 22 players used by Sven-Göran Eriksson. He then featured as a 'sub' in another friendly against Argentina a couple of years later. That was it. Konchesky, who played in four Youth and 15 U21 internationals, loves to attack down the wing and when given the chance can deliver a telling cross as well as fire in a bullet shot. He reached the personal milestone of 400 club appearances in 2011 and he held the record for being the youngest-ever debutant for Charlton until Jonjo Shelvey came along in April 2008.

LABONE, Brian Leslie 1962-70 (26)

Born: Liverpool, 23 January 1940
Died: Liverpool, 26 April 2005
Career: Liverpool Collegiate School, Everton (amateur, June 1955, professional, July 1957, retired, June 1972); went into the insurance business, later worked in Everton's commercial department (mid-1970s).

Taking over from Tottenham's Maurice Norman, centre-half Brian Labone made his England debut against Northern Ireland in October 1962. Over the eight years he added a further 25 caps to his tally, producing several outstanding performances at the heart of the defence. He did, however, have the misfortune to score a late 'own goal' to hand West Germany a 1-0 win in Hanover in June 1968, deflecting Franz Beckenbauer's 82nd minute shot past 'keeper Gordon Banks.
    A legend in the blue shirt of Everton, centre-half Labone was a one-club footballer. Though predominantly right-footed, he was a rugged tackler who surprisingly withdrew from Alf Ramsey's World Cup squad in 1966 because of his impending marriage. He played in three of the four games in the 1970 tournament in Mexico.
    Twice a League championship winner in 1963 and 1970, he also helped Everton win the FA Cup in 1966 and during his 15 years at Goodison Park, he appeared in 534 first-class games and scored two goals. Labone, who was described by his club manager Harry Catterick as 'the last of the great Corinthians' died suddenly outside his home in 2005 after returning from a fans' awards dinner.

LAMPARD, Frank James 1999-2013 (97) (29)

Born: Romford, Essex, 20 June 1978
Career: West Ham United (apprentice, June 1994, professional, July 1995), Swansea City (loan, October-November 1995), Chelsea (£11m, July 2001).

In October 1999, Frank Lampard junior followed in the footsteps of his father, Frank senior (opposite page) by representing England in a full international. He was selected for the friendly with Belgium at Sunderland and played well before being substituted in the second-half by Dennis Wise in a 2-0 win.
    With stamina, passing ability, brilliantly-timed forward runs and a goalscoring technique, Lampard is regarded by some as the 'complete midfield player.' He has been a regular in the England team over the last six years, forming an excellent partnership with Steven Gerrard.
    First selected for England by manager Peter Taylor, Lampard made

Frank Lampard

his debut in the U21 international against Greece in November 1997. He went on to win 19 caps at this level, and scored nine goals, a total bettered only by Alan Shearer and Francis Jeffers.

He had to wait almost four years before scoring his first senior goal, in a 3-1 win over Croatia in August 2003. Overlooked for Euro 2000 and the 2002 World Cup, he had to wait until Euro 2004 to participate in his first major international competition. England reached the quarter-finals with Lampard netting three times in four matches, equalising in the 112th minute against Portugal, only for England to lose on penalties. After his excellent performances in that competition, he was duly named in the team of the tournament by UEFA.

A regular in the squad since Paul Scholes' retirement from international football, Lampard was voted England's 'Player of the Year' in 2004 and 2005 and though he played every minute of his country's 2006 World Cup matches, he failed to get on the scoresheet. Surprisingly he was booed by the fans when he came on as a second-half substitute during the Euro 2008 qualifier against Estonia in October 2007. Thankfully, he shrugged that off and at long last, finally found his scoring boots again by netting his first international goal for two years in a 4-0 win over Slovakia in March 2009. This goal, in fact, was the 500th scored by England at Wembley. Six months later he struck twice in a 5-1 win over Croatia which secured a place at World Cup 2010. Unfortunately at the finals in South Africa, neither Lampard nor England played well, although 'Lamps' did have a 'goal' disallowed against Germany!

Named captain of his country for the first time for the friendly with Denmark in February 2011, Lampard had played very well before being replaced by Scott Parker halfway through the second-half of a 2-1 win.

Later appointed captain of his country, he scored a 'six-inch' headed winner against the reigning European and World champions Spain at Wembley in November 2011. Unfortunately injury ruled him out of the Euro 2012 tournament – and England certainly missed him! He has since added to his tally of caps and his now in sight of his 100th senior international appearance.

As a club footballer, Lampard has now netted 243 goals in 804 appearances, including 38 in 186 outings for his first club, West Ham and a record 203 in 608 games for Chelsea.

In March 2010, he weighed in with the first four-timer of his career, helping Chelsea whip Aston Villa 7-1 in a home Premiership game.

Since his big-money transfer to Stamford Bridge, he has so far helped Chelsea win thirteen trophies in 12 years - three Premiership, the Champions League, four FA Cups, two League Cups, the Europa League and two Charity Shields. His uncle is Harry Redknapp, the current manager of QPR.

LAMPARD, Frank Richard George 1972-80 ②

Born: East Ham, London, 20 September 1948
Career: East London Schools, West Ham United (juniors, then professional, September 1965, Southend United (August 1985, retired, May 1986); West Ham United (assistant-manager, June 1994-May 2001, serving under Harry Redknapp, his brother-in-law); out of the game for a while, returning in 2008, as football consultant at Watford, later holding the same position with Reading (both jobs under manager Brendan Rogers).

A resilient, hard-tackling and resourceful left-back, Frank Lampard made his England debut under manager Alf Ramsey in the 1-1 draw with Yugoslavia in October 1972, taking over from the injured Emlyn Hughes. However, he had to wait eight years before collecting his second cap, in a 2-1 friendly win against Australia in Sydney. Lampard also represented his country at Youth and U23 levels, gaining four caps in the latter category. Regarded as being one of the greatest players in West Ham's history, he made 665 senior appearances for the club in 18 years (1967-85), gaining two FA Cup

winner's medals and helping the Hammers win the Second Division championship in 1981. On leaving Upton Park, Lampard teamed up with his former playing colleague Bobby Moore who was manager at Southend. Lampard is, of course, the father of Frank junior (left).

LANGLEY, Ernest James 1957-58 ③

Born: Kilburn, London, 7 February 1929
Died: Yiewsley, Hillingdon, 9 December 2007
Career: Evelyn's Senior School Kilburn, Yiewsley (August 1943), Hounslow Town (May 1944), Uxbridge (August 1945), Hayes (June 1946), Brentford (signed amateur forms, August 1946), Ruislip (briefly, January 1947), Guildford City (July 1947), Leeds United (professional, June 1952), Brighton & Hove Albion (July 1953), Fulham (February 1957), Queens Park Rangers (June 1965), Hillingdon Borough (player-manager, September 1967, retired May 1971); Crystal Palace (trainer/coach, August 1971), Hillingdon Borough (club administrator, seasons 1973-76), Dulwich Hamlet (manager, January-May 1977).

Replacing Roger Byrne (sadly killed in the Munich air crash) Jim Langley was a nimble, yet rugged left-back who made a commendable debut in England's 4-0 win over Scotland at Hampden Park in April 1958, but eighteen days later he missed a penalty in a 2-1 win over Portugal at Wembley…the fourth spot-kick miss in a row at the Empire Stadium. Despite this, he still kept his place as Don Howe's partner for a third game against Yugoslavia a month before the start of the World Cup. Unfortunately Langley was teased and tormented all through that game by winger Petacavic as England lost 5-0 in Belgrade. His international career ended there and then as Bolton's Tommy Banks replaced him in the squad for Sweden. He also played in three B internationals and also represented the Football League.

A League Cup and Third Division championship winner with QPR in 1967, Langley made 650 appearances at club level, spending his best years with Fulham (356 outings: 1956-65). In 1965 he became only the second full-back to score 50 or more League goals.

LANGTON, Robert 1946-51 ⑪ ①

Born: Burscough, Lancs, 8 September 1918
Died: Wisbech, 15 December 1996
Career: Burscough Victoria (September 1933), Blackburn Rovers (amateur, September 1938, professional, November 1938), Preston North End (£10,000, August 1948), Bolton Wanderers (£22,500, November 1949), Blackburn Rovers (£2,500, September 1953), Glentoran (guest, 1955), Ards (June 1956), Wisbech Town (July 1957), Kidderminster Harriers (July 1959), Wisbech Town (player-coach, October-December 1959), Colwyn Bay (October 1960-May 1962); King's Lynn (trainer-coach, July 1962-May 1963), Wisbech Town (coach, July 1963-April 1968), Burscough Rangers (manager, May 1968-June 1970); also represented the Army while on national service in India; was a licensee in Wisbech, initially from October 1961.

A speedy, clever left-winger with a strong shot, Bobby Langton came into great prominence in season 1946-47 when he was capped against Ireland, the Republic of Ireland, Wales, Holland and France, scoring on his debut in a resounding 7-2 win over Ireland when he also had a hand in three of the other six goals.

Unfortunate in the respect that Tom Finney was the regular No. 11 in the England team, Langton missed out on the 1950 World Cup in Brazil, Jimmy Mullen of Wolves joining Finney and Stan Matthews as the named wingers.

A Second Division championship winner with Blackburn in 1939, Langton also played in the 1953 FA Cup final for Bolton v. Blackpool and represented England in four B internationals and played for the Football League. He scored over 90 goals in 425 appearances during his professional career: 1938-57.

LATCHFORD, Robert Dennis 1977-79 ⑫ ⑤

Born: King's Heath, Birmingham, 18 January 1951
Career: Brandwood Secondary School, South Birmingham &
Warwickshire Schools, Birmingham City (apprentice, May 1967,
professional, August 1968), Everton (£350,000, February 1974 in
a deal involving Howard Kendall and Archie Styles both of whom
moved to St Andrew's), Swansea City (£125,000, July 1981),
NAC Breda/Holland (February 1984), Coventry City (June 1984),
Lincoln City (July 1985), Newport County (loan, January-May 1986),
Merthyr Tydfil (August 1986, retired May 1987); became a director
of Alvechurch FC (late 1980s); Birmingham City (Football in the
Community Officer 1996-99, club coach season 1999-2000);
now lives in Germany with his family; makes regular trips back to
England to speak on the after-dinner circuit

Everton's burly striker Bob Latchford was substituted in the second-
half of his England debut in a 2-0 World Cup qualifying win over
Italy at Wembley in November 1977. Left out for the next game
by manager Ron Greenwood against West Germany, he scored in
his third international when Wales were defeated 3-1 and soon
afterwards he netted a 'disputed' goal which helped England beat
Denmark 4-3 in a European Championship qualifier in Copenhagen
in September 1978.

A month later, Latchford scored with a smart header in the 1-1
draw with the Republic of Ireland in Dublin and in February 1979 he
netted twice when Northern Ireland got blitzed 4-0 at Wembley.

Overall his strike record for his country was very good but he
struggled at times against better opposition and after failing to find
the net in any of his last five internationals he was not chosen after
June 1979.

Also capped at Youth and U23 levels, Latchford helped
Birmingham gain promotion to the First Division in 1972 and won
the Welsh Cup with both Swansea (twice) and Merthyr Tydfil. He hit
84 goals in 194 games for Birmingham and 138 in 289 outings for
Everton, earning himself £10,000 from the *Daily Express* for scoring
30 in the League in 1978-79, when he was also the First Division's
top marksman.

His two brothers, Dave and Peter, both goalkeepers, played for
Blues, and West Bromwich Albion and Celtic respectively.

LATHERON, Edwin Gladstone 1912-14 ② ①

Born: Grangetown, Yorkshire, 22 December 1887
Died: Passchendaele, Belgium, 14 October 1917
Career: South Bank Corinthians (August 1902), Grangetown Athletic
(June 1904), Blackburn Rovers (professional, March 1906-October
1917); also Blackpool (WW1 guest)

Eddie Latheron was a First Division championship winner with
Blackburn in 1912 and 1914 and during that time was regarded
by many as the one of the finest inside-lefts in the country. Blessed
with wonderful ball control, he created chances aplenty for his
team-mates and found ample time to score himself, netting 120
goals in 303 appearances during his years at Ewood Park: 1906-
17. He was also on target when he made his England debut. Playing
alongside his Blackburn team-mate Joe Hodkinson he starred in
a 4-3 win over Wales in Bristol in March 1913. Unfortunately, he
missed two clear chances in his second game a year later when
Ireland won 3-0 at Middlesbrough. Joe Smith of Bolton seemed to
have the edge on him in respect of England calls. Latheron was
killed at the Battle of Passchendaele while serving as a gunner with
the Royal Field Artillery. He was just 29 years of age.

LAWLER, Christopher 1970-72 ④ ①

Born: Liverpool, 20 October 1943
Career: Liverpool & District Schools, Liverpool (amateur, May 1959,
professional, October 1960), Portsmouth (free, October 1975),
Stockport County (free, August 1977), Bangor City (July 1978-May
1980); coached in Norway (from October 1980), Wigan Athletic
(assistant-manager/coach, October 1981-May 1983), Liverpool
(reserve team coach, July 1983-June 1985, later engaged as a
local scout); also worked in Skelmersdale, coaching young children.

A former Schoolboy international, right-back Chris Lawler decorated
his England debut with a spectacular long-range goal from fully 30
yards in the 5-0 win over Malta at Wembley in May 1971. But with
Paul Madeley and then Mick Mills ahead of him in the selection
stakes, the Liverpool star added only three more caps to his tally,
his last coming against Switzerland in a European Championship
qualifier in October 1971.

Tall, strong in the tackle and quick over the ground, Lawler scored
a remarkable number of goals for a defender, total 64, with 61
coming in 549 senior appearances for Liverpool whom he served for
16 years: 1959-75. One of the greatest full-backs in the Merseyside
club's history, Lawler helped the Reds win the FA Cup, UEFA Cup and
two First Division championships, and he also represented his country
at Youth and U23 levels and played twice for the Football League.

LAWTON, Thomas 1938-49 ㉓ ㉒

Born: Moses Gate, Bolton, 6 October 1919
Died: Nottingham, 6 November 1996
Career: Tonge Moor Council, Castle Hill & Faulds Road Schools/Bolton,
Bolton Schools, Lancashire Boys, Hayes Athletic (season 1932-33),
Rossendale United (amateur, season 1933-34), Bolton Wanderers
(amateur, August 1934), Sheffield Wednesday (amateur, September
1934), Burnley (amateur, May 1935, professional, October 1935),
Everton (£6,500, December 1936); joined Army (January 1940);
Wartime guest for Tranmere Rovers (December 1940) and Greenock
Morton (January 1941); Chelsea (£11,500, November 1945), Notts
County (record £20,000, November 1947 - Bill Dickson, valued at
£2,500, moved to Stamford Bridge in same deal), Brentford (£12,000,
March 1952, appointed player-manager, January 1953), Arsenal
(£10,000 plus Jimmy Robertson, September 1953), Kettering Town
(£1,000 as player-manager, February 1956), Notts County (manager,
May 1957-July 1958), licensee of Magna Charta Inn, Lowdham, Notts
(October 1958-October 1962); Wolverhampton Wanderers (part-time
scout, briefly in 1963), Kettering Town (manager, October 1963-April
1964; then club director to October 1968), Notts County (coach and
chief scout, October 1968-April 1970); also played cricket for Burnley
(Lancashire League); columnist for *Nottingham Evening Post* (1985-96).

In their book *The Essential History of England* writers Andrew
Mourant and Jack Rollin wrote: 'Lawton combined brawn and
delicacy; one moment a blood-and-thunder centre-forward, the next
executing some manoeuvre of wit and subtlety.' 'He was' said one
contemporary, 'the lightest mover of any big man who ever played
football.' Another wrote: 'Everything about him was a threat: from his
coolness, to the jut of his head on a muscular neck that could flick a
heavy ball into goal like a stone from a catapult.'

Tommy Lawton was a dynamic centre-forward, six feet tall, blessed
with a wonderful physique who could head a ball as powerfully as
some players could kick one. Indeed, he was unrivalled in the air,
having an elastic neck which he seemed to stretch in all directions to
get to the ball. He also had a short back-swing for his shooting which
he did with authority and direction. If the ball was in the goalmouth he
would get it. He had marvellous timing in his preferred right foot and

England colleague Stanley Matthews said: "Tommy Lawton possessed a rocket of a shot and, like all great players, could hit the ball equally well with either foot. He was lethal in the air and, most surprisingly for a centre-forward of the time, had all the ball skill and creative prowess of the most mercurial of inside-forwards. He was a goal-getter, a towering athlete with a seemingly elasticated neck that enabled him to rise that inch or so above defenders, which he did often to devastating effect. With his shirt unbuttoned so that it appeared to be sliding off his shoulders, a sharp flint-like face, hair greased back to form a black V off his forehead and long stringy legs protruding from his baggy shorts, he cut an unmistakable figure on the pitch. He knew a centre-forward was expected to run through a brick outhouse if need be and he never shirked from his responsibilities. His dominance in the air was unsurpassed and he would often hurl himself at the opposing goalkeeper and centre-half when the odds were against him winning the ball. If he didn't win the ball, neither did the goalkeeper. What resulted was a scramble in the goalmouth between him and the defenders, reminding me of the scrummage to get on the last tram of the night."

Fellow international Wilf Mannion recalled: "I cannot recall any centre half who could keep him in check in his international days. He was the complete centre forward who made goals and scored them with monotonous regularity. With his head or with his feet, they came all the same."

And Blackpool's ace striker Stan Mortensen stated: "At his very best, he was only a fraction behind Ted Drake in my estimation. With his tremendous shooting power and wonderful knack of heading the ball from a high centre, he was marvellously equipped for the job of leading a forward line. I have heard people say that he was lucky, and that success came easily to him. They forget those hours of practice; the heart-breaking days when the shots wouldn't connect; the hard labour of striving to make his left foot do the job which nature thought should be done with the right."

the only player who could match him for this technique was Stoke's Freddie Steele.

He scored virtually a goal a game for England, starting off with one in each of his first six internationals, including the winner against Scotland in Glasgow in April 1939 when, with just two minutes remaining, he rose majestically to send a crashing header past Jimmy Dawson from Stan Matthews' terrific cross.

He struck a four-timer (which might have been six) in an 8-2 win over Holland on a rain-soaked pitch at Huddersfield in November 1946. After this game, the Dutch FA President, Karel Lotsy told Lawton: "You are the world's greatest centre-forward."

Lawton netted another four-timer, which could and should have been a six pack, in a 10-0 romp over Portugal in Lisbon in May 1947. In fact, his first goal in this game was scored after just 17 seconds - the fastest-ever by an England player. After his 23rd and final game for his country (a 0-0 draw with Denmark in September 1948) Lawton, in his own words, said "I had a stinker, was dropped and never chosen again. I deserved it."

Lawton bagged another 24 goals in 23 Wartime internationals, striking a hat-trick in a 5-4 defeat by Scotland in April 1942 and a four-timer (including a first-half hat-trick in 10 minutes) in an 8-0 thumping of Scotland at Maine Road in October 1945. He also appeared in two unofficial games against Switzerland in Berne and Zurich in July 1945, represented the Football League on three occasions (scoring four goals in an 8-1 win over the Irish League in Belfast in September 1938) and won the Third Division (South) title with Notts County. His professional club career spanned 20 years (1936-56) during which time he scored 235 goals in 383 League games. He was certainly one of the greatest strikers of his era – despite having flat feet!

LE SAUX, Graeme Pierre 1993-2001 ㊱ ①

Born: St Helier, Jersey, 17 October 1968
Career: St Paul's FC/Jersey (August 1984), Chelsea (professional, September 1986), Blackburn Rovers (£750,000, March 1993), Chelsea (£5m, August 1997), Southampton (£500,000, plus Wayne Bridge, July 2003, retired, injured, May 2005); became a soccer pundit on TV and radio and also participated in TV reality programmes.

Left wing-back Graeme Le Saux didn't score too many goals during his career but the one he netted for England was superb – a crashing volley against the reigning World champions Brazil in a 3-1 defeat at Wembley in June 1995. Small and stocky with good speed over 20-30 yards, he made his international debut at senior level against Denmark in March 1994. After being sidelined for a year with a broken ankle and ruptured tendons, he came back strongly and was always in the reckoning despite there being some very useful players challenging for the same position, among them Stuart Pearce and Phil Neville. In 1998, after an excellent World Cup, he was rated 'so good' that the likes of Barcelona and Juventus were chasing his signature but in the end he remained in England and went on to amass a fine club record of 586 appearances (36 goals). He helped Blackburn win the Premiership in 1995.

LE TISSIER, Matthew Paul 1993-97 (8)

Born: St Peter Port, Guernsey, 14 October 1968
Career: Vale Recreation FC/Guernsey, Southampton (apprentice, October 1986, professional, April 1987, retired, May 2002); later engaged as an ambassador at St Mary's (Southampton FC); also match summariser/reporter for Sky Sports. Appointed president of Guernsey FC in 2011 for whom he played a few games in April-May 2013.

Despite scoring a hat-trick in a B international against Russia, Matt Le Tissier did not make the full England squad for the 1996 European Championships, nor did he figure in the 1998 World Cup. He failed to reproduce his club form in the six internationals prior to Euro '96 and realistically was never a strong contender to travel to France in 1998.

Making his senior debut as a substitute against Denmark at Wembley in March 1994 (won 1-0), his first start followed seven months later in the 1-1 draw with Romania. He actually came on as a 'sub' five times in his England career. A one club man, Le Tissier scored 210 goals (some of them with spectacular long range shots) in 540 appearances for Southampton: 1986-2001. He also had the pleasure of scoring the last-ever goal at Saints' old ground at The Dell.

LEACH, Thomas 1930-31 (2)

Born: Wincobank near Sheffield, 23 September 1903
Died: Sheffield, 20 July 1970
Career: Wath Athletic (July 1924), Sheffield Wednesday (professional, October 1925), Newcastle United (£1,000, June 1934), Stockport County (£300, June 1936), Carlisle United (February 1937), Lincoln City (September 1938, retired, May 1939).

Initially a forward, Tom Leach developed into a very efficient centre-half, his lithe physique being a distinctive factor in his defensive play. Twice a League championship winner with Sheffield Wednesday, he also helped Stockport lift the Third Division (North) title and during his professional career (1926-39) he appeared in well over 300 club matches. He gained two England caps as an 'Owl' in 'big wins' over Ireland (5-1) and Wales (4-0) in October and November 1930. Taking over from Webster of Middlesbrough, he played alongside his Hillsborough defensive clubmates Blenkinsopp and Strange and produced two excellent performances.

LEAKE, Alexander 1903-05 (5)

Born: Small Heath, Birmingham, 11 July 1871
Died: Harborne, Birmingham, 29 March 1938
Career: Jenkins Street & Little Green Lane Schools/Bordesley Green, Hoskins & Sewell FC (season 1887-88), King's Heath Albion (seasons 1888-91), Saltley Gas Works FC (August 1891), Singers FC/Coventry (briefly, April 1893), Old Hill Wanderers (1893), Small Heath Alliance (July 1894), Aston Villa (June 1902), Burnley (December 1907-May 1910), Wednesbury Old Athletic (July 1910, retired, May 1912), Crystal Palace (trainer-coach, July 1912-May 1915), Merthyr Town (trainer-coach, October 1919-July 1920), Walsall (trainer, September 1932-May 1933); was a blacksmith by trade.

An FA Cup winner with Aston Villa in 1905, Alex Leake was a conformed humorist on and off the field and the dressing room was always a happy place to be when he was around – even in defeat! On the pitch, Leake was equally at home in the centre-half and left-half positions, being safe, sound and solid most of the time. Blessed with tremendous stamina, he always played to the gallery and collected his five England caps between March 1904 and April 1905, making his international debut against Ireland. He was actually selected by England as a 'standby' reserve at the age of 40 when engaged as a player-coach with Crystal Palace.

LEE, Ernest Albert 1903-04 (1)

Born: Bridport, Dorset, 10 May 1879
Died: Southampton, 14 January 1958
Career: Bridport AFC (April 1894), Poole (August 1898), Southampton (July 1900), Dundee (May 1906), Southampton (player-trainer, May 1911, retired May 1916, became club trainer, July 1919-May 1935); later helped his son's radio business as a salesman.

A 'dashing' right-half, full of energy and commitment, Ernie Lee was a fine player who won three Southern League Championship medals with Southampton and helped Dundee lift the Scottish Cup in 1910. He gained his only England cap against Wales in February 1904, when he deputised for Harry Johnson (Sheffield United) in a 2-2 draw at Wrexham.

LEE, Francis Henry 1968-72 (27) (10)

Born: Westhoughton near Bolton, Lancs, 29 April 1944
Career: Lancashire Schools, Bolton Wanderers (amateur, July 1959, professional, May 1961), Manchester City (£60,000, October 1967), Derby County (£110,000, August 1974, retired, May 1976); became a millionaire via the paper business and also a successful racehorse trainer, gaining his National Hunt licence in 1984 and a Flat racing licence in 1987; served as Manchester City's Chairman (February 1994-January 1998)

Francis Lee was 16 years old when he made his League debut for Bolton Wanderers (alongside Nat Lofthouse) in November 1960. Bubbly and diminutive, Lee was a 'real livewire' whether it was down the right flank or directly through the middle, who was much-admired by England boss Alf Ramsey. An effervescent character, stocky, well-built, confident on the ball with a booming right foot shot, he had a direct approach, gave defenders plenty to think about and won penalties by whatever means possible! He was once accused by Norman Hunter (Leeds United) of diving to earn a penalty in a League match in 1975 and it resulted in the two of them engaging in a notorious fist fight.

But his conversion rate from the spot was near perfect...once awarded a penalty, he often found the net, although he did miss two 12-yard kicks playing for England! In fact, in 1971-72, Lee scored a record 15 penalties for Manchester City (13 in the League), with whom he won First Division, FA Cup and League Cup winner's medals. He then went on to gain a second League Championship medal with Derby. For his three clubs, Lee amassed a total of 622 appearances and scored 284 goals, including 148 in 329 games for Manchester City.

Lee made his England debut, alongside his Manchester City team-mate Colin Bell, in the 1-1 draw with Bulgaria in December 1968. He actually netted three times in his first six internationals, which all ended in wins (v. Northern Ireland, Wales and Uruguay) but after Astle had been fouled, he missed from the spot in the 1-0 win over Portugal.

Nevertheless, he had made a fine start to his international career, but Ramsey was quickly on the scene, and although praising him for his efforts, he told Lee that he risked being dropped, like everyone else, if things went to 'his head.'

After scoring in a 2-0 warm-up win over Ecuador in Quito, Lee played in the 1970 World Cup in Mexico and in the opening game received some vicious attention from rugged Romanian defender Mocanu which went unpunished. In the third group game against Brazil, he should have equalised - if he had been more alert when a diving header from Hurst dropped to him near the far post in the 78th minute. And then in the quarter-final defeat by West Germany, Ramsey should have played him on the left instead of the right, and he never really figured, being marked out of it by Schnellinger.

Besides his games for England, Lee also played for his country at Youth team level, represented the Football League and starred for a United Kingdom XI in 1969.

After retiring from football, Lee became a successful businessman and millionaire…by running his paper recycling business - F.H. Lee Ltd. He also became a racehorse trainer, over the sticks and on the flat before becoming a major shareholder and then Chairman of his former club Manchester City, stepping down after four years.

LEE, John 1950-51 ① ①

Born: Sileby, Leics, 4 November 1920
Died: Rugby, Warwickshire, 15 January 1995
Career: Quorn Methodists FC (April 1937), Leicester City (professional, December 1940), Derby County (June 1950), Coventry City (November 1954, retired, May 1955); played County cricket for Leicestershire in 1947.

A two-footed inside-right or centre-forward, with strong shot, Jack Lee's career was plagued by injury and he also lost six years of his time due to WW2. He played in the 1949 FA Cup final for Leicester but was forced to retire in 1955. He scored in his only game for England, in a 4-1 win over Northern Ireland in Belfast in October 1950 when he played up front alongside Blackpool's Stan Mortensen.

LEE, Robert Martin 1994-99 ㉑ ②

Born: West Ham, London, 1 February 1966
Career: Hornchurch (April 1981), Charlton Athletic (trial, May 1982, signed as a professional, July 1983), Newcastle United (£700,000, September 1992), Derby County (£250,000, February 2002), West Ham United (August 2003), Oldham Athletic (briefly, one game in 2004), Wycombe Wanderers (March 2005, retired June 2006); became a TV pundit on Singapore's football channel.

Midfielder Rob Lee's equalizing goal on his England debut salvaged a 1-1 draw against Romania at Wembley in December 1994. His second goal came in his 10th international, a 2-1 win over South Africa at Old Trafford in May 1997. An efficient, hard-working midfielder, his centre-field partners in international matches included Paul Ince, David Platt, Paul Gascoigne, Paul Scholes and David Batty, and he always gave a competent performance. Unfortunately along with Les Ferdinand, he missed from the spot in the penalty shoot-out defeat by Belgium in the King Hassan II Cup in Casablanca in May 1998.

Lee – nicknamed 'Lurker' – scored a total of 123 goals in 837 club appearances, including 65 in 343 outings for Charlton and 56 in 381 games for Newcastle, whom he helped gain promotion to the Premiership under manager Kevin Keegan.

LEE, Samuel 1982-86 ⑭ ②

Born: Liverpool, 7 February 1959
Career: Liverpool (apprentice, May 1972, professional, April 1976), Queens Park Rangers (£200,000, August 1986), FC Osasuna/Spain (£200,000, June 1987), Southampton (free, January 1990), Bolton Wanderers (free, October 1990, retired, May 1991); Liverpool (coach, July 1992), England (senior coach, July 2004), Bolton Wanderers (assistant-manager/coach, June 2005, manager, April-October 2007), Liverpool (assistant-manager/coach, May 2008-June 2011).

Midfielder Sammy Lee appeared in 295 first-class matches and scored 19 goals in his 11 years as a player at Anfield (1975-86), helping Liverpool win three League titles, the League Cup four times and the European Cup. Blessed with a terrific engine that never over-heated, at times he looked just as fresh at the end of a game as he did at the start. A manager's dream, Lee gave nothing less than 100 per cent each and every time he took the field and scored with a scorching free-kick in the first of his 14 outings for England in a European Championship qualifier against Greece in November

1982. His second goal came in another 3-0 victory, this time over Hungary in 1983. 'Little Sammy' who also gained Youth and U21 honours, became a respected coach, especially at Anfield.

LEIGHTON, John Edward 1885-86 ①

Born: Nottingham, 26 March 1865
Died: Nottingham, 15 April 1944
Career: Nottinghamshire schools football, Nottingham Forest (seasons 1884-88); also played for Corinthians (seasons 1885-89); was a wholesale stationer and paper merchant in Nottingham

A leading outside-right of the 1880s, Ted Leighton was fast, clever and industrious but for all his efforts gained only one England cap – lining up against Ireland in Belfast in March 1886, having a hand in two of Ben Spilsbury's four goals.

A passionate supporter of Forest, he died watching his favourite club against Northampton Town in a wartime Regional League game at The City Ground in 1944.

LENNON, Aaron Justin 2006-13 ㉑

Born: Chapeltown, Leeds, 16 April 1987
Career: Boston Spa School, Leeds United (Academy, June 2001, apprentice, June 2003), Tottenham Hotspur (£1m, July 2005)

Blessed with pace and trickery, Aaron Lennon can beat his man on the outside but occasionally ruins all his good work with a poor cross. He certainly gives England width and was in good form in the 2008 European Championships. Injuries, however, disrupted his form in 2009-10 yet he was still named in Fabio Capello's squad for the World Cup finals in South Africa. Honoured for the first time at senior level as a second-half substitute in the 6-0 win over Jamaica in June 2006, he has also two B and five U21 caps to his credit. Lennon began his professional career at Elland Road and was the youngest player ever to appear in the Premier League at the age of 16 years and 129 days, when he came off the bench for Leeds against his future club Tottenham Hotspur in a 2-1 defeat at White Hart Lane in August 2003. Lennon's family is of Irish, English and Jamaican descent.

LESCOTT, Joleon Patrick 2007-13 ㉖ ①

Born: Quinton, Birmingham, 16 August 1982
Career: Four Dwellings High School/Birmingham, Wolverhampton Wanderers (apprentice, June 1998, professional, August 1999), Everton (£5m, June 2006), Manchester City (£23m, August 2009)

Capped twice by England at U21 level, versatile defender Joleon Lescott was given his senior international debut in a 3-0 win over Estonia in October 2007, replacing Rio Ferdinand at half-time. His second cap - and his first start - followed in the Euro 2008 qualifier against Russia, which England lost 2-1. However, with John Terry, Matthew Upson and Ferdinand always seemingly ahead of him in the selection stakes, Lescott bided his time and even when Gary Cahill came on the scene, he still remained a vital member of the senior squad, taking his tally of full caps past the 25 mark.

Unfortunately Lescott does have the temptation to go long and waste possession, but he's a sturdy, resolute defender who gives very little away... He made 235 appearances for Wolves and 142 for Everton before moving to Manchester City in the summer of 2009. Injury ruled him out of contention for the 2010 World Cup finals but he was John Terry's defensive partner at Euro 2012, scoring England's first goal of the tournament v. France.

LILLEY, Henry Edward 1891-92 ①
Born: Sheffield, 6 June 1873
Died: Lincoln, 20 July 1953
Career: Staveley (May 1888), Sheffield United (August 1890), Gainsborough Trinity (July 1904, retired, May 1906).

A well-built, strong-kicking left-back, Harry Lilley made only 65 appearances for the Blades in four years. He gained his only England cap in a 2-0 win over Wales at Wrexham in March 1892 when he deputised for the injured Bob Holmes.

LINACRE, James Henry 1904-05 ②
Born: Ashton-on-Trent, Derbyshire, 20 June 1880
Died: Nottingham, 11 May 1957
Career: Loughborough Grammar School, Ashton-on-Trent FC (May 1895), Draycott Mills (August 1896), Derby County (December 1898), Nottingham Forest (professional, August 1899, retired, injured, May 1909); went into partnership with his brother-in-law Frank Forman as a building contractor in West Bridgford, Nottingham.

A Second Division championship winner with Nottingham Forest in 1907, goalkeeper Jimmy Linacre had a tremendous reach and brilliant reflexes. On his day he was one of the best in the country and made over 300 appearances for Forest but managed only two caps for England, performing well in victories over Wales (3-1) in March 1905 and Scotland (1-0) a month later. At the time England were seeking a replacement for Tom Baddeley and it was 1909 before an adequate replacement was found - Sam Hardy.

LINDLEY, Tinsley, OBE 1885-91 ⑬ ⑭
Born: Nottingham, 27 October 1865
Died: Nottingham, 31 March 1940
Career: Nottingham High School, Leys School, Cambridge University (Caius College, seasons 1884-89); Nottingham Forest (first registered, August 1883, remained as a signed-up player until April 1892); also played for Corinthians (seasons 1885-94), Casuals (1885-86), Notts County (1891), Crusaders (1891), Swifts (briefly) and Preston North End (February 1892); played county cricket for Nottinghamshire (1888) and Cambridge University and rugby for Old Leysians and Notts RUFC; called to the Bar in 1889, he practised on the East Midland circuit and was a Law Lecturer at Nottingham University and also a County Court judge; he was awarded the OBE in 1918 for his work as Chief Officer in the Nottingham Special Constabulary.

One of the greatest forwards of his era, Tinsley Lindley's goal against Scotland at Hampden Park in March 1886 is believed to be one of the 'longest' scored for England at full international level. His 40-yard effort put his side ahead in the 35th minute only for the Scots to hit back and earn a 1-1 draw. This was his third game for his country, having made his debut against Ireland earlier in the month at the age of 19, followed by an outing against Wales. In February 1887 he bagged a hat-trick in a 7-0 win over the Irish at Bramall Lane, Sheffield, and scored twice when Wales were crushed 4-0 three weeks later. He actually scored in nine consecutive internationals from his debut through to March 1888 (a record that still stands today) and went on to average more than a goal a game for his country, claiming his last two in his final outing when Ireland were thrashed 6-1 at Molineux in March 1891.
  Clever and accurate with his passing, Lindley 'held the team together' perfectly yet surprisingly never won a single honour at club level.

LINDSAY, Alec 1973-75 ④
Born: Bury, 27 February 1948
Career: Bury Schoolboys, Bury (apprentice, April 1963, professional, March 1965), Liverpool (£67,000, March 1969), Stoke City (loan, August 1977, signed for £25,000, September 1977), Oakland Stompers/USA £7,000, March 1978), Toronto Blizzard/Canada (May 1980), Newton FC (North West Counties League, October 1982, retired, May 1983); became a scrap metal dealer; also ran a pub and fish and chip shop.

Attacking full-back Alec Lindsay made his England debut (alongside his Liverpool team-mate Emlyn Hughes) in the 2-2 draw with Argentina at Wembley in May 1974. He did well against strong opposition and went on to play in three more internationals later in the year, against East Germany, Bulgaria and Yugoslavia. At club level, he gained League, FA Cup and UEFA Cup winner's medals during his time at Anfield, making 248 appearances for the Merseysiders.

LINDSAY, William 1876-77 ①
Born: Benares, India, 3 August 1847
Died: Rochester, Kent, 15 February 1923
Career: Winchester College (season 1872-73), Old Wykehamists (seasons 1873-76); also played for the Civil Service (seasons 1874-76), Wanderers (seasons 1876-78), Crystal Palace (briefly in 1877), Gitanos FC (1879), South Norwood (1880) and Surrey (1870s); played cricket for Devon and Surrey (1876-82); served in the India Office for 33 years up to 1900.

Versatile Bill Lindsay actually played for Scotland in all five unofficial internationals against England between March 1870 and February 1872 before switching countries and appearing for England in a 3-1 defeat by the Scots at The Oval in April 1877. Sure-footed and a strong kicker, he occupied seven different positions during his career, winning his England cap at right-back. He was a three-time FA Cup winner with the Wanderers. In 1867 he started work as a junior clerk in the store department of the India Office and from 1877 to 1881 was private secretary to the Under-secretary of State before becoming senior clerk in 1882. His father and most of his family were killed at the Siege of Cawnpore during the Indian Rebellion of 1857.

LINEKER, Gary Winston, OBE 1984-92 ⑧⓪ ④⑧
Born: Leicester, 30 November 1960
Career: Leicester City (apprentice, July 1977, professional, December 1978), Everton (£800,000 plus £250,000 from any subsequent transfer, June 1985), CF Barcelona/Spain (£2.75m, July 1986), Tottenham Hotspur (£1.2m, June 1989), Grampus 8 Nagoya/Japan (£946,000, November 1991, retired, April 1994); also played cricket, scoring a century for Leicestershire 2nd XI; became a TV pundit/commentator (several sports) and presenter of BBC's *Match of the Day*. He carried the Olympic torch through part of his native Leicester in 2012.

One of football's gentlemen, throughout his professional career, Gary Lineker was never sent off nor did he receive a yellow card. A silent man off the field, on it he was deadly especially inside the penalty-area.
  First capped by England against Scotland at Hampden Park in May 1984 (coming on as a substitute for the injured Tony Woodcock) he scored his first international goal in the 2-1 win over the Republic of Ireland at Wembley in March 1985, following up soon afterwards with his first hat-trick in a resounding 5-0 victory over Turkey at Wembley.
  Then, a year or so later, he played most of the 1986 World Cup tournament wearing a lightweight cast on his forearm, yet still

Gary Lineker

finished up as the tournament's top scorer with six goals, thus winning the 'Golden Boot', the first and to this day, the only English player to do so. He netted a first-half hat-trick in the final group game against Poland to send England through to the second phase and after grabbing a brace in a 3-0 win over Paraguay he weighed in with England's consolation goal in the quarter-final defeat by Argentina when Diego Maradona scored twice for the opposition, his first being the infamous 'Hand of God' goal, his second one of the best ever seen in World Cup football.

Lineker scored 19 goals in 13 internationals for England between June 1986 and March 1988, including a terrific four-timer in a 4-2 win over Spain on a muddy pitch at the Bernabeu stadium Madrid in February 1987 and a stunning hat-trick in an 8-0 win over Turkey at Wembley eight months later.

Then, sadly, he had a rather lack-lustre European Championship when he suffered badly from a bout of hepatitis. England lost all three games.

Duly regaining full fitness, he did very well in Spain with Barcelona and when the 1990 World Cup came round he was bang in form again. He netted four times in a string of draws and narrow wins as England reached the semi-finals where they would meet their arch-rivals West Germany in Turin. After Andreas Brehme had gleefully fired the Germans ahead, Lineker notched an equalizer, but in the end it was disappointment all round as the Germans won the penalty shoot-out before going on to win the trophy.

Shortly after the World Cup, Lineker was named England captain by Graham Taylor and he celebrated by scoring the only goal of the game from six yards against Hungary at Wembley in September 1990. A year later he scored his second international four-timer, which included his quickest goal for his country – after just 42 seconds – in a 4-2 win over Malaysia in Kuala Lumpur in June 1991. But after disappointing in the European Championships the following year, and having moved into Japanese football, he bowed out of the international arena, ending with a final overall goal-tally of 48, just one behind Bobby Charlton's all-time record...although it must be said that Sir Bobby took 26 more matches to score his one extra goal.

In what proved to be his last England match, in the 2-1 defeat by Sweden at Euro 92, Lineker was in fact, controversially substituted by boss Graham Taylor in favour of Arsenal striker Alan Smith, ultimately denying him the chance to equal — or even better — Charlton's scoring record. He had earlier missed a penalty that would have brought him level, in a pre-tournament friendly against Brazil, and was visibly upset at the decision to take him off, not looking at Taylor as he took the bench.

In the summer of 1994, Lineker announced his retirement as a player, having scored well over 300 goals at club and international level, including 103 for Leicester and 80 for Spurs with whom he won the FA Cup in 1991, despite missing a penalty in the final against Nottingham Forest - the second player at that time to fluff a spot kick in the final; Liverpool's John Aldridge v. Wimbledon in 1988 was the first.

Also capped at B team level, Lineker won the Second Division Championship with Leicester in 1980 and gained promotion to the top flight again in 1983 and was voted both the PFA and FWA 'Footballer of the Year' in 1986, the same season he finished up as leading marksman in the country with 40 goals for Everton. He then moved to Barcelona where he won the Copa del Rey and the European Cup Winners' Cup in successive seasons, 1988 and 1989, and in 1992 was voted FWA 'Footballer of the Year' for a second time,

while also receiving the OBE for services to football in the New Year's Honours List.

After taking off his shooting boots, Lineker developed a career in the media, initially on BBC Radio 5, then as the anchorman for football coverage, including their flagship football television programme *Match of the Day*. He was a team captain on the acerbic sports game show *They Think It's All Over* (1995-2003).

He followed Steve Rider as presenter for the BBC's golf coverage and also presented a six-part TV Series for the BBC in 1998 called *Golden Boots*.

In 2003, Lineker was inducted into the English Football Hall of Fame. Two years later he was sued for defamation by Harry Kewell over comments made writing in his column in the *Sunday Telegraph*. The jury failed to reach a verdict.

With Austin Healey in 2008, Lineker won £50,000 for the Nicholls Spinal Injury Foundation on the ITV1 programme *Who Wants To Be A Millionaire* and since 1995 he has advertised Walkers Crisps. He has four sons from his first marriage and is now married to former model Danielle Bux. In 2009, Leicester City fans voted Lineker as the club's greatest ever player. He received 37% of votes - more than double that of his closest competitor, the legendary goalkeeper Gordon Banks.

OLINTOTT, Evelyn Henry 1907-09 ⑦

Born: Godalming, Surrey, 2 November 1883
Died: River Somme, France, 1 July 1916
Career: King Edward VI Grammar School/Guildford, Guildford FC (briefly, season 1904-05), St Luke's Training College/Exeter (September 1905), Woking (season 1905-06), represented Surrey County (seasons 1904-08), Plymouth Argyle (briefly, August 1907), Queens Park Rangers (September 1907, professional, May 1908), Bradford City (November 1908), Leeds City (July 1912, retired, May 1915); Chairman of the Players' Union (seasons 1909-11); a schoolteacher by profession.

A very efficient left-half, vigorous and clever, Harry Lintott was also a precise tackler and very rarely committed a foul. A Southern League championship winner with QPR in 1908, he gained the first of his seven full England caps whilst with the London club, playing well in the 3-1 win over Ireland in Belfast in February 1908. Lintott, who also played in five amateur internationals for his country (1905-07), was killed while serving with the 1st Yorkshire Regiment.

LIPSHAM, Herbert Broughall 1901-02 ①

Born: Chester, 29 April 1878
Died: Toronto, Canada, 12 August 1932
Career: Chester (May 1894), Crewe Alexandra (July 1898), Sheffield United (February 1900), Fulham (November 1907), Millwall Athletic (July 1910, then player-manager, August 1913-May 1921); West Norwood (coach, August 1921), Northfleet (manager, July 1922-February 1923); emigrated to Canada (March 1923).

A wonderfully consistent and clever outside-left, Bert Lipsham spent almost eight years with Sheffield United (from February 1900) making 259 appearances (34 goals scored) and playing in successive FA Cup finals, gaining a winner's medal in 1902. He failed to reproduce his club form for England and as a result

Gary Lineker

won only one cap, versus Wales in March 1902. He did, however, represent both the Southern League and Football League. He lost a hand while working in a saw mill in Canada and soon afterwards was killed in a train crash.

LITTLE, Brian 1974-75 ①
Born: Peterlee, County Durham, 25 November 1953
Career: Durham County Schools, East Durham Senior Schools, Durham County Youths; trials with Burnley, Leeds United, Manchester City, Newcastle United, Stoke City, Sunderland, West Bromwich Albion (August 1968-May 1969); Aston Villa (trial, then apprentice, July 1969, professional, June 1971, retired, injured, May 1982; worked in club's Development Association officer, then acted as coach, season August 1985-January 1986); Wolverhampton Wanderers (coach, January 1986, caretaker-manager, August-October 1986), Middlesbrough (coach, July 1987-January 1989), Darlington (manager, February 1989-May 1991), Leicester City (manager, May 1991-November 1994), Aston Villa (manager, November 1994-February 1998), Stoke City (manager, February 1998-August 1999), West Bromwich Albion (manager, September 1999-March 2000), Hull City (manager, August 2000-February 2002), soccer pundit and summariser on Sky Sports (season 2002-03), Tranmere Rovers (manager, October 2003-May 2006), Wrexham (manager, November 2007-May 2008), Gainsborough Trinity (manager, September 2009, sacked, August 2011)

Brian Little played just 19 minutes for England. He came on as a substitute for Mick Channon in the 71st minute of the 2-2 Home International draw with Wales at Wembley in May 1975. Two months earlier, the sprightly forward had helped Aston Villa win the League Cup, adding two more League Cup winner's medals to his collection, in 1977 (as a player) and 1996 (as a manager). The scorer of 82 goals in 302 senior appearances, he also gained an FA Youth Cup winner's medal. He guided Darlington back into the Football League as manager as Conference champions in 1990. His brother Alan also played for Villa.

LIVERMORE, Jake 2012-13 ①
Born: Enfield, Middlesex, 14 November 1989
Career: Tottenham Hotspur (trainee, July 2005, professional, July 2005), Milton Keynes Dons (loan, February-March 2008), Crewe Alexandra (loan, July-September 2008), Derby County (loan, August-December 2009), Peterborough United (loan, January-March 2010), Ipswich Town (loan, September 2010-January 2011), Leeds United (loan, March-May 2011)

Central midfielder Jake Livermore had played in only 25 Premiership games for Tottenham before making his England debut as a substitute (for Frank Lampard) against Italy in Berne, Switzerland in August 2012. An aggressive competitor, highly rated by several fellow professionals, he took over from Luca Modric in the Spurs line-up.

LLOYD, Laurence Valentine 1970-80 ④
Born: Bristol, 6 October 1948
Career: Bristol Rovers (juniors, August 1965, professional, July 1967), Liverpool (£60,000, April 1969), Coventry City (£240,000, August 1974), Nottingham Forest (£60,000, October 1976), Wigan Athletic (player-manager/coach, March 1981, retired as a player, March 1983), Notts County (manager, July 1983-October 1984); became a publican in Nottingham, now living in Spain.

Larry Lloyd put the 'stop' into stopper - he was a beast of a man but there's no escaping the defender's shocking England record! He had some horrid games and never really produced his club form for his

country. He made his international debut in the 0-0 draw with Wales in May 1971, played in the European qualifier against Switzerland six months later (1-1) and had a 'stinker' on the night Northern Ireland won 1-0 at Wembley in May 1972. Dropped for nine years, he returned to play in the 4-1 defeat by Wales in Wrexham in May 1980 but wasn't called on again. At club level, Lloyd appeared in almost 600 first-class matches (218 for Liverpool, 214 for Forest), gaining a UEFA Cup winner's medal with the Merseysiders in 1973 and helping Brian Clough's side win the First Division championship, the League Cup twice and the European Cup on two occasions, all within the space of three years. An England Youth international, he also won eight U23 caps.

LOCKETT, Arthur Henry 1902-03 ①
Born: Alsager Bank, Staffs, 11 August 1875
Died: Crewe, 23 October 1957
Career: Alsager's Bank FC (August 1894), Crewe Alexandra (May 1897), Stoke (May 1900), Aston Villa (£40, April 1903), Preston North End (September 1905), Watford (July 1908), Port Vale (May-December 1912); played non-League football until 1915.

A very swift and talented left-winger, Arthur Lockett's only fault was that he held onto the ball far too long! Nevertheless he had an excellent career and amassed over 350 appearances at club level, scoring 27 goals. Capped by England in a 4-0 win over Ireland at Molineux in February 1903, he also represented the Football League.

LODGE, Lewis Vaughn 1893-96 ⑤
Born: Newton Aycliffe, County Durham, 21 December 1872
Died: Burbage, Derbyshire, 21 October 1916
Career: Durham School, Cambridge University (seasons 1892-96); also played for Casuals (season 1893-94), Corinthians (seasons 1894-98); played cricket for Durham and Hampshire; became a teacher at Horris Hill School, Newbury.

Although prone to rashness at times, after four decent performances for England, unfortunately right-back Lewis Lodge was 'indecisive' against Scotland at Celtic Park in April 1896 and was dropped for the next match v. Ireland. He was never selected again. He made his debut in a 5-1 win over Wales at Wrexham in March 1894.

LOFTHOUSE, Joseph Morris 1884-90 ⑦ ③
Born: Bank Top, Witton, Blackburn, 14 April 1865
Died: Blackburn, 10 June 1919
Career: St Luke's School/Witton, Blackburn Grammar School, King's Own/Blackburn (May 1881), Blackburn Rovers (August 1882), Accrington (August 1888), Blackburn Rovers (July 1889), Darwen (June 1892), Walsall (December 1893, retired, injured, May 1895); out of football for a while; then Magyar Athletic club/Budapest (coach, February 1902), New Brompton, Kent (trainer, June 1902), Everton (assistant-trainer, August 1903-May 1908), Blackburn Rovers (briefly as a scout).

Joe Lofthouse made an impressive debut for England, scoring in a 4-0 win over Ireland at Manchester in February 1885 at the age of 19. After another sound performance against Wales, he starred again in the 1-1 draw with Scotland at The Oval in March 1885. Linking up with his Blackburn team-mate James Brown, he gave his country 'a degree of style and comprehension' said the *Bell's Life* reporter. Lofthouse scored in each of his last two internationals - 6-1 and 9-1 wins over Ireland in 1889 and 1890.

LOFTHOUSE, Nathaniel, OBE 1950-59 ㉝ ㉚

Born: Bolton, 27 August 1925

Died: Bolton, 15 January 2011

Career: Brentwood and Castle Hills Schools/Bolton, Lomax's XI (August 1938), Bolton Wanderers (initially in August 1939, professional, August 1942, retired, injured, January 1960; appointed assistant-coach, March 1960, re-signed as a player, July 1960, finally retired, July 1961; then assistant-coach, reserve team trainer, chief coach, June 1967, acting manager, then manager, December 1968, general manager November 1970, chief scout, August 1971-June 1972; later manager of the Burnden Park Executive Club and then club president, until his death; also played for Mosley Common Colliery (as a Bevin Boy, 1943-45) and was briefly Arsenal's Lancashire-based scout.

A one club man throughout his senior career, Nat Lofthouse joined Bolton Wanderers as 14 year-old and went on to serve the club as a player for over 20 years, retiring from the game in November 1960 due to a knee injury, suffered against Birmingham City eleven months earlier.

He scored twice on his debut in a 5-1 Wartime Regional League victory over Bury at the age of 15 years, 207 days and over the next two decades he amassed a grand total of 640 first team appearances and notched 380 goals. At senior level alone his record for the Burnden Park club was magnificent - 285 goals in 503 outings. He scored in both the 1953 and 1958 FA Cup finals, gaining a winner's medal in the latter v. Manchester United when he controversially shoulder-charged 'keeper Harry Gregg and the ball over the line. Sometime after that game, while having a drink with his team-mate, goalkeeper Eddie Hopkinson, the barman refused to take any money from 'Hoppy' saying "We don't charge goalkeepers in here!"

Lofthouse also helped Bolton win the Wartime League Cup in 1945 but unfortunately he never won a prize for his efforts (or Bolton's) in the Football League, although in season 1955-56 he topped the First Division scoring charts with 32 goals.

He also found the net 30 times in 33 games for England and in the 1950s was rated one of the best centre-forwards in world football....ask a few centre-halves about that!

His international team-mate and captain Billy Wright once said: "I'd rather play with Nat than against him. He had a never-say-die approach to the game, was brave and scored some terrific goals."

A Bolton man through and through, he was born in the town in 1925 and played locally for Lomax's XI before joining the Trotters as a youngster in 1939. Conscripted in 1943, he worked at Mosley Common Colliery as a Bevin Boy during the war, before starting his professional career in earnest in 1945.

He played his heart out for the Trotters and after 'taking off' his shooting boots in 1960, nurtured several younger players at the club as well as serving as caretaker-manager, twice as team manager and also as the club's general manager.

Lofthouse announced his arrival on the international stage with both goals in a five-minute spell halfway through the first-half of England's 2-2 draw with Yugoslavia at Highbury in November 1950. He then notched two more in his third game against Northern Ireland a year later, having netted once against Austria at Wembley in November 1951.

The return fixture against the Austrians was played in Vienna in May 1952 and it was one that stirred the blood and rekindled patriotic pride.

England's 3-2 victory was immortalized by the display of Lofthouse which earned him a place in folklore. Once again he scored two stupendous goals, but on claiming his second was knocked out by the advancing Austrian 'keeper who tried to block his dashing 50-yard run which had started near the halfway line. After lengthy treatment Bolton's brave-hearted centre-forward returned to the action in a marauding style, head held high, tail up, hungry for a hat-trick. He tore into the Austrian defence, had two near misses before signing off with a booming shot that almost split the crossbar.

He was dubbed 'The Lion of Vienna' following that swashbuckling performance and after that he led England's line in the next 12 internationals, scoring 13 goals, including two 'beauties' in a 6-3 win over the USA in June 1953, and two braces in 5-2 and 4-1 victories over Wales in November 1952 and October 1953, giving centre-half Ray Daniel a tough time in both matches.

Frank Brennan of Scotland had also been 'severely tested and frequently disturbed' when England were held to a 2-2 draw at Wembley in 1953, shortly before Nat was voted 'Footballer of the Year' and had scored in that memorable 'Matthews Cup final' at Wembley when Blackpool beat Bolton 4-3.

In the 4-4 World Cup draw with Belgium in Basle in June 1954, Bolton's legend scored a cracking goal, a flying header from Tom Finney's cross. He netted a second in extra-time but his efforts failed to earn victory.

In a bad-tempered 1-1 draw with Spain in Madrid in May 1955, Nat had his shirt ripped off his back in the first-half and played the second 45 minutes in a numberless jersey. Always a fighter, no matter what the circumstances, or the opposition, he continued to torment defenders all over the world and grabbed another five goals for his country including two as a substitute (for Tommy Taylor) in a 5-1 win over Finland in Helsinki in May 1956.

He eventually quit the international scene after his farewell performance against Wales at Villa Park in November 1958.

Besides his senior outings for his country, he also played in one 'B' international and represented the Football League, netting a hat-trick in a 9-0 win over the Irish League in March 1952 and a six-timer in a 7-1 win over the same opposition six months later. Lofthouse was the recipient of various honours after retiring from the game. On 2 December 1989, he was made a Freeman of Bolton and on 1 January 1994, he was appointed an OBE (for his bold and brave efforts as a footballer and his service to Bolton Wanderers Football Club and England). Three years later, on 18 January 1997, Bolton chose to name their East Stand at their new Reebok Stadium after him. Then, on 7 April 1993, he appeared as a special guest on the TV guest show This Is Your Life.

Tributes were paid to Nat Lofthouse as he celebrated his 80th birthday, including a party at the Reebok. A campaign backed by former Bolton player and the Chief Executive of the Professional Footballers' Association, Gordon Taylor, was started, aiming to get Nat knighted. Sadly that never materialised but he was an Inaugural Inductee into the English Football Hall of Fame in 2002. He died from Alzheimer's disease at the age of 85.

LONGWORTH, Ephraim 1919-23 ⑤
Born: Halliwell, Lancs, 2 October 1887
Died: Liverpool, 7 January 1968
Career: Bolton & District Schools, Bolton St Luke's (August 1901), Halliwell Rovers (August 1902), Chorley Road Congregationalists (July 1904), Bolton St Luke's (August 1906), Halliwell Rovers (September 1906), Hyde St George (briefly), Hyde (professional, April 1907), Bolton Wanderers (June 1907), Leyton (October 1908), Liverpool (May 1901, retired, May 1928, remained at Anfield as a coach, thereafter was a key member of club's general backroom staff).

Twice a League championship winner with Liverpool in the early 1920s, right-back Eph Longworth was bow legged – a wonderful subject for the cartoonist! A brave footballer who never shirked a tackle, he gained the first of his five England caps against Scotland at Hillsborough in April 1920. Coming in to partner Jesse Pennington, he had a tough baptism but ended up on the winning side, 5-4. Two of his four other caps came against Belgium. Collecting his last v. Scotland in April 1923, he was given a tough time by left-winger Alan Morton in a 3-2 defeat at Hampden Park. Longworth, who also represented the Football League and toured South Africa with the FA party in 1920, made 371 appearances for Liverpool between 1910 and 1928.

LOWDER, Arthur 1888-89 ①
Born: Blakenhall, Wolverhampton, 11 February 1863
Died: Taunton, 4 January 1926
Career: St Luke's School/Blakenhall, Wolverhampton Wanderers (September 1882, professional, August 1885, retired, injured, October 1891); coached in France, Germany and Norway; Chairman of the Brewood Parish Council (from 1924 until his death).

A light-weight left-half, extremely hard but fair tackler, Arthur Lowder was a surprise choice by England for the game against Wales in February 1889. Replacing his club-mate Harry Allen, he played his part in a 4-1 win. He made 71 senior appearances for Wolves and appeared in the 1889 FA Cup final defeat by Preston.

LOWE, Edmund 1946-47 ③
Born: Halesowen, 11 July 1925
Died: Nottingham, 10 March 2009
Career: Halesowen & Stourbridge Schools, Goshill & Chambers FC, Napier Aircraft Company; WW2 guest for Millwall (amateur), Finchley FC, Walthamstow Avenue, Kynochs Works/Birmingham; Aston Villa (professional, May 1945), Fulham (£15,000 with brother, Reg, May 1950), Notts County (player-manager, July 1963, retired April 1965); later managed an international boiler & central heating firm in Nottingham; worked down the pit as a Bevin Boy during WW2.

Eddie Lowe made an impressive debut for England in a 3-0 win over France at Highbury in May 1947. He sent three defenders the wrong with one outrageous dummy before setting up Raich Carter who gleefully put away the third goal. A tall, commanding left-half with a receding hairline, he was an exceptionally hard worker who added two more caps to his collection later in the month, in a 1-0 defeat in Switzerland and a 10-0 victory over Portugal, when he assisted in two of the goals. Lowe made almost 650 appearances during his 21-year club career, 511 for Fulham (1950-63). He came fourth in the 1963 'Footballer of the Year' poll.

LUCAS, Thomas 1921-26 ③
Born: St Helens, 20 September 1895
Died: Stoke Mandeville, Buckinghamshire, 11 December 1953
Career: Sherdley Villa (May 1910), Sutton Commercial (August 1912), Heywood United (May 1913), Peasley Cross (September 1914), Eccles Borough (August 1915), Liverpool (professional, June 1916), Clapton Orient (July 1933, retired, May 1934); Ashford (manager, season 1935-36); became licensee at Stoke Mandeville.

A League championship winner with Liverpool in 1922, Tom Lucas was a fine full-back, stocky in build, strong in volleying and an expert at covering. Initially a 'reserve' to Jesse Pennington in the England set up, he was one of twelve different left-backs called up for international duty in the space of five years during the early 1920s, winning his first cap against Ireland in Belfast in October 1921 and his last v. Belgium in Antwerp in May 1926. He made 366 appearances during his 17 years at Anfield (1916-33).

LUNTLEY, Edwin 1879-80 ②
Born: Croydon, Surrey, 28 April 1857
Died: Nottingham, 1 August 1921
Career: Nottingham Castle FC (July 1876), Nottingham Forest (November 1878-January 1883); played cricket for Radcliffe; also founder member of the Chilwell Manor Golf Club; a lace manufacturer by profession.

A resolute right-back with a good turn of foot, Ed Luntley's two England caps were won against Scotland (lost 5-4) and Wales (won 3-2) in March 1880. He spent five years with Forest (1878-83) along with two of his brothers.

LYTTELTON,
Reverend, the Hon. Alfred, QC, KC, MP 1876-77 ② ①
Born: Westminster, London, 7 February 1857
Died: Chiswick, London, 5 July 1913
Career: Eton College (seasons 1874-76), Trinity College/Cambridge University (seasons 1876-79), Old Etonians (seasons 1879-81); played cricket for England v. Australia in four Tests (1880-84), also for Cambridge University (1876-79), Worcestershire and Middlesex (scored over 4,500 first-class runs); was President of the MCC (1897-98); gained a University Blue at football, cricket, rackets and real tennis; called to the Bar in 1881, later became KC and MP for Warwick (1895-1906); thence for the constituency of St George's, Hanover Square, London; also Secretary of State for the Colonies (1902-05), also a Knight Commander and barrister.

Alfred Lyttelton was, a contemporary assessment in the Football Annual noted: "...a very strong and fast forward, a splendid shot at goal, and perhaps the most dangerous forward out. A weighty, forceful, hard-shooting player, hard to knock off the ball, he lacked close ball control but he was nonetheless a very useful footballer."

Edward Lyttelton (next column) wrote the following about his brother in the late 1870s: "There have been other players more deft at dribbling, there have been a few, very few, of greater speed, and there have been heavier players, but I never knew one who combined the three great essentials, and added to them a surprising accuracy at kicking goals and 'bunting' his opponents. This last faculty he exercised by dint of a jerk of his hips, not as ordinarily by lowering the shoulder, and so the aggressor could see no sign of the terrific impact coming. Once playing against Royal Engineers I saw him make a run down from one end of the field to the other and floor four men on the way - the last two having charged him simultaneously from both sides, and both rebounding on their backs - and shoot the goal at the end."

Lyttelton's principal weapon as a forward was a unique and generally successful goalscoring technique that appears, from contemporary sources, to have been a primitive version of the 1970s Johan Cruyff. Edward explained: "He would run towards the corner and then swiftly turn inwards, running parallel to the back line, and some ten yards from it. At this point he was pursued probably by three of the opponents, barely keeping up. This continued till he got opposite the further goal post, and then one huge foot was smartly dropped on the ball, stopping it dead, and of course the pursuers all ran a yard or so too far, not suspecting the sudden pull up; thus he had a clear shot at the goal."

Lyttelton's only England cap came against Scotland in March 1877 when he scored a fine goal from Lindsay Bury's well-taken free-kick in a 3-1 defeat at The Oval. However, his team-mates were highly critical of his attempts to dribble through the entire Scotland defence by himself, and Sheffield's Billy Mosforth ventured to draw his colleague's attention to this failing. He was silenced by an imperious put-down that has been cited as exemplifying the attitude of the earliest amateurs: 'I play,' the unabashed Lyttelton sneered back, 'for my own pleasure.'

He played for Old Etonians in the 1876 FA Cup final (beaten by the Royal Engineers).

As a cricketer, Lyttelton's most notable Test Match was against Australia at The Oval in 1884. In the course of the game, Australia reached a total – all but unheard of at the time – of 500-6 and the England captain, Lord Harris, was so desperate for a breakthrough that he asked his wicket-keeper, Lyttelton, to bowl. W.G. Grace went behind the stumps, while Lyttelton sent down a succession of underarm lobs, succeeding, remarkably, in taking the last four Aussie wickets for only 19 runs in the course of a dozen overs. He was the brother of Edward (see below).

LYTTELTON, Hon. Edward 1877-78 ①

Born: Westminster, London, 23 July 1855
Died: Norwich, 26 January 1942
Career: Eton College (season 1872-73), Trinity College/Cambridge University (seasons 1873-76), Old Etonians (1870s), Hagley FC (briefly); also played cricket for Hertfordshire, Middlesex and Worcestershire; Master at Wellington College (1880-82), Eton (1882-89), headmaster of Haileybury School (for five years: 1890-95) and later Eton College (1905-16); Curate of St Martins in the Fields (1916-18), Rector of Sidestrand, Norfolk (1918-20); Dean of Whitelands College, Chelsea (for nine years, from 1920-29); thence officiate of the diocese of Norwich (1929 until his death).

Rugged defender Edward Lyttelton made full use of his weight, being difficult to pass but unfortunately he lacked pace. He won his only England cap a year after his brother, but struggled against Scotland, like the rest of his colleagues, to contain hat-trick hero John McDougall and two-goal Henry McNiel in a humiliating 7-2 defeat at the Queens Park Ground, Glasgow.

Four more Lyttelton brothers, namely Arthur, Charles, George and Robert, all played first-class cricket, as did their father, George, and nephews John and Charles Lyttelton.

MABBUTT, Gary Vincent, MBE 1982-88 ⑯ ①

Born: Bristol, 23 August 1961
Career: Bristol Schools, Avon Schools, Bristol Rovers (apprentice, August 1977, professional, January 1979), Tottenham Hotspur (August 1982, retired, May 1998); was an ambassador for the 2010 World Cup finals in South Africa; also worked with the Deloitte Street Child World Cup (training and encouraging street children and ex-street children in football and for street children's rights in Durban, South Africa – all run by the Amos Trust); also a TV football analyst; runs his own sports management company and is a member of the FA Video Review Advisory Panel and the FA International Development Committee.

Playing at right-back, Gary Mabbutt came close to scoring on his England debut – hitting a post in the 2-1 defeat by West Germany at Wembley in October 1982. He then played in eight more internationals up to October 1983 but was then out of the limelight for the next three years, returning for the 2-0 European Championship qualifying win over Yugoslavia in November 1986, when he celebrated the occasion by scoring the first goal in the 21st minute. His 16th and last England appearance was against Czechoslovakia in 1992.

Mabbutt, who was diagnosed with diabetes early in his career, made his debut for Spurs at Wembley, in the FA Charity Shield game against Liverpool in 1982. He then helped Spurs win the UEFA Cup in 1984 before returning to the Empire Stadium in 1987 as Spurs' captain, only to score at both ends of the field in a 3-2 FA Cup final defeat by Coventry City. Four years later he gained a winner's medal by leading Spurs to victory over Nottingham Forest in the same competition. Also the recipient of seven U21 and nine B caps, Mabbutt suffered a broken leg on the opening day of the 1996-97 season, and this unfortunately paved the way for an early retirement after he had made 619 appearances for Spurs as a full-back, central defender and midfielder. By the time of his retirement, he was the club's longest-serving player. His final appearance was against Southampton on the last day of the 1997-98 season.

His father Ray and brother Kevin also played for Bristol Rovers.

McCALL, Joseph 1912-21 ⑤ ①

Born: Kirkham, Lancs, 6 July 1886
Died: Wrea Green, Blackpool, 3 February 1965
Career: Kirkham FC (August 1901), Preston North End (professional, July 1906, retired, May 1925); became a smallholder and poultry farmer at Wrea Green.

A Second Division championship winner and FA Cup finalist with Preston in 1913 and 1922 respectively, Joe McCall was relatively small for a centre-half. But despite his lack of height, he was a fine defender, strong in the air and in the tackle and clever at switching play with a long, accurate pass.

He made his England debut against Wales in March 1913, scoring in a 4-3 win at Bristol. He then produced a sturdy display when Scotland were defeated 1-0 at Chelsea three weeks later but was well below par when the Scots gained revenge with a 3-1 win at Hampden Park in April 1914. His last two full caps came after the war, 5-4 and 2-0 wins over the Scots and the Welsh in April and October 1920.

McCall, who also played in two Wartime internationals and four England trials, made 328 appearances for Preston between 1906 and his retirement in 1925. He was also awarded two benefits: 1913 and 1920.

Gary Mabbutt MBE

McCANN, Gavin Peter 2000-01 ①
Born: Blackpool, 10 January 1978
Career: YMCA Juniors/Lytham St Anne's, Everton (apprentice, June 1994, professional, July 1995), Sunderland (£500,000, November 1998), Aston Villa (£2.25m, July 2003), Bolton Wanderers (£1m, June 2007; in February 2008, he launched his own Football Academy in Lytham St Anne's, the first one on the Fylde coast; named The Milligan-McCann Academy, it caters for 8-12 year-olds and is based at King Edward VII and Queen Mary School.

Called into Sven-Göran Eriksson's first squad for the friendly with Spain in February 2001, midfielder Gavin McCann came on as a second-half substitute for Nicky Butt to earn his one and only England cap. Manager David O'Leary's first signing for Aston Villa at £2.25m in 2003, he reached the personal milestone of 350 club appearances in 2009 whilst at Bolton, but injury seriously interrupted his career soon afterwards.

MACAULAY, Reginald Heber 1880-81 ①
Born: Hodnet, Shropshire, 24 August 1858
Died: Poplar, London, 15 December 1937
Career: Eton College (seasons 1878-80), Kings College/Cambridge University (seasons 1880-83); played for Old Etonians (seasons 1880-84); also AAA high jump champion; worked in India from 1884-1901; became an East India merchant in the City of London with Wallace & Co.

A quick-moving, hard-working utility forward with a powerful right foot shot, Reg Macaulay made his only appearance for England in the 6-1 defeat by Scotland at The Oval in March 1881. One reporter wrote: "He was marked out of the game by the Queen's Park duo of Campbell and Davidson." Macaulay won the FA Cup with Old Etonians in 1882.

McDERMOTT, Terence 1977-82 ㉕ ③
Born: Kirkby, Liverpool, 8 December 1951
Career: Liverpool & Merseyside Schoolboy football, Bury (apprentice, April 1967, professional, October 1969), Newcastle United (£22,000, February 1973), Liverpool (£170,000, November 1974), Newcastle United (£100,000, September 1982-September 1984); later with Cork City (January-March 1985), Apoel Nicosia/Cyprus (July 1985, retired, April 1987); returned to Newcastle United (as coach/assistant-manager, February 1992-May 1998 and again from September 2005-September 2008); Huddersfield Town (assistant-manager/coach, December 2008-May 2012), Birmingham City (assistant-manager/coach, June 2012)

Midfielder Terry McDermott ended England's near eight-hour goal famine with a cracking effort (from Steve Coppell's pass) in a 2-1 defeat by Switzerland in Basle in May 1981. Fours years earlier, he had made his international debut in a dull 0-0 draw with the same country at Wembley, lining up with five of his Liverpool team-mates. A regular for club and country, he won his 25 caps over a period of five years, scoring his other two goals in a 4-0 win over Norway in September 1980.
    A player with great drive and determination and known as the 'Black Box', McDermott, after moving from Newcastle to Anfield in 1974, linked up splendidly with Kevin Keegan and Ray Kennedy and over the next eight years won two European Cup, four League Championship and League Cup winner's medals (plus several runners-up prizes) and was also voted both FWA and PFA 'Footballer of the Year' in 1980. Also capped once at U23 level, 'Mac' made almost 600 appearances for his three English clubs including 168 for Newcastle (24 goals) and 329 for Liverpool (81 goals).

McDONALD, Colin Agnew 1957-59 ⑧
Born: Tottington, Bury, 15 October 1930
Career: Bury Technical College, Hawkshaw St Mary's FC (August 1946), Burnley (amateur, August 1948, part-time professional, October 1948), Headington United (loan, season 1950-51); returned to Burnley (professional, July 1952, retired, injured, May 1961); Wycombe Wanderers (coach, August-September 1961), Bury (chief scout, October 1961-January 1965), Altrincham (signed as player-coach, January 1965, finally retired, May 1967), Bolton Wanderers (chief Scout, May 1967-October 1968), Bury (administrative manager, August 1969, general manager, May 1970); later Oldham Athletic (coach), Tranmere Rovers (coach).

Named by Walter Winterbottom in England's 1958 World Cup squad, goalkeeper Colin McDonald made his debut in a friendly against the USSR in Moscow shortly before the start of the tournament in Sweden. Replacing Eddie Hopkinson who had conceded five goals in the previous international against Yugoslavia, he played well in a 1-1 draw and kept his place in the team, playing in all four World Cup matches - a 2-2 draw v. the Soviet Union, a 0-0 stalemate v. Brazil, when he pulled off three brilliant saves, another 2-2 draw with Austria and a 1-0 reverse in the play-off against the Russians. Unfortunately he was unsighted when Korner's swerving 30-yard drive flew past him to give the Austrians victory. Nevertheless McDonald was still voted best goalkeeper in the competition. After playing in three more internationals during the first half of the 1958-59 season, Burnley's number one fractured his right leg in three places during a League game against West Ham United on St Patrick's Day, March 1959. Complications set in and he contracted pneumonia. Thankfully he recovered his health and played a few games in the reserves before retiring, although he returned later and had a few outings with Altrincham. He made 201 appearances during his 11 years at Turf Moor.

MACDONALD, Malcolm Ian 1971-76 ⑭ ⑥
Born: Fulham, London, 7 January 1950
Career: Queen's Manor Primary School/Fulham and Sloane Grammar School/Chelsea, Barnet (junior, April 1965), Knowle Park Juniors (July 1966), Tonbridge (July 1967), Crystal Palace (trial, May 1968), Fulham (professional, August 1968), Luton Town (£17,500, July 1969), Newcastle United (£180,000, May 1971), Arsenal (£333,333, July 1976), Djurgardens IF/Sweden (loan, July-August 1979); returned to Arsenal and immediately retired, injured knee; Fulham (marketing executive, September 1979, then team manager, November 1980-March 1984, also club director from August 1981),licensee in Worthing, Sussex (May 1984), Huddersfield Town (manager, October 1987-May 1988), South Kinson FC/South Africa (player, April-May 1990), Lusitano FC/South Africa (player, September-October 1990); ran a hotel business before moving to Italy in 1991; lived in Milan and worked for Auditel, setting up the equivalent of the UK 0890 service until the Italian government declared such lines illegal; also acted as a football agent, was engaged as an after-dinner speaker, worked on Real Radio and wrote a column for a North-East newspaper; was later declared bankrupt following a failed business venture and became an alcoholic; now lives in Jesmond near Newcastle.

'Super Mac' as he was called, became the first player to score five goals in a competitive game at Wembley when he went 'nap' for England against Cyprus in April 1975. Four of his goals came from headers in an extraordinary display of finishing. Afterwards Macdonald said: "To be honest I should have had eight. I managed to miss three easy chances." Amazingly, a few weeks later, against the same opposition in Limassol, he hardly had a kick. Funny old game, football! Some three years earlier, in May 1972, the bold, brave striker, made

McFARLAND, Roy Leslie 1970-76 (28)

Born: Liverpool, 5 April 1948
Career: Edge Hill Boys Club (August 1962), Tranmere Rovers (apprentice, June 1964, professional, July 1966), Derby County (£24,000, August 1967), Bradford City (player-manager, May 1981), Derby County (player/caretaker-manager, November 1982, assistant-manager, June 1984, then manager October 1993-June 1995); Bolton Wanderers (manager, June 1995), Cambridge United (manager, December 1996-February 2001), Torquay United (manager, July 2001-April 2002), Chesterfield (manager, June 2003-March 2007), Burton Albion (assistant-manager, January 2009, then manager to May 2009).

Partnering Bobby Moore in the centre of the defence, Roy McFarland made his England debut against Malta in a European Championship qualifier in February 1971. He played 'fairly well' in a dour 1-0 win and kept his place for the next three matches before Larry Lloyd was given a chance. However, McFarland was soon back as first choice pivot and produced some excellent displays, although he struggled in the World Cup qualifier against Wales in January 1973. Failing to catch Leighton James and John Toshack offside, the latter duly netted to earn the Welsh a 1-1 draw. Later playing alongside Norman Hunter and his derby team-mate Colin Todd, McFarland won his last cap in a 2-0 World Cup qualifying defeat by Italy in Rome in November 1976. He was replaced at centre-half by Dave Watson. A club professional from 1967 to 1983, McFarland won a Second and two First Division championship medals with Derby in the early 1970s and all told appeared in more than 600 first-class matches for his three English League clubs, 530 coming with Derby (two spells). He also played in five U23 internationals and as a manager, guided Bradford City, Cambridge City and Burton Albion to promotion, steering the latter into the Football League, after succeeding Nigel Clough.

McGARRY, William Harry 1953-56 (4)

Born: Stoke-on-Trent, 10 June 1927
Died: Bophuthatswana, South Africa, 15 March 2005
Career: Northwood Mission/Hanley (July 1943), Port Vale (professional, June 1945), Huddersfield Town (£10,000, March 1951), Bournemouth (£2,000 as player-manager, March 1961-June 1963); Watford (manager, July 1963-October 1964), Ipswich Town (manager, October 1964-November 1968), Wolverhampton Wanderers (manager, November 1968-May 1976), Saudi Arabia (coach, June 1976-October 1977), United Arab Emirates (national coach, briefly), Newcastle United (manager, November 1977-August 1980), Brighton & Hove Albion (scout, season 1980-81), Power Dynamo/Zambia (coach), Zambia national team (coach), Wolverhampton Wanderers (manager, September-November 1985 – 61 days), Bophuthatswana, South Africa (coach, seasons 1986-95).

Huddersfield's Bill McGarry made his international debut in the World Cup-tie against Switzerland in Berne in June 1954. Brought into a reshuffled half-back line following an injury to Syd Owen, he did well for an hour against moderate opposition before fading in the sweltering heat as England qualified for the quarter-finals with a 2-0 win. He played in the next game v. Uruguay and won his last two caps in October 1955 against Denmark and Wales when he stepped in following an injury to Duncan Edwards.

An inside-right originally before finding his true milieu as a right-half, McGarry was a thoroughly competent performer, strong in the tackle, who amassed over 500 appearances at club level. He also played for England B and as a manager took Wolves into the 1972 UEFA Cup final and to League Cup glory two years later. He was with Ronnie Allen at Northwood Mission and Port Vale.

a 'bright' international debut in a 3-0 win over Wales in Cardiff, but was substituted by Martin Chivers in his second game 72 hours later. He headed his first England goal in a 2-0 win over West Germany in the 100th international played at Wembley in March 1975. Initially a full-back, Macdonald was converted into a centre-forward by Fulham manager Bobby Robson and went on to have a fine career as a striker, netting 256 goals in a total of 482 appearances for his four Football League clubs, having his best time without a doubt at Newcastle (138 goals in 258 outings). Whilst at Arsenal, he was the First Division's joint top scorer in 1976-77 with 25 goals.

He also played in four U23 internationals and in two losing Cup finals with Newcastle and one with Arsenal. A serious leg injury ended his career in 1979.

In 1975, MacDonald took part in the Superstars tournament and stunned everybody by running the 100m in 10.9 seconds. He held the European record for seven years until Des Drummond clocked 10.85 seconds in the 1982 International Superstars in Hong Kong.

McGUINNESS, Wilfred 1958-59 ②

Born: Manchester, 25 October 1937
Career: Mount Carmel School, Manchester & Lancashire Boys,
Blackley FC (July 1952), Manchester United (amateur, June 1953,
professional, November 1954, retired, injured, December 1961;
appointed assistant-trainer, made brief comeback, to no avail, in
1967; also England Youth team (trainer-coach, seasons 1963-
69); Manchester United (manager, June 1969-December 1970,
then assistant-trainer until February 1971, Aris Salonika/Greece
(manager-coach, July 1971-May 1973); Panaraiki Patras FC/Greece
(coach, season 1973-74), Everton (scout, August-November 1974),
York City (manager, February 1975-October 1977), Hull City (coach,
July 1978-December 1979), Everton (scout, late 1979), Bury
(coach, August 1980, later assistant-manager/physiotherapist, acted
as caretaker-manager, March-April 1989); quit football in July 1991
and became an accomplished, witty after-dinner speaker.

Twenty-two year-old wing-half Wilf McGuinness, one of the many
Busby Babes capped by England, made an impressive international
debut in the 3-3 draw with Northern Ireland in Belfast in October
1958. Then he was one of a number of players seriously affected
by the searing heat during a tour game against Mexico in May 1959
and had to receive an emergency intake of oxygen. An attack-
minded, stocky, tireless wing-half, McGuinness's career came to an
abrupt end after breaking his leg in a Central League match early in
the 1959-60 season. He had a disappointing spell as manager at
Old Trafford. Capped by England at Schoolboy, Youth team and U23
levels, he won three FA Youth Cup winner's medals with United.

McINROY, Albert 1926-27 ①

Born: Walton-le-Dale, Lancs, 23 April 1901
Died: Newcastle-upon-Tyne, 7 January 1985
Career: St Thomas High School/Preston, Upper Walton FC (seasons
1917-19), Cophull Central (August 1919), Preston North End
(amateur, August 1921), High Walton United (December 1921),
Great Harwood (April 1922), Leyland Motors (November 1922),
Sunderland (professional, May 1923), Newcastle United (£2,750,
October 1929), Sunderland (free, May 1934), Leeds United (May
1935), Gateshead (June 1937-May 1944), Stockton (May 1945,
retired April 1946); became a licensee in Newcastle.

An FA Cup winner with Newcastle in 1932, Albert McInroy was a
sound, reliable, agile and highly consistent goalkeeper who amassed
almost 550 appearances (160 for Newcastle, 227 for Sunderland)
during an 18-year career. His only England cap was against Northern
Ireland in October 1926 when he was surprisingly criticised for two
of the goals in a 3-3 draw at Anfield. He was, in fact, one of eight
different 'keepers used by England in the space of two years.

McMAHON, Stephen Joseph 1987-91 ⑰

Born: Halewood near Liverpool, Lancashire, 20 August 1961
Career: Everton (apprentice, June 1977, professional, August
1979), Aston Villa (£300,000, May 1983), Liverpool (£350,000,
September 1985), Manchester City (December 1991), Swindon Town
(player-manager, November 1994, retired, October 1999), Blackpool
(manager, January 2000-May 2004), Perth Glory/Australia (manager,
seasons 2004-06); later a pundit for ESPN Star Sports in the Far
East and served on the board of the Profitable Group; appointed
coach of Liverpool's Football Academy in India (October 2011).

Midfielder Steve McMahon made his England debut in the 0-0 draw
with Israel on a waterlogged pitch in Tel Aviv in February 1988.
Occasionally hot-headed, he was in and out of the team after that

before having a nightmare in his last international against the Republic
of Ireland in the World Cup in Cagliari in June 1990. Coming on as a
substitute for Peter Beardsley, his first touch he lost control and
looked on as his Everton club-mate Kevin Sheedy planted a left-footer
into the net for the equaliser (1-1). Soon afterwards he was booked!

Also capped at B and U21 levels, McMahon scored almost 90 goals
in more than 700 club games, 66 of his strikes coming in 364 outings
for Liverpool. Unfortunately he failed to do the business as a manager.

McMANAMAN, Steven 1994-2002 ㊲ ③

Born: Kirkdale, Lancs, 11 February 1972
Career: Liverpool (apprentice, April 1988, professional, February
1990), Real Madrid (free, July 1991), Manchester City (free, August
2003, retired, May 2005); became an ESPN analyst for the 2010 FIFA
World Cup in South Africa; also engaged as an English based in-game
analyst alongside Ian Darke for ESPN's USA and UK coverage of the
FA Premier League, FA Cup and Major League Soccer games; also an
associate producer on the film Goal! 2; invested in several racehorses
with Robbie Fowler; appointed Birmingham City's technical adviser in
2009-10 by the club's Chinese owners.

Steve McManaman made history by
becoming the first player, without first
team experience, to play for England
at U21 level, being handed his debut
by Lawrie McMenemy against Wales at
Tranmere in October 1990, two months
before he made his debut for Liverpool's
first XI. In February 1993, he captained the
U21s for the first time against San Marino
and scored the last goal in a 6-0 win.

A wide-midfielder (a good, old-fashioned winger really)
McManaman despite being forever an international enigma, was
one of England's best players in Euro '96 (earning praise from
Pele) but played only once in the World Cup finals two years later.
Fast, clever and direct, he made his international debut under Terry
Venables, as a substitute for Robert Lee in the friendly with Nigeria
at Wembley in November 1994 and, injuries permitting, was virtually
a regular for seven years. The last of his 37 caps came in 2001
when Sven-Göran Eriksson utilised him for his first games in World
Cup qualifiers, but then apparently left a message on McManaman's
answer-phone, informing him that he was not going to be in the
squad for the 2002 World Cup finals. Many fans and media critics
believed that McManaman's non-fruition at International level was a
combination of a failure by managers to find an effective position for
him and despite being a right footed player he was often placed on
England's problematic left-side at the time.

Two of his three international goals came in a 6-0 win over
Luxembourg in 2000; his third came in a 3-2 defeat by Portugal
later in the year.

McManaman who also played in one unofficial international,
won the FA Cup with Liverpool in 1992 and the League Cup three
years later, before going on to become the most decorated English
footballer, in terms of trophies won, to have played for a foreign
club, namely Real Madrid. He gained two La Liga championships,
two Champions League winner's medals and a Super Cup medal.
The first British player to win the UEFA Champions League title
twice, he was also the first Englishman to score for a foreign club in
a major European final - doing so for Real in their 2000 European
Champions League final victory over Valencia - and was the first
Englishman to win the Champions League with a non-English club.

'Macca' or 'Shaggy' as he was sometimes called was replaced
by David Beckham at the Bernabeu Stadium. He made almost 500
appearances at club level (60 goals scored).

McNAB, Robert 1968-69 ④

Born: Huddersfield, 20 July 1943
Career: Rawthorpe CSM/Huddersfield (April 1958), Moldgreen Civic Youth Club/Huddersfield (April 1959), Huddersfield Town (amateur, June 1961, professional, April 1962) Arsenal (£50,000, October 1966), Wolverhampton Wanderers (free, July 1975), San Antonio Thunder/USA (May 1976), Barnet (August 1977), Vancouver Whitecaps (coach, November 1978-May 1979, and again November 1980-May 1981); Tacoma Stars/US Indoor League (player-manager, later assistant-manager, seasons 1983-85); out of football for a while; San Jose Grizzlies (manager, season 1994-95), Portsmouth (caretaker-manager, December 1999-January 2000); also worked as a licensee in Tottenham; now a property developer, living in California.

Competent, quick-tackling left-back Bob McNab made his England debut as a substitute for Tommy Wright in the 0-0 draw with Romania in Bucharest in November 1968. Although playing 'out of position' on the right, he gave a 'sound display' in what was a dreary defence-dominated match. His other three caps, gained later that same season were all on the left flank, against Bulgaria and Romania at Wembley and Northern Ireland in Belfast. McNab made over 500 appearances during his playing career, 365 for Arsenal, whom he helped win the Fairs Cup in 1970 and complete the double in 1971. McNab, who also played in one unofficial international for England, later moved to Los Angeles. In 1999 he was part of a consortium led by Milan Mandaric that took over Portsmouth and briefly came out of retirement to act as caretaker-manager at Fratton Park following the sacking of Alan Ball. McNab's daughter, Mercedes, is a Hollywood actress.

McNEAL, Robert 1913-14 ②

Born: Hobson Village, County Durham, 19 January 1891
Died: West Bromwich, 12 May 1956
Career: Hobson Day School/Durham, Hobson Wanderers (August 1907), West Bromwich Albion (professional, June 1910, retired, injured, May 1925; then coach to May 1927); guest for Fulham, Middlesbrough, Notts County and Port Vale during WW1; became a publican in West Bromwich.

A rock solid, uncompromising left-half, stylish at times with a footballing brain, Bobby McNeal who was only 5ft 6ins tall, made 403 appearances for West Bromwich Albion between 1910 and 1925, gaining both Second and First Division championship medals either side of the Great War. He played in two Home Internationals at the end of the 1913-14 season. He had a fine game in a 2-0 win over Wales but struggled in the 3-1 defeat by Scotland in front of 127,000 spectators at Hampden Park, where he was given a difficult time by Celtic's clever inside-right Jimmy McMenemy. McNeal also represented the Football League on four occasions.

McNEIL, Michael 1960-62 ⑨

Born: Middlesbrough, 7 February 1940
Career: Middlesbrough Technical College, Cargo Fleet Juniors (June 1953), Middlesbrough (amateur, on schoolboy forms, June 1954, professional, February 1957), Ipswich Town (June 1964), Cambridge City (March 1972, retired, May 1974); later ran a chain of sports shops in Ipswich.

Left-back Mick McNeil worked as an analytical chemist before joining Middlesbrough as a professional in 1957. Powerfully built, strong in the air and a solid tackler, he made his England debut in place of the injured Ray Wilson in a 5-2 win over Northern Ireland in Belfast in October 1960, looking comfortable against the speedy

Billy Bingham and hardly putting a foot wrong. As partner to Jimmy Armfield, eight more caps came his way over the next year but he missed out on the 1962 World Cup when Armfield, Don Howe and Wilson were the preferred full-backs. McNeil made a total of 366 appearances for his two Football League clubs.

MacRAE, Stuart 1882-84 ⑤

Born: Port Bannatyne, Bute, Scotland, 12 December 1855
Died: Marylebone, London, 27 January 1927
Career: Edinburgh Academy (played rugby, seasons 1871-75), Edinburgh Academicals (rugby, seasons 1875-77), Newark (season 1877-78), Bolton Association (mid-1870s), Notts County (November 1879-February 1887); also played for Corinthians (seasons 1883-90); worked as a malster in Newark with Grilstrap Earl & Co.

Although a rugby international trialist as a three-quarter-back for Scotland, Stuart MacRae went on to win five England caps at football between February 1883 and March 1884, playing twice against his country of birth, twice against Ireland and once v. Wales. He had two outstanding games against the Irish, setting up goals in both games which resulted in 7-0 and 8-1 wins. A clever centre-half with a 'fighting weight' of 14st, MacRae possessed a powerful kick and presented a formidable barrier to opposing forwards.

MADELEY, Paul Edward 1970-77 ㉔

Born: Leeds, 20 September 1944
Career: Yorkshire League football, Farsley Celtic (April 1960), Leeds United (professional, May 1962, retired, May 1980); opened a sports shop in Leeds, also kept interest in the family's DIY retail business which was sold in a multi-million deal in December 1987.

Paul Madeley could, and would, play anywhere! Among the best versatile footballers from the 1970s, he occupied eight different positions during his long and successful association with Leeds United whom he served from 1962 to 1981, making 711 appearances. He helped Don Revie's team win two League championships, two Fairs Cup finals, the League Cup and also the FA Cup as well as gaining 24 England caps. He made his international debut in May 1971 in a 1-0 win over Northern Ireland. He then played his part in helping England qualify for the 1972 European Championships and after that produced some brilliant performances for his country, starring in resounding victories over Scotland (5-0), Austria (7-0), Cyprus (5-0) and Finland (4-1). Injury forced him into retirement at the age of 37. In 1992 he had a benign brain tumour removed, suffered a heart attack in 2002, had a hip replacement in late 2004 and now has Parkinson's disease.

MAGEE, Thomas Patrick 1922-25 ①

Born: Widnes, Lancs, 6 May 1899
Died: Widnes, 4 May 1974
Career: St Mary's School/Widnes, Appleton Hornets (Rugby League, season 1912-13), St Helens Recreation Club (Rugby League, season 1913-14), Widnes Athletic (amateur, season 1914-15); served in the Army; West Bromwich Albion (professional, January 1919), Crystal Palace (free, player-coach, May 1934), Runcorn (player-manager, July 1935, then manager-coach from April 1936, retired, May 1947); later worked in engineering in Widnes.

Standing just 5ft 2½ ins tall, 'Wee' Tommy Magee in one of the smallest players ever to win a full England cap. He occupied the right-half, outside-right and inside-right positions for West Bromwich Albion between 1919 and 1934, appearing in 434 games. Nicknamed the 'Mighty Atom' and 'Pocket Hercules' he gained League and FA Cup winner's medals and helped the Baggies complete the unique double of promotion and Cup glory in 1931. First capped in March 1923 against Wales, he played in the next international against Sweden, was outstanding when Belgium were battered 4-0 on his home ground at The Hawthorns in December 1924, grafted without success in a 2-0 defeat by Scotland at Hampden Park in April 1925 and had a 'decent 90 minutes' in his last outing when France were defeated 3-2 in Paris a month later. Magee, who twice toured Canada with the FA in 1926 and 1931, was signed by Albion whilst serving with the Army in France in January 1919.

MAKEPEACE, Joseph William Henry 1905-12 ④

Born: Middlesbrough, 22 August 1881
Died: Bebington, Cheshire, 19 December 1952
Career: Liverpool Schools, Everton (professional, April 1902, retired, May 1915, later coach at Goodison Park); played county cricket for Lancashire and Test cricket for England; also engaged as Lancashire CCC coach.

Covering the Scotland-England game at Hampden Park in April 1906, the *Daily Mail* reporter wrote: "Menzies struck England's wing-half Makepeace to the ground with a tackle that by all accounts was one of the most comprehensive yet seen in international football." This was, in fact, Joe Makepeace's first cap and it would be another four years before he gained his second cap, also against Scotland in April 1910. Two more followed in March 1912 before he slipped out of the frame.

As a lively, fearless and hard-working left-half, Makepeace gained both FA Cup and League Championship winner's medals with Everton in 1906 and 1915 respectively, while scoring 23 goals in 336 appearances for the club over a period of 15 years: 1903-18. As a Lancashire and England cricketer, 1906-30, he amassed 25,799 runs, including 44 centuries, with a top-score of 203. He played in four Tests against Australia in 1920-21 and overall appeared in 503 first-class matches. Makepeace is one of only 12 double internationals who have represented England at both cricket and football.

MALE, Charles George 1934-39 ⑲

Born: West Ham, London, 8 May 1910
Died: Toronto, Canada, 19 February 1998
Career: West Ham Schools, Clapton (amateur, May 1927), Arsenal (amateur, November 1929, professional, May 1930); served in Palestine with RAF during WW2; retired as a player, May 1948; became a coach at Highbury, later served club as chief scout and held several administration positions to May 1975); emigrated to Canada with his son.

Initially a left-half, George Male was successfully converted into an England international right-back by Arsenal manager Herbert Chapman. Well-built, clean-kicking and a fine positional player, Male proved the near perfect partner to Eddie Hapgood both at Highbury and for England. Capped for the first time, alongside six of his Arsenal team-mates, in a rough, tough 3-2 victory over Italy on his own ground at Highbury in November 1934, Male remained a regular in the England team until May 1939. Always giving his all, no matter what the circumstances, between 1930 and 1948, he made over 500 appearances for Arsenal (184 during the War), gaining three League championship, and FA Cup and Wartime League (South) Cup winner's medals. He was associated with the Gunners for 48 years.

MANNION, Wilfred James 1946-52 ㉖ ⑪

Born: South Bank, Middlesbrough, 16 May 1918
Died: Middlesbrough, 14 April 2000
Career: St Peter's Secondary School/South Bank, South Bank Juniors (April 1933), South Bank St. Peter's (August 1935), Middlesbrough (professional, September 1936-June 1954), Hull City (December 1954-May 1955), Poole Town (player-coach, September 1955-March 1956), Cambridge United (August 1956), Kings Lynn (May 1958), Havenhill Rovers (October 1958-May 1959); worked at and played for Vauxhall Motors/Luton (June 1959-October 1960), Earlstown (player-manager, October 1960, retired, aged 44, October 1962); returned to Teesside where he lived until his death.

Wilf Mannion was part of an exuberant, free-scoring post WW2 England forward-line under the country's 'first' official manager Walter Winterbottom and his hat-trick in the 7-2 win over Northern Ireland in Belfast in September 1946 was described in the press as 'stunning'. He deserved far more than the 26 full and four Wartime caps he gained for his country, his arresting presence and unmistakable class proved this. Making his international debut against Scotland in a Wartime encounter at Newcastle in February 1941, he 'played with all the assurance of an established international, holding the ball long enough to create an opening – perhaps too long – moving into surprising positions to the confusion of the opposition and showing rare craftsmanship in ball play' wrote Frank Carruthers in the *Daily Mail*.

Tom Finney said Mannion was 'a beautiful exponent of touch football...the ultimate player's player, always reading intentions and moving into position.'

He could turn on a sixpence, had a dummy which could shift anyone and on his day there were few who could touch him for skill. So nice and so modest, his understanding with Finney was rarely displayed better than in the 10-0 drubbing of Portugal in Lisbon in May 1947. Their combined interplay was a joy to watch and between them they set up five goals, Mannion's genius guaranteeing a big victory.

In the 2-2 draw with Northern Ireland at Goodison Park six months later, Mannion had a 70th minute penalty saved by Fulham 'keeper Eddie Hinton – and the roar from the home fans in the near 68,000 crowd could be heard back in Belfast!

Unfortunately when they played together against the USA in the World Cup in Belo Horizonte in 1950, they couldn't do a thing right as England lost 1-0 – one of the biggest upsets ever in top-class football.

Mannion, however, was sorely missed in the Scotland game of April 1951. He had started brilliantly but suffered a fractured cheekbone in the 11th minute and was carried off on a stretcher. Despite Matthews and Finney pairing up on the right-wing, the

Scots still won 3-2 – their second successive win on English soil.

An entrancing inside-forward, a text book footballer who could do anything with the ball, unfortunately Mannion never won a major prize at club level despite scoring 110 goals in 368 games for Middlesbrough (1936-54).

MARINER, Paul 1976-85 ㉟ ⑭

Born: Farnworth near Bolton, 22 May 1953
Career: Horwich County Secondary School, St Gregory's Boys' Club, Chorley (April 1971), Plymouth Argyle (professional, May 1973), Ipswich Town (£220,000 plus Terry Austin and John Peddelty, September 1976), Arsenal (£150,000, February 1984), Portsmouth (free, August 1986), Wollongong City/Australia (loan, 1988), San Francisco Bay Blackhawks/USA (1989, loan), Chorley (May 1989), Albany Capital/USA (player-coach, three spells between 1989 and 1992); also played for Bury Town (briefly); Naxxar Lions/Malta (between September 1990-May 1991 when he retired); Colchester United (Commercial manager, 1991-93); also served with SC Del Sol Phoenix/USA (coach), Juventus FC, Arizona/USA (Director of football), Havard University/USA (soccer assistant-coach); New England Revolution/USA (assistant-coach), Paradise Valley Club/USA (head coach), University of Arizona/USA (part-time coach); Plymouth Argyle (Technical Director, May 2009, manager June 2009-May 2010), Toronto FC/Canada (Director of Player Development, January 2011).

Centre-forward Paul Mariner had an excellent club career and he also performed well at international level, averaging more than a goal every three games for England. He made his debut as a substitute (for Joe Royle) in the 5-0 win over Luxembourg in a World Cup qualifier in March 1977, scored his first goal in the return game seven months later (won 2-0) and netted a real beauty in the 4-0 defeat of Norway at Wembley in September 1980 when he skilfully deceived three defenders before firing the ball majestically into the net with his left foot. He also bagged an important 16th minute winner against Hungary at Wembley in November 1981 and bagged the only goal of the game against Scotland at Hampden Park in May 1982, his brave 13th minute header clinching the Home International championship. This latter effort gave him the record of scoring in six consecutive matches.

His 13th and 14th goals were scored in October and November 1983 against Hungary (3-0) and Luxembourg (4-0) respectively, both in European Championship qualifiers.

The recipient of FA Cup and UEFA Cup winner's medals with Ipswich Town, under manager Bobby Robson, Mariner's playing record with his four English clubs was impressive - 214 goals in 561 first-class matches spread over 15 years. He netted 252 goals in all games. He was replaced as Plymouth's manager by former England international Peter Reid.

MARSDEN, Joseph Thomas 1890-91 ①

Born: Darwen, winter, 1868
Died: Liverpool, 18 January 1897
Career: Darwen (August 1886), Everton (professional, July 1891), retired due to injury and poor health, April 1892)

A very reliable right-back, the lightly-built Joe Marsden was the last Darwen player to win a full cap for England, lining up against Ireland at Molineux in March 1891. Six months later he was injured in his only League game for Everton v. West Bromwich Albion and never played again.

MARSDEN, William 1929-30 ③

Born: Silkworth, County Durham, 10 November 1901
Died: Sheffield, 20 September 1983
Career: Durham junior football, Sunderland (November 1921), Sheffield Wednesday (£450, May 1924, retired, injured, October 1931); Gateshead (trainer-coach, August 1934-April 1935), Be Quick FC/Holland (coach, seasons 1935-37), Hermes DWS/Holland (coach, season 1937-38); also Dutch FA (coach), Sheffield Wednesday (part-time coach, August 1942-April 1944), Doncaster Rovers (manager, April 1944-January 1946); later Worksop Town (caretaker-manager and coach, May 1953-June 1954); was also a licensee in Sheffield.

Bill Marsden, initially an inside-forward who was converted into a very useful left-half, was forced to quit football at the age of 28 due to a spinal injury and broken neck suffered in a collision with his team-mate Roy Goodall when playing in his third international for England in the 3-3 draw with Germany in Berlin in May 1930. He didn't appear for the second-half. Earlier in the season he had been capped in 6-0 and 5-2 wins over Wales and Scotland, playing exceptionally well in the latter game in front of 87,375 fans at Wembley.

MARSH, Rodney William 1970-72 ⑨ ①

Born: Hatfield, Herts, 11 October 1944
Career: Hackney Schools, Alexander Boys' Club (August 1959), West Ham United (amateur, seasons 1960-62), Fulham (professional, October 1962), Queens Park Rangers (£15,000, March 1966), Manchester City (£200,000, March 1972), Cork Hibernians (loan, 1976), Tampa Bay Rowdies/USA (£45,000, January 1976), Fulham (free, August 1976-February 1977), Tampa Bay Rowdies (March 1977-April 1980), New York United/USA (manager, season 1980-81), Carolina Lightnin'/USA (manager, seasons 1981-83), Tampa Bay Rowdies/USA (Indoor League, seasons 1984-86, then Chief Executive to 1989); became a soccer pundit on TV.

Rodney Marsh – a Third Division Championship and League Cup winner with QPR in 1967 – made his England debut as a substitute for Francis Lee, in the 1-1 draw with Switzerland at Wembley in November 1971…Sir Alf Ramsey responding to the crowd chants of 'Rod-Nee, Rod-Nee.'

He went on to appear in eight more internationals, up to January 1972, scoring just one goal, in a 3-0 win over Wales in May 1972 before his England career ended prematurely after he made a sarcastic comment to Ramsey. In an interview in 2005, Marsh stated that Ramsey told him "I'll be watching you for the first 45 minutes and if you don't work harder I'll pull you off at half-time," to which Marsh replied: "Crikey, Alf, at Manchester City all we get is an orange and a cup of tea." He was never selected again.

Also capped twice at U23 level, Marsh was a real character and excellent footballer, skilful, entertaining, with a terrific bodyswerve. One of a generation of highly talented 'maverick' players that emerged during the 1960s and '70s, he never quite fulfilled his potential yet still netted 270 goals in 606 appearances at club level, 134 of his goals coming in 242 appearances for QPR and another 56 in 144 outings for Manchester City. He played alongside George Best at Fulham.

MARSHALL, Thomas 1879-81 ②

Born: Withnell, Lancs, 12 September 1858
Died: Blackburn, 29 April 1917
Career: Darwen (seasons 1877-86), Blackburn Olympic (August 1886, retired May 1887); became a cotton mill worker.

A very fast and clever outside-right who passed with deadly accuracy, Tom Marshall played in successive internationals against Wales in March 1880 and February 1881, setting up a goal for Francis Sparks in the 3-2 win at Wrexham on his debut.

MARTIN, Alvin Edward 1980-87 ⑰

Born: Bootle, Lancs, 29 July 1958
Career: Everton (schoolboy forms, seasons 1972-74), West Ham United (apprentice, June 1974, professional, July 1976), Leyton Orient (May 1996, retired, April 1997); Southend United (manager, seasons 1997-99); became a soccer pundit on TalkSport and Sky Sports.

Centre-half Alvin Martin made 586 senior appearances for West Ham in a successful 22-year career at Upton Park (1974-96), in which he became one of only two players, along with Billy Bonds, to be awarded two testimonials. Nicknamed 'Stretch' he played alongside Bonds in the centre of the Hammers' defence, winning the FA Cup and Second Division championship in successive seasons at the start of the '80s. Manager Ron Greenwood, who signed Martin as a youngster for West Ham, awarded him his first England cap in May 1981 against Brazil at Wembley. However, injury ruled him out of the 1982 World Cup finals in Spain, but he was playing some of the finest football of his career when England's next manager, Bobby Robson, included him in his squad for the 1986 tournament in Mexico. Martin played in the victory over Paraguay, but was surprisingly dropped for the next game, the quarter-final defeat by Argentina and the infamous 'Hand of God' goal. The last of his 17 appearances for England came in the 1-0 defeat by Sweden in Stockholm in September 1986.

In April 1986, Martin achieved the rare feat of scoring a hat-trick against three different Newcastle United goalkeepers — Martin Thomas, who was then injured, and outfield players Chris Hedworth and Peter Beardsley — in a Division One match. His sons, David and Joe, are both footballers.

MARTIN, Henry 1913-14 ①

Born: Selston, Nottinghamshire, 5 December 1891
Died: Nottingham, summer 1974
Career: Sutton Junction (August 1909), Sunderland (January 1912), Nottingham Forest (WW1 guest, seasons 1915-19, signed May 1922), Rochdale (June 1925. retired June 1929, appointed trainer, then caretaker-manager, July-August 1930); Mansfield Town (trainer-coach, November 1933, manager, December 1933-March 1935), Swindon Town (trainer, June 1935; remained on staff at The County Ground until 1955).

A League championship winner with Sunderland in 1913, Harry Martin was unusually tall for a left-winger at almost 6ft. With a long, raking stride, he charged past defenders with consummate ease and could deliver a telling cross on the run. He gained his only full cap for England (as partner to Blackburn's Eddie Latherton) in a 3-0 defeat by Ireland at Middlesbrough in February 1914. Martin also appeared in two Victory internationals in 1919 and represented the Football League.

MARTYN, Antony Nigel 1991-2002 ㉓

Born: St Austell, Cornwall, 11 August 1966
Career: St Blazey FC/Cornwall (August 1984), Bristol Rovers (professional, August 1987), Crystal Palace (£1m, November 1989), Leeds United (£2.25m, July 1996), Everton (£5,000, July 2003, retired, June 2006); Bradford City (goalkeeping coach, March 2007-May 2009).

Replacing Chris Woods as a second-half substitute, goalkeeper Nigel Martyn made his England debut in the 2-2 draw with the CIS in Moscow in April 1992. He did well and retained his place for the next game v. Hungary but was then substituted by manager Graham Taylor in favour of the returning Seaman. After that Martyn, a fine shot-stopper, who commanded his area with authority, was basically second choice behind David Seaman, yet continued to add more caps to his tally, winning his 23rd and last ten years after his first, in the 2-2 friendly draw with Cameroon in Kobe in May 2002.

He was outstanding in the goalless draw with Poland in Warsaw in September 1999, produced several good saves in the 2-0 win over Ukraine at Wembley a year later and played exceedingly well in draws with Sweden in November 2001 and Holland three months later. He also played in 11 U21 and six B internationals and during his club career he appeared in 846 first-class matches, 349 for Palace and 207 for Leeds.

MARWOOD, Brian 1988-89 ①

Born: Seaham Harbour, 5 February 1960
Career: Seaham Secondary Modern School, Hull City (apprentice, June 1976, professional, February 1978), Sheffield Wednesday (£115,000, August 1984), Arsenal (£600,000, March 1988), Sheffield United (£350,000, September 1990), Middlesbrough (loan, October 1991), Swindon Town (non-contract, March 1993), Barnet (free, August 1993, retired, May 1994); also Chairman of the PFA (1990-93); Radio 5 Live, Sky Sports and Star Sport football summariser; then Manchester City (Football Administrator).

Brian Marwood's international career lasted just nine minutes. He came on as a late substitute (for Chris Waddle) in the 1-1 draw with Saudi Arabia in Riyadh in November 1988, making him one of five Arsenal players used in that game. His club-mate Tony Adams scored England's goal. In his 15-year professional career (1978-93), wide man Marwood scored just over 100 goals in almost 400 appearances for his seven clubs, having his best spells with Hull City and Sheffield Wednesday. He helped Arsenal win the League title in 1989.

MASKREY, Harry Mart 1907-08 ①

Born: Dronfield, Derbyshire, 8 October 1880
Died: Derby, 21 April 1927
Career: Ripley Athletic (August 1900), Derby County (professional, May 1903), Bradford City (October 1909), Ripley Town (June 1911), Burton All Saints (1913), Derby County (September 1920), Burton All Saints (August 1922, retired, December 1922); ran his own business in Derby.

A well-built, courageous and athletic goalkeeper, Harry Maskery – a former miner – played once for England, deputising for Sam Hardy in a 3-1 win over Ireland in Belfast in February 1908. He also played for the Football League and made 222 appearances in his two spells with Derby County. He played his last game of football at the age of 42.

MASON, Charles 1886-90 ③

Born: Wolverhampton, 13 April 1863
Died: Wolverhampton, 3 February 1941
Career: St Luke's School/Wolverhampton, Wolverhampton Wanderers (August 1877, retired May 1892); also West Bromwich Albion (guest, May 1988).

A lithe and indomitable full-back who knew no fear, Charlie Mason was the first Wolves player to win a full cap – lining up for England in the 7-0 win over Ireland at Bramall Lane in February 1887. His other two caps followed against Wales in February 1888 (won 5-1) and versus Ireland again (won 9-1) in March 1890. He played in the 1889 FA Cup final v. double winners Preston and also appeared in Wolves' first-ever League game v. Aston Villa in September 1888. He made 108 appearances for Wolves and as a guest for WBA, played in the 'Championship of the World' encounter against Renton (Scotland) in 1888.

MATTHEWS, Reginald Derrick 1955-57 ⑤

Born: Coventry, 20 December 1933
Died: Coventry, 7 October 2001
Career: Barkers Butt School/Coventry, Modern Machines FC/ Coventry (August 1945), Coventry City (groundstaff, December 1947, professional, May 1950), Chelsea (£22,500, November 1956), Derby County (£12,000, December 1961), Rugby Town (player-manager, August 1968-May 1969); later worked 20 years for Massey Ferguson (Coventry), retiring through ill-heath in 1990.

Goalkeeper Reg Matthews made his international debut against Scotland in front of 134,000 fans at Hampden Park in April 1956 while with Coventry City – thus becoming the first player since WW2 to be capped from outside the top two Divisions. Flattened in an early challenge, he had a sniff of smelling salts and quickly pulled himself round to go on and play very well in the 1-1 draw, pulling off at least five good saves including one beauty from Graham Leggat.

A month or so later Matthews played well in a 4-2 win over Brazil under the Wembley lights, kept a clean-sheet in the draw against Sweden in a near gale-force wind in Stockholm, helped England beat the reigning World champions West Germany 3-1 but blamed himself for Jimmy McIlroy's equalizing goal in his final international against Northern Ireland in Belfast in October 1956. "I palmed a long throw from Peter McParland into his path when I should have punched the ball clear," he said.

Matthews, who smoked like a trooper, made 116 appearances for Coventry, 148 for Chelsea and 246 for Derby. He was also honoured by England at B and U23 levels.

MATTHEWS, Sir Stanley, CBE 1934-57 (54) ⑪

Born: Hanley, Stoke-on-Trent, 1 February 1915
Died: Stoke-on-Trent, 23 February 2000
Career: Wellington Road School/Hanley, Stoke St Peter's (May 1927), Stoke City (office boy/amateur, September 1930, professional, February 1932); WW2 guest for Airdrieonians, Arsenal, Blackpool, Crewe Alexandra, Manchester United, Greenock Morton, Rangers and Wrexham; joined Blackpool (£11,500, May 1947); Waterford & Bohemians XI (guest, 1953); represented Nigeria FA XI (1957), Toronto City (loan, summer, 1961); Stoke City (£2,500, October 1961-May 1965), Toronto City (June 1965, retiring on his return to England); Port Vale (general manager, July 1965, honorary manager July 1968-May 1969); moved to Malta; Hibernians/Malta (manager, April 1970-May 1971); thereafter coached in Egypt, Soweto/South Africa and the Middle East; also Walton & Hersham FC (President); Stan's Men/ Soweto (coach); also coached in Australia, Canada and USA; became a Life Member and President of Stoke City (until his death); also Blackpool (Honorary vice-President) and City of Vale Club (President).

Football's first knight (honoured in January 1965) and 'a name of unsurpassed lustre' Stanley Matthews was an outside-right of pure genius whose body-swerve, change of pace, exquisite close ball control and general wing-wizardry enchanted football supporters the world over. His captain in the 1950s, Billy Wright, said: "He was the easiest man in the world to play with… probably the greatest footballer of all time."

A unique talent from the start, his playing days started in earnest when he joined Stoke City in 1930, and ended with the same club 25 years later, having assisted Blackpool in between times.

Matthews's international career – at times so magical as to strain credulity – spanned a record 22 years and 228 days (some two years longer than Peter Shilton). He made a scoring debut for England at the age of 19 in September 1934 against Wales at Ninian Park and played his last game – his swansong - in a World Cup qualifier against Denmark in Copenhagen in May 1957. He is, of course, the oldest player ever to appear in a full England international, aged 42 years and 103 days. He is also the oldest outfield player to line up for England in the World Cup – aged 39 years, 145 days in June 1954 – and is one of only eight players to have won caps in three different decades (1930s, '40s, and '50s)

Covering his first game in the Principality, one reporter stated: 'He showed great promise and scored in a 4-0 victory.'

But the barbarous game against Italy at Highbury a year later set him back considerably. In his autobiography, published in 1989, he said: "I was only 19 and it was one of the roughest games of my life. In the dressing room at half-time Tom Whittaker, our trainer insisted that we should go out and try to play football. I felt relieved, because trying to play the Italians at their own game would have led to a blood-bath. It took me a while to get back to my normal game after that match."

Matthews, who was suffering from nerves and shock of being in such a ruthless match, was dropped from the next four internationals. "I was glad to be out of the news for a while," he said.

Some say his best performance for England was against Belgium in Brussels in September 1947. The 'Master of Dribble' laid on all the goals in a 5-2 win and at the end of the game received a standing ovation from the Belgium crowd. He started the slaughter as early as the 35th second, crossing for Tommy Lawton to power home a header. And, in pouring rain, no fewer than five home defenders tried to get the ball off him as he weaved his way through to set up the fourth goal for Tom Finney. Matthews certainly put on an astonishing show.

Soon afterwards, when Wales were beaten 3-0 at Ninian Park, full-back Wally Barnes was given a real 'roasting' by Matthews. After the game the Arsenal defender admitted that "Stan had run me dizzy."

Matthews missed that disastrous 1-0 World Cup defeat by the USA in 1950. After the game he said: "The will to win was sadly lacking. I blame the defeat on a pre-match talk on playing tactics that had been introduced for the first time by our new team manager."

Some say if he had played, England would have won. Maybe, but it was a result that shock the world.

Recalled for the next game against Spain, Matthews caused turmoil down the right in the first-half but all his good work went to waste. The Spaniards grabbed a goal on 50 minutes and England went out of the competition at the first attempt. Matthews left the pitch in Rio, his head hung in shame. "That was the worst day of my football career," he said.

After a terrific performance in a 4-2 win over Brazil under the lights at Wembley in May 1956, Nilton Santos, the Brazilian full-back, one of the best in the world at that time, said to Matthews "You are a king."

Matthews's 11th and last goal for England was perhaps his best. It came after just two minutes in the 1-1 draw with Northern Ireland in Belfast in October 1956. Jackie Blanchflower, the Irish defender, said: "Why does he pick on us? When I was a schoolboy in 1948, I saw him score against Ireland in a 6-2 win – now he's done it again. Can't grumble really - he's such a great player."

Matthews was 41 years, 248 days old when he netted against the Irish – making him England's oldest-ever marksman.

During his exciting and wonderful career, 'Sir Stan' - the 'Master of dribble' who played in his last match for charity at Grangemouth in 1981, aged 66 – appeared in 1,127 football matches (he thought it was nearer 2,000 including all those for charity). He starred in 701 League games (332 for Stoke and 369 for Blackpool) and netted 80 goals. He also played in 86 FA Cup-ties (9 goals scored), appeared in 13 Inter-League games (2 goals), in 24 Wartime and five Victory internationals (2 goals), twice represented Great Britain (in 1947 and 1956) and why he won only 54 full caps, no-one really knows!

A Football League War Cup and FA Cup winner with Blackpool in 1943 and 1953 respectively, the latter after two runner's-up medals, he also gained two Second Division championship winner's medals with Stoke in 1933 and 1963, was twice voted FWA 'Footballer of the Year' in 1948 and 1963, captured the 'European Footballer of the Year' award in 1956 and was made a CBE a year later.

His testimonial match, staged at The Victoria Ground in April 1965, attracted a crowd of 35,000 and featured his own Stoke City XI against an International XI, the latter winning 6-4.

In 1987, 'Sir Stan' was awarded an honorary degree from Keele University in Staffordshire. Twenty-eight years earlier, Matthews was the first celebrity to feature on the BBC TV programme *This Is Your Life* with Eamonn Andrews.

His son, Stanley junior, was a fine tennis player who won the Wimbledon Boys' singles title in 1962 and represented Great Britain in the Davis Cup in 1971.

MATTHEWS, Vincent 1927-28 ②

Born: Aylesbury, 15 January 1896
Died: Oxford, 15 November 1950
Career: St Frideswade FC/Aylesbury (May 1914), Oxford City (August 1919), Bournemouth & Boscombe Athletic (August 1921), Bolton Wanderers (January 1923), Tranmere Rovers (May 1925), Sheffield United (June 1927), Shamrock Rovers (May 1931), Shrewsbury Town (1932), Oswestry Town (player-manager, season 1933-34); Morris Motors FC (player-coach, season 1934-35); worked at the Morris Motor Car factory, Cowle, and coached works football team from 1948 until his death.

A late developer, centre-half Vince Matthews, at 6ft tall and 13st in weight, was rated as one of the best central defenders of the late 1920s. A strong tackler with a powerful kick, he played twice for England on their end of season 1928 tour, starring in 5-1 and 3-1 wins over France in Paris and Belgium in Brussels. He made over 300 appearances in his club career, 212 in the Football League with Bolton, Tranmere and Sheffield United.

MAYNARD, William John 1872-76 ②

Born: Kensington, London, 18 March 1853
Died: Durham, 2 September 1921
Career: 1st Surrey Rifles (from summer 1870), Wanderers (season 1876-77); represented Surrey County (1870s); after retiring, served as District Registrar of Durham (1903-21).

Bill Maynard played as a forward for the opening 45 minutes of England's first-ever international against Scotland in November 1872. Then, during the interval, he swapped places with Bob Barker and kept goal throughout the second period. Both 'keepers' kept clean-sheets in the 0-0 draw. He won his second cap as a left-winger in a 3-0 defeat by the Scots at Partick in March 1876. His son, Alfred, played for England at rugby union before losing his life during WW1.

MEADOWS, James 1954-55 ①

Born: Didsbury, 21 July 1931
Died: Manchester, 11 January 1994
Career: Bolton YMCA (from April 1944), Southport (amateur, October 1948, professional, March 1951), Manchester City (March 1951, retired, injured, October 1957; trainer at Maine Road from June 1959, trainer-coach, August 1960-April 1965); Stockport County (trainer-coach, January 1966, then manager, October 1966-April 1969), Bury (assistant-manager, July-September 1969), Blackpool (trainer, September 1969, acting manager October 1970, assistant-manager, December 1970), Bolton Wanderers (manager for 81 days, January-April 1971), Southport (manager, May 1971-May 1974), Stockport County (May 1974-August 1975), Blackpool (caretaker-manager, February-May 1978); later Kuwait Sporting Club (assistant-manager/coach, seasons 1978-80); also coached in Sweden with GIF Sundsvall.

Jimmy Meadows won his only England cap as Roger Byrne's full-back partner, in a 7-2 Wembley victory over Scotland in April 1955, a few weeks before he was carried off injured in the Manchester City's FA Cup final defeat by Newcastle United. Once a forceful right-winger, and useful centre-forward, Meadows was forced to retire in October 1957, aged 26. As a manager, he guided both Stockport (1967) and Southport (1973) to the Fourth Division championship.

MEDLEY, Leslie Dennis 1950-51 ⑥ ①

Born: Edmonton, London, 3 September 1920
Died: London, 22 February 2001
Career: Edmonton Schools, London Schools, Middlesex Schools, Tottenham Juniors (September 1933), Tottenham Hotspur (amateur, May 1935), Northfleet (loan, seasons 1935-37); returned to Tottenham Hotspur (signed professional, February 1939); WW2 guest for Aldershot, Clapton Orient, Millwall and West Ham United; also represented Greenbacks/Canada, Ulster United/Canada; returned to Tottenham Hotspur (January 1948, retired, May 1953), assisted Randfontein FC/South Africa (as player-coach, seasons 1958-61).

First registered with the club at the age of 14, Les Medley was a fast and tricky outside-left who became a key member of Tottenham Hotspur's famous 'push and run' side that won the Second and First Division championships in 1950 and 1951. He gained his first England cap in a 4-2 win over Wales at Sunderland in November 1950, partnering his Spurs team-mate Eddie Baily. Despite there being several other good outside-lefts around at the same time, he added five more to his tally over the next 12 months, having a terrific game in the 2-0 win over Northern Ireland at Villa Park in November 1951. Medley retired in May 1953, having scored 74 goals in 254 appearances for Spurs.

MEEHAN, Thomas 1923-24 ①

Born: Harpurhey, Manchester, 4 March 1896
Died: Wandsworth, London, 18 August 1924
Career: Harpurhey Boys Club (April 1910), Newton FC (August 1912), Walkden Central (April 1915), Rochdale Town (January 1917), Manchester United (£1,500, June 1917), Atherton (loan), WW1 guest for Rochdale, season 1918-19; Chelsea (£3,300, December 1920 until his death).

Although standing only 5ft 5ins tall and weighing just 9st 8lbs, Tommy Meehan battled it out with the roughest and toughest players in the game. A very competitive and purposeful left-half he was awarded his only England cap v. Ireland in October 1923, having a 'moderate' game in a 2-1 defeat in Belfast. Sadly Meehan died of polio in St George's Hospital, London, whilst at the peak of his career. Over 2,000 mourners attended his funeral after which a fund was set up which realised £1,850 for his family.

MELIA, James John 1962-63 ② ①

Born: Liverpool, 1 November 1937
Career: St Anthony's School/Liverpool, Liverpool Boys, Liverpool Schools, Liverpool (groundstaff, April 1953, amateur, May 1954, professional, November 1954), Wolverhampton Wanderers (£55,000, March 1964), Southampton (£30,000, December 1964), Aldershot (£9,000, player-coach, November 1968, player-manager, April 1969-January 1972), Crewe Alexandra (player-player/coach, May 1972, retired as a player, May 1973, remained as manager, until December 1974); Southport (manager, July-September 1975); coached in Middle East (from October 1975); California Lasers/USA (coach and scout, late 1970s); Brighton & Hove Albion (scout and coach, 1980, then manager, March-October 1983); FC Belenenses/ Portugal (manager, October 1983-November 1985), Stockport County (manager, July-November 1986); Kuwait (coaching, seasons 1987-90), Dallas/Texas (indoor soccer coach, seasons 1991-93).

Clever, scheming inside-forward Jimmy Melia was completely overshadowed by Jim Baxter when he made his England debut (with his Liverpool club-mate Gerry Byrne) in April 1963, in the 2-1 defeat by Scotland at the 'new' Wembley with its brand new £500,000 roof which swept all round the stadium. Despite having a 'poor game', the 'Scouser'. with his receding hairline, was called up again two months later – and scored in an 8-1 win over Switzerland in Basle.
    Also capped by England at Schoolboy and Youth team levels and a Football League representative, Melia scored 105 goals in a career tally of 571 appearances, gaining both Second and First Division championship winning medals with Liverpool in the space of two years: 1962-64. He also helped Southampton clinch promotion from Division Two and as a manager took Brighton to the 1983 FA Cup final.

MERCER, David William 1922-23 ② ①

Born: St Helens, Lancs, 20 March 1893
Died: Torbay, Devon, 4 June 1950
Career: Prescot Athletic (April 1908), Skelmersdale United (August 1911), Hull City (professional, January 1914), Sheffield United (£4,500, December 1920), Shirebrook (November 1928), Torquay United (June 1929, retired, May 1930); continued to live and work in Torquay.

After an unbroken run of 200 appearances for Hull City during WW1, fast-raiding outside-right David Mercer gained two England caps as Jimmy Seed's wing partner in season 1922-23, lining up against Ireland at The Hawthorns (won 2-0) and scoring in the 6-1 victory over Belgium at Highbury. Mercer was an FA Cup winner with Sheffield United in 1925. His son played for Torquay after WW2.

MERCER, Joseph, OBE 1938-39 ⑤

Born: Ellesmere Port, Cheshire, 9 August 1914
Died: Manchester, 9 August 1990
Career: Ellesmere Port & Cheshire Schools, Elton Green (April 1927), Shell Mex FC (September 1928), Chester (briefly, late 1928), Runcorn (April 1929), Blackburn Rovers (trial), Ellesmere Port Town (1930), Bolton Wanderers (trial), Everton (amateur, August 1931, professional, September 1932); WW2 guest for Aldershot and Chester; Arsenal (£7,000, November 1946, retired, injured, May 1953; returned, but retired for good, May 1954); ran grocery shop in the Wirral for a year; Sheffield United (manager, August 1955-December 1958), Aston Villa (manager, December 1958-July 1964); out of football for a year; Manchester City (manager, July 1965-October 1971, then general manager, to June 1972), Coventry City (general manager, June 1972-July 1975, also director from April 1975-July 1981); England (caretaker-manager, May 1974).

Spindly, lean and light, Joe Mercer was a tireless performer at left-half and his cultured, wobbly legs, became legendary. He loved to take the ball through to his front-men, eventually supplying the perfect pass, although, said one reporter: 'He occasionally carried the leather too far upfield before choosing to get rid of it.'
    A fine all-rounder, aware and clever, like many players of his generation, Mercer lost out on seven seasons of football due to the Second World War. He became a sergeant-major in the Army and played in 27 Wartime internationals, scoring one goal v. Scotland at Wembley in February 1944 (the only defender to find the net in the 36 Wartime internationals played by England). He also starred in two unofficial internationals v. Switzerland in Berne and Zurich in July 1945.
    He partnered Stan Cullis, who was born in the same town, in 15 of his wartime games.
    Mercer's five senior caps all came in season 1938-39 when he helped Everton win the League Championship. He made an impressive debut in a 7-0 win over Ireland in the November but then his manager at Goodison Park, Theo Kelly, accused him of 'not trying' in the next game against Scotland. But in reality Mercer had sustained a severe cartilage injury a week earlier and had consulted an orthopaedic specialist. Although in some pain, he played well, helping England record a 2-1 victory. The Everton management, however, refused to believe him, and Mercer had to pay for the surgery himself. After 184 games for Everton, 'Jovial Joe' went on to captain Arsenal, helping the Gunners win the League title in 1948 and 1953 and the FA Cup in 1950, when he was also voted FWA 'Footballer of the Year'. Also a Football League representative, a double fracture of his left leg, suffered in a First Division game against Liverpool at Highbury, ended his career in 1954 after he had made 275 appearances for Arsenal.
    As a manager, Mercer won the First and Second Division Championships, FA Cup, League Cup and European Cup Winners' Cup, all with Manchester City, and the Second Division title and League Cup with Aston Villa. His first game in charge of England was against Wales in Cardiff in May 1974, celebrating with a 2-0 win. He gave Keith Weller his debut in this game and he set up a goal for Stan Bowles.
    Awarded the OBE for services to football in 1976, Mercer suffered with Alzheimer's disease late in life and died, sitting in his favourite armchair, on his 76th birthday in 1990.

MERRICK, Gilbert Harold 1951-54 (23)

Born: Sparkhill, Birmingham, 26 January 1922
Died: Sparkbrook, Birmingham, 3 February 2010
Career: Acocks Green Council School, Fenton Rovers (August 1935), Shirley Juniors (May 1936), Olton Sports (August 1937), Shirley Juniors (September 1938), Birmingham City (amateur, August 1938 – played on loan for Solihull Town in season 1938-39 – professional at St Andrew's, August 1939, retired, May 1960; then team manager, June 1960-May 1964); had guested for Northampton Town, Nottingham Forest and West Bromwich Albion during WW2; Bromsgrove Rovers (manager, August 1967-May 1970); Atherstone Town (manager, July 1970-May 1972); became personnel manager of a Midland Stores Group.

Gil Merrick was England's unfortunate goalkeeper who conceded 13 goals against the 'Magical Magyars' of Hungary when they recorded 6-3 and 7-1 victories in November 1953 at Wembley and May 1954 in Budapest.

In the World Cup in Switzerland soon afterwards, Gil Merrick was certainly responsible for two of Uruguay's goals in their 4-2 quarter final victory in Basle. He allowed a speculative long-range volley from the centre-half Varela to elude him with the scores level at 1-1 and was caught flat-footed when Schiaffino made it 3-1 from a direct free-kick early in the second-half. These errors proved fatal, not only for England but also for Merrick, who was never chosen again.

Those mistakes in Switzerland were highlighted by Stan Matthews in his autobiography. "He disappointed me in the quarter-final...when we were playing well and had a chance," said Stan. "He let in two, maybe three at the near post," said the winger.

Merrick made his England debut (in place of fellow Midlander Bert Williams) in a 2-0 win over Northern Ireland at Villa Park in November 1951, producing two brilliant saves to deny Eddie McMorran and Sammy Smyth. Two years later he prevented John Charles from netting a hat-trick in England's 4-1 win over Wales in October 1953.

A one-club man, Merrick served Blues for 21 years as a player, amassing a record 551 first-class appearances (720 overall), gaining a Football League South and two Second Division championship winner's medals in the process. After retiring he became manager at St Andrew's and led Blues into the final of the Inter Cities Fairs Cup in 1961 and to victory in the League Cup final two years later. He also represented the Football League on 11 occasions.

Before his death, Merrick penned the foreword to my book: *The Complete Record of Birmingham City* (published in 2010 by DB Publishing, Derby).

MERSON, Paul Charles (21) (3)

Born: Harlesden, London, 20 March 1968
Career: Brent Schools, Ealing & District Boys, Middlesex Schools, Forest United (season 1980-81); had trials for Chelsea, Queens Park Rangers and Watford during season 1981-82; Arsenal (schoolboy forms, April 1982, apprentice, July 1984, professional, December 1985), Brentford (loan, January-February 1987), Middlesbrough (£4.5m, July 1997), Aston Villa (£6.75m, September 1998), Portsmouth (free, August 2002), Walsall (free, August 2003, player-caretaker-manager, March 2004, player-manager, May 2004, retired as a player, May 2005, continued as manager until February 2006); Tamworth (one game, retired March 2006); wrote column in the Arsenal official programme, now a soccer pundit on Sky Sports and Arabic TV

A darting, skilful forward with good pace and ability, Paul Merson won four Youth, four U21, four B (some as captain) and 21 full caps for England, gaining his first in the senior category as a second-half substitute for Trevor Steven in a 1-0 friendly defeat by Germany at Wembley in September 1991 and his last in a 2-0 win over the Czech Republic in November 1998, having played against Argentina in the World Cup finals in France five months earlier. He netted his first international goal in the 2-2 draw with Czechoslovakia in Prague in February 1992; his second earned a 1-1 draw with Switzerland in Berne in March 1998 and his third came in his last match against the Czechs.

Merson's career was put on the line in November 1994 when he admitted to being an alcoholic and cocaine addict. After a three-month rehabilitation programme organised by the FA he returned to action with Arsenal in February 1995 and under caretaker-manager Stewart Houston, helped the Gunners reach the Cup Winners' Cup final for the second season in a row. Unfortunately his addiction to drinking and also to gambling continued for quite some time. When he was sold to Middlesbrough for £5m in 1997, he became the most expensive player ever signed by a non-Premiership club. Merson won two Premiership titles, the League Cup, the FA Cup and ECWC with Arsenal for whom he scored 99 goals in 423 senior games. His professional career overall realised 152 goals in 773 club appearances.

METCALFE, Victor 1950-51 (2)

Born: Barrow-in-Furness, 3 February 1922
Died: Huddersfield, 6 April 2003
Career: West Riding Schools, Ravensthorpe Albion (April 1938), Huddersfield Town (amateur, January 1940, professional, December 1945), Hull City (June 1958, retired, February 1960); Huddersfield Town (Youth team coach, June 1961-October 1964), Halifax Town (coach/scout, December 1964, then manager, June 1966-November 1967).

Vic Metcalfe was a very effective, hard-working, strong-running outside-left who had a fine career with Huddersfield Town for whom he scored 87 goals in 434 League appearances between 1945 and 1958. He partnered his club-mate Harold Hassall in his two England games in May 1951 v. Argentina at Wembley (won 2-1) and Portugal at Goodison Park (won 5-2). He twice represented the Football League.

MEW, John William 1920-21 (1)

Born: Sunderland, 30 March 1889
Died: Barton-upon-Irwell, Eccles, Manchester, 16 January 1963
Career: Marley Hill Council School, Church Choir FC (May 1905), Marley Hill St Cuthbert's (August 1907), Blaydon United (June 1909), Marley Hill United (August 1911), Manchester United (amateur, July 1912, professional, September 1912), Barrow (September 1926, retired, August 1927), Lyra FC/Belgium (trainer-coach, October 1927), Lima FC/Peru (coach, June 1928-May 1930); later worked in a Manchester factory before going into a business partnership with former England and Lancashire cricketer Cecil Parkin.

Blessed with a safe pair of hands, strong wrists and excellent positional sense, goalkeeper Jackie Mew appeared in 199 games and received two benefits from Manchester United between 1912 and 1926. Replacing Sam Hardy for his only international outing, he starred in a 2-0 win over Ireland at Roker Park in October 1920.

MIDDLEDITCH, Bernard 1896-97 ①

Born: Highgate, London, 5 November 1871
Died: Aldwich, London, 3 October 1949
Career: Educated privately; Jesus College/Cambridge University (seasons 1894-97); played for Corinthians (seasons 1895-1905); Master at University School/Hastings (1895-1900), at Malvern Public School (1900-03) and Harrow (from 1903 until retiring in 1932).

A clever, industrious half-back, Bernard Middleditch played in 82 games in ten years for the Corinthians, winning his only England cap in February 1897 v. Ireland at Nottingham when he assisted in two goals in a 6-0 victory.

MILBURN, John Edward Thompson 1948-56 ⑬ ⑩

Born: Ashington, County Durham, 11 May 1924
Died: Ashington, 8 October 1988
Career: Welfare Rangers (August 1939), REC Rangers (April 1940), Hirst East Old Boys (August 1941), Ashington ATC (April 1942), Newcastle United (professional, August 1943); WW2 guest for Sheffield United (1944-45) and Sunderland (1944-45); Linfield (player-manager, June 1957 in part-exchange deal involving J. Hill), Yiewsley (player, November 1960, then player-manager, December 1960-May 1962); Reading (briefly as part-time coach), Carmel College/Wallington (coach, October 1962), Ipswich Town (manager, January 1963-September 1964); Gateshead (manager, November 1965-May 1966); later a columnist of the News of the World.

Jackie Milburn was a terrific centre-forward, strong and mobile who could also play equally as well on the right-wing. Unfortunately, many thought he didn't have a change of pace which sometimes is essential, but nevertheless he certainly produced the goods for Newcastle and to a certain extent for England.
   'Wor Jackie' announced his England debut with a neatly headed goal in a 6-2 win over Northern Ireland at Windsor Park in October 1948 and after found the net at regular intervals on the international circuit as he did for his club (Newcastle). He bagged a smart hat-trick in a 4-1 win over Wales in a World Cup qualifier in October 1949 and also netted with confidence in wins over Switzerland (6-0), Argentina (2-1), Portugal (5-2) and Wales again (4-2), while his effort against Scotland at Wembley in April 1949 was to no avail as the visitors won 3-1. The recipient of three FA Cup winner's medals with Newcastle in five years, he scored with a brilliant first minute header in the 1955 victory over Manchester City. Milburn spent 14 years at St James' Park (1943-57) during which time he notched 239 goals in 494 appearances for the Geordies. He also played three times for the Football League, had four outings for the Irish League, won the Irish Cup in 1960 with Linfield for whom he scored 102 goals in two seasons and was voted Ulster 'Footballer of the Year' in 1958. Later rewarded with the Freedom of the City of Newcastle, Milburn died of cancer and virtually the whole population turned out for his funeral. A statue on Newcastle's main thoroughfare now recognizes the footballing achievements of the 'working man's hero' Jackie Milburn.
   Milburn was the son of Alexander Milburn, the uncle of the four professional brothers, namely John Milburn (Leeds United and Bradford City), George Milburn (Leeds United and Chesterfield), Jimmy Milburn (Leeds United and Bradford City) and Stan Milburn (Chesterfield, Leicester City and Rochdale). Also related to the Milburn family are the England international brothers Jack and Bobby Charlton.

MILLER, George Brian 1960-61 ①

Born: Hapton, Burnley, Lancs, 19 January 1937
Died: Burnley, 7 April 2007
Career: St Mary's College/Blackburn, Blackburn Schools, Burnley (professional, February 1954, retired, injured, April 1968; became first team coach, then trainer, had two spells as manager, October 1979-January 1983 and July 1986-January 1989, also served club as chief scout).

Replacing Bobby Robson, and playing out of position on the right, wing-half Brian Miller made his England debut, along with his Burnley team-mate John Angus, in a 3-1 defeat by Austria in Vienna in May 1961, being responsible for a late goal that sealed the game. Also capped three times at U23 level, he was a strapping player who appeared in 455 games for Burnley between 1954 and 1967, gaining a League championship winner's medal in 1960. As manager he guided the Clarets to the Third Division title in 1982 and spent well over 25 years at Turf Moor – a wonderful and dedicated clubman.

MILLER, Harold Sydney 1922-23 ①

Born: Watford, 20 May 1902
Died: Watford, 24 October 1988
Career: Villa Juniors/Herts (July 1917), St Albans City (amateur, September 1919), Charlton Athletic (amateur, January 1922, professional, December 1922), Chelsea (£1,500, June 1923), Northampton Town (free, June-September 1939), Wellingborough Town (briefly during the 1945-46 season).

A workmanlike winger who later switched to left-half, Harold Miller's career covered 16 years during which time he made well over 400 appearances for his three major clubs, scoring 44 goals in 363 outings for Chelsea. Partnering Middlesbrough's Tom Urwin on the left-flank, he produced a competent display on his England debut in a 3-1 win over Sweden in Stockholm in May 1923. He was with Third Division (S) side Charlton Athletic at the time.

MILLS, Daniel John 2000-04 ⑲

Born: Norwich, 18 May 1977
Career: Norwich City (apprentice, June 1993, professional, November 1994), Charlton Athletic (£350,000, March 1998), Leeds United (£4.1m, May 2000), Middlesbrough (loan, August 2000-May 2004), Manchester City (free, June 2004), Hull City (loan, September-November 2006), Charlton Athletic (loan, March-May 2007), Derby County (loan, January-May 2008; retired, August 2009); became a TV soccer pundit.

Shaven-haired right-back Danny Mills made the strange admission in an interview that he disliked football and would never watch it once he stopped playing. Despite his odd attitude, he managed 19 caps, angering many budding footballers by playing every minute of England's 2002 World Cup campaign, prompting the question on many people's lips: 'why not me?' Following a series of impressive performances for Leeds, Mills made his international debut in May 2001, as a substitute in a friendly against Mexico at Pride Park, Derby. His first start followed in March 2002 in a friendly against Italy. Next came his appearances in the World Cup before winning his last few caps in 2003-04. All of Mills' England games were away from Wembley, a record in the modern era. In August 2009, he announced his retirement from all football during an appearance on BBC Five Live. He made 387 appearances for his seven League clubs (6 goals), winning the League Cup with Middlesbrough. He also collected three Youth, one England B and 14 U21 caps. Keeping himself fit, Mills ran in the Brighton marathon in 2010 in an excellent time of 2 hours 43 minutes.

MILLS, George Robert 1937-38 ③ ③
Born: Deptford, London, 29 December 1908
Died: Deptford, 15 July 1970
Career: Arthur Street School/Peckham, Emerald Athletic (April 1923), Bromley (September 1925), Chelsea (£10, December 1929, retired, May 1943; returned to Stamford Bridge after the War as a coach); later worked for a printing firm in London.

A well-built, direct, forceful and hard-shooting inside or centre-forward, George Mills spent 15 years with Chelsea (1929-44) during which time he scored 123 goals in 239 first-team appearances. Capped by England three times in 1937-38, he notched a hat-trick on his debut in a 5-1 win over Ireland in Belfast and followed up with useful displays in 2-1 and 5-4 victories over Wales and Czechoslovakia, having a hand in one of Stanley Matthews' three goals in the latter game at White Hart Lane.

MILLS, Michael Denis, MBE 1972-82 ④
Born: Godalming, Surrey, 4 January 1949
Career: Portsmouth (junior, June 1964), Ipswich Town (amateur, May 1965, professional, February 1966), Southampton (£50,000, November 1982), Stoke City (player-manager, July 1985, retired as a player, May 1986, continued as manager until November 1989); Colchester United (manager, January-May 1990), Middlesbrough (scout, 1990), Coventry City (assistant-manager/coach, November 1990-November 1991); Sheffield Wednesday (chief scout), Birmingham City (coach, assistant-manager, also caretaker-manager, briefly, October 2001); awarded the MBE for services to football in 1984; now technical director of Galaxy Sports Management, a sports management company.

It was tough luck on full-back Mick Mills who was handed his international debut by Alf Ramsey against the famed and feared Yugoslavian winger Djazic at Wembley in October 1972. It was a baptism of fire for the Ipswich player who was given a tough time in the 1-1 draw. He took quite a while to recover and it was some two-and-a-half years before he gained his second cap. After that – and despite challenges from Phil Neal, Kenny Sansom, Colin Todd, Dave Clement and Trevor Cherry - he became a regular in the team, produced several outstanding performances, featured in some rousing matches, among them wins over Hungary 4-1, Northern Ireland 4-0 and 5-1 and Scotland 3-1, and captained his country eight times.

Mills was also capped by his country at Youth and U23 levels, played in one unofficial international and appeared twice for the Football League. Known as 'Captain Fantastic' at club level, he made over 900 appearances (in all competitions) between 1965 and 1989, including a record 591 in the League for Ipswich, with whom he won the FA Cup in 1978 and the UEFA Cup in 1981, under Bobby Robson's management.

MILNE, Gordon 1962-65 ⑭
Born: Preston, 29 March 1937
Career: Preston Amateurs (April 1952), Morecambe (August 1953), Preston North End (professional, January 1956), Liverpool (£16,000, August 1960), Blackpool (£30,000, May 1967), Wigan Athletic (player-manager, January 1970-May 1972); England (Youth team coach, August 1971); Coventry City (manager, June 1972, executive manager, May 1981-August 1982), Leicester City (manager, August

1982, general manager, June 1986-May 1987), Besiktas JK/Turkey (manager, July 1987-May 1994), Nagoya Grampus Eight/Japan (manager, seasons 1994-96), Bursaspor/Turkey (manager, season 1996-97), Trabzonspor/Turkey (manager, season 1998-99); Newcastle United (Director of Football, seasons 1999-2003); League Managers' Association (Chief Executive); Besiktas JK/Turkey (Director of Football, seasons 2006-08).

Well built, with plenty of muscle, Gordon Milne was an excellent right-half, hard to knock off the ball, whose international debut came in a prestigious 1-1 friendly draw with Brazil at Wembley in May 1963. Described in some quarters as a 'master tactician' he produced three outstanding performances in successive victories over Wales (4-0), the Rest of the World (2-1) and Northern Ireland (8-3) later in the year and, linking up with George Eastham in midfield, he was terrific when Portugal were defeated 4-3 in Lisbon in May 1964. During his time at Anfield (1960-67) Milne scored 18 goals in 282 appearances, gaining a Second Division and two First Division championship winning medals. Unfortunately he missed Liverpool's 1965 FA Cup final triumph through injury. As a manager he guided Leicester into the First Division and was a great success with Besiktas, winning three Turkish League titles. His father, Jimmy, also played for Preston.

MILNER, James 2009-13 ㊳ ①
Born: Wortley, Leeds, 4 January 1986
Career: Rawden FC (April 2001), Leeds United (apprentice, March 2002, professional, February 2003), Swindon Town (loan, September-October 2003), Newcastle United (£3.6m, July 2004), Aston Villa (loan, August 2005-May 2006; signed for £12m, August 2008), Manchester City (£13m, plus Stephen Ireland, August 2010)

An all-purpose footballer, with good pace and a fair bit of skill, James Milner is able, and willing, to play at full-back, in the centre of midfield, out on the flanks and even through the middle. He represented England at U15, U17, U19, U20 and U21 levels (scoring nine goals in a record 46 appearances in the latter category) before making his full international debut in August 2009, as a second-half substitute in the friendly against Holland. He did very well and outran defender John Heitinga to set up the equalizer for Jermain Defoe in a 2-2 draw.

He played twice more for his country the following month against Slovenia and Croatia, helping England win the latter match 5–1 to secure a place in the 2010 World Cup finals and later named in the 23-man squad, Milner played in the opening group game against the USA and later crossed for Defoe to net the only goal of the game against Slovenia.

He always puts in a good shift, is forever tracking back and helping out his defence, making him an extremely hard worker whose commitment cannot be faulted. Played in all of England's games at Euro 2012.

At club level, Milner scored five goals in 54 games for Leeds, two in six for Swindon, 11 in 136 for Newcastle and 21 in 125 for Aston Villa before his big-money move to Manchester City with whom he gained an FA Cup winner's medal in 2011 and a Premiership winner's medal twelve months later.

MILTON, Clement Arthur, MA 1951-52 ①

Born: Bristol, 10 March 1928
Died: Bristol, 25 April 2007
Career: Cotham Grammar School/Bristol, Bristol & Gloucestershire Schools (football & cricket), Arsenal (amateur, April 1945, professional, July 1946); National Service in the Royal Army Ordnance Corps (1946-48), Bristol City (February 1955, retired from football, July 1955); played county cricket for Gloucestershire (1948-74) and England; Oxford University (cricket coach); worked as a Bristol postman until he was 60.

An injury to Tom Finney enabled outside-right Arthur Milton to win his one and only England cap against Austria at Wembley in November 1951. Partnering Ivor Broadis on the wing, he put in an 'adequate' performance in the 2-2 draw. He had appeared in just 10 League games for Arsenal, making him the least-experienced England player at that time to make his full international debut. Afterwards he went on to score 22 goals in 90 outings for the Gunners before moving to Bristol City.
    Milton played in 585 cricket matches for Gloucestershire up to 1974, scoring over 32,000 runs for an average of 33.60. He topped 1,000 runs on 16 occasions and he also took 758 catches. He appeared in six Tests Matches and was the first Englishman to remain on the pitch for the duration of a Test – batting and fielding for all five days against New Zealand at Headingley in 1958. Milton was the last player capped by England at cricket and football. And besides being a fine footballer and excellent cricketer, he was also a very useful golfer, driving off the tee with a handicap of 4.

MILWARD, Alfred Weatherell 1891-97 ④ ③

Born: Great Marlow, Bucks, 12 September 1870
Died: Winchester, 1 June 1941
Career: Sir William Borlase's Grammar School/Marlow, Old Borlasians (seasons 1884-86), Marlow AFC (September 1886), Everton (May 1888), New Brighton Tower (£200, May 1897), Southampton free, (May 1899), New Brompton (July 1901), Southampton Cambridge FC (July 1903, retired, April 1905); later a licensee of the Diamond Jubilee pub, Orchard Lane, Southampton; also a qualified referee, officiating in Southampton FA fixtures (1909-10).

Having established himself at Everton, outside-left Alf Milward scored on his international debut against Wales in March 1891 at the age of 20. A month later he was one of five players from Goodison Park who helped England defeat Scotland 2-1 at Blackburn in April in 1891. He was surprisingly out of the team for six years, returning in March 1897 with two goals in a 4-0 victory over Wales before gaining his last cap against Scotland a week later. A hard worker, Milward forged a great partnership with Edgar Chadwick at Everton for whom he scored 96 goals in 224 appearances (1888-97), collecting a League championship and two FA Cup winner's medals in the 1890s. He later won the Southern League title with Southampton.

MITCHELL, Clement 1879-85 ⑤ ⑤

Born: Cambridge, 20 February 1862
Died: Aldrington, Hove, Sussex, 6 October 1937
Career: Felsted School XI/Cambridge (seasons, 1877-80); also played for Upton Park (late 1870s), Essex County (1879-82), Corinthians (seasons 1882-90)

'Clem' Mitchell was a tough, hard running centre-forward who set up one of England's goals in a 3-2 win over Wales on his international debut in March 1880, aged 18 years, 23 days – the

second youngest England player at that time. A year later he was by far his country's best player when Scotland won 6-1 at The Oval and two years after that he became the first Englishman to score an international hat-trick when the Welsh were defeated 5-0, also at the Oval. He went on to score in each of his last two matches, a 3-2 defeat by Scotland and a 1-1 draw with Wales.
    Mitchell, who also played for Kent CCC between 1890 and 1892, spent several years working in India.

MITCHELL, James Frederick 1924-25 ①

Born: Manchester, 18 November 1897
Died: Manchester, 30 May 1975
Career: Arnold Grammar School/Blackpool, Manchester University (September 1914), Blackpool (professional, April 1915), Northern Nomads (1918), Preston North End (October 1920), Manchester City (May 1922), Leicester City (October 1926, retired, May 1927); later secretary of Stead & Simpson Sports Club.

Hefty goalkeeper Fred Mitchell earned his only international cap as a Manchester City player, starring in a 3-1 win over Ireland at Goodison Park in October 1924. Mitchell wore spectacles in that game, and to date remains as the only player capped for England while wearing spectacles. He played for Preston in the 1922 FA Cup final and later made 109 appearances for Manchester City. He also represented his country in six amateur internationals and played for Great Britain in the 1920 Summer Olympics.

MOFFAT, Hugh 1912-13 ①

Born: Congleton, Cheshire, January 1885
Died: Congleton, 14 November 1952
Career: Congleton Town (April 1901), Burnley (professional, June 1903), Oldham Athletic (May 1910), Chesterfield Municipal (player-manager, July 1919-May 1921).

A competent, well-built right-half, Hugh Moffat won his only England cap v. Wales in March 1913. He didn't have the greatest of games, being at fault for one of the goals in a 4-3 win. He made 201 League appearances for Burnley and 162 for Oldham.

MOLYNEUX, George Murdoch 1901-03 ④

Born: Liverpool, 10 August 1875
Died: Rochford, Essex, 14 April 1942
Career: Third Grenadiers, South Shire FC/Blackpool (April 1893), Kirkdale (August 1894), Wigan County (briefly), Everton (March 1896), Wigan County (June 1897), Everton (May 1898), Southampton (free, May 1900), Portsmouth (May 1905), Southend United (May 1906, player-manager from August 1910-May 1912), Colchester Town (player-coach, July 1912-May 1914).

A three-time Southern League championship winner with Southampton (1901-04), left-back George Molyneux was a stalwart of all-round ability, being exceptionally good in the air. He partnered Bob Crompton in all four of his England games, producing his best display in the 2-2 draw with Scotland at Villa Park in May 1902 when he made two goal-line clearances. He also played in one unofficial international – the ill-fated Ibrox Park disaster game in April 1902.

MOON, William Robert 1887-91 ⑦

Born: Maida Vale, London, 27 June 1868
Died: Hendon, 9 January 1943
Career: Westminster School (seasons 1883-85), Old Westminsters (seasons 1885-87); also played for Corinthians (seasons 1886-1901); was a solicitor with the London-based firm Moon, Gilks and Moon.

A smart, accomplished goalkeeper, courageous, alert and able to use both feet, Billy Moon conceded eight goals in his seven internationals and was on the losing side just once, in a 3-2 defeat by Scotland in April 1889. He had made three excellent saves on his debut a year earlier when Wales were defeated 5-1 and he also produced a quality performance in the 2-1 win over the Scots in April 1891. Moon also played cricket for Middlesex.

MOORE, Henry Thomas 1883-85 ②

Born: Nottingham, 27 June 1861
Died: Sudbury-on-Thames, 24 September 1939
Career: Notts County (August 1881-May 1888); later ran an off-licence in Nottingham.

A reliable, strong-kicking full-back and a fine tactician, Harry Moore played for Notts County for seven years, retiring just when League football commenced in 1888. His two caps came two years apart – in the 7-0 win over Ireland in February 1883 when he had 'very little to do' and in the 1-1 draw with Wales in March 1885.

MOORE, James 1922-23 ①

Born: Handsworth, Birmingham, 11 May 1889
Died: Derby, 6 November 1972
Career: Quebec Albion/Handsworth (September 1905), Cradley Heath (seasons 1908-11), Glossop (professional, May 1911), Derby County (October 1913), Chesterfield (March 1926, retired, May 1927); returned with Mansfield Town (November 1927-May 1928), Worcester City (August 1928, retired April 1929).

A Second Division championship winner with Derby in 1915, Jim Moore was a clever inside-left and a regular marksman throughout his career. He had the pleasure of scoring on his international debut in a 4-2 win over Sweden in Stockholm in May 1923 when he played alongside his Derby colleagues, George Thornewell and Harry Bedford.

MOORE,
Robert Frederick Chelsea, OBE 1961-74 ⑩⑧ ②

Born: Barking, Essex, 12 April 1941
Died: London, 24 February 1993
Career: Barking & Leyton Schools, Woodford Youth Club (from August 1956), West Ham United (professional, June 1958), Fulham (£20,000, March 1974-May 1977); assisted San Antonia Thunder/USA (April-August 1976), Seattle Sounders/USA (July-August 1978), Herning FC/Denmark (player-coach, February 1978, retired as a player, September 1979); Oxford City (manager, December 1979), Eastern AA/Hong Kong (manager, August 1982); Southend United (chief executive, August 1983, manager, February 1984-April 1986, later director, August 1989); joined Capital Gold (as a football analyst).

Over a period of 11½ years, from May 1962 to November 1973, consummate defender Bobby Moore captained England 90 times (the same as Billy Wright) in his 108 internationals. He was unbeaten in 77 of those matches, 57 won, 20 drawn, and of course rejoiced in full glory with millions of others when he proudly held aloft the coveted Jules Rimet Trophy (the World Cup) on that exceptional day at Wembley in July 1966 when he and a few others around him, became legends!

A surprise selection for the 1962 World Cup in Chile, Moore seized his chance and never looked back. Bobby Robson, who cracked his ankle in training, made way for the West Ham star.

He had made his international debut, along with the Spurs' defender Maurice Norman, in a 4-0 warm-up win over Peru at dusty Lima in May 1962, and a year later was named captain, leading his country for the first time at the age of 22 years and 48 days against Czechoslovakia in Bratislava in May 1963 when he took over from Jimmy Armfield.

After recovering from testicular cancer, he got better and better and although his relationship with Alf Ramsey was not always easy, he was 'top man' as far as his manager was concerned.

Moore's first international goal earned England a 1-1 draw with Poland on a glue-pot pitch at Goodison Park in January 1966. He put the finishing touch to a late move started by the Burnley left-winger Gordon Harris, and carried on by Jack Charlton. A minute later he headed an Alan Ball centre against the crossbar. Five months later he notched his second England goal - a 25-yard 'screamer' in the 6-1 win over Norway in Oslo.

A wonderful reader of the game, he tackled with great precision and rarely committed a foul in the danger-zone. In fact, throughout his lengthy career he was seldom booked and only once sent off (in a League game for the Hammers). He could deliver a long or short pass with inch-perfect accuracy and was one of the best positional players in the game, showing coolness and composure, even under pressure.

Unfortunately Moore's occasional inability to command in the air caught him out several times.

In the tough European Nations Cup semi-final clash with Yugoslavia in Florence in June 1968, he missed a dipping cross, allowing the ball to drop down for Dzajic to fire home the winning goal. He was also caught out in the World Cup in Mexico and had a difficult time when having 'aerial battles' with the bulky and robust strikers from Switzerland, Poland and Italy.

Moore celebrated his 100th England cap with a 5-0 win over Scotland on a snow-covered pitch at Hampden Park in February 1973 but four months later, in the World Cup qualifier in Poland, he defended poorly for a free-kick. The ball bounced off him, Peter Shilton fumbled and England were 1-0 down. Two minutes after half-time Moore chose to dribble the ball out of his own penalty-area, and lost possession to Polish pace man Lubanski who cracked a low shot into the net: 2-0, game over.

In another game against Poland in Chorzow in June 1973 Moore scored an own-goal in a 2-0 defeat.

Going back to Mexico in 1970, he was alleged to have stolen a gold bracelet from a shopping area near to Colombia's plush Tequendama Hotel where the England party was staying ahead of the World Cup. Arrested and questioned at length for four days, he was allowed to play in the friendly in Ecuador but was then re-arrested when England arrived back in Colombia. However, after diplomatic intervention and with the case against him slowly unravelling, leading people to think it was a 'set up' Moore was released, his composure and dignity intact. But it affected him. There's no doubting that. And one suspects that he wasn't at his best during the tournament, although he played a 'blinder' in the 1-0 defeat by Brazil in the second game.

After the World Cup, Moore continued to serve England with passion and commitment, although he did have a few 'bad' games, including the 3-1 home defeat by the 'enemy' West Germany in the European Nations Cup qualifier at Wembley in May 1972 when his passing was 'well below standard.'

His 107th appearance for his country was against Italy in Turin in June 1973. He played well enough, but dithered around with Roy McFarland when anticipating an offside flag to allow a certain Fabio Capello to nip in and seal a 2-0 win. Six months later Moore bowed out with his final appearance, also against Italy, at Wembley – and once again he was on the losing side, Capello netting again to clinch a 1-0 victory.

Moore is only one of 10 players to have represented England in three World Cup Finals tournaments (1962-66-70).

Moore's boss in 1966, Sir Alf Ramsey, said: "My captain, my leader, my right-hand man. He was the spirit and the heartbeat of the team. A cool, calculating footballer I could trust with my life. He was the supreme professional, the best I ever worked with. Without him England would never have won the World Cup."

Besides his senior outings for his country, Moore also won six Youth and eight U23 caps. He also played 12 times for the Football League and in 1976 starred against his homeland, for Team America in a prestige and unofficial friendly in Philadelphia.

At club level, Moore helped West Ham win the FA Cup in 1964, the European Cup Winners' Cup in 1965 and reach the League Cup final in 1966. He scored 28 goals in 642 appearances for the Hammers, making his debut in August 1958 against Manchester United (League).

He joined Fulham for £20,000 in March 1974 and remained at Craven Cottage for three seasons, scoring once in 150 appearances and playing against his former club in the 1975 FA Cup final. After that Moore had spells in the NASL with San Antonia Thunder (1976, 24 appearances, one goal) and Seattle Sounders (1978, seven appearances) and also assisted Herning FC in Denmark (as player-coach). He then moved into management with Oxford City, December 1979-May 1981, having Harry Redknapp as his assistant. There followed a six-week spell in charge of the Hong Kong-based club Eastern A (August-September 1982) before he ended his career in football with Southend United, initially as the club's chief executive, August 1983, then team manager from February 1984 to April 1986 and finally as a director, 1989-90.

Three years later, in mid-February 1993, Moore announced publicly that he was suffering from cancer and sadly, he died a few days later, aged 51.

On hearing of his death, the Brazilian maestro Pele said: "Bobby was my friend as well as the greatest defender I ever played against. The world has lost one of its greatest football players and an honorable gentleman."

Another World Cup star, the German Franz Beckenbauer, regarded Moore: "...as the best defender in the history of the game."

The stand which replaced the old south bank at West Ham's Upton Park ground, was named the Bobby Moore Stand shortly after his death.

There is also a statue close to the ground based on a famous photograph taken at Wembley after the World Cup celebrations, with Moore being held aloft, holding the trophy, by his Hammers team-mates and final goalscorers Geoff Hurst and Martin Peters, along with Everton's left back Ray Wilson.

In November 2003, to celebrate UEFA's Jubilee, he was selected as the 'Golden Player' of England by the FA as their most outstanding player of the past 50 years.

This bronze statue of Moore was erected outside the main entrance at the new Wembley Stadium in May 2007, to pay tribute to what he did for the game of football.

In August 2008, West Ham United officially retired the number 6 shirt as a mark of respect 15 years after his death.

The charity Cancer Research UK (CRUK) set up the Bobby Moore Fund to raise money for bowel cancer research in his memory: the Run for Moore races raise funds for this.

MOORE, William Gray Bruce 1922-23 ① ②
Born: Newcastle-upon-Tyne, 6 October 1894
Died: West Ham, London, 26 September 1968
Career: Seaton Delaval (amateur, August 1911), Sunderland
(professional, May 1913), West Ham United (May 1922, retired, May
1929; appointed club coach, then head trainer, May 1932-May 1960).

Lightly-built inside-forward William Moore played for West Ham in
the 1923 FA Cup final... a month later he scored twice in his only
international for England in a 3-1 win over Sweden in Stockholm. The
perfect partner to Jimmy Ruffel at Upton Park, he spent seven years
as a player with the Hammers (1922-29), netting 48 goals in 202
appearances. Moore also won four caps as an amateur in 1913-14.

MORDUE, John 1911-13 ②
Born: Edmondsley, County Durham, 13 December 1886
Died: Durham, 14 December 1957
Career: Sacriston FC (August 1901), Spennymoor United (April
1902), Barnsley (professional, August 1905), Woolwich Arsenal
(£300, April 1907), Sunderland (£750, May 1908); WW1 guest for
Hartlepools United; Middlesbrough (free, May 1920), Hartlepool
United (June 1922), Durham City (player-manager, February
1923-February 1924), Ryhope FC (May 1924, retired April 1926).

Speedy and effective on both wings, Jackie Mordue scored 82 goals
in 294 appearances for Sunderland in 12 years to 1920, winning
the League championship in 1913. They were also beaten FA Cup
finalists in the same year. He made an impressive England debut on
the left flank as partner to his club-mate George Holley in a 6-1 win
over Ireland in Dublin in February 1912 and collected his second
cap, also against the Irish, in Belfast a year later, when he played on
the right-wing, alongside his Sunderland colleague Charlie Buchan.
    At Arsenal, he played with his brother-in-law, England goalkeeper
Jimmy Ashcroft. A penalty expert, Mordue scored over 25 goals
from the spot.

MORICE, Charles John 1872-73 ①
Born: Kensington, London, 27 May 1850
Died: Hammersmith, London, 17 June 1932
Career: Harrow School, Harrow Chequers (September 1868), Barnes
FC (seasons 1869-74); served on the FA Committee (seasons
1873-77), later a member of the Stock Exchange.

A fast and clever lightweight utility forward, Charlie Morice played in
England's first-ever international match against Scotland at Partick
in March 1873. According to *Bell's Life*, he had only two chances to
score, shooting wide in the first-half and having a 10-yard toe-poke
saved by goalkeeper Bob Gardner in the second.

MORLEY, William Anthony 1981-83 ⑥
Born: Ormskirk, Lancs, 26 August 1954
Career: Ormskirk & District Schools, Arsenal (trial, May 1969),
Preston North End (apprentice, July 1969, professional, August
1972), Burnley (£100,000, February 1976), Aston Villa (£200,000,
June 1979), West Bromwich Albion (£75,000, December 1983),
Birmingham City (loan, November-December 1984), FC Seiko/
Japan (August 1985), ADO Den Haag/Holland (July 1986), Walsall
(trial, June 1987), Notts County (trial, July 1987), West Bromwich
Albion (free, August 1987), Burnley (loan, October-November 1988),
Tampa Bay Rowdies/USA (free, March 1989), Hamrun Spartans/
Malta (April 1990); New Zealand football (seasons 1990-92), Sutton
Coldfield Town (August 1992), Bromsgrove Rovers (player-coach,
January 1995), Stratford Town (March 1995, retired May 1996);

also coached in Australia and Hong Kong and played for both Aston
Villa and West Bromwich Albion Old Stars (1990s).

A fast-raiding, skilful and penetrative left-winger, Tony Morley made
his England debut (as a substitute for Steve Coppell) in the 1-0 win
over Hungary at Wembley in November 1981. Five more caps followed
during the next twelve months but he was not picked for any of the
games at the 1982 World Cup... despite his manager Ron Greenwood
supposedly favouring attacking football! Morley enjoyed the best days
with Aston Villa. Seen initially as a wayward genius, he was moulded
by his boss Ron Saunders into one of the most dangerous players in
the game, developing a technique of scoring spectacular goals – the
one against Everton at Goodison Park in 1980-81 was voted 'Goal of
the Season'. He helped Villa win the League Championship in 1981
and the European Cup and Super Cup after that. In fact, it was his
cross, after a brilliant touchline dribble, which gave Peter Withe the
chance to sweep in the winning goal against Bayern Munich in the
European Cup final. Morley, who also won two B caps, scored 67
goals in more than 450 career appearances at club level.

MORLEY, Herbert 1909-10 ①
Born: Kiveton Park, Sheffield, 1 October 1882
Died: Skegness, 16 July 1957
Career: Kiveton Park (August 1897), Grimsby Town (September
1904), Notts County (March 1907, retired, injured, May 1917;
became a scout for County).

A Second Division championship winner with Notts County in 1914,
Bert Morley was a tall and hefty right-back, brilliant in the air but
sometimes erratic on the ground. He won his only England cap
in the 1-1 draw with Ireland in Belfast in February 1910 when he
replaced the injured Bob Crompton. It is believed that Morley was the
innovator of the offside manoeuvre, which was made law in 1925
and made effective by Newcastle United defender Bob McCracken.

MORREN, Thomas 1897-98 ① ①
Born: Middlesbrough, 3 February 1871
Died: Hunter's Bar, Sheffield, 31 January 1929
Career: Middlesbrough Victoria (April 1887), Middlesbrough
Ironopolis (May 1890), Middlesbrough (August 1891), Barnsley
St Peter's (April 1892), Sheffield United (April 1895; retired, May
1904); later ran a newsagents shop in Sheffield.

A diminutive but very effective centre-half, Tommy Morren was,
at times, caught out of position and this could be the reason why
he only received one cap for England. That came against Ireland
in March 1898 when, taking over from Crawshaw, he scored the
opening goal in a 3-2 win at Solitude, Belfast. He made well over
250 appearances at club level, 190 in League and FA Cup for
Sheffield United with whom he gained First Division championship
and FA Cup winner's medals in 1898 and 1899 respectively and
also played in the losing Cup final of 1901. He was an FA Amateur
Cup winner with Middlesbrough in 1895.

MORRIS, Frederick 1919-21 ② ①
Born: Tipton, Staffs, 27 August 1893
Died: Tipton, 4 July 1962
Career: Bell Street Primitives (August 1907), Tipton Victoria
(September 1908), Redditch (September 1910), West Bromwich
Albion (professional, May 1911); WW1 guest for Fulham, Watford,
Tipton Excelsior; transferred to Coventry City (£625, August 1924),
Oakengates Town (£50, August 1925, retired, May 1930); lived and
worked in Tipton until his death.

Fred Morris 'played well' on his international debut against Scotland at Sheffield in April 1920. A report of the match stated: 'He brought the scores level at 4-4 before passing to his left-wing partner Quantrill who, in turn, crossed to Kelly to win the game nine minutes from time.' His second cap was against Ireland at Sunderland six months later, having a hand in Billy Walker's goal in a 2-0 win. A prolific marksman from the inside-left position with West Bromwich Albion, Morris possessed a powerful right foot shot and headed the Football League list with 37 goals in 1919-20 when the Baggies won the First Division title. He went on to score 118 times in 287 appearances during his 13 years at The Hawthorns: 1911-24.

MORRIS, John 1948-50 ③ ③
Born: Radcliffe, Lancs, 27 September 1923
Died: Bolton, 6 April 2011
Career: St John's School/Radcliffe, Radcliffe FC (September 1937), Mijacs FC (season 1938-39), Manchester United (amateur, August 1939, professional, March 1941); WW2 guest for Bolton Wanderers, Charlton Athletic, Everton and Wrexham; Derby County (£24,000, March 1949), Leicester City (October 1952), Corby Town (player-manager, May 1958), Kettering Town (player-manager, May 1961), Rugby Town (player-manager, October 1961-January 1962), Great Harwood (manager, May 1964), Oswestry Town (manager, October 1967-January 1969); became a tyre salesman in Lancashire.

An expert dribbler, not easily dispossessed despite being on the small side, inside-right Johnny Morris scored on his England debut in a 4-1 win over Norway in Oslo in May 1949 and then just four days later, he netted twice in his second game to stun the home side as France were humbled 3-1 in Paris. He also played in one B international and represented the Football League five times.
   An FA Cup winner with Manchester United in 1948 and twice a Second Division championship winner with Leicester, in 1954 and 1957, Morris scored 116 goals in 452 club appearances during his career which began in earnest with Manchester United in 1939 and ended in 1962 by which time he was occupying the right-half position. After a disagreement with Matt Busby at Old Trafford, Morris was sold to Derby County for a then record fee of £23,850 in 1949. His younger brother, William, played for Rochdale in season 1952-53.

MORRIS, William Walter 1938-39 ③
Born: Handsworth, Birmingham, 26 March 1913
Died: Dudley, 20 August 1995
Career: Handsworth New Road & Nineveh Road Schools/Handsworth, Handsworth Old Boys (April 1928), West Bromwich Albion Colts (August 1929), Halesowen Town (May 1931), Wolverhampton Wanderers (professional, May 1933); WW2 guest for Wrexham; Dudley Town (June 1947, retired, May 1949); lived in a nursing home for several years before his death.

Able to play at full-back or centre-half, Bill Morris certainly slipped through Albion's net as he went on to play in 265 first team games for Wolves (1933-47), collecting an FA Cup runners-up medal in 1939 (v. Portsmouth). Well built and strong in the tackle, he perhaps lacked pace but more than made up for this deficiency with his enthusiasm and commitment. Replacing the injured Bert Sproston (Spurs), he gained his first England cap at right-back in a 7-0 win over Ireland in November 1938 and after a fine display added two more to his tally, lining up in the 2-1 win over Scotland in April 1939 when a record crowd of 149,269 packed into Hampden Park, and the 2-0 victory over Romania in Bucharest a month later. His Wolves team-mate Stan Cullis played alongside him in the latter two internationals.

MORSE, Harold 1878-79 ①
Born: Edgbaston, Birmingham, 4 March 1859
Died: New York, USA circa 1932
Career: Derby Wanderers (rugby, seasons 1876-78), Notts County (September 1878-October 1882); also assisted Notts Rangers (1880s); emigrated to USA in 1891.

Capped for the only time as a 19 year-old in April 1879, in a 5-4 friendly win over Scotland at The Oval, Harry Morse was a solid defender who had the tendency to over-kick his front men, often sending the ball 20 yards ahead of them! Nevertheless he was a good footballer, one of the best of his era. In 1881 he moved into the centre-forward position and scored a hat-trick for Notts County in an 8-1 FA Cup win over Sheffield FC.

MORT, Thomas 1923-26 ③
Born: Kearsley, Bolton, 1 December 1897
Died: Wigan, 6 June 1967
Career: Farnworth Council School, Kearsley St Stephen's FC/Bolton (April 1912), Newton Lads' Club (August 1913), Lancashire Fusiliers (army football, seasons 1915-18), Altrincham (December 1918), Rochdale (professional, June 1921), Aston Villa (April 1922, retired, May 1935); became a businessman in Wigan.

Left-back Tommy Mort made 368 appearances for Aston Villa between 1922 and 1935, gaining an FA Cup winner's medal in 1924. A well-built defender, he believed in safety first and regularly hoofed the ball 50-60 yards downfield to clear his lines...sometimes to the annoyance of his colleagues! He did, though, possess a singularly effective sliding tackle which the fans at Villa Park loved!
   The first of his three England caps came in a surprise 2-1 defeat by Wales at Blackburn in March 1924 when he partnered his club-mate Tommy Smart. Known as 'Death and Glory' they had been outstanding at club level, but unfortunately they didn't do the business against the Welsh! Mort's second cap followed in a 3-1 win over France in Paris two months later when he played alongside Liverpool's Tom Lucas, and his third was against Scotland at Old Trafford in April 1926 when he mastered the threat of Huddersfield's outside-right Alex Jackson, although finishing on the losing side 1-0.
   Mort also featured in three England trials, 1924-26.

MORTEN, Alexander 1872-73 ①
Born: Eltham, Middlesex, 15 November 1831
Died: Earls Court, London, 24 February 1900
Career: No Names FC/Kilburn (seasons 1863-65), Wanderers (seasons 1865-74); also played for Crystal Palace (during seasons 1866-74); Middlesex County FA (Committee member and match umpire); also a London stockbroker; played for Crystal Palace CC.

Alex Morten was the first (and oldest) goalkeeper to captain England and holds the twin distinctions of having been born at an earlier date than any other international footballer, and of being older than any other England player on his international debut. He was aged 41 years and 113 days old when he made his solitary appearance in a 4-2 win over Scotland at The Oval ion 8 March 1873.
   The FA secretary, Charles Alcock, wanted Morten to play in the first international against Scotland in November 1872, but injury prevented this. Rated as perhaps the 'best goalkeeper in the world' during the early 1870s (according to *Football Annual*) Morten's motto was 'Toujours prêt' (always ready). He never lost concentration, even under the most trying circumstances, and was always urging his colleagues on to greater things.
   The oldest player ever to represent England has been Stanley Matthews, who was aged 42 years 103 days when he played in his final international in May 1957.

MORTENSEN, Stanley Harding 1946-54 ㉕ ㉔

Born: South Shields, 26 May 1921
Died: Blackpool, 22 May 1991
Career: St Mary's School/South Shields, South Shields ex-Schools XI, Blackpool (amateur, May 1937, professional, May 1938); WW2 guest for Bath City and Arsenal; Hull City (November 1955), Southport (February 1957), Bath City (July 1958, retired, May 1959); came out of retirement to play for Lancaster City (November 1960-March 1962); Blackpool (manager, February 1967-April 1969); later a Blackpool businessman and local town councillor.

Englishman Stan Mortensen made his international debut against England! Named as a reserve for the Wartime clash with Wales at Wembley in September 1943, he was sitting on the bench in his RAF uniform when Ivor Powell, the Welsh left-half damaged his collar bone. At half-time 'Morty' was asked if he would like to go on in his place as Wales hadn't got a 12th man. "No problem," he said, "I'd love to." Playing up front he gave Cliff Britton and Stan Cullis plenty to think about although he did finish on the losing, 8-3! Five months later 'Morty' played for England v. Wales at Anfield – the first of three Wartime caps (3 goals scored).

The all-action Blackpool centre-forward entered the full international arena in tremendous style, scoring four times on his England debut against Portugal in Lisbon in May 1947. He opened his account in the very first minute and never looked back. Indeed, he could well have netted six goals that day, as two other efforts scraped the woodwork with the 'keeper beaten.

He was a 'real miracle man' wrote one reporter and the record books show that he was one of only four players in the twentieth century to score a hat-trick on their England debut. 'Morty' continued to hit the target, bagging 14 goals in his first eight matches, including two more hat-tricks, in a 4-2 victory over Sweden at Highbury six months after his efforts in Lisbon and in a 6-2 win over Northern Ireland in Belfast in October 1948. In the Swedish game he should have bagged a four-timer but late on he refused to take a penalty, allowing Tommy Lawton to score from the spot instead. And against the Irish, it was his club-mate Stanley Matthews who, after scoring the first goal himself, laid on all three of his goals 'on a plate.'

Mortensen then had the pleasure of scoring England's first goal in the World Cup finals proper when he headed in Jimmy Mullen's cross in the 27th minute of the 2-0 opening group game against Chile in Rio de Janeiro in June 1950.

Mortensen played in only four more internationals after the World Cup – unable to get into the team because of the form being produced by Jackie Milburn and Nat Lofthouse. But when he did play, he certainly made his mark, scoring both goals in a 2-1 win over Argentina in 1951 and finding the net in the 4-4 draw with the Rest of the World and in the 6-3 defeat by Hungary in 1953. Even in the 3-2 Wembley reverse against Scotland before the Argentinian game, he refused to leave the field after being knocked unconscious four minutes before half-time. With England already down to 10 men (Mannion had gone off with a fractured cheek-bone) 'Morty' although dazed, chose to come out for the second-half to 'do his best'...this was the spirit of the man.

Mortensen spent the majority of his career with Blackpool (19 years in all). He scored 222 goals in 354 appearances for the Seasiders (in League and FA Cup competitions) and had the pleasure of netting a hat-trick in the 1953 FA Cup final win over Bolton Wanderers, having been a runner-up in the 1948 and 1951

finals. Besides his full England honours, he also played in two B internationals (netting a hat-trick in a 5-1 win over Switzerland B in May 1948) and represented the Football League on five occasions.

After suffering several set-backs with his club (Blackpool) and almost losing his life when his Wellington bomber caught fire and crashed on a training exercise with the RAF, a head full of stitches did not deter this electrifying centre-forward who possessed a devastating burst of speed, could jump as high as anyone and packed one of the most powerful shots in the game. His Blackpool team-mate Stan Matthews said: "He was a fast as a whippet...so courageous...and would usually arrive at the ground ten minutes before kick-off, ready for action and rarin' to go."

Mortensen was born in May, turned professional in May, made his full England debut in May, scored an FA Cup final hat-trick in May and died in May.

MORTON, John Randall 1937-38 ① ①

Born: Sheffield, 26 February 1914
Died: London, 8 March 1986
Career: Sheffield Schools, Woodhouse Alliance (April 1930), Gainsborough Trinity (professional, May 1931), West Ham United (December 1931; retired during WW2); became a London-based bookmaker.

Although on the frail side, Jackie Morton was a deceptively quick and tricky left-winger whose only full England cap was gained against Czechoslovakia at White Hart Lane in December 1937. He deputised for Eric Brook and celebrated the occasion with a goal in a 5-4 victory. Two years earlier he played in an unofficial international against Scotland at Hampden Park.

He scored 57 goals in 275 senior appearances for the Hammers between 1931 and 1939.

MOSFORTH, William 1876-82 ⑨ ③

Born: Ecclesfield, Sheffield, 2 January 1858
Died: Sheffield, 11 July 1929
Career: Ecclesfield (April 1873), Sheffield Wednesday (August 1875), Lockwood Brothers (season 1886-87), Sheffield Albion (May 1888), Hallam (seasons 1888-90), Heeley (1890), Providence FC (1892), Sheffield United (briefly); represented Sheffield County FA (1880s); retired 1894; became a Sheffield licensee.

Billy Mosforth was a wily, fast-moving, line-hugging outside-left who spent his entire playing career in Sheffield. A great favourite with the watching public, he possessed a superb screw-kick, was a smart dribbler and could centre with precision whilst travelling at top speed. The nine internationals in which he played produced a total of 54 goals. England lost six times but there was no blame placed on Mosforth, for he played well in most matches and scored in the 5-4 win over Scotland in April 1879, in the revenge defeat by the same score a year later and also in the 5-3 loss to Wales in his last game in March 1882. Five years earlier he had made an impressive international debut when the Scots won 3-1 at The Oval, the *Bell's Life* reporter stating: "Mosforth had two or three good runs at the visitors' defence and a foul on him by Campbell led to England's goal, scored by Lyttelton."

Mosforth helped Lockwood Brothers reach the semi-finals of the FA Cup in 1887.

MOSS, Frank 1921-24 ⑤
Born: Aston, Birmingham, 17 April 1895
Died: Worcester, 15 September 1965
Career: Burlington Street School/Aston, Aston Manor (April 1909), Walsall (August 1911), Aston Villa (February 1914); WW1 guest for Bellis & Morcom FC, Aston Park Rangers (August 1919), Smethwick Carriage Works (1919) and Bradford City (1919), Cardiff City (£2,500, January 1929), Oldham Athletic (July 1929), Bromsgrove Rovers (player-manager, September 1929), Worcester City (player-coach, August 1932; retired, May 1934); was licensee of the Grosvenor Arms, Worcester for 35 years until his death.

Sports journalist Archie Ledbrooke, covering the England-Italy international of 1934, wrote: "Moss was outstanding. He had a fine game despite twice being bowled over by strong challenges from the Juventus players Serantoni and Ferrari."
  A tall blond wing-half, strong and resilient, excellent in the air, Frank Moss, nicknamed 'Snowy', captained both his club, Aston Villa, in a 2-0 FA Cup final defeat by Newcastle United, and England in the 1-1 draw with Scotland, on successive Saturdays at Wembley in April 1924. Four years earlier he had helped Villa win the Cup, playing a 'blinder' against Huddersfield Town. A real athlete, Moss won the first of his five caps in the 1-1 draw with Ireland in October 1921, but with several other quality half-backs around at the same time, he was never a first-choice with the selectors, despite producing a sterling performance every game he played in. Moss, who also represented the Football League on two occasions, made 283 appearances for Villa. Seriously injured during WW1 while serving as a corporal with the 4th Lincolnshire Regiment at Bouchezenes, France, Moss fathered two sons, Amos and Frank junior, both of whom went on to play for Aston Villa.

MOSS, Frank 1933-35 ④
Born: Leyland, Lancs, 5 November 1909
Died: Heswall, Cheshire, 7 February 1970
Career: Farrington Villa (April 1924), Lostock Hall (August 1925), Leyland Motors (July 1926), Preston North End (professional, October 1927), Oldham Athletic (£1,000, May 1929), Arsenal (November 1931, retired February 1937); Heart of Midlothian (manager, March 1937-May 1940); WW2 service as an Army engineer; later a licensee in Chorley, Lancs until his death.

Frank Moss was a very capable goalkeeper, keen and agile, who gained three League championship winner's medals with Arsenal in the mid-1930s. Taking over from the injured Harry Hibbs, he made his international debut in a 3-0 win over Scotland at Wembley in April 1934, reporter Arthur Simmons of the *Daily Express* writing: "Moss was at his best, judgment and pluck...he made excellent saves from Hughie Gallacher and Marshall." Moss played in the next two England games, versus Hungary in Budapest and Czechoslovakia in Prague, both ending in 2-1 defeats, and he also featured in that epic battle with Italy on his home ground at Highbury, in November 1934 when he pulled off four superb second-half saves as England held on for a 3-2 win. However, with Ted Sagar (Everton) also pushing for a place in the team, coupled with an irritating shoulder injury which dogged him for several years, Moss never got another chance.
  He made 161 appearances for Arsenal (1931-36) and scored one goal v. Everton in March 1935 after moving to the wing following an injury.

MOSSCROP, Edwin 1913-14 ②
Born: Southport, 16 June 1892
Died: Southport, 14 March 1980
Career: Blowick FC (August 1906), Shepherd's Bush (September 1908), Middlesex County (season 1909-10), Southport YMCA (August 1911), Southport Central (February 1912), Burnley (amateur, June 1912, professional, September 1912, retired through illness, November 1922); WW1 guest for Reading; was a schoolteacher by profession.

A small, rather lightweight left-winger, with good pace and useful skills, Eddie Mosscrop won the FA Cup and the League championship with Burnley in 1914 and 1921 respectively. Quite outstanding in the 1913-14 season, his form earned him two England caps against Wales at Cardiff (won 2-0) and Scotland at Hampden Park (lost 3-1). He partnered Bolton's Joe Smith on the left-flank in both games and was unlucky not to score against the Scots, Jim Brownlie saving his low drive with 10 minutes remaining.
  Mosscrop, who also represented the Football League, was forced to retire at the age of 30 due to health problems. He made 198 appearances for Burnley (20 goals).

MOZLEY, Bertram 1949-50 ③
Born: Derby, 21 September 1923
Career: Derby Schools, Shelton United (August 1938), Nottingham Forest (amateur, February 1944), Derby County (March 1945, retired, January 1955); Emigrated to Canada (played for Western Canada All Stars).

A cool, calculated defender with a precise tackle and smart distribution skills, Bert Mozley made his England debut on his 26th birthday, in the surprise 2-0 defeat by the Republic of Ireland at Goodison Park. With Alf Ramsey, Bill Ellerington and Eddie Shimwell also seeking to establish themselves in the team at right-back, his opportunities were therefore limited to just three internationals, his other two games coming later in the year in World Cup qualifying victories over Wales at Cardiff (4-1) and Northern Ireland at Maine Road (9-2). He played very well against the Welsh but in truth had very little to cope with against the Irish! Mozley made 321 League and FA Cup appearances for Derby (1946-55) and toured Canada with the FA Party in 1950, obviously taking a liking to that country!

MULLEN, James ⑫ ⑥

Born: Newcastle-upon-Tyne, 6 January 1923
Died: Wolverhampton, 23 October 1987
Career: Wolverhampton Wanderers (junior, July 1937, professional, January 1940); WW2 guest for Leicester City, Newcastle United and Darlington; retired, May 1960; later ran his own sports shop in Wolverhampton.

Jimmy Mullen became England's first substitute in a major international when he replaced Jackie Milburn after just 11 minutes in a 4-1 victory over Belgium at the Heysel Stadium, Brussels in May 1950. The International Football Association Board had authorized substitutions by advance agreement between opponents in friendly matches in 1932, but substitutions in international play generally were not approved until the 1970 World Cup. Mullen scored in that game and therefore was also the first 'sub' to find the net for England. It would be six years before the next scoring 'sub' – Nat Lofthouse v. Finland.

A fast-raiding left-winger with a powerful shot, Mullen played in two World Cups and, along with his clubmates Bert Williams and Billy Wright, was in the team that lost 1-0 to the USA in Brazil in 1950. Four years later, he was superb along with another Wolves colleague, Dennis Wilshaw, and both players found the net in a 2-0 win over Switzerland in Berne. However, with Tom Finney around it was always tough for Mullen to hold down a regular place in the England team but he made the most of his opportunities and produced some exciting performances, one of his best coming against Scotland at Hampden Park in April 1954 when he set up a goal for Ronnie Allen and then netted himself with a powerful header in a 4-2 victory.

Also the recipient of three Wartime caps, the first against Wales on his home ground at Molineux in October 1942, Mullen represented the Football League and played in three B internationals. He joined Wolves in 1937, turned professional on his 17th birthday, and remained with the club for 23 years. He scored 112 goals in 486 senior appearances, added another 25 goals to his tally in 97 Wartime games, and won FA Cup and three League championship winner's medals between 1949 and 1959. As a 16 year-old he played in the 1939 Cup semi-final victory over Grimsby Town.

During the War, Mullen served as a soldier in the Army, based at Farnborough, Catterick and Barnard Castle. After retiring from football, he ran a sports shop in Wolverhampton until shortly before his death.

MULLERY, Alan Patrick, MBE 1964-72 ㉟ ①

Born: Notting Hill, London, 23 November 1941
Career: West London Schools, Middlesex Schools, Fulham (groundstaff, June 1957, professional, December 1958), Tottenham Hotspur (March 1964), Fulham (loan, March-April 1972; signed permanently, June 1972, retired, May 1976); Brighton & Hove Albion (manager, July 1976-June 1981), Charlton Athletic (manager, July 1981-May 1982), Crystal Palace (manager, June 1982-May 1984), Queens Park Rangers (manager, June-December 1984), Brighton & Hove Albion (manager, mid-1986-January 1987); later Sky TV and radio football analyst; Football consultant at Crawley Town; also engaged as a matchday corporate host by Tottenham Hotspur and Fulham.

Forced to pull out of England's 1964 summer tour of South America with a muscle spasm (suffered while shaving) Alan Mullery finally made his international debut against Holland in December of that year. Doing well alongside his Spurs team-mate Terry Venables, the pair combined to set up a late goal for their club-mate Jimmy Greaves to earn a 1-1 draw.

An experimental choice by manager Alf Ramsey, he didn't feature in subsequent England squads, nor was he selected for the final 22 who competed at the 1966 World Cup.

In fact, Mullery had to wait two-and-a-half years before gaining his second cap, taking over from the pugnacious Nobby Stiles against Spain in May 1967 – four days after he had helped his club, Spurs, win the FA Cup on the same Wembley pitch. He subsequently played in the European Championships of 1968 when England reached the semi-finals only to be beaten 1-0 by Yugoslavia.

In fact, disaster and ignominy struck Mullery in the game against the Yugoslavs in Florence. Never a dirty player, he was surprisingly sent off for 'retaliation' after he had been fouled once too often by Trivic. This was the first time an England player had been dismissed in a senior international. "It was the worst moment of my career," said Mullery. "I felt as if I had not only let England down but also my wife and family. The player I kicked out at had been hacking at me throughout the game. I just lost my temper."

Stiles played in the third place play-off victory over USSR as Mullery served his suspension, but Ramsey kept faith with the Spurs player and reinstated him in the side for most of the friendly matches as England prepared to defend their World Cup crown in Mexico.

A grafter in midfield, Mullery had the knack of breaking up attacks, bursting forward and scoring spectacular goals – although he only netted once for his country, in the disappointing 3-2 quarter-final defeat by West Germany in the 1970 World Cup.

Two years earlier, in a 3-1 win over Sweden in May 1968, Mullery thought he was going to break his scoring duck but goalkeeper Larsson bravely dived at his feet, suffered a fractured skull in the process, but prevented a goal. Mullery never forgot the incident.

Continuing in England's midfield after the 1970 tournament, Mullery was now being pressurised by the likes of Colin Bell and Peter Storey for the central midfield role and after captaining the side to a 1-0 win over Malta on a bone-hard pitch in Valletta in February 1971, he made his 35th and final appearance for his country eight months later in a 3-2 victory over Switzerland.

Mullery also gained three U23 caps and represented the Football League and made over 800 appearances at club and international level, including 374 for Spurs and 412 for Fulham. Besides his 1967 Cup final medal, he also helped Spurs win the League Cup (scoring a decisive goal in the two-legged final v. Wolves) and the UEFA Cup, and was voted FWA 'Footballer of the Year' in 1975 when he played in the losing FA Cup final for Fulham.

MURPHY, Daniel Benjamin 2001-04 ⑨ ①

Born: Chester, 18 March 1977
Career: Manchester United (junior trialist, season 1992-93), Crewe Alexandra (apprentice, May 1993, professional, March 1994), Liverpool (£1.5m, July 1997), Crewe Alexandra (loan, February-May 1999), Charlton Athletic (£2.5m, August 2004), Tottenham Hotspur (£2m, January 2006), Fulham (undisclosed fee, August 2007), Blackburn Rovers (free, June 2012)

Hard-working, creative midfielder Danny Murphy, was bang in form and all set to play at the 2002 World Cup (as Steve Gerrard's replacement) but had to withdraw from the squad after suffering a metatarsal injury, similar to that which had affected England team-mates David Beckham and Gary Neville in the run-up to the tournament.

He made his international debut in November 2001, in the 1-1 friendly draw with Sweden at Old Trafford when he came on as a 58th minute substitute. His ninth and last cap for his country followed two years later in a 3-2 defeat by Denmark, also at Old Trafford, when once again he appeared as a second-half substitute.

Three months later Neal conceded an own-goal as England were held to a 1-1 draw by Australia in Melbourne - manager Bobby Robson describing it as a "game of little value to anybody."

The unfortunate Neal then gave away a penalty in his last game against Denmark in 1983, allowing Allan Simonsen to win the game for the Danes. And for the record, this appearance against the Danes made him England's most capped right-back at that time. Earlier, Neal had the pleasure of captaining his country in the 1-1 draw with Iceland in Reykjavik in June 1982 and in that summer's World Cup in Spain he came on as a late, late substitute v. France with a second remaining. As he stepped onto the field (on place of Kenny Sansom), so the referee blew the final whistle. Obviously he never touched the ball!

During a wonderful playing career which spanned some 20 years, Neal appeared in 915 competitive games and scored 94 goals. With Liverpool alone, he featured in 650 first-class matches (417 consecutively from 1974-83) and struck 60 goals, helping the Reds win four European Cups, eight League Championships, four League Cups, five Charity Shields, the UEFA Cup and the European Super Cup. One of the most consistent right backs Liverpool has ever had, he was at Anfield for over ten years and was the team captain on that ill-fated night of the 1985 European Cup final tragedy at the Heysel Stadium.

After leaving Anfield Neal spent six years at Bolton before taking charge of Coventry City, Cardiff City and then Manchester City. He also assisted England boss Graham Taylor as a senior coach. He has written two autobiographies, being *Attack From The Back* in 1981 and *Life At The Kop* in 1986.

NEEDHAM, Ernest 1893-1902 ⑯
Born: Whittingham Moor, Chesterfield, 21 January 1873
Died: Chesterfield, 8 March 1936
Career: Waverley FC (August 1888), Staveley (October 1889), Sheffield United (April 1891, retired, May 1913); also played cricket for Derbyshire.

Ernest 'Nudger' Needham was, without doubt, the finest left-half in England before the Great War, although surprisingly he made a rather 'undistinguished' international debut against Scotland in Glasgow in 1894, the *Daily Mail* reporter stating 'Needham was slow to react at times and was certainly at fault when the Scots scored their second goal. He tried to do too much.'

In an interview about his role in the team, Needham said: 'Keep your eye on the wing man, and lend what help you can to the centre-half now and then.' This belied his wealth of talent. He was brilliant when the Scots were defeated 3-1 in 1898...'playing ingenious clever triangles with forwards Fred Wheldon and Fred Spiksley, he displayed great confidence and positional awareness.'

Fast and brave with great endurance, in defence he rarely committed himself early, relying on his exceptional timing. He could pass the ball diligently, would curl in an awkward shot when least expected and in short, was the 'Prince of half-backs.'

Four years later, in March 1902, his penalty miss in the 0-0 draw with Wales at Wrexham, effectively ended England's marvellous run of having scored at least one goal in 52 consecutive internationals. This, in fact, was his last appearance in an England shirt. Needham, who represented the Football League on ten occasions, won the FA Cup and two League Championships with Sheffield United for whom he scored 65 goals in 554 appearances in 22 years from 1891 to 1913.

Besides being a superb footballer, Needham was also a fine batsman and between 1901 and 1912, scored 6,375 runs in 186 matches (average 20.15) for Derbyshire in the County Cricket championship.

Murphy, who gained Schoolboy honours for his country, has also played in six U18, four U20 and five U21 internationals. He helped Liverpool win five different trophies in the year 2001 and added a second League Cup winner's medal to his collection with the same club in 2003. At the end of the 2012-13 season, Murphy had amassed 736 club appearances, including 158 for Crewe, 246 for Liverpool and 198 for Fulham. He had also netted almost 120 goals.

NEAL, Philip George ㊿ ⑤
Born: Irchester, Northamptonshire, 20 February 1951
Career: Irchester FC (April 1966), Northampton Town (apprentice, July 1967, professional, December 1968), Liverpool (£66,000, October 1974), Bolton Wanderers (player-manager, December 1985, retired as a player, May 1989, continued as manager until May 1992), Coventry City (assistant-manager, July 1992, manager October 1993-February 1995), Cardiff City (manager, February-November 1996), Manchester City (November 1996-May 1997, as coach, assistant-manager, caretaker-manager), Peterborough United (assistant-manager, July 1997-March 1998); also part-time England coach; has worked in media from 2001.

Right-back Phil Neal made his full England debut against Wales in March 1976 and gained his 50th and last cap seven years later against Denmark on a sodden Wembley pitch in September 1983. His first goal for his country was scored 20 seconds before half-time in the game against Northern Ireland at Wembley in May 1978. It proved to be the winner. His next strike followed almost five years later – a 78th minute penalty which earned his country a scrambled 2-1 victory over Wales at Wembley in February 1983. This spot-kick conversion came just four days after he had missed from 12 yards when playing for Liverpool in an FA Cup-tie.

NEVILLE, Gary Alexander 1994-2008 ⑧⑤

Born: Bury, Lancs, 18 February 1975
Career: Manchester United (apprentice, July 1991, professional, January 1993, retired, June 2011); entered into punditry as a commentator for Sky Sports; appointed England coach (April 2012, appointed assistant-manager/coach May 2013).

Right-back Gary Neville made his first appearance for England in June 1995, selected by Terry Venables for the friendly against Japan. A year later, in May 1996, he was joined in the England team by his brother Phil for the match against China; they had also appeared together in the FA Cup final two weeks earlier and by doing so became the first pair of brothers to play together in a Cup winning side and for England in the same season since Hubert and Francis Heron lined up against Scotland in March 1876.

Selected for his country by five different managers (coaches) at one point, in 2009, Neville was set to become England's most capped full back, taking over the mantle from Kenny Sansom who played 86 times for his country. But this never happened as Fabio Capello chose his Manchester United colleague Wes Brown and then Liverpool's Glen Johnson ahead of him.

The youngest player in the England team at Euro '96, Neville's first tournament, he played in every game up to the semi-final, when he was suspended and watched England knocked out by the eventual winners, Germany. He also played in the 1998 World Cup and in Euro 2000 but a broken foot ruled him out of the 2002 World Cup. Plucky and gutsy as he is, Neville regained full fitness and quickly returned to the side, becoming first choice right back by the time Euro 2004 came round. Unfortunately he missed the latter stages of the qualification campaign for the 2006 World Cup through injury but was back in the team in March 2006 for a friendly with Uruguay. Duly named in the squad for the World Cup, he played in the opening Group B game against Paraguay but tweaked his calf in training and missed the next three fixtures before playing in the quarter-final defeat by Portugal. That was his 81st appearance in an England shirt, moving him ahead of Gary Lineker and Michael Owen. He also took the captain's armband during the course of that game.

After the World Cup, Neville said he would continue to be available for selection under new coach Steve McClaren and added that, unlike some former international team-mates, he would not ever make the decision to retire from the England set-up, stating: "That decision is not Gary Neville's to make."

In October 2006, Neville was involved in a game-changing incident during the Euro 2008 qualifier against Croatia when his backpass took an unfortunate bounce and caused goalkeeper Paul Robinson to miss the ball which rolled into the empty net. Neville was officially credited with an own-goal, the second of his international career!

In February 2007, Neville won his 85th cap in a 1–0 friendly defeat by Spain, shooting up to eighth place in the all-time appearances list for his country. However, an ankle injury suffered the following month while playing for Manchester United robbed him of the chance to equal Sansom's record, as he was forced to miss the Euro 2008 qualifiers against Israel and Andorra. Then he was stunned when surgery on his ankle ruled him out of two summer internationals at the new Wembley, and to make things worse a calf muscle injury delayed his recovery in the autumn. Although he was included in Fabio Capello's squad for the 2010 World Cup qualifiers against Kazakhstan and Andorra, he was not used and at that juncture Neville's international career ended.

He does, however, hold a few England records: (a) the most capped right-back, (b) 11 appearances in the European Championship finals (over three tournaments: 1996-2000-2004), (c) most appearances by an outfield player without scoring a goal

(for England), (d) he and Phil are England's most capped brothers, with 144 appearances between them (Phil's appearance as a substitute against Israel in 2007, a game for which Gary was injured, breaking the previous record held by the Charltons, Bobby and Jack) and (e) the Nevilles have made the most appearances in the same England team as a pair of brothers, 31.

Neville joined Manchester United straight from school, made his League debut in 1994 and up to his retirement in January 2011, made almost 600 senior appearances for the Reds, exactly 400 in the Premiership.

He gained eight Premiership, three FA Cup, two League Cup, two Champions League, three Charity Shield, Intercontinental Cup, World Club championship and FA Youth Cup winner's medals, and also represented England in five Youth internationals.

Neville's sister Tracey plays netball for England, his mother Jill is the receptionist at Bury's Gigg Lane ground and his father was a Lancashire cricketer.

NEVILLE, Philip John 1995-2008 (59)

Born: Bury, Lancs, 21 January 1977
Career: Manchester United (apprentice, June 1993, professional, June 1994), Everton (£3.5m, August 2005-May 2013)

Able to perform comfortably in both full-back positions, in the centre of defence or as a midfield anchorman-cum-destroyer, Phil Neville is just the sort of player a manager dreams about. Known as 'Mr Versatility' in the footballing community, at the end of the 2012-13 season he retired from playing football. Capped for the first time as a 19 year-old against China in Beijing in May 1996, he was only briefly a regular in the side at left back in 2000 under Kevin Keegan and then had his work cut out with the likes of Wayne Bridge and Ashley Cole around. But he stuck in there, nonetheless, and actually captained the side in a friendly when four different players donned the armband. Despite being in the England squad for the 1996, 2000 and 2004 European Championships, and gaining a total of 59 caps (23 as a substitute), Neville never played in the World Cup.

He was the youngest member of Terry Venables' squad for Euro 96, though he never kicked a ball and was one of the players omitted at the last minute by Glenn Hoddle prior to the 1998 World Cup. It must be said that Hoddle's decision left Neville in tears, though media attention was almost entirely devoted to the exclusion of another player, Paul Gascoigne. It was revealed afterwards that 'Gazza', not usually noted for his maturity, took Neville under his wing and consoled him.

Playing at left back in Euro 2000, Neville received criticism and a large proportion of blame for England's exit, when he committed a late foul on Viorel Moldovan which led to a penalty for Romania which Ionel Ganea scored to win the match. Neither of the Neville brothers went to the 2002 World Cup – Phil was left out, while Gary was injured. Both were back in the squad, however, for Euro 2004 and they played together for the first time in seven years in a 1-0 friendly defeat by Spain in February 2007. Not included in Sven-Göran Eriksson's squad for the 2006 World Cup, he was named in the stand-by group and remained a squad member when newly-appointed England manager Steve McClaren took over. In fact, he started at right back against Andorra but has not been called up since 2007.

Neville made 386 appearances for Manchester United, gaining Youth Cup, six Premiership, three FA Cup, a European Champions League and three FA Charity Shield winner's medals before transferring to Everton. He went on to appear in 303 first-class matches for the Merseysiders in eight seasons.

NEWTON, Keith Robert 1965-70 (27)

Born: Manchester, 23 June 1941
Died: Burnley, Lancs, 15 June 1998
Career: Manchester Youth football, Bolton Wanderers (trial, January 1957), Blackburn Rovers (amateur, April 1957, professional, October 1958), Everton (£80,000, December 1969), Burnley (June 1972), Morecambe (August 1978-May 1979), Clitheroe (season 1979-80).

Keith Newton made his international debut at left-back in place of Ray Wilson against West Germany at Wembley in February 1966. Although substituted he had a 'fair' game but six weeks later was 'tortured' by impish winger Jimmy Johnstone at Hampden Park when Scotland were defeated 4-3 in one of the best games seen at Hamden Park for many a year. Hugh McIlvanney, writing for *The Observer*, said 'Newton never got to grips with the pace and trickery of the Celtic winger.'

Although named in the 40-strong squad for the World Cup and then in the 'probable list' of 27, in the end Newton missed out altogether as Alf Ramsey went for Wilson and Gerry Byrne as his two left-backs. "It was disappointing," said Newton, "but I knew there would be another chance as I was only 25 at the time."

Things were different, however, four years later when he was taken to the World Cup finals in Mexico. Almost 'kicked' out of the tournament in the opening game, by some ruthless challenges by certain Romanians, he missed the defeat by Brazil but played in the last two games, against Czechoslovakia and West Germany, with Terry Cooper as his partner. In the quarter-final clash with the Germans in Leon he played 'his best game' for England, linking up splendidly with Alan Mullery down the right. In fact, he set up the midfielder's goal on 30 minutes and then early in the second-half, after taking Geoff Hurst's pass in his stride, he charged down the right again and swung over a superb cross for Martin Peters to make it 2-0.

That, in fact, was Newton's last game for his country. He continued playing top-line football until 1978, quitting the game two years later.

He made 700 appearances for his four major clubs, including 357 for Blackburn and 252 for Burnley, with whom he won a Second Division championship medal in 1973. And besides his 27 full England caps, Newton also gained four at U23 level and represented the Football League. He sadly died from lung cancer, aged 57.

NICHOLLS, John 1953-54 (2) (1)

Born: Heath Town, Wolverhampton, 3 April 1931
Died: West Bromwich, 1 April 1995
Career: Prestwood Road, Holy Trinity & Springfield Road Schools/Wolverhampton, Heath Town FC/Wolverhampton (1945), West Bromwich Albion (trial, July-September 1946), Heath Town Wesley (October 1946), Heath Town United (May 1948), Wolverhampton Wanderers (trial, August-September 1949), West Bromwich Albion (amateur, August 1950, professional, August 1951), Cardiff City (£4,000, May 1957), Exeter City (free, November 1957), Worcester City (August 1959), Wellington Town (February 1961), Oswestry Town (July 1961), GKN Sankey Works (August 1962, retired, May 1963); Henry Meadows FC/Wolverhampton (technical adviser, season 1963-64), Red Dragon FC/West Bromwich League (part-time player, late 1960s); also played for West Bromwich Albion All Stars (seasons 1969-73).

Johnny Nicholls celebrated his 23rd birthday by scoring on his England debut in a 4-2 win over Scotland at Hampden Park in April 1954. He raced fully 30 yards to get on the end of Tom Finney's pin point centre to send a flying header past 'keeper George Farm for the second goal. Despite his goal, 'he had a moderate match' wrote Roy Peskett in the *Daily Mail*. His second England game ended in a disappointing 1-0 defeat in Yugoslavia. His West Brom team-mate Ronnie Allen played alongside him in both internationals and at club level they were superb. In 1953-54 when the Baggies won the FA Cup and came runners-up in the First Division, they scored 66 goals between them and in two seasons (1953-55) they bagged a total of 105. Nicholls, known as the 'Poacher,' spent seven years at The Hawthorns during which time he netted 64 times in 145 appearances. He also represented England at B and U23 levels. He sadly died while driving home after watching the WBA-Middlesbrough League game at The Hawthorns in 1995.

NICHOLSON, William Edward, OBE 1950-51 ① ①

Born: Scarborough, 26 January 1919
Died: Potters Bar, Hertfordshire, 23 October 2004
Career: Scarborough Boys' High School, Young Liberals FC (season 1932-33), Scarborough Working Men's Club (August 1934), Tottenham Hotspur (amateur, March 1936); played for Northfleet FC/Tottenham's nursery team (seasons 1936-38); Tottenham Hotspur (professional, August 1938; retired, August 1955); WW2 guest for Darlington, Fulham, Hartlepool United, Manchester United, Middlesbrough, Newcastle United and Sunderland; Tottenham Hotspur (coach, December 1955; assistant-manager, August 1957, then manager, October 1958-September 1974); served as England coach and assistant-manager at the World Cup in Sweden in summer, 1958; West Ham United (scout, October 1974-July 1976); Tottenham Hotspur (consultant, July 1976, then chief scout, 1980s and finally club President from May 1991 until his death).

Bill Nicholson, a strong, well-equipped right-half, scored after just 19 seconds with a well-struck 18-yard shot on his England debut against Portugal at Goodison Park in May 1951. This is believed to have been the fastest goal scored by an England player from the start of a game. Despite some enterprising performances for Tottenham with whom he won the Second and First Division championships in successive seasons (1950 and 1951) he failed to win another cap, yet was named reserve for his country no less than 22 times (a record). A no frills, rugged, strong-tackling wing-half, he was a wonderful club man who, after making 395 first-team appearances as a player (357 at senior level) went on to manage Spurs to the double in 1961, to two more FA Cup triumphs in 1962 and 1967, European Cup Winners' Cup glory in 1963, two League Cup final victories in 1971 and 1973 and success in the UEFA Cup in 1972. He was presented with an OBE in 1975 and the PFA Merit Award in 1984. 'Bill Nick' as he was called, served Spurs (in various capacities) for some 60 years. He was Spurs' manager for 823 matches (unbeaten in 596 - 401 wins and 195 draws).

NISH, David John 1972-74 ⑤

Born: Burton-on-Trent, 26 September 1947
Career: Measham Imperial (seasons 1961-63), Leicester City (apprentice, August 1963, professional, July 1966), Derby County (£225,000, August 1972), Tulsa Roughnecks/USA (£10,000, February 1979), Seattle Sounders/USA (seasons 1980-81; played in the outside and indoor leagues), Shepshed Charterhouse (June 1982), Gresley Rovers (player-manager, August 1983), Stapenhill FC (briefly); Middlesbrough (youth coach, season 1988-89), Derby County (coach, briefly, season 1986-87), Leicester City (coach, then Youth Development Office, to 1995).

David Nish was a teenage prodigy, capped by England at Youth team level, who was once chosen as first-team substitute by Leicester City while still at school. Initially a creative midfielder, he later settled in as an international left-back and in 1969 became the youngest-ever FA Cup final captain at 21. He rarely missed a game for Leicester for five years during which time he also appeared in 10 England U23 matches and represented the Football League. He scored 31 goals in 272 appearances for the Foxes who he helped climb back into the top flight in 1971. He looked all set for a lengthy career at Filbert Street when reigning champions Derby County came in with a British record fee of £225,000 to take him to the Baseball Ground.

Nish gained five full England caps – the first v. Northern Ireland in May 1973 when he replaced Emlyn Hughes at left-back, and the other four at right-back (as partner to Mike Pejic) against Portugal, Wales, Ireland (again) and Scotland over a six-week period at the end of the season. He won a League championship medal with the Rams in 1975 but a series of knee injuries led to him leaving the UK for the less demanding sphere of the NASL.

He eventually rejoined former Derby team-mates Bruce Rioch and Colin Todd on the coaching staff at Middlesbrough (1988) before returning to Leicester as Youth Development Officer, also assuming responsibility for coaching the Youth team in the mid-1990s.

NORMAN, Maurice 1961-65 ㉓

Born: Mulbarton, Norfolk, 8 May 1934
Career: Mulbarton & Wymondham Secondary Modern School, Wymondham Miners FC (August 1949), Mulbarton FC (September 1950), Norwich City (groundstaff, July 1951, professional, September 1952), Tottenham Hotspur (November 1955; retired, injured, May 1967); became assistant-manager of a North London garage and then ran a shop in Frinton-on-Sea; now living in Felixstowe.

Having used Trevor Smith, Ken Brown, Bill Slater and then Peter Swan at centre-half following the retirement of Billy Wright in 1959, England manager Walter Winterbottom turned to the giant 6ft 3in Spurs defender Maurice Norman to make the number five shirt his own in the 1962 World Cup in Chile. Already an U23 international with three caps to his name, he played very well in a pre-tournament friendly against Peru and also in the group matches against Hungary, Argentina and Bulgaria, but in his fifth international, against the reigning champions Brazil, he struggled. Beaten in the air by one of the smallest players on the pitch, Garrincha, for Brazil's first goal, he then failed to close down the 'Little Bird' who scored from 25 yards in the 61st minute to make it 3-1. In between times he had seen Garrincha swerve a free-kick into goalkeeper Springett's chest, Vava netting the rebound after the Spurs defender had failed to react. Afterwards Norman said: "We'd never seen anything like it...you could not believe anyone could bend a ball so far."

In the European Nations Cup qualifier against France at Hillsborough in October 1962 – the first game after the World Cup – Norman was booed every time he touched the ball on the ground of Peter Swan, the man he replaced at centre-half!

Nevertheless Norman continued as England's centre-half and he had some excellent games over the next two years, playing quite brilliantly in the 1-1 draw with Brazil at Wembley in May 1963, doing likewise against the Rest of the World five months later and also producing a terrific display against Portugal in Sao Paulo June 1964.

In between times he had a few dodgy matches – like all players – but was generally a fine defender who loved to join the attack – sometimes to the annoyance of his manager!

After 23 internationals as England's number one pivot, Norman was replaced by Jack Charlton for the game against Scotland at Wembley in April 1965...having admitted publicly that his form 'had slumped dramatically over the past year or so.'

Six months later, while playing in a friendly for Spurs against a Hungarian XI, Norman suffered a double fracture of the tibia and fibula. The compound fracture would keep him out for three years, thus ending his international career. "I would have been in the World Cup," said Norman. "I was told that by Alf Ramsey."

Initially a right-back, Norman made 411 senior appearances for Spurs (453 all games), gaining League, two FA Cup and European Cup Winners' Cup medals when he was part of Bill Nicholson's great attacking side that won the double in 1961.

NUGENT, David James 2006-07 ① ①

Born: Huyton, Liverpool, 2 May 1985
Career: Bury (apprentice, May 2001, professional, March 2003), Preston North End (January 2005), Portsmouth (£6m, July 2007), Burnley (loan, September 2009-May 2010), Leicester City (July 2011).

David Nugent is the last player from a club outside the top flight of League football (including the Premiership) to win a full cap for England, which he won against v. Andorra in March 2007. He had already scored four goals in 14 U21 internationals and came on as a late substitute and marked the occasion by netting the final goal in an easy 3-0 victory over moderate opposition.

In an after-match press interview, Nugent expressed genuine satisfaction over having accomplished a 'one goal, one cap' national team record... for he hasn't been chosen since!

He was the first Preston North End player to play for England since Tom Finney some 49 years previously and was also the first player outside the top-flight to win a full cap since goalkeeper David James of West Ham in 2003. And he became the first non-Premier League outfield player since Michael Gray (Sunderland) in 1999 to win a full cap.

Nugent made his U21 debut against Wales two years earlier and he was part of the team that advanced into the play-off round of the UEFA European U21 Championship, netting his third goal at this level in a 2-2 draw with Spain in February 2007 - Stuart Pearce's first game as coach. An FA Cup winner with Portsmouth in 2008, at the end of the 2012-13 season, Nugent had scored 115 goals in 430 first-class appearances for his four English clubs. And for the record book, he is one of only three players to have made just one substitute appearance and scored one goal for England. The others are Paul Goddard and Franny Jeffers.

NUTTALL, Henry 1927-29 ③

Born: Bolton, 9 November 1897
Died: Bolton, 12 April 1969
Career: Bolton St Mark's (August 1910), Fleetwood (September 1911), Bolton Wanderers (professional, December 1920), Rochdale (May 1932), Nelson (August 1933, retired May 1935); Bolton Wanderers (groundstaff, August 1935, assistant-trainer, July 1946, kitman and later club factotum until May, 1964).

Harry Nuttall was 'Bolton Wanderers' through and through – he was born in the cottage within the confines of Burnden park where his father was groundsman.

A studious, attack-minded wing-half he had a terrific engine and was invariably in the right place at the right time. He made 326 appearances during his 12 years as a player with Bolton, gaining three FA Cup winner's medals in the space of six years.

Unfortunately he was on the losing side in each of his three England games – against Ireland in October 1927 (0-2), versus Wales a month later (1-2) and against Scotland in April 1929 (0-1). In the latter he was given a testing time by the right-wing pairing of Jackson and Cheyne, the latter scoring the only goal.

Nuttall served Bolton Wanderers in various capacities for some 40 years.

OAKLEY, William John 1894-1901 ⑯

Born: Shrewsbury, 27 April 1873
Died: Wokingham, Berks, 20 September 1934
Career: Shrewsbury County School (seasons 1887-93), Oxford University (seasons 1893-97); also played for Corinthians (seasons 1894-1903; joint secretary of club with G. O. Smith, seasons 1898-1902), Casuals (briefly 1898-99); President of Oxford University Athletic Club (1895); a schoolteacher by profession (headmaster of Ludgrove School, Berkshire).

An all-round sportsman, Bill Oakley participated in cricket, rugby and soccer, was a decent track athlete, a champion long jumper and hurdler, a fine rower, a keen tennis player and useful swimmer. A close friend of G.O. Smith, Oakley was one of the 'swiftest backs' of his day, two-footed, quick and clever. At times he a let fly from fully 30 yards with one of his rocket shots, but more often than not the ball was nowhere near its target!

Capped for the first time against Wales at The Queens Club, London in March 1895, he held his position, either on the right or left, relatively unchallenged for seven years, only missing games through injury. He captained England against Ireland at The Dell, Southampton in March 1901 before playing in his final international 12 days later, in a 2-2 draw with Scotland at Crystal Palace. That afternoon, he partnered Jimmy Iremonger (Nottingham Forest) and had a 'fine game against a very tricky winger in Johnny Walker' wrote 'Albion' in *The Times*. Oakley died from injuries received in a motor cycling accident in 1934.

O'DOWD, James Peter 1931-33 ③

Born: Halifax, 26 February 1908
Died: Westminster, London, 8 May 1964
Career: St Bees Grammar School/Bradford, Apperley Bridge FC (May 1923), Selby Town (August 1925), Blackburn Rovers (amateur, September 1926, professional, December 1926), Burnley (March 1930), Chelsea (November 1931), Valenciennes/France (September 1935), Torquay United (March 1937, retired June 1937); later ran a drapery business for many years.

Effective and reliable as a wing-half or centre-half, Peter O'Dowd gained the first of his three England caps against Scotland at Wembley in April 1932 (won 3-0). His second followed six months later in a 1-0 win over Ireland and his last came in May 1933 when Switzerland were thumped 4-0 in Berne. He had an excellent game against the Scots, as the *Daily Mail* correspondent wrote in his report: "Here is a cool and resourceful player whose control in the middle of the field is a sheer delight." Around this time O'Dowd was acclaimed as being one of the best England defenders in the game.

A Football League representative in 1932, O'Dowd, who spent his best years with Chelsea, retired prematurely after breaking a leg in a trial match in 1937.

OGILVIE, Robert Andrew Muter Macindoe 1873-74 ①

Born: Brentwood, Essex, 30 November 1852
Died: Newham, London, 5 March 1938
Career: Brentwood School, Upton Park (September 1870), Clapham Rovers (seasons 1871-75); served on FA Committee (seasons 1874-81); also an official FA referee; Member of Lloyds (Chairman of Institute of Lloyds Underwriters 1910-11); Underwriter to Alliance Assurance Company (1911-14); also worked in the Government's War Risks Department (1914-19).

Robert Ogilvie played in successive FA Cup finals for Clapham Rovers, gaining a winner's medal in his second (1880). Equally at home at right-back or right-half, he was a hard-tackler whose displays were often marred by a degree of uncertainty. He won his only England cap in a 2-1 defeat by Scotland at the local cricket ground, Partick, in March 1874 when, wrote the *Bell's Life* reporter: "He (Ogilvie) kicked well under pressure and was always a willing worker." Ogilvie refereed the Scotland-England international at The Oval in March 1877.

O'GRADY, Michael 1962-69 ② ③

Born: Leeds, 11 October 1942
Career: Corpus Christi School/Leeds, Huddersfield Town (amateur, June 1958, professional, November 1959), Leeds United (£30,000, October 1965), Wolverhampton Wanderers (£80,000, September 1969), Birmingham City (on loan, February 1972), Rotherham United (free, November 1972, retired, through injury, May 1974); later worked for Yorkshire TV (as a grip) before becoming mine host of The Royal Oak, Aberford near Wetherby; also played for Leeds Old Stars.

The scorer of two goals in a 3-2 win over Northern Ireland on his international debut in October 1962, versatile winger Mike O'Grady was recalled to the England team by manager Alf Ramsey after seven years in the wilderness to add 'impetus down the left' for the home clash with France in March 1969. And to celebrate the occasion, he scored again, this time with a 'searing volley' from Geoff Hurst's headed knock-down to help clinch a 5-0 victory. Yet, after producing a fine display, the unfortunate O'Grady was not chosen again.
The fifth son of an Irishman, O'Grady had a useful career in top-class football (1959-74), during which time he amassed 363 club appearances and scored 52 goals. With Leeds, he won the Inter Cities Fairs Cup and successive League Championships: 1968 and 1969. He was also capped three times at U23 level.

OLIVER, Leonard Frederick 1928-29 ①

Born: Fulham, London, 1 August 1905
Died: Kensington, London, 4 August 1967
Career: London & District Schools, Fulham Schools, Alma Athletic (May 1920), Tufnell Park (August 1922), Fulham (professional, July 1924, retired, May 1935), Letchworth (briefly, August 1935), Arlesey Town (August 1936), Cliftonville/Ireland (player-coach, seasons 1937-39); Army PT Instructor during WW2; had worked as a clerk in a London store before joining Fulham; lived in Hertfordshire for many years.

Right-half Len Oliver was as efficient in defence as he was in attack. Hard-working and with a stirring tackle, he captained Fulham for seven years and helped them win the Third Division (South) title in 1932. He made 434 appearances for the Cottagers (1924-35) but for all his efforts gained only one England cap, against Belgium in May 1929 when he assisted in two of George Camsell's four goals in a resounding 5-1 win in Brussels.

OLNEY, Benjamin Albert 1927-28 ②

Born: Holborn, London, 30 March 1899
Died: Derby, 23 September 1943
Career: Farley's Athletic (April 1914), Aston Park Rangers (August 1915), Brierley Hill Alliance (September 1918), Stourbridge (August 1919), Derby County (professional, £800, April 1921), Aston Villa (£2,000, December 1927), Bilston United (player-manager, July 1930), Walsall (August 1931), Shrewsbury Town (August 1932), Moor Green (reinstated as an amateur, August 1934, retired, May 1935); later licensee of The Horse & Jockey/Bilston, also worked at the Rolls Royce factory (Derby).

A very tidy and capable goalkeeper, clever in anticipation and highly consistent, Ben Olney made 240 appearances for Derby, helping the Rams gain promotion from Division Two in 1926. Replacing Tommy Jackson, he made nearly 100 appearances for his next League club, Aston Villa, winning his two caps in 5-1 and 3-1 wins over France in Paris and Belgium in Brussels on England's end-of-season tour in May 1928. Known as 'Big Ben', Olney also played in two unofficial internationals (Test Matches) against South Africa in 1929.

OSBORNE, Frank Raymond 1922-26 ④ ③

Born: Wynberg, South Africa, 14 October 1896
Died: Epsom, Surrey, 8 March 1988
Career: Gymnasium School/South Africa, Netley FC (April 1911), Bromley (amateur, July 1919), Fulham (professional, November 1921), Tottenham Hotspur (January 1924), Southampton (June 1931, retired, May 1933); became a Fulham director (March 1935, manager, September 1948, retired October 1964); also served as general manager at Craven Cottage.

An accomplished outside-right or centre-forward, Frank Osborne netted 18 goals in 70 games for Fulham before spending seven years with Spurs for whom he amassed 219 appearances and scored 82 goals. He won his first two caps with Fulham, starring in a 2-0 win over Ireland at West Brom's Hawthorns ground in October 1922 and in a resounding 4-1 victory over France in Paris in May 1923. After 18 months in the wilderness he was returned to international duty against Belgium, playing his part in an excellent 4-0 win again at The Hawthorns in December 1924, and five months later he was outstanding as he cracked in a hat-trick when the Belgians were beaten 5-3 in a return fixture in Antwerp. Osborne is the fourth oldest player ever to win a full cap for England, aged 39 years and 221 days. His younger brother Reg (below) and Harry, who played for Norwich City, were also professional footballers.

OSBORNE, Reginald 1927-28 ①

Born: Wynberg, South Africa, 23 July 1898
Died: Hounslow, Middlesex, 26 June 1977
Career: Gymnasium School/South Africa; played for the Army while serving with the Royal Army Medical Corps (seasons 1917-22); worked for the Watling Street Boot Company/Leicester (1922); joined Leicester City (professional, February 1923, retired, May 1933), returned with Folkestone (November 1933-May 1934).

Younger brother of Frank, Reg Osborne was a quite fearless left-back, solid in the tackle, strong in kicking who played in two amateur internationals in 1921-22 before winning his only England cap in a 2-1 defeat by Wales at Burnley in November 1927 when he deputised for Blackburn's Harry Jones. This game had two own-goals and a missed penalty by Goodall of England. A Second Division championship winner with Leicester in 1925, Osborne made 249 appearances for the Foxes in 10 years: 1923-33.

OSGOOD, Peter Leslie 1969-74 ④

Born: Windsor, 21 February 1947
Died: Slough, 1 March 2006
Career: Windsor Under-11s, Spital Boys' Club (April 1960), Windsor & Eton (July 1962), Chelsea (amateur, April 1964, professional, September 1964), Southampton (£275,000, March 1974), Norwich City (loan, November 1976), Philadelphia Fury/USA (December 1977), Chelsea (£25,000, December 1978-September 1979), Spitals & Aldwyck Bay Rowdies/Gambia (season 1979-80); coach in Gambia, the Far East and at Butlins (seasons 1980-85); Portsmouth (youth team coach, June 1986-June 1988); became licensee of The Union Inn, Windsor (with ex-Chelsea player Ian Hutchinson); also a sports promotions manager (1990); later engaged as a match-day host at Stamford Bridge and was also a respected after-dinner speaker.

A striker perhaps 'too mercurial for his own good' Peter Osgood was, in some people's mind, a surprise choice for the 1970 World Cup finals in Mexico. But at the time he was in the 'form of his life' and was one of four main 'goal-getters' (the others being Jeff Astle, Allan Clarke and Geoff Hurst) in Alf Ramsey's squad.

However, Ramsey, who apparently disapproved of his playboy life-style, only used him twice as a substitute, in 1-0 wins over Romania and Czechoslovakia.

Earlier Osgood had made a 'satisfactory' international debut, alongside Hurst, in the 3-1 win over Belgium on a quagmire of a pitch in Brussels in February 1970 and his last cap came in a 1-0 defeat at the hands of Italy at Wembley in November 1973 – Bobby Moore's 108th and final game in an England shirt.

Osgood loved to hover around the edge of the penalty area. He was extremely mobile, physically strong, two-footed, possessed a ferocious shot and scored 150 goals in 380 appearances for Chelsea in two spells, 1964-1974 and 1978-79, gaining FA Cup and European Cup Winners' Cup winning medals in 1970 and 1971. In 1976 he added a second FA Cup winner's medal to his collection with Southampton for whom he netted 36 goals in 157 games.

His autobiography *Ossie – King of Stamford Bridge* was published in 2003 and a year later Osgood appeared in a cameo role in the British film *The Football Factory*. A former apprentice bricklayer, he was only 59 when he collapsed and died while attending a funeral at Slough crematorium.

OSMAN, Leon 2012-13 ②

Born: Billinge Higher End, Wigan, 17 May 1981
Career: Up Holland High School, Winstanley College, Everton (trainee, July 1997, professional, May 1999), Carlisle United (loan, October 2002-January 2003), Derby County (loan, January-May 2004)

Everton midfielder Leon Osman was 31 years and 181 days old when he made his full England debut in the 4-2 friendly defeat in Sweden in November 2012. He was the third over 30 year-old to make his bow for the senior team since WW2, following Leslie Compton (38) in 1950 and Kevin Davies (33) in 2011. He had earlier worn the 'Three Lions' shirt five times at U16 level.

Hard-working with a terrific engine, Osman thoroughly deserved his call-up after some enterprising displays in the Premiership for David Moyes' side. He won an FA Youth Cup winner's medal with the Blues having earlier represented his country at schoolboy and youth team levels. At November 2012, he had scored 51 goals in 347 club appearances, with more to come.

Osman was born to a Turkish-Cypriot father and an English mother.

OSMAN, Russell Charles 1979-80 ⑪

Born: Repton, Derbyshire, 14 February 1959
Career: Ipswich Town (apprentice, May 1974, professional, March 1976), Leicester City (£225,000, July 1985), Southampton £325,000, June 1988), Bristol City (£50,000, October 1991, manager, summer 1993-May 1994), Sudbury Town (August 1994), Plymouth Argyle (loan, March-May 1995), Brighton & Hove Albion (non-contract, September 1995), Cardiff City (non-contract, February 1996, manager, December 1996-January 1998), Bristol Rovers (caretaker-manager, briefly, 2003-04), Bristol City (coach, seasons 2004-06); set up the Russell Osman Academy, also pursued media work, and became the first ex-professional footballer to commentate on the game in India (working on the Asian Cup in Qatar); Exeter City (assistant-manager/coach, November 2007), Ipswich Town (Academy coach, February 2011, then assistant-manager/coach, June 2011).

England boss Ron Greenwood handed Russell Osman his international debut (along with his Ipswich Town defensive colleague Terry Butcher) in a 2-1 friendly win over Australia in Sydney in May 1980. He played well and as a result won ten further caps over the next three years,

including three more appearances against the Aussies.

The son of a former Derby County player (Rex) Osman played 319 times for Ipswich Town, helping the Tractor Boys win the FA Cup in 1978 and UEFA Cup in 1981 (under Bobby Robson's management). He made well over 700 club appearances in total and also represented his country in two B and seven U21 internationals.

Osman also played one of the prisoner-of-war footballers in the 1981 film *Escape To Victory* which also featured Bobby Moore, Brazilian legend Pele, Mike Summerbee, American star Sylvester Stallone, British actor Michael Caine, Argentinian World Cup winner Ossie Ardiles and several of his Ipswich Town team-mates including John Wark, Kevin Beattie, Rob Turner and goalkeeper Paul Cooper.

OTTAWAY, Cuthbert John 1872-74 ②

Born: Dover, Kent, 20 July 1850
Died: Kensal Green, London, 2 April 1878
Career: Eton College, Brasenose College/Oxford University (seasons 1869-76); also played for Old Etonians (season 1874-75); FA Committee (season 1872-73); obtained a First in moderations and a Third in classics, he was called to the Bar in 1876; a cricketer for Oxford University (1870-74), South of England, Gentlemen (v. Players), Eton (v. Harrow), the MCC, Kent (seasons 1869 and 1870) and Middlesex (seasons 1874-76); he also played Real Tennis and rackets and was a fine track athlete.

Described as being a 'rampant, individualistic and versatile forward, elegant in style with great ability', Cuthbert Ottaway captained England in their first-ever international against Scotland in November 1872. The game, held at The West of Scotland cricket ground, Partick, ended in a 0-0 draw.

Ottaway did not play in the return fixture in March 1873, but captained his country again in the third England-Scotland international, also at Partick in March 1874 which ended in a 2-1 win for the Scots.

When Charles Alcock, the original captain, met with an accident, Ottaway was unanimously selected by the Englishmen as 'best worthy to take the command' of the team. Ottaway played in three FA Cup finals, losing two and winning with Oxford University in 1874. As a cricketer, Ottaway scored a total of 1,691 first-class runs at an average of 27.27. He achieved an incredible amount during his tragically short life which ended when he was only 27 years of age.

OWEN, John Robert Blayney 1873-74 ①

Born: St Leonard's, Buckinghamshire, 14 June 1848
Died: Chelmsford, Essex, 13 June 1921
Career: Queen's College/Oxford University (seasons 1869-74); also played for Sheffield FC (seasons 1871-74), Sheffield County FA (1870s), Nottinghamshire (1870s), Maldon FC (seasons 1871-72), Essex County (1870s); second Master of Trent College (later Headmaster); Master in charge of Hawkshead Grammar School; ordained in 1876; became Vicar of Toftrees and Rector of Bradwell-on-Sea, Essex.

A fleet-footed forward who was one the best 'poachers' in the game during the 1870s, John Owen won his only England cap against Scotland at the West of Scotland Cricket Ground in Partick in March 1874, playing on the left-wing in a 2-1 defeat. He found it 'hard going against a rugged defence' reported *Bell's Life*.

OWEN, Michael James 1997-2008

Born: Chester, 14 December 1979

Career: Rector Drew Primary School/Hawarden, North Wales, Deeside Primary, Mold Alexandra (from August 1987), Hawarden High School; had talks with Chelsea, Manchester United and Arsenal as a 15 year-old; attended FA School of Excellence (from 1994); Liverpool (apprentice, April 1995, professional, December 1996), Real Madrid (£11m, August 2004), Newcastle United (£16m, August 2005), Manchester United (free, July 2009, released, June 2012), Stoke City (free, August 2012), retired from senior football (May 2013)

After a highly successful record at Schoolboy and Youth levels, Owen moved up the ladder and played for England's U20 team in the 1997 FIFA World Youth Championship, scoring three goals in four games. After that he netted in an U21 win over Greece at Carrow Road, Norwich before making his senior debut in a 2–0 friendly defeat by Chile in February 1998 at the age of 18 years and 59 days, thus becoming the youngest player to represent England in the 20th century.

Three months later, Owen became the youngest player to score an international goal for England when he obliged against Morocco in Casablanca in May, aged 18 years and 164 days. This record was surpassed by Wayne Rooney in 2003.

Although he was selected in Glenn Hoddle's 1998 World Cup squad, he was named as a substitute in the first two games, coming on in the second to score in a 2–1 defeat by Romania, when he also hit the post and almost salvaged a point for England. His goal against the Romanians gave him the record of being England's youngest-ever scorer in the World Cup.

After that, Hoddle played him from the start, and in England's second round match against Argentina, Owen scored a sensational individual goal. Moving forward at speed, he beat defenders Ayala and Chamot before striking the ball home from just outside the penalty box. It was a truly great goal.

England drew that match and went out of the tournament on penalties, but Owen had sealed his place as his country's first choice striker. His popularity increased greatly and at the end of the year, he was voted BBC Sports Personality of the Year by the public.

Owen went on to play in Euro 2000 and 2004 and also in the 2002 World Cup, scoring goals in all three tournaments... making him the only player to ever have netted in four major tournaments for England.

In April 2002, Owen, aged 22 years and 124 days, was named captain of England for the friendly against Paraguay on his home patch at Anfield. Taking over from the injured David Beckham, he became the youngest England skipper since Bobby Moore in 1963, and to celebrate the occasion, he scored in a 4-0 win.

During the following few seasons he often led his country during the absence of the regular captain.

Owen played for England B in a friendly against Belarus in May 2006, as part of his return to match fitness ahead of the 2006 World Cup. He captained the team and played for 61 minutes before being substituted.

Owen thus became one of only a handful of England players to appear in three World Cup tournaments when he played in South Korea and Japan in 2006, although this time he failed to score and was injured in the final group game.

He didn't look quite right in the opening games against Paraguay and Trinidad & Tobago

and then shock, horror, as he played only 51 seconds of the third match against Sweden. He badly twisted his left knee and was forced to leave the pitch, and the match, on a stretcher. A scan carried out later confirmed that he had torn the anterior cruciate ligament in his knee. Sent home, his World Cup, and to a certain extent England's chances of winning it, were over.

Owen subsequently underwent successful reconstruction surgery, carried out by Dr Richard Steadman in early September 2006. Unfortunately the injury sidelined him until April 2007, meaning he missed England's first six qualifying matches for Euro 2008.

He returned for a B international against Albania and was named in the full squad for the games against Brazil and Estonia at which point Owen, with 80 caps already under his belt, said: "I feel sharp and, if given the chance, I feel confident when in front of goal."

He played in both matches and scored against Estonia, breaking Gary Lineker's record for most goals in competitive internationals for England.

Then, by netting twice in a 3–0 win over Russia in September 2007, he became the first player to score international goals at both the old and new Wembley Stadiums.

For Owen 2008 proved to be a tough year. He was excluded from the World Cup qualifiers against Andorra, Croatia, Kazakhstan and Belarus despite, at times, being in good goalscoring form and having a positive work-rate in a poor Newcastle side.

Many fans and pundits called for Owen to be reinstated in the national team but Fabio Capello had other ideas and although the Italian manager hinted that 'he would consider picking him if he was playing and scoring regularly for his club' injuries began to interrupt his game and that was bad news for Owen whose England career effectively ended there and then... although he, himself, seriously believed he still had a good chance of making the squad for the World Cup in South Africa in 2010, especially after playing and scoring in the League Cup final for Manchester United.

Owen was capped 89 times by England. He also netted 40 goals, a tally which took him into fourth place in the list of all-time top scorers for England at senior level, behind Bobby Charlton (49 goals), Lineker (48) and Jimmy Greaves (44). He claimed a record 26 goals for his country in all competitive matches (World Cup and European Championship games and qualifying fixtures for those two tournaments) and was named skipper on seven occasions.

Owen has had a terrific career in football. He joined Liverpool at the age of 16, turned professional in December 1996 and went on to score 158 goals in 297 games for the Merseyside club. He then hit 16 goals in 45 games for Real Madrid, bagged another 30 goals in 79 appearances for Newcastle and netted 17 times in 52 outings for Manchester United, as well as his record for England at senior level.

At Anfield, Owen helped Liverpool win seven trophies (the FA Youth Cup, the FA Cup, the League Cup twice, FA Charity Shield, the UEFA Cup and the European Super Cup). Voted PFA 'Young Player of the Year' in 1998, he was awarded the 'Golden Boot' (jointly) in both 1998 and 1999 (with 18 PL goals), claimed the Ballon d'Or in 2001 and won the Premiership and League Cup with Manchester United before his release from Old Trafford in the summer of 2012.

Owen scored 97 goals playing for Deeside Primary School - beating the previous record holder Ian Rush by 25 goals.

OWEN, Sidney William 1953-54 ③

Born: Birmingham, 29 September 1922
Died: Manchester, 12 January 1999
Career: Birmingham YMCA (August 1938), Birmingham City
(professional, October 1945), Luton Town (June 1947, retired May
1959, having been initially appointed player-manager, April 1959;
continued as manager until April 1960); Leeds United (coach,
May 1960), Birmingham City (assistant-manager/coach, October
1975-September 1977), Hull City (coach, December 1977-February
1978), Manchester United (Youth team coach, May 1978-April 1982).

After failing to establish himself with Birmingham City, centre-half
Sid Owen made over 400 appearances for Luton Town (388 in the
Football League) up to May 1959 when he retired, having captained
the Hatters in that season's FA Cup final (v. Nottingham Forest) and
been voted as FWA 'Footballer of the Year."

A polished, upright defender, who always tried to play football, very
rarely committing a foul, Owen gained three England caps at the age
of 31, all 'away' from home in May/June 1954, against Yugoslavia,
Hungary and Belgium, the latter in the World Cup on Switzerland.

His debut ended in a 1-0 defeat in Belgrade after he had become
the eleventh centre-half used by Walter Winterbottom since Neil
Franklin's defection to the Colombian League four years earlier.

Then, he was 'far from convincing' in his second game when
Hungary won 7-1 in Budapest. In an interview after the match
a bewildered Owen said: "It was like playing people from outer
space." This is still England's record defeat.

In his third international, the opening match of the World Cup
against Belgium, Owen pulled a muscle and was forced to spend
the last 15 minutes hobbling on the left-wing. The game ended 4-4.

Twice a Football League representative, he helped Birmingham
win the League (South) championship in 1946 and was a highly-
regarded coach under Don Revie at Leeds.

OXLADE-CHAMBERLAIN, Alexander Mark David 2011-12 ⑫ ③

Born: Portsmouth, 15 August 1993
Career: St John's College/Southsea, Southampton (Academy junior,
aged seven in 2000, apprentice, August 2009, professional, August
2010), Arsenal (£12m + August 2011)

Alex Oxlade-Chamberlain made his Football League debut for
Southampton at the age of 16 years 199 days, as a substitute
in a 5–0 victory over Huddersfield Town in March 2010 to
become the club's second youngest ever appearance-maker
behind Theo Walcott. Nicknamed 'The Ox' (from his school
days) he netted 10 goals in his first full season with Saints,
helping them gain promotion. He was also named in the
PFA League One Team of the Year for 2010–11 and was
immediately the subject of transfer speculation, with Arsenal
showing a great deal of interest. And on 8 August 2011 he
joined the Gunners for an initial fee believed to be around £12
million which could rise to £15 million with various add-ons.
He made his debut as a substitute three weeks later, in that
embarrassing 8–2 defeat at Manchester United, and in doing
so became the 150th player to represent Arsenal in the Premier
League. Within a month he had scored his first goal for the
Emirates club in a League Cup match against Shrewsbury Town
and thereafter things simply got better. He became the youngest
Englishman to score in the Champions League and in early February
2012, he celebrated his first two Premier League goals in a home
game against Blackburn Rovers which Arsenal won 7-1.

He played for England's U18 team in a 3-0 victory over Poland in

November 2010 and was then called up to the U19 squad to face
Germany in February 2011 but was promoted into the U21 side
instead for a friendly in Italy, a game England lost to an 88th minute
penalty. After several impressive displays at intermediate level, which
included a hat-trick in a 3-0 U21 win in Iceland Oxlade-Chamberlain
was named by new head coach Roy Hodgson in his 23-man senior
England squad for Euro 2012 and before the tournament started
he was handed his full international debut as a substitute for Ashley
Young, in a 1—0 win over Norway, making his first senior start shortly
afterwards in another single-goal victory against Belgium at Wembley.

Then, on 11 June, he made his major tournament debut when
he started in England's opening Euro 2012 game against France
to become the second youngest in this competition behind Wayne
Rooney. He has subsequently added further caps to his tally, while
also scoring his first goal – a smartly taken effort in a 5-0 win over
San Marino in a World Cup qualifier at Wembley in October 2012.

As a schoolboy, Oxlade-Chamberlain enjoyed playing rugby (as
a scrum half or full-back) but in the end he chose the round ball
game as opposed to the oval one. He is the son of former Stoke City,
Portsmouth and England international winger Mark Chamberlain, while
his uncle, Neville Chamberlain, was also a professional footballer.

PAGE, Louis Antonio 1926-28 ⑦ ①

Born: Kirkdale, Lancs, 27 March 1899
Died: Prenton, Birkenhead, 12 October 1959
Career: St Alexander School, Sudley Schooboys, Liverpool
Schoolboys, Sudley Juniors (August 1912), Everton (trial, August
1913), South Liverpool (August 1915), Stoke (professional, May
1919), Northampton Town (July 1922), Burnley (May 1925),
Manchester United (March 1932), Port Vale (October 1932), Yeovil
& Petters United (player-manager, July 1933-May 1935); Newport
County (manager, June 1935-September 1937), Glentoran (trainer-
coach, December 1938-May 1944), Carlton FC/Liverpool (manager,
seasons 1944-45), Swindon Town (manager, July 1945-May 1953),
Chester (manager, June 1953-June 1956), Leicester City (scout,
August 1956 until his death).

Louis Page played most of his football on the left-wing. Quick and
elusive, he was blessed with a powerful shot and in October 1926,
scored six goals for Burnley in a League game against Birmingham
after being switched to centre-forward in an emergency. He won
his seven England caps in successive games between February
and November 1927. He helped set up one of Dixie Dean's two
goals in a 3-3 draw with Wales on his debut, scored once, with a
fine drive on 63 minutes, and laid on three more goals in a 9-1
victory over Belgium in his third game and assisted in goals scored
by George Brown and Dean again in a 6-0 victory over France in
his fifth outing. A total of 37 goals were scored in Page's seven
internationals.

For his main League club, Burnley, whom he served for seven
years, Page netted 115 goals in 259 appearances.

*Besides his football activities, Page also represented England at
baseball (along with his brother).*

PAINE, Terence Lionel, MBE 1962-66 ⑲ ⑦

Born: Winchester, 23 March 1939
Career: All Saints School/Winchester, Winchester & District Schools,
Highcliffe Corinthians (August 1953), Winchester City (June 1954),
Southampton (amateur, August 1956, professional, February 1957),
Hereford United (free, as player-coach, August 1974); Kazma FC/
Kuwait (coach, summer 1977); Coventry City (appointed scout, May
1980), Cheltenham Town (manager-coach, November 1980), Witts
University/South Africa (coach, July 1983), Coventry City (Youth
team coach, May 1988), Witts University (coach, April-September

1991); became licensee of the Prince of Wales pub (Cheltenham), engaged as a Southampton Borough councillor; latterly worked as a football presenter on digital satellite TV sports channel Supersport in South Africa, appearing alongside former Manchester United and England goalkeeper Gary Bailey; during the run up to South Africa's successful bid to stage the 2010 World Cup, Paine was part of the country's delegation in Zurich when 'victory' was announced.

Outside-right Terry Paine played four times for England at U23 level and on 19 occasions for the seniors. He won his first full cap in a 4-2 win over Czechoslovakia in May 1963 when, having taken over from Bryan Douglas, he made one of the goals and afterwards received praise from his manager Alf Ramsey for his 'all round contribution.' Six months later he scored a hat-trick in an 8-3 victory over Northern Ireland at Wembley to become the first right-winger to score three times for England since Stanley Matthews in 1937. Furthermore, no forward wearing the no. 7 shirt has ever scored a hat-trick at Wembley.

After that and despite fellow winger Peter Thompson being around, he was a regular in the England set-up and added two more goals to his tally in a 10-0 win over the USA in May 1964 and scoring the winner against West Germany in May 1965.

Imbued with a keen, competitive spirit, he was a clever ball player with good pace, could shoot with both feet and was also able to deliver a measured cross from out on the flank.

A member of Alf Ramsey's squad at the 1966 World Cup, Paine played in only one match, against Mexico. This, in fact, was his last and 19th outing for his country and to make things worse he got injured! Ramsey, of course, had now found little use for the 'old-fashioned' winger and it was Alan Ball who took over on the right.

Paine was one of four players to play for England in the tournament without appearing in the final itself, the others being Jimmy Greaves, John Connelly and Ian Callaghan.

Paine made a record 713 League appearances (out of an overall total of 808) during his 17-year association with Southampton for whom he also scored 185 goals. He then added another 111 League appearances to his tally with Hereford to bring his career total up to 824, placing him fifth in the all-time list of League appearance-makers. A Third Division championship winner with Saints in 1960, six years later Paine helped the club climb into Division One for the very first time.

PALLISTER, Gary Andrew 1987-1997 ㉒

Born: Ramsgate, Kent, 30 June 1965
Career: Billingham Town (August 1982), Middlesbrough (professional, November 1984), Darlington (loan, October-November 1985), Manchester United (£2.3m, August 1989), Middlesbrough (£2m, July 1998, retired, May 2001); became a TV summariser/reporter/pundit.

Centre-half Gary Pallister had the rare achievement of representing England at senior level before appearing in top flight League football. Already regarded as one of the most respected defenders in the game, he proved this beyond all doubt by making an impressive full international debut alongside Tony Adams in the 0-0 draw with Hungary in Budapest in April 1988. Later in the year he helped his club, Middlesbrough, clinch promotion for the second successive season and reach the First Division, some two years after almost going out of business. Standing 6ft 5ins tall and tipping the scales at 13st, Pallister was the right height and build for a central defender. Dominant in the air, keen and robust in the tackle, he was never really given a 'hard time' by an opposing striker and, in fact, in most of his England games he proved to be one of the more reliable defenders. A regular in the national side until 1997, he won four League, three FA Cup, League Cup and European Cup Winners' Cup winner's medals with Manchester United and was also voted PFA 'Footballer

of the Year' in 1992. He made 250 appearances in his two spells with Middlesbrough and 437 for United. Besides his 22 senior appearances for England, Pallister also played in nine B internationals.

PALMER, Carlton Lloyd 1991-94 ⑱ ①

Born: Rowley Regis, West Midlands, 5 December 1965
Career: Rowley Regis & District Boys, Newton Albion (August 1980), Netherton Town (seasons 1981-82), Dudley Town (season 1982-83), West Bromwich Albion (apprentice, July 1983, professional, December 1984), Sheffield Wednesday (£750,000, in deal involving Colin West, February 1989), Leeds United (£2.6m, June 1994), Southampton (£1m, September 1997), Nottingham Forest (£1.1m, January 1999), Coventry City (£500,000, September 1999), Watford (on loan, December 2000-January 2001), Sheffield Wednesday (on loan, February-May 2001), Stockport County (free, player-manager, November 2001-September 2003), Darlington (non-contract, November 2003), Cork City (on loan, February-March 2004), Dublin City (August-October 2004), Mansfield Town (player/caretaker-manager, November 2004, full-time manager, March-September 2005); became a soccer pundit and analyst on BBC's Final Score, and Dish TV; he owns the Dam House in Sheffield, and has also featured on Ten Sports (a mid-East Asian sports channel which broadcasts in the UAE, India, Pakistan, Bangladesh and Sri Lanka); has worked as a PE teacher/sports master at Repton School and in Dubai, has been a guest presenter on Showsports, starred in a Paddy Power advert and won a one-off football special of Come Dine With Me, collecting a cheque for £1,000 which went to a chosen charity.

A tall, lanky midfielder who also played at centre-half, Carlton Palmer could be abrasive, awkward and argumentative in the dressing room, yet determined, hard-working and persistent on the pitch where his long legs made him difficult to play against. He made an impressive international debut against the CIS in Moscow in April 1992. Two months later he was outstanding in the European Championship opener against Denmark in Malmo when, accompanying Trevor Steven and David Platt in midfield, he came close to scoring on two occasions in the 0-0 draw.

Palmer eventually found the net in February 1993, scoring with a splendid diving header in the 6-0 World Cup qualifying win over the minnows from San Marino at Wembley. A regular in the England team for 18 months, during which time he missed only two games against Germany and Poland, he was a member of the team that competed in the 1992 European Championships in Sweden.

Palmer made over 700 senior appearances at club level, including 591 in the League competition alone, and 205 for Sheffield Wednesday whom he helped win promotion and reach both the FA Cup and League Cup finals. He was also capped on four occasions at U21 level and five times by England B.

PANTLING, Harry Harold 1923-24 ①

Born: Leighton Buzzard, Bedfordshire, 2 February 1891
Died: Sheffield, 22 December 1952
Career: Luton Schools, Watford (amateur, July 1908, professional, 1911), Sheffield United (March 1914), Rotherham United (May 1926), Heanor Town (November 1927, retired May 1929); was a licensee in Sheffield until his death.

A well-built, strong-tackling right-half with good distribution skills, Harry Pantling won the FA Cup with Sheffield United in April 1925, having gained his only England cap in a 2-1 defeat by Ireland in Belfast in October 1923. He made 368 appearances during his 12 years at Bramall Lane. In 1917-18, Pantling became the first Sheffield United player to be sent off twice in the same season.

PARKER, Paul Andrew 1988-94 ⑱

Born: West Ham, London, 4 April 1964
Career: Essex & Havering Schoolboys, Fulham (associated schoolboy forms, June 1978, apprentice, May 1980, professional, April 1982), Queens Park Rangers (£300,000, June 1987), Manchester United (£2m, August 1991), Derby County (free, August 1996), Sheffield United (free, November 1996), Fulham (free, January 1997), Chelsea (free, March 1997), Farnborough Town (free, July 1997, retired, May 1998); Chelmsford City (assistant-manager, August 2000, manager, June 2001), Welling United (manager, season 2002-03); now employed as an ambassador for the Blue Square Premier League; has also ventured into media punditry.

Paul Parker made his international debut as a substitute in the 5-0 World Cup qualifying win over Albania at Wembley in March 1989, before starting his first England game a month later v. Chile when he partnered Stuart Pearce at full-back.

A very competent, hard-working defender with attacking instinct, Parker was selected as Gary Stevens' back-up for the 1990 World Cup in Italy but after Stevens had produced a disappointing display in the opening 1–1 draw with the Republic of Ireland, Parker took over the number 2 shirt, just five caps into his career.

He played well and stayed there, producing some fine displays behind Chris Waddle as England progressed through to the semi-finals, where they met West Germany. Here two incidents would define Parker's career. With the score at 0–0, the Germans won a free-kick just outside the penalty-area early in the second-half. The ball was tapped to Andreas Brehme who fired a shot at goal. The ball struck Parker as he broke from the wall and looped over goalkeeper Peter Shilton and into the net. The goal was credited to Brehme, but Parker managed to make amends with fewer than ten minutes to play. Collecting the ball wide down the right flank, he looked up and whipped over a high cross towards Gary Lineker. The German defenders got in each other's way and Lineker found room to score with a far post shot. The game ended 1–1 but sadly England lost the penalty shoot-out. Eventually Arsenal's Lee Dixon took over at right-back in the national team, soon after Parker had joined Manchester United. Unfortunately his five-year career at Old Trafford was plagued by injury and as the Reds started to dominate the English game, he struggled to maintain his fitness and left in 1996, leaving Gary Neville to take over on a permanent basis. Parker won the League Cup, two Premiership titles and the FA Cup with United for whom he made 146 senior appearances, followed by 185 for Fulham and 160 for QPR. During his career he played in well over 500 club games and in eight U21 and three B internationals.

PARKER, Scott Matthew 2003-12 ⑱

Born: Lambeth, London, 13 October 1980
Career: FA School of Excellence/Lilleshall (summer 1996), Charlton Athletic (apprentice, August 1997, professional, October 1997), Norwich City (loan, October-November 2000), Chelsea (£10m, January 2004), Newcastle United (£6.5m, July 2005), West Ham United (£7m, June 2007), Tottenham Hotspur (£6m, August 2011)

Hard-working and skilful central midfielder Scott Parker has represented England at every level from Under-15 upwards, and besides his tally of senior caps, he has collected eleven with the U21 team. His senior debut came in mid-November 2003, as a 66th minute substitute for Wayne Rooney in a 3–2 defeat by Denmark at

Old Trafford. His brilliant club form then earned him a place in the starting line-up for the European Championship qualifier away to Croatia but he was restricted to tracking back and covering when the more attacking players like Frank Lampard and Steven Gerrard ventured forward. England boss Steve McClaren specifically told Parker to 'chase the wingers and assist the two wing backs, Gary Neville and Ashley Cole' and in his own words after the match, Parker said: "I was knackered, well and truly knackered." At the end of a superb season, he was named PFA 'Young Player of the Year'. Having made only one further 'sub' appearance for his country (in September 2006) he had to wait until May 2010 before tasting the possibility of another England cap when he was named in Fabio Capello's 30-man preliminary squad for that summer's World Cup. In the end he missed out on a trip to South Africa. Thankfully though after some terrific club performances Parker re-appeared on the international scene as a second-half substitute for Frank Lampard in England's impressive 2-1 friendly win over Denmark in February 2011. Later in the year he helped his country qualify for the 2012 European Championship, winning his eighth cap in eight years with five different clubs. In November 2011 he was named 'Man of the Match' when England beat the reigning European and World champions Spain 1-0 in a friendly at Wembley, his brilliant late, but precise challenge, denying the visitors a draw. Parker then did exceedingly well at Euro 2012, showing great commitment and drive from midfield, as always.

At May 2013, he had made 435 club appearances (30 goals).

PARKER, Thomas Robert 1924-25 ①

Born: Peartree Green, Southampton, 19 November 1897
Died: Southampton, 1 November 1987
Career: Shotley Rangers (April 1911), Shotley Athletic (August 1912), Woolston St Marks (September 1913), Southampton (amateur, August 1918, professional, May 1919), Arsenal (£3,250, March 1926; retired, March 1933); Norwich City (manager, April 1933-February 1937); Southampton (manager, February 1937-May 1943), surveyor with Lloyds Registry (June 1943), Ministry of Transport (Marine Division, from 1946); Norwich City (manager, April 1955-March 1957); Southampton (chief scout, ten seasons, 1963-73).

Right-back Tom Parker, according to The Alphabet of the Saints was not the fastest of players but had wonderful positional sense and his tackling was always well-timed.

He made 292 first-class appearances for Southampton (24 goals) before going on to amass a further 297 for Arsenal (17 goals). After gaining a Third Division (South) championship winner's medal with Saints in 1922, Parker had the misfortune to concede an own-goal, miss a penalty and get in a muddle with his 'keeper which led to the deciding goal in the 1925 FA Cup semi-final defeat by Sheffield United. During his time at The Dell, the likeable and dependable Parker won his solitary cap for England in a 3-2 win over France in Paris in May 1925, performing very well alongside Bill Felton (Sheffield Wednesday).

PARKES, Philip Benjamin Neil Frederick 1973-74 ①

Born: Sedgley, West Midlands, 8 August 1950
Career: West Midlands Schools, Walsall (juniors, August 1966, professional, January 1968), Queens Park Rangers (£18,500, June 1970), West Ham United (£560,000, February 1969), Ipswich Town (August 1990, retired May 1991); later goalkeeping coach at West Ham United, Queens Park Rangers and Ipswich Town; now involved in the hospitality department at Upton Park and also an after dinner speaker.

Giant goalkeeper Phil Parkes who appeared in one B, one U21 and six U23 internationals, gained his only senior cap against Portugal in April 1974 when he deputised for Peter Shilton in the 0-0 draw in Lisbon. Unfortunately with Shilton and Ray Clemence around, he never got another chance for his country, although manager Don Revie selected him as a substitute v. Wales in April 1976 and told him that he would 'go on after half-time' but never left the bench! When he joined West Ham from QPR in 1969, it was for a then world record fee for a goalkeeper. He helped the Hammers win the League Cup in 1980 and the Second Division championship in 1981 and during his career amassed over 900 club appearances, including 344 in the League for both West Ham and QPR.

PARKINSON, John 1909-10 ②
Born: Bootle, 12 September 1883
Died: Liverpool, 13 September 1942
Career: Hertford Albion (August 1897), Valkyrie FC/Liverpool (July 1900), Liverpool (amateur, September 1901, professional, April 1903), Bury (July 1914, retired, 1918); later ran two newsagents and a tobacconist shop in Bury.

Injury-prone centre-forward Jack Parkinson represented the Football League on three occasions and gained a Second Division championship winner's medal in 1905 but missed out on a First Division medal and an FA Cup final appearance because of knee and ankle problems. One feels that if he had remained fit, he would have won more than the two England caps he received. Taking over from Vivian Woodward (Spurs) he found it hard going in a 1-0 win over Wales at Cardiff and a 2-0 defeat by Scotland at Hampden Park in March/April 1910. Generally Parkinson's displays were always full of vigour and commitment. He had a good eye for goal and during his career netted over 130 times in almost 250 senior appearances for his two Football League clubs.

PARLOUR, Raymond 1999-2001 ⑩
Born: Barking, 7 March 1973
Career: Arsenal (associated schoolboy forms, January 1988, apprentice, July 1989, professional, March 1991), Middlesbrough (free, July 2004), Hull City (free, February 2007, retired, June 2007); now a pundit on television, as well as on radio stations BBC Radio 5 Live and Talksport.

Energetic midfielder Ray Parlour, despite showing excellent form for Arsenal, missed out on the 1998 World Cup, coach Glenn Hoddle preferring Spurs' wide man Darren Anderton instead. Parlour finally made his England debut as a second-half substitute in the Euro 2000 qualifier against Poland in March 1999. He went on to gain ten senior caps for his country, but failed to score a single goal. The closest he came was in the 2002 World Cup qualifying clash against Finland in October 2000 when his thumping 30-yard drive hit the crossbar, bounced down over the line but to his and England's dismay, the 'goal' was not given by the assistant referee (linesman). The match finished 0-0. Parlour did not feature in any tournament finals, a knee injury forcing him to withdraw from England's squad for Euro 2000. His final cap came in a friendly against Italy in November 2000, although afterwards he was named in Sven-Göran Eriksson's squad several times, but never made it onto the pitch under the Swede.
    Also capped once at B and on twelve occasions by England at U21 level, Parlour made 466 appearances for Arsenal (32 goals), 60 for Middlesbrough and 15 for Hull.

PARR, Percival Chase 1881-82 ①
Born: Bickley, 2 December 1859
Died: Bromley, Kent, 3 September 1912
Career: Winchester College (seasons 1876-78), New College/Oxford University (seasons 1878-84); also represented Kent County (1880s), West Kent (1880s); FA Committee member (seasons 1881-84); Barrister (from 1885); partner in WH Allen & Co., publishers and later Editor of the *National Observer* and *Ladies Field*; also played cricket for The Gentleman (of Kent).

Besides being a big, brave and very effective inside-forward, Percy Parr at times played in goal. He won his only England cap as Harry Cursham's wing partner in a 6-3 defeat by Wales at Wrexham in March 1882. Two years earlier Parr was an FA Cup runner-up with Oxford University.

PARRY, Edward Hagarty 1878-82 ③ ①
Born: Toronto, Canada, 24 April 1855
Died: Slough, 19 July 1931
Career: Charterhouse School (seasons 1871-74), Exeter College/Oxford University (seasons 1874-78), Old Carthusians (seasons 1878-83); also, between 1876 and 1883 played for Swifts, Remants FC, Stoke Poges, Windsor FC and Berks & Bucks; FA Committee member (seasons 1881-82); Schoolmaster at Felsted (1879-80) and Stoke House School, Slough (1881-92), then headmaster of the latter School (1892-1918).

An FA Cup finalist in 1877 and a winner with Old Carthusians in 1881, Edward Parry was a clever dribbler with good speed who became the butt of constant 'charging' by opposing defenders, much to his annoyance! A left-half, capped for the first time in a 2-1 victory over Wales at The Oval in January 1879, he had to wait over three years before gaining his second and third appearances for England, lining up in 5-1 and 5-3 away defeats by Scotland and Wales in March 1882, scoring in his last international.
    The first Canadian ever to represent England at senior level, it was almost 120 years before the next one appeared – Owen Hargreaves v. Holland in August 2001.

PARRY, Raymond Alan 1959-60 ② ①
Born: Derby, 19 January 1936
Died: Bolton, 23 May 2003
Career: Bolton Wanderers (amateur, September 1950, professional January 1953), Blackpool (£20,000, October 1960), Bury (£6,000, October 1964, then player-coach September 1970, retired as a player in May 1972; New Brighton (coach, seasons 1973-77); also qualified FA coach.

Ray Parry played in the same England Schoolboys team as Duncan Edwards. Slightly-built, he was a forceful all-purpose inside or outside-left who spent ten years with Bolton, appearing in 299 games, scoring 79 goals, gaining an FA Cup winner's medal in 1958 and being the youngest-ever First Division debutant at the age of 15 years and 267 days v. Wolves in October 1951. Deputising for Bobby Charlton, he found the net on his full international debut in a 2-1 win over Northern Ireland in November 1959 but was denied by the woodwork in his second game, a 1-1 draw with Scotland at Hampden Park five months later. Parry also won nine Schoolboy, five Youth and U23 caps.

PATCHITT, Basil Clement Alderson 1922-23 ②

Born: London, 12 August 1900
Died: Johannesburg, South Africa, 2 July 1991
Career: Charterhouse School (seasons 1916-19), Trinity College/Cambridge University (seasons 1920-23); also played for Corinthians (from August 1922), Castleford Town (November 1923-May 1924); emigrated to South Africa, circa 1928.

A versatile amateur footballer, able to play at full-back, centre-half and wing-half, Basil Patchitt was one of the last true Corinthians to represent England. He gained his two caps in successive wins over the same country, Sweden, in Stockholm, in May 1923, lining up at right-half and left-half in the space of three days.

PAWSON, Francis William 1882-85 ② ①

Born: Sheffield, 6 April 1861
Died: Ecclesfield, Sheffield, 4 July 1921
Career: Sheffield Collegiate School (seasons 1877-81) Caius College/Cambridge University (seasons 1881-86); also played for Sheffield FC, Casuals, Surrey, Corinthians; FA Committee member (season 1882-83); ordained in 1886, he was curate of Battersea (1886-90), of Bexhill-on-Sea (1890-99), then Rector of Lewes (1900-03) and Vicar of Ecclesfield, Sheffield (1902-21).

A mobile, enthusiastic outside-right or centre-forward, with a good strike record, Frank Pawson scored on his England debut in a 7-0 win over Ireland at Liverpool in February 1883. His second cap was also gained against the Irish in February 1885 at Manchester (won 4-0). Unfortunately he broke his right leg playing for Corinthians against Cambridge University in 1886 and although he recovered full fitness, he was never the same player again.

PAYNE, Joseph 1936-37 ① ②

Born: Brimington Common, Chesterfield, 17 January 1914
Died: Bedford, 22 April 1975
Career: Bolsover Colliery (April 1929), Luton Town (professional, July 1934), Biggleswade Town (on loan, season 1934-35), Chelsea (£5,000, March 1938), West Ham United (December 1946), Millwall (September 1947), Worcester City (October 1952, retired May 1953).

Despite a terrific scoring record at club level, centre-forward Joe Payne gained only one full England cap, against Finland in Helsinki in May 1937, netting twice in an 8-0 win. Initially a wing-half, Payne was unlucky inasmuch that there were so many other great marksmen around at the same time, including Tommy Lawton, Freddie Steele, Len Goulden, George Mills, Willie Hall and Frank Broome. He will, however, always be remembered (especially by Luton supporters) for scoring ten goals in the Hatters' 12-0 League victory over Bristol Rovers in April 1936. Two-footed, strong in the air and blessed with a powerful right-foot shot, he helped Luton win the Third Division (S) championship the following season and Chelsea lift the FL (South) Wartime Cup in 1945.
A plaque commemorating Payne's footballing career, is affixed to the outside of the Miner's Arms public house in Brimington Common, adjacent the site of the house, now demolished, where he used to live.

PEACOCK, Alan 1961-66 ⑥ ③

Born: Middlesbrough, 29 October 1937
Career: Lawson Secondary Modern School/Middlesbrough, Middlesbrough (amateur, May 1953, professional, November 1954), Leeds United (February 1964), Plymouth Argyle (October 1967, retired, March 1968); returned to Middlesbrough where he ran a newsagents shop for several years; now deeply involved with the Middlesbrough ex-players' association.

Powerful Middlesbrough centre-forward Alan Peacock was drafted into the forward-line in place of Inter Milan's Gerry Hitchens for the crucial group 4 World Cup game against Argentina in Chile. The selectors' wisdom to play Peacock was vindicated. His 17th minute goal-bound header was handled by defender Navarro, allowing Ron Flowers to net from the spot, and then he helped Greaves 'steal' a third in a 3-1 win.
Chosen for the next game v. Bulgaria, he was then omitted (replaced by Gerry Hitchens) for the vital clash with Brazil and had to wait four months for his third cap v. Northern Ireland in Belfast. He then scored twice in his fourth international when Wales were hammered 4-0 at Wembley and after a moderate showing against the Principality three years later (0-0), he netted in his final England game, a 2-1 win over Northern Ireland in November 1965.
Peacock, who was capped at Youth team level, scored a total of 173 goals in 315 first-class appearances for his three major clubs, 141 coming in 238 outings for Middlesbrough, many as partner to Brian Clough. As a Leeds player, he won a Second Division championship medal and played in the 1965 FA Cup final defeat by Liverpool.

PEACOCK, John 1928-29 ③

Born: Wigan, 15 March 1897
Died: Wigan, 4 March 1979
Career: Atherton FC (April 1914), Everton (professional, July 1919), Middlesbrough (September 1927), Sheffield Wednesday (August 1930), Clapton Orient (July 1931), Sliepner FC/Sweden (player-coach, March 1933; retired as a player, April 1934, remained as coach until April 1938); Wrexham (trainer, July 1938-September 1948).

Called 'Joe' throughout his career, Peacock occupied several positions but admitted that his best was at left-half from where he displayed fine ball control. Taken on England's 1929 end-of-season European tour, he played against France (won 4-1), Belgium (won 5-1) and Spain (lost 4-3), having a hand in goals against the French in Paris and Spain in Madrid. Peacock made over 300 appearances during his career, including 161 for Everton and 85 for Middlesbrough whom he helped win the Second Division title in 1929.

PEARCE, Stuart, MBE 1986-99 ⑦⑧ ⑤

Born: Hammersmith, London, 24 April 1962
Career: Fryent Primary School, Kingsbury/North West London (1976), Claremont High School/Kenton, Queens Park Rangers (trial, August 1977), Hull City (trial, July-August 1978), Wealdstone (April 1979), Coventry City (£25,000, October 1983), Nottingham Forest (£450,000, June 1985; later player-manager and also caretaker-manager), Newcastle United (free, July 1997), West Ham United (free, August 1998), Manchester City (free, July 2001, retired, May 2002; appointed coach, then manager, March 2005-May 2007); England U21 manager-coach (February 2007-June 2013); also acted as England senior team coach (briefly); Great Britain football team manager at the 2012 London Summer Olympics.

The oldest outfield player ever to appear for England in the European Championships, Stuart Pearce – nicknamed 'Psycho' – was 34 years and 63 days old when he lined up against Germany at Wembley in June 1996. The fierce-tackling left-back was a real lion-hearted defender who wasn't afraid to put his head on the block after doing something wrong! Remember that penalty miss against the Germans in the World Cup semi-final shoot-out in Turin in July 1990 when England lost 4-3. It took him months to get over

recall for the 36-year-old for two qualifying games for Euro 2000, and surprisingly, during the match against Luxembourg, Pearce had a goal disallowed for an offside! His last England outing was against Poland in September 1999 before a broken leg effectively ended his international career with a total of 78 caps under his belt. Indeed, for a time he was in the all-time top ten appearance-makers for his country.

During his one match tenure, head coach Peter Taylor appointed Pearce as assistant-manager when England lost to Italy in Turin. Only two left-backs, Ashley Cole, 100+ and Kenny Sansom with 86 have made more appearances for England than Pearce. However, in a 2000 poll to find England's greatest XI, the public overwhelmingly voted Pearce as their left back.

A top player, a top man, Pearce made 942 appearances at club level (570 in the FL/Premiership) and netted a total of 119 goals – the most for a full-back ever! And if his England outings are added to his tally, then his career realised well over 1,000 games.

Pearce, who also played in one unofficial international, skippered Forest several times, helping them twice win the League Cup, lift the FMC on two occasions and reach the 1991 FA Cup final (beaten by Spurs). He later won the InterToto Cup with West Ham, was also a beaten FA Cup finalist with Newcastle and gained a Nationwide Division One championship medal with Manchester City.

Pearce, who replaced Kevin Keegan as manager of Manchester City in 2005, was awarded the MBE for services to football in the 1999 New Year's Honours List.

PEARSON, Harold Frederick 1931-32 ①

Born: Tamworth, Staffs, 7 May 1908
Died: West Bromwich, 2 November 1994
Career: Tamworth & Amington Schools; then, between August 1921 and May 1925 played, in turn, for Glascote United, Glascote Methodists, Belgrave Working Men's Club, Belgrave United, Two Gates FC, Nuneaton Borough and Tamworth Castle; joined West Bromwich Albion (amateur, April 1925, professional, May 1927), Millwall (£300, August 1937, retired May 1940); WW2 guest for West Ham United (season 1939-40); West Bromwich Albion (coach, seasons 1948-52, then scout seasons 1953-55); worked for West Bromwich firm WJ & S Lees, iron-founders, for over 20 years.

Harold 'Algy' Pearson, at 6ft 2in tall and 13st 5lbs in weight, was a sound rather than showy goalkeeper. He had a huge pair of hands, could kick vast distances and in effect, made the art of goalkeeping look easy. He never really got a chance with England, due to the form of his cousin, Harry Hibbs, who he played against in the 1931 FA Cup final. Limited to just one cap, against Scotland at Wembley in April 1932, when he played behind his Albion team-mate George Shaw, Pearson kept a clean sheet in a comfortable 3-0 victory. James Freeman, the *Daily Mail* reporter, stated: "The England defence was rarely troubled after the first ten minutes during which time Pearson made important saves from Alan Morton and Neil Dewar."

Pearson made 303 first-class appearances for WBA, gaining an FA Cup winner's medal in 1931, the same season the Baggies completed the unique double by also gaining promotion from Division Two. The recipient of a runners-up medal after the 1935 Cup final defeat by Sheffield Wednesday, he admitted he was to blame for two of the Owls' goals. He won the Third Division (S) Championship with Millwall.

Pearson's father, Hubert, also a goalkeeper, was registered as a player with West Bromwich Albion at the same time as Harold (1925-26). He was chosen to play for England against France in 1923 but had to cry off through injury.

that agony...but he was first in line to take the next spot-kick!

Pearce made his senior debut in place of Kenny Sansom against Brazil in the Rous Cup at Wembley in May 1987, to become the 999th player to represent England at senior level, scored plenty of goals during his career, five for England, with his best possibly coming against Poland at Wembley in September 1993 when he blasted home a well-worked free-kick from 22 yards to seal a 3-0 win. Two months later, however, as team captain, he was embarrassed and certainly at fault when his weak back-pass after just nine seconds play in a World Cup qualifier in San Marino, was intercepted by Davide Gualtieri who scored what is believed to be the fastest goal ever recorded against England who went on to win the game 7-1. As before he quickly got over that mishap and produced some brilliant displays in Euro 96, smashing in a penalty in the shoot-out victory over Spain to wipe out the memory of his miss six years earlier.

Pearce, who had intended to retire from international football after Euro 96, but was persuaded to change his mind by new boss Glenn Hoddle, continued his international career until 1999. He was not selected for the 1998 World Cup, but the appointment of Kevin Keegan to the England job and his club form for West Ham prompted a

PEARSON, James Stuart 1975-77 ⑮ ⑤

Born: Hull, 21 June 1949
Career: East Riding Schools, Hull City (amateur, May 1956,
professional, July 1968), Manchester United (£200,000, May
1974), West Ham United (£220,000, August 1979); played in the
NASL and South Africa; Stockport County (coach, season 1985-86),
Northwich Victoria (manager, May-December 1986), West Bromwich
Albion (assistant-manager/coach, November 1988), Bradford City
(assistant-manager, July 1992-May 1994); also played Rugby Union
for Sale (late 1980s); now lives in Spain.

Having made a 'competent' international debut against Wales in
May 1976, striker Stuart Pearson scored in his second England
game, a 4-0 home win over Northern Ireland in May 1976. He went
on to net three more goals for his country… in a 4-1 win over
Finland the following month, another versus the Republic of Ireland
later in the year and one against Argentina in June 1977.
    A consistent marksman throughout his career, 'Pancho' Pearson
netted 120 goals in a total of 358 senior appearances including
66 in 179 games for Manchester United whom he helped win the
Second Division championship (1975) and the FA Cup (1977). He
was also an FA Cup winner with West Ham in 1980.

PEARSON, John Hargreaves 1891-92 ①

Born: Crewe, 25 January 1868
Died: Crewe, 22 June 1931
Career: Crewe Alexandra (amateur, August 1881, retired April
1893); was a Football League referee (seasons 1893-1915); later
worked for London & North Western and London, Midland & Scottish
Railways, up to December 1930.

Inside-right Jack Pearson joined his hometown club Crewe
Alexandra as a 13 year-old but was forced to retire with a serious
knee injury in 1893. At that point he took up refereeing and in 1911
took charge of the FA Cup final between Barnsley and Newcastle
United. He won his only England cap against Ireland in March 1892
when, as Charlie Athersmith's right-wing partner, he had a hand in
one of Harry Daft's two goals in a 2-0 win in Belfast.

PEARSON, Stanley Clare 1948-52 ⑧ ⑤

Born: Salford, Lancs, 15 January 1919
Died: Prestbury, Manchester, 20 February 1997
Career: Adelphi Lads' Club (April 1934), Manchester United
(professional, May 1936); WW2 guest for Brighton & Hove Albion
and Queens Park Rangers; Bury (February 1954), Chester (October
1957, player-manager, April 1959, retired as a player, May
1959; resigned as manager, May 1961); became a newsagent in
Prestbury, Manchester; Prestbury FC/East Cheshire League (coach/
manager, seasons, 1961-63).

Stan Pearson made his England debut against Scotland in front of
135,376 fans at Hampden Park in April 1948, and after a 2-0 win,
told reporters that he was 'shocked by the viciousness of the home
side's tackling.'
    Six months later Pearson scored in a 6-2 win over Northern
Ireland and then found the net twice in a 9-2 victory over the same
country in November 1949.
    In April 1952, and by now playing as a schemer, he scored both
goals in another win (2-1) over the Scots on their home soil. His
first, on eight minutes was a superb hook shot while his second,
shortly before half-time, was a low drive from 12 yards.
    In between his international calls, Pearson won the FA Cup and

First Division championship with Manchester United for whom he
scored 149 goals in 345 appearances before moving to Bury. In
1958, he helped Chester win the Welsh Cup.
    Pearson also played in one B international.

PEASE, William Harold 1926-27 ①

Born: Leeds, 30 September 1899
Died: Middlesbrough, 2 October 1955
Career: Played Rugby League at school; served in the Royal
Northumberland Fusiliers (from 1915); Leeds City (amateur,
December 1918), Northampton Town (professional, October 1919),
Middlesbrough (May 1926), Luton Town (June 1933, retired, injured,
January 1935); became a licensee in the Middlesbrough area.

Twice a Second Division championship winner with Middlesbrough
(1927 and 1929), Bill Pease was a fast and direct outside-right who
could cross inch-perfect, whether on the run or not. He drew up a fine
goal tally during his career, especially for Middlesbrough. Taking over
from Joe Spence (Manchester United) on the right-wing, he created
one of the goals for England in his only international, a 3-3 draw with
Wales at Wrexham in February 1927. He certainly deserved more
caps but there were some extra-special wingers around at the same
time including Joe Hulme (Arsenal), Hugh Adcock (Leicester City),
Jack Bruton (Blackburn Rovers) and Sammy Crooks (Derby).

PEGG, David 1956-57 ①

Born: Doncaster, 20 September 1935
Died: Munich, Germany, 6 February 1958
Career: Doncaster Schoolboys, Manchester United (amateur, August
1951, professional, September 1952, until his tragic death).

Manchester United winger David Pegg played his only game for
England against the Republic of Ireland in Dublin in May 1957. With
Stan Matthews out, Tom Finney was switched to the right flank to
accommodate Berry who, with his Old Trafford team-mates Roger
Byrne, Duncan Edwards and Tommy Taylor, helped his country
scramble a 1-1 draw. Sadly, along with several of his fellow United
colleagues, friends and passengers, he perished in the Munich air
crash just nine months later.
    A brilliant ball playing outside-left, fast, upright, direct with an
eye for goal, raven-haired Pegg, who was capped five times as a
Schoolboy, won two FA Youth Cup, a League Championship and
FA Cup runners-up medals with Manchester United for whom he
scored 28 goals in 148 appearances.

PEJIC, Michael 1973-74 ④

Born: Chesterton, Staffs, 25 January 1950
Career: Chesterton & North Staffs Schools, Corona Drinks FC (August
1965), Stoke City (apprentice, June 1966, professional, January
1968), Everton (£135,000, February 1977), Aston Villa (£250,000,
September 1979, retired, with pelvic injury, May 1980); became a
farmer (unsuccessfully); Leek Town (player-manager, season 1981-
82), Northwich Victoria (manager, season 1982-83), Port Vale (Youth
coach, July 1986; senior coach, December 1987-March 1992); FA
North-east coach and player development officer; Kuwait (coach),
Chester City (manager, June 1994-February 1995), Stoke City (Youth
coach, 1955-99); Selangor FC (Malaysia, manager, 1999-2000);
also taught FA coaching courses at NWHC in Nuneaton; Plymouth
Argyle (Head of Youth Coaching, seasons 2007-10), Ipswich Town
(Head of Youth Coaching, season 2010-11).

Mike Pejic made four appearances for England…and was reportedly dropped by Joe Mercer because he didn't smile enough! He made his first start in the 0-0 draw with Portugal in April 1974 and a month later, did well in 2-0 and 1-0 wins over Wales and Northern Ireland but conceded an own-goal in a 2-0 defeat by Scotland at Hampden Park. The son of a Yugoslavian (Serbian) immigrant miner, Pejic was a strong and aggressive tackler who cleared his lines precisely, without too much finesse. He made over 400 club appearances during his career, 336 for Stoke whom he helped win the League Cup in 1972. He also played in eight U23 internationals.

Pejic's brother, Mel, played for Stoke City, Hereford United and Wrexham, and Shaun Pejic, son of Mel and nephew of Mike, plays for CP Baltimore and Wales U21s.

PELLY, Frederick Raymond 1892-94 ③

Born: Upminster, 11 August 1868
Died: Marylebone, London, 16 October 1940
Career: Forest School XI (seasons 1881-86), Old Foresters (seasons 1886-89); also played for London FA, Essex County, Casuals, Corinthians (seasons 1891-98); became senior partner in the commercial firm, Mann George & Co.

A well-built, studious left-back, 6 feet tall and weighing 15 stones, Fred Pelly was a well-respected amateur footballer who starred for two of the better clubs of his time, Casuals and Corinthians. Very dependable, he won his first England cap in a 6-1 win over Ireland in Birmingham in February 1893. Thirteen months later he was outstanding in a 5-1 victory over Wales at Wrexham and the following month played in a 2-2 draw with Scotland at Parkhead, Glasgow, the *Daily Mail* reporter stating: "He found it difficult at times against Billy Guilliand who made several sharp dashes down the England left."

In fact, in the first-half, the Scottish right-winger helped set up Lambie for 'the most brilliant goal of the match.'

PENNINGTON, Jesse 1907-20 ㉕

Born: West Bromwich, 23 August 1883
Died: Kidderminster, 5 September 1970
Career: Summit Star/Smethwick (August 1898), Smethwick Centaur (May 1899), Langley Villa (February 1890), Langley St Michael's (October 1890), Dudley Town (season 1901-02), Aston Villa (amateur, August 1902), Dudley Town (November 1902), West Bromwich Albion (professional, April 1903-May 1922); played briefly for Kidderminster Harriers (following a pay dispute with WBA: August-September 1910); Oldbury Town (guest, season 1915-16); Notts County (guest 1916); Birmingham (guest season 1916-17); West Bromwich Albion (coach, May 1922-August 1923); Kidderminster Harriers (coach, September 1923-June 1925); also football coach at Malvern College (season 1938-39), also Wolverhampton Wanderers (scout, during season 1938-39); Rafman FC/Kidderminster (manager, season 1939-40); out of football for ten years; returned as West Bromwich Albion (scout, August 1950-May 1961); later a poultry farmer, at Hartlebury near Stourport, Worcs.

The first outfield player to represent England in three decades (1900s, 1910s, 1920s) Jesse Pennington, along with goalkeeper Sam Hardy, was also the first to win caps either side of WW1. In fact, Pennington's international career spanned 13 years and 23 days (up to April 1920) and only four players have bettered that - Stanley Matthews, Tony Adams, David Beckham and Raich Carter.

In fact, Pennington is the oldest full-back ever to win a full England cap, aged 35 years, 230 days in April 1920 (v. Scotland). Known around West Bromwich as 'Peerless Pennington', he was

a superbly-equipped left-back, scrupulously fair, notably quick in recovery and blessed with beautiful balance and a strong kick. He was also a wonderful captain who made 496 senior appearances for WBA, gaining Second and First Division championship winning medals in 1911 and 1920 respectively. Unfortunately, he missed out on an FA Cup winner's medal when he failed to 'foul, obstruct or impede' Barnsley's Harry Tufnell who, with a minute remaining of extra-time in the 1912 final replay at Sheffield, raced clear and scored the only goal of the game.

Universally regarded as the nonpareil of West Brom and England left-backs, he formed a superb partnership at international level with Blackburn's Bob Crompton, the pair playing together 23 times for their country.

Pennington was a regular in the England team from the day of his debut v. Wales in March 1907 until his 25th and final appearance against Scotland at Sheffield in 1920 when, as skipper he was outstanding on a squelchy pitch in a 5-4 victory.

Capped nine times against the Scots, he was on the losing side just twice, and produced masterful displays when the old enemy was defeated 2-0 at Crystal Palace in April 1909 and 1-0 at Stamford Bridge four years later. He also played brilliantly when England beat Ireland 3-1 in February 1908 and Wales 2-0 in March 1909.

In 1913, Pennington was the subject of a bribe scandal whereby he was approached by a man who offered him £55 in cash to 'fix' the result of a League game between his club, WBA, and Everton so that the Merseysiders would not lose! A very shrewd character, Pennington informed the club and the police. A trap was set and the culprit, Samuel Johnson, alias Frederick Pater, was arrested, charged and subsequently found guilty at Stafford Assize Court where he was sentenced to six months' imprisonment.

PENTLAND, Frederick Beaconsfield 1908-09 ⑤

Born: Wolverhampton, 29 July 1883
Died: Poole, Dorset, 16 March 1962
Career: Avondale Juniors (August 1898), Willenhall Swifts (June 1899), Small Heath/Birmingham (August 1900), Blackpool (June 1903), Blackburn Rovers (October 1903), Brentford (May 1906), Queens Park Rangers (May 1907), Middlesbrough (June 1908), Halifax Town (August 1912), Stoke (February 1913), Halifax Town (March 1913, retired, April 1914); German Olympic team (coach, season 1914-15); France Olympic team (coach, four months in 1920), Racing de Santander/Spain (coach, season 1920-21), Athletic Bilbao/Spain (coach, seasons, 1922-25), Atletico Madrid/Spain (coach, season 1925-26), Real Oviedo/Spain (coach, season 1926-27), Atletico Madrid/Spain (coach, two seasons 1927-29), Spain (national team coach, May-August 1929), Athletic Bilbao/Spain (coach, September 1929-May 1933), Atletico Madrid/Spain (coach, seasons 1935-36); Brentford (training staff, July 1936-December 1937), Barrow (assistant-manager/coach, January 1938, manager, January 1938-September 1939).

Before joining his first League club, Small Heath (Birmingham), Fred Pentland worked as a gunmaker's assistant and played for several junior clubs. After helping Queens Park Rangers win the Southern League championship in 1908 and appearing in the FA Charity Shield game against League champions Manchester United, he moved to Middlesbrough where he won his five England caps, lining up alongside Vivian Woodward and helping his country win the Home International Championship in 1909.

A quick and clever outside-right, Pentland was guilty at times of over-dribbling, but on his day was a very clever, enterprising footballer who made his debut in a 2-0 win over Wales at

Nottingham in March of that year and played in the 2-0 victory against Scotland at The Crystal Palace the following month. His other three caps came on the summer tour against Hungary (twice) and Austria, 'making' goals for Woodward in all three matches, reports stating 'he was a constant threat on England's right-wing.'

A knee injury, suffered when playing for Halifax against Heckmondwike in April 1914, ended Pentland's playing career. He scored 55 goals in more than 250 appearances at club level.

After retiring as a player, Pentland went to Berlin in 1914 to take charge of the German Olympic soccer team. However, within a few months, WW1 broke out and he was subsequently interned at Ruhleben, a civilian detention camp in the Spandau district of Berlin. The camp contained between 4,000 and 5,500 prisoners. Gradually a mini-society evolved and football became a popular activity. Cup and League competitions were organised and as many as 1,000 attended the bigger games. Pentland was prominent in organising and playing football within the camp. He became Chairman of the Ruhleben Football Association and regularly contributed to football articles in the camp magazine.

He was one of several former professional footballers at Ruhleben. Others included former club-mates and fellow England internationals Sam Wolstenholme and Steve Bloomer, veteran Sheffield Wednesday star Fred Spiksley, Scottish international, John Cameron, a German international Ted Dutton and John Brearley, once of Everton and Tottenham Hotspur.

In early May 1915, an England XI featuring Pentland, Wolstenholme, Brearley and Bloomer played a World XI, captained by Cameron. Towards the end of the war, an international triangular tournament called the Coupe de Alies, featuring teams representing Britain, France and Belgium, was organised. Pentland remained in the camp until the end of the war and then returned to England. While recuperating in the West Country he met and later married his nurse, a war widow working as a VAD.

In 1920, Pentland guided the French Olympic soccer team into the semi-finals, only to lose 4-1 to Czechoslovakia. The final stages of the tournament descended into farce and as a result France missed out on the opportunity to win the silver medal. The host nation, Belgium, won the gold medal by default after Czechoslovakia walked off in protest during the final, unhappy with the performance of the referee. As a result they were disqualified and a second consolation tournament was organised to decide the silver and bronze medalists. However, France and Pentland, presuming the competition was over, had already returned home and Spain went on to take the silver medal.

As a coach/manager in Spain, he led Bilbao to victory in the Copa del Rey, took Atletico Madrid to the Copa final in 1926 and to victory in the Campeonato del Centro two years later. He was also in charge of Madrid during the inaugural La Liga season and in May 1929, was coach of Spain (under manager José María Mateos) when they beat England 4-3 in Madrid's Metropolitano Stadium, to become the first non-British team to beat England.

After rejoining Bilbao, Pentland subsequently led them to La Liga/Copa del Rey doubles in 1930 and 1931 and in fact to four Copa del Rey titles in a row, 1930-33, while also seeing his team finish second in La Liga in 1932 and 1933. In 1931, the much-admired Pentland masterminded Bilbao's emphatic 12-1 victory over FC Barcelona, the latter club's worst ever defeat. Pentland returned to England at the outbreak of the Spanish Civil War. There's no doubt that he had a wonderful career in football.

PERRY, Charles 1889-93 ③

Born: West Bromwich, 3 January 1866
Died: West Bromwich, 2 July 1927
Career: Christ Church School/West Bromwich, West Bromwich Strollers (August 1880), West Bromwich Albion (amateur, March 1884, professional August 1885, retired May 1896; became a director of the club: seasons 1896-1902); also a Director of the local brewery firm, Arnold & Bates, for whom he worked; licensee of The Golden Cup, West Bromwich.

Charlie Perry, tall and strong, was a wonderful centre-half with a polished style who marshalled his defence superbly. He played in four FA Cup finals for WBA, winning in 1888 and 1892, but missed the 1895 final through injury which eventually led to his retirement. He scored 16 goals in 219 appearances for West Brom for whom his brothers, Tom and Walter also played.

Capped twice by England against Ireland in March 1890 and March 1891, Perry played in his third international against Wales in March 1893. He was outstanding in all three matches, helping England to 9-1, 6-1 and 6-0 victories respectively. Johnny Holt (Everton) and Harry Allen (Wolves) were his main challengers for the centre-half spot. He also played twice for the Football League.

PERRY, Thomas 1897-98 ①

Born: West Bromwich, 5 August 1871
Died: West Bromwich, 18 July 1927
Career: Christ Church School/West Bromwich, Christ Church FC (August 1885), West Bromwich Baptist (September 1887), Stourbridge (August 1888), West Bromwich Albion (professional, July 1890), Aston Villa (£100, October 1901, retired, injured, May 1902); later worked as an accountant.

A highly efficient half-back, enthusiastic, hardworking, full of vim and vigour, Tom Perry was unlucky to win only one cap for England, lining up against Wales in March 1898 when he starred in a 3-0 win at Wrexham.

Perry, who represented the Football League on three occasions and also played for a League Select XI, scored 15 goals in 291 appearances for WBA. He died just two weeks after his brother, Charlie.

PERRY, William 1955-56 ③ ②

Born: Johannesburg, South Africa, 10 September 1930
Died: Blackpool, 27 September 2007
Career: Johannesburg Rangers/South Africa (August 1946), Blackpool (professional, October 1949), Southport (June 1962), Hereford United (July 1963), South Coast United, Australia (July-October 1964), Holyhead Town (April 1966, retired, May 1967); Fleetwood Town (Director, seasons 1967-70).

Bill Perry scored the injury-time winning goal for Blackpool against Bolton Wanderers in the 1953 FA Cup final. A sturdy, strong-running outside-left with a powerful shot, he scored 129 goals in 436 appearances during his 13 years with the Seasiders, playing on the opposite flank to Stanley Matthews with Stan Mortensen in the centre.

Perry scored 20 goals in 1955-56 including a hat-trick in two West Lancashire derbies in the space of 24 hours, helping Blackpool to their highest-ever League position of runners-up in Division One. And his bold efforts earned him three England caps.

He made an impressive debut in a 3-0 win over Northern Ireland at Wembley in November 1955, scored twice, one a real cracker, in an exciting 4-1 victory over Spain on the same pitch four weeks later and put in a solid performance in the 1-1 draw with Scotland at Hampden Park in April 1956. In fact, in the latter match, he linked up with Roger Byrne and helped set up a late equaliser for Johnny Haynes, which stunned the home fans in the near 133,000 crowd.

With Tom Finney, Frank Blunstone and Colin Grainger all contesting the left-wing position, Perry was certainly satisfied to get three outings for his country.

PERRYMAN, Stephen John, MBE 1981-82 ①

Born: Ealing, London, 21 December 1951
Career: Ealing Schools' FA XI, Middlesex Schools' FA & London Schools' FA, Tottenham Hotspur (apprentice, July 1967, professional, January 1969), Oxford United (March 1986), Brentford (player/assistant-manager, November 1986, player-manager, February 1987, retired as a player, May 1989, remained as manager to August 1990), Watford (manager, November 1990-94), Tottenham Hotspur (caretaker-manager, November 1994), IK Start/ Norway (manager, season 1995-96), Shimizu S-Pulse/Japan (coach, seasons 1996-2000), Exeter City (advisory capacity, season 2000-01), Kashiwa Reysol/Japan coach, season 2001-02), Exeter City (Director of Football, May 2002); lent his name to a brand of Sports stores in the 1980s, concentrated in the West London area and sporting the Tottenham Hotspur cockerel; later opened stores in Ruislip, Greenford and Hayes (Middlesex) and Bergen, Norway.

A hardworking midfielder and occasional defender, Steve Perryman scored 52 goals in 1,021 first-team appearances for Tottenham, including a club record 854 at competitive level (39 goals) during his 19 years at White Hart Lane. Captain of the team on many occasions, he won two UEFA Cup, two FA Cup and two League Cup winner's medals, and in 1982 became only the third man in history to lift the FA Cup two years running, and the second Spurs legend to do so after 'double winning' skipper Danny Blanchflower in 1961 and 1962.

For all his efforts, Perryman was rewarded with only one England cap, appearing as a 70th minute substitute in a low-key friendly against Iceland in June 1982, just after he had been voted FWA 'Player of the Year'. Two years later he was awarded the MBE for services to football.

Perryman also played in four Schoolboy and four Youth internationals for his country before going on to win a then record 17 England U23 caps.

As coach of Shimizu S-Pulse, he won the J-League championship, 2nd stage, in 1999 and the Asian Cup Winners' Cup in 2000.

Perryman lent his name to a brand of sports stores in the 1980s which were mainly concentrated in the West London area and sported the Tottenham Hotspur cockerel. There were outlets in Ruislip, Greenford and Hayes (Middlesex). A store in Bergen, Norway, opened in the early 1980s, is still operating

PETERS, Martin Stanford ⑥⑦ ⑳

Born: Plaistow, London, 8 November 1943
Career: Dagenham & District Schools, West Ham United (apprentice, May 1959, professional, November 1960), Tottenham Hotspur (£200,000, March 1970, deal involving Jimmy Greaves), Norwich City (March 1975), Sheffield United (August 1980, as a player, then player-manager), Gorleston (season 1981-82); ran a fruit machine company in East Anglia and later worked in insurance (until 2001); Tottenham Hotspur (director, 1998-99); also engaged as a matchday host at Tottenham and West Ham.

Goalkeeper Gordon Banks described Martin Peters as '...a drifter, all smoothness and style – a real player's player' and in 1966, Ron Greenwood, his manager at West Ham, thought he was ten years ahead of his time!

Blessed with an ideal temperament for the game of football, when in full flow, Peters was an elegant, even-tempered player who could ghost in unnoticed and score a vital goal, or two. If required he could work box-to-box as well as anyone in the game but is best remembered for being the 'man in the middle' of the midfield triangle when England won the World Cup in 1966. He scored against West Germany that afternoon at Wembley – probably his most important goal for his country – and he celebrated like a 'spoiled child' when the Jules Rimet was lifted by his Hammers club-mate Bobby Moore.

For a good period of time when Alf Ramsey was running the England side, Peters was always one of the first names on his team-sheet. He was a tremendous all-purpose player who had the built-in knack of grabbing a goal when least expected – by defenders anyway!

Ramsey had seen Peters' potential quickly, giving the young midfielder his England debut against Yugoslavia at Wembley in May 1966 when he impressed with his industry and exuberance around the park.

In the final preparation period ahead of the World Cup, Peters played in the warm-up games against Finland (when he scored) and Poland and subsequently made Ramsey's 22-man squad for the competition, as did his West Ham colleagues Bobby Moore and Geoff Hurst.

Peters did not play in the opening group 0-0 draw with Uruguay but after Ramsey had changed his team formation, doing away with a direct winger, he inserted Peters as an attacking midfielder. The ideal player for the 4-1-3-2 system, he became a star in Ramsey's "Wingless wonders".

He played in the last two group victories over Mexico and France, his late cross set up Hurst's header for the only goal against ruthless Argentina in the quarter-finals and then he played his part in the semi-final victory over Portugal, before putting in a sterling performance against the Germans in the final.

Four years later Peters, now an established international with 38 caps to his name, played in England's three group games of the 1970 World Cup in Mexico, but then tasted disappointment as Germany gained revenge for that 1966 defeat with a 3-2 extra-time win in the quarter-finals. Peters scored early in the second half – a superb and typical 'ghosting' goal - to give England a commanding 2–0 lead, but Ramsey committed the tactical faux-pas of taking off both Peters and Bobby Charlton and the Germans took heart and went on to win 3-2.

Peters remained an England regular while also picking up his first domestic winners' medal in 1971 when Spurs won the League Cup. Later that same year, Peters gained his 50th cap in a qualifier for the 1972 European Championships by beating Switzerland 3–2. But unfortunately England failed to make progress after another defeat by Germany, who went on to win the tournament. For Peters, this set-back was tempered mildly by more club success as Spurs won the UEFA Cup in 1972 and the League Cup again in 1973. Peters then scored his 20th and last international goal as Scotland were beaten 1-0 at Wembley and after England had stuttered in their qualifying campaign for the 1974 World Cup, they needed to defeat Poland at Wembley to qualify for the finals in Germany. Peters captained the side for this crucial game which ended 1-1, England's goal coming from Allan Clarke's penalty, gained by Peters who admitted in his autobiography (*The Ghost of '66*), that he had dived to win the spot-kick. So there was no third successive World Cup competition for Peters.

After playing in his 67th international, a 2-0 defeat by Scotland at Hampden Park in May 1974, Peters' illustrious international career came to an end. He managed one more season with Spurs – losing the 1974 UEFA Cup final – before moving to Norwich City. And whilst at Carrow Road, Peters was rewarded with a testimonial against an all-star team which included most of England's 1966 World Cup winning XI.

Canaries' 'Player of the Year' two years running (1976 and 1977), Peters ended an excellent career with spells at Sheffield United and non-League Gorleston. In all, he made 882 club appearances and scored 220 goals. In the Football League, he struck 175 goals in 724 games - 81 in 302 starts for West Ham, 44 in 207 for Norwich, 46 in 189 for Spurs and four in 24 for Sheffield United.

PHELAN, Michael Christopher 1989-90 ①

Born: Nelson, Lancs, 24 September 1962
Career: Nelson & Colne Town Schools, Lancashire Schools, Barrowford Celtic Boys' Club (April 1976), Burnley (associated schoolboy forms, July 1977, apprentice July 1979, professional, July 1980), Norwich City (May 1985), Manchester United (£750,000, July 1989), West Bromwich Albion (free, July 1994), Norwich City (player/reserve team coach, December 1995), Blackpool (non-contract player, 1996), Stockport County (player/assistant-manager), Norwich City (reserve team manager, July 1998), Manchester United (School of Excellence coach, July 1999, then assistant-manager/coach, August 2001 to June 2013)

Hardworking midfielder Mike Phelan gained his only England cap as a Manchester United player, coming on as a second-half substitute for his Old Trafford team-mate Bryan Robson in a 0-0 draw with Italy at Wembley in November 1989. In a useful career, Phelan gained Youth international honours as a teenager, helped Burnley win the Third Division championship and then won the Premiership title, the FA Cup,

League Cup and European Cup Winners' Cup with Manchester United. He made over 570 appearances at club level (485 in the League), his best return coming with Burnley: 13 goals in 208 games.

PHILLIPS, Kevin Mark 1999-2002 ⑧

Born: Hitchin, Herts, 25 July 1973
Career: Southampton (apprentice/youth, August 1989, released May 1992), Baldock Town (August 1992), Watford (£10,000, as a professional, December 1994), Sunderland (£325,000, July 1997), Aston Villa (£750,000, July 2005), West Bromwich Albion (£700,000, August 2006), Birmingham City (free, August 2008), Blackpool (free, July 2011), Crystal Palace (loan, January-May 2013)

Despite his scoring record at club level, Kevin Phillips failed to find the net in his eight outings for England. He was never given a full 90 minutes for his country, and the closest he came to scoring was in a 2-1 friendly win over Malta in Valletta in June 2000 when he rounded the goalkeeper only to hit the side-netting. Phillips, who was three times an unused substitute during the group stage of the Euro 2000 finals, made his final appearance for England against Holland in Amsterdam in February 2002.

One of the finest strikers of his era, Phillips is a member of the band of elite marksmen who have netted 250 goals in first-class football. He helped Sunderland win the First Division title in 1998-99 and the following season collected the PL's Golden Boot award for most League goals scored, 23, being the last Englishman to achieve the honour. He also starred for WBA when they won the Championship in 2008. On 2 April 2011, he became the oldest Premiership goalscorer when he netted for Birmingham City against Bolton Wanderers. Phillips, who also has one England B cap to his name, reached the milestone of 600 club appearances when playing for Blackpool in May 2012 (271 goals scored).

His 105th minute winning penalty v Watford in the 2013 Championship play-off final, earned Crystal Palace £120m and a place in the Premier League.

PHILLIPS, Leonard Horace 1951-55 ③

Born: Shoreditch, 11 September 1922
Died: Portsmouth, 9 December 2011
Career: Hackney Boys (September 1935), Hillside Youth club (from August 1936; also served in Royal Marines, from September 1940); Portsmouth (amateur, February 1946, professional, September 1946), Poole Town (August 1956), Chelmsford City (June 1959), Bath City (May 1963-May 1964), Ramsgate Athletic (August 1964, retired May 1965); thereafter worked as a lathe operator at De Havilland's in Portsmouth for many years.

Originally an inside-forward, Len Phillips developed into a fine, inventive right-half. He spent his entire senior career with Portsmouth, gaining successive League Championship winning medals in 1949 and 1950 and making 270 appearances during his time at Fratton Park (55 goals). He enjoyed limited international success, playing in only three full internationals over a period of three years. He made his debut in a 2-0 win over Northern Ireland in November 1951, starred in a 3-1 victory over Wales in November 1954 and 'created three chances' (none taken) in the 3-1 defeat of the reigning World Champions West Germany at Wembley a month later.

Whilst a serving marine, Phillips was involved in the D-Day landings during WW2.

PICKERING, Frederick 1964-65 ③ ④

Born: Blackburn, 19 January 1941
Career: Blackburn junior football, Blackburn Rovers (amateur, August 1956, professional, January 1958), Everton (£85,000, March 1964), Birmingham City (£50,000, August 1967), Blackpool (free, June 1969), Blackburn Rovers (free, March 1971), Brighton & Hove Albion (trial, February 1972); retired from football, May 1973; later worked as a fork-lift truck driver for a plastics company in Blackburn.

Three days before commencing a tournament in Brazil in May 1964, England played a friendly against the USA in New York and manager Alf Ramsey gave a debut to the Everton centre-forward Fred Pickering. Well, what a start he made to his international career! He cracked in a hat-trick, assisted in three other goals and played very well in a 10-0 win, albeit against moderate opponents. But for all his efforts, he was then left out of the next three matches, replaced by Johnny Byrne. In the autumn, however, Pickering was back on international duty, scoring in a 4-3 win over Northern Ireland in Belfast and having a decent game in the 2-2 draw with Belgium at Wembley. After that he was snubbed by Alf Ramsey despite some excellent club performances which resulted in him netting a total of 201 goals in 418 senior appearances, 168 coming in 354 League games. He helped Everton reach the 1966 FA Cup final (which he missed through injury) and Birmingham City reach the 1967 League Cup and 1968 FA Cup semi-finals.

PICKERING, John 1932-33 ①

Born: Mortomley, Yorkshire, 18 December 1908
Died: Bournemouth, 10 May 1977
Career: Mortomley St Saviour's (seasons 1923-25), Sheffield United (May 1925, retired, May 1948).

Long-striding inside-left Jack Pickering, a one club man, made his 356th and final appearance for the Blades in a League game against Portsmouth at Bramall Lane on New Year's Day, 1948 at the age of 39. He scored 110 goals (101 in the League) in all competitions, played in the 1936 FA Cup final defeat by Arsenal and helped United win the Football League (N) title in 1946. Surprisingly Pickering won only one England cap against Scotland at Hampden Park in April 1933 when he assisted in a 25th minute equaliser of a 2-1 defeat, the *Daily Mail* reporter writing: "Out of nowhere came Pickering. His fast ground pass to Hunt was accurate enough.... and he drove the ball with his left foot at a pace too great for the headlong dive of Jackson."

Pickering had trained as an accountant, and when he cut his formal links with football he took over a hotel in Bournemouth.

PICKERING, Nicholas 1982-83 ①

Born: South Shields, 4 August 1963
Career: North Shields (August 1978), Sunderland (apprentice, July 1979, professional August 1981), Coventry City (£120,000, January 1986), Derby County (August 1988), Darlington (October 1991), Burnley (loan, signed March 1993, retired, May 1993); since 1994 has been involved in youth coaching, and working on the radio in the North East.

A hard-working, strong-running midfielder, Nick Pickering was capped once by England in the 1-1 draw with Australia in Melbourne in June 1983. He was also part of his country's U21 team that won the 1984

European U21 Championship and reached the semi-final of the same competition two years later. As a Coventry player he gained an FA Cup winner's medal in 1987. He made over 400 appearances at club level before retiring in 1994. He has been involved in youth coaching, and working on the radio in the North East for the past 16 years or so.

PIKE, Thelwell Mather 1885-86 ①

Born: Andover, Hants, 17 November 1866
Died: Margate, Kent, 21 July 1957
Career: Malvern School (seasons 1883-85), Clare College/Cambridge University (seasons 1886-89), Old Malvernians (season 1889-90), Crusaders (season 1890-91), Brentwood FC (season 1891-92), Swifts (1893), Thanet Wanderers (1894); also played for Corinthians (seasons 1886-91); county cricketer for Worcestershire (seasons 1886-95); became a schoolteacher on leaving university; headmaster of Weybridge Preparatory School (1897-1906), later headmaster of Thanet School (Margate).

A fast-raiding outside-right with good skills and vision, Thelwell Pike won his only cap in a 6-1 victory over Ireland at Ballynafiegh Park, Belfast, in March 1886, when his fellow Cantabrians, Ralph Squire and Ben Spilsbury, played centre-half and inside-left respectively. Spilsbury scored four goals, two of which were created by Pike.

PILKINGTON, Brian 1954-55 ①

Born: Farringdon near Leyland, Lancs, 12 February 1933
Career: Leyland Motors (April 1950), Burnley (professional, April 1951), Bolton Wanderers (March 1961), Bury (February 1964), Barrow (January 1965), Chorley (November 1967; retired through injury, January 1968); returned as a player with Leyland Motors (August 1969, appointed manager, April 1970-May 1973); now Vice-Chairman of Chorley Football Club and President of the Central Lancs Clarets (Burnley supporters club).

A League Championship winner with Burnley in 1960, outside-left Brian Pilkington was fast, direct and an excellent goalscorer. He netted 77 goals in 340 appearances for Burnley and gained his only England cap with the Clarets, lining up alongside Johnny Haynes against Northern Ireland in Belfast in October 1954, 'doing quite well' in a 2-0 win. He also played in two B internationals, and amassed over 500 appearances for his four League clubs whose names all began with the letter 'B'.

PLANT, John 1899-1900 ①

Born: Bollington, Cheshire, 15 July 1871
Died: Darwen, Lancs, circa 1950
Career: Denton (August 1886), Bollington FC (September 1888), Bury (professional, April 1890), Reading (June 1898), Bury (May 1899, retired, April 1907).

Fleet-footed outside-left Jack Plant helped Bury win the Second Division Championship in 1895 and the FA Cup twice, in 1900 and 1903. During his two spells at Gigg Lane, he appeared in 371 League games and was perhaps unlucky to win only one England cap... in a 4-1 defeat by Scotland at Celtic Park in April 1900. That afternoon he struggled against a fine, close-marking full-back in Alex Smith (Rangers), although he did set up a good scoring chance which was missed by the usually reliable Steve Bloomer.

PLATT, David Andrew 1989-96 ⁶² ²⁷

Born: Chadderton near Oldham, Lancs, 10 June 1966
Career: Chadderton FC (April 1981), Manchester United (apprentice,
June 1982, professional, July 1984), Crewe Alexandra (free, February
1985), Aston Villa (£200,000, February 1988), Bari (Italy, £5.5m,
July 1991), Juventus (Italy, £6.5m, June 1992), Sampdoria (Italy,
£5.25m, August 1993), Arsenal (£4.75m, July 1995), Sampdoria
(free, player, also coach, then manager, August-November 1998),
Nottingham Forest (player-manager, August 1999, retired, July 2001);
England U21 (coach-manager, July 2001-May 2004); media pundit
(2004-10); Manchester City (coach/joint assistant-manager, July
2010-May 2013); has also been the proprietor of a night club and
owns racehorses.

David Platt was effective all over the pitch. The perfect replacement
in the England team for Bryan Robson, he was always likely to score
and gave some exceptionally fine performances in midfield.
He made his international debut against Italy in November 1989
and a year later played in the World Cup finals in Italy, scoring a
stoppage time winner (1-0) against Belgium to take England into
the quarter-finals. He struck again in the next match v. Cameroon in
Naples (won 3-2) but was devastated when West Germany won the
semi-final penalty shoot-out 4-3 in Turin.
　Platt then found the net with one of the best headers of the
whole tournament as England lost 2-1 to Italy in the 3rd place play-
off game in Bari. This was also Bobby Robson's last game in charge.
　Although he bagged four goals when England blitzed hapless
San Marino 6-0 in a World Cup qualifier at Wembley in February
1993, he had the chance to equal his country's all-time record of
five goals in an international but fluffed a late penalty.
　Platt netted again in the next game – his 10th goal for England
in 10 internationals – when Turkey were beaten 2-0 in Izmir.
　Over the next three years he was, for the majority of the time,
outstanding – certainly one of the team's better players – and he
continued to find the net on a regular basis. One of his best came in
the 1-1 draw with Brazil in the US Cup in Washington in June 1993;
he also struck winners against Denmark and Nigeria at Wembley in
March and November 1994 and netted a penalty to secure a 2-1
victory over Japan in the Umbro Trophy in June 1995.
　Injury at times interrupted his performances but generally he was
always one of the first names to be inserted on to the team-sheet.
　In Euro '92, England failed to win any of their group games and
crashed out, with Platt scoring their only goal of the competition
in a 2–1 defeat by Sweden. The squad then failed, despite Platt's
continuing drive from midfield, to qualify for the 1994 World Cup.
Manager Graham Taylor quit and was replaced by Terry Venables
who kept faith with Platt who had the pleasure of scoring the first
England goal in the Venables era, but by the time Euro '96 came
round, Platt was on the bench as Paul Ince and Paul Gascoigne
were ahead of him in the pecking order for the midfield places.
　In fact, Platt appeared as a substitute in most of the Euro '96 games,
and started the quarter-final against Spain when Ince was suspended. In
the semi-final, he scored in the penalty shoot-out against Germany, but
equally similarly, ended up on the losing side. And rather disappointed,
he retired from international football soon afterwards.
　Platt, who played in one unofficial international, also represented
England in three B and three U21 internationals. At club level he
accumulated 585 appearances (all competitions) and scored 201
goals, having his best return with Aston Villa (68 goals in 155
outings). He won the UEFA Cup with Juventus in 1993 and the
Coppa Italia with Sampdoria in 1994 (under Sven-Göran Eriksson)
and the Premiership and FA Cup double with Arsenal in 1998.

PLUM, Seth Lewis 1922-23 ①

Born: Edmonton, London, 15 July 1899
Died: Tottenham, 29 November 1969
Career: Page Green School/Tottenham, Mildway Athletic (August
1912), Tottenham Park Avondale FC (July 1913); served in Royal
Navy during WW1; Barnet (September 1919), Charlton Athletic
(amateur, August 1922), Chelsea (professional, March 1924),
Southend United (May 1927, retired April 1929); later lived and
worked (as a petrol pump attendant) in Tottenham.

A very capable, hard-working and creative wing-half, Seth Plum
helped England beat France 4-1 in Paris in May 1923, having a
hand in one of Ken Hegan's two goals. At club level, he amassed
less than 100 senior appearances, having his best spell with
Chelsea. He was with Third Division (S) side Charlton when he won
his only cap, lining up with his club-mate Harold Miller.

POINTER, Raymond 1961-62 ③ ②

Born: Cramlington, 10 October 1936
Career: Cramlington Modern School, Dudley Welfare Juniors (August 1952), Burnley (amateur, April 1955, professional, August 1957), Bury (August 1965), Coventry City (December 1965), Portsmouth (January 1967), Havant & Waterlooville (May 1968, retired May 1969); Portsmouth (coach, seasons 1969-73); later Burnley (coach, from 1978), Bury (coach).

Dynamic and tireless centre-forward Ray Pointer had a long and successful playing career, scoring 179 goals in 421 League appearances for his four major clubs. He won his three caps whilst with Burnley, netting twice - on his debut in September 1961 in a 4–1 win over Luxembourg and in the 2-1 World Cup qualifying victory over Portugal a month later. In between times he played in the 1-1 draw with Wales at Cardiff. With so many other champion goalscorers around at the same time, and doing well, Pointer found it tough even to get into the England squad. But he made the most of his opportunities. He helped Burnley win the League title in 1960 and reach the FA Cup final two years later.

PORTEOUS, Thomas Stoddard 1890-91 ①

Born: Newcastle, 12 December 1864
Died: Sunderland, 23 February 1919
Career: Heart of Midlothian (August 1881), Kilmarnock (August 1884), Sunderland (May, 1889), Rotherham Town (June 1894), Ardwick/Manchester City (January-March 1896), Rotherham Town (March 1896, retired, May 1896).

Right-back Tom Porteous' only England call-up was against Wales at Newcastle Road, Sunderland, in March 1891, partnering Jackson (Oxford University) in a 4-1 win. This international was the first to be staged in Sunderland.
   Twice a League Championship winner with Sunderland (1892 and 1893) Porteous played with 'proficiency and great steadiness' and made 93 appearances during his five-year stay on Wearside.

POWELL, Christopher George Robin 2000-05 ⑤

Born: Lambeth, London, 8 September 1969
Career: Crystal Palace (junior, September 1985, professional, December 1987), Aldershot (loan, January-March 1990), Southend United (free, August 1990), Derby County (£750,000, January 1996), Charlton Athletic (£825,000, July 1998), West Ham United (free, September 2004), Charlton Athletic (free, July 2005), Watford (free, July 2006), Charlton Athletic (free, August 2007), AFC Bournemouth (trial, July 2008), Leicester City (August 2008, then player/first team development coach from July 2009, retired as player, May 2010; continued as coach, then caretaker-manager, October 2010), Charlton Athletic (manager, January 2011); since November 2005 he also has been Chairman of the Professional Footballers' Association and in October 2009, was named as one of 50 ambassadors for England's 2018 World Cup bid.

Left-back Chris Powell had an excellent career, scoring eight goals in a total of 763 club appearances and winning five caps for England. Whilst at Charlton, for whom he made 206 first team appearances and helped to win the First Division title in 2000, he evidently caught the eye of England boss Sven-Göran Eriksson who selected him for international duty in February 2001, at the unusually late age of 31. In fact, when he lined up against Spain he became the oldest England debutant since Syd Owen in 1954. His other four caps were awarded against Finland, Mexico and two v. Holland.
   He often delighted the crowds at The Valley with his exuberant leaps of celebration when the Addicks registered a win!
   After making his last League appearance on 26 January 2010 in Leicester's 1-0 defeat to Barnsley Powell was 40 years of age, and after the game confessed: "I still love football... it's a great sport."

PRIEST, Alfred Ernest 1899-1900 ①

Born: Guisborough, 23 June 1875
Died: Hartlepool, 5 May 1922
Career: Darlington (July 1892), South Bank (April 1894), Sheffield United (May 1896), Middlesbrough (player/assistant-trainer, May 1906), Hartlepool United (player-manager, July 1908, retired, May 1912); remained Hartlepool where he became licensee of the Market Hotel.

Standing 5ft 10ins tall and weighing 11st, Fred Priest was a clever ball-player who gained a League Championship (1898) and two FA Cup (1899 and 1902) winner's medals with Sheffield United for whom he served for 10 years, scoring 86 goals in 248 appearances, many of them as Bert Lipsham's left-wing partner. He was awarded his only England cap (in place of Nottingham Forest star Fred Forman) against Ireland in March 1900, when he partnered fellow debutant Charlie Sagar (Bury) on the left-wing in a 2-0 win in Dublin. Priest was Hartlepool United's first-ever manager.

PRINSEP, James Frederick McLeod 1878-79 ①

Born: India, 27 July 1861
Died: Nairn, Scotland, 22 November 1895
Career: Charterhouse School XI (autumn 1874-April 1878), Clapham Rovers (seasons 1878-80), Sandhurst (Army, February 1881), Surrey (season 1880-81); played for Old Carthusians (season 1881-82) and Corinthians (1882-84); commissioned into the Essex Regiment in May 1882, he saw action in the Mahdist War; in 1886, as a Lieutenant, was seconded to the Egyptian Army; later promoted to captain and then sub-Inspector General in the Egyptian Coastguard Service in 1890.

A fine, safe, sure-kicking half-back, always cool, very strong in the tackle, James Prinsep held two England 'youngest player' records for almost 125 years, before they were both broken within the space of just over a year.
   He made his international debut (and only appearance) against Scotland in April 1879, at the age of 17 years and 252 days, which made him England's youngest-ever player at that time. He held this record for almost 124 years, until Wayne Rooney made his debut at the age of 17 years and 111 days against Australia on 12 February 2003.
   Prinsep was also the youngest player ever to appear in an FA Cup final when he lined up for Clapham Rovers in their 1-0 defeat by Old Etonians in the 1879 final at the age of 17 years and 245 days. This record was broken not long after his England record, by the Millwall youngster Curtis Weston who played in the 2004 final, aged 17 years and 119 days.
   A strong, well-proportioned half-back with good kicking ability, Prinsep made up for his earlier disappointment by gaining an FA Cup winner's medal with Old Carthusians in 1881.
   He was a fine track athlete, competing in the 220 and 440 yards and the long jump. He also enjoyed golf, rackets, rugby and cricket, once scoring 150 for the Free Foresters team and topping the batting averages three years running while at Charterhouse School. He was awarded the Royal Humane Society's bronze medal (the Albert Medal) for his bravery on the River Nile near Khartoum, two days before Christmas in 1884 for saving a Sudanese sailor from drowning in the Shaban Cataract. He also received the prestigious clasp of honour and an Egyptian decoration, the 4th Class Osmanieh.
   Prinsep died from blood poisoning and kidney failure after being taken ill on a golf course. His eldest son, Col. Evelyn Prinsep, lived to see England win the World Cup in 1966.

PUDDEFOOT, Sydney Charles 1925-26 ②

Born: Bow, London, 17 October 1894
Died: Rochford, Essex, 2 October 1972
Career: Park School/West Ham, East London Schools, Conder Athletic (August 1909), Limehouse Town (June 1911), West Ham United (amateur, July 1912, professional, November 1912), Falkirk (WW1 guest, signed for record £5,000, February 1922), Blackburn Rovers (£4,000, February 1925), West Ham United (February 1932, retired, May 1933); Fenerbahce, Turkey (coach, 1933-34), Galatasaray, Turkey (coach, August 1934), Northampton Town (manager, March 1935-March 1937); Istanbul, Turkey (coach, April 1937-September 1940); joined Blackpool Borough Police Force during the war; later a Civil Servant, retiring in 1963; Southend United (scout, June 1963-May 1965); also played county cricket for Essex (seasons 1922-23).

Despite top-scoring for England with four goals in three Victory internationals in 1919, Syd Puddefoot had to wait another six years before winning his first full cap against Ireland in October 1925, adding a second to his tally v. Scotland at Old Trafford in April 1926 when, wrote *The Times* reporter: "Most of his efforts lacked steam."
Puddefoot was a very unorthodox centre-forward who played with 'dash and enthusiasm' and brought the best out of his attacking colleagues. He scored 98 goals in 126 Football Combination League and Cup games during the First World War, including a record seven against Crystal Palace in November 1918. Ten years later he helped Blackburn win the FA Cup, scoring in the very first minute by bundling the Huddersfield Town goalkeeper Billy Mercer into the net. In all Puddefoot netted 254 goals in a career total of 612 appearances (all levels).

PYE, Jesse 1949-50 ①

Born: Treeton, Yorkshire, 22 December 1919
Died: Blackpool, 19 February 1984
Career: Catliffe FC/Sheffield (Rotherham & District League, August 1934), Treeton FC (August 1937), Sheffield United (amateur, December 1938), Notts County (professional, August 1945), Wolverhampton Wanderers (£10,000, May 1946), Luton Town (£9,000, July 1952), Derby County (£5,000, October 1954), Wisbech Town (free, July 1957, then player-manager, March 1960, retired as a player, 1961, continued as manager to December 1966); became the proprietor of a hotel in Blackpool.

After wartime service with the Royal Engineers in North Africa and Italy, centre-forward Jesse Pye played in the transitional League season with Notts County and scored for England in a Victory International against Belgium in January 1946 before joining First Division Wolves. He made an instant impact at Molineux, bagging a hat-trick on his debut in a 6-1 win over Arsenal in the first game of the season. Strong and mobile, Pye continued to find the net on a regular basis and in 1949 netted twice when Wolves beat Leicester City in the FA Cup final.
His prowess in front of goal won him his only senior cap in September 1949, but he was kept relatively quiet as the Republic of Ireland won 2-0 at Goodison Park to inflict upon England her first defeat on home soil by a non-Home nation.
Pye, who also represented his country in three 'B' internationals and played for the Football League, continued playing at club level until 1960. He scored 160 goals in almost 350 appearances in major League and Cup action, including 95 in 209 games for Wolves.
Playing for the 556th Coy RE against Italian opponents in the Tripoli Army League in 1943, Pye scored seven goals (three penalties) in a 9-0 win.

PYM, Richard Henry 1924-26 ③

Born: Topsham, Devon, 2 February 1893
Died: Topsham, Devon, 16 September 1988
Career: Topsham St Margaret's (April 1909), Exeter City (professional, November 1911), Bolton Wanderers (£5,000, June 1921), Yeovil & Petters United (May 1931, retired, July 1937); Exeter City (assistant-trainer, August 1937-September 1939); later enjoyed a prolonged life, fishing at Topsham.

Dick Pym, calm and unruffled with excellent anticipation and positional sense, kept goal for Bolton Wanderers in the first-ever Wembley Cup final, starring in a 2-0 win over West Ham United. He later added two more Cup winner's medals to his tally (in 1926 and 1929) and played three times for England, twice against Wales (in February 1925 and March 1926) and against Scotland (in April 1925). He was unlucky that there were at least six other top-class 'keepers chasing the number one spot in the international team and in the end he lost out to Jack Brown (Sheffield Wednesday).
Nicknamed 'Pincher Pym' he made 336 appearances for Bolton and was the last-surviving member of that historic Cup-winning 1923 team, living until he was 95, which at the time made him the oldest England footballer.

QUANTRILL, Alfred Edward 1919-21 ④ ①

Born: Rawalpindi, Punjab, India, 22 January 1897
Died: Trefriw, Conwy, Wales, 19 April 1968
Career: Boston Swifts (August 1912), Derby County (November 1914), Preston North End (June 1921), Chorley (August 1924), Bradford Park Avenue (September 1924), Nottingham Forest (May 1930, retired May 1932); became a successful insurance broker.

Alf Quantrill played on both wings but won all of his four England caps on the left. Quick over the ground with a powerful shot, he helped Derby gain promotion to Division One in his first season at the club, but his career was severely interrupted by the First World War when he served in the Derbyshire Yeomanry, only to be sent home after contracting malaria in Salonika.
He made his England debut in a 2-1 defeat by Wales in March 1920, scored the second goal (a squirter through the mud) in a 5-4 victory over Scotland at Sheffield a month later and played in the Home Internationals against Ireland and Wales the following season.
A Third Division (North) championship winner with Bradford in 1928, he scored 58 goals in 191 League games for the Yorkshire club, striking over 100 goals in more than 350 games during his career.
Quantrill was married to Hetty Winifred Bloomer, the eldest daughter of former England centre-forward Steve Bloomer.

QUIXALL, Albert 1953-55 ⑤

Born: Sheffield, 9 August 1933
Career: Sheffield Wednesday (amateur, May 1948, professional, August 1950), Manchester United (£45,000, September 1958), Oldham Athletic (£7,000, September 1964), Stockport County (free, July 1966), Altrincham (free, September 1967), Radcliffe Borough (briefly during season 1968-69; retired May 1969); later worked as a scrap metal dealer in Manchester.

Albert Quixall was the 'Golden Boy' of the 1950s. With his good looks, blond Teddy-boy haircut and wearing the shortest of close-fitting shorts, he was, without doubt, a teenage idol.
Highly talented, with a wonderful bodyswerve, he made his England debut as a 20 year-old in the 4-1 World Cup/Home International win over Wales at Cardiff in October 1953, creating

a goal for fellow debutant Dennis Wilshaw. He then played – and played well – in the next two games, a 4-4 draw with the Rest of Europe at Wembley and a 3-1 victory over Northern Ireland at Goodison Park. Not chosen in the team which lost 6-3 home to Hungary in late November, he gained his fourth and fifth caps on tour in May 1955, against Spain in Madrid and as a substitute (for Nat Lofthouse) v. Portugal in Lisbon. He had twice represented his country as a schoolboy, played in one U23 and one 'B' international and made four appearances for Football League XIs.

Quixall joined Manchester United for a then British record fee in 1958, being one of Matt Busby's major recruits in building a new team in the aftermath of the Munich air crash. His only medal with the Reds came in the 1963 FA Cup final win over Leicester. Earlier, he had twice helped Sheffield Wednesday win the Second Division title (1952 and 1956), scoring 65 goals in 260 appearances for the Owls. He then added 56 goals to his tally in 183 games during his time at Old Trafford.

RADFORD, John 1968-72 ②

Born: Pontefract, Yorks, 22 February 1947
Career: Hemsworth Youth Club (season 1961-62), Bradford City (amateur, August 1962), Arsenal (apprentice, October 1962, professional, February 1964), West Ham United (£80,000, December 1976), Blackburn Rovers (£20,000, February 1978), Bishop's Stortford (player, then player-manager); also ran a pub in Essex.

A big, strong inside or centre-forward, excellent in the air, John Radford had already won four caps for England's U23 side before making his senior debut in a friendly against Romania in January 1969. However, he was not a favourite of manager Sir Alf Ramsey and collected only one more cap, against Switzerland on 13 October 1971.

Radford spent most of his career with Arsenal for whom he scored 149 goals in 481 first-class appearances. Prolific at youth and reserve team levels, he made his League debut against West Ham in March 1964 and ten months later became the youngest player ever to claim a hat-trick for the Gunners when he netted three times against Wolves in January 1965, at the age of 17 years and 315 days, a record that remains to this day.

The recipient of a Fairs Cup winner's medal in 1970, the following year he starred in Arsenal's 'double' winning team, forming an excellent partnership with Ray Kennedy and Charlie George.

RAIKES, Reverend George Barkley 1894-96 ④

Born: Carleton-Forehoe, Wydmondham, Norfolk, 14 March 1873
Died: Shepton Mallet, Somerset, 18 December 1966
Career: Shrewsbury School XI (season 1891-92), Oxford University (seasons 1892-96), Wydmondham FC (1893), Norfolk (1893), Corinthians (seasons 1893-96); also a cricket blue (at Oxford), played cricket for Norfolk (1890-97 and 1904) and Hampshire (1900-02); ordained in 1897, became curate of Portsea (to 1903); Chaplain to the Duke of Portland 1905-20 and Rector of Bergh Apton, Norfolk from 1920-36.

George Raikes was a fine goalkeeper, quick, alert, with safe hands and a strong kick. He shared the number one position in the England team over a 12-month period with John Sutcliffe, his four caps coming in the 1-1 draw with Wales at the Queens Club, London in March 1895, in the 2-0 win over Ireland in Belfast the following year, in a 9-1 victory over Wales at Cardiff in March 1896

and in a 2-1 defeat by Scotland at Celtic Park three weeks later. He made four important saves on his debut but was left stranded when conceding the two goals against the Scots.

Raikes, who in 1912, had starred for an England XI against Australia at cricket, was one of the oldest cricketers at the time of his death in 1966, aged 93.

His brother Ernest and nephew Thomas also played first-class cricket.

RAMSEY, Sir Alfred Ernest 1948-55 ㉝ ③

Born: Dagenham, Essex, 22 January 1920
Died: Ipswich, 28 April 1999
Career: Becontree Heath School/Dagenham, Dagenham Schools, Essex County Schools, Five Elms FC (June 1939), Portsmouth (amateur, January 1940), Southampton (amateur, October 1943, professional, August 1944), Tottenham Hotspur (£21,000, May 1949, retired, January 1954), Elton Manor FC (part-time manager, February 1954); Ipswich Town (manager, August 1955-April 1963), England (officially appointed team manager, October 1962; effective from May 1963-May 1974); Birmingham City (director, January 1976, manager, September 1977-March 1978); suffered a stroke in 1998 and entered a Suffolk nursing home where he subsequently died from prostate cancer a year later.

A clean-kicking right-back with good positional sense, Alf Ramsey was a finesse player who also had flair. He wasn't fast but made up for it with superb positional sense. Always a thinker, he made great use of the ball.

Making his international debut in a comprehensive 6-0 win over Switzerland at Highbury in December 1948, Ramsey was on the winning side in his first six games before tasting defeat as the USA beat England 1-0 in the World Cup in Brazil in June 1950.

One snappy reporter asked Ramsey after this humiliating defeat in Belo Horizonte: "Did you play?" Ramsey replied: "Yes... I was the only bloody one who did."

He retained his place, despite having several different partners in Bill Eckersley, Johnny Aston and Lionel Smith, and actually took over the captaincy from Billy Wright for England's game against Portugal at Goodison Park in May 1951, when most unRamsey-like, he handed the visitors a second equalizer with a mishit back-pass early in the second-half. Thankfully, England went on to win 5-2.

Six months later at Wembley he scored from the penalty spot and laid on a goal for Nat Lofthouse with a pin-point free-kick to earn a draw with Austria.

Ramsey's last minute penalty for England salvaged a 4-4 draw with the Rest of Europe at Wembley in the FA's 75th anniversary match in October 1953. However, a month later he struggled to contain Honved's flying winger Budai as Hungary won 6-3 on the same pitch, when once again he found the net with a 60th-minute penalty with the score already standing at 6-2.

This, in fact, proved to be his last game for his country as a player.

A vital member of Tottenham's elegant push-and-run side of the early 1950s, Ramsey won Second and First Division Championship winner's medals in 1950 and 1951 and during his time at White Hart Lane, he appeared in 283 first-team games for Spurs (all levels), scoring 30 goals.

As manager, he guided Ipswich to the Third Division (South), Second Division and First Division Championships in 1957, 1961 and 1962 respectively, before leading England to World Cup glory in 1966....which duly earned him a Knighthood in January 1967. (See under England managers).

RAWLINGS, Archibald 1920-21 ①

Born: Leicester, 2 October 1891
Died: Preston, Lancs, 11 June 1952
Career: Shirebrook Juniors (August 1905), Wombwell (July 1906), Shirebrook (December 1906), Barnsley (February 1907), Darfield United (April 1907), Shirebrook (August 1907), Northampton Town (May 1908), Barnsley (August 1911), Rochdale (July 1914), Dundee (September 1919), Preston North End (£1,500, June 1920), Liverpool (March 1924), Walsall (June 1926), Bradford Park Avenue (February 1927), Southport (July 1928), Dick Kerr's XI/Preston (December 1928), Burton Town (August 1931, retired May 1933); then Preston North End (assistant-trainer, seasons 1933-35).

A footballing nomad, Archie Rawlings, at six feet, was unusually tall for an outside-right but he was extremely mobile, dangerous (when in the right frame of mind) and could shoot with both feet. However, for all his noble efforts for Preston and Liverpool, he was rewarded with only one England cap, deputising for Sam Chedgzoy in a 2-0 win over Belgium in Brussels in May 1921.

RAWLINGS, William Ernest 1921-22 ②

Born: Andover, Hants, 3 January 1896
Died: Chandlers Ford, 25 September 1972
Career: Andover FC (April 1914), Southampton (amateur, August 1918, professional, May 1919), Manchester United (March 1928), Port Vale (November 1929), New Milton (May 1930), Newport Isle-of-Wight (October 1930, retired July 1932); pub licensee for 10 years, followed by 25 as a civil servant with the Admiralty.

A very lively, all-action centre-forward, Bill Rawlings had an eye for goal and loved to shoot, from any distance! He was 'useful' on his England debut in a 1-0 win over Wales at Goodison Park in March 1922 but was 'not in the game' in his second international, a 1-0 defeat by Scotland at Villa Park three weeks later, when he was 'dominated throughout' by the big Celtic centre-half Billy Cringan. In his ten years with Southampton, Rawlings scored 193 goals in 364 first-class appearances, gaining a Third Division (South) Championship medal in 1922.

RAWLINSON, John Frederick Peel 1881-82 ①

Born: New Alresford, Hants, 21 December 1860
Died: Cambridge, 14 January 1926
Career: Eton College (seasons 1878-81), Trinity College/Cambridge University (seasons 1881-83), Old Etonians (1883), Corinthians (original committee member, 1882); FA Committee member 1885-86; qualified as a barrister and called to the bar in 1884; became a QC in 1897; recorder of Cambridge University (1898-1926); Member of Parliament for Cambridge (1906-26); Privy Counsellor (1923-26).

An FA Cup winner with Old Etonians in 1882 and a losing finalist twice, in 1881 and 1883, John Rawlinson was a well-balanced, highly efficient goalkeeper who, it has to be said, could be rather 'too casual' in his approach at times!
   He won his only England cap in a rather one-sided 13-0 victory over Ireland in February 1882, one reporter stating: "He was rarely troubled, spending most of the game talking to spectators behind his goal."

RAWSON, Herbert Edward 1874-75 ①

Born: Port Louis, Mauritius, 3 September 1852
Died: London, 18 October 1924
Career: Wallace's School/Cheltenham, Westminster School/London (seasons 1869-72), also played for Royal Engineers (briefly, in

season 1871-72), Royal Military Academy/Woolwich (joined in 1972); Royal Engineers (August 1872, retired May 1909, having attained the rank of Colonel); also played cricket for Kent as a wicketkeeper in 1873.

Herbert Rawson was a clever dribbler, a fine crosser of the ball and a useful goalscorer who played for England, alongside his brother William, in the 2-2 draw with Scotland at The Oval in March 1875 – this being the first occasion on which two brothers had ever played for the same England team.
   An FA Cup loser in 1874 and a winner in 1875 with the Royal Engineers, William played against him for Oxford University in the first final.

RAWSON, William Stepney 1874-75 ②

Born: Cape Town, South Africa, 14 October 1854
Died: Essex, 4 November 1932
Career: Westminster School (seasons 1870-73), Oxford University (seasons 1874-77), Old Westminsters (season 1877-78), Wanderers (season 1878-79); FA Committee member (seasons 1876-77 and 1879-80); refereed the 1876 FA Cup final; also played lacrosse.

The younger brother of Herbert (above) William Rawson was a half-back who gained an FA Cup winner's medal in 1874 and a loser's prize in 1877. Short and stocky, he possessed great judgment and always looked in control of the ball. He played twice for England, with his brother in the 2-2 draw with Scotland in March 1875 and in a 3-1 defeat by the same country at The Oval two years later when, stated the reporter for *Bell's Life,* "He was one of several players who selfishly kept hold of the ball until it was too late."

READ, Albert 1920-21 ①

Born: Ealing, 24 February 1899
Died: Chiswick, London, summer, 1964
Career: Tufnell Park (August 1919), Queens Park Rangers (May 1921), Reading (July 1922, retired, injured, May 1923).

Capped twice by England as an amateur, Albert Read was an unobtrusive yet very effective footballer who played equally well in the right half and centre-half positions.
   He appeared in one full international – against Belgium in Brussels in May 1921 – playing well behind Jimmy Seed and Charlie Buchan down the right in a 2-0 win.

READER, Joseph 1893-94 ①

Born: West Bromwich, 27 February 1866
Died: West Bromwich, 8 March 1954
Career: Beeches Road & St Phillip's Schools/West Bromwich, Carter's Green FC/West Bromwich (August 1883), West Bromwich Albion (amateur, January 1885, professional, August 1885, retired, April 1901; became trainer-coach at The Hawthorns, later engaged as a ground steward until 1950).

Believed to be the last goalkeeper to discard the long white trousers, doing so in 1896, Joe Reader was an excellent custodian who used his legs to great effect. He made 370 appearances for West Bromwich Albion, the club he served for 65 years. He played in two FA Cup finals, winning in 1892, losing in 1895, and was the only player to have served the club at three of their grounds – Four Acres, Stoney Lane at The Hawthorns. Nicknamed 'Kicker' Reader, he gained his only England cap in a 2-2 draw with Ireland in Belfast in March 1894 when he deputised for Leslie Gay. He replaced another England international, Bob Roberts, between the Albion posts.

REANEY, Paul 1968-71 ③

Born: Fulham, London, 22 October 1944
Career: South Leeds FC (seasons 1959-61), Leeds United (trial, then professional, October 1961), Bradford City (free, June 1978), Newcastle KB United/Australia (season 1980-81); later ran coaching courses for the World in Sport organisation; was a partner in the Classic Portrait Company, also ran coaching sessions at Potters Leisure Resort, Norfolk.

A tremendously effective over-lapping right-back, Paul Reaney was an unsung but truly vital part of Don Revie's feared and admired Leeds United team of the 1960s/70s.

He won the first of his three England caps as a substitute for Keith Newton in the 1-1 draw with Bulgaria at Wembley in December 1968. His appearance, however, assumed greater importance in later years. At the time he was regarded as a 'white' player but in today's world he would be viewed by many as 'black' or mixed race. Therefore, his international debut came nine years before that of Viv Anderson, who is widely credited as the first black man to play senior competitive football for England.

Reaney's two other caps followed against Portugal in December 1969 and Malta in February 1971. He was unfortunate inasmuch that he had the likes of Newton, Tommy Wright and Cyril Knowles all wanting to wear the number two shirt at the same time!

During his 17 years at Elland Road, Reaney who made his senior debut at the age of 18 helped Leeds win the Second Division title in 1964, the League Cup in 1968, the Fairs Cup in 1968 and 1971, the Football League Championship in 1969 and 1974 and the FA Cup in 1972. He was also an FA Cup, European Cup and Fairs Cup losing finalist and had the ill-luck to miss the 1970 FA Cup final with a broken leg, which also kept him out of that year's World Cup in Mexico.

Reaney, who also played in five U23 internationals, made 748 appearances for Leeds (only Jack Charlton and Billy Bremner have made more) and he was voted Australia's 'Player of the Year' in 1981.

In 1993, burglars broke into Reaney's home and stole a safe containing his collection of medals, though left behind his trophies, caps and other honours.

REDKNAPP, Jamie Frank 1995-2000 ⑰ ①

Born: Barton-on-Sea, Hampshire, 25 June 1973
Career: Tottenham Hotspur (associated schoolboy forms, July 1988), Bournemouth (apprentice, June 1989, professional, June 1990), Liverpool (£350,000, January 1991), Tottenham Hotspur (free, April 2002), Southampton (free, January 2005, retired, injured, August 2005); produced *Ikon* magazine (about footballer's lifestyles) with Tim Sherwood; Sky Sports soccer pundit; also worked on TV adverts.

Jamie Redknapp, on his England international debut, had his goalbound shot kept out by the acrobatics of the Colombian 'keeper Rene Higuita during the 0-0 draw at Wembley in September 1995. The midfielder's snap shot fired in from some distance, looked a goal all the way but as everybody inside the stadium looked on, open mouthed, the eccentric figure of Higuita performed a double overhead clearance almost off his goal-line to steer the ball to safety. His brilliant effort was later referred to as the 'scorpion save'.

Two years later, having established himself the midfield engine-room and playing in his eighth full international, he broke an ankle in the 2-1 win over South Africa at Old Trafford and this knocked him back considerably. He eventually recovered but a series of other niggling pulls and twists severely handicapped his progress in the England team and although he went on to win 17 caps in total, he played only 39 minutes in major tournaments - during Euro '96. Injury also ruled him out of contention for both the 1998 World Cup

and 2000 European Championships.

Redknapp's only international goal came in the 2-1 friendly victory over Belgium at the Stadium of Light, Sunderland in October 1999. His last appearance in a 'Three Lions shirt' came in the 1-0 home defeat by Scotland later that same year.

At club level Redknapp amassed almost 400 appearances (315 in the League) and scored close on 50 goals, having by far his best years with Liverpool for whom he netted 39 times in exactly 300 first-class matches. On 23 October 1991, he became the youngest Liverpool player to appear in major European competition, at 18 seasons 120 days when making his debut against Auxerre in the UEFA Cup.

His only career winners' medals came in the 1995 League Cup when Liverpool beat Bolton Wanderers in the final and in FA Charity Shield and Super Cup triumphs in 2001.

Besides his full international honours, Redknapp also won one B and 18 U21 caps (scoring five goals). And in late June 2006, he hand picked a squad of eight semi-professional players to represent England in an International World Cup 6 v 6 in Germany. However, Vigan Qehaja was the only player to go on and play professional football.

The son of Harry Redknapp, who played outside-right for Bournemouth and West Ham and is now manager of Queen's Park Rangers, having previously been in charge at Portsmouth, Southampton,Bournemouth and Tottenham, Jamie was actually signed by his father for Bournemouth but after failing to agree a long-term contract with the Cherries, he moved to Anfield while his father was sacked from his position at Dean Court!

Redknapp junior married the former Eternal singer Louise Nurding in the summer of 1998.

REEVES, Kevin Philip 1979-80 ②

Born: Burley, Hampshire, 20 October 1957
Career: Bournemouth (apprentice, June 1974, professional, July 1975), Norwich City (£50,000, January 1977, Manchester City (£1.25 million, March 1980), Burnley (£125,000, July 1983, retired, injured, June 1984; appointed coach); Swansea City (coach, December 1984-December 1985), Birmingham City (coach, January 1986-May 1987); Wrexham (assistant-manager/coach, December 1989-October 2001), Swansea City (assistant-manager/coach, November 2001-December 2003); scout Stoke City (scout, January 2004-May 2006), Swansea City (scout, seasons 2006-08); Wigan Athletic (advisory coach, seasons 2009-11)

Goalscoring forward Kevin Reeves made his debut in the mid-1970s for Bournemouth but his League career lasted only eight years before a hip injury forced him to retire at the age of 26 after he had netted more than 150 goals in almost 400 appearances for his four clubs. He was Norwich City's first £1 million player and scored a penalty for Manchester City in the 1981 FA Cup final v. Spurs which went to a replay.

He played under manager John Bond at each of his four clubs and was coach under him at Turf Moor and St Andrew's.

The recipient of six U21 and three B caps, Reeves made his senior international debut in the 2-0 European Championship qualifying win over Bulgaria in November 1979 when he played 'up front' with Trevor Francis and Tony Woodcock. His second game was in the 1-1 draw with Northern Ireland in May 1980 when he was substituted in the second-half by Paul Mariner. After retiring as a player, he became a highly-respected coach with the aforementioned Bond and also with former Welsh international Brian Flynn.

REGIS, Cyrille, MBE 1981-88 ⑤

Born: Maripiasoula, French Guyana, 9 February 1958
Career: Kensal Rise Primary & Cardinal Hinsley RC Secondary
Schools/London, Borough of Brent Boys (August 1973), Ryder Brent
Boys (October 1973), Oxford & Kilburn Boys (March-May 1974),
Ryder Brent Valley (again, August 1974), Mosley (Athenian League,
August 1975), Hayes (semi-professional, July 1976), West Bromwich
Albion (£5,000, May 1977 + another £5,000 after 20 appearances),
Happy Valley FC/Hong Kong (guest, summer 1980); Coventry City
(£300,000, October 1984, appointed player-coach, April 1988), Aston
Villa (free, July 1991), Wolverhampton Wanderers (free, August 1993),
Wycombe Wanderers (free, August 1994), Chester City (free, May
1995, retired, injured, October 1996); West Bromwich Albion (reserve
team manager/coach, February 1997, joint caretaker-manager,
July-August 1999, with John Gorman, and again, on his own, January
2000; left club later that same month); became a football agent.

A powerhouse centre-forward, strong and mobile, blessed with
a cracking right-foot shot and great heading ability, 'Smokin Joe'
Regis made his England debut as a substitute (for Trevor Francis)
in the 4-0 win over Northern Ireland at Wembley in February 1982.
He was inches away from scoring with a diving header and the Irish
were overwhelmed.

Four more caps followed for the West Brom striker, three over a
six-month period later in 1982 v. Wales, Iceland and West Germany,
and his last against Turkey in a European Championship qualifier
in October 1987 when he was came on as a substitute for Peter
Beardsley in an 8-0 win at Wembley.

Also capped three times at B team level and on six occasions by
the U21s (three goals), Regis scored 112 times in 302 games for
WBA and 62 in 274 outings for Coventry City with whom he won the
FA Cup in 1987. He did a good job as a stop-gap striker with each
of his last four clubs, eventually ending a fine career with over 200
goals under his belt in 700 senior appearances. He was voted PFA
'Young Footballer of the Year' in 1979 and was runner-up to Steve
Perryman in the 'Footballer of the Year' poll in 1982.

One of the 'Three Degrees' with WBA in the late 1970s (the
others being Brendon Batson and Laurie Cunningham) Regis
returned to The Hawthorns in a coaching capacity under manager
Ray Harford in 1997 and stayed on with Denis Smith.

Awarded an honorary fellowship by the University of
Wolverhampton in 2001, Regis and his wife Julia visited water-
related projects in Ethiopia in 2007 as part of their continued
support for WaterAid. Then in the 2008 Birthday Honours, he
received the MBE (for services to football). As a youngster Regis was
offered a trial by Chelsea but had to withdraw due to a hamstring
injury. A year later he joined West Brom.

*Regis' brother, Dave, was also a professional footballer while his
cousin John Regis MBE, is a former athlete who still holds the UK
record for the 200 metres.*

REID, Peter 1984-88 ⑬

Born: Huyton, Lancs, 20 June 1956
Career: Huyton Boys (season 1969-70), Bolton Wanderers
(apprentice, July 1971, professional, May 1974), Everton (£60,000,
December 1982, player-coach, June 1987-February 1989), Queens
Park Rangers (February 1989), Manchester City (player-coach,
December 1989, player-manager, November 1990-September
1993), Southampton (player, non-contract, October 1993), Notts
County (non-contract, February 1994), Bury (non-contract, July
1994); Sunderland (manager, March 1995-October 2002); also
England U21 (manager, appointed for 1999-2000 season), Leeds
United (manager, March 2003-May 2004), Coventry City (manager,

May 2004-January 2005), Thailand (national team manager/coach,
September 2008-September 2009); worked as a TV pundit; Stoke
City (assistant-manager, September 2009-May 2010), Plymouth
Argyle (manager, July 2010, sacked, September 2011); Kolkata
Camelians FC/India (manager, August 2012)

Hard-working midfielder Peter Reid made his full international debut
as a second-half substitute as England tired in the high altitude when
losing 1-0 to Mexico in Mexico City in June 1985. It was a tough
baptism as he hardly got a kick against tough opponents. Reid went
on to win 12 more caps, many due to injuries to other players.

Replacing Bryan Robson (injured) he became the linchpin of
the team in the 1986 World Cup finals, producing some excellent
performances, none better than in the 3-0 win over Poland.
However, in the game against Argentina in the quarter-finals, he was
one of the players left behind by Diego Maradona as he burst from
inside his own half to score his second goal to add to his first he
netted with his hand!

His last international appearance came in May 1988, in a 3-0
friendly win over Switzerland in Lausanne.

Reid also played in six U21 internationals and was voted PFA
'Footballer of the Year' in 1985 when with Everton. He broke his
leg in 1979 and was out of action for over a year but came back
strongly and had an excellent career, making 657 club appearances
in major competitions (41 goals scored), helping Bolton win the
Second Division title in 1978 and Everton the FA Cup in 1984, the
League Championship in 1985 and 1987 and the European Cup
Winners' Cup, also in 1985, plus four FA Charity Shields.

He twice guided Sunderland into the Premiership as manager
and saw Thailand win the T & T Championship in Vietnam. He
replaced Paul Mariner as manager of Plymouth but was sacked
after the team suffered eight successive defeats at the start of the
2011-12 season and were 92nd in the 'League'. Kolkata Camelians
bought Reid at auction for £128,000 ahead of the inaugural Indian
Premier League season.

REVIE, Donald George, OBE 1954-56 ⑥ ④

Born: Middlesbrough, 10 July 1927
Died: Edinburgh, 26 May 1989
Career: Newport Boys' Club/Middlesbrough (seasons 1940-42),
Middlesbrough Swifts (August 1942), Leicester City (amateur,
August 1944, professional, July 1945), Hull City (£20,000,
November 1949), Manchester City (£13,000 plus a player, October
1951), Sunderland (£23,000, November 1956), Leeds United
(player, £14,000, December 1958, player-manager March 1961,
retired as a player, May 1963, continued as manager to July 1974);
England (manager, July 1974-July 1977), UAE (manager-coach,
July 1977-May 1980), Al-Nassr/Egypt (manager, June 1980-July
1984), Al-Ahly/Egypt (manager, August 1984-May 1985); Leeds
United (on a consultancy basis, seasons 1985-87).

Don Revie made his England debut, along with Johnny Haynes,
against Northern Ireland in Belfast in October 1954…and both
players scored in a 2-0 win. There were, in fact, seven debutants in
this game – the first after the World Cup in Switzerland.

He was on target again in his second match – a 7-2 win over
Scotland at Wembley in April 1955. He also assisted in two of the
four goals scored by the Wolves striker Dennis Wilshaw in this game.

Then, after having a rather 'indifferent' game in a 1-0 defeat in
France, he sparkled in a rare Sunday fixture in October 1955, which
was played in front of the King and Queen of Denmark and 53,000
fans in Copenhagen. Having just started playing as a deep-lying
centre-forward for his club Manchester City, he scored twice,
including a penalty, in a resounding 5-1 win over the Danes. He won

two more caps after that – a 2-1 defeat by Wales in October 1955 and a 1-1 draw with Northern Ireland a year later when he helped create a rare goal for Stanley Matthews after just two minutes.

Revie, who also played once for England B and twice for a Football League XI, had a solid career as a player. He made almost 500 club appearances (474 in the Football League) and scored just over 100 goals. He missed the 1949 FA Cup final due to a severe nose bleed, and was a runner-up in the same competition in 1955 before collecting a winner's medal in 1956.

Voted FWA 'Footballer of the Year' in 1955, he was perhaps responsible for developing the 'deep-lying' centre-forward role (although Ronnie Allen of West Brom played in a similar position). During the mid 1950s Manchester City drew up the 'Revie Plan' which, it is said, had enormous significance in the development of football, moving from the old 2-3-5 formation to 3-3-4 which, as we know, was followed by 4-2-4, 4-3-3 and 2-5-3 and so on.

After retiring as a player, manager Revie produced a thoroughbred-sort of team at Elland Road, steering Leeds to the Second Division Championship (1964), to two First Division titles (1969 and 1974), to FA Cup glory (1972), to a League Cup victory (1969), to two Fairs Cup successes (1968 and 1971) and numerous runners-up prizes. He developed some brilliant footballers, far too many to mention, and although not always the fans' favourite manager because of the tactics used by his players in certain matches, he certainly made Leeds buzz.

Following the 1973-74 season, when Leeds won their League Championship, Revie was widely acknowledged as one of the most successful managers in the country and was considered one of the leading candidates to take over as the English boss.

Alf Ramsey had just departed after the team had failed to qualify for the World Cup finals and in July of 1974, Revie accepted the manager's job after Joe Mercer had turned it down because of his advanced years. The FA, particularly Ted Croker, were impressed with Revie's personality and ideas.

However, he was unable to reproduce the success he had enjoyed at Leeds. England failed to qualify for the 1976 European Championships and looked like failing to qualify for the 1978 World Cup when Revie secretly negotiated a massively-paid coaching job in the United Arab Emirates, believed to be worth £60,000 a year. He was bitterly criticized by the FA and the national Press – although he did sell the story of his departure to a national newspaper before telling the FA – and was later suspended from British soccer until he was willing to face a charge of bringing the game into disrepute. In fact, he was later banned for ten years from English football but later won a High Court battle against the FA and was guaranteed an injunction quashing the ban. He later returned to Leeds United as a consultant.

Awarded the OBE in 1970, Revie was struck down by motor neuron disease in 1987 and was confined to a wheelchair for the last two years of his life. (See under England managers.)

REYNOLDS, John 1891-97 (8) (3)

Born: Blackburn, 21 February 1869
Died: Sheffield, 12 March 1917
Career: Park Road FC/Blackburn (August 1882), Witton FC/Blackburn (September 1883), Blackburn Rovers (reserves, seasons 1884-86), Park Road FC (August 1886), East Lancashire Regiment (December 1886, posted to Ireland, demobbed, December 1889), Distillery (guest, May 1888-December 1889), Ulster (June 1890), West Bromwich Albion (March 1891), Droitwich Town (loan, 1892), Aston Villa (£50, April 1892), Celtic (free, May 1897), Southampton (free, January 1898), Bristol St George (free, July 1898), Gafton FC/New Zealand (seasons 1899-1902); coached in New Zealand (season

1902-03), Stockport County (September 1903), Willesden Town (October 1903, retired, April 1905); Cardiff City (coach, season 1907-08); subsequently employed as a miner at a colliery near Sheffield.

Wing-half Jack 'Baldy' Reynolds was a stumpy man who mastered every trick in the book, sometimes bewildering his own team-mates with his clever flicks.

He played five times for Ireland in 1890-91 (twice v. England, twice v. Wales and once v. Scotland) before it was realised he had been born in Blackburn and went on to win another eight caps for the country of his birth, the first against Scotland at Ibrox Park in April 1892 when he 'impressed with his tenacity' in a comprehensive 4-1 win.

He scored his first of three international goals in his second outing, in a 6-0 win over Wales at Stoke in March 1893 – netting with a well-struck drive from 25 yards.

His second goal followed two weeks later, in another excellent win over Scotland, this time by 5-2 at the Richmond Athletic ground, Surrey. This time he thumped a low hard shot past Renton's 'keeper John Lindsay.

After playing in the 2-2 draw with Ireland a year later, he nagged his third goal in a 2-2 draw with Scotland at Celtic Park in April 1894, the *Daily Mail* reporter stating (with England attacking) "The leather, however, did not get past Reynolds, who nursed it so well that he made a long shy at goal. The ball hit the bar and after bouncing back, went over Haddow's head just into the net."

Reynolds then starred in another fine win over the Scots (4-0 in April 1895) and followed up by helping his team beat Wales 4-0 in March 1897 before ending his international career with a 2-1 defeat at the hands of Scotland five days later.

At club level, he gained three FA Cup winner's medals in five years, one with West Brom, two with Aston Villa. He helped the latter win the double in 1897 and added two more League winner's medals to his tally in 1894 and 1896. A Scottish Cup winner with Celtic in 1898, he also represented the Football League on four occasions, the Professionals (v. Amateurs) three times and appeared in one England trial. Reynolds scored West Brom's first-ever penalty v. Nottingham Forest in April 1893

Three other players, John Hawley Edwards, Bob Evans and Stuart Macrae, all played for England and one other country at full international level.

RICHARDS, Charles Henry 1897-98 (1)

Born: Burton-on-Trent, 9 August 1875
Died: Nottingham, circa 1959
Career: Gresley Rovers (April 1891), Newstead Byron (August 1892), Notts County (July 1894), Nottingham Forest (January 1896), Grimsby Town (January 1896), Leicester Fosse (June 1901), Manchester United August 1902), Doncaster Rovers (March 1903, retired May 1905); became a licensee (albeit briefly).

With an eye-for-goal, rugged inside-forward Charlie Richards won his only England cap in March 1898, in a 3-2 victory over Ireland in Belfast when he partnered Charlie Athersmith on the right flank. He made over 200 appearances at club level, gaining an FA Cup winner's medal with Nottingham Forest in 1898 and a Second Division Championship medal with Grimsby Town in 1901.

RICHARDS, George Henry 1908-09 ①

Born: Castle Donington, Leicestershire, 10 May 1880
Died: Derby, 1 November 1959
Career: Castle Donington Juniors (seasons 1896-98), Whitwick
White Cross (August 1898), Derby County (professional, April 1902,
retired, injured, May 1914).

Initially an inside-forward, left-half George Richards was a clever,
consistent footballer, a sportsman both on and off the field, whose
only cap was gained against Austria in Vienna when, playing in front
of Jesse Pennington and behind winger Arthur Bridgett, he 'assisted
in two of the goals' in an impressive 8-1 victory. He made over 300
appearances for Derby, collecting an FA Cup runners-up medal in
1903 and Second Division Championship winner's medal in 1912.
He toured South Africa with the FA in 1910.

RICHARDS, John Peter 1972-73 ①

Born: Warrington, 9 November 1950
Career: Wolverhampton Wanderers (apprentice July 1967,
professional, July 1969), Derby County (loan, November
1982-January 1983), Club Sport Maritimo/Madeira (August
1983-April 1984); worked for Wolverhampton Leisure Services
Department; then Wolverhampton Wanderers (Director, August
1995, managing-Director, October 1997-May 2000); currently
works as operations director of Pitchcare, a Wolverhampton-based
online service for groundsmen.

The Wolves striker made his only England appearance, alongside
two-goal Martin Chivers, in a 2-1 win over Northern Ireland at
Goodison Park in May 1973. He didn't perform all that well in what
was a disappointing display by Sir Alf Ramsey's men.
However, with the acknowledged talent England possessed at the
time in the form of Kevin Keegan, Chivers and Allan Clarke, this
ensured that Richards became a 'one-cap wonder'.
Virtually a one-club man who spent 16 years at Molineux,
Richards made 486 appearances for Wolves and netted 194 goals
(only Steve Bull has scored more). He helped the team reach the
1972 UEFA Cup final, scored the winner in the 1974 League Cup
final victory over Manchester City, added a second League Cup
winner's prize to his collection in 1980 and was a key member of
Wolves' Second Division Championship winning team in 1977,
forming a terrific strike-force initially with Derek Dougan and later
with Andy Gray. Capped as a schoolboy, Richards also played
for England in three B, two U21 and six U23 internationals and
represented the Football League.
*Richards scored one of the fastest-ever goals by a Wolves
player – 12 seconds after the start of the League game at Burnley
in November 1975.*

RICHARDS, Micah Lincoln 2006-12 ⑬ ①

Born: Birmingham, 24 June 1988
Career: Leeds United (schoolboy forms, August 2000), Leeds City
Boys (seasons 2000-02), Oldham Athletic (junior, May 2002),
Manchester City (apprentice, July 2003, professional, June 2006)

In November 2006, following an injury to regular full-back Gary
Neville, Micah Richards was named in the England team for the
friendly against Holland, having played only 28 senior matches for
Manchester City. As a result he became England's youngest-ever
defender at the age of 18 years and 144 days, breaking the record
previously held by Rio Ferdinand.

He played well enough in the 1-1 draw
in Amsterdam and added more caps to
his tally as his game developed, eventually
scoring his first international goal in the
Euro 2008 qualifier against Israel at
Wembley in September 2007.
His last cap to date came against
Croatia in November 2007. Since then,
injury has affected his game at both club
and international level, but he will be
looking to increase his number of caps over the coming years.
Besides his senior appearances for his country, the versatile
Richards, who can also play in the centre of the defence, has
represented his country in two U16, three U19 and 14 U21
internationals. He had appeared in 234 games for Manchester City
at May 2013, gaining FA Cup and Premiership winner's medals in
2011 and 2012. He was also a member of the Great Britain team at
the London Olympics in 2012.
*As a youngster, Richards attended the Brazilian Soccer Schools
scheme and still retains strong links with this programme. His
father, Lincoln, runs a Brazilian Soccer School in Chapeltown, Leeds.*

RICHARDSON, James Robert 1932-33 ② ②

Born: Ashington, 8 February 1911
Died: Bexley Heath, Kent, 28 August 1964
Career: Blyth Spartans (August 1925), Newcastle United (£200,
April 1928), Huddersfield Town (£4,000, October 1934), Newcastle
United (£4,500, October 1937), Millwall (£4,000, March 1938);
WW2 guest for Fulham (season 1941-42), Aldershot (season 1942-
43), Charlton Athletic (season 1942-43), Leyton Orient (season
1944-45), joined Orient (as player-trainer, January 1948, retired as
a player, June 1951; senior trainer, June 1951-June 1955); worked
in engineering (July 1955-November 1956); Millwall (assistant-
trainer, November 1956-May 1957).

A tenacious, hard-working, clever dribbling inside-forward, Jimmy
Richardson was the player deeply involved in the famous 'over-the-
line' goal in the 1932 FA Cup final. At the time Newcastle United
were trailing Arsenal 1-0 when Richardson chased a long ball down
the wing to the byline before crossing for Jack Allen to score. The
referee ruled that the ball had not gone out of play, even though
photographic evidence later showed it had actually crossed the line.
The goal stood and Newcastle went on to win 2-1.
For some bold and honest performances during the 1932-33
season, Richardson was awarded two caps at the end of that
campaign, the first in a 1-1 draw with Italy in Rome, the second
against Switzerland when he scored twice in a 4-0 win in Berne. His
brother, John, played for Oldham Athletic.
*In March 2003, Richardson's 1932 FA Cup-winning medal sold
for £6,462 in an auction at Christies.*

RICHARDSON, Kevin 1993-94 ①

Born: Newcastle-upon-Tyne, 4 December 1962
Career: Montagu & North Fenham Boys Club (seasons 1976-78),
Everton (apprentice, June 1978, professional, December 1980),
Watford (£225,000, September 1986), Arsenal (£200,000, August
1987), Real Sociedad, Spain (£750,000, July 1990), Aston Villa
(£450,000, August 1991), Coventry City (£300,000, February
1995), Southampton (£150,000, September 1997), Barnsley
(£300,000, July 1998), Blackpool (loan, January-February 1999,
signed March 1999, retired, May 2000); Sunderland (youth team
manager, season 2000-01), Stockport County (assistant-manager,
seasons 2001-03), Sunderland (reserve team coach, 2004, first

team coach under a consortium headed by Niall Quinn; Newcastle United (Academy team coach), Darlington (assistant-manager, October 2009)

A highly competitive midfielder, Kevin Richardson made more than 700 appearances during a nomadic career. He was capped just once by England in May 1994, in a comfortable 5–0 friendly victory over Greece at Wembley when fewer than 24,000 fans were present. Richardson won the League Championship (1984) and the FA Cup (1985) with Everton, a second League title with Arsenal (1989) and the League Cup (1994) with Aston Villa. He also played in Everton's 1984 Charity Shield winning team.

RICHARDSON, Kieran Edward 2004-07 ⑧ ②
Born: Greenwich, London, 21 October 1984
Career: West Ham United (youth player, seasons 1998-2001), Manchester United (apprentice, April 2001, professional, October 2002), West Bromwich Albion (loan, January-May 2005), Sunderland (£5.5m, July 2007), Fulham (£2m, August 2012)

A versatile footballer, able to play equally as well on the left-wing, in midfield or at full-back, Kieran Richardson won his first cap for the England U21 team in February 2005, during his loan spell with West Brom. After a series of convincing performances for the Baggies, he gained his first full cap against the USA at the end of that season, celebrating the occasion by scoring twice, including one direct from a free kick, in a 2-1 win in Chicago. His performance that day earned high praise from manager Sven-Göran Eriksson, who described it as 'fantastic.' He also came on as a substitute in England's second match of that summer tour against Colombia. He then made two further substitute appearances in World Cup qualifiers against Wales in Cardiff and Austria at Old Trafford but was not selected by Sven-Göran Eriksson in the 2006 World Cup squad.

But he did play for Steve McClaren afterwards, making more appearances off the bench.

In between times, Richardson returned to U21 duty and played in both legs of the England crucial European Championship qualifier against France U21s which they lost 3–2 on aggregate. The decisive goal came from an 85th minute penalty in the second leg after the unfortunate Richardson had brought down Lassana Diarra inside the box. Besides his eight full caps, Richardson has also gained a total of 11 at U21 level.

He made 81 appearances for Manchester United, gaining an FA Youth Cup winner's medal in 2003, helped West Brom retain their Premiership status and played 149 games for Sunderland before moving to Fulham.

RICHARDSON, William 1934-35 ①
Born: Framwellgate Moor, County Durham, 29 May 1909
Died: Small Heath, Birmingham, 29 March 1959
Career: Framwellgate Moor & Easington Colliery Boys, Durham Schools, Horden Wednesday FC (August 1927), United Bus Company/Hartlepool (April 1928), Hartlepools United (August 1928), West Bromwich Albion (£1,250, June 1929); WW2 guest for Derby County and Walsall; Shrewsbury Town (£250, November 1945, retired May 1946); West Bromwich Albion (assistant-trainer/coach, June 1946 until his death in March 1959).

A quick, sharp and decisive centre-forward, 'W.G.' Richardson had a wonderful 16-year career with West Bromwich Albion for whom he scored 328 goals (202 in the Football League) in 444 first-team appearances (including wartime football). He netted twice in Albion's 1931 FA Cup Final win over Birmingham and later that year struck four goals in five minutes at the start of a League game at West Ham. He also claimed a club record 40 goals in season 1935-36 (39 in the League). But for all his efforts, he gained only one cap for England, in the 1-0 win over Holland in Amsterdam. One must remember though, that the likes of Ted Drake, Bob Gurney, George Camsell, Ray Westwood and Freddie Steele were all around at the same time.

Richardson, who died while playing in a charity match at the BSA sports ground in Birmingham, was called 'W.G.' to distinguish from another Bill Richardson who was at West Brom at the same time.

RICKABY, Stanley 1953-54 ①
Born: Stockton-on-Tees, 12 March 1924
Career: Stockton & District Schools, South Bank FC (August 1940), Middlesbrough (amateur, July 1941, professional, July 1946), West Bromwich Albion (£7,500, February 1950), Poole Town (player-manager, June 1955), Weymouth (player, August 1960-April 1961), Newton Abbot Spurs (August 1963, retired July 1964); ran an ice-cream business before becoming an accountant; emigrated to Australia in 1969; now residing at North Beach, Perth.

Replacing Alf Ramsey and partnering Bill Eckersley, raven-haired, hard-tackling right-back Stan Rickaby made his only England appearance in the 3-1 win over Northern Ireland at Goodison Park in November 1953. He played in over 200 games for West Bromwich Albion, but missed the Baggies' 1954 FA Cup Final triumph through injury. He was replaced at The Hawthorns by future England star Don Howe. Rickaby is one of the oldest former England players alive today.

His autobiography – Upover and Downunder - was published in 2003 by Britespot Solutions, Cradley Heath, West Midlands.

RICKETTS, Michael Barrington 2001-02 ①
Born: Birmingham, 4 December 1978
Career: Walsall (apprentice, April 1995, professional, September 1996), Bolton Wanderers (£500,000, July 2000), Middlesbrough (£3m, January 2003), Leeds United (free, June 2004), Stoke City (loan, February-May 2005), Cardiff City (loan, August 2005-January 2006), Burnley (loan, January–May 2006), Southend United (June 2006), Preston North End (free, January 2007), Oldham Athletic (July 2007), Walsall (loan, November 2007-January 2008), Columbus Crew/USA (trial), San Jose Earthquakes/USA (trial), Oldham Athletic (March 2008), Walsall (free, July 2008), Tranmere Rovers (free, August 2009, contract cancelled by mutual consent, February 2010).

'One-cap wonder' Michael Ricketts played 45 minutes in England's 1-1 friendly draw with Holland in Amsterdam in February 2002. He was never really considered again!

A useful striker at club level, he netted 37 goals in 98 League games for Bolton but after that, he never stayed long enough with any one club to make an impact. When he left Tranmere in 2010 he had amassed over 400 appearances and netted 96 goals.

On 17 January 2011, Ricketts pleaded guilty to a charge of common assault after punching and head butting his ex-girlfriend. He was sentenced to a 12 month community order and fined £200 and ordered to pay £85 costs.

RIGBY, Arthur 1926-28 (5) (3)

Born: Chorlton-cum-Hardy, Manchester, 7 June 1900
Died: Crewe, 25 March 1960
Career: Manchester & Salford Schoolboy football, Stockport County (August 1915), Crewe Alexandra (April 1919), Bradford City (February 1921), Blackburn Rovers (April 1925), Everton (November 1929), Middlesbrough (May 1932), Clapton Orient (August 1933), Crewe Alexandra (August 1935, retired, May 1937).

A goalkeeper during his teenage years, Arthur Rigby developed into a very talented and lively outside-left who, as a Blackburn player, also appeared at inside-left. He won his first cap in the Home International Championship match against Scotland at Hampden Park, in April 1927, playing his part in a 2–1 win. One newspaper report stated: 'Rigby exchanged passes with Bishop who sent Dean dashing through to score England's first goal.'
    Rigby scored twice himself in his second game when Belgium were battered 9-1 a month later and he added a third goal to his tally when France were beaten 6-0 in May 1927.
    An FA Cup winner with Blackburn in 1928, a Second Division Championship winner with Everton in 1931 and a Welsh Cup winner with Crewe in 1936, Rigby made a total of 467 League appearances during his career, scoring 108 goals.

RIMMER, Ellis James 1929-32 (4)

Born: Birkenhead, 2 January 1907
Died: Formby, Lancashire, 16 March 1965
Career: Parkside FC/Birkenhead (August 1919), Northern Nomads (August 1921), Everton (amateur, July 1922), Whitchurch (September 1923), Tranmere Rovers (professional, August 1924), Sheffield Wednesday (£1,850, February 1928), Ipswich Town (August 1938, retired, February 1939); became a licensee, first in Sheffield, later in Formby.

Ellis Rimmer was a tricky left-winger, fast and direct with a powerful shot who scored twice on his England debut in a 5-2 win over Scotland at Wembley in April 1930. He had a superb game that afternoon, netting with a cracking drive from Sammy Crooks' centre in the 30th minute (to make it 2-0) and again in the 55th minute when he steered the ball home after an excellent move involving his club colleague Alf Strange and Joe Bradford. Two other Wednesday players, Bill Marsden and Ernie Blenkinsop also starred against the Scots. Rimmer played in three more internationals, his last against Spain in December 1931 when he assisted in three goals in a 7-1 win and also knocked over one of the linesmen (Sir) Stanley Rous during a mazy run down the wing.
    He also scored twice late on in the 1935 FA Cup Final to earn Sheffield Wednesday a 4-2 victory over West Bromwich Albion. Twice a League Championship winner with the Owls (1929 and 1930) he netted 140 goals in 418 appearances during his ten years at Hillsborough. He played with future legends 'Dixie' Dean and 'Pongo' Waring at Tranmere. Rimmer was also a talented musician who regularly played the piano at public venues.

RIMMER, John James 1975-76 (1)

Born: Southport, 10 February 1948
Career: Southport & Merseyside Schools, Manchester United (amateur, May 1963, apprentice, September 1963, professional, May 1965), Swansea City (loan, October 1973-February 1974), Arsenal (£40,000, February 1974), Aston Villa (£65,000, August 1977), Swansea City (August 1983), Hamrun Spartans/Malta (August 1986), Luton Town (briefly, late 1986); Swansea City (coach,

July 1987-May 1988); became manager of a golf complex in Swansea; also coached in China; now lives and works in Canada.

Agile, positive and a fitness fanatic, goalkeeper Jimmy Rimmer had a wonderful career, accumulating over 550 appearances, 470 in the Football League. Taking over from the 'rested' Ray Clemence, he gained his only England cap in the US Bi-centennial Tournament against Italy in New York in May 1976, being replaced in the second-half by Joe Corrigan in a 3-2 win. He already had two U23 caps under his belt. He won the League Championship, European Cup (although he was only on the pitch for a few minutes before hurting his back) and European Super Cup with Aston Villa and was a substitute for Manchester United when they lifted the European Cup in 1968. He was reserve to internationals Alex Stepney at Old Trafford and Pat Jennings at Highbury.

RIPLEY, Stuart Edward 1993-95 (2)

Born: Middlesbrough, 20 November 1967
Career: Middlesbrough (apprentice, June 1984, professional November 1985), Bolton Wanderers (loan, February-March 1986), Blackburn Rovers (£1.3m, July 1992), Southampton (£1.5m, June 1998), Barnsley (loan, November 2000-January 2001), Sheffield Wednesday (loan, from March-May 2002, when he retired); later set up the Castleford Physiotherapy & Sports Injury Clinic, providing physiotherapy to nearby Rugby League teams, as well as local football teams; he also graduated from the University of Central Lancashire in 2007, with a first class combined honours degree in Law and French. He became a qualified solicitor in 2010.

A blond wide midfielder, with good pace, Stuart Ripley gained his two England caps as a Blackburn player, making his debut in a one-sided 7-1 World Cup qualifying victory over San Marino in November 1993. Four years later he played in the 4-0 win over Moldova. A Premier League winner with Blackburn in 1995 (under Kenny Dalglish) he also helped Middlesbrough rise from the Third to the First Division inside five years. Ripley, who also gained eight U21 caps, made 511 League appearances for his six clubs. His son, Conner, was a goalkeeper with Middlesbrough.

RIX, Graham 1980-84 (17)

Born: Doncaster, 23 October 1957
Career: Campsmount School/Doncaster, Doncaster & Yorkshire Schools, Yorkshire Youths, Askern Schools, Askern Juniors (seasons 1972-74), Leeds United (trial, August 1973), Arsenal (apprentice June 1974, professional, January 1975), Brentford (loan, December 1987-January 1988), CM Caen/ France (June 1988), Le Havre/ France (free, August 1990), Dundee (free, July 1992), Chelsea (non-contract player/youth team coach, March 1994; retired as a player, June 1994; served six months of a 12-month prison sentence for a sex offence (March-September 1999); on release rejoined Chelsea as first team coach, September 1999-January 2001; acted as caretaker-manager for four days in September 2000); Portsmouth (manager, February 2001-March 2002), Oxford United (manager, March 2004; appointed Director of Football, November 2004), Heart of Midlothian (manager, November 2005-March 2006); now coach at The Glenn Hoddle Soccer Academy, near Malaga, Southern Spain.

First selected for the full England team by manager Ron Greenwood v. Norway in September 1980, midfielder Graham Rix played well in a 4-0 win and did likewise against Holland and Finland ahead of the 1982 World Cup. A clever footballer with a terrific engine, he spent his best years with Arsenal, gaining an FA Cup winner's medal in

1979. During his career, Rix amassed 473 League appearances and scored 52 goals. He also won one B and seven U21 caps. He worked under managers Glenn Hoddle, Ruud Gullit and Gianluca Vialli at Chelsea and saw the Blues win the FA Cup in 1997 and the League and European Cup Winners' Cups in 1998 and after returning to Stamford Bridge coached the team that won the FA Cup in 2000.

After his prison sentence, Rix was placed on the sex offenders' register for ten years, and banned by the FA from working with youth players under the age of 16.

ROBB, George 1953-54 ①

Born: Finsbury Park, London, 1 June 1926
Died: Ardingly, Hayward's Heath, 25 December 2011
Career: Finchley (August 1942), Tottenham Hotspur (amateur, December 1951, professional, June 1953, retired, injured, May 1958); also an English teacher at St. Mary's C. of E. Primary School, Crouch End, Hornsey (before 1951), sports-master at Christ's College, Finchley (1952-64) and English teacher/sports-master at Ardingley College, Haywards Heath, West Sussex (from 1964).

George Robb, a well-built, purposeful and direct left-winger, was called up as a late replacement for Tom Finney for the home friendly with Hungary in November 1953. Unfortunately he was completely out of his depth in the 6-3 defeat and was never chosen again. Before turning professional at the age of 27, he had represented his country 17 times as an amateur and also played for Great Britain at the 1952 Olympics in Helsinki, scoring in a 5-3 defeat by Luxembourg. During his time at White Hart Lane he played 200 games and scored 58 goals.

ROBERTS, Charles 1904-05 ③

Born: Darlington, 6 April 1883
Died: Manchester, 7 August 1939
Career: Rise Carr Rangers (April 1898), Darlington St Augustine's (season 1899-1900), Sheffield United (trial, April-May 1900), Bishop Auckland (amateur, August 1900), Grimsby Town (professional, May 1903), Manchester United (£600, April 1904), Oldham Athletic (£1,500, August 1913; retired during WW1, appointed manager, June 1921, resigned, December 1922), Manchester Central (coach, seasons 1923-25).

A strong, skilful, fast centre half and a rebel to boot, Charlie Roberts flouted FA rules by wearing his shorts above the knee and was politically minded in favour of the unionisation of professional footballers. He helped Manchester United win two League titles (in 1908 and 1911) as well as the FA Cup in 1909 and scored 23 goals in 299 appearances for the Reds. He was also United's first England international, capped three times in the space of five weeks (February-April 1905) he he was outstanding his last game, a 1-0 win over Scotland at Crystal Palace. Journalist William McGregor wrote in the *Daily Mail*: 'Roberts, the Manchester United pivot, was one of England's outstanding players... he is a born tackler.'

On 2 December 1907, Roberts and Billy Meredith were instrumental in setting up the Players' Union. The organisation was not recognised by the FA but it did attract considerable support from fellow League clubs. In August 1909, the FA threatened to suspend any player who admitted to being a member of the Union, following which Roberts and his Manchester United's team-mates were summoned to a meeting with the club's management. The players refused to relinquish their Union membership, forcing the club to contact their first opponents of the new season, Bradford City, to cancel the fixture, as it could not field a team. The FA's threat had seen the membership of the Union fall so that the only members were the Manchester United players, who called themselves 'The Outcasts'. It was only after Everton's Tim Coleman renewed his support by siding with 'The Outcasts' that the FA relented and Roberts' Union was saved.

ROBERTS, Frank 1924-25 ④ ②

Born: Sandbach, Cheshire, 3 April 1894
Died: Cheshire, 23 May 1961
Career: Sandbach Villa (May 1910), Sandbach Ramblers (August 1911), Crewe Alexandra (May 1912), West Ham United (briefly, March-April 1913), Bolton Wanderers (August 1914), Manchester City (£3,400, October 1922), Manchester Central (June 1929), Horwich RMI (August 1930, retired May 1932); became a licensee.

Opportunist centre-forward Frank Roberts made an impressive international debut alongside Joe Bradford and Billy Walker in England's 4-0 win over Belgium in December 1924. He scored twice in his second game, a 2-1 victory over Wales in late February 1925 and played well in the 2-0 defeat by Scotland before helping his side beat France 3-2 in Paris in his last outing in May.

Roberts, who netted 116 goals in 216 League games for Manchester City, was suspended and transfer listed (and subsequently sold) by Bolton in 1922 'for taking over one of the principal hotels in that town'.

ROBERTS, Graham Paul 1982-84 ⑥

Born: Southampton, 3 July 1959
Career: Southampton & Hampshire Schools, Sholing Sports FC (August 1972), Southampton (associate schoolboy, August 1973), Bournemouth (apprentice, August 1975), Dorchester Town (loan, August 1976, signed permanently, October 1976), Portsmouth (apprentice, February 1977, professional, March 1977), Weymouth (August 1979), Tottenham Hotspur (£35,000 May 1980), Glasgow Rangers (£450,000, May 1986), Chelsea (May 1988, player-coach from November 1989), West Bromwich Albion (free, November 1990), Enfield (player-manager, March 1992), Chesham (briefly, 1994), Slough Town (season 1994-95), Stevenage Borough (1995), Yeovil Town (player-manager, January 1995-February 1998), Hertford Town (manager, August 1998), Borehamwood (manager, February 2001), Carshalton (manager season 2002-03); soccer coach in Marbella/Spain (seasons 2003-05), Clyde (manager, May 2005-August 2006); also ran his own sports management company; Pakistan (national team manager, season 2010-11); in 2009, teamed up with *Daily Record* journalist Colin Duncan to write his autobiography, *Hard As Nails*.

A rugged, no-nonsense defender or midfielder, Graham Roberts collected his six England caps over a period of twelve months between May 1983 and June 1984. He had a decent debut in the 0-0 draw with Northern Ireland and did not let his country down in any of his games. He had a fine playing career, amassing more than 500 club appearances, helping Spurs win the FA Cup in 1981 and 1982 and the UEFA Cup in 1984, Rangers the League title in 1987 and League Cup in 1987 and 1988 and Chelsea the Second Division title in 1989.

ROBERTS, Henry 1930-31 ①

Born: Barrow-in-Furness, 1 September 1907
Died: Torbay, Devon, 12 October 1984
Career: Barrow Schools, Barrow Wireworks FC (August 1922), RASC (seasons 1923-25), Barrow (December 1925), Chesterfield (June 1926), Lincoln City (August 1928), Port Vale (£100, June 1930), Millwall (April 1931), Sheffield Wednesday (trial, April 1935), Peterborough United (August 1935), Spalding United (seasons 1936-39); retired to Devon after WW2.

A bustling, thickset inside-right with clever tricks, Harry Roberts was capped by England in a friendly against Belgium in May 1931. One feels he might have done better if he had been with a more fashionable club.

ROBERTS, Herbert 1930-31 ①

Born: Oswestry, 19 February 1905
Died: France, 19 June 1944
Career: Oswestry Town (August 1920); also played for Oswestry Police team (seasons 1923-26), Arsenal (£200, December 1926, retired, injured, January 1938); Margate (trainer/coach, February-May 1939); also engaged on coaching staff at Highbury; died of erysipelas while serving with the Royal Fusiliers during the war.

Regarded as one of the first 'third back' defenders, introduced as such to combat the new offside rule in 1925 by Arsenal manager Herbert Chapman, red-haired Herbie Roberts was the 'best player' on the pitch when he made his only start for England in a 2-0 defeat by Scotland at Hampden Park in March 1931. Unfortunately he never got another chance at international level, despite making over 300 first-class appearances for Arsenal with whom he won four League titles and the FA Cup between 1931 and 1936. Referred to as the Gunners' 'policeman or stopper centre-half' Roberts was one of nine Arsenal players who perished during WW2.

ROBERTS, Robert John 1886-90 ③

Born: West Bromwich, 9 April 1859
Died: Byker, Newcastle-upon-Tyne, 28 October 1929
Career: George Salter Works (from May 1873), West Bromwich Albion (amateur, September 1879, professional, August 1885), Sunderland Albion (May 1890), West Bromwich Albion (May 1891), Aston Villa (May 1892, retired June 1893); became a shop-keeper in Byker, Newcastle.

West Brom's first international, goalkeeper Bob Roberts had 'a very poor first game for his country', fumbling twice while conceding two goals in a 3-2 defeat by Scotland at Ewood Park in March 1887. The *North British Daily Mail* reporter stated: "His mistakes lost England the match…he was too far off his line for the second goal."
Nevertheless, Roberts went on to win two more caps, both in comprehensive 5-1 and 9-1 victories over Ireland, in 1888 and 1890 respectively.
Tall and distinguished, he wore a size 13 boot and made over 400 first-team appearances for West Brom (84 at senior level), gaining an FA Cup winner's medal in 1888, having been a losing finalist in the previous two years. He was one of only two players to have featured in West Brom's first FA Cup-tie and the clubs, first League game.

ROBERTS, William Thomas 1923-24 ② ②

Born: Handsworth, Birmingham 29 November 1898
Died: Preston, 13 October 1965
Career: Kentish Rovers/Handsworth (August 1912), Boyce Engineers FC/Smethwick (May 1912), Lord Street FC/Birmingham (August 1913), Soho Villa/Handsworth (September 1914), Leicester Fosse (January 1915), West Bromwich Albion (trial, May 1915); WW1 guest for Southport Vulcan; Preston North End (May 1919), Burnley (October 1924), Preston North End (July 1926), Tottenham Hotspur (May 1928), Dick Kerr's XI (August 1929), Chorley (October 1930, retired, May 1931); became a publican in Preston (for 30 years).

Tommy Roberts, a dashing, wholehearted, big-shooting centre-forward, played twice for England. His first match was in the 2-2 draw with Belgium in Antwerp in November 1923 and his second in a 2-1 defeat by Wales at Blackburn four months later. He scored in both matches but with so many other excellent strikers around at the same time including David Jack, Joe Bradford, Billy Walker, Charlie Buchan, Jack Cock and his namesake Frank Roberts, he never got another chance. He netted 178 goals in a total of 307 League games. He broke an arm in a motor accident in 1927 and was never the same player afterwards.

ROBINSON, John 1936-39 ④ ③

Born: Shiremoor, Northumberland, 10 August 1917
Died: Shiremoor, 30 July 1972
Career: Shiremoor FC (April 1932), Sheffield Wednesday (£20, August 1934); WW2 guest for Darlington, Hartlepool United, Newcastle United, Middlesbrough; Sunderland (October 1946), Lincoln City (October 1949, retired, injured, January 1950).

Jackie Robinson made a goalscoring debut for England in an 8-0 win over Finland in May 1937. A year he went on an end-of-season tour of continental Europe and played in the first game against Germany in Berlin and the second against Switzerland in Zurich. The game against the Germans was infamous because the England players were forced to give the Nazi salute. None of them actually wanted to effect the salute but the British Ambassador insisted they did so… to keep the crowd in a good frame of mind! The game itself resulted in a fine 6-3 victory for England with Robinson scoring twice. He had a moderate game in a 2-1 defeat by the Swiss.
One more international appearance followed, against Wales in October 1938, when he partnered Stan Matthews on the right-wing in a 4-2 defeat at Cardiff.
Robinson was a graceful, eye-catching, close-dribbling, scheming and goalscoring inside-right who scored 39 goals in 119 appearances for Sheffield Wednesday.

ROBINSON, John William 1896-1901 ⑪

Born: Derby, 22 April 1870
Died: Derby, 28 October 1931
Career: Derby Midland (May 1886), Lincoln City (January 1889), Derby County (June 1891), New Brighton Tower (August 1897), Southampton (May 1898), Plymouth Argyle (May 1903), Exeter City (October 1905), Millwall (December 1905), Green Waves FC/Plymouth (August 1907), Exeter City (September 1908), Stoke (May 1909), Rochester FC/New York, USA (October 1912, retired March 1913); also played baseball; later ran a hotel and worked as an insurance salesman.

Jackie Robinson was noted, during his playing career, for his reliability and was, according to author Francis Hodgson, among the first goalkeepers to dive full length to make saves. Well-built, he always wore a bright cream sweater and a huge floppy cap. He was a 'smiling man', extra-large with powerful shoulders who often rushed out, with superb judgment, to whip the ball off the toes of a forward. He made his name with Southampton in the palmy days of C B Fry, the famous cricketer. To him a penalty never seemed very fearsome; he saved plenty during his time.

Robinson made eleven appearances for England, the first against Ireland in February 1897 when he had 'little to do' in a 6-0 victory at Nottingham.

In his next game, six weeks later, he was outstanding in a 2-1 defeat by Scotland at Crystal Palace, '...keeping the visitors at bay with several fine saves' wrote *The Times* correspondent.

Seven of his next nine internationals, played over a three-year period, ended in victories. He performed superbly in 3-0 and 4-0 wins over Wales, and likewise in 3-1 and 2-1 successes over Scotland but had a difficult time against the Scots at Celtic Park in April 1900 when he was beaten four times, blaming himself for two of the goals.

He eventually lost his place in the team in March 1901 but over the next two years, England used five different goalkeepers in the next seven matches, before settling with Tom Baddeley.

Robinson made well over 400 club appearances during his career, playing in two losing FA Cup finals with Southampton whom he helped win three Southern League titles.

As a baseball player, he represented the Derby County Baseball Club with Steve Bloomer and helped them become British champions twice in the 1890s.

In December 1922, Robinson fell from an upstairs window and suffered, as a result of the fall, from epilepsy.

ROBINSON, Paul William 2003-09 ㊶
Born: Beverley, Yorkshire, 15 October 1979
Career: Leeds United (apprentice, July 1996, professional, May 1997), Tottenham Hotspur (£1.5m, May 2004), Blackburn Rovers (£3.5m, July 2008).

A solid-enough goalkeeper, with good reflexes, Paul Robinson made stupid mistakes - like a lot of others. Once revered as the definitive number one, in October 2006, his career took a nosedive after his 'miss-hit' at Gary Neville's back-pass in the World Cup qualifier against Croatia saw England fall two goals behind.

Afterwards Robinson described the incident as 'a freak.'

Prior to that, he had produced many fine displays, saving a penalty in the 1-0 defeat by Spain in Madrid in November 2004, having been a member of England's squad at the 2004 European Championships (as cover for David James). He was later in the squad for the 2006 World Cup qualifiers when he replaced James as first choice 'keeper.

Subsequently named in the World Cup squad for Germany, he was an ever-present during the campaign, keeping four clean sheets in five games. However, despite this he was criticised for being very indecisive on crosses, missing three against Trinidad & Tobago.

In August 2007, Robinson gifted Germany their first goal in England's first defeat at the new Wembley (1-2). He was substituted at half-time by James, although before the game, manager Steve McClaren stated that he would make this change.

Then, after palming the ball into the path of Roman Pavlyuchenko who scored for Russia in another 2–1 defeat soon afterwards, manager Robinson was dropped for the final qualifier, and return match with Croatia, Scott Carson taking over.

Recalled to the squad by new coach Fabio Capello for the 2010 World Cup qualifiers against Kazakhstan and Andorra, due to an injury to James, Robinson sat on the bench as cover for Robert Green, to the annoyance of his boss at Blackburn, Sam Allardyce, who publicly stated that his player (Robinson) is England's 'number one - due to his impressive club form.'

Unfortunately Robinson failed to make the squad for World Cup,

Joe Hart, James and Green going to South Africa instead.

In August 2010, with 41 caps under his belt, Robinson announced his retirement from international football, after pulling out of the squad for the friendly with Hungary, saying: "Only now have I been able to make this decision as previously I haven't been in contention for selection. I don't see myself as a number three or four keeper and find that role very frustrating."

'Robbo' made 119 appearances for Leeds and 175 for Spurs, scoring a goal for each club and at the end of the 2012-13 season had played in 172 first-class games for Blackburn. He also won eleven U21 caps and helped Spurs lift the League Cup in 2008.

ROBSON, Bryan, OBE 1979-91 ⑨⓪ ㉖
Born: Chester-le-Street, County Durham, 11 January 1957
Career: Chester-le-Street Council & Birtley Comprehensive Schools, Washington & Chester-le-Street Schools, Chester-le-Street Cubs FC, Burnley (trial, May 1971), Coventry City (trial, July 1971), Newcastle United (trial, August 1971), West Bromwich Albion (apprentice, April 1972, professional, August 1974), Happy Valley/Hong Kong (guest, July 1980), Manchester United (£1.5m, October 1981), Middlesbrough (player-manager, May 1994, retired as a player, May 1997, manager to June 2001), Bradford City (manager, November 2003-May 2004), West Bromwich Albion (manager, November 2004-September 2006), Sheffield United (manager, June 2007-February 2008), Manchester United (Global Ambassador, June 2008); Thailand (national team manager/coach, September 2009, resigned, June 2011); also has a stake in the Birthday chain of card shops; turned down the position of Nigeria national team coach, October 2003.

'Captain Marvel' Bryan 'Pop' Robson skippered England on 65 occasions - only Billy Wright and Bobby Moore had led their country more times. Often willing to play through the pain barrier, he was an inspirational midfielder, certainly one of the best players on the international circuit during the 1980s.

Called up to the youth team for the mini World Cup in the summer of 1975, he played centre-half during the tournament, which England won, beating Finland 1–0 in the final. After being selected for the U21s for the first time in March 1977, Robson was withdrawn from the squad by his club, West Bromwich Albion, who needed him for a League match against Manchester United at Old Trafford. The game ended 2–2 and Robson was on the scoresheet.

In February 1979, he finally made his England U21 debut in a 1-0 win over Wales at Swansea, albeit as an overage player (he was 22 at the time) and four months later he featured in a B international against Austria. And despite scoring after just five minutes in Klagenfurt, the match was abandoned after 60 minutes with England leading 1-0.

He won four B caps in all, captaining the side in his final game, a 0–0 with Algeria's A team in Algiers on 11 December 1990.

Some ten years earlier, in February 1980, Robson made his full international debut, and his first appearance at Wembley as England beat the Republic of Ireland 2–0 in a European Championship qualifier. His second cap came in the final preparation game for the finals, a 2–1 win over Australia in Sydney, but he didn't feature in the tournament itself, from which England were eliminated in the first round.

In September 1981 Robson marked his 13th cap by scoring his first goal for England, in a 2–1 defeat by Norway in Oslo. This match is remembered mainly for Norwegian commentator Bjorge Lillelien's taunting of England following the final whistle.

Manager Ron Greenwood, who had always been an admirer of Robson, started to play him regularly in midfield, selecting him for the first dozen internationals after the 1980 European Championships had ended, including all eight of the qualifying games for the 1982 World Cup in Spain, through which England earned a place in the finals.

In England's first group game against France in Bilbao, Robson entered the record books where he would remain for 20 years, by scoring after just 27 seconds of the match. He later headed a second goal in the 3-1 victory. His quick-fire opener is now the second-fastest in World Cup finals history, Hakan Sükür having scored after ten seconds for Turkey in the third-place match against South Korea in 2002.

For his achievement, Robson received an inscribed gold watch.

Given the captain's armband for the first time in November 1982, he immediately led England to a 3–0 win over Greece in Salonika. A month later he was brilliant when Luxembourg were hammered 9-0 at Wembley and in November 1984, in an 8–0 World Cup qualifying victory over Turkey in Istanbul, he became the first England captain since Vivian Woodward in 1909 to score a hat-trick at senior level.

Then, when winning his 50th cap against Israel in Tel Aviv in February 1986, Robson celebrated the occasion by scoring both goals in a 2-1 win.

Captain Marvel, as he was nicknamed, then played his part in helping England qualify for the 1986 World Cup in Mexico. Considered at the time by his manager Bobby Robson to be the best player in England, possibly in Europe, his hopes of glory were crushed when he re-aggravated an existing shoulder injury in England's second game of the group stages against Morocco. He took no further part in the tournament and with his fellow midfielder Ray Wilkins also missing (through suspension following a sending-off) England battled on and played well to reach the quarter finals where the 'Hand of God' from Argentina, knocked them out!

Robson's shoulder troubled him for several weeks after the competition and if the truth be known, it lingered on for five years!

Robson was fit enough, however, to lead England through the qualifying stages of the 1988 European Championships, playing exceedingly well as always and scoring a fine individual goal against the eventual champions Holland. But for all his efforts, England went out early after losing all three of their group games.

Robson scored the fastest goal in a Wembley international in December 1989 – netting 38 seconds into the game with Yugoslavia. He later added a second goal in England's 2-1 win, which was, in fact, their 100th victory at Wembley.

His international career continued for another two years. He helped England reach the 1990 World Cup finals, giving him the honour of appearing in three tournaments (1982-86-90), though his role was limited in Italy when once again he suffered an injury, this time in the second match draw with Holland in Cagliari, which kept him out of the team, David Platt taking his place. In fact, it came to light that Robson injured a toe 'messing around' with Paul Gascoigne and he also had a niggling Achilles tendon problem.

Even more ironically, for the second World Cup in succession, England's revamped formation played better without their captain and reached the semi-finals, only to lose on penalties to West Germany in Turin.

Robson 'retired' from the international arena with only Peter Shilton (125), Bobby Moore (108), Bobby Charlton (106) and Billy Wright (105) ahead of him in England's all-time list of cap winners.

As a club player, Robson scored 46 goals in 249 appearances for West Bromwich Albion and 100 in 465 games for Manchester United with whom he gained medals galore, including two

Premiership triumphs, three FA Cup final victories and European Cup Winners' Cup success.

He also played in seven U21 games for his country and when he called it a day as a player in 1997, he had appeared in 832 competitive matches, scoring 172 goals – brilliant.

Robson did reasonably well as manager, leading Middlesbrough into the Premiership twice and taking them to three domestic Cup finals. He also lifted West Brom into the top flight and then pulled off the 'Great Escape' a season later.

Sadly, in March 2011, Bryan was diagnosed with throat cancer and underwent an emergency operation to remove a tumour in Bangkok.

His younger brother, Gary, also played as a professional at The Hawthorns (1981-93).

Robson was the subject on the TV programme This Is Your Life in January 2005.

ROBSON, Sir Robert William 1957-62 (20) (4)

Born: Sacriston, County Durham, 18 February 1933
Died: Newcastle, 31 July 2009
Career: Langley Park Juniors (April 1947), Chester-le-Street FC (briefly, May 1947), Middlesbrough (amateur, August 1948), Southampton (trial, May 1949), Fulham (amateur, April 1950, professional, May 1950), West Bromwich Albion (£25,000, March 1956), Fulham (£20,000, August 1962; released June 1967); assisted Oxford University (trainer-coach, season 1965-66); Vancouver Royals/Canada (player-manager, August 1967), Fulham (manager, January 1968-November 1968), Chelsea (scout, December 1968-January 1969), Ipswich Town (manager, January 1969-July 1982), England B (manager, January 1978-July 1982), England (manager July 1982- July 1990), PSV Eindhoven/Holland (manager, July 1990-June 1992), Sporting Lisbon/Portugal (manager, July 1992-December 1993), FC Porto/Portugal (manager, January 1994-July 1996), CF Barcelona/Spain (manager, July 1996-June 1997, general manager, July 1997-June 1998), PSV Eindhoven (manager, July 1998-June 1999), Newcastle United (manager, September 1999-August 2004); later Ipswich Town (honorary President); Republic of Ireland (support role as International Football Consultant under manager Steve Staunton, January 2006-November 2007); also a former vice-President of the League Managers' Association (a non-executive role).

During his first spell at Fulham, Bobby Robson participated in two ambassadorial Football Association tours, to the West Indies in 1955 and South Africa in 1956. However, it was during his time with West Bromwich Albion that he graduated to the full England squad, winning his first cap against France at Wembley in November 1957, scoring twice in a 4-0 win. Surprisingly he was dropped for the next game against Scotland, Bobby Charlton being preferred in attack. His manager at The Hawthorns, Vic Buckingham, had played for England during the war. He advocated the famous 'push and run' game and was instrumental in switching Robson from an attacking wing-half into a scheming, goalscoring inside-right in an excellent team which included England internationals Ronnie Allen, Ray Barlow, Don Howe and Derek Kevan.

Robson went on to make 20 appearances for his country, being selected ahead of several fine players. He was one of England's best players in Sweden and thought he had scored the winner in

Bryan Robson OBE

Sir Bobby Robson

the final pool 2 game against Russia but his effort was ruled out for handball, when in fact the ball hit his stomach.

He and his colleagues returned home disappointed, as England lost in a group play-off match. Following the World Cup, Robson became an established member of Walter Winterbottom's squad and enjoyed considerable success between October 1960 and May 1961 when he starred in seven victories, including a 9-0 demolition of Luxembourg, a record 9-3 win over Scotland and an 8-0 walloping of Mexico.

He set the ball rolling and the Scots tumbling, as early as the 9th minute by netting with a crisply-struck right-foot shot past 'keeper Frank Haffey from 20 yards and he also scored against the Mexicans.

Selected for the 1962 World Cup in Chile, unfortunately he sustained an ankle injury in a pre-tournament friendly against a Chilean club side which ruled him out of the tournament. Recalled Robson: "I never played for England again...my international career was unfulfilled. It was annoying as I felt I was in excellent form at the time."

During his playing career, Robson scored 151 goals in 673 club appearances, including 141 in 627 first-class games for Fulham and West Brom and 133 in a total of 583 League matches. He gained one B and one U23 cap, represented the Football League on five occasions and also played in the 1962 FA Charity Shield game for the FA against Tottenham Hotspur.

After leaving Fulham (for the second time in 1967) he effectively entered management in Canada. He then returned to London as boss of Fulham and then guided Ipswich Town to FA Cup and UEFA Cup glory in 1978 and 1981 as well as seeing the Tractor Boys finish runners-up in the League Championship. He did well as England's manager, taking the team to the semi-finals of the 1990 World Cup, and after that was also admired for his efforts with PSV Eindhoven (winning the Dutch League title in 1992), Sporting Lisbon, FC Porto (whom he led to victory in the Cup of Portugal and twice winning the Portuguese League title), Barcelona (whom he steered to glory in the Spanish Super Cup, Copa Del Rey and European Cup Winners' Cup) and to a certain extent with Newcastle. Created a Knight Bachelor in 2002, he was inducted as a member of the English football Hall of Fame in 2003, was also made a Freeman of Ipswich and received a special lifetime achievement from UEFA.

From 1991 onwards he suffered recurrent medical problems with cancer and in March 2008, put his name and efforts into the Sir Bobby Robson Foundation, a cancer research charity. In August 2008, his lung cancer was confirmed to be terminal at which he said: "My condition is described as static and has not altered since my last bout of chemotherapy. I am going to die sooner rather than later. But then everyone has to go sometime and I have enjoyed every minute." Sadly he died eleven months later (See under England managers).

ROCASTLE, David Carlyle 1988-92 (14)
Born: Lewisham, London, 2 May 1967
Died: London, 31 March 2001
Career: Roher Manwood's Boys' School/London, Arsenal (schoolboy forms, May 1982, apprentice, June 1983, professional, May 1985), Leeds United (£2m, August 1992), Manchester City (£2m, December 1993), Chelsea (£1.25m, August 1994), Hertha Berlin/Germany (trial), Aberdeen (trial), Norwich City (loan, January-March 1987), Hull City (loan October-November 1997), CF Selangor Sabah/Malaysia (August 1998, retired, May 1999); diagnosed with non-Hodgkin's lymphoma in February 2001.

Arsenal's attacking wide midfielder David 'Rocky' Rocastle made his England debut in a friendly against Denmark at Wembley in September 1988, doing well in the 1-0 win. He was a regular in the team over the next two years, but surprisingly failed to make the squads for either the 1990 World Cup or Euro 92 tournaments, Rangers' Trevor Steven being preferred instead. Still chosen afterwards, he went on to win 14 caps, collecting his last against Brazil in May 1992 when, ironically, he replaced Steven as a second-half substitute. In a fine career, had his best spell with Arsenal (34 goals in 280 outings) with whom he gained a League Cup (1987), two League Championship winner's medals (1989 and 1991) and FA Charity Shield winner's medals.

RODWELL, Jack Anya Nii Mensah 2011-12 (3)
Born: Southport, Merseyside, 11 March 1991
Career: Everton (junior, July 2000, apprentice, May 2007, professional, March 2008), Manchester City (£12m, August 2012)

Born to an English father and a Nigerian mother, Jack Rodwell joined Everton's youth system at the age of seven, making his U18s debut at 14 and his second XI debut at the age of 15. He then broke a record on his senior debut by becoming the youngest player to represent Everton in Europe when he came on as a substitute against the Dutch side, AZ Alkmaar, aged 16 years and 284 days. In March 2008, he came off the bench for his Premiership bow, making his first professional start against Blackburn Rovers five months later. He scored his first senior goal for Everton in an FA Cup-tie against Aston Villa in February 2009 and he hasn't looked back since, celebrating his first goal in the Premiership in a 3-1 win over Manchester United.

Although primarily deployed as a defensive midfielder, Rodwell is just at home as a centre-back while during the second half of the 2009-10 season, he was regularly employed as a more attacking midfielder. Unfortunately he was sent off in the 23rd minute of the 216th Merseyside derby in October 2011 after making what appeared to be a legitimate challenge on Luis Suarez. Everton lodged a successful appeal to the FA and his red card was rescinded.

In December 2006, Rodwell captained the England U16 side and four months later he netted the first winning goal at the 'new' Wembley, in a 1-0 win over Spain. Then, in late March 2008, he scored for England's U17s v. France in a 2008 European U17 Championship qualifier, played for his country's U21 team and gained a call up to the senior squad in November 2011 for the friendlies against Spain and Sweden, making his debut as a second-half substitute for Phil Jones in the 1-0 win over the reigning European and World Champions at Wembley and then starting against the Swedes. He also modelled Great Britain's 2012 Olympic Football kit along with Gareth Bale and Aaron Ramsey. Rodwell is the nephew of the former Blackpool winger, Tony Rodwell.

ROONEY, Wayne Mark 2003 to date (83) (36)
Born: Croxteth, Liverpool, 24 October 1985
Career: De La Salle School/Liverpool, Liverpool Schools, Everton (apprentice, April 2002, professional, February 2003), Manchester United (£25.6m, August 2004)

Wayne Rooney was actually 'signed' by Everton as an associate schoolboy/youth player at the age of 10...he was that good at the time! Progressing through the ranks, he made his Premiership debut in 2002 and then scored a dramatic winning goal against the reigning League champions Arsenal five days before his 17th birthday, thus ending the Gunners' 30-match unbeaten run. He also became the youngest goalscorer in Premier League history, a record since bettered, first by James Milner and then by another Everton player, James Vaughan. At the end of the 2001-02 season the 'star of the future' was named BBC Sports' 'Young Personality of the Year'. Rooney remained at Goodison Park until the summer of 2004 when

Wayne Rooney

he joined Manchester United... and what a tremendous start he made to his Old Trafford career, claiming a hat-trick on his debut in a 6–2 Champions League group win over Fenerbahçe.

Since then, he has helped the Reds win three Premier League titles, the UEFA Champions League, two League Cups and two FA Community Shields, and in 2010 was voted both the PFA and FWA 'Footballer of the Year'.

A stocky, all-action, robust and at times, a seriously controversial and moody striker, he became the youngest player to appear for England at senior level when winning his first cap in a friendly against Australia in February 2003 at the age of 17 years and 111 days. England's youngest debutant prior to Rooney was James Prinsep of Clapham Rovers, who started his international career in April 1879, aged 17 years and 253 days. Soon after that opener against the Aussies, the now loveable and likeable Rooney became the youngest player to score for his country.

Arsenal's Theo Walcott then broke Rooney's appearance record by 36 days in June 2006.

One interesting fact is that Rooney wore a different numbered shirt in each of his first four internationals – nos. 23, 18, 9 and 21 – all as a substitute.

Tasting tournament action for the first time at Euro 2004 during which he become the youngest player ever to appear for England in a major competition (age 18 years and 232 days v. France in Lisbon) he then became the youngest-ever scorer in the same competition when, on 17 June 2004, he netted twice against Switzerland. However, this record was topped four days later by Swiss midfielder Johan Vonlanthen. Rooney later suffered an injury in the quarter-final tie against Portugal as England were eliminated on penalties.

Struck down with a foot injury (a dreaded broken metatarsal) in April 2006, Rooney faced a race to get fit for the 2006 World Cup finals. England's medical staff hastened his recovery with the use of an oxygen tent, thus allowing him to play in the group match against Trinidad & Tobago and in the next match against Sweden. However, he never really got going as England bowed out in the quarter-finals, again on penalty kicks, this time to Portugal, after Rooney had been red-carded in the 62nd minute for stamping on defender Ricardo Carvalho as both attempted to gain possession of the ball. The incident occurred right in front of referee Horacio Elizondo. Rooney's club-mate Cristiano Ronaldo openly protested his actions and was, in turn, pushed by Rooney. Elizondo sent Rooney off, after which Ronaldo was seen winking at his colleagues and coach on the Portuguese bench.

In a statement afterwards, Rooney denied intentionally targeting Carvalho, saying: "I bear no ill feeling to Cristiano but I'm disappointed that he chose to get involved. I suppose I do, though, have to remember that on that particular occasion we were not teammates."

Referee Elizondo confirmed that Rooney was dismissed solely for the infraction on Carvalho.... not for getting involved with Ronaldo! A regular in the England squad since then (when fit and available) he failed miserably at the 2010 World Cup (along with his team-mates) and as he and his team-mates were booed as they walked off the pitch at the of the 0-0 draw in a group game with Algeria, Rooney, in front of the television cameras said: "Nice to see your home fans boo you, that's loyal supporters." He later apologised for the comment, made during another lacklustre tournament for England who were eliminated in the second round.

Then, in a European Championship qualifier in Montenegro on 8 October 2011 he was shown a red card for again losing self-control 17 minutes from time when he kicked out at Miodrag Dzudovic. He received a three-match ban (later reduced to two), which meant he would miss the opening games of Euro 2012. He returned for the third game and scored the only goal versus Ukraine, but was sadly out of touch against Italy in the quarter-finals. Since then, though, he's regained some of his firepower and after scoring against San Marino in October 2012 he moved into fifth place in England's all-time scoring list behind Charlton (49), Lineker (48), Greaves (44) and Owen (40).

No doubt one of the world's greatest footballers – when on song – Rooney who netted 17 times in 77 outings for Everton, had scored 197 goals in exactly 400 appearances for Manchester United (up to the end of the 2012-13 season) and, on average, he's bagged a goal in less than every three games for England – with more to come one hopes!

Rooney has endorsement deals with Nike, Nokia, Ford, Asda and Coca-Cola. He has also appeared on five straight UK-version covers of Electronia Arts' FIFA Series from FIFA 2006 (2005) to FIFA 11 (2010)

ROSE, William Crispin 1883-91 ⑤

Born: St Pancras, London, 3 April 1861
Died: Bordesley Green, Birmingham, 4 February 1937
Career: Small Heath/Birmingham (briefly in season 1881-82), Swifts/London (season 1882-83); represented Wiltshire, Shropshire and London (seasons 1883-85); Preston North End (season 1885-86), Stoke (August 1886), Wolverhampton Wanderers (January 1889), Loughborough Town (July 1894), Wolverhampton Wanderers (August 1895, retired, May 1896); became a licensee in Birmingham and Wolverhampton, and ran a general stors in Bordesley Green, Birmingham, near to the St Andrew's football ground.

Tall, brave and competent in everything he did and rightly regarded as one of the finest goalkeepers of his era, Bill Rose had a 'quiet' international debut when England beat Ireland 8-1 in February 1884, but a month later he played 'exceedingly well' in a 1-0 defeat by Scotland, earning praise from one match reporter who wrote: 'It is difficult to find a better goalkeeper.'

Owing to the presence, and availability, of so many other quality goalkeepers who were around at the same time, Rose collected his five caps over a period of seven years and he never had a bad game, although the opposition in his last three internationals was relatively poor as Wales (4-0) and Ireland (twice by 6-1) were all defeated comfortably.

Rose made over 250 club appearances during his career, 155 for Wolves, with whom he won the FA Cup in 1893 and played in the losing final of 1896.

Rose also attempted to form a Footballers' Union in 1894, of which his club, Wolves, disapproved! He was sacked along with four other players, Dickie Baugh, Harry Allen, George Kinsey and George Swift, the first three England internationals, like Rose.

ROSTRON, Thurston 1880-81 ②

Born: Darwen, Lancs, 21 April 1863
Died: Darwen, 3 July 1891
Career: Helmshore FC (May 1878), Old Wanderers (August 1881), Darwen (August 1882), Great Lever (September 1883), Blackburn Rovers (December 1884-February 1885), Darwen (March 1885 until his death); represented Lancashire at both football and athletics.

'Tot' Rostron was a small, skilful inside-right who could deliver a marvellous 'screw' kick. He won his two caps towards the end of the 1880-81 season against Wales at Blackburn and Scotland at The Oval. He was the second youngest England debutant at that time, behind James Prinsep, at the age of 17 years and 311 days when he lined up against the Welsh, performing reasonably well in a 1-0 defeat. Unfortunately Rostron was completely 'out of his depth' in his next game, a 6-1 defeat by the Scots. He was only 28 when he died suddenly while working as a bowling green keeper.

ROWE, Arthur Sydney 1933-34 ①

Born: Tottenham, London, 1 September 1906
Died: Norbury, South London, 8 November 1993
Career: Tottenham Hotspur (amateur, April 1923), loaned out to Cheshunt & Northfleet (seasons 1923-29), Tottenham Hotspur (professional, May 1929, retired with knee injury, May 1939); coached in Hungary (briefly), Chelmsford City (manager, July 1945), Tottenham Hotspur (manager, May 1949, resigned, through ill-health, May 1955, remained at club for twelve months); West Bromwich Albion (scout, part-time coach, July 1957-October 1958), Crystal Palace (assistant-manager, October 1958, manager, April 1960, resigned November 1962; appointed general manager, March 1963; caretaker-manager January-April 1966, then assistant-manager to May 1967-May 1971); secretary of Football's Hall of Fame (London) until its disbandment in December 1971; Leyton Orient (consultant, January 1972-May 1978), Millwall (consultant, June 1978-May 1979); also served on the Board of Directors at Crystal Palace.

An easy-going centre-half, clever at turning defence into attack, Arthur Rowe always tried to pass the ball rather than hoof it downfield. Injuries affected his game considerably and as a result he gained only one cap for England, in a 4-1 win over France on his home ground, White Hart Lane, in December 1933.
    As manager of Spurs, Rowe signed Alf Ramsey from Southampton and then guided the team to the Second and First Division Championships in 1950 and 1951.

ROWLEY, John Frederick 1948-50 ⑥ ⑥

Born: Wolverhampton, 7 October 1920
Died: Shaw near Oldham, June 1998
Career: Dudley Old Boys, Wolverhampton Wanderers (amateur, November 1935); played for Cradley Heath (loan, September-November 1936) and Bournemouth & Boscombe Athletic (loan, February-April 1937); Manchester United (£3,500, October 1937); guest for Aldershot, Tottenham Hotspur, Wolves and Distillery during World War Two; Plymouth Argyle (player-manager, February 1955, retired as a player, May 1957, remained as manager until March 1960); Oldham Athletic (manager, July 1960-May 1963), Ajax Amsterdam (coach, August 1963-July 1964), Wrexham (manager, January 1966-April 1967), Bradford Park Avenue (manager, March 1967-October 1968), Oldham Athletic (manager, October 1968-December 1969).

Jack Rowley scored with a terrific goal – later described as a 'masterpiece' – on his England debut against Switzerland at Highbury in December 1948, the ball never rising more than a yard off the turf from boot to net. Billy Wright sent a long pass through to him and at first it seemed as though the Manchester United star had lost control when he slipped over. But he landed on one knee, got up quickly and unleashed a thunderous drive from fully 35 yards past the stunned Swiss 'keeper. England went on to win the game 6-0.
    In November 1949, having failed to score against Sweden, Norway and France, hot-shot Rowley netted four times in a 9-2 win over Northern Ireland at Maine Road, two of his strikes flashing past hapless 'keeper Hugh Kelly from 'some distance.' He then scored again in his last international when Italy succumbed 2-0 a fortnight later.
    An aggressive, powerfully-built forward, able to play in any position and nicknamed 'Gunner' because of his lethal, direct shooting, Rowley scored 208 goals in 422 appearances (163 in 317 League games) for Manchester United, bagging a couple in a 4-2 FA Cup final win over Blackpool in 1948. Earlier he helped Wolves win the League War Cup in 1942 and then, in 1952 was in the Manchester United side that won the First Division Championship. Capped once by England during the war, Rowley represented his country in one B international

and also played for the Football League. As a manager he won the Third Division title with Plymouth in 1959 and four years later gained promotion from the same Division with Oldham.
    Rowley's brother, Arthur, who surprisingly never won an England cap, holds the record for scoring most League goals in a career – 434 in 619 games – while playing for West Bromwich Albion, Fulham, Leicester City and Shrewsbury Town (1946-65).

ROWLEY, William 1888-92 ②

Born: Hanley, Stoke-on-Trent, 16 July 1865
Died: Florida, USA, 12 June, 1939
Career: Hanley Orion (as a centre-forward, April 1880), Stoke reserves (August 1883), Port Vale (April 1884), Stoke (professional, August 1886; reclaimed amateur status, May 1893; became player/secretary-manager, May 1895, retired as a player, May 1896, remained as manager to August 1897, then engaged solely as club secretary); Leicester Fosse (secretary-manager, August-October 1898), also represented Staffordshire; later a licensee in Stoke-on-Trent before emigrating to the USA.

Billy Rowley was a very capable goalkeeper, smart, safe and agile, who had few equals. He made 143 appearances for the Potters and played twice for England, in 6-1 and 2-0 wins over Ireland in March 1889 and March 1892, saving Sam Torrans' penalty in the latter. In August 1898, Rowley transferred himself to Leicester Fosse but the forms were not accepted by the Football Association and two months later he was suspended in connection with the matter.

ROYLE, Joseph 1969-73 ⑥ ②

Born: Liverpool, 8 April 1949
Career: Liverpool Schools, Everton (amateur, July 1964, professional, August 1966), Manchester City (£200,000, December 1974), Bristol City (loan, December 1977-May 1978), Norwich City (£60,000, August 1980, retired, injured, April 1982); Oldham Athletic (manager for 12½ years: July 1982 to November 1994), Everton (manager, November 1994, resigned, March 1997), Manchester City (manager, February 1998-May 2001), Ipswich Town (manager, November 2002-May 2006), Oldham Athletic (manager, March-May 2009).

Striker Joe Royle was excellent in the air and pretty useful on the ground! He served Everton very well for a decade, scoring 119 goals in 270 appearances, gaining a League Championship medal in 1970. In fact, he made his League debut for the Merseyside club at the age of 16 and held the record of being the youngest player to appear at senior level for Everton until James Vaughan beat it by 11 days in April, 2005. Royle, who was a League Cup winner with Manchester City in 1976, netted 152 goals in a career total of 473 League games and as an influential manager, guided Oldham into the top flight of English football and to the League Cup final in 1990, won the FA Cup and Charity Shield with Everton in 1995 and steered Manchester City to promotion in 2000. He was in charge of 1,096 matches as a club manager, 608 with Oldham.
    He made his England bow against Malta in a European Championship qualifier in February 1970, but missed out on the summer's World Cup in Mexico, manager Alf Ramsey choosing Jeff Astle, Allan Clarke and Peter Osgood as his main front men.
    Royle's two goals for England were both scored at Wembley - against Yugoslavia in October 1972 (1-1) and Finland in October 1976 (won 2-1). His second was a splendid winning header from Mick Channon's precise centre.
    Royle who represented his country at both schoolboy and youth team levels, also won ten U23 caps and played for the Football League.

RUDDLESDIN, Herod 1903-05 ③
Born: Birdwell, Yorkshire, 11 January 1876
Died: Birdwell, 26 March 1910
Career: Birdwell FC (April 1892), Barnsley (January 1876), Sheffield Wednesday (May 1898, retired, ill-health, December 1906); hoping to make a comeback, he joined Northampton Town in August 1908, but never played a game for the Cobblers.

Herod Ruddlesdin, a neat and clever wing-half with an uncomplicated style, made his first appearance for England, alongside his Sheffield Wednesday team-mate Tom Crawshaw, in a 2–2 draw with Wales in February 1904. Both players did well and retained their places for the next match against Ireland two weeks later, which ended in a 3–1 victory. Ruddlesdin gained his last cap the following year in a 1–0 victory over Scotland at Crystal Palace.
Unfortunately health problems seriously affected his game. He made 286 appearances (7 goals scored) in his ten years with Sheffield Wednesday, helping the Owls win the Second Division Championship in 1900 and two First Division titles, in 1903 and 1904. His brother, Bill, also played for Barnsley.

RUDDOCK, Neil 1994-95 ①
Born: Wandsworth, London, 9 May 1968
Career: Millwall (associate schoolboy forms, July 1981, apprentice, May 1984, professional, March 1986), Tottenham Hotspur (April 1986), Millwall (£300,000, June 1988), Southampton (£250,000, February 1989), Tottenham Hotspur (£75,000, July 1992), Liverpool (£2.5m, July 1993), Queens Park Rangers (loan, March-May 1998), West Ham United (£100,000, July 1998), Crystal Palace (July 2000), Swindon Town (player-coach, August 2001, retired, May 2002); became a radio presenter on TalkSport; is a full-qualified UEFA coach (B badge); team member on BBCs TV show *Question of Sport*; now coaching young footballers, released from Academies, at his own 'Pass and Move' Soccer School.

Teak-tough defender Neil 'Razor' Ruddock, the lovable rogue who promised so much as a young Millwall talent and delivered very little really, gained his one cap against Nigeria in November 1994. He and another debutant, Steve Howey, did reasonably well as a centre-back duo in the 1-0 victory at Wembley, but neither Terry Venables nor his successors selected him again. He also gained one B and four U21 caps, captaining the team against Ireland B at Anfield.
Throughout his career Ruddock battled with weight problems and was often criticised for being unfit; this is often thought to be one of the reasons he only ever gained one full cap.
He made well over 400 appearances at club level (358 in the League) and was a League Cup winner with Liverpool in 1995.

RUDDY, John Thomas Gordon 2012-13 ①
Born: St Ives, Cambridgeshire, 24 October 1986
Career: Cambridge United (junior, August 2002), Manchester United (trial, summer 2004), Cambridge United (professional, September 2004), Everton (£250,000, May 2005), Walsall (loan, September-October 2005), Rushden & Diamonds (loan, November-December 2005), Chester City (loan, December 2005-January 2006), Stockport County (loan, September-December 2006), Wrexham (loan, February-March 2007), Bristol City (loan, April 2007), Stockport County (loan, February-March 2008), Crewe Alexandra (loan, January-May 2009), Motherwell (loan, July 2009-May 2010), Norwich City (£1m, July 2010)

A big, strong goalkeeper, with great agility and anticipation, John Ruddy made his England debut as a second-half substitute for young Jack Butland in the 2-1 friendly win over Italy in Berne, Switzerland

in August 2012. As a teenager he played in 43 senior games for his 'home' club Cambridge United before joining Everton for whom he appeared just once – as a substitute in a Premiership game at Blackburn in February 2006 when Iain Turner was sent off. Over a period of four years, 2005-09, he amassed around 100 appearances as a loanee, spread all over the UK before becoming first-choice 'keeper at Norwich, whom he helped gain promotion to the Premiership in 2011, playing in 45 out of 46 Championship matches.

RUFFELL, James William 1925-30 ⑥
Born: Barnsley, 8 August 1900
Died: Chelmsford, Essex, 5 September 1989
Career: Manor Park School/London, Fullers FC (September 1914); played for Chadwell Heath United, Manor Park Albion, East Ham, Wall End Albion and the Ilford Electricity Board (between August 1915 and May 1918); West Ham United (professional, March 1920), Aldershot (June 1938, retired February 1939); became a brewery representative and later a licensee in Essex.

Jimmy Ruffell played for West Ham in the 1923 FA Cup final defeat by Bolton. Three years later he made his international debut in a 1-0 defeat by Scotland at Manchester, taking over on the left-wing from Jimmy Dimmock. He won another five caps for his country, having a wonderful game against Wales at Stamford Bridge in November 1929 when he assisted in three of the goals in a 6-0 victory. Unfortunately, competition from the likes of Cliff Bastin, Eric Houghton, Billy Smith and Len Barry kept him out of the team. He also represented the Football League on three occasions.
Blessed with exceptional speed, Ruffell was also a brilliant dribbler and given time and space he could destroy a defence! He scored 166 goals in 549 senior appearances for the Hammers – only Bobby Moore has played in more games.

RUSSELL, Bruce Bremner 1882-83 ①
Born: Chiswick, London, 25 August 1859
Died: Basingstoke, 13 May 1942
Career: Cheltenham Public School, Royal Military College, Woolwich/London (August 1876), Royal Engineers (April 1878-May 1907, attaining the rank of Colonel; rejoined the Engineers in 1914, served until 1918).

Bruce Russell was a strong-kicking left-back, highly dependable, who played for the Royal Engineers until he was 45 years of age. He gained his only England cap in a 5-0 win over Wales at The Oval in February 1883 – the 100th player to represent his country.

RUTHERFORD, John 1903-08 ⑪ ③
Born: Percy Main, 12 October 1884
Died: Neasden, London, 21 April 1963
Career: Willington Athletic (November 1899), Newcastle United (£75, January 1902), Woolwich Arsenal (£800, October 1913); guest for Chelsea and Fulham during the war; Stoke (player-manager, March-April 1923), Arsenal (September 1923, retired January 1926); returned to game with Clapton Orient (August 1926, retired permanently, June 1927); Tufnell Park FC (coach, seasons 1926-29); became a licensee in Neasden, London (1932-39).

The recipient of three League Championship winning medals in four years (1905-09), 'Jock' Rutherford won the FA Cup with Newcastle in 1910. A top-quality right-winger, fast, cunning with a powerful shot, he had an excellent playing career, scoring 90 goals in 336 appearances for Newcastle and 31 in 255 for Arsenal. He made an impressive debut for England in a 1-0 win over Scotland in April 1904 and, in fact, was never on the losing side in his eleven internationals. He made two goals in the 7-1 win over Wales in March 1898 and two more in the 6-1 victory over Austria in June 1908 before scoring himself in each of his last three internationals v. Austria, again (won 11-1), Hungary (7-0) and Bohemia (4-0). His inside partner in his last seven England games, from February 1908 when the team scored 39 goals, was Vivian Woodward of Tottenham Hotspur; prior to that it had been Steve Bloomer. Rutherford also represented the Football League and won the London War Cup with Chelsea in April 1919, scoring twice in a 3-1 win over Fulham in the final. He left Stoke after a row with a director. His brother, Sep, played for Portsmouth.

SADLER, David 1967-71 ④

Born: Yalding, Kent, 5 February 1946
Career: Maidstone United (junior, August 1961), Manchester United (apprentice, November 1962, professional, February 1963), Miami Toros, USA (loan, 1973), Preston North End (November 1973, retired, injured, May 1977); helped form and is now secretary of the former Manchester United Players' Association; also worked with Charlton Athletic in corporate hospitality and managed a Building Society in Hale, Greater Manchester.

The versatile David Sadler – who actually started out as a centre-forward - made his England debut at centre-half in place of Jack Charlton in the 2-0 win over Northern Ireland at Wembley in November 1967. He did well and kept his place for the next game against the USSR. A year later he was superb alongside Bobby Moore when England beat East Germany 3-1 at Wembley. However, with so many other exceptionally fine defenders around, all good enough to play international football, Sadler was limited to just four caps. He scored 27 goals in 333 appearances during his time at Old Trafford, helping United win two League Championships (1965 and 1967) and the European Cup (1968). He was also an FA Youth Cup winner and was also capped twice by England at amateur level as a Maidstone player. Bobby Charlton signed him for Preston.

SAGAR, Charles 1899-1902 ② ①

Born: Daisy Hill, Edgworth, Lancashire, 28 March 1878
Died: Bolton, 4 December 1919
Career: Edgworth Rovers (1893), Turton St Anne's/Bolton League (1894), Turton Rovers (1896), Bury (professional, May 1898), Manchester United (May 1905), Atherton FC (June 1907), Haslingden FC (March 1909, retired, injured, May 1910).

Twice an FA Cup winner with Bury, Charlie Sagar was described as being a 'shrewd forward craftsman, employing good footwork.' Able to lead the attack and play inside-left, he scored in his first game for England, sewing up a 2-0 win over Ireland in Dublin in March 1900 and a year later he added a second cap to his collection v. Wales when he played alongside Steve Bloomer in a 0-0 draw at Wrexham.
    Sagar and Wayne Rooney are the only players to have scored a hat-trick on their debuts for Manchester United, Sager v. Bristol City in September 1905 and Rooney v. Fenerbahce in September 2004.

SAGAR, Edward 1935-36 ④

Born: Moorends, Thorne, Doncaster, 7 February 1910
Died: Liverpool, 16 October 1986
Career: Thorne Colliery, Hull City (trial, 1928), Everton (March 1929, retired, May 1953); was landlord of the Blue Anchor pub, Aintree for many years.

Ted Sagar looked slim and underweight to be a goalkeeper, especially in the days when it was legitimate for a tough, tall, robust centre-forward to bounce both 'keeper and ball into the net. But Sagar avoided all this battering, simply because he was highly skilful, had an uncanny ability to judge a high, floating cross from either flank and he was completely unafraid. He was undemonstrative and gave confidence to the defenders in front of him. Spending a record 24 years and five weeks at Goodison Park (the longest any one player has served a club without a break) he made 499 first-class appearances for Everton (463 in the League) and only fellow goalkeeper Neville Southall has more (750). A First Division Championship winner with the Merseysiders in 1932 and 1939, he also gained an FA Cup winner's medal in 1933. It was surprising then to see that he only gained four caps for England – due without doubt to the form showed by Harry Hibbs (at first) and then by Frank Moss and Harry Holdcroft.
    Replacing Hibbs, Sagar made his international debut against Ireland in Belfast in October 1935, pulling off four fine saves in a 3-1 win. He then kept the Scots at bay for long periods in a 1-1 draw at Wembley in April 1936 before suffering two defeats against Austria in Vienna (2-1) and Belgium in Brussels (3-2) over a period of three days early in May, being at fault (by his own admission) for one of the goals in the latter game. Sagar also kept goal for Northern Ireland against Southern Ireland while stationed at Portadown during the Second World War. He also played for a Football League XI during the hostilities. Aged 76 when he died, his ashes were spread in the Gwlady's Street goalmouth at his beloved Goodison Park.

SALAKO, John Akin 1990-92 ⑤

Born: Ibadan, Oyo State, Nigeria, 11 February 1969
Career: Wildernesse School/Sevenoaks, Crystal Palace (apprentice, April 1985, professional, November 1986), Swansea City (loan August-November 1989), Coventry City (£1.5m, August 1995), Bolton Wanderers (free, March 1998), Fulham (free, July 1998), Charlton Athletic (£150,000, August 1999), Reading (£75,000, November 2001), Brentford (briefly, retired, May 2004); now coaches Crystal Palace's U13 team with former team-mate Mark Bright.

Basically a left-winger, John Salako made his England debut as a second-half substitute for David Hirst in the 1-0 win over Australia in Sydney in June 1991. A player with excellent technique, good pace and energy, he added three more caps to his tally on that same tour, playing in the 1-0 and 2-0 wins over New Zealand in Auckland and Wellington (when two other Crystal Palace players took part – Geoff Thomas and Ian Wright) and in the 4-2 victory over Malaysia in Kuala Lumpur, assisting in one of Gary Lineker's four goals. His final international was in the disappointing 1-0 home defeat by Germany at Wembley in the September. After that the preferred wide men were Chris Waddle, Andy Sinton and Tony Daley.
    At club level, Salako amassed a total of 532 appearances (510 in the Football League) and scored 85 goals. He won two First Division Championship medals in 1994 and 2000.

John Salako

SANDFORD, Edward Albert 1931-32 ①

Born: Handsworth, Birmingham, 22 October 1910
Died: Great Barr, Birmingham 12 May 1995
Career: Tantany Athletic, Overend Wesley, Birmingham Carriage Works FC, Smethwick Highfield, West Bromwich Albion (amateur, October 1929, professional, May 1930), Sheffield United (£1,500, March 1939), Morris Commercial FC (April 1941, retired, May 1943); West Bromwich Albion (coach, seasons 1950-57, scout seasons 1961-67); ran a café next to The Hawthorns for 15 years.

A rock-solid performer, firstly at inside-left and then at centre-half, Teddy Sandford was only 20 when he helped West Bromwich Albion complete the unique double of FA Cup and promotion in 1931 and two years later was capped by England against Wales at Wrexham when he deputised for inside-left Tommy Johnson of Everton in a 0-0 draw.

Not at all flashy, he had great stamina and scored 75 goals in 317 appearances during his ten years at The Hawthorns.

SANDILANDS, Rupert Renorden 1891-96 ⑤ ①

Born: Thrapston, Northamptonshire, 7 August 1868
Died: Chatham, Kent, 20 April 1946
Career: Westminster School, Old Westminsters (seasons 1887-89), Corinthians (August 1889-May 1897); also represented London and Kent; worked for the Bank of England for many years

Rupert Sandilands, a well-built winger who loved to 'head for goal' was a fine dribbler with a strong shot who, at times, was too clever for his own colleagues!

He scored on his England debut in a 2-0 win over Wales at Wrexham in March 1892 but with Dennis Hodgetts, John Southworth and Fred Spiksley all eager to cement their position on the left flank, Sandilands managed only four more caps over the next four years. He had an excellent game against Ireland at Villa Park in February 1893 when he assisted in two of the goals in a 6-1 win and also against the Welsh at Cardiff in March 1896 when he was involved in four of the goals in a resounding 9-1 victory.

SANDS, John 1879-80 ①

Born: Nottingham, 4 March 1859
Died: Nottingham, 29 February 1924
Career: Trent Valley (1875), Nottingham Forest (August 1878-May 1883)

Goalkeeper John Sands joined Nottingham Forest as a 19 year-old and in his first season helped the club reach the semi-finals of the FA Cup (lost 2–1 to Old Etonians), repeating the act a year later (beaten 1–0 by Oxford University). Shortly before the 1880 semi-final Sands was selected for his only appearance for England against Wales at Wrexham in mid-March, one of six players who made their debut in this match which resulted in a 3-2 victory. Under pressure during the second-half after left-back Tom Brindle had gone off injured, Sands pulled off a series of fine saves to keep his side in front. Little can be found about his life outside football.

SANSOM, Kenneth Graham 1978-88 ⑧⑥ ①

Born: Camberwell, Surrey, 26 September 1958
Career: Beaufoy School, South London Schools, Surrey Schools, London & District Schools, Leeds United (trial, July-August 1973),

Crystal Palace (apprentice September 1973, professional, December 1975), Arsenal (£1.35m, August 1980, exchange deal involving Clive Allen), Newcastle United (£300,000, December 1988), Queens Park Rangers (£340,000, May 1989), Coventry City (£100,000, March 1991), Everton (free, February 1993), Brentford (free, March 1993), Barnet (August 1993), Partick Thistle (trial, September 1993), Chertsey Town (December 1993), Watford (player-coach, July 1994, assistant-manager, August 1995-February 1996), Croydon FC (season 1996-97); suffered from gambling and alcohol problems, now works as a media pundit and hosts Arsenal legends tours at the Emirates Stadium; now lives in Bromley, Kent.

Confident on the ball, a good tackler, Kenny Sansom was, however, caught out of position from time to time after embarking on one of his sorties downfield, causing some concern in the England defence. Keeping Derek Statham (WBA), a far better attacking player, out of the team, Sansom is England's most-capped full-back of all-time and appeared in his the first international in May 1979, in a 0-0 draw with Wales at Wembley.

Sansom gave away a 'dubious' 75th minute penalty against Romania in Bucharest in October 1980. Iordanescu picked himself up to score from the spot and earn his side a 2-1 win. He was rarely out of the team, however and played in the 1982 World Cup in Spain in which he and England exited in the second group phase.

Sansom continued to produce some excellent performances, both at home and away, perhaps one of his best coming on the day he won his 50th cap against Romania in May 1985 (0-0), one reporter stating 'England's left-back gave a polished display.'

He was still the first-choice left back for the 1986 World Cup in Mexico, playing well in most of the matches up to and including the quarter final defeat by Argentina, the game when he was one of the players 'left behind' by Diego Maradona as he burst from inside his own half to score his second goal without the use of his hand!

One blemish came in the 1-0 defeat by Portugal in Monterrey when his 'horrid' mistake handed Carlos Manuel the winning goal.

In fact, Sansom missed only a handful of England matches in eight years up to 1988, sitting out games so that coaches Ron Greenwood and Bobby Robson could check on potential replacements including the aforementioned Statham, Alan Kennedy and even Nick Pickering in the event of the Arsenal player suffering from a serious injury or chronic loss of form! Neither happened, but the first genuine sign of competition came in 1987, when tough-tackling Nottingham Forest left-back captain Stuart Pearce was given his senior debut against Brazil. He did very well and set up England's goal for Gary Lineker. However, Sansom was still selected as England's regular left-back during the successful qualifying stages for the 1988 European Championships.

The finals themselves were a disaster, for Sansom and England who lost all three group games, including a humiliating 1-0 defeat to the Republic of Ireland whose manager was Jack Charlton, Sansom's horrible error leading to Ray Houghton's headed goal.

Sansom played in the other two group fixtures but after the tournament Pearce replaced him as first-choice left back. So, after nine years and a then record number of caps (86) plus one goal, scored in a World Cup qualifier against Finland in 1984, Sansom's international career ended just a few months before his 30th birthday. His successor (Pearce) went on to win 78 caps and it was not until 2010 that Sansom's record of 86 was surpassed – by Ashley Cole.

Sansom made 867 appearances at club and international level. A League Cup winner with Arsenal in 1987, he also represented England at Youth, U23 and 'B' team levels and was often seen impersonating Norman Wisdom!

SAUNDERS, Frank Etheridge 1887-88 ①

Born: Brighton, 26 August 1864
Died: Fricksburg, Orange River Colony, South Africa, 14 May 1905
Career: Repton School (seasons 1881-84), Cambridge University, Swifts (seasons 1884-88); also played for Corinthians (seasons 1885-91), St Thomas's Hospital, Sussex County; a Licentiate of the Worshipful Society of Apothecaries of London, he emigrated to South Africa in 1900.

A Cambridge University 'blue' in 1885, 1886 and 1887, Frank Saunders occupied all three half-back positions, preferring to play in the middle where his physical strength set him apart from his colleagues. He won his only cap against Wales in February 1888 when he assisted in one of Fred Dewhurst's two goals in a 5-1 win at Crewe.

SAVAGE, Arthur Henry Patrick 1875-76 ①

Born: Sydney, Australia, 18 October 1850
Died: Bayswater, 15 August 1905
Career: Crystal Palace (seasons 1872-78), Surrey County (1870s).

Archie Savage kept goal against Scotland in Glasgow in March 1876. On a waterlogged pitch, he made two early saves (one with his right leg) but was deceived soon afterwards by Angus McKinnon's overhead kick. Later he was beaten by Henry McNeill's close range header (from a free-kick) and left-foot shot from 20 yards by James Heriot. Unfortunately, Savage tended to 'balloon' the ball downfield far too often!

SAYER, James Bernard 1886-87 ①

Born: Mexborough, 11 July 1862
Died: Stoke-on-Trent, 1 February 1922
Career: Mexborough (1878), Heeley FC/Sheffield (1879), Sheffield Wednesday (1880), Sheffield FA (1881), Stoke (August 1883), Mexborough Town (May 1890, retired, injured, April 1894); became secretary and director of Fielding Limited, makers of Devon Pottery, Stoke-on-Trent.

A terrific sprinter, especially over 30-40 yards, Jimmy Sayer was outstanding in his only England game, a 7-0 hammering of Ireland in February 1887. Known as the 'greyhound' he was also aggressive and made over 120 appearances for Stoke at various levels.

SCALES, John Robert 1994-96 ③

Born: Harrogate, Yorkshire, 4 July 1966
Career: Leeds United (apprentice, July 1982, professional, July 1984), Bristol Rovers (free, July 1985), Wimbledon (£70,000, July 1987), Liverpool (£3.5m, September 1994), Tottenham Hotspur (£2.6m, December 1996), Ipswich Town (free, July 2000, retired, April 2001); helped with sponsorship for schools to purchase football kits; runs 'Be Sport', a company promoting sports merchandising; coach for the Danone Nations Cup in 2007 and coached England's beach soccer team; is a member of the Wimbledon Old Players Association and has played for the Dons in Masters' XI football.

John Scales partnered David Unsworth at the heart of the defence when making his England debut in a 2-1 win over Japan at Wembley in June 1995. He played in the next two games against Sweden (3-3) and Brazil (lost 3-1) before slipping out of the limelight and back into club football. Well-equipped and very adaptable, he could also play at full-back and made 412 League appearances, 240 for Wimbledon, helping the Dons cause a major shock by defeating Liverpool 1-0 in the 1988 FA Cup final. He won the League Cup with Spurs in 1995.

SCATTERGOOD, Ernald Oak 1912-13 ①

Born: Riddings, Derbyshire, 29 April 1887
Died: Bradford, 2 July 1932
Career: Alfreton (1890), Riddings St James' (1892), Ripley Athletic (1894), Derby County (£11, April 1907), Bradford Park Avenue (October 1914, retired, July 1925).

Rather on the small side at 5ft 8in, Ernald Scattergood was nevertheless a fine goalkeeper, with an exceptionally powerful 'punch' who made his England debut in place of 'Tim' Williamson in a 4-3 win over Wales at Bristol in March 1913, holding his hand up to two of the visitors' goals, one due to bad judgment, another down to mishandling. With Sam Hardy also available for international duty, he never got another chance.

A Second Division Championship winner with Derby in 1912, he made almost 200 appearances for the Rams in seven years. His son, Ken, went on to keep goal for Stoke and Derby.

SCHOFIELD, Joseph Alfred 1891-95 ③ ①

Born: Hanley, Stoke-on-Trent, 1 January 1871
Died: Hartshill, Stoke-on-Trent, 29 September 1929
Career: Hanley Hope Sunday School FC, Stoke (professional, August 1891, retired, April 1899; joined office staff; appointed club director in 1908; acted as secretary-manager, May 1915-January 1919), Port Vale (secretary-manager, March 1920, then manager, March 1927 until his death).

Within a few months of joining Stoke, outside-left Joe Schofield made a goalscoring debut in a League game against Burnley. A lightly-built player 'of well-balanced judgment', he quickly became a regular in the Potters side and remained so for seven seasons, before ill-health caused his retirement at the age of 28. He made 230 appearances for Stoke and scored 94 goals.

He gained the first of three England caps against Wales in March 1892; scored in his second international against the same country a year later (on his home patch, The Victoria Ground) and made his last appearance against Ireland in March 1895.

As a manager he became the players' 'friend, confidant and counsellor' with a knack of discovering and developing promising players. He sadly died while still in charge at Port Vale who at the time were sitting on top of the League. His win percentage of 49.56% over 266 games is the highest of any manager in Vale's history.

SCHOLES, Paul 1997-2004 ⑥⑥ ⑭

Born: Salford, Greater Manchester, 16 November 1974
Career: Langley Furrows, Great Britain National Schools, Manchester United (apprentice, December 1990, professional, January 1993, retired, May 2011; joined club's coaching staff), returned to playing (January 2012), retired for a second time, (May 2013)

Paul Scholes made his international debut as a second-half substitute for Teddy Sheringham in a 2-1 friendly win over South Africa at Old Trafford in May 1997. He played well, as he did in his next two games, against Italy and Brazil in the Tournoi de France a month later.

Continuing to perform at both club and international level, he was chosen in England's 1998 World Cup squad, and in the group match against Tunisia, it was his late goal which sealed a 2–0 victory. Picking up a pass from Paul Ince just outside the penalty area, he pushed the ball slightly to his right and hit a right-foot shot which curled into the top right-hand corner of 'keeper Chokri El Quaer's net. It was a fine effort. Unfortunately England were eliminated from the competition by Argentina on penalties in the first knock-out round.

In March 1999, Scholes, winning his 16th cap, was a hat-trick hero in a 3-1 European Championship victory over Poland at Wembley and three months later, became the seventh England player to take an early bath in a major international when he was shown the red card in another European Championship qualifier against Sweden for what was described as a 'reckless challenge.'

Some eight months earlier Paul Ince had been dismissed against the same opponents in the same competition!

This indiscretion apart, Scholes had earlier scored both goals in a 2–0 win over Scotland at Hampden Park in the Euro 2000 play-off first leg, sealing a 2–1 aggregate win and qualification for the finals tournament.

Around the turn of the century, Scholes had become a prominent player in England's midfield, an automatic choice by his manager, his game seemed to get better and better and he was duly selected for the 2002 World Cup finals.

However, after that tournament, which ended with a quarter-final defeat by Brazil, Scholes saw his opportunities in the team decline due to Sven-Göran Eriksson choosing to play him out of position on the left side of midfield, so as to accommodate the pairing of Steven Gerrard and Frank Lampard in the centre.

Still annoyed, Scholes announced his retirement from international football in August 2004, citing his family life and his club career with Manchester United as being more important than representing England!

In July 2006, following Eriksson's departure, there was talk of Scholes making himself available for international duty again under new boss Steve McClaren but nothing materialised and four years later, in May 2010, Fabio Capello approached him again, about a return to international football in the run-up to the World Cup in South Africa, but the player rejected the offer, stating he'd prefer to spend time with his family.

Then, in early June, Scholes revealed that Capello had asked him if he would consider playing at international level again, and having the chance of winning the World Cup. Again he said 'no'... yet soon afterwards admitted that he may have made a mistake!

Interestingly, Scholes was substituted 38 times in his 66 games for England – a record.

As a Manchester United player – and a great one at that – Scholes reached two personal milestones for the club in 2010, making his 650th appearance and scoring his 150th goal. The recipient of 11 Premier League, three FA Cup, two League Cup, two UEFA Champions League, one Intercontinental Cup, one FIFA Club World Cup and five FA Community Shield winner's medals, he helped England win the UEFA Under 18 Youth tournament in 1993. A player who never courted much fuss, Scholes was a thoroughbred among professional footballers who will go down as a Manchester United legend, having scored 155 goals (107 in the Premiership) in 718 senior appearances for the club.

Xavi, the Barcelona star and Spanish international, admitted that Scholes was 'a pass master, much appreciated in Spain'... Zinedine Zidane, the former French star, said "P.S. was undoubtedly the greatest midfielder of his generation. He had so much natural ability" ... and Kevin Keegan thought he was 'different to anything else in English football.'

SCOTT, Lawrence 1946-49 (17)

Born: Sheffield, 23 April 1917
Died: Sheffield, 10 July 1999
Career: Attercliffe Church of England School/Sheffield, Sheffield Schools, Edgar Allen's FC/Sheffield (1930), Bradford City (amateur, July 1931, professional, April 1934), Arsenal (February 1937), Crystal Palace (player-manager, October 1951, retired as a player, August 1953, continued as manager to September 1954), Hendon (manager, November 1954-May 1957), Hitchin Town (manager, August 1957-May 1957); became a sales representative for a hardware store owned by the Crystal Palace chairman; later returned to live in Sheffield.

Laurie Scott started out as an outside-right with Bradford City and was at Valley Parade when the Second World War broke out. He served in the RAF as a PT Instructor during the hostilities (playing football whenever and wherever possible) and by the time peace returned he was regarded as one of the country's most assured and composed full-backs. A tiger in the tackle, he used the sliding to good effect and for a little fellow was also exceptionally good in the air. But his real asset was his speed on the turn. He could match the fastest wingers in the game and very rarely was he given a roasting by an opponent.

He made his senior debut for Arsenal against West Ham in an FA Cup-tie in January 1946, with his League baptism following on the first day of the 1946-47 season. He played in his first full international for England against Ireland in September 1946 and the following season helped the Gunners win the First Division title. Unfortunately after that Scott was blighted by injury; he was stricken with a bout of appendicitis in the summer of 1948 and suffered a badly injured knee in the 25th minute of England's 1-0 win over Wales at Villa Park in the November, sidelining him for four months.

He missed the rest of that season and thereafter his appearances for Arsenal were limited for quite some time afterwards. However, he still helped the Gunners win the 1950 FA Cup final and after a successful four-match run in the England B side, he was selected for the 1950 World Cup, at the age of 33. He had not played for his country for two years – and he sat and watched as Alf Ramsey played in every game in Brazil. A re-occurring injury troubled him during the first part of 1950-51 and he was no longer an automatic first-team choice at Highbury. He eventually left the Gunners, having made 316 appearances (all levels). And besides his full England caps, he also appeared in 16 Wartime internationals and in the two unofficial games against Switzerland in Berne and Zurich in July 1945. He also helped Arsenal win the FL (South) Cup in 1943.

Scott had little success as player-manager of Crystal Palace, the club having to apply for re-election to the Football League in May 1954. He twice reached the semi-finals of the FA Amateur Cup with Hitchin Town.

SCOTT, William Reed 1936-37 (1)

Born: Willington Quay, Northumberland, 6 December 1907
Died: London, 18 October 1969
Career: Howden Bridge British Legion, Middlesbrough (professional, July 1927), Brentford (£1,500, May 1932), Aldershot (August 1947), Dover (August 1948, retired May 1949).

A Third Division (S) and then Second Division Championship winner with Brentford in 1933 and 1935, inside-right Billy Scott was a clever player who had a good scoring record throughout his career. One feels that if he had been with a much bigger club he would have gained more than the one England cap he received – that against Wales at Cardiff in October 1936 when he partnered Sammy Crooks of Derby County on the right-wing in a 2-1 defeat. He made a then club record 273 League appearances for Brentford.

SEAMAN, David Andrew, OBE 1988-2003 (75)

Born: Rotherham, 19 September 1963
Career: Kimberworth Comprehensive School/Rotherham, Leeds United (apprentice, September 1979, professional, September 1981), Peterborough United (£4,000, August 1982), Birmingham City (£100,000, October 1984), Queens Park Rangers (£225,000, August 1986), Arsenal (£1.3m, May 1990), Manchester City (free, July 2003, retired, January 2004); Arsenal (assisted on coaching staff, seasons 2005-07).

A commanding figure between the posts, England's second most-capped goalkeeper David Seaman was brave, agile, had a safe pair of hands and rarely had a bad game for England. Indeed, he made very few mistakes on the international circuit... but when he did the whole world was watching!

Probably his worst mistake for his country came against Brazil in the quarter-finals of the 2002 World Cup when he allowed Ronaldinho's looping free-kick to sail over his head and into the net, thus knocking England out of the competition!

He was also at fault against Czechoslovakia in Prague in March 1992 when he fumbled two early efforts and was then responsible for an appalling error which led to a goal on the hour mark. He lost his place as England's number two in the European Championship squad after this horror show. But he battled on and regained his place. However, in his 75th and final international match, he conceded a goal directly from a corner taken by Artim Sakiri in the 2–2 draw which earned him a lot of press criticism. Sven-Göran Eriksson immediately dropped him in favour of David James. And that was the end of his England career.

It must be said in all fairness, that in Euro '96 he was brilliant between the posts as England reached the semi-finals under manager Terry Venables. He saved Gary McAllister's penalty in the 2-0 win over Scotland, made three superb saves in the 4-1 victory over Holland and was majestic again when Spain were defeated 4-2 on penalties. Indeed, in normal play he was par excellence and was 'spot on' in the shoot-out as well. His magnificent form continued against Germany in the semi-final but in the end he slumped to his knees when the penalty shoot-out went in favour of the Germans 6-5.

Making his senior debut for England against Saudi Arabia in Riyadh in November 1988 (in place of Peter Shilton) he did 'okay' in the 1-1 draw but with Chris Woods also challenging for the number one spot, he was third in line for the 1990 World Cup, and in fact, had to wait until September 1993 before making the goalkeeping position his own. In fact, from the day of his debut until he effectively replaced Woods, he won only 10 caps in almost five years during which time England fulfilled 59 internationals.

From 1993 until his last outings for his country, a Euro 2004 qualifier in October 2002 against Macedonia, he was virtually top man. However, in his final match, he let in a goal directly from a corner by Artim Sakiri in the 2–2 draw which earned him a lot of press criticism. Sven-Göran Eriksson immediately dropped him in favour of David James.

At times Seaman was quite brilliant between the posts, producing breathtaking performances against Norway (1994 and 1995), Croatia and Poland (1996), against France and in the World Cup qualifier v. Italy (1997), v. Portugal and Colombia in the World Cup finals of 1998, v. Bulgaria, the Czech Republic and Sweden in 1999, v. Argentina, Germany (twice) and Finland in 2000, v. Greece, Germany (again) and Albania in 2001 and against Nigeria and Argentina in the 2002 World Cup. But it all had to come to an end some time! Seaman, who was 39 years old and 27 days old when he lined up in his last full England game in October 2002 and played under seven different managers, also represented his country in one unofficial, six 'B' and ten U21 internationals and overall at senior level, for clubs and England, he amassed a grand total of 1,050 appearances, 712 in the Football League and Premiership alone. Known for his brilliant handling of the ball, Seaman towards the end of his career, started to sign his autograph 'safe hands.'

He gained all his medals with Arsenal, helped the Gunners win the First Division Championship, the Premiership twice, the FA Cup four times and the League Cup and European Cup Winners' Cup once. He has also appeared on the BBC TV shows *Strictly Come Dancing* and *Dancing on Ice* and received the OBE in 1997.

Seaman played under seven different England managers - Bobby Robson, Graham Taylor, Terry Venables, Glenn Hoddle, Howard Wilkinson, Kevin Keegan and Sven-Göran Eriksson.

SEDDON, James 1922-29 ⑥
Born: Bolton, 20 May 1895
Died: Southport, 21 October 1971
Career: Hamilton Central (1911), Bolton Wanderers (amateur, October 1913, retired, May 1932); Dordrecht, Holland (coach/trainer, July 1932-May 1935); Altrincham (trainer, June 1935-May 1936), Southport (trainer, June 1936-May 1939), Liverpool (training staff, July-September 1939); later assistant-manager, then manager of the Scarisbrick Hotel, Southport.

In 1913, centre-half Jimmy Seddon was standing on the platform of a train station when he was asked to play for Bolton Wanderers reserves who were a man short! He accepted the offer, did well, and was later offered a professional contract before going on to appear in 375 first team games for the club, gaining three FA Cup winner's medals (1923-26-29) and playing in six internationals for England.

Despite contracting the infamous 'trench foot' while serving in the Army during the Great War, at the peak of his career Seddon was a no frills defender who believed in the direct approach... 'clear your lines first, ask questions later.' Replacing George Wilson of Sheffield Wednesday, he made his debut for England against France in Paris in May 1923, having a 'decent game' in a 4-1 win. He played twice more during that end-of-season tour, holding his own in back to back matches against Sweden in Stockholm. His final appearance in an England shirt was in the 1-0 defeat by Scotland at Hampden Park in April 1929 when, wrote Albion in the *Daily Express*: "He was given a hard time by the Newcastle United centre-forward Hughie Gallacher."

SEED, James Marshall 1920-25 ⑤ ①
Born: Blackhill, County Durham, 25 March 1895
Died: 16 July 1966
Career: Whitburn (1911), Sunderland (professional, April 1914), Mid-Rhondda (July 1919), Tottenham Hotspur (February 1920), Sheffield Wednesday (August 1927, retired April 1931); Clapton Orient (secretary-manager, April 1931-May 1933), Charlton Athletic (manager, May 1933-September 1956), Bristol City (advisor to Pat Beasley, January 1957, then acting manager in January 1958), Millwall (manager, January 1958-July 1959; advisor then a director from January 1960 until his death).

Just two months after playing a vital role in Tottenham's 1921 FA Cup final win over Wolverhampton Wanderers, goalscoring inside-right Jimmy Seed won the first of his five England caps against Belgium in Brussels. Unfortunately, despite his excellent club form, and due to the fact that there were several other quality players of similar style around at the same time, he never got a long run in the international side, playing his final game in April 1925. He scored his only England goal in a 6-1 beating of the Belgians in March 1923. Toured South Africa with the FA in 1929, he netted 77 times in his 254 senior appearances for Spurs and 37 in 147 outings for Wednesday with whom he won successive League Championships in 1929 and 1930. During his 23-year reign as Charlton manager, Seed guided the Addicks to the Division Three (S) title in 1935, to promotion from Division Two the following year and to the FA Cup final ten years later. By far the greatest manager in the London club's history, he came so close to winning the League Championship in 1937 and when he left The Valley he was a bitter man!

SETTLE, James 1899-1903 ⑥ ⑥
Born: Millom, Cumberland, June 1875
Died: Lancashire, circa 1950
Career: Bolton junior football, Bolton Wanderers (August 1894), Halliwell (May 1895), Bury (January 1897), Everton (April 1899), Stockport County (May 1908, retired May 1909).

A speedy inside or outside-right with good skill, Jimmy Settle could be rather lethargic and selfish at times and could well have been a sprint champion if he had not taken up football. Three years after moving to Goodison Park he was the First Division's top-scorer in 1901-02 with 18 goals, the lowest seasonal total achieved by a player in the English top-flight to date. He won the FA Cup with the Toffees in 1906 and went on to net 97 times for the Merseysiders in 269 appearances (84 in 237 League games). While at his peak, Settle represented England on six occasions, scoring a hat-trick on his international debut in a 13-2 win over Ireland in February 1899. He netted three more times, twice v. Scotland in 1899 (won 2-1) and 1902 (drew 2-2) and once more v. Ireland, also in 1902 (won 1-0) before collecting his sixth and final cap against the Irish in February 1903 when he and his club-mate Jack Sharp helped set up a goal for Vivian Woodward in a 4-0 win.

SEWELL, John 1951-54 ⑥ ③

Born: Kells Village, Whitehaven, 24 January 1927
Career: Kells Centre, Whitehaven Town; guest for Carlisle United
and Workington during the Second World War; Notts County
(semi-professional, October 1944, professional, August 1945),
Sheffield Wednesday (£34,500, March 1951), Aston Villa (£20,000,
December 1955), Hull City (October 1959), Lusaka City/Zambia
(player-coach, September 1961-May 1964); Zambia national team
(coach, seasons 1968-71), Belgian Congo (coach, July 1972-May
1973); worked as a car salesman for Bristol Street Motors, West
Bridgford, Nottingham (1973-87).

A prolific goalscorer with Notts County where he played alongside
Tommy Lawton, and also with Sheffield Wednesday, who signed him
for a then record fee of £34,500 in 1951, inside-right Jackie Sewell
helped the Magpies win the Third Division (S) Championship in
1950 and Wednesday the Second Division title in 1952. In fact, the
Owls were well on their way to claiming the Second Division crown
again when Sewell was transferred to Aston Villa halfway through
the 1955-56 season. An FA Cup winner in 1957 (with Villa over
double-chasing Manchester United) he continued playing English
club football until 1961, scoring almost 250 goals in a total of 551
matches (228 in 510 League games).

He won the first of his six England caps in a 2-0 win over
Northern Ireland in November 1951 and his last two came against
the mighty Hungarians, who won 6-3 at Wembley in November
1953 and 7-1 in Budapest in May 1954.

His 15th minute equalizer in that historic game at Wembley was,
wrote Geoffrey Green in *The Times*: "...worthy of any international...
his low shot the finale of a rapid incisive counter attack from
defence by Harry Johnston and Stan Mortensen."

Sewell also represented the Football League and toured Canada
and North America with the FA in June 1950, notching six goals in
seven games including a hat-trick in a 9-0 win over Alberta. Sewell
suffered relegation four times, twice with Wednesday and once with
Villa and Hull.

SEWELL, William Ronald 1923-24 ①

Born: Middlesbrough, 19 July 1890
Died: Lincoln, 4 February 1945
Career: Wingate Albion (June 1908), Gainsborough Trinity (July
1911), Burnley (February 1913), Blackburn Rovers (February 1920,
retired May 1927); became a licensee in Lincoln.

Billy Sewell was a well-built, shrewd goalkeeper whose physique
set him in good stead for many years. The dressing room comedian,
he played for Burnley in the 1914 FA Cup final (against Liverpool)
and after the war made 248 appearances for Blackburn as well as
gaining an England cap in a 2-1 defeat by Wales in March 1924 on
his home ground at Ewood Park.

SHACKLETON, Leonard Francis 1948-55 ⑤ ②

Born: Bradford, 3 May 1922
Died: Grange-over-Sands, Cumbria, 28 November 2000
Career: Bradford Schools, Kippax United (August 1937), Arsenal
(groundstaff, August 1938), London Paper Mills (loan, September-
November 1938), Enfield (loan, December 1938-March 1939), Bradford
Park Avenue (professional, December 1940; guest for Bradford City
during the war; Newcastle United (£13,000, October 1946), Sunderland
(£20,050, February 1948, retired, injured ankle, August 1957); became
a journalist; was a director of Fulham FC (albeit briefly); played cricket
for Lidgett Green (Bradford League) and Northumberland (Minor
Counties League); and was a qualified boxing referee.

Nicknamed 'The Clown Prince of Soccer' Len Shackleton
first tasted international football in a Victory international against
Scotland at Hampden Park in April 1946 when 139,468 spectators
saw the Scots win 1-0.

"It wasn't the greatest day of my life, really," said Len. "The
Football Association only allowed me a third class railway ticket to
travel to Glasgow. My match fee was thirty shillings (£1.50) and I
took my wife to the game. She paid her own expenses – rail fare
and hotel accommodation!"

Shackleton was a big personality and prodigious talent. He
made his full international debut in the 0-0 draw with Denmark in
Copenhagen in September 1948. In fact, he thought he had scored
in this game - only for the ball to stick in the mud a few inches
from the goal-line. He then played twice against Wales during the
next twelve months, firstly in a 1-0 Home International victory and
then in a World Cup qualifier in Cardiff when he laid on a goal for
Jackie Milburn after a brilliant 50-yard dribble in England's 4-1
win. Surprisingly, though, it would be another five years before
Shackleton was chosen to represent his country again, this time
for the home clash with Wales at Wembley when he scored in a
3-1 win. Soon afterwards he starred against the reigning World
Champions West Germany at the same venue, once more finding
the net, this time with an impudent chip shot over the 'keeper
Herkenrath in another 3-1 win.

"This was one of his finest displays in an England shirt I have
ever seen. He did little wrong and his goal was brilliant" wrote Rex
Bellamy in the *Birmingham Gazette*.

After this match 'Shacks' was given a third-class rail ticket for
the overnight sleeper back to Sunderland. He said to the bowler-
hatted man who handed him the ticket: "Couldn't you raise enough
money for a first-class one?" The FA official replied, "Sorry, but all
the first-class tickets have been sold." When Shackleton got on the
train at Kings Cross, he had no problem whatsoever in transferring
into a first-class compartment.

"There was plenty of space and I was happy to pay the five pounds difference…but by the time I had paid my taxes and expenses I was left with just £20 out of my £50 match fee," he said. The gate receipts for the England-Germany game amounted to £50,000…and Shackleton remarked: "We footballers, who had drawn the crowd and the money, were considered third-class by those blinkered fools who ran the Football Association."

Why wasn't he selected more times for his country? He had his own opinion. "I was told, off the record, that my prolonged absence was caused by selectors' reluctance to play individualists. It was considered, I feel, an unforgivable sin for a player like Stan Matthews or myself to beat an opponent by employing any skill we might possess as ball players."

Yet England eventually, yet grudgingly, did select individualists - far too late though for the likes of Shackleton to benefit.

Shackleton was a touch-player, an entertainer, two-footed with wonderful ball control but was reluctant to track-back and tackle. He certainly loved playing to the gallery and often poked fun at people in high places. "He had nearly everything as an inside-forward except the ability, or inclination, to get stuck in" wrote Maurice Edelston and Terence Delaney, co-authors of *Masters of Soccer*.

In his book, entitled *The Clown Prince of Soccer* published in 1955, Shackleton upset a lot of football folk, including the England selectors, when one page with the heading 'The Average Director's Knowledge of Football' was left completely blank.

A schoolboy international (capped against Ireland, Scotland and Wales in 1936) Shackleton also played for England 'B', the FA and twice represented the Football League (1948-49). He accumulated a supreme record with Bradford for whom he netted 170 goals in 217 wartime games plus four in seven League outings and one in his eight FA Cup matches. He followed up with 29 goals in 64 appearances for Newcastle, scoring a double hat-trick (six goals) on his Geordies League debut in a 13-0 home win over Newport County in 1946. He then proceeded to assemble some exquisite statistics for Sunderland – bagging another 100 goals in 348 League and FA Cup outings during his near 10-year spell at Roker Park… and all this after being released by Arsenal!

Shackleton was a truly great footballer…I know, I saw him play! Journalist Malcolm Hartley, who compiled a history of Bradford Park Avenue, confirmed this about Shackleton: "Apart from the adhesive ball control and breathtaking body swerve, 'Shack' could hit a ball. His slender legs could crack the ball like a Bofors gun."

Tom Finney considered him to be 'a footballing genius who at times could make the ball talk.'

And Stanley Matthews thought he was a 'complete showman, blessed with every trick in the book' while 'his' England manager Walter Winterbottom admitted that during the early 1950s, he made many unsuccessful attempts to 'tame' him for the England set up. "If only he had come half-way to meet the needs of the team, there wouldn't be many to touch him," he said.

On Christmas Day 1940, Shackleton played for Bradford Park Avenue in the morning and for Bradford City in the afternoon (scoring twice v. Huddersfield Town). He simply loved his football!

Top UK musical group Chumbawamba included a song entitled "Song for Len Shackleton" on their 2002 album *Readymades*.

SHARP, John 1902-05 ②

Born: Hereford, 15 February 1878
Died: Wavertree, Liverpool, 27 January 1938
Career: Clyde Henry School/Hereford, Violet Boys' Club (seasons 1892-95), Hereford Thistle (August 1895), Aston Villa (£100, April 1897), Everton (£500, August 1899, retired, injured, May 1910); also played cricket for Lancashire, Herefordshire and England; by profession he was a sports outfitter in Liverpool who became a

millionaire; along with his brother Bert (also ex-Villa and Everton) was a director of Everton FC, August 1922-August 1932, later Chairman at Goodison Park (until his death).

Jack Sharp was a short, thick-set outside-right who played in two FA Cup finals for Everton, winning in 1906, losing in 1907. During the first decade of the 20th century, he was highly-rated in the Football League, yet he only played for England twice, against Ireland in February 1903 and Scotland in April 1905, and also represented the Football League on three occasions. Very quick, clever and unusually tough for a winger, he scored almost 100 goals during a career total of 366 senior appearances.

As a cricketer between 1899 and 1925, he amassed more than 22,700 runs, including 38 centuries, took 440 wickets and held 223 catches. He played in three Test Matches for England against Australia in 1909, hitting 105 at The Oval.

SHARPE, Lee Stuart 1990-94 ⑧

Born: Halesowen, Worcs, 27 May 1971
Career: Edghill School/Kinver, Hagley High School/Halesowen & Stourbridge Schools, Birmingham City (schoolboy forms, July 1986), Torquay United (apprentice, August 1987, professional, May 1988), Manchester United (£185,000, June 1988), Leeds United (£4.5m, August 1996), Sampdoria/Italy (loan December 1998-January 1999), Bradford City (loan, March 1999, signed for £200,000, May 1999), Portsmouth (loan, February-May 2001), Grimsby Town (trial, season 2001-02), Exeter City (free, August 2002), FC Grindourink/Iceland (March-April 2003), Hoobrook Crown FC/Kidderminster (briefly), Garforth Town (September 2004, retired, injured, May 2005); football pundit for ESPN Star and *Match of the Day 2*; took part in TV's *Dancing On Ice*, *Coronation Street* and *Celebrity Love Island*; now a respected after-dinner speaker.

One of the few England internationals to play for two major Devon clubs (Torquay and Exeter) wide-man Lee Sharp had an excellent career which spanned 17 years during which time he scored over 40 goals in 352 first-class appearances, including 35 in 324 League games.

In March 1991, when he gained his first full cap (v. the Republic of Ireland), he became the youngest player to appear for England since Duncan Edwards in 1955. Initially he looked the part, but in the end managed only eight appearances for his country – perhaps because there were several players similar to Sharpe who could do the same job, among them John Barnes, Tony Daley, John Salako and Andy Sinton, plus the fact he suffered with injuries!

Voted PFA 'Young Player of the Year' in 1991 Sharpe also played in one 'B' and eight U21 internationals. He helped Manchester United win the European Cup Winners' Cup, the League Cup and three Premiership titles.

SHAW, George Edward 1931-32 ①

Born: Swinton, 13 October 1899
Died: Doncaster, 10 March 1973
Career: Swinton Schools, Bolton-on-Deane (1914), Rossington Main Colliery (1915), Doncaster Rovers (professional, August 1919), Gillingham (March 1920), Huddersfield Town (£1,000, February 1924), West Bromwich Albion (£4,100, November 1926), Stalybridge Celtic (player-manager, May 1938), Worcester City (player-manager, March 1939), FC Floriana/Malta (player-manager/coach, August 1948-June 1951); later worked at Hamworth Colliery near Doncaster.

Right-back George Shaw made 29 appearances for Huddersfield and 425 for WBA, missing only five out of 306 League games for the Baggies between December 1926 and January 1934.

Nicknamed 'Teapot', the 'Singer' and 'Cocky' he helped the Terriers win three successive First Division championships (1924-25-26) and was a key member of West Brom's promotion and FA Cup winning team of 1931 and he also played in the 1935 Cup final. A wonderful volleyer and expert penalty-taker, he formed a terrific partnership with Bert Trentham and then Bob Finch at The Hawthorns. Replacing the injured Roy Goodall, he gained his only England cap in the 3-0 home international victory over Scotland at Wembley in April 1932. Playing in front of his club goalkeeper Harold Pearson, he had a solid game against the brilliant left-winger Alan Morton who was playing his last game for his country. James Freeman, reporting for the *Daily Mail*, wrote: "Shaw played with fine keenness and cleared his lines accurately."

Shaw also represented the Football League and went on the FA tours to Belgium, France and Spain in 1929 and Canada in 1931. He won the Maltese Cup twice with Floriana.

SHAW, Graham Laurence 1958-63 ⑤
Born: Sheffield, 9 July 1934
Career: Southey Green Secondary School/Sheffield, Oaks Fold FC (1950), Sheffield United (professional, July 1951), Doncaster Rovers (September 1967), Scarborough (player-manager, March 1968-January 1969); was an ABA boxing champion as a teenager.

Replacing Tommy Banks at left-back, Graham Shaw made an impressive international debut in England's 5-0 win over the USSR at Wembley in October 1958. A firm tackler, dependable and totally committed, he played in the next three games as Don Howe's partner and collected his fifth and final cap against Wales in November 1962 when he replaced the injured Ray Wilson in a 4-0 home win.

Basically a one-club footballer, he served Sheffield United for 16 years, making his League debut in January 1952, in the 'Steel City' derby, when a post-war record crowd of 65,384 packed into Hillsborough to witness the 3-1 victory achieved by the Blades. He went on to amass a total of 498 senior appearances for the Blades, gaining a Second Division championship winner's medal in 1953 along with his brother Joe who was the team's centre-half. Shaw didn't score too many goals, 15 in all, but one is worth recalling, a well-struck 50-yard free-kick while playing for Sheffield United against Portsmouth in September 1960.

SHAWCROSS, Ryan 2012-13 ①
Born: Chester, 4 October 1987
Career: Elfed High School, Buckly Town, Flintshire Boys, Wrexham (trial, March 2003), Manchester United (trial, April 2003, signed as a trainee June 2003, professional, July 2006), Royal Antwerp/Belgium (loan, January-May 2007), Stoke City (loan, August 2007, signed permanently for £1 million, January 2008; agreed new deal, January 2013)

The tall Stoke City defender made his England debut as a second-half substitute for Steven Caulker in the 4-2 defeat by Sweden in Stockholm in November 2012. And he admitted afterwards that he was at fault for the second goal scored by Zlatan Ibrahimovic, who went on to add two more to finish up with a four-timer. Previously named in Roy Hodgson's squad for the World Cup qualifiers against Poland and San Marino, he deservedly won his first cap after some impressive performances at the heart of the Potters' defence. Shawcross, who represented Wales at schoolboy level and also played twice for England's U21 team, is renowned for his tough tackling and it was his challenges on the Arsenal duo of Emmanuel Adebayor and Aaron Ramsey in 2008 and 2010 respectively which hit the headlines of the sporting press. In fact, Ramsey broke his tibia and fibula in the same leg but afterwards said that Shawcross's challenge "…was not malicious, just mistimed."

SHEA, Daniel 1914-15 ②
Born: Wapping, London, 6 November 1887
Died: Wapping, London, 25 December 1960
Career: Manor Park Albion, Builders Arms (London pub team), West Ham United (professional, November 1907), Blackburn Rovers (£2,000, January 1913), Celtic (briefly), West Ham United (May, 1920), Fulham (November 1920), Coventry City (May 1923), Clapton Orient (March 1925), Sheppey United (October 1926, retired May 1927); coached Zurich FC/Switzerland (1927-29); became a London licensee.

An artful schemer and delicate dribbler, Danny Shea had the knack of wheeling suddenly when near goal and unleashing a thunderbolt shot. He scored 103 goals in 166 games for West Ham and 61 in 97 games for Blackburn, helping Rovers win their second League Championship in 1914, the same year he gained his first England cap against Ireland. Despite having 'an average game' in a surprise 3-0 defeat at Middlesbrough, he retained his place for the game against Wales. However, the outbreak of the First World War brought an abrupt end to Shea's international career. He continued to play whenever possible during the hostilities and after brief spells with Celtic and West Ham (again) he netted 23 goals in 100 appearances for Fulham.

SHEARER, Alan, OBE ㉖ ㉚
Born: Newcastle, 13 August 1970
Career: Newcastle & Northumberland Schools, Southampton (apprentice, July 1986, professional, April 1988), Blackburn Rovers (£3.6m, July 1992), Newcastle United (£15m, July 1996, retired, May 2006; acted as caretaker-manager, for 54 days, April-May 2009); worked in the media and is now a respected pundit on BBC's *Match of the Day* programme.

Angular, combative, single-minded, decidedly quick over short distances, fearless in a 50-50 challenge, cool and composed when in possession, strong in the air and deadly with his finishing, especially with his right-foot rockets, Alan Shearer was, without doubt, one of the best strikers in world football during the early-to-mid 1990s. His record proves that – 379 goals in 734 club appearances alone!

His international career began in 1990 when he was called up to the England U21 squad by manager Dave Sexton. During his time with the squad, he scored 13 times in 11 games; a joint record return (with Francis Jeffers) which is still to be beaten.

Shearer's goals at this level, coupled with those for his club, meant he was soon promoted to the senior squad by coach Graham Taylor, marking his debut with a 44th minute goal in a 2–0 win over France at Wembley in February 1992.

A month later he made his only appearance for his country's B team and although Gary Lineker announced his retirement, Shearer played only intermittently in the qualifying campaign for the 1994 World Cup due to injury as England failed to reach the finals in USA. Thankfully, Euro 96 was a more positive experience for both Shearer and England, who being the host nation had a free passage into the finals.

Shearer – known as 'Big Al' – had not scored in 12 games in the 21 months prior to the Championships but he found the net in the 22nd minute of the first game against Switzerland (1-1), scored in the following game against Scotland (won 2-0) and netted twice in a splendid 4–1 victory over the Netherlands in the third game as England progressed to the next stage in front of their own fans at Wembley.

In the quarter finals, England were outplayed by Spain but scraped through on penalties after a goalless draw. Shearer smashed in the first spot-kick to send England on their way to a semi-final clash with Germany. Shearer headed his team into the lead after just three minutes, but the Germans quickly equalised and the match

went to penalties again. This time, Germany won the shoot-out; despite another successful 12-yard kick from Shearer, whose tally of five goals made him the competition's top scorer, and together with his England colleagues David Seaman and Steve McManaman, he was named in the official UEFA team of the tournament.

Named captain by the new England manager Glenn Hoddle for the 1998 World Cup qualifier against Moldova in September 1996, he retained the armband for the next game against Poland when he scored twice in a 2-0 win.

England then beat Georgia twice, Moldova and Poland again and lost and drew with Italy to qualify for the finals in France. However, Shearer was sidelined for much of season 1997–98 but recovered to play in the World Cup with Michael Owen as his strike partner. Shearer scored England's first goal of the tournament, in a 2–0 win over Tunisia and later an equaliser from the penalty-spot against Argentina in the second round before David Beckham was sent off. In the final minutes of the game Sol Campbell headed in what could have been the winning goal only for the referee to disallow it due to Shearer having elbowed goalkeeper Carlos Roa. With the score level at 2-2, the game went to penalties. Shearer scored again, but England were eliminated after David Batty saw his effort saved. This was Shearer's only World Cup tournament.

In September 1999, Shearer scored his only international hat-trick, in a Euro 2000 qualifier against Luxembourg. This helped England reach a play-off against Scotland which England won over two legs, thus qualifying for the European Championships. By now, Shearer was fast-approaching his 30th birthday and he publicly announced that he intended to retire from international football after Euro 2000.

He failed to score in an opening 3–2 defeat by Portugal but struck the winner against Germany in Chaleroi – England's first win over the arch-rivals since the 1966 World Cup final. To remain in the tournament, only a draw was required against Romania in the final group match but after Shearer had scored a penalty, Romania hit back to win 3–2 and England's tournament was over... along with Shearer's international career.

In his 63 internationals, he captained the team 34 times, scored thirty goals, placing him joint-fifth in England's all-time goalscoring list, and missed only one penalty, striking a post in a 2-0 World Cup qualifier victory in Poland in May 1997.

Shearer remained in international retirement despite speculation of a return during the 2002 World Cup and 2004 European Championship campaigns, and he further declined an offer to be assistant-manager to Steve McClaren after the 2006 World Cup - a position ultimately filled by Terry Venables.

Shearer became the youngest player (at 17 years, 240 days) to score a hat-trick in the First Division when he obliged with a treble for Southampton against Arsenal in April 1988 and when playing for Blackburn against Spurs in December 2003 he had the pleasure of netting the 12,000th goal in Premiership football.

He went on to net 43 goals in 158 appearances for Saints, followed up with 130 in 171 first-class outings for Blackburn whom he helped win the Premiership title in 1995, and rounded things off by bagging a club record 206 goals in 404 games for Newcastle.

The first player to reach the milestone of 100 Premiership goals, he also set a new record by notching five hat-tricks in one season.

He claimed 13 goals in eleven U21 internationals, was awarded the OBE in 2001 (for services to football) and was also the first player to score a century of Premiership goals for two different clubs: Blackburn and Newcastle.

Named FWA 'Player of the Year' in 1994 and the PFA 'Footballer of the Year' in 1995 and 1997, Shearer was voted Premiership 'Player of the Decade' by the PFA in 2003. Other awards and records include: Golden Boot Winner at Euro 96 (five goals); UEFA Cup top-scorer in 2003–04, 2004–05; scorer of most Premiership goals in total (260); Premier League Golden Boot winner in 1995, 1996 and 1997; is joint record holder with Andy Cole for scoring most Premier League goals in a 42-game season, 34 in 1994–95; he has netted more European goals for Newcastle than any other player (30); was inducted into the English Football Hall of Fame in 2004... and he's listed among Pele's greatest living footballers.

After quitting the game, Shearer raised substantial amounts of money for various national and local charities, both within and outside of sports. He is also a deputy Lieutenant of Northumberland, a Freeman of Newcastle-upon-Tyne and an honorary Doctor of Civil Law of Northumbria and Newcastle universities.

- His own testimonial match in 2006, watched by 54,000 at St James' Park, raised £1.64m for 14 worthwhile causes, including a donation of £400,000 to the NSPCC and £320,000 towards the completion of the 'Alan Shearer Centre', a respite care facility based in West Denton, Newcastle.
- In October 2006, he became an ambassador for the NSPCC, describing it as "The kick-off to my most important role yet."
- He has also worked with the charity 'The Dream Foundation' and in 2006, founded the 'Alan Shearer Academy Scholarship' to aid the development of promising young players in the region.
- In 2008, he raised over £300,000 for Sport Relief by cycling the full length of Great Britain, with fellow BBC *Match of the Day* presenter Adrian Chiles.
- In September 2008, Shearer scored twice in a Soccer Aid match featuring celebrities and ex-players at Wembley Stadium to raise money for UNICEF.

SHELLITO, Kenneth John 1962-63 ①

Born: East Ham, London, 18 April 1940
Career: Sutton School/Hornchurch, London & Essex Schools, Chelsea (junior, March 1956, professional April 1957, retired, injured, January 1969; appointed youth team coach at Stamford Bridge: June 1969; youth team manager, December 1969; first team manager, July 1977-December 1978; Queens Park Rangers (coach/assistant-manager, May 1979-April 1980), Crystal Palace (coach, July 1980-May 1981), Preston North End (assistant-manager, July-December 1981), Crystal Palace (assistant-manager, June 1982-November 1983), Wolverhampton Wanderers (coach, January-February 1985), Cambridge United (manager, March-December 1985); coached in Malaysia (seasons 1986-89), Tonbridge Wells (general manager, season 1990-91); Kuala Lumpur (coach, season 1994-95), Perak FA (coach, seasons 1995-97), Sabah FA (season 1998-99); a Malaysian permanent resident, he now works in a coaching role for the Asian Football Confederation, based in Kuala Lumpur.

Full-back Ken Shellito made an 'impressive' international debut in the 4-2 win over Czechoslovakia in Bratislava in May 1963. A beautifully balanced player who could match the speed of the quickest winger, he was forced to retire prematurely with a knee injury after just 123 games for Chelsea. An FA Youth Cup winner (v. Wolves) in 1958, he also played in three U23 internationals.

Alan Shearer OBE

SHELTON, Alfred 1888-92 ⑥

Born: Nottingham, 11 September 1865
Died: Nottingham, 24 July 1923
Career: Notts Rangers (amateur, August 1882), Notts County (July 1888), Loughborough Town (May 1896), Ilkeston (July 1897; reinstated as an amateur in June 1898); later employed at Cammell Laird Works, Nottingham; sadly killed when a crane collapsed.

An FA Cup runner-up with Notts County in 1891 and a winner in 1894, Alf Shelton was a hard-working, industrious left-half with a big heart. Never on the losing side in his six internationals, he had an excellent debut in a 6-1 win over Ireland in March 1889, and also played well in the 4-1 wins over Wales in March 1891 and Scotland at Ibrox Park in April 1892, having a hand in John Goodall's 25th minute goal in the latter.

SHELTON, Charles 1887-88 ①

Born: Nottingham, 22 January 1864
Died: Nottingham, 23 February 1899
Career: Notts Rangers (August 1881), Notts County (July 1888, retired through ill-health, May 1892).

A typically strong half-back who enjoyed playing in the middle, Charlie Shelton had a 'solid game' when making his only England appearance in a resounding 5-1 win over Ireland in March 1888. Elder brother of Alf (above) both men played with future England international Fred Geary at Notts Rangers.

SHELVEY, Jonjo 2012-13 ①

Born: Romford, Essex, 27 February 1992
Career: Arsenal (youth team), West Ham United (youth team), Charlton Athletic (apprentice, July 2007, professional, February 2009), Liverpool (£1.7m, May 2010), Blackpool (loan, September-November 2011).

A well-balanced, hard-working, goalscoring midfielder who played for and captained England's U16, U17, U19 and U21 teams before winning his first senior cap as a second-half substitute in the World Cup qualifier against San Marino in October 2012.

He became Charlton's youngest-ever player, aged 16 years and 59 days old when he made his League debut against Barnsley in April 2008, beating the previous record set by Paul Konchesky. Nine months later he became the London club's youngest-ever goalcorer when he netted against Norwich City in a 3rd round FA Cup-tie. Shelvey suffers from Alopecia Totalis – which has resulted in a complete loss of hair.

SHEPHERD, Albert 1905-11 ② ②

Born: Great Lever near Bolton, 10 September 1885
Died: Bolton, 8 November 1929
Career: Bolton Schools, St Mark's Sunday School/Bolton, Bolton Temperance, Bolton Wanderers (amateur, July 1902), Bolton St Luke's (December 1902), Blackburn Rovers (amateur, August 1903), Bolton Wanderers (professional, July 1904), Newcastle United (£850, November 1908), Bradford City (£1,500, July 1914, retired, May 1917); became a licensee in Bolton.

A Football League Championship winner with Newcastle in 1909, dashing centre-forward Albert Shepherd then helped the Magpies win the FA Cup the following year but withdrew from the 1911 final through injury – and how Newcastle missed him!

The scorer of a late consolation goal on his international debut in a 2-1 defeat by Scotland in April 1906, he didn't have a good game at Hampden Park, the *Daily Record* stating: "Raisbeck practically blotted out the Saxon centre (Shepherd)."

On the mark in his second game five years later, to earn a 2-1 win over Ireland in February 1911, he was unfortunate that there were so many players of similar stature and style around at the same time, that he was virtually fourth choice in the England pecking order.

He scored four times for the Football League XI in a 6-2 win over the Scottish League in March 1906.

SHERINGHAM, Edward Paul, MBE (51) ⑪

Born: Higham's Park, 2 April 1966
Career: Leytonstone & Ilford FC, Tottenham Hotspur (trial), Leyton Orient (trial), Crystal Palace (junior), Millwall (apprentice, June 1982, professional, January 1984), Aldershot (loan, February-April 1985), Djurgärdens IF/Sweden (loan, late 1985), Nottingham Forest (£2m, July 1991), Tottenham Hotspur (£2.1m, August 1992), Manchester United (£3.5m, July 1997), Tottenham Hotspur (free, July 2001), Portsmouth (free, June 2003), West Ham United (July 2004), Colchester United (July 2007-May 2008); out of football for 16 months; Beckenham Town (briefly, September 2009).

Teddy Sheringham was superb at times alongside Alan Shearer in the England team, and indeed, he was pretty useful with several other main strikers as well! He scored some wonderful goals for club and country, with his deadly right foot and he was not bad with his head either. Something of a late developer on the international scene, he did not win his first cap until the age of 27 in a World Cup qualifier against Poland in May 1993.

However, he had to wait two years before netting his first England goal - a beauty in the 3-3 draw with Sweden at Elland Road in June 1995.

Under the reign of manager Terry Venables (1994–96) Sheringham was the preferred strike partner for Shearer yet during this time there was a wealth of talented marksmen to choose from, among them Andy Cole, Ian Wright, Robbie Fowler and Les Ferdinand. The Shearer-Sheringham partnership became famous at international level, as they complemented each other's strengths: Shearer was the out-and-out goalscorer, big, strong and powerful, Sheringham just 'dropped off' his colleague, finding spaces, creating play and providing key passes, forming a superb link between attack and midfield. The pairing came to be known as 'The SAS' ('Shearer And Sheringham') although Shearer was a member of another 'SAS' at Blackburn, himself and Chris Sutton.

Sheringham's most successful time in the England team came in Euro 96. He was terrific in the 4–1 victory over Holland in the opening group stage, scoring twice against one of the strongest teams in the tournament. Despite being knocked out in the semi-finals, many believed that that squad of players such as Sheringham and his contemporaries including Shearer (of course), Paul Gascoigne, Steve McManaman, Tony Adams, Paul Ince and goalkeeper David Seaman had done the nation proud.

Sheringham continued to be a first choice selection under the new England boss Glenn Hoddle (1996–99) but after that he was pressed all the way by new teenage superstar Michael Owen. Although he began the 1998 World Cup with Owen on the bench, Sheringham's front line international career was slowly coming to an end.

He was not selected at all for the 2000 European Championships by manager Kevin Keegan but the retirement from international football of Shearer, who was at the time four years younger than Sheringham, after that tournament and the arrival of another new

Manchester United as they won three Premierships crowns, 1999-2000-2001, the FA Cup in 1999, the FA Charity Shield in 1997, the European Champions League in 1999 (when he scored a dramatic late equaliser against Bayern Munich in the final) and the Intercontinental Cup, also in 1999.

In 1992-93, Sheringham won the Barclays League 'Golden Boot' and was awarded the MBE for services to football in June 2003.

In season 2011-12 his son, Charlie, was on the books of AFC Bournemouth.

Upon his retirement from professional football in 2008, Sheringham has been a noticeable figure on the world poker scene, playing in various competitions worldwide. He made the final table in the €5,000 No Limit Hold 'em Main Event in the EPT Vilamoura, finishing 5th out of a field of 384 players, winning €93,121. He vowed to donate his winnings to charity, though later admitted to the Daily Mail he decided to put the money towards a new Aston Martin DB9 he had been shown at a local dealer.

SHERWOOD, Timothy Alan 1998-99 ③
Born: St Albans, Herts, 6 February 1969
Career: Watford (apprentice, April 1985, professional, February 1987), Norwich City (£175,000, July 1989), Blackburn Rovers (£500,000, February 1992), Tottenham Hotspur (£3.8m, February 1999), Portsmouth (free, January 2003), Coventry City (free, August 2004, retired, injured, May 2005); Tottenham Hotspur (part-time coach, then technical co-ordinator and assistant first-team coach, seasons 2008-11).

Hard-working midfielder Tim Sherwood was handed his England debut at the age of 30 by manager Kevin Keegan in a 3-1 European Championship qualifying victory over Poland at Wembley in March 1999. His other two caps followed soon afterwards, against Hungary in a friendly (1-1) and Sweden in another 'Euro' qualifier (0-0). At club level he amassed a total of 550 appearances (483 at League level) and scored 65 goals. He helped Blackburn win the Premiership title in 1995 and Portsmouth the League Championship in 2003. He also played in one B and four U21 internationals.

SHILTON, Peter Leslie, MBE, OBE 1970-90 ⑫⑤
Born: Leicester, 18 September 1949
Career: King Richard III Boys School/Leicester, Leicester & District Schools, Leicester City (apprentice, June 1964, professional, September 1966), Stoke City (£325,000, November 1974), Nottingham Forest (£270,000, September 1977), Southampton (£300,000, August 1992), Derby County (£90,000, July 1997), Plymouth Argyle (player-manager, March 1992-December 1994), Wimbledon (non-contract, January-February 1995), Bolton Wanderers (non-contract, March 1995), Coventry City (free, July 1995), West Ham United (free, January 1996), Leyton Orient (November 1996, retired, May 1997).

By far England's most capped player to date, and the second oldest (behind Stanley Matthews) to win a full cap, Peter Shilton appeared in three World Cup tournaments (1982-86-90) and two European Championships in a goalkeeping career spanning three decades. Shilton's international career alone covered almost 20 years, from November 1970 until July 1990 - only Stanley Matthews played longer: 22 years 228 days. In that time 'Shilts' appeared in 125 matches – a record which will take some beating. He also holds the record for most appearances in World Cup finals (17) and, in fact, is the oldest England player ever to appear in the World Cup, aged 40 years and 292 days in 1990 and also in the European Championships, aged 38 years and 271 days in 1988. He's the

manager, Sven-Göran Eriksson, saw a return to international favour for him. He was often deployed as a tactical substitute late in games by Eriksson, valued for his ability to hold the ball up and create intelligent play. In 2001, Sheringham scored an important goal for England against Greece in a World Cup qualifier, 15 seconds after coming off the bench (the fastest-ever goal by an England substitute) although this effort is generally overlooked by David Beckham's brilliant 93rd minute equaliser. Sheringham 'won' a free-kick 20 yards from goal and at the time suggested to the England captain that he take it as Beckham had missed several already in the match, but Beckham decided to have another go – and scored to take England through.

He was selected in Eriksson's 2002 World Cup squad after an impressive 2001–02 season, and played in the famous 1–0 win over Argentina. He made his final England appearance at the age of 36 as a substitute in the 2–1 quarter-final defeat by Brazil in Japan. His twelve appearances for Eriksson were all as a substitute and, in fact, Sheringham's overall total of 21 'sub' appearances for England is a national record.

During his exciting career which spanned 25 years, Sheringham, who also played in one B international and in one unofficial England game, scored 372 goals in 979 club and international appearances (at all levels). Finding the net 288 times in 755 Premiership/League games, he had his best spells with Millwall (111 goals in 262 senior outings), Tottenham (124 in 277) and Manchester United (46 in 153). His 13 goals helped Djurgårdens win Sweden's Division Two (North) title in 1985, Millwall the Second Division Championship in 1988 and Nottingham Forest the Simod Cup in 1992 before starring for

youngest goalkeeper (aged 21) and oldest (40) ever to appear for England in a senior international.

Sir Alf Ramsey gave Shilton his international debut against East Germany in November 1970, when he conceded a 25-yard dipping goal in the second-half of a 3-1 win.

His second cap followed six months later, in a goalless draw with Wales at Wembley; and his first competitive match for his country was his third appearance as England drew 1–1 with Switzerland in a 1972 European Championship qualifier.

At this stage, Gordon Banks was still England's first choice 'keeper, but when the back-ups from the 1970 World Cup in Mexico, Peter Bonetti and Alex Stepney, were cast aside, Shilton moved forward to become his country's number two at the age of 22.

His international career progressed smoothly as he collected his fourth and fifth caps towards the end of 1972, although England failed to qualify for the European Championships. Then a tragic incident suddenly propelled 'Shilts' into the limelight as the country's number one.

In October 1972, Banks was involved in a serious car crash which resulted in the loss of the sight in one eye and thus ended his career. Liverpool goalkeeper Ray Clemence was called up to make his debut a month later in England's opening qualifier for the 1974 World Cup, a 1–0 win over Wales. Ultimately, this caused the FA continual selection headaches as the choice between Shilton and Clemence was not an easy one. In the end, Shilton ended up with over 100 caps compared to Clemence's 61 and is generally acknowledged to be the better of the two by a small margin.

Shilton performed with aplomb during the summer of 1973 as England defeated Northern Ireland 2-1, Wales 3-0, Scotland 1-0 (denying Peter Lorimer and Kenny Dalglish with breathtaking saves) and USSR 2-1, and drawing 1-1 with Czechoslovakia.

This latter match saw Shilton collect his 10th cap and was a warm-up to a crucial World Cup qualifier against Poland in Chorzów a week later. This went badly for England, with Shilton powerless to stop both goals in a 2–0 defeat and therefore making victory in the final qualifier, against the same opposition at Wembley four months later, a necessity if England were to make the finals.

Selected for the return match against the Poles, he spent a good proportion of the game watching the action at the other end of the field as his opposite number, Jan Tomaszewski, stopped everything which was fired at him. Then disaster struck! Midway through the second-half, Norman Hunter inexplicably trod on the ball near the touchline and Poland broke, with Grzegorz Lato feeding the ball across to the onrushing Jan Domarski. He shaped to hit the ball first time, and as Shilton got himself into position to be able to block the shot, the ball was struck beyond Emlyn Hughes' challenge and speared low into the net just inside Shilton's near post. 'Shilts' said afterwards that he dived awkwardly and fractionally late but should have saved the shot.

He also claimed in his autobiography that this is the only mistake he made in his 125 international appearances for England.

Although Allan Clarke levelled things up late on, when Shilton famously turned his back on the ball at the opposite end because he could not bear to look, England failed to qualify for the World Cup. The Poles went on to finish third!

With Clemence still battling to become England's top goalkeeper, both he and Shilton were given their share of caps up to April 1975. However, Clemence seemed to be getting the edge and played in twelve consecutive internationals up to May 1976 under manager Don Revie.

In fact, in May 1976, with just 21 caps to his credit, Shilton withdrew from the squad to face Scotland at Hampden Park, telling the selectors 'not to pick him again.' However, three months later he changed his mind, and although not chosen immediately, he

eventually regained his place between the posts against Northern Ireland in May 1977, only to give away a penalty in his next game, a 1-0 defeat by Wales at Wembley.

England then fought in vain to reach the 1978 World Cup finals in Argentina despite some terrific displays by Shilton.

Invariably Shilton managed to produce at least one brilliant save every game he played in. Against Sweden in Stockholm in June 1979 (when he had three of his Forest team-mates in front of him, namely Viv Anderson, Trevor Francis and Tony Woodcock) he made four to earn England a 0-0 draw and then in April 1981, he stopped three goal-bound efforts as Romania pressed for a winner at Wembley. One was described as 'unbelievable' when he somehow scooped the ball clear whilst on the ground with two forwards racing in for the kill. The game ended 0-0.

He played in all five games in the 1982 World Cup in Spain, conceding only one goal (v. France) as England slipped out in the second round. And when he made his 50th appearance, in a 2-0 win over Scotland in June 1983, he produced a stunning diving save to thwart Gordon Strachan.

In June 1985, in a tournament in Mexico, Shilton made his only penalty save for England, stopping Andreas Brehme's spot-kick in a 3-0 win over West Germany.

A year later in the World Cup back in Mexico, he was again outstanding, especially against Morocco (drew 0-0) and Poland (won 3-0) but, along with his colleagues, he was disgusted, annoyed and stunned when the referee allowed Diego Maradona's 'Hand of God' goal to stand in the quarter-final defeat by Argentina. "That was an absolutely disgraceful decision" said Shilton.

Between September 1986 and his last England outing in the 2-1 defeat by Italy in the third-place play-off match in the 1990 World Cup when he captained the team at the age of 40 years and nine months – which was also Bobby Robson's last game as manager – Shilton played in 38 out of 46 internationals, keeping 19 clean-sheets. He won his 100th cap in the 3-1 European Championship defeat by Holland in Dusseldorf in June 1988, having earlier become England's most capped goalkeeper when starring in his 75th international in the 0-0 draw against Northern Ireland at Wembley in November 1985

Over a period of 30 years, 1966-96, Shilton played in no less than 1,390 football matches (1,375 at first-class level). His last outing was as a second-half substitute for Bolton, appropriately against his first club, Stoke City, in March 1995.

He made 1,005 appearances in the Football League alone, topping the century mark with five different clubs: Leicester City 286, Stoke City 110, Nottingham Forest 202, Southampton 188 and Derby County 175. He also scored one goal – for Leicester in a 5-1 League win against his future club, Southampton, at The Dell in October 1968.

An FA Cup runner-up and Second Division Championship winner with Leicester in 1969 and 1971 respectively, he helped Nottingham Forest win the League title in 1978, the League Cup in 1979, two European Cup finals in 1979 and 1980, the European Super Cup, also in 1979, and the FA Charity Shield. He was voted PFA 'Footballer of the Year' in 1978 – only the second goalkeeper to win this award.

Honoured with the MBE and later the OBE, for services to football, in 1990, following his retirement from the international arena, Shilton was awarded the prestigious Order of Merit by the PFA, and a year later received the Football Writers' Tribute Award.

He was made an inaugural inductee of the English Football Hall of Fame in 2002 in recognition of his impact on the game and being one of England's greatest goalkeepers.

Shilton was the last player born in the 1940s to play in the Football League and also for England in a senior international.

SHIMWELL, Edmond 1948-49 ①

Born: Wirksworth, Derbyshire, 27 February 1920
Died: Derby, 3 October 1988
Career: Wirksworth FC (1937), Sheffield United (professional, June 1939); WW2 guest for Southampton (season 1943-44); Blackpool (December 1946), Oldham Athletic (May 1957), Burton Albion (player-manager, July 1958), Matlock Town (player-manager, August 1959, retired, May 1960); became a proprietor of the Royal Volunteer pub, Clay Cross, Derbyshire.

With at least four quality right-backs to choose from, England manager Walter Winterbottom selected Eddie Shimwell just once, for the friendly with Sweden in May 1949. Unfortunately he didn't have a great game in a 3-1 defeat in Stockholm.
    Well-built, resolute and strong-kicking with a distinguished trait, he played in three FA Cup finals for Blackpool, gaining a winner's medal in 1953 along with Tom Garrett, Stanley Matthews, Harry Johnston, Ernie Taylor, Stan Mortensen and Bill Perry, all of whom played for England. Shimwell made 324 appearances for Blackpool and, in fact, was the first full-back to score in an FA Cup final, from the penalty spot for the Seasiders against Manchester United in 1948.

SHOREY, Nicholas 2006-07 ②

Born: Romford, 19 February 1981
Career: Leyton Orient (apprentice, June 1997, professional July 1999), Reading (£25,000, February 2001), Aston Villa (£3.5m, August 2008), West Bromwich Albion (free, August 2010).

Included in England's B team against Albania at Turf Moor in May 2007, he was substituted after 73 minutes by Joleon Lescott but immediately the pundits suggested that Nicky Shorey could make the step up to the senior squad. He did just that, named by Steve McClaren in his squad to face Brazil and Estonia the following month. He made his full debut in a 1–1 draw against the Brazilians at Wembley, impressing many, but did not make the bench for the Estonia match. Two months later, the crisp-tackling Shorey earned his second cap in a 2–1 friendly defeat by Germany, also at Wembley. He hasn't figured since on the international scene. He made 296 appearances for Reading, helping them win the League Championship in 2006.

SHUTT, George 1885-86 ①

Born: Stoke-on-Trent, 30 October 1861
Died: Hanley, Stoke-on-Trent, 6 August 1936
Career: Stoke Priory (seasons 1877-80), Stoke (amateur, August 1880, professional August 1885), Hanley Town (May 1889), Burslem Port Vale (August 1891), Hanley Town (March-April 1893, retired); qualified as a referee in 1891 – and became the youngest on the Football League list in 1893; later ran a pub and then the Borough Exchange Hotel in Stoke.

Tough and reliable, rugged centre-half George Shutt earned his only England cap in a 6-1 win over Ireland in March 1886. One of his long clearances led to a goal for Ben Spilsbury. Shutt also played for Staffordshire on 12 occasions, represented the Birmingham FA, the Players' XI and The North of England (v The South) in an international trial. He played in Stoke's first FA Cup-tie and the club's first League game.

SILCOCK, John 1921-23 ③

Born: Wigan, 15 January 1898
Died: Manchester, 28 June 1966
Career: Aspull Juniors (1909), Atherton (1912), Manchester United (amateur, April 1916, professional, September 1917), Oldham Athletic (trial, May 1934, not retained, retired June 1934; became a licensee in Manchester.

Left-back John Silcock made 449 senior appearances for Manchester United and gained his three England caps over a period of two years. A player with classic ability, he made his international debut against Wales in March 1921, played against Scotland the following month and won his last cap against Sweden in May 1923. He deserved more, but he did have the likes of Sam Wadsworth, Fred Titmuss, Jack Harrow and Tom Lucas to contend with!

SILLETT, Richard Peter 1954-55 ③

Born: Southampton, 1 February 1933
Died: Ashford, Kent, 12 March 1998
Career: Hampshire County Youths, Normansland FC (1947), Southampton (amateur, April 1948, professional, June 1950), Chelsea (£12,000, May 1953), Guildford City (free, June 1962), Ashford United (player-manager, July 1965-December 1973), Folkestone Town (manager, August 1974-April 1975), Ashford United (manager, January-February 1976), Hereford United (scout, seasons 1976-78), Hastings United (manager, August 1978-June 1983), Coventry City (scout, August 1983-March 1985), Ashford United (manager, April 1985-May 1987), Poole Town (manager, June 1987, unable to take up position due to poor health); Hastings United (manager, seasons 1987-91); thereafter confined to his Ashford home with an arthritic knee which prevented him from walking.

A powerful full-back who could send a free-kick 100 yards downfield, Peter Sillett (stepping in for the injured Jimmy Meadows) conceded a 36th minute penalty on his England debut against France in Paris in May 1955. Raymond Kopa scored from the spot to win the game 1-0. Three days later he played in the 1-1 draw with Spain and soon after that appeared in the 3-1 defeat in Portugal.
    He captained Young England v England in 1955, just after helping Chelsea win the League Championship and scored 34 goals, most of them penalties or free-kicks, in 288 appearances in his nine years at Stamford Bridge. His brother, John, also played for Chelsea and later, along with co-manager George Curtis, guided Coventry City to victory in the 1987 FA Cup final. Sillett died from cancer at the age of 65.

SIMMS, Ernest 1921-22 ①

Born: Easington, County Durham, 23 June 1891
Died: Biggleswade, 11 October 1971
Career: South Shields Adelaide (1906), Murton Colliery (1908), Barnsley (professional, August 1912), Luton Town (July 1913); served in Army during WW1; South Shields (March 1922), Stockport County (January 1924), Scunthorpe United (June 1926), York City (August 1928), Vauxhall Motors FC (April 1929, retired, May 1931).

Ernie Simms received his first call into an England squad in October 1920, but had to settle for being a non-playing reserve against Ireland. However, a year later he gained his only cap (in October 1921) when he played against the Irish in a 1-1 draw at Windsor Park, Belfast - becoming the first Third Division centre forward ever to play for England. Two of Simms' club-mates at Luton, Louis Bookman and Allan Mathieson, lined up for Ireland. He was only 5ft 9ins tall, yet had a fine career overall, netting over 150 goals including 109 in 160 League games for the Hatters. He also captained the FA touring team in Australia in 1925. While serving with the Diehards battalion attached to the Middlesex regiment during the Great War he suffered a savage disabling leg wound which left him with serious muscle damage and a permanent limp. Simms was deemed no more use as a soldier, and was sent home in 1916. He continued playing football for another 15 years!

SIMPSON, John 1912-14 ⑧ ①

Born: Pendleton, Lancashire, 25 December 1885
Died: Falkirk, 4 January 1959
Career: Laurieston Villa (1900), Grange Rovers (1903), Glasgow Rangers (trial, 1905), Falkirk (professional, November 1906), Blackburn Rovers (January 1911); WW1 guest for Falkirk (seasons 1916-19); Falkirk Amateurs (May 1922-April 1924), Falkirk Orient (seasons 1924-26); became mine host of the Horse Shoe Inn on Falkirk High Street.

'Jock' Simpson was a celebrity outside-right who was occasionally used as an emergency centre-forward. Although born in Lancashire, his parents were Scottish and by the time he was three years old the family had returned to their native home at Laurieston near Falkirk where Simpson spent his formative years. After an unsuccessful trial at Ibrox Park, he signed for Falkirk at the age of 19. He went on to score 110 goals in senior competition for The Bairns, but became increasingly frustrated when the SFA stuck to their guns by refusing to pick a player born outside of Scotland, while at the same time the FA would not accept a player who was registered with a club outside England!

Early in January 1911, Simpson was linked with a move to Blackburn and amazingly, just seven days before his transfer to Ewood Park, he was selected to play in an England international trial match - for the 'Stripes' against the 'Whites' at White Hart Lane - making him the first Scottish-based footballer to play in a representative match wearing the colours of England!

He became a star at Blackburn, helping Rovers twice win the Football League Championship in 1912 and 1914, during which time he took his tally of full England caps to eight. Having made an impressive debut in a 2-1 win over Ireland in February 1911, he followed up with another excellent display in a 3-0 victory over Wales a month later before playing his part in a creditable 1-1 draw with Scotland at Goodison Park. His only England goal helped thrash Ireland 6-1 in February 1912 and after playing in the other Home Internationals that season (v. Wales 2-0 and Scotland 1-1) he ended with two solid performances against Scotland (1-0) in April 1913 and Wales (2-0) a year later. During the First World War Simpson played as a guest for Falkirk, adding another 13 League goals to his tally, and when footballing normalcy arrived he returned to Blackburn, but by this time a leg injury was severely curtailing his appearances, and he was released in April 1922 having made a total of 151 League appearances for the Ewood Park club, scoring 16 goals. He attempted a return with Falkirk, but deep down he knew his senior career was over and after the odd appearance for Falkirk Amateurs and Falkirk Orient in the Falkirk District Wednesday Afternoon Shopworkers League, he eventually retired in 1928. His son played for St Johnstone for a short while.

SINCLAIR, Trevor Lloyd 2001-04 ⑫

Born: Dulwich, London, 2 March 1973
Career: Blackpool (apprentice, August 1989, professional, August 1990), Queens Park Rangers (£600,000, August 1993), West Ham United (£2.7m combined deal involving Iain Dowie and Keith Rowland), Manchester City (£3.3m, July 2003), Cardiff City (July 2007, retired on release, May 2008).

Four of Trevor Sinclair's 12 England caps came in the 2002 World Cup in Japan and Korea. A late replacement for the injured Danny Murphy, he took over in midfield from Owen Hargreaves who was also injured early in the competition. Widely regarded as one of England's best players in the tournament, and playing in the 'problem left hand side' position, he had a fine game as a substitute against Argentina (1-0), played very well in the 0-0 draw with Nigeria, laid on a goal in the 3-0 win over Denmark but was replaced by Kieron Dyer against Brazil when England were 2-1 down and chasing the game. He made his international debut in November 2001 against Sweden at Old Trafford (1-1) and added seven more to his tally after the World Cup.

He made 659 club appearances, scoring 83 goals, having his best years with Blackpool (16 goals in 140 outings) and QPR (21 in 190). He had the pleasure of scoring the first goal at The City of Manchester Stadium (for Manchester City against TNS in a UEFA Cup game in 2003) and his brilliant bicycle kick strike for QPR against Barnsley in a 4th round FA Cup-tie in January 1997, was voted BBC *Match of the Day's* 'Goal of the Season'. Also capped once at B and 13 times (5 goals scored) at U21 levels, Sinclair played in the 2008 FA Cup final for Cardiff. He currently lives in Dubai.

SINTON, Andrew 1991-93 ⑫

Born: Cramlington near Newcastle, 19 March 1966
Career: Cambridge United (apprentice, June 1981, professional, April 1983), Brentford (£25,000, December 1985), Queens Park Rangers (£350,000, March 1989), Sheffield Wednesday (£2.75m, August 1993), Tottenham Hotspur (£1.5m, January 1996), Wolverhampton Wanderers ('Bosman' free, July 1999), Burton Albion (August 2002-May 2004), Bromsgrove Rovers (August-September 2004), Fleet Town (player and Football Development Officer, September 2004-May 2005, player-manager, June 2005-May 2010), AFC Telford United (manager, May 2010).

It was clearly not Andy Sinton's fault that manager Graham Taylor selected him in front of the supremely gifted Chris Waddle! Oh yes he did.

The wide midfielder made his England debut (with fellow wide man Tony Daley) in the 1-1 draw with Poland in Poznan in November 1991, the point securing a place in the 1992 European Championships. Surprisingly, to a lot of people, he went on to play in eleven more internationals over the next two years, and to be fair, he had some useful games, including the 2-0 win over Turkey in a World Cup qualifier in Izmir in March 1993, the 1-1 draw with Brazil in the US Cup in Washington in June 1993 and the 7-1 victory over the minnows from San Marino in another World Cup qualifier in Bologna in November 1993, which was his last England game. He also played against France and Sweden during the disappointing European Championship campaign. It must be said, however, that niggling injuries didn't help matters at times.

A wide midfielder with good pace and a powerful right-foot shot, Sinton scored 89 goals in a total of 777 club appearances covering more than 20 years. He had his best spell with QPR (25 goals in 191 games).

SLATER, William John, OBE, CBE, BSc 1954-60 (12)

Born: Clitheroe, Lancashire, 29 April 1927
Career: Lancashire & District Youths, Blackpool (amateur, April 1944); also played for Yorkshire Amateurs and Leeds University (seasons 1945-48); Brentford (amateur, December 1951), Wolverhampton Wanderers (amateur, August 1952, part-time professional, February 1954), Brentford (June 1963), Northern Nomads (August 1964, retired November 1964); became deputy director of the Crystal Palace Sports centre and later worked as a director of Physical Education at both Liverpool and Birmingham Universities; in 1982 he was awarded the OBE for services to sport and in 1998 received the CBE; from 1984-89 he was director of the National Services and in July 1989 was elected president of the British Gymnastics Association, later serving on the National Olympic Committee and has also sat on the panel of the National Lottery.

After impressing on his England debut against Wales in November 1954 and doing likewise in his next game against West Germany, wing-half Bill Slater was then given the impossible job of replacing Duncan Edwards for the away clash with Scotland in April 1958. He did okay, assisted in one of the goals in a 4-0 win, and as a result was named in the squad for the World Cup finals in Sweden that summer. Chosen for all four matches, along with his Wolves team-mates Eddie Clamp and Billy Wright, he completed the half-back line in three of them v USSR, Brazil and Austria, actually finishing the 0-0 draw with the ultimate winners, Brazil, in Gothenburg with several heavy bruises on the inside of both knees where he had banged them together in an effort to stop Didi pulling off his favourite trick of nutmegging his opponent.

Back in England, unfortunately it was Slater's suicidal back-pass which led to Scotland's goal in the 1-1 draw at Hampden Park in April 1960, bringing to an end his six-year international career.

A three-time League Championship winner with Wolves (1954-58/59) he captained the Molineux club to a 3-0 FA Cup final victory over Blackburn in 1960, having collected a runners-up medal with Blackpool nine years earlier. Also capped 21 times by England at amateur level, and once by Great Britain (in 1952) Slater was voted FWA 'Footballer of the Year' in 1960.

He made over 400 appearances in club football, 339 for Wolves. He holds the record, jointly with James Quinn, for the fastest goal ever scored by a Blackpool player – 11 seconds v. Stoke City in December 1949.

His daughter Barbara is a former national gymnast champion who represented Great Britain in the 1976 Olympic Games and later worked for Central TV.

SMALLEY, Thomas 1936-37 (1)

Born: Kinsley near Barnsley, Yorkshire, 13 January 1912
Died: Wolverhampton, 12 April 1984
Career: South Kirby Colliery, Wolverhampton Wanderers (professional, May 1931), Norwich City (£4,500, August 1938); WW2 guest for West Bromwich Albion; Northampton Town (October 1941-May 1951); Lower Gornal (player-coach, July 1952-May 1953); also played local club cricket.

An utterly reliable and tenacious midfielder (a wing-half) Tom Smalley made 179 appearances for First Division Wolverhampton Wanderers before joining Norwich City. He proved to be an excellent capture for the Canaries, and it was something of a rarity for the Carrow Road club to have an England international on its staff, for Smalley had played for England in a 2-1 defeat by Wales at Ninian Park, Cardiff in October 1936. Named as Norwich's captain for the 1938-39 season, he played in every game before the war came

along and disrupted his career, along with those of so many other players up and down the country. He returned to League action after the hostilities and made over 400 appearances for Northampton before entering non-League football at the age of 39.

SMALLING, Christopher 2011-12 (6)

Born: Greenwich, London, 22 November 1989
Career: Chatham Grammar School, Millwall (Academy), Kent Schools, Maidstone United (season 2007-08), Middlesbrough (May 2008 – contract cancelled, June 2008), Fulham (professional, June 2008), Manchester United (pre-contract agreement, January 2010, signed for £10m, July 2010)

Manchester United's utility defender Chris Smalling made his England senior debut at right-back in a 3-0 European Championship qualifying victory over Bulgaria in Sofia in September 2011. In his own words he said: "I enjoyed the occasion and I believe I played well." He was the 1,175th player to gain a full cap and quickly added a second to his tally when playing against Wales in another qualifier at Wembley four days later (won 1-0).

A Premiership winner in his first full season at Old Trafford (2010-11) and again in 2012-13, Smalling made only 13 top-flight appearances for Fulham before his surprise transfer to the Reds. He has also played five times for England Schools at U18 level, once for the U20 team and 14 times at U21 level. Unfortunately injuries sidelined him for long periods in 2012.

SMART, Thomas 1920-30 (5)

Born: Blackheath, Staffs, 20 September 1896
Died: Brierley Hill, Staffs, 10 June 1968
Career: Rowley Regis Schools, Blackheath Town (1913); Army service and football (seasons 1915-18), Halesowen (July 1919), Aston Villa (professional, January 1920), Brierley Hill Alliance (May 1934), then player-coach, July 1935-May 1938), Blackheath Town (player-coach, August 1938-September 1939); later worked at Marsh & Baxter sausage and pork factory for 17 years.

Three months after joining Aston Villa, right-back Tommy Smart collected an FA Cup winner's medal when Huddersfield Town lost 1-0 in the final at Stamford Bridge. Barrel-chested, nicknamed 'Tic' he owned a ferocious tackle, was built like a buffalo and kicked like a mule - and when clearing his lines, he always yelled out a famous war cry of 'Thik Hai' (Hindustani language) which he picked up in India. He made great strides in the game and went on to appear in 452 first-class games for Villa, scoring eight goals over a period of 14½ years.

He won the first of his five England caps in a 3-0 defeat by Scotland at Hampden Park in April 1921 when, despite the result, he coped well with Rangers' flying winger Alan Morton.

Wrote John Crockett in the *Daily Mail*: "He (Smart) and Bert Smith (Tottenham) were up against probably the finest left-wing in the three countries, certainly the cleverest."

Smart also played well in his next two games in March and April 1924 against Wales (lost 2-1) and Scotland (again, 1-1) but wasn't at his best in the 0-0 draw with Ireland in October 1925. However, along with his team-mates, he had an excellent game in his last international in November 1929, when Wales were battered 6-0 at Stamford Bridge – one of his favourite grounds! Smart, who also played in two international trials, served in Greece, Belgium and India during the Great War with the South Staffs Regiment.

His brother Len played for Port Vale, Luton, Wolves and Bournemouth.

SMITH, Alan 2000-07 (19) (1)

Born: Rothwell, West Yorkshire, 28 October 1980
Career: FA School of Excellence (season 1996-97), Leeds United (apprentice April 1997, professional March 1998), Manchester United (£7.1m, May 2004), Newcastle United (£6m, August 2007, given free transfer, June 2011), MK Dons (loan, January-May 2012, signed permanently, July 2012)

The general consensus seems to be that it's his attitude that jars people when they realise that Alan Smith won 19 caps for his country. And his sending-off in a Euro 2004 qualifier against Macedonia was a particular low-point in his six-year international career.

Hardly known for the calmness of his temperament, Smith was dismissed in a shambles of a match which ended in a 2-2 draw and, in fact, in leaving the pitch early, he became the ninth England player to take an early bath in a competitive game.

Initially a striker, and later a midfielder, he was a youth international at multiple levels, before receiving his first call into the England senior squad for the friendly against Italy in November 2000. Surprisingly, he later withdrew in order to rest (after injury)! Forgiven, he eventually earned his first cap in May 2001 against Mexico but did not make the final cut for the 2002 World Cup finals, yet continued representing the U21s. He had the pleasure of scoring on his full senior debut against Portugal in September 2002, being set up by his Leeds team-mate Lee Bowyer. Then came that red card against Macedonia (for a foul on Aleksander Vasoski).

In October 2002, Smith came on as a substitute in injury-time against Slovakia in Bratislava in the European Championship preliminary match just as the ball ran dead behind David Seaman's goal. As the 'keeper took the goal kick, so the referee blew for time. Smith never touched the ball.

In August 2005, he attracted a lot of criticism when he withdrew from the England squad to play Denmark in Copenhagen, so that he could play for Manchester United reserves. The Danes won the game 4-1.

After a prolonged absence from international duty, Smith was selected for an England B match against Albania in May 2007, scoring the first goal in a 3-1 victory. The next day he was named in the senior team to face Brazil the following month – his 19th and last cap.

Smith, who has been sent off seven times in Premiership football and once in the Champions League, played in his 400th club game in September 2010. He helped Manchester United win the title in 2007 and three years later starred for Newcastle in their Championship-winning campaign. He also scored three times in ten U21 internationals for his country.

SMITH, Alan Martin 1988-92 (13) (2)

Born: Birmingham, 21 November 1962
Career: Birmingham City (April 1978), Alvechurch (August 1979), Leicester City (£22,000, professional, June 1982), Arsenal (£850,000, March 1987, retired on medical advice, May 1994); become a journalist (with the help of a PFA grant, studied at the London School of Journalism); now a soccer pundit for Sky TV.

Striker Alan Smith had seven largely successful seasons at Arsenal but his international career was less auspicious. He scored just two goals in 13 appearances – both at Wembley – his first a low right-foot shot early on in a 5-1 win over the USSR in May 1991 and his second, a smart header to earn a 1-0 victory over Turkey in a European Championship qualifier five months later. He is, however, probably best remembered for being a member of the England side that failed so miserably in Euro 92.

He made his international debut as a substitute against Saudi Arabia in November 1988 and played his 13th and last game against Sweden in Stockholm in June 1992.

Smith formed a very useful partnership with Gary Lineker at Leicester whom he helped win promotion to the top flight while scoring 84 goals in 217 appearances. He later won two League titles, the FA Cup, League Cup and European Cup Winners' Cup with Arsenal for whom he netted 115 goals in 345 appearances. He represented England at semi-professional level while with Alvechurch and won the English 'Golden Boot' in 1989 with 23 top-flight goals.

SMITH, Albert 1890-93 (3)

Born: Nottingham, 23 July 1869
Died: Nottingham, 18 April 1921
Career: Notts Rangers (June 1883), Long Eaton Rangers (October 1883), Derby County (1884), Nottingham Forest (October 1888), Notts County (February 1890), Nottingham Forest (October 1890), Blackburn Rovers (November 1891), Nottingham Forest (March 1892, retired April 1894); later worked as a shoe/boot maker in Nottingham.

Albert Smith was described as being 'a plucky, indefatigable right-half, possessing forcefulness and a fair tackle.' However, at times his passing left a lot to be desired!

He gained his three England caps between March 1891 and February 1893, playing in excellent victories over Wales (won 4-1), Scotland (2-1) and Ireland (6-1). In the win over the Scots at Blackburn, he was outstanding behind Billy Bassett, The Times reporter stating: "Smith defended with determination and commitment."

SMITH, Bertram 1920-22 (2)

Born: Higham, Kent, 7 March 1892
Died: Biggleswade, 8 September 1969
Career: Vanbrugh Park, Crawford United, Metrogas FC, Army football, Huddersfield Town (professional, April 1913); WW1 guest for Tottenham Hotspur (signed permanently in August 1919), Northfleet (player-coach, May 1930), Sheppey United (September 1931), Young Boys of Berne/Switzerland (player-coach, September 1931-May 1934), Harwich & Parkeston (manager-coach, August 1934), Stevenage Town (briefly as coach), Hitchin Town (trainer-coach, July 1937-August 1939; later returned to club as groundsman and part-time trainer, retiring from football, October 1966, aged 74).

An energetic and virile right half, Bert Smith won the Second Division Championship (1920) and the FA Cup (1921) in his first two seasons at White Hart Lane, going on to make made 319 appearances in all competitions for Spurs. However, he was involved when a major fracas broke out after a Spurs goal against Arsenal in September 1922. The reporter from The Sunday Evening Telegram recorded that: "After the Spurs goal came the most disgraceful scene I have witnessed on any ground at any time. Players pulled the referee, blows with fists were exchanged, and all the dignity that appertains in the referee was rudely trampled on." In the aftermath, following a Commission of Inquiry, Tottenham's Bert Smith was found to have used "filthy language" and suspended for a month. Arsenal's Alex Graham was censured for retaliating instead of reporting matters to the ref, and Stephen Dunn (Arsenal's goalkeeper) for his conduct after Tottenham's goal was allowed to stand.

Smith's international career comprised just two games for England. He debuted in April 1921 in a 3-1 defeat by Scotland and played against Wales in March 1922.

SMITH, Charles Eastlake 1875-76 [1]

Born: Colombo, Ceylon (now Sri Lanka) 12 February 1850
Died: France, 10 January 1917
Career: Rossall School XI (seasons 1867-70), Crystal Palace (seasons 1870-75); also played for Wanderers and Surrey County (1870s); FA Committee member (season 1875-76); also a good cricketer; cousin of G. O. Smith (below).

An eagle-eyed forward with a strong shot in both feet, Charlie Smith was also a smart dribbler who played for England in a 3-0 defeat by Scotland at The West of Scotland FC ground, Partick, in March 1876, the *Bell's Life* reporter stating that '...once or twice H. Heron, Smith and Jarrett shaped an open space, but the gap was speedily filled.' He was killed while serving with the British Army in France in 1917.

SMITH, Gilbert Oswald 1892-1901 [20] [11]

Born: Croydon, Surrey, 25 November 1872
Died: Lymington, Hampshire, 6 December 1943
Career: Charterhouse School XI (seasons 1889-92), Keble College/Oxford (seasons 1893-96, captain and blue); also played for Old Carthusians and Corinthians (seasons 1892-1903, being joint secretary of the latter club with W. J. Oakley from 1898-1902); cricket blue (Oxford, 1895-96, scoring 132 v. Cambridge University in 1896); also played for Surrey CCC and Herts CC; schoolmaster at Ludgrove from 1896; became joint headmaster after retiring from football in 1902; later headmaster of Sunningdale School.

An FA Amateur Cup finalist with Old Carthusians in 1895 and a winner two years later, G. O. Smith was justifiably regarded the greatest centre-forward in England during the period 1892-1902. Not over-big, he packed a deadly shot and his brilliant passes constantly out-manoeuvred defenders. 'On the wettest, muddiest day, when the ball was heavy with clay or as greasy as a Christmas pudding, his passes never went astray' wrote commentators Gibson and Pickard. Not the fastest of forwards, he perhaps lacked the physique and height to play the hard, bruising game, but nevertheless he endured the shoulder-charging and rough challenges of the tough, uncompromising defenders without flinching a muscle. In their book, *The Essential History of England*, the authors (Andrew Mourant and Jack Rollin) wrote of Smith: 'He opposed subtlety to force, intellect to mere strength... in full cry... you saw a king among athletes.'

He scored on his international debut against Ireland in February 1893 (won 6-1), repeated the dose against the same opposition three years later (2-0) and when the Irish were demolished 13-2 at Sunderland in February 1899, Smith bagged four of the goals while assisting in five others. Two months later, as captain, he found the net again, this time with a wonderful 20-yard lofted drive in the 2-1 victory over Scotland at Villa Park, this being his eighth competitive game in ten days.

Playing against Scotland in April 1900 (lost 4-1) and March 1901 (drew 2-2) – his last two internationals – he came close to scoring three times in each game, almost cracking a post with one rasping drive in the latter game at Crystal Palace when he received some rough treatment from the Liverpool centre-half Alec Raisbeck on a heavy, soggy pitch.

He scored goals at will – and although it is difficult to ascertain how many he did register during a fine career, one can readily state it was over 100...a brilliant footballer.

SMITH, Herbert 1904-06 [4]

Born: Witney, Oxford, 22 November 1879
Died: Oxford, 7 January 1951
Career: Oxford County School, Beccles School, Witney Town (August 1894), Oxford City (May 1895), Richmond (April 1896), Stoke (November-December 1902), Reading (January 1903), Oxford City (February 1903), Reading (August 1903), Derby County (guest, April 1907), Clapton Orient (1908), Richmond (1909); also played for Oxfordshire; was President of the Oxfordshire FA from 1912 until his death in 1951.

Herbert Smith, a burly, muscular left-back, made his international debut for England against Wales (won 3-1) at Goodison Park in March 1905 as a Reading player. He remained in the team for the next three matches, putting in a terrific performance in the 1-0 win over Scotland at Crystal Palace. However, from November 1906 onwards he chose to play for the England amateur team, eventually winning 17 caps at this level.

An FA Amateur Cup finalist with Oxford City in 1903, five years later Smith won an Olympic Games football gold medal with the United Kingdom, partnering Walter Corbett in the final against Denmark.

SMITH (Schmidt),
James Christopher Reginald 1938-39 [2] [2]

Born: Battersea, London, 20 January 1912
Died: Cape Town, South Africa, 6 January 2004
Career: Hitchin Town (April 1930), Crystal Palace (trial, 1931), Tottenham Hotspur (amateur, June 1932), St Albans City (August 1933), Millwall (professional, September 1935); WW2 guest for West Ham United, Luton Town, Dundee, Partick Thistle, Watford, Chelsea and Tottenham Hotspur; Dundee (£1,000, March 1946), Corby Town (player-manager, August-October 1948), Dundee (player/trainer-coach, August 1949, retired as a player, May 1951, continued as trainer-coach to June 1954); Dundee United (manager, September 1954-December 1955), Falkirk (manager, January 1956-May 1959), Millwall (manager, July 1959-January 1961), Addington FC/South Africa (coach, March-May 1961), Durban City (manager, July-November 1961), Bedford Town (manager, December 1961-September 1963), Addington FC/South Africa (manager-coach, December 1963-October 1970), Bedford Town (manager, November 1971-June 1972), Stevenage Town (manager, season 1972-73).

The son of a South African rugby union international who was a member of the first-ever Springboks team that toured England in the 1920s, Reg Smith began his career as an amateur with Hitchin Town before turning professional with Millwall. After a slow start he helped the Lions reach the FA Cup semi-final in 1937 - the first time a team from the third tier of English football had reached that stage - and in 1937-38 he and Millwall enjoyed even greater success by winning the Third Division (South) Championship and also lifting the London FA Challenge Cup.

An inside or outside-left, Smith was the last Millwall player to win a full England cap, making his debut against Norway in November 1938, scoring twice in a 2-0 win at St James' Park, Newcastle. Seven days later he played – and played well – in a 7-0 victory over Northern Ireland at Manchester. He also played in three Wartime internationals.

When the Second World War broke out in 1939, Smith, like many other footballers, found his career disrupted. He joined the RAF and continued to appear sporadically for Millwall when his military schedule allowed. Transferred to RAF Leuchars in Fife, in 1944, he subsequently played for Dundee as a guest in the Wartime North-Eastern League. When the hostilities were over, he joined the Dens Park club on a permanent basis in 1946, helping them to the Scottish 'B' Division in his first season. Returning to South Africa in the late 1980s, he was almost 92 when he died.

SMITH, John William 1931-32 ③ ④

Born: Whitburn, County Durham, 28 October 1898
Died: London, 19 January 1977
Career: Whitburn (seasons 1915-17), North Shields Athletic (seasons 1917-19), South Shields (£5, August 1919), Portsmouth (£250, December 1927), Bournemouth & Boscombe Athletic (free, May 1935), Clapton Orient (October 1936, retired, injured, February 1937).

A leading tactician and quality marksman, Jack Smith's senior career spanned 18 years during which time he scored well over 160 goals in more than 600 appearances, 147 of his goals coming in 569 League appearances. He gained two FA Cup runners-up medals with Portsmouth in 1929 and 1934.

He scored in each of his three internationals in 1931, against Ireland in mid-October (won 6-2); v. Wales a month later (won 3-1) and twice versus Spain (won 7-1) two weeks before Christmas. His brother, Septimus Smith, also played for England.

SMITH, Joseph 1912-20 ⑤ ①

Born: Dudley Port, Staffs, 25 June 1889
Died: Blackpool, August 1971
Career: Newcastle St Luke's (1906), Bolton Wanderers (professional, May 1908), Stockport County (March 1927), Darwen (June 1929), Manchester Central (July 1930, retired April 1931); Reading (manager, July 1931-August 1935), Blackpool (manager, August 1935, retired, April 1958).

A Second Division Championship winner in 1909, inside-left Joe Smith won the first of his five England caps in February 1913 in a 2-1 defeat by Ireland in Belfast. His other four international appearances followed against Wales, won 2-0, in March 1914 (when he scored the opening goal), a 3-1 reverse against Scotland in April 1914, a 1-1 draw with Ireland in October 1919 and another 2-1 defeat, this time by Wales in March 1920. After that Smith twice helped Bolton win the FA Cup, in 1923 (the first Wembley final) and in 1926. Possessing one of the hardest shots in football, he scored 277 goals in 492 appearances during his 21 years at Burnden Park. As a manager, he guided Blackpool to FA Cup glory over his former club Bolton in 1953 and overall was in charge of his two clubs for a total of 914 matches.

SMITH, Joseph 1919-22 ②

Born: Darby End, Dudley, 10 April 1890
Died: Wolverhampton, 9 June 1956
Career: Halesowen Road Council School/Netherton in Dudley, Netherton St Andrew's, Darby End Victoria/Dudley, Cradley St Luke's (August 1908), West Bromwich Albion (professional, May 1910); served in the Army in WW1, also guest for Everton and Notts County; Birmingham (free, May 1926), Worcester City (player-manager, May 1929, retired, July 1932); became a licensee in Darby End, later worked at Lloyds Proving House, eventually becoming chief tester.

Right-back Joe Smith made 471 appearances for West Brom, several of them as partner to Jesse Pennington. He helped the Baggies win the Second and then First Division Championships in 1911 and 1920 and gained an FA Cup runners-up medal in 1912.

A relatively small man, he was a strong tackler who gained a remarkable level of consistency, missing only five League games out of a possible 252 between 1919 and 1925. A junior international in 1909, he won his two full caps both against Ireland, the first in Belfast in October 1919 (1-1), the second three years later on his home ground at The Hawthorns (won 2-0). He also played in the 2-0 Victory international win over. Wales at Stoke in October 1919. Smith perhaps deserved more honours, but was up against some exceptionally fine full-backs, all challenging for an England place!

SMITH, Leslie George Frederick 1938-39 ①

Born: Ealing, Middlesex, 23 March 1918
Died: Lichfield, Staffs, 20 May 1995
Career: St John's Grammar School/Brentford, West London Schools, Petersham FC (1932), Brentford (junior and office clerk, June 1933), Wimbledon (August 1934), Hayes (July 1935), Brentford (amateur, late 1935, professional March 1936); WW2 guest for Chelsea, Leicester City, Manchester City and West Bromwich Albion; Aston Villa (£7,500, October 1945), Brentford (£3,000, June 1952), Kidderminster Harriers (player-manager, August 1953-June 1954), Wolverhampton Wanderers (scout, seasons 1954-56); later Aston Villa Old Stars (manager, seasons 1960-65); ran an electrical goods business in Aston for many years.

After gaining his one and only full cap for England against Romania in Bucharest in May 1939 as a Brentford player, 'will-o'the wisp', hard-shooting outside-left, Les Smith went on to star in 13 Wartime/Victory internationals (three goals) and in two unofficial matches against Switzerland in Berne and Zurich in July 1945. He also represented the FA on tour to Romania, Italy and Yugoslavia and played for both the RAF and Combined Services during the hostilities.

A runner-up with Wimbledon in the 1935 FA Amateur Cup final (aged 17); he won the London Wartime Cup with Brentford in 1942 and the Football League (South) title with Chelsea in 1945. He appeared in over 80 games for Brentford and 197 for Villa, for whom he netted 37 goals.

SMITH, Lionel 1950-53 ⑥

Born: Mexborough, Yorkshire, 23 August 1920
Died: Stoke Newington, London, 8 November 1980
Career: Mexborough Albion (1934), Yorkshire Tar Distillers (1935), Denaby United (1937), Arsenal (amateur, August 1939, professional, November 1939); Army service; Watford (June 1954), Gravesend & Northfleet (player-manager, May 1955-April 1960).

A tall, slim, stylish left-back, Lionel Smith was known for his pace and the quality of his distribution – always trying to use the ball rather than simply bang it aimlessly downfield! An FA Cup winner with Arsenal in 1950, he gained his England cap in November of that same year, in a 4-2 win over Wales at Roker Park, Sunderland when he partnered Alf Ramsey. Making his debut at the relatively late age of 30, he went on to play in five more internationals, in the 1-1 draw with Wales and the 2-0 victory over Northern Ireland the following year before gaining his last three caps in 1952-53 against Wales, again (won 5-2), Belgium (won 5-0) and Scotland (drew 2-2). Smith, who battled for a place in the England team with Bill Eckersley, made 198 appearances for the Gunners (all games), collecting an FA Cup runners-up medal in 1952. He served as a sapper in the Royal Engineers during the Second World War.

SMITH, Robert Alfred 1960-64 ⑮ ⑬

Born: Lingdale, County Durham, 22 February 1933
Died: Enfield, Middlesex, 18 September 2010
Career: Lingdale School, Redcar Boys Club (1947), Chelsea (groundstaff, May 1949, professional May 1950), Tottenham Hotspur (December 1955), Brighton & Hove Albion (May 1964-October 1965), Hastings United (October 1965, retired, March 1967); later worked as a van delivery driver on the south coast before becoming a painter and decorator; he died in hospital following a short illness.

Spurs' centre-forward Bobby Smith scored with his second kick in international football – banging home Johnny Haynes' short free-kick to set up a convincing 5-2 win over Northern Ireland on his debut in Belfast in October 1960.

Later in the same month, when Spain were defeated 4-2 at Wembley, Smith scored twice, his first being a delicate chip over the 'keeper's head from 20 yards.

However, the chunky striker rated England's 9-3 win over Scotland at Wembley six months later as one of his most 'memorable moments' in his entire football career. In a game of all-out attack by both teams, England played brilliantly to win the game 9-3. Smith scored twice, his second being the ninth.

Two years later, in this same fixture, Smith was involved in an early crunching tackle with the Rangers full-back Eric Caldow. Both players were carried off on stretchers. Smith returned but Caldow didn't. He sadly broke his leg and was out of action for several months. In May 1963, when England defeated the World Cup runners-up from the previous year Czechoslovakia 4-2 in Bratislava, Smith was superb, scoring once while assisting in one of Jimmy Greaves' two goals.

His final England appearance followed six months later, against Northern Ireland at Wembley, when he scored in an 8-3 victory.

At club level the burly Smith, robust, brave with a powerful shot, linked up superbly well at Spurs with first Les Allen and then Jimmy Greaves. All three players (and others) fed off the delights provided by John 'The Ghost' White.

Smith scored 251 goals in 359 first-team appearances during his time at White Hart Lane, helping Spurs in the League and FA Cup double in 1961, the FA Cup for a second time in 1962 and the European Cup Winners' Cup in 1963. Two years later he helped Brighton win the Fourth Division Championship. Smith had two hip replacements later in life - the legacy of being an all-action striker - a good old-fashioned English centre-forward. He was 77 when he died.

SMITH, Septimus Charles 1935-36 ①

Born: Whitburn, County Durham, 15 March 1912
Died: Leicester, 28 July 2006
Career: Whitburn Church of England School, Leicester City (professional, March 1929, retired, injured May 1949; remained at Filbert Street as a coach until May 1950); later worked as a fitter in Leicester.

Wing-half 'Sep' Smith was the first substitute called into action by England – albeit in the unofficial Jubilee international against Scotland at Hampden Park in August 1935. He replaced Jackie Bray of Manchester City at half-time in the 4-2 defeat. A Second Division Championship winner with Leicester in 1937, he always played a forceful game, being strong in the tackle and deliberate with his passing,

yet above all he was totally committed. He won just one full cap for England, competing honestly to the last in a 3-1 win over Ireland in Belfast in October 1935. One felt he deserved more honours.

SMITH, Stephen 1894-95 ① ①

Born: Abbots Langley, Staffs, 14 January 1874
Died: Benson, Oxfordshire, 19 May 1935
Career: Cannock & Rugeley Colliery (1889), Cannock Town (July 1889), Rugeley Ceal FC (May 1890), Hednesford Town (September 1891), Aston Villa (professional, August 1893), Portsmouth (May 1901), New Brompton (July 1906, player-manager from December 1906, retired, May 1908); lived in Portsmouth until 1932; then owned and managed the Roke Stores, Benson, Oxfordshire until his death.

A five times League winner with Aston Villa (1894-96-97-99-1900), he also gained an FA Cup winner's medal in 1895 but injury forced him to miss the final of 1897, the year Villa completed the double. Despite his brilliance on the left-wing, Smith won only one England cap, netting an impressive 3-0 win over Scotland at Goodison Park in April 1895. The *Daily Mail* reporter wrote: 'Smith closed the scoring with an angled shot which gave the Scottish 'keeper no chance.'

SMITH, Thomas, MBE 1970-71 ①

Born: Liverpool, 5 April 1945
Career: Cardinal St John's & Archbishop Godfrey High Schools/ Liverpool, Liverpool Schools, Liverpool (apprentice, May 1960, professional, April 1962), Tampa Bay Rowdies/USA (summer 1976), Los Angeles Aztecs/USA (player-manager, summer 1978), Swansea City (free, as player, August 1978, appointed player-coach, August-October 1979); Liverpool (coach, seasons 1979-81); engaged as a weekly columnist for the *Liverpool Echo* for 25 years; also briefly ran a pub in Billinge, Wigan called 'The Smithy'.

Tommy Smith started out as a deep lying inside-left before becoming one of the hardest and toughest defenders in the game. With his no-nonsense tackling, he was part and parcel of a great Liverpool team under Bill Shankly who once said: "Tommy Smith wasn't born, he was quarried."

The recipient of four League, two FA Cup, two European Cup, a European Super Cup, two UEFA Cup and three FA Charity Shield winner's medals between 1965 and 1978, Smith also collected his fair share of runners-up prizes while scoring 48 goals in 638 appearances during his 18 years at Anfield.

For all his commitment, he won only one England cap, in the 0-0 draw with Wales at Wembley in May 1971. Liverpool team-mates, Chris Lawler, Larry Lloyd and Emlyn Hughes, also played in this game and the four 'Reds' formed England's defence.

Smith, who gained youth honours for his country in 1963 and played for Team America with Bobby Moore and Pele against England in May 1976, was awarded the MBE in 1978, for services to football.

In June 2007, Smith suffered a heart attack at his Liverpool home. Thankfully he recovered after a six-way heart bypass and now supplements his income as an after-dinner speaker. In March 2008, he published his autobiography, *Anfield Iron*.

In May 1977, two days after winning the European Cup in Rome, Smith had his testimonial game at Anfield, when a Liverpool XI took on Bobby Charlton's Select XI. A crowd of 35,694 saw an enthralling 9-9 draw in which Reds' goalkeeper Ray Clemence and 'Smithy' himself both scored twice!

SMITH, Trevor 1959-60 ②

Born: Brierley Hill, Staffs, 13 April 1936
Died: Dagenham, Essex, 9 August 2003
Career: Quarry Bank Secondary Modern School/Brierley Hill, Brierley Hill, Sedgley & District Schools, Dudley Boys (trial), Birmingham City (amateur, July 1951, professional, April 1953), Walsall (October 1964, retired, injured, February 1966); became a licensee at Stonnall near Lichfield; was a permit player in the Lichfield League; Mile Oak Rovers (manager, season 1970-71); later manager of Threshers Wine Store, first in Birmingham's Bull Ring, then in Dagenham.

When Billy Wright retired from international football in May 1959, the 23-year-old Smith was chosen as his replacement, making his England debut against Wales at Ninian Park, Cardiff the following October. However, a calf injury sustained early on hampered his movement and meant he failed to do himself justice in the 1-1 draw which was played in driving wind and incessant rain, making the playing conditions intolerable. In fact he held up his hands for being responsible for Graham Moore's equalising goal.

Smith kept his place for the next match, against Sweden later in the month, but both he and England as a whole, performed poorly, the defence failing to cope with eager-beaver forward Agne Simonsson who caused problems aplenty as the Swedes won 3-2 at Wembley. Smith wasn't called upon again, England chief Walter Winterbottom preferring Peter Swan instead.

As a matter of interest, Brian Clough's England career was also restricted to these same two games.

Of strong build, sure and solid in defence Smith, who made 430 appearances for Birmingham City (three goals), gained a Second Division Championship winner's medal in 1955 and runners-up medals in the 1955 FA Cup and 1960 and 1961 Inter Cities Fairs Cup finals, before skippering Blues to victory in the 1963 League Cup over arch-rivals Aston Villa. He also played in 15 U23 and two B internationals and twice represented the Football League.

As a youngster Smith played with and against Duncan Edwards at schoolboy level and in 1951 captained Brierley Hill, Sedgley & District Schools in the final of the English Schools FA trophy which they lost to Liverpool Schools 5–3 on aggregate. He had the misfortune to concede an own-goal on his debut for Birmingham against Derby County.

After retiring to Walton-on-the-Naze, Essex, early in 2002, he sadly died 18 months later from lung cancer.

SMITH, William Henry 1921-28 ③

Born: Tantobie, County Durham, 23 May 1895
Died: Doncaster, 13 April 1951
Career: West Stanley Seniors (season 1909-10), Hobson Wanderers (April 1910), Tantobie FC (May 1911), Huddersfield Town (professional, October 1913-May 1934), Rochdale (player-coach, July 1934, then trainer and manager to November 1935).

A Huddersfield Town legend, outside-left Billy Smith spent most of his career with the Yorkshire club, forming an excellent wing-partnership with Clem Stephenson. In fact, to this day, Smith is still the Yorkshire club's record scorer with a total of 126 goals in 574 appearances made between 1913 and 1934, winning three First Division Championship medals in succession (1924-25-26) and netting the Terriers' controversial penalty winner in the 1922 FA Cup final against Preston North End at Stamford Bridge. Two years earlier he had missed Huddersfield's Cup final defeat by Aston Villa after being sent off in a League game at Stoke three weeks previous.

Smith's three England caps were gained against Wales at Goodison Park in March 1922 (won 1-0), against Scotland a month later at Villa Park (lost 1-0) and versus Scotland again at Wembley in March 1928, when the 'Blue Devils' dazzled in a magnificent 5-1 victory. Three of his Huddersfield team-mates also played for England – Roy Goodall, Bob Kelly and Tommy Wilson.

In his second international against the Scots, Smith was given 'very little chance to show what he could do' wrote the *Daily Mirror* reporter. In fact, he was marked out of the game by right-back Jock Marshall (Middlesbrough) and in his last he 'hardly got a kick' against the brilliant Jimmy Nelson of Cardiff City.

Smith represented the Football League on three occasions, played for the FA in 1934 and featured in four international trials between 1922 and 1928. He was also the first player to score a goal direct from a corner, netting from the flag for Huddersfield in the home League game against Arsenal in October 1924.

Smith and his son, Conway (Huddersfield, QPR and Halifax Town) were the first father and son to score 100 goals each in senior football. His grandson, Robert Smith, played in the last ever match at Huddersfield's old Leeds Road ground before it was knocked down in 2004.

Smith died of cancer in 1951, after having his left leg amputated due to a mistreated football injury.

SORBY, Thomas Heathcote 1878-79 ① ①

Born: Sheffield, 16 February 1856
Died: Scarborough, 13 December 1930
Career: Cheltenham College, Thursday Wanderers/Sheffield (1876), Sheffield FC (seasons 1877-80); also played for Sheffield FA (1870s); became a wealthy businessman in Scarborough.

Versatile forward Tom Sorby was prone to dribbling with his head down – to the annoyance of his team-mates! He scored 20 minutes into his England debut against Wales at The Oval in January 1879. He then had a hand in Herbert Whitfield's goal in a 2-1 win.

SOUTHGATE, Gareth 1995-2004 (57) ②

Born: Watford, 3 September 1970
Career: Crystal Palace (apprentice, January 1987, professional January 1989), Aston Villa (£2.5m, July 1995), Middlesbrough (£6.5m, July 2001, retired as player, May 2006; then manager, June 2006-October 2009); appointed FA's Head of Elite Development to work alongside Sir Trevor Brooking, January 2011, quit in May 2012); also engaged as an ITV soccer pundit.

Defender Gareth Southgate had the ill luck to miss a crucial penalty in the shoot-out at the end of England's Euro 96 semi-final encounter with Germany at Wembley. With the spot-kick count level after five kicks apiece, he saw his weak effort saved by 'keeper Kopke and as a result the Germans went into the final with a 6-5 victory.

Putting that bitter disappointment behind him, Southgate battled on and helped his country reach the 1998 World Cup finals in France, but after appearing in the opening match he was injured in training and missed the rest of the tournament. Thankfully he recovered full fitness and was a key figure in the qualifying campaign for Euro 2000.

Southgate made his international debut as a second-half substitute against Portugal in December 1995 and went on to win 57 caps in nine years, collecting his last in March 2004 v. Sweden. The first of his two England goals came in the 3-0 win over Luxembourg in a Euro 2000 qualifier in October 1998 (a 90th minute effort), his second followed in the 2-1 friendly match victory over South Africa in May 2003, getting his team off to a flier in the very first minute!

Southgate, who amassed a total of 637 club appearances (504 in the Premiership/League), helped Crystal Palace win the First Division title in 1994 and both Aston Villa (1994) and Middlesbrough (1996) lift the League Cup. He also played for the latter club in the 2002 UEFA Cup final. Captain of Villa, Middlesbrough and England (for 45 minutes v. South Korea in May 2002), he was manager at The Riverside Stadium for exactly 150 matches.

SOUTHWORTH, John 1888-92 ③ ③
Born: Blackburn, 11 December 1866
Died: Manchester, 16 October 1956
Career: Inkerman Rangers (aged 11, August 1878), Brookhouse Rangers (season 1881-82), Brookhouse Perseverance FC (August 1882), Higher Walton (February 1883), Chester (April 1883), Blackburn Olympic (August 1883, professional, August 1886), Vale of Lune (guest, early 1887), Blackburn Rovers (£50, September 1887), Everton (£400, August 1893, retired, injured, April 1895).

Jack Southworth scored once in each of his three internationals, all of which ended in 4-1 victories. He won his first two caps against Wales, in February 1889 and March 1891, and claimed his last against Scotland at Ibrox Park in April 1892. He swapped wings (from left to right) and crossed for Edgar Chadwick to score a first minute goal against the Scots before bagging 'a special goal of his own' following a mazy dribble in the 23rd minute.

Arguably the finest marksman in the Football League during its early years, Southworth was dubbed the 'Prince of Dribblers'. A truly great footballer, highly talented, he had everything a centre-forward needed – and more.

A write-up of him in the late 1880s stated: 'His dodging, his neat passing, his speed and general accuracy in shooting won the hearts of the spectators at the Leamington ground (Blackburn's home ground at the time). He is built for speed, he plays an unselfish game; he's good at tackling and has excellent judgment.'

After doing well with Blackburn Olympic (4 goals in 4 FA Cup-ties and 70 in all games including six against Leigh as a 16 year-old) he was then twice an FA Cup winner with Blackburn (1890 and 1891) he made 133 senior appearances and scored a staggering 122 goals during his time at the club. He struck Rovers' first-ever League hat-trick (v. Burnley in November 1888) and went on to claim a record 13 trebles.

As an Everton player, he cracked in a six timer in a 7-1 League win over West Bromwich Albion in December 1893 but injuries seriously affected his game at Goodison Park where he remained for just two seasons during which time he still notched 36 goals in only 32 outings.

Taking his full record at senior level (clubs and country) Southworth has the best ratio of goals per game than any other footballer....165 goals in 172 appearances. That's some record! And it must be said that his skills were not confined to the football field; far from it. He was an accomplished musician and pursued a career as a professional violinist with the Halle Orchestra in Manchester. His brother, James, was the conductor! He was almost 90 when he died.

SPARKS, Francis John 1878-80 ③ ③
Born: Billericay, Essex, 4 July 1855
Died: Islington, London, 13 February 1934
Career: St Albans Pilgrims (1873), Brondesbury (1874), Upton Park/London and also Hertfordshire Rangers (seasons 1876-78), Clapham Rovers (seasons 1879-82); also represented Essex County and London; FA Committee member (seasons 1876-80)

A useful forward, not the quickest but willing and able, Frank Sparks was an FA Cup winner with Clapham Rovers in 1880, having already gained three caps for England. He made his international debut in the thrilling 5-4 victory over Scotland in April 1879, scored his side's third goal in his next game, a 5-4 defeat by the Scots in March 1880, and as captain, was on the mark twice in a 3-2 win over Wales just two days later.

SPENCE, Joseph Walter 1925-27 ②
Born: Throckley, Northumberland, 15 December 1898
Died: Chesterfield, 31 December 1966
Career: Throckley School, Bluchers Juniors, Throckley Celtic (1914); served in the Army as a machine gunner during WW1; Scotswood (August 1918), Manchester United (March 1919), Bradford City (June 1933), Chesterfield (May 1935, retired, May 1938); Manchester United (scout/coach, 1945-48); Chesterfield (part-time scout, seasons 1948-60); also worked for the Chesterfield Tube Company until 1965.

Despite his success at club level, Joe Spence won only two full caps for England. No-one knows why! A bustling, all-action, lion-hearted inside or centre-forward with terrific shooting ability, he was a huge favourite at Old Trafford where the fans regularly shouted 'Give it to Joe.' Known also as 'Mr Soccer' he scored 168 goals in 510 first-class appearances for Manchester United, 481 of his games coming in the Football League, a record that stood for 37 years, until Bill Foulkes surpassed it in 1970.

Spence won the Third Division (North) Championship with Chesterfield in 1936. His son, also named Joe, was on the books of Buxton, Chesterfield, York City and Gainsborough Trinity (1946-56). Spence senior was the cousin of George Brown (ex-England international).

SPENCE, Richard 1935-36 ②
Born: Platts Common near Barnsley, 18 July 1908
Died: Fulham, London, 12 March 1983
Career: Thorpe Colliery (1923), Platts Common WMC (1927), Barnsley (professional, February 1932), Chelsea (£5,000, October 1934, retired May 1950, joined coaching staff, remained at Stamford Bridge until 1975); served in the Metropolitan Police during the Second World War.

A smart, two-footed outside-right, full of tricks with a strong shot, Dick Spence took over from Sammy Crooks on England's end-of-season tour, making his debut in a 2-1 defeat by Austria in Vienna in May 1936 when six Arsenal players figured in the England team. Spence's second cap followed three days later in a 3-2 reverse at the hands of Belgium in Brussels. He didn't figure at all after that – simply because there were so many other right-wingers around at the same time, with Stanley Matthews ready to step forward. After helping Barnsley win the Third Division (N) Championship, Spence scored 62 goals in 221 appearances for Chelsea, the club he served for over 40 years.

He was the great uncle of the honourable Tom Simpson, Earl of Derbyshire.

SPENCER, Charles William 1923-25 ②
Born: Washington, County Durham, 4 December 1899
Died: York, 9 February 1953
Career: Glebe Rovers, Washington Chemical Works FC, Newcastle United (October 1921), Manchester United (£3,250, July 1928), Tunbridge Wells Rangers (player-manager, May 1929), Wigan Athletic (player-manager, August 1932), Grimsby Town (manager, March 1937-April 1951), Hastings United (manager, August 1951-July 1952), York City (manager, November 1952 until his death).

Although billed as a 'stopper centre-half' Charlie Spencer had a lot of skill, always endeavouring to get his attack moving with deliberate passes. He made his England debut in the 1-1 draw with Scotland in April 1924 - the first international played at Wembley Stadium. His second cap followed ten months later in a 2-1 win over Wales at Swansea. He also toured Australia with the FA in 1925 (playing in five Test Matches), twice represented the Football League and played in one England trial. An FA Cup winner and

League Championship winner with Newcastle (in 1924 and 1927 respectively), Spencer made 175 appearances during his eight years at St James' Park.

SPENCER, Howard 1896-1905 ⑥

Born: Edgbaston, Birmingham, 23 August 1875
Died: Four Oaks, Sutton Coldfield, 14 January 1940
Career: Albert Road School/Handsworth, Birmingham, Stamford FC (August 1890), Birchfield All Saints (August 1891), Birchfield Trinity (January 1892), Aston Villa (amateur, April 1892, professional, June 1894, retired, November 1907; then club director, July 1909-May 1936).

Howard Spencer was an incredibly gifted player and renowned sportsman to boot. Known as the 'Prince of full-backs', during his hugely successful time with Aston Villa he won four League Championships in 1896, 1897, 1899 and 1900 and three FA Cups, captaining the side to its 1905 victory over Newcastle United. A key member of the Villa's double-winning side of 1896-97, he continued to serve the club after his playing days were over, serving as a director for 27 years. His association with the Birmingham club covered 42 years. He made 295 appearances. Surprisingly, Spencer was capped only six times by England, which many felt was paltry reward for a player of his quality. He made his international debut in a 4-0 win over Wales in March 1897, following up with his second cap five days later in a 2-1 defeat by Scotland. It was then three years before he played again, in a 1-1 draw with Wales in March 1900, and it was another three years before he played in his fourth game, a comprehensive 4-0 victory over Ireland. His last two England calls came in March and April 1905 v. Wales (3-1) and Scotland (1-0). Linesman of the *Daily Chronicle*, reporting on the latter game at Crystal Palace, said: "Spencer was too good for Wilson and did nothing wrong."

SPIKSLEY, Frederick 1892-98 ⑦ ⑤

Born: Gainsborough, 25 January 1870
Died: Goodwood, Sussex, 28 July 1948
Career: Holy Trinity School/Gainsborough, Eclipse FC, Gainsborough Working Men's Club, Gainsborough Wednesday, Jubilee Swifts/Gainsborough (season 1886-87), Gainsborough Trinity (August 1887), Sheffield Wednesday (January 1891), Glossop (October 1904), Leeds City (briefly, March 1905), Southern United (April-May 1905), Watford (August 1905 retired, May 1906); AIK Stockholm/Sweden (coach, July 1911), then briefly coach/manager of the Swedish national team (1913); TSV 1869 Munich/Germany (coach, July 1913), 1FC Nuremberg/Germany (coach, April 1914); interned at the Ruhleben P-o-W detention camp near Berlin (August 1914; escaped February 1915); returned to England, then sailed to USA in mid-1915 (worked in a munitions factory in Pittsburgh); coached in Spain (season 1918-19), in the USA (two years, 1919-21); then Reformat AC/Mexico (coach, season 1921-22); Real Club Español/Spain (coach, seasons 1922-24); Fulham (assistant-coach, August 1924-May 1926); 1FC Nuremberg/Germany (coach, June 1926-May 1928); Lausanne Sports/Switzerland (coach, seasons 1928-30); later football coach at King Edward VII School, Sheffield (August 1933-May 1936); became a bookmaker.

Fred Spiksley helped England win the British Home International Championship in both 1893 and 1898. He scored twice with 'crisp finishes' on his debut against Wales at The Victoria Ground, Stoke in March 1893 when England won 6-0, and a month later he struck twice more with brilliantly taken headers within a minute of each other, both from right-wing crosses by Billy Bassett, when Scotland were defeated 5-2 at the Richmond Athletic ground, Surrey.

He notched his fifth goal in his third game, a 2-2 draw with Ireland in March 1894.

In March 1903, ten years after his international debut, Spiksley scored for the Football League in a 3–0 win over the Scottish League at Celtic Park. He played in one other Inter-League game and also represented Lincolnshire on three occasions in the late 1880s.

One of the great players in Sheffield Wednesday's history, outside-left Spiksley was certainly one of the star players of the 1890s. Fast, cunning with great dribbling skills, he packed a terrific shot and seemed to be on hand – in the right place at the right time – to score important goals. An FA Cup winner in 1896 and Second Division and then First Division Championship winner in 1900 and 1903 respectively, Spiksley notched 126 goals in 337 appearances for the Owls. As coach (manager) he guided AIK Stockholm to the Swedish League title in 1912, Real Club Español to the Mexican Primera Fuerza League Championship in 1924 and 1 FC Nuremberg to the Bundesliga title in 1927.

He was interned with several other footballers, including three England internationals – Fred Pentland, Sam Wolstenholme and Steve Bloomer. He scored no less than 31 goals in just six local Cup games for Jubilee Swifts in 1886-87 and actually turned down Accrington FC to join Sheffield Wednesday in 1891.

Spiksley collapsed and died at a Goodwood race meeting at the age of 78.

It must be pointed out that over the years Spiksley's goal-scoring record for England has been disputed several times via different sources. In his book 50 Years of Football 1884-1934, Sir Frederick Wall, secretary of the FA, claims that he scored a hat-trick against Scotland in 1893. However, newspaper reports from that game give the scorers as Spiksley (2), Goodhall, Bassett, Reynolds and Schofield. Brian James, in his book England v Scotland (published in 1969) also states that Spiksley scored twice, as does author Nick Gibbs in his book England – The Football Facts (published 1988). And all club publications give Spiksley's England goal count as five (2, 2, 1).

SPILSBURY, Benjamin Ward 1884-86 ③ ⑤

Born: Findern, Derbyshire, 1 August 1864
Died: Vancouver, Canada, 15 August 1938
Career: Rossall School, Repton College (seasons 1881-83), Jesus College/Cambridge University (1883-87); assisted the Corinthians (seasons 1885-88), Derby County (engaged between August 1884-April 1889); also played cricket for Derbyshire CCC; emigrated to Vancouver, Canada, 1891.

A quick, sure-footed player, sharp at times, Ben Spilsbury occupied the outside and inside-right positions. Making his England debut against Ireland in February 1885, he partnered Jim Brown of Blackburn Rovers on the right-wing and scored the second goal in a 4-0 win at Manchester. Then, a little over a year later, in March 1886, he was quite brilliant, claiming a four-timer in a resounding 6-1 victory in Belfast, two of his efforts being 'powerful shots from 'distance'. He rounded off his international career in the 1-1 draw with Scotland two weeks later.

An all-round athlete who engaged in football, cricket and athletics, Spilsbury was the Repton School champion four times in the long jump, while in 1882 he broke the all-time record. Spilsbury, who scored the first recorded Derby goal in 1884, became an estate agent in Canada.

SPINK, Nigel Philip 1982-83 ①

Born: Chelmsford, Essex, 8 August 1958
Career: Chelmsford City Schools/Boys, West Ham United (schoolboy forms, August 1974), Chelmsford City (semi-professional, August 1975), Aston Villa (£4,000, January 1977), West Bromwich Albion (free, January 1996), Millwall (£50,000, September 1997-May 2000); goalkeeping coach at West Bromwich Albion (briefly), Birmingham City, Swindon Town, Northampton Town; Forest Green Rovers (coach, then joint-manager, season 2002-03); then goalkeeping coach, under manager Steve Bruce, at Birmingham City (2003-04), Wigan Athletic (seasons 2007-09) and Sunderland (coach, June 2009).

Goalkeeper Nigel Spink had been at Villa Park for five-and-a-half years before he got his big break in the first team – on one of the biggest stages of all – in the European Cup final. Ten minutes into the 1982 showdown with Bayern Munich in Rotterdam, Villa's first choice 'keeper and former England international, Jimmy Rimmer was injured in the 8th minute and as a result Spink came on as a substitute, having made only two previous appearances in the first XI. He performed superbly, keeping a clean sheet, as Villa won the game 1-0. He also helped Villa win the Super Cup (1983) and League Cup (1994) and made 460 senior appearances during his time at Villa Park. He then became the oldest goalkeeper ever to appear for the Baggies when, at the age of 39 years and 19 days, he played in a League Cup-tie against Cambridge United in August 1997. Tremendously effective and a good shot-stopper, at 6ft 2ins tall and 14st 10lbs in weight, Spink could withstand the strongest of challenges. He played just 45 minutes for England as a second-half substitute for Peter Shilton in the 1-1 draw with Australia in Melbourne in June 1983. Although he later took part in two B internationals in 1988, Spink was never going to be England's number one!

SPOUNCER, William Alfred 1899-1900 ①

Born: Gainsborough, Lincolnshire, 1 July 1877
Died: Southend-on-Sea, 31 August 1962
Career: Gainsborough Grammar School (seasons 1891-93), Gainsborough Trinity (August 1893), Sheffield United (July 1894), Nottingham Forest (£125, May 1897, retired, June 1910); later coach of CF Barcelona/Spain, also other clubs in Europe.

A skilful outside-left who centred with perfection, when given the time, Alf Spouncer won the FA Cup and Second Division Championship with Forest in 1898 and 1907 respectively. In between times he gained his only England cap, in the 1-1 draw with Wales at Cardiff in March 1900 – chosen at a time when the outside-left position was causing something of a problem! In fact, a different winger was used on the left flank in each of nine consecutive internationals played over a period of three years: March 1899-March 1902. Spouncer scored 51 goals in 338 senior games for Forest.

SPRINGETT, Ronald Deryk George 1959-66 ㉜

Born: Fulham, London, 22 July 1935
Career: Victoria United (August 1950); served in Egypt with Army (1951-52); Queens Park Rangers (professional, February 1953), Sheffield Wednesday (£10,000, March 1958), Queens Park Rangers (£16,000, June 1967), Valley United (July 1969, retired May 1971); later ran a sports shop and then a decorating and landscape/gardening business in London.

On his day, Ron Springett was an excellent goalkeeper with cat-like ability and superb anticipation. He marked an impressive first game for England by saving Jimmy McIlroy's penalty in a 2-1 victory over Northern Ireland at Wembley in November 1959.

Maintaining his form, he continued to play well but was responsible for Portugal's goal in the 1-1 World Cup qualifying draw in Lisbon in May 1961. He failed to give Bobby Robson a call and it proved fatal.

In May 1962, during England's penultimate warm-up game before the World Cup in Chile, Springett made four stunning saves as Switzerland were defeated 3-1 at Wembley. Then, two weeks later, he kept a clean-sheet in a 4-0 win over Peru, saving another penalty, this time from Oscar Montalvo. However, in the World Cup, he had mixed fortunes. He was caught cold by Tichy's 25-yard drive which set Hungary on their way to a 2-1 win in the opening group 4 game and in the crucial match with Brazil, he was at fault when Garrincha's powerful free-kick struck him in the chest and rebounded out for Vava to head home in a 3-1 defeat in Vina del Mar.

The Wednesday 'keeper then had a real 'stinker' in a 5-2 defeat by France in a European Championship qualifier in Paris in February 1963 - Alf Ramsey's first game in charge. He was held responsible for three goals, with his mostly costly error coming after England had clawed back from 3-0 down to 3-2. These lapses cost him his place in the team…and Gordon Banks stepped in for the next game against Scotland.

Later recalled for the game against Wales in Cardiff in October 1965, he impressed in the 0-0 draw and went on to win two more caps while also being named as one of two reserve goalkeepers to Gordon Banks in the 1966 World Cup. Only the 11 players on the pitch during the 4-2 win over West Germany received medals but following an FA-led campaign to persuade FIFA to award medals to all the winners' squad members, Springett duly received his from PM Gordon Brown at a ceremony at 10 Downing Street in June 2009.

At club level, Springett – who also represented the Football League – helped Sheffield Wednesday win the Second Division Championship in 1959 and reach the FA Cup final seven years later. He made 384 appearances for the Owls and 123 in his two spells with QPR. His brother, Peter, also played for Wednesday and QPR and both goalkeepers 'swapped' clubs in 1967. Together the Springetts amassed 1,120 appearances in senior football.

SPROSTON, Bert 1936-39 ⑪

Born: Elworth near Sandbach, Cheshire, 22 June 1915
Died: Bolton, 27 January 2000
Career: Sandbach Ramblers (1931), Huddersfield Town (trial, 1932), Leeds United (professional, May 1933), Tottenham Hotspur (£9,500, June 1938), Manchester City (£9,500, November 1938); WW2 guest for Aldershot, Millwall, Port Vale and Wrexham; Ashton United (August 1950, retired May 1951); Bolton Wanderers (trainer, July 1951, later club scout and then team attendant to 1984).

Bert Sproston was a very efficient, hard-working, strong-willed right-back, especially quick in recovery and a player who gave 110 per cent every time he took the field.

Replacing the injured George Male, he made his England debut in a 2-1 defeat by Wales at Cardiff in October 1936. He had a decent game but had to wait twelve months before winning his second cap, in a 5-1 win over Ireland in Belfast. Chosen for the next nine games in a row (ahead of Male), he hardly put a foot wrong and produced excellent performances in 6-3 and 4-2 wins over Germany in Berlin and France in Paris in May 1938 and in the 2-1 victory over a strong FIFA XI at Highbury five months later.

Sproston also played for England in two Wartime internationals. The first was against Scotland in May 1940. He recalled: "I travelled up to Glasgow by train and at Crewe station news came through that the Germans had started their bombing and that Austria was on fire. Lord Haw Haw, in one of his German radio propaganda broadcasts, said he hoped the people of Scotland would enjoy half the match as the Germans would bomb the ground at half-time. We could see

British fighter planes circling the stadium during the match but the 75,000 fans inside never budged and saw us gain a 1-1 draw."

He made almost 300 senior appearances during his club career, including 140 for Leeds and 134 for Manchester City whom he helped win the Second Division Championship in 1947.

SQUIRE, Ralph Tyndall 1885-86 ③
Born: Marylebone, London, 10 September 1864
Died: Chatham, Kent, 22 August 1944
Career: Westminster School (1880-82), Cambridge University (Trinity Hall, Blue 1884 and 1886; football secretary in 1885); Old Westminsters (seasons 1885-86), Clapham Rovers (also 1886), registered to play for Corinthians (seasons 1886-92; treasurer for many years from 1903); FA Committee member (seasons 1884-87).

A fine, versatile footballer, able to play at right-back and centre-half, Ralph Squire was quick over the ground and possessed a strong, reliable kick. He made his three international appearances in the same month, March 1886, starring in wins over Ireland (6-1) and Wales (3-1) and in the 1-1 draw with Scotland. He also played several times for London in representative matches.

STANBROUGH, Morris Hugh 1894-95 ①
Born: Cleobury, Shropshire, 2 September 1870
Died: Broadstairs, Kent, 15 December 1904
Career: Charterhouse School (seasons 1887-89), Caius College/ Cambridge University (1889-92, captain in 1892), Old Carthusians (seasons 1893-95); played for Corinthians (seasons 1890-94), Eastbourne FC (season 1895-96); a schoolteacher in turn at Elstree, Stanmore and Eastbourne, he was engaged at St Peter's School, Broadstairs at the time of his death.

A positive outside-right, regarded by many as one of the best in his position in the early 1890s, Hugh Stanbrough made his England debut at senior level in the 1-1 draw with Wales at the Queen's Club, London in March 1895, having a hand in the build-up to G.O. Smith's goal.

Stanbrough, who also played in one unofficial international, was an FA Amateur Cup winner with Old Carthusians in 1895 – just after winning his only cap.

STANIFORTH, Ronald 1953-55 ⑧
Born: Newton Heath, Manchester, 13 April 1924
Died: Sheffield, summer 1988
Career: Hague Street School (Newton Heath), Manchester Schools (1938-39); served in the Royal Navy during the war; Newton Albion (August 1945), Stockport County (amateur, August 1946, professional, October 1946), Huddersfield Town (£1,000, May 1952), Sheffield Wednesday (July 1955), Barrow (player-manager, October 1959, retired as a player, May 1961, continued as manager until July 1964); Sheffield Wednesday (assistant-coach, July 1960, chief coach, March 1971, later youth team coach to 1976).

Stylish, uncomplicated and sure-kicking right-back Ron Staniforth had an excellent game on his debut for England in a 4-2 victory over Scotland at Hampden Park in April 1954. He produced a similar performance in his next international in Yugoslavia but, like the rest of his team-mates, he had a rough time against Hungary a week later when the Magyars won 7-1 in Budapest. However, Staniforth was named in Walter Winterbottom's squad for that summer's World Cup finals, partnering Manchester United's Roger Byrne in all three matches against Belgium, the host country Switzerland and Uruguay. He made two more appearances before the turn of the year, against Wales and the reigning World champions West

Germany, before losing his place.

Staniforth made well over 500 appearances at club level, 473 in the League alone, and was twice a Second Division Championship winner with Sheffield Wednesday in 1956 and 1959. He also played three times for England B.

STARLING, Ronald William 1932-37 ②
Born: Pelaw-on-Tyne near Gateshead, 11 October 1909
Died: Sheffield, 17 December 1991
Career: Durham County Schools, Newcastle United (trial, November 1923), Usworth Colliery (January 1924), Washington Colliery (September 1924), Hull City (amateur, June 1925, professional, August 1927), Newcastle United (£3,750, May 1930), Sheffield Wednesday (£3,250, June 1932), Aston Villa (£7,500, January 1937); Wartime guest for Northampton Town (1939-40), Hereford United (1940), Nottingham Forest (1939-40 and 1941-42), Walsall (1939-42) and Sheffield Wednesday (1940-41); Nottingham Forest (player-coach, July 1948-June 1950), Beighton FC (February-April 1951); later ran a newsagents shop near the Hillsborough ground.

Ronnie Starling's first-class career lasted for 25 years: 1925-50. A creative inside-forward who possessed all the tricks in the book, his ball carrying ability earned him the nickname of 'Fluttering Feet.' He made 431 appearances in all competitions but was never a prolific marksman, scoring just 65 goals. He captained Sheffield Wednesday to FA Cup glory in 1935 and helped Aston Villa win the Second Division Championship in 1938. He also made almost 200 appearances in Wartime football (136 for Villa).

In April 1933, Starling won his first England cap, playing at inside right in the 2–1 defeat by Scotland at Hampden Park. Surprisingly he had to wait four years before gaining his second, also against the Scots in Glasgow in April 1937, when a record crowd of 149,547 saw the home side win 3-1. He starred for an International XI against a District XI in September 1940 and had the distinction of playing in an FA Cup semi-final with four different clubs: Hull (1930), Newcastle (1932), Wednesday (1935) and Villa (1938). He could also preach a sermon as good as any vicar!

STATHAM, Derek James 1982-83 ③
Born: Whitmore Reams, Wolverhampton, 24 March 1959
Career: St Mary's and St Edmund's Schools (Wolverhampton), West Bromwich Albion (apprentice, July 1975, professional, April 1976), Southampton (£100,000, August 1987), Stoke City (£50,000, July 1989), Aston Villa (trial, July 1991), Walsall (August 1991-May 1993), Telford United (briefly during 1993-94), King's Lynn (two weeks, retired May 1994); West Bromwich Albion Old Stars (1995-99); now runs a spa (hot tub) business in Casares near Malaga, Spain.

Derek Statham was an attacking left-back, who, said his manager at West Bromwich Albion, Ron Atkinson: "Was miles better than Kenny Sansom." He made his England debut against Wales at Wembley in February 1983 and four months later added two more caps to his collection when chosen twice against Australia, first in Sydney, then in Brisbane. He deserved far more – but unfortunately Sansom rarely had a bad game for his country.

Statham, who also represented England in four Youth, two B (2 goals scored v. Spain and USA in 1980-81) and in six U21 internationals, made 555 appearances during his career (378 for WBA), yet for all his efforts, he never won a major competition with any of his clubs, losing in one League Cup and two FA Cup semi-finals and in a European Cup Winners' Cup quarter-final, all with the Baggies. His first senior goal was a beauty, driven hard and low past Stoke and England 'keeper Peter Shilton on his League debut in December 1976. He was voted Midland 'Young Player of the Year' in 1978.

Statham was set to join Liverpool for £250,000 in 1987 but the deal broke down on medical grounds.

STEELE, Frederick Charles 1936-37 ⑥ ⑧

Born: Hanley, Stoke-on-Trent, 6 May 1916
Died: Newcastle-under-Lyme, Staffs, 23 April 1976
Career: Hanley Council School, Stoke City (amateur, July 1931); played for Downings Tileries FC (seasons 1931-33, while still registered with Stoke), Stoke City (professional, June 1933); WW2 guest for Sheffield United, Northampton Town, Notts County, Leicester City, Doncaster Rovers, Bradford Park Avenue, Leeds United, Arsenal, Nottingham Forest and Fulham; Mansfield Town (£1,000, player-manager, June 1949), Port Vale (£1,500, player-manager, December 1951, retired as a player, May 1953, continued as manager until January 1957); became a licensee; Port Vale (manager again, October 1962-February 1965); South Africa (footballer advisor and part-time coach); a fine track athlete for Staffordshire, he ran 100 yards in 11.5 seconds, competed in the men's 4x100 yards relay and participated in the 110 hurdles.

Centre-forward Freddie Steele had a wonderful change of pace which made him a great player – and that's no exaggeration. Brave and committed, he could shoot with both feet but was unlucky to receive a bad knee injury when at his peak playing for Stoke against Charlton Athletic in October 1937 which knocked him back considerably, although he continued to play for another 16 years!

Quicker than Tommy Lawton by far, some said he may well have been better, given the chance, and one suspects that if he had been with a 'bigger' club, then more caps would certainly have come his way. It was perhaps unfortunate for Steele that there were some many high-quality centre-forwards around at the same time – for he was certainly one of the best in the late 1930s. Nicknamed 'Nobby' he failed to score in his first two internationals (v. Wales and Ireland in October and November 1936) but netted eight times in his next four, including a superb first-half hat-trick in a 4-0 win in Sweden in May 1937. He scored 159 goals in 251 first-class appearances for Stoke, plus another 81 in 95 Wartime fixtures. He also represented the Football League against The Irish League in Belfast in September 1936. As a manager, he guided Port Vale to the Third Division (North) Championship and FA Cup semi-finals in 1954. He was the uncle of David Steele, the former Northants and England Test cricketer.

STEIN, Brian 1983-84 ①

Born: Cape Town, South Africa, 19 October 1957
Career: Edgware Town (August 1974), Luton Town (£1,000, professional, October 1977), Stade Malherbe de Caen/France (June 1988), FC Annency/France (June 1990), Luton Town (July, 1991), Barnet (non-contract, August 1992, retired, May 1993); Luton Town (reserve team coach, seasons 1993-2000, then caretaker-

manager, March-May 2007), Grimsby Town (chief scout, then first team coach, November 2008, being reunited with his former Luton Town colleague, Mike Newell; appointed assistant-manager, May-November 2009); now runs a chain of fish restaurants including a 'chippy' in Padstow, Cornwall.

Striker Brian Stein partnered his Luton team-mate Paul Walsh in attack when making his England debut in the 2-0 defeat by France in Paris in February 1984. That same year he helped England win the European U21 Championship, playing in three games. During his two spells with the Hatters, Stein netted 127 goals in 388 League appearances, gaining Second Division Championship and League Cup winner's medals in 1982 and 1988 respectively, his two late goals defeating Arsenal 3-2 in the final of the latter competition.

One of nine children born to a father who was under house arrest because he opposed the apartheid system, Stein's elder brother, Mark, also a striker, played for Luton (1982-88), Aldershot, QPR, Oxford United, Stoke City, Chelsea, Ipswich Town and Bournemouth, scoring 123 goals in almost 350 League games: 1984-98.

STEPHENSON, Clement 1923-24 ①

Born: New Delaval, County Durham, 6 February 1890
Died: Huddersfield, 24 October 1961
Career: Bedlington Boys (1904-05), West Stanley (1905-06), New Delaval Villa (July 1906), West Stanley (August 1908), Blyth Spartans (November 1908-February 1909), Aston Villa (£175, March 1910), Stourbridge (loan, August 1910-February 1911); served in the Royal Navy for two years (PT Instructor at Crystal Palace); Wartime guest for Leeds City (February 1919), South Shields & District (also in 1919), Huddersfield Town (£3,000, March 1921, retired, May 1929; became manager at Leeds Road, a position he held until June 1942); became a caterer in Huddersfield.

One of three brothers who played for Aston Villa, Clem Stephenson was an expert schemer, a true and precise passer of the ball using both feet. He was quick over the ground and could shoot, from long distances!

Stephenson played in four FA Cup finals and managed in two more. He was a winner in 1913, 1920 and 1922 but collected runners-up medals in 1928, 1930 and 1938. He actually dreamed that Villa would win the 1913 final 1-0 (v. Sunderland) with Tommy Barber heading the only goal. And that is precisely what happened! He was certainly unlucky to win only one England cap, appearing in the 2-1 defeat by Wales at Blackburn in March 1924. He scored 96 goals in 216 appearances for Villa and 50 in 275 outings for Huddersfield with whom he won three successive League Championships, 1924-25-26.

STEPHENSON, George Ternent 1927-31 ③ ②

Born: Horton, Northumberland, 3 September 1900
Died: Derby, 18 August 1971
Career: Blyth Secondary School Juniors, County Durham Schools, Northumberland County Boys, Blyth Secondary School Seniors, New Delaval Juniors, New Delaval Villa, Leeds City (professional, August 1919), Aston Villa (£250, November 1919), Stourbridge (loan, August 1920-March 1921), Derby County (£2,000, November 1927), Sheffield Wednesday (£2,500, February 1931), Preston North End (£1,500, July 1933), Charlton Athletic (£660, May 1934, retired, injured, May 1937; joined coaching staff at The Valley, later scout and assistant-manager); Huddersfield Town (manager, August 1947-March 1952); became licensee of the Sportsman's Inn near Huddersfield (1954-56); worked at Rolls Royce factory, Derby (1957-58); Derby County (A team coach, 1961-63).

Brother of Clem (above) George Stephenson was small in stature with a big heart; a brainy, cultured inside-left who played for England in a junior international before gaining three full caps, the first against France in Paris in May 1928 when he netted twice in a 5-1 win, the second against Belgium in Antwerp two days later (won 3-1) and the third v. France again in Paris, in May 1931 (lost 5-2). He partnered Len Barry (Leicester) on the left-wing in his first two outings and outside-right Sammy Crooks (Derby) in his last.

Stephenson's club career realised almost 350 appearances (319 in the Football League, 120 goals). He won the Third Division (South) Championship with Charlton in 1935.

His son, Robert (Bobby), played for Derby County, Shrewsbury Town and Rochdale in the 1960s, and was also a cricketer with Derbyshire and Hampshire.

STEPHENSON, Joseph Eric, Major 1937-39 ②
Born: Bexleyheath, Kent, 12 September 1914
Died: Burma, 8 September 1944
Career: Tom Hood School/Leytonstone, Harrogate FC (1931), Leeds United (amateur, January 1933, professional, September 1934; killed in action while serving as a Major in the Gurkha Rifles in Burma).

Capped by England at both schoolboy and youth team levels, Eric Stephenson was a clever inside-forward who linked up superbly with his wing-half and outside-left. Making his international debut against Scotland at Wembley in April 1938, he assisted Cliff Bastin on the left flank but was generally kept under control by the well-educated Preston duo of Bill Shankly and Tommy Smith. He had just one chance during the 1-0 defeat, firing over after some good work by Stan Matthews.

Stephenson's second outing came against Ireland seven months later when he had an outstanding game, assisting in two of Willie Hall's seven goals in an emphatic 7-0 victory at Maine Road. He scored 22 goals in 115 appearances for Leeds – and may well have doubled his goals and games tallies had he not lost his life serving his country.

STEPNEY, Alexander Cyril 1967-68 ①
Born: Mitcham, Surrey, 18 September 1944
Career: Surrey Schoolboys, London Schoolboys, Achilles FC/Surrey, Fulham (trial, May 1958), Tooting & Mitcham United (August 1958), Millwall (amateur, March 1962 professional, May 1963), Chelsea, (£50,000, May 1966), Manchester United (£55,000, August 1966-February 1979), Dallas Tornado/USA (March 1979-May 1980), Altrincham (player-coach, August 1979), Dallas Tornado/USA (April-August 1980); worked in Stockport County and Rochdale Commercial Departments; acted as a Northern-based scout for Exeter City and Southampton (while managing a car/van rental business in Rochdale); was a licensee (briefly); Manchester City (goalkeeping coach, season 2000-01); an after-dinner speaker and hosted The Legends Football Phone in on 105.4 Century Radio.

Highly competent goalkeeper Alex Stepney won his only England cap a week after helping Manchester United lift the European Cup. Taking over from Gordon Banks, he played well in the 3-1 victory over Sweden at Wembley in May 1968.

He starred in 546 first-class games for Manchester United, kept 175 clean sheets, made a club record 92 consecutive appearances (later broken by Steve Coppell) and scored two goals! Besides his European Cup triumph, Stepney won a First Division Championship winner's medal in 1967 and played in successive FA Cup finals (losing in 1976 and winning in 1977). A goalkeeper who shouted more than most (to his defenders) he was once taken to hospital with a dislocated jaw – for opening his mouth too wide when yelling instructions to his centre-half Bill Foulkes!

STERLAND, Melvyn 1988-89 ①
Born: Sheffield, 1 October 1961
Career: Middlewood Rovers/Sheffield, Sheffield Wednesday (apprentice, June 1977, professional, October 1979), Glasgow Rangers (£800,000, March 1989), Leeds United (July 1989, contract cancelled, January 1994), Boston United (player-manager, seasons 1994-96), Denaby United (season 1996-97), Stalybridge Celtic (manager, December 1997), Hallam FC/Sheffield (briefly, season 1998-99).

Full-back Mel Sterland - as tough as nails - made just one appearance for his country, doing 'okay' as one reporter stated, in the 1-1 friendly draw with Saudi Arabia in November 1988. Nicknamed 'Zico' by his fans (due to his ferocious shooting power) Sterland scored 69 goals in almost 500 League and Cup appearances during his club career, helped Wednesday gain promotion to the top flight in 1984, Rangers win the Scottish Cup in 1989 and Leeds the Second Division and First Division titles in 1990 and 1992.

His autobiography, entitled *Boozing, Betting & Brawling* (Green Umbrella Publishing), was co-written with Sheffield-based journalist Nick Johnson and was published in August 2008.

STERLING, Raheem Shaquille 2012-13 ①
Born: Maverley, Kingston, Jamaica, 8 December 1994
Career: Copeland High School (Wembley), Queen's Park Rangers (academy, July 2005), Liverpool (£600,000, rising to £5m, February 2010; turned professional, December 2011)

After some excellent displays for Liverpool in the Premiership and in Europe during the first four months of the 2012-13 season, right-winger Raheem Sterling was given his senior international debut by England boss Roy Hodgson in the 4-2 friendly defeat in Sweden in November 2012. He was on the field for virtually the duration of the game and although he lost possession at times, he produced a decent performance, helping set up a goal for Danny Welbeck with a sweeping pass out to the left for Ashley Young, who then picked out his Manchester United team-mate with an inch-perfect cross. Sterling was 17 years and 332 days old when he lined up in Stockholm, making him only the fifth seventeen year-old ever to play at senior level for England, behind Theo Walcott (the youngest debutant, aged 17 years and 75 days), Wayne Rooney, James Prinsep and Thurston Rostron.

Previously capped a total of 25 times for England at U16, U17, U19 and U21 levels, Sterling was actually featured on the front page of Jamaica's national newspaper, *The Gleaner*, at the age of 14 – as a star footballer of the future.

STEVEN, Trevor McGregor 1984-92 ㊱ ④
Born: Berwick-on-Tweed, 21 September 1963
Career: Burnley (apprentice, June 1980, professional, September 1981), Everton (£300,000, July 1983), Glasgow Rangers (£1.5m, July 1989), Olympique Marseille/France (£5.5m, August 1991), Glasgow Rangers (£2.4m, September 1992, retired, May 1999); became a football agent, then TV soccer pundit, latterly for RTÉ Sport in Ireland; also worked for aviation company, Cloud9.

Trevor Steven won the first of his 36 England caps in the 1-0 World Cup qualifying win over Northern Ireland in Belfast in February 1985. In his second game he scored his first goal in the 2-1 win over the Republic of Ireland and then grabbed another goal in the 5-0 win over the USA four months later. After firing home his third goal – which was England's 1,500th at senior level to set up a 4-0 win over Egypt in Cairo in January 1986 - he had to wait over six years before his fourth and final effort, in the 2-2 draw with the C.I.S. in Moscow in April 1992. This last strike saved the match for England. Generally a hard-working right-sided midfielder, his international career spanned eight years and he was initially called up by Bobby Robson. He partnered his Everton team-mate Gary Stevens at times before linking up with Chris Waddle and John Barnes.

He played in the 1986 World Cup, the disastrous 1988 European Championships and also the 1990 World Cup. Remaining a key member of the team over the next two years, he eventually slipped out of favour once Paul Ince had bedded himself in alongside David Batty and David Platt.

Steven made over 600 appearances for his four major clubs (scoring 107 goals). He had his best spell with Everton (58 goals in 298 outings), gaining FA Cup, two League Championship, a European Cup Winners' Cup and four FA Charity Shield winner's medals. During his two spells north of the border, he collected seven League, four League Cup and two Scottish Cup winner's medals with Rangers while also adding a Ligue winner's medal to his collection with Marseille in 1992.

STEVENS, Gary Andrew 1984-86 ⑦

Born: Hillingdon, 30 March 1962
Career: West Suffolk Schools, Suffolk Schools, Ipswich Town (schoolboy forms), Brighton & Hove Albion (professional, October 1979), Tottenham Hotspur (£350,000, June 1983), Portsmouth (loan, January 1990, signed for £250,000, March 1990, retired, injured, May 1992); became a media commentator and presenter.

After some excellent performances for Spurs, versatile defender Gary Stevens made his England debut as a second-half substitute in a 5-0 win over Finland at Wembley in a World Cup qualifier in October 1984. He played well enough but a serious knee injury sidelined him until March 1985. Returning to the squad, he was in good form through to the 1986 World Cup finals in Mexico and played against Morocco and Paraguay. However, another series of injury problems ruined his game and also ended his international career after just seven games.

An FA Cup runner-up with Brighton in 1983, he helped Spurs in the UEFA Cup the following year and during his career made almost 400 club appearances, 332 in the League.

STEVENS, Michael Gary 1985-92 ㊻

Born: Barrow-in-Furness, 27 March 1963
Career: Everton (apprentice, April 1979, professional, March 1981), Glasgow Rangers (£1.2m, July 1988), Tranmere Rovers (£350,000, September 1994, retired, May 1988); graduated in 2002 from the University of Salford with a degree in Physiotherapy; Bolton Wanderers (Academy physiotherapist), Chester City (coach); then worked as a physiotherapist at Ellesmere Port Cottage Hospital, Cheshire.

Only 8,000 spectators witnessed Gary Stevens' England debut at right-back, in a 2-1 defeat by Italy in Mexico in June 1985. The Everton star, who had been in fine form throughout the 1984-84 season, quickly established himself as first choice right back for his country.

Named in the squad for the 1986 World Cup finals in Mexico, (along with his namesake from Tottenham, Gary A. Stevens, above), he played in all five games as England reached the quarter-finals, where they were beaten, albeit controversially, by Argentina and the 'Hand of God'. Remaining in the team, he then helped England qualify for Euro '88 but by now one or two critics had started to scorn him for some poor positional play and ball distribution, but his coaches at club and international level kept resolute faith in him. Unfortunately, Euro '88 proved to be a disaster for both Stevens and England who lost 1-0 to the Republic of Ireland and 3-1 to the Netherlands. Stevens was certainly at fault for the first goal in the defeat by the Dutch for whom Marco Van Basten scored a hat-trick. He was caught napping wide on the flank by Ruud Gullit but showed good speed and determination to get back and also stop Van Basten's shot from finding the net.

When England qualified for the 1990 World Cup finals in Italy, Stevens was named in the squad, though again a handful of critics had been scathing of his displays. However, he was in the side which again faced the Republic of Ireland in the opening game which ended 1-1. Not a disaster - but there were clear problems with the England personnel and tactics and manager Bobby Robson made several changes for the next game. Stevens was replaced by Parker, who played so well (despite being more usually a central defender for QPR) that he kept his place up to and including England's dramatic semi-final exit on penalties against West Germany, the eventual winners. Stevens was then recalled for the third place play-off defeat by Italy.

Parker's emergence - plus that of Arsenal's Lee Dixon - left Stevens looking over his shoulder at international level and following Robson's departure, he only received occasional starts and the odd substitute appearance under new coach, Graham Taylor. He was also left out of the squad for Euro '92 in favour of Dixon but when the Arsenal man Dixon got injured, Stevens was recalled, only for him to suffer an injury which led to his withdrawal, leaving England without a recognised right back... and they exited in the group stage. Stevens wasn't chosen again and he ended his international career with 46 caps in his locker.

Stevens made 680 appearances for his three clubs – 284 for Everton, 245 for Rangers and 151 for Tranmere. Twice a League Championship winner at Goodison Park, he also won the FA Cup and European Cup Winners' Cup with the Merseysiders, and followed up by helping the 'Gers win six League titles, the Scottish Cup and three League Cups.

STEWART, James 1906-11 ③ ②

Born: Gateshead, 24 April 1883
Died: Gateshead, 23 May 1957
Career: Todd's Nook FC/Newcastle, Gateshead North Eastern Railway (seasons 1898-1902), Sheffield Wednesday (professional, May 1902), Newcastle United (£1,000, August 1908), Glasgow Rangers (£600, September 1913), South Shields (player-manager, May 1914, retired from football during the Great War); worked as a commercial traveller for many years.

Inside-forward 'Tadger' Stewart helped Sheffield Wednesday win the FA Cup in 1907 and gained a League Championship medal with Newcastle two years later before collecting a runners-up medal after defeat to Bradford City in the 1911 FA Cup final.

Clever in footwork, Stewart was also a fine header of the ball who scored on his England debut in the 1-1 draw with Wales in March 1907. He played in the next game in April, starring in a 1-1 with Scotland, but had to wait until April 1911 before collecting his third cap, when once again he found the net in another 1-1 draw v. Scotland. He fired England ahead in the 20th minute but missed a good chance to make it 2-0 just after half-time. 'More composure was required' reported the *Daily Mail*.

STEWART, Paul Andrew 1991-92 ③

Born: Manchester, 7 October 1964
Career: Blackpool (junior, June 1980, professional, October 1981), Manchester City (£200,000, March 1987), Tottenham Hotspur (£1.7m, June 1988), Liverpool (£2.3m, July 1992), Crystal Palace (loan, January-March 1994), Wolverhampton Wanderers (loan, September-November 1994), Burnley (loan, February-March 1995), Sunderland (loan, August-September 1995, signed on a free, March 1996), Stoke City (June 1997), Workington (August 1998, retired May 2000); in 2006 was inducted into the Hall of Fame at Bloomfield Road, when it was officially opened by former Blackpool player Jimmy Armfield; he now lives in Poulton-le-Fylde

Attacking midfielder Paul Stewart played alongside Paul Gascoigne at Tottenham for whom he missed a penalty on his debut v. Manchester United in October 1988. Three years later he scored in Spurs' FA Cup final victory over Nottingham Forest and soon afterwards gained the first of his three England caps, having a moderate game in the 1-0 defeat by Germany at Wembley in September 1991. He claimed his second cap (as a sub) in a 2-2 draw with Czechoslovakia in March 1992 and the following month appeared in his last international, again as a sub, in another 2-2 draw, this time with CIS in Moscow.

One of a band of attack-minded midfield players chosen for international duty in the early 1990s, Stewart was not one of the best! He tried his hardest but with Neil Webb, David Platt, Carlton Palmer and Trevor Steven all getting a game or two, he quickly faded into insignificance. At club level, albeit with ten different employers, he netted 155 goals in more than 650 senior appearances over a period of 20 years. He helped Blackpool (with whom he had his best spell: 225 games, 62 goals) win promotion and Palace the First Division Championship. A Youth international with Blackpool, he was capped once at U21 level and five times by his country's B team.

STILES, Norbert Peter, MBE 1965-70 ㉘ ①

Born: Manchester, 18 May 1942
Career: St Patrick's School/Manchester, Manchester & Lancashire Schools, Manchester United (amateur, September 1957, professional, June 1959), Middlesbrough (£20,000, May 1971), Preston North End (£20,000, August 1973; chief scout, August 1975, manager July 1977-June 1981); Vancouver Whitecaps/ Canada (assistant-manager/coach, seasons 1981-84), West Bromwich Albion (youth team coach, February 1984, then assistant-manager, briefly, and manager, October 1985-February 1986), Manchester United (youth coach, seasons 1989-91); became an after-dinner speaker and charity committee member; suffered a mild heart attack in 2002 and a stroke in 2010 – but said with a smile on his face (as always): "Don't panic, I'm okay."

In 1965, Alf Ramsey, in desperate need of a ball-winner, chose the Manchester United firebrand 'Nobby' Stiles to fill that role for England. He did a terrific job in what would become a well-balanced, highly-efficient five-pronged centre-field diamond in the national team. It comprised Bobby Moore as the defensive passer, Stiles in front of him, Alan Ball as the creator, and Roger Hunt and Bobby Charlton as the two receivers up front.

Four months before the 1966 World Cup, Stiles was asked (nicely) if he would like to play centre-forward! "No problem," he said. Although basically occupying a withdrawn role, he went out and scored the only goal of the game – and of his international career – to beat the West Germans at Wembley...Was that an omen I wonder?

Stiles made his international debut in the 2-2 draw with Scotland in April 1965 and, Brian James in the *Daily Mail* thought he was the

outstanding player: 'More skilled...than I had rated him; his tackles on club-mates Crerand and Law proved that for him, England's cause was paramount.'

A month later, while training ahead of a friendly with Sweden in Gothenburg, Stiles lost his contact lenses and a special lubricant had to be flown out from London on the day of the match so that he could wear a spare pair. On a treacherous surface, he and Alan Ball went out and controlled the midfield, helping England win a fiercely-competitive game by 2-1.

An inspirational footballer, known as 'Happy', he certainly became the nation's favourite son in 1966 after playing a huge part in England's World Cup victory – and I for one will never forget him dancing around, trophy lid on his head, socks down by his ankles, celebrating joyously with his team-mates after that extra-time 4-2 victory over West Germany.

He played in four England games in 1966-67 but was out of the international limelight for 14 months before returning (for the suspended Alan Mullery) against USSR in the European Championships in Rome in June 1968 ... and with a typical tigerish display, he helped England win 2-0.

He managed three more outings for his country after that, appearing for the last time in a 0-0 draw with Scotland in April 1970.

Twice a League Championship winner with Manchester United (1965 and 1967), he also helped the Reds win the European Cup in 1968, and during his playing days at Old Trafford, he amassed 392 first-class appearances and scored 19 goals. Capped by England as a schoolboy (five times in 1957-58) and also at youth team level (1959), Stiles appeared three times for the U23s.

Stiles worked under his brother-in-law, Johnny Giles, at Vancouver Whitecaps and West Bromwich Albion. In October 2010, he sold his World Cup and European Cup winner's medals to his former club, Manchester United, for £188,000 and £49,000 respectively. They are now on display in the Old Trafford museum.

STOKER, Lewis 1932-34 ③

Born: Wheatley Hill, County Durham, 31 March 1910
Died: Birmingham, 26 May 1979
Career: Bearpark Council School, Brandon Juniors, Esh Winning Juniors, Bearpark FC, West Stanley, Birmingham (trial, June 1930, signed, professional, September 1930), Nottingham Forest (May 1938, retired, injured, May 1943); worked as a charge hand at Wimbush's bakery in Birmingham for many years.

A talented right-half and 'feeder of the attack' Lew Stoker spent most of his professional career with Birmingham for whom he made 246 appearances in all competitions, including 230 in the First Division. The recipient of three England caps over a period of 18 months, he made his international debut in a 0-0 draw with Wales in November 1932, played superbly well (behind Sammy Crooks and Raich Carter) in a 3-0 victory over Scotland at Wembley in April 1934 and had a final call in a 2-1 defeat by Hungary in Budapest the very next month. He also represented the Football League.

His younger brother, Bob Stoker, played for Bolton and Huddersfield Town in the 1930s.

STONE, Steven Brian 1995-97 ⑨ ②

Born: Gateshead, 20 August 1971
Career: Nottingham Forest (apprentice, June 1987, professional, May 1989), Aston Villa (£5.5m, March 1999), Portsmouth (loan, October-November 2002, signed free, December 2002), Leeds United (June, 2005, retired, December 2006); Newcastle United (reserve team coach, July 2010, first team coach, December 2010).

Steve 'Bulldog' Stone made his England debut as a second-half substitute for Dennis Wise in the 0-0 draw with Norway in Oslo in October 1995. He brought tremendous energy to the midfield and went on to win nine full caps, scoring two goals in successive matches in the space of four weeks, against Switzerland (won 3-1) and a stunning 25-yarder v. Portugal (1-1) in November and December 1995.

A real workaholic in the engine-room, he had a fine career, and despite breaking his leg three times during his spell with Nottingham Forest, he amassed over 400 League appearances, helping Forest win the First Division Championship in 1997 and Portsmouth likewise in 2003. He played for Villa in the 2000 FA Cup final.

STORER, Harry 1923-28 ② ①

Born: West Derby, Liverpool, 2 February 1898
Died: Derby, 1 September 1967
Career: Heanor Secondary School, Heanor Weslyans, Marehay FC, Codnor Park FC, Riddings St James', Eastwood Bible Class, Ripley Town, Eastwood Town, Notts County (amateur, 1918), Grimsby Town (February 1919), Derby County (£2,500, March 1921), Burnley (£4,250, February 1929, retired, May 1931); Coventry City (manager, June 1931-June 1945), Birmingham City (manager, June 1945-November 1948), Coventry City (manager, again, November 1948-December 1953), Derby County (manager, June 1955-May 1962); Everton (scout, 1963-68); also played cricket for Derbyshire (1920-36), scoring 13,485 runs, including 17 centuries.

Able to play left-half and inside-left, Harry Storer was immense in either position, being brainy, unselfish, confident in the tackle,

comfortable on the ball and strong in shooting. He gained his two England caps three-and-a-half years apart, his first against France in Paris in May 1924 when he scored in a 3-1 win, his second versus Ireland in October 1927 when he twice scraped the woodwork in a 2-0 defeat. As a manager, Storer saw Coventry win the Third Division (South) title in 1936, Birmingham reach the FA Cup semi-finals and lift the Football League (South) title in 1946 and clinch two Second Division Championships, in 1946 and 1948, and Derby claim the Third Division (N) prize in 1957. One interesting fact is that Storer signed Martin O'Donnell three times - for Coventry, Birmingham and Derby.

STOREY, Peter Edwin 1970-73 ⑲ ①

Born: Farnham, Surrey, 7 September 1945
Career: Aldershot Schoolboys (seasons 1959-61), Arsenal (apprentice, May 1961, professional, September 1962), Fulham (£11,000, March 1977, retired, injured, November 1977); ran a market stall, a pub (The Nag's Head), a brothel (for which he was fined) and served time in prison for a variety of crimes including involvement with a coin counterfeiting ring, car theft and illegally importing pornographic videos; now lives in France with his third wife where he runs a small farm.

After playing consistently for double-winners elect Arsenal, Peter Storey was handed his first England cap against Greece at Wembley in April 1971. Lining up out of position at right-back, he played well in a 3-0 win. Thirteen months later, in a 0-0 draw with West Germany in Berlin, Storey and Norman Hunter literally made their presence felt in midfield by committing 27 fouls between them, with Storey being described by the German manager Helmut Schoen as 'brutal.'

In between times the rugged midfielder, who effectively took over from Nobby Stiles, starred in a 3-1 win over Scotland and over the course of three years he played in 19 full internationals, having further outstanding games in a resounding 5-0 win over the Scots in February 1973, a 3-0 victory over Wales three months later and in the 2-1 success over the Soviet Union in June 1973. In fact, Storey had a longer international career than any other player in Arsenal's 1971 double-winning team – and featured in 11 wins and five draws. Unfortunately he never played in a major tournament.

Besides his double-success with the Gunners, Storey was also an Inter Cities Fairs Cup winner in 1970, having previously played for his country as a schoolboy (1960-61) and twice for the Football League. He scored 17 goals in 501 senior outings for Arsenal and lies eighth in the Gunners' all-time list of appearance-makers.

In September 2010, Storey released a no-holds-barred autobiography called True Storey: My Life and Crimes as a Football Hatchet Man.

STOREY-MOORE, Ian 1969-70 ①

Born: Ipswich, 17 May 1945
Career: Lincoln Gardens Primary & Westcliffe Secondary Modern Schools, Scunthorpe junior football, Ashby Juniors (season 1960-61), Nottingham Forest (amateur, February 1961, professional, May 1962), Manchester United (£200,000, March 1972, retired, on medical advice, December 1973); returned with Burton Albion (player-manager, September 1974); Chicago Sting/USA (1975), Shepshed Charterhouse (player-manager, season 1976-77); also played briefly in South Africa; Aston Villa (chief scout, seasons 2003-06).

Ian Storey-Moore, a hard-working, penetrative left-winger with good pace, made just one appearance in an England shirt, in the 0-0 draw with Holland at Wembley in January 1970. Although he had a headed 'goal' disallowed, he didn't have the greatest of games in a rather slip-shod performance by Alf Ramsey's much-changed side, the crowd showing their disapproval with a bout of slow-handclapping in the second-half.

Regarded as 'one of the most dangerous wingers in the game' during the early 1970s, Storey-Moore netted 118 goals in 272 appearances for Forest, top-scoring in four out of five seasons between 1966-67 and 1970-71. He then bagged just 11 goals in 39 games for Manchester United. He also won two England U23 caps.

STRANGE, Alfred Henry 1929-34 ⑳

Born: Ripley, Derbyshire, 2 April 1900
Died: Ripley, 20 October 1978
Career: Marehay Colliery (1919), Portsmouth (professional, December 1922), Port Vale (£1,000, October 1924), Sheffield Wednesday (player-exchange deal, February 1927), Bradford Park Avenue (May 1935, retired, May 1936); became a poultry farmer in his native Ripley.

Initially an inside-forward, swift-tackling right-half Alf Strange represented the Football League three times before receiving his first England cap in April 1930. Lining up against Scotland at Wembley, he was outstanding in a 5-2 win with his Wednesday team-mate Ellis Rimmer scoring twice, Strange and Joe Bradford setting up his second goal and England's fifth. Two other Owls players – Ernie Blenkinsopp and William Marsden – also helped beat the Scots.

At the end of that season (May 1930) Strange accompanied England on a European tour where he played in the drawn matches against Germany and Austria, and on his return to England he missed a penalty in a 5-1 win over Ireland. He continued to be selected for his country over the next few years, and captained the team in a 5-2 defeat by France in Paris in May 1931 and also in a 3-1 victory over Wales six months later. Then he was one of the 'best players on the pitch' when Spain got hammered 7-1 in December 1931 and he was also in 'fine form' in the 3-0 and 4-3 wins over Scotland and Austria in April and December 1932. His 20th and final England appearance came at White Hart Lane in December 1933, when he and his colleagues gained 'revenge' for that earlier defeat by whipping France 4-1, Strange setting up a goal for George Camsell.

Twice a League Championship winner with Sheffield Wednesday - 1929 and 1930 - Strange made 273 appearances for the Owls during his eight years at Hillsborough. He had earlier helped Portsmouth win the Third Division (South) title in 1923-24.

STRATFORD, Alfred Hugh 1873-74 ①

Born: Kensington, London, 5 September 1853
Died: Pittsburg, USA, 2 May 1914
Career: Malvern College (seasons 1871-74), Wanderers (seasons 1875-78); also played for Swifts, Middlesex; cricketer for Middlesex and represented the MCC (1877-1880); immigrated to USA, October 1880; later played cricket in both Canada and USA.

On his day Alf Stratford was a top-class defender but surprisingly appeared in only one full international - a 2-1 defeat by Scotland at the West of Scotland Cricket Ground, Partick in March 1874, being given a hard game by the lively Queen's Park inside-right Harry McNeil.

A member of three Wanderers' FA Cup winning teams (1876-77-78) he decided to concentrate on cricket (rather than football) and became a star player with Middlesex, for whom he scored almost 600 runs and took 83 wickets. His best performance with the ball came in 1878 when he took 12 Surrey wickets at The Oval - finishing with 6-41 in the first innings and 6-113 in the second. After moving

to America, Stratford continued playing cricket, assisting Winnipeg, Pittsburgh, New York and Newark. In 1884, four years after his last first-class appearance in England, he played alongside his brother, Frederick, for the USA against the Gentlemen of Philadelphia.

STRETEN, Bernard Reginald 1949-50 ①

Born: Gillingham, Norfolk, 14 January 1921
Died: North Walsham, Norfolk, 6 May 1994
Career: Beccles Boys (Norfolk), Wartime guest for Wolverhampton Wanderers (season 1943-44); Notts County (amateur, August 1946), Shrewsbury Town (briefly, early, 1947), Luton Town (amateur, July 1947, professional, 1948), Kings Lynn (July 1957), Wisbech Town (July 1959), Cambridge City (January 1961-November 1962), North Walsham FC/Norfolk (January 1963, retired, May 1964).

Bert Williams declared himself unfit for the World Cup qualifier against Northern Ireland at Maine Road in November 1949 and into his place stepped Luton Town's agile goalkeeper Bernard Streten. He didn't have a great deal to do as the Irish were whipped 9-2. This was his only cap in a career that spanned some 20 years (all levels). A friendly chap, always chatting to the fans behind his goal, Streten made 301 appearances for Luton (276 in the League). Before joining the Hatters, he also played in six amateur internationals for England.

STURGESS, Albert 1910-14 ②

Born: Etruria, Stoke-on-Trent, 21 October 1882
Died: Sheffield, 16 July 1957
Career: Tunstall Crosswells, Stoke (amateur, July 1900, professional, October 1900), Sheffield United (June 1908); served in the Army during the First World War; Norwich City (August 1923, retired, April 1925); later ran a crockery shop in Eccleshall, Sheffield.

Honest-to-goodness defender Albert Sturgess won his two caps as a Sheffield United player. He made his debut at left-half in the 2-1 win over Ireland in February 1911 and played in his second international three years later in a 3-1 defeat by Scotland in front of 127,000 fans at Hampden Park. He occupied the right-half berth that afternoon, and was given a testing time by Jimmy Croal (Falkirk).

A strong kicker, with anticipation second to none, he was totally reliable and made 135 appearances for Stoke before going on to add a further 512 for the Blades for whom he occupied every position on the field. An FA Cup winner in 1915, Sturgess played his last game for Norwich against Millwall in February 1925, aged 42 years and 116 days. He was also a fine crown green bowler, winning several local competitions.

STURRIDGE, Daniel Andre 2011-13 ⑥ ①

Born: Birmingham, 1 September 1989
Career: Aston Villa (junior, September 2001), Coventry City (June 2002), Manchester City (Academy, aged 13, October 2003, apprentice, September 2005, professional, September 2006 when City were ordered to pay Coventry £30,000 with £170,000 to follow at a later stage depending on appearances/goals), Chelsea (January 2010 for an initial fee of £3.5m with additional payments of £500,000 after each of 10, 20, 30 and 40 first-team competitive appearances, plus a further payment of £1m for a first full international appearance), Bolton Wanderers (loan, January-May 2011), Liverpool (£12m, January 2013)

Utility forward Daniel Sturridge has occupied all 'five' front-line positions so far in his career. He has admitted that he prefers to play on the right which gives him the opportunity to cut inside and take shots with his favoured left foot – and he's done that exceptionally well!

After playing intermediate level with Aston Villa and Coventry City, he signed for Manchester City where his development was rapid. He played in two FA Youth Cup finals and made his senior debut in the 2007-08 season, thus becoming the only player ever to score in the FA Youth Cup, FA Cup and Premier League in the same season. After netting five goals in 21 PL games for City he joined Chelsea and was then loaned to Bolton Wanderers for the second half of the 2010–11 season, scoring eight goals in 12 appearances. He returned to Stamford Bridge a 'far better and more mature player' and was given more chances by new boss André Villas-Boas and as a result gained his full England cap as a second-half substitute in the 1-0 win over Sweden at Wembley in November 2011. And here's an interesting stat... he was one of nine players that night that had been associated with Aston Villa. Sturridge has represented his country at U16, U17, U18, U19, U20 and U21 levels, scoring four times in 15 appearances for the latter. From a footballing family, he is the nephew of former strikers Simon Sturridge and Dean Sturridge.

Sturridge played in five games for Team GB at the 2012 Olympics, scoring two goals.

SUMMERBEE, Michael George 1967-73 ⑧ ①
Born: Cheltenham, 15 December 1942
Career: Swindon Town (amateur, August 1959, professional, December 1959), Manchester City (£35,000, August 1965), Burnley (£25,000, June 1975), Blackpool, Stockport County (player-manager, March 1978-December 1979), Mossley FC (January 1980, retired, May 1982); owned a boutique with George Best in Manchester.

Mike Summerbee made a quietly impressive international debut on England's right wing in the 2-2 draw with Scotland on a slippy Hampden Park pitch in February 1968, having a hand in Martin Peters' goal. He played in two more games in April and June of that year (v. Spain and West Germany) but had to wait three-and-a-half years before winning his fourth cap against Switzerland in a European Championship qualifier in November 1971, scoring in a 1-1 draw at Wembley.

A very competitive footballer, always involved in the action, Summerbee made his next four appearances over a period of 13 months between May 1972 and June 1973, having a fine game in a 3-0 victory over Wales in his sixth international.

Summerbee, who also played in one U23 game and represented the Football League, made 716 League appearances during his career (92 goals scored). He played in almost 250 games for Swindon and 443 for Manchester City, helping the latter win the Second and First Division Championships (1965 and 1968), FA Cup (1969) and League Cup (1970). He was former England left-half and future manager Joe Mercer's first signing for City.

SUNDERLAND, Alan 1979-80 ①
Born: Conisbrough, Yorkshire, 1 July 1953
Career: Wolverhampton Wanderers (apprentice, July 1969, professional, June 1971), Arsenal (£240,000, November 1977), Ipswich Town (loan, February 1984, signed permanently, July 1984), Derry City (August 1985, retired May 1986); opened a pub in Ipswich, before emigrating to Malta, where he coached local team, Birkirkara (up to 2006); also an occasional soccer pundit on BBC TV.

Bubble-permed inside-forward Alan Sunderland made his England debut, along with the Ipswich Town duo of Terry Butcher and Russell Osman, Brighton's Peter Ward and Southampton's David Armstrong in a 2-1 friendly win over Australia in Sydney in May 1980. Tentative

in his approach for long periods, he was actually substituted by Ward. And ironically neither player gained another cap!

At club level, Sunderland was a League Cup and Second Division Championship winner with Wolves in 1974 and 1977, played in three successive FA Cup finals for Arsenal, 1978-80, scoring a dramatic late winner against Manchester United (3-2) in 1979. He also played in the 1980 European Cup Winners' Cup final and represented England in seven B internationals as well as in one U21 and one U23 game. He scored 34 goals in 198 appearances for Wolves and 101 in 321 outings for the Gunners.

SUTCLIFFE, John William 1892-1903 ⑤
Born: Shibden near Halifax, 14 April 1868
Died: Bradford, 7 July 1947
Career: played rugby for Bradford RUC and Heckmondwike RUC; Bolton Wanderers (professional, September 1889), Millwall Athletic (April 1902), Manchester United (May 1903), Plymouth Argyle (January 1905, retired May 1911), Southend United (coach, season 1911-12), Heckmondwike AFC (February 1913), FC Arnhem/Holland (coach, season 1914-15); Bradford City (trainer, May 1919-May 1923).

Rightly listed among England's finest goalkeepers, 'John Willie' Sutcliffe was equally effective saving high or low shots and quite often used his feet to keep the ball out of the danger-zone. Surprisingly he won only five caps and only had one 'bad day' for his country. That was in March 1901 when he was clearly at fault for Scotland's first goal scored by Jock Campbell in the 2-2 draw at Crystal Palace. "I simply misjudged the flight of the ball," he said. Sutcliffe made 364 appearances for Bolton, helping them win the FA Cup in 1894.

Tall, with a waxed, sergeant-major style moustache and voice to match, he was a strong kicker and often cleared his lines with an almighty toe-poke, sending the ball flying 100 yards downfield! He also represented England against New Zealand at rugby in 1889, making him only one of three men to have represented England at both rugby and soccer.

SUTTON, Christopher Roy 1997-98 ①
Born: Nottingham, 10 March 1973
Career: Norwich City (apprentice, April 1989, professional, July 1991), Blackburn Rovers (£5m, July 1994), Chelsea (£10m, July 1999), Celtic (£6m, July 2000), Birmingham City (January-May 2006), Aston Villa (October 2006, retired, July 2007), Lincoln City (manager, September 2009, resigned, September 2010); in October 1999, Sutton was involved in a fracas in a Soho restaurant and was subsequently found guilty of twice spitting in the face of the trainee barrister. He was fined on two charges of common assault and ordered to pay costs of £200 with £200 compensation to Richard Partridge.

Tall and positive in the air, Chris Sutton's club form for Blackburn Rovers, alongside his Ewood Park 'SAS' strike partner Alan Shearer, earned him his only England cap in November 1997 against Cameroon (won 2-0). However, he was subsequently left out of Glenn Hoddle's 1998 World Cup squad. In fact, he was demoted to the B team before that, but refused to play at that level, claiming: "It is a waste of time... I should have been selected for the first team." This boycott ended Sutton's chances of ever playing for the full national team again.

During his club career, Sutton scored 192 goals in 537 senior appearances, including 151 in 410 League matches. A huge favourite at Parkhead, he spent his best years with Celtic, netting 86 goals in 199 outings, gaining three Premier League, one League Cup and three

Scottish Cup winner's medals. A Premiership winner with Blackburn in 1995 and FA Cup winner with Chelsea in 2000, he also scored once in 13 U21 internationals and played twice for England B. He also shared the PL Golden Boot award with Michael Owen and Dion Dublin (with 18 goals) in 1998. He was the most expensive footballer in Great Britain when he joined Blackburn in 1994 and third highest when he signed for Chelsea. His father, Mike Sutton, played for Norwich City.

SWAN, Peter 1959-62 ⑲

Born: South Elmsall, Yorkshire, 8 October 1936
Career: Doncaster Schools, Sheffield Wednesday (amateur, May, 1952, professional, December 1953; suspended from May 1965, re-signed, June 1972), Bury (August 1973), Matlock Town (player-manager, July 1974-May 1976), Buxton (season 1977-78), Worksop Town (manager, seasons 1978-80), Matlock Town (manager, November 1980-December 1981); later a publican in Chesterfield.

Replacing Bill Slater who had been dropped after a 'poor' game against Scotland three weeks previous, centre-half Peter Swan had a tough first game for England, struggling at times to contain a lively Yugoslav attack in the 3-3 draw at Wembley in May 1960. He was 'stranded' in no man's land when a clever back-heel by Galic gave Kosctic the chance to make it 3-2 with 10 minutes to go. Thankfully Johnny Haynes popped up with an equalizer.
 In the 1-1 draw with Wales at Ninian Park, Cardiff in October 1961, Swan lost his right boot as he tackled David Ward. The ball dropped invitingly for Graham Williams to give the Welsh the lead on 30 minutes. Swan said to reporters after the match: "That was one of the toughest games of football I ever played in."
 Swan went on to play in 19 full internationals, but missed out on the 1962 World Cup, and during his time as an England player, the defence conceded no less than 29 goals, including 10 in his first three internationals. He was a 'stopper' centre-half, big and strong, hard to beat whose promising career came to an abrupt end!
 He was involved (with two of his Sheffield Wednesday colleagues, Tony Kay and David Layne) in an infamous betting scandal revolving round an away League game at Ipswich on 1 December 1962. It was agreed between parties that Wednesday would lose at Portman Road – and they did by 2-0.
 After the betting ring was uncovered, and publicised as a major article in The People newspaper, the whole incident went to court. And in April 1964, just as he was preparing to play against Tottenham that evening, Swan was found guilty and was later handed a four-year jail sentence (in Lincoln prison) while also being banned from football for life. He was replaced in the Wednesday team by Vic Mobley.
 In an interview with The Times newspaper, some 42 years later, in July 2006, Swan admitted: "We lost the game fair and square, but I still don't know what I'd have done if we'd been winning. It would have been easy for me to give away a penalty or even score an own goal. Who knows?"
 Many people believe that Swan would have been in the England squad for the 1966 World Cup... having been told by Alf Ramsey that he was 'top of the list'.
 Swan successfully appealed against his life ban and was back in action (with Wednesday) after seven years, going on to amass a total of 291 senior appearances for the Owls with whom he had earlier gained a Second Division championship winner's medal in 1959. Capped at Youth team level, Swan also played three times for England's U23 side, and managed Matlock Town to an FA Trophy final victory at Wembley in 1975. After quitting the pub trade, Swan retired and is sadly suffering from Alzheimer's disease. He released a book in September 2006 called Setting The Record Straight written in conjunction with Nick Johnson. Tragically, Swan's 39 year-old son Gary died of stomach cancer in 1998.

SWEPSTONE, Harry Albemarle 1879-83 ⑥

Born: Stepney, London, 1 September 1859
Died: Bethnal Green, London, 7 May 1907
Career: Chigwell School, Clapton (seasons 1874-78), Pilgrims FC (seasons 1878-84); also played for Ramblers FC (1876), Essex County (1877); founder member of the Corinthians and proposer of that club's name; FA Committee member (season 1883-84); admitted a solicitor in 1881, he practised at Bethnal Green, London from 1881-92, thereafter in Bishopsgate.

Rated one of the best goalkeepers of his day, Harry Swepstone had a nightmare debut for England in a 5-4 defeat by Scotland in March 1880. One effort, from William Ker, flew past him like a 'cricket ball' reported the North British Daily Mail.
 Two years later the Scots struck five more goals past him and soon afterwards Wales did likewise (15 goals conceded by the big man in his first three internationals). But he battled on and played superbly when the Welsh were defeated 5-0 in February 1883 and Ireland 7-0 three weeks later.
 Then, in his sixth and final international the very next month, Swepstone pulled off two brilliant saves on a frozen pitch at Sheffield as the Scots won 3-2.

SWIFT, Frank Victor 1946-49 ⑲

Born: Blackpool, 26 December 1913
Died: Munich, Germany, 6 February 1958
Career: Blackpool Schools, Blackpool Gas Works FC (1927-29), Fleetwood (from August 1929), Manchester City (amateur trialist, October 1932, signed professional, November 1932, retired May 1949; returned to play a few games during early part of 1949-50 season); guest for Aldershot, Charlton Athletic, Fulham, Hamilton Academical, Liverpool and Reading during WW2; became a chief reporter for the News of the World.

Being the first goalkeeper to captain England, Frank Swift was brilliant between the posts when England thrashed the reigning World champions Italy 4-0 in the cauldron of Turin in May 1948. He pulled off three terrific saves early in the second-half with the score at 2-0 and was in action again late to thwart Loik and Gabetto as the Italians tried, in vain, to get back into the match. At the final whistle Swift was carried aloft from the pitch on the shoulders of his team-mates.

Swift conceded 17 goals in 19 full internationals, three of them against Scotland at Wembley in April 1949. Jim Mason struck the first, which flew into the net via Johnny Aston's boot and an upright, Billy Steel whipped in the second through a crowd of players and Lawrie Reilly's effort took a slight deflection off Neil Franklin. The final scoreline could well have been doubled, but Swift played brilliantly after the break, pulling off several fine stops.

In the 2-0 win over the Scots at Hampden Park twelve months earlier 'Swift was outstanding and when Delaney, Steel and Liddell created sheer panic in every defender, Swift was there to save the day' wrote Clifford Webb in the *Daily Herald*.

Occasionally, like all great goalkeepers, the imperturbable Swift made mistakes, like in three Wartime internationals against Wales twice and Scotland which all resulted in goals. But he always seemed to balance his errors with a series of great saves, once diving full length to stop Matt Busby's penalty kick against the Scots in April 1945 when England won 6-1.

In another international against Ireland at Goodison Park in November 1947, England were leading 2-1 with just ten seconds remaining when a long ball pumped into the danger-zone by Irish winger Tommy Eglington was heading straight into the arms of 'Swifty' but up popped his former Manchester City team-mate, Peter Doherty, who beat Neil Franklin in the air and nodded in the equalizer. Doherty, who collided heavily with Franklin, collapsed in a heap on the ground near the edge of the penalty-area. Swift ran over to him, picked him up and congratulated him. Too dazed to know what had happened, Docherty was visited in the dressing room after the game by Swift who repeated his congratulations and to make sure the great Irish forward had recovered.

Swift himself was knocked out during the 2-0 win over Scotland at Hampden Park in April 1948 (after a collision with Billy Liddell) but he quickly recovered and stunned the 135,000 plus crowd with a series of terrific saves. On his return to Manchester's railway station later that evening, Swift, still wobbly, was wheeled along the platform on a porter's trolley to a waiting ambulance. An examination revealed he was 'fine' except that he had also broken two ribs.

Swift's final appearance for his country was in the 3-1 win over France in Paris in May 1949. The game was played under a boiling hot sun and on a pitch seemingly made out of concrete.

Universally popular with his natural good humour, Swift's presence on the field was immense while his formidable physique included a hand span of 11½ inches. His England team-mate Raich Carter thought '…he had frying pan hands' while Stan Matthews said; "He had hands like spades, and would also occasionally head goalbound shots away. He was an excellent shot-stopper."

In fact, he was one of the first 'keepers to throw the ball out to a colleague rather than kick it aimlessly downfield. He was a big man and a big talent, the bravest of the brave. The crowds loved his goalkeeping aerobatics and although he was terrific with high shots and long range efforts he was, at times, caught out with quickly-taken ground shots, and once, in a League game against West Bromwich Albion in 1934, he conceded seven goals, six fired low into the net from inside the penalty-area. The recipient of 14 Wartime caps, Swift also played in the four unofficial, 10 WW2 and four Victory internationals, made four appearances with the FA XI and won the FA Cup and gained First and Second Division Championship winner's medals with Manchester City for whom he made 511 appearances (375 in the Football League).

He was sadly killed in the Munich air crash in 1958 while working as a journalist covering Manchester United's European Cup game with Red Star in Yugoslavia.

TAIT, George 1880-81 ①

Born: Edgbaston, Birmingham, 2 February 1859
Died: Moseley, Birmingham, late 1882
Career: Birmingham Excelsior (eight seasons: 1874-82); worked as a city bank manager.

A utility forward, tall, strong and mobile, George Tait won his only England cap in a 1-0 defeat by Wales at Blackburn in February 1881 when he led the attack owing to the absence of Mitchell and Sparks. He died suddenly at the age of 23.

TALBOT, Brian Ernest 1976-80 ⑥

Born: Ipswich, 21 July 1953
Career: Ipswich & Suffolk Schools, Ipswich Town (amateur, July 1969, professional, July 1972), Toronto Metros/Canada (loan, 1971 and 1972), Arsenal (£450,000, January 1979), Watford (£150,000, June 1985), Stoke City (£25,000, October 1986), West Bromwich Albion (£15,000, January 1988, player-caretaker manager October 1988, player-manager November 1988-January 1991), Fulham (non-contract player, March 1991), Aldershot (non-contract, April 1991, manager season 1991-92), Sudbury Town (player-manager/coach, briefly, 1992), Marsaxlokk FC/Malta (player-manager/coach, 1992-94), Hibernians/Malta (player-coach, seasons 1994-96), Marsaxlokk FC/Malta (manager-coach, season 1996-97), Rushden & Diamonds (guest player, May 1997, manager, August 1997), Oldham Athletic (manager, March 2004-March 2005), Oxford United (manager, May 2005-March 2006), Marsaxlokk FC/Malta (manager, June 2006-May 2008; now Technical Director of club).

Midfielder Brian Talbot made his England debut as a 66th minute substitute for Ray Wilkins against Northern Ireland in Belfast in May 1977. He was excellent and after Pat Jennings had denied him a goal with a brilliant diving save, the Ipswich star crossed for Dennis Tueart to head the winner with just four minutes remaining (2-1). Full of energy, he was the driving force in centre-field and feels he deserved more than the six caps he received – although it must be said that there were plenty of other quality midfield players around at the same time.

Talbot's other four England games ended in draws against Brazil (0-0), Argentina (1-1) and Uruguay (0-0) while a 2-1 victory was chalked up over Australia in 1980.

He made 533 club appearances during his 22-year career. He won the FA Cup with Ipswich in 1978 and Arsenal in 1979 and led Rushden & Diamonds to the Nationwide Conference Championship in 2001 and Marsaxlokk to the Maltese League title in 1993, 1994 and 1997.

TAMBLING, Robert Victor 1962-66 ③ ①

Born: Storrington, Sussex, 18 September 1941
Career: Havant Town (season 1956-57), Chelsea (groundstaff, July 1957, professional, September 1958), Crystal Palace (loan, January-March 1969, signed for £40,000, June, 1970), Cork Celtic (October, 1973, player-manager June 1974-June 1977), Waterford United (player, August 1977-May 1978), Shamrock Rovers (August-October 1978), Cork Alberts FC (October 1978-February 1979); later Cork City (manager, August-October 1984), Crosshaven FC (manager-coach, from early 1985 onwards); now an after-dinner speaker, he lives in Crosshaven, Cork.

The record books show that Chelsea's utility forward Bobby Tambling was the last England player to be capped by a committee (after Walter Winterbottom's reign as manager had come to an end and before Alf Ramsey officially took charge). He made his debut in an emphatic 4-0 win over Wales at Wembley in November 1962 when only 27,500 hardy supporters bothered to turn up. Three months later he scored in Ramsey's first game as boss – in a disastrous 5-2 defeat by France in Paris. His third and last cap was gained against Yugoslavia in May 1966, shortly before the World Cup began. He did well in a 2-0 win but didn't make the final squad of 22, Jimmy Greaves, Bobby Charlton, Geoff Hurst and Roger Hunt being chosen as the main goalscoring forwards.

At club level, especially with Chelsea, Tambling was brilliant. He scored a club record 202 goals (since beaten by Frank Lampard) in 370 first-class appearances, was an FA Youth Cup and League Cup winner in 1960 and 1965, and played in the 1967 FA Cup final defeat by Tottenham.

He struck 12 goals in 68 League games for Palace before spending ten years in Ireland, winning the League of Ireland League Championship in his first season with Cork Celtic.

Besides representing England at senior level, Tambling played in seven Schoolboy and 13 U23 internationals. He also represented the League of Ireland v. Argentina as a Waterford player in April 1978. He played under Johnny Giles at Shamrock Rovers and was the first-ever manager of Cork City in 1984, but his reign lasted only 13 games.

Tambling has a suite named after him at Stamford Bridge in honour of his status at Chelsea and features in the club's greatest ever XI.

TATE, Joseph Thomas 1931-33 ③

Born: Old Hill, Staffs, 4 August 1904
Died: Cradley Heath, West Midlands, 18 May 1973
Career: Stourbridge Council School, Birch Coppice Primitives, Grainger's Lane Primitives, Round Oak Steelworks/Brierley Hill (1920), Cradley Heath (April 1923), Aston Villa (£400, professional, April 1925), Brierley Hill Alliance (player-manager, May 1935, retired May 1937); Birmingham University (football coach, September 1937-May 1944); thereafter ran a tobacconist shop in Brierley Hill (started initially in 1936); also played cricket for Warwickshire club and ground.

Joe Tate was an outstanding wing-half, a fine tactician who attempted to play the ball on the ground rather than hoofing it skywards! Strong in attack and quick in recovery, he made 193 appearances for Aston Villa before injury forced him to quit League football in 1935. Two years later he broke his right leg playing for Brierley Hill against Moor Green and retired immediately. An international trialist in 1925, he made his England debut in a 5-2 defeat by France in Paris in May 1931, played in the 4-1 win over Belgium two days later and made his third and last appearance in a 0-0 draw with Wales in November 1932.

TAYLOR, Edward Hallows 1922-26 ⑧

Born: Liverpool, 7 March 1891
Died: Manchester, 5 July 1956
Career: Marlborough Old Boys/Liverpool (1908), Liverpool Balmoral (1910), Oldham Athletic (professional, February 1912), Huddersfield Town (June 1922), Everton (February 1927), Ashton National (September 1928), Wrexham (November 1928, retired May 1929); became a cotton worker in Manchester.

Although not all that tall, Ted Taylor was a very confident, quick-thinking goalkeeper, a fine shot-stopper who had few weaknesses. Twice a League Championship winner with Huddersfield (1924-26) and added a third medal to his collection with Everton in 1928. During his career Taylor made almost 300 appearances for his four

major clubs and conceded ten goals in his eight internationals. He made an impressive start to his England career in a 2-0 win over Ireland in October 1922 but let the ball slip away from him during the 2-2 draw with Scotland at Hampden Park in April 1923, allowing Andy Cunningham to tap home. A year later he played very well in the first international at Wembley when the Scots forced a 1-1 draw. No less than 11 different goalkeepers were used by England between October 1922 and May 1926, Taylor being one of them, such was the competition for the number one spot.

TAYLOR, Ernest 1953-54 ①

Born: Sunderland, 2 September 1925
Died: Birkenhead, 9 April 1985
Career: Hylton Colliery Juniors, Newcastle United (£10, September 1942); WW2 guest for Plymouth Argyle (season 1945-46); Blackpool (£25,000, October 1951), Waterford & Bohemians XI (guest, 1953), Manchester United (£6,000, February 1958), Sunderland (£6,000, December 1958), Altrincham (May 1961), Derry City (December 1961-February 1962); emigrated to New Zealand; New Brighton FC/Christchurch/New Zealand (coach, February 1964), East Coast Bays/Auckland (player-coach, season 1965-66); returned to England, 1967; Heswall FC/Cheshire (consultant); also assisted Carshalton Athletic; later worked at Vauxhall Motors, Hooton, Cheshire.

Inside-forward Ernie Taylor's career covered nineteen years, during which time he played for four League clubs, scored over 100 goals in almost 500 senior appearances, gained two FA Cup winner's medals – with Newcastle in 1951 and Blackpool in 1953 – and in 1958, after the Munich air crash, helped a rebuilt Manchester United team reach the FA Cup final (beaten by Bolton).

After Blackpool's defeat by Newcastle in the 1951 final, Stanley Matthews asked his manager Joe Smith to sign Taylor... five months later he did just that.

A former naval submariner, Taylor, just 5 ft 4 in tall, was able to deliver defence-splitting passes to perfection and caused problems for every defender in the game. It was his cheeky back-heel that set up one of Jackie Milburn's goals in that '51 final.

He spent seven years with Blackpool, linking up brilliantly with Matthews on the right-wing. In November 1953, the pair played together for England in that 6-3 home demolition by Hungary at Wembley. This was Taylor's only international appearance. He deserved more.

TAYLOR, James Guy 1950-51 ②

Born: Hillingdon, Middlesex, 5 November 1917
Died: Hayes, Middlesex, 6 March 2001
Career: Hillingdon Town (1935), Fulham (professional, March 1938), Queens Park Rangers (April 1953), Tunbridge Wells Rangers (player-manager, May 1954, retired, may 1958), Yiewsley (manager, June 1958-March 1959), Uxbridge (manager, season 1959-60).

Jim Taylor – a non-playing member of England's squad at the 1950 World Cup in Brazil – was 33 years and 185 days old when he made his England debut at centre-half in place of Billy Wright in the 2-1 win over Argentina at Wembley in May 1951. He added a second cap to his tally against Portugal soon afterwards, assisting in one of Jackie Milburn's two goals in a 5-2 victory. Initially an inside-right, Taylor developed into a strong, quick-tackling and constructive defender who made 278 appearances for Fulham, gaining a Second Division Championship winning medal in 1949.

TAYLOR, Peter John 1975-76 ④ ②

Born: Southend-on-Sea, Essex, 3 January 1953
Career: Canvey Island (August 1968), Southend United (professional, January 1971), Crystal Palace (October 1973), Tottenham Hotspur (£400,000, September 1976), Leyton Orient (November 1980), Oldham Athletic (loan, January 1983), Maidstone United (August 1983), Exeter City (non-contract, October 1983), Maidstone United (player-manager, seasons 1984-86), Dartford (player-manager, seasons 1986-90); Southend United (manager, August 1993-February 1995), Dover Athletic (May 1995-July 1996), England U21 (manager, July 1995-June 1999), Gillingham (manager, July 1999-June 2000), Leicester City (manager, June 2000-September 2001), England (caretaker-manager, November 2000 – one match), Brighton & Hove Albion (manager, October 2001-May 2002), Hull City (manager, October 2002-June 2006), England U21 (manager, 2004-January 2007), Crystal Palace (manager, June 2006, sacked October 2007), Stevenage Borough (manager, November 2007-April 2008), Wycombe Wanderers (manager, May 2008-October 2009), Bradford City (manager, February 2010-March 2011), Bahrain FA (coach, July 2011-October 2012), England (U20 coach, March 2013).

Crystal Palace striker Peter Taylor became the first Third Division player to win a full England cap since Johnny Byrne in 1961, when he made his debut in the 2-1 win over Wales at Wrexham in March 1976. A second-half substitute for Mick Channon, he scored the clinching goal ten minutes from time. In fact, Taylor was one of seven players who made their England debuts in this game.

Taylor found the net in his second international against Wales two months later (won 1-0) but played in only two more matches after that, against Northern Ireland (won 4-0) and Scotland (lost 2-1), both in May 1976. He had earlier won caps as a semi-professional and played in four U23 internationals.

A pacy winger, he scored over 100 goals in more than 450 club appearances (87 in 388 League games). Up to 2011 he had managed eleven different football clubs, steering Gillingham to a play-off final win in 2000, Brighton to the Second Division Championship in 2002 and Hull City to successive promotions in 2004 and 2005. Besides his two spells as boss of England's U21 team, he also acted as caretaker-boss of the senior team for one match v. Italy in November 2000 (England's 775th full international), whilst managing Leicester. Unfortunately England lost 1–0 to Italy in Turin as he handed David Beckham the captain's armband for the first time and used six players then still eligible for the U21s: Gareth Barry, Jamie Carragher, Kieron Dyer, Rio Ferdinand, Emile Heskey and Seth Johnson.

TAYLOR, Philip Henry 1947-48 ③

Born: Bristol, 18 September 1917
Died: 1 December 2012
Career: Greenbank School/Bristol, Bristol Rovers (junior, August 1932, professional, March 1935), Liverpool (£5,000, plus Billy Hartill, March 1936); WW2 guest for Bristol Rovers, Brighton & Hove Albion, Leeds United and Newcastle United; (retired, July 1954; became Liverpool coach, then manager, May 1956, resigned November 1959); later a sales representative; also played cricket for Gloucestershire.

Phil Taylor joined Liverpool as a young inside-forward with a lot of potential but was converted into a wing-half by manager George Kay, developing into a stylish, composed defender. A member of the Reds' 1946-47 League Championship winning team and captain of their beaten 1950 FA Cup final side, Taylor won three caps for England. He made his debut in October 1947 against Wales at Cardiff, lining up alongside Neil Franklin and Billy Wright and behind legends Stan Matthews, Tom Finney, Stan Mortensen and Tommy

Lawton in a 3-0 win. His other caps followed a month later, in a 2-2 draw with Northern Ireland and a 4-1 win over Sweden.

Honoured by his country as a schoolboy, Taylor scored 34 goals in 345 appearances for Liverpool and also played in two B internationals and represented the Football League. He helped coach several promising players at Anfield and was manager there for three years before resigning through ill-health to allow in Bill Shankly. A decent cricketer, Taylor played in one county match for Gloucestershire in 1938. At the time of his death, aged 95, Taylor was the oldest former League and England international footballer.

TAYLOR, Thomas 1952-58 ⑲ ⑯

Born: Smithies, Yorkshire, 29 January 1932
Died: Munich, 6 February 1958
Career: Smithies United (1947), Barnsley (professional, July 1949), Manchester United (£29,999, March 1953-February 1958).

Tommy Taylor broke into the England team, unaided. Described as 'a jinking, dribbling talent, dominant in the air and altogether a forceful presence' he made his debut in the abandoned tour game against Argentina in May 1953, scored in his next two internationals against Chile and Uruguay but didn't fare too well in the 1954 World Cup. However, he kept his place and found the net in the first floodlit game at Wembley when Brazil were defeated 4-2 in May 1956 while his brilliant hat-tricks in 5-2 and 5-1 wins over Denmark and the Republic of Ireland respectively in December 1956 and May 1957 saw Walter Winterbottom's side qualify for the World Cup finals unbeaten. Taylor also netted twice in the return fixture with the Danes and struck twice in his last international, a 4-0 win over France at Wembley in November 1957. Many thought that Taylor would have been England's centre-forward for the next ten years but sadly he lost his life in the Munich air disaster, having scored 16 goals in just 19 games for his country and 128 in just 189 senior appearances for Manchester United, with whom he won two League Championship medals and played in the 1957 FA Cup final defeat by Aston Villa. He also played for England B and represented the Football League.

Regarding Taylor's transfer fee of £29,999: Manchester United manager Matt Busby did not want to burden the youngster as being a '30,000 pound player' so he took out a £1 note from his wallet and handed it to the lady who had been serving up the teas in the boardroom!

TEMPLE, Derek William 1964-65 ①

Born: Liverpool, 13 November 1938
Career: Dovecot Secondary Modern School/Liverpool, Everton (groundstaff, July 1955, professional, August 1956), Preston North End (September 1967), Wigan Athletic (July 1970, retired May 1973); went into business in Wigan.

Flying left-winger Derek Temple was called into England's injury-weakened team for the game against West Germany in Nuremburg in May 1965. And it was his surging run and cross from the left that laid on the 37th minute winning goal for Terry Paine. This was his only senior cap, although he had represented his country at Schoolboy (English Schools winner, 1954) and Youth team levels.

Blessed with terrific firepower and intricate footwork, Temple scored Everton's winning goal in the 1966 FA Cup final v. Sheffield Wednesday and overall netted 84 times in 277 appearances during his 12 years at Goodison Park.

TERRY, John George 2003-13 (78) (6)

Born: Barking, Essex, 7 December 1980
Career: Senrab FC (London Sunday League team), Chelsea (apprentice, April 1996, professional, March 1998), Nottingham Forest (loan, March-April 2000)

Courageous, strong in both boxes and a decent distributor (when unchallenged) John Terry is a terrific leader but at times has been caught out by a lack of pace.

After representing England in nine U21 internationals, the 6ft tall central defender gained his first full cap against Serbia & Montenegro in June 2003 and since then, when fit and free from suspension, he has been first choice at centre-back for his country, having many different partners in the process.

He scored his first England goal in a 3-1 win over Hungary in May 2006 and despite an injury scare in the friendly with Jamaica, he recovered to play in the opening World Cup fixture next month against Paraguay (won 1–0).

In the second match v. Trinidad & Tobago, he made a terrific goal-line clearance from Stern John's scruffy header which helped England reach the quarter-finals. They lost 3-1 on penalties to Portugal and Terry and his colleagues were left in tears.

Named as his country's full-time captain at the start of the 2006-07 season, succeeding David Beckham, Terry received this praise from his manager Steve McClaren: "Choosing a captain is one of the most important decisions a coach has to make. I'm certain I've got the right man in John Terry. I'm convinced he will prove to be one of the best captains England has ever had."

However, with Terry as leader, England failed to qualify for Euro 2008. Midway through the qualification campaign, Terry had accepted that he would 'bear full responsibility' should England fail to qualify!

In June 2007, Terry became the first player in the senior England team to score an international goal at the new Wembley Stadium, a header from Beckham's free-kick in a 1–1 draw with Brazil. Almost a year later, in May 2008, he bagged a similar headed goal from another Beckham free-kick to put England 1–0 up against the USA.

He went on to lead England in qualifying for the 2010 World Cup but was given a torrid time by Milan Baros in a 2-2 draw with the Czech Republic.

His first competitive England goal was scored against Ukraine in the qualifiers for the 2010 World Cup - a late winner after earlier conceding a free kick from which his former Chelsea team-mate Andriy Shevchenko equalised. Early in 2010, following allegations regarding Terry's private life, England boss Fabio Capello announced that Terry had been removed as captain of the national team, replaced by fellow defender Rio Ferdinand.

England disappointed everyone in the 2010 World Cup in South Africa and Terry was one player who received heavy criticism from the media. Two days after the Algeria game he hinted at dissatisfaction with Capello's team selection and stated that the players were bored with little to do in the evenings at their training base; he also said that a clear-the-air team meeting would take place that evening. The next day Capello responded by saying that Terry had made 'a very big mistake' in challenging his authority to the media. But all was forgiven and forgotten back home when qualification started for the 2012 European Championships.

In January 2010, a super-injunction was imposed by a High Court judge preventing the media from reporting that Terry had had a four-month affair in late 2009 with Vanessa Perroncel, the former girlfriend of Wayne Bridge, his former Chelsea and England teammate. The injunction was lifted a week later and the British media — especially the tabloid press — covered it in depth in the days following. Capello then dropped Terry from the England captaincy in February 2010,

replacing him with Rio Ferdinand. Thirteen months later, however, he was re-appointed as his country's skipper and led the team into the 2012 European Championships.

Terry is one of a very small band of footballers who have been paid more than £1m for their autobiography. Chris Nathaniel of NVA Management, negotiated a deal with publisher Harper Collins in 2004.

THICKETT, Henry 1898-99 (2)

Born: Hexthorpe near Doncaster, 3 June 1872
Died: Trowbridge, 15 November 1920
Career: Haxthorpe FC (1889), Sheffield United (professional, August 1890), Rotherham Town (May 1892), Sheffield United (December 1893), Bristol City (player-manager, May 1904, retired as a player, May 1905, continued as manager until 1910); was a licensee in Trowbridge from 1910 until his death.

A League Championship winner (1898) and the recipient of two FA Cup winning medals (1899 and 1902) with Sheffield United, right-back Harry Thickett was brave, strong-kicking and quick over the ground. Unfortunately at times he was far too reckless with his tackling, conceding over 20 penalties during his career. He made almost 300 senior appearances in his two spells at Bramall Lane (261 in the League).

His two outings for England were against Wales at Bristol in March 1899 (won 4-0) and Scotland in Birmingham the following month (won 2-1). He partnered Billy Williams (WBA) on his debut and James Crabtree (Aston Villa) in his second game when he held his own against Celtic's tricky left-winger Johnny Bell. He also cleared a late effort from Bob McColl off the line to preserve England's lead. Thickett also represented the Football League on two occasions and played for the Sheffield FA in several inter-city games. As a manager he took Bristol City to the 1909 FA Cup final and to the runners-up spot in the First Division (1907). It is also reported that when Thickett played in the 1899 FA Cup final v. Derby County, he had 50 yards of bandages strapped round in body to protect two broken ribs. He weighed 26 stone at the time of his death.

THOMAS, Daniel Joseph, M.D. 1982-83 ②

Born: Worksop, Notts, 12 November 1961
Career: Sheffield United (trial), Leeds United (trial), Coventry City (apprentice, April 1977, professional, December 1978), Tottenham Hotspur (£250,000, June 1983; suffered serious knee injury in March 1987, retired in January 1988); completed a degree in physiotherapy and with the assistance of the PFA, completed a Masters Degree; worked first as a 'physio' at Tottenham, then West Bromwich Albion; now runs his own practice in Coventry.

Attacking right-back Danny Thomas made his England debut as a substitute in the 0-0 draw with Australia in Sydney in June 1983, gaining his second cap as a substitute against the Aussies in Melbourne a week later.

A Schoolboy international, he also played for his country seven times at U23 level.

A UEFA Cup winner with Spurs in 1984, he worked as a 'physio' under manager Ossie Ardiles at White Hart Lane and The Hawthorns.

THOMAS, David 1974-76 ⑧

Born: Kirkby-in-Ashfield, 5 October 1950
Career: Burnley (apprentice, February 1966, professional, October 1967), Queens Park Rangers (£165,000, October 1972), Everton (£200,000, August 1977), Wolverhampton Wanderers (£325,000, October 1979), Vancouver Whitecaps (August 1981), Middlesbrough (March 1982), Portsmouth (July 1982, retired, May 1985; became youth team coach at Fratton Park); later engaged as a PE teacher at the Bishop Luffa School, Chichester for several years.

Dave Thomas was an extremely skilful left-winger, fast and elusive whose trademark was playing without shin pads. He had a long and successful career, spanning almost 20 years during which time he amassed over 500 club appearances, making his League debut for Burnley at the age of 16 years, 220 days v. Everton in 1967.

He won his eight England caps as a QPR player – the first awarded by manager Don Revie in October 1974 against Czechoslovakia when as a substitute he set up the first goal in a 3-0 win. He was outstanding in a 5-0 victory over Cyprus in April 1975 and played very well when Scotland got thumped 5-1 a month later. His last England outing was in the 1-1 European Championship qualifying draw with Portugal in November 1975.

Capped at schoolboy and youth team levels, Thomas also played eleven times for his country's U23 team. The fee paid by QPR to Burnley in 1972 was a record for a Second Division club.

THOMAS, Geoffrey Robert 1990-92 ⑨

Born: Manchester, 5 August 1964
Career: Littleborough FC (1981), Rochdale (professional, August 1982), Crewe Alexandra (March 1984), Crystal Palace (£50,000, June 1987), Wolverhampton Wanderers (£800,000, June 1993), Nottingham Forest (free, May 1997), Barnsley (July 1999), Notts County (March 2001), Crewe Alexandra (August 2001, retired May 2002); he is the founder of the Geoff Thomas Foundation, a charity that raises funds to fight cancer, a disease from which Thomas has suffered.

Grafting midfielder Geoff Thomas scored 67 goals in 550 League appearances during a career which lasted 20 years. He helped Crystal Palace gain promotion and skippered the London club in the 1990 FA Cup final.

After representing England in three B internationals, he won his first full cap as a substitute in a 1-0 win over Turkey in a European Championship qualifier in Izmir in May 1991, starting his first senior game three weeks later in a 3-1 win over USSR at Wembley when he played alongside David Platt and Dennis Wise. Over the next nine months he added seven more caps to his tally, starring in wins over Australia in Sydney, New Zealand in Auckland and Wellington and Malaysia in Kuala Lumpur, having a hand in one of Gary Lineker's four goals in the latter.

After a good, honest performance in a 1-1 draw with Poland in Poznan in November 1991, Thomas made his final appearance for his country in a 2-0 friendly win over France at Wembley in February 1992.

After a year in retirement, the footballing world was shocked, in June 2003, when Thomas revealed he had been diagnosed with chronic myeloid leukaemia, from which he later recovered. In 2005, he won the BBC Sports Personality of the Year Helen Rollason Award, after raising over £150,000 for the Leukaemia Research charity by cycling 2,200 miles in 21 days, completing the route of all 21 stages of the 2005 Tour de France a few days ahead of the race itself.

In April 2006, the players from the 1990 FA Cup final all took part in a re-run of the match, in aid of Leukemia Research, at Selhurst Park. Manchester United beat Palace 3-1. Eleven months later, in March 2007, a 'Geoff Thomas Foundation Charity XI' took on a team of celebrities in the first-ever match at the new Wembley Stadium. Thomas published his biography *Riding Through The Storm* in 2008.

THOMAS, Michael Lauriston 1988-90 ②

Born: Lambeth, London, 24 August 1967
Career: Henry Thornton School/London, South London Schools, Arsenal (schoolboy forms, September 1982, apprentice, August 1983, professional, December 1984), Portsmouth (loan, January 1987), Liverpool (£1.15m, December 1991), SL Benfica/Portugal (free, May 1997), Middlesbrough (loan, February-May 1998), Wimbledon (July 2000, retired May 2001); now runs his own security firm in Liverpool.

Strong-running and purposeful midfielder Michael Thomas (who started out as an attacking right-back) is best remembered for scoring a dramatic last minute goal in the final game of the 1988-89 season which earned Arsenal the League title ahead of Liverpool whom he later joined!

During his time with the Gunners, Thomas achieved something of a record by representing England at five different levels – schoolboy, youth, U21, B and full. He made his senior international debut (under Bobby Robson) in the 1-1 draw with Saudi Arabia in Riyadh in November 1988 and added a second cap to his tally in December 1989, playing in a 2-1 friendly win over Yugoslavia at Wembley.

During his club career, Thomas scored 33 goals in 315 League games. He gained a second Championship medal in 1991 and won both the FA Cup and League Cup with Liverpool.

THOMPSON, Alan 2003-04 ①

Born: Newcastle-upon-Tyne, 22 December 1973
Career: Newcastle United (apprentice, June 1990, professional, March 1991), Bolton Wanderers (£250,000, July 1993), Aston Villa (£4.5m, June 1998), Celtic (£2.5m, September 2000), Leeds United (loan, January-May 2007; signed permanently, August 2007), Hartlepool United (loan, January-February 2008); retired, May 2008; Newcastle United (Academy coach, July 2008), Celtic (first team coach, June 2010).

Left-sided midfielder Alan Thompson gained one cap for England, selected by Sven-Göran Eriksson for a friendly with Sweden in March 2004. He played for an hour before being substituted. He had earlier played for his country at youth and U21 levels.

A deadball specialist, he scored over 100 goals in more than 450 club appearances including 84 in 408 League matches. He won the First Division Championship with Newcastle in 1993 and Bolton in 1997 and with Celtic gained four Premier League, three Scottish Cup and two League Cup winner's medals in the space of five years: 2001-06.

THOMPSON, Peter 1963-70 ⑯

Born: Carlisle, 27 November 1942

Career: Preston North End (amateur, August 1958, professional, November 1959), Liverpool (£37,000, August 1963), Bolton Wanderers (loan, December 1973, signed permanently for £18,000, January 1974, retired, May 1978); became a director of a garage business; later ran a caravan park and a hotel in the Lake District.

Manager Alf Ramsey selected Peter Thompson in his initial squad of 40 for the 1966 World Cup but in the end went for three wingers, Ian Callaghan, John Connelly and Terry Paine. Thompson had already played in twelve full internationals, having made his debut against Portugal in Lisbon in May 1964 when he had an 'excellent 90 minutes on a very warm day.'

He also starred in a 10-0 win over the USA later that month, had a 'terrific game' on the left flank when Northern Ireland were defeated 4-3 in the October and played well in the next five games, none of which were lost.

Two years after missing out on possible World Cup glory, Thompson was recalled to the England team by Ramsey for the European Nations qualifier against Northern Ireland. He was told: 'I want you to play like you do for Liverpool – yet not hold the ball.' "It was like asking me to play with my legs tied together. That was a ridiculous ask," said Thompson. But he did what he was told – or tried to anyway – as England won 2-0. Three further outings for the national team followed before his England career just prior to the 1970 World Cup tournament, thus having the misfortune to be omitted for the second successive World Cup. In fact, as a member of Ramsey's initial squad ahead of the finals in Mexico, Thompson was involved in the Bogota bracelet incident. By some accounts he was in or around the Green Fire jewellery shop when Bobby Moore was alleged to have taken a bracelet.

Thompson, who also represented his country in three Schoolboy and four U23 internationals and played five times for the Football League, scored 31 goals in 143 appearances for Preston, 55 in 416 games for Liverpool and two in 132 outings for Bolton, winning two League Championships and the FA Cup with the Merseysiders and the Third Division title with Bolton.

THOMPSON, Philip Bernard 1975-83 ㊷ ①

Born: Liverpool, 21 January 1954

Career: Liverpool (apprentice, April 1970, professional February 1971), Sheffield United (December 1984, retired May 1986); Liverpool (coaching staff, July 1986-May 1992, and again, July 1999-May 2004; also caretaker-manager for six months during 2001-02); now a Sky Sports football reporter/summariser/analyst and a regular Visiting Fellow at the University of Liverpool where he teaches on their Football Industries MBA (FIMBA).

Phil Thompson was the proud young 'Kopite' who became Bill Shankly's last great prodigy. A Liverpool fan from the age of five, 'Thommo' was without doubt, the sorcerer's apprentice, who went on to captain club (Liverpool) and country, lifted the European Cup and won every domestic honour in the game. Indeed, between 1973 and 1983 he helped the Merseyside club win seven League titles,

two UEFA Cups, the FA Cup, three European Cups, the European Super Cup, three League Cups and six FA Charity Shields. He also appeared in 466 senior games for the Reds (340 in the League).

Regarded (by many) as one of the finest centre-backs the club has had since WW2, Thompson won one U23, one B and 42 full caps for England, making his senior debut against Wales in March 1976, lining up with four of his Anfield colleagues, Ray Clemence, Phil Neal, Kevin Keegan and Ray Kennedy in a 2-1 win.

A regular in the team over the next six months, he was outstanding in three fine wins over Northern Ireland (4-0), Italy (3-2 in New York, when he scored his only international goal with a powerful header from Gordon Hill's left-wing corner) and Finland (4-1).

However, he slipped out of favour for two years (when Dave Watson was preferred) but came back as strong as ever in 1978 and held his position for four years, forming a wonderful partnership at the back with the aforementioned Watson.

Unfortunately he had the occasional off-day and conceded an own-goal in a 4-1 defeat by Wales at Wrexham in May 1980. He played his last game in an England shirt in November 1982 when Greece was defeated 3-0 in a European Championship qualifier in Salonika. That day he was joined in defence by Alvin Martin who kept his position as Terry Butcher's partner as 'Thommo' waved farewell.

After retiring as a player in May 1986, having played 45 games for Sheffield United, he became a member of the famous Anfield 'boot room' coaching staff, only to be axed by his former team-mate, then manager Graeme Souness in 1992. But like a red phoenix from the flames, Thompson rose again, and came back to Liverpool as Gerard Houllier's assistant, acting as caretaker-boss for six months during the 2001-02 season when his new mentor was preparing for life-saving heart surgery.

Forget the sky-high salaries and cynicism that dominate today, Thompson would have played football for peanuts... he loved the game – and still does.

Few characters in football have stirred up as much emotion and controversy as the former Liverpool and Sheffield United defender Phil Thompson. Indeed, his profile is as powerful as ever due to his regular appearances as a respected and outspoken pundit on Sky Sports. Thompson's autobiography, Stand Up Pinocchio, will bring a smile to the faces of all fans. It's the greatest football story ever told!

THOMPSON, Thomas 1951-57 ②

Born: Fencehouses near Houghton-le-Spring, County Durham, 10 November 1929

Career: Lumley YMCA (1943), Newcastle United (£15, August 1946), Aston Villa (£12,000, September 1950), Preston North End (£28,500, June 1955), Stoke City (£10,000, July 1961), Barrow (£5,000, March 1963, retired, May 1965); returned to live in Preston where he became a carpenter, assisting Tom Finney at times.

Inside-forward Tommy Thompson played inside-right to two of the greatest wingers in English football – Tom Finney (at Preston) and Stanley Matthews (at Stoke).

A shade on the small side, he was nevertheless a keen, clever and thrustful footballer who netted six goals in 20 appearances for Newcastle and 76 in 165 outings for Aston Villa before moving to Deepdale to partner Finney. He scored after just 90 seconds of his debut for the Lillywhites in a 4–0 win over Everton and went on to claim 117 goals in 188 starts during his six years with North End (including 117 in 188 League matches). Then, with Matthews alongside him, he struck 18 times in 46 games for Stoke whom he helped gain promotion to the First Division in 1963 and added another 16 goals in 46 appearances for Barrow, retiring with 224 goals to his credit in 451 competitive games.

Deputising for Wilf Mannion, and linking up with Finney for the first time at international level, Thompson made his England debut in the 1-1 draw with Wales in October 1951, but he then had to wait 5½ years before collecting his second cap, in a 2-1 victory over Scotland at Wembley in April 1957 when his right-wing partner was Stan Matthews. Thompson, nicknamed 'Toucher' also represented the Football League (he netted four goals in a 9-0 win over the League of Ireland in October 1951) and England B.

THOMSON, Robert Anthony 1963-65 ⑧

Born: Smethwick, 5 December 1943
Died: Dudley, 19 August 2009
Career: Crocketts Lane Junior & Lyndon High Schools (Smethwick), Cape Hill Juniors, Wolverhampton Wanderers (apprentice, June 1959, professional, July 1961), Birmingham City (£40,000, March 1969), Walsall (loan, November-December 1971), Luton Town (July 1972), Hartford Bicentennials/USA (April 1976), Port Vale (October 1976), Connecticut Bicentennials/USA (player-coach, April 1977), Worcester City (briefly, in 1978), Memphis Rogues/USA (March 1979), Stafford Rangers (player-manager, August 1979); later assisted Brewood, Solihull Borough and Tipton Town, retiring in May 1987; ran a sports shop in Sedgley near Dudley; played in local charity matches until he was 47; he also played cricket in the Birmingham League.

Left-back Bobby Thomson's baptism for England came as a 19 year-old in an 8-3 demolition of Northern Ireland at Wembley in November 1963 when he partnered skipper Jimmy Armfield. He had a 'sound game' behind Bobby Moore and one of his long measured clearances down the wing led to one of Jimmy Greaves's four goals.

His next cap (with George Cohen to his right) came in a 10-0 win over USA in May 1964 and following another 'solid performance' he retained his place for the next six games, producing fine displays in victories over Northern Ireland (4-3) and Wales (2-1). Ray Wilson replaced him in the national team.

Thomson, elegant and speedy, made over 500 club appearances (477 in the League), having his best years with Wolves (300 outings). He also represented England 15 times at U23 level and played for the Football League on four occasions.

Thomson died of prostate cancer at Russell's Hall Hospital in Dudley. He had defeated a first occurrence of the illness, only to succumb after suffering a relapse.

THORNEWELL, George 1922-25 ④ ①

Born: Romiley, Cheshire, 8 July 1898
Died: Derbyshire, 6 March 1986
Career: St James' Road School/Derby, Rolls Royce FC/Derby (1913), Nottingham Forest (amateur, season 1917-18), Derby County (amateur, May 1918, professional, May 1919), Blackburn Rovers (December 1927), Chesterfield (August 1929, retired, May 1932).

A smart, tricky outside-right who rarely lost the ball, George Thornewell was an FA Cup winner with Blackburn in 1928 and a Third Division (N) winner with Chesterfield three years later.

Playing alongside two of his Derby team-mates, inside-right Moore and centre-forward Bedford, he scored on his England debut in a 4-2 win over Sweden in Stockholm in May 1923 and three days later starred in a 3-1 victory over the same country at the same venue. Twelve months on, Thornewell gained his third cap when France were beaten 3-1 in Paris before playing in his last international, also in France in May 1925 (won 3-2).

He was desperately unlucky not to have won more caps... as there were so many other talented right-wingers around at the same time.

THORNLEY, Irvine 1906-07 ①

Born: Hayfield, Derbyshire, 23 February 1883
Died: Glossop, 24 April 1955
Career: Glossop Villa (1898), Glossop St James' (1899), Glossop North End (professional, August 1901), Manchester City (£800, April 1904), South Shields (August 1912), Hamilton Academical (July 1919), Houghton FC (May 1920, retired April 1922).

A powerful, lively, all-action centre-forward, difficult to contain, Irvine Thornley gained his only England cap in a 1-1 draw with Wales in March 1907. He helped Manchester City win the Second Division championship in 1910 and played twice for the Football League.

Thornley, who initially combined playing football with a career as a butcher, was a controversial character, being sent off at least eight times during his career. One of the players present at the first ever meeting of the Professional Footballers' Association in 1907, he scored 93 goals in 204 appearances for Manchester City and netted no less than 154 in 130 games in three seasons with South Shields.

Soon after his transfer to Manchester City, the FA carried out an investigation into the financial activities of the club. City's manager, Tom Maley, was interviewed and admitted that he had followed what seemed like 'standard English practice' by making additional payments to all his players. He claimed that if all First Division clubs were investigated, not four would come out 'scatheless'. As a result of their investigation, the FA suspended Maley from football for life while seventeen players were fined and suspended until January 1907.

As a reward for his service to Manchester City, Thornley was rewarded with a benefit match in 1912. Over 40,000 fans turned out and a record £1,036 was raised for the player.

TILSON, Samuel Frederick 1933-36 ④ ⑥

Born: Swinton, South Yorkshire, 19 April 1903
Died: Manchester, 21 November 1972
Career: Barnsley Schools, Regent Street Congregationalists (Barnsley), Barnsley (professional, March 1926), Manchester City (£6,000, with Eric Brook, March 1928), Northampton Town (March 1938), York City (May 1939, retired during WW2); Manchester City (coach from 1946, then assistant-manager to July 1965, later chief scout, August 1965-April 1968).

Described as being 'a quick thinker with an elusive body-swerve and excellent shot', inside-left Fred Tilson, who also starred at centre-forward, was an FA Cup and League Championship winner with Manchester City in 1934 and 1937 respectively. He was unfortunate with injuries - he missed the 1933 Cup final - yet nevertheless netted 132 goals in 273 senior appearances during his playing career at Maine Road (including a club record 22 in the FA Cup, two of them coming in the 1934 final v. Portsmouth).

A scorer on his England debut in a 2-1 defeat by Hungary in Budapest in May 1934, he then found the net in each of his next three internationals – in a 2-1 defeat by Czechoslovakia in Zlin, six days after the Hungary game, twice in a 4-0 win over Wales at Cardiff in September 1934 and two more in a 3-1 victory over Ireland in Belfast a year later. His close pal Brook played on the left-wing in each of his four England games

Tilson, one feels, would have surely won more caps but for injury, and it must be pointed out that he also faced stiff competition from George Camsell, Ted Drake and 'Pongo' Waring. He served Manchester City for a total of 32 years.

TITMUSS, Frederick 1921-23 ②

Born: Pirton, Herts, 15 February 1898
Died: Plymouth, 2 October 1966
Career: Pirton United (August 1914-April 1915), Hitchin Town (during WW1 when he served with the Lancashire Fusiliers, playing regularly for the Army team), Southampton (professional, May 1919), Plymouth Argyle (£1,750, February 1926-May 1932), St Austell FC (briefly in season 1932-33); was a licensee in Plymouth (until his death).

A left-back of great merit, sure-footed with precise timing in his tackle and kicking, Fred Titmuss made his international debut in a 1-0 win over Wales at Goodison Park in March 1922, the same day as his Southampton colleague, Bill Rawlings. This was the first time that two players from a Third Division club had appeared in the same England side, and the only occasion on which two players from the same Third Division club had played together for their country. He added a second cap to his tally, also against Wales, a year later, a 2-2 draw at Cardiff.

A defender who specialised in the sliding tackle, Titmuss was also a wonderful positional player who made 237 appearances for Saints whom he helped win the Third Division (S) Championship in 1922. Eight years later he helped Plymouth Argyle win the same Division. He had 173 outings for the Pilgrims in six years.

TODD, Colin 1971-77 ㉗

Born: Chester-le-Street, County Durham, 12 December 1948
Career: Chester-le-Street Boys, Sunderland (apprentice, July 1964, professional, December 1966), Derby County (£180,000, February 1971), Everton (£333,000, September 1978), Birmingham City (£300,000, September 1979), Nottingham Forest (£70,000, August 1982), Oxford United (February 1984), Vancouver Whitecaps/Canada (May-October 1984), Luton Town (October 1984, retired May 1985); Whitley Bay (manager, season 1985-86), Middlesbrough (youth team coach, May 1986, assistant-manager, May 1987, manager, March 1990-June 1991), Bradford City (assistant-manager, January 1992), Bolton Wanderers (assistant-manager, May 1992, joint-manager with Roy McFarland, June 1995-January 1996, then sole manager to September 1999), Swindon Town (manager, May-November 2000), Derby County (assistant-manager, December 2000, manager October 2001-January 2002), Bradford City (assistant-manager, March 2003, manager June 2004-February 2007), Randers FC/Denmark (manager, June 2007-January 2009), Darlington (manager, May-September 2009).

Scrupulously fair, blessed with a sure tackle, discernment and a brilliant reader of the game, Colin Todd made his England debut at right-back in the 1-0 defeat by Northern Ireland at Wembley in May 1972. This, in fact, was the first international since 1966 that England had started without one of their World Cup winning heroes in the line-up. Martin Peters later came on as a substitute. In his fourth international Todd had the misfortune to concede an own-goal in a 2-0 defeat by Scotland at Hampden Park.

He also played 'exceptionally well' when he came on as a make-shift left-back in the 0-0 draw with Portugal at Wembley in November 1974 and was a regular in the England defence for the next two years, having more outstanding games in victories over Bulgaria (1-0), West Germany (2-0), Cyprus (5-0), Scotland (5-1 at Wembley), Northern Ireland (4-0) and Finland (4-1 in a World Cup qualifier) and draws with Argentina (2-2), Portugal (0-0 and 1-1 in European Championship qualifiers) and the Republic of Ireland (1-1).

He won his 27th and last cap in a 2-1 victory over Northern Ireland in May 1977.

As a youngster, Todd had opportunities to sign for Newcastle United and Middlesbrough, but chose Sunderland 'because of their

tradition for youth'. Under coach Brian Clough, he played a major part in the Wearsiders' FA Youth Cup triumph in 1967, having already made his League debut against Chelsea in October 1966 - the first of more than 800 appearances he would make at club level.

Todd later rejoined Clough at Derby who signed him for a then British record fee of £180,000. He won two League titles with the Rams in 1972 and 1975 and the Texaco Cup, also in 1972, forming a formidable partnership with Roy McFarland at both club and international levels. He helped Birmingham gain promotion to the top flight in 1980 (under manager Jim Smith) while as manager he took Bolton in and out of the Premiership in 1997 and 1998 respectively.

In 1984, at the age of 35 years, four months, he became the oldest player to appear in a League game for Oxford United. A youth international who also played in one unofficial England game, earned 14 U23 caps and represented the Football League on three occasions, Todd was highly regarded in English football circles and was voted PFA 'Footballer of the Year' in 1975. He was in charge of 525 games as a manager.

His son, Andy, has played as a defender for Middlesbrough, Swindon, Bolton, Charlton, Grimsby, Blackburn Rovers, Derby County and Perth Glory in Australia.

TOONE, George 1891-92 ②

Born: Nottingham, 10 June 1868
Died: Nottingham, 1 September 1943
Career: Forest Olympic/Nottingham (1883), St Saviour's/Nottingham (1884), Lincoln City (briefly, 1886), Nottingham Jardine (1887), Notts Rangers (1888), Notts County (August 1899), Bedminster (August 1899), Bristol City (May 1900), Notts County (December 1901, retired, April 1902; re-signed, August 1903, retired again, November 1903); was a licensee in Nottingham for many years.

Cool and confident goalkeeper George Toone made an impressive debut for England when Wales were defeated 2-0 at Wrexham in March 1892. A month later he did not touch the ball for the first 30 minutes of the game against Scotland, but after half-time he was 'frequently under siege but held out gallantly, making several great saves' in a 4-1 victory at Ibrox Park.

After missing the 1891 FA Cup final through injury, he celebrated three years later with a winner's medal and in 1897, helped the Magpies clinch the Second Division. He made 308 appearances during his two spells at Meadow Lane. His son, George junior, played for Notts County, Sheffield Wednesday and Watford.

TOPHAM, Arthur George 1893-94 ①

Born: Ellesmere Port, Cheshire, 19 February 1869
Died: Eastbourne, 18 May 1931
Career: Oswestry Council School, Keble College/Oxford University (seasons 1889-92); also played for Casuals, Eastbourne, Chiswick Park and the Corinthians (during seasons 1892-97); brother of R. Topham (below); a schoolmaster by professional, he was co-proprietor of Lynchmere School (Eastbourne) and later taught at Ascham St Vincent's School (1912-25).

An amateur right-half, strong and competitive in the tackle, Arthur Topham could be somewhat erratic with his kicking at times, but was generally a fine defender. He played with his brother for England against Wales in March 1894, starring in a 5-1 win. That very same year he appeared in the FA Amateur Cup final for the Casuals.

TOPHAM, Robert 1892-93 ②

Born: Ellesmere Port, Cheshire, 3 November 1867
Died: Canterbury, Kent, 31 August 1951
Career: Oxford University (seasons 1884-87); also played for Oswestry FC (season 1886-87), Casuals (seasons 1887-94), Chiswick Park (season 1889-90), Wolverhampton Wanderers (between August 1891 and April 1896), Corinthians (seasons 1894-98, retiring in May 1898); a schoolmaster at Brighton College (1892-1905), he later became a hop grower in Kent.

Elder brother of Arthur (above) Bob - sometimes called Dick - Topham played outside-right in the 6-1 victory over Ireland in February 1893 and the 5-1 win against Wales in March 1894, having previously been selected to represent Wales against Scotland in 1885, an offer he refused!

A Welsh Cup finalist with Oswestry in 1885, FA Cup winner with Wolves in 1893 and an Amateur Cup finalist with Casuals in 1894, he was described as being 'difficult to contain, had speed, dribbling ability and middled the ball with skill.'

TOWERS, Mark Anthony 1975-76 ③

Born: Manchester, 13 April 1952
Career: Manchester & Lancashire Schools, Manchester City (July 1967, professional, April 1969), Sunderland (£100,000, plus Mick Horswill, March 1974), Birmingham City (£140,000, July 1977), Montreal Manic/Canada (March 1981), Tampa Bay Rowdies/USA (seasons 1983-84), Vancouver Whitecaps/Canada (August 1984), Rochdale (non-contract, February-March 1985, retired May 1985).

Influential midfielder Tony Towers – who went on to play as a central defender – made his League debut as a 17 year-old for Manchester City against Southampton in 1970. He helped City win the European Cup Winners' Cup final v. Gornik Zabrze in Vienna and four years later played in the League Cup final defeat by Wolves. He later won the Second Division championship with Sunderland in 1976.

He gained his three England caps as a Sunderland player, lining up in successive wins over Wales, Northern Ireland and Italy, all in May 1976, having earlier starred in four schoolboy, three youth and eight U23 internationals. Towers made 159 appearances for Manchester City, 124 for Sunderland but was a huge disappointment at St Andrew's, despite making a further 103 appearances.

TOWNLEY, William John 1888-90 ② ②

Born: Blackburn, 14 February 1866
Died: Blackpool, 30 May 1950
Career: Blackburn Olympic (May 1884), Blackburn Rovers (professional, August 1887), Stockton (July 1892), Darwen (July 1894), Manchester City (September 1896, retired, May 1897); a schoolmaster by profession, he football coached abroad from 1909 to 1933, engaged by Deutscher FC Prag/Germany (briefly in 1909), Karlsruher FV/Germany (seasons 1909-11), SpVgg Fürth/Austria (four spells: April 1911-December 1913, April-May 1914, August-October 1914 and May 1926-September 1927), Bayern Munich/Germany (three spells: January-April 1914, August-November 1914, season 1919-20), FC St. Gallen/Switzerland (twice, August 1920-January 1921 & August 1923-February 1925), SV Waldhof Mannheim/Germany (January-March 1921), SC Victoria Hamburg/Germany (June 1921-May 1923), the Netherlands national team (March-June 1924), Union Niederrad 07/Germany (August 1924-May 1927), FSV Frankfurt/Germany (August 1927-April 1930), Eintracht Hannover FC/Germany (briefly in 1932) and finally, Armenia Hannover/Germany (season 1932-33).

Twice an FA Cup winner with Blackburn, he became the first player to score a hat-trick in a final when he bagged a treble in Rovers' 6-1 win over Sheffield Wednesday in 1890. A year later he collected his second winners' medal.

A prolific goalscoring outside-left, Bill Townley possessed a stunning long-range shot, was also a smart header of the ball and was most elusive when racing down the flank.

Capped twice by England, first against Wales in February 1889 (won 4-1) and then against Ireland in March 1890 (won 9-1), he scored twice and had a hand in three other goals in his second international in Belfast. He bagged 51 goals in 124 senior appearances for Blackburn Rovers. As a coach/manager – and a brilliant one at that – Townley guided Karlsruher to the League title in 1910, SpVgg Fürth to five League championships (1912, 1913, 1914, 1926 and 1931), Bayern Munich to the Southern Bavarian title, Netherlands to fourth place in the 1924 Olympic Games and Armenia to the North German (South District) championship in 1933.

TOWNROW, John Ernest 1924-26 ②

Born: West Ham, London, 28 March 1901
Died: Harrogate, Yorkshire, 11 April 1969
Career: Pelly Memorial School/West Ham, West Ham & District School, Fairburn House FC, Clapton Orient (semi-professional, August 1919), Chelsea (£5,000, February 1927), Bristol Rovers (May 1932, retired June 1933); later groundsman and coach at Fairburn House and also worked at Becton Gasworks and later as a licensee; returned to the game to manage Harrogate Town for two seasons (1964-66).

A tall, well-built centre-half, cool and collected, Jack Townrow was also a fine passer of the ball. He played 265 times for Orient, 140 for Chelsea and ten for Bristol Rovers. A schoolboy international v. Scotland and Wales in 1915, he gained his two full caps against Scotland in April 1925 (lost 2-0) and Wales in March 1926 (lost 3-1). Unfortunately there were far too many good centre-halves around at the same time for Townrow to win any more caps.

TREMELLING, Richard Daniel 1927-28 ①

Born: Mansfield Woodhouse, Notts, 13 November 1897
Died: Birmingham, 15 August 1970
Career: Langwith Colliery Junction Wagon Works FC (from 1912), Shirebrook (season 1917-18), Lincoln City (professional, August 1918), Birmingham (May 1919), Bury (May 1932); Birmingham (assistant-trainer, June 1936-May 1941); later in the licensing trade.

Dan Tremelling played initially as a full-back for his local team, before becoming a goalkeeper…taking over the job during an injury crisis! He did well, so much so that in 1918, he was recruited by Lincoln City. A permanent fixture at St Andrew's for ten years, he went on to make 395 first-class appearances for Blues. He lost his place to future England 'keeper Harry Hibbs in 1929–30. Brilliant at catching and handling the ball, he helped Blues win the Second Division title in 1921 and played for England in a 2-1 defeat by Wales at Burnley in November 1927, holding his hands up for conceding the deciding goal.

TRESADERN, John 1922-23 ②

Born: Leytonstone, 26 September 1890
Died: Tonbridge, 26 December 1959
Career: Wanstead (1909), Barking Town (August 1912), West Ham United (July 1913), Burnley (October 1924), Northampton Town (player-manager, May 1925, retiring as a player, December 1926 after breaking his leg, continuing as manager until September

1930); Crystal Palace (manager, October 1930-June 1935), Tottenham Hotspur (manager, June 1935-April 1938), Plymouth Argyle (manager, April 1938-November 1947); Aston Villa (scout, season 1948-49), Chelmsford City (manager, June 1949-November 1950), Hastings United (manager, December 1951-May 1957), Tonbridge (manager, April 1958 until his death).

A member of the West Ham squad which gained election to the Football League in 1919, Jack Tresadern, a small, dapper, terrier-like left-half, became a regular in the first team immediately and went on to appear in 160 senior games for the club (five goals scored) before transferring to Burnley. A year earlier he had made his England debut in the 2-2 Home International draw with Scotland in April 1923... But admitted he wasn't exactly enamored with his performance. "I was the best player Scotland had on the field" he said! His second international appearance followed a month later, in a 4-2 win over Sweden in Stockholm, when he assisted in one of Billy Walker's two goals.

Playing for the Hammers against Bolton Wanderers in the first-ever Wembley FA Cup final, he became entangled in the crowd while taking a throw-in after just two minutes. Unable to return to the pitch immediately, he saw David Jack score the first goal in a 2-0 win for the Lancashire club.

TUEART, Dennis 1974-77 ⑥ ②

Born: Newcastle-upon-Tyne, 27 November 1949
Career: Newcastle Boys, Sunderland (apprentice, April 1966, professional, August 1967), Manchester City (£275,000, March 1974), New York Cosmos/USA (£250,000, February 1978), Manchester City (£150,000 January, 1980), Stoke City (free, July 1983), Burnley (free, December 1983), Derry City (briefly, in season 1985-86); became a successful businessman in corporate hospitality in Manchester; also a director of Manchester City (up to July 1997).

Able to play on both wings, Dennis Tueart, in his third international, fired England into a third minute lead against Finland at Wembley in October 1976. A 'horrid' game ended in a 2-1 win. Seven months later, in May 1977, he scored again, this time in another 2-1 victory over Northern Ireland in Belfast, stooping low to head home a cross from debutant Brian Talbot in the 86th minute.

Tueart, who made his international debut as a substitute for Kevin Keegan in a 1-0 European Championship qualifying victory over Cyprus in Limassol in May 1975, played his last game for his country in a 2-1 defeat by Scotland at Wembley in June 1977 when again he was used as a second-half substitute, this time for Ray Kennedy.

An FA Cup winner with Sunderland (v. Leeds United) in 1973, Tueart scored with a brilliant overhead kick when Manchester City beat Newcastle in the 1976 League Cup final. He also played in the 1981 FA Cup final defeat by Spurs. Honoured by England at U23 level, as an over-aged player v. Scotland in December 1974, he also netted for the Football League in a 5-0 win over the Scottish League. In his 17-year senior career (1967-84) Tueart bagged well over 150 goals in almost 500 club appearances, 137 coming in 420 League games. His polished and exciting play was certainly appreciated by the fans.

TUNSTALL, Frederick Edward 1922-27 ⑦

Born: Low Valley, Wombwell, Yorks, 29 March 1901
Died: Boston, Lincolnshire, 18 November 1965
Career: Darfield St George's (August 1918), Scunthorpe & Lindsey United (professional, March 1920), Sheffield United (£1,000, December 1920), Halifax Town (January 1933), Boston United (June 1936, retired May 1939; remained with club until his death in 1965, having three separate spells as manager, four as trainer and two as coach).

An FA Cup winner with Sheffield United in 1925 when he hit the deciding goal v. Cardiff City, live-wire and direct outside-left Fred Tunstall who could unleash a ferocious shot, scored 135 goals in 491 senior appearances for the Blades during his career at Bramall Lane.

He won his seven England caps as a Sheffield United player, having a superb debut in the 2-2 draw with Scotland at Hampden Park in April 1923 when he crossed for both Bob Kelly and Vic Watson to score. He was also in good form when the Scots forced a 1-1 draw in the first international at Wembley in April 1924. *The Times* reporter wrote: "Tunstall played an excellent game at outside-left and centred accurately without wasting time."

A month later he had another splendid game when England defeated France 3-1 in Paris. Aston Villa's Arthur Dorrell, West Ham's Jimmy Ruffell and Tom Urwin of Newcastle were all challenging Tunstall for the left-wing position during the mid-1920s.

TURNBULL, Robert Joseph 1919-20 ①

Born: South Bank near Middlesbrough, 17 December 1895
Died: Middlesbrough, 18 March 1952
Career: South Bank Schools, South Bank East End (1910), Bradford Park Avenue (professional, January 1918), Leeds United (May 1925), Rhyl Athletic (September 1932, retired May 1933); thereafter worked at the Dorman Long steel factory, Middlesbrough until his death.

A goalscoring inside-left and occasional outside-right, Bob Turnbull was a direct, no-frills and consistent footballer who scored 46 goals in 215 appearances during his seven years at Elland Road. Having previously played in three Victory internationals (one goal), he gained his only cap for England against Ireland in October 1919 when he partnered a former South Bank East End colleague, Jack Carr, on the right-wing. He toured South Africa with the FA Party in 1920 and 1929, making five appearances in total.

TURNER, Arthur Donald 1899-1901 ②

Born: Hartley Wintney, Hampshire, 1877
Died: Farnborough, 4 April 1925
Career: Aldershot North End (July 1892), South Farnborough (August 1894), Camberley St Michael's FC (June 1896), Brentford (trial, 1897), Reading (trial, 1898), Southampton (professional, May 1899), Derby County (May 1902), Newcastle United (January 1903), Tottenham Hotspur (February 1904), Southampton (May 1904), Bristol City (loan briefly, 1904), South Farnborough FC (June 1905, retired, May 1914).

In his first season with reigning Southern League champions Southampton, outside-right Archie Turner played in a losing FA Cup final, Saints being swept aside 4–0 by Bury. He also achieved the then unique distinction of being called up to play for England in his first season in top-class football, starring in a 2-0 win over Ireland in Dublin in March 1900 and in a 3-0 victory over the same country a year later – making him the first Hampshire-born player to represent England.

His rapid rise to prominence made Turner a target for opposing full-backs and as a result he received some rough treatment. Despite this, he continued to produce exciting wing play down the right-hand side and in Holley & Chalk's *The Alphabet of the Saints*, was described as being 'A master of delivering accurate centres; if he had a fault it was a reluctance to shoot, preferring instead to find a colleague who perhaps would not be in such a promising position.'

Turner - a Southern League Championship winner in 1900-01 - played in his second FA Cup final when Saints lost to Sheffield United in a replay in 1902.

He played alongside Steve Bloomer at Derby but he wasn't a success with the Rams, nor with Newcastle or Tottenham Hotspur.

Returning to Southampton in 1904, his career was virtually over and on quitting Saints in May 1905, he joined Farnborough Athletic, and in the summer played cricket for the local team. At the age of 28, he entered the family business in Farnborough.

His brother, Harry Turner, also played for Southampton (1903-05).

TURNER, Hugh 1930-31 (2)
Born: Wigan, 6 August 1904
Died: Durham, 16 May 1997
Career: Felling Colliery (1920), Darlington (amateur, August 1924), High Fell FC/Gateshead (January 1925), Huddersfield Town (professional, April 1926), Fulham (May 1937, officially retired, May 1945)

An astute goalkeeper, very consistent, Hugh Turner made 364 League appearances for Huddersfield, gaining an FA Cup runners-up medal in 1930. He took over between the posts from Harry Hibbs when winning his two England caps...having a 'nightmare' (wrote one reporter) in Paris in May 1931 when France won 5-2 but played well in a 4-1 win over Belgium in Brussels 48 hours later.

TURNER, James Albert 1892-98 (3)
Born: Black Bull, Stoke-on-Trent, 11 January, 1866
Died: Stoke-on-Trent, 9 April 1904
Career: Black Lane Rovers/Radcliffe, Radcliffe FC (briefly, season 1887-88), Bolton Wanderers (professional, July 1888), Derby County (£70, June 1896), Stoke (£100, August 1898, retired through injury, May 1899).

Initially an outside-right, he was subsequently converted into a half-back and made over 100 appearances for Bolton.

A Football League representative, he gained his first England cap in a 6-0 win over Wales at Stoke in March 1893, assisting in two goals. His second cap came in a resounding 9-0 win over Ireland at Derby two years later but it wasn't until March 1898 that he collected his third and last cap, in a hard-earned 3-2 win over the Irish in Belfast.

Turner also played in the 1898 losing FA Cup final for Derby against Nottingham Forest, having missed the 1893 one with Bolton through injury. He made well over 200 League appearances during his career.

His brother, Dick Turner, also played for Bolton.

TWEEDY, George Jacob 1936-37 (1)
Born: Willington, County Durham, 8 January 1913
Died: Grimsby, 23 April 1987
Career: Durham & District Schools, Willington Town (April 1928), Grimsby Town (professional, August 1931); WW2 guest for Arsenal and Hibernian; back to Grimsby Town (as a player, acted as assistant-manager, July 1950-January 1951; then caretaker-manager, retired as a player, May 1953, aged 40); was later heavily associated with the family furniture business in Grimsby.

Regarded as Grimsby Town's greatest-ever goalkeeper, George Tweedy's only game for England was in December 1936 against Hungary at Highbury when he 'played effectively and well' in a 6-2 win. He was, one feels, prevented from gaining more caps owing to his club status, as well as the fact he was in competition with four more excellent 'keepers in Ted Sagar (Everton), Holdcroft (Preston), Vic Woodley (Chelsea) and Harry Hibbs (Birmingham). Always unruffled and a wonderful club man, he served the Mariners for almost 22 years, making 372 appearances.

UFTON, Derek Gilbert 1953-54 (1)
Born: Crayford, Kent, 31 May 1928
Career: Dartford Grammar School, Borough United (Kent), Dulwich Hamlet, Cardiff City (as an amateur while serving in the forces), Bexleyheath & Welling United (1946), Charlton Athletic (September 1948, retired, injured, May 1960); Tooting & Mitcham (coach, January 1962), Plymouth Argyle (coach, September 1964, manager May 1965-February 1968); worked as a photographic model and was manager of the Sporting Club (in London's West End) in 1972; also played cricket for Kent (1949-62); Charlton Athletic (director, August 1984, later club's vice-President, 1993 to date); appointed Chairman of the Lord's Taveners cricket team (April 1990); he was vice-Chairman of the TTT Trust from 1993 to 2005.

Cultured and stylish, with a solid tackle, centre-half Derek Ufton dislocated his shoulder 20 times during his 12 years at The Valley yet still made 277 appearances for Charlton.

A big favourite with the Addicks supporters, he was captain of the team in an extraordinary home League match with Huddersfield Town in December 1957. Reduced to ten men after Ufton had gone off injured, the visitors held a 5-1 lead with just 27 minutes remaining. At that point, uncapped winger Johnny Summers burst into life! Switched to centre-forward, he scored four goals and set up another to send Charlton into a 6-5 lead. Then, after the Terriers had equalised, Summers set up Ryan for a 90th minute winner to earn his side a stunning 7-6 victory. This was the first and only time a team has scored six goals in a Football League match – or indeed any other professional match – and lost!

Capped by England in the 4-4 draw with the Rest of Europe at Wembley in October 1953, when he deputised for the injured Harry Johnston, Ufton was given a testing time by some talented opponents. A recurring shoulder injury surely prevented him from winning more honours.

Initially coach to Malcolm Allison at Plymouth, he then upset the fans by selling some star players and recruiting inferior ones to Home Park. Later in life, he played an important role in Charlton's return to The Valley in December 1992.

On the cricket field, Upton was a batsman-wicketkeeper who played in 148 games for Kent, scoring 3,919 runs and claiming 314 victims (271 caught, 43 stumped). Ufton is one of the oldest former Charlton players alive today.

UNDERWOOD, Alfred 1890-92 (2)
Born: Hanley, Stoke-on-Trent, 2 August 1867
Died: Stoke-on-Trent, 8 October 1928
Career: Hanley Tabernackle FC/Stoke, Etruria FC, Stoke (July 1887, retired, injured, May 1893; remained at club as coach for one extra season); a potter by trade, he was chronically ill for 25 years until his death in 1928.

A rock-hard, durable and highly-effective full-back, Alf Underwood was utterly reliable with a prodigious kick who at times 'tackled far too recklessly.' He helped Stoke win the Football Alliance Championship in 1891, the same year he gained the first of his two England caps in a 6-1 win over Ireland at Wolverhampton. In March 1892, along with his Stoke colleagues Billy Rowley (in goal) and Tommy Clare (as left-back partner), Underwood won his second cap in a 2-0 victory in Belfast. He made 131 senior appearances for the Potters before injury forced him into early retirement at the age of 25.

UNSWORTH, David Gerald 1994-95 ①

Born: Chorley, Lancs, 16 October 1973
Career: Everton (apprentice, April 1990, professional, June 1992), West Ham United (£1m, August 1997), Aston Villa (£3m, July 1998), Everton (£3m, August 1998), Portsmouth (free July 2004), Ipswich Town (loan, January-May 2005), Sheffield United (free, August 2005), Wigan Athletic (free, January 2007), Burnley (free, August 2007), Huddersfield Town (free, August 2008, retired, April 2009); Preston North End (Development coach, June 2009, then first team coach).

The lack of competitive qualifiers ahead of Euro '96 meant that England boss Terry Venables could experiment with the side in warm-up tournaments such as the Umbro Trophy in 1995. He picked out Everton's centre-back David Unsworth for his one appearance for his country. The experiment wasn't a success! Unsworth didn't have a great game as England beat Japan 2-1 at Wembley in front of just 21,142 fans. He also played seven times for the U21 side between 1994 and 1995.

Associated with nine different League clubs during his career, Unsworth - nicknamed 'Rhino' - made a total of 509 senior appearances, scoring 53 goals. He won the FA Cup with Everton in 1995.

UPSON, Matthew James 2002-11 ㉑ ②

Born: Hartismere, Eye, Suffolk, 18 April 1979
Career: Luton Town (apprentice, May 1994, professional April 1996), Arsenal (£1m, May 1997), Nottingham Forest (loan, December 2000), Crystal Palace (loan, March-April 2007), Reading (loan, September-December 2002), Birmingham City (£2m, January 2003), West Ham United (£6m, January 2007), Stoke City (free, August 2011), Brighton & Hove Albion (loan, January-May 2013)

Centre-back Matthew Upson always leads by example and although rated below John Terry, Rio Ferdinand and Ledley King in the England pecking order, wherever he pulls on his country's 'three lions' shirt, he is totally committed.

A Youth international, he had eleven U21 caps to his credit (2 goals scored) before his excellent performances for Birmingham City led to his selection for the senior squad. He made his debut against South Africa in May 2003. However, he was out of favour for quite a while before being named in Fabio Capello's first provisional international squad in February 2008 for the friendly with Switzerland at Wembley, starting the game alongside Ferdinand in a 2-1 victory.

Outstanding and a goalscorer in a 2-1 win over Germany in November 2008, he was subsequently voted ITV's 'Man of the Match.'

Included in England's 2010 World Cup squad in South Africa, he played in the third group match against Slovenia and scored against Germany in the devastating 4-1 defeat which eliminated England from the tournament in the round of 16.

A Premiership winner in 2002 with Arsenal, Upson who has now made well over 350 appearances at club level, teamed up with fellow England centre-back Jonathan Woodgate at Stoke in 2011.

URWIN, Thomas 1922-26 ④

Born: Haswell, County Durham, 5 February 1896
Died: Sunderland, 7 May 1968
Career: Monkwearmouth Colliery School, Sunderland Schools, Fulwell FC, Lambton Star (1911), Shildon FC (amateur, August 1913, professional February 1914), Middlesbrough (May 1914), Newcastle United (£3,200, August 1924), Sunderland (£525, February 1930,

retired, May 1936); Sunderland (coach, seasons 1936-39); after WW2 worked as a clerk in Sunderland hospital until February 1962).

A First Division championship winner with Newcastle in 1927, Tom Urwin was a crafty, midget winger who played on both flanks and could cross a ball with either foot.

He spent 22 years playing with all three top clubs in the North East of England, amassing a total of 455 appearances, 200 with both Middlesbrough and Newcastle. He made his England debut on the left-flank in a 4-2 win over Sweden in Stockholm in May 1923, played against the same country three days later (won 3-1) and won his third cap in a 2-2 draw with Belgium in Antwerp in November 1923. He then had to wait until March 1926 for his fourth England outing, in a 3-1 defeat by Wales at Selhurst Park when he lined up on the right wing. Urwin also represented the Football League.

UTLEY, George 1912-13 ①

Born: Elsecar, near Barnsley, Yorks, 23 April 1887
Died: Blackpool, 8 January 1966
Career: Elsecar-Wentworth FC, Sheffield Wednesday (amateur, June 1906), Elsecar (1907), Barnsley (May 1908), Sheffield United (£2,000, November 1913), Manchester City (September 1922, retired, May 1923); Bristol City (trainer, July 1923), Sheffield Wednesday (trainer/coach, May 1924), Fulham (trainer, July 1925-May 1927); also engaged as an assistant cricket coach at Rossall School (seasons 1911-31) and acted as the school's assistant groundsman (1929-31).

In February 1913, long-throw expert George Utley played left-half for England in their first-ever defeat by Ireland, 2-1 in Belfast. A battler through and through, he was one of the most competitive footballers of his era and was twice an FA Cup winner, with Barnsley in 1912 and Sheffield United in 1915. He made a total of 278 appearances in League football, 170 coming with Barnsley.

In early 1920, Utley authored articles for boys' magazines including: Football by Prominent Players: 'Captaining the Cup-Winners' (The Boys' Friend) and 'The Complete Half-Back' (The Boys' Realm)

VASSELL, Darius 2001-04 ㉒ ⑥

Born: Sutton Coldfield, 13 June 1980
Career: Yenton Primary and John Willmott Schools, Romulus FC/Sutton Coldfield (1995), Aston Villa (School of Excellence, June 1996, professional, April 1998), Manchester City (£2m, July 2005), Ankarangucu/Turkey (July 2009-May 2010), Leicester City (October 2010-June 2012)

Striker Darius Vassell made his England debut in February 2002, scoring with a 60th minute bicycle kick in a 'Man of the Match' performance in a 1-1 draw with Holland in Amsterdam.

Subsequently included in England's 2002 World Cup squad in Korea/Japan, he played in three matches but started just once, against Sweden in the opening group game.

A positive, forceful forward, he missed the crucial last spot kick in the penalty shoot-out of the quarter-final encounter with Portugal at Euro 2004, having replaced the injured Wayne Rooney early in the game.

He won all his 22 full England caps under Sven-Göran Eriksson whom he served under at both Manchester City and Leicester. Vassell also played in eleven U21 internationals.

An InterToto Cup winner with Aston Villa in 2001, he had scored 77 goals in 373 appearances up to the end of the 2011-12 season. A practising Christian, Vassell credits his faith for his survival of a serious car accident.

VAUGHTON, Oliver Howard 1881-84 ⑤ ⑥

Born: Aston, Birmingham, 9 January 1861
Died: Birmingham, 6 January 1937
Career: Waterloo FC (seasons 1874-76), Birmingham FC (seasons 1876-78), Wednesbury Strollers (seasons 1878-80), Aston Villa (August 1880, retired, injured, May 1888); became managing-director of the Birmingham-based jewellery and silversmith company which manufactured the second FA Cup for £25; Aston Villa (vice-president, August 1923, president, June 1924, director September 1924-December 1932); then life member of club from February 1933 until his death.

A utility forward with Aston Villa before the Football League was formed, Howard Vaughton was an FA Cup winner in 1887 and played in 26 matches in that competition, hitting 15 goals.

He was also Villa's first senior international, capped by England five times. He scored six goals; five coming in an emphatic 13-0 win over Ireland in Belfast in February 1882 when his Villa team-mate Arthur Brown bagged a four-timer. With Malcolm Macdonald (5 v. Cyprus 1975), Vaughton shares the record for most goals scored by one player in an England match. His other four caps were gained against Scotland in March 1882 (scored in 5-1 defeat), v. Wales in March 1882 (lost 5-3), v. Scotland in March 1884 (lost 1-0) and v. Wales, also in March 1884 (won 4-0).

Said to be 'The people's favourite' by Villa fans, he was adept at every form of indoor and outdoor sport. He dribbled with great skill and could shoot from any distance. Whatever he did he did well, and was neatness personified. A keen judge of most games, Vaughton was a thorough sportsman who won the all-England ice-skating title, played cricket for Warwickshire and Staffordshire, participated in field hockey for Staffordshire, was a racing cyclist and also a first-class swimmer.

One of his descendants, Jonny Vaughton, played Rugby Union for the Ospreys and competed for Wales' 7's team in the 2006 Commonwealth Games in Australia.

VEITCH, Colin Campbell McKechnie 1905-09 ⑥

Born: Heaton, Newcastle-upon-Tyne, 22 May 1881
Died: Berne, Switzerland, 26 August 1938
Career: Heaton Council School, Larkspur Juniors/Newcastle, Dalton Juniors/Newcastle, Malcolm Juniors/Newcastle, Rutherford College/Newcastle, Newcastle United (amateur, January 1899, professional April 1899; retired in May 1915; appointed coach until May 1926); Bradford City (secretary-manager, August 1926-January 1928); became a producer and actor and briefly chairman of the People's Theatre in Newcastle; also worked as a journalist from 1929 until his death.

Renowned for his versatility, half-back Colin Veitch captained Newcastle United to three League Championship victories in 1905, 1907 and 1909, to FA Cup glory in 1910 and in four losing Cup finals in 1905, 1906, 1908 and 1911. He scored 49 goals in 322 appearances during his time at St James' Park and represented England in six full internationals, gaining his first cap in a 5-0 win over Ireland in February 1906, when he was outstanding, and his last in a 2-0 victory over Wales in March 1909.

Following a dispute with Newcastle in 1911, Veitch continued to play for the club until the outbreak of WW1 after which he returned to St James' Park as a coach. In 1924 he formed the junior side, Newcastle Swifts, the pioneers of the current Newcastle United juniors system, but was sacked two years later, thus ending a 27-year association with United.

For a short spell in the early 1900s, Veitch considered giving up football to pursue an academic career, but after a spell in the reserves, when he played under the pseudonym of 'Hamilton' he changed his mind.

VEITCH, John Gould 1893-94 ① ③

Born: Kingston Hill, Surrey, 19 July 1869
Died: London, 3 October 1914
Career: Old Westminsters (August 1885-April 1888), Cambridge University (seasons 1888-91), Corinthians (August 1889, retired, ill-health, May 1898); employed in the family horticultural business as company secretary until his death.

For the match against Wales at Wrexham in March 1894, the England selectors decided to field a team consisting entirely of players with Corinthian connections, handing three their international debuts, one being astute dribbling inside-left John Veitch who played alongside his Old Westminster colleague, Rupert Sandilands.

After going 1-0 down, England fought back to equalise through Veitch who, playing superbly, went on to complete an excellent hat-trick in the 80th minute, thus joining a select band of players to score three times on their international debut. England ran out comfortable 5-1 victors. Veitch is also one of five players to have scored a treble for his country in his only appearance. He also scored 63 goals in just 72 games for the Corinthians. Veitch unfortunately had weak lungs and suffered from premature deafness.

VENABLES, Terence Frederick 1964-65 ②

Born: Bethnal Green, London, 6 January 1943
Career: Lennards Secondary School, Dagenham Schools, Chelsea (amateur, July 1958, professional, August 1960), Tottenham Hotspur (£80,000, May 1966), Queens Park Rangers (£70,000, June 1969), Crystal Palace (September 1974, player-coach February 1975), St Patrick's Athletic (April 1976), Crystal Palace (manager, June 1976, resigned, October 1980), Queens Park Rangers (manager, October 1980-May 1984), CF Barcelona (manager, May 1984-September 1987), Tottenham Hotspur (manager, November 1987-July 1991, then Chief Executive until sacked in May 1993); England (manager, January 1994-June 1996), Portsmouth (Consultant, July 1996, then Chairman), Australia (national team manager, November 1996-May 1997), Crystal Palace (manager, March 1998-January 1999), Middlesbrough (Head of Football, December 2000, then joint manager with Bryan Robson to June 2001, also acted as chief scout, briefly), Leeds United (manager, July 2002, sacked March 2003), England (assistant-manager, to Steve McClaren, July 2006-November 2007); Cambrian Sky Blues FC/Rhondda (Chairman, 2010).

Alf Ramsey experimented with a new left-wing pairing of Terry Venables and Alan Hinton for England's friendly with Belgium at Wembley in October 1964. Personally for Venables, selection completed a unique collection of England caps at five different levels – schoolboy, youth, amateur, U23 (4) and full. He gave a good account of himself in the 2-2 draw but appeared in only one more international after that, the 1-1 draw with Holland in Amsterdam two months later.

An FA Youth Cup and League Cup winner with Chelsea in 1960 and 1965 and an FA Cup victor with Spurs in 1967, Venables made 649 appearances for his four London clubs including 237 for Chelsea and 226 for QPR. He also represented the Football League and as a manager won the Second Division title in 1979 and 1983 with Crystal Palace, the FA Cup in 1991 with Spurs and Spain's La Liga with Barcelona in 1985. He also reached other Cup finals and claimed several runners-up prizes. He was coach under Malcolm Allison at Selhurst Park and saw the Eagles twice win the FA Youth Cup in 1977 and 1978.

By November 1993, the England team was at a low point, having failed to qualify for the 1994 World Cup finals under previous manager Graham Taylor. Venables, though not active in the game, seemed to have the presence and charisma that could re-ignite some patriotic pride and achievement. He was appointed manager in late January 1994. However, the speculation coincided with Venables coming under scrutiny and censure in connection with several of his business dealings. The FA struggled to identify an alternative candidate but their discomfort with his soiled reputation for probity was articulated in their appointment of him as England 'coach' rather than under the traditional title of 'manager'. However, Venables decided in January 1996 that he was going to leave the England job after the European Championships that summer, as he wanted to concentrate on clearing his name in connection with off-the-field business dealings.

As hosts, England did not need to qualify for Euro 96 and there were plenty of highs and lows during the finals. Three of their five games (including one on penalties) were won, the best, a thumping 4–1 defeat of Holland in the final group game. However, England suffered penalty shoot-out heartache (again) in the semi-finals, losing to Germany as they had done in the 1990 World Cup six years earlier. During his 23 match tenure as England boss, Venables saw the team lose only one game. Alan Shearer spoke highly of Venables' tenure as England chief, stating: "The best England team I played in was the one under Terry Venables at Euro 96. Terry's knowledge and tactical know-how were spot-on and he knew how to get the best out of us too. We responded to him, believed in him and played some outstanding football in that tournament."

Venables' first game in charge of England saw the reigning European champions Denmark beaten 1-0 at Wembley in March 1994, skipper David Platt steering in the all-important goal in the 16th minute.

Venables combined his duties with that of managing Australia as consultant and then chairman at Portsmouth. He purchased a 51% controlling interest in the club for £1 in February 1997, but left in controversial circumstances 11 months later. His company Vencorp received a £300,000 bonus in the summer of 1997 and he is thought to have been paid around £250,000 upon leaving the club, but left the team bottom of Division One. Although relegation was avoided in 1998, the club's financial situation worsened and Pompey were in real danger of bankruptcy until being taken over by Milan Mandaric in late 1999. In mid-January 1998 Venables was disqualified by the high court from acting as a company director for seven years under section 8 of the Company Directors' Disqualification Act 1986 for mismanagement of four companies - the London drinking club Scribes West Ltd, Edenote plc, Tottenham Hotspur plc and Tottenham Hotspur Football and Athletic Company Ltd.

The case was brought by the Department of Trade and Industry who cited instances of bribery, lying, deception, manipulation of accounts and taking money that should have been given to creditors.

Venables has been involved in many court battles (relating to football) during his lifetime but has always come up smiling!

An accomplished singer, in 2010 Venables recorded a cover of the Elvis Presley hit 'If I Can Dream' in association with *The Sun* newspaper. It featured a 60-piece Royal Philharmonic Orchestra with Harry Redknapp and Ian Wright and was filmed at Wembley Stadium. The song reached number 23 in the UK charts in June 2010.

Also an excellent author/writer, over the years Venables co-authored four novels with writer Gordon Williams and is credited as co-creator of the ITV detective series *Hazell*. Having been a football pundit for the BBC since the mid-1980s, he left for ITV in 1994, following a legal dispute with the corporation over

allegations made against him in a *Panorama* programme. In 1990 Venables co-devised the board game: 'Terry Venables invites you to be The Manager.' This is a football management game and is a cross between the Game of Life, Risk and Trivial Pursuit. In 1995, a photograph of Venables from his playing days appeared on the cover of the Morrissey single 'Dagenham Dave'. In 2002, Venables recorded a single for the World Cup with the band Rider entitled 'England Crazy' which reached number 46 in the UK charts. In May 2006, he guided the England Legends and Celebrities squad to victory in the annual Charity Soccer Aid programme.

VENISON, Barry 1994-95 ②

Born: Consett, County Durham, 16 August 1964
Career: Consett & District Schools, Stanley Boys (seasons 1977-79), Sunderland (apprentice, May 1979, professional, January 1982), Liverpool (£250,000, July 1986), Newcastle United (£250,000, July 1992), Galatasaray/Turkey (£275,000, June 1995), Southampton (£850,000, October 1995, retired with back injury, October 1996); became a soccer pundit for Sky Sports and ITV; now lives in Southern California.

Versatile defender Barry Venison was 30 years of age when he was selected to represent his country by Terry Venables. The call-up came as a surprise, not least to Venison, but he played well in each of two internationals – a 2–0 friendly victory over the USA in September 1994 and a 0-0 draw with Uruguay in March 1995, both games being staged at Wembley.

Venison, who also represented his country at Youth and U21 levels, gaining 10 caps in the latter category, helped Sunderland reach the 1985 League Cup final when he became the competition's youngest ever final captain, aged 20 years and seven months. He won two League championships with Liverpool (1989 and 1990) and the FA Cup (1989) as well as gaining a First Division Championship medal with Newcastle (1993). He made well over 500 appearances at club level, 428 in League competition. A player with Graeme Souness at Liverpool, he later played under Souness in Turkey and at Southampton.

VIDAL, Robert Walpole Sealy 1872-73 ①

Born: Cornborough near Bideford, Devon, 3 September 1853
Died: Abbotsham, Devon, 5 November 1914
Career: Westminster School (seasons 1870-72), Christ Church College/Oxford University (seasons 1872-75); played for Wanderers (seasons 1871-76); also Old Westminsters (season 1875-76); FA Committee member (1872 and 1874); an Oxford University rugby blue (1873); ordained in 1877; was the Vicar of Abbotsham, Devon 1881 until his death; was also a fine golfer at Devon's Westward Ho! course.

An adroit and mobile forward, Robert Vidal was one of the 'finest dribblers that ever played football' and once scored three goals in a match without the other team touching the ball – this was when the rule stated that the team that scored also kicked off afterwards. The only player to appear in each of the first three FA Cup finals, one match report states that he 'looped the ball across the field' for Morton (MP) Betts to score the first-ever Cup final goal for the Wanderers in their victory over the Royal Engineers in 1872. As result Vidal became the only player to receive a Cup winners' medal whilst still at school. He then set up Charles Mackarness's goal in Oxford University's 2-0 final victory in 1874.

For all his efforts on the pitch Vidal gained only one England cap... starring in a 4-2 victory over Scotland in March 1873, twice having efforts saved by the Scots goalkeeper and captain Bob Gardner. He was later known as R. W. Sealy.

VILJOEN, Colin 1974-75 ②

Born: Johannesburg, South Africa, 20 June 1948
Career: Johannesburg Rangers Colts (seasons 1961-63), Southern Transvaal/South Africa (August 1963), Ipswich Town (amateur, July 1965, professional, August 1967), Manchester City (August 1978), Chelsea (£60,000, March 1980, contract cancelled, May 1982), Southall FC (July 1982, retired, June 1983); became a licensee of a pub near Heathrow airport.

Having qualified for British citizenship in 1971, South African-born midfielder Colin Viljoen made his England debut in the 0-0 draw with Northern Ireland in Belfast in May 1975 and played his second game against Wales at Wembley four days later when he was joined by his Ipswich team-mate David Johnson.
    Viljoen scored a hat-trick on his League debut for Ipswich v. Portsmouth in March 1967; the following year he helped the Portman Road club win the Second Division championship. He scored 54 goals in 372 appearances during his 11 years with the 'Tractormen.'

VIOLLET, Dennis Sydney 1959-62 ③ ①

Born: Manchester, 20 September 1933
Died: Florida, USA, 6 March 1999
Career: St Margaret's Central School Whalley, Manchester Schools, Manchester United trial, autumn 1947, amateur, September 1949, professional, September 1950), Stoke City (£25,000, January 1962), Baltimore Bays/USA (loan, April 1967-May 1968), Witton Albion (January 1969), Linfield (player-coach-manager, August 1969), Preston North (coach, July 1970), Crewe Alexandra (coach, February 1971, manager August-November 1971), Washington Diplomats/USA (coach, April 1974-June 1977), New England Teamen (assistant-coach, seasons 1978-81); Jacksonville Teamen (assistant-coach, season 1981-82, then head coach, seasons 1982-90); Jackson University Dolphins (coach, seasons 1990-94), Richmond Kickers (coach, seasons 1994-97), Jacksonville Cyclones (coach, September 1997 until his death).

Manchester United's quick and clever inside-forward Dennis Viollet won the first of his two England caps in the 2-0 defeat by Hungary in Budapest in May 1960. With better luck he may well have scored but one feels the nerves got to him on such a big occasion.
    His second international outing followed in September 1961, when, as left-wing partner to his Manchester United team-mate Bobby Charlton, he netted in a 4-1 win over Luxembourg in a World Cup qualifier at Highbury.
    Viollet formed a lethal strike-force with Tommy Taylor during his first years at Old Trafford, gaining successive League Championship winner's medals in 1956 and 1957 but missed the FA Cup final defeat by Aston Villa in the latter year through injury. He survived the Munich air crash and in 1959-60 netted 32 League goals in 36 games to set a United record which still stands today. He went on to bag a total of 179 goals in 293 appearances for the Reds before helping Stoke City (with Stanley Matthews) win the Second Division title in 1963. He hit 66 goals in 207 games for the Potters and in 1970 lifted the Irish Cup with Linfield. As a coach he won the USISL 'double' (Premier and Open Cup titles) with Richmond Kickers.
    Viollet, who was capped five times as a Schoolboy and represented the Football League on three occasions, sadly died from a brain haemorrhage in a Florida hospital, aged 65.
    Viollett's daughter, Rachel, became the British number one ranked tennis player when she reached the second round of Wimbledon in 1996. During her career, she won one ITF singles tournament and one ITF doubles tournament.

VON DONOP, Pelham George 1872-75 ②

Born: Southsea, Hampshire, 28 April 1851
Died: Richmond, Surrey, 7 November 1921
Career: Somerset College Bath, Royal Military Academy Woolwich, Royal Engineers (April 1871 to May 1883, remained in the Army until 1899, attaining the rank of Captain, Major and then Lt. Colonel to 1899); was Inspecting Officer of Railways (1899-1913, then Chief Inspecting Officer, 1913-16).

One of the early corner-kick specialists, George Von Donop who could play equally well as a forward or half-back gained his two England caps in friendly matches against Scotland. He made his international debut in March 1873, at left-half in the second official match played between the two countries, which England won 4–2.
    Described as a 'stalwart of the Royal Engineers team' he made his second international appearance two years later at centre-half in a 2-2 draw in March 1875. He also appeared in two FA Cup finals, losing in 1874, winning in 1875.
    Von Donop, whose younger brother Stanley served in the Boer War, was godfather to Pelham, the son of writer P. G. Wodehouse.

WACE, Henry 1877-79 ③

Born: Shrewsbury, 21 September 1853
Died: Shrewsbury, 5 November 1947
Career: Shrewsbury School (seasons 1868-73), St John's College Cambridge (seasons 1873-75), Wanderers (seasons 1876-79); also played briefly for Clapham Rovers and Shropshire Wanderers and was a Cambridge rugby union player (season 1874-75); qualified as a barrister and called to the Bar in 1879 and became an acknowledged expert in bankruptcy law.

Twice an FA Cup winner with the Wanderers in 1877 and 1878, and the son of a Shrewsbury solicitor, Harry Wace was a quick, plucky, tenacious forward who often tended to 'station' himself too far upfield – to the annoyance of his team-mates.
    He struggled, as did his colleagues, when making his England debut in a 7-2 defeat by Scotland in March 1878. He showed improvement in his second game, a 2-1 victory over Wales in January 1879 and was one of the team's 'better players' when the Scots were defeated 5-4 three months later.

WADDLE, Christopher Roland 1984-92 62 6

Born: Felling near Hepworth, County Durham, 14 December 1960
Career: Pelaw Juniors, Whitehouse SC, Mount Pleasant SC, HMH Printing, Pelaw SC, Leam Lane SC, Clarke Champions, Tow Law Town (May 1978), Newcastle United (£1,000, July 1980), Tottenham Hotspur (£590,000, July, 1985), Olympic Marseille (£4.5m, July 1989), Sheffield Wednesday (£1.25m, July 1992), Falkirk (September 1996), Bradford City (October 1996), Sunderland (£75,000, March 1997), Burnley (player-manager, May 1997-May 1998), Torquay United (September 1998); Sheffield Wednesday (coach, July 1999-June 2000), Worksop Town (player, seasons, 2000-02); later played non-League football for Devonshire Arms FC, Glapwell, Gedling Town, Stocksbridge Park Steels, Staveley Miners' Welfare, South Normanton Athletic, HSBC FC and Teversal Grange FC (player-coach); also a BBC Radio Five summariser and TV pundit with Setanta and ESPN.

When on form Chris Waddle was great, when he was 'off the pace' he was poor! Nevertheless, overall he was a fine touchline-hugging winger who never quite fulfilled his international potential, despite producing some excellent displays, at times!

After making his England debut in a 2-1 win over the Republic of Ireland in March 1985, he came on as a substitute or was substituted in seven of his first 10 outings and in 17 of his first 24. He never shirked, moaned or complained about the manager's decisions; he simply got on with the game.

He netted his first England goal in a 5-0 win over Turkey in a World Cup qualifier in October 1985 but his return in the goal stakes was relatively poor – only six scored in his 62 appearances.

He also had the misfortune, along with Stuart Pearce, to miss from the spot in the penalty shoot-out against West Germany in the World Cup semi-final in Turin in July 1990 when England lost 4-3. In the last minute of normal time Waddle struck a German post.

His last cap came during Graham Taylor's reign, in a 1-0 win over Turkey in a European Championship qualifier at Wembley in October 1991.

Waddle also played in one U21 international and at club and international level, appeared in a total of 806 first-class matches, bagging 153 goals, 119 of which came in exactly 600 League games. Surprisingly, though, very few winners' medals came his way. He won the French League title with Marseille three seasons in succession (1990-92) and helped Bradford City clinch the League Championship in 1997. He was a runner-up in European Cup, League Cup and two FA Cup finals and in 1993 was voted FWA 'Player of the Year'.

Waddle's son, Jack, played for Chesterfield and his cousin, Alan Waddle, for Halifax Town, Liverpool, Leicester City, Swansea City, Newport County, Mansfield Town, Hartlepool United and Peterborough United.

In 1987, Waddle teamed up with his Spurs team-mate Glenn Hoddle to record the song 'Diamond Lights' which reached number 12 in the UK charts.

WADSWORTH, Samuel John 1921-27 ⑨

Born: Darwen, Lancs, 13 September 1896
Died: Eindhoven, Holland, 1 September 1961
Career: Darwen (amateur, May 1912, professional, September 1912), Blackburn Rovers (July 1914), Nelson (May 1919), Huddersfield Town (April 1921), Burnley (September 1929), Lytham (May 1931; retired, injured, May 1933; Delfit FC/Holland (coach, July 1934-April 1935), PSV Eindhoven/Holland (coach, June 1935-July 1938), DWS/Holland (coach, August 1938-October 1940), PSV Eindhoven (coach, August 1945-June 1951), Brabantia FC/Holland (coach, August 1951-October 1955); quit football at the age of 59, remained in Holland until his death.

A prominent figure in a long line of Huddersfield Town international defenders, Sam Wadsworth was an excellent left-back, being fast and constructive who kicked long and accurate and rarely committed a 'nasty' foul.

One of the first players signed by Herbert Chapman for Huddersfield, he helped the Terriers win the FA Cup (1922) and carry off three successive League championships (1924-26). During his eight years at Leeds Road, he appeared in 312 first-class matches, scoring just four goals.

He made his England debut in a 1-0 defeat by Scotland at Villa Park in April 1922 - the *Daily Mirror* reporting stating 'He performed yeoman service against a brilliant attack' - and won his last cap in a 3-3 draw with Ireland in October 1926. In between times he was outstanding in a 6-1 victory over Belgium in March 1923 and likewise when the Irish were defeated 3-1 in October 1924. He also played six times for the Football League and was reserve in four other senior internationals.

WAINSCOAT, William Russell 1928-29 ①

Born: East Retford, Notts, 28 July 1898
Died: Barnsley, 10 July 1967
Career: Maltby Main Colliery (August 1912), Barnsley (professional, March 1920), Middlesbrough (£3,750, December 1923), Leeds United (£2,000, March 1925), Hull City (October 1931, retired, injured, May 1934); later worked on the Yorkshire railway, ran a corner shop and was a licensee.

Russell Wainscoat was a big, strong, hard-running and aggressive inside-left who toured Canada with the FA in May/June 1926. He played in nine games, scoring 13 goals, five coming in a 9-0 win over New Ontario at Fort William. He eventually won his only England cap in a 1-0 defeat by Scotland at a gusty Hampden Park in April 1929. 'Albion' in the *Daily Express*, gave a special mention to Cooper, skipper Edwards and Wainscoat 'for some determined play against the lucky Scots'.

A Third Division (N) Championship winner with Hull City in 1933, Wainscoat had a brilliant club career which realised almost 500 appearances and nearly 200 goals. He netted 93 times in 226 games for Leeds.

WAITERS, Anthony Keith 1963-65 ⑤

Born: Southport, 1 February 1937
Career: Bishop Auckland (amateur, August 1953), Macclesfield Town (amateur, June 1958), Blackpool (amateur, July 1959, professional, October 1959, retired, May 1967); FA's North-west coach (August 1967-June 1969), Liverpool (coach, July 1969-June 1970), Burnley (player, July 1970, retired, officially, May 1971); Coventry City (Director of Coaching, June 1971-October 1972), also engaged as England's Youth team coach; Plymouth Argyle (manager, October 1972-April 1977), Vancouver Whitecaps/Canada (manager-coach, May 1977); later Canada's national team coach (seasons 1981-86 and 1990-91); created his company – World of Soccer – in the 1980s, producing a complete series of coaching books and soccer equipment; was appointed the first Director of the National Soccer Coaches Association of America's (NSCAA) Goalkeeping Institute, stepping down in 2006. He remains a National Staff Coach of the NSCAA and U.S. Soccer.

Tony Waiters, tall and athletic, and a lifeguard on the beach when he was not keeping goal for Blackpool, was given his England debut by Alf Ramsey against the Republic of Ireland in Dublin in May 1964, replacing the 'dropped' Gordon Banks. He conceded a goal but produced some fine saves in a 2-1 win.

Six days later he was under fire for long periods when Brazil blitzed England 5-1 in Rio and in October of the same year, he played well in a 2-2 draw with Belgium. His last two games for his country ended in a 2-1 win over Wales in November 1964 and a 1-1 draw with Holland three weeks later. When with Bishop Auckland, Waiters played once for England as an amateur and he also had one outing for the Football League in 1963.

As Blackpool's number 1, Waiters appeared in 286 competitive games during his eight years at Bloomfield Road. He came out of retirement to play 38 times for Burnley.

As England youth team coach, he led his team in the European Youth Championship in Italy in 1973, and two years later, as Plymouth's manager, he guided the Devon club to the Third Division Championship. Later he took Canada to the 1984 Olympic Games and also to the 1986 World Cup finals in Mexico.

WALCOTT, Theo James 2005-13 ㉝ ④

Born: Stanmore, Middlesex, 16 March 1989
Career: The Downs School/Newbury, AFC Newbury (season 2003-04), Swindon Town (junior, August 2004), Southampton (apprentice, February 2005), Arsenal (March 2006... for an initial fee of £5m, rising to £12m depending on appearances made for club and country. The original fee was payable by instalments – £5m, £5m and £2m, but this was revised to a total of £9.1m by a compromise settlement agreed on 31 March 2008)

Sven-Göran Eriksson arranged only one B international during his time as England boss, in late May 2006 against Belarus as a World Cup warm-up game. Theo Walcott was in the team that lost 2-1 and was the youngest player to play for his country at this level. Soon afterwards, he became the youngest player at senior level when he appeared in the 3-1 friendly win over Hungary at Old Trafford at the age of 17 years and 75 days, taking over the mantle from James Prinsep.

A surprise inclusion in Eriksson's squad for the 2006 World Cup, selected over several established Premier League stars including Darren Bent (the highest-scoring Englishman in the Premier League in 2005-06), Andy Johnson, Dean Ashton and Jermain Defoe, he did not play at all during the tournament. Eriksson defended his decision, claiming 'The experience has served him well for future tournaments.'

At the end of the World Cup, Eriksson was replaced by Steve McClaren, who quickly named Walcott in the U21 team to play Moldova at Portman Road in August 2006. He quickly made a point by becoming the youngest player ever to score at this level when he netted a third-minute opener in a 2–2 draw. He later struck twice against Germany to seal qualification for England to the U21 European Championships.

In September 2008, Walcott made his first competitive start for his country in a World Cup qualifier against Andorra, and later in the same month, against Croatia, he became the youngest-ever England player to score a hat-trick, producing a wonderful show of pace and individualism against worthy opponents.

During the summer of 2009, Walcott played in the U21 European Cup campaign, despite protests from his Arsenal manager, Arsene Wenger, who complained that his participation in the tournament, as well as matches with the senior squad, would lead to burn out and injury. Walcott went on to win 21 caps at this level.

Surviving some tough matches, for club and country, he returned to full international action in March 2010 for the friendly with Egypt - his first senior start for nine months. He faded after a bright start and was replaced by Shaun Wright-Phillips after 57 minutes as England recovered from a goal down to win 3-1 at Wembley.

His performance in that game was criticized by Chris Waddle who said: "I've never seen him develop. He just doesn't know when to run inside a full back or when to play a one-two. It's all off the cuff. I just don't think he's got a football brain. He's going to have problems. Let's be honest, good defenders would catch him offside every time."

Walcott laughed those comments off, yet after playing well in friendly victories over Mexico and Japan in May 2010, he was left out of England's 23-man World Cup squad by Fabio Capello. Argentinian star Lionel Messi said he was shocked by Walcott's exclusion, believing he would have made a huge difference against Germany and Algeria. In the Euro 2012 qualifying match against Switzerland in September 2010, Walcott was stretchered off after being clipped in the build-up to Rooney's opening goal in the 10th minute. He was sidelined for six weeks before storming back with some terrific displays for Arsenal. Two years later he was crunched early on in a World Cup qualifier against San Marino at Wembley and once again took an early bath!

Fast and direct with good skills and powerful right foot shot, he looks set for an excellent future in the game... if he can avoid serious injury.

Voted BBC's 'Young Sports Personality of the Year' in 2006, by May 2013 his record with Arsenal was excellent - 63 goals in 263 appearances.

Walcott also holds the record as Southampton's youngest-ever player, aged 16 years and 143 days, when appearing as a substitute in a 0-0 home draw with Wolves in 2005.

His older sister, Holly, is a bodybuilder who came second in the British Natural Bodybuilding Federation Central Championships in July 2010.

Theo Walcott

WALDEN, Frederick Ingram 1913-22 ②

Born: Wellingborough, 1 March 1888
Died: Northampton, 3 May 1949
Career: Victoria School/Wellingborough, Wellingborough White Cross (1904), Wellingborough All Saints (1905), Wellingborough Redwell (1906), Wellingborough Town (1907), Northampton Town (professional, May 1909), Tottenham Hotspur (£1,700, April 1913), Northampton Town (July 1924, retired May 1927); played in 258 first-class cricket matches for Northamptonshire (1910-29), scoring 7,538 runs with five centuries and taking 119 wickets; he became a first-class umpire (1934-39), standing in 212 County matches and 11 Tests.

Standing a fraction over 5ft 2in tall – the smallest player ever to represent England – 'Fanny' Walden was often described as a 'diminutive winger' and known for his 'darting jinking runs down the right flank'. He could wriggle past a defender like an eel, was difficult to catch when clear and his small stature also accounted for his nickname which was in common use during his time to describe those of 'dainty physique'.

He helped Spurs win the Second Division title in 1920 but the following year unfortunately missed the FA Cup final victory over Wolves due to injury. He went on to play in 324 first-team games (46 goals scored) during his time at White Hart Lane before returning to Northampton Town.

Walden won the first of his two England caps in April 1914 against Scotland in front of 127,037 fans at Hampden Park. Partnering Harry Fleming (Swindon) on the right-wing, he got little joy against the strong-tackling Joe Dodds (Celtic) in a 3-1 defeat.

His second cap followed eight years later, in March 1922, in a 1-0 win over Wales at Goodison Park. Unsurprisingly, Walden holds the record for being the smallest ever footballer to represent England at senior level.

WALKER, Desmond Sinclair 1989-94 ⑤⑨

Born: Hackney, London, 26 November 1965
Career: Tottenham Hotspur (trialist, June 1980), Aston Villa (trialist, June 1980), Birmingham City (trialist, July 1980), Nottingham Forest (apprentice, June 1982, professional, December 1983), Sampdoria/Italy (£1.2m, May 1992), Sheffield Wednesday (£2.7m, July 1993), Burton Albion (briefly), New York Metros/USA (in their 9/11 benefit matches), Nottingham Forest (July 2002, left January 2005); played in the Hong Kong Soccer Sevens (2009), Manchester City (coach, briefly); also has an interest in property developing.

Exceptionally quick over the ground, Des Walker had the pace to match the fastest forwards in the game – and he could spot danger before it happened! At times he was 'sloppy' with his distribution yet he was probably one of the best markers and timers of the tackle of all time, clearly demonstrated by a remarkably low amount of bookings despite often dispossessing opponents with sliding challenges from all directions. Not the tallest centre-half in the game, nevertheless he could leap to beat the tallest forwards in the air. Overall he was a fine defender.

After an impressive international debut as substitute for Tony Adams in a 1-0 friendly win over Denmark in September 1989, he became a rock at the heart of the England defence over the next three years or so, despite competition from the aforementioned Adams, Terry Butcher and Mark Wright.

At Italia 90, he started all seven games in which England played, gaining international acclaim which was only overshadowed by another new young star, namely Paul Gascoigne. Playing in a three-man defence, he shrugged off knocks and fatigue to enjoy a superb tournament, which ended when England were knocked out on penalties by West Germany in the semi-finals.

Unfortunately his game suffered somewhat when he went to Sampdoria where he was often played out of position (occasionally at full-back). However, he retained his England place and performed with a great deal of confidence, going on to celebrate his 50th appearance with a 'faultless display of defending' in a resounding 4-0 win over Turkey in a World Cup qualifier at Wembley in November 1992.

Like all footballer, he did have his off days! He gave away an 85th minute penalty to concede two World Cup qualifying points in a 2-2 draw with Holland at Wembley in April 1993; had a poor performance against Poland, twice conceding possession and nearly gifting his opponents a second goal and in a vital game against Norway, he stopped, anticipating the referee's whistle, to allow Leonhardsen to score and was then out-paced (a rarity) as Bohinen netted a second goal in a 2-0 defeat in Oslo five week later.

Walker was included in Taylor's last match in November 1993. It proved to be one of the most infamous, as San Marino scored the fastest World Cup goal ever after just eight seconds. England won 7-1 but failed to make the 1994 finals in America in 1994 (they had needed to win by seven clear goals and hope that Holland lost in Poland, but the Dutch won anyway so England's result was academic).

It also proved to be Walker's last game for England, although he continued to play professionally at club level for the next 11 years.

For his clubs, Walker did exceptionally well, making almost 900 senior appearances (660 at League level). A League Cup winner with Forest in 1989 and 1990, he conceded an own goal in the 1991 FA Cup final defeat by Spurs. He also gained seven England U21 caps.

At the height of his career, Forest and Owls fans frequently chanted 'You'll never beat Des Walker.' This was turned into 'You'll never meet Des Walker' as a private joke among journalists, commenting on the defender's refusal to talk to the press at this point.

WALKER, Ian Michael 1995-2004 ④

Born: Watford, Herts, 31 October 1971
Career: Great Cornard Upper School & Technology College, Tottenham Hotspur (apprentice, April 1988, professional, October 1989), Oxford United (loan, August-September 1990), Gillingham (loan, October-November 1990), Ipswich Town (loan, December 1990), Leicester City (£2.5m, July 2001), Bolton Wanderers (June 2005, contract cancelled by mutual consent, December 2008); moved to South Florida; returned to Bishop Stortford (manager, March 2011)

Goalkeeper Ian Walker and his Spurs team-mate Sol Campbell, made their England debuts as substitutes in a comfortable 3-0 win over Hungary at Wembley in May 1996. Another Spurs player, Darren Anderton scored two of the goals. He then did well in another 3-0 victory over China before pulling off some excellent saves against Italy when Gianfranco Zola's goal was enough to inflict upon England their first-ever World Cup defeat at Wembley.

He backed up David James at Euro 2004 but was overtaken by others in the pecking order. However, despite his club, Leicester, suffering relegation from the Premier League, Walker played his first international in seven years, and his last, as a 61st minute substitute for Paul Robinson in a 6–1 win over Iceland in June 2004.

He also won one B and nine U21 caps and made over 500 club appearances, including 319 for Spurs and 156 for Leicester. He won the League Cup with Spurs in 1999.

Walker's father, Mike, kept goal for Shrewsbury Town, York City, Watford (137 League appearances), Charlton and Colchester United (451 League games) and Wales U23s. He also managed Norwich City and Everton.

WALKER, Kyle 2011-13 (5)

Born: Sheffield, 28 May 1990
Career: Sheffield United (junior, aged seven, recommended by Football Unites, Racism Divides; apprentice, May 2006, professional, May 2008), Northampton Town (loan, November 2008-January 2009), Tottenham Hotspur (July 2009, with Kyle Naughton for a combined fee of £9m), Sheffield United (loan, August 2009-May 2010), Queens Park Rangers (loan, July 2010-January 2011), Aston Villa (loan, January-May 2011)

In February 2009, before he had made a single League appearance for Sheffield United, right-back Kyle Walker was capped by England at U19 level against Spain and then, two years later, after showing excellent form for Tottenham in the Premiership, he was called up to the senior squad but did not feature in any of the games, mainly due to injury. However, at the end of the 2010–11 season, Walker was named in England's U21 team which competed in the 2011 European U21 Championships in Denmark and despite a poor showing by Stuart Pearce's side, he was named in the 'Team of the Tournament'. And things got even better for Walker when he made his full international debut as a late substitute for his Spurs colleague Scott Parker in the 1-0 victory over the reigning European and World champions Spain at Wembley in November 2011. He had made less than 100 first-class appearances at club level before winning his first full cap. On 2 October 2011, Walker scored a 25-yard winning goal for Spurs in the 2-1 North London derby victory over Arsenal.

WALKER, William Henry 1920-33 (19) (9)

Born: Wednesbury, Staffs, 29 October 1897
Died: Sheffield, 28 November 1964
Career: King's Hill School/Wednesbury, Walsall Boys (1909), Fallings Heath (1910), Hednesford Town (junior, 1911), Darlaston (1912), Wednesbury Old Park (season 1912-13), Aston Villa (trial, summer 1913), Wednesbury Old Athletic (August 1913), Aston Villa (amateur, March 1915, professional, June 1920, retired November 1933); WW1 guest for Birmingham (season 1916-17) and Wednesbury Old Park (1916-18); Sheffield Wednesday (manager, December 1933-November 1937), Chelmsford City (manager, January-October 1938), Nottingham Forest (manager, March 1939-July 1960; remained on the club's committee until his death); played cricket for Warwickshire Club & Ground and was also a fine golfer, winning the Robin Hood Bowl and 36-hole Open Championship in June 1930.

One of Aston Villa's true legends, Billy Walker spent 20 years with the Birmingham club during which time he scored a record 244 goals (including a hat-trick of penalties v. Bradford City in 1921) in 531 appearances, won the FA Cup in 1920 and lost in the final four years later.

As a youngster, the well-built, strong running, hard-shooting and powerful heading inside-left or centre-forward, netted 80 goals in the Walsall Boys' League in 1910-11 and he never really stopped scoring!

He celebrated his England debut with a goal in a 2-0 win over Ireland in October 1920, netted twice in his fifth game, a 4-2 victory over Sweden in May 1923, was on target in the 1-1 draw with Scotland, England's first goal in their first international at Wembley in April 1924, and in the 3-1 win over Ireland in October of that same year, fired in two more (including a net-busting penalty) in a 4-0 romp over Belgium six weeks later and claimed his last two goals in the annual games against Wales in 1926 (lost 3-1) and 1927 (drew 3-3). His last England game was against Austria at Stamford Bridge in December 1932. During the game he was sent flying by a robust yet perfectly legitimate shoulder charge by right-half Nausch. Sat on the ground and looking quizzically at his opponent, Walker said: "I was told there wouldn't be any charging." The Austrian replied: "I didn't say that – you did." Walker shrugged that incident aside and played his part in a famous 4-3 win.

An international trialist, he also captained the Staffordshire Jubilee side against the Football League in 1926.

After retiring, Walker became a successful manager, bringing FA Cup glory to both Sheffield Wednesday in 1935 and Nottingham Forest in 1959. He also guided the latter club to promotion from Division Three (S) in 1951 and Division Two in 1957. He was the only manager to win the FA Cup before and after the Second World War. And during the hostilities, he actually played in six games for Forest as an emergency goalkeeper!

WALL, George 1906-13 (7) (2)

Born: Boldon Colliery, County Durham, 20 February 1885
Died: Manchester, 21 February 1962
Career: Boldon Royal Rovers (August 1899-May 1901), Whitburn (August 1901-October 1902), Jarrow (September 1903), Barnsley (professional, November 1903), Manchester United (April 1906); served with the Black Watch Regiment during WW1; Oldham Athletic (£200, March 1919), Hamilton Academical (June 1921), Rochdale (June 1922), Ashton National (August 1923-May 1926); played for Manchester Ship Canal team in 1926-27 while working in Manchester's dockland.

In March 1907, outside-left George Wall gained his first of his seven England caps in a 1-1 draw with Wales. The following year he played in England's 3-1 and 7-1 victories over Ireland and Wales in February and March and scored both goals in 2-0 win over Scotland at Crystal Palace in April 1909, the first from a third minute corner, the second after a dazzling run down the line before cutting in to fire past 'keeper Jim Brownlie.

His other three caps came against Wales in March 1910 (won 1-0), v. Scotland, the following month (lost 2-0) and v. Ireland in February 1913 (lost 2-1). Arthur Bridgett (Sunderland), Albert Hall (Aston Villa) and Harold Hardman (Everton) were also vying for the left-wing position at the same time as Wall.

A smart dribbler, very fast with a strong shot, Wall had a wonderful knack of cutting inside a defender and getting in a shot when least expected. He was also a wonderful crosser of the ball who twice won the League Championship with Manchester United (1908 and 1911) as well as the FA Cup (1909). He netted 98 goals in 316 appearances for the Reds and had five outings for the Football League.

WALLACE, Charles William 1912-20 (3)

Born: Southwick near Sunderland, 20 January 1885
Died: Birmingham, 7 January 1970
Career: Sunderland & District Schools, Southwick FC (1903), Crystal Palace (July 1905), Aston Villa (£500, May 1907), Oldham Athletic (£1,000, May 1921, retired, April 1923); became a printer & decorator, also worked part-time at Villa Park (in club's boot-room, as kit man, scout and steward); also mentor to junior Ordnance team in the late 1930s.

Charlie Wallace, a speedy right-winger, direct in his approach, loved taking on defenders 'down the line' before whipping in a dangerous cross, given the opportunity.

An international trialist who represented the Football League on five occasions, he won the first of his three England caps in a 4-3 win over Wales in March 1913. His Villa team-mate Harry Hampton played centre-forward.

His second game followed in February 1914 (a 3-0 defeat by Ireland) and his last was against Scotland at Sheffield in April 1920 when he assisted in two of the goals in an exciting 5-4 victory on a saturated pitch.

Wallace, who helped Aston Villa win the League title in 1910 and the FA Cup in 1913 and 1920, missed a penalty in the 1913 final against Sunderland before laying on the winner for Edgeley. He scored 57 goals in 350 appearances during his 14 years with Villa whom he served, in various capacities, for 50 years.

WALLACE, David Lloyd 1985-86 ①

Born: Greenwich, London, 21 January 1964
Career: West Greenwich School, Deal Town (junior), Southampton (initially as an associate schoolboy, February 1977, apprentice, July 1980, professional, January 1982), Manchester United (£1.2m, September 1989), Millwall (loan, March-May 1993), Birmingham City (£250,000, October 1993), Wycombe Wanderers (May 1994, retired, ill-health, June 1996); his career was ended prematurely by the effects of multiple sclerosis.

Small, compact, and highly explosive, 'Danny' Wallace had an impressive career at Southampton for whom he scored 79 goals in 317 first-class appearances. On 22 October 1988, his two brothers, Rod and Ray, joined him in the Saints' team for the home League game against Sheffield Wednesday; this was the first time three brothers had played in the same team in English professional top-flight football since 1920. The Wallace brothers continued to play together for the remainder of the 1988–89 season, with Danny and Rod playing in attack alongside Alan Shearer and Matt Le Tissier.

Wallace won his only full England cap as a 'Saint' in January 1986 against Egypt in January 1986, celebrating with a goal in a 4-0 victory. He also played in one B and 14 U21 internationals.

After leaving The Dell, he didn't do half so well with Manchester United, although he remained their first choice left-winger in 1989-90, gaining an FA Cup winner's medal. His opportunities were reduced when Lee Sharpe arrived on the scene and more so in 1992 once Ryan Giggs had started to perform. He missed the 1991 League Cup and European Cup Winners' Cup finals, but as a squad member he did collect a winner's medal as a non playing substitute in the latter. A year later he added a League Cup winner's medal to his collection.

After a series of injuries and a puzzling loss of form which meant he rarely played during his last two years at Old Trafford, Wallace was sold to Birmingham. There it soon became obvious that he was far from fit, and after 18 months he moved to Wycombe.

The reason for his problems was discovered in 1996 when he was diagnosed with multiple sclerosis and as a result was forced to retire from football.

In 2006, Wallace completed the London Marathon in five-and-a-half days. His goal in running in the marathon was to raise money for the Danny Wallace Foundation, which provides aid for those suffering from multiple sclerosis. He was greeted at the finish line by former boxer Michael Watson, who himself completed the marathon in seven days after suffering brain injuries in a 1991 boxing match.

Wallace made his League debut (in place of the injured Kevin Keegan) at the age of 16 years and 313 days against Manchester United at Old Trafford in November 1980, thus becoming the youngest player to be picked for Southampton, a record subsequently taken from him by Theo Walcott in August 2005.

WALSH, Paul Anthony 1982-84 ⑤ ①

Born: Plumstead, London, 1 October 1962
Career: Blackheath Schools, South London Schools, Charlton Athletic (professional, October 1979), Luton Town (£400,000, July 1982), Liverpool (£700,000, May 1984), Tottenham Hotspur (£500,000, February 1988), Queens Park Rangers (loan, September-November 1991), Portsmouth (£400,000, June 1992, in deal involving Darren Anderton), Manchester City (£750,000, March 1994-September 1995), Portsmouth (April 1994, retired, injured, June 1996); became a players' agent, TV soccer pundit and Ambassador for FIFA.

Paul Walsh's impish, natural predatory instincts around the penalty area earned him five full caps. His first three (under manager Bobby Robson) came during England's summer tour of Australia in June 1983. After a 0-0 draw in Sydney on his debut (as a substitute), he scored the only goal of the game in Brisbane and was unlucky not to net again in a third-match draw in Melbourne. His two other caps followed against France in Paris in February 1984 and versus Wales at Wrexham two months later. He also scored four times in four U21 internationals.

His all-round ability was recognised by his fellow professionals who voted him as the PFA 'Young Player of the Year' in 1984 when he also helped England lift the UEFA European U21 Championship.

During his lengthy career – ended by a knee injury – Walsh scored 168 goals in 633 League and Cup games for his seven professional clubs. He helped Liverpool (37 goals in 112 games) win the First Division Championship and Screen Sport Super Cup in 1986 and Spurs (21 in 155 outings) lift the FA Cup in 1991. He also collected six runners-up medals during his time at Anfield where he played alongside Ian Rush and Kenny Dalglish. His Spurs partner at times was Gary Lineker.

WALTERS, Arthur Melmoth 1884-90 ⑨

Born: Ewell, Surrey, 26 January 1865
Died: Minnickwood, Holmwood, Surrey, 2 May 1941
Career: Charterhouse School (seasons 1879-83), Trinity College Cambridge (seasons 1883-88); also played for Corinthians (August 1883-April 1893), Old Sheen (briefly), Old Carthusians (seasons 1892-95) and Surrey County (1890s); qualified as a solicitor in November 1889, later engaged in the family business in London (Walters & Co.); served in the Army, attaining the rank of lieutenant with the 3rd Surrey Rifles.

'A M' Walters – known as 'Morning' – formed a tremendous full-back partnership with his brother 'P M' who was called 'Afternoon'. Occupying the right flank in the main, he could kick with both feet, was strong and confident and hardly shirked a tackle. Rated one of the best 'defenders' of the 1880s, he won the FA Amateur Cup with Old Carthusians in 1894 and was a beaten finalist a year later. First choice for England (when fit) from February 1885, he made his debut with his brother in a 4-0 win over Ireland at Whelley Grange, Manchester. Walters made his last international appearance in April 1890, in a 1-1 draw with Scotland at Hampden Park. In an early drawn game with the Scots in March 1886, nine of the eleven players (including the Walters brothers) were members of the Corinthian club, although all had their primary affiliation with other clubs.

Walters quit football for a short time in 1893 following the sudden death of another brother.

WALTERS, Mark Everton 1990-91 ①
Born: Aston, Birmingham, 2 June 1964
Career: Hampton Junior & Holte Grammar Schools/Birmingham, Aston & District Boys, Birmingham Schools, Aston Villa (apprentice, June 1980, professional, May 1982), Glasgow Rangers (£600,000, December 1987), Liverpool (£1.25m, August 1991), Stoke City (loan, March-April 1994), Wolverhampton Wanderers (loan, September-October 1994), Southampton (free, January 1996), Swindon Town (free, July 1996), Bristol Rovers (non-contract, November 1999), Ilkeston Town (July 2002); Coventry Preparatory School (Saturday morning football coach, February 2003, later head coach); played briefly for Dudley Town (September 2003); Aston Villa (junior coach; returned to school, obtained teaching qualifications; now Head of Languages at Aston Villa's Academy).

Out-and-out left-winger Mark Walters was given his only England cap by his former Villa Park manager Graham Taylor, in the 1-0 win over New Zealand in Auckland in June 1991. With so many other 'similar players' available including John Barnes, Chris Waddle and John Salako, he was never going to get another chance!
Fast, clever and direct in his approach, Walters had one personal trick whereby he used to drag his foot over the ball, swivel and leave his opponent standing. He scored 48 goals in 225 appearances for his first club, Aston Villa, with whom he won the FA Youth Cup and European Super Cup. In Scotland, he made 143 appearances and netted 51 goals for Rangers, helping them win three Premier League titles and two League Cup finals. He was then an FA Cup and two-times League Cup winner with Liverpool for whom he struck 19 goals in 125 outings. He followed up by claiming 28 goals in 128 games for Swindon and 14 in 96 appearances for Bristol Rovers. Walters, who also represented England in six Youth, one B and nine U21 internationals, bagged almost 170 goals in more than 750 club games during his extended career.
Walters has been referred to as the first black player to sign for Rangers. However, Walter Tull joined the Glasgow club during the First World War but was killed in the conflict before he could play.

WALTERS, Percy Melmoth 1884-90 ⑬
Born: Ewell, Surrey, 30 September 1863
Died: Ashtead, Surrey, 6 October 1936
Career: Charterhouse School (seasons 1877-80), Oriel College Oxford (seasons 1881-85), Old Carthusians (mid-to-late 1880s), East Sheen (1884), Epsom (season 1884-85), Ewell FC (founder member, with his brother and John Henry Bridges, 1890); registered with Corinthians (seasons 1885-92); also played for Surrey County; FA Committee member (season 1885-86, vice-President 1891 and 1892); also served in the Army and in June 1886, was promoted to the rank of lieutenant in the 3rd Surrey Rifles; called to the Bar at Lincoln's Inn, 1888.

Strong, courageous, a fine judge of pace, who kicked long and true, Percy Walters made his England debut at left-back alongside his younger brother (above) in February 1885 in a 4–0 victory over Ireland. Just over a year later he captained his country in his third appearance, against Ireland in March 1886, in the absence of the regular skipper, Norman Coles Bailey and starred in a 6–1 victory. In March 1888, Walters played at left-back (alongside Bob Howarth of Preston North End) when England achieved their first victory over Scotland since 1879. In 'a brilliant display of attacking football' England won 5–0 with Walters having a hand in one of the goals, his long clearance starting the move.
Walters captained his country five times and, like his brother, made his farewell appearance in the 1-1 draw with the Scots in

April 1890. Of the thirteen internationals he played in, eight were won and three drawn (all against Scotland).
As an Old Carthusian, he lined up in the losing 1895 FA Amateur Cup final and also made one appearance on the cricket field for Oxford University against the MCC in May 1885, as a wicket-keeper.

WALTON, Nathaniel 1889-90 ①
Born: Preston, 12 March 1867
Died: Blackburn, 3 March 1930
Career: Witton (seasons 1883-85), Blackburn Rovers (professional, August 1885), Nelson (July 1892-May 1895); later Blackburn Rovers (trainer, May 1898-May 1906); became a Blackburn licensee.

An FA Cup winner with Blackburn in 1886 and 1891, Nat Walton was among the most versatile of the early leading footballers, enabling him to occupy virtually any outfield position as well as keeping goal in an emergency. Big and strong, he was best as an inside-forward and loved to run at defenders. His only England cap was gained against Ireland in Belfast in March 1890 when he starred with four of his Blackburn team-mates (Barton, Forrest, Lofthouse and Townley) in an emphatic 9-1 win. He didn't score but had a hand in three of the goals.

WARD, James Thomas 1884-85 ①
Born: Blackburn, 28 March 1865
Died: Blackburn, circa 1899
Career: Furthergate School/Blackburn, Little Harwood (seasons 1879-81), Blackburn Olympic (August 1881), Blackburn Rovers (semi-professional, July 1886, retired, injured, May 1890); became a licensee in Blackburn.

A part-time footballer and FA Cup winner with Blackburn Olympic in 1883, quick-moving, strong-tackling left-back Jim Ward was selected to play for England against Wales at the Leamington Road ground, Blackburn in March 1885. He replaced Arthur Walters in the 1-1 draw.
A cotton machine operator by trade, Ward also played for a team of tradesmen and weavers who achieved a small level of success in the 1880s. The team's coach was former England international Jack Hunter.

WARD, Peter David 1979-80 ①
Born: Derby, 27 July 1955
Career: Burton Albion (semi-professional, August 1972), Brighton & Hove Albion (£4,000, May 1975), Nottingham Forest (£400,000, October 1980... in a three way deal which saw Gary Birtles leave Forest for Manchester United and Andy Ritchie switch from United to Brighton), Seattle Sounders/USA (loan, April-June 1982), Brighton & Hove Albion (loan, October 1982), Seattle Sounders/USA (loan, April-June 1983), Vancouver Whitecaps/USA (September 1983), Cleveland Force/USA Indoor League (October 1984), Tacoma Stars/USA Indoor League (June 1987), Tampa Bay Rowdies/USA (June 1989), Witchita Wings/USA Indoor League (September 1989), Baltimore Blast/USA Indoor League (January 1990), Tampa Bay Rowdies/USA (April 1991, retired, May 1992); became Director of Training at Tarpon FC/USA... and played at amateur level, complete with titanium knee, until 2010; now lives in Tampa Bay, Florida.

Peter Ward, then of Brighton, came on as an 86th minute substitute for England in a 2-1 win over Australia in May 1980. There were three minutes added time at the end of the game and therefore Ward's international career was over after just seven minutes. Three years earlier, he fired in a hat-trick in a 6-0 victory over Norway in an U21 international and as a result was selected for the full England squad to play Luxembourg a month later but didn't make it onto the pitch.

During his career in the Football League, hot-shot striker Ward netted 88 goals in 227 appearances, following up with 186 goals in 274 American Indoor matches.

His book - He Shot He Scored, It Must Be Peter Ward - was published in 2010.

WARD, Timothy Victor 1947-49 ②

Born: Cheltenham, 17 October 1917
Died: Barton-under-Needwood, 28 January 1993
Career: Charlton Kings Boys' School, Cheltenham Schools, Charlton Kings FC (season 1932-33), Cheltenham Town (August 1933), Leicester City (trial, 1934), Derby County (trial, March 1937, signed for £100, April 1937, professional August 1937); WW2 guest for Hamilton Academical, Leeds United, Notts County; Barnsley (£1,000, March 1951, retired May 1952; appointed club's A team coach for season 1952-53), Exeter City (manager for eight days, March 1953), Barnsley (manager, March 1953-February 1960), Grimsby Town (manager, February 1960-June 1962), Derby County (manager, June 1962-May 1967), Carlisle United (manager, June 1967-September 1968); became a representative for Douglas Concrete firm near Burton-on-Trent; Nottingham Forest (scout, August 1969-May 1971); later Chairman of the Former Derby County Players' Association.

A quick, smooth-running, attacking left half, Tim Ward replaced England international defender Errington Keen at Derby but like many other footballers of his generation, his career was adversely affected by the outbreak of World War II. While serving in the Army he made guest appearances for three senior clubs and also played for the Scottish Army XI before going to fight in Europe. After the hostilities had ended, Ward played for the BAOR team in Germany before being demobbed.

Unfortunately he missed all but one game of Derby's 1946 FA Cup campaign and was philosophical on missing the final, saying "So many of my friends were killed in the War and I regarded myself lucky to emerge from it, rather than unlucky to miss Wembley." On his return to England, despite Arsenal offering £10,000 for his services, Derby found him a position at right-half. He won his two England caps in that position, making his debut in a 5-2 win over Belgium at the Heysel Stadium, Brussels in September 1947 and later lining up in a 1-0 win over Wales at Villa Park in November 1948. He was also part of the FA Tour of Canada in 1950, representing an FA XI v. World Cup XI in the 1950 Charity Shield game. As a manager, he won the Third Division (N) Championship with Barnsley in 1955 and gained promotion from Division Three with Grimsby in 1962.

Ward scored with the first kick of his first trial match with Derby County 'A', and convinced George Jobey to pay Cheltenham £100. He played his last game of football for the Derby County Old Stars – former Rams – team at the age of 72!

WARING, Thomas 1930-32 ⑤ ④

Born: High Tranmere, Birkenhead, 12 October 1906
Died: Liverpool, 20 December 1980
Career: Mersey Park Council School, Birkenhead & District Schools, Tranmere Colts (August 1922), Tranmere Celtic (July 1923), Tranmere Rovers (professional, February 1926), Aston Villa (£4,700, February 1928), Barnsley (November 1935), Wolverhampton Wanderers (July 1936), Tranmere Rovers (October 1936), Accrington Stanley (November 1938-July 1939), Bath City

(August-September 1939), WW2 guest for New Brighton (seasons 1939-42), Wrexham (seasons 1940-43), Everton (season 1941-42), Crewe Alexandra (season 1942-43), Aston Villa (February 1944); also played for Grayson's FC/South Liverpool (1945), Ellesmere Port Town (August 1946), Birkenhead Dockers FC (July 1948), Harrowby FC (August 1949-May 1950); worked at and played for the Hercules Motor Cycle Company in Aston, Birmingham (1928-35) and was also employed in Merseyside docks.

A crowd of 23,440 saw dynamic centre-forward Tom 'Pongo' Waring make his debut for Aston Villa in a reserve team game against local rivals Birmingham in February 1928 – and immediately he became a hero, by scoring a hat-trick in a 6-3 wi.

Tall, long-striding, six feet of sinew, muscle and bone, he went on to net a total of 167 goals (including ten hat-tricks) in 226 first-class appearances for Villa. He struck a club record 49 League goals in the 1930-31 season, 50 goals in all competitions. A legend at Villa Park, a reputation buoyed by his captain Billy Walker, who, in his autobiography, wrote: "There were no rules for 'Pongo'. Nobody knew what time he would turn up for training - ten o'clock, eleven o'clock, twelve o'clock, it made no odds. Nobody on the staff could do anything with him, although I think I can claim, as the captain in his days, to be the only person able to handle him. He was a funny lad indeed. We started the week's training on Tuesday mornings and every Tuesday he followed a habit which he could never break. He would go round all the refreshment bars on the ground and finish off the lemonade left in the bottles! Then he would start a little of his training - but that seldom lasted very long."

Capped five times by England, Waring scored on his debut in a 5-2 defeat by France in Paris in May 1931. He then played exceedingly well without scoring in a 4-1 victory over Belgium two days later and was on target twice when Ireland were thumped 6-2 in October of the same year. His remaining caps came in the other two Home Internationals in season 1931-32, against Wales (won 3-1) and Scotland (won 3-0). It was a pity in a way that Waring was scoring goals at the same time as three other terrific centre-forwards – namely 'Dixie' Dean, George Camsell, Gordon Hodgson, Fred Tilson and Jimmy Hampson – who all played for England in the early 1930s.

In November 1935, when he moved to Barnsley, around 5,000 angry Villa fans demonstrated, demanding Waring's return. He never did... going on to play for another Midland-based club instead, Wolves!

After his death at the age of 74, Waring's ashes were scattered in the Holte End goal mouth at Villa Park before a game against Stoke City.

As a Tranmere player, he scored six times in an 11-1 win over Durham City in a Third Division (N) game in January 1928.

WARNER, Conrad 1877-78 ①

Born: Cripplegate, London, 19 April 1850
Died: New York, USA, 10 April 1890
Career: Quaker School, Tottenham/London, Upton Park (seasons 1872-79); also played rugby for Cheshunt, hockey for Southgate, cricket for Winchmere Hill and lawn tennis for London and Middlesex; worked as a mechant for Partridge & Cooper in the City of London; he died from pneumonia whilst on a business trip to America.

Goalkeeper Conrad Warner had a 'torrid time' between the posts when England lost 7-2 to Scotland at the Queen's Park ground, Glasgow in March 1878. One reporter wrote: 'He was caught out of position time and again, and seemed to be heavy-legged when dealing with high balls.'

Apart from this horror show, he regularly produced some fine performances, being calm, assured and precise with his kicking.

WARNOCK, Stephen 2007-10 ②

Born: Ormskirk, Cheshire, 12 December 1981
Career: Liverpool (apprentice, September 1997, professional, April 1999), Bradford City (loan, September-October 2002), Coventry City (loan, July 2003-May 2004), Blackburn Rovers (£1.5m, January 2007), Aston Villa (undisclosed fee, August 2009), Bolton Wanderers (loan, September-December 2012), Leeds United (January 2013)

Left-back Stephen Warnock – who was once described by his manager, Martin O'Neill, as a 'warrior' – made his senior debut as an 84th minute substitute for Wayne Bridge in the friendly international against Trinidad & Tobago in June 2008. Two years later, after Bridge had told Fabio Capello he didn't want to be considered for the World Cup, he was named in the final 23 for South Africa (as cover for Ashley Cole) but did not feature in any game. However, soon after the competition had ended he won his second cap versus France at Wembley.

Warnock, who made 67 appearances for Liverpool and 109 for Blackburn before moving to Villa Park, played for England at Schoolboy and Youth team levels.

WARREN, Benjamin 1905-11 ㉒ ②

Born: Newhall, Derbyshire, 1879
Died: Derbyshire, 15 January 1917
Career: Newhall Town (seasons 1894-97), Newhall Swifts (seasons 1897-99), Derby County (professional, May 1899), Chelsea (£1,500, August 1908, retired, ill-health, February 1912).

An FA Cup winner with Derby in 1903, Ben Warren was an intuitive right-half. Although a tad slow at times, he had perfect timing, a clean tackle and good passing ability who was a regular choice for England for three full years, appearing in 19 consecutive internationals in the process.

He made an impressive debut in a 5-0 win over Ireland in February 1906 and was again outstanding in the victories over Wales (1-0) the following month, Ireland (3-1) in February 1908 and Wales again (7-1) four weeks later.

In the four end-of-season tour games in June 1908, when England twice beat Austria 6-1 and 11-1 (one goal scored), Hungary 7-1 and Bohemia 4-0, he never put a foot wrong. And he continued to shine in season 1908-09 when England beat Ireland 4-0, Wales 2-0 and Scotland 2-0 to win the Home International Championship.

On another European tour, in May/June 1909, the irrepressible Warner played his part once more in wins over Hungary 4-2 and 8-2 and Austria 8-1 (one goal scored) before having a quiet two years! He returned for his last three England games in February, March and April 1911, against Ireland (won 2-1), Wales (3-0) and Scotland (1-1) respectively. He was only once on the losing side in his 22 England games (a 2-1 defeat by Scotland in April 1906). He made 269 appearances for Derby (33 goals) and 101 for Chelsea (five goals).

WATERFIELD, George Smith 1926-27 ①

Born: Swinton, Yorkshire, 2 June 1901
Died: Yorkshire, circa 1975
Career: Mexborough (May 1919), Burnley (professional, October 1923), Crystal Palace (June 1935, retired, May 1937).

An outside-left with Mexborough, George Waterfield was later converted into a very positive, workmanlike left-back at Burnley and as a result of some fine performances, gained an England cap in a 3-3 draw with Wales at Wrexham in February 1927.

He was never called upon again, despite making a total of 394 appearances during his twelve years at Turf Moor.

WATSON, David 1983-88 ⑫

Born: Liverpool, 20 November 1961
Career: Liverpool (apprentice, April 1977, professional, May 1979), Norwich City (£100,000, November 1980), Everton (£900,000, August 1986; appointed player/caretaker-manager, March-May 1997); played for Hong Kong Golden FC (1996); retired as a player, May 2001), Tranmere Rovers (manager, April 2001-September 2002), Birmingham City (scout, during seasons 2003-07), Wigan Athletic (youth team manager, April 2008).

Norwich City centre-half Dave Watson made his England debut against Brazil in the Maracana Stadium, Rio de Janeiro in June 1984. Replacing appendicitis-victim Graham Roberts, he had a 'good game' as England caused a major upset by winning 2-0.

He played in the next two internationals (v. Uruguay and Chile) but with Alvin Martin, Graham Roberts, Terry Fenwick, Terry Butcher and Mark Wright ahead of him in the selection table, he had to wait a year before gaining his fourth cap v. Mexico (away).

Basically a reserve to the aforementioned quintet, plus Tony Adams, Watson collected his last eight caps over a period of two years, his last coming in June 1988 against USSR in the European Championship finals in Frankfurt.

A strong, well-balanced, hard-tackling defender with a big heart, Watson made 256 appearances for Norwich and 529 for Everton (38 goals scored). He won the League Cup and Second Division Championship with the Canaries in 1985 and 1986 and the First Division title and FA Cup with the Merseysiders in 1986 and 1995. The transfer fee paid by Norwich in 1980 was made in two £50,000 instalments. His brother, Alex Watson, was also a professional footballer with Liverpool and AFC Bournemouth.

WATSON, David Vernon 1973-82 ㉕ ④

Born: Stapleford, Notts, 5 October 1946
Career: Stapleford Old Boys, Notts County (professional, January 1967), Rotherham United (£25,000, January 1968), Sunderland (£100,000, December 1970), Manchester City (£275,000 plus Jeff Clarke, June 1975), Werder Bremen/Germany (£100,000, June 1979), Southampton (£200,000, October 1979), Stoke City (£50,000, January 1982), Vancouver Whitecaps/USA (free, April 1983), Derby County (free, September 1983), Vancouver Whitecaps (loan, briefly, early 1984), Fort Lauderdale Strikers/USA (free, May 1984), Notts County (free, as player-coach, September 1984), Kettering Town (August 1985, retired, May 1986); later ran his own business in Nottingham.

Dave Watson holds the record for being the player with most England caps never to have appeared in the World Cup. The rugged centre-half made his international debut against Portugal in Lisbon in April 1974 (0-0) and played his 65th and last game as Russell Osman's partner in the 1-1 draw in Iceland in June 1982, ahead of the World Cup finals. He didn't make the 22-man squad for Spain, Steve Foster (Brighton) being preferred.

His four goals all came in 1979 – in 4-0 and 2-0 wins over Northern Ireland and in 3-0 and 2-0 victories over Bulgaria. Unfortunately he gave away a last minute free-kick against West Germany in Munich in February 1978 and while England's defence was still forming a wall, Rainer Bonhof ran up and fired the ball past Ray Clemence to give the reigning World champions an undeserved 2-1 win.

Three months later Watson was a 'tower of strength' at the back when England beat Scotland 1-0 at Hampden Park – making it a miserable send-off to the World Cup finals for the Scots.

In the autumn of 1975, Watson sustained an injury to his back which resulted in him having a laminectomy at the end of the season. As a result he missed on further England calls, failing to win a single cap during the calendar year of 1976 and sat out three qualifying games for the 1978 World Cup.

At the beginning of 1977, Liverpool's centre-back Phil Thompson was sidelined through injury and Watson, now 30 years old and back to full health, was recalled to the heart of the England defence. He played every minute of every game that year, including World Cup qualifying victories over Luxembourg (twice) and Italy. However, the Italians had earlier defeated England and had a better scoring record against Luxembourg. As a result England missed out on the finals for a second successive tournament.

Watson continued to play well for his country before eventually handing over his position, on a permanent basis, to Terry Butcher.

During his club career Watson made well over 800 club appearances including 660 in the Football League (65 goals). He had his best spells with Sunderland (177 games) with whom he won the FA Cup in 1973 and Manchester City, for whom he starred in their 1976 League Cup winning side.

Watson was all set to go on to the 'illegal' tour to South Africa in 1983 but pulled out at the last minute. His wife, Penny, wrote a novel entitled: *My Dear Watson*.

WATSON, Victor Martin 1922-30 ⑤ ④

Born: Girton, Cambridgeshire, 10 November 1897
Died: Girton, Cambridgeshire, 3 August 1988
Career: Girton FC (1910), Cambridge Town (1912), Peterborough & Fletton United (1914), Brotherhood Engineering Works FC (1918), Wellingborough (August 1919), West Ham United (£50, as a professional, March 1920), Southampton (June 1935, retired, May 1936); became a market gardener at Girton where he remained until his death.

Dashing, all-action centre forward Vic Watson scored 326 goals in 505 first-class appearances for West Ham over a period of 16 years. Initially signed as cover for Syd Puddefoot, his goal-tally was second to none and included a six-timer in an 8-2 home League win over Leeds in February 1929, three four-goal hauls and 13 hat-tricks. Yet despite his magnificent record, Watson gained only five England caps, lining up against Wales in March 1923 (one goal scored in a 2-2 draw), versus Scotland the following month (one goal in another 2-2 draw), v. Scotland again in April 1930 (two goals in a 5-2 win), in Germany in May 1930 (drew 3-3) and in Austria four days later (drew 0-0). He was top scorer in his only season with Southampton and played in the first-ever Wembley FA Cup final of 1923.

In June 2010 a plaque honouring Watson was unveiled in his native Girton.

WATSON, William 1912-20 ③

Born: Southport, 11 September 1890
Died: Southport, 1 September 1955
Career: All Saints Wennington Road School/Southport, Blowick Wesleyans (1905), Southport Central (August 1907, professional, September 1908), Burnley (March 1909), Accrington Stanley (May 1925, retired, May 1927); Blackburn Rovers (coach, November 1926-March 1927); became an ironmonger, later a decorator in Southport; also had two spells as a Liberal councillor at Southport, the second from May 1955 until his death.

Billy Watson was described as being a 'polished left-half' whose main attributes were his defensive play and remarkable level of consistency. He appeared in 380 first-class games (20 goals) during his 16 years at Turf Moor, helping Burnley win the FA Cup and League Championship in 1914 and 1921 respectively.

Making his England debut in front of Jesse Pennington in April 1913 in a 1-0 win over Scotland at Stamford Bridge, he came close to scoring on two occasions before going off injured with 15 minutes remaining. He played the full 90 minutes of his second game, a 3-0 defeat by Ireland at Middlesbrough in February 1914 and was reported to have been one of the 'better forwards' in a disappointing 1-1 draw with the Irish in October 1919 in Belfast. Watson was one of five different players selected at left-half by England in ten matches either side of WW1.

WATSON, William 1949-51 ④

Born: Bolton-on-Dearne, 7 March 1920
Died: Johannesburg, South Africa, 24 April 2004
Career: Paddock Council School/Huddersfield, Huddersfield & District Schools; played local junior football in Huddersfield; Huddersfield Town (professional, October 1937); served in and played for the Army during WW2; Sunderland (£8,000, April 1946-May 1954); Halifax Town (£4,000, player-manager, November 1954-April 1956; manager again, September 1964-April 1966), Bradford City (manager, April 1966-January 1968), Wanderers FC Johannesburg/South Africa (manager, April 1968-May 1972); also first-class cricketer with Yorkshire and Leicestershire between 1939 and 1962, playing in 468 County games and 23 Test Matches, accumulating 26,549 runs, with 57 centuries and a top score of 257; became a Test selector.

Willie Watson was only 19 when WW2 broke out and after a number of games for the Army, he scored and laid on a goal for Tom Finney, from the left-wing position for England in an unofficial international against Switzerland in Zurich in July 1945 and played well in the Victory international versus Wales at The Hawthorns three months later. However, he had to wait until November 1949, before gaining his first full cap – starring at right-half in a comfortable 7-2 win over Northern Ireland at Maine Road when he set up goals for Jack Rowley and Stan Pearson. Soon afterwards he helped England beat Italy 2-0 and the following season, after World Cup disappointment, played in a 4-2 win over Wales on his home ground, Roker Park, and also in the 2-2 draw with Yugoslavia. Watson also appeared in three B internationals.

A cultured wing-half, he scored 16 goals in 223 appearances for Sunderland in his seven seasons at the club. As Bradford City's manager, he laid the foundations of a promotion-winning team. As a cricketer he made his Test debut v. South Africa in 1951 and went on to captain Leicestershire. Along with Trevor Bailey, he batted for almost six hours, scored 109 not out and helped save the second Test v. Australia at Lord's in 1953. England went on to win the Ashes. Twelve months later he was voted Wisden 'Cricketer of the Year'. In 1963, he was player-manager of the MCC touring party to South Africa. His father, William senior, also played for Huddersfield Town (1912-26).

WEAVER, Samuel 1931-33 ③

Born: Pilsley, Derbyshire, 8 February 1909
Died: Mansfield, 15 April 1985
Career: Pilsley Red Rose, Sutton Junction (trial), Sutton Town (August 1926), Hull City (£100, March 1928), Newcastle United (£2,500, November 1929), Chelsea (£4,166, August 1936), WW2 guest for Leeds United; Stockport County (December 1945, retired, May 1947); Leeds United (trainer/coach, August 1947-June 1949); Millwall (coach, July 1949-January 1954); steward of Oxo Sports

Club/Bromley (February 1954-August 1955), Mansfield Town (coach, September 1955, manager, June 1958-January 1960, coach briefly, then assistant-trainer, and chief scout, 1967, caretaker-manager, November 1971); also played cricket for Derbyshire and Somerset; became Derbyshire CCC masseur (1956).

Sam Weaver was a polished and stylish left-half, aggressive when called for, who also possessed an exceptionally long throw, sometimes hurling the ball up to 40 yards. He played three times for England, gaining his first cap in April 1932, in a 3-0 victory over Scotland at Wembley, a few weeks before helping Newcastle win the FA Cup. He played splendidly against the Scots, the *Daily Mail* reporter stating "While Morton (Scotland) was bowing out, a new star was born on the home side – Newcastle left-half Weaver, whose fine display was enhanced by his remarkably long thrown-in – setting a pattern for many generations of wing-halves to come."

His other England games were against Ireland at Blackpool in October 1932 (won 1-0) and Scotland at Hampden Park in April 1933 when he played well below par in a 2-1 defeat.

Weaver made over 400 appearances at club level, including 230 for Newcastle (43 goals) and 125 for Chelsea (4 goals).

WEBB, George William 1910-11 ② ①
Born: Poplar, London, 10 February 1887
Died: Harlesden, London, 28 March 1915
Career: Shaftsbury Road School, Ilford Alliance, West Ham United (August 1905), Manchester City (July 1912, retired, October 1912); worked in the family toy manufacturing business.

Although he scored on his England debut against Wales at Millwall in March 1911 (won 3-0), big, bold centre-forward George Webb, with hefty physique, had a 'poor game' in the 1-1 draw with Scotland at Goodison Park a month later, being completely 'bottled up' by Jimmy Low of Newcastle United. He quickly disappeared from the international scene, never to re-appear.

A year earlier he had represented England at amateur level against Switzerland and also in 1911 played at this level against Wales, Belgium, Germany and Holland. Webb died of consumption at the age of 28.

WEBB, Neil John 1987-92 ㉖ ④
Born: Reading, 30 July 1963
Career: Reading (apprentice, June 1979, professional, November 1980), Portsmouth (£87,500, July 1982), Nottingham Forest (£250,000, July 1985), Manchester United (£1.5m, July 1989), Nottingham Forest (£800,000, November 1992), Swindon Town (loan, October-November 1994), Instant-Dictionary FC/ China (1995), Grimsby Town (non-contract, August-October 1996), Exeter City (briefly, early 1997), Weymouth (player-coach, June-December 1997), Aldershot Town (1998), Merthyr Tydfil (February-May 2000), Reading Town (manager, season 2000-01), Weymouth (manager, briefly, 2001), also played for England Veterans XI; fell on hard times and sold programmes outside the Madejski Stadium; also worked as a postman, for a transport company and Charlton Athletic (staff); now a part time soccer pundit.

Midfielder Neil Webb was the 1,000th player to be capped by England when he came on as a substitute for Glenn Hoddle in the 64th minute against West Germany in Dusseldorf in September 1987. England lost the game 3-1.

Webb was in good form after that, but in his 11th international against Sweden at Wembley in October 1988, he suffered a serious Achilles tendon injury which sidelined him for almost three months. During his career, Webb, a strong-running midfielder, scored 134 goals in 566 club appearances, gaining League Cup and FA Cup winner's medals with Nottingham Forest (1989) and Manchester United (1990) respectively.

WEBSTER, Maurice 1929-30 ③
Born: Blackpool, 13 November 1899
Died: Middlesbrough, 10 February 1978
Career: Bloomfield Villa, South Shore Wednesday/Blackpool, Fleetwood, Lytham, Stalybridge Celtic (October 1921), Middlesbrough (April 1922), Carlisle United (June 1935, retired May 1936), Middlesbrough (trainer, seasons 1936-037), Carlisle United (trainer, May 1937-September 1939); worked as a plumber after the war.

A Second Division Championship winner with Middlesbrough in 1929, centre-half Maurice Webster was relatively small for a defender but he was, nevertheless, able to compete with the toughest and even the tallest centre-forwards in the game. He was quick over the ground and could pass the ball with pace and precision.

Taking over from Ernie Hart of Leeds United, he made his England debut in a 5-2 win over Scotland at Wembley in April 1930, having a solid game between the Sheffield Wednesday duo of Alf Strange and Bill Marsden. His second and third caps were gained on the end of season tour against Germany and Austria. Webster also represented the Football League. He made 262 League appearances for Middlesbrough.

WEDLOCK, William John 1906-14 ㉖ ①
Born: Bedminster, 28 October 1880
Died: Bristol, 24 January 1965
Career: Masonic Rovers/Bedminster (1895), Arlington Rovers (1897), Bristol City (amateur, May 1898), Gloucester County (seasons 1898-1901), Aberdare (professional, June 1901), Bristol City (May 1905, retired May 1921); became a licensee near to Bristol City's Ashton Gate ground.

Also known as 'Fatty' and the 'India Rubber Man' Billy Wedlock played professional football for 20 years. A centre-half, he was only 5ft 4ins tall but his short and stout stature belied his natural talent and his only rival for the pivotal position was Charlie Roberts of Manchester United. He played in 26 out of the 30 England games staged during his ten-year international career. He won his first caps against Ireland in February 1907 and his last against Wales in March 1914. He was on the losing side only once (in a 2-0 defeat by Scotland in 1910) and his only international goal came in a 7-1 victory over Wales in 1908.

Described in the press as a player who put his 'heart and soul in to the game' Wedlock appeared in successive losing Welsh Cup finals for Aberdare, before helping Bristol City win the Second Division championship in 1906 and reach the FA Cup final in 1909. He made 403 appearances during his time with Bristol City.

The East End stand at the club's Ashton Gate ground is named after Wedlock whose grandson is the folksinger, Fred Wedlock.

Neil Webb

WEIR, David 1888-89 ②

Born: Aldershot, 7 June 1863
Died: Edinburgh, Scotland, 7 November 1933
Career: Hampton FC (1870), Maybole FC/Glasgow (1875), Glasgow
Thistle (1879), Halliwell (1887), Bolton Wanderers (professional,
July 1888), Ardwick/Manchester City (May 1890), Bolton Wanderers
(February 1893-May 1895); Maybole FC (player-coach, August
1895, retired as a player, May 1896, remained as coach and
assistant-manager until 1900); Glossop (manager, October
1909-April 1911), Stuttgart/Germany (coach, April 1911-May 1914).

Born the son of an officer's batman, Davie Weir was a strong
attacking player who occupied the centre-half and three inside-
forward positions with total commitment. Unfortunately he was
not liked by his colleagues being described as too much of an
'individualist'. He actually missed the 1894 FA Cup final due to his
unpopularity with other players!
   He lined up at centre-half in his first England game, a 6-1 victory
over Ireland in March 1889, and played inside-left in his second,
a 3-2 defeat by Scotland a month later. He scored 41 goals in just
92 appearances during his two spells with Bolton, lining up in the
Wanderers' first-ever League game against Derby County at Pike's
Lane in September 1888.

WELBECK, Daniel Nii Tackie Mensah 2010-13 ⑯ ④

Born: Longsight, Manchester, 26 November 1990
Career: Manchester United (apprentice, May 2007, professional,
July 2008), Preston North End (loan, January-March 2010),
Sunderland (loan, August 2010-May 2011)

A Youth international at the age of 17, Danny Welbeck made four
appearances for England's U21 team before gaining his first cap as
a second-half substitute in the 1-1 home friendly draw with Ghana
at Wembley in March 2011.
   With so many highly talented versatile forwards in the senior
squad at Old Trafford, Welbeck spent quite some time on loan,
initially at Preston where he was 'signed' by Sir Alex Ferguson's son,
Darren. He then did well with Sunderland during 2010-11, linking
up exceedingly well with Asamoah Gyan, the Ghanaian World Cup
striker who he played against at Wembley on his England debut.
Then, with the Mexican Hernandez out injured, he played a key part
in United's excellent start to the 2011-12 season. Welbeck's parents
were both born in Ghana and were at Wembley to see their son in
action – one perhaps supporting England, the other Ghana!
   Coincidentally, Jack Rodwell was also christened Nii Mensah.

WELCH, Reginald de Courtenay 1872-74 ②

Born: Kensington, London, 17 October 1851
Died: Guildford, Surrey, 4 June 1939
Career: Harrow School (seasons 1870-72), Harrow Chequers
(1872); also played for Wanderers (seasons 1870-74), Remnants
FC, Middlesex County; FA Committee member (seasons 1873-75
and 1879-80); Army tutor (years 1883-95); thence Principal of the
Army College, Heath End at Farnham, Surrey.

Twice an FA Cup winner with Wanderers in 1872 and 1873, Reginald
Welch's two England caps were won in different positions! He made his
England debut at left-back against Scotland in Glasgow in November
1872 (the first ever full international between the two countries which
ended 0-0) and played his second game in goal against the Scots,
also in Glasgow, in March 1874 when he was on the losing side, 2-1.
Capable in both positions, he preferred to keep goal and was regarded
one of the best in the country between 1873 and 1875.

WELLER, Keith 1973-74 ④ ①

Born: Islington, London, 11 June 1946
Died: Seattle, USA, 12 November 2004
Career: Tottenham Hotspur (apprentice, June 1962, professional,
January 1964), Millwall (June 1967), Chelsea (£100,000, May
1970), Leicester City (£100,000, September 1971), New England
Teamen/USA (loan, January 1979, signed for £40,000, February
1979), Fort Lauderdale Strikers/USA (December 1980), Dallas
Sidekicks/USA (coach, season 1981-82); remained in America,
based in Seattle, where he became a driver for an outside
broadcasting unit for a TV company; later ran a coffee shop.

Manager Joe Mercer awarded winger Keith
Weller his four England caps in May 1974...
the first against Wales in Cardiff, where he
had a sound game, setting up a goal for Stan
Bowles in a 2-0 win; the second against
Northern Ireland when he scored with a
late header to clinch a 1-0 win at Wembley;
the third in a 2-0 defeat by Scotland at
Hampden Park and his fourth in a 2-2 draw
with Argentina, again at Wembley.
   A lively player, with plenty of pace and good skills, Weller tended
to drift in and out of the game but on his day was a fine footballer
who helped Chelsea win the European Cup Winners' Cup in
1971 before moving to Filbert Street. He scored 47 goals in 305
appearances for Leicester, having previously netted 77 goals in 210
outings for his three London clubs, Spurs, Millwall and Chelsea. He
was only 58 when he died.

WELSH, Donald 1937-39 ③ ①

Born: Manchester, 25 February 1911
Died: Stevenage, 2 February 1990
Career: Princes Road School/Manchester, Manchester & Lancashire
Schools, Royal Navy football (1926-28); assisted FC Valletta/Malta
(1928); Naval Barracks/Devonport, Devon; Torquay United (amateur,
April 1933, professional, July 1934), Charlton Athletic (£3,250,
February 1935); WW2 guest for Southend United, Aldershot,
Brighton & Hove Albion, Chester, Liverpool, Manchester City and
Liverpool; returned to Charlton (retired, November 1947); Brighton
& Hove Albion (secretary-manager, November 1947-March 1951),
Liverpool (manager, March 1951-May 1956); also ran a hotel in
Bovey Tracey, Devon for two years (mid 1950s); Bournemouth &
Boscombe Athletic (manager, July 1958-February 1961), Clubland
Youth Centre/Camberwell (manager, May 1961), Wycombe
Wanderers (manager, July 1963-November 1964), (manager),
Charlton Athletic (administration staff, December 1964-May 1965);
played club cricket for Torquay and was also a keen hockey player.

The versatile Don Welsh was a 'complete
and inspirational player' who won the Third
Division (S) Championship and the FA Cup
with Charlton in 1935 and 1947. He also
played in the losing Cup final of 1946 and
in two Wartime Cup finals for the Addicks,
for whom he scored 50 goals in 216
League and Cup games plus 100 goals in
118 wartime appearances. As a guest for
Liverpool during the hostilities he netted six
times in a 12-1 win over Stockport County in December 1940.
   Replacing Wilf Copping at left-half, he made an impressive
debut for England against Germany in Berlin in May 1938, having
a hand in two of the goals in a 6-2 win. He kept his place for the next

game, a 2-1 defeat by Switzerland in Zurich but had to wait twelve months before earning his third and last cap, in a 2-0 win over Romania in Bucharest when his goal clinched victory.

Welsh also had the honour of netting the first international hat-trick in WW2 football – in England's 4-1 win over Wales at The City Ground, Nottingham in April 1941. He struck a total of 11 goals in nine Wartime games for England and added two more in one unofficial international. He also played once for the Football League.

WEST, Gordon 1968-69 ③

Born: Darfield, Barnsley, 24 April 1943
Died: Liverpool, 10 June 2012
Career: Don & Dearne Schools/Barnsley, Everton (amateur, May 1958, professional, April 1960), Everton (£27,000, March 1962, retired, May 1973); returned with Tranmere Rovers (1975; later worked on groundstaff at Prenton Park); subsequently employed as a security officer at RAF Woodvale, Formby, Lancashire (1983-92).

Goalkeeper Gordon West made an impressive debut for England in the 1-1 draw with Bulgaria at Wembley in December 1968… but had no chance whatsoever when Asparoukov equalised with a magnificent solo goal. He then produced a solid display in a 2-1 win over Wales in May 1969 and was outstanding in the 0-0 draw in Mexico the following month before admitting to boss Alf Ramsey that he suffered so much from homesickness that he didn't feel he could play for his country again – refusing in effect to join the World Cup squad! His international career ended there and then.

A strong, well-built and competent goalkeeper with a pair of good, safe hands West made his League debut for Blackpool at the age of 17. And after 33 games for the Seasiders, he joined Everton in March 1962 for £27,000, a British record for a goalkeeper at that time. A regular for the Merseysiders until 1972, he won two League Championships and the FA Cup and made 402 appearances for Everton before retiring in 1973. He returned briefly with Tranmere late on. Also capped by his country at youth team level, West was refused a job on the Barnsley groundstaff as a youngster – so he joined Everton instead! He lived in Brighton-le-Sands prior to his death, in hospital from cancer, at the age of 69.

WESTWOOD, William Raymond 1934-37 ⑥

Born: Kingswinford near Dudley, 14 April 1912
Died: Brierley Hill, 8 January 1982
Career: Brierley Hill Schools, Stourbridge, Brierley Hill Alliance, Bolton Wanderers (professional, March 1930), Chester (December 1947), Darwen (May 1949, retired May 1950); became a licensee in Brierley Hill.

Initially a left-winger, Ray Westwood developed into a swift-moving inside or centre-forward with a lethal right-foot shot. Noted for his direct approach, his go-for-goal dashes were something to savour as far as the Bolton fans were concerned, for he scored some smashing goals during his 17 years at Burnden Park. Indeed, he netted 144 times in 333 senior appearances for the Wanderers.

He won the first of his six England caps against Wales in September 1934. Replacing Cliff Bastin at inside-left, he had a decent game, setting up a goal for Sam Tilson in a 4-0 win. His second international appearance followed against Scotland in April 1935 when he was well contained by some sturdy defenders in a 2-0 defeat in Glasgow. He then partnered West Brom's 'W.G.' Richardson

in attack when Holland were defeated 1-0 in Holland before assisting in another Tilson goal in a 3-1 win over Ireland in Belfast.

Westwood's fifth and sixth caps came in a 3-0 win over Germany at Tottenham in November 1935 and a 2-1 defeat by Wales in Cardiff ten months later. One can honestly say that there were far too many other players of similar style to that of Westwood's around in the late 1930s - hence his low tally of caps. He also played in one unofficial international (one goal scored) and was a Second Division promotion winner with Bolton in 1935.

WHATELEY, Oliver 1882-83 ② ②

Born: Coventry, 8 August 1861
Died: Edgbaston, Birmingham, 10 October 1926
Career: Gladstone Unity/Coventry (1878), Aston Villa (July 1880, retired with face cancer, May 1888); underwent successful operation in 1911 and during WW1 worked for the YMCA in Rouen, France; was an artist and designer by trade.

Variable in performance, at his best Olly Whateley was a formidable amateur inside or outside left. He was aggressive and packed a powerful right-foot shot, reputed to be one of the hardest of his day. Nicknamed 'Daisy-cutter' – because a lot of his efforts skimmed along the turf – he scored twice on his England debut in a 7-0 win over Ireland in February 1883 and was unlucky not to figure on the scoresheet in his second international a fortnight later when Scotland won 3-2 on a very slippery, icy pitch at Sheffield.

He scored nine goals in 19 FA Cup appearances for Aston Villa.

WHEELER, John Edward 1954-55 ①

Born: Crosby, Lancs, 26 July 1928
Career: St Leonard's School/Bootle, Carlton FC/Liverpool, Tranmere Rovers (amateur, August 1944, professional, April 1946), Bolton Wanderers (in exchange for Vince Dillon plus £1,500, February 1951), Liverpool (£9,000, September 1956), Bury (assistant-trainer, May 1963, head trainer, July 1967, assistant-manager, September 1969-September 1970); was offered the player-manager's job at New Brighton in May 1963 but did not take up the appointment.

Captain of Bolton's 1953 FA Cup final team, Johnny Wheeler was a strong, hard-tackling right-half with tremendous stamina. He also played at inside-right and centre-forward and once scored a hat-trick for his club v. Blackpool. During his club career he amassed nearly 500 appearances, including 105 for Tranmere, 205 for Bolton and 177 for Liverpool. His only England cap came in a 2-0 win over Ireland in Belfast in October 1954 when he took over from Bill McGarry. Wheeler also played in five 'B' internationals and represented the Football League.

WHELDON, George Frederick 1896-98 ④ ⑥

Born: Langley Green, Oldbury, 1 November 1869
Died: St George's, Worcester, 13 January 1924
Career: Chance's Infants & Langley St Michael's Council Schools/ Oldbury, Rood End White Star, Langley Green Victoria, West Bromwich Albion (trial, October-November 1888), Small Heath (February 1890), Aston Villa (June 1896), West Bromwich Albion (£100, August 1900), Queens Park Rangers (£400, December 1901), Portsmouth (£150, August 1902), Worcester City (July 1904, retired, January 1907); played cricket for Worcestershire (1899-1906) and Carmarthenshire; later a publican in Worcester.

The youngest of ten children, Fred 'Diamond' Wheldon was a brilliant footballer, an exceptional talent, a tremendous goalscorer who went on to great things with club and country. Often seen wearing a pair of golfing stockings (instead of football socks) Wheldon scored 84 goals in 134 games for Small Heath, helping them win the Second Division championship and gain promotion in successive seasons (1893 and 1894). In fact he scored the club's first-ever League goal v. Burslem Port Vale in September 1892 and also netted the Birmingham club's first penalty. He moved to Aston Villa for a record fee and went on to net 74 goals in 140 games, gaining one FA Cup and three League championship winner's medals, being a key figure in Villa's double-winning season of 1896-97. During his time with Villa, he won four England caps. It should have been more. He scored a hat-trick on his debut in a 6-0 win over Ireland in February 1897, starred in a 3-2 win over the Irish a year later, netted twice in a 3-0 victory over Wales in March 1898 and ended with another goal in a 3-1 triumph over Scotland at Celtic Park shortly afterwards. Playing alongside Steve Bloomer, he had a hand in all three goals against the Scots. He opened the scoring from club-mate Charlie Athersmith's short pass on 10 minutes, set up Bloomer for the second goal halfway through the first-half and sent Wreford-Brown speeding away down the right before Frank Forman lined up Bloomer for the third.

Wheldon also played in four Inter-League games and when he joined West Brom, he became the first player to appear for all three major Birmingham-area clubs.

As a Worcestershire county cricketer, he scored almost 5,000 runs at an average of 22.54 per innings in 138 matches. He struck three centuries and also took 95 catches as a wicket-keeper. His brother, Sam, also played for West Brom and his son, Norris, for Liverpool.

WHITE, David 1992-93 ①

Born: Urmston, Manchester, 30 October 1967
Career: Salford Boys, Manchester City (apprentice, April 1983, professional, October 1985), Leeds United (£2m, December 1993), Sheffield United (loan, November 1995, signed for £500,000, January 1996, retired, injured, May 1997).

One of manager Graham Taylor's follies, David White, the strong, hard-running Manchester City winger, made his only England appearance in the 1-0 defeat by Spain in Santander in September 1992. In the first few minutes, he rounded the goalkeeper but missed the target, and was later substituted by Paul Merson, never to be seen in the Three Lions shirt again. It was a night he would rather forget.

White made a total of 394 League appearances for his three League clubs (101 goals scored). He helped Manchester City win the FA Youth Cup in 1986 and gain promotion from Division Two in 1988. He also played for his country at Youth, 'B' and U21 levels.

WHITE, Thomas Angus 1932-33 ①

Born: Pendleton, Manchester, 29 July 1908
Died: Liverpool, 13 August 1967
Career: Southport Council School, Southport Schools, Trinity Old Boys, Southport (amateur, August 1923, professional, September 1925), Everton (February 1927), Northampton Town (trial, October 1937), New Brighton (February 1938, retired, May 1938); worked at Liverpool docks and died as a result of injuries received whilst working there.

A League Championship and FA Cup winner with Everton in 1932 and 1933, Tom White was not the tallest of centre-halves but his discerning distribution could not be faulted. He also played at inside-right and centre-forward and in fact scored some important goals. His only England cap came in the 1-1 draw with Italy in Rome in May 1933. Deputising for Ernie Hart at the heart of the defence, he had a solid game and came close to scoring when a header from Cliff Bastin's left-wing corner clipped the outside of a post. Also in 1933, White toured the continent with the FA. He was also a good swimmer and played golf and tennis at a high level.

WHITEHEAD, James 1892-94 ②

Born: Church, Lancs, 23 June 1870
Died: Manchester, 7 August 1929
Career: Church FC (1886), Peel Bank FC (1888), Accrington (professional, July 1890), Blackburn Rovers (June 1893), Manchester City (September 1897, retired, injured, July 1899).

Jim Whitehead was described as being "too lightly built for bustling tactics. He was a spruce, lively inside-right, adroit in evading weightier opponents." He won the first of his England caps against Wales at Stoke in March 1893, assisting in one of Fred Spiksley's two goals in a 6-0 win. His second cap followed a year later in a 2-2 draw with Ireland in Belfast. He was injured on the hour mark and hobbled on the wing for the last 30 minutes. He was forced to retire at the age of 29.

WHITFIELD, Herbert 1878-79 ① ①

Born: Lewes, Sussex, 25 November 1858
Died: Chailey near Lewes, 6 May 1909
Career: Eton College (seasons 1875-78), Trinity College/Cambridge University (seasons 1878-81); also played for Old Etonians (seasons 1878-85); also played cricket for Cambridge University and Sussex (seasons 1878-89); was a local director of Barclays Bank.

An FA Cup winner with Old Etonians in 1879 and a finalist in 1881, Bertie Whitfield was a never-say-die left-winger with pace and skill. He was one of the best of his era yet won only one England cap, scoring in a 2-1 defeat by Wales at The Oval in January 1879 when he deputised for Bill Mosforth. Besides being a fine cricketer (75 appearances and 2,400 runs for Sussex), he also starred on the athletics track and played Real Tennis for his University.

WHITHAM, Michael 1891-92 ①

Born: Ecclesfield, Yorkshire, 6 November 1867
Died: Brentford, Middlesex, 6 May 1924
Career: Ecclesfield FC, Rotherham Swifts (professional, September 1885) Sheffield United (June 1890, retired, injured, May 1898; appointed club trainer); later employed as first team trainer at Gainsborough Trinity (two spells), Rotherham County, Huddersfield Town and Brentford (until his death in May 1924); also played for Sheffield FA

A resilient full-back, especially strong in the air, Mike Whitham surprisingly made his only England appearance at left-half against Ireland in March 1892. This was when England played two games on the same day – the other was against Wales at Wrexham – hence there were 22 players on international duty. Whitham made 160 appearances in eight years with Sheffield United.

WHITWORTH, Stephen 1974-77 ⑦

Born: Coalville, Leicestershire, 20 March 1952
Career: Leicester City (associated schoolboy forms, April 1966, apprentice, May 1967, professional, November 1969), Sunderland (£180,000, March 1979), Bolton Wanderers (October 1981), Mansfield Town (August 1983), Barnet (player-coach, June 1985, assistant-manager/player-coach, June 1986, retired, May 1989).

A very useful overlapping right-back, strong in the tackle with a good technique, Steve Whitworth gained Schoolboy honours for England before joining Leicester City. He made rapid progress and went on to amass 415 senior appearances for the Foxes, helping them win the Second Division title in 1971. During his time at Filbert Street, he also represented England at youth team level and played in six U23 internationals before gaining his seven senior caps (under manager Don Revie), the first (in place of Paul Madeley) in a 2-0 win over West Germany in March 1975. He collected his other six over the next eight months, playing against Cyprus in a European Championship qualifier (won 1-0), Northern Ireland (0-0), Wales (2-2), Scotland (a 5-1 victory at Wembley), Switzerland (2-1) and Portugal (1-1). He never let his country down in any of the seven games he played, but in the end the right-back position went to Colin Todd with Dave Clement and Mick Mills in reserve.

WHYMARK, Trevor John 1977-78 ①

Born: Burston, Norfolk, 4 May 1950
Career: Diss Town (August 1965), Ipswich Town (apprentice, May 1968, professional, May 1969), Vancouver Whitecaps/Canada (£150,000, February 1979), Sparta Rotterdam/Holland (£50,000, September 1979), Derby County (loan, November 1979), Grimsby Town (£80,000, December 1980), Southend United (free, January 1984), Peterborough United (free, August 1985), Diss Town (loan, October 1985), Colchester United (non-contract, October 1985), Diss Town (January 1986, retired, injured, May 1986); out of football for several years; Norwich City (U13 coach, season 1999-2000), Ipswich Town (U12 coach, seasons 2000-03).

Striker Trevor Whymark was given his England debut by manager Ron Greenwood against Luxembourg in Stad Letzenuerg in October 1977. He came on as a second-half substitute for Terry McDermott in a bid to increase the pressure on the home defence. England eventually scrambled a 2-0 win. He was never selected again, although he did play in seven U23 internationals.

At club level, Whymark scored well over 150 goals in more than 500 senior appearances including 104 in 335 outings for Ipswich. He helped Vancouver Whitecaps win the NASL in 1979.

WIDDOWSON, Sam Weller 1879-80 ①

Born: Hucknall Torkard, Notts, 16 April 1851
Died: Beeston, Notts, 9 May 1927
Career: Hucknall Torkard Council School, People's College/Nottingham, Nottingham Forest (August 1866, retired May 1879; was then club Chairman until August 1884); FA Committee member (seasons, 1888-92 and 1893-94); became a first-class referee; also played cricket for Nottinghamshire; was a lace manufacturer by trade.

A centre-forward, quick off the mark with a strong right-foot shot, Sam Widdowson made his only appearance for England in a 5-4 defeat by Scotland in Glasgow in March 1880. Wrote The Times correspondent: "Widdowson was prominent on several occasions... and was in the ruck of players which helped E. C. Bambridge force the ball over the Scottish line in the late revival which almost earned a share of the match honours."

Widdowson is credited with inventing players' shin guards in 1874 when he cut down a pair of his old cricket pads and strapped them outside his stockings. Initially the concept was ridiculed but it soon caught on with other players and shin pads are now part and parcel of the game. As a referee, he was in charge of the first-ever match when goal nets were used (for an exhibition game in Nottingham). He was also a fine athlete in the 200 and 400 yard races and 100 yards hurdles.

Widdowson also pioneered early floodlighting for night games by using gas lamps. However, his idea was dropped due to the gas running out, and fears for crowd safety, but when electricity was more readily available in 1909 he, now retired, returned to the City Ground to attempt electric lighting.

WIGNALL, Francis 1964-65 ② ②

Born: Chorley, Lancs, 21 August 1939
Career: Horwich RMI (1957), Everton (professional, May 1958), Nottingham Forest (£20,000, June 1963), Wolverhampton Wanderers (£50,000, March 1968), Derby County (£20,000, February 1969), Mansfield Town (£8,000, February 1971-May 1973), King's Lynn (player-manager, July 1973), Burton Albion (manager, August 1974), Qatar (coach, October 1975, national team manager/coach, October 1980), Shepshed Charterhouse (manager, July 1981-March 1983); now lives in Ruddington and helps coach the Ruddington Colts team which includes his grandson.

Frank Wignall, playing between strikers Roger Hunt and Johnny Byrne, netted twice on his England debut in a 2-1 win over Wales at Wembley in November 1964. Three weeks later he had an 'off day' in the 1-1 draw in Holland and was never selected again – although he did represent the FA v. Mexico and played for the Football League XI.

The scorer of 107 goals in 323 League games for his four clubs, he broke his leg as a Nottingham Forest player but recovered and played on for another 10 years.

WILCOX, Jason Martin 1995-2000 ③

Born: Farnsworth, Lancs, 15 July 1971
Career: Blackburn Rovers (apprentice, July 1987, professional June 1989), Leeds United (£3m, December 1989) Leicester City (free, June 2004), Blackpool (loan, November-December 2005, signed on a free transfer, January 2006 retired, May 2006).

Jason Wilcox's career was thrown into doubt during the summer of 1993 when he contracted legionnaire's disease which sidelined him for several weeks. Thankfully he recovered full fitness and was awarded his first England cap against Hungary at Wembley in May 1996. He hit the bar in the first minute in a 3-0 win.

He had a fine game against the Magyars and many tipped him to make the squad for Euro '96 but in the end he was left out by boss Terry Venables who described the decision as one of the toughest of his career. He did, however, make the squad for Euro 2000 but did not play. Wilcox went on to add two more caps to his tally, playing against France in February 1999 (lost 2-0) and Argentina a year later (0-0). He also made two appearances for England's B team v. Chile and Hong Kong and appeared in one unofficial international.

Initially it was thought that Wilcox was the answer to England's left-wing problem, but he never had the opportunity to impress, due to a long list of injuries, which some say restricted his potential as a player.

He made almost 300 League appearances during his career, spending his best years with Blackburn. Unfortunately his days with Leeds were fraught with injuries.

Jason Wilcox

WILKES, Albert 1900-02 ⑤ ①

Born: Birmingham, 18 October 1874
Died: Stoke-on-Trent, 9 December 1936
Career: Walsall Street School/West Bromwich, West Bromwich
Baptists, Oldbury Town, West Bromwich Albion (trial, 1894), Walsall
(professional, April 1895), Aston Villa (May 1898), Fulham (June
1907), Chesterfield (February 1909, retired, May 1909); became
a Football League referee and from 1934 until his death was a
Director of Aston Villa.

As a straight-as-a-die, no-nonsense defender, Albert Wilkes was
renowned for his competitiveness and hard work. He possessed a
formidable tackle and was a fine helpmeet to his full-back, being
scrupulously fair. He won two League Championship medals with
Aston Villa (1899, 1900) and made 159 appearances for the
Birmingham club. He gained his five England caps consecutively
between March 1901 and May 1902, making his debut in a 6-0
defeat of Wales and scoring, with a beautifully executed lob 'over
the heads of friends and foes alike' in his last outing to earn his side
a 2-2 draw with Scotland on his home ground at Villa Park. Wilkes
had many interests outside football including painting, literature and
music. Indeed, he was a quality singer and delighted thousands at
music halls with his strong baritone voice. He was also awarded
the Humane Society's Award after diving into the sea off Aberdovey,
Wales to save a child from drowning.
    Wilkes later established a flourishing photography business in
West Bromwich, specializing at first in teams groups before going
on to concentrate on individual players. His son, Albert junior, ran the
business for many years after his death, which occurred at the age
of 61 from pneumonia.

WILKINS, Raymond Colin, MBE 1975-86 ⑧④ ③

Born: Hillingdon, Middlesex, 14 September 1956
Career: Middlesex Schools, London & District Schools, Chelsea
(apprentice, September 1971, professional, October 1973),
Manchester United (£825,000, August 1979), AC Milan/Italy
(£1.5m, June 1984), Paris St Germain (July 1987), Glasgow
Rangers (November 1987), Queens Park Rangers (November
1989), Crystal Palace (May 1984), Queens Park Rangers (player-
manager, November 1994-September 1996), Wycombe Wanderers
(non-contract, September 1996), Hibernian (free, September
1996), Millwall (free, January 1997), Leyton Orient (non-contract,
February 1997), Fulham (manager, September 1997-May 1998);
Chelsea (assistant-manager/coach, June 1998, caretaker-manager,
September 2000 for 4 days), Watford (assistant-manager, July
2001), Millwall (coach, September 2002, assistant-manager,
December 2003, later co-caretaker-manager), Chelsea (coach,
September 2008, caretaker-manager, February 2009 for six days;
sacked as coach, November 2010).

Ray 'Butch' Wilkins had made his international debut against Italy
in New York in May 1976. He accompanied Tony Towers and Trevor
Brooking in midfield and starred in a 3-2 win. One of his best goals
for his country came against Belgium in a crowd-troubled European
Championship encounter in Turin in June 1980. He put England
ahead in the 22nd minute by collecting a clearance, lobbing the ball
over advancing defenders and then running round to hook a shot
into the roof of the net. The final score was 1-1. Maligned in some
quarters for 'negative' play (he was deemed more likely to pass a
ball sideways rather than forwards – earning him semi-affectionate
nicknames like Squareball and The Crab), Wilkins nevertheless
became one of his country's most sought-after players. His first

season at Old Trafford was uneventful, with domestic honours
continuing to elude him, but he achieved one of his career highs after
helping England qualify for the European Championship finals in Italy
in 1980...the first tournament England had reached for a decade.
    In a tight group game against Belgium, Wilkins scored a stunning
individual goal when he lobbed the ball over the entire opposing
defence and, in one movement, ran on to his own pass, thereby
breaching the obvious offside trap, before delivering a second lob,
this time over the head of the goalkeeper and into the net to put
England ahead. The Belgians swiftly equalised and a disappointing
England failed to make progress from their group. Wilkins remained
a fixture for his country, playing well during a successful campaign
to qualify for the 1982 World Cup finals in Spain which England
exited at the second group stage.
    Over the next two seasons, Wilkins continued to play for England
under Bobby Robson but the team failed to qualify for Euro '84. That
same summer, United accepted an offer 'they couldn't refuse' from
AC Milan and Wilkins went off to Italy. Wilkins played well below par
in Serie A and was allowed to leave in 1987 to join Paris St Germain.
    Still an England regular, he was chosen for the squad which
qualified for the 1986 World Cup in Mexico and played in the
opening defeat against Portugal but didn't last the full 90 minutes in
the next group game against Morocco after receiving a red card for
the only time in his career, making him the first England player to be
sent off in a World Cup finals match. In disagreeing with a decision

made by the fussy referee, Wilkins threw the ball towards the official – but hit him with it. He was suspended for the next two games and was not reinstated by the time the quarter final against Argentina came round, which England lost 2–1. Wilkins made his 84th and final England appearance in November 1986. He had scored three international goals and had captained his country on ten occasions. In a playing career spanning 26 years (1971-97) Wilkins accumulated more than 900 club and international appearances (608 in the Football League alone), and scored 64 goals. He also represented England at Schoolboy, Youth, U21 and U23 levels.

In 1983, he scored for Manchester United in the FA Cup final against Brighton to put his side 2–1 up. It was a strike of great quality and also some rarity as it had taken Wilkins three years to get his first goal for the Reds. The game ended 2–2 after extra-time but Wilkins got his winner's medal when United won the replay 4–0.

He also won the Scottish League and League Cup double with Rangers in 1989. He was Chelsea's youngest-ever captain in April 1975 (age 18) and was awarded the MBE in the Queen's Birthday honours list in June 1993 for services to the game of football. George, his father played for several League clubs whilst his two brothers, Dean and Graham also enjoyed League careers.

WILKINSON, Bernard 1903-04 ①

Born: Thorpe Hesley, Yorkshire, 12 September 1879
Died: Sheffield, 28 May 1949
Career: Thorpe Hesley FC, Shiregreen FC/Sheffield (1897), Sheffield United (professional, July 1899), Rotherham Town (May 1913, retired May 1915); became a successful businessman in Sheffield; also played cricket for Yorkshire.

An FA Cup winner with Sheffield United in 1902, centre-half Bernard Wilkinson was short in stature but big in heart! He loved to attack and had a clever back-heel technique, often setting up his forwards with a deliberate flick.

He was awarded his only England cap against Scotland in April 1904 when he replaced Steel-city neighbour Tom Crawshaw from Sheffield Wednesday. He did well against a below-par centre-forward Bobby Walker and, wrote Bedouin in the *Daily Record*: "In the middle line Leake of Aston Villa was the mainspring... but Wolstenholme and Wilkinson played their part in a 1-0 victory."

WILKINSON, Leonard Rodwell 1890-91 ①

Born: Highgate, London, 15 October 1868
Died: Dulwich, London, 9 February 1913
Career: Charterhouse School (seasons 1886-88), Christ Church College/Oxford University (seasons 1888-92); also played for Corinthians (seasons 1890-93); Old Carthusians (seasons 1890-98); called to the Bar in 1893.

Twice an FA Amateur Cup winner with Old Carthusians (1894 and 1897), Len Wilkinson was a very capable goalkeeper, lithe in movement who at times pulled off some breathtaking saves, with hands, arms, body and feet... he seemed to throw himself at the ball whenever he could.

Called up by England for the game against Wales at Sunderland in March 1891, he didn't let his side down, produced three outstanding saves and also, from one of his long downfield clearances, a goal was scored as England won 4-1. Wilkinson, in fact, was one of four different goalkeepers used by England between March 1890 and April 1901.

He died at the relatively young age of 44.

WILLIAMS, Bert Frederick, MBE 1948-56 ㉔

Born: Bradley, Bilston, 31 January 1920
Career: Bilston & District Schools, Thompson's FC/Wolverhampton, Walsall (amateur, August 1936, professional, April 1937), Wolverhampton Wanderers (£3,500, September 1945, retired, May 1957); served in the RAF during WW2; ran a sports outfitters in Bilston for many years, also opened a goalkeeping school for local youngsters, and in December 2011, a Leisure Centre in Bilston was named and opened after him (The Bert Williams Leisure Centre).

Bert Williams was between the posts when England lost 1-0 to the USA in a World Cup group game in Belo Horizonte in June 1950. Recalling the match quite vividly, the Wolves goalkeeper said: "There were about seven minutes remaining before half-time. Tom Finney had just hit a post and I thought, here we go, we are on our way. But then the Americans launched an attack and I seemed well-positioned to collect a harmless-looking shot from Bahr, only for Gaetjens, a Haitian-born centre-forward, to suddenly arrive in front of me to divert the ball with his head into the net. I couldn't believe it, nor could my team-mate Billy Wright or Lawrie Hughes who looked at each other aghast."

Shortly before the World Cup tournament, Williams had produced one of the finest one-handed saves ever seen at Hampden Park when he stopped Billy Liddell's pile-driver at full length to earn England a 1-0 win and with it qualification for the World Cup.

In the 3-2 international Championship defeat by Scotland at Wembley in April 1951, Williams had the ball literally kicked out of his hands by Hibs' striker Lawrie Reilly. It bounced down nicely for Billy Liddell to score and give the Scots a 3-1 lead. And then against France at Highbury in the October of that same year, his brilliant late save from Jacques Grumellon enabled England to earn a 2-2 draw.

Capped initially against France in May 1949 - when he replaced Frank Swift - Williams remained first-choice for England until October 1951, appearing in 18 out of 19 internationals. Ousted by Gil Merrick, he later returned to take his tally of full caps to 24.

Nicknamed the 'Cat' for his acrobatic performances in goal, Williams was alert, confident and fearless and made 420 appearances for Wolves, helping the Molineux club win the FA Cup in 1949 and the First Division championship in 1954.

The oldest former England international alive today, he was awarded the MBE (for services to sport and the Alzheimer's Society) in the Queen's Birthday honours list in June 2010.

WILLIAMS, Owen 1922-23 ②

Born: Ryhope, County Durham, 3 September 1896
Died: Durham, 9 December 1960
Career: Sunderland Schools, Ryhope Colliery, Sunderland (trial, 1912), Manchester United (amateur, May 1913), Easington Colliery Welfare, Clapton Orient (professional, July 1919), Middlesbrough (£3,000, February 1924), Southend United (£250, July 1930), Shildon FC (May 1931, retired, May 1933).

A canny outside-left, Owen Williams made almost 400 appearances at club level during an 18-year career. He helped Middlesbrough twice win the Second Division title in 1927 and 1929 and before gaining his two full caps, he had played for England at schoolboy level. He made his international debut in a 2-0 win over Ireland at The Hawthorns in October 1922 when he replaced Billy Smith (Huddersfield). He did well and played in the next game, a 2-2 draw with Wales at Cardiff. Unfortunately for Williams there were at last six other outside-lefts doing the business in the Football League during the early 1920s and he was never selected for his country again.

WILLIAMS, Steven Charles 1982-85 ⑥

Born: Romford, Essex, 12 July 1958
Career: St Edward's Church of England School/Romford, Chadwell
Heath, Havering Schools, London Selection Centre (Southampton
Academy), Crystal Palace (associated schoolboy, 1972), Southampton
(apprentice, September 1974, professional, July 1976), Arsenal
(£550,000, December 1984), Luton Town (£300,000, July 1988),
Southampton (trial, July 1991), Exeter City (player/assistant-manager,
August 1991-January 1993), Derry City (briefly in season 1993-94);
after retiring he went into the magazine publishing business in Exeter
which he eventually sold out to a partner; in 2003, he was involved in
property development in South Devon.

Hard-working midfielder Steve Williams made his England debut – as
did four other players – in the 0-0 draw with Australia in Sydney in June
1983. The press agreed that he had a 'decent game' alongside Mark
Barham, John Gregory and Gordon Cowans in a 4-4-2 system.
   He lined up in the next game, also against the Aussies three
days later, and went on to play against France in February 1984 and
East Germany, Finland and Turkey, the latter two being World Cup
qualifiers, during the first half of the 1984-85 season. Before being
substituted against the Turks, he assisted in one of Bryan Robson's
three goals in an emphatic 8-0 victory.
   A self-confessed 'bad loser' Williams was somewhat
temperamental but when he put his mind to it, he could be
outstanding, driving forward with confidence. Besides his six
England senior appearances, he also played in four 'B' and 14 U21
internationals. He helped Arsenal win the League Cup in 1987 and
made over 470 club appearances (349 for Southampton).
   He was assistant-manager to his former Southampton team-
mate and fellow England international Alan Ball at Exeter.

WILLIAMS, William 1896-99 ⑥

Born: West Smethwick, 20 January 1876
Died: West Bromwich, 11 January 1929
Career: Oldbury Road School/Smethwick, West Bromwich Hawthorn
(1888), West Smethwick FC (1889), Hawthorn Villa/West Bromwich
(1891), Old Hill Wanderers (1892), West Bromwich Albion (£20,
professional, May 1894, retired, injured, June 1901; retained as
club trainer, later engaged as coach; left The Hawthorns in 1902);
became a licensee on the Smethwick/West Bromwich border, near
to the Albion ground.

A brilliant, clean-kicking, sure-footed
left-back, Billy Williams' career was cut
short due to a tedious cartilage injury. He
was only 25 at the time of his enforced
retirement. He made 208 appearances
for West Bromwich Albion and gained six
England caps between February 1897 and
March 1899, lining up in victories over
Ireland (6-0 and 3-2), Wales (3-0), Scotland
(3-1), Ireland again (13-2) and Wales (4-0).
   In that record breaking win over the Irish at Sunderland in
February 1899, he set up a goal for G.O. Smith and made two last-
gasp tackles to deny the visitors early in the first-half.

WILLIAMSON, Ernest Clarke 1922-23 ②

Born: Murton Colliery, County Durham, 24 May 1890
Died: Norwich, 30 April 1964
Career: Murton Red Star (August 1906), Wingate Albion (May
1909), Croydon Common (June 1913); served with the Footballers'
Battalion RASC during WW1; Arsenal (guest, August 1916-April
1919, signed for £200, May 1919), Norwich City (June 1923,

retired, May 1926); was a licensee in Norwich for 24 years; also a
first-class cricketer.

A cool, efficient goalkeeper, Ernie Williamson made 235 first-team
appearances (at all levels) for Arsenal, having his best seasons
at Highbury in 1921-22 and 1922-23. At the end of the latter he
gained his two England caps, both against Sweden, in 4-2 and 3-1
wins in Stockholm during the May tour. At the time Edward Taylor
(Huddersfield Town) was England's first-choice 'keeper. Williamson
also played in one unofficial international.

WILLIAMSON, Reginald Garnet 1904-12 ⑦

Born: North Ormesby, Yorkshire, 6 June 1884
Died: Middlesbrough, 11 August 1943
Career: Coatham Grammar School near Redcar, Redcar Crusaders
(1899), Middlesbrough (July 1901, retired, May 1924); became an
engineer's draughtsman.

The first goalkeeper to score an own-goal in an international match
was England's 'Tim' Williamson (Middlesbrough) who conceded
against Ireland in February 1905, doing so on his own ground
(Ayresome Park). The game ended in a 1-1 draw.
   Williamson was also clearly at fault for Scotland's goal, scored by David
Wilson, in the 1-1 draw at Hampden Park in March 1912. The reporter
stated that he 'would have saved the shot 99 times out of 100.'
   In between times he had performed with a 'fair degree of
competence' in a 2-1 victory over the Irish in February 1911, in
successive victories over Wales (3-0 and 2-0) and also in another
1-1 draw with the Scots in April 1911 when he had a fine game, the
Daily Mail correspondent writing: "He was never once at fault."
   Williamson made a club record 563 League appearances for
Middlesbrough.

WILLINGHAM, Charles Kenneth 1936-39 ⑫ ①

Born: Sheffield, 1 December 1912
Died: Leeds, 10 May 1975
Career: Yorkshire Schools, Ecclesfield, Worksop Town, Huddersfield
Town (amateur, April 1930, professional, November 1931), Sunderland
(December 1945), Leeds United (player-coach, March 1947, retired as
a player, June 1948, remained as coach until May 1950), Halifax Town
(coach, seasons 1950-52); became a licensee in Leeds.

A terrier of a wing-half, small and aggressive, mainly defensive but a
good passer of the ball, Ken Willingham scored on his England debut
in a resounding 8-0 win over Finland in May 1937. Thereafter, he
had a 'quiet' game against Scotland (lost 1-0) but starred alongside
his Huddersfield team-mate Alf Young in a thrilling 6-3 victory over
Germany in Berlin in May 1938. He then played his part in wins over
France (4-2), FIFA (3-0), Norway (4-0), Ireland (7-0) and Scotland (2-1).
However, he found it tough against Italy (2-2) and was off the pace in
the 2-1 defeat by Yugoslavia in May 1939, which brought him his last
full cap, although he did play in six Wartime internationals.
   Willington also represented the Football League on six occasions
and made 270 appearances during his 14 years with Huddersfield.
Also an exceptionally talented sportsman, as a schoolboy he set
several records on the running track.

WILLIS, Arthur 1950-51 ①

Born: Denaby Main, Yorkshire, 2 February 1920
Died: Haverfordwest, Wales, 7 November 1987
Career: Tottenham Hotspur (amateur, August 1938); loaned out to
Northfleet and Finchley during seasons 1938-39; Tottenham Hotspur
(professional, January 1944), WW2 guest for Millwall; Swansea Town
(player-coach, September 1954), Haverfordwest (player-manager,
May 1960-June 1962).

A really tough left-back, strong in all areas of defensive play, Arthur Willis formed a fine partnership at White Hart Lane with Alf Ramsey and, in fact, they lined up together for England against France at Highbury in October 1951, both having decent games in the 2-2 draw. Bill Eckersley (Blackburn), Lionel Smith (Arsenal) and Tom Garrett (Blackpool) were also vying for the left-back position at that time.

Willis spent over a decade as a senior squad member with Spurs for whom he made 273 first-team appearances at various levels. He played for Swansea in the 1956 Welsh Cup final.

WILSHAW, Dennis James 1953-57 ⑫ ⑨
Born: Stoke-on-Trent, 11 March 1926
Died: Stoke-on-Trent, 10 May 2004
Career: Hanley High School/Stoke-on-Trent, Packmoor Boys Club, Wolverhampton Wanderers (professional, March 1944); Walsall (loan, May 1946-September 1948); WW2 guest for Port Vale (1946); Stoke City (December 1957, retired, injured, July 1961); was a schoolteacher by profession, he was a scout for Stoke City during the late 1960s.

A centre-forward or inside-left, strong and mobile, Dennis Wilshaw scored with two brilliant headers either side of half-time in England's 4-1 win over Wales in October 1953 and then, just 18 months later he created a record by becoming the first player to net four times in an international at Wembley when England thrashed Scotland 7-2 in April 1955.

Stanley Matthews was the engineer and Wilshaw the executioner in this annihilation of the Scots. He cracked in his first goal after just 55 seconds and his other three came in the space of 13 minutes during the last third of the game.

He later netted twice in a 3-0 win over Northern Ireland in November 1955 and once in a 5-1 victory over Finland in May 1956. Goalless in his other eight England games – and that wasn't for the want of trying – he played exceptionally well alongside the likes of Tommy Taylor (Manchester United) and Nat Lofthouse (Bolton) and was desperately unlucky not to score in the 1-1 draw with Spain in Madrid in May 1955, twice striking the outside of the woodwork and having a fine header saved.

He scored 117 goals in 232 appearances for Wolves whom he helped win the First Division Championship in 1954 and followed up with another 50 in 100 games for Stoke. Wilshaw unfortunately broke his leg in an FA Cup-tie against Newcastle in 1961, having made his League debut for Wolves against the Geordies 12 years earlier.

WILSHERE, Jack 2010-13 ⑦
Born: Stevenage, Herts, 1 January 1992
Career: Whitehill Junior & Priory Senior Schools, Arsenal (apprentice, April 2008, professional May 2008), Bolton Wanderers (loan, January-May 2010)

Energetic, all-action and skilful midfielder Jack Wilshere was 18 years and 223 days old when made his senior England debut as a late substitute for Steven Gerrard in the 2-1 friendly win over Hungary at Wembley in August 2010.... and before he had touched the ball, so pumped up was he that he was lucky to be yellow-carded and not shown a red! He made his first start for his country in February 2011, playing the first 45 minutes of a 2-1 win in Denmark. Wilshere, highly-rated by his manager at Arsenal, Arsene Wenger, suffered a stress fracture of the ankle which sidelined him for 14 months. Nevertheless, he came back with all guns blazing (he was even sent off against Manchester United) and after a handful of outings for the Gunners, he returned to international duty with England in the 4-2 friendly defeat in Sweden in November 2012. Voted PFA Young Footballer of the Year for 2011, he looks set for an excellent career at both club and international level.

WILSON, Charles Plumpton 1883-84 ②
Born: Roydon, Norfolk, 12 May 1859
Died: East Dereham, Norfolk, 9 March 1938
Career: Uppingham School (1874), Marlborough College (seasons 1875-77, played rugby), Trinity College/Cambridge (seasons 1877-81, rugby and cricket blue, not football); played for Hendon, Casuals, Corinthians during 1880s; represented Norfolk County (seasons 1881-85); also a good road and track cyclist; brother of G. P. Wilson (below); Master at Elstree School (years 1881-98), then joint-headmaster at Sandroyd School, Cobham, Surrey (years 1898-1920).

A wing-half blessed with strength and stamina, strong at heading, Charles Wilson was playing for Hendon when he made his England debut in the 1-0 defeat by Scotland at Cathkin Park, Glasgow in March 1884. He is one of only three players, the others being John Sutcliffe and Reg Birkett, who have won full caps for England at both rugby union and football.

WILSON, Claude William 1878-81 ②
Born: Banbury, Oxon, 9 September 1858
Died: Brighton, 7 July 1881
Career: Brighton College (seasons 1876-78), Exeter College/Oxford (seasons 1879-81), also played for Old Brightonians (season 1880-81) and Sussex County (seasons 1879-81)

An FA Cup finalist with Oxford University in 1880, Bill Wilson was a fine full-back whose life ended when he was only 22 years old. A lively, attacking player with powerful kick, he won his first cap against Wales at The Oval in January 1879 (won 2-1) and his second against Scotland two years later, also at The Oval (lost 6-1).

WILSON, Geoffrey Plumpton 1899-1900 ② ①
Born: Bourne, 21 February 1878
Died: Camberwell, London, 30 July 1934
Career: Rossall School (seasons 1894-96), Corinthians (seasons 1897-1902); also played for Casuals (briefly), Southampton (season 1901-02) and London Hospital (seasons 1902-15); qualified as a physician and surgeon in 1902.

The younger brother of Charles Wilson (above), Geoff Wilson was a neat and accomplished dribbling inside-left who loved to run with the ball. He scored on his England debut against Wales in March 1900, salvaging a point from a 1-1 draw in Cardiff. A month later he had a poor second game (v. Scotland, lost 4-1) and was never selected again.

WILSON, George 1920-24 ⑫
Born: Blackpool, 14 January 1892
Died: Blackpool, 25 November 1961
Career: Sacred Heart School/Blackpool, Catholic College/Preston, Kirkham Sunday School football/Preston; Morecambe FC (1910), Blackpool (professional, February 1912), Sheffield Wednesday (£3,000, March 1920), Nelson (£2,000, July 1925, retired, May 1930); was a licensee for 30 years, retiring from the Mere Park Hotel, Blackpool, in May 1961.

Rated the best centre-half in Britain during the early 1920s, George Wilson was fast over the ground, had excellent control and was terrific in the air. For all his efforts, however, he gained only 12 caps in four seasons, winning his first against Wales in March 1921 and his last against France in Paris in May 1924. He had Frank Moss, Jimmy Seddon and Harry Healless contesting the pivotal role with him. He also had four games for the Football League and during his career amassed well over 450 club appearances (434 in the Football League, 37 goals scored).

WILSON, Ramon 1959-68 (63)

Born: Shirebrook, Yorkshire, 17 December 1934
Career: Shirebrook Central Secondary Modern School, Langwith Boys Club, Langwith Junction Imperials, Huddersfield Town (amateur, May 1952, professional, August 1952), Everton (June 1964), Oldham Athletic (June 1969), Bradford City (player-coach, August 1970, retired, May 1971, became assistant-manager, then caretaker-manager, September-December 1971); became a funeral director; now retired, living in Slaithwaite near Huddersfield.

Early in his career, left-back Ray Wilson looked 'ordinary' when his opponent was a line-hugging winger with pace and skill. Indeed, one reporter said 'he could be made to look silly by a magician working the flank.' But Wilson worked at his game and in the mid-to-late 1960s was regarded as one of the best players in his position in Europe!

After four different left-backs had been given the chance to succeed Roger Byrne, Wilson entered the international scene against Scotland in April 1960, breaking his nose in the second minute, before returning to put on a fine display. He had got a sniff of the action and once in position, he stayed put, indicating that there was precious little chance of anyone else getting a call-up for the next eight years. During that time he had a couple of bad days! Perhaps his worst was when he was teased and tormented by the Russian winger Chislenko (who was also an international ice hockey player) on a snow-covered pitch at Wembley in December 1967.

Ray admitted that it was his mistake which led to West Germany's first goal in the 1966 World Cup final. He failed to clear his lines on the wet surface, allowing Helmut Haller to drive in the 13th minute opener. Thankfully, after that, he played exceedingly well and duly collected his winner's medal.

A niggling injury brought Wilson's England career to an end in 1968. He made 437 appearances at club level (283 for Huddersfield, 154 for Everton), gaining FA Cup winner's and loser's medals with the Merseysiders in 1966 and 1968 respectively. Only Kenny Sansom (86) and Ashley Cole (101), have won more caps than Wilson in the left-back position.

WILSON, Thomas 1927-28 (1)

Born: Seaham, County Durham, 6 April 1896
Died: 2 February 1948
Career: Sunderland Schools, Seaham Colliery, Sunderland, Seaham Colliery (season 1918-19), Huddersfield Town (June 1919), Blackpool (November 1931), Huddersfield Town (assistant-trainer, June 1932-August 1945); during the war he worked for British Dyes and from September 1945 until his death was trainer at Barnsley.

Tom Wilson helped Huddersfield Town win three successive League titles (1924-25-26) and the FA Cup (1922) while also playing in two losing finals (1920 and 1930). A real 'stopper' centre-half with outstanding heading ability, he was a good, precise passer of the ball and during his 12 years at Leeds Road made exactly 500 first-class appearances. Surprisingly he gained only one England cap, lining up against Scotland in March 1928 when, along with his team-mates, he was given a right real roasting by the 'Wembley Wizards' who won 5-1 on a sodden pitch.

WINCKWORTH, William Norman 1891-93 (2) (1)

Born: Earls Court, London, 9 February 1870
Died: Exeter, Devon, 9 November 1941
Career: Westminster School/London (seasons 1884-88), Old Westminsters (seasons 1888-94); also played for Corinthians (seasons 1890-94); retired May 1894, emigrated to Calcutta, India in 1895 where he went into business (until 1914); returned to England after the Great War.

Able to play at centre-half or inside-left, Bill Winckworth made a 'solid' international debut in a 2-0 win over Wales at Wrexham in March 1892 and followed up by scoring from his defensive position in his second game, a rousing 6-1 win over Ireland at Perry Barr, Birmingham in February 1893. Described as being 'dexterous, diligent, judicious and adept at heading' he often upset his team-mates by being somewhat over-elaborate with his passing.

WINDRIDGE, James Edwin 1907-09 (8) (7)

Born: Small Heath, Birmingham 21 October 1882
Died: Small Heath, 23 September 1939
Career: Small Heath Alma (amateur, August 1897), Small Heath FC/Birmingham junior, June 1899, professional, July 1901), Chelsea (£190, August 1905), Middlesbrough (£100, November 1911), Birmingham (free, April 1914, retired, June 1916); also played three games for Warwickshire CCC (1909-13)

Jimmy Windridge scored in six consecutive internationals (seven goals in total) over a three-month period from March to June 1908. Included in his haul was a fine equalizer in the 1-1 draw with Scotland in early April when his wicked right foot shot hit the underside of the crossbar before bouncing down over the line. He also netted with two fine strikes in the 11-1 demolition of Austria in June. An artful, skilful forward, he was strong, had an eye for goal and was always on the move. He scored a total of 89 goals in 289 senior games for his three League clubs, having his best spell with Chelsea, for whom he netted 58 times in 152 outings.

WINGFIELD-STRATFORD,
Cecil Vernon, CBE, CMG, CB 1876-77 (1)

Born: West Malling, Kent, 7 October 1853
Died: London, 5 February 1939
Career: Royal Military Academy/Woolwich, Royal Engineers (player, seasons 1873-1888; soldier until retiring in 1910, with the rank of Brigadier General; recalled to service during World War One; awarded the CMG in 1916, the CB two years later and the CBE after the War); also represented Kent (at football, seasons 1875-80)

The player with the longest name (29 letters in total) ever to play for England, centre-forward Cecil Wingfield-Stratford made his only international appearance in a 3-1 defeat by Scotland at The Oval in March 1877. He won the FA Cup with the Royal Engineers in 1875.

WINTERBURN, Nigel 1989-93 (2)

Born: Nuneaton, Warwickshire, 11 December 1963
Career: Birmingham City (apprentice, April 1980, professional, May 1981), Oxford United (free transfer, April 1983), Wimbledon (free transfer, August 1983), Arsenal (£350,000, May 1987), West Ham United (free, June 2000, retired, June 2003); became a TV soccer pundit.

Attacking left-back Nigel Winterburn, despite winning Youth honours for England, never played a senior game for Birmingham City. After a brief spell with Oxford, he helped Wimbledon gain promotion to the First Division and added U21 caps to his collection before moving to Highbury where, after replacing Kenny Sansom, he formed a wonderful partnership with Lee Dixon at Arsenal. He helped the Gunners win three League titles, two FA Cups, the League Cup and European Cup Winners' Cup while making a total of 587 senior appearances and collecting two England caps, both as a substitute, the first against Italy at Wembley in November 1990 (when he replaced Stuart Pearce) and the second against Germany in Detroit in June 1993 when he took over from Lee Sharpe.

A model of consistency, he remained a regular in the Arsenal side until 2000 when he was released to join London neighbours West Ham.

WISE, Dennis Frank 1991-2001 ㉑ ①
Born: Kensington, London, 15 December 1966
Career: Southampton (apprentice, April 1983), Wimbledon (professional, March 1985), Grebbestads IF (loan, autumn, 1985), Chelsea (£1.6m, July 1990), Leicester City (£1.6m, June 2001), Millwall (free, September 2002, then player-manager from October 2003-May 2005), Southampton (free, August 2005, acted as caretaker-manager briefly), Coventry City (free, January 2006, retired, May 2006); Swindon Town (manager, May-October 2006), Leeds United (manager, October 2006-January 2008), Newcastle United (Technical Adviser, January 2008-April 2009)

Aggressive, hard-working midfielder Dennis Wise celebrated his England debut with the only goal of a vital European Championship qualifier against Turkey in Izmir in May 1991. He somehow managed to scramble the ball over the line in the 32nd minute of a rather undistinguished game.

Selected initially by manager Graham Taylor, he was in and out of the national team during the next decade, averaging just two games per season. But when called into action, he certainly put himself about. He was in the squad for Euro 2000 and played in all three group games, against Portugal (lost 3-2), Germany (won 1-0) and Romania (lost 3-2).

Wise, who captained five of his six League clubs, had by far his best spells with Wimbledon and Chelsea and also with Millwall. He helped Dave Bassett's 'Crazy Gang' with Vinnie Jones & Co. win the FA Cup in 1988, played in two more FA Cup winning teams with Chelsea, as well as gaining League Cup and European Cup Winners' Cup medals, and developed and spotted some quality players at The New Den while leading the Lions to their first-ever FA Cup final in 2004. All told, Wise amassed 760 club appearances (593 in the Premiership/Football League) and scored 128 goals. He also played in one U21 and three B internationals, netting once for the latter.

WITHE, Peter 1981-85 ⑪ ①
Born: Liverpool, 30 August 1951
Career: Skelmersdale, Southport, Barrow (trial), Portland Timbers/USA, Port Elizabeth/South Africa, Acadia Shepherds/South Africa, Wolverhampton Wanderers, Birmingham City, Nottingham Forest, Newcastle United, Aston Villa, Sheffield United, Birmingham City (loan), Wimbledon (manager), Huddersfield Town (assistant-manager/coach), Aston Villa (Youth team coach); managed Thailand and Indonesia; now lives on the Joondalup Golf Resort, Joondalup, Perth, Western Australia.

Striker Peter Withe made his England debut in the 1-0 defeat by Brazil at Wembley in May 1981 – just after he had helped his club, Aston Villa, win the League title. And he came mighty close to equalising when his last minute header struck an upright. Two years later Withe topped a powerhouse performance by scoring a terrific goal in a 2-0 home win over Hungary, chesting down a Sammy Lee pass before rifling the ball home with a vicious cross-shot. He gained his last cap against Turkey in November 1984.

A tall, strong, combative striker, he had a nomadic career early on before settling down to help Nottingham Forest gain promotion to the First Division. Soon after that he became Ron Saunders' final piece in his championship and European Cup winning teams of 1981 and 1982 when he scored the winner against Bayern Munich in the latter.

WOLLASTON, Charles Henry Reynolds 1873-80 ④ ①
Born: Flepham, Sussex, 31 July 1849
Died: London, 22 June 1926
Career: Lancing College XI (seasons 1863-68), Trinity College/Oxford University (seasons 1868-70); also played for Clapham Rovers (season 1870-71), Lancing Old Boys (periodically), Wanderers (seasons 1871-78) and Middlesex County (during 1870s); engaged as a solicitor (from 1875); also worked as assistant-secretary and later secretary of the Union Bank, London (20 years: 1878-98).

The recipient of five FA Cup winner's medals, all with Wanderers in 1872, 1873, 1876, 1877 and 1878, Charles Wollaston had consummate skill in dribbling and possessed a stunning, precise right-foot shot and was, without doubt, one of the finest inside-forwards in the 1870s. He played in four full internationals, all against Scotland, the first ending in a 2-1 defeat at Partick in March 1874 when unfortunately he suffered a leg injury and was a passenger for 75 minutes. A year later he scored in the 2-2 home draw with Scotland at The Oval and in his last game, he captained the team in a nine-goal thriller at First Hampden which ended in a 5-4 defeat. Wollaston also appeared in one unofficial international.

WOLSTENHOLME, Samuel 1903-05 ③
Born: Little Lever, Lancs, 5 June 1878
Died: Wigan, 10 January 1933
Career: Darley Dale FC, Farnworth, Farnworth Alliance, Horwich (1896), Everton (1897), Blackburn Rovers (May 1904), Croydon Common (August 1908), Norwich City (May 1909), Chester (June 1913, retired, April 1914); Norddeutscher Futball-Verband FA/Germany (team coach/manager); interned at P-o-W camp in Ruhleben near Berlin during WW1.

Sam Wolstenholme was given a tough time by the partisan crowd on his international debut against Scotland at Celtic Park in April 1904 as some of the home players had reason to feel aggrieved by the reckless style in which they were tackled.

The *Daily Record* reporter wrote: "He is none too particular in the manner in which he meets his opponents."

Nevertheless Wolstenholme had a useful game and helped set up Steve Bloomer's winning goal, although a miskick by the home full-back Jimmy Watson handed the Derby striker an easy chance.

His other two caps came towards the end of the 1904-05 season, in a 1-1 draw with Ireland at Middlesbrough and a 3-1 win over Wales at Anfield. Wolstenholme never retreated at club or international level and throughout his career was regarded as one of the toughest defenders in the game. Brainy and thoughtful as well as being as hard as nails, he was rarely given the runaround by an opposing inside-forward and was usually able to counter the wiles of the trickiest of players. He made 170 appearances for Everton, 114 for Blackburn and 45 for Norwich and was interned along with fellow internationals Bloomer, Fred Pentland and Fred Spiksley during WW1, although all four persuaded the commandant to allow them to organise a League tournament among fellow prisoners. In addition to his three full caps, Wolstenholme played in two international trials (North v South) and represented the Football League.

Dennis Wise

WOOD, Harry 1889-96 ③ ①

Born: Walsall, 26 June 1868
Died: Portsmouth, 5 July 1951
Career: Walsall Town Swifts (1884), Wolverhampton Wanderers (professional, August 1885), Walsall (May 1891), Wolverhampton Wanderers (November 1891), Southampton (May 1898), Portsmouth (player-trainer, May 1905, retired as a player, September 1905, continued as trainer at Fratton Park until May 1912); became landlord of the Milton Arms, 200 yards from the Portsmouth ground.

Inside-left Harry Wood was regarded as a 'perfect gentleman and model professional' on the pitch and more so off it. He made an impressive England debut against Wales in March 1890 when he partnered Harry Daft on the left-wing and three weeks later scored a fine opening goal, in off the far post, in the 1-1 draw with Scotland at Hampden Park. It was then six years before he gained his third cap, in a 2-1 defeat by the Scots in Glasgow in April 1896 when he came in as a late replacement for Steve Bloomer.
    Nicknamed 'Wolf', Wood helped Wolves win the FA Cup in 1893 and also played in two losing finals, those of 1889 and 1896. After leaving the Black Country club he gained four Southern League championship medals with Southampton and played in two more losing Cup finals.
    He made a total of 380 club appearances and scored 194 goals, his best 'stats' coming with Wolves: 126 goals in 289 outings in two spells. His son played in goal for Southampton and Clapton Orient.

WOOD, Raymond Ernest 1954-56 ③

Born: Hebburn-on-Tyne, 11 June 1931
Died: Bexhill, East Sussex, 7 July 2002
Career: Newcastle United (amateur, May 1948), Darlington (professional, September 1949), Manchester United (December 1949), Huddersfield Town (December 1958), Toronto Roma FC/Canada (May 1965), Bradford City (October 1965), Barnsley (August 1966, retired, May 1967); went on to coach/manage in USA (Los Angeles Wolves), Canada, Zambia, Greece (Apoel), Kuwait and the UAE; also managed the national teams of Cyprus and Kenya; left football in 1982.

Ray Wood had far too many other fine goalkeepers to contend with when he was in his prime and ready to represent his country. The Manchester United number 1 managed just three senior appearances for England, played in one B and one U23 international and also starred in three games for the Football League XI. Replacing Gil Merrick after the summer World Cup in Switzerland, he made a satisfactory international debut in a 2-0 win over Northern Ireland in Belfast in October 1954 and a month later pulled off three terrific saves as England battled to beat Wales 3-2 at Wembley. His final cap came in May 1956 when, deputising for Reg Matthews, he was hardly troubled as England romped to a 5-1 win over Finland in Helsinki.
    He took over from Reg Allen at Old Trafford and over the course of nine years helped United win two League Championships and reach the FA Cup final in 1957. In the latter game he suffered a fractured cheek-bone as early as the sixth minute and played on the wing for virtually the remainder of the game as Aston Villa denied United the double by winning 2-1. The following year, after surviving the Munich air disaster, Wood, who had been replaced between the posts at Old Trafford by Harry Gregg, moved to Huddersfield where he stayed until 1965. He made well over 500 senior appearances during his career, 205 with United and 223 for the Terriers. He did extremely well as a coach/manager (worldwide).

WOODCOCK, Anthony Stewart 1977-86 ㊷ ⑯

Born: Eastwood, Nottingham, 6 December 1955
Career: Nottingham Forest (apprentice, June 1972; professional, January 1974), Lincoln City (loan, February-March 1976), Doncaster Rovers (loan, September 1976), 1FC Koln/Germany (for a German record fee of £650,000, October 1979), Arsenal (£500,000, June 1982), 1FC Koln (£140,000, July 1986), Fortuna Dusseldorf/Germany (free, June 1988; retired, June 1991; coach to May 1993); Vfb Leipzig/Germany (manager/coach, seasons 1993-95); Eintracht Frankfurt/Germany (coach, season 1995-96); became TV soccer pundit while living in Cologne; later returned to England where he started a sports media business with Viv Anderson.

Goalscoring forward Tony Woodcock made his international debut against Northern Ireland at Wembley in May 1978. He played 'efficiently well' and came close to scoring on two occasions in a hard-earned 1-0 win. Some 18 months later, against the same opposition, he was outstanding, scoring twice in a 5-1 win in Belfast.
    Woodcock then netted the winner (2-1) in the European Championship encounter against Spain in Naples in June 1980 and two-and-a-half years later, wearing a pair of borrowed boots, he struck twice in a 3-0 win over Greece in Salonika. One of his best England goals, however, followed in May 1984, a brilliant equaliser from the edge of the box in the 1-1 draw with Scotland at Hampden Park before an injury saw him replaced by debutant Gary Lineker. He was also capped twice by England B.
    In 1977-78, Woodcock proved the perfect foil to Peter Withe at Nottingham Forest, both strikers scoring 19 goals as the Reds won the League title. He later linked up splendidly with Gary Birtles and Trevor Francis at The City Ground and after leaving England for Germany, spent three excellent seasons with 1FC Koln. After returning to the UK, he was Arsenal's leading marksman in each of his four seasons at Highbury and in the away League game against Aston Villa in October 1983 he scored five of his side's six goals. At League level, Woodcock netted a total of 139 goals in 437 appearances.

WOODGATE, Jonathan Simon 1998-2008 ⑧

Born: Nunthorpe, Middlesbrough, 22 January 1980
Career: Middlesbrough (juniors, 1995), Leeds United (apprentice,
April 1996, professional, May 1997), Newcastle United (£9m,
January 2003), Real Madrid (£13.4m, August 2004), Middlesbrough
(loan, August 2006, signed for £7m, August 2007), Tottenham
Hotspur (£7.8m, January 2008), Stoke City (free transfer, July 2011)

There is no doubt that injury and controversy have seriously
affected Jonathan Woodgate's career. A tall, rugged, hard-tackling
defender, he did well at both Leeds and Newcastle and, in fact,
his performances at St James' Park led to Spanish giants Real
Madrid signing him for a huge fee in the summer of 2004. Injuries
blighted his time at the Bernabeu and he failed to make a single
appearance during the entire 2004–05 season. He then endured
an awful debut in La Liga, conceding an own goal and being sent
off for two bookable offences. He went on to play just 14 times for
Los Blancos before joining his home town club Middlesbrough and
then Tottenham for whom he scored the winning goal in the 2008
League Cup final victory over Chelsea. Sadly, more injury problems
virtually ruled him out of action for two seasons when he made only
four appearances before his departure to Stoke City on a pay-as-
you-play deal in July 2011.

Having represented his country at U16, U18 and U21 levels, he
made his England senior debut against Bulgaria in June 1999 under
manager Kevin Keegan, being the first player born in the 1980s to
win a full cap. He went on to play in eight full internationals, making
his last appearance in 2008.

WOODGER, George 1910-11 ①

Born: Croydon, Surrey, 3 September 1883
Died: Surrey, June 1961
Career: Thornton Heath Wednesday FC, Croydon Glenrose, Croydon
Wanderers, Surrey County, Crystal Palace (November 1905,
professional, July 1906), Oldham Athletic (£800, September 1910),
Tottenham Hotspur (May 1914, retired, injured, February 1915)

Able to play inside or outside-left, George 'Lady' Woodger was a
clever ball player who at times could be deceptively dangerous.
His only England appearance was against Ireland at The Baseball
Ground, Derby in February 1911 when he partnered one of the
goalscorers, Bob Evans, on the left-wing. He scored 115 goals in
229 League appearances for Oldham.

WOODHALL, George 1887-88 ② ①

Born: West Bromwich, 5 September 1863
Died: West Bromwich, 29 September 1924
Career: Hateley Heath School/West Bromwich, West Bromwich
Saints, Wednesbury Town (guest, 1881), Churchfield Foresters,
West Bromwich Albion (amateur, May 1883, professional, August
1885), Wolverhampton Wanderers (July 1892), Berwick Rangers/
Worcestershire non-League club (May 1894), Oldbury United
(October 1894, retired, May 1898).

George 'Spry' Woodhall scored in the 71st minute – England's
100th goal at senior level - and assisted with two others on his
international debut in a 5-1 win over Wales at Crewe in February
1888. This, in fact, was an away game, switched from Wrexham
due to the state of the pitch. A month later, he had a helping hand in
all five goals when Scotland were hammered 5-0 at Hampden Park.
Two of his pin-point corner-kicks were headed home by Lindley and
Hodgetts early in the game and soon afterwards he and Goodall
set up Dewhurst to make it 3-0. Woodall himself then touched on

a free-kick for Goodall to claim a fourth before half-time. The fifth
goal, also scored by Dewhurst, came from Woodhall's clever, angled
pass between Gow and Kelso, halfway through the second-half.

An FA Cup winner and scorer for West Bromwich Albion v. Preston
North End in the 1888 final, Woodhall and his club partner and fellow
England international Billy Bassett were regarded as the best right-
wing combination in the first two seasons of League football.

WOODLEY, Victor Robert 1936-39 ⑲

Born: Slough, Bucks, 26 February 1910
Died: Bradford-on-Avon, Wiltshire, 23 October 1978
Career: Chippenham (seasons 1925-28), Windsor & Eton (seasons
1928-31), Chelsea (professional, May 1931), Bath City (December
1945), Derby County (January 1946), Bath City (player-manager,
May 1947, retired, December 1949); worked as a licensee in
Bradford-on-Avon for many years.

A goalkeeper who came off his line more than most, Vic Woodley
was good at going down to deal with ground shots and was also
a fine shot-stopper at close quarters. He made his 19 senior
appearances for England in consecutive internationals between
April 1937 and May 1939. He made his debut against Scotland in
front of 149,547 spectators at Hampden Park (lost 3-1), and was
then on the winning side in 13 of his next 18 games, producing
brilliant performances in victories over Wales (2-1 at Middlesbrough
in November 1937), versus France (4-2 in Paris in May 1938) and
against Romania (2-0) in his last outing in Bucharest.

He also had a fine game when England beat the Rest of Europe
3-0 at Highbury in October 1938 but on his own admission, 'gave
away silly goals' in the 2-1 defeat in Switzerland in May 1938, in
the 4-2 Home International loss to Wales five months later and a
2-1 reverse against Scotland at Hampden Park in April 1939 when
once again the attendance topped 149,000.

Woodley also played for his country in two Wartime internationals
(v. Wales in November 1939 and Scotland in May 1940). He made
272 appearances for Chelsea and gained an FA Cup winner's medal
with Derby in 1946.

WOODS, Christopher Charles Eric 1984-93 ㊸

Born: Boston, Lincolnshire, 14 November 1959
Career: Nottingham Forest (apprentice, April 1975, professional,
December 1976), Queen's Park Rangers (£250,000, July 1979),
Norwich City (loan, March 1981, signed permanently for £225,000,
May 1981), Glasgow Rangers (£600,000, July 1986), Sheffield
Wednesday (£1.2m, August 1991), Reading (loan, October 1995),
Colorado Rapids/USA (free, May 1996), Southampton (free,
November 1996), Sunderland (non-contract, March 1997), Burnley
(free, July 1997, retired, August 1998); Rangers (goalkeeping coach
seasons 1999-2003), Everton (goalkeeping coach, since 2003).

Manager Bobby Robson awarded
goalkeeper Chris Woods his first cap
against the USA in Los Angeles in June
1985. He had very little to do in a 5-0
win. In and out of the team after that, he
finally established himself as a regular in
the senior squad following Peter Shilton's
retirement in 1990 and did very well until
David Seaman eventually took control. One
of Woods' finest displays for his country
was against France in the European Championships in Malmo in
June 1992. That day he pulled off four superb saves, one quite
magnificent from Papin's free-kick. Ironically he made his 43rd and

final England appearance against the USA in Boston in June 1993 – exactly eight years after his debut against the same country.

Woods, aged 18, was thrust into the spotlight in 1978 when he replaced the cup-tied Peter Shilton against Liverpool in the 1978 League Cup final. Still to make his Football League debut, he did exceedingly well and helped Brian Clough's team lift the trophy. Later he won the League Cup for a second time with Norwich City (1985). When he joined Rangers, the fee involved was a record paid by a Scottish club and the highest in British football for a goalkeeper. He helped the 'Gers win four Premiership titles and four League Cup finals. And between 26 November 1986 and 31 January 1987, the excellent Woods set a British first-class goalkeeping record by going 1,196 minutes without conceding a goal. As well as his 43 senior appearances, Woods also represented England at Youth, B and U21 levels, winning six caps in the latter category. A very capable goalkeeper, agile, courageous and consistent, he made almost 750 senior appearances during his lengthy career, 603 at League level.

WOODWARD, Vivian John 1902-11 ㉓ ㉙
Born: Kensington, London, 3 June 1879
Died: Ealing, London, 31 January 1954
Career: Ascham College, Clacton, Harwich & Parkeston, Chelmsford City (2 spells), Tottenham Hotspur (player, later a director), The Pilgrims (touring team), Chelsea (player, then director); an architect who played tennis and cricket (for Essex); he later became a gentleman farmer.

Vivian Woodward was a tall, elegant, upright forward, who had the complete armoury of skills – passing ability, strong shot, close ball control, speed, body swerve – and he was once described as 'The human chain of lightning, the footballer with magic in his boots.' His only deficiency was perhaps a lack of physical strength…but he made up for that with his cleverness on and off the ball, one contemporary saying 'Woodward has the power of thinking in his legs.'

One of the most celebrated players of his era, besides his full England career, he appeared in 67 amateur internationals (41 at competitive level, 44 goals scored), twice captained the United Kingdom to victory in the Olympic Games (1908 and 1912, scoring in the final of the first against Denmark), represented both the Football League and Southern League, toured South Africa with the FA in 1910 (scoring a total of 27 goals) and the Army gave him 'special leave' to play for Chelsea in the 1914 FA Cup final.

A prolific marksman throughout his career, scoring over 400 goals in total, including 100 in almost 200 games for Spurs and 34 in 116 starts for Chelsea, Woodward feasted on easy pickings a great deal. He netted seven times (some reference books say eight) in a 15-0 amateur international victory over France in 1906 and bagged a double hat-trick (six goals) in a 9-1 win over Holland three years later, giving him the honour of becoming the first player ever to score a double hat-trick in two games for his country.

In 1908 he claimed a four-timer when Austria were hammered 11-1 in Vienna in a full international. In fact, he scored in 14 of his 23 full internationals, including two on his debut against Ireland in February 1903 and two in his last outing against Wales in March 1911.

His tally of 29 goals for England in just 23 outings (14 as captain, 12 wins, giving him a 92.86 per cent success rate) remained a record for 47 years, until Tom Finney bettered it in 1958.

Remaining an article of faith to amateurism throughout his career, it is known that Woodward declined Spurs' offer of the bus fare to and from White Hart Lane and while in hospital in 1950, he uttered the word 'shocking' when informed that a player (Tommy Lawton) had been transferred for £20,000!

WOOSNAM, Maxwell 1921-22 ①
Born: Liverpool, 6 September 1892
Died: London, 14 July 1965
Career: Winchester College (seasons 1908-11), Trinity College/Cambridge University (seasons 1912-14), Chelsea (season 1914-15); served with the Montgomery Yeomanry and Royal Welsh Fusiliers during WW1; Cambridge University (seasons 1919-21), also played for Corinthians (seasons 1913-21, later becoming club president); Manchester City (seasons 1919-25), Northwich Victoria (June 1925, retired, May 1926); worked for ICI for 31 years (initially joining in 1919 and becoming personnel manager); was a fine golfer and rackets player, and was a champion at both Real and Lawn tennis (winning the men's Wimbledon doubles title with R. Lycett in 1921, while reaching the mixed doubles final that same year); also represented Great Britain in the 1920 and 1924 Olympic Games at Lawn tennis, winning gold and silver medals in the former in Antwerp.

Dubbed the Admirable Crichton of his day, Max Woosnam was in the same class as C.B. Fry. A courageous, hard as nails centre-half with a solid shoulder charge, he surprisingly played in only one full international, lining up against Wales at Anfield in March, 1922. He proved an able deputy for George Wilson and never put a foot wrong in a 1-0 win. Earlier in his career he had won caps as an amateur for both England and Wales and in 1922 suffered a serious leg injury from which he recovered to continue playing for another four years. His League career realised less than 100 appearances (93 coming with Manchester City).

His nephew, Phil Woosnam, played for Leyton Orient, West Ham, Aston Villa and Wales before moving to the USA where he was a key figure in establishing the NASL.

Seriously injured his leg (not broken) in April 1922.

WORRALL, Frederick Joseph 1934-37 ② ②
Born: Warrington, 8 September 1910
Died: Cheshire, 13 April 1979
Career: Witton Albion (season 1925-26), Nantwich Town (August 1927), Bolton Wanderers (briefly – illegally signed, early December 1928), Oldham Athletic (professional, mid-December 1928), Portsmouth (October 1931); WW2 guest for Crewe Alexandra (signed, April 1946); Stockport County (free, September 1946, retired, May 1947); Chester (coach, July 1948), later Warrington Rugby League club (trainer), Stockton Heath FC (manager, seasons 1953-55).

An FA Cup finalist with Portsmouth (1934) and later a winner in the same competition (1939), Fred Worrall was a fast, direct winger who hardly ever had a bad game. Despite his lack of inches, he was tough and willing and was described as a veritable 'Jack-in-the-Box.' After netting the only goal of the game on his England debut v. Holland in Amsterdam in May 1935, he had to wait 18 months, until November 1936, before gaining his second cap, scoring again, this time in a 3-1 victory over Ireland at Stoke when he also helped create a goal for Raich Carter. Worrall scored 90 goals in 424 League appearances during his career, bagging 71 goals in 337 first-team games for Portsmouth.

WORTHINGTON, Frank Stuart 1973-75 ⑧ ②

Born: Halifax, Yorks, 23 November 1948
Career: Liverpool (trial, June 1964), Huddersfield Town (apprentice, July 1964, professional, November 1966), Leicester City (£70,000, August 1972), Bolton Wanderers (£87,000, September 1977), Philadelphia Fury/USA (loan, April-November 1981), Birmingham City (£150,000, November 1979), Tampa Bay Rowdies/USA (loan, 1982), Leeds United (March 1982), Southampton (£30,000, June 1983), Brighton & Hove Albion (May 1984), Tranmere Rovers (player-manager, July 1985), Preston North End (player, February 1987), Stockport County (loan, November 1987, signed, March 1988), Cape Town Spurs/South Africa (April 1988), Chorley (October 1988), Stalybridge Celtic (December 1988), Galway United (February 1989), Weymouth (early 1990), Radcliffe Borough (season 1990-91), Guiseley (season 1991-92), Hinckley Town (player-manager-coach, July 1992), Cemaes Bay (briefly, 1993), Halifax Town (player-coach, mid-1993), Swindon Town (coach, December 1993-May 1994); became an after-dinner speaker.

Elvis Presley fanatic Frank Worthington was regarded by some of his team-mates as a 'maverick' in the England camp. A tremendously gifted striker, his appearances in an England shirt were limited to just eight games. Why? I honestly don't know.
He made his debut as a substitute for Stan Bowles against Northern Ireland at Wembley in May 1974 and played his last international against Portugal six months later. He netted two goals – the first in a 2-2 draw with Argentina a week after his debut, while his second beat Bulgaria in Sofia in early June.
He also played twice for England U23s and represented the Football League and during his extensive career (in the UK and abroad) he netted 298 goals in 905 club appearances (236 coming in 757 Football League games). He had his best years with Leicester (72 goals in 210 outings) and actually scored in each of 22 consecutive League seasons (1966 to 1988 inclusive). One can only speculate what he might have achieved if he had joined Liverpool instead of Huddersfield! Because, as a 15 year-old, Worthington was rejected by Anfield boss Bill Shankly who told him "You haven't got enough skill to make it with us – sorry."

WREFORD-BROWN, Charles 1888-98 ④

Born: Clifton, Bristol, 9 October 1866
Died: London, 26 November 1951
Career: Charterhouse School (seasons 1884-87), Oriel College/Oxford University (seasons 1888-91); also played for Old Carthusians (seasons 1893-98), Corinthians (seasons 1887-1903); served on FA Committee (seasons 1892-93 and 1895-1902); vice-President of FA from 1941 until his death; also international team selector; awarded Oxford cricket Blue in 1887 but withdrew through injury; played county cricket for Gloucestershire (seasons 1896-98); admitted a solicitor in 1895, he practised in London with baker, Jenkins & Co.

It is thought that Charles Wreford-Brown was the man who introduced the word 'soccer.' Around 1888, he was talking 'sport' with some colleagues when, asked if he was going to play rugger, he replied "No, soccer." Some anoraks say he took the letters 'SOC' out of Association to form the word soccer.
A centre-half with exceptional ability, he was ranked among the best ever and certainly enjoyed playing to the 'gallery.' He won the

FA Amateur Cup with Old Carthusians in 1894 and 1897 and gained the first of his four England caps against Ireland in March 1889 (won 6-1). He had to wait until March 1894 for his second (v. Wales, won 5-1), followed by his third v. Wales again in March 1895 and his fourth and last v. Scotland at Celtic Park in April 1898 when he played superbly in a 3-1 win.
Wreford-Brown's younger brother, Oswald Eric, toured Austria and Germany with the FA in 1899.

WRIGHT, Edward Gordon Dundas 1905-06 ①

Born: Earlsfield Green, Surrey, 3 October 1884
Died: Johannesburg, South Africa, 5 June 1947
Career: St Lawrence School/Ramsgate, Ramsgate FC; Queen's College/Cambridge University (seasons 1903-06); went on to play for Royal School of Mines, Worthing Reigate Priory, Leyton (two spells), Portsmouth (season 1905-06), Hull City (three spells, from February to 1910) and Corinthians (season 1906-10); also played for Sussex County; Hymer's College/Hull (lecturer); emigrated to USA in 1913, later resided in South Africa until his death.

The recipient of 20 England amateur caps, outside-right Ted Wright – the son of a clergyman – was one of the finest crossers of the ball when travelling at high speed. He also possessed fine footwork and had a tactical brain. He played in his only senior game for England against Wales at Cardiff in March 1906, having a 'decent game' in a 1-0 win.
There remains a doubt over which affiliation E.G.D. Wright belonged to in 1906 - Douglas Lamming quotes his clubs as being Cambridge University, Corinthians, Hull City and Portsmouth in 1906, yet nevertheless, lists Wright as being Hull City's first ever international.

WRIGHT, Ian Edward, MBE 1990-99 ㉝ ⑨

Born: Woolwich, London, 3 November 1963
Career: Ten-em-Bee FC/Woolwich (1978), Millwall (trial), Southend United (trial), Brighton & Hove Albion (trial), Greenwich Borough (1984), Dulwich Hamlet (early 1985), Crystal Palace (professional, August 1985), Arsenal (£2.5m, September 1991), West Ham United (£750,000, July 1998), Nottingham Forest (loan, August-October 1999), Celtic (free, October 1999), Burnley (free, February 2000, retired, May 2000); Ashford Town (Director of Football Strategy, March 2007), MK Dons (first team coach 2012); also engaged as a Sky Sports and BBC match summariser and TV presenter, and columnist for the *Sun* newspaper.

Ian Wright was handed his England debut by manager Graham Taylor in February 1991. He started in the 2–0 victory over Cameroon at Wembley and helped his country reach the finals of Euro 1992 in Sweden. Despite the fact that his international career spanned eight years (87 matches played under three different full-time managers) he only started 17 times and was a used substitute on 16 occasions.
In each of the seven seasons that followed the 1990 World Cup in Italy, Wright never scored fewer than 23 goals a season for his club but despite these feats, the most number of games he started for England consecutively was three, something he only did twice. Taylor, who became England's manager after the World Cup, only handed Wright nine starts and seven substitute appearances, as he opted instead to use a whole host of less prolific strikers, including Nigel Clough, Paul Stewart, David Hirst and Brian Deane. Wright did not make it into the squad for Euro 1992, missing out to Clough,

Ian Wright MBE

Gary Lineker, Alan Shearer, Alan Smith and Paul Merson. This was particularly surprising as Wright had been the highest goalscorer in England's top Division that season.

Five of Wright's nine international goals were scored under Taylor's management. These included an 84th minute equaliser in a 1–1 away draw against Poland in Katowice in May 1993 and four goals in the 7–1 away win against San Marino in Bologna, Italy, in November 1993, the final match of Taylor's reign as manager. Both of these matches were qualifiers for the 1994 World Cup in the USA, but England failed to qualify for the first time since 1978. Terry Venables replaced Taylor as national boss after the unsuccessful World Cup qualifying campaign but Wright's appearances in the side became even more limited. Despite featuring in four of the first five matches under Venables, albeit three times as a substitute, Wright never played under his management again. Ultimately, it cost Wright a place in the squad for Euro '96, where England reached the semi-finals as the host nation. Venables was subsequently replaced by Glenn Hoddle and having been in international exile for 21 consecutive matches, Wright was surprisingly recalled to the team by Hoddle in November 1996 when he came off the bench in a 2–0 World Cup qualifying victory in Georgia.

Four of Wright's nine international goals were scored under Hoddle's management... the winner in a 2–1 friendly win against South Africa at Old Trafford in May 1997 (although he later admitted that he handled the ball before netting)... the opener a month later in a 2–0 victory over Italy in the Tournoi de France.... two in the 4–0 World Cup qualifying victory over Moldova at Wembley in September 1997. He then produced arguably his best performance for his country in the vital 0–0 draw in Italy a month later, which secured his country's passage through to the finals. Unfortunately Wright missed out on the finals due to a recurrence of the hamstring injury which had ruled him out for much of Arsenal's double-winning campaign.

Following the 1998 World Cup, Wright appeared twice more for England as a West Ham player. He came on as a substitute in the 3-0 Euro 2000 qualifying victory in Luxembourg in October 1998 before winning his 33rd and final cap, a month later, in a 2-0 friendly win over the Czech Republic at Wembley, which also turned

out to be Hoddle's last game as manager.

Wright, who won his last cap at the age of 35, missed out on playing in Euro 2000 and in fact, only Mick Channon played more times for England without being selected for a World Cup or European Championships squad. At club level, Wright was outstanding, scoring 333 goals in 661 senior appearances including 117 in 277 outings for Palace and a then record 185 in 290 games for Arsenal, a total which was later beaten by Thierry Henry who netted 226 times in 370 appearances.

While he was still a professional footballer at Arsenal, Wright published his autobiography, *Mr Wright*. It was first published in hardback in 1996 by Collins Willow when Wright was still a professional player at Arsenal. It was then published in paperback in 1997 which included a brand new up-dated chapter.

In 1993, Wright wrote and released a single called "Do The Right Thing". The song was co-written and produced by Chris Lowe (of the Pet Shop Boys) and reached number 43 in the UK singles charts. And ten years later he was voted Crystal Palace's greatest-ever player.

WRIGHT, John Douglas 1938-39 ①

Born: Southend-on-Sea, 29 April 1917
Died: Bedlington, 28 December 1992
Career: Chelmsford (1935), Southend United (professional, July 1936), Newcastle United (£325, May 1938), Lincoln City (£600, December 1948), Blyth Spartans (player-trainer, December 1954, player-manager, May 1955, retired, May 1957, then club secretary, May 1957-November 1960).

Capped against Norway in November 1938, left-half Doug Wright had 'an enchanting artistry in ball control' which, to the annoyance of his colleagues and certainly his manager, he exercised far too frequently near his own penalty area! He captained Lincoln with grim determination, leading the Sincil Bank club to the Third Division (North) Championship in 1952. He made 338 League appearances during his career, including 74 for Newcastle and 233 for the Imps.

WRIGHT, Mark 1983-96 (45) (1)

Born: Berinsfield, Oxfordshire, 1 August 1963
Career: Oxford United (apprentice, August 1979, professional, August 1980), Southampton (£140,000, player-exchange deal, March 1982), Derby County (£760,000, August 1987), Liverpool (£2.2m, July 1991, retired, back injury, September 1998); Southport (manager, December 1999-June 2001), Oxford United (manager, June-December 2001), Chester City (manager, January 2002-May 2004), Peterborough United (manager, May 2005, sacked for gross misconduct, January 2006), Chester (manager, March 2006-May 2007 and again from November 2008).

Mark Wright had a disastrous debut for England in the 1-0 defeat by Wales at Wrexham in May 1984. He failed to get to grips with Mark Hughes who rose above him to head the only goal of a poor game.

Wright's solitary international goal himself was the winner in the World Cup encounter against Egypt (1-0) in June 1990 which catapulted England into the second phase of the World Cup tournament in Cagliari, Italy. He went forward to head home Paul Gascoigne's brilliantly flighted free-kick in the 59th minute.

His impressive performances at centre-back and sweeper during that World Cup competition were one of the reasons why Liverpool bought him from Derby. He was originally a surprise selection for the tournament as he was ahead of the higher-rated Tony Adams, who was not fully fit when the squad was named. Some suspected he was an emotion-driven choice, as he had missed the 1986 World Cup with a broken leg. However, his inclusion was justified as he was one of England's many stars that year as they reached the semi-final only going out to the eventual winners, Germany, on penalties.

Wright was subsequently selected in the Euro 92 championship squad. However, unknown to manager Graham Taylor and the rest of the England staff, Wright had aggravated an old Achilles tendon injury in a recent friendly, which his club, Liverpool, had kept quiet. In fact, the England boss was not notified until the day before the England squad was scheduled to leave for Sweden. In fact, Wright did not show up at the airport on the morning of departure and an anxious Taylor waited patiently for word on his fitness. When it became clear he would not play, Taylor applied to UEFA for permission to replace him with Tony Adams but was refused. Martin Keown replaced Wright in the team. Wright then struggled over the next four years to get back into the squad.

Wright ended up with 45 England caps to his credit but would surely have passed the 50 mark if it hadn't been for injury problems prior to the Euro 96 championship in England. His performances for Liverpool had alerted manager Terry Venables who gave him a shock recall for the international friendly with Croatia in April 1996 - four years after his previous cap. He also played in the friendly with Hungary the following month, which was to be his final international appearance, before he got injured.

During his lengthy career Wright amassed 664 club appearances (536 at League level). He played in 216 senior games for Southampton and 211 for Liverpool with whom he gained an FA Cup winner's medal in 1992.

Unfortunately Wright failed as a football club manager, his only honour coming in 2004 when Chester City won the Conference championship.

WRIGHT, Richard Ian 2000-01 (2)

Born: Ipswich, 5 November 1977
Career: Ipswich Town (apprentice, April 1993, professional, January 1995), Arsenal (£6m, July 2001), Everton (£3.5m, July 2002), West Ham United (free, July 2007), Southampton (loan, March-May 2008), Ipswich Town (free, July 2008), Sheffield United (non-contract, retired September 2010, retired, May 2011).

On his day Richard Wright was a pretty decent goalkeeper but nowhere near as good as several people thought he would be. He had the misfortune to concede an own-goal on his England debut against Malta in June 2000. He gave away a 31st minute penalty which was taken by Dave Carabott whose shot struck a post; the ball bounced out, hit Wright and rolled back over the line. Wright made amends later on by saving a second spot kick as England scraped home 2-1. He was a member of the Euro 2000 squad, where he was third-choice behind David Seaman and Nigel Martyn, and later won his second cap as a substitute in a friendly against the Netherlands in 2001.

His career at club level realised a total of 447 appearances. He made 342 appearances for Ipswich (in two spells), only 22 for Arsenal (as reserve to Seaman) and 71 for Everton. He was also honoured by his country at Youth, B and U21 levels.

WRIGHT, Thomas James 1967-70 (11)

Born: Liverpool, 21 October 1944
Career: Liverpool and Merseyside Schools, Everton (amateur, August 1961, professional, March 1963, retired, May 1974); later worked in the Merseyside docks.

Right-back Tommy Wright was handed his England debut in the European Championship third place play-off against Russia in Rome in June 1968. Reserve to Keith Newton, he later played in the 1970 World Cup in Mexico, when he was perhaps the least known of Alf Ramsey's squad, collecting his last cap in the 1-0 defeat by Brazil in Guadalajara. His performance in that game was his best in an England shirt. Unfortunately he was forced to retire with a serious injury in 1972 and took up a new career working in the docks on Merseyside. Also capped by his country at Youth, B and U21 levels, Wright played in one unofficial international and appeared in 374 first-class games during his time at Goodison Park, gaining FA Cup and League Championship winner's medals in 1966 and 1970 respectively.

WRIGHT, William Ambrose, CBE 1946-59 (105) (3)

Born: Ironbridge, Shropshire, 6 February 1924
Died: Barnet, 3 September 1994
Career: Madeley Schools, Wolverhampton Wanderers (trial, March 1938), Cradley Heath (briefly), Wolverhampton Wanderers (groundstaff, June 1938, professional August 1945, retired, August 1959); WW2 guest for Leicester City; England U23 (manager), Arsenal (manager), Wolverhampton Wanderers (director, May 1990 until his death); also worked for ATV (Birmingham) for many years, becoming Head of Sport.

Wrote one newspaper reporter: "Billy Wright, amid the shifting sands of half-backs who came and went, assumed an unflappable and at times heroic indispensability at the heart of England's defence."

Among the many players who achieved greatness on the international scene, Wright was the first footballer in the world to win 100 caps for his country, gaining a record 70 in succession between October 1951 and May 1959. Indeed, he skippered England no less than 90 times (a figure later matched by Bobby Moore) and led his country for the first time in October 1948 when Northern Ireland went

Billy Wright CBE

down 6-2 at Windsor Park. He was only 24 years and 245 days old at the time. England won 49 and drew 22 of the internationals when Wright was captain.

Wright's first international goal came in Frank Swift's last international – in a 3-1 win over France in Paris in May 1949 and, in fact, it was the first scored by an English defender since WW2.

Six months later, Wright was on target again, this time in a 2-0 win over Italy at White Hart Lane. It was a 'goal in a million' for the captain and it clinched the victory. He simply lobbed the ball forward from the halfway line towards the visitors' penalty-area and as the Italian 'keeper came out to collect, a gust of wind caught it and sent it sailing over his head and into the unguarded net.

His third and final England goal was scored against Northern Ireland in October 1950 – a shot that flew through the legs of 'keeper Hugh Kelly in a 4-1 win at Windsor Park.

Wright was dropped from the England for the first time in May 1951 when Jim Taylor of Fulham played against Portugal. Quickly back in the team, he never suffered that humiliation again.

The first time Wright appeared at centre-half was in the 5-2 victory over Wales in November 1952. He was given a tough time by the fiery Trevor Ford but came through with flying colours. He also had a few hard tussles with John Charles, the giant Welsh centre-forward. In a terrific battle at Wembley in November 1954, Wright managed to shut out the big man for most of the game but Charles took his two chances well yet couldn't stop England from winning 3-2.

Wright was one of several England defenders who were bemused by the brilliance of the Hungarian forwards when they rattled in 13 goals when winning 6-3 at Wembley and 7-1 in Budapest in the space of six months: November 1953-May 1954. As he came off the pitch in Hungary, his face was as a white as a sheet….like a man who had just seen a ghost come back to haunt him….but in all honesty he had just been given the runaround for the second time by the 'Galloping Major' himself, Ferenc Puskas. "I couldn't get near him," said the England skipper.

Wright conceded two penalties playing for England. His second proved crucial when Jimmy McIlroy's rebound went in off 'keeper Eddie Hopkinson to set up Northern Ireland's 3-2 win at Wembley in November 1957.

Wright became the first footballer ever to win 100 caps for his country when he led England to victory over Scotland at Wembley in April 1959.

His last England game was against the USA in May 1959 when he starred in an 8-1 win at the Wrigley Field stadium in Los Angeles. A crowd of 57,000 had seen his debut in 1946, but there were only 13,000 present to see him say farewell.

During a period of uncertainty, the team relied on players like the Wolves defender whose style was undemonstrative and highly efficient, and although he had many critics, many from the London Press, but also a team-mate, none other than Stanley Matthews, who said "He never inspired me when I played with him in international matches."

Wright's senior international career lasted for 12½ years and he participated in three World Cups: 1950-54-58.

A one-club man, he amassed a grand total of 541 appearances for Wolves and scored six goals. Married to Joy Beverley (one of the famous singing sisters) he was associated with the Black Country club (as a player and director) for 25 years. A £5m stand at Molineux was named in his honour and today a statue of the former Wolves and England defender stands proudly outside the main entrance to the club's ground.

WRIGHT-PHILLIPS, Shaun Cameron 2004-12 (36) (6)

Born: Lewisham, London, 25 October 1981

Career: Haberdashers' Aske's Hatcham College, New Cross Gate/London; Nottingham Forest (junior, 1993, apprentice, April 1997, professional, October 1998), Manchester City (October 1999), Chelsea (£21m, July 2005), Manchester City (£9m, August 2008), Queens Park Rangers (August 2011)

Shaun Wright-Phillips made his England debut as a substitute against Ukraine in August 2004, scoring a fine late goal in a 3-1 win. A real bundle of energy, he was frequently called upon throughout England's World Cup qualifying campaign. However, after a decline in form, especially a poor performance away to Northern Ireland, and a lack of games following his move to Chelsea, he missed out on a place in the 2006 World Cup squad. Mainly a right-sided midfielder (a winger really) he played on the flank during England's two Euro 2008 qualifiers against Macedonia and Croatia and in the 2-1 friendly defeat by Germany at the new Wembley Stadium when he was named 'Man of the Match' by the sponsors after an impressive performance. Selected to start against Israel in early September, he scored the first goal in the 3–0 victory and again took the 'Man of the Match' award. On target in a 3-0 victory over Estonia soon afterwards, he was then substituted (by David Beckham) during the second-half of the critical Euro 2008 qualifying game against Croatia, which was eventually lost 3-2 and with it a place in Euro 2008.

Further appearances for his country followed against Germany in Berlin and Belarus at Wembley (when he scored) when perhaps surprisingly, with Wayne Rooney absent, he was joined by Tottenham Hotspur's Aaron Lennon, meaning England played with two recognised wingers. He then netted versus Egypt in March 2010, and set up Peter Crouch for the third as England came from behind to win 3–1. He was selected for England's final 23 man squad for the 2010 World Cup in South Africa. This came as a shock to many journalists who had thought that the dropped Theo Walcott would be in the squad instead.

Once described as being one of 'the most exciting talents in the game' inconsistency has let Wright-Phillips down many times. Nevertheless, in 2011-12 he reached the personal milestone of 400 club appearances, having already won the First Division (2002) and FA Cup (2011) with Manchester City and the Premiership (2006) and FA Cup and League Cup double (2007) with Chelsea. He has also played in six U21 internationals.

Shaun Wright-Phillips

WYLIE, John George 1877-78 ① ①

Born: Shrewsbury, 2 June 1854
Died: Wandsworth, London, 30 July 1924
Career: Shrewsbury School (April 1866-May 1870); Shropshire Wanderers (seasons 1870-72); trained as a solicitor in Sheffield and played for Sheffield FC; also represented the Sheffield FA (1870s); Wanderers (January 1875-November 1879); later joined a practice in Putney, London.

An FA Cup winner with Wanderers in 1878, Jack Wylie was strong, fast and enterprising and could play in any forward position. Perhaps a shade too individualistic at times for his team-mates, he collected his only England cap against Scotland in March 1878, and despite scoring, he had, according to the *Bell's Life* reporter, '...a rather quiet game' in a humiliating 7-2 defeat at the Queen's Park Ground, Glasgow. He was described by C. W. Alcock in the 1879 'Football Annual' as being 'a good centre, with pace and strength (who) should play for his side more'.
  A very capable athlete, Wylie took part in the National Olympian Games held at Shrewsbury in 1879, when he won a cup presented for the Pentathlon by King George I of Greece. He was also joint winner in the high jump, won a heat in the quarter-mile handicap, and came third in heats of 100 yards and 120 yards hurdles and finished third in pole leaping.

YATES, John 1888-89 ① ③

Born: Blackburn, summer, 1861
Died: Blackburn, 1 June 1917
Career: Accrington (August 1879), Blackburn Olympic (August 1880), Accrington (February 1886), Burnley (July 1888, retired, May 1894); was a cotton weaver by profession; also a licensee.

A positive left-winger, full of aggression and a useful goalscorer, Jack Yates won the FA Cup with Blackburn Olympic in 1883 and gained his only England cap six years later, having a brilliant game against Ireland at Anfield when he struck a hat-trick in a resounding 6-1 win. Everything went right for Yates, four shots, three goals and one assist, but surprisingly he was never chosen again. Licensee of the Brickmaker's Arms pub near Turf Moor for many years, he died from cancer, aged 56.

YORK, Richard Ernest 1921-26 ②

Born: Hockley, Birmingham, 25 April 1899
Died: Handsworth, Birmingham, 9 December 1969
Career: Icknield Street School/Birmingham, King Edward Grammar School/Birmingham, local junior and Army and RAF football, Aston Villa (amateur, March 1915, semi-professional, May 1915, professional, August 1919), Port Vale (June 1931), Brierley Hill Alliance (August 1935); Aston Villa (third team coach, seasons 1934-38); later worked as a plumber and decorator in Birmingham.

An FA Cup finalist with Aston Villa in 1924, Dicky Yorke was a fast-raiding right-winger, strong and direct who could cross a ball inch-perfect. Perhaps too eager to release the ball at times, he was nevertheless, a wholehearted club man who scored 86 goals in 390 games during his 12 years with Villa. His two England outings both ended in 1-0 defeats at the hands of Scotland, the first on his home ground (Villa Park) in April 1922, the second four years later at Old Trafford.

YOUNG, Alfred 1932-39 ⑨

Born: Sunderland, 4 November 1905
Died: Huddersfield, 30 August 1977
Career: Durham City (amateur, May 1926), Huddersfield Town (professional, January 1927), York City (November 1945); Køge

Boldklub/Denmark (coach, April 1946-May 1948), Huddersfield Town (coach, August 1948-May 1952), Bradford Park Avenue (manager, December 1957-November 1958), FC Esbjerg/Denmark (coach, November 1958-November 1960), Huddersfield Town (coach, December 1960-May 1964, then chief scout, June 1964-July 1965).

As strong as an ox, centre-half Alf Young 'would hurt you in the tackle' said Stan Matthews. An unflagging worker, confident on the ball, he was a terrific defender who would often carry the ball a long way upfield before either having a shot or turning round and passing it 30 yards back to a team-mate. He rarely wasted it! An FA Cup finalist in 1938 when he 'unwittingly' conceded a late penalty winner against Preston, Young won the first of his nine England caps in a 0-0 draw with Wales at Wrexham in November 1932, but with so many other talented pivots around at the same time, it was four years before he gained his second (v. Hungary at Highbury in December 1936). Although pushed hard by Stan Cullis after that he made a further seven appearances over the next two years before the Wolves centre-half took over on a regular basis.
  Young, a former colliery worker, who represented the Football League on three occasions, made 309 senior appearances for Huddersfield.

YOUNG, Ashley Simon 2010-13 ㉙ ⑦

Born: Stevenage, Herts, 9 July 1985
Career: Watford (apprentice, July 2001, professional, July 2002), Aston Villa (£9.65m, January 2007), Manchester United (£16m, June 2011)

Most of the time Ashley Young plays on the left wing, but during the 2009-10 and 2010-11 seasons he was handed the role of a 'roaming forward' with his club, Aston Villa, and after some very impressive displays, was called up to play the same role by England boss Fabio Capello. And he went out and scored his first international goal against Denmark in February 2011, striking home a 68th minute winner in a 2-1 victory over Denmark, having come on as a second-half substitute for Wayne Rooney. After that he was in and out of the team but when called up he never let the team down.
  He made 110 appearances for Watford (22 goals) and 190 for Aston Villa (38 goals) before his big-money move to Old Trafford. Young's younger brother, Lewis, joined Northampton Town in July 2011.

YOUNG, Gerald Morton 1964-65 (1)

Born: South Shields, 1 October 1936
Career: Croft Terrace School/Jarrow, Hawthorn Leslie Juniors/
Newcastle, Newcastle United (amateur 1953), Sheffield Wednesday
(amateur, May 1955, retired, May 1971; became reserve team
trainer-coach, then caretaker-manager, December 1973; remained
at Hillsborough until October 1975); Barnsley (coach, 1976-77);
went into business with former Wednesday player John Quinn
opening a sports and trophy shop on Middlewood Road which
stayed in business for many years

Left-half Gerry Young completely misjudged a through ball in the
second-half of the 1966 FA Cup final which led to Derek Temple
racing on to strike the winning goal for Everton after Sheffield
Wednesday had led 2-0. It was heartbreak for Young who prior to
that had been immense in a determined and resolute Owls defence.
   The previous season he had gained his solitary England cap
in a 2-1 win over Wales at Wembley in November 1964 when he
deputised for Bobby Moore. He made 335 appearances during his
16-year playing career at Hillsborough.

YOUNG, Luke Paul 2004-06 (7)

Born: Harlow, Essex, 19 July 1979
Career: Tottenham Hotspur (apprentice, July 1995, professional,
July 1997), Charlton Athletic (£3m, July 2001), Middlesbrough
(£2.5m, August 2007), Aston Villa (£5m, August 2008), Queens Park
Rangers (August 2011)

Luke Young snubbed Fabio Capello after being recalled to the
England squad for the game against Brazil in November 2009. The
attacking full-back had already won 17 U21 and seven full caps
for his country but had officially announced his retirement from
international football long before being chosen again for his country.
He had made his senior debut as a substitute in a 2-1 win over the
USA in Chicago in May 2005 and played his last England game
against Argentina in Geneva six months later, doing well in a 3-2
victory. Young made 76 appearances for Spurs, 210 for Charlton, 42
for Middlesbrough and 89 for Villa.
   *Young's 17 year old brother, Andre, was found dead on 12
August 2009 whilst on holiday, in Mali, Crete after sustaining head
injuries. "He was a tremendous and talented person and a diligent
student and this is such a waste of a promising life," said Luke.*

ZAHA, Dazet Wilfried Armel 2012-13 (1)

Born: Abidjan, Ivory Coast, 10 November 1992
Career: Crystal Palace (trainee, April 2007, professional, November
2009), Manchester United (£15m, January 2013); Crystal Palace
(loan, January-May 2013)

After representing England at U19 and U21 levels, wide midfielder
Wilfried Zaha was introduced by manager Roy Hodgson as a late
second-half substitute for Raheem Sterling in the 4-2 friendly
defeat in Sweden in November 2012 to become the first Crystal
Palace player to win a full England cap since striker Andy Johnson
v. FYR of Macedonia in September 2006. And he thoroughly
deserved his call-up after two excellent seasons for the Eagles in
the Premiership, being named the Football League's 'Young Player
of the Year' in March 2012. There's more to come from this young,
talented, aggressive midfielder, mark my words!

ZAMORA, Robert 2010-11 (2)

Born: Bromley, Kent, 16 January 1981
Career: Bristol Rovers (apprentice, April 1997, professional, July 1999),
Brighton & Hove Albion (loan, February-March 2000), Tottenham
Hotspur (£1.5m, July 2003), West Ham United (February 2004),
Fulham (July 2008), Queen's Park Rangers (£4.5m, January 2012)

Striker Bobby Zamora made his senior debut for England as a
second-half substitute in the 2-1 friendly win over Hungary at
Wembley in August 2010, having earlier in the year helped Fulham
reach the final of the Europa League. Strong in the air, unfortunately
he has suffered with injuries over the last three seasons but when fit
he can be a handful for the best defenders in the game. At the end
of the 2012-13 season, his club record was pretty good - 174 goals
in 482 senior appearances.

NOTES
* *Although the friendly against Argentina in Buenos Aires on 17 May
  1953, was abandoned in the 23rd minute due to a waterlogged
  pitch, caps were still awarded to the eleven England players who
  participated. The scoresheet was blank when the game ended
  prematurely.*
* *The international match, played in Dublin on 15 February 1995,
  between the Republic of Ireland and England, was abandoned in
  the 27th minute due to crowd violence with the Republic leading
  1-0 thanks to David Kelly's goal. Again, full caps were awarded for
  this fixture, yet no official result was declared.*
* *The FA refused to award caps to the 16 players who appeared
  for England against a selected Hong Kong XI in Hong Kong on 26
  May 1996. In the end the game was declared 'unofficial'.*

333

PLAYERS WHO APPEARED IN WARTIME/VICTORY INTERNATIONALS BUT DID NOT WIN A FULL CAP

(Figures in circles indicate the number of wartime caps won)

World War 1 - 1915-19

BALL, William
Dudley-born right-back Billy Ball of Birmingham was injured in the first-half of his only international against Wales at Cardiff in October 1919 and failed to take the field after the interval. He formed a great full-back partnership at St Andrew's with Frank Womack and helped Blues win the Second Division Championship in 1921.

BARNES, Horace
Capped once during the war, inside-left Horace Barnes scored 226 goals in 450 League appearances while playing for Derby County, Manchester City, Preston North End and Oldham Athletic between 1908 and 1927.

BROOKS, Samuel Ernest
Tricky left-winger Sammy Brooks scored 51 goals in 217 appearances for Wolverhampton Wanderers before going on to play for Tottenham Hotspur, Kidderminster Harriers and Southend United.

DUCKWORTH, Fred
Left-back Fred Duckworth won his two caps in 1919. He spent twelve years with Blackburn Rovers before retiring in 1922.

FLEETWOOD, Thomas ②
Right-half Tom Fleetwood also played in two internationals in 1919. Initially with Rochdale, he spent 12 years with Everton (1911-23) before rounding off his career with Oldham Athletic and Chester.

GRENYER, Alan ②
Left-half Alan Grenyer, who played against Wales at Cardiff in October 1919, served Everton for 14 years (1910-24) before assisting South Shields. He helped Everton win the Football League title in 1915.

HENDREN, Elias Henry
Outside-right 'Patsy' Hendren was with Brentford when he starred against Wales at Cardiff in October 1919. He also played for Manchester City and Coventry City but was more famous for his cricketing ability, appearing in 581 matches for Middlesex and in 51 Tests for England between 1907 and 1937. In all he scored 57,611 runs (amassing over 3,000 in a season three times) with a top-score of 301 not out for Middlesex against Worcestershire in 1933.

HILDITCH, Clarence George ①
'Lal' Hilditch, the Manchester United centre-half, was capped against Wales at Cardiff in October 1919. He also toured South Africa with the FA in 1920 and spent 16 years at Old Trafford (1916-32), acting as player-manager in 1926-27.

PARKER, Charles William
Centre-half Charlie Parker played against Wales on his home ground at Stoke in October 1919. He also represented the Football League and Southern League and after leaving the Potters in 1920 he signed for Sunderland, later assisting Carlisle United.

VOISEY, William
Right-half Bill 'Banger' Voisey played against Wales at Cardiff in October 1919 and then, twenty years later, when manager-trainer of Millwall, he was named as spongeman by England for several of their WW2 and Victory matches. During an extended career, he also played for Bournemouth & Boscombe Athletic, was trainer-coach at Leytonstone and trainer at Fulham.

WHITTINGHAM, Robert ①
A strong, forceful centre or inside-forward, Bob Whittingham played for Crewe Alexandra, Blackpool, Bradford City, Chelsea and Stoke between 1905 and 1920 and scored in his only international in the 2-0 win over Wales on his home patch at The Victoria Ground, Stoke in October 1919. He also represented the Football League and during his career netted 139 goals in 231 appearances. He died of TB in 1926 at the age of 37.

World War 2 - 1939-46

BACUZZI, Giuseppe Luigi Davide
Fulham right-back 'Joe' Bacuzzi made way for England's first-ever substitute – Jim Lewis – when he went off injured against Wales at Cardiff in November 1939. In February 1941, Bacuzzi conceded a headed own-goal to give Scotland a 3-2 victory over England at Hampden Park. The only player to appear in England's first and last WW2/Victory internationals, Bacuzzi made his final appearance against France in May 1946. His son, David, played for Arsenal, Manchester City and Reading in the 1960s.

BALMER, John
A League Championship winner with Liverpool in 1947, inside-forward Jack Balmer netted 111 goals in 313 appearances in peacetime football for the Merseysiders whom he served from 1935 to 1952. He netted a hat-trick in three successive League games in November 1946, against Portsmouth, Derby and Arsenal. He also scored in his only wartime game for England v. Wales at Cardiff in November 1939. He was the nephew of brothers William and Robert Balmer who played for Everton in the Edwardian era.

BARTRAM, Samuel
Making his England wartime debut against Wales at Wembley in April 1940, the Charlton goalkeeper was seriously at fault for the winning goal scoffed by Arsenal's Bryn Jones. Willie Hall had the chance to equalise but missed a penalty.

Bartram was selected against Scotland at Hampden Park the following month but the RAF refused him leave and Vic Woodley (Chelsea) was drafted into the team. Charlton's number one for over 20 years, Bartram made 623 senior appearances for the London club (1934-56), gaining Third Division (South) and FA Cup winner's medals in 1935 and 1947 respectively. He went on to manage both York City and Luton Town.

BROWN, Robert Albert John

Rugged inside-forward Albert 'Sailor' Brown played in one Test Match while on tour with the FA in South Africa in 1939, scored four goals in six Wartime internationals and won the FA Cup with Charlton (and Sam Bartram) in 1947. He also assisted Nottingham Forest and Aston Villa and was player-manager of Gorleston Town. Brown also scored in the unofficial international v. Switzerland in Berne in July 1945.

BUCKINGHAM, Victor Frederick

Capped twice in Wartime football (v. Wales in April and June 1941) left-back or left-half Vic Buckingham played for Tottenham Hotspur (1931-51) and after retiring managed Bradford Park Avenue, West Bromwich Albion, Ajax Amsterdam (two spells), Sheffield Wednesday, Fulham, Ethnikos/Greece (two spells), CF Barcelona and FC Sevilla. Also coach of Pegasus and the Middlesex FA, he guided WBA to FA Cup Final glory over Preston in 1954.

CLIFTON, Henry

Utility forward Harry Clifton scored in his only wartime international, a 2-1 win over Scotland at St James' Park, Newcastle in December 1939. An amateur with West Bromwich Albion, he played his League football for Chesterfield, Newcastle United and Grimsby Town, and also assisted Goole Town.

COMPTON, Denis Charles Scott, CBE

Scorer of two goals in 12 wartime games for England, outside-left Denis Compton was associated with Arsenal for 18 years from 1932, gaining League Championship and FA Cup winner's medals in 1948 and 1950 respectively. More famous for his cricketing ability than his football skills, he accumulated almost 39,000 runs for Middlesex CCC, cracking a record 18 centuries in 1947 when he finished with an amazing average of 90.85. He also appeared in 78 Test Matches for England (5,807 runs) and was awarded the CBE in 1958. His brother Leslie was capped at senior level by England.

CROOK, Walter

A League championship winner with Blackburn Rovers in 1939, left-back Wally Crook played in one Wartime international (v. Wales at Wrexham in November 1939). He joined Bolton Wanderers in 1947 and after retiring became manager-coach of Ajax Amsterdam, later managing both Accrington Stanley and Wigan Athletic as well as being a coach at Preston North End and back in Holland.

EDELSTON, Maurice

Inside-forward Maurice Edelston scored once in five England games during the hostilities, having previously played in nine amateur internationals and also for Great Britain in the 1936 Olympic Games v. China. At League level he played for Fulham, Brentford, Reading and Northampton Town before becoming a respected BBC radio commentator.

ELLIOTT, William Bethwaite

Speedy right-winger Billy Elliott made over 300 appearances for West Bromwich Albion (1938-51) after being rejected by Carlisle United and then Wolves. He won two Wartime caps and helped the Baggies gain promotion from the Second Division in 1949.

FENTON, Edward Benjamin A.

An England Schoolboy international centre-forward, Benny Fenton played left-half in his only Wartime international v. Wales at Cardiff in November 1939. A West Ham player from 1930 to 1946, he went on to manage Colchester United, his old club West Ham and Southend United. He also toured South Africa with the FA in 1939 (playing in three Test Matches) and appeared in the unofficial international against Switzerland in Zurich in July 1945.

FINCH, Lester Charles

Outside-left Lester Finch played twice for Great Britain in the 1936 Olympic Games soccer tournament, on 16 occasions for England at amateur level and in two Test Matches for the FA on tour in South Africa in 1939 before gaining a Wartime cap v. Wales in June 1941. Five years later he won the FA Amateur Cup with Barnet whom he served for 20 years from 1928. A clever footballer, he also assisted West Bromwich Albion, Wolves, Chelsea, Nottingham Forest, Walsall and Bournemouth as a Wartime guest and was registered briefly with Arsenal in the mid-1930s but never played.

FISHER, Frederick William

Outside-right Fred Fisher who played League football for Barnsley, Chesterfield and Millwall before the war, won his only cap against Wales in April 1940. He was killed in action in September 1944.

FLEWIN, Reginald

The Portsmouth central defender became the first serviceman from the Royal Navy to be selected by England during the war. He lined up at centre-half in the 2-2 draw with Wales at Anfield in September 1944. Flewin, who gained successive League Championship winning medals with Pompey in 1949 and 1950, also toured Canada and Australia with the FA in 1950 and 1951. After retiring as a player he managed Stockport County, Bournemouth and Hastings United.

GIBBONS, Albert Henry

'Jack' Gibbons represented Middlesex County and appeared in two Test Matches when touring South Africa with the FA in 1939 before gaining his only Wartime cap against Wales in October 1942. A player with Tottenham Hotspur, Brentford (two spells) and Bradford Park Avenue, he later travelled the world as a coach.

GOSLIN, Henry A.

Capped four times in wartime internationals as a Bolton Wanderers player, right-half Harry Goslin had spent 13 years at Burnden Park before he was killed in action in December 1943.

GREENHALGH, Norman
A First Division Championship winner with Everton in 1939, left-back Norman Greenhalgh also represented the Football League and played in one Wartime game for England v. Scotland in December 1939. He also assisted New Brighton and Bangor City at club level.

HANSON, Adolphe Jonathan
'Alf' Hanson played League football for Liverpool and Chelsea and won his only Wartime cap v. Scotland at Newcastle in February 1941. He went on to become player-manager of Shelbourne (Ireland) and Ellesmere Port Town.

HARPER, Bernard
Half-back Bernie Harper appeared in 228 first-class games for Barnsley before becoming player-manager of Scunthorpe United in 1946. He represented England against Scotland at Newcastle in December 1939.

JOHNSON, William Herbert
Capped twice by England in Victory internationals against France and Switzerland in May 1946, left-half Bill Johnson played the majority of his football for Charlton Athletic and Cambridge United before becoming a respected scout with Leicester City, Nottingham Forest, Derby County and Southampton.

KINSELL, Thomas Henry
Left-back 'Harry' Kinsell made both of his appearances in Victory Internationals against Ireland and Wales in September and October 1945. He also played in the unofficial international against Switzerland in Zurich in July 1945. A Football League player with West Bromwich Albion, Bolton Wanderers, Reading and West Ham United, he represented the FA, the Army, Combined Services and Western Command and during a lengthy career made almost 300 club appearances.

LEWIS, James William
Jim Lewis (of Walthamstow Avenue) became England's first-ever substitute when he replaced the injured Joe Bacuzzi (Fulham) in the international against Wales at Ninian Park, Cardiff in November 1939. This was his only 'cap'. Lewis played League football for QPR in the early 1930s. His son won the First Division title with Chelsea in 1955.

MAPSON, John
Goalkeeper Johnny Mapson spent 18 years with Sunderland (1936-54) during which time he made 345 appearances, gained an FA Cup winner's medal in 1937, toured South Africa with the FA in 1939 (playing in two Test Matches) and played for England in the Wartime international against Wales at The City Ground, Nottingham, in April 1941. Two months later he was chosen to keep goal against Wales at Cardiff but withdrew, choosing to play for Reading in the London Wartime Cup Final instead. He had a fine game, helping his side beat Brentford 3-2. In a lengthy career, Mapson also assisted Swindon Town, Reading and Guildford.

MARKS, William George
Arsenal goalkeeper George Marks was injured early on in England's game with Wales at Cardiff in May 1942. With no 'reserve' or 'substitute' available, he carried on bravely with heavy strapping around his stomach and back. England lost 1-0.

In all, Marks won eight Wartime caps between October 1941 and February 1943. He was with the Gunners for ten years (1936-46) and after leaving Highbury played for Blackburn Rovers, Bristol City and Reading.

MARTIN, John Rowland
A lively forward, Jackie Martin spent 14 years with Aston Villa (1935-49) during which time he made only 53 first-team appearances (22 goals scored). He guested for several clubs during the war and played for England against Wales (when he scored) and Scotland in season 1939-40.

MASON, George William
Tough-tackling Coventry City centre-half George Mason played against Scotland and Wales at the end of the 1941-42 season. He was at Highfield Road for 21 years (1931-52), helping the Sky Blues win the Third Division (S) title in 1936. He also played once for England at schoolboy level.

MOUNTFORD, Reginald Charles
An FA Cup winner with Huddersfield Town, whom he served for 15 years (1929-44) left-back Reg Mountford played in England's 3-2 home defeat by Scotland in February 1941. During the hostilities he guested for six different clubs and later coached the Danish national side at the 1948 Olympic Games.

OAKES, John
A solid centre-half who played for Nottingham Forest, Crook Town (two spells), Southend United, Spennymoor United, Aldershot, Charlton Athletic (1936-47) and Plymouth Argyle, John Oakes made his England debut in the first Wartime international v. Wales at Cardiff in November 1939. He won the FA Cup with Charlton in 1946. He was 87 when he died in Perth, Australia, in 1992.

PEARSON, Thomas Usher
Tom Pearson, a Scot, was a late replacement for car-crash victim Eric Brook against Scotland at St James' Park, Newcastle in December 1939. The Newcastle United outside-left was later capped for his home country against England and Belgium in 1947 and also represented the Scottish League as an Aberdeen player.

Brook and his Manchester City club-mate Sam Barkas were travelling together for the wartime game at Newcastle when they were involved in a three-car collision near Wath-on-Dearne, Yorkshire. Joe Richardson (next entry) stepped in for Barkas.

RICHARDSON, Joseph (1)
Newcastle United star Joe Richardson stepped in as a late replacement for Sam Barkas against Scotland on his home pitch (St James' Park) in December 1939. He served Newcastle for 48 years, as a player (from 1929) and then as assistant-trainer from 1944 until his death in 1977.

ROOKE, Ronald Leslie (1)
Centre-forward or inside-left Ronnie Rooke had a long and varied career which ran from 1928 until 1961. He had a trial with Stoke City and then served, in turn, with Woking, Guildford City, Crystal Palace, Fulham, Arsenal, Crystal Palace (again, this time as a player-manager), Bedford Town (two spells, the first as player-manager, the second as manager). He won the League Championship with Arsenal in 1948.

ROXBURGH, Alexander White (1)
A capable goalkeeper who played his club football for Manchester City (as an amateur), Blackpool, Barrow and Hyde United, Alex Roxburgh appeared for England against Wales in front of 80,000 fans at Wembley in September 1943, doing well in an 8-3 win.

SMITH, George Casper (1)
A pre-war centre-half with Bexley Heath & Welling and Charlton Athletic, George Smith served with Brentford, Queens Park Rangers, Ipswich Town and Chelmsford City after the hostilities and later managed Eastbourne United, Sutton United, Crystal Palace and Portsmouth, the latter from 1961-70. He was capped by England against Wales at Cardiff in May 1945 and captained QPR when they won the Third Division (S) Championship three years later.

SOO, Hong Yi (9)
'Frank' Soo was born in Liverpool and played for England eleven times - in seven Wartime, two Victory and two unofficial internationals, the latter against Switzerland in Berne and Zurich in July 1945.

A terrific wing-half with Stoke City (1933-45), he guested for Brentford, Chelsea and Everton during the War and went on to assist Leicester City, Luton Town (as player-coach) and Chelmsford City, and coached in Israel, Sweden and Italy as well as managing Scunthorpe United (1959-60) and St Albans City.

STUBBINS, Albert (1)
Between 1937 and 1946, red-haired centre-forward Albert Stubbins scored 194 goals in 261 appearances for Newcastle United (only six of them in 30 peacetime games). He also netted 83 times in 180 games for Liverpool with whom he won the League title (1947) and played in the FA Cup (1950). He gained his only England cap against Wales at The Hawthorns in October 1945 and represented the Football League on four occasions, scoring five times in a 6-3 win over the Irish League in October 1950. Later engaged as a scout at Anfield, he was the USA national team coach in 1960-61.

SWINBURNE, Thomas Anderson (1)
Newcastle United goalkeeper Tom Swinburne played in the third Wartime international against Scotland on his home ground at St James' Park in December 1939. He had trials with West Ham United and Hull City before spending 13 years with Newcastle (1934-47). Both of his sons, Trevor and Alan, became professional goalkeepers.

TAYLOR, Frank (1)
Left-back Frank Taylor played for Wolverhampton Wanderers in the 1939 FA Cup final defeat by Leicester City before representing England against Scotland at Hampden Park in April 1944, his only cap. He joined Wolves in 1933 but was forced to retire through injury in 1944. Assistant-manager of Hull City (1947-48), he later managed Scarborough (1948-50) and Stoke City (1952-60), having been coach and assistant-manager at Leeds United in between times.

WESTCOTT, Dennis (4) (5)
Initially with New Brighton, Dennis Westcott turned into a scoring-machine with Wolverhampton Wanderers (1936-48), Blackburn Rovers (1948-50), Manchester City (1950-52) and Chesterfield (1952-53), netting 172 goals in 259 League games, and he also struck four times for Wolves in their 1939 FA Cup semi-final win over Grimsby Town, yet failed to hit the target against Portsmouth in the final. Westcott bagged five goals in his four Wartime games for England, including a hat-trick in his second, a 5-3 win over Wales at Wembley in February 1943. Westcott, who made his international debut against the Principality in April 1940 and who later played for Stafford Rangers, died suddenly in 1960 at the age of 43.

PLAYERS WHO APPEARED IN THE FIVE UNOFFICIAL INTERNATIONALS AGAINST SCOTLAND: 1870-72

(Appearances made & goals scored in brackets)
*Later played for England at senior level

Player	Club(s)	Apps	Goals
C W Alcock*	Old Harrovians/Wanderers/Pilgrims	5	
A J Baker	N.N./Wanderers	3	1
T S Baker	Clapham Rovers	1	
M P Betts*	West Kent/Harrow Chequers	2	
A G Bonsor*	Wanderers	1	
E E Bowen	Wanderers	1	
W C Butler	Barnes/Civil Service	2	
T N Carter	Eton College	1	
C J Chenery*	Crystal Palace	1	
J C Clegg*	The Wednesday Sheffield	1	1
J Cotterell	Brixton	2	
W P Crake	Harrow School/Barnes/Harrow Chequers	4	
E Freeth	Civil Services	1	
T C Hooman	Wanderers	3	
J Kenrick	Clapham Rovers	1	
E Lubbock	Old Etonians/West Kent	5	
A Nash	Clapham Rovers	1	
W B Paton	Harrow School	1	
H J Preston	Eton College	1	
J C Smith	Crusaders	1	
C W Stephenson	Westminster School/Wanderers	3	
A C Thompson	Eton Cambridge Club/Wanderers	2	
A H Thornton	Old Harrovians	1	
R W S Vidal*	Westminster School	5	
R S F Walker	Clapham Rovers	3	4
P Weston	Barnes	2	
C H R Wollaston*	Oxford University	1	

NB: A Morten and W Lindsay played for Scotland in March 1870 and F B Maddison and A K Smith in the February 1871 game. All four players later won full caps for England.

PLAYERS WHO APPEARED FOR ENGLAND IN 'UNOFFICIAL' INTERNATIONALS: 1891-2010

Appearances include those made in World Wars One and Two (1915-19 & 1939-46 inclusive) and also those as a substitute.
NB: For 1916 read season 1915-16 and 1940 read 1940-41 etc.

Player	Club(s)	Season(s)	Apps	Goals
L Abrams	Chelsea	1916	1	1
T A Adams	Arsenal	1996	1	
G E Ainsley	Leeds United	1939	1	
V Anderson	Manchester United	1988	1	
D R Anderton	Tottenham Hotspur	1996	1	
J Armfield	Blackpool	1962	1	
L Armitage	Stoke City	1929	2	
J Astle	West Bromwich Albion	1970	3	7
W C Athersmith	Aston Villa	1899	1	
R W Ayre	Charlton Athletic	1956	1	1
J D Bacuzzi	Fulham	1941-46	13	
J J Bagshaw	Derby County	1920	1	
A J Ball	Everton	1970	2	
W Ball	Birmingham	1920	1	
J Balmer	Liverpool	1940	1	1
J Bamber	Liverpool	1920	2	1
H C Bamford	Bristol Rovers	1951	5	
T Barber	Aston Villa	1918	1	
H Barnes	Derby County	1914	1	2
H Barnes	Manchester City	1920	1	
J Barnes	Liverpool	1988	1	
M Barrass	Bolton Wanderers	1946	1	
A F Barrett	Fulham	1929	2	
S Bartram	Charlton Athletic	1939-51	6	
H G Batten	Plymouth Argyle	1925	5	10
P A Beardsley	Liverpool	1988	1	4
A Beasley	Huddersfield Town	1939	2	1
C Bell	Manchester City	1970	2	
R W Benson	Sheffield United	1910	3	
A Berry	Everton	1910	1	1
H A Betmead	Grimsby Town	1939	2	
R J E Birkett	Newcastle United	1941	1	1
W Blackburn	Oxford University	1902	1	
S Bloomer	Derby County	1902	1	2
J F Bond	West Ham United	1956	1	
P P Bonetti	Chelsea	1970	1	
I Boocock	Bradford City	1914-16	2	
E R Bowden	Arsenal	1935	1	
W E Boyes	West Bromwich Albion	1936	1	
T W Boyle	Burnley	1916	1	
H Bradshaw	Tottenham Hotspur	1899	1	
J Bray	Manchester City	1936	1	
J Brennan	Manchester City	1916	1	
S T Briggs	Clapton	1899	1	
C S Britton	Everton	1936-44	16	
A K Brook	Casuals	1892	1	
E F Brook	Manchester City	1939-40	2	
T D Brooking	West Ham United	1976	1	
S E Brooks	Wolverhampton Wanderers	1920	1	
F H Broome	Aston Villa	1940-51	3	3
E D Brown	Clapton	1899	1	
R A J Brown	Charlton Ath/Nottm Forest	1939-46	7	5
C M Buchan	Sunderland	1916-20	2	
V F Buckingham	Tottenham Hotspur	1941	2	
J Bulcock	Crystal Palace	1910	2	
E Burgin	Sheffield United	1951-56	7	
J J Byrne	West Ham United	1962	1	1
W C Caesar	Dulwich Hamlet	1925	1	

Name	Club	Year		
J Calvey	Nottingham Forest	1902	1	3
S J Campbell	Tottenham Hotspur	1996	1	
J Carragher**	Liverpool	2010	1	
M Carrick	Manchester United	2010	1	
H S Carter	Sunderland/Derby County	1936-46	18	19
A Chadwick	Southampton	1899	1	
H Chambers	Liverpool	1918	1	
A Chandler	Leicester City	1929	3	6
F Channell	Tottenham Hotspur	1935	1	
M R Channon	Southampton	1976	1	
J Charlton	Leeds United	1970	3	
R Charlton	Manchester United	1962-70	2	
S Charlton	Exeter City	1925	5	1
T Cherry	Leeds United	1976	1	
A J Clarke	Leeds United	1970	1	2
I Clarke	Portsmouth	1951	5	10
R N Clemence	Liverpool	1976	1	
H Clifton	Newcastle United	1940	1	
R Coates	Tottenham Hotspur	1970	2	
J G Cock	Huddersfield Town	1920	1	
A Cole	Chelsea	2010	1	
J J Cole	Chelsea	2010	1	1
D C S Compton	Arsenal	1940-46	12	2
L H Compton	Arsenal	1940-44	5	
W Copping	Leeds United	1940	1	
G H Cotterill	Old Brightonians	1892	1	1
J D Cox	Derby County	1892	1	
J W Crabtree	Aston Villa	1899	1	
W J Crayston	Arsenal	1935-40	2	
W Crook	Blackburn Rovers	1940	1	
R Crompton	Blackburn Rovers	1902	1	
P Crouch	Tottenham Hotspur	2010	1	
S Cullis	Wolverhampton Wanderers	1940-44	20	
A S Davies	Swindon Town	1920	3	
H A Davies	Stoke City	1929	2	
H Davis	Birmingham St George	1892	1	
J E Davison	Sheffield Wednesday	1925	3	
M R Dawson	Tottenham Hotspur	2010	1	
J Defoe	Tottenham Hotspur	2010	1	1
E G Ditchburn	Tottenham Hotspur	1944	2	
A Dixon	Oldham Athletic	1918	1	
A R Dorigo	Chelsea	1988	1	
J Dorsett	Manchester City	1914	1	
B Douglas	Blackburn Rovers	1962	1	
M Doyle	Manchester City	1976	1	
F Duckworth	Blackburn Rovers	1919	2	
R Duckworth	Manchester United	1910	1	
M Edelston	Reading	1941-43	5	1
J W Elkes	Tottenham Hotspur	1925	5	2
W B Elliott	West Bromwich Albion	1944-46	2	
J R Elvey	Luton Town	1920	3	
J English	Sheffield United	1918	1	
A S Farnfield	Casuals	1902	1	2
J Fay	Bolton Wanderers	1914	1	
S N Fazackerley	Sheffield United	1914-20	3	6
E B A Fenton	West Ham United	1939-40	4	
M Fenton	Middlesbrough	1939-46	4	5
L Ferdinand	Newcastle United	1996	1	1
W Fielding	Everton	1946	1	
L C Finch	Barnet	1939-41	3	2
T Finney	Preston North End	1946	2	1
F W Fisher	Millwall	1941	1	
J Fitchett	Bolton Wanderers	1901	1	
T Fleetwood	Everton	1919	2	
H J Fleming	Swindon Town	1910	2	3
R Flewin	Portsmouth	1945-51	5	
R Flowers	Wolverhampton Wanderers	1962	1	
R E Foster	Old Malvernians	1902	1	6
R B Fowler	Liverpool	1996	1	
G C J Francis	Queens Park Rangers	1976	1	1
C F Franklin	Stoke City	1945-46	10	
C B Fry	Oxford University	1892	1	
K J Gadsby	Leeds United	1939	1	
L H Gay	Cambridge University	1892	1	
W George	Aston Villa	1902	1	
S G Gerrard	Liverpool	2010	1	
A H Gibbons	Brentford/Tottenham Hot.	1939-43	3	3
R Glendinning	Bolton Wanderers	1914	1	
H A Goslin	Bolton Wanderers	1940-42	4	
H Gough	Sheffield United	1918-20	3	
L A Goulden	West Ham United	1940-45	6	3
L Graham	Millwall	1925	5	
R Green	West Ham United	2010	1	
N H Greenhalgh	Everton	1940	1	
B Greenhoff	Manchester United	1976	1	
A Grenyer	Everton	1920	1	
A Grimsdell	Tottenham Hotspur	1919	2	2
R Gurney	Sunderland	1936	1	1
J Hagan	Sheffield United	1941-51	19	18
L Hales	Crewe Alexandra	1902	1	1
G W Hall	Tottenham Hotspur	1935-42	4	
M Hamill	Manchester United	1914	1	
J Hamilton	Crystal Palace	1925	4	
H Hampton	Aston Villa	1916	1	1
C Hannaford	Clapton Orient	1925	3	1
J H Hannah	Norwich City	1925	4	
A J Hanson	Chelsea	1941	1	
E A Hapgood	Arsenal	1935-43	15	
G F M Hardwick	Middlesbrough	1941-46	17	
H Hardy	Stockport County	1925	2	
S Hardy	Aston Villa	1919-20	3	
B Harper	Barnsley	1940	1	
P P Harris	Portsmouth	1956	3	3
A Harrison	Nottingham Forest	1929	1	
E A Hart	Leeds United	1929	3	1
J Hart	Manchester City	2010	1	
C Harvey	Everton	1970	2	
M Hateley	AS Monaco	1988	1	
J N Haynes	Fulham	1962	1	1
E H Hendren	Brentford	1920	1	
A G Henfrey	Corinthians	1892	1	1
E W Heskey	Aston Villa	2010	1	
W Hibbert	Bury	1910	1	3
H E Hibbs	Birmingham	1929-36	2	
C G Hilditch	Manchester United	1920	4	
G A Hitchens	Cardiff City	1956	3	3
J Hodkinson	Blackburn Rovers	1920	1	
H H F Hobbis	Charlton Athletic	1935	1	
G Hoddle	AS Monaco	1988	1	
G H Holley	Sunderland	1910-18	4	3
J Holliday	Brentford	1935	1	
R Holmes	Preston North End	1899	1	
S N Howey	Newcastle United	1996	1	
F C Hudspeth	Newcastle United	1920	1	
E W Hughes	Liverpool	1970	2	
G S Hunt	Tottenham Hotspur	1946	1	
N Hunter	Leeds United	1970	2	
G Hurst	Charlton Athletic	1951	5	4
P E C Ince	Inter Milan	1996	1	
J Iremonger	Nottingham Forest	1901	1	
G Jackson	Everton	1939	3	
A C Jephcott	West Bromwich Albion	1914	1	
B A G Jezzard	Fulham	1956	2	

G Johnson	Liverpool	2010	1	
W H Johnson	Charlton Athletic	1946	2	
J E Jones	Everton	1939	2	
B Joy	Casuals/Arsenal	1935-45	2	
J K Keegan	Liverpool	1976	1	2
A E Keeping	Southampton	1929	3	
B Kidd	Manchester United	1970	1	
L V Kieran	Tranmere Rovers	1951	1	
J W King	Stoke City	1956	3	1
L B King	Tottenham Hotspur	2010	1	
H F Kinsell	West Bromwich Albion	1946	2	
A J Kirchen	Arsenal	1941-42	3	
A E Knight	Portsmouth	1920	1	
F J Lampard	Chelsea	2010	1	
J Landells	Millwall	1929	1	
E J Langley	Brighton & Hove Albion	1956	4	
R Langton	Bolton Wanderers	1951	4	1
T Lawton	Everton/Chelsea	1940-46	25	25
A Leake	Small Heath/Birmingham	1902	1	
J Leeming	Brighton & Hove Albion	1910	1	
A Lennon	Tottenham Hotspur	2010	1	
L Leuty	Notts County	1946	1	
J W Lewis	Walthamstow Avenue	1939-40	3	3
J M Lewis	Walthamstow Avenue	1946	1	
J Lievesley	Sheffield United	1910	3	
G Lineker	Barcelona	1988	1	1
F W Lock	Charlton Athletic	1951	1	
E Longworth	Liverpool	1919-20	5	
J McCall	Preston North End	1919	2	
J W McCue	Stoke City	1951	4	
W McCracken	Newcastle United	1914-18	2	
W H McGarry	Huddersfield Town	1956	4	1
S McMahon	Liverpool	1988	1	
S McManaman	Liverpool	1996	1	
J McMullan	Partick Thistle	1918	1	
R McNab	Arsenal	1970	3	
J R McNaught	Tottenham Hotspur	1899	1	
M McNeil	Middlesbrough	1962	1	
J Mahon	Huddersfield Town	1939	1	
C G Male	Arsenal	1936	1	
W J Mannion	Middlesbrough	1941-46	5	
J Mansell	Portsmouth	1956	1	
J Mapson	Sunderland	1939-41	3	
G W Marks	Arsenal	1942-43	8	
T Marshall	Bishop Auckland	1902	1	
H Martin	Sunderland	1919	2	
J R Martin	Aston Villa	1940	2	1
G W Mason	Coventry City	1942	2	
S Matthews	Blackpool	1940-46	30	2
D W Mercer	Hull City	1920	1	1
J Mercer	Everton	1940-46	30	1
J W Mew	Manchester United	1920	1	
H Miller	Chelsea	1935	1	
W Millership	Sheffield Wednesday	1936	1	
M D Mills	Ipswich Town	1976	1	
J Milner	Manchester City	2010	1	
F Mitchell	Birmingham City	1946	1	
W G B C Moore	West Ham United	1970	1	
W A Morgan	Birmingham	1918	1	
S H Mortensen	Blackpool	1945-46	3	3
J R Morton	West Ham United	1935-36	2	
R H Morton	Luton Town	1956	2	
E Mosscrop	Burnley	1916	1	1
R C Mountford	Huddersfield Town	1941	1	
J Mullen	Wolverhampton Wanderers	1943-46	3	
A P Mullery	Tottenham Hotspur	1970	1	
P J Neville	Manchester United	1996	1	
J Oakes	Charlton Athletic	1939-40	2	
B A Olney	Aston Villa	1929	2	
P L Osgood	Chelsea	1970	1	
S W Owen	Luton Town	1951-56	4	
C Parker	Stoke	1920	1	
D Parker	West Ham United	1951	3	
A Parsons	Clapton	1902	1	
S Pearce	Nottingham Forest	1996	1	
T U Pearson	Newcastle United	1940	1	
W H Pease	Middlesbrough	1929	2	
F R Pelly	Old Foresters	1892	1	
W Perry	Blackpool	1956	4	1
M Peters	Tottenham Hotspur	1970-76	3	
G E Petheridge	Bristol Rovers	1956	3	
D Platt	Arsenal	1996	1	
C Poynton	Tottenham Hotspur	1925	1	
W J Price	Fulham	1929	1	
S C Puddefoot	West Ham United	1919-20	3	4
J Pye	Notts County	1946	1	1
L W Quested	Huddersfield Town	1956	4	
L E Raine	Glossop North End	1910	2	
P Reid	Everton	1988	1	
C Roberts	Oldham Athletic	1914	1	
G H Richards	Derby County	1910	2	
J R Richardson	Newcastle United	1940	1	
A C Robinson	Birmingham	1916	1	
B Robson	Manchester United	1988	1	
J Robson	Burnley	1962	1	
R W Robson	West Bromwich Albion	1956-61	5	2
D Rogers	Swindon Town	1920	1	1
D Rogers	Swindon Town	1970	1	
J Rogers	Newcastle United	1899	1	
R L Rooke	Fulham	1943	1	
W Rooney	Manchester United	2010	1	1
J F Rowley	Manchester United	1944	1	
A W Roxburgh	Blackpool	1944	1	
C F Ryder	Old Carthusians	1902	1	
K Sansom	Arsenal	1988	1	
L Scott	Arsenal	1942-46	18	
D A Seaman	Arsenal	1996	1	
J M Seed	Sheffield Wednesday	1929	2	
J Sewell	Sheffield Wednesday	1951	5	10
G S Seymour	Morton/Newcastle United	1918-25	4	
L F Shackleton	Bradford Park Avenue	1946	1	
J Shaw	Sheffield United	1951	5	
D Shea	Blackburn Rovers	1919	2	
A Shearer	Newcastle United	1996	1	
S Shelbourne-Taylor	Cambridge Unv/Corinthians	1899	1	
F A Shelley	Southampton	1929	2	
E P Sheringham	Tottenham Hotspur	1996	1	
P L Shilton	Leicester/Derby County	1969-88	3	
W A Silto	Swindon Town	1910	1	
E Simms	Stockport County	1925	5	8
J Simpson	Blackburn Rovers	1918	1	
G C Smith	Charlton Athletic	1945	1	
G O Smith	Corinthians	1902	1	2
J Smith	Bolton Wanderers	1916-20	7	4
J Smith	West Bromwich Albion	1920	1	
J C R Smith	Millwall	1940-41	3	
L G F Smith	Brentford	1940-46	15	3
S C Smith	Leicester City	1936	1	
T Smith	Tottenham Hotspur	1899	1	1
W Smith	Manchester City	1902	1	
W Smith	Nottingham Forest	1892	1	4
W E Smith	Manchester City	1914	1	
W H Smith	Birmingham City	1951	1	1
F Soo	Stoke City	1942-46	10	
C W Spencer	Newcastle United	1925	5	
R Springett	Sheffield Wednesday	1962	1	

B Sproston	Manchester City	1940	2	
M H Stanbrough	Cambridge University	1892	1	
T M Steven	Everton	1988	1	
M G Stevens	Everton	1988	1	
N P Stiles	Manchester United	1970	2	
S B Stone	Nottingham Forest	1996	1	
A Stubbins	Newcastle United	1946	1	
A Sturgess	Sheffield United	1910	2	
J W Sutcliffe	Bolton Wanderers	1899	1	
P Swan	Sheffield Wednesday	1962	1	
F V Swift	Manchester City	1940-46	17	
T A Swinburne	Newcastle United	1940	1	
F Taylor	Wolverhampton Wanderers	1944	1	
P J Taylor	Crystal Palace	1976	1	
J Terry	Chelsea	2010	1	
F Thompson	Nottingham Forest	1892	1	
P Thompson	Liverpool	1970	1	
P B Thompson	Liverpool	1976	1	
W P Thompson	Nottingham Forest	1929	2	
H Thwaites	Corinthians	1902	1	
C Todd	Derby County	1976	1	
A G Topham	Casuals	1892	1	
R J Turnbull	Bradford PA/Leeds United	1919-29	8	4
M Upson	West Ham United	2010	1	
H Vickers	Casuals	1902	1	
W Voisey	Millwall	1920	4	
C R Waddle	Tottenham Hotspur	1988	1	
F A Walden	Tottenham Hotspur	1916	1	
G Wall	Manchester United	1910	3	1
W Waller	Richmond Association	1899	1	
J A Walsh	Liverpool	1925	3	
J Walton	Manchester United	1946	1	
S Warnock	Aston Villa	2010	1	
D V Watson	Everton	1988	1	1
W Watson	Burnley	1920	1	
W Watson	Huddersfield Town	1946	1	1
N J Webb	Nottingham Forest	1988	1	
H Webster	Bolton Wanderers	1951	1	3
W J Wedlock	Bristol City	1910	3	
A C Weller	Everton	1916	1	
D Welsh	Charlton Athletic	1940-46	10	14
D Westcott	Wolverhampton Wanderers	1940-43	4	5
R W Westwood	Bolton Wanderers	1936	1	1
S E Wharton	Small Heath/Birmingham	1902	1	1
A Whittaker	Blackburn Rovers	1902	1	
R Whittingham	Chelsea	1920	1	1
W Wigmore	Gainsborough Trinity	1899	1	
J M Wilcox	Blackburn Rovers	1996	1	
B F Williams	Walsall/Wolverhampton W.	1945-46	4	
J J Williams	Stoke City	1929	2	
W Williams	West Bromwich Albion	1899	1	
W D Williams	West Ham United	1925	2	
E C Williamson	Arsenal	1920	1	
C K Willingham	Huddersfield Town	1940-42	6	
G R Wilson	Corinthians	1899	1	
H Wood	Southampton	1899	1	
C Woods	Rangers	1988	1	
W Woodcock	Manchester City	1920	2	1
J Woodhouse	Brighton & Hove Albion	1920	1	
V R Woodley	Chelsea	1940	2	
V J Woodward	Chelsea	1910	3	4
W Wooldridge	Wolverhampton Wanderers	1902	1	4
C Wreford-Brown	Old Carthusians	1899	1	
H E Wright	Charlton Athletic	1935	1	
M Wright	Derby County	1988	1	
T Wright	Everton	1970	3	
W A Wright	Wolverhampton Wanderers	1946	5	
S Wright-Phillips	Manchester City	2010	1	

FACTS

* Reg Foster scored his six goals in England's 12-0 friendly win over Germany at White Hart Lane in September 1901.

* Billy Wooldridge netted his four goals in England's 10-0 victory over the Germans at Hyde Road, Manchester four days after the game at Tottenham (above).

* Jackie Sewell equalled Foster's double hat-trick feat with six goals in a 17-0 win over Australia in Sydney in June 1951.

* Ike Clarke (4 goals) and Jimmy Hagan (3) joined Sewell in that goal spree against the Aussies.

* Don Welsh's ten goals included a four-timer in England's 4-1 Wartime victory over Wales at The City Ground, Nottingham in April 1941.

* G.O. Smith bagged his four goals in a 6-1 win over Canada at The Oval in December 1891.

* Stan Fazackerley scored four of his six goals in a 9-1 tour win over South Africa in Cape Town in July 1920.

* Bert Batten scored all his goals in tour Test Matches against Australia in 1925 including a five-timer in an 8-2 win in Maitland.

* Tommy Lawton netted four times in England's 8-0 Wartime victory over Scotland at Maine Road in October 1943; he also struck hat-tricks in a 5-4 defeat by Scotland in April 1942 and in a 6-2 victory over the Scots at Wembley in October 1944.

OFFICIAL FA/ENGLAND TOUR SQUADS

Details of players who went on tour with the FA and/or England.

1899 – Austria and Germany
Phil Bach (Sunderland)
Billy Bassett (West Bromwich Albion)
Stanley Briggs (Clapton)
Edward D. Brown (Clapton)
Edgar Chadwick (Burnley)
Jimmy Crabtree (Aston Villa)
Jack Cox (Derby County)
Fred Forman (Nottingham Forest)
Johnny Holt (Reading)
Joe Rogers (Newcastle United)
Stanley Shelbourne-Taylor
(Cambridge University/Corinthians)
Wilfred Waller (Richmond Association)
Geoffrey Wilson (Corinthians)
Oswald Eric Wreford-Brown (Old Carthusians)

1910 – South Africa
Bob Benson (Sheffield United)
Arthur Berry (Everton)
Joe Bulcock (Crystal Palace)
Dick Duckworth (Manchester United)
Harold Fleming (Swindon Town)
Vince Hayes (Manchester United)
Billy Hibbert (Bury)
George Holley (Sunderland)
Joe Leeming (Brighton and Hove Albion)
Joe Lievesley (Sheffield United)
James Raine (Glossop)
George Richards (Derby County)
Ivan Sharpe (Glossop)
Billy Silto (Swindon Town)
Albert Sturgess (Sheffield United)
George Wall (Manchester United)
Billy Wedlock (Bristol City)
Vivian Woodward (Chelsea)
Gordon Wright (Hull City)

1920 – South Africa
Jack Bamber (Liverpool)
Thomas Burn (London Caledonians)
Bert Davies (Swindon Town)
Joe Edelston (Hull City)
John Elvey (Luton Town)
Stan Fazackerley (Sheffield United)
Harold Gough (Sheffield United)
Bill Harvey (Sheffield Wednesday)
Clarrie Hilditch (Manchester United)
Ephraim Longworth (Liverpool)
David Mercer (Hull City)
Jack Mew (Manchester United)
David Rogers (Swindon Town)
Billy Sage (Tottenham Hotspur)
Joe Smith (Bolton Wanderers)
Cyril Treasure (Bristol City)
Bobby Turnbull (Bradford Park Avenue)
Bill Voisey (Millwall Athletic)
Wilf Woodcock (Manchester United)
Jack Woodhouse (Brighton and Hove Albion)

1925 – Australia
Bert Batten (Plymouth Argyle)
Bill Caesar (Dulwich Hamlet)
Stan Charlton (Exeter City)
Teddy Davison (Sheffield Wednesday)
Jack Elkes (Tottenham Hotspur)
Len Graham (Millwall)
Jimmy Hamilton (Crystal Palace)
Charlie Hannaford (Clapton Orient)
Joe Hannah (Norwich City)
Harry Hardy (Stockport County)
Cecil Poynton (Tottenham Hotspur)
Billy Sage (Tottenham Hotspur)
Stan Seymour (Newcastle United)
Ernie Simms (Stockport County)
Charlie Spencer (Newcastle United)
Jimmy Walsh (Liverpool)
Tom Whittaker (Arsenal)
Billy Williams (West Ham United)

1926 – Canada
Ned Barkas (Huddersfield Town)
John Booker (Nunhead)
George Clifford (Portsmouth)
Benny Cross (Burnley)
Harry Foxall (Portsmouth)
Tommy Gale (Barnsley)
George Harkus (Southampton)
Wallace Harris (Birmingham)
David Jack (Bolton Wanderers)
Mike Keeping (Southampton)
Tommy Magee (West Bromwich Albion)
Bill Rawlings (Southampton)
Ronnie Sewell (Blackburn Rovers)
Joe Smith (Bolton Wanderers)
Fred Tunstall (Sheffield United)
Russell Wainscoat (Leeds United)
Jimmy Waugh (Sheffield United)
Owen Williams (Middlesbrough)

1929 – South Africa and Rhodesia
Len Armitage (Stoke City)
Bert Barrett (Fulham)
Arthur Chandler (Leicester City)
Harry Davies (Stoke City)
Albert Harrison (Nottingham Forest)
Ernie Hart (Leeds United)
Harry Hibbs (Birmingham)
Mike Keeping (Southampton)
Jack Landells (Millwall)
Ben Olney (Aston Villa)
Reg Osborne (Leicester City)
Billy Pease (Middlesbrough)
Johnny Price (Fulham)
Jimmy Seed (Sheffield Wednesday)
Albert Shelley (Southampton)
Bill Thompson (Nottingham Forest)
Bobby Turnbull (Leeds United)
Joey Williams (Stoke City)

1931 – Canada
Stan Alexander (Hull City)
Len Barry (Leicester City)
Ray Bowden (Plymouth Argyle)
Austen Campbell (Huddersfield Town)
Jimmy Cookson (West Bromwich Albion)
Harry Hibbs (Birmingham)
Ernie Hine (Leicester City)
Harold Houghton (Exeter City)
Jack Jennings (Middlesbrough)
Tommy Magee (West Bromwich Albion)
Joe McClure (Everton)
Peter O'Dowd (Burnley)
Len Oliver (Fulham)
George Roughton (Huddersfield Town)
George Shaw (West Bromwich Albion)
Jack Smith (Portsmouth)
Ken Tewkesbury (Birmingham University)
Tommy Urwin (Sunderland)

1939 – South Africa
George Ainsley (Leeds United)
Sam Bartram (Charlton Athletic)
Pat Beasley (Huddersfield Town)
Harry Betmead (Grimsby Town)
Cliff Britton (Everton)
Eric Brook (Manchester City)
Robert 'Sailor' Brown (Charlton Athletic)
Micky Fenton (Middlesbrough)
Ted Fenton (West Ham United)
Lester Finch (Barnet)
Ken Gadsby (Leeds United)
Jackie Gibbons (Brentford)
George Jackson (Everton)
Jack Jones (Everton)
Jim W. Lewis Sr (Walthamstow Avenue)
Jack Mahon (Huddersfield Town)
Johnny Mapson (Sunderland)
Jack Oakes (Charlton Athletic)

1950 – Canada and USA
Frank Bowyer (Stoke City)
Bill Ellerington (Southampton)
Reg Flewin (Portsmouth)
Jimmy Hagan (Sheffield United)
Johnny Hancocks (Wolverhampton Wanderers)
Stan Hanson (Bolton Wanderers)
Harry Johnston (Blackpool)
Nat Lofthouse (Bolton Wanderers)
Stanley Matthews (Blackpool)
Les Medley (Tottenham Hotspur)
Stan Milburn (Chesterfield)
Bert Mozley (Derby County)
Eddie Russell (Wolverhampton Wanderers)
Jackie Sewell (Notts County)
Jim Taylor (Fulham)
Charlie Vaughan (Charlton Athletic)
Eddie Wainwright (Everton)
Tim Ward (Derby County)

1951 – Australia and USA
Harry Bamford (Bristol Rovers)
Sam Bartram (Charlton Athletic)
Frank Broome (Notts County)
Ted Burgin (Sheffield United)
Ike Clarke (Portsmouth)
Reg Flewin (Portsmouth)
Jimmy Hagan (Sheffield United)
Gordon Hurst (Charlton Athletic)
Len Kieran (Tranmere Rovers)
Bobby Langton (Bolton Wanderers)
Frank Lock (Charlton Athletic)
John McCue (Stoke City)
Syd Owen (Luton Town)
Derek Parker (West Ham United)
Jackie Sewell (Sheffield Wednesday)
Joe Shaw (Sheffield United)
Bill Smith (Birmingham City)
Harry Webster (Bolton Wanderers)

1955 – Bermuda, Jamaica, Trinidad and Curacao
Ted Bennett (Watford)
Geoff Bradford (Bristol Rovers)
Tony Emery (Lincoln City)
Peter Goring (Arsenal)
Vic Groves (Leyton Orient)
Grenville Hair (Leeds United)
Jeff Hall (Birmingham City)
Ron Heckman (Bromley)
John Hoskins (Southampton)
Jimmy Hill (Fulham)
Bedford Jezzard (Fulham)
Jimmy Kelly (Blackpool)
Jimmy Langley (Brighton & Hove Albion)
Gordon Nutt (Cardiff City)
Syd Owen (Luton Town)
Stan Pearson (Bury)
Bobby Robson (Fulham)
Harry Sharratt (Bishop Auckland)

1956 – South Africa and Rhodesia
Bobby Ayre (Charlton Athletic)
John Bond (West Ham United)
Ted Burgin (Sheffield United)
Peter Harris (Portsmouth)
Gerry Hitchens (Cardiff City)
Bedford Jezzard (Fulham)
Johnny King (Stoke City)
Ray King (Port Vale)
Jimmy Langley (Brighton & Hove Albion)
Jack Mansell (Portsmouth)
Bill McGarry (Huddersfield Town)
Bob Morton (Luton Town)
Syd Owen (Luton Town)
Bill Perry (Blackpool)
George Petherbridge (Bristol Rovers)
Len Quested (Huddersfield Town)
Bobby Robson (West Bromwich Albion)
Jackie Teasdale (Doncaster Rovers)

1958 – Nigeria and Ghana
George Brown (Willington)
Herbert Edward Dodkins (Ilford)
Jack Dougal (Pegasus)
Grenville Hair (Leeds United)
Gilbert Hamm (Woking)
George Hannah (Lincoln City)
Ron Heckman (Millwall)
Johnny Hills (Tottenham Hotspur)
Tommy Jones (Everton)
Roy Littlejohn (Woking)
Charlie Mortimore (Woking)
Pat Neil (Corinthian-Casuals)
Mike Pinner (Pegasus)
Walter Robinson (Sutton United)
Derek Saunders (Chelsea)
Dennis Syrett (Wycombe Wanderers)
Johnny Wheeler (Liverpool)

1961 – Malaya, Singapore, Hong Kong, New Zealand and USA
Alan A'Court (Liverpool)
Colin Appleton (Leicester City)
Bobby Brown (Fulham)
Laurie Brown (Northampton Town)
Ray Charnley (Blackpool)
Fred Else (Preston North End)
Johnny Fantham (Sheffield Wednesday)
Tom Finney (ex-Preston North End)
Mike Greenwood (Corinthian-Casuals)
Grenville Hair (Leeds United)
George Hannah (Manchester City)
Jim L. Lewis Jr (Walthamstow Avenue)
Hugh Lindsay (Kingstonian)
Bobby Moore (West Ham United)
Mike Pinner (Manchester United)
Graham Shaw (Sheffield United)
Gerry Summers (Sheffield United)
Bryan Thurlow (Norwich City)

1965 – Gibraltar
Ronnie Clayton (Blackburn Rovers)
Tony Hateley (Aston Villa)
Don Howe (Arsenal)
Howard Kendall (Preston North End)
Hugh Lindsay (Wealdstone)
Tony Macedo (Fulham)
Jimmy Melia (Southampton)
Bobby Noble (Manchester United)
Alan Ogley (Manchester City)
Don Rogers (Swindon Town)
David Sadler (Manchester United)
John Sissons (West Ham United)
Bob Thursby (Crook Town)
Mick Wright (Aston Villa)

1969 – Tahiti, New Zealand, Singapore, Hong Kong and Thailand
Jimmy Armfield (Blackpool)
John Charles (Leytonstone)
Colin Dobson (Huddersfield Town)
George E. Eastham Jr (Stoke City)
Keith Eddy (Watford)
Chris Gedney (Alvechurch)
Tony Hateley (Coventry City)
Graham Hawkins (Preston North End)
Alan Hodgkinson (Sheffield United)
Ken Knighton (Preston North End)
Don Megson (Sheffield Wednesday)
Ian Morgan (Queens Park Rangers)
David Payne (Crystal Palace)
Norman Piper (Plymouth Argyle)
Bruce Rioch (Luton Town)
Jim Shippey (Oxford City)
Keith Weller (Millwall)

1971 – Republic of Ireland and Australia
Jim Barron (Nottingham Forest)
Barry Bridges (Millwall)
Chris Chilton (Hull City)
Keith Eddy (Watford)
Chris Garland (Bristol City)
Peter Grummitt (Sheffield Wednesday)
Peter Hindley (Nottingham Forest)
Mike Keen (Luton Town)
George McVitie (West Bromwich Albion)
Mick Mills (Ipswich Town)
Dennis Mortimer (Coventry City)
Norman Piper (Portsmouth)
Alan Stephenson (West Ham United)
Ken Wagstaff (Hull City)
Peter Wall (Crystal Palace)
Dave Watson (Sunderland)

INTERNATIONAL TRIALS

January 1878	Probables	4	3	Improbables	(The Oval)
February 1879	Probables	0	0	The Rest	(The Oval)
March 1879	England	4	3	The Rest	(Victoria Ground)
December 1879	The North	0	0	The South	(The Oval)
March 1880	The North	0	0	The South	(The Oval)
February 1881	The North	1	2	The South	(Bramall Lane)
March 1881	England XI	5	4	Birmingham & District XI	(Aston Lower Grounds)
January 1882	The North	1	3	The South	(The Oval)
March 1882	Probables	4	4	Improbables (Lancashire XI)	(Pikes Lane, Bolton)
January 1883	The North	0	4	The South	(Aston Lower Grounds)
January 1884	The North	2	4	The South	(The Oval)
January 1885	The North	2	1	The South	(County Cricket Ground, Derby)
January 1886	The North	0	3	The South	(The Oval)
January 1886	Amateurs	1	0	Professionals	(Deepdale)
March 1886	Amateurs	1	2	Professionals	(The Oval)
December 1886	Amateurs	2	0	Professionals	(County Ground, Stoke)
January 1887	The North	4	2	The South	(Aston Lower Grounds)
January 1888	The North	3	1	The South	(The Oval)
January 1889	The North	1	2	The South	(Newcastle Road, Sunderland)
January 1890	The North	1	3	The South	(The Oval)
March 1890	Whites	2	2	Stripes	(Gregory Road, Nottingham)
January 1891	The North	3	0	The South	(Town Ground, Nottingham)
February 1892	Whites	4	2	Stripes	(Perry Barr, Birmingham)
March 1894	Whites	2	1	Stripes	(Richmond Athletic Ground, Surrey)
March 1894	Amateurs	2	1	Professionals	(County Cricket Ground, Derby)
March 1895	Amateurs	0	7	Professionals	(Trent Bridge Cricket Ground)
March 1896	Amateurs	2	0	Professionals	(Essex Cricket Ground, Leyton)
March 1897	Amateurs	1	3	Professionals	(Queen's Club, West Kensington)
February 1899	The North	3	1	The South	(Crystal Palace)
March 1900	The North	4	4	The South	(Crystal Palace)
February 1901	The North	3	3	The South	(Crystal Palace)
February 1902	The North	2	0	The South	(Crystal Palace)
January 1903	The North	2	1	The South	(White Hart Lane)
January 1904	The North	4	0	The South	(Manor Road, Plumstead)
January 1905	Amateurs of the South	1	1	Professionals of the South	(White Hart Lane)
February 1905	The North	3	1	The South	(Ashton Gate)
January 1906	Amateurs of the South	0	1	Professionals of the South	(Craven Cottage)
January 1906	The North	0	2	The South	(Elland Road)
March 1906	Amateurs	2	3	Professionals	(Owlerton, Sheffield)
January 1907	The North	4	1	The South	(Stamford Bridge)
January 1908	The North	4	4	The South	(Hyde Road, Manchester)
January 1909	The North	0	0	The South	(Craven Cottage)
January 1910	Whites	1	1	Stripes	(Anfield)
January 1911	Whites	4	1	Stripes	(White Hart Lane)
January 1912	Whites	1	0	Stripes	(Ewood Park)
November 1912	England	1	3	The South	(White Hart Lane)
January 1913	England	0	5	The North	(Hyde Road, Manchester)
October 1913	Amateurs	2	7	Professionals	(The Den)
November 1913	England	3	1	The South	(Craven Cottage)
January 1914	England	4	2	The North	(Roker Park)
April 1919	The North	4	1	The South	(Stamford Bridge)
February 1920	England	2	1	The South	(The Hawthorns)
February 1920	England	5	3	The North	(St James' Park)
February 1921	England	1	1	The South	(White Hart Lane)
February 1921	England	1	6	The North	(Turf Moor)

January 1922	England	0	1	The North	(Valley Parade)
February 1922	England	1	3	The South	(Craven Cottage)
February 1923	England	1	0	The South	(The Den)
October 1923	Amateurs	0	2	Professionals	(Stamford Bridge)
January 1924	The North	5	1	The South	(Elland Road)
February 1924	England	1	1	The Rest	(White Hart Lane)
October 1924	Amateurs	1	3	Professionals	(Highbury)
January 1925	The North	1	3	The South	(Stamford Bridge)
February 1925	England	2	2	The Rest	(Maine Road)
October 1925	Amateurs	6	1	Professionals	(White Hart Lane)
January 1926	England	0	1	The Rest	(The Den)
February 1926	England	3	4	The Rest	(St James' Park)
October 1926	Amateurs	6	2	Professionals	(Maine Road)
February 1927	England	7	3	The Rest	(Stamford Bridge)
February 1927	England	2	3	The Rest	(Burnden Park)
January 1928	England	5	1	The Rest	(The Hawthorns)*
February 1928	England	8	3	The Rest	(Ayresome Park)*
February 1929	England	4	3	The Rest	(Hillsborough)
March 1929	England	1	2	The Rest	(White Hart Lane)
October 1929	Amateurs	0	3	Professionals	(The Den)
March 1930	England	1	6	The Rest	(Anfield)
March 1931	England	3	2	The Rest	(Highbury)*
March 1932	England	1	4	The Rest	(Leeds Road)
March 1933	England	1	5	The Rest	(Fratton Park)
March 1934	England	1	7	The Rest	(Roker Park)
March 1935	England	2	2	The Rest	(The Hawthorns)
March 1936	Probables	3	0	Possibles	(Old Trafford)
March 1937	Probables	2	0	Possibles	(Turf Moor)
October 1937	Probables	1	1	Possibles	(Goodison Park)
April 1946	FA XI	3	5	APTC XI	(Wembley)
September 1946	FA XI	2	2	Combined XI	(City Ground)

*Dixie Dean scored three at West Bromwich, five at Middlesbrough and three at Highbury

ENGLAND v. YOUNG ENGLAND

April 1954	England over 30s	2	1	Young England	(Highbury)
May 1955	England	5	0	Young England	(Highbury)
May 1957	England	1	2	Young England	(Highbury)
May 1958	England	4	2	Young England	(Stamford Bridge)
May 1959	England	3	3	Young England	(Highbury)
May 1960	England	2	1	Young England	(Highbury)
May 1961	England	1	1	Young England	(Stamford Bridge)*
May 1962	England	3	2	Young England	(Highbury)
May 1963	England	3	3	Young England	(Highbury)
May 1964	England	3	0	Young England	(Stamford Bridge)
April 1965	England	2	2	Young England	(Highbury)
May 1966	England	1	1	Young England	(Stamford Bridge)
May 1967	England	0	5	Young England	(Highbury)
May 1968	England	1	4	Young England	(Highbury)
April 1969	England	0	0	Young England	(Stamford Bridge)

*There was a record 46,661 crowd at Chelsea for this annual match

ENGLAND MANAGERS

The team was run and chosen by an FA Committee from 11 November 1872 to 24 May 1939, and also during WW2 and indeed, right up until the appointment of England's first full-time manager, Walter Winterbottom, in September 1946.

Managers' Records

Name	From	To	Played	Won	Drawn	Lost
Committee	11 November 1872	27 September 1946	226	138	37	51
Walter Winterbottom	28 September 1946	21 November 1962	140	78	34*	28
Alf Ramsey	27 February 1963	3 April 1974	113	69	27	17
Joe Mercer	11 May 1974	5 June 1974	7	3	3	1
Don Revie	4 July 1974	12 July 1977	29	14	8	7
Ron Greenwood	7 September 1977	5 July 1982	55	33	12	10
Bobby Robson	22 September 1982	7 July 1990	95	47	30	18
Graham Taylor	12 September 1990	17 November 1993	38	18	13	7
Terry Venables	9 March 1994	26 June 1996	24	11	11	2*
Glenn Hoddle	1 September 1996	18 November 1998	28	17	6	5
Howard Wilkinson**	1 February 1999	26 March 1999	1	0	0	1
Kevin Keegan	27 March 1999	7 October 2000	18	7	7	4
Howard Wilkinson**	11 October 2000	14 November 2000	1	0	1	0
Peter Taylor**	15 November 2000	25 November 2000	1	0	0	1
Sven-Göran Eriksson	12 January 2001	20 July 2006	67	40	17	10
Steve McClaren	20 July 2006	22 November 2007	18	9	4	5
Fabio Capello	1 December 2008	8 February 2012	41	28	7	6
Stuart Pearce**	9 February 2012	29 February 2012	1	0	0	1
Roy Hodgson	1 May 2012	2 June 2013	17	9	7	1
Totals:	**11 November 1872**	**2 June 2013**	**921**	**527**	**225***	**175***

* Includes one abandoned match
** Caretaker manager

NB: Matches decided in a penalty shoot-out have been recorded as draws.

Managerial Fact File

• Eight players who won full caps have so far gone on to manage England.
• Walter Winterbottom was officially appointed as Director of Coaching to the FA in 1946, having never managed any other team (club or country). Under his guidance England won the Home International Championship seven times and played in four World Cups (1950, 1954, 1958 and 1962). He also awarded 'first' England caps to future managers Alf Ramsey, Don Revie and Bobby Robson. His assistant at the 1962 World Cup was Burnley's captain Jimmy Adamson. In 1942, Winterbottom represented the FA (v. the RAF) and was also named reserve for England v. Scotland at Wembley.
• Don Revie's England team did not concede a single goal in any of his first six internationals in charge. Wales was the first country to score against a Revie team, drawing 2-2 in May 1975.
• Alf Ramsey said to his players just before England started the first period of extra-time against West Germany in the 1966 World Cup: "You've beaten them once... now go out and bloody beat them again."
• Ramsey, reacting to the dirty play by certain Argentinians during the 1966 World Cup match, said: "England's best football will come against the right type of opposition – a team who come to play football and not act like animals!"
• Bobby Robson rejected the notion of divine intervention in Maradona's first goal for Argentina in the 1986 World Cup finals. "It wasn't the 'Hand of God'. It was the hand of a rascal. God had nothing to do with it," said the England boss.
• Excluding penalty shoot-outs, Terry Venables tasted defeat only once as England chief – a 3-1 reverse to Brazil at Wembley in 1995. Venables' reign as boss excludes the abandoned game v. The Republic of Ireland in February 1995.

Milestones

• England's 100th full international resulted in a 2-0 win over Wales at The City Ground, Nottingham, in March 1909.
• England's 200th international ended in a 3-0 win over Germany at White Hart Lane in December 1935.
• England beat Wales 4-1 in their 250th International match at Ninian Park, Cardiff in October 1949.
• The 500th international took place at Hampden Park in May 1976 when Scotland beat England 2-1.
• The 750th England game ended in a penalty shoot-out defeat by Argentina in a World Cup game in France in June 1998.

WHAT THE MANAGER SAID!

Napoleon wanted his generals to be lucky. I don't think he would have wanted me.
Graham Taylor, 1993

I think I have the best job in the country. I'm an honest, straightforward guy and I've found some criticism hard to take. It's what got me the England job.
Bobby Robson, 1985

This is a great job... until a ball is kicked.
Terry Venables, 1995

I made the first move; they didn't contact me. I fancied being England boss.
Don Revie, 1974

Look at Jesus; he was an ordinary, run-of-the-mill, sort of guy who had a genuine gift, just as Eileen has.
Glenn Hoddle singing the praises of faith healer, Eileen Drewer, 1998

I do not get mad, I get even.
Glenn Hoddle
(after two Liverpool players had pulled out of his squad), 1997

Oh misery, misery; what's going to become of me.
Graham Taylor, after England lose a two-goal lead v. Holland, 1993

He played with tremendous joy and his spirit stimulated the whole team.
Walter Winterbottom on the death of Duncan Edwards, Munich 1958

He's ten years ahead of his time.
Alf Ramsey on Martin Peters, 1968

What can I say about Peter Shilton? Peter Shilton is Peter Shilton, and he has been Peter Shilton since the year dot.
Bobby Robson, 1986

He should have been the cool captain who keeps everyone away; instead he got involved and got another red card.
Glenn Hoddle after Paul Ince's sending-off in Valencia, 1998

He's as daft as a brush.
Bobby Robson on Paul Gascoigne, 1990

We have still to produce our best football. It will come against a team who come to play football and not act like animals.
Alf Ramsey after England's 1-0 World Cup win over Argentina, 1966

Tell your friend out there that he's just got me the sack.
What Graham Taylor said to the linesman after Holland's Ronald Koeman was allowed to stay on the pitch after a professional foul on David Platt and score a vital goal in the crucial World Cup qualifier against Holland, 1993

Bloody hell, I'll have to stop that.
Graham Taylor, after England had strung together 13 passes in a build-up to a goal, 1991

I expect to win. Let me do the worrying – that's what I'm paid for.
Graham Taylor's message to the fans before England's European Championship flop, 1992

I can smell the blood of an Englishman, and this Englishman's name is Graham Taylor.
Graham Taylor, under pressure, before England's European Championship qualifier with Poland, 1991

I was a victim of the tabloid newspaper war. I had watched this cancer spread over the eight years I had been in the job. It was ugly and damaging.
Bobby Robson, stepping down as England manager, 1990

Hitler didn't tell us when he was going to send over the doodlebugs, did he?
Bobby Robson refusing media requests to announce his team ahead of a World Cup qualifier in Sweden, 1989

I've nothing to say - this is my day off.
Alf Ramsey's comments to reporters on the Sunday after England had won the World Cup in 1966.

We are delighted to be in Mexico and the Mexican people are wonderful, despite having to put up with a band playing outside our hotel at full blast until 5 o'clock in the morning, having no police escort to the stadium (after arranging one) and our players being jeered as they practised on the pitch.
Alf Ramsey after England's goalless draw with Mexico, 1969

He's a stubborn bugger.
Brian Clough on Sir Alf Ramsey, 1971

The first ninety minutes are the most important.
Bobby Robson, 1985

I want to be here, in charge, for a long time.
Kevin Keegan, 48 hours before his resignation, 2000

A mistake is only a mistake when it's done twice; it becomes a nightmare when it's done three times!
Sven-Göran Eriksson, 2003

We were half decent at times, hopeless the rest of the game.
Fabio Capello, 2011

ENGLAND FACT FILE

Abandoned matches

England have been involved in just three abandoned matches in their long history. The first was in Buenos Aires on Sunday 17 May 1953 when a friendly against Argentina was halted after 23 minutes with the score at 0-0 when heavy rain resulted in a waterlogged pitch. The last, more recently, was on Wednesday 15 February 1995, when England's friendly in Dublin against the Republic of Ireland was abandoned after 27 minutes due to rioting within an English section of the crowd. England trailed 1-0 at the time.

In between times, the only time a competitive fixture involving England has been abandoned was against Czechoslovakia in Bratislava on Wednesday 29 October 1975. The European Championship qualifier was called off after 17 minutes due to fog with the score 0-0. The match was staged the following day and England lost 1-2, England's first defeat with Don Revie as manager.

Old stagers

The average age of the England team that played against Scotland at Sheffield in April 1920 was 30 years, 217 days - the oldest on record! This was the team with their respective ages: Sam Hardy (36 years, 227 days); Eph Longworth (32, 190), Jesse Pennington (35, 230); Andy Ducat (34, 54), Joe McCall (33, 265), Arthur Grimsdell (26, 18); Charlie Wallace (35, 80), Bob Kelly (26, 146), Jack Cock (26, 148), Fred Morris (26, 227) and the youngest, Alf Quantrill (23, 79).

Short careers

Many players have appeared in just one senior international for England – several enjoying just a few minutes on the pitch. Here are the top twelve who have had very short careers: Stephen Warnock 6 mins, Martin Kelly 7 mins, Peter Ward 7 mins, Jim Barrett 8 mins, Wilfried Zaha 9 mins, Joey Barton 11 mins, Peter Davenport 17 mins, Seth Johnson 17 mins, Jay Bothroyd 18 mins, Brian Little 19 mins, Kevin Davies 20 mins, Matt Jarvis 21 mins.

Several players were introduced as a late substitute and therefore added time at the end of a game has been taken into consideration.

Long careers

Many players have had 'long' careers with England, several of whom won their last cap some years after making their debut. Here are those who have represented England, off and on, for more than eleven years at senior international level: Stanley Matthews 22 yrs 229 days, Peter Shilton 19 yrs 224 days, David Seaman 13 yrs 334 days, Frank Lampard 13 yrs 239 days, Tony Adams 13 yrs 232 days, Rio Ferdinand 13 yrs 200 days, David James 13 yrs 91 days, David Beckham 13 yrs 43 days, Raich Carter 13 yrs 34 days, Jesse Pennington 13 yrs 23 days, Steven Gerrard 13 yrs 6 days, Billy Wright 12 yrs 242 days, Stuart Pearce 12 yrs 112 days, Ashley Cole 12 yrs 70 days, Bobby Charlton 12 yrs 56 days, Bob Crompton 12 yrs 32 days, Tom Finney 12 yrs 24 days, Bryan Robson 11 yrs 253 days, Gary Neville 11 yrs 249 days, Sol Campbell 11 yrs 186 days, Bobby Moore 11 yrs 178 days, Michael Carrick 11 yrs 149 days, Ian Callaghan 11 yrs 98 days, Emile Heskey 11 yrs 60 days, Jamie Carragher 11 yrs 51 days, Ron Flowers 11 yrs 45 days, Ray Clemence 11 yrs one day.

Unchanged

It took England more than 35 years and 98 internationals before they fielded an unchanged team in consecutive matches. The team that played in the 98th game v. Bohemia on 13 June 1908 in Prague (won 4-0) was: Bailey (Leicester Fosse); Crompton (Blackburn), Corbett (Birmingham); Warren (Derby County), Wedlock (Bristol City), Hawkes (Luton Town); Rutherford (Newcastle United), Woodward (Tottenham Hotspur), Hilsdon (Chelsea), Windridge (Chelsea), Bridgett (Sunderland). This same eleven had beaten Hungary 7-0 in the previous match.

Most senior appearances (75 or more)

Peter Shilton 125, David Beckham 114, Bobby Moore 108, Bobby Charlton 106, Billy Wright 105, Steven Gerrard 102, Ashley Cole 101, Frank Lampard 95, Bryan Robson 90, Michael Owen 89, Kenny Sansom 86, Gary Neville 85, Ray Wilkins 84, Rio Ferdinand 81, Gary Lineker 80, John Barnes 79, Stuart Pearce 78, Terry Butcher 77, Wayne Rooney 77, John Terry 77, Tom Finney 76, David Seaman 75.

Youngest debutants

Theo Walcott, 17 yrs 75 days, May 2006; Wayne Rooney, 17 yrs 111 days, February 2003; James Prinsep, 17 yrs 252 days, April 1879; Thurston Rostron, 17 yrs 311 days, February 1881; Raheem Sterling, 17 yrs 332 days, November 2012; Clement Mitchell, 18 yrs 23 days, March 1880; Michael Owen, 18 yrs, 60 days, February 1998; Micah Richards, 18 yrs 144 days, November 2006; Duncan Edwards, 18 yrs 183 days, April 1955; James Brown, 18 yrs 2010 days, February 1881; Jack Wilshere, 18 yrs 223 days, August 2010; Alex Oxlade-Chamberlain, 18 yrs 285 days, May 2012; Arthur Brown, 18 yrs 328 days, February 1904.

Most consecutive appearances

Billy Wright, 70, 3 October 1951 to 28 May 1959

Most appearances as a substitute

Owen Hargreaves, 25, 1 September 2001 to 6 February 2008

Most appearances as a substitute without starting a game

Ugo Ehiogu, 4, 23 May 1996 to 27 March 2002

Most goals scored for England (25 goals or more)

Bobby Charlton 49, Gary Lineker 48, Jimmy Greaves 44, Michael Owen 40, Wayne Rooney 35, Tom Finney 30, Nat Lofthouse 30, Alan Shearer 30, Vivian Woodward 29, Steve Bloomer 28, Frank Lampard 28, David Platt 27, Bryan Robson 26.

Most goals in a game

5 – by Howard Vaughton v. Ireland, 18 February 1892; by Steve Bloomer v. Wales, 16 March 1896; Willie Hall v. Ireland, 16 November 1938; by Malcolm Macdonald v. Cyprus, 16 April 1975

Longest England career

Stanley Matthews, 22 years 228 days, 29 September 1934 to 15 May 1957

Shortest England career

Stephen Warnock, 6 minutes, 1 June 2008

Youngest outfield player

Theo Walcott, 17 years 75 days, 30 May 2006 v. Hungary

Youngest goalkeeper
Jack Butland, 19 years, 158 days, 15 August 2012 v. Italy

Oldest player
Stanley Matthews, 42 years 103 days,
15 May 1957, 4–1 v. Denmark

Oldest debutant
Alexander Morten, 41 years 114 days, 8 March 1873, 4-2 v.
Scotland

Most appearances at the World Cup Finals
Peter Shilton, 17, 16 June 1982 to 7 July 1990

Most appearances without ever playing in the World Cup Finals
Dave Watson, 65, 3 April 1974 to 2 June 1982

Appearances at three World Cup Finals tournaments
Tom Finney, 1950, 1954 and 1958
Billy Wright, 1950, 1954 and 1958
Bobby Charlton, 1962, 1966 and 1970
Bobby Moore, 1962, 1966 and 1970
Peter Shilton, 1982, 1986 and 1990
Bryan Robson, 1982, 1986 and 1990
Terry Butcher, 1982, 1986 and 1990
David Beckham, 1998, 2002 and 2006
Michael Owen, 1998, 2002 and 2006
Sol Campbell, 1998, 2002 and 2006

Most non-playing selections for the World Cup Finals
George Eastham, 2, 1962 and 1966
Viv Anderson, 2, 1982 and 1986
Chris Woods, 2, 1986 and 1990
Nigel Martyn, 2, 1998 and 2002
Martin Keown, 2, 1998 and 2002
David James, 2, 2002 and 2006

Oldest player to feature at the World Cup Finals
Peter Shilton, 40 years, 292 days, 7 July 1990

Oldest outfield player to feature at the World Cup Finals
Stanley Matthews, 39 years, 145 days, 26 June 1954

Youngest player to feature at the World Cup Finals
Michael Owen, 18 years, 183 days, 15 June 1998

First player to debut at the World Cup Finals
Laurie Hughes, 2-0 v. Chile, 25 June 1950

Last player to debut at the World Cup Finals
Allan Clarke, 1-0 v. Czechoslovakia, 7 June 1970

Most appearances at the European Championship Finals
Gary Neville, 11, 8 June 1996 to 24 June 2004

**Most consecutive appearances at the
European Championship Finals**
Stuart Pearce, 8, 11 June 1992 to 26 June 1996
Alan Shearer, 8, 8 June 1996 to 20 June 2000

**Most appearances without ever playing at the
European Championship Finals**
Terry Butcher, 77, 31 May 1980 to 4 July 1990

**Appearances at three
European Championship Finals tournaments**
Tony Adams, 1988, 1996 and 2000
Alan Shearer, 1992, 1996 and 2000
Gary Neville, 1996, 2000 and 2004
Sol Campbell, 1996, 2000 and 2004

**Most non-playing selections for the
European Championship Finals**
Tony Dorigo, 2, 1988 and 1992
Ian Walker, 2, 1996 and 2004

Oldest player to feature at the European Championship Finals
Peter Shilton, 38 years, 271 days, 15 June 1988

**Oldest outfield player to feature at the
European Championship Finals**
Stuart Pearce, 34 years, 63 days, 26 June 1996

Youngest player at the European Championship Finals
Wayne Rooney, 18 years, 232 days, 13 June 2004

First player to debut at the European Championship Finals
Tommy Wright, 0-1 vs. Yugoslavia, 8 June 1968

**Most appearances on aggregate at the World Cup
and European Championship Finals**
Peter Shilton, 20, 12 June 1980 to 7 July 1990
David Beckham, 20, 22 June 1998 to 1 July 2006

**Most appearances without ever playing at the World Cup Finals
or the European Championship Finals**
Emlyn Hughes, 62, 5 November 1969 to 24 May 1980

**Fewest appearances while still playing at the World Cup Finals
and European Championship Finals**
Tommy Wright, 11, 8 June 1968 to 7 June 1970

**Most appearances without ever being in a World Cup or
European Championship Finals squad**
Mick Channon, 46, 11 October 1972 to 7 September 1977

Most consecutive years of appearances
David Seaman, 15, 1988 to 2002 inclusive

Longest wait between appearances
Ian Callaghan, 11 years 49 days, 20 July 1966, 2-0 v. France to 7
September 1977, 0-0 v. Switzerland

Most tournaments appeared in consecutively
Sol Campbell, 6, 1996 European Championships - 2006 World Cup

Appearances in three separate decades
Sam Hardy, 1900s, 1910s, 1920s
Jesse Pennington, 1900s, 1910s, 1920s
Stanley Matthews, 1930s, 1940s, 1950s
Bobby Charlton, 1950s, 1960s, 1970s
Emlyn Hughes, 1960s, 1970s, 1980s
Peter Shilton, 1970s, 1980s, 1990s
Tony Adams, 1980s, 1990s, 2000s
David Seaman, 1980s, 1990s, 2000s

**First player to make tournament appearances
in three separate decades**
Tony Adams, 1988 European Championships; 1996 European
Championships and 1998 World Cup; 2000 European
Championships

Most appearances on aggregate by a set of brothers
Gary and Philip Neville, 144, 1995 - 2007

Most appearances in same team by a set of brothers
Gary and Philip Neville, 31, 23 May 1996 to 7 February 2007

Most consecutive appearances by an unchanged team
6, 23 July 1966 to 16 November 1966

First player capped who had never been with an English club
Joe Baker, of Hibernian, 18 November 1959

First player to debut as a substitute
Norman Hunter, v. Spain, 8 December 1965

Last appearance by a player from outside the top division
David Nugent, v. Andorra, 26 March 2007

Most captains in a single match
Four - in the 2-1 friendly match against Serbia and Montenegro at
Walkers Stadium in Leicester on 3 June 2003, four players wore
the captain's armband, including three Liverpool players. There was
widespread dismay in the media and among some former England
stars that three players deemed undeserving of the captaincy -
Emile Heskey of Liverpool, Phil Neville of Manchester United and
Jamie Carragher of Liverpool - were handed the captain's armband
as a result of the spate of substitutions that followed the half-time
retirement of Liverpool's Michael Owen, who had started the match
as captain in the absence of regular captain David Beckham. Only
Owen is listed as captain in the official match records, however. The
three who took over the armband were merely acting as temporary
custodians.

England's 500th win
England recorded their 500th win at full international level against
Egypt at Wembley in March 2010. Fabio Capello's men beat the
African Cup of Nation champions 3-1 in a friendly.

Aston Villa link
Nine players in the England-Sweden game at Wembley in November
2011, had links with Aston Villa: Scott Carson, Darren Bent, James
Milner, Daniel Sturridge, Gareth Barry, Kyle Walker, Stewart Downing
and Gary Cahill of England and Olof Mellberg of Sweden had all
worn the claret and blue strip at various levels. Also, the Swedish
assistant manager Marcus Allback played for Villa as did co-TV
presenter Gareth Southgate. That's a full team!

ENGLAND IN THE WORLD CUP FINALS

The FIFA World Cup tournament started in 1930 but it was 20 years before England first entered, doing so in Brazil in 1950 under manager Walter Winterbottom, who was appointed into office in 1946.

They won their opening game, 2-0 v. Chile but then suffered an embarrassing 1-0 defeat at the hands of underdogs and no-hopers the USA before losing their final pool 2 game, also by 1-0 to Spain.

In 1954, with Winterbottom still at the helm, England reached the quarter-finals, only to lose 4-2 to the 1930 champions Uruguay. Earlier they had drawn 4-4 with Belgium and defeated the host country Switzerland 2-0.

Winterbottom was again in charge four years later in Sweden when England took second place in pool 2 behind the subsequent champions Brazil but then lost in a play-off 1-0 to Russia.

Unfortunately in Chile in 1962 - Winterbottom's last World Cup - England fared no better, losing once more in a play-off, this time 3-1 to Brazil, having taken second spot in group 4 behind Hungary.

In 1966, the nation celebrated joyously as Alf Ramsey's wingless wonders lifted the coveted Jules Rimet Trophy for the first time at the fifth attempt.

Solid throughout the competition, England remained unbeaten. They topped group 1 with five points out of six, beat a tough Argentinian side 1-0 in the quarter-finals, saw off Eusebio's Portugal in the semis and then, courtesy of Geoff Hurst's hat-trick, defeated West Germany 4-2 after extra-time in the final at Wembley in front of 96,924 spectators.

The winning team was: Banks; Cohen, Wilson; Stiles, J Charlton, Moore (captain); Ball, Hurst, R Charlton, Hunt, Peters.

Joint favourites to retain the trophy in the stifling heat of Mexico in 1970, England looked well on course to win back-to-back World Cups after qualifying in second place in group 3. However, in the quarter-final, after leading their arch-rivals West Germany 2-0 in Leon, they were eventually pegged back before losing the tie 3-2 after extra-time, Gerd Muller scoring the deciding goal past stand-in 'keeper Peter Bonetti who was deputising for stomach-bug victim Gordon Banks.

To everyone's annoyance England failed to qualify for the 1974 and 1978 tournaments in Germany and Argentina respectively and when they re-entered in 1982, they looked good to win the competition under Ron Greenwood in Spain.

Group 4 victories over France, Czechoslovakia and Kuwait, took England through to the second phase. They earned a battling 0-0 draw with West Germany and had to beat the host nation Spain, to qualify for the knockout stage. This didn't happen and on a frustrating day in Madrid, Greenwood's men had to settle for another goalless draw and as a result slipped out of the competition.

Moving on four years to Mexico in 1986, Bobby Robson's England squeezed in to the second round by finishing runners-up in group F on goal difference, courtesy really of Gary Lineker's hat-trick in a 3-0 win over Poland. England then bowled over Paraguay to set up an intriguing quarter-final clash with the 1978 World champions Argentina.

A crowd of 114,580 packed into the Aztec Stadium in Mexico City to see the 'Hand of God' belonging to Diego Maradona do the dirty on England who lost 2-1 to bow out of the tournament which the players believed they could have won.

Chris Waddle said afterwards: "We were too angry for tears."

Few turned on manager Robson after this defeat... the villains were the feeble Tunisian referee and the diabolical Maradona himself!

England's next World Cup exploits took them to Italy in 1990 and again Bobby Robson was at the helm.

The supporters, the press and the players were confident of doing well but surprisingly the team struggled in Group F with draws against the Republic of Ireland and Holland before edging to the second round with a hard-earned 1-0 win over Egypt with Mark Wright's glancing header.

David Platt's late effort put out the Belgians and Gary Lineker netted twice in a nervous 3-2 quarter-final win over Cameroon in Naples to take England through to meet West Germany for a place in the final.

A tense contest in Turin ended 1-1 after extra-time and then, dramatically, both Stuart Pearce and Chris Waddle missed from the spot in the vital penalty shoot-out which resulted in England's elimination. It was a sad occasion.

It would be another eight years before England played again in the World Cup, as they failed to qualify for the 1994 tournament in the USA.

It was to be another bitterly disappointing end to their campaign in France in 1998.

Group G wins over Tunisia and Colombia and defeat by Romania meant a second round encounter – and a great chance of revenge – against Argentina in St Etienne. But despite a brilliant goal by Michael Owen, England, who had David Beckham sent-off, were held to a 2-2 draw. And then, like it was in 1990, they succumbed 4-3 in a penalty shoot-out after Paul Ince and David Batty both missed from the spot.

In 2002, in the Far East, England looked good at times. They drew with Sweden, beat Argentina with a Beckham penalty and shared the spoils with Nigeria before knocking out Denmark 3-0 in the second round. But a flukey goal – although David Seaman held up his hands to say he was to blame – helped Brazil to a 2-1 quarter-final victory in Shizuoka to leave England thinking 'what might have been' yet again.

In 2006 in Germany, 'Sven's Men' looked competent and determined as they beat Paraguay 1-0, Trinidad & Tobago 2-0 and drew 2-2 with Sweden to win Group B and so clinch a second round tie with Ecuador whom they went on to defeat 1-0. This took them through to meet Portugal for a place in the semi-finals, but after Beckham went off injured and Wayne Rooney got sent-off, the firepower went out of the team and the game flittered out to a 0-0 draw. England then had their seemingly usual blips from the spot with Frank Lampard, Steven Gerrard and Jamie Carragher all missing as the Portuguese, with Cristiano Ronaldo doing his business, won 3-2 on penalties.

So it was off to South Africa in 2010 and the irritating vuvuzelas. England spluttered along with disappointing group draws against the USA (thanks to Rob Green's goalkeeping blunder) and Algeria and an unconvincing 1-0 win over Slovenia to scrape a place in the last 16 and a meeting with the deadly foe, Germany.

It turned out to be an especially bad night ...if you were English!

Lampard had a perfectly good goal 'not given' and with some woeful defending and sloppy midfield play, the Germans capitalized to the full and stormed to a 4-1 victory, their biggest-ever over England at senior level.

England had been poor... the players knew it, Capello knew it and the press and the diehard supporters certainly knew it. Let's hope it will be better in 2014.

England's Full Record in the World Cup Finals

Knockout	P	W	D	L	F	A	Position
1950	3	1	0	2	2	2	8th
1954	3	1	1	1	8	8	¼ finals
1958	4	0	3	1	4	5	11th
1962	4	1	1	2	5	6	¼ finals
1966	6	5	1	0	11	3	winners
1970	4	2	0	2	2	4	4th
1982	5	3	2	0	6	1	2nd

Group	P	W	D	L	F	A	Position
1986	5	2	1	2	7	3	¼ finals
1990	7	3	3	1	8	6	4th
1998	4	2	1	1	7	4	9th
2002	5	2	2	1	6	3	¼ finals
2006	5	3	2	0	6	2	¼ finals
2010	4	1	2	1	3	5	13th
Totals	**59**	**26**	**19**	**14**	**77**	**52**	

World Cup Squads

1950 (Brazil)

Manager	Walter Winterbottom
Goalkeepers	Bert Williams (Wolves)
	Ted Ditchburn (Tottenham Hotspur)
Full-backs	Johnny Aston (Manchester United)
	Alf Ramsey (Tottenham Hotspur)
	Bill Eckersley (Blackburn Rovers)
	Laurie Scott (Arsenal)
Defenders	Billy Wright (Wolves)
	Jimmy Dickinson (Portsmouth)
	Bill Nicholson (Tottenham Hotspur)
	Laurie Hughes (Liverpool)
	Willie Watson (Sunderland)
Midfielders	Henry Cockburn (Manchester United)
	Wilf Mannion (Middlesbrough)
	Jim Taylor (Fulham)
	Eddie Baily (Tottenham Hotspur)
Wingers	Stanley Matthews (Blackpool)
	Tom Finney (Preston North End)
	Jimmy Mullen (Wolves)
Forwards	Jackie Milburn (Newcastle United)
	Stan Mortensen (Blackpool)
	Roy Bentley (Chelsea)
Reserves	Bill Jones (Liverpool)
	Johnny Hancocks (Wolves)
	Bert Mozley (Derby County)

1954 (Switzerland)

Manager	Walter Winterbottom
Goalkeepers	Gil Merrick (Birmingham City)
	Ted Burgin (Sheffield United)
Full-backs	Ron Staniforth (Huddersfield Town)
	Roger Byrne (Manchester United)
	Ken Green (Birmingham City)
Defenders	Billy Wright (Wolves)
	Syd Owen (Luton Town)
Midfielders	Jimmy Dickinson (Portsmouth)
	Bill McGarry (Huddersfield Town)
Wingers	Tom Finney (Preston North End)
	Stanley Matthews (Blackpool)
	Jimmy Mullen (Wolves)
Forwards	Ivor Broadis (Newcastle United)
	Nat Lofthouse (Bolton Wanderers)
	Tommy Taylor (Manchester United)
	Albert Quixall (Sheffield Wednesday)
	Dennis Wilshaw (Wolves)
Reserves	Ken Armstrong (Chelsea)
	Joe Kennedy (West Bromwich Albion)
	Allenby Chilton (Manchester United)
	Johnny Haynes (Fulham)
	Ronnie Allen (West Bromwich Albion)

1958 (Sweden)

Manager	Walter Winterbottom
Goalkeeper	Colin McDonald (Burnley)
	Eddie Hopkinson (Bolton Wanderers)
Full-backs	Don Howe (West Bromwich Albion)
	Tommy Banks (Bolton Wanderers)
	Peter Sillett (Chelsea)
Defenders	Billy Wright (Wolves)
	Maurice Norman (Tottenham Hotspur)
	Bill Slater (Wolves)
	Ronnie Clayton (Blackburn Rovers)
Midfielders	Johnny Haynes (Fulham)
	Eddie Clamp (Wolves)
	Bobby Robson (West Bromwich Albion)
	Peter Broadbent (Wolves)
Wingers	Tom Finney (Preston North End)
	Bryan Douglas (Blackburn Rovers)
	Peter Brabrook (Chelsea)
	Alan A'Court (Liverpool)
Forwards	Bobby Charlton (Manchester United)
	Derek Kevan (West Bromwich Albion)
	Bobby Smith (Tottenham Hotspur)
Reserves	Eddie Hopkinson (Bolton Wanderers)
	Jim Langley (Fulham)
	John Atyeo (Bristol City)

1962 (Chile)

Manager	Walter Winterbottom
Goalkeepers	Ron Springett (Sheffield Wednesday)
	Alan Hodgkinson (Sheffield United)
Full-backs	Jimmy Armfield (Blackpool)
	Don Howe (West Bromwich Albion)
	Ramon Wilson (Huddersfield Town)
Defenders	Bobby Moore (West Ham United)
	Peter Swan (Sheffield Wednesday)
	Maurice Norman (Tottenham Hotspur)
Midfielders	Ron Flowers (Wolves)
	Bobby Robson (West Bromwich Albion)
	Stan Anderson (Sunderland)
Wingers	Bryan Douglas (Blackburn Rovers)
	John Connelly (Burnley)
Forwards	Johnny Haynes (Fulham)
	George Eastham (Arsenal)
	Jimmy Greaves (Tottenham Hotspur)
	Gerry Hitchens (Inter Milan)
	Bobby Charlton (Manchester United)
	Roger Hunt (Liverpool)
	Alan Peacock (Middlesbrough)
Reserves	Graham Shaw (Sheffield United)
	Brian Labone (Everton)
	Ray Crawford (Ipswich Town)

1966 (England)

Manager	Alf Ramsey
Goalkeepers	Gordon Banks (Leicester City)
	Ron Springett (Sheffield Wednesday)
	Peter Bonetti (Chelsea)
Full-backs	George Cohen (Fulham)
	Jimmy Armfield (Blackpool)
	Ramon Wilson (Everton)
	Gerry Byrne (Liverpool)
Defenders	Nobby Stiles (Manchester United)
	Bobby Moore (West Ham United)
	Jack Charlton (Leeds United)
	Norman Hunter (Leeds United)
Midfielders	Ron Flowers (Wolves)
	Alan Ball (Blackpool)
	George Eastham (Arsenal)
	Martin Peters (West Ham United)
Wingers	John Connelly (Manchester United)
	Ian Callaghan (Liverpool)
	Terry Paine (Southampton)
Forwards	Roger Hunt (Liverpool)
	Bobby Charlton (Manchester United)
	Geoff Hurst (West Ham United)
	Jimmy Greaves (Tottenham Hotspur)
Reserves	Peter Thompson (Liverpool)
	Gordon Milne (Liverpool)
	Keith Newton (Blackburn Rovers)
	Bobby Tambling (Chelsea)
	Barry Bridges (Chelsea)
	Johnny Byrne (West Ham United)
	Fred Pickering (Everton)
	Brian Labone (Everton)

1970 (Mexico)

Manager	Sir Alf Ramsey
Goalkeepers	Gordon Banks (Stoke City)
	Peter Bonetti (Chelsea)
	Alex Stepney (Manchester United)
Full-backs	Keith Newton (Everton)
	Tommy Wright (Everton)
	Terry Cooper (Leeds United)
Defenders	Jack Charlton (Leeds United)
	Brian Labone (Everton)
	Nobby Stiles (Manchester United)
	Emlyn Hughes (Liverpool)
	Bobby Moore (West Ham United)
	Norman Hunter (Leeds United)
Midfielders	Alan Mullery (Tottenham Hotspur)
	Martin Peters (Tottenham Hotspur)
	Alan Ball (Everton)
	Colin Bell (Manchester City)
Forwards	Bobby Charlton (Manchester United)
	Francis Lee (Manchester City)
	Peter Osgood (Chelsea)
	Geoff Hurst (West Ham United)
	Jeff Astle (West Bromwich Albion)
	Allan Clarke (Leeds United)
Reserves	Tony Brown (West Bromwich Albion)
	David Sadler (Manchester United)
	Ralph Coates (Tottenham Hotspur)
	John Kaye (West Bromwich Albion)

1982 (Spain)

Manager	Ron Greenwood
Goalkeepers	Ray Clemence (Tottenham Hotspur)
	Joe Corrigan (Manchester City)
	Peter Shilton (Nottingham Forest)
Full-backs	Vivian Anderson (Nottingham Forest)
	Phil Neal (Liverpool)
	Kenny Sansom (Arsenal)
	Mick Mills (Ipswich Town)
Defenders	Terry Butcher (Ipswich Town)
	Phil Thompson (Liverpool)
	Steve Foster (Brighton & Hove Albion)
Midfielders	Trevor Brooking (West Ham United)
	Glenn Hoddle (Tottenham Hotspur)
	Ray Wilkins (Manchester United)
	Terry McDermott (Liverpool)
	Graham Rix (Arsenal)
	Bryan Robson (Manchester United)
Winger	Steve Coppell (Manchester United)
Forwards	Kevin Keegan (Southampton)
	Paul Mariner (Ipswich Town)
	Tony Woodcock (Arsenal)
	Peter Withe (Aston Villa)
	Trevor Francis (Manchester City)
Reserves	Cyrille Regis (West Bromwich Albion)
	Dave Watson (Stoke City)
	Tony Morley (Aston Villa)
	Alan Devonshire (West Ham United)

1986 (Mexico)

Manager	Bobby Robson
Goalkeepers	Peter Shilton (Southampton)
	Chris Woods (Norwich City)
	Gary Bailey (Manchester United)
Full-backs	Gary Stevens (Everton)
	Kenny Sansom (Arsenal)
	Vivian Anderson (Arsenal)
Defenders	Alvin Martin (West Ham United)
	Gary Stevens (Tottenham Hotspur)
	Terry Fenwick (Queens Park Rangers)
	Terry Butcher (West Ham United)
Midfielders	Glenn Hoddle (Tottenham Hotspur)
	Bryan Robson (Manchester United)
	Peter Reid (Everton)
	Trevor Steven (Everton)
	Steve Hodge (Aston Villa)
	Ray Wilkins (AC Milan)
	Chris Waddle (Tottenham Hotspur)
	John Barnes (Watford)
Strikers	Mark Hateley (AC Milan)
	Gary Lineker (Everton)
	Peter Beardsley (Newcastle United)
	Kerry Dixon (Chelsea)
Reserves	Mark Wright (Southampton)
	Dave Watson (Norwich City)
	Gordon Cowans (Bari)
	Trevor Francis (Sampdoria)

1990 (Italy)

Manager	Bobby Robson
Goalkeepers	Peter Shilton (Derby County)
	Chris Woods (Glasgow Rangers)
	David Seaman (Arsenal)
Full-backs	Gary Stevens (Glasgow Rangers)
	Stuart Pearce (Nottingham Forest)
	Paul Parker (Queens Park Rangers)
	Tony Dorigo (Chelsea)
Defenders	Des Walker (Nottingham Forest)
	Terry Butcher (Glasgow Rangers)
	Mark Wright (Derby County)
Midfielders	Neil Webb (Manchester United)
	Bryan Robson (Manchester United)
	Steve McMahon (Liverpool)
	David Platt (Aston Villa)
	Steve Hodge (Nottingham Forest)
	Paul Gascoigne (Tottenham Hotspur)
	Trevor Steven (Glasgow Rangers)
Forwards	Chris Waddle (Olympique de Marseille)
	Peter Beardsley (Liverpool)
	Gary Lineker (Tottenham Hotspur)
	John Barnes (Liverpool)
	Steve Bull (Wolverhampton Wanderers)
Reserves	Dave Beasant (Chelsea)*
	Lee Dixon (Arsenal)
	Tony Adams (Arsenal)
	David Rocastle (Arsenal)
	Replaced the injured David Seaman.

1998 (France)

Manager	Glenn Hoddle
Goalkeepers	David Seaman (Arsenal)
	Nigel Martyn (Leeds United)
	Tim Flowers (Blackburn Rovers)
Full-backs	Graeme Le Saux (Chelsea)
	Gary Neville (Manchester United)
Defenders	Sol Campbell (Tottenham Hotspur)
	Tony Adams (Arsenal)
	Gareth Southgate (Aston Villa)
	Martin Keown (Arsenal)
	Rio Ferdinand (West Ham United)
Midfielders	Paul Ince (Liverpool)
	David Beckham (Manchester United)
	David Batty (Newcastle United)
	Steve McManaman (Liverpool)
	Darren Anderton (Tottenham Hotspur)
	Paul Scholes (Manchester United)
	Rob Lee (Newcastle United)
Strikers	Alan Shearer (Newcastle United)
	Teddy Sheringham (Manchester United)
	Paul Merson (Middlesbrough)
	Les Ferdinand (Tottenham Hotspur)
	Michael Owen (Liverpool)
Reserves	Dion Dublin (Coventry City)
	Nicky Butt (Manchester United)
	Phil Neville (Manchester United)
	Ian Wright (Arsenal)

2002 (South Korea/Japan)

Manager	Sven-Goran Eriksson
Goalkeepers	David Seaman (Arsenal)
	Nigel Martyn (Leeds United)
	David James (West Ham United)
Full-backs	Danny Mills (Leeds United)
	Ashley Cole (Arsenal)
	Wayne Bridge (Southampton)
Defenders	Rio Ferdinand (Leeds United)
	Sol Campbell (Arsenal)
	Wes Brown (Manchester United)
	Martin Keown (Arsenal)
	Gareth Southgate (Middlesbrough)
Midfielders	Steven Gerrard (Liverpool)
	Danny Murphy (Liverpool)
	Trevor Sinclair (West Ham United)
	David Beckham (Manchester United)
	Paul Scholes (Manchester United)
	Joe Cole (West Ham United)
	Nicky Butt (Manchester United)
	Owen Hargreaves (Bayern Munich)
	Kieron Dyer (Newcastle United)
Forwards	Robbie Fowler (Leeds United)
	Michael Owen (Liverpool)
	Emile Heskey (Liverpool)
	Teddy Sheringham (Tottenham Hotspur)
	Darius Vassell (Aston Villa)
Reserves	Gary Neville (Manchester United)
	Phil Neville (Manchester United)
	Chris Powell (Charlton Athletic)
	Kevin Phillips (Sunderland)

2006 (Germany)

Manager	Sven-Goran Eriksson
Goalkeepers	Paul Robinson (Tottenham Hotspur)
	David James (Manchester City)
	Richard Green (Norwich City)
Full-backs	Gary Neville (Manchester United)
	Ashley Cole (Arsenal)
	Wayne Bridge (Chelsea)
Defenders	Rio Ferdinand (Manchester United)
	John Terry (Chelsea)
	Sol Campbell (Arsenal)
	Jamie Carragher (Liverpool)
Midfielders	David Beckham (Real Madrid)
	Michael Carrick (Tottenham Hotspur)
	Frank Lampard (Chelsea)
	Steven Gerrard (Liverpool)
	Owen Hargreaves (Bayern Munich)
	Jermaine Jenas (Tottenham Hotspur)
	Stewart Downing (Middlesbrough)
	Joe Cole (Chelsea)
	Aaron Lennon (Tottenham Hotspur)
Forwards	Wayne Rooney (Manchester United)
	Michael Owen (Newcastle United)
	Peter Crouch (Liverpool)
	Theo Walcott (Arsenal)
Reserves	Scott Carson (Liverpool)
	Luke Young (Charlton Athletic)
	Nigel Reo-Coker (West Ham United)
	Jermain Defoe (Tottenham Hotspur)
	Andrew Johnson (Crystal Palace)

2010 (South Africa)

Manager	Fabio Capello
Goalkeepers	Robert Green (West Ham United)
	David James (Portsmouth)
	Joe Hart (Manchester City)
Full-backs	Glen Johnson (Liverpool)
	Ashley Cole (Chelsea)
	Stephen Warnock (Aston Villa)
Defenders	John Terry (Chelsea)
	Matthew Upson (West Ham United)
	Rio Ferdinand (Manchester United)
	Jamie Carragher (Liverpool)
	Ledley King (Tottenham Hotspur)
Midfielders	Steven Gerrard (Liverpool)
	Frank Lampard (Chelsea)
	Gareth Barry (Manchester City)
	Michael Carrick (Manchester United)
	Joe Cole (Chelsea)
	James Milner (Aston Villa)
	Aaron Lennon (Tottenham Hotspur)
	Shaun Wright-Phillips (Manchester City)
Forwards	Wayne Rooney (Manchester United)
	Peter Crouch (Tottenham Hotspur)
	Jermain Defoe (Tottenham Hotspur)
	Emile Heskey (Aston Villa)
Reserves	Theo Walcott (Arsenal)
	Leighton Baines (Everton)
	Adam Johnson (Manchester City)
	Tom Huddlestone (Tottenham Hotspur)
	Scott Parker (West Ham United)
	Michael Dawson (Tottenham Hotspur)
	Darren Bent (Sunderland)

NOTE: With tactical formations such as 4-2-4, 4-4-2 and 4-3-3 etc, being introduced in the mid-1960s, for easy reference, players named in the 1950-54-58-62 World Cup squads, who were, at the time, referred to as half-backs at club level, have been listed under midfielders to link up with inside-forwards.

ENGLAND'S UNDER-21 TEAM

England's Under-21 team is considered to be a feeder for the full international side.

The team is for players aged under 21 at the start of the calendar year in which a two-year European U21 Football Championship campaign begins. Therefore, certain players can remain with the squad until they reach the age of 23.

In fact, as long as they are eligible, players can play for England at any level, making it possible to feature for the U20s, the U21s and even the senior side before they are 23 as goalkeeper Jack Butland, Tom Cleverley, Jake Livermore, Ryan Bertrand and Danny Welbeck have done in recent years.

It's also possible for a player to represent one country at youth team level and another at senior level, providing the player is eligible of course.

The U21 team came into existence in 1976, following the realignment of UEFA's youth competitions. England's first U21 international ended in a goalless draw with Wales in a friendly at Molineux in December 1976.

England U21s do not have a permanent home. The team plays throughout England, in an attempt to encourage younger fans in all areas of the country to get behind their national team. Because of the smaller demand compared to the senior national team, lower capacity grounds are regularly used.

U21 Team Fact File

- England's biggest wins have been 8-1 v. Finland at Boothferry Park, Hull in October 1977 and 7-0 v Azerbaijan at the MK Stadium, Milton Keynes in June 2009.

- The three heaviest defeats have all been by 4-0 versus Romania (away) in October 1980, v. Spain at St Andrew's in February 2001 and v Germany in Malmo, Sweden, in June 2009.

- The record attendance for an England U21 match was set on 24 March 2007, when 59,876 spectators at the brand new Wembley Stadium, witnessed the England v Italy U21 encounter. This is also a record attendance for an U21 game anywhere in the world. The match itself was one of the required two 'ramp up' events the stadium hosted in order to gain its safety certificate in time for its full-capacity opening for the 2007 FA Cup Final in May.

- At June 2013, more than 625 players had represented England at U21 level.

- The most capped players are: James Milner 46, Tom Huddlestone 33, Fabrice Muamba 33, Michael Mancienne 30, Scott Carson 29, Steven Taylor 29, Jamie Carragher 27, Gareth Barry 27, David Prutton 25, Jermaine Pennant 24.

- Top ten goalscorers: Francis Jeffers 13, Alan Shearer 13, Darren Bent 9, Frank Lampard 9, James Milner 9, Carlton Cole 8, Mark Hateley 8, Mark Robins 7, Shola Ameobi 7, Jermain Defoe 7.

- U21 coaches/managers: 1977-90 Dave Sexton; 1990-93 Lawrie McMenemy; 1994-96 Dave Sexton; 1996-99 Peter Taylor; 1999 Peter Reid; 1999-2001 Howard Wilkinson; 2001-04 David Platt; 2004-07 Peter Taylor; since 2007 Stuart Pearce.

ENGLAND'S UNDER-23 TEAM

Having initiated a 'B' team, Walter Winterbottom then decided to form an England U23 team in 1953, with the emphasis on developing younger players from an early age, although he did confirm that the country's youth team would still be in evidence.

U23 Team Fact File

- England's first U23 international took place on 20 January 1954 in Bologna when they lost 3-0 to the host country Italy. The first home game in the UK was played on 8 February 1955 in Glasgow when Scotland were defeated 6-0.

- England's biggest U23 wins were 7-1 v. Israel at Elland Road on 9 November 1961, 8-0 v. Wales at Molineux on 12 October 1966, 6-0 v. Scotland in Glasgow on 8 February 1955 and 6-0 against Wales at Wrexham on 30 November 1966.

- Their heaviest defeat was 4-0, in Tel Aviv against Israel on 22 May 1960.

- Some 300 players were honoured by England at U23 level.

- Most U23 caps won: Martin Chivers 17, Steve Perryman 17, Maurice Setters 16, Bobby A Thomson 15, Colin Todd 14, Len Badger 13, Tony Currie 13, John McDowell 13, Vic Mobley 13, Peter Shilton 13, Trevor Smith 13, Bobby Tambling 13.

- Most U23 goals scored: Jimmy Greaves 13, Bobby Tambling 11, Johnny Haynes 8, Martin Chivers 7, Allan Clarke 7, Johnny Byrne 6, Freddie Hill 6, Alan Hinton 6, Bobby Charlton 5, Duncan Edwards 5, Brian Kidd 5.

ENGLAND'S 'B' TEAM

Walter Winterbottom first discussed having an England 'B' team in 1947 - as a way of preparing players for the full international side. He arranged the first 'B' team game against Switzerland 'B' in Geneva on 21 February 1947 which finished goalless. However, it was two years before the second game took place – England beating Finland's 'B' team 4-0 in Helsinki on 15 May 1949.

Thereafter the frequency of the 'B' internationals depended almost entirely upon the manager of the senior team. For example, there were no 'B' games played under Sir Alf Ramsey or Don Revie; indeed there were none staged for 21 years, between 1957 and 1978.

Ron Greenwood reintroduced them and Bobby Robson arranged a few more regularly – in fact, nine 'B' team internationals were played in 1989 and 1990. This period saw the likes of Paul Gascoigne enter the England team via the 'B' squad.

Sven-Göran Eriksson arranged just one 'B' team match during his time in charge - on 25 May 2006 against Belarus as a World Cup warm-up game. England lost 2-1, with a goal from Jermaine Jenas.

Steve McClaren's only 'B' team match was against the Albania full side on 25 May 2007 at Turf Moor, Burnley. A crowd of 22,534 saw England win 3-1 as they prepared for a vital Euro 2008 qualifier against Estonia on 6 June.

McClaren's squad included a recovering Michael Owen, who captained the side, as well as seven uncapped players, five of whom latter gained full international caps.

Fabio Capello did not arrange a 'B' team match.

'B' Team Fact File

- England's 'B' international record: played 57, won 37, drawn 10, lost 9, one game abandoned.

- Biggest win is 8-0 v. Singapore on 18 June 1978 at National Stadium, Singapore.

- Heaviest defeat is 7-1 v. France in Le Havre on 22 May 1952.

- A 'B' international record crowd of 60,122 saw The Netherlands beat England in Amsterdam's Olympic Stadium in May 1950.

- The biggest 'home' crowd for a 'B' international is 43,068 at St James' Park, Newcastle when The Netherlands lost 1-0 on 22 February 1950.

- A total of 259 players have appeared in at least one 'B' international for England.

- Most 'B' caps won: 10 - Joe Corrigan (Manchester City, 1978-82), 9 - Gary Pallister (Manchester United, 1989-92), 9 - Gary Mabbutt (Tottenham Hotspur, 1984-92) and 8 - Brian Talbot (Ipswich Town/Arsenal, 1978-80).

- Most goal scored: 6 – Bedford Jezzard (Fulham, 1954-55), 4 – Tommy Taylor (Manchester United, 1956), 4 - Gordon Hill (Manchester United, 1978) and 4 - Alan Smith (Arsenal, 1990-92).

- Theo Walcott (Arsenal) is the youngest 'B' team player so far... aged 17.

ENGLAND'S INTERNATIONAL RECORD: 1872-2013

Opponents	P	W	D	L	F	A
Albania	4	4	0	0	12	1
Algeria	1	0	1	0	0	0
Andorra	4	4	0	0	16	0
Argentina+	14	6	6	2	21	15
Australia	6	3	2	1	6	5
Austria	18	10	4	4	58	27
Azerbaijan	2	2	0	0	3	0
Belarus	2	2	0	0	6	1
Belgium	21	15	5	1	70	25
Bohemia*	1	1	0	0	4	0
Brazil	25	5	10	11	23	34
Bulgaria	10	6	4	0	16	2
C.I.S.*	1	0	1	0	2	2
Cameroon	4	3	1	0	9	4
Canada	1	1	0	0	1	0
Chile	5	2	2	1	4	3
China PR	1	1	0	0	3	0
Colombia	5	3	2	0	10	3
Croatia	7	4	1	2	18	10
Cyprus	2	2	0	0	6	0
Czech Republic	2	1	1	0	4	2
Czechoslovakia*	12	7	3	2	25	15
Denmark	18	11	4	3	35	19
Ecuador	2	2	0	0	3	0
Egypt	3	3	0	0	8	1
Estonia	2	2	0	0	6	0
Finland	11	9	2	0	36	7
France	29	16	5	8	67	36
Georgia	2	2	0	0	4	0
Germany	12	5	2	5	24	19
Germany, East*	4	3	1	0	7	3
Germany, West*	16	7	3	6	24	19
Ghana	1	0	1	0	1	1
Greece	9	7	2	0	23	3
Hungary	22	15	2	5	56	30
Iceland	3	1	2	0	7	2
Ireland (1872-1920)*	35	29	4	2	154	25
Ireland, Northern	63	46	12	5	169	56
Ireland, Republic of #	15	5	7	3	20	14
Israel	4	2	2	0	5	1
Italy	24	8	7	9	30	27
Jamaica	1	1	0	0	6	0
Japan	3	2	1	0	5	3
Kazakhstan	2	2	0	0	9	1
Kuwait	1	1	0	0	1	0
Liechtenstein	2	2	0	0	4	0
Luxembourg	9	9	0	0	47	3
Macedonia FYR	4	2	2	0	5	3
Malaysia	1	1	0	0	4	2
Malta	3	3	0	0	8	1
Mexico	9	6	1	2	23	4
Moldova	3	3	0	0	12	0
Montenegro	3	0	3	0	3	3
Morocco	2	1	1	0	1	0
Netherlands	19	5	9	5	28	24
New Zealand	2	2	0	0	3	0
Nigeria	2	1	1	0	1	0
Norway	11	6	3	2	27	7
Paraguay	3	3	0	0	8	0
Peru	2	1	0	1	5	4
Poland	18	10	7	1	28	11
Portugal	22	9	10	3	45	25
Rest of Europe	2	1	1	0	6	5
Rest of the World	1	1	0	0	3	0
Romania	11	2	6	3	10	10
Russia	2	1	0	1	4	2
San Marino	4	4	0	0	26	1
Saudi Arabia	2	0	2	0	1	1
Scotland	110	45	24	41	192	169
Serbia/Montenegro*	1	1	0	0	2	1
Slovakia	3	3	0	0	8	2
Slovenia	2	2	0	0	3	1
South Africa	2	2	0	0	4	2
South Korea	1	0	1	0	1	1
Spain	23	12	3	8	39	24
Sweden	24	8	9	7	38	32
Switzerland	22	14	5	3	52	19
Trinidad & Tobago	2	2	0	0	5	0
Tunisia	2	1	1	0	3	1
Turkey	10	8	2	0	31	0
U.S.A.	10	7	1	2	36	9
U.S.S.R.*	11	5	3	3	19	13
Ukraine	6	4	1	1	9	3
Uruguay	10	3	3	4	10	13
Wales	101	66	21	14	245	90
Yugoslavia*	14	5	5	4	23	20
86 opponents	**921**	**521**	**225**	**175**	**2039**	**922**

* Country no longer exists
+ Includes abandoned match on 17 May 1953 (0-0)
# Includes abandoned match on 15 Feb 1995 (0-1)

NATIONS CUP/EUROPEAN CHAMPIONSHIP

The UEFA European Football Championship is the main football competition governed by UEFA (the Union of European Football Associations). Held every four years since 1960, in the even-numbered year between World Cup tournaments, it was originally called the European Nations Cup, changing to the current name in 1968. Starting with the 1996 tournament, specific championships are often referred to in the form of 'Euro 2008' or whichever year is appropriate.

Prior to entering the tournament all countries, other than the host nation(s) who qualify automatically, compete in a qualifying process. The championship winners earn the opportunity to compete in the following FIFA Confederations Cup, but are not obliged to do so.

England has staged the tournament just once, in 1996, when they reached the semi-final stage before losing on penalties to Germany at Wembley. In their group games, under the guidance of manager Terry Venables, England defeated Scotland 2-0 and Holland 4-1, and drew 1-1 with Switzerland. Spain were then defeated on penalties in the quarter-final.

After finishing third in 1968, England next qualified for the finals in 1980, but failed to progress beyond the group stage after losing to the host country Italy, drawing with Belgium and beating bottom team Spain.

After missing out in 1984, four years later in Germany, they qualified for the finals for the second time but once more failed to impress in their group, losing all three games against the Republic of Ireland, Holland and the USSR.

It was a similarly dismal story in 1992 in Sweden. England scored just one goal as they drew 0-0 with both Denmark and France and lost 2-1 to the home nation in pool 2.

Then, after a reasonably successful 1996 tournament, it was back down to earth in Holland in 2000 when England lost 3-2 to both Portugal and Romania and beat Germany 1-0 as they failed to qualify from group A.

England participated in the tournament in Portugal in 2004 and qualified well from group B with 3-0 and 4-2 wins over Switzerland and Croatia respectively and a 2-1 defeat against France. But in the quarter-finals they succumbed 6-5 on penalties (after a 2-2 draw) with the usually reliable David Beckham and Darius Vassell both missing from the spot.

Unfortunately England failed to make it into the finals in 2008 under manager Sven-Goran Eriksson, but four years on, with Italian Fabio Capello at the helm, they qualified in style for the tournament in Poland/Ukraine, only to get knocked out at the quarter-final stage by Italy on penalties.

England's record in the finals of the Nations Cup/European Championship
(qualifying & preliminary games not included)

Venue	P	W	D	L	F	A
Home	5	2	3	0	8	3
Away	4	1	1	2	4	5
Neutral	18	6	5	7	24	23
Totals	27	9	9*	9	36	311

Includes four draws, all of which went to a penalty shoot-out. England won one v. Spain in 1996, but lost to Germany, also in 1996, Portugal in 2004 and Italy in 2012

Fact File

- In all England, up to and including the 2012 tournament in Poland and Ukraine, has so far played a total of 117 games (including 90 qualifiers and preliminary fixtures) in the Nations Cup/European Championships since first entering in 1962. They have won 65, drawn 33 and lost 19, scored 226 goals and conceded 86.
- England did not enter the inaugural tournament in 1960 but since then they have qualified from the group stage in 1968, 1980, 1988, 1992, 2000, 2004 and 2012. They did not have to qualify in 1996, being the host nation in 1996, but failed to reach the finals in 1964, 1972, 1976, 1984 and 2008.
- England has finished third on two occasions, in 1968 and 1996 (shared with France).
- England's first Nations Cup game ended in a 1-1 draw with France at Hillsborough, Sheffield on 3 October 1962, Ron Flowers of Wolves, with a penalty, scoring the first goal.
- England has played most games in this tournament against Bulgaria, Northern Ireland, Turkey, Switzerland and Wales – all six – and they have met both the Republic of Ireland and Scotland on five occasions.
- The youngest player to play in a European Championship finals game for England is Wayne Rooney, aged 18 years and 234 days old v. France in Portugal in 2004.
- England's oldest player to play at a European Championship finals is goalkeeper Peter Shilton, aged 38 years and 272 days v. Holland in Germany in 1988. This was also his 100th cap.

Players chosen for the finals:

1968 – A Ball, G Banks, P Bonetti, J Charlton, R Charlton, R Hunt, N Hunter, G Hurst, C Knowles, B Labone, R Moore, A Mullery, K Newton, M Peters, N Stiles, M Summerbee, R Wilson, T Wright. Manager: Alf Ramsey

1980 – V Anderson, G Birtles, T Brooking, T Cherry, R Clemence, S Coppell, G Hoddle, D Johnson, K Keegan, R Kennedy, T McDermott, P Mariner, D Mills, P Neal, K Sansom, P Shilton, P Thompson, D Watson, R Wilkins, A Woodcock. Manager: Ron Greenwood

1988 – T Adams, J Barnes, P Beardsley, M Hateley, G Hoddle, G Lineker, S McMahon, B Robson, K Sansom, P Shilton, T Steven, G Stevens, C Waddle, N Webb, C Woods, M Wright. Manager: Bobby Robson

1992 – D Batty, K Curle, A Daley, G Lineker, M Keown, P Merson, C Palmer, S Pearce, D Platt, A Shearer, A Sinton, A Smith, T Steven, D Walker, N Webb, C Woods. Manager: Graham Taylor

1996 – T Adams, D Anderton, N Barmby, S Campbell, R Fowler, P Gascoigne, P Ince, S McManaman, G Neville, S Pearce, D Platt, J Redknapp, D Seaman, A Shearer, E Sheringham, G Southgate, S Stone. Manager: Terry Venables

2000 – T Adams, N Barmby, D Beckham, S Campbell, S Gerrard, E Heskey, P Ince, M Keown, S McManaman, N Martyn, G Neville, P Neville, M Owen, D Seaman, P Scholes, A Shearer, G Southgate, D Wise. Manager: Kevin Keegan

2004 – D Beckham, S Campbell, A Cole, K Dyer, S Gerrard, O Hargreaves, E Heskey, D James, L King, F Lampard, G Neville, P Neville, M Owen, W Rooney, P Scholes, J Terry, D Vassell. Manager: Sven-Goran Eriksson

2012 – A Carroll, A Cole, J Defoe, S Gerrard, J Hart, J Henderson, G Johnson, J Lescott, J Milner, A Oxlade-Chamberlain, S Parker, W Rooney, J Terry, T Walcott, D Welbeck, A Young. Manager: Roy Hodgson

Unofficial England Matches

(including Wartime/Victory internationals)
(Caps not awarded)

England 1 Scotland 1
Friendly, 5 March 1870 (The Oval)

England 1 Scotland 0
Friendly, 19 November 1870 (The Oval)

England 1 Scotland 1
Friendly, 25 February 1871 (The Oval)

England 2 Scotland 1
Friendly, 18 November 1871 (The Oval)

England 1 Scotland 0
Friendly, 24 February 1872 (The Oval)

England 6 Canada 1
Friendly, 19 December 1891 (The Oval)

England XI 1 Scotland XI 2
Friendly, 12 May 1899 (The Oval)
(In aid of the Players' Union Fund)

England 12 Germany 0
Friendly, 21 September 1901 (London)

England 10 Germany 0
Friendly, 25 September 1901 (Manchester)

Scotland 1 England 1
Home International, 5 April 1902 (Ibrox Park)
(This match was long and widely regarded as unofficial because, after the collapse of an Ibrox Park stand killed 25 spectators and injured hundreds more, it was replayed at Villa Park in Birmingham on 3 May 1902)

South Africa 0 England 3
Tour game, 29 June 1910 (Durban)

South Africa 2 England 6
Tour game, 23 July 1910 (Johannesburg)

South Africa 3 England 6
Tour game, 30 July 1910 (Cape Town)

Scotland 0 England 2
Friendly, 20 April 1914 (Ibrox Park)
(In aid of the Players' Union Fund)

England 4 Scotland 3
Friendly, 13 May 1916 (Goodison Park)
(Billed as a Military International)

Scotland 2 England 0
Friendly, 10 June 1918 (Hampden Park)
(In aid of World War Two Fund)

England 2 Scotland 2
Wartime, 26 April 1919 (Goodison Park)

Scotland 3 England 4
Wartime, 3 May 1919 (Hampden Park)

Wales 2 England 1
Wartime, 11 October 1919 (Ninian Park)

England 2 Wales 0
Wartime, 18 October 1919 (The Victoria Ground, Stoke)

South Africa 1 England 3
Tour game, 19 June 1920 (Durban)

South Africa 1 England 3
Tour game, 26 June 1920 (Johannesburg)

South Africa 1 England 9
Tour game, 17 July 1920 (Cape Town)

Australia 1 England 5
Tour game, 27 June 1925 (Brisbane)

Australia 1 England 2
Tour game, 4 July 1925 (Sydney)

Australia 2 England 8
Tour game, 11 July 1925 (Maitland)

Australia 0 England 5
Tour game, 18 July 1925 (Sydney)

Australia 0 England 2
Tour game, 25 July 1925 (Melbourne)

South Africa 2 England 3
Tour game, 15 June 1929 (Durban)

South Africa 1 England 2
Tour game, 13 July 1929 (Johannesburg)

South Africa 1 England 3
Tour game, 17 July 1929 (Cape Town)

England 0 Anglo-Scots 1
Friendly, 8 May 1935 (Highbury)
(In aid of King George V Jubilee Fund)

Scotland 4 England 2
Friendly, 21 August 1935 (Hampden Park)
(In aid of King George V Jubilee Fund)

South Africa 0 England 3
Tour game, 17 June 1939 (Johannesburg)

South Africa 2 England 8
Tour game, 24 June 1939 (Durban)

South Africa 1 England 2
Tour game, 1 July 1939 (Johannesburg)

Wales 1 England 1
Wartime, 11 November 1939 (Ninian Park)

Wales 2 England 3
Wartime, 18 November 1939 (Racecourse Grd, Wrexham)

England 2 Scotland 1
Wartime, 2 December 1939 (St James' Park, Newcastle)

England 0 Wales 1
Wartime, 13 April 1940 (Wembley)

Scotland 1 England 1
Wartime, 11 May 1940 (Hampden Park)

England 2 Scotland 3
Wartime, 8 February 1941 (St James' Park, Newcastle)

England 4 Wales 1
Wartime, 26 April 1941 (City Ground, Nottingham)

Scotland 1 England 3
Wartime, 3 May 1941 (Hampden Park)

Wales 2 England 3
Wartime, 7 June 1941 (Ninian Park)

England 2 Scotland 0
Wartime, 4 October 1941 (Wembley)

England 2 Wales 1
Wartime, 25 October 1941 (Villa Park)

England 3 Scotland 0
Wartime, 17 January 1942 (Wembley)

Scotland 5 England 4
Wartime, 18 April 1942 (Hampden Park)

Wales 1 England 0
Wartime, 9 May 1942 (Ninian Park)

England 0 Scotland 0
Wartime, 10 October 1942 (Wembley)

England 1 Wales 2
Wartime, 24 October 1942 (Molineux)

England 5 Wales 3
Wartime, 27 February 1943 (Wembley)

Scotland 0 England 4
Wartime, 17 April 1943 (Hampden Park)

Wales 1 England 1
Wartime, 8 May 1943 (Ninian Park)

England 8 Wales 3
Wartime, 25 September 1943 (Wembley)

England 8 Scotland 0
Wartime, 16 October 1943 (Maine Road)

England 6 Scotland 2
Wartime, 19 February 1944 (Wembley)

Scotland 2 England 3
Wartime, 22 April 1944 (Hampden Park)

Wales 0 England 2
Wartime, 6 May 1944 (Ninian Park)

England 2 Wales 2
Wartime, 16 September 1944 (Goodison Park)

England 6 Scotland 2
Wartime, 14 October 1944 (Wembley)

England 3 Scotland 2
Wartime, 3 February 1945 (Villa Park)

Scotland 1 England 6
Wartime, 14 April 1945 (Glasgow)

Wales 2 England 3
Wartime, 5 May 1945 (Ninian Park)

Ireland 0 England 1
Wartime, May 1945 (Windsor Park)

England 2 France 2
Friendly, 26 May 1945 (Wembley)

Switzerland 3 England 1
Friendly, July 1945 (Berne)

Switzerland 'B' 0 England 3
Friendly, July 1945 (Zurich)

Ireland 0 England 1
Wartime, September 1945 (Windsor Park)

England 0 Wales 1
Wartime, 20 October 1945 (The Hawthorns)

England 2 Belgium 0
Friendly, 19 January 1946 (Wembley)

Scotland 1 England 0
Friendly, 13 April 1946 (Hampden Park)

England 4 Switzerland 1
Friendly, 11 May 1946 (Stamford Bridge)

France 2 England 1
Friendly, 19 May 1946 (Paris)

England 2 Scotland 2
Friendly, 24 August 1946 (Maine Road)
(In aid of the Bolton Disaster Fund)

England 4 Canada 2
Friendly, 20 September 1950 (Stamford Bridge)

Australia 1 England 4
Tour, 26 May 1951 (Sydney)

Australia 0 England 17
Tour, 30 June 1951 (Sydney)

Australia 1 England 4
Tour, 7 July 1951 (Brisbane)

Australia 1 England 6
Tour, 14 July 1951 (Sydney)

Australia 0 England 5
Tour, 21 July 1951 (Newcastle, NSW)

South Africa 3 England 4
Tour, 23 June 1956 (Johannesburg)

South Africa 2 England 4
Tour, 30 June 1956 (Durban)

South Africa 0 England 0
Tour, 9 July 1956 (Cape Town)

South Africa 1 England 4
Tour, 14 June 1956 (Salisbury)

England XI 2 Tottenham 3
Charity Shield, 12 August 1961 (White Hart Lane)
(England team was 'officially' an FA XI)

Team America 1 England 3
Friendly, 30 May 1976 (Philadelphia)
(USA Bi-Centennial tournament; Bobby Moore and Pele played for
Team America)

England 4 Korean Republic 1
Friendly, 14 May 1986 (Denver, USA)

Bradford City XI 2 England 1
Friendly, 14 December 1986 (Valley Parade)
(In aid of the Bradford Fire Disaster Fund)

Aylesbury Utd 0 England 7
Friendly, 4 June 1988 (Aylesbury)

Hong Kong Select XI 0 England 1
Friendly, 26 May 1996 (Hong Kong)

Caen XI 0 England XI 1
Friendly, 9 June 1998 (Caen)
(World Cup warm-up game, played behind closed doors)

Platinum Select 0 England XI 3
Friendly, 2 August 2010 (South Africa)

TONY MATTHEWS
The world's most prolific author of football books

Tony was born and bred in West Bromwich, in the heart of the Black Country. An avid Baggies supporter, having played for Albion as an amateur, he served as the club's statistician/historian for 35 years and opened the Hawthorns museum.

Besides his footballing exploits which also saw him play in Switzerland and briefly for Coventry City and Shrewsbury Town, Tony has also been a policeman (based in Handsworth, Birmingham), a swimming instructor and a PE and art teacher, and is now engaged as a reporter/correspondent for the EWN and Spectrum Radio in Spain as well as being a local quiz-master and fund-raiser.

The world's most prolific author of factual books on one single subject - football - he is still producing the goods, with this, the 120th publication of his career, Tony having delivered his first book - on wartime football - in 1975.

His previous books have covered Arsenal, Aston Villa, Birmingham City, Chelsea, Everton, Huddersfield Town, Leicester City, Liverpool, both Manchester City and United, Nottingham Forest, the two Sheffield clubs, Stoke City, Tottenham Hotspur (of which the original, bound in navy blue leather with silver lettering, sold at £125 per copy), Walsall, WBA and Wolves; individual players Ronnie Allen, Cyrille Regis and Gary Lineker (digital); 100 Years at The Hawthorns (WBA's ground: 1900-2000); England in the World Cup (to be updated next year); Scotland - The Team (with Kevin Gallacher); Midlands Soccer At War (1939-45); Football Firsts & Football Oddities; several Miscellany books and various catalogues and magazines.

Tony, who saw his first 'live' England match in 1958 (v. Wales at Villa Park) is now living in Cabrera, Andalucia, Spain with his wife, Margaret.

DEDICATION

I dedicate this book to Sunderland-born Mr Charles William Alcock, the first secretary of the Football Association and the instigator of the first ever international football match (England v. Scotland) and also to the 1,194 players who, over the last 140 seasons, have represented England through thick and thin while proudly wearing their country's famous white shirt with the Three Lions logo.

Tony Matthews